DICTIONARY OF
American History

Third Edition

EDITORIAL BOARD

DICTIONARY OF
American History

Third Edition

Stanley I. Kutler, *Editor in Chief*

Volume 2
Cabeza to Demography

CHARLES SCRIBNER'S SONS

New York • Detroit • San Diego • San Francisco • Cleveland • New Haven, Conn. • Waterville, Maine • London • Munich

Dictionary of American History, Third Edition

Stanley I. Kutler, *Editor*

© 2003 by Charles Scribner's Sons
Charles Scribner's Sons is an imprint
of The Gale Group, Inc., a division of
Thomson Learning, Inc.

Charles Scribner's Sons® and Thomson
Learning™ are trademarks used herein
under license.

For more information, contact
Charles Scribner's Sons
An imprint of the Gale Group
300 Park Avenue South
New York, NY 10010

For permission to use material from this
product, submit your request via Web at
http://www.gale-edit.com/permissions, or you
may download our Permissions Request form
and submit your request by fax or mail to:

Permissions Department
The Gale Group, Inc.
27500 Drake Rd.
Farmington Hills, MI 48331-3535
Permissions Hotline:
248-699-8006 or 800-877-4253, ext. 8006
Fax: 248-699-8074 or 800-762-4058

LIBRARY OF CONGRESS CATALOGING-IN-PUBLICATION DATA

Dictionary of American history / Stanley I. Kutler.—3rd ed.
    p.   cm.
Includes bibliographical references and index.
   ISBN 0-684-80533-2 (set : alk. paper)
   1. United States—History—Dictionaries.   I. Kutler, Stanley I.
E174 .D52   2003
973'.03—dc21

Printed in United States of America
10 9 8 7 6 5 4 3 2 1

C

CABEZA DE VACA EXPEDITIONS. Born in Andalucia (Spain) sometime between 1485 and 1492, Álvar Núñez Cabeza de Vaca arrived in the New World as treasurer of the Pánfilo de Narváez expedition, which attempted to colonize the territory between Florida and the western Gulf Coast. This territory had been claimed by Ponce de León but remained unsettled by Europeans and mostly unknown to them. After arriving in Tampa Bay in early April 1528, the expedition moved west, facing several Indian attacks. The explorers were scattered, and Cabeza de Vaca sailed along the coast with a small group from September to November, finally disembarking near Galveston Island. Enslaved by Natives, Cabeza de Vaca remained there during the winter of 1528–1529. In early 1530 he moved down the coast and reached Matagorda Bay, becoming a trader among the Natives. He was accompanied by Alonso del Castillo, Andrés Dorantes, and the Moorish slave Estebanico.

In the summer of 1535 Cabeza de Vaca and his companions traveled inland across modern Texas, finding bison and minerals along the way. Their journey was eased by the fact that the Natives believed they had curing powers. After reaching the Pamoranes Mountains, they moved northwest to the San Lorenzo River, continued up the Oriental Sierra Madre, and finally arrived at the conjuncture of the Grande and Conchos Rivers. By late autumn they changed to a southwest direction, and in early 1536 they went down the Yaqui and Chico Rivers into Mexico, where they received news about other Spaniards in the area. Moving south, they met the Spaniards at the Petatlan River by late April and arrived in Culiacán in May.

Back in Spain, Cabeza de Vaca published an account of his journey entitled *Relacion* (1542). His explorations contributed to the mapping of the greater Southwest and northern Mexico, and his descriptions of southwestern Indian civilizations motivated the expeditions of Marcos de Niza (1539) and Francisco Vázquez de Coronado (1540–1542).

La Relacion. The cover of Álvar Núñez Cabeza de Vaca's 1542 account of his extraordinary travels across what is now the southern United States. ARTE PZBLICO PRESS

BIBLIOGRAPHY

Adorno, Rolena, and Patrick Charles Pautz. *Alvar Núñez Cabeza de Vaca: His Account, His Life, and the Expedition of Pánfilo de Narváez.* 3 vols. Lincoln: University of Nebraska, 1999.

Hallenbeck, Cleve. *Álvar Núñez Cabeza de Vaca: The Journey and Route of the First European to Cross the Continent of North America, 1534–1536.* Glendale, Calif.: Clark, 1940.

Hickerson, Nancy Parrott. *The Jumanos: Hunters and Traders of the South Plains.* Austin: University of Texas Press, 1994.

Hoffman, Paul E. "Narváez and Cabeza de Vaca in Florida." In *The Forgotten Centuries: Indians and Europeans in the American South, 1521–1704.* Edited by Charles Hudson and Carmen Chaves Tesser. Athens: University of Georgia Press, 1994, 50–73.

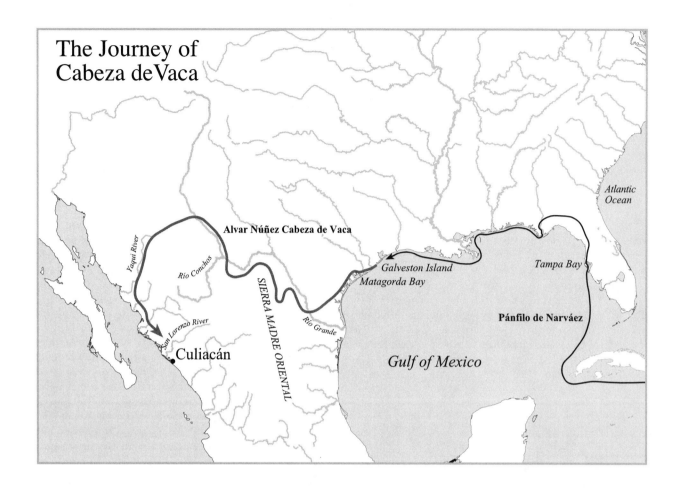

The Journey of Cabeza de Vaca

Atlantic Ocean

Yaqui River

Río Conchos

Alvar Núñez Cabeza de Vaca

SIERRA MADRE ORIENTAL

San Lorenzo River

Río Grande

Culiacán

Galveston Island
Matagorda Bay

Tampa Bay

Pánfilo de Narváez

Gulf of Mexico

Reinhartz, Dennis, and Gerald D. Saxon, eds. *The Mapping of the Entradas into the Greater Southwest.* Norman: University of Oklahoma Press, 1998.

Grover Antonio Espinoza

See also **Coronado Expeditions; Explorations and Expeditions: Spanish.**

CABINET. This body, which has existed since the presidency of George Washington, rests on the authority of custom rather than the Constitution or statute. During Washington's presidency the cabinet consisted of only four positions: secretary of state, secretary of the treasury, secretary of war, and attorney general. The size of the cabinet has grown steadily since. By the early 2000s, it was composed of the heads of the major federal administrative departments: STATE, TREASURY, DEFENSE, JUSTICE, INTERIOR, AGRICULTURE, COMMERCE, LABOR, HEALTH AND HUMAN SERVICES, HOUSING AND URBAN DEVELOPMENT, TRANSPORTATION, VETERANS AFFAIRS, and EDUCATION. In terms of money spent, number of persons employed, and scope of legal authority, these are the most significant units of the administration. The heads of these departments are presidential appointees, subject to CONFIRMATION BY THE SENATE and serving at the choice of the president.

Although all presidents have, periodically, held formal cabinet meetings, the role of the cabinet in presidential decision making has generally been limited. The importance of the cabinet varies depending on the particular president (for example, Dwight D. Eisenhower and Lyndon B. Johnson relied on the cabinet more than Franklin D. Roosevelt or John F. Kennedy did), but as a collective body it does not play a central role in any administration. Frequently cabinet meetings are largely symbolic; they are held because of the expectation that such meetings take place. The cabinet collectively may lack significance, but individual members can have great influence in an administration because of their expertise, political skill, or special relationship to the president. Examples of this kind of influence were noted with the service of John Mitchell as attorney general under Richard M. Nixon; Secretary of Defense Robert McNamara under Kennedy and Johnson; Attorney General Robert Kennedy under Kennedy; and Secretary of State James Baker under George H. W. Bush.

Frequently and increasingly, the expanding White House staff (personal assistants to the president) has overshadowed cabinet members. Also of considerable importance in any administration are informal advisers to and confidants of the president. In no area have cabinet members found their influence with the president more severely challenged than in the realm of foreign affairs. In particular, the post of national security adviser, a non-cabinet position, has consistently generated conflict and rivalry with the secretary of state. Although the secretary of state technically holds a higher-ranking position, the national security adviser typically enjoys comparable access to the president, and in some cases even greater access, as during the administrations of Kennedy and Nixon. Similar rivalries continue to characterize the cabinet's relationship with the ever-expanding White House staff.

The cabinet in the United States, unlike that in most parliamentary systems, does not function as a collegial executive; the president clearly is the chief executive. Cabinet members in the course of their work find that their survival and success generally do not depend on their colleagues or on any sense of collegiality; rather, they must often fend for themselves. Particularly crucial are their own relationships to the president, the clientele of their agency, the Congress, and the national media. Also in contrast to parliamentary systems, U.S. cabinet members may not serve concurrently in the legislative body. If a person is a member of Congress when appointed to the cabinet, that person must resign the congressional seat.

BIBLIOGRAPHY

Fenno, Richard F. *The President's Cabinet: An Analysis in the Period from Wilson to Eisenhower.* Cambridge, Mass.: Harvard University Press, 1959.

Neustadt, Richard E. *Presidential Power and the Modern Presidents: The Politics of Leadership from Roosevelt to Reagan.* New York: Maxwell Macmillan, 1990.

Dale Vinyard/A. G.

See also **Council of National Defense; Environmental Protection Agency; Federal Agencies; National Security Council; President, U.S.**

CABLE NEWS NETWORK. *See* **Television.**

CABLES, ATLANTIC AND PACIFIC. Telegraphy had barely been established on land in the mid-1840s when thoughts turned to bridging the Atlantic Ocean. The development of large ocean-going steamships and the plastic material gutta-percha, for insulating copper wires, made the idea feasible. When cables were successfully laid across the English Channel and the Mediterranean in the 1850s, investors grew optimistic about the chances for more ambitious ventures.

British interests dominated the early cable projects. The American paper wholesaler Cyrus Field financed a line up to and across Newfoundland, but the money and expertise for the ocean route were to be found among London, Liverpool, and Manchester merchants. The British and American governments supplied guaranteed subsidies for a working cable as well as ships for the laying operations. After an unsuccessful attempt the year before, in 1858 British and American steamships met at midocean to try again. The line broke three times—each time requiring a new start—before, on August 5, a single-wire connection was made between Valencia, Ireland, and Trinity Bay, Newfoundland. The event was greeted with great excitement; during the celebration, fireworks lit atop New York city hall sparked a blaze that destroyed most of the building's roof. Unfortunately, attempts to use high-voltage pulses aggravated flaws in the cable, and it failed entirely by October 20.

The Civil War emphasized the need for rapid transoceanic communications. In 1865 the entire length of a transatlantic cable was loaded on board the *Great Eastern*. It broke two-thirds of the way across. On 27 August 1866, a renewed attempt was successful; the 1865 cable was then picked up and completed. Another cable was laid in 1869.

In 1884 the mining mogul John W. Mackay and James Gordon Bennett of the *New York Herald* laid the first two American-sponsored cables. Many others followed. New techniques were developed to clarify the blurred signal that came through these 2,000-mile spans. Two systems emerged, one developed by the Eastern Company (British) with its long chains of cables to the Far East, the other by Western Union (American) with its dominance—in the twentieth century—of the high-density North Atlantic routes. The first (British) Pacific cable was not laid until 1902; it ran from Vancouver to Australia and New Zealand. In 1903 the first link of an American Pacific cable (promoted by Mackay) was completed between San Francisco and Hawaii; it was extended to Guam and the Philippines. In 1956 procedures were finally perfected for submerging repeaters, or amplifiers, with the cable; this greatly increased the information capabilities, making telephone transmission possible. American companies, especially the American Telephone and Telegraph Company, led cable advances in the twentieth century.

Submarine cables proved immeasurably important politically and commercially. Their effect was often psychological, reducing U.S. separation from the rest of the world from weeks to seconds. They also were valuable in wartime; during World War I, German U-boats attempted (unsuccessfully) to knock out the cable link between Washington and London by sinking explosive charges on the western terminus of the cable just off Cape Cod, Massachusetts. Despite the rise of radio, satellite, and wireless telephones, transoceanic cables, using fiber-optic technology, remained crucial links into the twenty-first century.

BIBLIOGRAPHY

Coates, Vary T., and Bernard Finn. *A Retrospective Technology Assessment: Submarine Telegraphy: The Transatlantic Cable of 1866.* San Francisco: San Francisco Press, 1979.

Dibner, Bern. *The Atlantic Cable.* New York: Blaisdell, 1964.

The Eighth Wonder of the World. Kimmel and Forster's 1866 lithograph allegorically celebrates the first successful transatlantic cable, linking the British lion and the American eagle. Cyrus Field is depicted at top center. Library of Congress

Finn, Bernard S. *Submarine Telegraphy: The Grand Victorian Technology.* London: Science Museum, 1973.

Bernard S. Finn / a. r.

See also **AT&T; Electronics; Intelligence, Military and Strategic; Radio; Telegraph; Western Union Telegraph Company.**

CABOT VOYAGES. Early in 1496 a petition was placed before King Henry VII of England in the name of John Cabot, an Italian navigator, and his three sons, Sebastian, Lewis, and Sanctius, for the privilege of making explorations in the New World. The king granted letters patent, dated 5 March 1496, to the Cabots. In the spring of 1497 they sailed west from Bristol, England, setting a southward course on a single ship, the *Mathew*, with a crew of only eighteen. They discovered, it is believed, the present-day Canadian provinces of Newfoundland and Nova Scotia, although the exact location of landing is a matter of much controversy. After a month of exploration, during which time the elder Cabot staked England's claim to the land, the *Mathew* and crew set sail for home, reaching Bristol in early August.

John Cabot received a pension of twenty pounds per year as a reward, and the following year he received letters patent authorizing him to make further explorations along the eastern coast of North America. The discoveries made on this voyage were supposedly recorded on a map and globe made by the explorer. Both are now lost.

Because there is no firsthand data concerning the Cabot voyages, Sebastian Cabot has often been confused

4

Sebastian Cabot. A late portrait of the explorer. LIBRARY OF CONGRESS

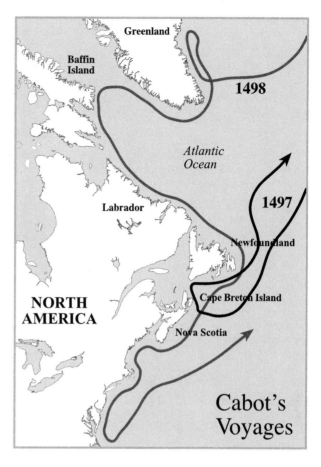

Cabot's Voyages

with his father, John. The Cabots made important contributions to the geographical knowledge of North America, although the descriptions of the regions they explored apply to no portion of the United States.

BIBLIOGRAPHY

Maestro, Betsy, and Giulio Maestro. *The Discovery of the Americas*. New York: Lothrop, Lee and Shepard, 1991.

Williamson, James A. *The Cabot Voyages and Bristol Discovery under Henry VII*. Cambridge: Cambridge University Press, 1962.

Lloyd A. Brown / Shelby Balik

See also **Exploration of America, Early; Explorations and Expeditions, British; Northwest Passage.**

CADDO. The Caddo cultural pattern developed among groups occupying conjoining parts of Arkansas, Louisiana, Oklahoma, and Texas from A.D. 700 to 1000. These groups practiced agriculture, hunting, and trading and lived in dispersed family farmsteads associated with regional temple mound centers. Their elite leadership institutions and an emblematic material culture distinguished these groups. Caddos were first contacted by members of Hernando de Soto's expedition in 1542, when their population may have included as many as 200,000 people. Sub-

sequent accounts portray a well-organized society, one that traced ancestry through the mother's line, that filled leadership positions by male inheritance, that had a calendar of ceremonies associated with important social and economic activities, and that had widely extending alliances. Access to European goods stimulated production of commodities for colonial markets, and Caddo leaders played important roles in colonial diplomacy. By the nineteenth century, European diseases had reduced the Caddo population to about 500 individuals, and families had been removed to reservations in Texas and Oklahoma. In this region, the Caddo preserved key social, political, and religious institutions, despite their diminishing circumstances. In 2002, about 4,000 people represented the Caddo Nation of Oklahoma, where at a tribal complex near Binger, a variety of health, education, economic development, social service, and cultural programs were maintained.

BIBLIOGRAPHY

Carter, Cecile Elkins. *Caddo Indians: Where We Come From*. Norman: University of Oklahoma Press, 1995.

LaVere, David. *Caddo Chiefdoms: Caddo Economics and Politics, 800–1835*. Lincoln: University of Nebraska, 1998.

Newkumet, Vynola B., and Howard L. Meredith. *Hasinai: A Traditional History of the Caddo Confederacy*. College Station: Texas A&M University Press, 1988.

Perttula, Timothy K. *The Caddo Nation: Archaeological and Ethno-historic Perspectives.* Austin: University of Texas Press, 1992.

Smith, F. T. *The Caddo Indians: Tribes at the Convergence of Empires, 1542–1854.* College Station: Texas A&M University Press, 1995.

———. *The Caddos, the Wichitas, and the United States, 1846–1901.* College Station: Texas A&M University Press, 1996.

George Sabo III

See also **Tribes: Southeastern, Southwestern.**

CAHOKIA MOUNDS. This prehistoric settlement on the alluvial plain of the Mississippi River valley about four miles northeast of present-day East Saint Louis is the largest archaeological site north of central Mexico. Excavations at Cahokia began in the mid-twentieth century as salvage operations preceding construction of a highway. Major archaeological investigations were initiated in 1984 by the Illinois Historic Preservation Agency and its chief archaeologist for the site, Thomas Emerson. A focus of development of the Mississippian culture in the Midwest between A.D. 700 and 1350, Cahokia's population, estimated at between 10,000 and 25,000, probably peaked from A.D. 1000 to 1100. The site, covering six square miles and featuring at least 120 mounds (some ceremonial, some burial), was carefully laid out with horizontal compass orientations in mind. The ceremonial Monks Mound, the largest platform mound north of Mexico, towers about 98 feet high, with a base of about 984 feet by 656 feet. Many conical burial mounds have been excavated, showing clear signs of social stratification in the form of elaborate grave goods, sometimes imported from great distances. In one mound, a high-status male was buried on a platform of 20,000 cut shell beads.

While Cahokia was surrounded by an enormous log palisade 13 to 16 feet high and perhaps 2.4 miles in length, its decline does not seem to have resulted from outside

Cahokia Mound. A 1907 photograph of one of the numerous ceremonial and burial mounds at this prehistoric settlement in present-day southwestern Illinois. LIBRARY OF CONGRESS

attack. Nor does any evidence exist to suggest that Cahokia engaged in wars of conquest. A chiefdom (lacking a standing army or police force) rather than a state, Cahokia may have declined for simple environmental reasons. While the maize agriculture introduced into the area around A.D. 750 sparked the rapid growth of the community and supported a relatively large population, it did not provide a balanced diet to the average Cahokian. Soil erosion may have also cut into productivity over time. Further, the enormous palisade required perhaps 20,000 large trees, which were replaced several times during Cahokia's heyday. This huge structure, plus the daily firewood needs of the Cahokians, put considerable strain on local woodlands. In addition, satellite communities arose, increasing the general area's population and placing still more demands on the local environment. Gradually, over perhaps fifty to seventy-five years, the population may have simply overwhelmed local resources. The anthropologist Timothy Pauketat of the University of Illinois, however, argues that political and religious failures by Cahokia's leaders were the primary reasons for the population's dispersal. For whatever reason, by 1350 Cahokia was abandoned.

BIBLIOGRAPHY

Fowler, Melvin L. *The Cahokia Atlas: A Historical Atlas of Cahokia Archaeology.* Springfield: Illinois Historic Preservation Agency, 1989.

Mehrer, Mark W. *Cahokia's Countryside: Household Archaeology, Settlement Patterns, and Social Power.* DeKalb: Northern Illinois University Press, 1995.

Young, Biloine Whiting, and Melvin L. Fowler. *Cahokia: The Great Native American Metropolis.* Urbana: University of Illinois Press, 2000.

Guy Gibbon
Robert M. Owens

See also **Indian Mounds.**

CAHUENGA, TREATY OF. *See* **Mexican-American War.**

CAIRO CONFERENCES. On their way to the Teheran Conference, President Franklin D. Roosevelt and Prime Minister Winston Churchill met with Generalissimo Chiang Kai-shek at Cairo in November 1943 to discuss the war against Japan. During the meeting at Cairo, Roosevelt hoped to provide symbolic—rather than additional material—support to Chiang's embattled regime. In contrast, Chiang hoped to use the conference as a forum to persuade Roosevelt to devote more Allied resources to the fighting on the Asian mainland, particularly in China and Burma. The three conferees issued a declaration of intent: to take from Japan all of the Pacific islands occupied by it since 1914; to restore to China all territory seized by Japan, such as Manchuria, Formosa, and the Pescadores Islands; and to give Korea its independence "in due course." Despite the broad statement of war aims, however, the main focus of the Allied military effort against Japan remained the islands of the Central and South Pacific, rather than the expulsion of Japanese forces from China.

Returning from Teheran, Roosevelt and Churchill met in December with President Ismet Inönü of Turkey at the second Cairo Conference and unsuccessfully attempted to persuade him to declare war on the Axis powers.

BIBLIOGRAPHY

Dallek, Robert. *Franklin D. Roosevelt and American Foreign Policy, 1932–1945.* New York: Oxford University Press, 1979.

Smith, Gaddis. *American Diplomacy During the Second World War, 1941–1945.* New York: Wiley, 1965.

Charles S. Campbell/A. G.

See also **Japan, Relations with; Teheran Conference.**

CAJUNS. *See* **Acadia.**

CALDER V. BULL, 3 U.S. 386 (1798). The Connecticut legislature, which also served as the state's highest appellate court, set aside a probate court decision involving a will and ordered a new trial, which upheld the will and awarded the property in question to the Bulls. The Calders, who had initially been awarded the property, claimed this amounted to an ex post facto law, which was prohibited by the U.S. Constitution. The Supreme Court held that an ex post facto law could only apply to laws that retroactively criminalized previously legal behavior, not to a case involving property or in a civil matter. Although agreeing on the outcome, Justices Samuel Chase and James Iredell set out quite different views of the role of the judiciary and of the basis for judicial review.

Chase argued that legislative acts were limited by the "great first principles of the social compact," and that an act that violated these principles "cannot be considered a rightful exercise of legislative authority." Chase implied that courts might overturn legislative decisions that violated basic republican principles. For example, the Court could overturn a state law "that takes property from A, and gives it to B." Having set out these examples, Chase found that this act of the Connecticut legislature did not in fact violate these principles.

Iredell, however, argued that the courts could not declare a statute "void, merely because it is . . . contrary to the principles of natural justice." Rather, Iredell argued for a strict textual reading of the Constitution that would give judges little latitude in deciding cases and prevent them from overturning acts of the legislature because they denied fundamental rights or violated natural law.

Paul Finkelman

See also **Judicial Review.**

CALIFORNIA, whose name derives from a fifteenth-century Spanish romance, lies along the Pacific Coast of the United States. Formidable natural barriers, including the Sierra Nevada and the Cascade Mountains to the east and the north and the Sonoran Desert to the south and southeast, isolate it from the rest of the continent. Streams plunging down from the mountains form the Sacramento and San Joaquin Rivers in the Great Central Valley, while coastal ranges divide the littoral into isolated plains, valleys, and marine terraces. The state contains a wide variety of ecologies, from alpine meadows to deserts, often within a few miles of each other. San Francisco Bay, near the center of the state, is the finest natural harbor in the eastern Pacific.

The first known people came to California thousands of years ago, filtering down from the north in small bands. In the varied geography, especially the many valleys tucked into the creases of the coastal mountains, these early immigrants evolved a mosaic of cultures, like the Chumash of the southern coast, with their oceangoing canoes and sophisticated trading network, and the Pomo, north of San Francisco Bay, who made the beads widely used as money throughout the larger community.

Spanish California

Spain claimed California as part of Columbus's discovery, but the extraordinary hardships of the first few voyages along the coast discouraged further exploration until Vitus Bering sailed into the northern Pacific in 1741 to chart the region for the czar of Russia. Alarmed, the viceroy in Mexico City authorized a systematic attempt to establish control of California. In 1769, a band of Franciscan monks under Fray Junipero Serra and a hundred-odd soldiers commanded by Gaspar de Portola traveled up the peninsula of Baja California to San Diego with two hundred cattle. From there de Portola explored north, found San Francisco Bay, and established the presidio at Monterey. Spanish California became a reality.

Spanish policy was to Christianize and civilize the Native peoples they found. To do this, Serra and his followers built a string of missions, like great semifeudal farms, all along what came to be called El Camino Real and forced the Indians into their confines. Ultimately, twenty-one missions stretched from San Diego to Sonoma. The missions failed in their purpose. Enslaved and stripped of their cultures, the Native people died by the thousands of disease, mistreatment, and despair. From an estimated 600,000 before the Spanish came, by 1846 their population dropped to around 300,000.

The soldiers who came north to guard the province had no place in the missions, and the friars thought them a bad influence anyway. Soldiers built the first town, San Jose, in 1777, and four years later, twenty-two families of mixed African, Indian, and Spanish blood founded the city of Los Angeles. The settlers, who called themselves Californios, planted orange trees and grapevines, and their cattle multiplied.

In 1821, Mexico declared its independence from Spain, dooming the mission system. By 1836, all the missions were secularized. The land was to be divided up among the Natives attached to the missions but instead fell into the hands of soldiers and adventurers. The new Mexican government also began granting large tracts of land for ranches. In 1830, California had fifty ranches, but by 1840 it had more than one thousand. Power gravitated inevitably to the landholders. Mexico City installed governors in Monterey, but the Californio dons rebelled against anybody who tried to control them.

When the Swiss settler Johann Sutter arrived in 1839, the government in Monterey, believing the land was worthless desert and hoping that Sutter would form a barrier between their holdings and greedy interlopers, gave him a huge grant of land in the Sacramento Valley. But in 1842, when a band of nineteen American immigrants came over the Sierras, Sutter welcomed them to his settlement and gave them land, tools, and encouragement. John Charles Frémont, a U.S. Army mapmaker, on his first trip to California also relied on Sutter's help. Frémont's book about his expedition fired intense interest in the United States, and within the next two years, hundreds of settlers crossed the Sierras into California. Many

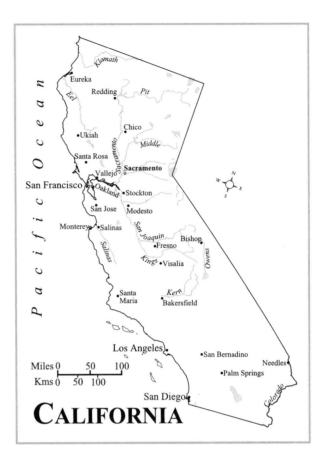

CALIFORNIA

more came by ship around Cape Horn. By 1846, Americans outnumbered the Californios in the north.

The U.S. government itself had long coveted California. In 1829, President Andrew Jackson tried to buy it. When Mexico indignantly declined, American interest turned toward taking it by force. The argument with Mexico over Texas gave the United States the chance. In May 1846, U.S. forces invaded Mexico. On 7 July 1846, Commodore John Drake Sloat of the U.S. Navy seized Monterey, and Frémont raised the American flag at Sonoma and Sacramento. The Spanish period was over; California had become part of the United States.

The Americans Take Over

Signed on 20 May 1848, the Treaty of Guadeloupe Hidalgo officially transferred the northern third of Mexico to the United States for $15 million. Because of the gold rush, California now had a population sufficient to become a state, but the U.S. Congress was unwilling even to consider admitting it to the Union for fear of upsetting the balance between slave and free states. In this limbo a series of military governors squabbled over jurisdictions. Mexican institutions like the alcalde, or chief city administrator, remained the basic civil authorities.

Yet the American settlers demanded a functioning government. The gold rush, which began in 1848 and

CALIFORNIA ALIEN LAND LAW.

Responding to the strong anti-Asian sentiments among voters, the California legislature passed the Alien Land Law of 1913. The act was amended and extended by popular initiative in 1920 and by the legislature in 1923 and 1927. Aimed at the largely rural Japanese population, the law, with a few exceptions, banned individual aliens who were not eligible for citizenship (under the Naturalization Act of 1870 this included all persons of Asian descent born outside of the United States), as well as corporations controlled by such aliens, from owning real property. Similar laws were passed in other western states. The law was repealed in 1956 by popular vote.

BIBLIOGRAPHY

Daniels, Roger. *The Politics of Prejudice: The Anti-Japanese Movement in California and the Struggle for Japanese Exclusion.* Berkeley: University of California Press, 1962.

Ichioka, Yuji. "Japanese Immigrant Response to the 1920 Alien Land Law." *Agricultural History* 58 (1984): 157–78.

Thomas J. Mertz
P. Orman Ray

CALIFORNIA HIGHER EDUCATIONAL SYSTEM

is the largest in the nation, with over 2.1 million students and 140 campuses. It has a tripartite structure, composed of the state's three postsecondary institutions: the University of California, California State University, and the California Community College system. Its fundamental goals are to provide affordable access to higher education for all California residents and maintain world-class research capability. Although it has weathered many storms over the years, including friction among the three institutions, explosive population growth, economic swings, and varying levels of support from governors and state legislatures, its mission and structure have remained essentially unchanged. It remains one of the most studied and admired higher education systems in the world.

The origins of the California higher educational system lie in the Progressive Era, roughly 1900–1920. California educational reformers and the state legislature envisioned a tiered, geographically dispersed postsecondary system within financial and physical reach of every Californian. By 1920, the tripartite system was in place, composed of the public institutions of higher education then in existence: the University of California, the state teachers colleges, and the state junior colleges, the first of their kind in the nation. The three institutions coordinated their programs and admissions policies to avoid duplication: the university offered bachelor's, doctoral, and professional degrees to the top 15 percent of high school graduates; the teachers colleges offered two-year teacher-training programs with admissions standards varying by campus; and the junior colleges offered two-year liberal arts and vocational programs to all California high school graduates as well as the option to transfer to the university as third-year undergraduates.

The division of academic programs never sat well among the three institutions, and the ever increasing demand for college degrees encouraged the teachers colleges and the junior colleges to agitate for expanded degree programs and additional campuses. The university opposed these moves, arguing that they would lower academic standards, and in turn made attempts to absorb some teachers college campuses. As state legislators championed the campuses in their home districts or sought to have new campuses built, pork barrel politics and internecine squabbling seemed to be taking over the higher education planning process.

The California higher education system has undergone periodic review, with each review commission building upon previous recommendations, always keeping in mind the goals of universal, affordable education and rational growth. All three higher education institutions saw their number of campuses increase and their programs expand. The state colleges in particular grew to include a bachelor's degree in several liberal arts disciplines and a master's degree in education. Ultimately, the state colleges were officially renamed California State University in 1982.

In 1960 the higher educational system underwent its most sweeping review to date, and the resulting report, known as the "California Master Plan for Higher Education," remains the blueprint for both operation and growth. The Master Plan is not a single document, but a collection of some sixty agreements between all parties in the system. Most importantly, many of the key recommendations of the plan were written into law in the Donohoe Act of 1960.

The overall purpose of the Master Plan is to coordinate expansion and prevent duplication and competition among the three higher education institutions, while maintaining universal, inexpensive access to postsecondary education for all Californians. It confirmed California's traditional policy of free tuition for state residents, with low fees for noninstructional services only. The Master Plan also codified the mission of each of the three institutions. The University of California would offer bachelor's, master's, doctoral, and professional degrees, engage in theoretical and applied research and public service, and admit the top 12.5 percent of California high school graduates. The California State campuses would offer bachelor's and master's degrees, admit the top 33 percent of California students, and engage in applied research in its program areas and public service. The community colleges (formerly known as junior colleges) would offer an associate degree as preparation for a higher degree, as well as vocational and adult programs, and would be open to all California high school graduates.

The policies delineated in the Master Plan faced their biggest test in the austere economic environment of the 1990s. Budget shortfalls made painful inroads into both universal access and reasonable cost. The state has set enrollment caps at the community colleges, and the University of California campuses have reached capacity or are overenrolled. Although tuition remains free, fees for noneducational services have soared, challenging the notion of "reasonable cost." Hard choices are being debated, such as tightening residency requirements, giving enrollment priority to younger students, and penalizing undergraduates who take longer than four years to complete a bachelor's degree.

In 1999 California determined that a new Master Plan was needed that would address tightened economic conditions as well as the needs of an ethnically and linguistically diverse student body. In May 2002 the draft for a twenty-first-century Master Plan was released that built upon the existing plan, expanding it to include kindergarten through postsecondary education. Implementation of the new plan is expected in 2003.

BIBLIOGRAPHY

Douglass, John Aubrey. *The California Idea and American Education: 1850 to the 1960 Master Plan.* Stanford, Calif.: Stanford University Press, 2000.

Joint Committee to Develop a Master Plan for Education—Kindergarten Through University. *Framework to Develop a Master Plan for Education.* Available at http://www.sen.ca.gov/masterplan/framework.htm.

University of California History Digital Archives. *The History of the California Master Plan for Higher Education.* Available at http://sunsite.berkeley.edu/uchistory/archives_exhibits/masterplan/.

Nadine Cohen Baker

See also **Education, Higher: Colleges and Universities.**

CALIFORNIA INSTITUTE OF TECHNOLOGY.

In 1891, Amos Gager Throop, a self-made businessman and philanthropist, founded a small coeducational college in Pasadena that became one of the world's leading scientific institutions. Initially named Throop University, the school changed its name to Throop Polytechnic Institute in 1893. Throop was the first school west of Chicago to offer manual arts, teaching students of all ages—as its mandate proclaimed—"those things that train the hand and the brain for the best work of life." In 1907, the astronomer George Ellery Hale, the first director of

Mount Wilson Observatory, joined Throop's board that year and played a key role in the school's transformation. Hale, a visionary brimming with educational and civic ideas, set about rebuilding Throop. He persuaded its officers to abandon their secondary-school program and concentrate on developing the college along engineering school lines. He hired James A. B. Scherer, Throop's president from 1908 to 1920, and brought Arthur A. Noyes, former president of the Massachusetts Institute of Technology and the nation's leading physical chemist, to the campus part-time as professor of general chemistry. In hiring Noyes (once his own chemistry professor), Hale hoped both to bring chemistry at Throop College of Technology—as it was called after 1913—up to the level of that at the Massachusetts Institute of Technology and to raise Throop to national prominence.

The third member of this scientific troika was Robert A. Millikan, a renowned experimental physicist at the University of Chicago who in 1917 began spending several months a year at Throop, now an all-male school. Together in Washington, D.C., during World War I, the three recruited scientists to work on military problems, founded the National Research Council (NRC), and built an impressive network of contacts that would serve the school well. As first chairman of the NRC, Hale not only promoted the role of science in national affairs but also increased Throop's role in American science. He put Noyes in charge of the nitrate supply committee and asked Millikan to oversee the NRC's work in physics. Millikan proved an astute administrator, and his influence on American science grew in the postwar decades. Collectively ambitious for American science and determined to put Throop on the map, Hale, Millikan, and Noyes were a formidable scientific triumvirate and by Armistice Day were ready to transform the engineering school into an institution that emphasized pure science.

In 1919, Noyes resigned from MIT and accepted full-time appointment as Throop's director of chemical research. Throop changed its name to the California Institute of Technology (Caltech) the following year, and trustee Arthur Fleming turned over the bulk of his fortune—more than $4 million—to the institute in a successful bid to lure Millikan permanently to Pasadena. As director of the Norman Bridge Physics Laboratory and Caltech's administrative head, Millikan guided the school for the next twenty-five years, establishing the undergraduate requirement of two years of physics, two years of mathematics, and one of chemistry (a curriculum that remains virtually unchanged, with the signal exception of a required term of biology). He also put physics on the map in southern California. Albert Einstein's visits to the campus in 1931, 1932, and 1933 capped Millikan's campaign to make Caltech one of the physics capitals of the world.

Caltech in the early 1920s was essentially an undergraduate and graduate school in the physical sciences. Until 1925 it conferred doctorates only in physics, chemistry, and engineering. Geology joined the list of graduate studies in 1925, aeronautics in 1926, and biology and mathematics in 1928. In the 1930s, the work of Charles Richter in seismology, Theodore von Kármán in aeronautics, Linus Pauling in chemistry, and Thomas Hunt Morgan in biology spearheaded scientific research at the institute. Fiercely opposed to government funding of research, Millikan dealt directly with the heads of the Carnegie, Guggenheim, and Rockefeller Foundations and coaxed funds from a growing number of local millionaires.

In 1946, Lee A. DuBridge, head of MIT's wartime radar project, became Caltech's new president. Robert Bacher, a mainstay of the Manhattan Project, headed the physics division and later became the institute's first provost. Other distinguished scientists who joined the postwar faculty included theoretical physicists Richard Feynman and Murray Gell-Mann, astronomer Jesse Greenstein, psychobiologist Roger Sperry, and geochemist Clair Patterson. During DuBridge's tenure (1946–1969), Caltech's faculty doubled, the campus tripled in size, and new research fields flourished, including chemical biology, planetary science, nuclear astrophysics, and geochemistry. A 200-inch telescope was dedicated on nearby Palomar Mountain in 1948 and remained the world's most powerful optical telescope for over forty years. DuBridge, unlike Millikan, welcomed federal funding of science—and got it. Female students returned to the campus as graduate students in the 1950s, and in 1970, during the presidency of Harold Brown, as undergraduates.

BIBLIOGRAPHY

Florence, Ronald. *The Perfect Machine: Building the Palomar Telescope.* New York: HarperCollins, 1994.

Goodstein, Judith R. *Millikan's School: A History of the California Institute of Technology.* New York: Norton, 1991.

Kevles, Daniel J. *The Physicists: The History of a Scientific Community in Modern America.* New York: Knopf, 1978. Reprint, with a new preface, Cambridge, Mass: Harvard University Press, 1995.

Judith R. Goodstein

See also **California Higher Educational System; Education, Higher: Colleges and Universities; Engineering Education; Massachusetts Institute of Technology; Science Education.**

CALIFORNIA TRAIL was the name given to several routes used by settlers traveling to California in the nineteenth century. Several immigrant parties, setting out from towns along the Missouri River, attempted to reach California in the 1840s, after branching south off the Oregon Trail. Some of the early immigrant routes followed the Humboldt River, while the Stephens-Murphy party crossed the Sierra westward to the Truckee River. By 1846 the United States had acquired California in the war with Mexico, and large numbers of wagon trains en-

tered the territory, the most famous being the ill-fated DONNER PARTY.

BIBLIOGRAPHY

Morgan, Dale. *Overland in 1846: Diaries and Letters of the California-Oregon Trail.* Lincoln: University of Nebraska Press, 1993. The original edition was published in 1963.

Stewart, George Rippey. *The California Trail: An Epic with Many Heroes.* New York: McGraw-Hill, 1962.

Lansing B. Bloom / h. s.

See also **Oregon Trail; Overland Trail; Westward Migration.**

CALVINISM, in its broadest sense, is the entire body of conceptions arising from the teachings of John Calvin. Its fundamental principle is the conception of God as absolutely sovereign. More than other branches of Protestantism, Calvinism emphasizes the doctrine of predestination, the idea that God has already determined whom to save and damn and that nothing can change his decision. The 1618–1619 Synod of Dort produced five canons that defined Calvinist orthodoxy: total depravity, the belief that original sin renders humans incapable of achieving salvation without God's grace; unconditional election, that the saved do not become so as a result of their own virtuous behavior but rather because God has selected them; limited atonement, that Christ died only to redeem those whom God has already chosen for salvation; irresistible grace, that individuals predestined for salvation cannot reject God's grace; and perseverance of the saints, that those whom God has chosen for salvation cannot lose that grace. The statement of Calvinism most influential in the United States was the Westminster Confession of 1647. New England Congregationalists accepted its doctrinal portion and embodied it in their Cambridge Platform of 1648. American Presbyterians coming from Scotland and Northern Ireland were sternly Calvinistic. The Synod of Philadelphia, the oldest general Presbyterian body in the United States, passed the Adopting Act in 1729, which required all ministers and licentiates to subscribe to the Westminster Confession. Other Calvinistic bodies in the United States are the Dutch and German Reformed churches and all Presbyterian bodies.

BIBLIOGRAPHY

Cashdollar, Charles D. *A Spiritual Home: Life in British and American Reformed Congregations, 1830–1915.* University Park: Pennsylvania State University Press, 2000.

Hirrel, Leo P. *Children of Wrath: New School Calvinism and Antebellum Reform.* Lexington: University Press of Kentucky, 1998.

Howard, Victor B. *Conscience and Slavery: The Evangelistic Calvinist Domestic Missions, 1837–1861.* Kent, Ohio: Kent State University Press, 1990.

Pahl, Jon. *Paradox Lost: Free Will and Political Liberty in American Culture, 1630–1760.* Baltimore: Johns Hopkins University Press, 1992.

William W. Sweet/A. E.

See also **Baptist Churches; Cambridge Platform; Congregationalism; Presbyterianism; Puritans and Puritanism; Reformed Churches; Religion and Religious Affiliation.**

CAMBODIA, BOMBING OF. As part of the American involvement in the VIETNAM WAR, the U.S. military began secret bombing operations, code-named Operation Menu, in Cambodia on 9 March 1969. Initially conducted by B-52 bomber planes, the operations aimed to reduce the threat to U.S. ground forces, which were being withdrawn as part of President Richard M. Nixon's program to end U.S. ground involvement. At the time of the decision to begin the B-52 strikes, American casualties were occurring at a rate of about 250 a week. The North Vietnamese had established stockpiles of arms and munitions in Cambodian sanctuaries, from which they launched attacks across the border into South Vietnam against American troops. After quick strikes, enemy forces returned to their sanctuaries to rearm and prepare for further action. The air strikes, in conjunction with other factors—such as the reduction of the overall vulnerability of American forces as they relinquished the major combat roles to South Vietnamese forces—cut the number of American ground casualties in half.

Limited tactical air operations in Cambodia began on 24 April 1970, preparatory to ground operations during the American-Vietnamese incursion. The purpose of these strictly controlled operations, made with the acquiescence of the government of Cambodia but without the consent of the U.S. Congress, was to destroy long-standing North Vietnamese base areas and supply depots near the Cambodian border and cause the North Vietnamese to further disperse their forces.

In the United States the bombing of Cambodia became a subject of contention. Although the Nixon administration intended to keep it a secret, journalists quickly broke the story. The bombings became a major object of protest within the antiwar movement, with some labeling the covert operations foolish and others declaring them illegal. A protest against the bombing of Cambodia at KENT STATE University on 4 May 1970 turned violent, resulting in the death of four students after a National Guard unit, brought in to quiet the protesters, fired into the crowd.

The bombings were devastating to Cambodia's civilian population and proved to be a major source of political instability as well. General Lon Nol's coup in 1970, shortly after the American raids began, displaced Prince Norodom Sihanouk and sent the country into a period of political turmoil. This ultimately resulted in the rise to power of leader Pol Pot and the Khmer Rouge, a communist political and military group, in 1975.

After the withdrawal of U.S. ground troops from Cambodia on 30 June 1970, tactical air and B-52 strikes continued at the request of the Cambodian government. These missions were approved by Federal Armée National Khmer representatives prior to execution. Air strikes continued, again at the request of the Cambodian government, until the Senate Armed Services Committee held hearings on the bombing operations. After determining that Nixon had improperly conducted such operations in a country that Congress officially recognized as neutral, Congress voted to terminate the bombing—after some thirty-five hundred raids—as of midnight, 14 August 1973. The bombing operations lasted four and one-half years, but they represented only about 1 percent of the total U.S. air activity in the Vietnam War.

BIBLIOGRAPHY

Goldstein, Donald M., Katherine V. Dillon, and J. Michael Wenger. *The Vietnam War: The Story and Photographs.* Washington, D.C.: Brassey's, 1997.

Matusow, Allen J. *The Unravelling of America: A History of Liberalism in the 1960s.* New York: Harper and Row, 1984.

Michon, Michel M. *Indochina Memoir: Rubber, Politics, and War in Vietnam and Cambodia, 1955–1972.* Tempe: Arizona State University Program for Southeast Asian Studies, Monograph Series Press, 2000.

Philip D. Caine
Christopher Wells

See also **Air Power, Strategic; Antiwar Movements; Bombing; Vietnamization; War Powers Act.**

Cambodia. In this 1974 photograph by Françoise de Mulder, children in Phnom Penh, the country's capital, collect water from a bomb crater. © CORBIS

CAMBODIA INCURSION. On 18 March 1970, Cambodian General Lon Nol seized power from Prince Norodom Sihanouk while the royal leader was in Mos-

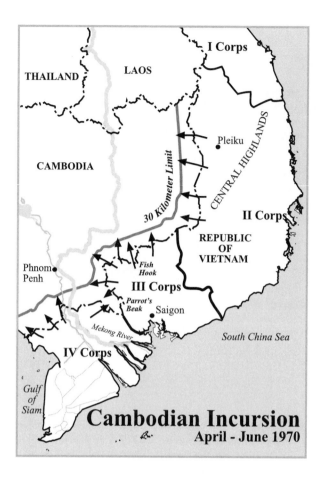

Cambodian Incursion
April - June 1970

while American troops would enter the "Fish Hook" area to the north. The United States hoped to destroy significant quantities of enemy supplies and locate the elusive enemy headquarters known as the Central Office for South Vietnam (COSVN).

The invasion began on 29 April, when three ARVN (Army of the Republic of Vietnam) columns of armor and infantry, totaling 8,700 men, crossed into the Parrot's Beak in Operation Toàn Thang (Total Victory) 42. On 12 May, 15,000 Americans and South Vietnamese invaded the Fish Hook region in Operation Rockcrusher/Toàn Thang 43. Subsequent operations were called Bold Lancer/Toàn Thang 44 and Tame the West/Binh Tay. The major enemy units opposing the allied forces included the Seventh Division of the People's Army of Vietnam and the Fifth Vietcong Division.

After a few sharp engagements, the enemy withdrew deeper into Cambodia. The allies captured large stores of equipment, including enough individual weapons to outfit seventy-four North Vietnamese army battalions and enough small-arms ammunition to supply the enemy's war effort for one entire year. Allied forces claimed 11,349 enemy killed in action and recorded 2,328 enemy captured or rallied. Allied losses came to 976 dead (338 Americans) and 4,534 (1,525 Americans) wounded. The last American ground forces pulled out of Cambodia on 30 June. The allied forces failed to locate the COSVN headquarters, which at that time was operating from the Central Highlands of South Vietnam. Despite losing substantial amounts of food and equipment, the enemy gradually replenished their base areas. The United States participation in the invasion of Cambodia re-energized the antiwar movement, stiffened congressional opposition to Nixon's White House, and widened the breech of trust between the media and the military.

BIBLIOGRAPHY

Nolan, Keith William. *Into Cambodia: Spring Campaign, Summer Offensive, 1970.* San Francisco: Presidio Press, 1990.

Shawcross, William. *Sideshow: Kissinger, Nixon, and the Destruction of Cambodia.* New York: Simon and Schuster, 1979.

Sorley, Lewis. *A Better War: The Unexamined Victories and Final Tragedy of America's Last Years in Vietnam.* New York: Harcourt Brace, 1999.

Erik B. Villard

See also **Vietnam War.**

cow. Unlike his predecessor, Lon Nol refused to tolerate the presence of tens of thousands of Vietnamese communists in the eastern part of Cambodia, where they maintained numerous base areas to support their war in South Vietnam. In addition, the communists received most of their supplies through the port of Sihanoukville. North Vietnam refused to acknowledge that it had any troops in Cambodia. The United States was reluctant to attack the bases with conventional ground forces, because invading an officially neutral country would incur serious diplomatic and domestic political risks. Determined to enforce his country's neutrality, Lon Nol tried to block the communists from using Sihanoukville and demanded that their troops leave his country. With their supply system threatened, the Vietnamese communist forces in Cambodia launched an offensive against Lon Nol's government. As the Cambodian forces faltered, the United States decided to mount a limited incursion to save Lon Nol's government. Destroying the communist base areas on the Cambodian border would also inhibit enemy operations in South Vietnam.

On 26 April, President Richard Nixon gave his approval for a multidivision offensive into Cambodia. He limited the incursion to 30 kilometers and imposed for U.S. troops a withdrawal deadline of 30 June. South Vietnamese troops would invade the "Parrot's Beak" region, a strip of land jutting from Cambodia toward Saigon,

CAMBRIDGE, a town in the Massachusetts Bay Colony originally known as Newtowne, was settled in 1630 by a group of seven hundred Puritans from England who were determined to create a pure religious foundation in the New World. Originally governed by John Winthrop, who abandoned the town for Boston, Newtowne was a well-organized town, with a system of streets laid out in a grid pattern, including a marketplace, Winthrop Square.

Harvard College. An early-eighteenth-century depiction of the oldest American college, founded in 1636. © CORBIS

At the beginning of the twenty-first century the town was bounded by Eliot Square, Linden Street, Massachusetts Avenue, and the Charles River. In 1636, Harvard College was founded to educate young men in the ministry. By the time of the American Revolution, Cambridge had become a farming community, but after the fighting began on 19 April 1775, more than twenty thousand armed militia members from New England arrived in Cambridge. Soldiers, including George Washington's army, camped on the Cambridge Commons and were quartered in the Harvard College buildings until April 1776.

In 1846, Cambridge became a city, unifying three towns: rural Old Cambridge; residential Cambridgeport, home to William Lloyd Garrison; and East Cambridge, developed in 1809 after the completion of the Canal Bridge. This town would be the chief industrial center of the city until the 1880s. The growth of urban housing and the influx of eastern European and Irish immigrants, as well as the construction of the East Cambridge jail, led to an impetus for prison reform, with Dorothea Dix at the forefront of this movement. Cambridge has always been an innovator, including the integration of its school system, which enticed many African Americans to move there. Harriet Jacobs, author of *Incidents in the Life of a Slave Girl*, ran a boardinghouse in the 1870s in Cambridge.

Twenty-first-century Cambridge has retained its charm and maintains a culturally diverse population of approximately ninety-five thousand. Home to Harvard, Radcliffe, Massachusetts Institute of Technology, and Lesley College, Cambridge attracts students from all over the world and has become a center for biotechnology and software research.

BIBLIOGRAPHY

Burton, John Daniel. *Puritan Town and Gown: Harvard College and Cambridge, Massachusetts, 1636–1800.* Ph.D. diss. Williamsburg, Va.: College of William and Mary, 1996.

———. "The Awful Judgements of God upon the Land: Smallpox in Colonial Cambridge." *New England Quarterly* 74 (September 2001): 495–507.

Paige, Lucius R. *History of Cambridge, Massachusetts, 1630–1877.* Boston: Houghton, 1877. Rev. ed. 1930.

Jennifer Harrison

See also **Harvard University; Massachusetts Bay Colony.**

CAMBRIDGE AGREEMENT. In Cambridge, England, on 26 August 1629, twelve Puritan members of the Massachusetts Bay Company led by John Winthrop signed an agreement in which they pledged to emigrate with their families to New England. The signers of the Cambridge Agreement insisted that the company charter be transferred to the New World and that it serve as the new colony's constitution. This was an unprecedented demand since, traditionally, a board in England governed chartered colonies. A few days later, the company's general court passed a motion to transfer the company and the charter to New England, thus making the Massachusetts Bay Company the only English colonizing company without a governing board in England. Subsequently, all stockholders who were unwilling to settle in America sold their shares to those who were willing to make the voyage. By taking the charter with them, the Puritans shifted the focus of the company from trade to religion, and they guaranteed that the Crown would not compromise their religious freedom in America.

In spring 1630, Winthrop and approximately one hundred followers set sail for the New World in the *Arbella*. The group arrived in Massachusetts in June 1630 and soon was joined by other English emigrants. By the end of the year, two thousand English-born colonists lived in Massachusetts. The voyage of the *Arbella* marked the beginning of a ten-year period of massive emigration from England known as the Great Migration. By the end of the decade, approximately eighty thousand men, women, and children had left England, and twenty thousand of them had settled in Massachusetts.

BIBLIOGRAPHY

Pomfret, John E., with Floyd M. Shumway. *Founding the American Colonies, 1583–1660.* New York: Harper and Row, 1970.

Jennifer L. Bertolet

See also **Great Migration; Massachusetts Bay Colony; Puritans and Puritanism.**

CAMBRIDGE PLATFORM,

a resolution drawn up by a synod of ministers from Massachusetts and Connecticut (August 1648), which met pursuant to a request of the Massachusetts General Court. The New England authorities desired a formal statement of polity and a confession of faith because of the current Presbyterian ascendancy in England and the activities of local Presbyterians such as Dr. Robert Child. The platform, written by Richard Mather, endorsed the Westminster Confession and for ecclesiastical organization upheld the existing Congregational practice. The Cambridge Platform remained the standard formulation in Massachusetts through the eighteenth century and in Connecticut until the SAYBROOK PLATFORM of 1708.

BIBLIOGRAPHY

Stout, Harry S. *The New England Soul: Preaching and Religious Culture in Colonial New England.* New York: Oxford University Press, 1986.

Perry Miller / A. R.

See also **Calvinism; Congregationalism; Presbyterianism.**

CAMDEN, BATTLE OF,

American Revolutionary battle taking place 16 August 1780. Following General Benjamin Lincoln's defeat and capture at Charleston, South Carolina, General Horatio Gates was given command of the American army in the southern department, consisting of 1,400 regulars and 2,052 unseasoned militia. Marching southward from Hillsboro, North Carolina, Gates met an army of two thousand British veterans under Lord Charles Cornwallis near Camden, South Carolina, early in the morning of 16 August. At the first attack, the militia fled. The regulars, standing their ground, were surrounded and almost annihilated. The Americans lost 2,000 killed, wounded, and captured; 7 cannon; 2,000 muskets; and their transport. The British loss was only 324. Gates fled to Hillsboro and vainly attempted to rally his demoralized army. On 2 December he was replaced by Nathanael Greene. Many Americans fled to the swamps and mountains and carried on guerrilla warfare.

BIBLIOGRAPHY

Hoffman, Ronald, Thad W. Tate, and Peter J. Albert, eds. *An Uncivil War: The Southern Backcountry during the American Revolution.* Charlottesville: University Press of Virginia, 1985.

Lumpkin, Henry. *From Savannah to Yorktown: The American Revolution in the South.* Columbia: University of South Carolina Press, 1981.

Pancake, John S. *This Destructive War: The British Campaign in the Carolinas, 1780–1782.* University: University of Alabama Press, 1985.

Nelson Vance Russell / A. R.

See also **Eutaw Springs, Battle of; Revolution, American: Military History; Southern Campaigns.**

CAMELS IN THE WEST.

In 1855 Congress appropriated $30,000 to purchase camels for use on express routes across the 529,189 square miles of territory acquired during the MEXICAN-AMERICAN WAR. In 1856 and 1857, over one hundred camels carried mail across this desert country. They were sold at auction in 1864, most to carry freight to and from Nevada mines. Others remained in Texas in circuses and zoological gardens. Between 1860 and 1862, Otto Esche, a German merchant, brought forty-five camels from Siberia to San Francisco for use on eastbound express routes, although he sold most of them to a mining company in British Columbia. Years later, wild camels still roamed the Northwest, Nevada, and especially Arizona. Wild American camels are now extinct.

BIBLIOGRAPHY

Lesley, Lewis B., ed. "Uncle Sam's Camels." *California Historical Society Quarterly* (1930).

A. A. Gray / C. W.

See also **Mail, Overland, and Stagecoaches; Pack Trains.**

CAMP DAVID.

Situated on 142 acres in Maryland's Catoctin Mountains, about seventy miles northwest of Washington, D.C., Camp David has served as a weekend and summer retreat for United States presidents since 1942. Franklin D. Roosevelt chose the site he called Shangri-La for its eighteen-hundred-foot elevation, which made it considerably cooler than summers in the White House. He oversaw the remodeling of the camp, esti-

Camp David. President John F. Kennedy (*left*) is shown around the grounds of Camp David by his predecessor, Dwight D. Eisenhower, on 22 April 1961, during the Cuban Bay of Pigs crisis. © BETTMANN/CORBIS

mated to cost about $18,650, with sketches for the design of the presidential lodge and directions for changes to the landscaping. President Dwight D. Eisenhower renamed the site in 1953 after his father and his grandson, David.

Several important meetings with heads of state occurred at Camp David. During World War II, Roosevelt met there with British prime minister Winston Churchill, and in 1959 Eisenhower hosted Soviet premier Nikita Khrushchev at Camp David. However, the site is most often associated with the 1978 talks between Egyptian president Anwar el-Sadat and Israeli prime minister Menachem Begin. President Jimmy Carter brought both men to the retreat to forge a framework for Middle East peace, which resulted in the signing of the Camp David Peace Accords on 17 September 1978. Camp David continues to be utilized by American presidents for both leisure and official government business.

BIBLIOGRAPHY

Lesch, Ann Mosely, and Mark Tessler, eds. *Israel, Egypt, and the Palestinians: From Camp David to Intifada.* Bloomington: Indiana University Press, 1989.

Nelson, W. Dale. *The President Is at Camp David.* Syracuse, N.Y.: Syracuse University Press, 1995.

———. "Company in Waiting: The Presidents and Their Guests at Camp David." *Prologue* 28 (1996): 222–231.

Dominique Padurano

See also **Camp David Peace Accords.**

CAMP DAVID PEACE ACCORDS, a set of agreements between Egypt and Israel signed on 17 September 1978. The agreements were the culmination of years of negotiations for peace in the Middle East. Acting as a peace broker, President Jimmy Carter convinced Egyptian President Anwar el-Sadat and Israeli Prime Minister Menachem Begin to reach a compromise in their disputes.

Peace in the Middle East had been a goal of the international community for much of the preceding thirty years. After a year of stalled talks, President Sadat announced in November 1977 that he would visit Israel and personally address the Knesset, the Israeli parliament. Speaking to the Knesset, Sadat announced his desire for peace between Egypt and Israel. While a seemingly small statement, it was a substantial step forward in the Middle East peace process. Up to that point, Egypt and its Arab allies had rejected Israel's right to exist. Despite Sadat's gesture, the anticipated renewal of negotiations failed to materialize.

In the following months, after several unsuccessful attempts to renew talks, President Carter invited Begin and Sadat to the U.S. presidential retreat at Camp David, Maryland. After twelve days of talks, the leaders reached two agreements: "A Framework for Peace in the Middle East" and "A Framework for the Conclusion of a Peace Treaty Between Egypt and Israel." The first treaty addressed the status of the West Bank and Gaza Strip, areas of land that Israel had occupied since the 1967 Six-Day War. The agreement provided for a transitional period, during which the interested parties would reach a settlement on the status of the territories. The second accord provided that Egypt and Israel would sign a peace treaty within three months. It also arranged for a phased withdrawal of Israeli forces from the Sinai Peninsula and the dismantling of Israeli settlements there. In exchange, Egypt promised to establish normal diplomatic relations with Israel.

While the two nations faced difficulty implementing many details, the Camp David Peace Accords represented an important step in the Middle East peace process. On 26 March 1979, Israel and Egypt signed their historic peace treaty in Washington, D.C., hosted by President Carter. It was an important moment for Middle East peace and the crowning achievement in Carter's foreign policy.

BIBLIOGRAPHY

Dayan, Moshe. *Breakthrough: A Personal Account of the Egypt–Israel Peace Negotiations.* New York: Knopf, 1981.

Kamel, Mohamed Ibrahim. *The Camp David Accords: A Testimony.* London: KPI, 1986.

Quandt, William B. *Camp David: Peacemaking and Politics.* Washington, D.C.: Brookings Institution, 1986.

Stephanie Wilson McConnell

See also **Egypt, Relations with; Israel, Relations with.**

Camp David, 12 September 1978. President Jimmy Carter is flanked by Prime Minister Menachem Begin of Israel *(left)* and President Anwar el-Sadat of Egypt. HULTON ARCHIVE

CAMP FIRE GIRLS. The origin of the Camp Fire Girls belongs to a larger, complex history of scouting in America. Two early promoters of the scouting movement were Earnest Thompson Seton and Daniel Beard. Seton established an organization for boys called the Woodcraft Indians in 1902 and Daniel Beard began an organization for boys called the Sons of Daniel Boone in 1905. The themes of the two organizations varied, but both influenced the establishment of the Boy Scouts of America in 1910. The sister organization to the Boy Scouts became the Camp Fire Girls, initially evolving from a lone New England camp run by Luther and Charlotte Gulick.

Dr. Luther Gulick was a well-known and respected youth reformer. His wife, Charlotte Gulick, was interested in child psychology and authored books and articles on hygiene. After consulting with Seton, Mrs. Gulick decided on using his Indian narrative as a camp theme. The name of the camp and motto was "Wo-He-Lo," an Indian-sounding word that was short for "Work, Health, and Love." Following the Woodcraft model, Mrs. Gulick focused on nature study and recreation. That first year they had seventeen young girls in camp singing songs and learning crafts. A year later William Chauncy Langdon, poet, social worker, and friend of the Gulicks, established another girls' camp in Thetford, Vermont, that followed the Woodcraft model. He was the first to coin the name "Camp Fire Girls."

In 1911 Luther Gulick convened a meeting at the Horace Mann Teachers College to entertain the ways and means of creating a national organization for girls along the lines of the Boy Scouts. Seton's wife, Grace, and Beard's sister, Lina, were both involved in the early organization and lobbied for a program that adopted Indian and pioneer themes. In 1912 the organization was incorporated as the Camp Fire Girls, and chapters soon sprang up in cities across the country. In the summer of 1914 between 7,000 and 8,000 girls were involved in the organization and a decade and a half later there were nearly 220,000 girls meeting in 9,000 local groups. The Camp Fire Girls remained an important part of the scouting movement throughout the twentieth century. The name was changed to the Camp Fire Boys and Girls in the 1970s when boys were invited to participate, and in 2001 the organization became known as Camp Fire U.S.A.

BIBLIOGRAPHY

Deloria, Philip. *Playing Indian.* New Haven, Conn.: Yale University Press, 1998.

Eells, Eleanor. *History of Organized Camping: The First 100 Years.* Martinsville, Ind.: American Camping Association, 1986.

Schmitt, Peter J. *Back to Nature: The Arcadian Myth in Urban America.* New York: Oxford University Press, 1969.

Timothy Bawden

See also **Girl Scouts of the United States of America.**

CAMP MEETINGS. Spontaneous outdoor religious meetings figured importantly in evangelical revivals in

21

both England and America in the eighteenth century. Most accounts trace the origins of the regular American camp meeting to Cane Ridge, on the banks of the Gasper River in Kentucky. There, during the summers of 1800 and 1801, Presbyterian and Methodist preachers together staged massive revivals. Contemporaries credited (or blamed) the Cane Ridge revival for the subsequent wave of weeklong meetings throughout the upper South, the Northeast, and the Chesapeake region. In the 1820s, hundreds of these camp meetings were held across the United States.

In the trans-Appalachian West, evangelical denominations, Methodists in particular, used camp meetings as way stations for roving circuit preachers and to attract new converts. They located the encampments away from town, usually in a wood near a water supply, to highlight God's immanence in nature and to encourage soulful reflection. There were several services each day, with up to four or five ministers speaking.

In the South services were sharply segregated by race. For white people, an egalitarian spirit pervaded guests who succumbed to the constant exhortation and fell into vigorous and physical bouts of religious ecstasy (such as leaping and swaying), all of which evoked fears of cult worship and unleashed sexuality. Some accused the camp meetings of promoting promiscuity.

By the mid-nineteenth century, camp meetings offered a desired religious alternative to the secular, middle-class vacation resort. By 1889 most of the approximately 140 remaining camp meetings were located on railroad lines. Victorian cottages replaced tents, and permanent auditoriums were established. In the 1870s the religious resort concept merged with new impulses for popular education. Methodist campgrounds served as the template for the education-oriented resort communities of Ocean Grove, N.J., and Chautauqua, N.Y. By the 1910s, most of the camp meetings had failed or had been absorbed into Chautauqua assemblies or residential suburbs.

BIBLIOGRAPHY

Eslinger, Ellen. *Citizens of Zion: The Social Origins of Camp Meeting Revivalism.* Knoxville: University of Tennessee Press, 1999.

Johnson, Charles A. *The Frontier Camp Meeting: Religion's Harvest Time.* Dallas, Tex.: Southern Methodist University Press, 1955.

Weiss, Ellen. *City in the Woods: The Life and Design of an American Camp Meeting on Martha's Vineyard.* New York: Oxford University Press, 1987.

W. B. Posey
Andrew C. Rieser

See also **Chautauqua Movement; Circuit Riders; Evangelicalism and Revivalism.**

CAMPAIGN FINANCING AND RESOURCES.

Candidates were spending money in elections as early as the seventeenth century, long before anything resembling the modern campaign first made its appearance. There always has been money in elections, but it has not played the same role in every era.

The Colonial Period: Deferential Politics

Government and politics in colonial America were dominated by merchant and landed elites, so candidates for elective office usually were wealthy men who paid their own campaign expenses. The purpose of those expenses was less to attract the attention of voters than a form of noblesse oblige that reinforced the deferential relationship between voters and candidates. Treating—buying food and alcohol—was common, especially in the southern colonies. Northern merchants standing for election might make it a point to give more than the usual business to local artisans by ordering new barrels, or furniture, or repairs to their buildings and ships.

Candidates had other political resources as well. Although there were no formal methods for nominating candidates, aspiring politicians usually made sure that they had the support of influential members of their class. This kind of support attained some of the same ends that would later be achieved with large sums of money: discouraging rivals from entering a race and enlisting the support of those who are indebted to, or do not want to offend, a candidate's powerful backers.

The Early Nineteenth Century: The Spoils System and Business Contributions

This deferential style of politics gradually gave way to mass democracy and the spoils system. At a time when politicians were less likely than before to be wealthy, the spoils system became a form of government subsidy for emerging political parties. Although this system began under Andrew Jackson, executive patronage had long been a valuable political resource. George Washington, for example, while appointing to federal office men from the same elites that had dominated colonial politics, also made sure that these appointees shared his political views. To do otherwise, he wrote, "would be a sort of political suicide." Thomas Jefferson and his successors followed Washington's example, and also began the practice of dismissing officeholders to make room for appointees who were more reliable politically.

Jackson, however, was not satisfied with using government office as a reward for campaign work. He expected his appointees to continue their campaign activity while in office. By using the patronage power to staff and finance the fledgling Democratic Party, Jackson nationalized the spoils system that already had appeared in the state politics of Pennsylvania and New York. Jackson introduced another innovation: raising campaign funds by assessing appointees a percentage of their salaries. Political assessments were first made public in 1839 during an investigation by the House of Representatives of the U.S. customshouse in New York. Another House investigation in 1860 revealed that the practice had become well entrenched.

Business interests also began contributing in these years, although this source of funds is very poorly documented. Martin Van Buren attributed Democratic losses in the 1838 congressional elections in New York State to the "enormous sum of money" raised by "Whig merchants, manufacturers and . . . banks." In 1861, New York Republican boss Thurlow Weed confirmed that he had raised money for Abraham Lincoln's 1860 presidential campaign by engineering the passage of railroad bills in return for "legislative grants" from railroad companies.

The Late Nineteenth Century: Assessments, Reformers, and Corporate Contributions

Business corporations became a far more important source of campaign funds in the decades after the Civil War. But that did not happen until after assessments had become perhaps the largest source of campaign funds. The Republican Party's unbroken control of the White House in the twenty years after the end of the Civil War gave it almost exclusive access to civil service assessments. According to an 1880 Senate report, Republicans had levied a 2 percent assessment on federal civil servants in 1876, and had raised 88 percent of their 1878 campaign funds from 1 percent assessments on those same employees. Democrats may not have controlled federal government patronage, but they levied assessments on state government employees wherever they could.

These assessments became the target of a growing reform movement. Although campaign finance was only one concern of civil service reform, fear of losing assessment money was a powerful reason for members of Congress to resist the movement. Two factors permitted reformers to break down that resistance. One was the assassination of President James A. Garfield in 1881 by a man described as a disappointed office seeker, which energized the reform movement. The other was the large business corporations that grew up after the Civil War, which had begun to provide an alternative source of campaign funds.

The Early Twentieth Century: The Response to Corporate Funding

Business has been the largest source of campaign funds since the last years of the nineteenth century. This development was initially associated in the popular mind with one man: Marcus A. Hanna, the wealthy industrialist who managed William McKinley's 1896 presidential campaign. During that campaign, Hanna sought to institutionalize business support for the Republican Party by levying a new kind of assessment: banks and businesses were asked to contribute sums equal to one-quarter of 1 percent of their capital.

Reaction against this new source of political money came almost at once. In 1897, four states prohibited corporations from contributing to election campaigns. In 1905, the revelation that Theodore Roosevelt's 1904 presidential campaign had been largely underwritten by big corporations caused a nationwide scandal, attracting critical editorials even from Republican newspapers. In 1907, Congress responded by passing the first federal campaign finance law, a ban on political contributions by corporations.

Business showed a preference for the GOP from the start, but this preference became much more marked during the New Deal years. Democrats received 45 percent of business money in 1932, but by 1940 were receiving only 21 percent. At the same time, organized labor began to make its first substantial contributions to Democrats.

The Late Twentieth Century: Public Financing, Soft Money, and PACs

This New Deal pattern was still in evidence when the Watergate scandal erupted out of the 1972 presidential election campaign. Watergate was only partly a campaign finance scandal, but those elements of it—individual contributions, illegal corporate and foreign money, and evasion of new disclosure laws—prompted Congress to pass the most comprehensive set of campaign finance regulations in history. Post-Watergate legislation introduced public financing for presidential elections. The presidential campaign fund was a new source of political funds and the only one to be created by legislation.

Public financing had a rocky history after the first bill for establishing it was unsuccessfully introduced in 1904. Congress passed a public funding law in 1966, financed by an income tax checkoff, but repealed it the next year. Congress reinstated the checkoff in the 1971 Federal Election Campaign Act, but postponed its implementation to meet criticisms from President Richard Nixon, congressional Republicans, and key southern Democrats. Watergate then renewed congressional and public support for public financing. Although most Republicans still opposed it, enough of them switched positions to ensure passage.

Under the law, candidates who accept public funding agree not to raise or spend private money. But Ronald Reagan's 1980 presidential campaign, realizing that private money could be raised and spent under more lenient state laws, introduced what has come to be called "soft money," that is, money raised outside the limits of federal law. What began as backdoor private financing for publicly funded presidential campaigns eventually became a means of evading federal law in congressional campaigns as well. During this same period, taxpayer participation in the income tax checkoff began to decline, suggesting weakening popular support for the program.

Soft money and political action committees (PACs) attracted a great deal of attention in the decades after Watergate. Neither, however, introduced new sources of campaign finance. Rather, they were artifacts of federal law, legal innovations devised to get around restrictions on sources and amounts of campaign contributions. PACs were created by labor unions in the 1940s to evade Republican and southern Democratic attempts to prevent them from making political contributions. The explosive growth of business PACs in the late 1970s and early 1980s was a reaction to post-Watergate restrictions on the individual contributions that had long been the preferred vehicle for getting business money into campaigns. PACs made business and labor contributions far more visible. This increased visibility revealed what looked like a return to New Deal patterns of partisan support. As late as 1972, incumbent House Democrats, despite having been the majority party since 1955, still were receiving three times as much money from labor as from business PACs ($1.5 million from labor, $500,000 from business). But by 2000, when Democrats had been in the minority for five years, their House incumbents were getting half again as much money from business as from labor PACs ($41.7 million from business, $26.9 million from labor).

Partisan funding patterns may shift over time, but the sources of party and candidate funds has changed little. Even with the increase of small individual donations and the big jump in labor union giving in the 1990s, the great majority of campaign money, soft and hard, still came from corporations and wealthy individuals.

BIBLIOGRAPHY

Heard, Alexander. *The Costs of Democracy.* Chapel Hill: University of North Carolina, 1960.

Mutch, Robert E. *Campaigns, Congress, and Courts: The Making of Federal Campaign Finance Law.* New York: Praeger, 1988.

Overacker, Louise. *Money in Elections.* New York: Macmillan, 1932.

Pollock, James K. *Party Campaign Funds.* New York: Knopf, 1926.

Sikes, Earl R. *State and Federal Corrupt-Practices Legislation.* Durham, N.C.: Duke University Press, 1928.

Robert E. Mutch

See also **Patronage, Political; Political Action Committees; Soft Money; Spoils System.**

CAMPAIGN SONGS are partisan ditties used in American political canvasses and especially in presidential contests. In the nineteenth century the words of these songs were commonly set to established melodies, such as "Yankee Doodle," "Marching through Georgia," "Rosin the Bow," "Auld Lang Syne," "John Brown's Body," "Dixie," and "O Tannenbaum" ("Maryland, My Maryland"). They were also set to tunes that were widely popular at the time, such as "Few Days," "Champagne Charlie," "Wearing of the Green," or "Down in a Coal Mine" (which served for the campaign song "Up in the White House").

Perhaps the best known of them was "Tippecanoe and Tyler Too," in which words by Alexander C. Ross were adapted to the folk tune "Little Pigs." First heard at Zanesville, Ohio, this song spread rapidly across the country, furnishing a party slogan. The *North American Review* stated that what the "Marseillaise" was to Frenchmen, "Tippecanoe and Tyler Too" was to the Whigs of 1840. In 1872 an attempt was made to revive "Greeley Is the Real True Blue." Glee clubs were often organized to introduce campaign songs and to lead audiences and marchers in singing them. The songs were real factors in holding the interest of crowds, emphasizing issues, developing enthusiasm, and satirizing opponents.

In the twentieth century, with changes in campaigning methods, particularly the use of first radio and then television, the campaign song declined as a popular form of expression. In his 1932 presidential campaign, Franklin D. Roosevelt adopted the nonpolitical melody "Happy Days Are Here Again." By the 1960s campaign songs no longer introduced issues; instead, they presented an emotional feeling attached to a campaign. John F. Kennedy's campaign song was adapted from the popular tune "High Hopes" and for Lyndon Johnson's 1964 campaign, the theme song from the Broadway show *Hello, Dolly* became "Hello, Lyndon." A significant trend in the last twenty years of the twentieth century was the use of rock music by presidential candidates, such as the adoption of Fleetwood Mac's 1977 hit "Don't Stop" by Bill Clinton's 1992 campaign. This tactic, however, caused difficulties for some candidates, especially Ronald Reagan and George W. Bush, because musicians protested that using their songs inaccurately implies that the artists themselves support the political positions of those candidates.

BIBLIOGRAPHY

Boller, Paul F., Jr. *Presidential Campaigns.* New York: Oxford University Press, 1984.

Silber, Irwin. *Songs America Voted By.* Harrisburg, Pa.: Stackpole Books, 1971.

G. S. Bryan / A. G.

See also **Canvass; Elections; Elections, Presidential; Era of Good Feeling; "Full Dinner Pail"; Jingoism; "Tippecanoe and Tyler Too."**

CAMPAIGNS, POLITICAL. *See* **Elections.**

CAMPAIGNS, PRESIDENTIAL. *See* **Elections, Presidential.**

CANADA, CONFEDERATE ACTIVITIES IN. Confederate plots against northern ships, prison camps, and cities were coordinated from Canada in May 1864 by Jacob Thompson, J. P. Holcombe, and C. C. Clay. Efforts to seize federal ships on Lake Erie, a raid on Saint Albans, Vermont, in October, a train-wrecking effort near Buffalo in December, and schemes to release Confederate prisoners in northern prison camps uniformly failed. Fires meant to burn northern cities, including New York and Cincinnati, were similarly unsuccessful. Hoping to depress federal currency values, Confederates in Canada bought nearly $2 million in gold and sold it in England, with no permanent result. About $300,000 was spent by Confederates in Canada in promoting these various futile schemes.

BIBLIOGRAPHY

Headley, John W. *Confederate Operations in Canada and New York.* Alexandria, Va.: Time-Life, 1984.

Kinchen, Oscar A. *Confederate Operations in Canada and the North.* North Quincy, Mass.: Christopher, 1970.

Wilson, Dennis K. *Justice under Pressure: The Saint Albans Raid and Its Aftermath.* Lanham, Md.: University Press of America, 1992.

Charles H. Coleman/ A. R.

See also **Civil War; Confederate Agents; Northwest Conspiracy; Saint Albans Raid.**

CANADA, RELATIONS WITH.

The Canadian-American relationship is unusual in a number of ways. The two nations share one of the longest common borders in the world, nearly five thousand miles, including Alaska. This frontier is technically undefended, which gives rise to much discussion of how the two nations pioneered mutual disarmament, even though the lack of defense is more mythical than real. Canada and the United States are one another's best customers, with more goods moving across the Great Lakes than over any other localized water system in the world. Nonetheless, the cultural impact of the more populous nation upon the smaller has caused Canada to fear a "creeping continentalism," or "cultural annexation," by the United States. In the 1960s and 1970s, this fear led to strains in the Canadian-American relationship. Indicative of the cultural problem is Canadian resentment over the use of the term "American" as solely applicable to the United States, since Canadians are Americans too in the geographical sense.

Two Distinct Nations

To understand the Canadian-American relationship, one must be aware of three problems. The first is that, until the twentieth century, Americans tended to assume that one day Canada would become part of the United States, especially since it continued to be, and technically still is, a monarchy. Democratic Americans who espoused the notion of MANIFEST DESTINY felt Canada should be added to "the area of freedom." The second problem is that Canadians found themselves caught between the United States, which they feared would absorb them, and Great Britain, which possessed Canada as a colony. Thus, Canadian statesmen often used the cry of "Americanization" to strengthen ties with Britain. The third problem is that the Canadian population has been roughly one-third

French-speaking for nearly two centuries, and this bilingual and bicultural condition has complicated the North American situation.

In a sense, one cannot separate Canadian-American relations from Canadian history. This is especially so for two reasons. Of the two score or more distinct steps by which a colonial dependency of Britain became a self-governing colony—and then a fully independent nation—Canada took most of them first, or the distinct steps arose from a Canadian precedent or over a Canadian initiative. Thus, Canada represents the best and most complete example of progressive decolonization in imperial history, and one must understand that the Canadian-American relationship involves sharp contrasts between a nation (the United States) that gained its independence by revolution and a nation (Canada) that sought its independence by evolution. Further, despite similarities of geography, patterns of settlement, technology, and standards of living, Canadians came to differ in numerous and fundamental ways from Americans. The most important areas of difference, apart from those arising from Canada's bilingual nature, were: (1) that Canada did not experience a westward movement that paralleled the frontier of the American West; (2) that Canada's economy was, especially in the eighteenth and nineteenth centuries, dependent upon a succession of staples, principally fish, furs, timber, and wheat, which prevented the development of an abundant and diversified economy like that of the United States; and (3) that Canadians could not at any time become isolationists, as Americans did, since they felt under threat from an immediate neighbor, which the United States did not. Most Americans are ignorant of these basic differences in the histories of the two nations, which perhaps stands as the single greatest cause of friction in Canadian-American relations, for, as Canadians argue, they know much American history while Americans know little of Canadian history.

Early Hostilities

The history of the relationship itself includes periods of sharp hostility tempered by an awareness of a shared continental environment and by the slow emergence of a Canadian foreign policy independent of either the United Kingdom or the United States. This policy, moreover, gave Canada middle-power status in the post–World War II world. The original hostility arose from the four intercolonial wars, sometimes referred to as the Great War for Empire, in which the North American colonies of Britain and France involved themselves from 1689 until 1763. The English Protestant settlers of the thirteen seaboard colonies were at war with the French Catholic inhabitants of NEW FRANCE until, in the FRENCH AND INDIAN WAR, Britain triumphed and in 1763 Canada passed to the British by the Peace of Paris. Thereafter, Canadians found themselves on the fringes of the American Revolution. Benjamin Franklin traveled to Montreal in an unsuccessful attempt to gain revolutionary support there, and rebel privateers raided the Nova Scotian coast. In

1783 the Treaty of Paris created the new United States and left what thereafter came to be the British North American Provinces in British hands. The flight of nearly forty thousand Loyalists from the United States to the new provinces of Upper Canada (later Canada West and now Ontario) and New Brunswick, and to the eastern townships of Lower Canada (later Canada East and now Quebec). This assured the presence of resolutely anti-American settlers on the Canadian frontier, which increased tensions between the two countries.

Relations between the United States and Great Britain, and thus with Canada too, remained tense for over three decades. Loyalists in Canada resented the loss of their American property and, later, the renunciation by some American states of their debts for Loyalist property confiscated during the American Revolution. The British regained certain western forts on American soil, contrary to the treaty of 1783, to ensure control over the Indians, and American frontier settlers believed that the British encouraged Indian attacks upon them. Although Jay's Treaty of 1796 secured these forts for the United States, western Americans continued to covet Canada. In 1812 a combination of such war hawks, a controversy over British impressment of American seamen, and the problem of neutral rights on the seas led to an American declaration of war against Britain. A series of unsuccessful invasions of Canada nurtured anti-Americanism there, while the burning of York (now Toronto), the capital of Upper Canada, became an event for the Canadian imagination not unlike the stand at the Alamo and the sinking of the *Maine* to Americans. The Treaty of Ghent, signed in 1815, restored the status quo ante but ended British trade with American Indians, which removed a major source of friction. The Rush-Bagot Agreement of 1817 placed limitations on armed naval vessels on the Great Lakes and became the basis for the myth, since the agreement did not apply to land fortifications, that the United States and Canada henceforth did not defend their mutual border.

A second period of strain along the border began in 1837 and extended until 1871. The British government put down rebellions in both Canadas in the former year but not before American filibustering groups, particularly the Hunters Lodges, provoked a number of border incidents, especially over the ship the *Caroline*. Further, the leaders of the rebellion sought refuge in the United States. Two years later, a dispute over the Maine boundary led to a war scare. Although the Webster-Ashburton Treaty of 1842 settled the border, the Oregon frontier remained in dispute until 1846. In the 1850s, Canada flourished, helped in part by trade with the United States encouraged by the Elgin-Marcy Reciprocity Treaty of 1854. An abortive annexation manifesto released by a body of Montreal merchants had forced the British to support such trade.

During the American Civil War, relations again deteriorated. The Union perceived the Canadians to be anti-Northern, and they bore the brunt of Union resent-

ment over Queen Victoria's Proclamation of Neutrality. The *Trent* affair of 1861 brought genuine danger of war between the North and Britain and led to the reinforcement of the Canadian garrisons. Canadians anticipated a Southern victory and an invasion by the Northern army in search of compensatory land; therefore, they developed detailed defensive plans, with an emphasis on siege warfare and "General Winter." The *Alabama* affair; Confederate use of Canadian ports and towns for raids on Lake Erie, Johnson's Island, and Saint Albans; and the imposition of passport requirements along the border by U.S. customs officials gave reality to Canadian fears. Ultimately, Canada enacted its own neutrality legislation. Moreover, concern over the American threat was one of the impulses behind the movement, in 1864, to bring the Canadian provinces together into a confederation, as achieved by the British North America Act in 1867. In the meantime, and again in 1871, Fenians from the United States carried out raids. These raids and congressional abrogation of the reciprocity treaty in 1866 underscored the tenuous position of the individual colonies. Thus, the formation of the Dominion of Canada on 1 July 1867 owed much to the tensions inherent in the Canadian-American relationship.

Arbitration and Strengthening Ties

The Treaty of Washington in 1871 greatly eased these tensions. From this date on, the frontier between the two countries became progressively "unguarded," in that neither side built new fortifications. The treaty provided for the arbitration of the *Alabama* claims and a boundary dispute over the San Juan Islands. This agreement strengthened the principle of arbitration. Furthermore, for the first time, Canada, in the person of Sir John A. Macdonald, its prime minister, represented itself on a diplomatic matter. Nevertheless, the treaty was unpopular in Canada, and it gave rise to the oft-repeated charge that Britain was willing to "sell Canada on the block of Anglo-American harmony" and that Canada was an American hostage to Britain's good behavior in the Western Hemisphere. Significantly, Canadians then began to press for independent diplomatic representation.

Problems between Canada and the United States after 1871 were, in fact, more economic and cultural than strictly diplomatic. Arbitration resolved disputes over the Atlantic fisheries, dating from before the American Revolution, and over questions relating to fur seals in the Bering Sea. In 1878, as the United States refused to renew reciprocity of trade, Canada turned to the national policy of tariff protection. A flurry of rumors of war accompanied the Venezuela boundary crisis in 1895. In addition, the Alaska boundary question, unimportant until the discovery of gold in the Klondike, exacerbated old fears, especially as dealt with in 1903 by a pugnacious Theodore Roosevelt. Perhaps Canadians drew their last gasp of fear of direct annexation in 1911, when the Canadian electorate indirectly but decisively turned back President William Howard Taft's attempt to gain a new reciprocity treaty that many thought might lead to a commercial, and ultimately political, union. English-speaking Canada resented American neutrality in 1914, at the outbreak of WORLD WAR I, and relations remained at a low ebb until the United States entered the war in 1917.

Wartime Alliances

A period of improved Canadian-American relations followed. In 1909 an international joint commission emerged to adjudicate on boundary waters, and the Canadian government had welcomed a massive influx of American settlers onto the Canadian prairies between 1909 and 1914. With the coming of World War I, the economies of the two nations began to interlock more closely. In 1927 Canada achieved full diplomatic independence by exchanging its own minister with Washington; by 1931, when all dominions became fully autonomous and equal in stature, Canada clearly had shown the United States how it could take the lead in providing the hallmarks of autonomy for other former colonies as well. During the U.S. experiment with PROHIBITION, which Canada did not share, minor incidents arose, the most important of which was the American sinking of the Canadian vessel *I'm Alone* in 1929. Luckily, harmonious arbitration of this specific case in 1935, following the United States's repeal of Prohibition in 1933, eliminated the cause of the friction. Canadians were disturbed that the United States failed to join the LEAGUE OF NATIONS, but they welcomed U.S. initiatives toward peacekeeping in the 1920s and 1930s. With the outbreak of WORLD WAR II in Europe and the rapid fall of France in 1940, Canadians were willing to accept the protection implied by President Franklin D. Roosevelt in his Ogdensburg Declaration of 18 August, and Roosevelt and Prime Minister William Lyon Mackenzie King established the Permanent Joint Board on Defense, which continued to exist in the early 2000s.

Military cooperation continued during and after the United States's entry into World War II. Canada and the United States jointly constructed the Alaska Highway, Canadian forces helped fight the Japanese in the Aleutian Islands, and both Canada and the United States became charter members of the NORTH ATLANTIC TREATY ORGANIZATION (NATO) in 1949. The two countries constructed a collaborative series of three early-warning radar systems across Canada during the height of the COLD WAR, and in 1957 the North American Air Defense Command (NORAD) came into existence. Increasingly, Canada came to play the role of peacekeeper in the world: at Suez, in the Congo, in Southeast Asia, and in 1973 in Vietnam. Although Canada entered into trade relations with Cuba and Communist China at a time when the United States strenuously opposed such relations, diplomatic relations remained relatively harmonious. Nor did relations deteriorate when Canadians protested against U.S. nuclear testing in the far Pacific Northwest, or during the VIETNAM WAR, when Canada gave refuge to over forty thousand young Americans who sought to avoid military service.

Economic and Trade Relations

Nonetheless, increased economic and cultural tension offset this harmony. In the 1930s, the two countries erected preferential tariff barriers against one another, and despite an easing of competition in 1935, Canadians continued to be apprehensive of the growing American influence in Canadian industry and labor. In the late 1950s and early 1960s, disputes over the role of American subsidiary firms in Canada; over American business practices, oil import programs, and farm policy; and over the influence of American periodicals and television in Canada led to a resurgence of "Canada First" nationalism under Prime Minister John Diefenbaker. Still, Queen Elizabeth II and President Dwight D. Eisenhower in 1959 together opened the SAINT LAWRENCE SEAWAY, long opposed by the United States, and the flow of Canadian immigrants to the United States continued. Relations, while no longer "easy and automatic," as Prime Minister Lester B. Pearson once described them, remained open to rational resolution. The growth of a French-Canadian separatist movement; diverging policies over the Caribbean and, until 1972, the People's Republic of China; as well as U.S. ownership of key Canadian industries, especially the automobile, rubber, and electrical equipment sectors, promised future disputes.

Canada remained within the U.S. strategic orbit in the last decades of the twentieth century, but relations soured amidst world economic instability provoked by the Arab oil embargo in 1973, a deepening U.S. trade deficit, and new cultural and environmental issues. Canadians complained about American films, television shows, and magazines flooding their country; acid rainfall generated by U.S. coal-burning power plants; and environmental damage expected from the U.S. oil industry's activities in the Arctic. After the U.S. tanker *Manhattan* scouted a route in 1969 to bring Alaskan oil through the Canadian Arctic ice pack to eastern U.S. cities, the Canadian parliament enacted legislation extending its jurisdiction over disputed passages in this region for pollution-control purposes. Subsequently, the oil companies decided to pump oil across Alaska and ship it to U.S. West Coast ports from Valdez. Disputes over fisheries, a hardy perennial issue, broke out on both coasts. On the East Coast, a treaty negotiated with Canada during the administration of President Jimmy Carter that resolved disputed fishing rights in the Gulf of Maine fell through after protests by congressional representatives from Massachusetts and Maine. Ultimately, the World Court in The Hague, Netherlands, resolved the issue. On the West Coast, the two countries argued over salmon quotas. (Later, during the 1990s, when fish stocks had declined precipitously in both regions, the disputes broke out again with renewed intensity.) In response to these issues, Prime Minister Pierre Trudeau's government (1968–1979, 1980–1984) struggled to lessen Canada's dependency on the United States. It screened U.S. investment dollars, sought new trading partners, challenged Hollywood's stranglehold on cultural products, canceled tax advantages enjoyed by

U.S. magazines, and moved to reduce U.S. control over Canada's petroleum industry.

Free Trade and Unity against Terrorism

Relations improved notably in 1984 because of a startling convergence of personalities and policies. A new Canadian leader, Brian Mulroney (1984–1993), established affable relations with Presidents Ronald Reagan and George H. W. Bush. In an important demonstration of Canadian-American economic cooperation, Mulroney led Canada into a controversial, U.S.-initiated continental trade bloc via the Free Trade Agreement (1988) and the NORTH AMERICAN FREE TRADE AGREEMENT (1992). These treaties between the United States, Canada, and Mexico intended to eliminate all trade barriers between the countries.

Scrapping Trudeau's nationalist agenda, Mulroney endorsed the U.S. presidents' hard line toward the Soviet bloc, joined the U.S.-dominated Organization of American States, and participated in the U.S.-led Persian Gulf War of 1991. In the spring of 1999, under U.S. president Bill Clinton and Canadian prime minister Jean Chrétien, the United States and Canada, as members of NATO, cooperated in military action in Serbia. Following the terrorist attacks on New York and Washington, D.C., on 11 September 2001, Canada assisted the United States in searching for those responsible. It passed the Anti-Terrorism Act, which brought Canada's more liberal immigration policy into line with that of the United States in an attempt to prevent terrorists from using Canada as a staging ground for further aggression against the United States.

In the early 2000s, Canada and the United States depended more heavily on one another for trade than on any other nation. Canadians purchased between one-quarter and one-third of all U.S. exports, while the United States bought some 80 percent of Canada's exports. Similarly, each nation invested more capital across the border than in any other country, including Japan and Mexico.

BIBLIOGRAPHY

Aronsen, Lawrence R. *American National Security and Economic Relations with Canada, 1945–1954.* Westport, Conn.: Praeger, 1997.

Campbell, Colin. *The U.S. Presidency in Crisis: A Comparative Perspective.* New York: Oxford University Press, 1998.

Fatemi, Khosrow, ed. *North American Free Trade Agreement: Opportunities and Challenges.* New York: St. Martin's Press, 1993.

Martin, Pierre, and Mark R. Brawley, eds. *Alliance Politics, Kosovo, and NATO's War: Allied Force or Forced Allies?* New York: Palgrave, 2001.

Menz, Fredric C., and Sarah A. Stevens, eds. *Economic Opportunities in Freer U.S. Trade with Canada.* Albany: State University of New York Press, 1991.

Pendakur, Manjunath. *Canadian Dreams and American Control: The Political Economy of the Canadian Film Industry.* Detroit, Mich.: Wayne State University Press, 1990.

Rafferty, Oliver P. *The Church, the State, and the Fenian Threat, 1861–75.* Basingstoke, Hampshire, U.K.: Macmillan Press; New York: St. Martin's Press, 1999.

Rugman, Alan M. *Multinationals and Canada-United States Free Trade.* Columbia: University of South Carolina Press, 1990.

Savoie, Donald J. *Thatcher, Reagan, Mulroney: In Search of a New Bureaucracy.* Pittsburgh, Pa.: University of Pittsburgh Press, 1994.

Winks, Robin W. *The Civil War Years: Canada and the United States.* 4th ed. Montreal and Ithaca, N.Y.: McGill-Queen's University Press, 1998.

Robin W. Winks/A. E.

See also **Acid Rain; Canada, Confederate Activities in; Canadian-American Waterways;** *Caroline* **Affair; Fenian Movement; Klondike Rush; North American Free Trade, Foreign; Washington, Treaty of;** *and vol. 9:* **Address of the Continental Congress to Inhabitants of Canada.**

CANADIAN-AMERICAN RECIPROCITY, the mutual reduction of duties on trade between the United States and Canada, emerged as a significant issue in United States–Canadian relations in the late 1840s. When Britain withdrew imperial trade preferences in 1846, Canada naturally turned to the United States. However, lingering anti-British sentiment made it easy for northern protectionists and southern congressmen (who feared that reciprocity might induce Canada to join the United States as an anti-slave country) to defeat early proposals for an agreement.

The situation changed in 1852, when Canada restricted U.S. access to its east coast fisheries. Both Washington and London, anxious to avoid a confrontation, sought a comprehensive treaty that would resolve the reciprocity and fisheries issues. On 5 June 1854 Lord Elgin, Governor General of BNA, and William Marcy, U.S. Secretary of State, signed the Reciprocity Treaty, whose principal clauses guaranteed American fishermen access to Canadian waters and established free trade for products of "the land, mine and sea." It was approved by Congress in August.

The Treaty remained in force until March 1866, when it was abrogated by the United States in retaliation for Britain's pro-Confederate posture during the Civil War. Successive Canadian governments sought a renewed treaty but none succeeded until that of Prime Minister Wilfrid Laurier in 1911. The Reciprocity Agreement of 1911 provided for the free exchange of most natural products. It was approved by Congress but rejected in Canada, where many feared it would lead to annexation. With this rejection, reciprocity—free trade—ceased to be a prominent issue in Canadian-American relations until the 1970s.

BIBLIOGRAPHY

Masters, Donald C. *The Reciprocity Treaty of 1954.* 2nd Edition. Toronto: McClelland and Stewart, 1963.

Stacey, C.P. *Canada and the Age of Conflict: A History of Canadian External Policies, Volume I: 1867–1921.* Toronto: Macmillan of Canada, 1977.

Greg Donaghy

See also **Canada, Relations with; United States–Canada Free Trade Agreement (1988).**

CANADIAN-AMERICAN WATERWAYS.

The history of the boundary waters that flow along and across the borders of the United States and Canada reflects the status of the relationship between the dominant societies on either side of this border.

Soon after the establishment of competing English and French societies in North America, the waterways—the St. Lawrence Bay and River, Lake Champlain and the adjacent lakes that fed into and merged with it, and later the Great Lakes and western waters like the Allegheny, Monongahela, and Ohio Rivers—were routes for isolated raids, military attacks, and even major campaigns.

The waterways continued to be used as military highways through the War of 1812. During the four colonial wars in North America, there were frequent efforts to isolate French Canada by controlling the entrance into the St. Lawrence River and to threaten Montreal through the Lake Champlain waterways. The French were moving west for the fur trade, and their presence at the headwaters of the Ohio River (modern-day Pittsburgh) helped precipitate the last of these wars. During the American Revolutionary War, Americans attempted to attack north, and the British general John Burgoyne unsuccessfully attempted to move down the lakes, with complementary attacks coming down the Mohawk River Valley and up the Hudson, to cut off New England from the rest of the colonies. In the War of 1812, the United States fought against Britain and Canada on the Great Lakes, near modern-day Detroit, across the Niagara frontier, and toward Montreal.

Then came the Rush-Bagot Convention of 1817 that neutralized the U.S.-Canadian border and hence the boundary waters. Americans and Canadians alike now take for granted the world's longest undefended border, which, in its eastern half, consists mostly of waterways.

As the pace of settlement and industrialization in the mid-nineteenth century brought people to the great middle of the continent, interest turned to the transportation potential of these waters. Over the years, the two countries have turned from competition to cooperation. Upper Canadian interests, for example, built the Welland Canal connecting Lakes Ontario and Erie to counter the Erie Canal through New York. America opened Lake Superior during the Civil War via canals near Sault Sainte Marie.

But despite positive rhetoric, both nations favored economic competition over cooperation.

It took from the 1890s to 1954 to reach agreement, but eventually the U.S. Congress agreed to a 1951 Canadian proposal to construct the St. Lawrence Seaway, opening the border waters to oceangoing vessels. More recently, transportation and navigation have played a decreasing role in Canadian-American waterway considerations; more important are issues of pollution, water supply, flood control, and hydroelectric power. The two countries concluded the Water Quality Agreement in 1978, the Great Lakes Water Quality Agreement in 1987, and initiated another effort ten years later to clean up the Great Lakes. The North American Free Trade Agreement in 1988 has helped increase the flow of goods and services across this border, and thus Americans and Canadians take the border even more for granted—a far cry from its early days of providing easier means of invasion for armed parties of French Canadians and English Americans.

BIBLIOGRAPHY

Classen, H. George. *Thrust and Counterthrust: The Genesis of the Canada–United States Boundary.* Chicago: Rand McNally, 1967.

LesStrang, Jacques. *Seaway: The Untold Story of North America's Fourth Seacoast.* Seattle: Superior, 1976.

Willoughby, William R. *The St. Lawrence Waterway: A Study in Politics and Diplomacy.* Madison: University of Wisconsin Press, 1961.

Charles M. Dobbs

See also **Great Lakes; Saint Lawrence River; Saint Lawrence Seaway.**

CANALS.

Even before the Revolutionary War gave new impetus to American expansionism, the colonial political and economic elites were deeply interested in the improvement of inland transportation. Vessels that plied offshore waters, small boats and rafts on the streams down to tidewater, and local roads and turnpikes served the immediate commercial needs of farmers and townspeople in the Atlantic coastal area. But the loftier dreams of planters, merchants, and political leaders—as well as of the common farmers who constituted by far most of the free population in British America—looked beyond the "fall line" that separated the rivers flowing to the coast from those that ran to the Ohio-Mississippi basin. A vast area for settlement and productivity—and riches—lay in the interior, and by the early 1790s demands for diffusion of new transport technologies and for investment in internal improvements were voiced frequently in both state and national political forums.

It was widely recognized that unless bulk agricultural commodities, which were the staples of a commercialized and expanding farm economy, could be carried cheaply

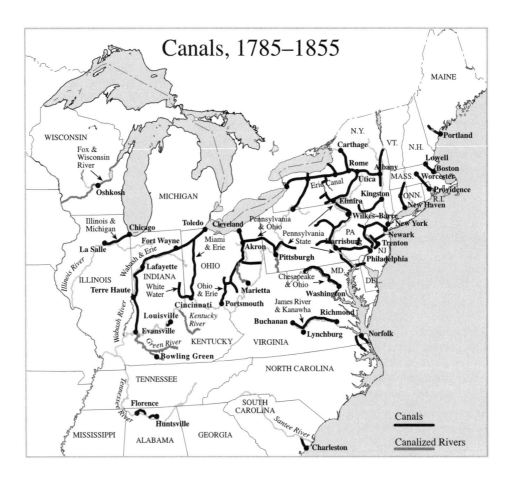

Canals, 1785–1855

and over long distances, settlement and economic growth would be badly hampered in the region beyond the Appalachian Mountains. Then, too, there were opportunities for construction of short lines on the Atlantic seaboard to link already developed areas (coal mines, farming and lumber regions, and rising industrial sites), with the promise of immediate traffic and revenues. The latter were "exploitative" projects, tapping existing trade routes and resources; but the major east-west projects were "developmental," promoted with the goal of opening newly or sparsely settled areas to economic opportunities. There was also a nationalistic or patriotic goal of canal promotion: to bind together far-flung sections of the young nation and to prove the efficacy of republican government.

And yet total canal construction in the United States up to 1816 totaled only 100 miles—the longest canal project being the Middlesex, which linked Boston's harbor with the farm region to the north. Other lines of some importance linked Norfolk, Virginia, to Albemarle Sound and connected the Santee River area to Charleston, South Carolina. Although many other canal projects were proposed up and down the Atlantic coast, progress was difficult because of shortages of capital and skepticism with regard to engineering feasibility projects. Moreover, regional or local jealousies notoriously worked against successful mobilization of governmental support in both the U.S. Congress and the state legislatures.

In the period from the mid-1820s to the Civil War, however, the United States underwent a vast expansion of canal construction, becoming the world's leading nation in both mileage of canals and the volume of tonnage carried on them. The canal lines were of crucial importance in the integration of a national economy, and they played a key role in the so-called "Transportation Revolution" that expedited both westward expansion and a robust industrialization process in the North and West.

Advantages, Disadvantages, and Construction Challenges

Canal technology proved especially attractive for several reasons. Since the 1760s, successful large-scale canal projects had been built in both Great Britain and France, and these canals had brought enormous economic advantages to the regions they served. The engineering advances pioneered in Europe gave American promoters confidence that they could build canals with equal success.

There was a downside to canal technology, too, though it was not always fully recognized in America. Difficult topography or uncertain water supply meant complex and highly expensive construction design. Canal building before the 1850s was mainly done with hand tools, augmented only by some primitive animal-powered machinery. A canal line had to be furnished with locks, permitting boats to pass through from one water level to another. The segments of line between the locks were of very gradual grade to permit controlled flow. At each lock, a gate at its higher level would be opened while the gate on the lower end was kept closed; once a boat entered the lock's chamber from the higher level, the upper gate was closed (holding the water flow back) while the lower gate was opened. As water ran out, the boat was carried down to the lower level, then passed through the open gate. For "upstream" movement, from the lower level to the higher, the process was reversed. The lock would be drained to the lower level, the boat would enter through the bottom gate, which was then closed, and water would then be admitted from the upper gate, lifting the boat up to the higher level. In steep areas, "flights" of locks, closely spaced, were necessary and often involved complex engineering; for transit of the boats, these series of locks meant a slow stretch and usually long waiting periods.

Locks varied in size. Lifts ranged from two to thirty feet, and there were great differences in the distances between gates as well as in the construction materials used. Masonry locks and metal or metal-trimmed gates were far more expensive—and more durable—than wooden gates and timber-supported rubble for the walls as found on some of the lines. The total rise and fall over an entire line was measured as "lockage," and served as an index of the difficulty of construction. For example, New York's Erie Canal route measured lockage of 655 feet, by contrast with Pennsylvania's lockage of 3,358 feet between Philadelphia and the Ohio River.

The size of the boats that could be accommodated, as well as the volume of water needed, were functions of the dimensions of the canal bed, or its "prism," as well as of the size of lock chambers. Prisms on American canals varied greatly, most of them ranging from forty to sixty feet in width at the top, with sloping sidewalls leading to a bottom of twenty-five to forty-five feet across. The Pennsylvania system was the most complex in engineering using inclined planes and steam-powered winches to drag boats out of the water and over some of the steepest hills.

To supply the line with flowing water, engineering plans had to include river connections, dams and reservoirs with feeder lines to the canals, and often massive culverts and aqueducts. Building the sidewalls to minimize loss of water through seepage was another challenging and expensive aspect of design. On many of the larger canals, such as the Ohio lines, engineers took advantage of fast-flowing feeder streams to design water-mill sites into the line.

Once a canal was in operation, moreover, maintaining navigation was a continuous challenge. Winter ice, droughts, floods, and breaches in the water-supply system would frequently cause navigational closings. Even in the best of circumstances, it was difficult to maintain regular schedules on the lines because of traffic bottlenecks at the locks and the continuous maintenance needed to keep water flowing.

Although steam-powered propeller craft were used on a few canal lines, this form of transport placed dangerous pressure on the canal walls. Hence, the use of horses or mules to haul canal boats was nearly universal, with the animals walking along the "towpath" alongside the line. Freight boats typically of 50- to 125-ton capacity operated at speeds of one to three miles per hour. On most lines they were owned by individuals or private companies, the line being a common carrier under the law.

In the short run, all the disadvantages of canal technology were more than offset by the cost savings for long-distance hauling, especially of bulk goods and produce. In the long run, however, innovations in steam technology and railroad engineering were destined to render many canals the losers in a new competitive age in transport that took shape in the late 1840s and the 1850s.

The Erie Canal
The great breakthrough came in 1817 with New York State's commitment to building the Erie Canal to connect the Hudson River at Albany with Buffalo on Lake Erie, a

Erie Canal. This engraving depicts the official opening of the historic canal—to the firing of cannon, the flying of the flag, and the cheers of spectators—on 26 October 1825; the celebration, which ran along the 360-mile length of the canal and culminated in fireworks in New York on 7 November, was reportedly the most exuberant in America since the Revolution. GETTY IMAGES

project far greater than any previously attempted in America. The Erie was important to subsequent canal development in several ways, most notably because it provided a model of public enterprise through its financing, administration, and implementation. The state raised capital through bond issues both in New York and in Europe, and supplemented these funds with tax revenues. Actual construction was overseen by a board of commissioners, some of whom were personally involved in the fieldwork, but the project became a celebrated "school for engineers," with most of the junior personnel learning their skills on the job under the tutelage of Benjamin Wright and James Geddes, two of less than twenty men who then constituted the profession in America. Many of the Erie engineers went on to direct canal surveys in other states.

The canal was divided into sections for purpose of construction, with private contractors taking on the work under the state engineers' supervision—a scheme that was emulated by nearly all the major canals subsequently built. It was an immediate commercial success once opened to its full length in 1825, leading the New York legislature to authorize a series of additional canals as well as the improvement and enlargement of the original line.

No nonmilitary enterprise in the United States had ever involved such expenditures as did the Erie, whose initial construction cost $6 million. The number of laborers employed was also unprecedented in any economic enterprise of the day. The state's construction expenditures energized local economies, giving part-time employment to farmers and creating sudden demand for stone, timber, mules, and oxen, and provisions for workers. Like canals and other public works throughout the country, moreover, the Erie attracted immigrant workers (mainly Irish and German) who were employed to do much of the most dangerous work.

The Erie's commercial impact on the rural countryside and on New York City's role as a center for trade with the interior and for exports to Europe—together with the rich stream of revenues from the tolls—heightened expectations everywhere in the country that other canals could produce equally spectacular fiscal and developmental results.

The Post-1825 Boom in Canal Building
Emulation of New York followed quickly. In 1825 Pennsylvania authorized a $10 million project, combining canal technology with the use of inclined planes. It was completed in 1834, tapping the Ohio Valley's farm country at Pittsburgh and giving Philadelphia trade advantages similar to those that its rival New York City had obtained from the Erie. The first of the western states to build a major line was Ohio, which authorized construction in 1825. Although still small in population and financial resources, Ohio, too, resorted to creation of a state enterprise and borrowed heavily both in the East and in Europe. Erie Canal engineers were brought in at first, but Alfred Kelley of Cleveland and Micajah Williams of Cin-

Chesapeake and Ohio Canal. The canal, which runs along the Potomac River about 200 miles to Cumberland, Md., was in use from 1850 to 1924 and is now a national historical park (including the adjacent towpath); these locks, photographed by Theodor Horydczak, are in the Georgetown section of Washington, D.C. LIBRARY OF CONGRESS

cinnati, local entrepreneurs with no prior engineering experience, took principal charge of overseeing construction once the technical plans were adopted. Although administrative incompetence and corruption plagued the Pennsylvania project, Ohio's record was widely admired for its efficiency and strength of design. One line, the Ohio Canal, was completed in 1834 and extended from Cleveland on Lake Erie to Portsmouth on the Ohio River—the first water link between the Great Lakes and the great Mississippi-Ohio basin. A second line, completed in the mid-1840s, linked Cincinnati with Toledo to the north.

Other important lines begun or fully built prior to 1840 included the Delaware and Hudson Canal, a successful private line in the Pennsylvania coal country; the Delaware and Raritan Canal, also private, linking Philadelphia and New York; and the Chesapeake and Delaware Ohio Canal, which with substantial state support built a line, surveyed by the engineer William Strickland, through Maryland to link Baltimore with the Philadelphia port.

In the period 1815–1834, $60 million was invested in 2,088 miles of canals, with 70 percent of the funds coming from governmental sources, mainly the states. Most of the funds were borrowed at home and abroad. Also, Congress authorized the Army Engineers to conduct surveys for the states and federal companies; made some direct federal investments; and gave several million acres of public lands to Ohio, Indiana, and Illinois to subsidize their canal projects during this period.

In the decade following, 1834–1844, the "canal enthusiasm" continued to animate state governments and private promoters. Rivalries among states and competition among cities were intense, feeding the spirit of optimism. A new wave of canal construction followed, with the projects again heavily financed by loans from Europe and the eastern cities. Almost 1,300 miles of canal were built during this ten-year period. They cost $72 million, of which 79 percent represented public funds. In addition to major new state canal systems begun in Illinois and in Indiana (where the Wabash and Erie line would open another link for direct trade between the Ohio River and Lake Erie), and in Illinois, three of the pioneering state projects—the Erie, Ohio's two main canals, and the Pennsylvania system—were further expanded to satisfy sections of their states that had been left out of the original system designs. As the new canals were generally of larger dimensions than the first ones to be built, the carrying capacity for canal traffic doubled between 1834 and 1844. Until 1839, conditions of prosperity and expansion sustained the canal-building movement, and expenditures for the new canals stimulated overall economic growth.

Financial Problems and Railroad Competition

The 1837 financial panic and the 1839–1843 depression created enormous fiscal problems for many canal states, leading to defaults on state debts in Pennsylvania and Indiana. Because many of the expansion projects and new lines produced toll revenues far below expectations, moreover, there was widespread disillusionment with state enterprise; and this became a factor favoring railroads as an alternative to canals, especially given the much greater reliability of rail transport. In the Ohio-Indiana-Illinois area, by 1848 the proliferation of canal lines also produced intensified competition between the various Great Lakes and Mississippi River routes, now also served by steamboat lines on these connecting waters. The east-west and local railroads of the 1850s made matters worse. The result was heavy downward pressure on canal rates, consequently reduced revenues, and, soon, a scenario of operating deficits that placed an unwelcome burden on taxpayers.

Transport competition drove down rates so much that the period from the mid-1840s to the Civil War formed a distinctive "second phase" of the Transportation Revolution. By 1850–1852, for example, western canal tolls were less than a third the level of the 1830s, creating still further fiscal problems for the canal states and companies. Where private investment had been invited on a matching basis for "mixed" canal enterprises, the costs fell hard on the capitalists as well. But while revenues fell, ton-miles of canal transportation continued to expand on all the major lines throughout the 1850s.

During the period 1844–1860, a last major cycle of canal construction produced 894 miles of line at a cost of $57 million. Here again, governmental activism was crucial, with public funds accounting for two-thirds of the total expended. Much of this increase constituted the completion or improvement of lines built earlier; in addition, the still-successful Erie system in New York was further enlarged and upgraded. A large expenditure was made, too, on the Sault Ste. Marie Ship Canal, a short but massive deepwater project that connected Lake Huron with Lake Superior.

Although much of the canal system experienced operating deficits in the 1850s, the impetus these new facilities had given the economy had clearly warranted most of the capital invested. Commercialization of agriculture in the western states and other interior had been made possible, while eastern manufacturers and importers were afforded economical access to interior markets. Coal-mining and iron centers were linked, and consumer prices fell where the transport facilities had proliferated. In sum, the areas served by canals were enabled to build on comparative economic advantage; and, at least in the northern states, processing of primary products carried by the canals served as the origin of manufacturing growth that augmented urban commercial activity.

Railroad competition led to many closings of once-important canals; indeed, more than 300 miles of line were abandoned by 1860. A few of the canals did continue to carry heavy traffic after the Civil War. The most important to commerce in the twentieth century was the Atlantic intra-coastal waterway, which permitted vessels to transit offshore waters safely from New England to Florida. The Erie retained importance as a barge canal, as did some of the shorter coal-carrying lines. Some of the old canal lines became rights-of-way for railroads or modern roads; others were absorbed into the changing landscape as development went forward. In scattered locations, a few segments of the great canal lines are today preserved or restored for enjoyment of citizens seeking a glimpse of the once-glorious era of canal transport in America.

BIBLIOGRAPHY

Fishlow, Albert. "Internal Transportation in the Nineteenth and Early Twentieth Centuries." In *The Cambridge Economic History of the United States.* Edited by Stanley L. Engerman and Robert E. Gallman. Volume 2. New York: Cambridge University Press, 2000.

Goodrich, Carter. *Government Promotion of American Canals and Railroads, 1800–1890.* New York: Columbia University Press, 1960. Reprint, Westport, Conn.: Greenwood Press, 1974.

Goodrich, Carter, ed. *Canals and American Economic Development.* New York: Columbia University Press, 1961.

Gray, Ralph D. *The National Waterway: A History of the Chesapeake and Delaware Canal, 1769–1965.* 2d ed. Urbana: University of Illinois Press, 1989. The original edition was published in 1967.

Larson, John Lauritz. *Internal Improvement: National Public Works and the Promise of Popular Government in the Early United States.* Chapel Hill: University of North Carolina Press, 2001.

Scheiber, Harry N. *Ohio Canal Era: A Case Study of Government and the Economy, 1820–1861.* 2d ed. Athens: Ohio University Press, 1987. The original edition was published in 1969.

Shaw, Ronald E. *Canals for a Nation: The Canal Era in the United States, 1790–1860.* Lexington: University of Kentucky Press, 1990.

Taylor, George Rogers. *The Transportation Revolution, 1815–1860.* New York: Rinehart, 1951. Reprint, Armonk, N.Y.: M. E. Sharpe, 1989.

Harry N. Scheiber

See also **Erie Canal; Illinois and Michigan Canal; Nicaraguan Canal Project; Panama Canal.**

CANCER remains one of the most feared diseases of our times. Every year 500,000 Americans die from tumors of one sort or another, up from about 30,000 at the beginning of the twentieth century. Part of the increase is due to population growth and the fact that people now live longer—and cancer is, generally speaking, a disease of the elderly. A smaller fraction of the increase is due to the fact that previously undetected cancers are now more likely to be diagnosed. But cancer risks have also grown over time, due to increased exposures to carcinogenic agents—notably new carcinogens in food, air, and water, such as pesticides and asbestos; the explosive growth of tobacco use in the form of cigarettes, which were not widely used until World War I; and exposure to various forms of radiation, such as X-rays and radioisotopes. Tobacco alone still causes nearly a third of all American cancer deaths—including 90 percent of all lung tumors—making it the single most important cause of preventable cancers.

Cancer is actually a cluster of several different diseases, affecting different parts of the body and different kinds of tissue. Leukemia is a cancer of the blood, myeloma a cancer of the bone marrow, melanoma a cancer of the skin, and so forth. Cancer can be seen as "normal" tissue growing out of control or in places where it should not. In the case of breast cancer, for example, the danger is not from cancer cells confined to the breast, but rather from cancerous breast cells spreading to other parts of the body ("metastasis"), where they grow and eventually interfere with other parts of normal bodily function. Cancerous growths seem to begin when the body's normal cellular "suicide" functions break down; malignant cells are immortal in the sense that they continue to divide instead of periodically dying off as healthy cells should.

A great deal of research has gone into exploring the genetic mechanisms of carcinogenesis, with the hope of finding a way to halt the growth of cancerous cells. The difficulty has been that cancer cells look very much like normal cells, the difference typically being only a few minor mutations that give the cell novel properties. That is why cancer is so difficult to treat. It is not like the flu or malaria, where a living virus or bacterium has infected the body. Cancer cells are often not even recognized as foreign by the body's immune system—which is why they can grow to the point that normal physiological processes are obstructed, causing disability and, all too often, death.

Cancer also has to be understood as a historical disease, since the kinds of cancer that are common in a society will often depend on what people eat or drink, what kinds of jobs or hobbies or habits are popular, what kinds of environmental regulations are enforced, the environmental ethics of business leaders and labor activists, and many other things as well. Cancer is a cultural and political disease in this sense—but also in the sense that different societies (or different people within the same society) can suffer from very different kinds and rates of cancer.

Stomach cancer was the number one cause of cancer death in America in the early years of the twentieth century, for example, accounting for about half of all American cancer deaths. By the 1960s, however, stomach cancer had fallen to fifth place in the ranks of cancer killers, as a result of food refrigeration and the lowered consumption of high-salt, chemically colored, and poorly preserved foods. Cancers of the lung, breast, and ovary are now the more common causes of death for women, as are cancers of the lung, colon, prostate, and pancreas among men. Lung cancer has become the leading cause of cancer death among both men and women, in consequence of the rapid growth of smoking in the middle decades of the twentieth century. The twenty- to thirty-year time lag between exposure and death for most cancers explains why the decline of smoking in the 1970s and 1980s only began to show up at the end of the century in falling lung cancer rates.

It is important to distinguish cancer *mortality* (death rates) from cancer *incidence* (the rates at which cancers appear in the population). Some cancers are fairly common—they have a high incidence—but do not figure prominently in cancer mortality. Cancer of the skin, for example, is the most common cancer among both men and women, but since few people die from this ailment, it does not rank high in the mortality tables. Most skin cancers are quite easily removed by simple surgery. Lung cancer survival rates, by contrast, are quite low. Mortality rates are tragically close to incidence rates for this particular illness.

Worries over growing cancer rates led President Richard Nixon to declare a "war on cancer" in his State of the Union address of 1971. Funding for cancer research has increased dramatically since then, with over $35 billion having been spent by the National Cancer Institute alone. Cancer activists have also spurred increased attention to the disease, most notably breast cancer activists in the 1980s and prostate cancer activists in the 1990s. Attention was also drawn to Kaposi's sarcoma from its association with AIDS. Cancer researchers have discovered a number of genes that seem to predispose certain individuals to certain kinds of cancer; there are hopes that new therapies may emerge from such studies, though such knowledge as has been gained has been hard to translate into practical therapies. Childhood leukemia is one case where effective therapies have been developed; the disease is now no longer the death sentence it once was. From the point of view of both policy and personal behavior, however, most experts agree that preventing cancer is in principle easier than treating it. Effective prevention often requires changing deeply ingrained personal habits or industrial practices, which is why most attention is still focused on therapy rather than on prevention.

We already know enough to be able to prevent about half of all cancers. The problem has been that powerful economic interests continue to profit from the sale of carcinogenic agents—like tobacco. With heart disease rates declining, cancer will likely become the number one cause of American deaths by the year 2010 or 2020. Global cancer rates are rapidly approaching those of the industrialized world, largely as a result of the increasing consumption of cigarettes, which many governments use to generate tax revenue. The United States also contributes substantially to this global cancer epidemic, since it is the world's largest exporter of tobacco products. Only about two-thirds of the tobacco grown in the United States is actually smoked in the United States; the remainder is exported to Africa, Europe, Asia, and other parts of the world. Cancer must therefore be regarded as a global disease, with deep and difficult political roots. Barring a dramatic cure, effective control of cancer will probably not come until these political causes are taken seriously.

BIBLIOGRAPHY

Epstein, Samuel S. *The Politics of Cancer Revisited.* Fremont Center, N.Y.: East Ridge Press, 1998.

Patterson, James T. *The Dread Disease: Cancer and Modern American Culture.* Cambridge, Mass.: Harvard University Press, 1987.

Proctor, Robert N. *Cancer Wars: How Politics Shapes What We Know and Don't Know About Cancer.* New York: Basic Books, 1995.

Robert N. Proctor

See also **Centers for Disease Control and Prevention; Smoking; Tobacco Industry.**

CANDLES lighted most American homes, public buildings, and streets until gas (1820s) and kerosene lamps (1850s) replaced them. Women in each family made many kinds of candles, from the common, made from tallow, to the expensive, made from beeswax. They also used a variety of other materials, such as bear grease, deer suet, bayberry, spermaceti, and well-rendered mut-

ton fat. Every autumn, they filled leather or tin boxes with enough candles to last through the winter. To make candles, women first prepared wicks from rough hemp, milkweed, or cotton spun in large quantity. Then they undertook the lengthy task of dipping or molding several hundred candles by hand.

Homemakers were the exclusive candle makers until the 1700s, when itinerant candle makers could be hired. Later, professional chandlers prospered in the cities. Although factories were numerous after 1750, home dipping continued as late as 1880. The West Indies provided a large market for sperm candles, purchasing over 500,000 pounds of sperm and tallow candles from the colonies in 1768. The total production of candles from both factories and homes was valued at an estimated $8 million in 1810. The New England factories, the largest producers, imported supplies of fat from Russia. Large plants also existed in New Orleans, Louisiana; St. Louis, Missouri; and Hudson, New York. South Carolina and Georgia produced quantities of seeds and capsules from tallow trees used extensively for candlemaking in the South. Allied industries grew rapidly for making metal and pottery candleholders.

BIBLIOGRAPHY

Cowan, Ruth Schwartz. *A Social History of American Technology.* New York: Oxford University Press, 1997.

Wright, Louis B. *Everyday Life in Colonial America.* New York: Putnam, 1966.

Lena G. FitzHugh / c. w.

See also **Hide and Tallow Trade; Kerosene Oil; Lamp, Incandescent; Whaling.**

CANNING INDUSTRY. While societies have preserved foods through drying, smoking, sugaring, freezing, and salting for hundreds of years, the ability to safely store and ship food in glass and metal canisters dates only to the early 1800s. During a series of military campaigns, Napoleon realized his troops were falling victim to scurvy and other diseases that resulted from poor diets, and he needed to provide a broader array of foods to troops often engaged in distant battles. In 1795, the French government promised to pay 12,000 francs for a process that would deliver safe and healthful food to its soldiers.

Nicolas Appert, a Frenchman with a background in brewing, distilling, and confectionary, began a series of food preservation experiments in the late 1790s. He packed an assortment of foods—vegetables, fruits, meats—into glass bottles that he sealed with corks held in place by wire. He then heated the bottles in boiling water, varying the amount of time in the water according to the specific type of food, and carefully let them cool. In 1805, he provided some bottles of broth to a French naval officer, who reported that the broth was still good three months later. Appert published his findings in 1810 in *L'Art de conserver, pendant plusiers années, toutes les substances animals et végé-tales* (The Book of All Households; or, The Art of Preserving Animal and Vegetable Substances for Many Years). In recognition of his work, the French government awarded him the prize.

Appert's work quickly spread to other countries. Translated into English, his book was printed in London in 1811 and in the United States in 1812. Within the next few years, several British firms began preserving meats and vegetables in tin cans as well as bottles. Initially, these goods were quite expensive, and the main buyers were wealthy individuals and military leaders. A few British entrepreneurs brought this emerging technology to the United States, where they packaged and sold preserved foods. American bookkeepers began to abbreviate the word "canister" as "can," a shortcut that soon gave rise to the word "canning," which came to refer to the process by which food was heated and then stored in airtight metal or glass containers.

The Canning Industry in Nineteenth-Century America

The canning industry grew rapidly, and by the 1850s, commercial canneries operated in Maine, New York, Delaware, Maryland, Pennsylvania, and New Jersey. Gail Borden developed a process to condense and seal milk and in 1856 opened the nation's first canned milk plant. While the range of canned products expanded, technical and economic concerns limited the overall size of the market. Although reasonably effective, Appert's method of sterilization was slow, cumbersome, and expensive. In 1860, Isaac Solomon, the manager of a tomato canning plant in Baltimore, introduced a new procedure for heating containers to a higher temperature, thus reducing the sterilization period from five or six hours to under an hour. Solomon's discovery led to higher production levels and lower prices, as factory output jumped from two thousand to three thousand cans a day to twenty thousand cans.

Solomon's innovation coincided with the beginning of the Civil War, which transformed the market for canned goods. Output rose from 5 million cans in 1860 to 30 million cans in 1865, a 600 percent increase. The federal government, recognizing the importance of canned foods, invested significant sums of money in canneries throughout the northern states. Equally important, however, was the change on the demand side of the equation. Until the 1860s, only the well-off could afford canned goods, but this quickly changed. The war greatly expanded the number of Americans who dined on canned meats, vegetables, and fruits, and cheaper production methods made them more widely available to consumers.

During the decades following the Civil War, a series of technological innovations, in concert with several broad social and cultural developments, led to a steadily increasing role for canned goods in American society. Two key technical advances stand out—the introduction of the pressure cooker and the invention of the sanitary can. In 1874, A. K. Shriver pioneered the retort, or pressure cooker, at a plant in Baltimore. By establishing consistent and measurable cooking times and temperatures for the wide range of products being canned, the pressure cooker provided faster and more uniform sterilization. The sanitary can, introduced around 1900, replaced the "hole and cap" can, an open-top container whose cover was soldered by hand after the container was filled. Unlike earlier containers, the sanitary can allowed firms to pack larger pieces of food with less damage. In addition, since a machine attached the lid, solder no longer came into contact with the food. By the 1920s, the sanitary can dominated the market for metal containers.

While these technical innovations spurred the supply side of the canning industry, demand also developed significantly. During the late nineteenth century, the United States underwent the dual transformations of urbanization and industrialization. Urban households had less space to grow fruits and vegetables and less time to preserve them, and, as a result, they bought increasing quantities of canned goods.

A number of businesspeople anticipated the opportunities these changes offered and enthusiastically entered the growing market. Henry Heinz, who grew up in Pittsburgh during the 1850s and 1860s, believed many households were going to begin buying foods they had traditionally prepared at home. He went into business selling cans of vegetables and fruits, along with jars of pickles, ketchup, and horseradish sauce. In 1888, he formed H. J. Heinz Company, a vertically integrated firm that packaged, distributed, and marketed its products throughout the nation. Heinz was one of the first American entrepreneurs to transform canning from a regional business into a national enterprise. His company sales rose from just under $45,000 in 1876 to over $12 million in 1914 and over $37 million in 1925.

While Heinz made his mark preparing a range of canned goods, other firms focused their energies more narrowly. Americans had made their own soups for generations, but the same trends leading households to replace home canning with store-bought foodstuffs were also leading them to substitute canned soup for home-made soup. Joseph Campbell worked for the Anderson Preserving Company for several years before leaving in 1876 to set up the Joseph Campbell Company. Initially, Campbell's company canned a wide range of goods, including peas and asparagus. In the 1890s, under the guidance of John Dorrance, a nephew of one of Campbell's partners, the firm began to produce concentrated soups. Removing the water, they reduced the size of the can and lowered their shipping and distribution costs. Their canned soups proved wildly popular. Sales rose from 500,000 cans in 1900 to 18 million by the early 1920s, and within a few years, the company spawned a number of competitors in the burgeoning market for soup.

The Canning Industry in Twentieth-Century America

The rapid achievements of Heinz, Campbell, and others marketing canned goods reflected the growing public acceptance of and dependence on packaged foodstuffs. Total production of canned vegetables rose from 4 million cases in 1870 to 29 million in 1904 and 66 million in 1919. Canned fruit production also rose rapidly during these years, increasing from 5 million cases in 1904 to 24 million in 1919. However, this very popularity generated concerns as well. In his novel *The Jungle* (1906), Upton Sinclair argued that the best meat was shipped in refrigerated railroad cars, while lower-quality and diseased meat often ended up being canned. Consumers could not readily evaluate canned foods as they could fresh produce, and reports of poisoning and adulteration, the practice of substituting filler goods, led state and local governments to pass labeling laws that required canners to specify their products' ingredients. In 1906, the federal government passed the Pure Food and Drug Act, which was intended, among other goals, to prevent the manufacture and sale of adulterated foods, drugs, and liquors.

Not coincidentally, canneries formed their first national trade association, the National Canners Association (NCA), in 1907. The NCA became the liaison between individual firms and government regulatory officials and agencies, such as the Food and Drug Administration. In 1978, the NCA became part of the National Food Processors Association (NFPA).

From the early 1900s through the end of the twentieth century, the canning industry grew tremendously. Part of the stimulus came from government contracts during World War I and World War II. The military bought large amounts of the industry's total production during the wars, and in the second war canned foods accounted for 70 percent of all the foodstuffs eaten by American troops. Yet consumer demand rose during peacetime as well, with significant increases in the overall production and consumption of canned juices, meats, vegetables, fruits, and soups. By the end of the twentieth century, canning had become a multibillion-dollar industry, with plants in nearly every state and tens of thousands of employees.

BIBLIOGRAPHY

Koehn, Nancy F. *Brand New: How Entrepreneurs Earned Consumers' Trust from Wedgwood to Dell.* Boston: Harvard Business School Press, 2001.

May, Earl Chapin. *The Canning Clan: A Pageant of Pioneering Americans.* New York: Macmillan, 1937.

National Canners Association, Communications Services. *The Canning Industry: Its History, Importance, Organization, Methods, and the Public Service Values of Its Products.* 6th ed. Washington, D.C.: National Canners Association, 1971.

Sim, Mary B. *Commercial Canning in New Jersey: History and Early Development.* Trenton: New Jersey Agricultural Society, 1951.

Smith, Andrew F. *Souper Tomatoes: The Story of America's Favorite Food.* New Brunswick, N.J.: Rutgers University Press, 2000.

Martin H. Stack

See also **Food and Cuisine; Food and Drug Administration; Food Preservation.**

CANOE. Native Americans constructed several kinds of canoes, including the birchbark canoe of the Eastern Woodland tribes; the dugout canoe, or pirogue, used by the Southeastern and many Western tribes; and the kayak of the Arctic Inuit. Light birchbark canoes were easily portaged, and they were responsive enough to be guided through rapids with precision. White explorers and fur trappers quickly adopted this remarkable watercraft for their travels across the continent. They also developed large trading canoes capable of carrying several hundred pounds of furs.

The pirogue, the traditional dugout canoe of the Indians of the Southeast, was usually shaped from the trunk of a cypress tree, hollowed out by burning and scraping. The pirogue drew only an inch or so of water, and it was well-suited to being poled through the vegetation-clogged bayous.

On the northern Pacific Coast of North America, elaborately carved and painted dugout canoes, some a hundred feet long, were made from the giant cedar and other light woods. The Chumash and Gabrielino Indians of the southern California coast and the offshore islands made plank canoes, the planks being lashed together and caulked with asphalt. The Inuit kayak is a specialized variant of the canoe, with a frame of whale ribs or driftwood, over which sealskins are stretched to make a watertight covering.

Fishing Camp—Skokomish. Edward S. Curtis's 1912 photograph shows two Indians with a dugout canoe in western Washington. LIBRARY OF CONGRESS

Until railroads and highways became common, the canoe was the principal form of transport wherever water routes allowed. As these newer forms of transportation and motorized boats became more common, most American Indians abandoned traditional canoes and the skills needed to make them.

BIBLIOGRAPHY

Roberts, Kenneth G. *The Canoe: A History of the Craft from Panama to the Arctic.* Toronto: Macmillan, 1983.

Kenneth M. Stewart/J. H.

See also **Indian Technology; River Navigation; Rivers; Waterways, Inland.**

CANVASS, to ascertain by direct personal approach how citizens intend to vote in a coming election or to seek public opinion on a candidate or issue. The practice was somewhat less common in the early 2000s because of polls made by local newspapers and by magazines of wide national circulation, as well as polls taken by more sophisticated methods used by professional polling services. More loosely, to canvass means to campaign for the support of a given candidate or for the political ticket supported by a given party. Canvass also refers to an official examination of ballots cast in an election to determine authenticity and to verify the outcome of the election.

Robert C. Brooks/A. G.

See also **Ballot; Blocs.**

CAPE COD is a narrow, sandy peninsula in southeastern Massachusetts bounded by Nantucket Sound, Cape Cod Bay, and the Atlantic Ocean. The Vikings may have visited in 1001. The Cape's sixty-five-mile arm—hooking into the ocean—was subsequently a landmark for many early European explorers. Giovanni da Verrazano sailed around it in 1524, Esteban Gomes arrived in 1525, and Bartholomew Gosnold named it in 1602 because of the abundant codfish in adjacent waters. Samuel de Champlain charted its harbors in 1606 and John Smith mapped Cape Cod in 1614. The Pilgrims landed at Provincetown in 1620 before settling at Plymouth and they established communities at Barnstable (1638), Sandwich (1638), Yarmouth (1639), and Eastham (1651).

The English colonists, who had peaceful relations with the native Wampanoag and Nauset people on Cape Cod, found the soil too poor for farming and turned to fishing and whaling. Harvesting clams and oysters and obtaining salt from the evaporation of seawater were industries before 1800 and cranberry bogs were first established in 1816. Shipbuilding flourished before the American Revolution and Sandwich was famous for glass making from 1825 to 1888. Many of the 100,000 Portuguese immigrants to New England, attracted by whaling,

Cape Cod. A storm lashes a beach where fences help keep sand dunes in place. GORDON S. SMITH/PHOTO RESEARCHERS, INC.

fishing, and shipping, had settled in Cape Cod communities as early as 1810.

Because of the many shipwrecks in the vicinity, the picturesque Highland Lighthouse was built on a scenic bluff in Truro in 1797. The *Whydah*, flagship of the Cape Cod pirate prince, Captain Samuel Bellamy, was wrecked in a storm off Orleans in 1717. The lighthouse and the Whydah Museum in Brewster are popular attractions for tourists visiting the Cape Cod National Seashore, established in 1961. The Cape Cod Canal, connecting Cape Cod with Buzzards Bay, was built in 1914 to shorten the often-dangerous voyage for ships sailing around Provincetown from Boston to New York City.

By 1835 Martha's Vineyard had attracted Methodist vacationers to summer campgrounds and tourism had become a cornerstone of the modern Cape Cod economy. Henry David Thoreau, who wrote *Cape Cod* in 1865, was one of many writers and artists attracted by the unique scenery of the Cape. Provincetown had a bohemian summer community by 1890, including an avant garde theater company, the Provincetown Players, in 1915. Summer theaters and art galleries continued to entertain visitors through the twentieth century. In Wellfleet, the ruins of Guglielmo Marconi's first transatlantic radio station in 1903 can be seen on the Cape Cod National Seashore's Marconi Beach.

The distinctive Cape Cod house, a one-story, center-chimney cottage built in the eighteenth century, is found across the United States. The moraines, high ground rising above the coastal plain, and sand dunes reveal a forest of pitch pine and scrub oak with marsh grasses, beach peas, bayberry shrubs, beach plums, and blueberry bushes. The naturalist Henry Beston described life on the Cape Cod dunes in *The Outermost House: A Year of Life on the Great Beach of Cape Cod* (1928). Most of the ponds and lakes on Cape Cod are kettles formed by melting glacial ice. Because the Gulf Stream tempers the New England climate on Cape Cod, retirement communities and tourism, as well as fishing and cranberry growing, are the major industries on Cape Cod.

BIBLIOGRAPHY

Adam, Paul. *Saltmarsh Ecology*. New York: Cambridge University Press, 1990.

Schneider, Paul. *The Enduring Shore: A History of Cape Cod, Martha's Vineyard, and Nantucket*. New York: Henry Holt, 2000.

Peter C. Holloran

See also **Exploration of America, Early; Martha's Vineyard; Provincetown Players; Tourism.**

CAPE HORN is at the southernmost tip of South America, on Horn Island, one of Chile's Wollaston Islands, which are part of the Tierra del Fuego archipelago. Storms, strong currents, and icebergs make passage of the cape extremely dangerous. The Dutch navigators Jakob Le Maire and Willem Schouten were the first to sail through Cape Horn, in 1616. Schouten named the point "Cape Hoorn" after the town of Hoorn in Holland, where he was born.

The discovery of gold at Sutter's Mill, California, in 1848, stimulated the use of the cape as a passageway from the Atlantic to the Pacific coast. Because of the rigors of Cape Horn on coast-to-coast voyages, American ship-

builders were compelled to produce fast, weatherly, and immensely strong vessels. The rapid growth of California trade stimulated production of American square-rigged ships. Famous Cape Horn ships of this period include the *Andrew Jackson*, which shared the record of eighty-nine days from New York to San Francisco, and the *James Baines*, which logged twenty-one knots, the fastest speed ever recorded under sail.

By the early 1900s, the rigors of the Horn passage, the growth of intercontinental trade, the greater development of the U.S. Navy, and the difficulty of adequately protecting the Pacific and the Atlantic coasts focused U.S. attention on the building of the Panama Canal, which opened in 1914. From that time, the importance of the route around Cape Horn, used previously only by freight ships, rapidly declined. The last American sailing ship to round Cape Horn was probably the schooner *Wanderbird* in 1936. Since that time, travel around the cape has mostly been limited to daring crews or individual sailors participating in races around the world.

BIBLIOGRAPHY

Knox-Johnston, Robin. *Cape Horn: A Maritime History*. London: Hodder and Stoughton, 1994.

Rydell, Raymond A. *Cape Horn to the Pacific: The Rise and Decline of an Ocean Highway*. Berkeley: University of California Press, 1952.

Alan Villiers / H. S.

See also **Chile, Relations with; Panama Canal; Schooner.**

CAPITAL PUNISHMENT. The history of capital punishment in the United States provides a means of understanding the dynamics of change and continuity. Changes in the arguments for and against capital punishment are indicative of larger developments regarding the saving and taking of human life by the state. The death penalty, optional or mandatory, is invoked for "capital crime," but no universal definition of that term exists. Usually capital crimes are considered to be treason or terrorist attacks against the government, crimes against property when life is threatened, and crimes against a person that may include murder, assault, and robbery. Criminal law is complex and involves many legal jurisdictions and social values. The existing statutory law and the circumstances of any case can mitigate the use of capital punishment. The power of a jury to decide for or against capital punishment is the dynamic element in its history.

Arguments for and Against Capital Punishment

The arguments for the death penalty and for its abolition have remained fairly constant since the seventeenth century. Advocates for the death penalty claim that the practice is justified for several reasons: retribution, social protection against dangerous people, and deterrence. Abolitionists' response is that the practice is not a deterrent; states without the practice have the same murder rates

Cape Horn. Natives observe the passage of the Dutch under Jakob Le Maire and Willem Schouten, who named the point at the southernmost tip of South America after his hometown in Holland. © CORBIS

over time as those with the law. Moreover, the imposition of the death penalty comes from many factors, resulting from cultural and social circumstances that might have demonstrated irrationality and fear on society's part. The result might be a miscarriage of justice, the death of an innocent person.

Religious groups have put forth several arguments regarding capital punishment. One argument states that perfect justice is not humanly possible. In the past God or his representatives had authority over life and death, but the people or their representatives (the state and the criminal justice system) have become God in that respect, an act of tragic hubris.

A secular argument against capital punishment is that historically the verdict for capital punishment has been rendered most frequently against the poor and against certain ethnic groups as a means of social control. Another argument claims that the death penalty is just an uncivilized activity.

The discovery of DNA provides an argument against capital punishment by stressing that the absence of a positive reading challenges other physical evidence that might indicate guilt. The finality of judgment that capital punishment serves is thus greatly limited. The fullest legal and judicial consequences are still evolving in American jurisprudence.

While these arguments whirl around the academy, the legal system, and public discourse, one method of understanding the issue is to examine its historical nature. Western societies in the seventeenth century slowly began replacing public executions, usually hangings, with private punishment. The process was slow because the number of capital crimes was great. By the nineteenth century, solitary confinement in penitentiaries (or reformatories) was the norm, with the death penalty reserved for first-degree murder.

History of Capital Punishment

Initially moral instruction of the populace was the purpose of public execution. As juries began to consider the causes of crime, the trend toward private execution emerged. In both cases the elemental desire for some sort of retribution guided juries' decisions.

Generally English law provided the definition of capital offenses in the colonies. The numbers of offenses were great but mitigating circumstances often limited the executions. The first execution of record took place in Virginia in 1608. The felon was George Kendall, who was hanged for aiding the Spanish, a treasonable act. Hanging was the standard method, but slaves and Indians were often burned at the stake.

Both the state and the church favored public executions in Puritan New England. Sermons touted the importance of capital punishment to maintain good civil order and prepare the condemned to meet his maker. He was a "spectacle to the world, a warning to the vicious."

Over time the event became entertainment and an occasion for a good time; much later vicious vigilante lynchings served a similar purpose. Order had to be maintained.

The American Revolution sparked an interest in reform of the death penalty as appeals for justice and equity became public issues. William Penn and Thomas Jefferson were early critics of capital punishment. The rebellion against Great Britain was more than a mere "political" event. Encouraged by Montesquieu's writings, Cesare Beccaria's *Essay on Crime and Punishment* (1764), and others, philosophers began the ideological critique of capital punishment. Benjamin Rush's *Enquiry into the Effects of Public Punishments upon Criminals and upon Society* (1787) was a pioneer effort toward reforming the method of executions.

For a time, events moved quickly in the young republic. Pennsylvania established the world's first penitentiary in 1790 and the first private execution in 1834. The adoption of the Bill of Rights in 1791 set the stage for the interpretative struggle over "cruel and unusual punishment [being] inflicted." John O'Sullivan's *Report in Favor of the Abolition of the Punishment of Death by Law* (1841) and Lydia Maria Child's *Letters From New York* (1845) were important items in antebellum reform. In 1847 Michigan abolished capital punishment. But the Civil War and Reconstruction pushed the issue off the national agenda for several years.

The Supreme Court

In 1879, the Supreme Court upheld death by firing squad as constitutional in *Wilkerson v. Utah*. By the end of the twentieth century Utah was the only state using that method. In 1890 in *re Kemmler*, the Supreme Court ruled death by electric chair to be constitutional. In a sense this case validated the use of private executions over public hangings. Enamored with the wonders of electricity, Gilded Age reformers believed this method was more humane. In 1947, the Supreme Court ruled in *Louisiana ex rel. Francis v. Resweber* that a second attempt at execution, after a technical failure on the first try, did not constitute cruel and unusual punishment. On humanitarian grounds, in 1921 Nevada passed the "Humane Death Bill" permitting the use of the gas chamber. The Supreme Court approved the bill and invoked *Kemmler* when Gee Jon appealed it. Jon then became the first person to die in the gas chamber on 8 February 1924.

With the rise of twentieth-century communications and the civil rights movement, public opinion slowly become more critical of execution. In a multitude of cases the issue was debated on two fronts: cruel and unusual punishment and the standard of due process and equity as stated in the Fourteenth Amendment. *Furman v. Georgia* (1972) created a flurry of legislative activity with its ruling that the administration of capital punishment violated both the Eighth and Fourteenth Amendments. Other cases, such as *Gregg v. Georgia* and *Woodson v. North Carolina* (1976), further confused the complex issue by once again allowing the constitutionality of capital punishment in some cases and not in others.

As membership on the Supreme Court changed, the prospect for the national abolition of capital punishment grew dimmer. Advocates of death by lethal injection came forward and claimed the method was humane, efficient, and economical. The Supreme Court has been hesitant to make a definitive statement as to whether or not capital punishment is constitutional. The result is a sizable body of cases dealing with due process. In 1995 the number of executions reached its highest level since 1957. The Society for the Abolition of Capital Punishment, established in 1845, was the first national organization to fight capital punishment. Their goal has yet to be reached.

BIBLIOGRAPHY

ABC-Clio. *Crime and Punishment in America: A Historical Bibliography.* Santa Barbara, Calif.: ABC-Clio Information Services, 1984. Excellent guide to the literature.

Brandon, Craig. *The Electric Chair: An Unnatural American History.* Jefferson, N.C.: McFarland, 1999. A candid narrative about the place of the "chair" in America.

Friedman, Lawrence. *Crime and Punishment in American History.* New York: Basic Books, 1993. First-rate account.

Lifton, Robert Jay, and Greg Mitchell. *Who Owns Death?: Capital Punishment, the American Conscience, and the End of Executions.* New York: William Morrow, 2000. The authors oppose capital punishment; however, the narrative regarding the conflicts among prosecutors, judges, jurors, wardens, and the public is informative.

Marquart, James W., Selfon Ekland-Olson, and Jonathan R. Sorensen. *The Rope, the Chair, and the Needle: Capital Punishment in Texas, 1923–1990.* Austin: University of Texas Press, 1994. A detailed and informative state study.

Masur, Louis P. *Rites of Execution: Capital Punishment and the Transformation of American Culture, 1776–1865.* New York: Oxford University Press, 1989. A brilliant cultural analysis.

Vila, Bryan, and Cynthia Morris, eds. *Capital Punishment in the United States: A Documentary History.* Westport, Conn.: Greenwood Press, 1997. With a chronology of events and basic legal and social documents, a basic source.

Donald K. Pickens

See also **Crime; Hanging; Punishment.**

CAPITALISM is an economic system dedicated to production for profit and to the accumulation of value by private business firms. In the fully developed form of industrial capitalism, firms advance money to hire wage laborers and to buy means of production such as machinery and raw materials. If the firm can sell its products for a greater sum of value than that originally advanced, the firm grows and can advance more money for a new round of accumulation. Historically, the emergence of industrial capitalism depends upon the creation of three prerequisites for accumulation: initial sums of money (or credit), wage labor and means of production available for purchase, and markets in which products can be sold.

Industrial capitalism entails dramatic technical change and constant revolution in methods of production. Prior to the British Industrial Revolution of the eighteenth and early nineteenth centuries, earlier forms of capital in Europe—interest-bearing and merchant capital—operated mainly in the sphere of exchange. Lending money at interest or "buying cheap and selling dear" allowed for accumulation of value but did not greatly increase the productive capabilities of the economic system. In the United States, however, merchant capitalists evolved into industrial capitalists, establishing textile factories in New England that displaced handicraft methods of production.

Capitalism is not identical with markets, money, or greed as a motivation for human action, all of which predated industrial capitalism. Similarly, the turn toward market forces and the price mechanism in China, Russia, and Eastern Europe does not in itself mean that these economies are becoming capitalist or that all industrial economies are converging toward a single form of economic organization. Private ownership of the means of production is an important criterion. Max Weber stressed the rational and systematic pursuit of profit and the development of capital accounting by firms as key aspects of modern capitalism.

In the United States the three prerequisites for capitalist accumulation were successfully created, and by the 1880s it surpassed Britain as the world's leading industrial economy. Prior to the Civil War, local personal sources of capital and retained earnings (the plowing back of past profits) were key sources of funds for industry. Naomi Lamoreaux has described how banks, many of them kinship-based, provided short-term credit and lent heavily to their own directors, operating as investment clubs for savers who purchased bank stock to diversify their portfolios. Firms' suppliers also provided credit. Capital from abroad helped finance the transport system of canals and railroads.

During the Civil War, the federal government's borrowing demands stimulated development of new techniques of advertising and selling government bonds. After the war, industry benefited from the public's greater willingness to acquire financial securities, and government debt retirement made funds available to the capital market. In the last decades of the century, as capital requirements increased, investment banks emerged, and financial capitalists such as J. P. Morgan and Kuhn, Loeb and Company organized finance for railroads, mining companies, and large-scale manufacturers. However, U.S. firms relied less on bank finance than did German and Japanese firms, and, in many cases, banks financed mergers rather than new investment.

Equity markets for common stock grew rapidly after World War I as a wider public purchased shares. Financial market reforms after the crash of 1929 encouraged further participation. However, internal finance remained a major source of funds. Jonathan Baskin and Paul Miranti noted (p. 242) that between 1946 and 1970 about 65 percent of funds acquired by nonfinancial corporate businesses was generated internally. This figure included retained earnings and capital consumption allowances (for depreciation). Firms' external finance included debt as well as equity; their proportions varied over time. For example, corporate debt rose dramatically in the late 1980s with leveraged buyouts, but in the 1990s net equity issuance resumed.

Labor for U.S. factories in the nineteenth century came first from local sources. In textiles, whole families were employed under the Rhode Island system; daughters of farm households lived in dormitories under the Waltham system. Immigration soared in the 1840s. Initially, most immigrants came from northern and western Europe; after 1880, the majority were from southern and eastern Europe. After reaching a peak in the decade before World War I, immigration dropped off sharply in the 1920s–1930s. It rose again in the 1940s and continued to climb in subsequent decades. The origins of immigrants shifted toward Latin America, the Caribbean, and Asia. Undocumented as well as legal immigration increased. For those lacking legal status, union or political activity was especially risky. Many were employed in the unregulated informal economy, earning low incomes and facing poor working conditions.

Thus, although an industrial wage labor force was successfully constituted in the United States, its origins did not lie primarily in a transfer of workers from domestic agriculture to industry. Gavin Wright (1988, p. 201) noted that in 1910 the foreign born and sons of the foreign born made up more than two-thirds of the laborers in mining and manufacturing. Sons of U.S. family farmers migrated to urban areas that flourished as capitalism developed, but many moved quickly into skilled and supervisory positions in services as well as industry, in a range of occupations including teachers, merchants, clerks, physicians, lawyers, bookkeepers, and skilled crafts such as carpentry. Black and white sharecroppers, tenant farmers, and wage laborers left southern agriculture and found industrial jobs in northern cities, particularly during World War II. But by the 1950s, job opportunities were less abundant, especially for blacks.

Family farms using family labor, supplemented by some wage labor, were dominant in most areas outside the South throughout the nineteenth century. But in the West and Southwest, large-scale capitalist agriculture based on wage labor emerged in the late nineteenth century. Mechanization of the harvest was more difficult for fruits, vegetables, and cotton than for wheat, and a migrant labor system developed, employing both legal and undocumented workers. In California a succession of groups was employed, including Chinese, Japanese, Mexican, and Filipino workers. Labor shortages during World War I led to federal encouragement of Mexican immigra-

tion, and Mexicans remained predominant in the 1920s. They were joined in the 1930s by migrants from Oklahoma and other Plains and southern states. Federal intervention during World War II and the 1950s established bracero programs to recruit Mexican nationals for temporary agricultural work.

An extraordinary home market enabled U.S. capitalists to sell their products and enter new rounds of accumulation. Supported by the Constitution's ban on interstate tariffs, preserved by Union victory in the Civil War, and served by an extensive transportation and communication network, the U.S. market by the 1870s and 1880s was the largest and fastest-growing in the world. Territorial acquisitions included the Louisiana Purchase of 1803, which nearly doubled the national territory, and the Mexican cession, taken by conquest in 1848 and including the area that became California. Although some acquisitions were peaceful, others illustrate the fact that capitalist development entailed violence and nonmarket coercion as well as the operation of market forces. Growth in government spending, particularly during and after World War II, helped ensure that markets and demand were adequate to sustain accumulation.

According to Alfred Chandler, the size and rate of growth of the U.S. market opened up by the railroads and telegraph, together with technological changes that greatly increased output, helped spawn the creation from the 1880s of the modern industrial enterprise, a distinctive institutional feature of managerial capitalism. Using the "visible hand" of salaried managers, large firms coordinated vast quantities of throughput in a sequence of stages of mass production and distribution. Chandler thought these firms were more efficient than their competitors, but other scholars argued their dominance rested at least partly on the deliberate creation of barriers to entry for other firms. These included efforts to monopolize raw materials and other practices restricting competition, such as rebates, exclusive dealing, tariffs, patents, and product differentiation.

Technological changes included the replacement of handicraft methods using tools and human or animal power by factories with specialized machinery and centralized power sources. Nineteenth-century U.S. capitalism was notable for two industrial processes: the American System of interchangeable parts, which eliminated the need for skilled workers to file parts (of firearms, for example) to fit together as they did in Britain; and continuous-process manufacture in flour mills and, later, factories with moving assemblies such as automobile factories. Public sector institutions played an important role in some technological developments. The Springfield armory promoted interchangeable parts in the early nineteenth century. Government funding of research and development for industry and agriculture assisted private accumulation by capitalist firms in the twentieth.

Organizational and technological changes meant that the labor process changed as well. In the last decades of the nineteenth century, firms employed semiskilled and unskilled workers whose tasks had been reduced to more homogenized activity. Work was closely supervised by foremen or machine paced under the drive system that many firms employed until the 1930s. "Scientific management," involving detailed analysis of individual movements, optimum size and weight of tools, and incentive systems, was introduced, and an engineering profession emerged.

In the early twentieth century, "welfare capitalism" spread as some firms provided leisure activities and benefits, including profit sharing, to their workers, partly to discourage unionization and reduce labor turnover. As Sanford Jacoby documented, higher worker morale and productivity were sought through new personnel management policies such as job promotion ladders internal to firms. Adoption of bureaucratic employment practices was concentrated in times of crisis for the older drive system—World War I and the Great Depression. In the 1930s, union membership also expanded beyond traditional craft unions, as strike tactics and the rise of industrial unions brought in less skilled workers. During and after World War II, union recognition, grievance procedures, and seniority rules became even more widespread. Capitalism rewarded relatively well those in primary jobs (with good wages, benefits, opportunities for promotion, and greater stability). But segmented labor markets left many workers holding secondary jobs that lacked those qualities.

Capitalism, the State, and Speculation

Capitalism involves a combination of market forces, nonmarket forces such as actions by the state, and what can be termed hypermarket forces, which include speculative activities motivated by opportunities for large, one-time gains rather than profits made from the repeated production of the same item. In some cases state actions created opportunities for capital gains by private individuals or corporations. In the United States, federal land grants to railroad companies spurred settlement and economic development in the West in the nineteenth century. Profits often were anticipated to come from increases in land values along railroad routes, particularly at terminal points or junctions where towns might grow, rather than from operating the railroads.

Similarly, from the mid-twentieth century, federal highway and dam construction and defense spending underpinned city building and capitalist development in the southern and western areas known as the U.S. Sun Belt. In the 1980s, real estate speculation, particularly by savings and loan institutions, became excessive and a threat to the stability of the system rather than a positive force. The corporate merger and takeover wave of the 1980s also showed U.S. capitalism tilting toward a focus on speculative gains rather than on increases in productive efficiency.

In the judicial sphere, the evolution of legal doctrines and conceptions of property in the United States during the nineteenth century promoted capitalist development. As Morton Horwitz explained, in earlier agrarian conceptions, an owner was entitled to absolute dominion and undisturbed enjoyment of a property; this could block economically productive uses of neighboring properties. At the end of the eighteenth century and beginning of the nineteenth century, the construction of mills and dams led to legal controversies over water rights that ultimately resulted in acceptance of the view that property owners had the right to develop properties for business uses. The taking of land by eminent domain facilitated the building of roads, canals, and railroads. Legal doctrines pertaining to liability for damages and public nuisance produced greater predictability, allowing entrepreneurs to more accurately estimate costs of economic improvements. Other changes affected competition, contracts, and commercial law. Horwitz concluded that by around 1850 the legal system had become much more favorable to commercial and industrial groups.

Actions by the state sometimes benefited industrial capitalism as an unintended consequence of other aims. Gavin Wright argued that New Deal farm policies of the 1930s, designed to limit cotton production, undermined the sharecropping system in the U.S. South by creating incentives for landowners to switch to wage labor. Along with minimum wage legislation, the demise of sharecropping led the South to join a national labor market, which fostered the region's development. Elsewhere, capitalist development was an explicit goal. Alice Amsden showed that beginning in the 1960s, the South Korean state successfully forged a reciprocal relation with firms, disciplining them by withdrawing subsidies if export targets were not met. It set priorities for investment and pursued macroeconomic stabilization policies to support industrialization.

State action also affected the relationship between capital and labor. In the United States, federal and state governments fiercely resisted unions during the late nineteenth century with injunctions and armed interventions against strikes. Federal legislation of the 1930s and government practices during World War II assisted unions in achieving greater recognition and bargaining power. But right-to-work laws spread in southern and western states in the 1940s and 1950s, the 1947 Taft-Hartley Act was a major setback for labor, and the federal government turned sharply against unions in the 1980s.

Varying combinations of ordinary market forces, state action, and speculative activity generated industrial capitalism by the late twentieth century in an increasing but still limited group of countries. Western Europe, which had seen a protracted transition from feudalism to capitalism, was joined in the nineteenth and early twentieth centuries by white settler colonies known as "regions of recent settlement," such as the United States, Canada, Australia, and New Zealand. Argentina and South Africa shared some features with this group. Capitalism in regions of recent settlement was less a transformation of existing economic structures than an elimination of native populations and transfer of capital, labor, and institutions from Europe to work land that was abundantly available within these regions.

However, capitalism was not simply imported and imposed as a preexisting system. Scholars have debated whether farmers in New England and the Middle Atlantic region in the seventeenth to nineteenth centuries welcomed or resisted the spread of markets and the extent to which accumulation of wealth motivated their actions. In their ownership of land and dependence on family labor they clearly differed from capitalist farms in England whose proprietors rented land and hired wage labor. Holding the independence of the farm household as a primary goal, these U.S. farmers also were determined to avoid recreating a European feudal social structure in which large landowners held disproportionate economic and political power.

A final group of late industrializers—Japan from the late nineteenth century and, after World War II, Korea, Taiwan, Brazil, India, Turkey, and possibly Mexico—took a path to capitalism based on what Amsden called "industrialization through learning." Like European latecomers such as Germany, Italy, and Russia, these countries took advantage of their relatively backward status. Generally, they borrowed technology rather than inventing or innovating, although Germany did innovate and Japan became capable of innovation in some areas.

Some late industrializers relied heavily on exports and benefited from participation in the international economy. But home markets were also important, and among the most successful Asian countries were those with land reforms and relatively equal income distributions. In this respect they resembled regions of recent settlement that were not dominated by concentrated landownership. For countries in the periphery, moreover, industrial capitalism could be fostered by delinking from the international economy. Some Latin American countries and Egypt saw their manufacturing sectors strengthen when the crises of the 1920s–1930s weakened their ties with the center. Delinking allowed them to follow more expansionary monetary and fiscal policies during the Great Depression than did the United States.

Capitalist and Noncapitalist Forms of Organization
The development of capitalism and free wage labor was intimately bound up with unfree labor forms and political subordination. Coexistence of capitalist forms with noncapitalist forms has continued into the twentieth century. Immanuel Wallerstein argued that during 1450–1640, a capitalist world-economy emerged that included very different labor forms: free labor (including yeoman farmers) in the core, slavery and coerced cash-crop labor in the periphery, and sharecropping in the semiperiphery. From the sixteenth to the nineteenth centuries, the Baltic grain trade provided food for western European cities while in-tensifying serfdom in eastern Europe. Eighteenth-century sugar plantations in the Caribbean using African slaves bought manufactured exports from Britain and food from the New England and Middle Atlantic colonies, which also then could import British manufactures.

In the United States, slavery, sharecropping, and petty production were noncapitalist forms that interacted with capitalist forms. Petty production is small-scale production that can be market-oriented but is not capitalist. It relies primarily on individual or family labor rather than wage labor, and producers own their means of production. Slavery, sharecropping, and petty production were especially important in agriculture, although some slaves were used in industry and the factory system did not universally eliminate artisan producers in manufacturing. In some sectors, specialty production by petty producers in industrial districts coexisted with mass production of more standardized products. Slaves and, after the Civil War, sharecroppers in the U.S. South produced the cotton that helped make textiles a leading industrial sector in both Britain and the United States. Slave owners purchased manufactured products produced by northern firms. Capitalist production and free wage labor thus depended on noncapitalist production for a key input and for some of its markets.

Petty producers in U.S. agriculture participated in markets and accumulated wealth, but unlike capitalist firms, accumulation was not their primary motivation. According to Daniel Vickers, U.S. farm families from initial settlement to the beginnings of industrialization held an ideal of "competency"—a degree of comfortable independence. They did not seek self-sufficiency, although they engaged in considerable production for their own use. They sold some of their produce in markets and could be quite interested in dealing for profit but sought to avoid the dependence on the market implied by a lifetime of wage labor.

As David Weiman explained, over the life cycle of a successful farm family more family labor became available and farm capital increased, allowing the household to increase its income and purchase more manufactured commodities. Farm households existed within rural communities that had a mix of private and communal social relations, some of which tended to limit market production and private accumulation of wealth. But over time the activities of petty producers contributed to a process of primitive accumulation—accumulation based on pre- or noncapitalist social relations, in which capital does not yet create the conditions for its own reproduction—which ultimately undermined the system of petty production in rural communities.

Noncapitalist forms of organization also include household production by nonfarm families and production by the state. These spheres have been variously conceived as supporting capitalism (for example, by rearing and educating the labor force), financially draining and undermining capitalism (in the case of the state), or providing an alternative to capitalism. Household production shrank over the nineteenth and twentieth centuries as goods and services formerly provided within households were supplied by capitalist firms. Production by the state expanded with defense spending, the rise of the welfare state, and nationalization in Western Europe and Latin America. Some of these trends contributed to the shift from manufacturing to services that was an important feature of capitalist economies in the twentieth century.

In addition to depending on noncapitalist economic forms, capitalism involved political subordination both domestically and internationally. In some countries, labor unions were suppressed. Political subordination of India within the British Empire was central to the smooth operation of the multilateral trade and payments network underlying the "golden age" of world capitalism that lasted from the last third of the nineteenth century to the outbreak of World War I in 1914. India's purchases of cheap manufactures and invisibles such as government services led to a trade deficit with Britain. Its trade surplus with India gave Britain the means to buy from other European countries such as Germany and France, stimulating their industrialization. On the monetary side, control of India's official financial reserves gave Britain added flexibility in its role as the world's financial center.

Uneven Capitalist Development

Both on a world scale and within individual countries, capitalist development is uneven: spatially, temporally, and socially. Some countries grew rapidly while others remained poor. Industrial leadership shifted from Britain to Germany and the United States at the end of the nineteenth century; they in turn faced new challengers in the twentieth. Within countries, industrial regions boomed, then often declined as growth areas sprang up elsewhere.

The textile industry in New England saw widespread plant closings beginning in the 1920s, and employment plummeted between 1947 and 1957. Production grew in southeastern states and was an important source of growth in the 1960s–1970s. But in the 1980s, textile production began shifting to even lower-cost locations overseas. Deindustrialization in the Midwest became a national political issue in the 1970s, as firms in the steel, automobile, and other manufacturing industries experienced competition from late industrializers and other U.S. regions. Growth in Sun Belt states was due to new industries and services as well as the relocation of existing industries.

Similarly, capitalism has been punctuated over time by financial crashes and by depressions with large drops in real output and employment. Epochs of growth and relative stability alternated with periods of stagnation and disorder. U.S. capitalism saw panics in 1819, 1837, 1857, 1873, 1907, and other years; particularly severe depressions occurred in the 1870s, 1890s, and 1930s. The post–World War II boom unraveled after 1973. Productivity growth was less rapid, and growth in median family income slowed markedly. Within periods of depression or

prosperity, the experience of different industries is highly uneven. As Michael Bernstein emphasized, even during the 1930s the U.S. petroleum and tobacco industries saw strong output growth, while the iron and steel, automobile, and rubber industries remained depressed.

Finally, capitalism has been associated with shifts in the position of social classes, and its effects on different groups of people have been enormously varied. The broad-brush picture for Europe includes the decline of a landed aristocracy whose wealth and status were land-based and inherited; the rise of a bourgeoisie or middle class of merchants, manufacturers, and professionals with earnings from trade and industry; and the creation of a working class of wage earners. The fate of the peasantry varied— it was eliminated in some countries (England) but persisted in others (France, Russia), with lasting implications for economic and political development.

This simple story requires qualification even for Britain, where scholars question whether the industrial bourgeoisie ever truly dominated and suggest that landed interests maintained their political presence in the late nineteenth and early twentieth centuries by allying with internationally oriented financial capital. In the United States and other regions of recent settlement, the class configuration included the sector of family farmers discussed above. One result was that debtor-creditor relationships were particularly important in generating social conflict and social movements in the United States.

Although one might expect the capital-labor relationship to be the main locus of conflict in capitalist economies, this was not always the case. The United States did have a long and at many times violent history of capital-labor conflict. Its labor movement succeeded in the twentieth century in achieving considerable material gains for unionized workers; it did not seriously limit capital's control over the production process. Although groups such as the Wobblies (Industrial Workers of the World) sought to overthrow capitalism in the years prior to World War I, the United States did not have a strong socialist movement that included labor, as did some European countries. Other groups, particularly farmers, were important in the United States in alliance with labor or on their own in opposing what they saw as negative effects of financial capital or monopoly.

Farmers typically incur debts to purchase inputs, machinery, or land. During times of deflation or economic downturn those debts become particularly difficult to service. In addition to opposing debt and tax collection and foreclosures, farmers supported monetary policies that would increase the amount of currency and generate inflation (which would erode the real value of their debts) rather than deflation. Armed resistance to debt collection occurred in 1786–1787 in Massachusetts (Shays's Rebellion) and other states. After the Civil War, a long period of deflation lasting until about 1896 led farmers to join farmers' alliances and the Populist Party, which united with silver producers and greenbackers in calling for increases in the money supply. Although there were some concessions to these forces, the defeat of William Jennings Bryan by William McKinley in the presidential election of 1896 signaled the triumph of "sound money" advocates.

The Populists, like other third-party movements in the United States, did not succeed in becoming a governing party, but they were an important source of agitation, education, and new ideas. Many Populist proposals eventually became law, including railroad regulation, the income tax, an expanded currency and credit structure, postal savings banks, and political reforms. While some criticize Populist efforts to redistribute income and wealth, others celebrate the alternative vision of a more democratic capitalism that these farmers and laborers sought to realize.

Conclusion

Capitalism has had a two-sided character from its inception. Free wage labor coincided with unfreedom. Although capitalism eventually delivered greatly improved standards of living, its impact on people's lives as producers rather than consumers often was less positive. Jobs were deskilled, working conditions could be dangerous, and independence and decision-making were transferred to the employer. With changes in technology and industrial location, new workers were drawn in but old workers were permanently displaced. Rapid economic growth produced harmful environmental effects. Large-scale firms contributed to rising productivity but created potentially dangerous concentrations of economic and political power. Evolution of banking and financial institutions both aided growth and added a source of potential instability to the economic system.

Eliminating negative features of capitalism while preserving positive ones is not a simple or straightforward matter. As Robert Heilbroner observed, a medical metaphor is inappropriate. It is not possible to "cure" capitalism of its diseases and restore it to full health. Moreover, measures that eliminate one problem can help produce the next. For example, if government spending and transfers provide a "floor" to soften depressions, inflationary tendencies can result. But a historical perspective helps underscore the fact that capitalism is not an immutable system; it has changed in the past and can continue to do so in the future.

BIBLIOGRAPHY

Amsden, Alice H. *Asia's Next Giant: South Korea and Late Industrialization.* New York: Oxford University Press, 1989.

Baskin, Jonathan Barron, and Paul J. Miranti Jr. *A History of Corporate Finance.* Cambridge, U.K.: Cambridge University Press, 1997.

Bernstein, Michael A. *The Great Depression: Delayed Recovery and Economic Change in America, 1929–1939.* Cambridge, U.K.: Cambridge University Press, 1987.

Braverman, Harry. *Labor and Monopoly Capital: The Degradation of Work in the Twentieth Century.* New York: Monthly Review Press, 1974.

Chandler, Alfred D., Jr. *The Visible Hand: The Managerial Revolution in American Business.* Cambridge, Mass.: Belknap Press, 1977.

Gerschenkron, Alexander. *Economic Backwardness in Historical Perspective: A Book of Essays.* Cambridge, Mass.: Belknap Press, 1962.

Gordon, David M., Richard Edwards, and Michael Reich. *Segmented Work, Divided Workers: The Historical Transformation of Labor in the United States.* Cambridge, U.K.: Cambridge University Press, 1982.

Heilbroner, Robert. "Inflationary Capitalism." *New Yorker* 55, no. 34 (8 Oct. 1979): 121–141.

Horwitz, Morton J. *The Transformation of American Law, 1780–1860.* Cambridge, Mass.: Harvard University Press, 1977.

Jacoby, Sanford M. *Employing Bureaucracy: Managers, Unions, and the Transformation of Work in American Industry, 1900–1945.* New York: Columbia University Press, 1985.

Kulikoff, Allan. *The Agrarian Origins of American Capitalism.* Charlottesville: University Press of Virginia, 1992.

Lamoreaux, Naomi. *Insider Lending: Banks, Personal Connections, and Economic Development in Industrial New England.* Cambridge, U.K.: Cambridge University Press, 1994.

Montgomery, David. *The Fall of the House of Labor: The Workplace, the State, and American Labor Activism, 1865–1925.* Cambridge, U.K.: Cambridge University Press, 1987.

Moore, Barrington, Jr. *The Social Origins of Dictatorship and Democracy: Lord and Peasant in the Making of the Modern World.* Boston: Beacon Press, 1966.

Nelson, Daniel. *Managers and Workers: Origins of the Twentieth-Century Factory System in the United States, 1880–1920.* 2d ed. Madison: University of Wisconsin Press, 1995.

Noble, David F. *America by Design: Science, Technology, and the Rise of Corporate Capitalism.* New York: Knopf, 1977.

Scranton, Philip. *Endless Novelty: Specialty Production and American Industrialization, 1865–1925.* Princeton, N.J.: Princeton University Press, 1997.

Vickers, Daniel. "Competency and Competition: Economic Culture in Early America." *William and Mary Quarterly*, 3d. Ser., 47, no. 1. (1990): 3–29.

Wallerstein, Immanuel. *The Modern World-System: Capitalist Agriculture and the Origins of the European World-Economy in the Sixteenth Century.* New York: Academic Press, 1974.

Weber, Max. *The Protestant Ethic and the Spirit of Capitalism.* New York: Scribners, 1958.

Weiman, David F. "Families, Farms and Rural Society in Preindustrial America." In *Agrarian Organization in the Century of Industrialization: Europe, Russia, and North America.* Edited by George Grantham and Carol S. Leonard. *Research in Economic History,* Supplement 5 (Part B). Greenwich, Conn.: JAI Press, 1989.

Weir, Margaret, and Theda Skocpol. "State Structures and the Possibilities for 'Keynesian' Responses to the Great Depression in Sweden, Britain, and the United States." In *Bringing the State Back In.* Edited by Peter B. Evans, Dietrich Rueschemeyer, and Theda Skocpol. Cambridge, U.K.: Cambridge University Press, 1985.

Wright, Gavin. *Old South, New South: Revolutions in the Southern Economy since the Civil War.* New York: Basic Books, 1986.

———. "American Agriculture and the Labor Market: What Happened to Proletarianization?" *Agricultural History* 62, no. 3 (1988): 182–209.

Carol E. Heim

See also **American System; Banking; Financial Panics; Industrial Revolution; Industrial Workers of the World; Labor; Populism; Right-to-Work Laws; Trade Unions; Welfare Capitalism.**

CAPITALS. Americans have had the opportunity to decide the location for fifty state capitals. The current array is the result of decisions made as early as the 1600s (Santa Fe, Boston, Annapolis) and as late as the 1970s, when Alaskans declined to build a new capital. The ways in which Americans have thought about capitals have been unavoidably influenced by the example of Washington, D.C., especially the principles of neutrality and centrality that determined the location of the federal district in the 1790s. The location of capitals also shows the effects of economic rivalries within territories and states.

In the early years of independence, many of the original states moved their capitals from seaboard to interior, following the westward movement of population and economic activity. Examples include Columbia, South Carolina; Raleigh, North Carolina; Richmond, Virginia; Harrisburg, Pennsylvania; Albany, New York; and Concord,

New Hampshire. Maryland and Massachusetts, in contrast, left their capitals at the seventeenth-century sites whose initial recommendation was easy access to waterborne commerce. In the 1960s and 1970s, Alaskans debated, and ultimately rejected, a similar shift from the tidewater town of Juneau to a site in the state's interior between Anchorage and Fairbanks. Centrality was also the key factor for Indianapolis, deliberately placed in the geographical center of Indiana in advance of European American settlement.

Neutrality was a more important principle for several other middle western states that split the difference between powerful cities. Frankfort, Kentucky, lay halfway between Lexington and Louisville. Columbus was not only central to Ohio but also midway between Cleveland, with its Great Lakes trade, and Cincinnati, with its Ohio River trade.

Local economic competition and promotion played a role in several capital locations. The Wisconsin promoter James Duane Doty finessed the rivalry among several Lake Michigan cities by offering territorial legislators prime town lots in a new community eighty miles west of the lake; the lawmakers soon discovered the merits of Madison as a capital. Coloradans in the 1860s aligned themselves between two factions of the Republican Party. The "Denver crowd" and the "Golden crowd" fought over political offices and over the designation of the ter-

Richmond, Va. A view, c. 1909, of the Virginia State Capitol, a 1780s Neoclassical building designed by Thomas Jefferson, with the help of Charles-Louis Clérisseau, and modeled after a Roman temple (now the Maison Carrée) in Nîmes, France. LIBRARY OF CONGRESS

Columbus, Ohio. The Ohio State Capitol, completed in 1861 and noted for its Greek Revival architecture. LIBRARY OF CONGRESS

ritorial capital, in the end secured by Denver. The choice of Pierre, South Dakota, represents the victory of the Chicago and Northwestern Railroad over towns favored by the rival Milwaukee, St. Paul, and Pacific Railroad.

Statehouses or capitol buildings occupy a prominent and often elevated site in most capital cities. Many of the buildings date from eras of statehouse building, from 1866 to 1886 and 1895 to 1924. During these years, state capitols grew from relatively modest colonial and antebellum origins to complex and formidable structures, often designed by leading architects such as Cass Gilbert and Charles Follen McKim. The typical statehouse draws on the U.S. Capitol and is a domed, low cross with symmetrically balanced wings for two legislative houses connected by a rotunda. Replacement buildings since the 1930s have tended toward simplified variations on the common themes.

Designation as a state capital has not guaranteed a city economic prominence. Atlanta, Boston, and Denver are the dominant city in their region, but only nine of thirty-seven cities that host Federal Reserve banks or branches are state capitals. Perhaps a dozen more state capitals, such as Hartford, Boise, Des Moines, Oklahoma City, and Phoenix, are the most prominent city in their state. But more commonly, the state capital is a second-tier or third-tier city even within its state, as shown by examples from Tallahassee, Florida, to Olympia, Washington.

BIBLIOGRAPHY

Goodsell, Charles T. *The American Statehouse: Interpreting Democracy's Temples.* Lawrence: University Press of Kansas, 2001.

Hitchcock, Henry-Russell, and William Seale. *Temples of Democracy: The State Capitols of the U.S.A.* New York: Harcourt Brace Jovanovich, 1976.

Carl Abbott

See also **Capitol at Washington; Washington, D.C.**

CAPITATION TAXES, or poll taxes, are levied on each person without reference to income or property. The U.S. Constitution, in Article I, Section 9, forbids the federal government from levying a capitation or other direct tax "unless in Proportion to the Census of Enumeration" provided for in Section 2. Section 9, however, in accord with colonial practices of placing taxes on the importation of convicts and slaves, permits a tax or duty to be imposed on persons entering the United States, "not exceeding ten dollars for each person."

The poll-tax restriction does not apply to the states. Following colonial precedents, the states employed this tax, generally placing a levy on all males above age twenty-one, or sometimes above age sixteen. Beginning in the late nineteenth century, southern states made payment of a poll tax a prerequisite to the exercise of suffrage. This requirement disqualified many African Americans who could not afford the tax, or subjected their votes to influence by those who paid the tax for them. The Twenty-fourth Amendment to the U.S. Constitution, ratified in 1964, outlawed the use of the poll tax in federal elections. In 1966 the Supreme Court ruled that the poll tax as a prerequisite for voting in a state election was unconstitutional under the Fourteenth Amendment.

BIBLIOGRAPHY

Kousser, J. Morgan. *The Shaping of Southern Politics: Suffrage Restriction and the Establishment of the One-Party South, 1880–1910.* New Haven, Conn.: Yale University Press, 1974.

Richard B. Morris/c. p.

See also **Disfranchisement; Poll Tax; Taxation.**

CAPITOL AT WASHINGTON. The United States was the first nation to plan and develop a city solely to serve as the seat of government. The country's founders selected the classical architecture of Greece and Rome as appropriate to express the new Republic's democratic ideals. Despite lingering disagreements over the design for the Capitol building, President George Washington laid the cornerstone on 18 September 1793. In 1800, Congress moved into the newly completed north wing. During the War of 1812, the British set fire to both wings, causing substantial damage. The rebuilt structure was completed in 1829 at a cost of approximately $2.5 million. It was 352 feet long, 283 feet wide, and 145 feet high to the top of the dome, and covered approximately 1.5 acres. By 1850 the Capitol had become too small. It took twenty years to complete wing extensions and a larger dome proportionate to the greater size. The dome alone required nine years to complete, at a cost of $1.25 million. By 1870, just under $13 million had been expended on the original construction and the enlargement.

L'Enfant's Plan

The Capitol was the focal point of Major Pierre Charles L'Enfant's 1791 plan for the new federal city. L'Enfant selected as the Capitol's site the western edge of Jenkin's Hill, ninety feet above the Potomac and with a commanding westward view. His plan aligned the Capitol due north-south, the midsection of the building at the center of a cruciform city plan with wide thoroughfares forming the long axes leading away from it in all four directions. Radial avenues overlaid the rectangular grid of city streets aligned with these axes. On a ridge northwest of Jenkin's Hill, L'Enfant sited the presidential residence, and linked it visually to the Capitol with a wide mall directly to the west and a diagonal avenue to the northwest.

L'Enfant's city plan sketched the Capitol building only in a rudimentary outline, although it indicated the north-south orientation and a large rotunda at the western edge. For refusing to make the details of his design for the Capitol and for other arbitrary, noncooperative acts, he was dismissed in March 1792, although his city plan was retained. Only in the twentieth century was the brilliance of L'Enfant's plan, with its centerpiece Capitol on the hill above a riverfront city of extraordinary coherence and expressiveness, fully realized.

Thornton's Design Chosen

After L'Enfant was dismissed, Jefferson and Washington responded positively to two designs, one by Dr. William Thornton, an Englishman, and the other by Stephen Hallet, a Frenchman. Both designs reflected the influence of the Italian Renaissance architect Andrea Palladio and consisted of a prominent center section where the members of Congress could confer together and where the president could meet with them. This section in both plans was flanked by the two wings for the separate deliberations by the two houses.

The concept of a circular room below a monumental dome was probably derived from L'Enfant's plan. However, Thornton's design was distinguished by two circular sections—although the two domes of the roofline at different levels would compromise the building's visual harmony. Nevertheless, Washington and Jefferson chose Thornton's design, with Hallet put in charge of construction. The latter was replaced first by George Hadfield and then by White House architect James Hoban, who by 1800 had completed the north wing. It was soon occupied by Congress, the Supreme Court, the Library of Congress, and the District of Columbia courts.

Latrobe's Changes

In 1803 Benjamin Henry Latrobe, a professional architect and engineer, began the construction of the House of

U.S. Capitol. A 1933 photograph by Walter Johnson. LIBRARY OF CONGRESS

Representatives wing and a reworking of the Senate wing, a project that took nine years. By 1806 he had completed a redesign of the center section. By 1811, Latrobe had completed the two legislative halls and bridged them temporarily with wooden scaffolding. On 24 August 1814, during the War of 1812, the British set fire to the Capitol, although a rainstorm prevented its complete destruction. From 1815 to 1819 Congress met in a building on First Street, N.E., later the site of the Supreme Court.

In 1817 Latrobe was charged with the reconstruction, to be based on his redesign. The dominant feature was to be the single central rotunda. Latrobe changed the overall design from baroque to Greek neoclassical. His neoclassical elements included uniquely American columns ornamented with ears of corn and tobacco leaves. Charles Bulfinch, a Boston architect, supervised the construction, which was completed in 1827.

Enlargement of the Capitol

By 1850 it had become clear that the Capitol was too small. In 1851 President Millard Fillmore selected Thomas U. Walter of Philadelphia to build two large wings on the north and south ends of the building. The new wing extensions, each 143 feet long and 239 feet wide, were constructed of white marble veined in blue. The corridors connecting these wings to the main building were each 44 feet long and 56 feet wide. The building's enlargement more than doubled its length. The extension of the wings of the building left the central dome out of proportion and in 1855 Congress voted to replace it with a cast iron dome twice as tall as Walter's design. The construction of the massive dome, begun six years before the Civil War, continued through the war.

A statue of the Goddess of Liberty, sculpted by Thomas Crawford, was placed on the top of the dome in 1863. It is 19.5 feet high and weighs nearly fifteen thousand pounds. On the statue's head is a "liberty cap" of eagle's feathers. In 1866 Constantino Brumidi's Rotunda canopy fresco, *The Apotheosis of Washington*, was completed. The Capitol extensions were completed in 1868.

The Modern Capitol

The landscape architect Frederick Law Olmsted, placed in charge of the Capitol grounds in 1874, added marble terraces on three sides of the building. Between 1958 and 1962, the Capitol was extended to the east by 32.5 feet with new marble walls. The extension added ninety new rooms. Between 1983 and 1987, the west front underwent a comprehensive stabilization of the deteriorating walls.

By 2000, the Capitol covered 175,170 square feet (about four acres). It was 751 feet long and, at its maximum, 350 feet wide. The building has five levels. Above the basement are the Old Supreme Court Chamber, the Hall of Columns, the Brumidi Corridors, and the Crypt under the Rotunda. The second floor contains the congressional chambers, the Rotunda, which is 180 feet high and 96 feet in diameter with a gallery of artwork portraying America's history, the National Statuary Hall, and the Old Senate Chamber. The third and fourth floors are mostly offices and other support space.

The Capitol building is the principal architectural symbol of the nation's political identity. At first, it was as a symbol of the federal union comprised of the separate states, freedom from monarchy and oppression, and a return to enlightenment. As the United States grew in power and influence, it also came to stand for the accomplishments and sacrifices the American people had experienced to preserve the freedoms of not only Americans, but of other nations as well.

BIBLIOGRAPHY

"The Architect of the Capitol." Available from http://www.aoc .gov.

Lowry, Bates. *Building a National Image: Architectural Drawings for the American Democracy, 1789–1912.* New York: Walker, 1985.

Gelernter, Mark. *A History of American Architecture: Buildings in Their Cultural and Technological Context.* Hanover, N.H.: University Press of New England, 1999.

Moore, Joseph West. *Picturesque Washington: Pen and Pencil Sketches.* Providence, R.I.: J. A. and R. A. Reid, 1890. This excellent older book contains highly detailed descriptions of the construction of the Capitol.

Partridge, William T. "L'Enfant's Methods and Features of His Plan for the Federal City." In *The Annual Report, National Capital Park and Planning Commission, 1930.* Washington, D.C.: National Capital Planning Commission, 1975.

Reed, Robert. *Old Washington, D.C. in Early Photographs, 1846–1932.* New York: Dover, 1980.

Judith Reynolds

See also **Architecture; Washington, D.C.; White House.**

CAPPER-VOLSTEAD ACT (18 February 1922), also known as the Cooperative Marketing Act. As a consequence of the depression of agricultural prices following World War I, farm organizations intensified their political activism and managed to get a farm bloc consisting of about twenty-five senators and one hundred representatives established in Congress. The Capper-Volstead Act was a key part of a new, moderate, businesslike farm legislative program, far removed from the agricultural radicalism of the Populist Era. The act exempted some types of voluntary agricultural cooperative associations from the application of antitrust laws. The secretary of agriculture was given the power to regulate these associations to prevent them from achieving and maintaining monopolies. He could hold hearings, determine facts, and issue orders ultimately subject to review by federal district courts. The act is an example of legislative aid to agricultural cooperatives and of the delegation of adjudicative power to an administrative agency.

BIBLIOGRAPHY

Guth, James L. "Farmers Monopolies, Cooperation and the Interest of Congress," *Agricultural History* 56 (January 1982): 67–82.

O'Brien, Patrick G. "A Reexamination of the Senate Farm Bloc, 1921–1933." *Agricultural History* 47 (July 1973): 248–263.

Saloutos, Theodore, and John D. Hicks. *Agricultural Discontent in the Middle West. 1900–1939.* Madison: University of Wisconsin Press, 1951.

Harvey Pinney / т. м.

See also **Cooperatives, Farmers'; Farmer-Labor Party of 1920; Populism.**

CAPTIVITY NARRATIVES. Rachel Parker Plummer, daughter of the Reverend James Parker, was captured along with her young son when Comanches attacked Fort Parker, Texas, on 19 May 1836. She witnessed the torture of her son James Pratt, who was taken from her, and she never learned his fate. The Comanches transported Plummer hundreds of miles, finally stopping in Santa Fe. While in captivity she gave birth to a daughter. Although Plummer was released in 1839, she died the next year. Describing her experiences, she wrote of her captors: "To undertake to narrate their barbarous treatment would only add to my present distress, for it is with feelings of the deepest mortification that I think of it, much less to speak or write of it." Her son James was ransomed in 1843. The Comanches adopted her daughter Cynthia Ann Parker, the mother of the Cherokee leader Quanah Parker. Cynthia Ann Parker was forcibly returned to white society in 1860 where she lived as a maid in her brother's house and died in 1870. These stories are part of the history, folklore, and myth of the American Southwest. Plummer's captivity narrative was published in two editions in 1839 and in 1844. Other stories, many based on historical events with similar themes and varia-

Taken Captive! The cover of this 1864 dime novel, *The Lost Trail*, depicts an ongoing fear of many white settlers. LIBRARY OF CONGRESS

tions, are part of the American saga of relationships among Euro-Americans and various Native groups. From the earliest British settlement came Captain John Smith's accounts of his own capture in 1607. Both Daniel Boone and his daughter Jamima were captives, the father in 1769 and the daughter in 1776. His story was told as a heroic experience; hers was told as a disaster from which she was rescued by her father.

The first and most well known incident of the Puritan era was of Mary White Rowlandson of Lancaster, Massachusetts, who was captured during King Philip's War in 1675 and published *A True History of the Captivity and Restoration of Mrs. Mary Rowlandson* (1682). John Williams, captured with his daughter Eunice Williams and hundreds of others in Deerfield, Massachusetts, in 1703, published his version as *The Redeemed Captive, Returning to Zion . . .* (1707). In New England between 1675 and 1763 Indian and French forces captured approximately 1,086 white people.

Captures continued after the Revolution and into the first half of the nineteenth century. In 1789 John Tanner was captured as a young boy. He lived with the Ottawa Ojibwas in Michigan for thirty years. His story was published in 1830. Sarah F. Wakefield and over one hundred other white women and children were captured by eastern Dakotas in the Dakota War along the Minnesota River in the late summer and early fall of 1862. Wakefield published two editions of her experiences (1863 and 1864). These are only a few of the thousands of men, women, and children caught up Indian wars over a three-hundred-year period. They were mostly white Anglo-Americans, but some were African Americans. French were captured in Canada, and Spanish were captured in Mexico and in the American and Spanish Southwest or Borderlands. The captives also included many Native American women and children, like Pocahontas, captured by the British in 1619.

Capture was both a historical experience and a genre of American historical adventure. The popularity of the white captive story was established in the British colonies with Rowlandson's work and continued down to twentieth-century films, such as *The Searchers* (1956) and *Dances with Wolves* (1990), whose female lead is a white captive turned Sioux.

Why all of this mayhem and exploitation? Indian captures were part of the Native ways of war. Printing and retelling these stories helped define the Anglo-American experience. Though Europeans defined American Indians as "savage" and "barbarian," European ways of war were brutal. In 1637, in the first major confrontation in New England between the Massachusetts Puritans and the Pequots of Connecticut and Rhode Island, British American men deliberately burned to the ground the fortress village of the Pequots. Women and children ran screaming from the flames, and many of the Pequots captured were sold into slavery in the West Indies.

Native tactics varied depending on region and tribal affiliation, but Native ways of war frequently consisted of the capture of neighboring hostile tribal members, either in the battle area or in the village. Men, women, and children were taken and marched overland to nearby or remote areas. The men and boys were tried by running the gauntlet, that is, they had to run between two lines of men, women, and children, who tried to beat them, throw things at them, and hurt them in any way possible. If the men or boys got through the process and did not die of injury, they might be put through tortures. But men, women, boys, and girls seen as brave and useful to the group were ceremonially adopted and became members of the tribe.

These adoptions were often the horrifying and exciting tales told to European and Euro-American readers. Some women who met this fate became famous, such as Eunice Williams, who was marched to New France, where many years later she married an Abenaki. Mary Jemison, a young girl captured on the Pennsylvania fron-

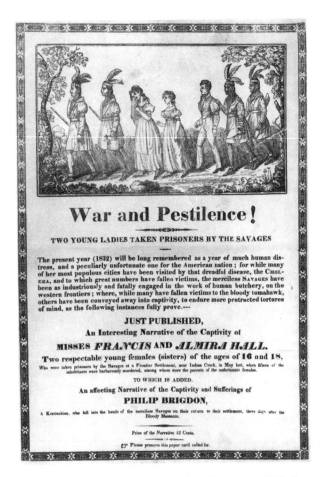

Tales of Captivity. This 1833 woodcut illustrates published narratives of the capture and brief captivity of the teenage sisters Frances and Almira Hall (real names, Rachel and Sylvia) and Philip Brigdon after an attack by Potawatomi warriors on the Illinois settlement of Indian Creek—leaving five men, three women, and seven children dead—during the Black Hawk War of early 1832. LIBRARY OF CONGRESS

tier by Shawnees and French in 1755, was traded to the Senecas, who adopted her. She first married a Delaware, but after her first husband died, she married a Seneca. In 1755 James Smith was an eighteen-year-old Anglo-American serving in the British army in western Pennsylvania, clearing a road in preparation for an attack on the French. Captured during the Battle of the Wilderness, he was taken to a Caughnawaga Mohawk village in the Ohio region, where he was ritually adopted. Smith lived with the Caughnawaga Mohawks and other Iroquois for five years and recalled that his new Delaware brother said they were happy to adopt him to take the place of other great men.

Men and women like Williams, Jemison, and Smith, called "White Indians," were to become new brothers and sisters to help increase the populations of the Native tribes. Their well-known experiences encouraged the white people of the colonies and the new nation to ex-

amine their prejudices against Indians as "wild," barbarous, untrained, and unrestrained. After his return, Smith wrote a small book telling of his experiences and urging the colonials to learn how to fight in the Indian way. After the orders were given, the men in the field fought alone and made their own decisions, as in guerrilla warfare.

The experiences of white captives varied. They were interpreted to emphasize notions of Indians as "savages" or as "noble savages." These experiences also provided lessons as to who was "civilized" and who was not and the expected roles of whites, Indians, and those of mixed descent.

BIBLIOGRAPHY

Axtell, James. *Natives and Newcomers: The Cultural Origins of North America.* New York: Oxford University Press, 2001. See especially Chapters 6 and 8.

Castiglia, Christopher. *Bound and Determined: Captivity, Culture-Crossing, and White Womanhood from Mary Rowlandson to Patty Hearst.* Chicago: University of Chicago Press, 1996.

Jennings, Francis. *The Invasion of America: Indians, Colonialism. and the Cant of Conquest.* New York: Norton, 1976.

Namias, June. *White Captives: Gender and Ethnicity on the American Frontier.* Chapel Hill: University of North Carolina Press, 1993.

Plummer, Rachel Parker. "Narrative of the Capture and Subsequent Sufferings of Mrs. Rachel Plummer, Written by Herself." In *Held Captive by Indians: Selected Narratives: 1642–1836.* Compiled by Richard VanDerBeets. Knoxville: University of Tennessee Press, 1973.

Rountree, Helen C. "Pocahontas: The Hostage Who Became Famous." In *Sifters: Native American Women's Lives.* Edited by Theda Perdue. New York: Oxford University Press, 2001.

Sayre, Gordon M., ed. *American Captivity Narratives: Selected Narratives with Introduction: Olaudah Equiano, Mary Rowlandson, and Others.* Boston: Houghton Mifflin, 2000.

Vaughan, Alden T., and Edward W. Clark, eds. *Puritans among the Indians: Accounts of Captivity and Redemption, 1676–1724.* Cambridge, Mass.: Belknap Press, 1981.

Vaughan, Alden T., and Daniel K. Richter. "Crossing the Cultural Divide: Indians and New Englanders, 1605–1763." *American Antiquarian Society* 90 (16 April 1980): 23–99.

Washburn, Wilcomb E., ed. *The Garland Library of Narratives of North American Indian Captivities.* 111 vols. New York: Garland Publishing, 1975–1983.

June Namias

See also **Indian Intermarriage; Indian Warfare.**

CARDIOVASCULAR DISEASE is the name of a group of ailments that affect the heart and blood vessels, including but not limited to hypertension, heart attack, stroke, congenital and rheumatic heart disease, and arrhythmia. The leading cause of death in America in the early twenty-first century, heart disease strikes both men and women across racial and ethnic lines, with people age

35 to 64 years old the most susceptible. Approximately one million Americans die of heart disease annually. For the millions of Americans with some form of heart disease, premature and permanent disability is a constant threat.

The diagnosis and treatment of heart disease developed slowly. In the eighteenth century one of the first steps toward diagnosis was Viennese scientist Leopold Auenbrugger's method of percussion. Striking the patient's chest to listen and feel the reverberation allowed Auenbrugger to estimate the size of the heart and the presence of fluid in the chest. Auenbrugger's method was improved by the invention of the stethoscope by French physician René Laënnec. These methods worked well for diseases that produced physical symptoms but not for ailments with no physical signs. Two other important eighteenth-century physicians were Englishmen William Heberden and John Hunter, who concentrated on the manifestation of the disease instead of the causes. The first to use the term "angina pectoris" in a 1772 lecture, Heberden separated myocardial infarction (heart attack) from other types of chest pain.

In 1902 Willem Einthoven, a Dutch physiologist, published the first electrocardiogram, which he recorded on a string galvanometer he had adapted for this purpose. This device was the forerunner of the electrocardiograph (EKG), a device that reads and records the heart's electrical activity. The EKG built on the work of English physicians James Mackenzie, developer of the polygraph, and Thomas Lewis. In Europe, physicians tended to de-emphasize the role of technology in diagnoses but American physician James Herrick saw the potential usefulness of the EKG in diagnosing conditions that could not be detected using the unaided senses. In 1912 Herrick was the first to describe coronary artery disease, or hardening of the arteries, as a form of heart disease.

In the spring of 1929, Werner Forssmann, a German physician, took another important step in cardiac research. Forssmann, fascinated by research conducted by nineteenth-century French doctors, inserted a urethral catheter into a main vein in his arm and guided the catheter into his own heart. Three years later two American doctors, Dickinson Richards, Jr. and André Cournand, moved Forssmann's research forward. Richards and Cournand began with the belief that the heart, lungs, and circulatory system were actually a single system. By 1942 the doctors successfully reached the right ventricle, and two years later they successfully inserted a catheter into a patient's pulmonary artery. Using a catheter, the doctors could measure hemodynamic pressure and oxygen in each side of the heart. Richards and Cournand received federal funds to continue their research.

With advances in technology, methods for treating patients suffering from heart disease increased. By 1938 the American Robert Gross had performed the first heart surgery, and by 1952 another American, F. John Lewis, performed the first open-heart surgery. In 1967 the South African surgeon Christiaan Barnard completed the first whole-heart transplant. One of the most striking medical advances is the artificial heart. The Jarvik-7, developed by the American doctor Robert K. Jarvik, was made to operate like a real heart. Made of aluminum, plastic, and Dacron polyester and needing a power source, the Jarvik-7 is bulky and meant to serve only as a temporary solution for those on a transplant list. Jarvik's heart, first used in the 1980s, was not the first artificial heart. In 1957 the Dutch physician Willem Kolff and his team tested an artificial heart in animals, and by 1969 another team led by Denton Cooley of the Texas Heart Institute kept a human artificial-heart patient alive for more than sixty hours. In 1982 the first Jarvik heart was transferred to Barney Clark by a team led by University of Utah's William DeVries. Clark lived for 112 days after the transplant.

Treatments less drastic than transplant surgery were also developed. For instance, in the late 1960s and early 1970s surgeons rerouted blood flow to the heart with coronary artery bypass surgery. Another less invasive procedure called percutaneous transluminal coronary angioplasty was developed in the late 1970s to open occluded cardiac arteries without opening the chest. Angioplasty uses a small device that is threaded through blood vessels to reach a blockage in the cardiac arteries. For patients suffering from abnormal or slow heart rhythm, doctors use a pacemaker, developed in the 1980s. Pacemakers, using lithium batteries lasting seven to ten years, are inserted in the body with wires attached to the heart. When the heart rhythm becomes dangerous the pacemaker delivers a shock to restore a normal heartbeat. The key to survival for heart attack victims is getting to the hospital quickly. Fortunately public awareness and widespread knowledge about CPR, cardiopulmonary resuscitation, greatly increases victims' chances.

Doctors and researchers have also identified certain risk factors that increase a person's chance of developing heart disease. In 1948 the Framingham Heart Study was initiated to track 5,209 people, examining each person every two years. The study's findings demonstrated that men, older people, and people with a family history of heart disease were more likely to develop heart problems. Further, the study indicated that those who smoke, have a poor diet, and lead sedentary lifestyles, are more likely to develop heart disease. The American Heart Association (AHA) was formed in 1924 to help doctors educate the public about heart disease. After launching a public awareness campaign in 1948, the AHA grew rapidly and remains one of the loudest voices for public health in America.

BIBLIOGRAPHY

Howell, Joel D. "Concepts of Heart-Related Diseases." In *The Cambridge World History of Human Diseases*. Kiple, Kenneth F., ed. New York: Cambridge University Press, 1993.

Lisa A. Ennis

See also **Epidemics and Public Health; Heart Implants; Medicine and Surgery; Transplants and Organ Donation.**

CARIBBEAN POLICY. The United States traditionally has had major national security interests in the Caribbean basin, loosely defined by U.S. policymakers as the Caribbean islands plus some Central American territories. Those interests are expressed not only in the military sphere but also in the political and economic arenas. In the early days of the republic, the United States engaged in trade with Caribbean territories, becoming the main trading partner of Spanish colonies like Cuba and Puerto Rico, from which it purchased sugar and molasses. In 1823 the proclamation of the MONROE DOCTRINE underscored the growing diplomatic role of the United States in the region. By the mid-nineteenth century, U.S. interest centered on the lush island of Cuba, but diplomatic overtures to purchase it from Spain failed. U.S. policymakers then turned their attention to the Dominican Republic, which the Grant administration tried to annex as a state of the union, but the 1870 annexation treaty failed to be ratified by the U.S. Senate.

In the 1890s, U.S. interest in the region was revitalized by the opportunity to build a canal across the Central American isthmus and also by the rekindling of the independence war in Cuba in 1895, which policymakers believed could cause Cuba to fall into the hands of another foreign power—most likely Great Britain—unless the United States intervened. As a result, U.S. foreign policy in the Caribbean basin became increasingly more aggressive, culminating in the Cuban-Spanish-American War of 1898. The war was short and easy for the United States. With the ratification of the 1898 Treaty of Paris, the United States became an imperial power through the acquisition of colonies in Puerto Rico, the Philippines, and Guam. Cuba was also acquired, and after four years of U.S. military occupation it was finally granted its independence in 1902, but only after the Cubans agreed to incorporate into their constitution the PLATT AMENDMENT, which gave the United States the unilateral right to intervene in Cuban affairs to protect its national interest.

Having become the new superpower in the region, the United States quickly moved to consolidate its status. After negotiations stalled with Colombia for rights to build the canal, the Theodore Roosevelt administration encouraged and supported a rebellion in the Colombian province of Panama in 1903. The United States immediately extended diplomatic recognition and military protection to Panama, which in turn granted the United States exclusive rights to build the canal. In 1905 the president issued the ROOSEVELT COROLLARY to the Monroe Doctrine, by which the United States would assume the role of the region's policeman. GUNBOAT DIPLOMACY and later DOLLAR DIPLOMACY would lead to further U.S. meddling in the region in order to protect perceived interests. Concerned about the practice of European powers of

sending warships into the region to force collection on debts, U.S. agents assumed control of the Dominican Republic's customs houses in 1905, paying the Dominican Republic's external debt to the European powers and establishing a payment schedule guaranteed by 50 percent of Dominican customs revenues.

The next logical step, political control, would be taken by the Wilson administration. After the inauguration of the PANAMA CANAL in 1914 and the start of World War I, U.S. military concerns over the region quickly escalated. In 1915, after political instability led to the assassination of Haiti's president by an angry mob, U.S. Marines invaded, leading to a prolonged and controversial military occupation (1918–1934). Shortly thereafter, the U.S. military occupied the Dominican Republic (1916–1924). These military occupations changed the face of these Caribbean nations as the marines modernized governmental administrations and infrastructure. On the other hand, the U.S. military repressed the local populations, censored the local press, limited freedom of speech, and created constabulary military forces to guarantee order after the marines' departure. In 1917, the United States purchased the Danish Virgin Islands and granted citizenship rights to Puerto Ricans, and in 1927 marines were landed in Nicaragua, beginning another long-term occupation in the region, which ended in 1932.

The Franklin D. Roosevelt administration established a new, noninterventionist policy toward the region known as the GOOD NEIGHBOR POLICY, which ended U.S. military occupations, abrogated the Platt Amendment in 1934, and favored diplomacy over military action. Unfortunately, the policy also happened to support strongmen in the region, as long as they remained friends of the United States, including Anastasio Somoza in Nicaragua, Fulgencio Batista in Cuba, and Rafael Trujillo in the Dominican Republic. World War II consolidated amicable relations with the region's nations, as the United States sought to forge a hemispheric defense shield against Nazi incursions in the region. A main outcome was the forging of a new working relationship with its colony in Puerto Rico, which became a U.S. commonwealth in 1952, giving Puerto Ricans control over their internal affairs while remaining a U.S. territory.

During the Cold War, U.S. relations with Caribbean nations were determined by the new political realities of a contest for world supremacy with the Soviet Union. In 1954, CIA-backed Guatemalan exiles overthrew the elected administration of Jacobo Arbenz, a moderate leftist who had been carrying out an ambitious land reform program that threatened the lands of the U.S.-owned United Fruit Company. On 1 January 1959, the triumph of the Cuban revolution presented a major challenge to U.S. national security interests in the region, as the administration of Fidel Castro quickly came at odds with the United States. After the Eisenhower administration implemented a trade embargo and cut off diplomatic relations in 1960, the Kennedy administration supported the BAY OF PIGS INVASION by CIA-trained Cuban exiles in 1961, which ended in a total fiasco. Castro then declared the revolution socialist and fully embraced the Soviet camp. This was followed by the tense standoff between the Soviet Union and the United States in the CUBAN MISSILE CRISIS of 1962. Elsewhere, concerns about a possible communist takeover led the Johnson administration to dispatch U.S. troops to the Dominican Republic in 1965 to quell the country's ongoing civil war. In the 1970s and 1980s, the United States watched with apprehension as military regimes in Central America were threatened by leftist insurgents. In Nicaragua, the Sandinista revolution in 1979 overthrew the Somoza dictatorship and quickly encountered the opposition of the Reagan administration, which isolated and undermined the Sandinistas through the support of counter-revolutionary armies while propping up besieged regimes in El Salvador and Guatemala with millions of dollars in military hardware and training. In 1983, similar concerns led to the GRENADA INVASION after the tiny island's self-styled "revolution" had established trade and aid relations with Cuba.

The end of the Cold War after 1989 led to a return to more traditional concerns about general instability in the region. In 1989, the George H. W. Bush administration ordered the PANAMA INVASION to capture strongman Manuel A. Noriega, who had been indicted on drug trafficking charges in the United States. In 1994, the Clinton administration sent U.S. troops into Haiti to depose the country's military junta and restore to office the democratically elected president, Jean-Bertrand Aristide, and a massive wave of Cuban rafters led to the signing of migratory accords with Cuba, ending the special status that Cubans had traditionally enjoyed as political refugees upon reaching U.S. shores. Concerns over a repetition of the 1980 MARIEL BOATLIFT, in which more than 125,000 Cubans had arrived to southern Florida, led to the change in policy.

At the beginning of the twenty-first century, U.S. policy toward the Caribbean basin continues to be characterized by its reliance on military over diplomatic solutions, by its reactive—rather than preventive—nature, by the growing asymmetry in power between the United States and Caribbean nations, and by the prevalence of dependent trade links with the United States among the region's nations. Today, however, after displacement of the European powers and later the Soviet Union, the United States is unquestionably the region's hegemonic power.

BIBLIOGRAPHY

Langley, Lester D. *The United States and the Caribbean in the Twentieth Century.* 4th ed. Athens: University of Georgia Press, 1989.

Maingot, Anthony P. *The United States and the Caribbean: Challenges of an Asymmetrical Relationship.* Boulder, Colo.: Westview Press, 1994.

Martínez-Fernández, Luis. *Torn Between Empires: Economy, Society, and Patterns of Political Thought in the Hispanic Carib-*

bean, 1840–1878. Athens: University of Georgia Press, 1994.

Ernesto Sagás

See also **Cuba, Relations with; Dominican Republic; El Salvador, Relations with; Guatemala, Relations with; Haiti, Relations with; Nicaragua, Relations with; Puerto Rico; Spanish-American War.**

CARLISLE INDIAN INDUSTRIAL SCHOOL,

the first off-reservation school for American Indians in the United States, was established in 1879 in Pennsylvania by army officer Capt. Richard H. Pratt. Following Pratt's injunction to "kill the Indian and save the man," the school uprooted students from their traditional cultures and reeducated them in the practices of white society. As presumptive wage workers at the lowest echelon of the industrial economy, boys learned agricultural and vocational skills and girls learned sewing, cooking, and other traditionally domestic occupations. Carlisle became a prototype for scores of other Indian schools. Its football team, led by the great Jim Thorpe, defeated many established college teams between 1907 and 1912. The school closed in 1918.

BIBLIOGRAPHY

Coleman, Michael C. *American Indian Children at School, 1850–1930.* Jackson: University of Mississippi Press, 1993.

Witmer, Linda F. *The Indian Industrial School, Carlisle, Pennsylvania, 1879–1918.* Carlisle, Pa.: Cumberland County Historical Society, 1993.

Mulford Stough / A. R.

See also **Education, Indian; Indian Policy, U.S.: 1830–1900; Indian Religious Life.**

CARNEGIE CORPORATION OF NEW YORK,

a private grant-making foundation, was created by Andrew Carnegie (1835–1919) in 1911 to "promote the advancement and diffusion of knowledge and understanding among the people of the United States." Capitalized with a gift of $135 million, the Carnegie Corporation has been influential in a number of areas, including education, race relations, poverty, and public policy. In 2001 the Carnegie Corporation had assets of around $2 billion, putting it in the top thirty of American foundations, making grants of around $60 million annually.

In 1889 Carnegie wrote "The Gospel of Wealth," in which he argued that wealth is a community trust, for the "man who dies rich dies disgraced." Carnegie's philanthropic activity became more systematic after his retirement in 1901, when he sold his steel companies to J. P. Morgan for $400 million. Carnegie set up a variety of philanthropic organizations, including the Carnegie Institute of Pittsburgh (1900), the Carnegie Institution of Washington (1902), the Carnegie Foundation for the Advancement of Teaching (1905–1905), the Carnegie Endowment for International Peace (1910), the Carnegie Corporation (1911), and several foundations in Europe. The Carnegie Corporation was his largest single endowment and was operated chiefly under his personal direction until his death. One of Carnegie's early interests was the establishment of free public libraries, a program he began in 1881 and continued through the corporation, building over 2,500 libraries. The corporation terminated the program in 1917 but supported library services for several decades thereafter.

In the mid–twentieth century the Carnegie Corporation, along with the Rockefeller and Russell Sage Foundations, shifted research funding away from independent institutes and bureaus into higher education, leading to the development of the research university. For example, after World War I the corporation reallocated resources away from advocacy groups, like social settlement houses, and instead began funding university-based sociology.

Under the presidency of Frederick P. Keppel (1923–1941), the corporation funded large-scale policy studies, including sociologist Gunnar Myrdal's study of racism, *An American Dilemma* (1944). After World War II, under John W. Gardner (1955–1965), the corporation experimented with funding liberal social movements and policy-related research. Gardner left the corporation to head the Department of Health, Education, and Welfare under President Lyndon Johnson, illustrating the ties between the corporation and the liberal policy establishment. Alan Pifer (1965–1982) continued this activist grant making, funding Common Cause and advocacy groups associated with Ralph Nader. The Carnegie Corporation provided major support for educational television, especially the children's show *Sesame Street*. In the 1970s the corporation joined with the Ford Foundation in providing significant funding for women's studies programs.

The Carnegie Corporation continued its program of activist grant making into the twenty-first century. It concentrated especially on education, electoral reform, international development, and peace studies.

BIBLIOGRAPHY

Carnegie Corporation of New York. Home page at http://www.carnegie.org.

Lagemann, Ellen Condliffe. *The Politics of Knowledge: The Carnegie Corporation, Philanthropy, and Public Policy.* Middletown, Conn.: Wesleyan University Press, 1989.

Rare Book and Manuscript Library, Columbia University. Home page at http://www.columbia.edu/cu/lweb/indiv/rare. Archive of Carnegie Corporation activities from 1911 to 1983.

Wall, Joseph Frazier. *Andrew Carnegie.* 2d. ed. Pittsburgh, Pa.: University of Pittsburgh, 1989.

Fred W. Beuttler

See also **Carnegie Foundation for the Advancement of Teaching; Carnegie Institution of Washington; Philanthropy.**

CARNEGIE FOUNDATION FOR THE ADVANCEMENT OF TEACHING (CFAT), a private foundation, was established in 1905 by Andrew Carnegie with an endowment of $15 million. One of the oldest of American foundations, CFAT, through its retirement programs and published research reports, was among the most important organizations shaping education in the twentieth century, helping create a national system of secondary, collegiate, graduate, and professional education.

In 1906 Congress chartered the foundation "to do and perform all things necessary to encourage, uphold, and dignify the profession of the teacher and the cause of higher education." One of Carnegie's purposes for the foundation was to counteract the perceived economic radicalism of professors by providing them with secure retirements. The pension fund fundamentally reoriented American higher education. Only nonreligiously affiliated schools were eligible, so many schools separated themselves from denominational control. The retirement fund eventually developed into the Teachers Insurance Annuity Association (TIAA), which, along with the College Retirement Equities Fund (CREF), became the largest pension system in the United States. Another qualification was an admission requirement of four years of high school, leading to the standardization of curricula based on the Carnegie Unit (1908), which measured the time students studied a subject.

The most influential Carnegie report was Abraham Flexner's *Medical Education in the United States and Canada* (1910). In his systematic survey of all medical training institutions in the country, Flexner severely criticized substandard programs, urging that medical schools be grounded in basic research and be affiliated with universities. He later joined the Rockefeller-funded General Education Board, where he directed grant activity toward its implementation. Flexner's report became a model of similar CFAT studies directed toward educational reform, such as in law, theology, and engineering, college athletics, teacher training, and educational administration.

From the 1920s through the 1940s CFAT sponsored research encouraging a national system. The Pennsylvania Study revealed the course-credit system's weakness as a measure of academic progress. CFAT supported the development of the College Board and the Educational Testing Service, which created and administered standardized college and graduate admission tests. In the 1960s and 1970s CFAT funded numerous publications of its Commission on Higher Education, research that led to dramatically increased federal support for higher education and federal financial aid for students.

In 1973 the Carnegie Foundation published its Classification of Institutions of Higher Education, subsequently updated, an oft-cited ranking of universities based on degrees awarded and research funding. Ernest Boyer (1928–1995) led CFAT from 1979 until his death, publishing numerous reports, including *High School* (1983), *College* (1987), and *The Basic School* (1995), and encouraging national debates on general education, core curricula, and "the scholarship of teaching."

BIBLIOGRAPHY

The Boyer Center. Home page at http://www.boyercenter.org.

Lagemann, Ellen Condliffe. *Private Power for the Public Good: A History of the Carnegie Foundation for the Advancement of Teaching.* Middletown, Conn.: Wesleyan University Press, 1983.

Wall, Joseph Frazier. *Andrew Carnegie.* 2d. ed. Pittsburgh, Pa.: University of Pittsburgh Press, 1989.

Wheatley, Stephen C. *The Politics of Philanthropy: Abraham Flexner and Medical Education.* Madison: University of Wisconsin Press, 1988.

Fred W. Beuttler

See also **Education, Higher: Colleges and Universities.**

CARNEGIE INSTITUTION OF WASHINGTON.

In 1901 Andrew Carnegie offered the federal government $10 million in bonds of the U.S. Steel Corporation as an endowment to finance the advancement of knowledge. His gift was declined, and he gave the money in 1902 to establish the private Carnegie Institution. In 1904 it received a congressional charter of incorporation and was renamed the Carnegie Institution of Washington. The wealthiest organization of its kind in the country, the institution was intended to encourage original research by providing opportunities to exceptional scholars and scientists. The trustees decided to accomplish this purpose by spending a small part of the institution's income on grants to individuals and the bulk of it on large, well-organized projects. Carnegie, pleased by this conception, added $2 million to the endowment in 1907 and another $10 million in 1911.

Under presidents Daniel Coit Gilman (1902–1904) and Robert S. Woodward (1904–1920), the institution created ten major departments in various fields of the physical and biological sciences as well as in history, economics, and sociology. Under presidents John C. Merriam (1920–1938), Vannevar Bush (1939–1956), Caryl P. Haskins (1956–1971), and Philip Abelson, the emphasis on large projects remained the standard policy of the institution, the last vestiges of the program of grants to individuals having been eliminated during Bush's tenure.

The ten departments evolved into six in different parts of the country, each distinguished in its field: the Mount Wilson Observatory; the Geophysical Laboratory; the Department of Terrestrial Magnetism; the Division of Plant Biology; the Department of Embryology; and the Department of Genetics. The facilities of the institution were mobilized for defense research in both world wars. After World War II the institution's administration chose to avoid major financing by federal grants and, receiving a new capital gift of $10 million from the Carnegie Cor-

poration of New York, the institution continued to operate almost wholly on income from endowment.

By the end of the twentieth century, the institution dedicated most of its expenditures to research carried on by employees in its own departments, although it also sponsored research programs at both predoctoral and postdoctoral levels for upcoming scholars. Through programs such as First Light, a Saturday school that teaches science to elementary school students, and the Carnegie Academy for Science Education, a summer school catering to elementary-school science teachers, the institution also promoted its program for science research and education to a broader audience.

BIBLIOGRAPHY

Good, Gregory A., ed. *The Earth, the Heavens and the Carnegie Institution of Washington.* Washington, D.C.: American Geophysical Union, 1994.

Haskins, Caryl Parker. *This Our Golden Age: Selected Annual Essays of Caryl Parker Haskins.* Washington, D.C.: Carnegie Institution of Washington, 1994.

Daniel J. Kevles/A. R.

See also **Foundations, Endowed; Geophysical Explorations; Laboratories; Philanthropy; Think Tanks.**

CAROLINA, FUNDAMENTAL CONSTITUTIONS OF,

drafted in 1669, reflected the Crown's attempts to establish a highly traditional social order in the American colonies and to undermine the considerable power of the existing General Assembly. While maintaining the right to religious liberty, the document regulated the proprietary colonies according to the legally established Church of England and placed control in the hands of gentry. It called for a manorial system in which serfs would be bound to land controlled by nobility and established a palatine's court composed of eight proprietors. The oldest lord proprietor in residence would be governor.

In North Carolina, which was settled primarily by poor farmers who had migrated from Virginia, the Fundamental Constitutions proved unenforceable. Settlers refused to live on manors and chose instead to manage their own small farms. Led by John Culpeper, farmers rebelled against taxes on their tobacco and annual quitrents; in 1677 they deposed the governor and forced the proprietors to abandon most of their land claims.

In South Carolina the Fundamental Constitutions fared no better. There, too, colonists refused to accept either the established laws or the quitrents and chose instead to forge their own economic system, dependent on enslaved African labor from Barbados. Slaves were used to raise cattle and food crops for trade with the West Indies. The Fundamental Constitutions were revised into obsolescence by the close of the seventeenth century.

BIBLIOGRAPHY

Craven, Wesley Frank. *The Colonies in Transition, 1660–1713.* New York: Harper and Row, 1968.

Kammen, Michael. *Deputyes & Libertyes: The Origins of Representative Government in Colonial America.* New York: Knopf, 1969.

Leslie J. Lindenauer

See also **Church of England in the Colonies; Feudalism.**

CAROLINE **AFFAIR.**   In November 1837, William Lyon Mackenzie launched a rebellion in Upper Canada. Defeated by government forces, his followers fled to Navy Island in the Niagara River. Sympathizers supplied them from the American side of the river, using the American-owned steamer *Caroline.* On the night of 29 December, Canadian troops crossed the river and seized the *Caroline,* killing an American in the ensuing struggle before towing the steamer into midstream, setting it afire, and turning it adrift. President Martin Van Buren lodged a protest at London, which was ignored. For a time feeling ran high, but the case dragged on for years before the WEBSTER-ASHBURTON TREATY settled the affair in 1842.

BIBLIOGRAPHY

DeConde, Alexander. *A History of American Foreign Policy.* New York: Scribner, 1978.

Milledge L. Bonham Jr. / c. w.

See also **Canada, Relations with; Great Britain, Relations with.**

CAROLINE ISLANDS.   In the American drive across the Central Pacific in World War II, Truk atoll, near the center of the Caroline Islands, was the target of attacks from carrier and land-based bombers in April 1944. Later that year, to protect the right flank of General Douglas MacArthur's return to the Philippines, key positions in the Palaus in the western Carolines were selected for amphibious landings. Pelelieu Island, strongly fortified and defended by about 13,000 Japanese, was assaulted on 15 September. Organized resistance ended on 27 November at the cost of almost 10,500 American casualties. Meanwhile, elements of the Eighty-first Infantry Division captured the neighboring island of Angaur and Ulithi atoll. Ulithi was promptly converted into a major U.S. naval base.

BIBLIOGRAPHY

Haynes, William E. "On the Road to Tokio." *Wisconsin Magazine of History* 76, no. 1 (1992): 21–50.

Ross, Bill D. *Peleliu: Tragic Triumph.* New York: Random House, 1991.

Smith, Robert Ross. *The Approach to the Philippines.* Washington, D.C.: U.S. Army Center of Military History, 1996. The original edition was published in 1953.

Philip A. Crowl / A. R.

See also **Peleliu; Philippine Sea, Battle of the; Philippines; World War II, Navy in.**

CARPET MANUFACTURE   is one of the few businesses that continue to maintain manufacturing plants in United States. The carpet manufacture industry produces carpets that cover 70 percent of floors in businesses and homes. Today, the carpet industry maintains its roots in Dalton, Georgia, known as "The Carpet Capital of the World." Eighty percent of U.S. carpet is manufactured within a sixty-five-mile radius of Dalton.

Until the early nineteenth century most carpets were manufactured on hand-operated machines. Erastus B. Bigelow, "father of the modern carpet industry," invented the power-driven ingrain loom in May 1842. The power loom increased productivity substantially into the early 1930s. By 1939 an oligopoly of carpet-manufacturing companies emerged, including Bigelow-Sanford, James Lees, Firth, Mohawk, and Alexander Smith.

Wool was the basic fiber used for carpet manufacture until World War II, when the government declared it a commodity and placed it on allocation. This caused a decline in carpet manufacturing, and most of the plants were converted to produce essentials for the war such as blankets. The allocation also prompted the manufacturers to conduct research for a new fiber. Firth and Bigelow-Sanford introduced a wool-rayon blend in 1940.

After World War II the consumer market for home products began expanding. Wool and other fibers were readily available and were usually imported. At the end of 1950, the finished price of carpet increased due to the Trading with the Enemy Act. This created an increase in synthetic fibers. Lees introduced carpets made from cellulose acetate rayon and blends with wools. DuPont introduced "Type 501" nylon yarn for carpets. Man-made fibers were well on their way by 1960, and the carpet industry was able to produce without relying heavily on wool.

The tufting process, developed in Dalton, changed the carpet industry dramatically in the 1950s. Tufting is similar to the sewing process, inserting thousands of pieces of yarn into woven backing and securing them with latex. New firms entering the carpet industry were the ones who adopted the tufting process. Most of them located near Dalton, where they had access to labor and inexpensive production, as opposed to settling in the North, where unions influenced production costs. By 1963, nearly 63 percent of the carpet mills were located within fifty miles of Dalton.

New markets emerged during the 1960s. Carpet was no longer used just in formal rooms or as a luxury but,

Mechanized Weaving. A worker at the Olsen Rug Company in Chicago operates an industrial loom strung with hundreds of wool threads, c. 1950. NATIONAL ARCHIVES AND RECORDS ADMINISTRATION

because of the improved durability, elsewhere in the home and even outdoors. Today carpet is a key decorative and functional element with a myriad of varieties. Brands of carpeting range from mainstays such as Mohawk to designer lines such as Ralph Lauren Home.

BIBLIOGRAPHY

Carpet and Rug Institute. Home page at http://www.carpet-rug.com.

Kirk, Robert W. *Carpet Industry Present Status and Future Prospects.* Philadelphia: University of Pennsylvania Press, 1970.

Patton, Randall L. *Carpet Capital: The Rise of a New South Industry.* Athens: University of Georgia Press, 1999.

Donna W. Reamy

CARPETBAGGERS. In the face of the dire financial collapse that followed the Union army's decimation of the physical and commercial infrastructure of the South, once-wealthy Southerners frequently found themselves thrust into abject poverty. An economy thus thrown into chaos made an attractive target for Northern speculators hoping to buy properties at a fraction of their pre-war values in exchange for ready cash. Known for their cheap, shoddy luggage indicative of the transient nature of their business travels, these "carpetbaggers" often enlisted local poor whites or newly freed slaves as their assistants. This invasion of their property by these geographic, economic, and/or racial outsiders insulted the Southern planters' love for tradition and heritage. During Reconstruction, these carpetbaggers formed the foundation of the Republican party in the South.

BIBLIOGRAPHY

Current, Richard Nelson. *Those Terrible Carpetbaggers.* New York: Oxford University Press, 1988.

Kennedy, Stetson. *After Appomattox: How the South Won the War.* Gainesville: University Press of Florida, 1995.

Barbara Schwarz Wachal

See also **Reconstruction; Scalawag.**

CARRIAGE MAKING. Horse-drawn vehicles were made in the North American colonies from the earliest days of settlement, although most travel was on horseback because of poor roads. Soon after American independence, the number of horse-drawn vehicles dramatically increased as a result of territorial expansion, a mobile population, and the democratization of travel.

Famous builders of wagons and stagecoaches established themselves at strategic points like Troy, New York, and Concord, New Hampshire. After carriages for the well-to-do ceased to meet the demand for personal wheeled transportation, private conveyances developed. The first example of this was the one-horse shay, or chaise, a light vehicle with two high wheels adapted to the rough roads and numerous fords of the undeveloped country. For fifty years these were so popular that proprietors of carriage shops were usually known as chaise makers.

By the middle of the eighteenth century, the chaise was superseded by the four-wheel buggy, the most typical American vehicle prior to the cheap motor car. It was simpler, lighter, stronger, and less expensive than other similar conveyances.

Carriage making reached the height of its development in 1904, then declined rapidly. The number of horse-drawn vehicles made in the United States in 1939 was less than 50,000, compared with 1,700,000 thirty years earlier. The number of wage earners engaged in making such vehicles in 1939 had fallen to less than 5 percent of the number at the opening of the century. By the 1950s the industry produced only racing sulkies and a few made-to-order buggies.

BIBLIOGRAPHY

Clark, Victor S. *History of Manufactures in the United States.* 3 vols. New York: McGraw-Hill, 1929. The original edition was published Washington, D.C.: Carnegie Institution, 1916–1928.

Moody, Ralph. *Stagecoach West.* New York: T. Y. Crowell, 1967.

Wooster, Harvey A. "Manufacturer and Artisan." *Journal of Political Economy* 34 (February 1926).

Victor S. Clark / T. D.

See also **Horse; Stagecoach Travel; Transportation and Travel; Wagon Manufacture.**

CARTER DOCTRINE.

In response to the 1979 overthrow of the shah of Iran and the Soviet invasion of Afghanistan the same year, President James Earl Carter warned in his January 1980 State of the Union address that "any attempt by any outside force to gain control of the Persian Gulf" would constitute a threat to vital U.S. interests, especially oil, and would be met by military action. Carter backed the declaration by creating a Rapid Deployment Force, boosting military spending, and cultivating expanded military ties from Pakistan to Egypt. In 1990, President George H. W. Bush invoked the doctrine in sending U.S. troops to confront Iraq during the Gulf War.

BIBLIOGRAPHY

Dumbrell, John. *The Carter Presidency: A Re-evaluation.* Manchester, U.K.: Manchester University Press, 1993.

Smith, Gaddis. *Morality, Reason, and Power: American Diplomacy in the Carter Years.* New York: Hill and Wang, 1986.

Max Paul Friedman

See also **Afghanistan, Soviet Invasion of; Arab Nations, Relations with; Iran, Relations with; Russia, Relations with.**

CARTER V. CARTER COAL COMPANY,

298 U.S. 238 (1936). The U.S. Supreme Court, by a 5–4 majority, struck down the Bituminous Coal Conservation Act of 1935, holding that its labor relations section was beyond the power of Congress to regulate interstate commerce and exclusively within state authority under the Tenth Amendment. Writing for the majority, Justice George Sutherland relied on specious distinctions between production and commerce and between direct and indirect effects on commerce. Ignoring the severability clause, he held the price-control title unconstitutional as well. The suit was collusive and thus improper for the Court to entertain. *Carter* was the penultimate and most emphatic rejection of the constitutionality of key New Deal measures.

BIBLIOGRAPHY

Currie, David P. *The Constitution in the Supreme Court: The Second Century, 1888–1986.* Chicago: University of Chicago Press, 1990.

William M. Wiecek

See also **Interstate Commerce Laws.**

CARTOGRAPHY.

The science of mapmaking in the United States has developed along two main lines, commercial and governmental, producing different kinds of maps for different purposes.

Commercial Mapping and Mapmaking

Commercial or nongovernmental mapping and mapmaking began immediately after the Revolution with proposals by William Tatham, Thomas Hutchins, Simeon De Witt, and other topographers and geographers who had served in the army to compile maps of the states and regions of the United States. Since then, the three most widely published types of commercial maps have been geographical national and world atlases, county atlases, and individual maps.

Geographical atlases and maps were first published in the United States in the early 1790s—for example, Matthew Carey's *American Atlas,* published in Philadelphia in 1795. By the 1820s the best work was being done by Henry C. Carey and Isaac Lea, Samuel E. Morse and Sidney Breese, Henry S. Tanner, and John Melish. Melish's *Map of Pennsylvania* (1822) and Herman Böÿe's *Map of the State of Virginia* (1826) are excellent examples of large-scale state maps. The principal centers of publication during most of the nineteenth century were Philadelphia, Boston, New York, and Chicago.

Prior to the introduction of lithography in about 1830, maps were printed from copper engravings. Use of lithography expedited publication of maps in variant

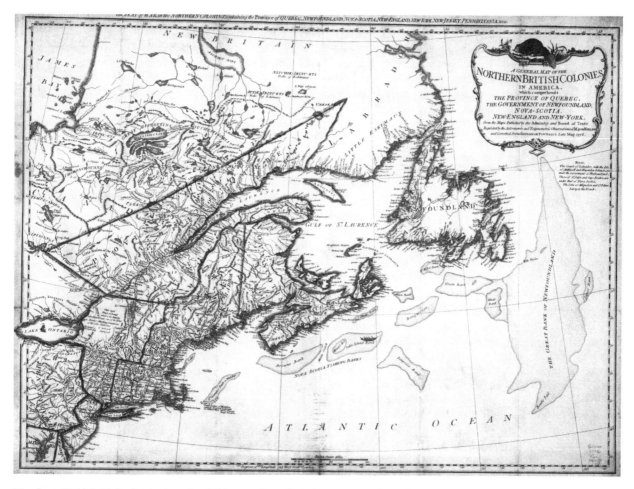

Northern British Colonies in America. This map shows British possessions from the French and Indian War to the American Revolution: Newfoundland, Quebec, Nova Scotia, the New England colonies, and New York. © CORBIS

forms and made them appreciably less expensive. These technical improvements rapidly increased commercial map publication. Meanwhile, the rapid expansion of white settlement into the West and the spread of American business interests abroad elicited a considerable interest in maps, either as individual state and county sheets or in atlases.

By midcentury, map publication was accelerated by the introduction of the rotary steam press, zinc plates, the transfer process, glazed paper, chromolithography, and the application of photography to printing. Two major map publishers, August Hoen of Baltimore and Julius Bien of New York, set the high standards of cartographic excellence during the second half of the nineteenth century. They produced many of the outstanding examples of cartographic presentation, especially those included in government publications. A. Hoen and Company was still making maps in the mid-1970s. Others who contributed significantly to the development of techniques of survey, compilation, and map reproduction were Robert Pearsall Smith and Henry Francis Walling. A uniquely American

form of commercial map publication in the second half of the nineteenth century was the county atlas and, to some extent, the city and town map. In addition, the fire insurance and underwriters map was developed during this period. The Sanborn Map Company perfected these maps in great detail and, until the 1960s, kept them up-to-date for most cities and towns of the United States.

During and after World War II commercial map production accelerated rapidly. Government mapping and mapmaking agencies contracted out to commercial map publishing firms large orders for many kinds of maps and atlases. Aerial and satellite photography, especially since World War II, has become a fundamental source of information in map compilation. Commercial map publication during the twentieth century expanded to include a wide variety of subjects, such as recreational, travel, road, airline, sports, oil and mineral exploration, and astronautical exploration maps, catering to a rapidly growing interest in graphic information. Using census and survey data, marketing firms have developed sophisticated maps to help them chart and predict consumer trends. In the late twentieth century, computer technology transformed the making and consumption of maps. Maps of high quality and detail, capable of being tailored to consumers' individual needs, became widely available in computer format. But computers and the Internet have also made it possible for noncartographers to produce and distribute maps of dubious accuracy.

Federal Mapping and Mapmaking

In a resolution of the Continental Congress on 25 July 1777, General George Washington was empowered to appoint Robert Erskine geographer and surveyor on Washington's headquarters staff. Under Erskine and his successors, Simeon De Witt and Thomas Hutchins, more than 130 manuscript maps were prepared. From these beginnings a considerable mapping program by the federal government has evolved that since the early days of World War II has literally covered the world, and since 1964, the moon.

In 1785 the Congress established a Land Ordinance to provide for the survey of public land, and in 1812 it created the General Land Office in the Department of the Treasury. The activity of this office has, in varying forms, continued to this day. Increase in maritime commerce brought about, in 1807, the creation of an office for the survey of the coasts, which, with several modifications and a lapse between 1819 and 1832, has continued through to the present as the U.S. Coast and Geodetic Survey. The rapid movement of population to the West and the large acquisition of lands by the LOUISIANA PURCHASE increased the need for exploration, survey, and mapping, much of which was accomplished by topographical engineer officers of the War Department.

Between 1818 and the eve of the Civil War, the mapping activities of the federal government increased greatly. A topographical bureau established in the War Department in 1818 was responsible for a nationwide program of mapping for internal improvements and, through detailed topographic surveying, for maps and geographical reports. A cartographic office that was set up in the U.S. Navy Depot of Charts and Instruments in 1842 was instrumental in the mapping of the Arctic and Antarctic regions and the Pacific Ocean and in supplying the navy with charts. In the 1850s the Office of Explorations and Surveys was created in the Office of the Secretary of War, with a primary responsibility for explorations, surveys, and maps of the West—especially for proposed and projected railroad routes to the Pacific coast.

During the Civil War the best European surveying, mapmaking, and map reproduction techniques were blended with those of U.S. cartographic establishments—especially in the Union and Confederate armies. By the end of the war, which had revealed the inadequacy of map coverage for military as well as civilian enterprise, U.S. mapmaking was equal to any in Europe. A few of the mapping agencies created between the Civil War and

World War I to serve the federal government's needs include the Bureau of the Census, which, beginning in 1874, published thematic demographic maps and atlases compiled principally from returns of the census; the Geological Survey, created in 1879 to prepare large-scale topographic and other maps, almost exclusively of the United States and its territories; the Hydrographic Office of the navy, established in 1866 to chart foreign waters; the Corps of Engineers, expanded greatly to undertake a major program of mapping and surveying for internal improvements; and the Weather Bureau, organized in 1870 in the Signal Office of the War Department to prepare daily, synoptic, and other kinds of weather maps.

World War I created a need for maps by the military, especially in Europe. Mapmaking and map reproduction units were organized and established in France. Some of the maps were made from aerial photographs and represented the beginning of modern quantitative mapping with a respectable degree of accuracy. New techniques of compilation and drafting and improved methods of rapid reproduction developed during the war accelerated and widened the opportunities for mapping during the 1920s and 1930s.

In part to provide work for unemployed cartographers and writers, during the Great Depression many specialized agencies were created to map a wide variety of cultural and physical features. Thematic and special-purpose maps—many of which were included with government reports—came into their own. Significant among the specialized agencies were the Bureau of Agricultural Economics, the Tennessee Valley Authority, the Climatic and Physiographic Division, the National Resources Committee and Planning Board, and the Federal Housing Administration. Geographers played a leading role in the development of techniques for presentation, especially in thematic and resource maps, and in field mapping.

Mapping agencies proliferated in the federal government during World War II. The principal types of maps of this period were topographic maps, aeronautical and nautical charts, and thematic maps. Several hundred geographers in Washington, D.C., alone were given responsibilities for mapmaking and geographical interpretation, particularly in the compilation of thematic maps. The wide use of aerial photography during the depression was expanded to universal application, especially for the making of large-scale topographic maps. The Aeronautical Chart and Information Service, the Hydrographic Office, and the Army Map Service, with their numerous field units, were the primary agencies of production.

The postwar period witnessed the spread of military and scientific mapping in all parts of the globe. The development of color-sensitive photographic instruments, of highly sophisticated cameras in space vehicles, of automated cartography combining electronics with computer technology, of sensing by satellites in prescribed earth orbits, and of a host of other kinds of instrumentation has made possible a wide variety of almost instantaneous mapping or terrain imaging of any part of the earth. By the 1980s and 1990s these sophisticated maps had assumed a central role in military reconnaissance and field operations. The U.S. military's reliance on maps was made all too clear during the 1999 NATO action in Yugoslavia, when an outdated map of Sarajevo resulted in the accidental bombing of the Chinese embassy there. As mapping has become an increasingly exact science, maps have become a fundamental source of information and a basic record in most agencies of the federal government.

BIBLIOGRAPHY

Brown, Lloyd A. *The Story of Maps.* Boston: Little, Brown, 1949.

Cumming, William P. *British Maps of Colonial America.* Chicago: University of Chicago Press, 1974.

McElfresh, Earl B. *Maps and Mapmakers of the Civil War.* New York: Abrams, 1999.

Ristow, Walter W. *American Maps and Mapmakers: Commercial Cartography in the Nineteenth Century.* Detroit, Mich.: Wayne State University Press, 1985.

Thompson, Morris M. *Maps for America: Cartographic Products of the U.S. Geological Survey and Others.* Reston, Va.: Department of Interior, Geological Survey, 1979.

U.S. National Archives. *Guide to Cartographic Records in the National Archives.* Washington, D.C.: U.S. Government Printing Office, 1971.

Wheat, James C. *Maps and Charts Published in America before 1800: A Bibliography.* 2d rev. ed. London: Holland Press, 1985.

Herman R. Friis/A. R.

See also **Coast and Geodetic Survey; Geography; Geological Survey, U.S.; Geophysical Explorations; Maps and Mapmaking; Printing Industry; Surveying.**

CARTOONS. In 1906, Vitagraph released the first animated film in the United States, *Humorous Phases of Funny Faces,* by cartoonist James Stuart Blackton. It featured a series of faces, letters, and words being drawn. This rudimentary foundation encouraged other cartoon pioneers, including Emil Cohl and Winsor McCay. Cohl produced *Drame Chez Les Fantoches* (A Drama in Fantoche's House) (1908), a film more like modern classics, both funny and with a well-developed plot. McCay's *Little Nemo* (1911), the first fully animated film, was based on his newspaper comic strip. His *Gertie the Dinosaur* (1914) was the first to use frame-by-frame animation, which produced fluid motion. *Gertie* also initiated fascination with a central character.

In the 1910s, animated cartoons were also being produced as series. John Randolph Bray had success with a number of them. Bray and other innovators developed ways of speeding up the drawing process using translucent paper, which enabled quicker drawing. The decade also witnessed the rise of the cell animation process and other important advances.

Mickey Mouse. *Steamboat Willie* (1928) was the second Mickey Mouse cartoon and the first cartoon ever to feature successfully synchronized sound (first introduced in motion pictures in Al Jolson's *The Jazz Singer* [1927]). A loose parody of Buster *Keaton's Steamboat Bill, Steamboat Willie* made a "star" out of Mickey Mouse, who quickly became one of the most beloved Disney characters. © THE KOBAL COLLECTION

Like early motion pictures, the cartoons were silent. Various methods of portraying speech were used, from balloons to dialogue on the screen, sometimes confusing the audience. In addition, the cartoonists lacked the resources to focus on story continuity. Often the cartoonist did all the work individually or with a small staff. Cartoons might have disappeared without sound.

Disney and Warner Brothers

The first sound cartoon, *Song Car-Tunes,* produced by Max and Dave Fleischer, appeared in 1924, three years before the first talking motion picture, Al Jolson's *The Jazz Singer.* Walt Disney introduced Mickey Mouse in 1928 in *Steamboat Willie.* In the 1930s, sound production fueled the growth of cartoons. In this period, Warner Brothers introduced the Looney Tunes series.

After the success of *Steamboat Willie,* Disney created the first full-color cartoon, *Flowers and Trees* (1932). Five years later, he scored with the first animated feature movie, *Snow White and the Seven Dwarfs.* It earned $8 million in its initial release, a success enabling Disney to build his empire. Disney established the idea that unique cartoon personalities would draw audiences. His company led the industry in cartoon development and Disney's success was widely copied. Disney also pushed merchandising, created the Disney theme parks in California in 1955 and Florida in 1971, and introduced a television show. He followed *Snow White* with a series of animated films that remain favorites, including *Pinocchio* (1940), *Fantasia* (1940), *Bambi* (1942), *Cinderella* (1950), and *Peter Pan* (1953). Drawing on universal themes, like good versus evil and family, the films featured songs, humor, slapstick, and emotion, all with intricate scenery, detailed drawing, and wonderful musical scores. Disney films were so triumphant that other animators essentially abandoned the field for twenty years.

Warner Brothers rivaled Disney in the early years of animated films. Cartoonist Chuck Jones popularized the wisecracking Bugs Bunny, who first appeared in the 1940 short, *A Wild Hare*. While at Warner from 1936 to 1962, Jones also created Elmer Fudd, Porky Pig, Road Runner, and Wile E. Coyote. Jones's favorite, however, was Daffy Duck, the daft everyman who first appeared in 1937. Jones is acknowledged as the inspiration of everything from the smart alecky Rugrats to the blockbuster movie *The Lion King* (1994). Except for Disney, no one had a more lasting influence on the development of cartoons.

The Television Age

In the 1950s, the rise of television and a decision by theater owners to stop paying extra for cartoon shorts reduced the importance of animated films. Studios began syndicating films for television. By the mid-1950s, more than four hundred TV stations ran cartoons, usually in the afternoons.

The first made-for-television series was *Crusader Rabbit*, which debuted in 1950. Bill Hanna and Joe Barbera introduced the cat and mouse team Tom and Jerry and later Yogi Bear, Huckleberry Hound, and Quick Draw McGraw. To maximize profits, Hanna and Barbera used limited animation, eliminated preliminary sketches, and recorded sound quickly.

The late 1950s and 1960s witnessed a plethora of all-cartoon series entering the market, from *Rocky and His Friends* (1959) to *Magilla Gorilla* (1964) and *Speed Racer* (1967). Cartoons began branching out into new areas, with some based on successful noncartoon shows. *The Flintstones* (1960), for example, was based on the sitcom *The Honeymooners*. Some animated series were based on comic books and strips like *Dick Tracy* and *Superman*.

In the 1960s, ABC put cartoons at the heart of its prime-time lineup, airing *The Flintstones* in 1960, followed by *The Bugs Bunny Show* (1960). In 1962, ABC added the space-age family *The Jetsons* and later *The Adventures of Johnny Quest* (1964). The first animated made-for-television special was NBC's 1962 *Mr. Magoo's Christmas Carol*, an adaptation of Dickens's famous story. The second holiday show was *A Charlie Brown Christmas* (1965), based on Charles Schulz's *Peanuts* comic strip. It attracted over half of the viewing audience. Theodore Geisel's *Dr. Seuss' How the Grinch Stole Christmas* appeared in 1966 on CBS.

Beginning in the 1963–1964 season, the networks ran cartoons on Saturday mornings. Large corporations like Kellogg's sponsored these cartoons and forced the networks to expand their selections. CBS executive Fred Silverman, who was responsible for the Saturday lineup, realized that both adults and children would watch. The

cartoons solidified the network's first-place standing in that time slot. ABC and NBC followed, and in 1970 the three networks made nearly $67 million in advertising revenue from their Saturday morning programming.

After the 1968 assassinations of Martin Luther King Jr. and Robert Kennedy, a public outcry against TV violence rocked the cartoon industry. Network censors cracked down. Comedy shows replaced action adventures, which drove away adult viewers. Cartoons were now seen as educational tools, not just entertainment.

The Rebirth of Animated Films

In the theaters, animated films for adults emerged. The Beatles' animated *Yellow Submarine* (1968) and the X-rated *Fritz the Cat* (1971), by Ralph Bakshi, proved that adults would view a less Disneyesque cartoon. Their success and that of later ones gave Disney its first serious competition in decades. The revival of animated films also included children's films such as *Charlotte's Web* (1972) and *Watership Down* (1978).

The demand for family-oriented films continued in the 1980s. Again, Disney led the industry, producing *Who Framed Roger Rabbit* (1988). Based on new characters, the film broke the magical $100 million mark in revenues.

In the 1990s, almost every animated movie became a hit and studios jumped in to battle Disney. In 1994 Disney released *The Lion King*, which became the highest grossing animated film of all time. The following year, Disney and Pixar released *Toy Story*, a technological masterpiece produced completely with computer animation. A string of computer-animated films followed. The Pixar

Animation Rebirth. In 1988, *Who Framed Roger Rabbit?* established a new standard in film cartoons when it seamlessly blended animated characters with real-life people and action. Starring Bob Hoskins (shown here with the character Jessica Rabbit) as a private detective who helped save the title character, the film grossed more than $100 million. © The Kobal Collection

film, *Monsters, Inc.* (2001), gave Disney another huge hit, the second all-time money earner for animated films.

The revival of animated films made it fashionable for actors to voice the characters. Major stars such as Mike Myers, Eddie Murphy, and Robin Williams have lent their voices to animated films. The growth of VHS and DVD sales has doubled the revenue of some animated films.

Television benefited from the rebirth of films, particularly in the adult market. In 1990, Fox introduced Matt Groening's *The Simpsons* in primetime, turning its characters into popular culture icons. MTV countered with *Beavis and Butt-Head* in 1993. The growth of cable television pushed cartoons in new directions. In 1990, Disney introduced a block of afternoon programming for the Fox Kids Network. The cable mogul Ted Turner created the twenty-four-hour Cartoon Network in the early 1990s. Opposition to animated violence, however, undermined the business. The Children's Television Act of 1990 required educational programs for children. Essentially, the act ended the traditional Saturday morning cartoon programming.

Cartoons continue to play an important role in popular culture and have a magnificent future. Using computer animation, Hollywood churns out hit film after hit film, while television audiences continue to grow. Video sales and rentals get subsequent generations of youngsters interested in traditional cartoons and characters while also promoting new films. As long as audiences want new animated films, television shows, and cartoons, the industry will respond.

BIBLIOGRAPHY

Grant, John. *Encyclopedia of Walt Disney's Animated Characters.* New York: Harper and Row, 1987.

Jones, Chuck. *Chuck Amuck: The Life and Times of an Animated Cartoonist.* New York: Farrar, Straus, Giroux, 1989.

Lenburg, Jeff. *The Encyclopedia of Animated Cartoons.* 2d ed. New York: Facts on File, 1999.

Maltin, Leonard. *Of Mice and Magic: A History of American Animated Cartoons.* New York: McGraw-Hill, 1980.

Peary, Danny, and Gerald Peary, eds. *The American Animated Cartoon: A Critical Anthology.* New York: Dutton, 1980.

Bob Batchelor

See also **Comic Books; Disney Corporation; Film.**

CASABLANCA CONFERENCE.

From 14 to 24 January 1943, President Franklin D. Roosevelt and Prime Minister Winston S. Churchill, together with their military staffs, met in Casablanca, French Morocco. The conferees agreed to pursue military operations in Sicily, to continue the heavy bombing offensive against Germany, and to establish a combined staff in London to plan a large invasion of France across the English Channel. They secured the promise of Charles de Gaulle, leader of the Free French, to cooperate with General Henri Giraud, whom Roosevelt was grooming as leader of the French forces in Africa. The leaders endorsed an UNCONDITIONAL SURRENDER policy, which they defined as "the total elimination of German and Japanese war power."

BIBLIOGRAPHY

Kimball, Warren F. "Casablanca: The End of Imperial Romance." In *The Juggler: Franklin Roosevelt as Wartime Statesman.* Princeton, N.J.: Princeton University Press, 1991.

———. *Forged in War: Roosevelt, Churchill, and the Second World War.* New York: William Morrow, 1997.

Justus D. Doenecke

See also **World War II.**

CASINOS. See **Gambling.**

CATAWBA.

Indians have been living beside the river of that name in the Carolina Piedmont since long before the first Europeans visited the region in 1540. The secret of the Catawbas' survival in their homeland is their ability to negotiate the "new world" that European and African intruders brought to America. Strategically located, shrewd diplomats, Catawbas became known as good neighbors. Even as their population fell from several thousand in 1540 to about 200 in the nineteenth century and rebounded to 2,600 by the end of the twentieth century, Catawbas kept their knack for getting along. Losing much of their aboriginal culture (including their Siouan language), they nonetheless maintained a native identity amid a sea of strangers. Some of that identity can be traced to enduring pottery traditions and a series of colorful leaders. Some is grounded in their land base, obtained from a grateful Britain after the French and Indian War, only to be lost and partially regained again and again over the next 250 years. Besides these visible traditions and this contested ground, in modern times Catawbas coalesced around the Mormon faith. A landmark 1993 agreement with state and federal officials assured governmental assistance that opened still another chapter in Catawba history.

BIBLIOGRAPHY

Blumer, Thomas J. *Bibliography of the Catawba.* Metuchen, N.J.: Scarecrow Press, 1987.

Hudson, Charles M. *The Catawba Nation.* Athens: University of Georgia Press, 1970.

Merrell, James H. *The Indians' New World: Catawbas and their Neighbors from European Contact Through the Era of Removal.* Chapel Hill: University of North Carolina Press, 1989.

James H. Merrell

See also **Tribes: Southeastern;** *and picture (overleaf).*

Catawbas. Descendants of Indians who have managed to stay in the Carolina Piedmont continuously since before 1540. LIBRARY OF CONGRESS

CATCH-22, a 1961 best-selling novel by Joseph Heller (1923–1999), set on a U.S. Air Force base in the Mediterranean during World War II. A work of comic genius, *Catch-22* represented not just a satire of life in the military but also a serious protest against the uselessness of both rationality and sentimentality in the face of unbridled power in any form.

The story recounts the efforts of the protagonist, Captain Yossarian, to gain a discharge despite the insane regulations of the military bureaucracy. The concept named in the title—which refers to a situation in which intentionally self-contradictory rules preclude a desired outcome—rapidly entered the American popular vocabulary and became widely used, without reference to the novel, to refer to any absurd situation in which rationality and madness are radically indistinguishable. By showing how catch-22 operated in every arena of authority, the novel staged a concerted assault on every truism and institution in America—including religion, the military, the legal and medical establishments, and big business. Heller's satire thus targeted not just the military during

World War II but also the complacent corporate conformism of the 1950s, the self-serving cynicism of the professions, Cold War militarism and patriotism, and above all the bureaucratic mindset.

Despite Heller's difficulty in finding a publisher and initial critical disdain, *Catch-22* quickly became one of the most popular American novels of all time. Its irreverence toward established authority helped make it one of the key literary inspirations of the culture of rebellion that erupted during the presidencies of Lyndon B. Johnson and Richard M. Nixon. In his every phrase and motive, including his manic wordplay and compulsive sexuality, Yossarian embodied the decade's spirit of anarchic dissent. The Vietnam War, which seemed to many to embody and even caricature the madness depicted in the novel, greatly enhanced *Catch-22*'s popularity.

> There was only one catch and that was Catch-22, which specified that a concern for one's own safety in the face of dangers that were real and immediate was the process of a rational mind. Orr was crazy and could be grounded. All he had to do was ask; and as soon as

he did, he would no longer be crazy and would have to fly more missions. Orr would be crazy to fly more missions and sane if he didn't, but if he was sane he had to fly them. If he flew them he was crazy and didn't have to; but if he didn't want to he was sane and had to. Yossarian was moved very deeply by the absolute simplicity of this clause of Catch-22 and let out a respectful whistle.

"That's some catch, that Catch-22," he observed.
"It's the best there is," Doc Daneeka agreed.

Nils Gilman

CATHOLICISM. Spanish and French explorers brought Roman Catholicism to what is now the United States in the sixteenth and seventeenth centuries. Spanish explorers founded St. Augustine, Florida, in 1565, and it became the site of the oldest Christian community in the United States. Missionary priests established mission towns that stretched from St. Augustine north to Georgia. Their goal was to Christianize and civilize the native population. The golden age of the missions was in the mid-seventeenth century, when seventy missionaries were working in thirty-eight missions. The missions then began to decline, and by the early eighteenth century St. Augustine was the only Catholic mission left in Florida. The mission era ended when the British gained control of Florida in 1763.

The French established a permanent settlement at Québec in 1608 that became the center of New France. Missionary priests traveled from Québec down the St. Lawrence River through the Great Lakes region seeking to evangelize the native population. This mission era endured through the first half of the eighteenth century, coming to an end when the British took over Canada in 1763. Throughout the Midwest, French missionaries and explorers left their mark in places like St. Ignace and Sault Ste. Marie, Michigan, and St. Louis, Missouri.

The Catholic presence in the Southwest was quite widespread. Spanish explorers settled Santa Fe in 1610 and then branched into what is now Arizona and Texas. In the eighteenth century Spanish missionaries, led by the Franciscan friar Junipero Serra, traveled the Pacific coast and founded a chain of twenty-one mission towns stretching from San Diego to San Francisco. The Mexican government took over the missions in 1833 in what marked the end of the Spanish mission era. The dissolution of the missions, however, did not mean the end of frontier Catholicism. The church survived, ministering to the needs of Hispanic Americans and Catholic Indians. When northern Mexico became part of the United States in 1848 as a result of the Mexican-American War, the Catholic Church there entered a new chapter in its history.

In 1634 Cecil Calvert, an English Catholic nobleman, and a small group of English colonists founded Maryland. That colony became the center of the Catholic colonial presence in the English colonies. St. Mary's City

John Carroll. Consecrated in 1790 as the first bishop of Baltimore—and the first in the United States—he later became Baltimore's first archbishop. LIBRARY OF CONGRESS

in southern Maryland became the capital of the colony, where Jesuit missionaries from England and Europe established farms. Worship services took place at these farms, which also became the home base for traveling missionaries who ministered to the needs of a rural population scattered about southern Maryland. Catholics were always a minority in Maryland, but they were in a position of prestige and power so long as the Calvert family was in control. That all changed in 1689 when William and Mary ascended to power in England and the Catholic Calverts lost ownership of the colony. Since Maryland was now a royal colony, England's penal laws became law in Maryland. These statutes discriminated against Catholics by denying them such rights and privileges as voting and public worship. Nonetheless, the Catholic population continued to grow, mainly because of the large numbers of Irish immigrants. By 1765, twenty-five thousand Catholics lived in Maryland; while another six thousand lived in Pennsylvania.

One of the most prominent families in colonial Maryland was the Carroll family. Irish and Catholic, Charles Carroll of Carrollton became a distinguished figure in the American Revolution. A delegate to the Continental Congress, he fixed his signature to the Declara-

Elizabeth Ann Seton. Founder of the first Catholic free school and other educational institutions, in the early nineteenth century; founder and first superior of a religious community of women; and, in 1974, the first native-born American saint. © CORBIS

tion of Independence. He also helped to write the new Maryland state constitution. Like Carroll, the vast majority of Catholics supported the Revolution of 1776.

The Early National Era and the Democratic Spirit

In 1790 John Carroll, an American-born and European-educated priest, was ordained as the first bishop of Baltimore. Only about 35,000 Catholics lived in the United States at that time. Carroll articulated a vision of Catholicism that was unique at this time. Together with many other Catholics he envisioned a national, American church that would be independent of all foreign jurisdiction and would endorse pluralism and toleration in religion; a church in which religion was grounded in the Enlightenment principle of intelligibility and where a vernacular liturgy was normative; and finally, a church in which the spirit of democracy, through an elected board of trustees, defined the government of parish communities.

The vital element in the development of American Catholicism was the parish. Between 1780 and 1820 many parish communities were organized across Catholic America. Perhaps as many as 124 Catholic churches, each one representing a community of Catholics, dotted the landscape in 1820. In the vast majority of these communities, laymen were very involved in the government of the parish as members of a board of trustees. The principal reason for such a trustee system was the new spirit of democracy rising across the land.

In emphasizing the influence of the democratic spirit on the Catholic parish, however, it is well to remember that tradition played a very important role in this development. When they sought to fashion a democratic design for parish government, American Catholics were attempting to blend the old with the new, the past with the present. The establishment of a trustee system was not a break with the past, as they understood it, but a continuation of past practices, adapted to a new environment. Lay participation in church government was an accepted practice in France and Germany, and English and Irish lay Catholics were also becoming more involved in parish government. Thus, when they were forced to defend their actions against opponents of the lay trustee system, Catholic trustees appealed to tradition and long-standing precedents for such involvement. This blending of the old with the new enabled the people to adapt an ancient tradition to the circumstances of an emerging, new society.

Mass Immigration and the Church

Once large-scale immigration began in the 1820s and 1830s, America's Catholic population increased dramatically. Many thousands of Irish and German Catholics arrived in the United States prior to the Civil War, marking the beginning of a new era in the history of American Catholicism. It was the age of the immigrant church. The republican model of Catholicism that defined the era of John Carroll went into decline as a more traditional, European model became normative as a result of the influx of foreign-born clergy who brought with them a monarchical vision of the church. Henceforth, the clergy would govern the parish.

In the closing decades of the century, Catholic immigrants from southern and eastern Europe settled in the United States. As a result, the Catholic population soared, numbering as many as seventeen million by 1920. It was a very ethnically diverse population, including as many as twenty-eight ethnic groups. The largest of these were the Irish, Germans, Italians, Polish, French Canadians, and Mexicans. Together they accounted for at least 75 percent of the American Catholic population. Each of these groups had their own national parishes. Based on nationality as well as language, these parishes became the hallmark of the urban church. A city neighborhood could have several different national parishes within its boundaries. Like separate galaxies, each parish community stayed within its own orbit. The Irish did not mix with the Poles. The Germans never mingled with the Italians. Some of these parishes were so large that their buildings (church, school, convent, and rectory) occupied an entire city block.

Because the public school culture was highly Protestant in the middle decades of the nineteenth century, Catholics began to establish their own elementary schools. John Hughes, the Irish-born archbishop of New York City, and John Purcell, the Irish-born archbishop of Cincinnati, were the two most prominent leaders championing parochial schools. The women religious were the key to the success of the schools. Like the clergy, most of these women were immigrants who worked within their own national or ethnic communities. In 1850 only about 1,344 sisters were at work in the United States. By 1900 their number had soared to 40,340, vastly outnumbering the 11,636 priests. This phenomenal increase in the number of women religious made the growth of schools possible, since they were the people who staffed the schools. Their willingness to work for low wages reduced the cost of schooling and made feasible an otherwise financially impossible undertaking.

In addition to the school, parishes sponsored numerous organizations, both religious and social. These organizations strengthened the bond between church and people. Hospitals and orphanages were also part of the urban church and women religious operated many of these institutions.

The Ghetto Mentality versus Americanization

In the antebellum period a Protestant crusade against Catholics swept across the nation. Anti-Catholic riots took place and convents as well as churches were destroyed. The crusade reached its height in the early 1850s when a new political party, the KNOW-NOTHINGS, gained power in several states. Their ideology was anti-immigrant and anti-Catholic. During this period Archbishop John Hughes became a forceful apologist on behalf of Catholics. Because of the discrimination they encountered, Catholics developed their own subculture, thus acquiring an outsider mentality. Often described as a ghetto mentality, it shaped the thinking of Catholics well into the twentieth century.

Some Catholics wanted the church to abandon this outsider mentality and become more American, less for-

James Gibbons. Seen here (*left*) with former president Theodore Roosevelt in 1918, the cardinal archbishop of Baltimore was a leading late-nineteenth-century advocate of reforms that Pope Leo XIII condemned as "Americanism."

eign. Isaac Hecker, a convert to Catholicism and a founder of the religious community of priests known as the Paulists, was the most prominent advocate of this vision in the 1850s and 1860s. Archbishop John Ireland of St. Paul, Minnesota, with support from James Gibbons, the cardinal archbishop of Baltimore, promoted this idea in the 1880s and 1890s. Advocating what their opponents labeled as an "American Catholicity," these Americanists endorsed the separation of church and state, political democracy, religious toleration, and some type of merger of Catholic and public education at the elementary school level. They were in the minority, however. Authorities in Rome were hostile to the idea of separation between church and state. They also opposed religious toleration, another hallmark of American culture, and were cool to the idea that democracy was the ideal form of government. As a result, in 1899 Pope Leo XIII issued an encyclical letter, *Testem Benevolentiae*, which condemned what he called "Americanism." The papal intervention not only ended the campaign of John Ireland, but also solidified the Romanization of Catholicism in the United States.

Devotional Catholicism

A distinguishing feature of the immigrant church was its rich devotional life. The heart of this devotional life was the exercise of piety, or what was called a devotion. Since the Mass and the sacraments have never been sufficient to meet the spiritual needs of the people, popular devotions have arisen throughout the history of Catholicism. In the nineteenth century some of the more popular of them were devotion to the Sacred Heart of Jesus, devotion to Jesus in the Eucharist through public exposition of the Blessed Sacrament, devotion to the passion of Jesus, devotion to Mary as the Immaculate Conception, recitation of the rosary, and of course, devotion to particular saints such as St. Joseph, St. Patrick, and St. Anthony. Prayer books, devotional confraternities, parish missions, newspapers, magazines, and the celebration of religious festivals shaped the cosmos of Catholics, educating them into a specific style of religion that can be described as devotional Catholicism. This interior transformation of Catholics in the United States was part of a worldwide spiritual revival taking place within Catholicism. The papacy promoted the revival by issuing encyclical letters promoting specific devotions and by organizing worldwide Eucharistic congresses to promote devotion to Christ.

Devotional Catholicism shaped the mental landscape of Catholics in a very distinctive manner. The central features of this worldview were authority, sin, ritual, and the miraculous. The emphasis on authority enhanced the prestige and power of the papacy at a time when it was under siege from Italian nationalists. Bishops and clergy also benefited from the importance attached to authority. Being Catholic meant to submit to the authority of God as mediated through the church—its pope, bishops, and clergy. Such a culture deemphasized the rights of the individual conscience as each person learned to submit to the external authority of the church. Catholic culture was also steeped in the consciousness of sin in this era. Devotional guides stressed human sinfulness and a multitude of laws and regulations sought to strengthen Catholics in their struggle with sin. Confession of sins became an important ritual for Catholics and priests spent long hours in the confessional. The Mass was another major ritual along with other sacraments such as baptism and marriage. Various devotions were associated with public rituals in church or with processions that marched through the streets of the neighborhood. In addition to such public rituals, people practiced their own private rituals of devotion. Fascination with the miraculous was another trait of devotional Catholicism. Catholics believed in the supernatural and the power of their heavenly patrons. Religious periodicals regularly reported cures and other miraculous events. Shrines such as Lourdes in France attracted much attention. In the United States many local shrines were associated with the healing powers of certain statues, relics, or pictures.

Consolidation

From the 1920s through the 1950s the church underwent a period of consolidation. Many new churches were built, the number of colleges grew, and record numbers of men and women entered Catholic seminaries and convents. In these years Catholicism still retained many features of the immigrant era. At the parish level Catholicism remained very ethnic and clannish into the 1940s. Devotional Catholicism remained the dominant ethos. Within the educated middle class, which was growing, there was a strong desire for Catholics to become more involved in the public life of the nation. What contemporaries called a Catholic renaissance took place in these years as Catholics began to feel more confident about their place in the United States. Catholics supported the New Deal and many worked in President Franklin D. Roosevelt's administration. Catholics also held influential positions in the growing labor movement. John Ryan, a priest and professor at the Catholic University of America, gained a national reputation as an advocate of social action and the right of workers to a just wage. Dorothy Day, a convert to Catholicism, founded the Catholic Worker movement in 1933 and her commitment to the poor and underprivileged inspired many young Catholics to work for social justice. In the 1950s Catholicism was riding a wave of unprecedented popularity and confidence. Each week new churches and schools opened their doors, record numbers of converts joined the church, and more than 70 percent of Catholics regularly attended Sunday Mass. The Catholic college population increased significantly. Bishop Fulton J. Sheen, an accomplished preacher, had his own prime time, Emmy Award–winning television show that attracted millions of viewers. In 1958 a new pope, John XXIII, charmed the world and filled Catholics with pride. The 1960 election of an Irish Catholic, John

F. Kennedy, to the presidency of the United States reinforced the optimism and confidence of Catholics.

Reform

In the 1960s the Catholic Church throughout the world underwent a period of reform. The catalyst was the Second Vatican Council (1962–1965). Coupled with the social changes that were taking place in the United States at this time, the reforms initiated by the Council ushered in a new age for American Catholicism. Change and dissent are the two words that best describe this era. The most dramatic change took place in the Catholic Mass. A new liturgy celebrated in English replaced an ancient Latin ritual. Accompanying changes in the Mass was a transformation in the devotional life of the people. People began to question the Catholic emphasis on authority and sin. The popular support for devotional rituals and a fascination with the miraculous waned. An ecumenical spirit inspired Catholics to break down the fences that separated them from people of other religious traditions. Catholics emerged from the cultural ghetto of the immigrant era and adopted a more public presence in society. They joined the 1960s war against poverty and discrimination, and were in the forefront of the peace movement during the Vietnam War. Also, the Catholic hierarchy wrote important pastoral letters that discussed war and peace in the nuclear age along with economic justice. An educated laity became more inclined to dissent, challenging the church's teaching on birth control, clerical celibacy, an exclusively male clergy, and the teaching authority of the pope. Other Catholics have opposed such dissent and have strongly defended the authority of the pope and the hierarchy. Such ideological diversity has become a distinguishing trademark of contemporary Catholicism.

Changes in the Ministry and the New Immigration

The decline in the number of priests and nuns in the late twentieth century also changed the culture of Catholicism. In 1965 there were 35,000 priests; by 2005 their numbers will have declined to about 21,000, a 40 percent decline in forty years. Along with this came a decline in the number of seminarians by about 90 percent from 1965 to the end of the century. In 1965 there were 180,000 sisters in the United States; in 2000 they numbered less than 100,000. This demographic revolution has transformed the state of ministry in the church. Along with this has come the emergence of a new understanding of ministry.

This new thinking about ministry emerged from the Second Vatican Council. The council emphasized the egalitarian nature of the Catholic Church, all of whose members received a call to the fullness of the Christian life by virtue of their baptism. This undermined the elitist tradition that put priests and nuns on a pedestal above the laity. This new thinking has transformed the church. By 2000 an astounding number of laypeople, 29,146, were actively involved as paid ministers in parishes; about 85 percent of them were women. Because of the shortage of priests many parishes, about three thousand, did not have a resident priest. A large number of these, about six hundred, had a person in charge who was not a priest. Many of these pastors were women, both lay women and women religious. They did everything a priest does except say Mass and administer the sacraments. They hired the staff, managed the finances, provided counseling, oversaw the liturgy, and supervised the educational, social, and religious programs of the parish. They were in charge of everything. The priest came in as a special guest star, a visitor who celebrated the Eucharist and left.

In addition to the changes in ministry, Catholicism is experiencing the impact of a new wave of immigration ushered in by the revised immigration laws starting in 1965. The church became more ethnically diverse than ever before. In 2000 Sunday Mass was celebrated in Los Angeles in forty-seven languages; in New York City thirty languages were needed to communicate with Sunday churchgoers. The largest ethnic group was the Spanish-speaking Latino population. Comprising people from many different nations, they numbered about 30 million in 2000, of whom approximately 75 percent were Catholic. It is estimated that by 2014 they will constitute 51 percent of the Catholic population in the United States. The new immigration transformed Catholicism in much the same way that the old immigration of the nineteenth century did.

At the beginning of the twenty-first century Catholicism in the United States is entering a new period in its history. No longer religious outsiders, Catholics are better integrated into American life. Intellectually and politically they represent many different points of view. The hierarchy has become more theologically conservative while the laity has become more independent in its thinking. An emerging lay ministry together with a decline in the number of priests and nuns has reshaped the culture of Catholicism. The presence of so many new immigrants from Latin America and Asia has also had a substantial impact on the shape of the church. Continuity with the past, with the Catholic tradition, will be the guiding force as the church moves into the twenty-first century.

In 2002 a major scandal shocked the American Catholic community, when it was revealed that some priests in Boston's Catholic community had sexually abused children over the course of several years. The crisis deepened with the revelation that church leaders had often reassigned accused priests to other parishes without restricting their access to children. The same pattern of secretly reassigning priests known to be sexual predators was discovered in other dioceses across the country. This unprecedented scandal of abuse and cover-up severely damaged the sacred trust between the clergy and the laity.

BIBLIOGRAPHY

Carey, Peter W. *People, Priests, and Prelates: Ecclesiastical Democracy and the Tensions of Trusteeism.* Notre Dame, Ind.: University of Notre Dame Press, 1987.

Dolan, Jay P. *The American Catholic Experience: A History from Colonial Times to the Present.* Garden City, N.Y.: Doubleday, 1985.

———. *In Search of an American Catholicism: A History of Religion and Culture in Tension.* New York: Oxford University Press, 2002.

Dolan, Jay P., and Allen Figueroa Deck, eds. *Hispanic Catholic Culture in the U.S.: Issues and Concerns.* Notre Dame, Ind.: University of Notre Dame Press, 1994.

Ellis, John Tracy. *The Life of James Cardinal Gibbons: Archbishop of Baltimore, 1834–1921.* 2 vols. Milwaukee, Wis.: Bruce Publishing, 1952.

Gleason, Philip. *Keeping the Faith: American Catholicism, Past and Present.* Notre Dame, Ind.: University of Notre Dame Press, 1987.

Greeley, Andrew M. *The American Catholic: A Social Portrait.* New York: Basic Books, 1977.

Hennesey, James, S.J. *American Catholics: A History of the Roman Catholic Community in the United States.* New York: Oxford University Press, 1981.

McGreevy, John T. *Parish Boundaries: The Catholic Encounter with Race in the Twentieth-Century Urban North.* Chicago: University of Chicago Press, 1996.

Morris, Charles R. *American Catholic: The Saints and Sinners Who Built America's Most Powerful Church.* New York: Times Books, 1997.

O'Toole, James M. *Militant and Triumphant: William Henry O'Connell and the Catholic Church in Boston, 1859–1944.* Notre Dame, Ind.: University of Notre Dame Press, 1992.

Jay P. Dolan

See also **Discrimination: Religion; Education: Denominational Colleges; Immigration; Religion and Religious Affiliation; Religious Liberty; Religious Thought and Writings; Vatican II.**

CATLIN'S INDIAN PAINTINGS. Born in Wilkes-Barre, Pennsylvania, in 1796, George Catlin worked briefly as a lawyer while he taught himself to paint portraits. From 1830 to 1838, Catlin roamed west of St. Louis, traveling thousands of miles and painting about 470 portraits and scenes of Native American life, most of which are at the SMITHSONIAN INSTITUTION. Beginning in 1837, he exhibited the paintings—which form a superb record of Native American life—in North America and Europe. He not only sketched his subjects and collected artifacts, but wrote a substantial text, *Letters and Notes on the Manners, Customs, and Conditions of the North American Indians,* issued in 1841. In 1844, he issued a portfolio of lithographs in London. Through exhibitions and his two publications, his work became well known.

BIBLIOGRAPHY

Catlin, George. *Letters and Notes on the Manners, Customs, and Condition of the North American Indians.* New York: Penguin Books, 1989. Originally published by the author in 1841.

Man Who Tracks. George Catlin's 1830 portrait of a chief (also called Pah-me-cow-ee-tah, one of several variant spellings) of the Peoria, a subtribe of the Illinois. SMITHSONIAN INSTITUTION

Catlin, George. *North American Indian Portfolio: Hunting Scenes and Amusements of the Rocky Mountains and Prairies of America.* New York: Abbeville Press, 1989. Originally published by the author in 1844.

Dippie, Brian W. *Catlin and His Contemporaries: The Politics of Patronage.* Lincoln: University of Nebraska Press, 1990.

Millichap, Joseph R. *George Catlin.* Boise, Idaho: Boise State University, 1977.

Troccoli, Joan Carpenter. *First Artist of the West: Paintings and Watercolors from the Collection of the Gilcrease Museum.* Tulsa, Okla.: Gilcrease Museum, 1993.

Truettner, William H. *The Natural Man Observed: A Study of Catlin's Indian Gallery.* Washington, D.C.: Smithsonian Institution Press, 1979.

Georgia Brady Barnhill

See also **Art: Painting.**

CATSKILL MOUNTAINS.

Part of the great Appalachian Mountain chain, the Catskill Mountains are located on the west side of the Hudson River, about one hundred miles northwest of New York City. Their heavily wooded terrain encompasses more than 6,000 square miles, with the highest peak of 4,204 feet at Slide Mountain. The area's most rapid growth came in the nineteenth century and accelerated with the building of rail lines, the first being the Canajoharie and Catskill Railroad, completed in 1828. Difficult to farm, the area developed commercially as a tanning and lumbering center while its peaks were excavated for bluestone and flagstone. In the late nineteenth century, the despoiling of the mountains led to one of the first conservationist movements, with large sections of the Catskills protected by state legislation beginning in 1885. Today almost 300,000 acres are designated as a preserve. Long famous as a vacation, resort, and camping center, the dense woods, dramatic waterfalls, splendid vistas, and clear mountain lakes of the Catskill Mountains continue to attract visitors, sportsmen, and vacationers.

BIBLIOGRAPHY

Adams, Arthur G. *The Catskills: An Illustrated Historical Guide with Gazetteer.* New York: Fordham University Press, 1994.

Kudish, Michael. *The Catskill Forest: A History.* Fleischmanns, New York: Purple Mountain Press, 2000.

Mary Lou Lustig

CATTLE

arrived in Florida before 1600 with early Spanish settlers. A shipment in 1611 initiated cattle raising in Virginia; the Pilgrims began with a few of the Devonshire breed in 1624. Black and white Dutch cattle were brought to New Amsterdam in 1625. John Mason imported large yellow cattle from Denmark into New Hampshire in 1633. Although losses of cattle during the ocean voyages were heavy, they increased rapidly in all the colonies and soon were exported to the West Indies, both live and as salted barreled beef.

Interest in improved livestock, based upon English efforts, came at the close of the American Revolution when Bakewell, or improved longhorn cattle, were imported, followed by shorthorns, sometimes called Durhams, and Devons. Henry Clay first imported Herefords in 1817. Substantial numbers of Aberdeen Angus did not reach the United States from Scotland until after the Civil War. By the 1880s, some of the shorthorns were being developed as dairy stock. By the 1860s other dairy breeds had been established—the Holstein-Friesian breed, based upon stock from Holland, and the Brown Swiss. Even earlier, Ayrshires, Jerseys, and Guernseys were raised as dairy cattle.

Cattle growers in the Northeast and across the Midwest relied on selective breeding, fencing, and haymaking, as well as built structures. Dairying began in New York State and spread across the northern regions of the country. Cheese production increased in the North during the Civil War. Butter making was a substantial source of income for many rural households. Cattle-raising techniques in the southern regions included open grazing, the use of salt and cow pens to manage herds, as well as dogs and whips to control animals. Southern practices included droving, branding, and roundups early in American history.

Chicago Stockyard. Cowboys bring their herd to the end of the trail (and rail line) in this photograph, c. 1900, by Ray Stannard Baker—later a noted *McClure's Magazine* muckraking journalist and adviser to (as well as authorized biographer of) President Woodrow Wilson. © CORBIS

During the Civil War, longhorn cattle, descendants of Spanish stock, grew up unchecked on the Texas plains. After other attempts to market these cattle failed, Joseph G. McCoy made arrangements to ship them from the railhead at Abilene, Kansas, and in 1867 the long drives from Texas to the railheads began. Midwestern farms diversified by fattening trailed animals on corn before shipping to market, leading to the feedlot industry. In 1868 iced rail cars were adopted, allowing fresh beef, rather than live animals, to be shipped to market. Chicago became a center for the meatpacking industry.

Overgrazing, disastrous weather, and settlement by homesteaders brought the range cattle industry to an end after 1887. The invention of BARBED WIRE by Joseph Glidden in the 1870s made fencing the treeless plains possible, ending free-ranging droving of cattle. Fencing allowed selective breeding and also minimized infection from tick fever by limiting the mobility of cattle.

While dairy breeds did not change, productivity per cow increased greatly. Dairy technology improved, and the areas of supply were extended. Homogenization, controls of butterfat percentage, and drying changed traditional milk production and consumption. The industry also became subject to high standards of sanitation.

By the 1980s, hormones and antibiotics were used to boost production of meat and milk while cutting costs to the producer. By 1998, 90 percent of all beef cattle were given hormone implants, boosting weight and cutting expenses by 7 percent. In the 1990s, mad cow disease, bovine spongiform encephalopathy, was identified in Britain. Related to a human disease, Creutzfeldt-Jakob disease, it was believed to be caused by feeding infected rendered animal products to cattle. Worldwide attention focused on cattle feeding and health. In 2001, foot-and-mouth disease swept through herds in many countries. Neither disease appeared in U.S. cattle.

Artificial insemination technology grew significantly. Eggs from prize cows were harvested and then fertilized in the laboratory, and the frozen embryos were implanted in other cows or exported to cattle-growing markets around the world. In 1998 the first cloned calf was created in Japan; by 2001, researchers at the University of Georgia had reproduced eight cloned calves. Cattle by-products from meat slaughter were significant in the pharmaceutical and health care industry. In 2001, artificial human blood was experimentally synthesized from cattle blood.

Grazing on public lands in the West was criticized in the 1980s, focusing attention on federal government–administered leases. At the same time, holistic grazing techniques grew in popularity, resulting from Allan Savory's work to renew desertified pastures through planned intensive grazing.

In 1998, slaughter cattle weighed 20 pounds more (with an average total of 1,194 pounds) than the year before; smaller numbers of cattle were going to market, but the meat yield was higher. The number of beef cattle slaughtered dropped 12 percent between 1998 and 2000. Per capita beef consumption dropped between 1980 and 2000 by 7 pounds, to 69.5 pounds per person, but began rising in 1998–1999. Total retail beef consumption rose from $40.7 billion in 1980 to $58.6 billion in 2000. In 1999, average milk production per dairy cow was 17,771 pounds per year; the total milk production was 163 billion pounds.

BIBLIOGRAPHY

Carlson, Laurie Winn. *Cattle: An Informal Social History.* Chicago: Ivan R. Dee, 2001.

Jordan, Terry G. *North American Cattle-Ranching Frontiers: Origins, Diffusion, and Differentiation.* Albuquerque: University of New Mexico Press, 1993.

Laurie Winn Carlson
Wayne D. Rasmussen

See also **Cowboys; Dairy Industry; Livestock Industry; Meatpacking.**

CATTLE ASSOCIATIONS,

organizations of cattlemen after 1865 on the western ranges. Local, district, sectional, and national in scope, they functioned on the edges of western Anglo-American settlement, much like miners' associations and squatters' claim clubs. The Colorado Cattle Growers' Association was formed as early as 1867. The Wyoming Stock Growers' Association was organized in 1873 and by 1886 had four hundred members from nineteen states. Its cattle, real estate, plants, and horses were valued in 1885 at $100 million. In 1884 the National Cattle and Horse Growers' Association was organized in St. Louis.

A president, secretary, treasurer, and executive committee administered each association's affairs and made reports at annual or semiannual meetings. Roundup districts were laid out, rules for strays or mavericks were adopted, and thousands of brands were recorded. Associations cooperated with local and state officials and urged favorable legislation by Congress.

BIBLIOGRAPHY

Dale, Edward Everett. *The Range Cattle Industry: Ranching on the Great Plains from 1865 to 1925.* New ed. Norman: University of Oklahoma Press, 1960. The original edition was published in 1930.

Peake, Ora Brooks. *The Colorado Range Cattle Industry.* Glendale, Calif.: Clark, 1937.

Pelzer, Louis. *The Cattlemen's Frontier: A Record of the Trans-Mississippi Cattle Industry from Oxen Trains to Pooling Companies, 1850–1890.* Glendale, Calif.: Clark, 1936.

Louis Pelzer / F. B.

See also **Cowboys; Livestock Industry.**

CATTLE BRANDS,

although traceable to ancient Egypt, are associated with cattle ranching and range horses. The brand is a mark of ownership, and every legitimate brand is recorded by either state or county, thus preventing duplication within a given territory. Ranchers use brands for stock in fenced pastures as well as on the open range. Brands guard against theft and aid ranchers in keeping track of livestock.

Brands can be made up of letters, figures, geometric designs, symbols, or representations of objects. Possible combinations are endless. Reading brands can be an art and requires discerning differences between similar marks. For example, a straight line burned into a cow's hide may be a "dash," a "bar," or a "rail." Brands usually signify something peculiar to the originator—a seaman turned rancher might use the anchor brand or a rancher might honor his wife, Ella, with the "E bar" brand. Because brands reduce the value of hides and also induce screw worms, in the early 2000s they were generally smaller and simpler than they were when cattle were less valuable.

BIBLIOGRAPHY

August, Ray. "Cowboys v. Rancheros: The Origins of Western American Livestock Law." *Southwest Historical Quarterly* 96 (1993).

Boatright, Mody C., and Donald Day, eds. *From Hell to Breakfast.* Publications of the Texas Folklore Society, no. 19. Dallas, Tex.: Southern Methodist University Press, 1944.

J. Frank Dobie / F. B.

See also **Cattle; Cattle Associations; Cattle Drives; Cowboys.**

CATTLE DRIVES.

Contrary to popular conception, long-distance cattle driving was traditional not only in Texas but elsewhere in North America long before anyone dreamed of the CHISHOLM TRAIL. The Spaniards, who established the ranching industry in the New World, drove herds northward from Mexico as far back as 1540. In the eighteenth and nineteenth centuries, Spanish settlements in Texas derived most of their meager revenue from contraband trade of horses and cattle driven into Louisiana. In the United States, herds of cattle, horses, and pigs were sometimes driven long distances as well. In 1790 the boy Davy Crockett helped drive "a large stock of cattle" four hundred miles, from Tennessee into Virginia. In 1815 Timothy Flint "encountered a drove of more than 1,000 cattle and swine" being driven from the interior of Ohio to Philadelphia.

Earlier examples notwithstanding, Texans established trail driving as a regular occupation. Before 1836, Texans had a "beef trail" to New Orleans. In the 1840s they extended their markets northward into Missouri. During the 1850s emigration and freighting from the Missouri River westward demanded great numbers of oxen, and thousands of Texas longhorn steers were broken for use as work oxen. Herds of longhorns were driven to Chicago and at least one herd to New York.

Under Spanish-Mexican government, California also developed ranching, and during the 1830s and 1840s a limited number of cattle were trailed from California to Oregon. However, the discovery of gold in California temporarily arrested development of the cattle industry and created a high demand for outside beef. During the 1850s, although cattle were occasionally driven to California from Missouri, Arkansas, and perhaps other states, the big drives were from Texas.

During the Civil War, Texans drove cattle throughout the South for the Confederate forces. At the close of the war Texas had some 5 million cattle—and no market for them. In 1866 there were many drives northward without a definite destination and without much financial success. Texas cattle were also driven to the old, but limited, New Orleans market.

In 1867 Joseph G. McCoy opened a regular market at ABILENE, Kansas. The great cattle trails, moving successively westward, were established, and trail driving boomed. Also in 1867, the Goodnight-Loving Trail opened New Mexico and Colorado to Texas cattle. They were soon driven into Arizona by the tens of thousands. In Texas, cattle raising expanded like wildfire. DODGE CITY, Kansas; Ogallala, Nebraska; Cheyenne, Wyoming, and other towns became famous because of trail-driver patronage.

During the 1870s the BUFFALO were virtually exterminated, and the American Indians of the Great Plains and the Rocky Mountains were subjugated. Vast areas were left vacant. They were first occupied by Texas longhorns, driven by Texas cowboys. The Long Trail extended as far as Canada.

In the 1890s, herds were still driven from the Panhandle of Texas to Montana, but by 1895 trail driving had virtually ended because of BARBED WIRE, RAILROADS, and settlement. During three swift decades it had moved more than 10 million head of cattle and 1 million range horses, stamped the entire West with its character, given economic prestige and personality to Texas, made the longhorn the most historic brute in bovine history, and glorified the cowboy throughout the globe.

BIBLIOGRAPHY

Dale, Edward Everett. *The Range Cattle Industry: Ranching on the Great Plains from 1865 to 1925.* New ed. Norman: University of Oklahoma Press, 1960. The original edition was published in 1930.

Gard, Wayne. *The Chisholm Trail.* Norman: University of Oklahoma Press, 1954.

Hunter, J. Marvin, compiler and ed. *The Trail Drivers of Texas: Interesting Sketches of Early Cowboys.* 2d ed. rev. Nashville, Tenn.: Cokesbury Press, 1925.

Osgood, Ernest Staples. *The Day of the Cattleman.* Minneapolis: University of Minnesota Press, 1929. New ed., Chicago: University of Chicago Press, 1970.

Worcester, Don. *The Chisholm Trail: High Road of the Cattle Kingdom.* Lincoln: University of Nebraska Press, 1980.

J. Frank Dobie / F. B.

See also **Cowboys; Dodge City Trail; Livestock Industry; Long Drive; Stampedes; Stockyards.**

CATTLE RUSTLERS, or cattle thieves, have been a problem wherever cattle are run on the range. Nineteenth-century rustlers drove off cattle in herds; present-day rustlers carry them off in trucks.

Rustlers' methods have varied from the rare forceful seizure of cattle in pitched battles, to the far more com-

Ella "Cattle Kate" Watson. Accused—perhaps falsely—of cattle rustling, she and the man she lived with were hanged by cattlemen on 20 July 1889, an early clash between ranchers and homesteaders that erupted in 1892 as the Johnson County War in the new state of Wyoming. WYOMING DIVISION OF CULTURAL RESOURCES

mon practice of sneaking away with motherless calves. While the former practice passed with the open range, the latter prevails in areas with widespread cattle ranching. Cattle are branded to distinguish ownership, but rustlers sometimes changed the old brand by tracing over it with a hot iron to alter the design into their own brand—a practice known as "burning brands." Rustlers also commonly took large and unbranded calves from cows and then placed them with their own brand.

The greatest deterrent to cattle rustling in the 1880s was the BARBED WIRE fence, which limited the rustlers' mobility. In the late twentieth century this deterrent became irrelevant as rustlers most commonly used automobiles and trucks. They killed cattle on the range and hauled away the beef, and they loaded calves into their trucks at night and drove hundreds of miles from the scene by morning.

Laws for recording brands to protect livestock owners have long been rigid. When the laws proved insufficient, however, cattle ranchers came together in posses, in vigilance committees, and finally in local and state associations to protect their herds.

BIBLIOGRAPHY

Evans, Simon M., Sarah Carter, and Bill Yeo, eds. *Cowboys, Ranchers, and the Cattle Business: Cross-Border Perspectives on Ranching History*. Boulder: University Press of Colorado, 2000.

Jordan, Terry G. *North American Cattle-Ranching Frontiers*. Albuquerque: University of New Mexico Press, 1993.

J. Evetts Haley / s. b.

See also **Chisholm Trail; Livestock Industry; Rustler War.**

CAUCUS, a face-to-face meeting of party members in any community or members of a legislative body for the purpose of discussing and promoting the affairs of their particular political party. Traditionally, the term "caucus" meant a meeting of the respective party members in a local community, for the purpose of nominating candidates for office or for electing delegates to county or state party conventions. Such a nominating caucus was used in the American colonies at least as early as 1725, particularly in Boston. Several clubs, attended largely by ship mechanics and caulkers, endorsed candidates for office before the regular election; these came to be known as caucus clubs. This method of nomination soon became the regular practice among the emerging political parties. It was entirely unregulated by law until 1866. Despite some legal regulation after that date, abuses had become so flagrant that control by party bosses came under increasing criticism. By the early 1900s the caucus had given way, first, to party nominating conventions and, finally, to the direct primary. By the late twentieth century a few states still permitted the use of caucuses for nomination of candidates for local offices or selection of delegates to larger conventions.

A second application of the term "caucus" is to the party caucus in Congress, which is a meeting of the respective party members in either house to organize, determine their position on legislation, and decide other matters. In general, this caucus has three purposes or functions: (1) to nominate party candidates for Speaker, president pro tem, and other House or Senate offices; (2) to elect or provide for the selection of the party officers and committees, such as the floor leader, whip, committee on committees, steering committee, and policy committee; and (3) to decide what action to take with respect to policy or legislation, either in broad terms or in detail.

Caucus decisions may be binding—that is, requiring members to vote with their party—or merely advisory. Whether formally binding or not, caucus decisions are generally followed by the respective party members; bolting is likely to bring punishment in the form of poorer committee assignments, loss of patronage, and the like. Party leaders have varied in their use of the caucus as a means of securing cohesive party action. During the late twentieth century all of the congressional caucuses or conferences underwent a revival, with much of the impetus for reform and reinvigoration coming from junior members.

A special application of the party caucus in Congress was the congressional caucus (1796–1824), which was the earliest method of nominating presidential candidates. No provision was made in the Constitution for presidential nomination, and no nominations were made for the first two presidential elections, since George Washington was the choice of all. But in 1796 the Federalist members of Congress met in secret conference and agreed to support John Adams and Thomas Pinckney for president and vice president, respectively; shortly afterward, the Republican members met and agreed on Thomas Jefferson and Aaron Burr. In 1800 the respective party members met again for the same purpose, and after that date the congressional caucus met openly as a presidential nominating caucus. In the 1830s the national convention system succeeded the congressional caucus as the method of selecting presidential nominees.

BIBLIOGRAPHY

Berhdahl, Clarence A. "Some Notes on Party Membership in Congress." *American Political Science Review* 43 (April 1949): 309–332; (June 1949): 492–508; (August: 1949): 721–734.

Bositis, David A. *The Congressional Black Caucus in the 103rd Congress*. Washington, D.C.: Joint Center for Political and Economic Studies, 1994.

Davis, James W. *U.S. Presidential Primaries and the Caucus-Convention System: A Sourcebook*. Westport, Conn.: Greenwood Press, 1997.

Peabody, Robert L. "Party Leadership Change in the United States House of Representatives." *American Political Science Review* 61 (1967).

Clarence A. Berdahl
Robert L. Peabody / A. G.

See also **Blocs; Canvass; Congress, United States; Lobbies; Majority Rule; Rules of the House.**

CAUCUSES, CONGRESSIONAL, informal groups of members of the U.S. House of Representatives. Although their history dates back to the late nineteenth century, congressional caucuses proliferated after World War II and have increased significantly in number since the early 1970s. Caucuses are created by groups of representatives who decide they have enough in common to meet and communicate regularly; they expire when members no longer find it in their interest to sustain them. The objective of caucus members is to exercise influence in Congress, determine public policy, or simply share social and professional concerns. Members create caucuses because their constituents share common economic concerns (Steel Caucus, Textile Caucus, Arts Caucus), regional interests (Northeast-Midwest Coalition, Sunbelt Caucus), ethnic or racial ties (Hispanic Caucus, Black Caucus), ideological orientation (Conservative Opportunity Society, Main Street Forum, Progressive Caucus), or partisan and policy ties (Chowder and Marching Society, Wednesday Group, Democratic Study Group).

One of the fastest-growing of these groups was the Congressional Caucus for Women's Issues, which admitted men in 1981. Caucuses range in size from a dozen members to, in a few instances, more than 150. Caucuses vary as to whether they have a paid staff, a formal leadership structure, division of labor among members, and a formal communications network. The larger groups have all of these features. Those that impose dues for paid staff are regulated by House rules. The two largest and most important caucuses are the majority and minority caucuses, which are made up of the members of the Republican and Democratic congressional delegations.

BIBLIOGRAPHY

Clay, William L. *Just Permanent Interests: Black Americans in Congress, 1870–1992.* New York: Amistad Press, 1992.

Gertzog, Irwin N. *Congressional Women: Their Recruitment, Integration, and Behavior.* New York: Praeger, 1984; Westport, Conn.: Praeger, 1995.

Schattschneider, E. E. *Party Government.* New York: Farrar and Rinehart, 1942.

Irwin N. Gertzog / A. G.

See also **Black Caucus, Congressional; Congress.**

CAUSA, LA ("The Cause"), a movement to organize Mexican American farm workers, originated in California's San Joaquin Valley in 1962. The movement's founder, César Estrada Chávez, initially brought workers and their families together through community organizing, the Catholic Church, and parades. Increasing support for the movement emboldened its leaders to mount labor strikes, organize boycotts of table grapes and wines in 1966, and establish the United Farm Worker Organizing Committee in 1967 (later the United Farm Workers of America, AFL-CIO), which sought health benefits and better wages and working conditions for its members. Despite opposition from growers, in 1975 the California legislature passed the Agricultural Labor Relations Act to allow farm workers the right to collective bargaining.

BIBLIOGRAPHY

Griswold del Castillo, Richard, and Richard A. Garcia. *César Chávez: A Triumph of Spirit.* Norman: University of Oklahoma Press, 1995.

Ferriss, Susan, and Ricardo Sandoval. *The Fight in the Fields: Cesar Chavez and the Farmworkers Movement.* New York: Harcourt Brace, 1997.

Donna Alvah

See also **United Farm Workers.**

CAVALRY, HORSE, a branch of the U.S. Army, used with varying effectiveness from the American Revolution through the Indian wars in the West. In 1775 and 1776 the Continental army fought with a few mounted militia commands as its only cavalry. In December 1776, Congress authorized three thousand light horse cavalry, and the army organized four regiments of cavalry, although the regiments never reached even half strength and became legions in 1780. The four legions and various partisan mounted units mainly went on raids and seldom participated in pitched battles. At the end of the war, all cavalry commands disbanded. For the next fifty years, regular cavalry units formed only for short periods and comprised a minute part of the army.

Indian trouble along the western frontier revived the need for mounted federal soldiers. In 1832, Congress authorized six Mounted Volunteer Ranger companies, which showed the value of mounted government troops in the West but also proved the need for a more efficient, less expensive, permanent force. On 2 March 1833, Congress replaced the Mounted Rangers with the Regiment of United States Dragoons, a ten-company force mounted for speed but trained to fight both mounted and dismounted. In May 1836 the Second Regiment of Dragoons formed to fight in the SEMINOLE WAR.

After the commencement of the MEXICAN-AMERICAN WAR, Congress augmented the two dragoon regiments with the Regiment of Mounted Riflemen, a third dragoon regiment, and several voluntary commands. Among the new organizations, only the Mounted Riflemen escaped standard reductions at the conclusion of hostilities. In 1855 the government enlarged the mounted wing with the First and Second Cavalry. By general orders these new regiments formed a distinct, separate arm of the army. Dragoons, mounted riflemen, and cavalrymen comprised mounted forces from 1855 until 1861.

Only during the CIVIL WAR did the U.S. Cavalry evolve into an efficient organization. In August 1861 the army redesignated the regular horse regiments as cavalry, renumbering them one through six according to seniority. Not until the Confederate cavalry corps demonstrated the efficiency of mass tactics and reconnaissances, however, did the Union cavalry begin to imitate the Southern horse soldiers. By the end of the war, the cavalry corps had demonstrated devastating effectiveness. After the Civil War, the six regiments failed to perform the many duties assigned, prompting Congress in July 1866 to authorize four additional regiments—the Seventh, Eighth, Ninth, and Tenth. The new regiments increased cavalry troops from 448 to 630 and the total manpower from 39,273 to 54,302. The Ninth and Tenth Cavalry, manned by black enlisted men and noncommissioned officers commanded by white officers, departed from past traditions. During the western Indian wars, the cavalry performed adequately under adverse conditions. Much of the time there were too few troops for so vast a region and such determined foes; a cost-conscious Congress rarely provided adequate support.

After the conclusion of the Indian wars in the early 1890s, the horse cavalry declined in importance. Some troops served as infantry during the Spanish-American War, and General John Pershing's punitive expedition into Mexico briefly revived the cavalry, but during WORLD WAR I only four regiments were sent to France, after which the mechanization of armies made the horse cavalry obsolete.

BIBLIOGRAPHY

Merrill, James M. *Spurs to Glory: The Story of the United States Cavalry*. Chicago: Rand McNally, 1966.

Prucha, Francis Paul. *The Sword of the Republic: The United States Army on the Frontier, 1783–1846*. New York: Macmillan, 1968.

Utley, Robert M. *Frontiersmen in Blue: The United States Army and the Indian, 1848–1865*. Reprint, Lincoln: University of Nebraska Press, 1981. The original edition was published New York: Macmillan, 1967.

———. *Frontier Regulars: The United States Army and the Indian, 1866–1891*. Reprint, Lincoln: University of Nebraska Press, 1984. The original edition was published New York: Macmillan, 1973.

Emmett M. Essin III / c. w.

See also **Black Horse Cavalry; Horse; Rangers.**

Oprah Winfrey. The hugely popular talk-show host, given to intertwining fame and intimacy in terms of her own life as well as the lives of guests, is emblematic of the celebrity culture at the turn of the twenty-first century. AP/WIDE WORLD PHOTOS

CELEBRITY CULTURE is an essentially modern phenomenon that emerged amid such twentieth-century trends as urbanization and the rapid development of consumer culture. It was profoundly shaped by new technologies that make easily possible the mechanical reproduction of images and the extremely quick dissemination of images and information/news through such media as radio, cinema, television, and the Internet.

Thanks to publications such as *People*, tabloids such as *Star* and *The National Enquirer*, and talk shows where both celebrities and supposedly ordinary people bare their lives for public consumption, there is a diminished sense of otherness in the famous. Close-up shots, tours of celebrity homes such as those originated by Edward R. Murrow's television show *Person to Person*, and intimate interviews such as those developed for television by Barbara Walters and by shows such as *Today* and *60 Minutes* have changed the public's sense of scale with celebrity. Americans are invited, especially through visual media, to believe they know celebrities intimately.

Celebrity culture is a symbiotic business relationship from which performers obtain wealth, honors, and social power in exchange for selling a sense of intimacy to audiences. Enormous salaries are commonplace. Multimillion-dollar contracts for athletes pale in comparison to their revenues from advertising, epitomized by basketball player Michael Jordan's promotion of footwear, soft drinks, underwear, and hamburgers. Celebrities also parade in public media events as they receive honors and awards ranging from the Cy Young Award for baseball, the Grammys for recording stars, and the Oscars for movie stars. Although it is certainly difficult to measure the social power accruing to celebrities, Beatle John Lennon's controversial assertion that "[The Beatles are] more popular than Jesus," suggests something of the sort of grandiosity that celebrity culture fosters.

For the fan, celebrity culture can produce intense identification at rock concerts, athletic arenas, and other displays of the fantasy object, whether live or recorded and mechanically reproduced. Such identifications can lead to role reversals where the fan covets the wealth, honors, and supposed power of the celebrity. Mark David Chapman, who murdered John Lennon in 1980, thought he was the real Beatle and that Lennon was an imposter. In 1981, when the Secret Service interviewed John Hinckley Jr., shortly after he shot President Ronald Reagan to impress actress Jodie Foster, the object of his fantasies, he asked: "Is it on TV?" Toward the end of the twentieth century, the excesses of celebrity came into question, notably in the examples of Princess Diana possibly pursued by paparazzi to her death in a car accident, and of the notoriety surrounding President Bill Clinton's relationship with congressional aide, Monica Lewinsky, a notoriety that threatened to eclipse any other reason for Clinton's celebrity status.

BIBLIOGRAPHY

Gamson, Joshua. *Claims to Fame: Celebrity in Contemporary America*. Berkeley: University of California Press, 1999.

Schickel, Richard. *Intimate Strangers: The Culture of Celebrity*. Garden City, N.Y.: Doubleday, 1985.

Hugh English

See also **Film; Music: Popular; Sports.**

CEMENT. In newly discovered lands, adventurers seek gold, while colonists seek limestone to make cement. American colonists made their first dwellings of logs, with chimneys plastered and caulked outside with mud or clay. To replace these early homes, the first bricks were imported. Brick masonry requires mortar; mortar requires cement.

Cement was first made of lime burned from oyster shells. In 1662 limestone was found at Providence, Rhode Island, and manufacture of "stone" lime began. Not until 1791 did John Smeaton, an English engineer, establish the fact that argillaceous (silica and alumina) impurity gave lime improved cementing value. Burning such limestones made hydraulic lime—a cement that hardens under water.

Only after the beginning of the country's first major public works, the ERIE CANAL in 1817, did American engineers learn to make and use a true hydraulic cement (one that had to be pulverized after burning in order to slake, or react with water). The first masonry on the Erie Canal was contracted to be done with common quick lime; when it failed to slake a local experimenter pulverized some and discovered a "natural" cement, that is, one made from natural rock. Canvass White, subsequently chief engineer of the Erie Canal, pursued investigations, perfected manufacture and use, obtained a patent, and is credited with being the father of the American cement industry. During the canal and later railway building era, demand rapidly increased and suitable cement rocks were discovered in many localities.

Cement made at Rosendale, New York, was the most famous, but that made at Coplay, Pennsylvania, the most significant, because it became the first American Portland cement. Portland cement, made by burning and pulverizing briquets of an artificial mixture of limestone (chalk) and clay, was so named because the hardened cement resembled a well-known building stone from the Isle of Portland. Soon after the CIVIL WAR, Portland cements, because of their more dependable qualities, began to be imported. Manufacture was started at Coplay, Pennsylvania, about 1870, by David O. Saylor, by selecting from his natural cement rock that was approximately of the same composition as the Portland cement artificial mixture. The Lehigh Valley around Coplay contained many similar deposits, and until 1907 this locality annually produced at least half of all the cement made in the United States. By 1900 the practice of grinding together ordinary limestone and clay, burning or calcining the mixture in rotary kilns, and pulverizing the burned clinker had become so well known that the Portland cement industry spread rapidly to all parts of the country. There were 174 plants across the country by 1971. Production increased from 350,000 barrels in 1890 to 410 million barrels in 1971.

At first cement was used only for mortar in brick and stone masonry. Gradually mixtures of cement, sand, stone, or gravel (aggregates) with water (known as concrete), poured into temporary forms where it hardened into a kind of conglomerate rock, came to be substituted for brick and stone, particularly for massive work like bridge abutments, piers, dams, and foundations.

BIBLIOGRAPHY

Andrews, Gregg. *City of Dust: A Cement Company in the Land of Tom Sawyer*. Columbia: University of Missouri Press, 1996.

Hadley, Earl J. *The Magic Powder: History of the Universal Atlas Cement Company and the Cement Industry*. New York: Putnam, 1945.

Lesley, Robert W. *History of the Portland Cement Industry in the United States*. Chicago: International Trade, 1924.

Nathan C. Rockwood/t. d.

See also **Building Materials; Housing.**

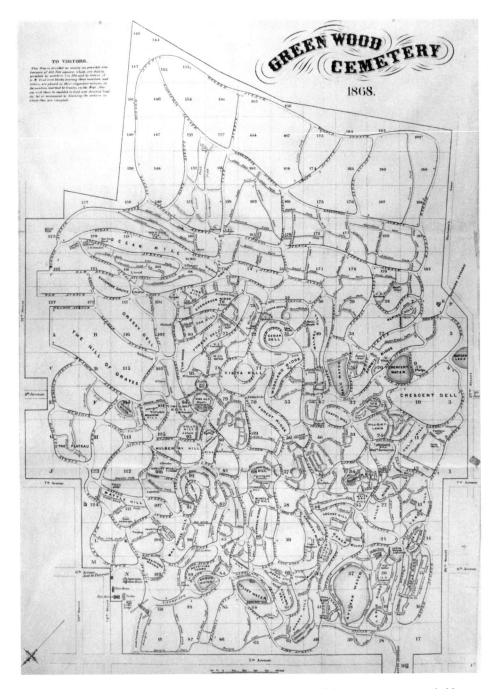

Green-wood Cemetery, Brooklyn. A map showing the layout of the cemetery as expanded by 1868.

CEMETERIES. The term "cemetery" entered American usage in 1831 with the founding and design of the extramural, picturesque landscape of Mount Auburn Cemetery. A non-denominational rural cemetery, Mount Auburn was an urban institution four miles west of Boston under the auspices of the Massachusetts Horticultural Society (1829).

With the exception of New Haven's New Burying Ground (1796, later renamed the Grove Street Cemetery), existing burial grounds, graveyards, or churchyards, whether urban or rural, public, sectarian, or private, had been unsightly, chaotic places, purely for disposal of the dead and inconducive to new ideals of commemoration. Most burials were in earthen graves, although the elite began to construct chamber tombs for the stacking of coffins in the eighteenth century. Most municipalities also maintained "receiving tombs" for the temporary storage of bodies that could not be immediately buried. New Or-

Spring Grove Cemetery, Cincinnati. Adolph Strauch's "landscape lawn plan": the cemetery as a park. 1845.

leans favored aboveground tomb structures due to the French influence and high water table.

Mount Auburn, separately incorporated in 1835, established the "rest-in-peace" principle with the first legal guarantee of perpetuity of burial property, although many notable families continued to move bodies around from older graves and tombs through the antebellum decades.

Mount Auburn immediately attracted national attention and emulation, striking a chord by epitomizing the era's "cult of the melancholy" that harmonized ideas of death and nature and served a new historical consciousness. Numerous civic leaders from other cities visited it as a major tourist attraction and returned home intent on founding such multifunctional institutions. Major examples include Baltimore's Green Mount (1838), Brooklyn's Green-Wood (1838), Pittsburgh's Allegheny (1844), Providence's Swan Point (1847), Louisville's Cave Hill (1848), Richmond's Hollywood (1848), St. Louis's Bellefontaine (1849), Charleston's Magnolia (1850), Chicago's Graceland (1860), Hartford's Cedar Hill (1863), Buffalo's Forest Lawn (1864), Indianapolis's Crown Hill (1864), and Cleveland's Lake View (1869). Most began with over a hundred acres and later expanded.

Prussian landscape gardener Adolph Strauch's "landscape lawn plan" brought a type of zoning to Cincinnati's Spring Grove (1845), which from 1855 on, in the name of "scientific management" and the park-like aesthetics of the "beautiful," was acclaimed as the "American system." Cemetery design contributed to the rise of professional landscape architects and inspired the making of the nation's first public parks.

Modernization

Inspired by Strauch's reform, cemetery managers (or cemeterians) professionalized in 1887 through the Association of American Cemetery Superintendents, later renamed the American Cemetery Association and then the International Cemetery and Funeral Association. The monthly *Modern Cemetery* (1890), renamed *Park and Cemetery and Landscape Gardening* in 1895, detailed the latest regulatory and technical developments, encouraged standardized taste and practices, and supplemented interchanges at annual conventions with emphasis on cemeteries as efficiently run businesses. Modernization led to mass production of memorials or markers, far simpler than the creatively customized monuments of the Victorian Era.

Forest Lawn Cemetery (1906) in Glendale, California, set up the modern pattern of the lawn cemetery or memorial garden emulated nationwide. Dr. Hubert Eaton, calling himself "the Builder," redefined the philosophy of death and exerted a standardized control at Forest Lawn after 1916, extending it to over 1,200 acres on four sites. Innovations included inconspicuous marker plaques set horizontally in meticulously manicured lawns and community mausoleums, buildings with individual niches for caskets, no longer called coffins.

Cremation offered a new, controversial alternative for disposal of the dead at the turn of the twentieth century. Mount Auburn installed one of the nation's first crematories in 1900, oven "retorts" for "incineration" to reduce the corpse to ashes or "cremains." Some larger cemeteries followed suit, also providing "columbaria" or niches for storage of ashes in small urns or boxes. Still, acceptance of cremation grew slowly over the course of the century and was slightly more popular in the West.

National Cemeteries

The War Department issued general orders in the first year of the Civil War, making Union commanders responsible for the burial of their men in recorded locations, sometimes in sections of cemeteries like Spring Grove and Cave Hill purchased with state funds. President Lincoln signed an act on 17 July 1862 authorizing the establishment of national cemeteries. On 19 November 1863, Lincoln dedicated the National Cemetery at Gettysburg, Pennsylvania, adjacent to an older rural cemetery, for the burial of Union soldiers who died on the war's bloodiest battlefield. In June of 1864, without ceremony, the Secretary of War designated the seized 200-acre estate of Confederate General Robert E. Lee in Arlington, Virginia, overlooking Washington, D.C., across the Potomac. Former Confederates dedicated grounds for their dead, often in large areas of existing cemeteries. By 1870, about 300,000 of the Union dead had been reinterred in national cemeteries; some moved from battlefields and isolated graves near where they had fallen.

After World War I, legislation increased the number of soldiers and veterans eligible for interment in national cemeteries. Grounds were dedicated abroad following both World War I and World War II. In 1973, a law expanded eligibility for burial to all honorably discharged veterans and certain family members. To accommodate veterans and the dead of other wars, Arlington grew to 408 acres by 1897 and to 612 acres by 1981. By 1981, with the annual burial rate exceeding 60,000 and expected to peak at 105,000 in 2010, new national cemeteries were needed, such as that dedicated on 770 acres at Fort Custer near Battle Creek, Michigan, in 1984.

Shiloh National Military Park. The national cemetery at Pittsburg Landing, Tenn., honors the 3,477 Union and Confederate soldiers who died in one of the bloodiest battles of the Civil War, 6–7 April 1862. ARCHIVE PHOTOS, INC.

BIBLIOGRAPHY

Hancock, Ralph. *The Forest Lawn Story.* Los Angeles: Academy Publishers, 1955.

Jackson, Kenneth T., and Camilo José Vergara. *Silent Cities: The Evolution of the American Cemetery.* Princeton: Princeton Architectural Press, 1989.

Linden-Ward, Blanche. *Silent City on a Hill: Landscapes of Memory and Boston's Mount Auburn Cemetery.* Columbus: Ohio State University Press, 1989.

Sloane, David Charles. *The Last Great Necessity: Cemeteries in American History.* Baltimore: The Johns Hopkins University Press, 1991.

Blanche M. G. Linden

See also **Arlington National Cemetery; Landscape Architecture.**

CEMETERIES, NATIONAL. Before the CIVIL WAR, military dead usually rested in cemetery plots at the posts where the men had served. The Civil War, however, demonstrated the need for more and better military burial procedures. Thus, War Department General Order 75 (1861) established for the first time formal provisions for recording burials. General Order 33 (1862) directed commanders to "lay off plots . . . near every battlefield" for burying the dead. Also in 1862, Congress authorized the acquisition of land for national cemeteries. Basically, two types developed: those near battlefields and those near major troop concentration areas, such as the ARLINGTON NATIONAL CEMETERY at Arlington, Virginia.

After the SPANISH-AMERICAN WAR, Congress authorized the return of remains for burial in the United States at government expense if the next of kin desired it rather than burial overseas. Of Americans killed in World War I, approximately 40 percent were buried abroad. Only 12.5 percent of the number returned were interred in national cemeteries. Beginning in 1930, the control of twenty-four cemeteries transferred from the War Department to the Veterans Administration, and after 1933 the Department of the Interior took over thirteen more. After WORLD WAR II approximately three-fifths of the 281,000 Americans killed were returned to the United States, 37,000 of them to be interred in national cemeteries. By 1951 the American Battle Monuments Commission oversaw all permanent overseas cemeteries. Eligibility requirements for interment have varied over the years, but now generally include members and former members of the armed forces; their spouses and minor children; and, in some instances, officers of the Coast and Geodetic Survey and the Public Health Service.

BIBLIOGRAPHY

Holt, Dean W. *American Military Cemeteries: A Comprehensive Illustrated Guide to the Hallowed Grounds of the United States, Including Cemeteries Overseas.* Jefferson, N.C.: McFarland, 1992.

Sloane, David Charles. *The Last Great Necessity: Cemeteries in American History.* Baltimore: Johns Hopkins University Press, 1991.

John E. Jessup Jr. / A. E.

See also **United States v. Lee; Unknown Soldier, Tomb of the; Veterans Affairs, Department of; War Memorials.**

CENSORSHIP, MILITARY. Military censorship was rare in the early Republic due to the primitive lines of communication in areas of American military operations. Reports from the front were more than a week removed from events and embellished with patriotic rhetoric, making the published accounts of little value to the enemy. Advances in communication during the nineteenth century brought an increased need for censoring reports of military actions. During the Civil War, the government federalized telegraph lines, suppressed opposition newspapers, restricted mail service, and issued daily "official" bulletins to control the flow of information and minimize dissent. Nevertheless, the public's voracious appetite for war news fueled competition among newspapers and gave rise to the professional war correspondent. Field reports were unfiltered and sometimes blatantly false; however, they demonstrated the press could serve as sources of intelligence and play a vital role in shaping public opinion. The Spanish-American War saw renewed attempts to control and manipulate the media's military coverage, though these efforts failed to prevent embarrassing reports of American atrocities and logistical mismanagement.

During World War I the government maintained strict control of transatlantic communications, including cable lines and mail. Media reports were subject to the Committee on Public Information's "voluntary" censorship regulations and the 1918 Espionage Act's restrictions seeking to limit antiwar or pro-German sentiment. With U.S. entry into World War II, the government established the Office of Censorship in mid-December 1941. The Office of Censorship implemented the most severe wartime restrictions of the press in the nation's history, reviewing all mail and incoming field dispatches, prohibiting pictures of American casualties, and censoring information for purposes of "national security." Reporters accepted these limits and practiced self-censorship, partly out of patriotic duty and partly to avoid rewriting heavily redacted stories.

The Vietnam War tested the relatively cordial rapport between the military and press. Limited in their ability to restrict information without a declaration of war, the government had to give the press virtually unfettered access to the battlefield. The military's daily briefings on Vietnam (derisively dubbed the "five o'clock follies") seemed overly optimistic and contradictory to field reports. Television broadcast the graphic conduct of the war directly into America's living rooms and exposed muddled U.S. policies in Vietnam. Thus, the "credibility gap" grew between the government and the public, particularly after the 1968 Tet Offensive and 1971 Pentagon Papers report. The military became increasingly suspicious of the press, blaming it for "losing" the war.

The emergence of live, continuous global news coverage forced a reevaluation of competing claims about the need for military security and the public's "right to know." After the controversial press blackout during the 1983 invasion of Grenada, the military developed a "pool" system that allowed small groups of selected reporters into forward-operating areas with military escorts. The pool system failed to meet media expectations during the 1989 invasion of Panama but was revised for the 1990–1991 Persian Gulf War and subsequent actions with only minor infractions of military restrictions.

BIBLIOGRAPHY

Denton, Robert E, Jr. *The Media and the Persian Gulf War.* Westport, Conn.: Praeger, 1993.

Hallin, Daniel C. *The "Uncensored War": The Media and Vietnam.* New York: Oxford University Press, 1986.

Knightly, Philip. *The First Casualty: From the Crimea to Vietnam: The War Correspondent as Hero, Propagandist, and Myth Maker.* New York: Harcourt Brace Jovanovich, 1975.

Vaughn, Stephen. *Holding Fast the Inner Lines: Democracy, Nationalism, and the Committee on Public Information.* Chapel Hill: University of North Carolina Press, 1980.

Sweeney, Michael S. *Secrets of Victory: The Office of Censorship and the American Press and Radio in World War II.* Chapel Hill: University of North Carolina Press, 2001.

Derek W. Frisby

See also **First Amendment.**

CENSORSHIP, PRESS AND ARTISTIC. Threats posed to power by free expression have prompted various forms of censorship throughout American history. Censorship is a consistent feature of social discourse, yet continued resistance to it is a testament to the American democratic ideal, which recognizes danger in systematic restraints upon expression and information access. Censorship is understood as a natural function of power—political, legal, economic, physical, etcetera—whereby those who wield power seek to define the limits of what ought to be expressed.

Censorship in Early America

Legal regulation of speech and press typified censorship in the American colonies. Strict laws penalized political dissent on the charge of "seditious libel." Printers needed government-issued licenses to lawfully operate their presses. Benjamin Franklin's early career took a turn, for instance, when his employer and brother, a Boston newspaper publisher, was jailed and lost his printing license for publishing criticism of the provincial government. British libertarian thought, especially *Cato's Letters*, popularized freedom of speech and the press as democratic ideals. Still, censorship thrived in the Revolutionary era, when British loyalists were tarred and feathered, for example, and freedom fighter Alexander McDougall led a New York Sons of Liberty mob out to smash Tory presses.

The First Amendment, ratified in 1791, provided a great legal counterbalance to censorship, although historians suggest it was intended more to empower states to punish libel than to guarantee freedom of expression. Then dominated by the Federalist Party, Congress passed the Alien and Sedition Acts in 1798, prohibiting "false, scandalous and malicious writing" against the government. After regaining a majority, congressional Republicans repudiated the Alien and Sedition Acts in 1802. Liberal, even coarse, speech and publication went largely unchecked by federal government for twenty-five years, although private citizens often practiced vigilante censorship by attacking alleged libelers.

Opposition to slavery revived government censorship in 1830, as Southern states passed laws restricting a free press that was said to be encouraging slave rebellion. Abolitionists in the North and South were censored by so-called vigilance committees. They included the Reverend Elijah Lovejoy, an Illinois newspaper editor killed by a mob in 1837, and Lexington, Kentucky, newspaper publisher Cassius M. Clay, whose press was dismantled and shipped away by a mob. Postal censorship also emerged when Southern states began to withhold abolitionist mail.

Military leaders and citizens of the North practiced "field censorship" during the Civil War (1861–1865) in response to publication of Union battle plans and strategy in newspapers. President Abraham Lincoln was a reluctant censor, closing newspapers and jailing "copperhead" editors who sympathized with the South, and giving credence to the notion that war necessitates compromises of free expression.

Widespread fraud and corruption inspired moral reflection in the Reconstruction era, when the U.S. Post Office dubiously assumed powers to categorize and withhold delivery of "obscene" mail. Postal censorship, which encountered early legal resistance, was based on an act of Congress in 1865, and the 1873 Comstock Law, named for New York anti-vice crusader Anthony Comstock. The U.S. attorney general then formally allowed Post Office officials censorship powers in 1890, forbidding delivery of any mail having to do with sex. Postal censors employed the "Hicklin test," whereby entire works were deemed "obscene" on the basis of isolated passages and words.

Censorship in the Early Twentieth Century

Federal censorship peaked during the early twentieth century, given the proliferation of "obscene" literature, political radicalism, and issues surrounding World War I (1914–1918). The U.S. Post Office added economic censorship to its methods by denying less expensive second-class postal rates to publications it found objectionable. Meanwhile, U.S. Customs prevented the import of books by literary artists charged as "obscene," such as Honoré de Balzac, Gustave Flaubert, James Joyce, and D. H. Lawrence. The rise of labor unions, socialism, and other ideological threats to government, business interests, and powerful citizens stimulated further suppression of dissent.

After President William McKinley's 1901 assassination by alleged anarchist Leon Czolgosz, President Theodore Roosevelt urged Congress to pass the Immigration Act of 1903, whereby persons were denied entry to the United States or deported for espousing revolutionary views. Controversy surrounding American involvement in World War I brought the Espionage Act of 1917, restricting speech and the press, and extending denial of second-class postal rates to objectionable political publications. Vigilante censorship thrived, as war effort critics were harmed, humiliated, and lynched by "patriotic" mobs. The success of the Russian Revolution also encouraged restraints upon free expression during this period.

Resistance to censorship continued, however, supported by the Supreme Court, politicians, and articulate citizens. Justice Oliver Wendell Holmes, Jr. effectively loosened speech controls under the "clear and present danger" test, and the 1925 *Gitlow v. New York* ruling used the Fourteenth Amendment to wrest federal powers back from the states regarding restraints upon free expression. The American Civil Liberties Union (ACLU) was founded in 1920, and First Amendment champion Theodore Schroeder notably fought censorship of literature involving sex and radical politics. Meanwhile, the new motion picture industry adopted a self-regulatory posture regarding objectionable movie content. The "Hicklin test" of obscenity suffered a major defeat in 1934 as a federal court ruled in *U.S. v. One Book Entitled Ulysses* (by James Joyce) that an entire work must be judged to determine obscenity, rather than isolated words and passages. Institutional censorship was resisted as well by the likes of *Free Speech in the United States* author Zechariah Chafee, New Mexico Senator Bronson Cutting, who effectively opposed Customs censorship, and Supreme Court Justice Louis D. Brandeis.

Governmental restraint on broadcast media appeared in 1934, as the Federal Communications Commission (FCC) was established to regulate radio. Reminiscent of press controls in the colonial period, the FCC gained licensing authority over the radio (and later television) broadcast spectrum. The FCC's charge to ensure that broadcasters operate in the public interest is understood as a kind of censorship. FCC regulation was challenged and justified in the Supreme Court through 1942 and 1969 cases citing that the number of would-be broadcasters exceeded that of available frequencies.

Censorship efforts increased at the onset of World War II (1939–1945), yet with diminishing effects. Responding to threats of fascism and communism, Congress passed the Alien Registration Act in 1940, criminalizing advocacy of violent government overthrow. Legal statistics reveal few prosecutions under this act, however. Then in 1946, the Supreme Court undermined postal censorship, prohibiting Postmaster General Robert E. Hannegan from denying second-class postal rates to *Esquire* magazine.

Charges of economic censorship also emerged with a trend toward consolidation of newspaper and magazine businesses. Activists asserted that press monopolies owned and operated by a shrinking number of moguls resulted in news troublesomely biased toward the most powerful economic and political interests. This argument was reinforced later in the century and into the new millennium.

Censorship in the Late Twentieth Century and After

Amid escalating fears of communism in the Cold War era, Congress passed the 1950 Internal Security Act (McCarran Act), requiring Communist Party members to register with the U.S. attorney general. That was despite a veto by President Harry Truman, who called it "the greatest danger to freedom of speech, press, and assembly since the Alien and Sedition Laws of 1798." Encouraged by the McCarran Act, Senator Joseph McCarthy chaired the Senate Subcommittee on Investigations in the 1950s, and harassed public figures on the basis of their past and present political views. Prosecutions for "obscenity" increased in the 1950s as libraries censored books by John Dos Passos, John Steinbeck, Ernest Hemingway, Norman Mailer, J. D. Salinger, and William Faulkner. The 1957 Supreme Court ruling in *Roth v. U.S.* ended obscenity protection under the First Amendment. Yet the Roth Act liberalized the definition of the term, saying: "the test of obscenity is whether to the average person, applying contemporary community standards, the dominant theme of the material taken as a whole appeals to prurient interest." As a result, American readers gained free access to formerly banned works such as D. H. Lawrence's *Lady Chatterley's Lover*, Henry Miller's *Tropic of Cancer*, and John Cleland's *Fanny Hill, or, Memoirs of a Woman of Pleasure*. Meanwhile, Cold War bureaucrats and government officials were increasingly being accused of hiding corruption, inefficiency, and unsafe practices behind a veil of sanctioned secrecy.

The turbulent 1960s brought more vigilante censorship, especially by Southern opponents of the civil rights movement; yet free expression protection and information access increased. The Warren Court, named for U.S. Supreme Court Chief Justice Earl Warren, loosened libel laws, and in 1965 rendered the Roth Act unconstitutional. Then in 1966, spurred by California Representative John Moss, Congress passed the Freedom of Information Act (FOIA). This was a resounding victory for the "people's right to know" advocates, such as Ralph Nader. The FOIA created provisions and procedures allowing any member of the public to obtain the records of federal government agencies. The FOIA was used to expose government waste, fraud, unsafe environmental practices, dangerous consumer products, and unethical behavior by the Federal Bureau of Investigation and Central Intelligence Agency. Supreme Court decisions beginning in the late 1960s further negated national obscenity statutes, but supported local governments' rights to set decency standards and to censor indecent material.

Television and movie censorship operated efficiently, as visual media were acknowledged to have profound psychological impact, especially on young and impressionable minds. The Motion Picture Producers Association censored itself in 1968 by adopting its G, PG, R, and X rating system. Television was highly regulated by the FCC, and increasingly by advertising money driving the medium. While seeking to avoid association of their products with objectionable programming, and by providing essential financial support to networks and stations serving their interests, advertisers directly and indirectly determined television content. Advertisers were in turn subject to Federal Trade Commission censorship, as cigarette and hard liquor ads, for example, were banned from television.

The 1971 Pentagon Papers affair revealed government secrecy abuses during the Vietnam War, and justification for the FOIA. Appeals to prevent publication of the classified Pentagon Papers were rejected by high courts, and the burden came upon government to prove that classified information is essential to military, domestic, or diplomatic security. The FOIA was amended in 1974 with the Privacy Act, curtailing government's legal ability to compile information about individuals, and granting individuals rights to retrieve official records pertaining to them.

Censorship issues in the 1980s included hate speech, flag burning, pornography, and popular music. Religious and parent organizations alarmed by increasingly violent, sexual, and otherwise objectionable music lyrics prompted Senate hearings in 1985. The Recording Industry of America responded by voluntarily placing warning labels where appropriate, which read: "Parental Advisory—Explicit Lyrics." Feminists unsuccessfully tried to ban pornography as injurious to women. President George H. W. Bush and Congress passed a ban on flag desecration, but the Supreme Court soon struck it down as violating the right to free and symbolic political speech. Bigoted expression about minorities, homosexuals, and other groups, especially on college campuses, was subject to censorship and freedom advocacy into the early 1990s, as were sex education and AIDS education in the public schools.

The explosive growth of the Internet and World Wide Web in the mid-1990s gave individuals unprecedented powers and freedom to publish personal views and images, objectionable or not, to the world from the safety of home computers. Predictably, this development brought new censorship measures. In 1996, President Bill Clinton signed into law the Communications Decency Act (CDA), providing broad governmental censorship powers, especially regarding "indecent" material readily available to minors. The CDA was rejected as unconstitutional by the U.S. Supreme Court in *Reno v. ACLU* (1997). Subsequent censorship measures were struck down as well, preserving the Internet as potentially the most democratic communication medium in the United States and the rest of the world.

Censorship in the new millennium centers on familiar issues such as obscenity, national security, and political radicalism. The Internet and the 11 September 2001 terrorist attacks against the United States presented new and complex constitutional challenges. Censorship and resistance to it continued, however. Third-party candidate Ralph Nader was not allowed to participate in nationally broadcast 2000 presidential debates. Globalization of the economy and politics inhibit free expression as well. Dissident intellectuals such as Noam Chomsky argued that media conglomeration and market and political pressures, among other factors, result in propaganda rather than accurate news, while self-censorship is practiced by journalists, so-called experts, politicians, and others relied upon to provide the sort of information needed to preserve a democratic society.

BIBLIOGRAPHY

Herman, Edward S., and Noam Chomsky. *Manufacturing Consent: The Political Economy of the Mass Media.* New York: Pantheon Books, 1988.

Levy, Leonard W., ed. *Freedom of the Press from Zenger to Jefferson.* Durham, N.C.: Carolina Academic Press, 1966.

Liston, Robert A. *The Right to Know: Censorship in America.* New York: F. Watts, 1973.

Nelson, Harold L., ed. *Freedom of the Press from Hamilton to the Warren Court.* Indianapolis: Bobb Merrill, 1967.

Post, Robert C., ed. *Censorship and Silencing: Practices of Cultural Regulation.* Los Angeles: Getty Research Institute for the History of Art and the Humanities, 1998.

American Civil Liberties Union. Home Page at http://www.aclu.org

The Nader Page. Home Page at http://www.nader.org

Ronald S. Rasmus

See also **First Amendment; Freedom of Information Act.**

Census Taker. Winnebago Indians stand near a man writing down census data in Wisconsin, 1911. LIBRARY OF CONGRESS

CENSUS, U.S. BUREAU OF THE. The U.S. Bureau of the Census, established in 1902, collects, compiles, and publishes demographic, social, and economic data for the U.S. government. These data affect business decisions and economic investments, political strategies and the allocation of political representation at the national, state and local levels, as well as the content of public policies and the annual distribution of more than $180 billion in federal spending. Unlike the information gathered and processed by corporations and other private sector organizations, the Census Bureau is commissioned to make its summary data publicly available and is legally required to ensure the confidentiality of the information provided by individuals and organizations for seventy-two years.

The Census Bureau employs approximately 6,000 full-time employees and hired 850,000 temporary employees to assist with the completion of the 2000 census. The president of the United States appoints the director of the Census Bureau, a federal position that requires confirmation by the U.S. Senate. The bureau's headquarters are located in Suitland, Maryland, a suburb of Washington, D.C. The bureau's twelve permanent regional offices are located across the United States, and its processing and support facilities are in Jeffersonville, Indiana.

The Census Bureau has several data gathering responsibilities: the original constitutional purpose from which it draws its names is the completion of the decennial census. Article I of the Constitution requires Congress to enact "a Law" providing for the completion of an "actual Enumeration" of the population of the United States every "ten years." The 1787 Constitutional Convention adopted this provision to facilitate a proportional division of state representation in the House of Representatives. The basis and method for apportioning representation were unresolved problems that divided the states throughout the early national years. Numerous solutions were proposed and debated. At the First Continental Congress in 1774, Massachusetts delegate John Adams recommended that "a proportional scale" among the colonies "ought to be ascertained by authentic Evidence, from Records." Congress subsequently requested that colonial delegates provide accurate accounts "of the number of people of all ages and sexes, including slaves." The population information provided to Congress during the Revolutionary War was gathered and estimated by the states from available sources, including state censuses, tax lists, and militia rolls. Before the 1787 convention, Congress never used this information to apportion congressional representation, rather it served as the basis for apportioning monetary, military, and material requisitions among the states.

After ratification of the Constitution, Congress and President George Washington enacted federal legislation authorizing the first national census in 1790. Sixteen U.S. marshals and 650 assistants were assigned the temporary task of gathering personal and household information from the 3.9 million inhabitants counted in this Census.

The secretary of state supervised the next four decennial censuses, and the Department of the Interior supervised it from 1850 through 1900. Beginning with the 1810 census, the information collected and published extended beyond population data to include tabular and graphic information on the manufacturing, mining, and agriculture sectors of the U.S. economy; on housing conditions, schools, and the achievement of students; and on water and rail transportation systems.

To expedite the collection and publication of the 1880 census, a special office was created in the Department of the Interior. With a number of endorsements, including ones from the American Economic Association and the American Statistical Association, Congress eventually enacted legislation in 1902 establishing the Census Office as a permanent executive agency. The legislation also expanded the mission of the new agency, authorizing an interdecennial census and surveys of manufacturers as well as annual compilations of vital statistics, and the collection and publication of data on poverty, crime, urban conditions, religious institutions, water transportation, and state and local public finance. In 1913 the Census Bureau was reassigned to and remains within the Department of Commerce.

With continued growth of the U.S. population and economy, the Census Bureau acquired new data collection and publication responsibilities in the twentieth century. In 1940, it initiated more detailed censuses of housing than previously available; in 1973, the Department of Housing and Urban Development contracted the bureau to complete the annual American Housing Survey. In 1941, the Bureau began collecting and tabulating official import, export, and shipping statistics; and since 1946 it has issued annual reports profiling the type, size, and payrolls of economic enterprises in every U.S. county. Among its other post–World War II statistical programs, the bureau has trained personnel and provided technical support for statistical organizations and censuses in other nations. Since 1957, the bureau also has completed censuses of state and local governments, a voluntary program of data sharing supplemented by annual surveys of public employee retirement programs and quarterly summaries of state and local government revenues. In 1963, the Census Bureau began a regular schedule of national transportation surveys. In 1969 and 1972 respectively, it started publishing regular reports on minority-owned and women-owned businesses, providing a statistical foundation for several federal affirmative action policies. Since the 1980s, it also provides quarterly and weekly surveys on the income and expenditures of American consumers for the Department of Labor.

Beyond the wealth of statistical information, the U.S. Census Bureau and its predecessors have additionally been supportive of several innovative and subsequently important technologies. A "tabulating machine" was employed in the 1880 census, completing calculations at twice the conventional speed. Herman Hollerith's electric punch card tabulating system, the computer's predecessor, replaced the tabulating machine in the 1890 census and ended the practice of hand tabulation of census returns. Subsequent censuses used improved versions of the punch card technology until the 1950 census, when the bureau received the first UNIVAC computer, the first commercially available computer, which completed tabulation at twice the speed of mechanical tabulation. Subsequent censuses have continued to employ the latest advances in computer technology, adopting optical sensing devices that read and transmit data from penciled dots on a mailed-in Census form and, in the 2000 Census, optical character recognition technology that reads an individual's hand-written responses.

BIBLIOGRAPHY

Anderson, Margo J. *The American Census: A Social History.* New Haven, Conn.: Yale University Press, 1988.

Anderson, Margo, ed., *Encyclopedia of the U.S. Census.* Washington, D.C.: CQ Press, 2000.

Eckler, A. Ross. *The Bureau of the Census.* New York: Praeger, 1972.

Factfinder for the Nation: History and Organization, U.S. Census Bureau, May 2000, accessed at: www.census.gov/prod/2000pubs/cff-4.pdf.

Robey, Bryant. "Two Hundred Years and Counting: 1990 Census," *Population Bulletin* 44, no. 1. Washington, D.C.: Population Reference Bureau, Inc., April 1989.

Charles A. Kromkowski

See also **Statistics.**

CENTENNIAL EXHIBITION, a grand world's fair, was held in Philadelphia in 1876 to mark the one hundredth anniversary of the Declaration of Independence, and was authorized by Congress as "an International Exhibition of Arts, Manufactures and Products of the Soil and Mine." Fifty-six countries and colonies participated, and close to 10 million visitors attended between 10 May and 10 November. As the first major international exhibition in the United States, the Centennial gave center stage to American achievements, especially in industrial technology. J. H. Schwarzmann designed the 284-acre fairground on which the exhibition's 249 buildings were located. The forty-foot-high Corliss Engine in Machinery Hall attracted marveling crowds. Less noted at the time, Alexander Graham Bell demonstrated his new invention, the telephone.

The Centennial celebration embodied the contours of American society. The fairground included a Woman's Building, organized by women for woman exhibitors, but Susan B. Anthony called attention to women's political grievances by reading "Declaration of Rights for Women" on 4 July at Independence Hall. The exhibition represented Native Americans as a declining culture, but news in early July of the Battle of Little Bighorn (25 June) con-

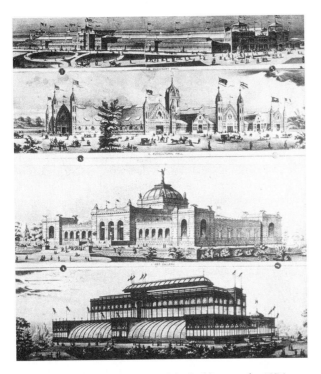

Centennial Exhibition. Four of the buildings at the 1876 world's fair in Philadelphia, held to celebrate the hundredth anniversary of the Declaration of Independence. LIBRARY OF CONGRESS

tradicted the image. Progress and its limitations were both on display as Americans took measure of their nation's first century.

BIBLIOGRAPHY

Post, Robert C., ed. *1876: A Centennial Exhibition: A Treatise upon Selected Aspects of the International Exhibition.* Washington, D.C.: Smithsonian Institution, 1976.

Rydell, Robert W. *All the World's a Fair: Visions of Empire at American International Expositions, 1876–1916.* Chicago: University of Chicago Press, 1984.

Charlene Mires

See also **World's Fairs.**

CENTERS FOR DISEASE CONTROL AND PREVENTION

(CDC), located in Atlanta, Georgia, is the largest federal agency outside the Washington, D.C., area, with more than eighty-five hundred employees and a budget of $4.3 billion for nonbioterrorism-related activities and another $2.3 billion for its emergency and BIOTERRORISM programs (2002). Part of the U.S. Public Health Service, the CDC was created in 1946 as successor to the World War II organization Malaria Control in War Areas. Originally called the Communicable Disease Center, it soon outgrew its narrow focus, and its name was changed in 1970 to Center (later Centers) for Disease Control. The words "and Prevention" were added in 1993, but the acronym CDC was preserved.

During the Cold War, the CDC created the Epidemic Intelligence Service (EIS) to guard against biological warfare, but quickly broadened its scope. The "disease detectives," as EIS officers came to be known, found the cause for the outbreak of many diseases, including LEGIONNAIRES' DISEASE in 1976 and TOXIC SHOCK SYNDROME in the late 1970s. In 1981, the CDC recognized that a half dozen cases of a mysterious illness among young homosexual men was the beginning of an epidemic, subsequently called AIDS. The CDC also played a leading role in the elimination of smallpox in the world (1965–1977), a triumph based on the concept of surveillance, which was perfected at the CDC and became the basis of public health practice around the world. From the 1950s to the 1980s, the CDC led the nation's immunization crusades against polio, measles, rubella, and influenza, and made major contributions to the knowledge of family planning and birth defects. Critics have faulted the CDC for its continuance of a study of untreated syphilis at Tuskegee, Alabama (1957–1972), and for a massive immunization effort against swine influenza in 1976, an epidemic that never materialized.

The CDC assumed an expanded role in maintaining national security after the terrorist attacks of 11 September 2001, and the subsequent discovery of deadly anthrax spores in the U.S. mail system. Responding to fears of biological, chemical, or radiological attacks, the CDC initiated new preparedness and response programs, such as advanced surveillance, educational sessions for local public health officials, and the creation of a national pharmaceutical stockpile to inoculate the public against bioterrorist attacks.

BIBLIOGRAPHY

Etheridge, Elizabeth W. *Sentinel for Health: A History of the Centers for Disease Control.* Berkeley: University of California Press, 1992.

Elizabeth W. Etheridge / A. R.

See also **Acquired Immune Deficiency Syndrome (AIDS); Epidemics and Epidemiology; Medical Research; Medicine and Surgery; Terrorism.**

CENTRAL EUROPE, RELATIONS WITH.

The concept of Central Europe evolved only in the twentieth century. When the United States was first forming, the Austrian empire controlled most of what is now Central Europe.

Many people in Mitteleuropa, as Central Europe was known, saw America as the hope for liberation of oppressed peoples. For Austria this created very strained relations with the United States. When Hungary revolted against Austrian rule in the 1848, America sympathized with the rebels and supported liberation movements within the Austrian empire.

In the late nineteenth century, millions of "Eastern Europeans" (people from areas east of Switzerland) migrated to America. Poles, who had already come in large numbers to the United States, were joined by Ukrainians, Gypsies, Slovaks, and especially Czechs. Czechs settled in the Midwest and made Cleveland, Ohio, a city with one of the world's largest Czech populations. These immigrants, often unwelcome, were characterized by some Americans as mentally and morally inferior to Americans of Western European ancestry. Nevertheless, America offered opportunities that were hard to find in Europe.

Creation of New Nations

During World War I the U.S. government favored the Allies (Russia, France, Britain, and, later, Italy), but many Americans supported the Germans and Austrians. Thus, President Woodrow Wilson was cautious in his support of the Allies. By 1917 conclusive evidence of Germany's effort to persuade Mexico to go to war against the United States made America's entrance into the war inevitable. By the summer of 1918 America was sending 250,000 troops per month to France and England. On 16 September 1918, at St. Mihiel, France, an American army of nine divisions fought and defeated the German forces, ensuring the eventual victory of the Allies.

Woodrow Wilson wanted to create a new Europe in which democracy would be brought to all Europeans, and it was through his efforts that Central Europe became a concept. It was a vague concept, however. Some political scientists saw its limits as Poland to the north, the Ukraine to the east, the Balkans to the south, and the eastern border of Switzerland to the west. Others saw it as consisting of Austria, Hungary, Czechoslovakia, western Ukraine, and sometimes Romania.

Woodrow Wilson argued that "self-determination" should govern the formation of new nations in Central Europe, although he agreed to cede Austria's German-speaking southeastern territories to Italy. Some historians regard this as a mistake, because it denied the people of those provinces their right to choose—the assumption being that they would have chosen to remain part of Austria, with which they had more in common than with Italy. But in 1918 Italy, though it had been the ally of Germany and Austria, had chosen to join the effort to defeat them, and the area ceded to Italy had been the site of horrendous battles in which the Italians had lost many lives. Making the region part of northern Italy seemed to be the only right choice. Thus on 12 November 1918 the Republic of Austria was established, minus its northern Italian holdings, Bohemia, Hungary, and parts of the Balkans and Poland.

With the Treaty of Versailles in 1919, Hungary, Poland, Transylvania, and Yugoslavia were established as independent nations. (Transylvania eventually became part of Romania.) Between the world wars Central Europe often was of little interest to America. Although Woodrow Wilson had pushed for the United States to be actively international in its outlook, many Americans believed that the best way to avoid being dragged into another European war was to stay out of European affairs. Meanwhile, the Central European nations dealt with the worldwide depression of the 1930s, as well as with an aggressive Soviet Union that was busily gobbling up its neighbors (e.g., Finland), and a resurgent and militaristic Germany that regarded all German-speaking peoples as properly belonging to Germany. Czechoslovakia fortified its borders against the possibility of a German invasion, hoping to hold out until Western European nations such as the United Kingdom could come to its aid. Instead, Britain and France gave the Sudetenland of Czechoslovakia to Germany to buy peace. Germany swept into Austria in March 1938, and in August 1939, Germany and the Soviet Union signed a treaty that included dividing Poland between them and giving Germany a free hand throughout Central Europe. Germany invaded the Soviet Union in June 1941, and many of the battles were fought on Central European land.

When the United States entered World War II, the Soviet Union hoped America would open a second front in Western Europe, taking on some of the Soviet Union's burden of fighting the war. That second front did not open until the Allied invasion of Normandy in June 1944. By May 1945 the American army reached Plzen (Pilsen) in Czechoslovakia, helping the Soviet Union to drive out the Germans.

On 27 April 1945 the Allies restored Austria to its 1937 borders. From 17 July to 2 August 1945, while meeting in Potsdam, Germany, the United States, the United Kingdom, and the Soviet Union agreed to treat Austria as a victim of the Germans rather than as a Nazi collaborator. The United States did not protect Central Europeans from Soviet domination. In early 1948 the Czechoslovakian Communist Party won a small plurality in elections, formed a multiparty government, then staged a coup in February; soon thereafter it began to execute thousands of possible anticommunists.

Blighted Lives

By 1955 almost all of Central Europe was under the control of the Soviet Union, and the United States and its World War II European allies had formed the North Atlantic Treaty Organization (NATO) to counter the Soviet military threat. The Central and Eastern European communist governments were tied together in the Warsaw Pact, a military arrangement intended more to formalize those nations as part of the Soviet empire than to counter Western European military threats. Austria, the lone holdout against communism in Central Europe, on 15 May 1955 ratified the Austrian State Treaty, which declared its perpetual neutrality in the Cold War.

During the Cold War, which lasted until 1989, the Central European states were expected to maintain harsh

Refugees. A group of Hungarians—among many more fleeing after the failed anticommunist uprising of 1956—celebrate their imminent freedom in the United States. © UPI/CORBIS-BETTMANN

totalitarian states that served the interests of the Communist Party. In 1956 Hungarians revolted against their communist government. When the Soviet Union invaded to suppress the rebellion, Hungarians held them at bay in heavy street fighting, in the hope that the United States would come to their aid. But the United States did not, and the revolt was suppressed.

In 1968 Czechoslovakia tried another approach to liberation. In the "Prague Spring," the communist government tried easing restrictions on dissent. The result was a short flowering of the arts, but the Soviet Union was intolerant of dissent, and in August 1968 it and the Warsaw Pact nations, especially Poland and Hungary, invaded Czechoslovakia. Alexander Dubcek, leader of Czechoslovakia's Communist Party, ordered his troops to surrender. There had been a faint hope that America might intervene, but America was embroiled in the Vietnam War and was not prepared to risk a nuclear war with the Soviet Union.

The Romanian government tried a dangerous diplomatic course. It created a foreign policy independent of the Soviet Union while maintaining a strict communist dictatorship as its domestic policy.

Modern Complexity

During the 1980s the Soviet Union's economy floundered. By 1989 the Soviet Union was nearing collapse,

and the nations of Central Europe were able to negotiate peaceful withdrawal of Soviet and other Warsaw Pact troops from their territories. The Warsaw Pact itself disintegrated in 1991.

The American government sent billions of dollars in medicine, food, and industrial investment. The Central European governments regarded this aid as owed to them for their forty years of oppression. For example, Romania's government remained both communist and suspicious of American motives. America's persistent support of the formation of opposition political parties in Romania was inevitably seen as hostile to the government. The nation experienced a health care crisis including an epidemic of AIDS among children, and sought medical and humanitarian aid to stabilize the situation before developing freer elections.

After years of oppression, Hungary seemed eager to embrace Western-style democracy. There and in Czechoslovakia, this created misunderstandings between America's intermediaries and the developing governments that favored parliamentarian governments in which the executive and legislative branches were linked (rather than three-branch democracy). Further, after decades of show trials, the new governments found the concept of an independent judiciary hard to understand. When the genocidal wars in Yugoslavia broke out, Hungary invited the United States to station troops near Kaposvar and Pecs in its south. This gave Hungary a chance to show that it belonged in NATO, boosted its local economy with American dollars, and created a sense of security.

Czechoslovakia came out of its communist era seemingly better prepared than its neighbors for joining the international community and building a strong international system of trade. The eastern part of the country had factories, but there was difficulty converting some military factories to other uses. Burdened with a huge military, Czechoslovakia freed capital for investment by paring back its army. There was unrest in eastern Czechoslovakia, where most of the Slovaks lived. The Slovaks believed most of the money for recovery was going to the western part of the country instead of to theirs. In what was called the "Velvet Divorce," the Slovaks voted to separate themselves from the Czechs. On 1 January 1993 Czechoslovakia split into the Slovak Republic and the Czech Republic.

The Slovak Republic, suspicious of Americans, was not entirely happy with American aid that was intended to help form a multiparty, democratic government. Part of this may have stemmed from a strong desire to find its own solutions to domestic challenges. On the other hand the Czech Republic privatized much of its industry, and America became an important trading partner. Americans invested in Czech industries, and America proved to be eager to consume Czech goods such as glassware and beer. The Czech Republic became a magnet for American tourists because of the numerous towns with ancient architecture. In 1999 the Czech Republic was admitted to NATO.

BIBLIOGRAPHY

Brook-Sheperd, Gordon. *The Austrians: A Thousand-Year Odyssey.* New York: Carroll & Graf, 1997.

Burant, Stephen R., ed. *Hungary: A Country Study.* 2d ed. Washington, D.C.: U.S. Government Printing Office, 1990.

Cornell, Katharine. "From Patronage to Pragmatism: Central Europe and the United States." *World Policy Journal* 13, no. 1 (Spring 1996): 89–86.

Knight, Robin. "Does the Old World Need a New Order?: No Longer Part of the East but Not Yet Part of the West, Central Europe Yearns for Security." *U.S. News & World Report,* 13 May 1991, pp. 42–43.

Newberg, Paula R. "Aiding—and Defining—Democracy." *World Policy Journal* 13, no. 1 (Spring 1996): 97–108.

"U.S. Assistance to Central and Eastern Europe." *U.S. Department of State Dispatch* 6, no. 35 (28 August 1995): 663–664.

Kirk H. Beetz

See also **Cold War; Immigration; World War I; World War II.**

CENTRAL INTELLIGENCE AGENCY.

World War II stimulated the creation of the first U.S. central intelligence organization, the Office of Strategic Services (OSS), whose functions included espionage, special operations ranging from propaganda to sabotage, counterintelligence, and intelligence analysis. The OSS represented a revolution in U.S. intelligence not only because of the varied functions performed by a single, national agency but because of the breadth of its intelligence interests and its use of scholars to produce finished intelligence.

In the aftermath of World War II, the OSS was disbanded, closing down on 1 October 1945, as ordered by President Harry S. Truman. The counterintelligence and secret intelligence branches were transferred to the War and State Departments, respectively. At virtually the same time that he ordered the termination of the OSS, Truman authorized studies of the intelligence structure required by the United States in the future, and the National Intelligence Authority (NIA) and its operational element, the Central Intelligence Group (CIG), were formed. In addition to its initial responsibility of coordinating and synthesizing the reports produced by the military service intelligence agencies and the Federal Bureau of Investigation, the CIG was soon assigned the task of clandestine human intelligence (HUMINT) collection.

CIA Organization

As part of a general consideration of national security needs, the National Security Act of 1947 addressed the question of intelligence organization. The act established the Central Intelligence Agency as an independent agency within the Executive Office of the President to replace the CIG. According to the act, the CIA was to have five functions: advising the National Security Council concerning intelligence activities; making recommendations to the National Security Council for the coordination of intelligence activities; correlating, evaluating, and disseminating intelligence; performing services of common concern as determined by the National Security Council; and performing "such functions and duties related to intelligence affecting the national security as the National Security Council may from time to time direct." The provisions of the act left considerable scope for interpretation, and the fifth and final provision has been cited as authorization for covert action operations. In fact, the provision was intended only to authorize espionage. The ultimate legal basis for covert action became presidential direction and congressional approval of funds for such programs.

The CIA developed in accord with a maximalist interpretation of the act. Thus, the CIA has become the primary U.S. government agency for intelligence analysis, clandestine human intelligence collection, and covert action. It has also played a major role in the development of reconnaissance and other technical collection systems employed for gathering imagery, signals, and measurement and signature intelligence. In addition, as stipulated in the agency's founding legislation, the director of the CIA serves as director of central intelligence (DCI) and is responsible for managing the activities of the entire national intelligence community. As a result, the deputy

DCI (DDCI) usually assumes the responsibility of day-to-day management of the CIA.

CIA headquarters is in Langley, Virginia, just south of Washington, D.C., although the agency has a number of other offices scattered around the Washington area. In 1991, the CIA had approximately 20,000 employees, but post–Cold War reductions and the transfer of the CIA's imagery analysts to the National Imagery and Mapping Agency (NIMA) probably reduced that number to about 17,000. Its budget in 2002 was in the vicinity of $3 billion. The CIA consists of three major directorates: the Directorate of Operations (known as the Directorate of Plans from 1952 to 1973), the Directorate of Intelligence, and the Directorate of Science and Technology (established in 1963). In addition, it has a number of offices with administrative functions that were part of the Directorate of Administration until 2000, when that directorate was abolished.

Directorate of Operations

The Directorate of Operations has three major functions: human intelligence collection, covert action, and counterintelligence. The directorate's intelligence officers are U.S. citizens who generally operate under cover of U.S. embassies and consulates, which provides them with secure communications within the embassy and to other locations, protected files, and diplomatic immunity. Others operate under "nonofficial cover" (NOC). Such NOCs may operate as businesspeople, sometimes under cover of working at the overseas office of a U.S. firm. The CIA officers recruit foreign nationals as agents and cultivate knowledgeable foreigners who may provide information as either "unwitting" sources or outside a formal officer-agent relationship.

During the Cold War, the primary target of the CIA was, of course, the Soviet Union. Despite the closed nature of Soviet society and the size and intensity of the KGB's counterintelligence operation, the CIA had a number of notable successes. The most significant was Colonel Oleg Penkovskiy, a Soviet military intelligence (GRU) officer. In 1961 and 1962, Penkovskiy passed great quantities of material to the CIA and the British Secret Intelligence Service, including information on Soviet strategic capabilities and nuclear targeting policy. In addition, he provided a copy of the official Soviet medium-range ballistic missile manual, which was of crucial importance at the time of the Cuban missile crisis.

In subsequent years, the CIA penetrated the Soviet Foreign Ministry, Defense Ministry and General Staff, GRU, KGB, at least one military research facility, and probably several other Soviet organizations. Individuals providing data to the CIA included some stationed in the Soviet Union, some in Soviet consulates and embassies, and some assigned to the United Nations or other international organizations. CIA HUMINT operations successfully penetrated a number of other foreign governments during the last half of the twentieth century, including India, Israel, the People's Republic of China, Taiwan, the Philippines, and Ghana.

The CIA also experienced notable failures. During 1987, Cuban television showed films of apparent CIA officers in Cuba picking up and leaving material at dead drops. It seemed a significant number of Cubans had been operating as double agents, feeding information to the CIA under the supervision of Cuban security officials. CIA operations in East Germany were also heavily penetrated by the East German Ministry for State Security. In 1995, France expelled several CIA officers for attempting to recruit French government officials. From 1984 to 1994, the CIA counterintelligence officer Aldrich Ames provided the Soviet Union and Russia with a large number of documents and the names of CIA penetrations, which resulted in the deaths of ten CIA assets.

CIA covert action operations have included (1) political advice and counsel, (2) subsidies to individuals, (3) financial support and technical assistance to political parties or groups, (4) support to private organizations, including labor unions and business firms, (5) covert propaganda, (6) training of individuals, (7) economic operations, (8) paramilitary or political action operations designed to overthrow or to support a regime, and (9) until the mid-1960s, attempted assassinations. Successes in the covert action area included monetary support to anticommunist parties in France and Italy in the late 1940s that helped prevent communist electoral victories. The CIA successfully engineered a coup that overthrew Guatemalan president Jacobo Arbenz Guzmán in 1954. In contrast, repeated attempts to eliminate Fidel Castro's regime and Castro himself failed. CIA covert action in cooperation with Britain's Secret Intelligence Service was crucial in restoring the shah of Iran to the throne in 1953, and, by providing Stinger missiles to the Afghan resistance, in defeating the Soviet intervention in Afghanistan in the 1980s. Such operations subsequently had significant detrimental consequences. The CIA also orchestrated a propaganda campaign against Soviet SS-20 missile deployments in Europe in the 1980s.

Counterintelligence operations conducted by the Directorate of Operations include collection of information on foreign intelligence and security services and their activities through open and clandestine sources; evaluation of defectors; research and analysis concerning the structure, personnel, and operations of foreign intelligence and security services; and operations disrupting and neutralizing intelligence and security services engaging in activities hostile to the United States. Successful counterintelligence efforts have included penetration of a number of foreign intelligence services, including those of the Soviet Union and Russia, the People's Republic of China, and Poland.

Directorate of Intelligence

The Directorate of Intelligence, established in 1952 by consolidating different intelligence production offices in

tocratic founders expected. They never dreamed it would also serve the recreational needs of a city of 8 million people.

BIBLIOGRAPHY

Olmsted, Frederick Law. *Creating Central Park, 1857–1861.* Baltimore: Johns Hopkins University Press, 1983.

Rosenzweig, Roy, and Elizabeth Blackmar. *The Park and the People: A History of Central Park.* Ithaca, N.Y.: Cornell University Press, 1992.

Jeremy Derfner

See also **City Planning; Landscape Architecture; Recreation.**

CENTRALIA MINE DISASTER. On 25 March 1947, an explosion at the Centralia Coal Company in Centralia, Illinois, killed 111 miners. Following the disaster, John L. Lewis, president of the United Mine Workers, called a two-week national memorial work stoppage on 400,000 soft-coal miners. A year earlier, against the opposition of coal operators, the Interior Department had issued a comprehensive and stringent Federal Mine Code, which tightened regulations governing the use of explosives and machinery and set new standards for ventilation and dust control in mining operations. Lewis, who since the 1930s had repeatedly campaigned to make coal-mine safety a federal concern, blamed the Department of the Interior for its lax enforcement of the mine code. Lewis claimed that the victims of the disaster were "murdered because of the criminal negligence" of the secretary, Julius A. Krug. Of the 3,345 mines inspected in 1946, Lewis argued, only two fully complied with the safety code. Lewis called for Krug's removal, but President Harry Truman, who regarded the mourning strike as a sham, rejected this demand.

Despite the president's chilly response, the disaster awakened officials to the need for improved mine safety. In August 1947, Congress passed a joint resolution calling on the Bureau of Mines to inspect coal mines and to report to state regulatory agencies any violations of the federal code. The resolution also invited mining states to overhaul and tighten their mine safety laws and enforcement. The Colorado Mine Safety Code of 1951 is among the most notable examples.

BIBLIOGRAPHY

DeKok, David. *Unseen Danger: A Tragedy of People, Government, and the Centralia Mine Fire.* Philadelphia: University of Pennsylvania Press, 1986.

Dubofsky, Melvyn, and Warren Van Tine. *John L. Lewis.* Urbana: University of Illinois Press, 1986.

Whiteside, James. *Regulating Danger.* Lincoln: University of Nebraska Press, 1990.

David Park

See also **Coal; Coal Mining and Organized Labor; Mining Towns; United Mine Workers of America.**

CENTURY OF DISHONOR. Written by Helen Maria Hunt Jackson and published in 1881, *Century of Dishonor* called attention to what Jackson termed the government's "shameful record of broken treaties and unfulfilled promises" and helped spark calls for the reform of federal Indian policy. Formerly uninvolved with reform causes, Jackson, a well-known poet, became interested in Indian issues after hearing of the removal of the Ponca tribe to Indian territory and the Poncas' subsequent attempt to escape and return to their homeland in Nebraska. A commercial success, *Century of Dishonor* also proved influential in shaping the thinking of reform organizations such as the Women's National Indian Association, the Indian Rights Association, and the Lake Mohonk Conference of the Friends of the Indians, all of which were founded between 1879 and 1883. Jackson distributed a copy of her book to each member of Congress. Believing that the United States was faced with a choice of exterminating or assimilating Indians, Jackson advocated greater efforts to Christianize and to educate Native Americans, as well as the passage of legislation to allot their lands to individual Indians.

BIBLIOGRAPHY

Mathes, Valerie Sherer. *Helen Hunt Jackson and Her Indian Reform Legacy.* Austin: University of Texas Press, 1990.

Prucha, Francis Paul. *American Indian Policy in Crisis: Christian Reformers and the Indians, 1865–1900.* Norman: University of Oklahoma Press, 1976.

Frank Rzeczkowski

See also **Dawes General Allotment Act; Indian Policy, U.S.: 1775–1830, 1830–1900;** and *vol. 9:* **A Century of Dishonor.**

CERAMICS. See **Art: Pottery and Ceramics.**

CEREAL GRAINS

Origins

Cereal grains are the seeds that come from grasses such as wheat, millet, rice, barley, oats, rye, triticale, sorghum, and maize (corn). About 80 percent of the protein and over 50 percent of the calories consumed by humans and livestock come from cereal grains. The United States is a major supplier of cereal grains to the rest of the world and some impoverished countries depend on gifts of both unmilled and processed grains from America to keep their people from starving.

Most archaeologists and paleoanthropologists agree that agriculture began around 10,000 B.C., when people near the Tigris and Euphrates Rivers in Mesopotamia (later Iraq) settled into villages and began cultivating and breeding wheat. By 8000 B.C., people in central Asia were cultivating millet and rice. By 7000 B.C., people in what is now Greece were cultivating not only wheat but barley

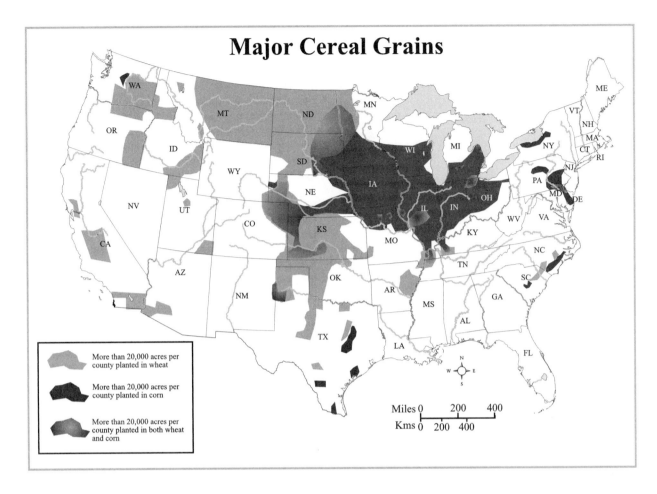

Major Cereal Grains

Legend:
- More than 20,000 acres per county planted in wheat
- More than 20,000 acres per county planted in corn
- More than 20,000 acres per county planted in both wheat and corn

Miles 0   200   400
Kms 0   200   400

and oats. By 6000 B.C., farmers were milling their cereal grains by hammering them with stone pestles and were toasting the milled grains. By 3000 B.C., people in South America, and probably Central America, too, were cultivating maize. Before 2500 B.C., ancient Egyptians were cultivating wheat and barley and fermenting them to make beer. Hand mills for grinding grain appeared by 1200 B.C., and continued in use in most seventeenth-century American colonies for processing cereal grains.

The Colonial Era: Survival and Beyond

Wheat was the staple of the European diet, especially valued when processed into flour for baking. Therefore, the first European colonists in eastern North America—the Dutch, English, Swedes, and Germans—brought with them wheat. However, they quickly ran into problems. In Virginia, high humidity promoted decay in stored wheat because the husks of wheat, high in fat, went rancid. That poisoned the fall harvest, making it useless for winter food. In New Amsterdam (later New York) and New England, the wheat had difficulty surviving in the cool climate, making the crops unproductive.

The Native Americans in New England were mostly farmers and their most important crop was maize, which came in many varieties and was hardy enough to tolerate cold weather. Using Native American stocks, the colonists took the highest-yielding stalks of maize and bred them in an effort to conserve their good qualities such as many ears per stalk, large kernels, and successful germination in anticipation of growing a better crop the next season. But maize is peculiar in that when it is inbred, the good qualities are always lost, making every successive crop worse than the previous one. In order for maize to remain hardy, its varieties must crossbreed. The failure of wheat and maize crops almost starved all the earliest settlers, but Native Americans shared their harvest, enabling many colonists to survive.

By the early 1700s, the cereal grains rice and oats had been imported from the Old World. The rice could grow on difficult terrain, as in the hilly, rocky region of western Pennsylvania. From 8000 B.C. until the nineteenth century, rice was raised on dry land, not in water-laden paddies. Thus, early American colonists grew a hardy dry land rice that was the ancestor of modern wild rice, beginning in South Carolina in 1695. Oats proved resistant to both drought and cold. The resistance to drought proved vital in the southern colonies, which suffered years-long droughts in the seventeenth and eighteenth centuries, and the resistance to cold made it almost as valuable as maize and, for a time, more valuable than wheat. During the seventeenth century, colonists had learned to make bread out of maize, and cornbread, or johnny cakes, became an everyday part of the American diet.

In 1769, the steamroller mill was introduced. Water mills and windmills used flowing water or wind to power huge stones to crush cereal grains, but the steamroller mill powered metal mills and could be built almost anywhere, not just by rivers or in windy areas. New immigrants constantly arrived in the colonies and they brought with them their preference for processed wheat; the steamroller mill made it possible to quickly process wheat before it decayed, encouraging the growing of wheat in Pennsylvania.

From the Revolution to 1900: Production Growth and Mechanization

By the end of the colonial era, cereal grains had become cash crops; that is, there was enough left over to sell after the farmers had fed themselves. In the early Republic, the federal and state governments tried to regulate and tax harvests. In the difficult countryside of western Pennsylvania, farmers distilled corn and rye into whiskey, a valuable product that was commercially viable when shipped east to cities. In 1791, however, the federal government placed a high tax on whiskey, forcing western Pennsylvania farmers to either ship their grain to the east through rough hills at high expense or give up making whiskey. They rebelled in 1794 and President George Washington raised and led an army that put down the rebellion.

During the first decade of the nineteenth century, rice became a major export crop for Georgia and South Carolina, and eventually would be a major crop in Louisiana and Texas. Wheat was being grown on flat lands in New York and Pennsylvania. Swedes began settling in the Midwest, bringing with them traditional methods of growing wheat and eventually turning Nebraska into a major wheat producer. In 1874, Russian immigrants brought seeds for Turkey Red Wheat to Kansas; a dwarf wheat, it was drought resistant and became a source for the many varieties of dwarf wheat grown in America.

America's capacity for nurturing cereal grains far outstripped its capacity to harvest it. In 1834 the mechanical revolution in farming began when Cyrus McCormick introduced his mechanical reaper, which allowed two field hands to do the work that had previously taken five to do. The reapers that followed relied on either humans or horses to pull them, but worked well on maize, wheat, and rye. The Great Plains, with their huge flat landscapes, were ideal for the mechanical reaper and its availability encouraged farmers to fill in the Plains with large fields of cereal grains. In the 1830s, Native Americans in the Midwest began cultivating wheat themselves. In 1847, McCormick patented another important farm implement, a disk plow that facilitated the planting of even rows of cereal grasses.

By 1874, mechanical planters had followed the mechanical reapers, allowing farmers to plant in a day what before had taken a week to do. A problem was that to work best, the mechanical planters required moist, plowed land. (This was one among many reasons why the federal government paid for irrigation canals in the Midwest during the 1920s and 1930s.)

In the 1890s, combine harvesters were introduced. At first pulled by teams of horses, these big machines with their turning blades like paddle wheels on steamboats could harvest and bale wheat and sort ears of maize. The result was another 80 percent jump in efficiency over the old mechanical harvesters. Soon, the combine harvesters would be powered by internal combustion engines and a single farm could harvest almost twenty times as much land as could have been harvested at the outset of the nineteenth century. That would make corporate farming possible.

The Twentieth Century and Beyond

In 1941, Dr. W. Henry Sebrell and others persuaded manufacturers of bread and other cereal grain products to mix thiamin, riboflavin, niacin, and iron into their baked goods. The federal government made this mandatory for the duration of World War II, but individual states extended it into the 1950s. Then, the Federal Food and Drug Administration (FDA) mandated the enrichment of flour. Incidents of malnutrition decreased for some two decades before a dramatic change in American diet, fad dieting, made malnutrition a growing problem during and after the late 1970s.

In the late 1950s, the federal government began one of what would become several campaigns to improve the way Americans ate, including food "triangles" or "pyramids" that made cereal grains the basis of a healthy diet, after many years of promoting dairy products and high-fat meats such as bacon (for energy). The triangles typically had grains and grain products such as bread at the base of the triangle, with dairy products such as milk and eggs in the middle of the triangle, and meats at the peak, meaning that a diet should consist mostly of grains, less of dairy products, and even less of meats. When eggs fell out of favor, because of their cholesterol, they were moved upwards. At first, fruits and vegetables were lumped in with grains, but were given their own category in the 1960s. By the year 2000, the FDA's pyramid was so confusing that almost no one understood it, although the federal government ran commercials promoting it during children's television shows. Always, cereal grains remained the foundation of the government's recommended diet. The status of cereal grains came under serious challenge in the mid-1980s, and soon after the turn of the twenty-first century some nutritionists were urging that vegetables high in vitamin C and roughage replace cereal grains, which had been linked to tooth decay.

BIBLIOGRAPHY

Cohen, John. "Corn Genome Pops Out of the Pack: Congress Is Poised to Launch a Corn Genome Project." *Science* 276 (1997): 1960–1962.

"Kansas Timelines." Kansas State Historical Society, Agriculture. Available from http://www.kshs.org.

Park, Youngmee K., et al. "History of Cereal-Grain Product Fortification in the United States." *Nutrition Today* 36, no. 3 (May 2001): 124.

Sebrell, W. Henry. "A Fiftieth Anniversary—Cereal Enrichment." *Nutrition Today* 27 no. 1 (February 1992): 20–21.

Siebold, Ronald. "From the Kansas River." *Total Health* 15, no. 3 (June 1993): 44–45.

"What Is Cereal?" Available from http://www.kelloggs.com.

Kirk H. Beetz

See also **Agriculture; Agriculture, Department of; Nutrition and Vitamins.**

CEREALS, MANUFACTURE OF.

In most of the world, the word "cereal" refers to the grains or seeds of cereal grasses. In the United States, however, it took on the additional meaning of "breakfast cereal" at the start of the twentieth century because products made from cereal grains were heavily advertised as food for breakfast. This had not always been the case in America. Before the late nineteenth century, Americans had preferred to eat pork, bacon, and lard for breakfast. In those days most Americans worked from dawn to past dusk at hard physical labor and the protein from pork and bacon and the calories from lard helped maintain muscle strength and provided energy. Early colonists who could not afford meat or lard ate porridge (boiled oats).

The Formation of Early Breakfast Cereal Manufacturers

The revolution in American eating habits that became a multibillion-dollar industry began in Akron, Ohio, in 1854, when German immigrant Ferdinand Schumacher began grinding oats with a hand mill in the back of his store and selling the results as oatmeal, suggesting that it be used as a substitute for pork at breakfast. This did not prevent people from dropping dollops of lard into their oatmeal, but the convenience of preparation made it popular. By the 1860s a health foods movement touted oatmeal as healthier than meats. Schumacher called his growing business the German Mills American Oatmeal Company; in 1877, he adopted the still-familiar Quaker trademark, which became one of the most successful symbols in history. He wanted to move away from the idea of oats as food for horses and the adoption of the Quaker symbol tied in nicely with the fundamentalist religious aspects of the health food movement. In 1888 his company merged with the Oatmeal Millers Association to become the American Cereal Company. In 1901 the company changed its name to the Quaker Oats Company.

Another successful entrepreneur was Henry Perky, who in 1893 began marketing shredded wheat, the earliest of the cold cereals; his Shredded Wheat Company was purchased in 1928 by the National Biscuit Company (abbreviated Nabisco). In the 1890s, William H. Danforth took over the Robinson Commission Company, and under the trade name Purina, the company produced a very successful line of food products for animals and a whole wheat cereal for people. By the 1890s cereal grains were touted as foods that made people healthier, even prolonging their lives, and health clubs that featured medical treatments, pseudoscientific treatments for ills, and special diets were popular. The Robinson Commission Company and Dr. Ralston health clubs merged to form Ralston-Purina, which during the 1890s was an outlet for introducing Americans to Purina breakfast foods.

In Michigan, Dr. John H. Kellogg experimented with ways to make healthy vegetarian foods for patients at his health clinic, the Adventist Battle Creek Sanitarium. In the early 1890s, he and his brother William K. Kellogg had developed a process whereby wheat grains would be mashed and then baked into flakes. In 1899, John Kellogg formed Kellogg's Sanitas Nut Food Company, but his narrow focus on producing foods just for patients proved frustrating for his younger brother. In 1895 the brothers discovered how to make corn flakes, which they sold by mail order. The corn flakes were popular, and in 1906, William Kellogg broke from his brother to found and run the Battle Creek Toasted Corn Flake Company. In the first year of the company's operation, it sold 175,000 cases of corn flakes. He soon changed the name of the company to W. K. Kellogg Company and the product was called Kellogg's Corn Flakes.

Among the many competitors that sprang up to rival Kellogg was C. W. Post, who in 1895 had invented Postum, a cereal beverage intended to be a coffee substitute. In 1897 he created Grape-Nuts breakfast cereal. In 1904 Post introduced a flaked corn breakfast cereal he called Elijah's Manna, which he later changed to Post Toasties. When Post died in 1914, his Postum Cereal Company began a series of mergers that resulted in the General Mills Company in 1928.

Expansion and Shifting Markets

Both William Kellogg and Post were canny marketers, aiming their advertising at busy adults who wanted something quick and easy to prepare for breakfast; corn flakes became their most popular products. Until his retirement in 1946, Kellogg was a relentless innovator. In 1928 he introduced Rice Krispies, whose crackling sounds enhanced its popularity. His company also introduced wax liners for cereal boxes, helping to keep the dry cereal dry and lengthen its shelf life. The Quaker Oats Company rapidly expanded its market in the 1920s. During the decade it introduced puffed wheat and rice; the manufacturing process involved steaming the grain under pressure and exploding them out of guns. Beginning in 1924, James Ford Bell used celebrities to market Wheaties, eventually focusing on athletes such as Olympic star Johnny Weissmuller to make Wheaties "the breakfast of champions." In 1937 General Mills introduced a new puffed cereal, Kix.

It was not until the late 1940s that breakfast cereals hit hard times. Physicians were telling their patients that eggs, bacon, and potatoes made for the healthiest breakfast, and as a result, adults bought less cereal. Kellogg's and General Mills compensated by targeting children as consumers. The new Kix slogan was, "Kix are for kids!" Kellogg's introduced Sugar Frosted Flakes and soon competitors followed suit with presweetened cereals.

The cereal manufacturers focused their advertising on children's television programs; for instance, Post advertised on *Fury*, pushing its sweet Raisin Bran cereal (introduced in 1942). During the 1960s surveys indicated that children made many of the decisions about what food to eat in American homes, encouraging cereal marketers to focus still more on commercials during cartoon shows and at hours that children were likely to be watching television.

In the early 1980s the federal government filed suit against Kellogg's, General Mills, and others for forming a trust that monopolized the breakfast cereal market. For a few years company profits declined, but in 1982 the suit was dropped. The cereal manufacturers found themselves in a marketplace driven by the same forces that had driven the market in the late nineteenth century. Eggs and bacon were condemned by physicians for having too much cholesterol and Americans were turning to "health food." Vitamin-fortified foods were developed not only for breakfast but for snacking and the term granola bar was attached to chewy, cereal grain snacks as well as cereals. The word sugar disappeared from labels as the cereal manufacturers once again targeted adults who wanted healthy diets. By 2002 the cereal market was about evenly divided between food marketed to children and food marketed to adults, and additives intended to prevent malnutrition among fad dieters were being included in adult cereals.

BIBLIOGRAPHY

Johnston, Nicholas. "Bowled Over: Dig In for a Spoonful of Cereal History." *Washington Post* 30 April 2001.

Lord, Lewis J. "Fitness Food Makes Good Business." *U.S. News and World Report* 100 (20 January 1986): 69.

Martin, Josh. "A Very Healthy Business." *Financial World* 155 (15 April 1986): 40.

Park, Youngmee K., et al. "History of Cereal-Grain Product Fortification in the United States." *Nutrition Today* 36, no. 3 (May 2001): 124.

Sebrell, W. Henry. "A Fiftieth Anniversary—Cereal Enrichment." *Nutrition Today* 27, no. 1 (February 1992): 20–21.

United States Food and Drug Administration. "Selling High-fiber Cereals." *FDA Consumer* 21 (September 1987): 6.

Kirk H. Beetz

See also **Health Food Industry.**

CHAIN GANGS, a type of convict labor that developed in the American South in the post–Civil War period.

Chain Gang. Inmates in Georgia take a moment off from their backbreaking rock-breaking work. © CORBIS-BETTMANN

Many penitentiaries and jails had been destroyed during the war and money was lacking to repair them or build new ones. The southern prison system lay in ruins and could not accommodate the influx of convicts moving through the court system. Chain gangs offered a solution to the problem since they generated revenue for the state and relieved the government of prison expenditures. They also eased the burden on the taxpayer. Southern states would lease convicts to private corporations or individuals who used the prisoners to build railroads, work plantations, repair levees, mine coal, or labor in sawmills. The lessees promised to guard, feed, clothe, and house the convicts. Convict leasing reached its zenith between 1880 and 1910 and proved to be extremely profitable.

The majority of convicts working on chain gangs were African Americans. Convict leasing was a tool of racial repression in the Jim Crow South as well as a profit-driven system. Some state legislatures passed laws targeting blacks that made vagrancy a crime and increased the penalties for minor offenses such as gambling, drunkenness, and disorderly conduct. As a result, arrests and convictions of African Americans (including children) shot up dramatically.

Life on the chain gang was brutal, and the mortality rate was extremely high. Many prisoners died of exhaustion, sunstroke, frostbite, pneumonia, gunshot wounds, and shackle poisoning caused by the constant rubbing of chains on flesh. Convicts were often transported to work camps in rolling cages where they slept without blankets and sometimes clothes. Sanitary conditions were appalling. Convicts labored from sunup to sundown and slow workers were punished with the whip. Chain gangs allowed white southerners to control black labor following the end of slavery.

County and municipal governments also used penal chain gangs to build roads in the rural South. In response to the "good roads movement" initiated during the Progressive Era, the state used convict labor to create a modern system of public highways. The goal was to modernize the South, and the use of chain gangs to build a transportation infrastructure contributed to commercial expansion in the region. Eventually, Progressive reformers began to focus on the atrocities of convict leasing. As a result, the private lease system was abolished. However, some southern states continued to use chain gangs on county and municipal projects until the early 1960s.

BIBLIOGRAPHY

Lichtenstein, Alex. *Twice the Work of Free Labor: The Political Economy of Convict Labor in the New South.* New York: Verso, 1996.

Mancini, Matthew J. *One Dies, Get Another: Convict Leasing in the American South, 1866–1928.* Columbia: University of South Carolina Press, 1996.

Oshinsky, David M. *Worse Than Slavery: Parchman Farm and the Ordeal of Jim Crow Justice.* New York: Simon and Schuster, 1996.

Natalie J. Ring

See also **Convict Labor Systems; Jim Crow Laws; Roads.**

CHAIN STORES are groups of retail stores engaged in the same general field of business that operate under the same ownership or management. Chain stores have come to epitomize the vertically integrated big businesses of modern mass distribution, and their strategies have shaped mass consumption.

Modern chain stores began in 1859, the year in which the Great Atlantic & Pacific Tea Company opened its first grocery store (A&P). F. W. Woolworth, the innovator of five-and-dimes, opened his first variety store in 1879 in Utica, New York. Chain-store firms grew enormously over the next few decades, both in sales and in numbers of stores, and by 1929 accounted for 22 percent of total U.S. retail sales. Growth was most dramatic in grocery retailing and in variety stores. But chains also proved successful in other fields, including tobacco stores (United Cigar Stores), drug stores (Liggett), and restaurants, like A&W root beer stands and Howard Johnson's.

The popularity of chains was not the result of extensive choice or services; executives limited the range of goods stores sold and kept tight control over store design and managers' actions in these relatively small-sized stores. Low price was the biggest drawing card, and ads prominently featured sale items. Lower costs and lower prices were the result of these firms' investments in their own warehouses and distribution networks and of "economies of scale"—lower unit costs through high-volume sales.

Growth also depended on several other important strategies. Chains lowered labor costs by adopting self-service, encouraging customers to choose goods for themselves rather than to go through a clerk who would procure goods from a storeroom or locked case. Firms also developed specialized techniques for choosing store sites. Executives fueled the real estate boom of the 1920s in their fevered search for sites that would attract the maximum possible number of potential customers—so-called 100 percent locations. Finally, in their ongoing attempts to increase sales, chain stores proved willing to sell in African American and white working-class neighborhoods. These actions won them the loyalty of shoppers who appreciated that chains' standardized practices generally translated into more equal treatment of customers than did the more personal, but sometimes discriminatory, service in grocery and department stores. Promises of autonomy and independence were especially compelling to the women customers targeted by grocery-store chains. Thus, social dynamics as well as low price help to explain the success of chain stores.

In the 1920s and 1930s, independent druggists and grocers urged Congress to pass legislation that might halt or slow the growth of chain-store firms. Neither the movement nor the resulting legislation—notably the Robinson-Patman Act (1936) and Miller Tydings Act (1937)—proved effective in stopping the growth of chains or, more importantly, in providing significant help to smaller, independently owned stores. Indeed, chain-store firms won government support by proving themselves useful partners in new attempts to regulate consumption in federal and state food-stamp and welfare programs, new sales taxes, and wartime rationing and price controls.

A more serious threat was the growth of a new kind of store—the supermarket. Supermarkets were often run as very small chains or as single-store independents and were physically much larger than chain stores. A single supermarket sold many more goods, and many more kinds of goods, than did most chain stores of the interwar era. These stores were often located in outlying urban areas and in the suburbs. Large chain-store firms at first balked at the notion of building fewer, but larger, stores. By the 1950s, however, most chain grocery firms were building supermarkets, and chain firms in other fields, particularly variety and housewares, also came to adopt these strategies. Large self-service stores built on the fringes of cities or in suburbs came to define mass retailing.

By 1997, the U.S. Census Bureau determined that "multi-unit" firms—firms that consisted of two or more retail establishments—made more than 60 percent of all

Five-and-Dime. Shown here is an early F. W. Woolworth store, with its easily recognizable red and white awning; note the goods on display in the window. The five-and-dime chain, also known as a dime store or variety store, was launched by namesake F. W. Woolworth in Utica, New York, in 1879. By 1929, just fifty years later, chain stores such as this one accounted for 22 percent of total U.S. retail sales. © ARCHIVE PHOTOS, INC.

retail sales. Even independently owned retail businesses were often affiliated through voluntary chains, cooperative wholesalers, or franchise systems that clearly recalled chain store firms. Thus many stores, regardless of the type of ownership, came to resemble one another in terms of the way they looked and the strategies they employed. Americans' experience of shopping had been transformed by the rise of chains.

BIBLIOGRAPHY

Cohen, Lizabeth. *Making a New Deal: Industrial Workers in Chicago, 1919–1939*. Cambridge, U.K., and New York: Cambridge University Press, 1990.

Deutsch, Tracey. "Untangling Alliances: Social Tensions at Neighborhood Grocery Stores and the Rise of Chains." In *Food Nations: Selling Taste in Consumer Societies*. Edited by Warren Belasco and Philip Scranton. New York: Routledge, 2001.

Tedlow, Richard. *New and Improved: The Story of Mass Marketing in America*. New York: Basic Books, 1990.

Tracey Deutsch

See also **Retailing Industry.**

CHALLENGER DISASTER.

Perhaps no tragedy since the assassination of President John F. Kennedy in 1963 had so riveted the American public as did the explosion of the SPACE SHUTTLE *Challenger* on 28 January 1986, which killed its seven-member crew. The horrific moment came seventy-three seconds after liftoff from Cape Canaveral, Florida, and was captured on live television and rebroadcast to a stunned and grieving nation.

Nearly nineteen years to the day after fire killed three *Apollo* astronauts during a launch rehearsal, the *Challenger* crew prepared for the nation's twenty-fifth space shuttle mission. Successes of the NATIONAL AERONAUTICS AND SPACE ADMINISTRATION (NASA) in shuttle missions had made Americans believe that shuttles were almost immune to the dangers of space flight. If not for the fact that a New Hampshire schoolteacher, Sharon Christa McAuliffe, had been chosen to be the first private citizen to fly in the shuttle, the launch might have received little attention in the nation's media.

The temperature on the morning of the launch was thirty-eight degrees, following an overnight low of twenty-four degrees, the coldest temperature for any shuttle launch. Liftoff occurred only sixteen days after the launch of the space shuttle *Columbia*, making this the shortest interval ever between shuttle flights. Sixty seconds after the launch, NASA scientists observed an "unusual plume" from *Challenger*'s right booster engine. A burn-through of the rocket seal caused an external fuel

Challenger. The space shuttle explodes just after liftoff from the Kennedy Space Center on 28 January 1986.

tank to rupture and led to an unforgettable flash—and then the sickeningly slow fall of flaming debris into the Atlantic Ocean. In addition to McAuliffe, the dead included *Challenger* pilot Michael J. Smith, a decorated Vietnam War veteran; flight commander Francis R. Scobee; laser physicist Ronald E. McNair, the second African American in space; aerospace engineer Ellison S. Onizuka, the first Japanese American in space; payload specialist Gregory B. Jarvis; and electrical engineer Judith A. Resnick, the second American woman in space. The diversity of the crew, reflecting that of the American people, made the tragedy an occasion for national mourning.

A commission led by former secretary of state William P. Rogers and astronaut Neil Armstrong concluded that NASA, its Marshall Space Flight Center, and the contractor Morton Thiokol, the booster's manufacturer, were guilty of faulty management and poor engineering. NASA's ambitious launch schedule, it was found, had outstripped its resources and overridden warnings from safety engineers. The successful launch of the space shuttle *Discovery* on 29 September 1988, more than two and a half years after the *Challenger* disaster, marked the nation's return to human space flight. The *Challenger* explosion had sobered the space agency, prompting hundreds of design and procedural changes costing $2.4 billion. The agency devoted the shuttle almost exclusively to delivering defense and scientific payloads. The SPACE PROGRAM, long a symbol of U.S. exceptionalism, continued to receive substantial, if less enthusiastic, support from the public.

BIBLIOGRAPHY

Hamilton, Sue L. *Space Shuttle: Challenger, January 28, 1986*. Edited by John C. Hamilton. Bloomington, Minn.: Abdo and Daughters, 1988.

Neal, Arthur G. *National Trauma and Collective Memory: Major Events in the American Century*. Armonk, N.Y.: M. E. Sharpe, 1998.

Vaughn, Diane. *The Challenger Launch Decision: Risky Technology, Culture, and Deviance at NASA*. Chicago: University of Chicago Press, 1996.

Bruce J. Evensen / c. w.

See also **Moon Landing.**

CHAMBERS OF COMMERCE. As early as the 1780s, businessmen realized they needed a commercial and trade organization to represent their interests in the wider community. Voluntary associations of local business leaders, usually culled from the service professions, chambers of commerce consider a wide variety of business, cultural, and community challenges. In addition to leadership development and fraternal aspects, chambers of commerce often focus on issues that directly involve local business leaders, such as zoning ordinances, property taxes, commercial development, and public relations efforts at promoting the business interests of the local area.

Chambers of commerce in the United States are modeled after similar organizations in England. Many chambers in older American cities evolved from two preceding associations: the Board of Trade and the Civic Association. While most chambers tackle a broad range of interests, many still cling to their roots and heavily promote trade and civic interests. Chambers of commerce also have an emphasis on charity work and raise money for the local community.

In 1912, a group of business leaders from local and regional chambers and trade associations founded the Chamber of Commerce of the United States. These leaders realized that they needed an organization in Washington, D.C., that would represent their interests regarding public policy issues. In 1926, they built a headquarters in the nation's capital in a building designed by the famous architect Cass Gilbert. By 1929, the chamber had more than 16,000 affiliated business organizations. The group worked closely with the government during World War I, organizing more than 400 War Service Committees to help coordinate business involvement in the war effort. The group remained supportive of the government until the New Deal. Like other business interests, they challenged President Franklin D. Roosevelt's policies, particularly over social security and public welfare. However, during World War II, the chamber once again rallied to aid the nation's efforts. After the war, the chamber once again fought expansion of the federal government and became a powerful lobbying force.

In 2002 there were 3 million businesses represented by the chamber, consisting of 3,000 state and local chambers, more than 800 business associations, and ninety-two American chambers of commerce overseas. Keeping with its tradition of representing local business leaders, 96 percent of its members were small businesses with 100 or fewer employees.

BIBLIOGRAPHY

Collins, Robert M. *The Business Response to Keynes, 1929–1964.* New York: Columbia University Press, 1981.

Werking, Richard Hume. "Bureaucrats, Businessmen, and Foreign Trade: The Origins of the United States Chamber of Commerce," *Business History Review* 52 (1978): 321–341.

Bob Batchelor

See also **Free Trade; Trade, Domestic; Trade, Foreign.**

CHAMPAGNE-MARNE OPERATION (15–18 July 1918).

In an effort to improve supply lines and distract the British from another offensive in Flanders during World War I, the German First, Seventh, and Third armies crossed the Marne River east of Château-Thierry, France, and advanced up the valley to Epernay. The attack was halted east of Reims on the first day by the Fourth French Army. Fourteen divisions crossed the Marne, but without artillery support, the attack soon bogged down. The Third, the Forty-second, and part of the Twenty-eighth American Divisions, consisting of approximately 85,000 soldiers, participated. The Thirty-eighth Infantry Regiment (Third Division) here won the sobriquet "Rock of the Marne."

BIBLIOGRAPHY

Coffman, Edward M. *The War to End All Wars: The American Military Experience in World War I.* New York: Oxford University Press, 1968.

Freidel, Frank. *Over There: The Story of America's First Great Overseas Crusade.* Boston: Little, Brown, 1964.

Girard L. McEntee/A. R.

See also **Aisne-Marne Operation; Belleau Wood, Battle of; Meuse-Argonne Offensive.**

CHAMPLAIN, SAMUEL DE, EXPLORATIONS OF.

Born about 1567 in the small French Atlantic port of Brouage, Samuel de Champlain had most likely already been to Spanish America when, in 1603, he embarked as an observer on a trading expedition to the St. Lawrence Valley. Hoping to find a shorter route to the Orient, he questioned Native people, notably Algonquins, whom he met at the summer trading rendezvous at Tadoussac, about the hydrography of the interior. They subsequently took him on a trip some fifty miles up the Saguenay River before showing him the St. Lawrence as far as the Lachine Rapids above present-day Montreal. The following year, Champlain joined Sieur de Monts, newly invested with the monopoly of the fur trade, as geographer on a venture to Acadia. After exploring parts of the Nova Scotia coastline, the party spent a difficult winter at Sainte-Croix

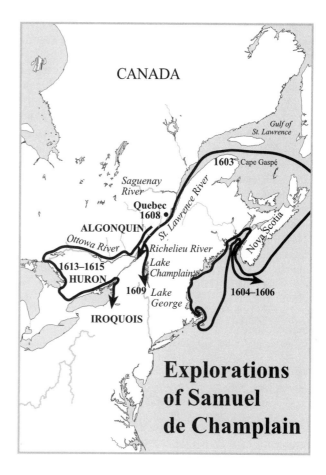

Explorations of Samuel de Champlain

(later St. Croix Island, Maine), before moving to Port-Royal (later Annapolis Royal, Nova Scotia). On two expeditions in 1605 and 1606, Champlain mapped the coast as far as Nantucket Sound, returning to France only in 1607.

Having convinced de Monts that the St. Lawrence Valley was more promising than Acadia for trade, exploration, and settlement, Champlain—along with a few dozen artisans and workers—established a base of operations at Quebec in 1608. The colony they founded would remain essentially a commercial and missionary outpost in the explorer's lifetime. (He died in 1635.) In 1609 Champlain and two compatriots accompanied a Native war party on a foray into Mohawk Iroquois territory, emerging victorious from an engagement at the southern end (near Crown Point, New York) of the lake to which Champlain gave his name. In 1613, the Algonquins invited Champlain to visit their country in the middle reaches of the Ottawa River. In 1615 and 1616, a similar invitation from the powerful Hurons took him east and south of Lake Huron and, on the occasion of a raiding party, to Iroquois villages probably situated between Lakes Oneida and Onondaga. While the allies permitted him to see their own and some of their neighbors' or enemies' territory, they refused him access to other parts of the interior, including the route northward to Hudson Bay he had learned about. Thus aided and constrained, Champlain explored much of the lower Great Lakes region. An energetic promoter of his colony, which he saw as a future customs station for the China trade, he published his *Voyages* in installments, illustrating them with carefully drafted maps. The 1632 cumulative edition of the *Voyages*, containing a remarkable map of New France, summarized the geographic and ethnographic observations of a long career.

In the history of French exploration in North America, Champlain is a pivotal figure, for it is with him that this enterprise began to venture inland toward the Great Lakes region and beyond. This great aboriginal domain he saw as the threshold to Asia and impatiently claimed as New France. To gain entry to it, Champlain had no choice but to obtain the permission and assistance of its Native inhabitants within the framework of the broader military and commercial alliance. Champlain was forced, aided above all by a few interpreters sent to live with the allied nations, to embark on explorations that were as much diplomatic as territorial.

BIBLIOGRAPHY

Champlain, Samuel de. *The Works of Samuel de Champlain.* Edited by H. P. Biggar. 6 vols. Toronto: Champlain Society, 1922–1936.

Heidenreich, Conrad. "Early French Exploration in the North American Interior." In *North American Exploration.* Vol. 2, *A Continent Defined.* Edited by John Logan Allen. Lincoln: University of Nebraska Press, 1997.

Kupperman, Karen Ordahl. "A Continent Revealed: Assimilation of the Shape and Possibilities of North America's East Coast, 1524–1610." In *North American Exploration.* Vol. 1, *A New World Disclosed.* Edited by John Logan Allen. Lincoln: University of Nebraska Press, 1997.

Trigger, Bruce. *Natives and Newcomers: Canada's "Heroic Age" Reconsidered.* Montreal: McGill-Queen's University Press, 1985.

Trudel, Marcel. "Champlain, Samuel de." *Dictionary of Canadian Biography.* Vol. 1, *1000–1700.* Toronto: University of Toronto Press, 1966.

———. *Histoire de la Nouvelle-France.* Vol. 2, *Le comptoir 1604-1627.* Montreal: Fides, 1966.

Thomas Wien

See also **Exploration of America, Early; Explorations and Expeditions: French.**

CHANCELLORSVILLE, BATTLE OF

CHANCELLORSVILLE, BATTLE OF (1–4 May 1863). In April 1863 Gen. Joseph Hooker, with almost 130,000 men, faced Gen. Robert E. Lee's army of 60,000 that was entrenched near Fredericksburg, Virginia. Beginning 27 April, Hooker moved four army corps to Lee's left flank and sent 20,000 men under John Sedgwick to Lee's right. On 1 May, Hooker advanced across the river beyond Chancellorsville, Virginia, threatening Lee's communications and forcing him to leave 10,000 men at Fredericksburg under Gen. Jubal A. Early and march the remainder of his troops toward Chancellorsville. Late in the day the opposing armies took battle position on lines nearly perpendicular to the Rappahannock. At night Lee and Gen. T. J. ("Stonewall") Jackson devised a daring measure: Jackson, with about 30,000 men, would march around Hooker's right flank, while Lee, with less than 20,000, would hold the front.

The army corps on Hooker's extreme right were unprepared when Jackson, late on 2 May, fell upon them furiously. Gen. O. O. Howard's corps was routed, and only a serious injury to Jackson inflicted by fire from his own troops halted the Confederate attack. On 3 May, a cannonball struck a pillar against which Hooker was leaning. Hooker quickly withdrew his troops to the banks of the river. Lee, meanwhile, turned back to deal with Sedgwick's corps, which had routed the force under Early and was rapidly approaching Chancellorsville. On 4 and 5 May, Lee's veterans forced both Sedgwick and Hooker to withdraw their forces north of the river. Hooker lost 17,287 men and Lee 12,764. But Lee suffered the irreparable loss of Jackson, who after days of intense suffering died of his wounds.

BIBLIOGRAPHY

Furgurson, Ernest B. *Chancellorsville 1863: The Souls of the Brave.* New York: Knopf, 1992.

Gallagher, Gary W., ed. *Chancellorsville: The Battle and Its Aftermath.* Chapel Hill: University of North Carolina Press, 1996.

Sears, Stephen W. *Chancellorsville.* Boston: Houghton Mifflin, 1998.

Alfred P. James / A. R.

See also **Army of Northern Virginia; Civil War; Fredericksburg, Battle of; Pennsylvania, Invasion of; Trenches in American Warfare.**

CHANUKAH, the Festival of Lights, celebrates Jewish religion and culture, candlelight symbolizing the beauty and warmth of JUDAISM. This minor holiday begins on the 25th day of the month of Kislev in the Jewish calendar, usually occurring in late December.

The festival marks the triumph of Judas Maccabeus over Greek ruler Antiochus IV and the rededication of the Temple in Jerusalem in 164 B.C. According to legend, in the Temple a lamp held enough oil for one day but burned for eight. This miracle is recalled by the eight-armed menorah, a candelabra, which also has an additional arm for a kindling light.

Chanukah is a family feast. For eight days, JEWS recite blessings and read from the Torah. They light the menorah after dusk, lighting the first candle on the right, then kindling an additional candle, moving from left to right each evening. Special holiday foods include cheese delicacies and latkes, potato pancakes. In the evenings family members may play games with a dreidl, a spinning top, for Chanukah gelt (chocolate coins).

In the United States the celebration of Chanukah has been increasingly commercialized. However, the marketing of Chanukah has not reached the levels associated with Christmas, a Christian holiday thoroughly exploited by retailers, due probably to the relatively small Jewish population and the tradition of giving only small gifts each night of the festival.

BIBLIOGRAPHY

Schauss, Hayyim. *The Jewish Festivals: A Guide to Their History and Observance*. New York: Schocken, 1996.

Trepp, Leo. *The Complete Book of Jewish Observance*. New York: Summit, 1980.

Regina M. Faden

CHAPBOOKS were cheap, popular pamphlets, generally printed on a single sheet and folded to form twenty-four pages or fewer, often crudely illustrated with woodcuts, and sold by chapmen. Published in the tens of thousands in America until about 1850, these books were most numerous between 1800 and 1825. For over a century, chapbooks were the only literature available in the average home except the Bible, the almanac, and the newspaper. They contained fairy tales, biographies of heroes and rascals, riddles, jests, poems, songs, speeches, accounts of shipwrecks and Indian activities, tales of highwaymen, deathbed scenes, accounts of executions, romances, astrology, palmistry, etiquette books, letters and valentines, and moral (and sometimes immoral) tales.

BIBLIOGRAPHY

Preston, Cathy Lynn, and Michael J. Preston, eds. *The Other Print Tradition: Essays on Chapbooks, Broadsides, and Related Ephemera*. New York: Garland, 1995.

R. W. G. Vail / A. E.

See also **Almanacs; Literature: Children's Literature, Popular Literature.**

CHAPPAQUIDDICK INCIDENT. During the evening and early morning hours of 18–19 July 1969, a young woman riding with Massachusetts Senator Edward M. Kennedy died in an automobile accident on Chappaquiddick Island, Massachusetts. After Kennedy and Mary Jo Kopechne left a reunion of workers from Robert Kennedy's 1968 presidential campaign, Kennedy drove his car off a narrow bridge that lacked guardrails. Kennedy suffered a concussion but managed to escape; Kopechne drowned. Kennedy said that he dove repeatedly to the car to try to rescue Kopechne. Many questioned Kennedy's behavior, however, because he had been drinking that night, had failed to report the accident until the police contacted him the next morning, and had given unsatisfying explanations of what happened. On 25 July, he pled guilty to leaving the scene of an accident and received a suspended sentence of two months.

The resulting scandal threatened Kennedy's political future. After entering his guilty plea, he gave a televised address to the people of Massachusetts, asking them for advice on whether he should resign his Senate seat. The public generally backed Kennedy, and he did not resign, but the Chappaquiddick incident permanently damaged Kennedy's presidential prospects. The issue arose frequently during his unsuccessful run for the Democratic presidential nomination in 1980.

BIBLIOGRAPHY

Clymer, Adam. *Edward M. Kennedy: A Biography*. New York: William Morrow, 1999.

Lange, James E. T., and Katherine DeWitt Jr. *Chappaquiddick: The Real Story*. New York: St. Martin's, 1992.

Mark Byrnes

CHAPULTEPEC, BATTLE OF (13 September 1847), took place at the western approaches to Mexico City, defended by Chapultepec, a 200-foot-high mesa crowned with stone buildings. During the MEXICAN-AMERICAN WAR, after vigorous bombardment, General Winfield Scott launched General G. J. Pillow's division against the southern slopes. Against desperate resistance, the Americans mounted the walls on scaling ladders and captured the summit. General John A. Quitman's and General William J. Worth's divisions then attacked the Belén and San Cosme gates, and the city surrendered the next morning. The American losses (for the day) were 138 killed and 673 wounded. Mexican casualties are unknown, but 760 were captured. At the war's end, the army briefly discredited Pillow after a public quarrel with Scott over credit for the victory.

BIBLIOGRAPHY

Bauer, K. Jack. *The Mexican War, 1846–1848*. New York: Macmillan, 1974.

Lavender, David S. *Climax at Buena Vista: The American Campaigns in Northeastern Mexico, 1846–47*. Philadelphia: Lippincott, 1966.

May, Robert E. *John A. Quitman: Old South Crusader*. Baton Rouge: Louisiana State University Press, 1985.

Charles Winslow Elliott / A. R.

See also **Mexico City, Capture of.**

CHARITY ORGANIZATION MOVEMENT emerged in the United States in the late nineteenth century to address urban poverty. The movement developed as a reaction to the proliferation of charities practicing indiscriminate almsgiving without investigating the circumstances of recipients. Inspired by a similar movement in Great Britain, the movement held three basic assumptions: that urban poverty was caused by moral deficiencies of the poor, that poverty could be eliminated by the correction of these deficiencies in individuals, and that various charity organizations needed to cooperate to bring about this change. The first charity organization societies (COS) in the United States were established in the late 1870s, and by the 1890s more than one hundred American cities had COS agencies. Journals like *Lend-a-Hand* (Boston) and *Charities Review* (New York) created a forum for ideas, while annual meetings of the National Conference of Charities and Corrections provided opportunities for leaders to discuss common concerns.

Supporters of the movement believed that individuals in poverty could be uplifted through association with middle- and upper-class volunteers, primarily Protestant women. Volunteers employed the technique of "friendly visiting" in homes of the poor to establish helping relationships and investigate the circumstances of families in need. Agency leaders were typically middle- and upper-class men, often clergymen. COS agencies did not usually give money to the poor; rather they advocated a more systematic and "scientific" approach to charity, coordinating various charitable resources and keeping records of those who had received charity in an effort to prevent duplicity and duplication.

Josephine Shaw Lowell, a national leader of the movement, was convinced that COS agencies were responsible for "moral oversight" of people in poverty. Although many leaders in the COS movement were religious persons, leaders cautioned against mixing evangelism with charity. Stephen Humphreys Gurteen, a clergyman and COS leader, warned workers in his *Handbook of Charity Organization* (1882) not to use their position for "proselytism or spiritual instruction."

As the movement grew, an insufficient number of volunteers led COS agencies to employ "agents," trained staff members who were the predecessors of professional social workers. Modernizers like Mary Richmond of the Boston COS and Edward T. Devine of the New York COS led the movement to train workers, which gave rise to the professionalization of social work in the early twentieth century. In 1898, Devine established and directed the New York School of Philanthropy, which eventually became the Columbia School of Social Work. The case method, later used by the social work profession, is rooted in charity organization philosophies and techniques.

BIBLIOGRAPHY

Boyer, Paul S. *Urban Masses and Moral Order in America, 1820–1920.* Cambridge, Mass.: Harvard University Press, 1978.

Katz, Michael. *In the Shadow of the Poorhouse: A Social History of Welfare in America.* 2d rev. ed. New York: Basic Books, 1996.

Popple, Phillip, and Leslie Leighninger. *Social Work, Social Welfare, and American Society.* 5th ed. Boston: Allyn and Bacon, 2002.

Richmond, Mary. *Friendly Visiting among the Poor: A Handbook for Charity Workers.* New York: Macmillan, 1899. Reprint, Montclair, N.J.: Patterson Smith, 1969.

T. Laine Scales

See also **Poverty; Social Work; Volunteerism.**

CHARITY SCHOOLS. During the colonial period, free EDUCATION generally meant instruction for children of poor families. Numerous schools were established in the American colonies and were organized and supported by benevolent persons and societies, a practice that served to fasten onto the idea of free education an association with poverty that was difficult to remove. The pauper-school conception came directly from England and persisted far into the nineteenth century. Infant-school societies and Sunday-school societies engaged in such work. Schools were sometimes supported in part by rate bills, charges levied upon parents according to the number of their children in school (with impoverished parents exempted). Charity schools provided food, clothes, and lodging, if little more than an elementary education, to destitute or orphaned children.

Charity schools demonstrated the importance of religious philanthropy in the early history of education in the United States. They also exemplified the related urge to preserve social order through benevolent campaigns to raise the moral, religious, and economic conditions of the masses. The inadequacy of charity schools to cope with the educational needs of European immigrants in the mid-nineteenth century contributed to the impetus for the development of public schools and compulsory attendance laws.

BIBLIOGRAPHY

Cremin, Lawrence A. *American Education, The National Experience, 1783–1876.* New York: Harper and Row, 1980.

Edgar W. Knight / A. R.

See also **Immigration; School, District; Schools, Private; Sunday Schools.**

CHARLES RIVER BRIDGE CASE, 11 Peters 420 (1837). In 1785, Massachusetts chartered a bridge over the Charles River, linking Boston and Charlestown. The Charles River Bridge proprietors completed the project the next year, and the bridge significantly enhanced commerce between the two areas.

The enterprise proved financially lucrative. The original charter provided the right to charge tolls for forty years, which later was extended to seventy. In the 1820s, political controversies, such as a fight over the Bank of the United States, focused on increasing opportunities in a market economy against the power of entrenched privilege. After extensive public criticism decrying the proprietors' "privileged monopoly," the Massachusetts legislature in 1828 chartered a new company to build a competing bridge, paralleling the existing one. The new Warren Bridge was to become toll-free after six years.

The proprietors of the first bridge, which included Harvard College, contended that the new bridge charter violated the Contract Clause (Article I, Section 10) of the United States Constitution as it unconstitutionally impaired the obligations of the original contract. The Massachusetts high court split on the issue in 1828, and the case went to the United States Supreme Court in 1831. Chief Justice John Marshall, in a significant deviation from his usual broad construction of the Contract Clause, favored sustaining the new charter, but the Court was sharply divided and lacked a full bench for a decisive ruling.

In 1837, however, recently appointed Chief Justice Roger B. Taney and his new colleagues sustained the Warren Bridge charter, with only one dissenting vote. Taney followed Marshall's formulation, strictly construing corporate charters in favor of "the rights of the community." The state, he determined, had never explicitly promised the Charles River Bridge proprietors the right to an exclusive bridge and toll.

Taney's opinion particularly emphasized the role of science and technology to promote material progress. The law, he insisted, must spur, not impede, such improvements. If the Charles River Bridge proprietors prevailed, Taney feared that turnpike corporations would make extravagant claims and jeopardize new innovations such as railroads. Taney cast the law with new entrepreneurs as the preferred agents for progress. "[T]he object and end of all government," he said, "is to promote the happiness and prosperity of the community which it established, and it can never be assumed, that the government intended to diminish the power of accomplishing the end for which it was created." Taney's opinion fit his times and reflected the American premium on the release of creative human energy to propel "progress" against the expansive claims of privilege by older, vested interests.

BIBLIOGRAPHY

Hurst, James Willard. *Law and the Conditions of Freedom.* Madison: University of Wisconsin Press, 1956.

Kutler, Stanley I. *Privilege and Creative Destruction: The Charles River Bridge.* Philadelphia: Lippincott, 1971. Reprint, Baltimore: Johns Hopkins University Press, 1992.

Stanley I. Kutler

CHARLESTON, S.C. Located on a peninsula where the Ashley and Cooper Rivers meet the Atlantic Ocean, Charleston was founded in 1680 by English colonists and enslaved Africans from Barbados. In its earliest years, the town was built on the provisioning trade, which sent Carolina livestock to Barbados to feed enslaved sugar workers. By the beginning of the eighteenth century, rice

Charleston. A view from Circular Church of some of the destruction, resulting from fire and Union bombardment, in the city where the Civil War began. LIBRARY OF CONGRESS

and indigo had become the principal exports from the town's expanding wharves.

In 1739, after a slave rebellion at nearby Stono, whites became alarmed at the town's growing black majority. In addition to enacting harsher codes to govern the slaves, Charleston made an effort to attract free settlers, eventually becoming home to sizable Huguenot and Jewish communities by the end of the century.

Charlestonians were ambivalent about the prospect of independence in the 1770s. While there had been some protests in response to British trade policies, Charleston's wealth was built largely on the export of rice and indigo to Great Britain. Nevertheless, the city resisted British efforts to capture it until 1780. After the Revolution, Charleston rebounded commercially but had to suffer the removal of SOUTH CAROLINA's capital to the upcountry town of Columbia. By the 1820s, the character of the city's social and commercial elite had begun to change. Merchants had long dominated the city but were increasingly marginalized by Low Country planters.

In the 1790s, the arrival of French refugees from Saint-Domingue (later named Haiti) coupled with an incipient slave rebellion led by a free black carpenter named Denmark Vesey, led to further restrictions on African Americans. These changes produced a social and intellectual climate that gave birth first to the doctrine of nullification in the 1830s and, in the 1860s, to secession.

The first shots of the Civil War were fired on Fort Sumter in Charleston harbor in April 1861. A fire that year and near-constant bombardment by Union forces reduced the city to a shadow of its former self by the time it surrendered in February 1865. The city struggled to recover in the years following the war, but was frustrated in 1886 by a devastating earthquake.

After 1901, the U.S. Navy provided an economic replacement for shrinking shipping activity. In decline for much of the twentieth century, the city's outlook had changed by the 1990s. Led by Mayor Joseph P. Riley Jr., Charleston rebounded economically and demographically. In 1990 the city had 80,414 residents, scarcely ten thousand more than twenty years before. By 2000 the city held 96,650.

BIBLIOGRAPHY

Coclanis, Peter A. *The Shadow of a Dream: Economic Life and Death in the South Carolina Low Country, 1670–1920.* New York: Oxford University Press, 1989.

Pease, Jane H., and William H. Pease. *The Web of Progress: Private Values and Public Styles in Boston and Charleston, 1828–1843.* Athens: University of Georgia Press, 1991.

J. Fred Saddler

See also **Sumter, Fort; Vesey Rebellion.**

CHARLESTON HARBOR, DEFENSE OF.

On 1 June 1776, during the American Revolution, a British squadron led by Sir Henry Clinton and Peter Parker anchored off Sullivan's Island, at the entrance to Charleston Harbor, CHARLESTON, S.C. The city of Charleston was defended by six thousand colonial militia, while a much smaller force, led by Colonel William Moultrie, was stationed on the island. On 28 June the British tried to batter down the island fort, only to find that their shots buried themselves in the green palmetto logs of the crude fortification. After the loss of one ship, the British retired and sailed for New York. Thus the Carolinas averted the threatened British invasion of the South.

BIBLIOGRAPHY

McCrady, Edward. *The History of South Carolina in the Revolution, 1775–1780.* New York: Macmillan, 1901.

Wates, Wylma Anne. "'A Flag Worthy of Your State'." *South Carolina Historical Magazine* 86:4 (1985): 320–331.

Hugh T. Lefler/A. R.

See also **Revolution, American: Military History; Southern Campaigns.**

CHARLESTON INDIAN TRADE.

As the largest English city on the southern coast, Charleston, South Carolina, became the center of trade between colonists and Indians from the time of its settlement in the late seventeenth century. English products such as woolens, tools, and weapons were cheaper and better than comparable Spanish and French items and became indispensable to the Indians. Carolinians not only amassed wealth through trade, but they created economic and military alliances with Indian trading partners, which helped them stave off Spanish and French control of Atlantic and Gulf Coast mercantile networks. After the FRENCH AND INDIAN WAR (1754–1763), Charleston lost prominence as the center of the southern Indian trade shifted westward, encompassing the newer British settlements of Savannah and Pensacola.

BIBLIOGRAPHY

Hatley, Tom. *The Dividing Paths: Cherokees and South Carolinians Through the Era of Revolution.* New York: Oxford University Press, 1995.

Merrell, James H. *The Indians' New World: Catawbas and Their Neighbors from European Contact Through the Era of Removal.* New York: Norton, 1989.

Usner, Daniel H., Jr. *Indians, Settlers, and Slaves in a Frontier Exchange Economy: The Lower Mississippi Valley Before 1783.* Chapel Hill: University of North Carolina Press, 1992.

R. L. Meriwether/s. b.

See also **Catawba; Cherokee; Colonial Commerce; Colonial Settlements; South Carolina.**

CHARLOTTE

(North Carolina). In the mid-eighteenth century, Scotch-Irish settlers moved west from the Carolina coastal plain, and German families traveled through the valley of Virginia to settle in the region called the Piedmont. There, a small town took shape at the intersection of two Indian trading paths. Settlers called it "Charlotte," after Queen Charlotte of Mecklenburg, Germany. By 1850, the modest settlement had fewer than 2,500 inhabitants. The arrival of the railroad connected the landlocked town with the markets of the Northeast and the fertile fields of the Deep South. After the Civil War (1861–1865), the city resumed railroad building, extending as many as five major lines from its borders. This transportation network and Charlotte's proximity to cotton fields prompted local engineer D. A. Tompkins to launch a mill campaign in the 1880s. With cheap electricity provided by James B. Duke's Southern Power Company, the town was transformed into a textile center by the mid-1920s. By 1930, Charlotte had become the largest city in the Carolinas.

As the textile empire expanded, so did the need for capital. This need was fulfilled by local banking institutions, leading the way for the city's emergence as a financial center. Charlotte's transportation network was improved by the opening of an expanded airport in 1941 and the convergence of interstates I-77 and I-85 in the 1960s. The city became a major distribution center in the Southeast.

During the first half of the 1900s, Charlotte experienced cordial race relations, though these existed within the strictures of Jim Crow. A substantial black middle class worked with white leaders to orchestrate a voluntary desegregation of public facilities in 1963. School desegregation occurred more fitfully. In the 1970 case of *Swann v. Charlotte-Mecklenburg School Board*, the U.S. Supreme Court ordered BUSING to desegregate the city's schools.

General U. S. Grant advanced his army slowly eastward. In September, W. S. Rosecrans's Union army was defeated at Chickamauga. Rosecrans retreated to Chattanooga, endured the siege of Confederate forces under General Braxton Bragg, and awaited Grant's assistance. Grant, placed in general command of all Union forces in the West, replaced Rosecrans with G. H. Thomas and instructed him to hold Chattanooga against Bragg's siege "at all hazards." Food was running short and supply lines were constantly interrupted. Grant's first act was to open a new and protected line of supply, via Brown's Ferry. Reinforcements arrived. Vigorous action turned the tables on Bragg, whose only act was to weaken himself unnecessarily by detaching General James Longstreet on a fruitless expedition to capture Knoxville. Bragg then awaited Grant's next move. President Jefferson Davis visited the army and tried, unsuccessfully, to restore confidence.

On 24 November 1863 Union General Joseph Hooker captured Lookout Mountain on the left of Bragg's line. The next day Grant attacked all along the line. The Confederate center on Missionary Ridge gave way; the left had retreated; only the right held firm and covered the retreat southward into northern Georgia. A brilliant rear-guard stand at Ringgold Gap halted Grant's pursuit. The Union troops returned to Chattanooga; the Confederate Army went into winter quarters at Dalton, Georgia.

BIBLIOGRAPHY
Cozzens, Peter. *The Shipwreck of Their Hopes: The Battles for Chattanooga*. Urbana: University of Illinois Press, 1994.

McDonough, James L. *Chattanooga: A Death Grip on the Confederacy*. Knoxville: University of Tennessee Press, 1984.

Sword, Wiley. *Mountains Touched with Fire: Chattanooga Besieged, 1863*. New York: St. Martin's, 1995.

Thomas Robson Hay / A. R.

See also **Chickamauga, Battle of; Civil War; Lookout Mountain, Battle on; Vicksburg in the Civil War.**

CHAUTAUQUA MOVEMENT. The institution that Theodore Roosevelt once called "the most American thing in America" occupies an honored place in American cultural mythology. From its inception in 1874, Chautauqua tailored its appeal to the patriotic, churchgoing, white, native-born, mostly Protestant, northern and Midwestern middle classes—a group whose claim to represent Americans as a whole has been alternatively championed and criticized. "He who does not know Chautauqua," wrote the journalist Frank Bohn in 1926, with knowing irony, "does not know America."

As millions across the nation flocked to Chautauqua's hundreds of summer assemblies and reading circles, few could deny that the Chautauqua movement had emerged as a leading educational, cultural, and political force in American life in the late nineteenth century. By the 1920s, however, the reform impulses of the social gospel and Progressive Era that had shaped Chautauqua's appeal had dissipated. Although no longer a source of new ideas, Chautauqua continued (and continues) to champion the major themes of modern liberal thought in America: humanistic education, religious tolerance, and faith in social progress.

Chautauqua's origins lie in a confluence of sacred and secular forces sweeping across America after the Civil War. Chautauqua's cofounder, John Heyl Vincent, began his career as a hellfire-and-brimstone preacher on the Methodist circuit in the 1850s. By the early 1870s Vincent came to feel that the spiritual awakenings experienced at the "holiness" revivals were too emotional, too superficial. A revitalized and more effective Sunday school, Vincent reasoned, would root evangelical Protestantism in the more solid foundation of biblical learning, secular study, and middle-class prosperity.

In 1873 Vincent joined forces with Lewis Miller, a wealthy manufacturer of farm implements from Akron, Ohio, to find suitable headquarters for their nascent National Sunday School Association. They settled on Fair Point, a cloistered Methodist camp meeting on the shores of Chautauqua Lake in western New York State. The following year, Vincent and Miller forbade impromptu proselytizing and opened Fair Point's doors to both serious students and fun-seeking vacationers—in essence, building on the camp meeting template while transforming it into a semipublic, ecumenical institute and vacation retreat devoted to teacher training. Vincent and Miller embraced the summer vacation as a fact of modern life and made it an integral part of their broader mission of spiritual and social renewal. They soon abandoned Fair Point and adopted the word "Chautauqua," cleverly hiding its evangelical roots behind an Indian place name.

By the 1880s, Chautauqua had evolved into the foremost advocate for adult education, sacred and secular. Its eight-week summer program combined Bible study with courses in science, history, literature, and the arts, while giving visibility to social gospel–minded academics, politicians, preachers, prohibitionists, and reformers. Through correspondence courses, university extension, journals like *The Chautauquan*, and especially reading circles, Chautauqua's influence spread far beyond its campus boundaries. In 1878, Vincent inaugurated the Chautauqua Literary and Scientific Circle (CLSC). Under the leadership of the director Kate F. Kimball, 264,000 people—three-quarters of them women—had enrolled in the CLSC by century's end. Students completing the four-year reading program received official (if symbolic) diplomas. Criticized by some as superficial, the CLSC nevertheless provided opportunities for thousands of mostly white, Protestant, middle-class women to develop stronger public voices and organizational experience.

Many CLSC women worked to establish independent Chautauqua assemblies in their own communities.

Independent assemblies developed close ties with local boosters, interurbans, and railroads, who saw them as profitable (yet moral) tourist attractions. By 1900, nearly one hundred towns, mainly in the Midwest, held assemblies on grounds patterned on the original Chautauqua. As assemblies proliferated in the early twentieth century, competition for guests grew fierce, forcing assemblies to hire more popular fare, such as musical acts, theater troupes, and inspirational speakers.

In 1904, the assemblies faced an even greater challenge: for-profit lyceum organizers that year introduced a network of mobile Chautauquas, or "circuits." Competition from circuit Chautauquas forced many independent assemblies to hire lecture bureaus to handle their programming, relinquishing the podium to big-city companies and hastening the assemblies' decline. To modernists like Sinclair Lewis, the circuit Chautauqua, with its "animal and bird educators" (i.e., pet tricks), William Jennings Bryan speeches, sentimental plays, and crude wartime patriotism, symbolized the shallowness of middle-class culture. Despite ridicule from the urban avant-garde, the circuits launched the careers of numerous performers and served as vital links to the outside world for some 6,000 small towns. In the mid-1920s, the rise of commercial radio, movies, automobiles, and an expanded consumer culture signaled the end of the circuits' popularity in rural America. The last tent show folded in 1933.

Although the wider Chautauqua movement was over, the original assembly on Lake Chautauqua thrived. The "Mother Chautauqua," as it was called, expanded steadily until a combination of overbuilding and the Great Depression pushed it to the brink of bankruptcy in 1933. Its survival hung in the balance until a timely gift from John D. Rockefeller returned the institution to sound footing in 1936. No longer a source of much new social or political thought, Chautauqua had discovered a secular principle to sustain it—the need for informed citizenship in modern democracy. Competing perspectives on virtually every major social issue of the twentieth century have at one time or another found their way to the Chautauqua platform. Its nearly utopian aesthetic continued to earn the admiration of urban planners nationwide. In 1989 the grounds were designated a National Historic Landmark.

BIBLIOGRAPHY

Bohn, Frank. "America Revealed in Chautauqua." *New York Times Magazine*, 10 October 1926, 3.

Kett, Joseph F. *The Pursuit of Knowledge Under Difficulties.* Stanford, Calif.: Stanford University Press, 1994.

Morrison, Theodore. *Chautauqua.* Chicago: University of Chicago Press, 1974.

Rieser, Andrew C. *The Chautauqua Moment.* New York: Columbia University Press, 2002.

Andrew C. Rieser

See also **Camp Meetings; Liberalism; Methodism; Progressive Movement; Social Gospel; Sunday Schools.**

CHECK CURRENCY denotes bank deposits against which the owner can write a check. Such deposits are called demand (or transaction) deposits in order to distinguish them from time deposits, against which checks cannot be written. Check currency is one of the two types of bank money, the other being bank notes. Whereas a check is an order to the bank to pay, a bank note is a promise by the bank to pay.

Although check currency was in use in New York and other large cities in the early nineteenth century, it was not until the National Banking Act of 1863 that it began to replace bank notes as the principal type of bank money. The twofold purpose of the National Banking Act was to finance the Civil War and to stop the widespread bankruptcies of state banks. State banks were failing because of the depreciation of the state bonds they held as reserves against the bank notes they issued. Both purposes of the National Banking Act could thus be accomplished by creating national banks that had to hold federal bonds as reserves for the bank notes they issued.

In March 1865, in an effort to compel state banks to become national banks, the government imposed a 10 percent tax on bank notes issued by state banks. The state banks responded by issuing check currency, which was not subject to the tax. So successful was this financial innovation that, by the end of the nineteenth century, it is estimated that from 85 to 90 percent of all business transactions were settled by means of check currency. And despite the widespread availability of electronic fund transfers, this was still true (for the volume of transactions, not their value) at the end of the twentieth century.

It is often argued that the amount of currency in circulation, including the amount of check currency, is exogenously (that is, externally) given by the government. It is then argued that the price level is determined by the amount of currency in circulation. This argument ignores the banks' capacity for financial innovations, like their creation of check currency to replace bank notes. Whenever the government tries to control one type of money (for example, bank notes with a penalty tax), the banks create another type of money (for example, check currency) that is not being controlled. Therefore, the amount of currency in circulation is endogenously (internally) determined by the banks, and the determinates of the price level must be sought elsewhere.

Until the Banking Act of 1933 (also known as the GLASS-STEAGALL ACT), banks generally paid interest on demand deposits with large minimum balances. From 1933 to 1973, there were no interest payments on demand deposits. Then money market funds came into widespread use, which in many ways marks a return to the pre-1933 situation of banks paying interest on demand deposits with large minimum balances.

BIBLIOGRAPHY

Dickens, Edwin. "Financial Crises, Innovations, and Federal Reserve Control of the Stock of Money." *Contributions to Political Economy*, vol. 9, pp. 1–23, 1990.

Friedman, Milton, and Anna J. Schwartz. *Monetary Trends in the United States and the United Kingdom: Their Relation to Income, Prices, and Interest Rates, 1867–1975.* Chicago: University of Chicago Press, 1982.

Mishkin, Frederic S. *The Economics of Money, Banking, and Financial Markets.* 6th ed. Boston: Addison Wesley, 2002.

Edwin T. Dickens

See also **Banking; Currency and Coinage; Money.**

CHECKERS SPEECH.

With the "Checkers" speech, Richard M. Nixon saved his 1952 Republican nomination for vice president. When news broke that Nixon had used a "secret fund" to pay for travel and other expenses, many people—including some advisers to Dwight D. Eisenhower, the Republican presidential candidate—wanted Nixon to leave the ticket. In a nationally televised speech on 23 September, Nixon denied any wrongdoing, but sentimentally admitted that his family had accepted the gift of a dog named Checkers. He declared that "the kids, like all kids, loved the dog and . . . we're going to keep it." The largely positive public reaction secured Nixon's position, and the Republican ticket went on to win the election.

BIBLIOGRAPHY

Ambrose, Stephen E. *Nixon: The Education of a Politician 1913–1962.* New York: Simon and Schuster, 1987.

Morris, Roger. *Richard Milhous Nixon: The Rise of an American Politician.* New York: Holt, 1990.

Nixon, Richard M. *Six Crises.* Garden City, N.Y.: Doubleday, 1962.

Mark Byrnes

See also **Corruption, Political.**

CHECKOFF

provisions in contract allow a union to collect dues through automatic payroll deduction on terms negotiated by the employees' exclusive bargaining agent (union) and the employer. Employees as individuals become third parties to the agreement. Federal law [29 USC §186 (c)(4), §320] permits the checkoff, conditional upon each employee in a bargaining unit signing a written authorization for the deduction. This authorization is of indefinite duration but may not be revoked for more than one year or the duration of the contract, whichever period is shorter. Under contractual terms, dues subsequently collected by the employer are transferred to the union.

Checkoff is controversial for two reasons: first, the arrangement promotes union security by bureaucratically stabilizing the labor unions' revenue streams and is therefore not accepted by anti-union workers and their allies. Second, the conjunction of dues checkoff with agency fee—whereby all employees in a bargaining unit must pay a service fee, equal in amount to regular union dues, whether or not they are union members—has sparked op-position among both employees who are disaffected with their unions and outsiders who oppose union activity in electoral politics. The separate, segregated fund prohibition clause of the 1996 Federal Election Campaign Act [2 USC §441b] distinguishes between dues assessed by unions to cover costs of collective bargaining and contract service and funds—often identified as dues to committees on political education (COPE)—which unions solicit separately from members for direct contributions to candidates seeking elective offices. Both kinds of dues may be collected through checkoff, but are not to be commingled.

In keeping with these distinctions, unions are not prohibited under the law from using general membership dues to engage in voter registration and mobilization drives, or to inform members about union positions on candidates and election issues. Critics, with growing intensity, have challenged the legitimacy of using the checkoff for such communications as being essentially political rather than related strictly to collective bargaining, and therefore illegal. During the 1990s these dissidents pursued legislative remedies proposed as "worker paycheck fairness," [HR 1625 (1997) and HR 2434 (1999)] but the effort died in Congress.

The checkoff first was negotiated in 1889 contracts between the nascent Progressive Miners' Union and Ohio bituminous coal mine operators, following strikes at five mines. In 1898, the United Mine Workers, a major national union, reached agreement with mining companies to introduce union dues checkoff. By 1910, miners union contracts provided for the checkoff in fourteen coal producing states.

Both parties stood to benefit from automatic dues deductions. The miners union intended to use the checkoff to routinize dues collection and to achieve the union shop, a contractual provision establishing that all employees in a bargaining unit must become union members within a specified period of time after employment. Shop stewards would thus be freed from the onerous task of contacting each member individually to collect dues and instead could concentrate on contract enforcement. Mine operators, meanwhile, anticipated that the unions would expend their enhanced resources on new organizing drives into hitherto nonunion mines, thereby eliminating the competitors' advantages of lower labor costs. Moreover, by administering the checkoff employers gained strategic information about a union's financial resources in advance of contract negotiations and potential strikes. Employers also benefited tactically in their ability to suspend the checkoff as leverage to break wildcat strikes.

While in the late nineteenth century the checkoff was written into some contracts negotiated locally and regionally, it was incorporated into national contracts only in the late 1930s and on into the World War II era, when the United Mine Workers and other unions made major contract gains under the oversight of the National War Labor Board. Employers conceded to such union security policies reluctantly, yielding to the policy objective of minimizing disruptions in industry to assure maximum production for the war effort. After the war, employers focused on full production, downplaying confrontational relations with labor; meanwhile, unions actively organized under the provisions in §7(a) of the National Labor Relations Act and swelled membership ranks. Yet, it was in the right-to-work states that the greatest proportion of agreements for checkoff were negotiated. Despite generalized hostility to organized labor in these states, unions and employers in bargaining often reached accommodation on union dues checkoff clauses.

Powerful antiunion and anticommunist currents in domestic politics of the postwar era paved the way for the passage of the Taft-Hartley Act in 1947, which altered the checkoff. While management was obliged to transfer automatic dues deductions to the unions, the act outlawed the closed shop—an arrangement between unions and management stipulating that only union members would be hired and employed on the job—and established that the checkoff was permissible only when workers individually signed written authorization cards. Subsequently, the Landrum-Griffin Labor-Management Reporting and Disclosure Act (1959) exempted employees in agency fee shops who belong to established religious groups and are conscientious objectors to joining or financially supporting labor organizations from paying union dues as a condition of employment. The act provided instead that comparable amounts would be deducted by checkoff and paid to nonreligious, nonlabor-organization charitable funds.

Checkoff increasingly has become a common feature in contracts. The United States Department of Labor's statistics from the 1980s indicate a steadily increasing proportion of checkoff agreements in almost all areas of the nation. Moreover, the difference in the number of contracts, including checkoff provisions in states without right-to-work laws and states with right-to-work laws, decreased between the late 1950s and the early 1980s.

BIBLIOGRAPHY

Beal, Edwin F. and Edward D. Wickersham. *The Practice of Collective Bargaining.* Homewood, IL: Richard D. Irwin, 1972.

King, F.A. "The Check-Off System and the Closed Shop Among The United Mine Workers." *Quarterly Journal of Economics* 25 (1911): 730-741.

Kingston, Paul J. "Checkoff—Does It Ever Die?" *Labor Law Journal* 21, no. 3 (March 1970): 159–166.

United States. Congress. House. Committee on Education and the Workforce. *Report of Worker Paycheck Fairness Act.* 105th Cong., 1st sess. Washington, D.C.: Government Printing Office, 1997.

United States. Congress. House. Committee on Education and the Workforce. *Worker Paycheck Fairness Act: Hearing before the Committee on Education and the Workforce.* 105th Cong., 1st sess., 9 July 1997. Washington, D.C.: Government Printing Office, 1997.

United States. Congress. House. Committee on Education and the Workforce. Subcommittee on Employer-Employee Relations. *Abuse of Worker Rights and H.R. 1625, Worker Paycheck Fairness Act: Hearing before the Subcommittee on Employer-Employee Relations of the Committee on Education and the Workforce.* 105th Cong., 2nd sess., 21 January 1988. Washington, D.C.: Government Printing Office, 1998.

United States. Congress. House. Committee on Education and the Workforce. *Report on Worker Paycheck Fairness Act of 1999.* 106th Cong., 2nd sess., 11 October 2000. Washington, D.C.: Government Printing Office, 2000.

U.S. Department of Labor. Bureau of Labor Statistics. *Major Collective Bargaining Agreements: Union Security and Dues Checkoff Provisions* (Washington, D.C., 1982), 1425-21.

Jonathan W. McLeod

See also **Labor; National Labor Union; Trade Unions.**

CHECKS AND BALANCES.

The term "checks and balances" is often invoked when describing the virtues of the Constitution of the United States. It is an Enlightenment-era term, conceptually an outgrowth of the political theory of John Locke and other seventeenth-century political theorists and coined by philosophes sometime in the eighteenth century. By the time the U.S. Constitutional Convention met in 1787, it was a term and a concept known to the founders. To them it meant diffusing power in ways that would prevent any interest group, class, or region, singly or in combination, to subvert the republic of the United States.

James Madison described a republic as "a government which derives all its power . . . from the great power of the people." Checks and balances were indispensable, he said, because it was vital to keep access to the full authority of the government "from an inconsiderable proportion [of the people], or a favored class of it; otherwise a handful of tyrannical nobles, exercising their oppressions by a delegation of their powers, might claim for their government the honorable title of republic" without its substance. Thus, he cautioned, it was necessary to check vice with vice, interest with interest, power with power, to arrive at a balanced or "mixed" government.

The balanced government derived from the brilliant compromises the founders drafted. First and foremost, a tyrannical federal government would be checked by limiting its sovereignty, granting sovereignty as well to the individual states. A host of crucial compromises followed this key one: federal power balanced among legislative, executive, and judicial branches; federal executive authority, in the form of a president elected every four years and accorded a veto, but with legislative ability to override; direct election of a president, but filtered through an electoral college of state representatives; legislative power checked in class and democratic terms by an elite upper house (Senate) pitted against a popularly elected House of Representatives; and a distant but powerful national judiciary headed by the Supreme Court, always appointed to life terms and understood from its inception to possess the power of judicial review over both executive and legislative actions.

Together this combination of checks and balances was meant to sustain the republic at all times, even in periods of great national stress. No political group, economic or social class, or region possessed the access to power capable of dominating all others in this most successful of "mixed" governments—which is not to say that all of the compromises made by the founders were just in themselves, as in the case of explicitly recognizing the constitutionality of slavery in an effort to placate some mostly southern delegates.

The secret of the system of checks and balances lay in its inherent flexibility of interpretation over the generations and the ability of the Constitution to mold itself to the times even as it retained its inherent invincibility as the law of the land. By the late twentieth century some Americans feared that this flexibility was a grave weakness, encouraging permissiveness in the national courts and a penchant for aggrandized reform in both the executive and legislative branches. These critics, adhering to a doctrine of strict interpretation and a significant lessening of constitutional flexibility, have sought as a recourse to pin down the founders' "original intent" in order to render the U.S. Constitution less open to interpretation or adaptation over time.

BIBLIOGRAPHY

Brant, Irving. *James Madison.* 6 vols. Volume 3: *Father of the Constitution, 1787–1800.* Indianapolis, Ind.: Bobbs-Merrill, 1950.

Fairfield, Roy, ed. *The Federalist Papers.* New York: 1981.

Jensen, Merrill, and Robert A. Becker, eds. *The Documentary History of the First Federal Elections, 1788–1790.* 4 vols. Madison: University of Wisconsin Press, 1976–1989.

Carl E. Prince

See also **Constitution of the United States; Federalist Papers; Judicial Review.**

CHEMICAL AND BIOLOGICAL WARFARE.

While limited use of chemicals and disease in warfare dates from ancient times, the origins of modern chemical and biological weapons systems date from the era of the two world wars. The term chemical warfare came into use with the gas warfare of World War I, and modern biological warfare dates from the weapons systems first introduced in the 1930s.

Early Gas Warfare

Following the first successful German gas attack with chlorine in the World War I battle at Ypres in 1915, the British, French, and, in 1918, the U.S. armies responded with gases including phosgenes, mustard gas, hydrogen cyanide, and cyanogen chloride. Initially spread from portable cylinders by the opening of a valve, delivery systems were extended to mortars and guns. In 1918 the U.S. War

Gas Masks. An American soldier demonstrates protection for himself and his horse during World War I, when both sides in the fighting commonly used a wide variety of poisonous gases.
NATIONAL ARCHIVES AND RECORDS ADMINISTRATION

Department established the Chemical Warfare Service (CWS) as part of the wartime, but not the regular, army.

The specter of future gas warfare left by the war revived earlier efforts to ban chemical warfare. Gas caused 1 million of 26 million World War I casualties, including over 72,000 of 272,000 U.S. casualties. The first attempt to ban gas warfare was a separate proposition to the first Hague Peace Conference in 1899. The United States didn't sign, arguing that there was no reason to consider chemical weapons less humane than other weapons, and that since there were no stockpiles of gas weapons it was premature to address the issue. Following World War I, the United States signed but the Senate failed to ratify the 1925 Geneva Protocol prohibiting chemical weapons, again arguing that they were as humane as other weapons and that the United States needed to be prepared. This direction was anticipated when the immediate postwar debate in the United States over chemical warfare resulted in the CWS becoming a part of the regular army in 1920. In 1932, chemical warfare preparedness became U.S. military policy.

The use of gas warfare in the 1930s by Italy in Ethiopia, Japan in China, and possibly elsewhere increased concern going into World War II. But the gas war of World War I did not recur. U.S. strategists apparently considered using gas during one crisis in the Pacific, but President Franklin D. Roosevelt, who declared a retaliation-only policy on chemical warfare at the beginning of the war, withheld his approval. The most significant development in chemical weapons during the war was the well-kept secret of German nerve gases.

Early Biological Warfare

Biological warfare received little attention in the United States prior to the outbreak of World War II. But with entry into the war, and growing awareness of other biological warfare programs, the United States established a large program and entered into a tripartite agreement with the programs of Canada and Great Britain.

These cooperating programs focused on antipersonnel weapons, while also doing anticrop and antianimal work. They experimented with a range of agents and delivery systems, and anthrax delivered by cluster bombs emerged as the first choice. A production order for an anthrax-filled bomb was canceled because the war ended. U.S. strategists considered using a fungus against the Japanese rice crop near the end of the war but dropped the plan for strategic reasons. Japan became the first nation to use a modern biological weapons system in war when it employed biological warfare against China.

Biological weapons introduced several new issues, including the ethical implications of the Hippocratic oath forbidding the use of medical science to kill. They also offered new military possibilities to be weighed in any debate over banning such warfare. The United States accepted the 1907 Geneva Regulations prohibiting biological weapons but subsequently joined Japan as the only nation not to ratify the ban in the 1925 Geneva Protocol. The United States again sidestepped the issue of biological weapons in the post–World War II United Nations negotiations to limit weapons of mass destruction. Meanwhile, U.S. strategic planners and their British partners advocated the tactical, strategic, and covert possibilities of biological weapons as well as their potential as weapons of mass destruction. They also emphasized the relatively low cost of such weapons and the fact that they did not destroy physical infrastructure, thus avoiding the costs of reconstruction.

The Cold War

In 1950 the U.S. government, concurrent with the growing tensions of the early Cold War, and especially the outbreak of the Korean War, secretly launched a heavily funded and far-ranging crash program in biological warfare. Gas warfare development expanded at an equal pace, especially work with nerve gas. Sarin was standardized in 1951, but emphasis shifted in 1953 to the more potent V-series nerve gases first developed by the British. VX was

standardized in 1957, though a standardized delivery system was not developed. But biological warfare had a higher priority than chemical: indeed, the biological warfare crash program introduced in 1950 shared highest-level priority with atomic warfare. The primary objective for biological weapons was to acquire an early operational capability within the emergency war plan for general war against the Soviet Union and China. By the time of the Korean War, an agent and bomb were standardized both for anticrop and antipersonnel use while research and development went forward with a broad range of agents and delivery systems. In the post–Korean War period many agents and several delivery systems were standardized, one of the more interesting being the standardization in 1959 of yellow fever carried by mosquito vectors. Further, the U.S. government secretly took over the Japanese biological warfare program, acquiring records of experiments with live subjects that killed at least 10,000 prisoners of war, some probably American. In exchange, the perpetrators of the Japanese program were spared prosecution as war criminals.

Another indication of the priority of biological warfare was the adoption in early 1952 of a secret first-use strategy. U.S. military strategists and civilian policymakers took advantage of ambiguities in government policy to allow the Joint Chiefs of Staff (JCS) to put a secret offensive strategy in place. Though the United States reaffirmed World War II retaliation-only policy for gas warfare in 1950, the JCS after some debate decided that it did not by implication apply to biological warfare. They concluded there was no government policy on such weapons, and the Defense Department concurred. Consequently the JCS sent directives to the services making first-use strategy operational doctrine, subject to presidential approval. During the Korean War, the United States also created a deeply buried infrastructure for covert biological warfare in the Far East. Data from the Chinese archives for the Korean War, corroborated by evidence from the U.S. and Canadian archives, builds a strong case for the United States experimenting with biological weapons during the Korean War. The issue remains controversial in the face of U.S. government denial. In 1956 the United States brought policy into line with strategic doctrine by adopting an official first-use offensive policy for biological warfare subject to presidential approval.

Escalation and the Search for Limits

In 1969, President Richard M. Nixon began changing U.S. policy with regard to chemical and biological warfare. In the midst of growing public and congressional criticism over the testing, storage, and transportation of dangerous chemical agents, Nixon resubmitted the 1925 Geneva Protocol, which the Senate ratified in 1974. But the United States decided there was evidence the Soviets had chemical weapons in their war plans, which set off efforts to reach agreement with the Soviets on a verifiable ban while at the same time returning to a posture of retaliatory preparedness. In 1993 the United States joined Russia and other countries in signing the Chemical Weapons Convention. The Senate delayed ratification because it was dissatisfied with the lack of "transparency" in the Russian and other programs. But negotiations continued and further agreements were reached between the U.S. and Russia.

Nixon also unilaterally dropped biological warfare from the U.S. arsenal in 1969, and in 1972 the United States signed the Biological Warfare Convention banning all but defensive preparations. The Senate ratified the convention in 1974. Negotiations to extend the 1972 convention to include an adequate inspection system continued with little progress through most of the 1990s, and early in his presidency George W. Bush withdrew from these negotiations.

Attempts to limit biological weapons under international law floundered for several reasons. There was no accord on the terms of an inspection agreement. Mutual suspicions were heightened by the Russian government's admission that their Soviet predecessors had violated the 1972 convention, and by charges and counter-charges of hidden capabilities across the international landscape.

This unrest was enhanced by a generation of growing use of biological and chemical weapons. The United States had used the biological anticrop AGENT ORANGE in the Vietnam War. Chemical weapons were used in the Iran-Iraq war and by Iraq against the Kurds. The Soviets apparently used chemical weapons in Afghanistan, and there were unconfirmed reports of the use of both chemical and biological weapons elsewhere.

Also highly controversial was the issue of whether provisions for defense against biological warfare under the 1972 convention provided an opening for research for offensive use. Concern in this respect increased with greatly expanded funding for defense against biological weapons; evidence of offensive work hiding under the rubric of defensive work; new possibilities with recombinant DNA and genetic engineering; and pressures for preparedness arising from the 11 September 2001 terrorist attack on the United States. At the beginning of the new millennium these considerations thickened the fog surrounding the question of whether biological and chemical warfare would be limited or extended.

BIBLIOGRAPHY

Brown, Frederic J. *Chemical Warfare: A Study in Restraints.* Princeton, N.J.: Princeton University Press, 1968. Reprint, Westport, Conn.: Greenwood Press, 1981.

Cole, Leonard. *The Eleventh Plague: The Politics of Biological and Chemical Warfare.* New York: Freeman, 1997.

Endicott, Stephen, and Edward Hagerman. *The United States and Biological Warfare: Secrets from the Early Cold War and Korea.* Bloomington: Indiana University Press, 1998.

Harris, Robert, and Jeremy Paxman. *A Higher Form of Killing: The Secret History of Chemical and Biological Warfare.* New York: Hill and Wang, 1982.

Harris, Sheldon H. *Factories of Death: Japanese Biological Warfare, 1932–45, and the American Cover-Up.* London and New York: Routledge, 1994. Rev. ed., New York: Routledge, 2002.

Miller, Judith, Stephen Engelberg, and William Broad. *Germs: Biological Weapons and America's Secret War.* New York: Simon and Schuster, 2001.

Edward Hagerman

See also **Bioterrorism.**

CHEMICAL INDUSTRY. U.S. chemical industry shipments total about $450 billion annually. The industry is a major provider of raw materials for consumers, manufacturing, defense, and exports (about 15 percent of the total). End markets include consumer products, health care, construction, home furnishings, paper, textiles, paints, electronics, food, and transportation. In fact, most industries use chemicals as their key raw materials. For example, the auto has about $1,500 of chemicals such as paints, lube oils, rubber tires, plastic, and synthetic fibers; a cell phone is feasible because of its use of silicon-based chemicals and a durable plastic assembly; microwave ovens are made with silicon chips, plastic housings, and fire-retardant plastic additives.

Chemical industry sales and profitability tend to follow the U.S. consumer economy, with peak sales and profits a few years after strong consumer economic growth periods and low points during recessions. While demand growth for the overall chemical industry has slowed since the 1960s, it is still better than annual gross domestic product (GDP) gains. Operating margins were about 6 percent in 2000 compared with a peak of almost 11 percent in 1995. Research and development and capital spending by the industry are about $30 billion each, or just under 7 percent of sales. The fastest growth areas are life sciences, specialties such as electronic chemicals, and select plastics. The overall employment level of the chemical and allied industries is over 1 million people, with about 600,000 in direct manufacturing. Most of the chemical industry's basic manufacturing plants are located in the Gulf Coast (primarily Texas and Louisiana) due to the proximity of key energy raw materials. Finished product manufacture, by contrast, is located closer to population centers on the East and West Coasts and in the Midwest.

Product Categories

External sales of the chemistry business can be divided into a few broad categories, including basic chemicals (about 35 to 37 percent of the dollar output), life sciences (30 percent), specialty chemicals (20 to 25 percent) and consumer products (about 10 percent).

Basic chemicals are a broad chemical category including polymers, bulk petrochemicals and intermediates, other derivatives and basic industrials, inorganic chemicals, and fertilizers. Typical growth rates for basic chemicals are about 0.5 to 0.7 times GDP. Product prices are generally less than fifty cents per pound. Polymers, the largest revenue segment at about 33 percent of the basic chemicals dollar value, includes all categories of plastics and man-made fibers. The major markets for plastics are packaging, followed by home construction, containers, appliances, pipe, transportation, toys, and games. The largest-volume polymer product, polyethylene (PE), is used mainly in packaging films and other markets such as milk bottles, containers, and pipe. Polyvinyl chloride (PVC), another large-volume product, is principally used to make pipe for construction markets as well as siding and, to a much smaller extent, transportation and packaging materials. Polypropylene (PP), similar in volume to PVC, is used in markets ranging from packaging, appliances, and containers to clothing and carpeting. Polystyrene (PS), another large-volume plastic, is used principally for appliances and packaging as well as toys and recreation. The leading man-made fibers include polyester, nylon, polypropylene, and acrylics, with applications including apparel, home furnishings, and other industrial and consumer use. The principal raw materials for polymers are bulk petrochemicals.

Chemicals in the bulk petrochemicals and intermediates segment are primarily made from liquified petroleum gas (LPG), natural gas, and crude oil. Their sales volume is close to 30 percent of overall basic chemicals. Typical large-volume products include ethylene, propylene, benzene, toluene, xylenes, methanol, vinyl chloride monomer (VCM), styrene, butadiene, and ethylene oxide. These chemicals are the starting points for most polymers and other organic chemicals as well as much of the specialty chemicals category. Other derivatives and basic industries include synthetic rubber, surfactants, dyes and pigments, turpentine, resins, carbon black, explosives, and rubber products and contribute about 20 percent of the basic chemicals external sales. Inorganic chemicals (about 12 percent of the revenue output) make up the oldest of the chemical categories. Products include salt, chlorine, caustic soda, soda ash, acids (such as nitric, phosphoric, and sulfuric), titanium dioxide, and hydrogen peroxide. Fertilizers are the smallest category (about 6 percent) and include phosphates, ammonia, and potash chemicals.

Life sciences (about 30 percent of the dollar output of the chemistry business) include differentiated chemical and biological substances, pharmaceuticals, diagnostics, animal health products, vitamins, and crop protection chemicals. While much smaller in volume than other chemical sectors, their products tend to have very high prices—over ten dollars per pound—growth rates of 1.5 to 6 times GDP, and research and development spending at 15 to 25 percent of sales. Life science products are usually produced with very high specifications and are closely scrutinized by government agencies such as the Food and Drug Administration. Crop protection chemicals, about 10 percent of this category, include herbicides, insecticides, and fungicides.

Specialty chemicals are a category of relatively high valued, rapidly growing chemicals with diverse end product markets. Typical growth rates are one to three times GDP with prices over a dollar per pound. They are generally characterized by their innovative aspects. Products are sold for what they can do rather than for what chemicals they contain. Products include electronic chemicals, industrial gases, adhesives and sealants as well as coatings, industrial and institutional cleaning chemicals, and catalysts. Coatings make up about 15 percent of specialty chemicals sales, with other products ranging from 10 to 13 percent.

Consumer products include direct product sale of chemicals such as soaps, detergents, and cosmetics. Typical growth rates are 0.8 to 1.0 times GDP.

Every year, the American Chemistry Council tabulates the U.S. production of the top 100 basic chemicals. In 2000, the aggregate production of the top 100 chemicals totaled 502 million tons, up from 397 million tons in 1990. Inorganic chemicals tend to be the largest volume, though much smaller in dollar revenue terms due to their low prices. The top 11 of the 100 chemicals in 2000 were sulfuric acid (44 million tons), nitrogen (34), ethylene (28), oxygen (27), lime (22), ammonia (17), propylene (16), polyethylene (15), chlorine (13), phosphoric acid (13) and diammonium phosphates (12).

The Industry in the Twentieth Century

While Europe's chemical industry had been the most innovative in the world in the nineteenth century, the U.S. industry began to overshadow Europe and the rest of the world in both developments and revenues by the mid-1900s. A key reason was its utilization of significant native mineral deposits, including phosphate rock, salt, sulfur, and trona soda ash as well as oil, coal, and natural gas. By 1914, just before World War I, the U.S. industry was already 40 percent larger than that of Germany. At that time, the fertilizer sector was the largest, at 40 percent of total chemical sales, with explosives the next largest sector. Much of the petroleum-based chemicals industry did not develop into a meaningful sector until the post–World War II period. In the 1970s and 1980s, chemical production began to grow rapidly in other areas of the world; the growth was fueled in the Middle East by local energy deposits and in Asia due to local energy deposits and by increased demand. At the end of the century, the United States was the largest producer of chemicals by a large margin, with the overall European and Asian areas a close second and third. On a country basis, Japan and Germany were a distant second and third.

In the early twentieth century, the availability of large deposits of sulfur spurred an innovative process development by Hermann Frasch in which hot water was piped into the deposits to increase recovery. Extensive power availability at Niagara Falls also enabled the growth of an electrochemical industry, including the production of aluminum from bauxite (via Charles Martin Hall's process),

therefore show how the transuranium elements fit into the periodic table. Seaborg's work on the transuranium elements led to his sharing the 1951 Nobel Prize in chemistry with Edwin McMillan. In 1961, Seaborg became the chairman of the Atomic Energy Commission, where he remained for ten years.

Perhaps Seaborg's greatest contribution to chemistry in the United States was his advocacy of science and mathematics education. The cornerstone of his legacy on education is the Lawrence Hall of Science on the Berkeley campus, a public science center and institution for curriculum development and research in science and mathematics education. Seaborg also served as principal investigator of the well-known Great Explorations in Math and Science (GEMS) program, which publishes the many classes, workshops, teacher's guides, and handbooks from the Lawrence Hall of Science. To honor a brilliant career by such an outstanding individual, element 106 was named Seaborgium.

Twentieth-Century Research and Discoveries

Research in the American chemical industry started in the early twentieth century with the establishment of research laboratories such as General Electric, Eastman Kodak, AT&T, and DuPont. The research was necessary in order to replace badly needed products and chemicals that were normally obtained from Germany. Industry attracted research chemists from their academic labs and teaching assignments to head small, dynamic research groups. In 1909, Irving Langmuir was persuaded to leave his position as a chemistry teacher at Stevens Institute of Technology to do research at General Electric. It was not until World War I that industrial chemical research took off. Langmuir was awarded a Nobel Prize for his industrial work. In the early 1900s, chemists were working on polymer projects and free radical reactions in order to synthesize artificial rubber. DuPont hired Wallace H. Carothers, who worked on synthesizing polymers. A product of Carothers's efforts was the synthesis of nylon, which would become DuPont's greatest moneymaker. In 1951, modern organometallic chemistry began at Duquesne University in Pittsburgh with the publication of an article in the journal *Nature* on the synthesis of an organo-iron compound called dicyclopentadienyliron, better known as ferrocene. Professor Peter Pauson and Thomas J. Kealy, a student, were the first to publish its synthesis, and two papers would be published in 1952 with the correct predicted structure. One paper was by Robert Burns Woodward, Geoffrey Wilkinson, Myron Rosenblum, and Mark Whiting; the second was by Ernst Otto Fischer and Wolfgang Pfab. Finally, a complete crystal structure of ferrocene was published in separate papers by Phillip F. Eiland and Ray Pepinsky and by Jack D. Dunitz and Leslie E. Orgel. The X-ray crystallographic structures would confirm the earlier predicted structures. Ferrocene is a "sandwich" compound in which an iron ion is sandwiched between two cyclopentadienyl rings. The discovery of ferrocene was important in many aspects of chemistry, such as revisions in bonding concepts, synthesis of similar compounds, and uses of these compounds as new materials. Most importantly, the discovery of ferrocene has merged two distinct fields of chemistry, organic and inorganic, and led to important advances in the fields of homogeneous catalysis and polymerization.

Significant American achievements in chemistry were recognized by the Nobel Prize committee in the last part of the twentieth century and the first years of the twenty-first century. Some examples include: the 1993 award to Kary B. Mullis for his work on the polymerase chain reaction (PCR); the 1996 award to Robert F. Curl Jr. and Richard E. Smalley for their part in the discovery of C60, a form of molecular carbon; the 1998 award to John A. Pople and Walter Kohn for the development of computational methods in quantum chemistry; the 1999 award to Ahmed H. Zewail for his work on reactions using femtosecond (10^{-14} seconds) chemistry; the 2000 award to Alan G. MacDiarmid and Alan J. Heeger for the discovery and development of conductive polymers; and the 2001 award to William S. Knowles and K. Barry Sharpless for their work on asymmetric synthesis. The outcomes of these discoveries are leading science in the twenty-first century. The use of PCR analysis has contributed to the development of forensic science. The discovery C60 and related carbon compounds, known as nanotubes, is leading to ideas in drug delivery methods and the storage of hydrogen and carbon dioxide. The computational tools developed by Pople and Kohn are being used to assist scientists in analyzing and designing experiments. Femtosecond chemistry is providing insight into how bonds are made and broken as a chemical reaction proceeds. Heeger and MacDiarmid's work has led to what is now known as plastic electronics—devices made of conducting polymers, ranging from light-emitting diodes to flat panel displays. The work by Knowles and Sharpless has provided organic chemists with the tools to synthesize compounds that contain chirality or handedness. This has had a tremendous impact on the synthesis of drugs, agrochemicals, and petrochemicals.

BIBLIOGRAPHY

Brock, William H. *The Norton History of Chemistry.* New York: Norton, 1993.

———. *The Chemical Tree: A History of Chemistry.* New York: Norton, 2000.

Greenberg, Arthur. *A Chemical History Tour: Picturing Chemistry from Alchemy to Modern Molecular Science.* New York: Wiley, 2000.

Servos, John W. *Physical Chemistry from Ostwald to Pauling: The Making of Science in America.* Princeton, N.J.: Princeton University Press, 1990.

Jeffrey D. Madura

See also **American Association for the Advancement of Science; Biochemistry; Chemical Industry; Petrochemical Industry.**

CHEMOTHERAPY is the treatment of diseases with specific chemical agents. The earliest efforts to use chemotherapy were directed at infectious diseases. Paul Ehrlich, known as the Father of Chemotherapy, reported the clinical efficacy of Salvarsan in 1910, the first agent to be shown effective against syphilis. In 1936, sulfonamides were introduced for the treatment of diseases, such as pneumonia, caused by bacteria. And in 1941, a team of scientists in Oxford, England, isolated the active component of the mold *Penicillium notatum*, previously shown by Alexander Fleming to inhibit growth of bacteria in culture media. Thereafter, penicillin was manufactured on a large scale in the United States and is still widely used in clinical practice. Subsequent research has led to significant discoveries such as the antibiotics streptomycin, cephalosporins, tetracyclines, and erythromycin, and the antimalarial compounds chloroquine and chloroguanide.

As control of infectious diseases improved, scientists turned their attention to malignant diseases. They sought compounds that would interfere with the metabolism of tumor cells and destroy them. The compounds they discovered work in various ways. Some, such as methotrexate, provide tumors with fraudulent substrates, while others, such as nitrogen mustards, alter tumor DNA to disrupt tumor metabolism and so destroy the malignant cells. Unfortunately, these latter compounds also affect normal tissues, especially those containing rapidly dividing cells, and cause anemia, stomatitis, diarrhea, and alopecia. By careful selection and administration of these chemotherapeutic agents, safer techniques are being developed to prevent the fatal effects of malignant tumors.

BIBLIOGRAPHY

Hardman, Joel G., and Lee E. Limbird, eds. *Goodman and Gilman's: The Pharmacological Basis of Therapeutics*. 10th ed. New York: McGraw-Hill, 2001.

Higby, Gregory J., and Elaine C. Stroud, eds. *The Inside Story of Medicines: A Symposium*. Madison, Wisc.: American Institute of the History of Pharmacy, 1997.

Markle, Gerald E., and James C. Petersen, eds. *Politics, Science, and Cancer: The Laetrile Phenomenon*. Boulder, Colo.: Westview Press, 1980.

Perry, Michael C., ed. *The Chemotherapy Source Book*. 2d ed. Baltimore: Williams and Wilkins, 1996.

Peter H. Wright/c. p.

See also **Cancer; DNA; Epidemics and Public Health; Malaria; Medical Research; Pharmacy; Sexually Transmitted Diseases.**

CHERBOURG. The capture of this French city during World War II by American forces three weeks after the Normandy landings of 6 June 1944 gave the Allies their first great port in northwestern Europe. Cherbourg had been held by the Germans since June 1940. General J. Lawton Collins's U.S. Seventh Corps, a part of General Omar N. Bradley's First U.S. Army, drove west from Utah Beach, cut the Cotentin Peninsula to isolate Cherbourg, and turned north against the well-fortified city. The Germans fought stubbornly, demolished the port, and blocked the harbor channels, but finally surrendered on 26 June. A vast rehabilitation program put the port back into working condition several weeks later.

BIBLIOGRAPHY

Breuer, William B. *Hitler's Fortress Cherbourg: The Conquest of a Bastion*. New York: Stein and Day, 1984.

Ruppenthal, Roland G. *Utah Beach to Cherbourg (6 June–27 June 1944)*. Washington, D.C.: Historical Division, Department of the Army, 1948. Reprinted 1984.

Martin Blumenson/A. R.

See also **D Day; Normandy Invasion; Saint-Lô.**

CHEROKEE, an American Indian tribe that, at the time of European contact, controlled a large area of what is now the southeastern United States. Until the later part of the eighteenth century, Cherokee lands included portions of the current states of Tennessee, Kentucky, Virginia, North and South Carolina, Georgia, and Alabama. Cherokees are thought to have relocated to that area from the Great Lakes region centuries before contact with Europeans, and their language is part of the Iroquian lan-

Sequoyah. The inventor of the Cherokee syllabary—giving his people a written language for the first time. Library of Congress

guage family. Although "Cherokee" probably comes from the Choctaw word meaning "people of the caves," Cherokees have often referred to themselves as Ani-yun-wiya, "real people."

Cherokee society was organized into seven matrilineal clans that structured their daily lives in villages along rivers. Each village had a red chief, who was associated with war and games, and a white chief, who was responsible for daily matters, such as farming, legal and clan disputes, and domestic issues.

The Cherokee economy was based on agriculture, hunting, and fishing. Tasks were differentiated by gender, with women responsible for agriculture and the distribution of food, and men engaged in hunting and gathering. After contact, trade with Europeans formed a significant part of the Cherokee economy.

During the eighteenth century, the Cherokee population was reduced by disease and warfare, and treaties with the English significantly decreased their landholdings. Cherokees fought in numerous military conflicts, including the Cherokee War against the British and the American Revolution, in which they fought against the rebels. Cherokees were known as powerful allies, and they attempted to use warfare to their benefit, siding with or against colonists when they perceived it to help their strategic position.

By the nineteenth century, Cherokee society was becoming more diverse. Intermarriage with traders and other Europeans created an elite class of Cherokees who spoke English, pursued education in premier U.S. institutions, and often held slaves. Missionaries lived within the nation, and an increasing number of Cherokees adopted Christianity.

Following European models of government, Cherokees wrote and passed their own constitution in 1827. Sequoyah invented a Cherokee alphabet in 1821, and the *Cherokee Phoenix*, a national newspaper, was founded in 1828.

In the 1820s and 1830s, the Cherokee nation was at the center of many important and controversial decisions regarding Native American sovereignty. American settlers living around the Cherokees were anxious to acquire tribal lands. The U.S. government, particularly during the presidency of Andrew Jackson, pressured the tribe to move west. As early as 1828, some Cherokees accepted land in INDIAN TERRITORY (now northeastern Oklahoma) and relocated peacefully.

After years of resistance to removal, a small faction of the Cherokee Nation signed the Treaty of New Echota in 1835, exchanging the tribe's land in the East for western lands, annuities, and the promise of self-government. Some moved west at that time, but most rejected the treaty and refused to leave their homes. U.S. troops entered Cherokee lands to force them to leave.

In 1838 and 1839, the majority of Cherokees were forced to make the journey, many on foot, from their

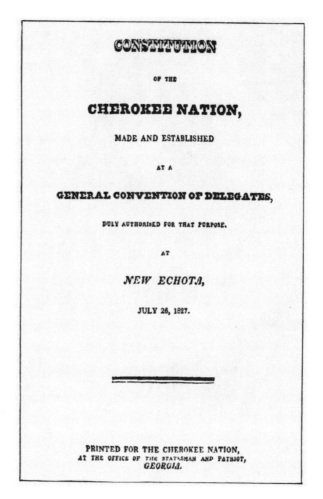

Cherokee Constitution. The title page of this 1827 document, based on European models. NORTH WIND PICTURE ARCHIVES

homes in the East to Indian Territory. Over 12,000 men, women, and children embarked upon the trail west, but over one-fourth of them died as a result of the journey. Due to the harsh conditions of the journey and the tragedy endured, the trip was named the TRAIL OF TEARS. The Cherokees' trauma has become emblematic of all forced removals of Native Americans from lands east of the Mississippi, and of all of the tragedies that American Indians have suffered at the hands of the U.S. government over several centuries.

A number of Cherokees separated from those heading west and settled in North Carolina. These people and their descendents are known as the Eastern Cherokee. Today, this portion of the tribe, in addition to the United Keetoowah Band and the Cherokee Nation, form the three major groups of contemporary Cherokees.

After the survivors of the Trail of Tears arrived in Indian Territory (they were commonly called the Ross party, due to their allegiance to their principal chief, John Ross), a period of turmoil ensued. Ross's followers claimed

Wilma Mankiller. The first woman to be the principal chief of the Cherokees, starting in 1985. AP/WIDE WORLD PHOTOS

the treaty signers had betrayed the nation, and conflict continued between the Old Settlers (those who had relocated voluntarily), the treaty party, and the Ross party. Although this conflict was eventually resolved, tension remained and was exacerbated by the Civil War. During the war the Cherokee Nation officially allied itself with the Confederacy, but many Cherokee men fought for the Union. The Civil War destroyed Cherokee lives and property, and the Union victory forced the tribe to give up even more of its land.

During the second half of the nineteenth century, members of the Cherokee Nation rebuilt their government. By the end of the century it boasted a national council, a justice system, and medical and educational systems to care for its citizens.

In the 1890s, the U.S. Congress passed legislation mandating the allotment of land previously held in common by citizens of the Cherokee Nation. In 1906, in anticipation of Oklahoma statehood, the federal government unilaterally dissolved the sovereign government of the Cherokee Nation. Many Cherokee landowners were placed under restrictions, forced to defer to a guardian to manage their lands. Graft and corruption tainted this system and left many destitute. Despite this turmoil, many played an active role in governing the new state of Okla-

homa, and Cherokees in Oklahoma and North Carolina kept their traditions alive.

In the 1960s, Cherokees pursued ways to commemorate their traditions and consolidate tribal affiliations. They formed organizations such as the Cherokee National Historical Society and initiated the Cherokee National Holiday, a celebration of their arts and government. In 1971, they elected a chief for the first time since Oklahoma statehood, beginning the process of revitalizing their government. In 1987, Wilma Mankiller was elected the first woman chief. The renewed interest in tribal politics and the strength of services continues in the Cherokee Nation.

BIBLIOGRAPHY

Ehle, John. *Trail of Tears: The Rise and Fall of the Cherokee Nation.* New York: Doubleday, 1988.

McLoughlin, William G. *After the Trail of Tears: The Cherokees' Struggle for Sovereignty, 1839–1880.* Chapel Hill: University of North Carolina Press, 1993.

Perdue, Theda. *Cherokee Women: Gender and Culture Change, 1700–1835.* Lincoln: University of Nebraska, 1998.

Woodward, Grace Steele. *The Cherokees.* Norman: University of Oklahoma Press, 1963.

Kerry Wynn

See also **Cherokee Language; Cherokee Nation Cases; Cherokee Wars.**

CHEROKEE LANGUAGE. The Cherokee homeland at the time of European contact was located in the highlands of what would later become the western Carolinas and eastern Tennessee. Contact with anglophone and, to a lesser extent, francophone Europeans came early to the Cherokee, and their general cultural response—adaptation while trying to maintain their autonomy—is mirrored in their language.

In the history of Native American languages, the singular achievement of Sequoyah, an illiterate, monolingual Cherokee farmer, is without parallel. Impressed by the Europeans' ability to communicate by "talking leaves," Sequoyah in the early nineteenth century set about, by trial and error, to create an analogous system of graphic representation for his own language. He let his farm go to ruin, neglected his family, and was tried for witchcraft during the twelve years he worked out his system. The formal similarity with European writing—a system of sequential groups of discrete symbols in horizontal lines—belies the complete independence of the underlying system. What Sequoyah brought forth for his people was a syllabary of eighty-four symbols representing consonant and vowel combinations, and a single symbol for the consonant "s." By about 1819, he had demonstrated its efficacy and, having taught his daughter to use it, what followed was a rapid adoption and development of literacy skills among the tribe. By 1828, a printing press had been set up, and a newspaper, *The Cherokee Phoenix*, and other publications in the Cherokee syllabary were produced for tribal consumption.

The removal of the Cherokees from their homeland to Oklahoma in 1838–1839 ("The Trail of Tears") necessitated the reestablishment of the printing press in the independent Cherokee Nation, where native language literacy continued to flourish, to the point where the literacy rate was higher than that of the surrounding white population. In 1906, Cherokee literacy was dealt a severe blow when the United States government confiscated the printing press, evidently as a prelude to incorporating the Cherokee Nation into the State of Oklahoma.

The Cherokee language is the only member of the Southern branch of the Iroquoian language family. The Northern branch—which includes Mohawk, Seneca, Cayuga, Oneida, Onondaga, and Tuscarora—is geographically fixed in the area of the eastern Great Lakes, and it seems likely that the ancestors of the Cherokee migrated south from that area to the location where they first contacted Europeans. Because of the substantial differences between Cherokee and the Northern languages, it may be inferred that the migration took place as early as 3,500 years ago.

Cherokee Writing. A page of the remarkable written language, a syllabary, that Sequoyah developed for his people in the early nineteenth century. UNIVERSITY OF OKLAHOMA PRESS

Today, there are about ten thousand who speak Cherokee in Oklahoma and one thousand in North Carolina. Most are over fifty years of age.

BIBLIOGRAPHY

Pulte, William and Durbin Feeling. "Cherokee." In *Facts About The World's Languages: An Encyclopedia of the World's Major Languages, Past and Present.* Edited by Jane Garry and Carl Rubino. New York: H. W. Wilson, 2001, 127–130.

Walker, Willard. "Cherokee." In *Studies in Southeastern Indian Languages.* Edited by James M. Crawford. Athens: University of Georgia Press, 1975, 189–196.

Gary Bevington

CHEROKEE NATION CASES. *Cherokee Nation v. Georgia* (1831) and *Worcester v. Georgia* (1832) arrived at the Supreme Court in a political setting of uncertainty and potential crisis. Andrew Jackson was reelected president in 1832, southern states were uneasy with the union, and Georgia, in particular, was unhappy with the Supreme Court. Within the Court, divisiveness marked relations among the justices. John Marshall, the aging chief justice, suffered the strains of his wife's death, his own illness, and tests of his leadership. At the same time, Americans craved the lands of resistant Native Americans, and armed conflict was always possible.

Cherokee Nation v. Georgia was the first controversy Native Americans brought to the Supreme Court. Until the late 1820s, the Cherokees were at peace with the United States. They had no desire and no apparent need for war. They were remaking their nation on the newcomers' model. They had a sound, agricultural economy. They adopted a constitution and writing as well as Western dress and religion. Treaties with the United States guaranteed protection of their territory. The Cherokees in north Georgia planned to remain in place and prosper, but the state and the United States had other plans. When Georgia ceded its claims to western territory in 1802, the federal government agreed to persuade southeastern tribes to move west of the Mississippi. Peaceful campaigns convinced most Cherokees in Tennessee to leave but had no effect on the majority in Georgia.

Cherokee territory proved vulnerable to illegal entry by Georgians. Violations escalated with the discovery of gold there in 1829. Federal defense of the borders was unavailing. The state grew aggressive and enacted legislation for Cherokee country as though it were Georgia. The president removed the troops. Congress voted to remove the tribes. The Cherokees hired a famous lawyer, William Wirt, to represent them. Wirt filed suit in the Supreme Court. *Cherokee Nation v. Georgia* asked the Court to forbid enforcement of state law in the nation's territory. Law and morality favored the Cherokees; Congress and the president sided with Georgia. A Court order against the state could produce a major constitutional crisis if the president refused to enforce it. The court

127

avoided the political risk without abandoning the law. Although the Cherokees had a right to their land, the chief justice said, the court had no authority to act because the Constitution allowed the Cherokee nation to sue Georgia only if it were a "foreign nation." Because it was instead what he termed a "domestic, dependent nation," the court lacked jurisdiction.

The crisis passed, but not for long. Wirt returned to the Court the following year, representing Samuel A. Worcester, a missionary to the Cherokees. Georgia had convicted Worcester and sentenced him to hard labor for his conscientious refusal to obey Georgia law within the Cherokee nation. Because Worcester was a U.S. citizen, the Court had jurisdiction over his appeal and could not escape a difficult judgment. The Cherokees had another chance.

Writing resolutely for a unanimous court, Marshall found that Georgia had acted unlawfully. The Cherokees, he said, were an independent people and a treaty-making nation. The decision was a triumph for the Cherokees and the chief justice. It would amount to little, however, without the president's support. According to popular story, Jackson responded: "John Marshall has made his decision, now let him enforce it."

A showdown never took place. Procedural delays intervened. In the interim, southern secessionists pressed toward a different crisis. Supporters of Worcester's mission feared for the union. They urged him to relieve pressure on Georgia by halting the legal proceedings. He did so and was released. The tribe's white allies also advised the Cherokees to strike a bargain. A minority of the tribe's leadership agreed to a sale, and the tribe was brutally herded west along the Trail of Tears. Georgia was ethnically cleansed of Native Americans.

Worcester v. Georgia continues to be important in American law and in Native American self-understanding because of its robust affirmation of tribal sovereignty, a familiar concern of modern Court cases. *Cherokee Nation v. Georgia* has currency because of Marshall's passing comment that tribes' relation to the United States resembles that of a ward to a guardian. Some judges and scholars find in this analogy a source for the modern legal doctrine that the United States has a trust obligation to tribes. Worcester himself reentered the news in 1992 when Georgia posthumously pardoned him.

BIBLIOGRAPHY

Ball, Milner S. "Constitution, Court, Indian Tribes." *American Bar Foundation Research Journal* 1 (1987): 23–46.

Breyer, Stephen. "'For Their Own Good.'" *The New Republic*, 7 August 2000: 32–39.

McLoughlin, William. *Cherokee Renascence in the New Republic.* Princeton, N.J.: Princeton University Press, 1986.

Milner S. Ball

See also **Cherokee; Georgia; Indian Land Cessions; Indian Removal; Trail of Tears.**

CHEROKEE STRIP, a 12,000-square-mile area in OKLAHOMA between 96 and 100 degrees west longitude and 36 and 37 degrees north latitude. Guaranteed to the Cherokees by treaties of 1828 and 1833 as an outlet—the term "strip" is actually inaccurate—it was not to be permanently settled. The treaty of 1866 compelled the Cherokee Nation to sell portions to friendly Indians.

The Cherokee Nation leased the strip in 1883 to the Cherokee Strip Livestock Association for five years at $100,000 a year. In 1891 the United States purchased the Cherokee Strip for $8,595,736.12. Opened by a land run on 16 September 1893, it became part of the Oklahoma Territory.

BIBLIOGRAPHY

Marquis, James. *The Cherokee Strip: A Tale of an Oklahoma Boyhood.* Norman: University of Oklahoma Press, 1993. Originally published New York: Viking Press, 1945.

Savage, William W. *The Cherokee Strip Live Stock Association: Federal Regulation and the Cattleman's Last Frontier.* Columbia: University of Missouri Press, 1973.

M. L. Wardell/c. w.

See also **Cherokee; Land Policy.**

CHEROKEE TRAIL, also known as the Trappers' Trail, was laid out and marked in the summer of 1848 by Lieutenant Abraham Buford as a way for both CHEROKEE and white residents in northeastern Arkansas to access the SANTA FE TRAIL on their way to the California gold fields. It had previously been followed by trappers en route to the ROCKY MOUNTAINS. It extended from the vicinity of Fort Gibson up the ARKANSAS RIVER to a point in the northwestern part of present-day Oklahoma. From there it ran west and joined the Sante Fe Trail.

BIBLIOGRAPHY

Agnew, Brad. *Fort Gibson: Terminal on the Trail of Tears.* Norman: University of Oklahoma Press, 1980.

Bieber, Ralph P., ed. *Southern Trails to California in 1849.* Glendale, Calif.: Arthur H. Clark, 1937.

Byrd, Cecil K. *Searching for Riches: The California Gold Rush.* Bloomington: Lilly Library, Indiana University, 1991.

Edward Everett Dale/h. s.

See also **Gold Rush, California.**

CHEROKEE WARS (1776–1781). The CHEROKEE Indians had generally been friendly with the British in America since the early 1700s, siding with them against the French in the FRENCH AND INDIAN WARS. Colonial encroachment by settlers provoked them into a two-year war with SOUTH CAROLINA (1759–1761), and the land cessions that ended the war fueled resentment that came to a head with the outbreak of the American Revolution.

Restless because of the continued encroachment on their lands by the colonists, encouraged and supplied with ammunition by British agents, and incited by Shawnee and other northern Indians, the Cherokee sided with the British during the Revolution. Cherokee raids against Patriot settlements in the summer of 1776 incited militias from Virginia, the Carolinas, and Georgia to respond in kind. Lacking anticipated support from the Creek Indians and the British, the Cherokees were decisively defeated, their towns plundered and burned. Several hundred Cherokees fled to British protection in Florida. Cherokee leaders sued for peace with revolutionary leaders in June and July 1777, ceding additional Cherokee lands.

Those unwilling to settle for peace split off from the majority of Cherokees and migrated down the Tennessee River to Chickamauga Creek. Under the leadership of Dragging Canoe, the Chickamauga group continued raiding frontier settlements for the next four years. Although the Cherokees suffered additional defeats at American hands, some Chickamaugas refused to make peace, instead moving further downstream in the early 1780s. Most Cherokee fighting ended with the Treaty of Hopewell in 1785, and the treaty's additional land cessions discouraged Cherokees from joining other conflicts between Indians and whites in succeeding decades.

BIBLIOGRAPHY

Calloway, Colin G. The *American Revolution in Indian Country: Crisis and Diversity in Native American Communities.* New York: Cambridge University Press, 1995.

Hatley, M. Thomas. *The Dividing Paths: Cherokees and South Carolinians through the Era of Revolution.* New York: Oxford University Press, 1993.

Woodward, Grace S. *The Cherokees.* The Civilization of the American Indian Series, no. 65. Norman: University of Oklahoma Press, 1963.

Kenneth M. Stewart / J. H.

See also **Indian Treaties, Colonial; Indians in the Revolution; Revolution, American: Military History.**

CHESAPEAKE COLONIES,

Maryland and Virginia, grew slowly from 1607 to 1630 due to the low-lying tidewater's highly malignant disease environment. Stagnant water, human waste, mosquitoes, and salt poisoning produced a mortality rate of 28 percent. Within three years of coming to the colony, 40 to 50 percent of the indentured servants, who made up the majority of the population, died from malaria, typhus, and dysentery before finishing their contracts. By 1700, settlement patterns tended toward the healthier Piedmont area, and the importation of slaves directly from Africa boosted the population.

As the tobacco colonies' populations increased, so did their production of tobacco, their principal source of revenue and currency. Plantations were set out in three-to-

ten-acre plots for tobacco along the waterways of Maryland and Virginia, extending almost 200 miles in length and varying from 3 to 72 miles in width, which gave oceangoing ships access to almost 2,000 miles of waterways for transporting hogsheads of tobacco. Ship captains searched throughout Chesapeake Bay for the larger planters' wharves with storehouses, called factories, to buy tobacco for merchants. Small planters also housed their crops at these large wharves. Planters turned to corn and wheat production in the eighteenth century.

The county seat remained the central aspect of local government, yet it generally held only a courthouse, an Anglican church, a tavern, a country store, and a sparse number of homes. A sense of noblesse oblige was conserved within the church government and the militia. Books and pamphlets imported from London retained the English culture and a sense of civic responsibility.

BIBLIOGRAPHY

Finlayson, Ann. *Colonial Maryland.* Nashville: Thomas Nelson, 1974.

Kulikoff, Allan. *Tobacco and Slaves: The Development of Southern Cultures in the Chesapeake, 1680–1800.* Chapel Hill: University of North Carolina Press, 1986.

Meyer, Eugene L. *Chesapeake Country.* New York: Abbeville, 1990.

Morgan, Phillip D. *Slave Counterpoint: Black Culture in the Eighteenth-Century Chesapeake and Lowcountry.* Chapel Hill: University of North Carolina Press, 1998.

Michelle M. Mormul

See also **Maryland; Virginia; Virginia Company of London;** *and vol. 9:* **An Act Concerning Religion; Speech of Powhatan to John Smith; Starving in Virginia, 1607–1610.**

CHESAPEAKE-LEOPARD INCIDENT,

one of the events leading up to the WAR OF 1812. On 22 June 1807 off Hampton Roads, Virginia, the American frigate *Chesapeake* was stopped by the British ship *Leopard*, whose commander demanded the surrender of four seamen alleged to have deserted from the British ships *Melampus* and *Halifax*. Upon the refusal of the American commander, Captain James Barron, to give up the men, the *Leopard* opened fire. The American vessel, having just begun a long voyage to the Mediterranean, was unprepared for battle, and to the repeated broadsides from the British replied with only one gun, which was discharged with a live coal from the galley. After sustaining heavy casualties and damage to masts and rigging, Barron surrendered his vessel (he was later court martialed for dereliction).

The British boarding party recovered only one deserter. In addition, three former Britons, by then naturalized Americans, were removed by force and impressed into the British navy to help fight its war with France. The British captain refused to accept the *Chesapeake* as a prize, but forced it to creep back into port in its crippled condition. The incident enflamed patriotic passions and spurred new calls for the protection of American sovereignty in neutral waters. Seeking to pressure England and France to respect American neutrality, President Thomas Jefferson pushed the EMBARGO ACT through Congress in December 1807. The embargo, which prohibited exports to overseas ports, hurt the domestic economy and did little to alter British practices. Negotiations over the *Chesapeake* incident continued until 1811 when England formally disavowed the act and returned two of the Americans—the third had died.

BIBLIOGRAPHY

Spivak, Burton. *Jefferson's English Crisis: Commerce, Embargo, and the Republican Revolution.* Charlottesville: University Press of Virginia, 1979.

Charles Lee Lewis
Andrew Rieser

See also **Impressment of Seamen; Navy, United States; Warships.**

CHESS. Records from the court of Baghdad in the ninth and tenth centuries represent the first well-documented history of the game of chess. The game entered Spain in the eighth century and had spread across western Europe by the year 1000. Benjamin Franklin advanced chess in the United States with his essay "The Morals of Chess" (1786), in which he stressed the importance of "foresight," "circumspection," "caution," and "perseverance." Popular interest in chess was also advanced by the publication of such books as *Chess Made Easy*, published in Philadelphia in 1802, and *The Elements of Chess*, published in Boston in 1805. By the mid-nineteenth century, the United States had produced its first unofficial national chess champion, Paul Morphy, who took Europe by storm

Chess. In this 1942 photograph, youths concentrate on their game at a camp in Interlochen, Mich. LIBRARY OF CONGRESS

in 1858, defeating grandmasters in London and Paris, but his challenge of British champion Howard Staunton was rebuffed. America's next world-championship aspirant was Harry Nelson Pillsbury, a brilliant player with prodigious powers of recall who died at age thirty-four.

In 1924, at a meeting in Paris, representatives from fifteen countries organized the Fédération Internationale des Échecs (or FIDE) to oversee tournaments, championships, and rule changes. The United States Chess Federation (USCF) was founded in 1939 as the governing organization for chess in America.

Since 1948, Russian-born players have held every world championship, with the exception of the brief reign (1972–1975) of American grandmaster Bobby Fischer, a child prodigy who captured the U.S. chess championship in 1958 at the age of fourteen. In 1972 Fischer defeated Soviet great Boris Spassky for the world championship in Reykjavík, Iceland, in the most publicized chess match in history. The irascible Fischer refused to defend his title in 1975, because of disagreements over arrangements for the match, and went into reclusive exile. He reappeared in the former Yugoslavia in 1992 and defeated Spassky, but no one took the match seriously.

Quick chess, which limited a game to twenty-five minutes per player, appeared in the mid-1980s and grew in popularity in the 1990s, after Fischer patented a chess clock for speed games in 1988. Computer chess began earlier, when, in 1948, Claude Shannon of Bell Telephone Laboratories delivered a paper stating that a chess-playing program could have applications for strategic military decisions. Richard Greenblatt, an undergraduate at the Massachusetts Institute of Technology, wrote a computer program in 1967 that drew one game and lost four games in a USCF tournament. Researchers from Northwestern University created a program that won the first American computer championship in 1970. Deep Thought, a program developed at Carnegie Mellon University and sponsored by International Business Machines, defeated grandmaster Bent Larsen in 1988. Deep Thought's successor, Deep Blue, played world champion Gary Kasparov in Philadelphia in February 1996. Kasparov won three games and drew two of the remaining games to win the match, 4–2. At a rematch in New York City in May 1997, after the match was tied at one win, one loss, and three draws, the computer program won the final game. Computer programs of the 1960s could "think" only two moves ahead, but Deep Blue could calculate as many as 50 billion positions in three minutes.

BIBLIOGRAPHY

Fischer, Bobby. *My Sixty Memorable Games.* Reissue, London: Batsford, 1995.

Hooper, David, and Kenneth Whyld. *The Oxford Companion to Chess.* 2d ed., New York: Oxford University Press, 1992.

Levy, David, and Monty Newborn. *How Computers Play Chess.* New York: Computer Science Press, 1991.

Louise B. Ketz
David P. McDaniel

See also **Toys and Games.**

CHEYENNE. The word "Cheyenne" is Siouan in origin, and traditional Cheyennes prefer the term "Tsistsistas." As a tribal nation, the Cheyennes were formed from several allied bands that amalgamated around the Black Hills in the early eighteenth century to become one of the most visible Plains Indian tribes in American history.

Their political unity has been based on respect for four Sacred Arrows that were brought to them "444 years ago" by the prophet Sweet Medicine. Each year, the Cheyennes conduct an arrow ceremony in honor of their prophet and a sun dance that allows tribal members to fast and sacrifice to secure blessings for themselves and their tribe. Their politico-religious structure, unlike that of any other Plains tribe, could require all bands to participate in military actions. Consequently, Cheyenne military leaders were able to mobilize their warriors to carve a territory for the tribe that reached from the Arkansas River to the Black Hills, a large territory for a nation of only 3,500 persons.

The Cheyennes first entered American documentary history as potential trading partners for U.S. interests, in the narratives of Meriwether Lewis and William Clark in 1806. Within a few decades, however, military confrontations had begun, ultimately resulting in Cheyenne victories at Beecher Island in 1868 and the Little Bighorn in 1876, and tragic defeats at Sand Creek in 1864 and Summit Springs in 1869.

In their long history, the Cheyennes mastered three different modes of subsistence. As foragers in Minnesota during the seventeenth century, they lived in wigwams. As corn farmers on the middle Missouri River, they lived in earthen lodges surrounded by palisades. As full-time nomadic buffalo hunters, they rode horses and lived in tipis. Each of these lifestyles had a characteristic social structure. As foragers, they lived in chief-led bands where both sexes made equal contributions to the economy. During the farming period, women came to dominate the economy, doing most of the agricultural work and preparing buffalo robes for trade. A council of chiefs comprised men who were important because they had many wives and daughters. About 1840, some Cheyenne men became oriented toward military societies, who emphasized raiding rather than buffalo hunting for subsistence. War chiefs began to challenge the authority of the peace chiefs.

At the beginning of the twenty-first century, the Cheyennes occupied two reservations, one in Oklahoma, which they shared with the Southern Arapahos, and another in Montana. The Cheyenne language was spoken

Cheyenne. A photograph of a tribal member in 1893, by which time the tribe had been confined to present-day Oklahoma after years of military confrontations with white settlers and the U.S. Army. LIBRARY OF CONGRESS

on both reservations, and they retained their major ceremonies.

BIBLIOGRAPHY
Grinnell, George Bird. *The Cheyenne Indians.* 2 vols. Reprint of the 1923 edition. New York: Cooper Square, 1962.
Moore, John H. *The Cheyenne.* Oxford: Blackwell, 1996.

John H. Moore

See also **Little Bighorn, Battle of; Sand Creek Massacre; Tribes: Great Plains;** *and vol. 9:* **A Century of Dishonor; Fort Laramie Treaty of 1851; Account of the Battle at Little Bighorn.**

CHICAGO, the largest city in the Midwest, is located at the southwest corner of Lake Michigan. In 1673, the French explorers Louis Jolliet and Father Jacques Marquette led the first recorded European expedition to the site of the future city. It was a muddy, malodorous plain the American Indians called Chicagoua, meaning place of the wild garlic or skunkweed, but Jolliet recognized the site's strategic importance as a portage between the Great Lakes and Mississippi River valley. The French government ignored Jolliet's recommendation to construct a canal across the portage and thereby link Lake Michigan and the Mississippi River. Not until 1779 did a mulatto fur trader, Jean Baptiste Point du Sable, establish a trading post along the Chicago River and become Chicago's first permanent resident. In 1803, the U.S. government built Fort Dearborn across the river from the trading post, but during the War of 1812, Indians allied to the British destroyed the fort and killed most of the white inhabitants. In 1816, Fort Dearborn was rebuilt and became the hub of a small trading settlement.

The state of Illinois revived Jolliet's dream of a canal linking Lake Michigan and the Mississippi Valley, and in 1830 the state canal commissioners surveyed and platted the town of Chicago at the eastern terminus of the proposed waterway. During the mid-1830s, land speculators swarmed to the community, anticipating a commercial boom once the canal opened, and by 1837 there were more than 4,000 residents. In the late 1830s, however, the land boom busted, plunging the young settlement into economic depression.

During the late 1840s, Chicago's fortunes revived. In 1848, the Illinois and Michigan Canal finally opened to traffic, as did the city's first rail line. By 1857, eleven trunk lines radiated from the city with 120 trains arriving and departing daily. Moreover, Chicago was the world's largest primary grain port and the point at which lumber from Michigan and Wisconsin was shipped westward to treeless prairie settlements. Also arriving by ship and rail were thousands of new settlers, increasing the city's population to 29,963 in 1850 and 109,260 in 1860. Irish immigrants came to dig the canal, but newcomers from Germany soon outnumbered them and remained the city's largest foreign-born group from 1850 to 1920. In the 1870s and 1880s, Scandinavian immigrants added to the city's diversity, and by 1890, Chicago had the largest Scandinavian population of any city in America.

Attracting the newcomers was the city's booming economy. In 1847, Cyrus McCormick moved his reaper works to Chicago, and by the late 1880s, the midwestern metropolis was producing 15 percent of the nation's farm machinery. During the 1860s, Chicago became the nation's premier meatpacking center, and in 1865 local entrepreneurs opened the Union Stock Yards on the edge of the city, the largest of its kind in the world. In the early 1880s, George Pullman erected his giant railroad car works and model industrial town just to the south of Chicago. Meanwhile, Montgomery Ward and Sears, Roebuck Company were making Chicago the mail-order capital of the world.

The Great Fire of 1871 proved a temporary setback for the city, destroying the entire central business district and leaving approximately one-third of the city's 300,000 people homeless. But Chicago quickly rebuilt, and during the 1880s and 1890s, the city's architects earned renown for their innovative buildings. In 1885, William Le Baron Jenney completed the first office building supported by a

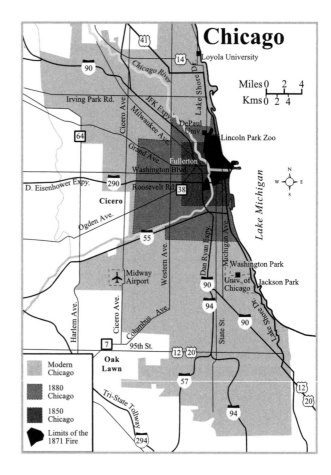

cage of iron and steel beams. Other Chicagoans followed suit, erecting iron and steel frame skyscrapers that astounded visitors to the city. Chicago's population was also soaring, surpassing the one million mark in 1890. In 1893, the wonders of Chicago were on display to sightseers from throughout the world when the city hosted the World's Columbian Exposition. An estimated 27 million people swarmed to the fair, admiring the neoclassical exposition buildings as well as enjoying such midway attractions as the world's first Ferris wheel.

Some Chicagoans, however, did not share in the city's good fortunes. By the last decades of the century, thousands of newcomers from eastern and southern Europe were crowding into slum neighborhoods, and disgruntled workers were earning the city a reputation for labor violence. The Haymarket Riot of 1886 shocked the nation, as did the Pullman Strike of 1894, during which workers in Pullman's supposedly model community rebelled against the industrialist's tightfisted paternalism. In 1889, Jane Addams founded Hull-House, a place where more affluent and better-educated Chicagoans could mix with less fortunate slum dwellers and hopefully bridge the chasms of class dividing the city.

Meanwhile, the architect-planner Daniel Burnham sought to re-create Chicago in his comprehensive city plan of 1909. A model of "city beautiful" planning, Burnham's scheme proposed a continuous strand of parkland stretching twenty-five miles along the lakefront, grand diagonal boulevards imposed on the city's existing grid of streets, and a monumental neoclassical civic center on the near west side. Although not all of Burnham's proposals were realized, the plan inspired other cities to think big and draft comprehensive blueprints for future development. It was a landmark in the history of city planning, just as Chicago's skyscrapers were landmarks in the history of architecture.

During the post–World War I era, violence blemished the reputation of the Midwest's largest city. Between 1915 and 1919, thousands of southern blacks migrated to the city, and white reaction was not friendly. In July 1919, a race riot raged for five days, leaving twenty-three blacks and fifteen whites dead. Ten years later, the St. Valentine's Day massacre of seven North Side Gang members confirmed Chicago's reputation for gangland violence. Home of the notorious mobster Al Capone, Prohibition-era Chicago was renowned for bootlegging and gunfire. The Century of Progress Exposition of 1933, commemorating the city's one-hundredth anniversary, drew millions of visitors to the city and offered cosmetic relief for the blemished city, but few could forget that in Chicago bloodshed was not confined to the stockyards.

In 1931, Anton Cermak became mayor and ushered in almost fifty years of rule by the city's Democratic political machine. The greatest machine figure was Mayor Richard J. Daley, who presided over the city from 1955 to his death in 1976. Under his leadership, Chicago won a reputation as the city that worked, unlike other American metropolises that seemed increasingly out of control. During the late 1960s and early 1970s a downtown building boom produced three of the world's tallest buildings, the John Hancock Center, the Amoco Building, and the Sears Tower. Moreover, the huge McCormick Place convention hall consolidated Chicago's standing as the nation's premier convention destination. And throughout the 1970s and 1980s, the city's O'Hare Field ranked as the world's busiest airport.

Yet the city did not necessarily work for all Chicagoans. The bitter demonstrations and "police riot" outside the 1968 Democratic National Convention signaled trouble to the whole world. By the 1970s, a growing number of African Americans felt that the Democratic machine was offering them a raw deal. A combination of black migration from the South and white migration to the suburbs had produced a marked change in the racial composition of the city; in 1940, blacks constituted 8.2 percent of the population, whereas in 1980 they comprised 39.8 percent. By constructing huge high-rise public housing projects in traditional ghetto areas, the machine ensured that poor blacks remained segregated residentially, and these projects bred as many problems as the slums they replaced. As the number of manufacturing jobs declined in rust belt centers such as Chicago, blacks suffered higher unemployment rates than whites. Mean-

while, the Democratic machine seemed unresponsive to the demands of African Americans who had loyally cast their ballots for the Democratic Party since the 1930s.

Rebelling against the white party leaders, in 1983 African Americans exploited their voting strength and elected Harold Washington as the city's first black mayor. Although many thought that Washington's election represented the dawning of a new era in Chicago politics, the mayor was forced to spend much of his four years in office battling white Democratic aldermen reluctant to accept the shift in political power. In any case, in 1989, Richard M. Daley, son of the former Democratic boss, won the mayor's office, a position he was to hold for the remainder of the century.

Despite the new skyscrapers, busy airport, and thousands of convention goers, the second half of the twentieth century was generally a period of decline during which the city lost residents, wealth, and jobs to the suburbs. Chicago's population peaked at 3,621,000 in 1950 and then dropped every decade until 1990, when it was 2,784,000. During the last decade of the century, however, it rose 4 percent to 2,896,000. Much of this growth could be attributed to an influx of Latin American immigrants; in 2000, Hispanics constituted 26 percent of the city's population. A growing number of affluent whites were also attracted to gentrifying neighborhoods in the city's core. But during the last two decades of the century, the African American component declined both in absolute numbers and as a portion of the total population. The black-and-white city of the mid-twentieth century no longer existed. Hispanics and a growing Asian American population had diversified the Chicago scene.

BIBLIOGRAPHY

Cronon, William. *Nature's Metropolis: Chicago and the Great West.* New York: Norton, 1991.

Green, Paul M., and Melvin G. Holli, eds. *The Mayors: The Chicago Political Tradition.* Carbondale: Southern Illinois University Press, 1987.

Mayer, Harold M., and Richard C. Wade. *Chicago: Growth of a Metropolis.* Chicago: University of Chicago Press, 1969.

Miller, Donald L. *City of the Century: The Epic of Chicago and the Making of America.* New York: Simon and Schuster, 1996.

Pacyga, Dominic A., and Ellen Skerrett. *Chicago, City of Neighborhoods: Histories and Tours.* Chicago: Loyola University Press, 1986.

Pierce, Bessie Louise. *A History of Chicago.* 3 vols. New York: Knopf, 1937–1957.

Jon C. Teaford

See also **Art Institute of Chicago; Chicago Riots of 1919; Chicago Seven; Haymarket Riot; Illinois; Midwest; Museum of Science and Industry; Sears Tower.**

CHICAGO FIRE. Modern Chicago, Illinois, began its growth in 1833. By 1871 it had a population of 300,000.

Across the broad plain that skirts the Chicago River's mouth, buildings by the thousand extended, constructed with no thought of resistance to fire. Even the sidewalks were of resinous pine, and the single pumping station that supplied the mains with water had a wooden roof. The season was excessively dry. A scorching wind blew up from the plains of the far Southwest week after week and made the structures of pine-built Chicago as dry as tinder. A conflagration of appalling proportions awaited only the igniting spark.

It began on Sunday evening, 8 October 1871. Where it started is clear, but how it started, no one knows. The traditional story is that Mrs. O'Leary went out to the barn with a lamp to milk her cow, the cow kicked over the lamp, and cow, stable, and Chicago became engulfed in one common flame. Nonetheless, Mrs. O'Leary testified under oath that she was safe abed and knew nothing about the fire until a family friend called to her.

Once started, the fire moved onward relentlessly until there was nothing more to burn. Between nine o'clock on Sunday evening and ten-thirty the following night, an area of five square miles burned. The conflagration destroyed over 17,500 buildings and rendered 100,000 people homeless. The direct property loss was about $200 million. The loss of human life is commonly estimated at between 200 and 300.

In 1997, in a nod to the city's history, Major League Soccer announced the formation of an expansion team called the Chicago Fire, which began play in 1998.

BIBLIOGRAPHY

Biel, Steven, ed. *American Disasters.* New York: New York University Press, 2001.

Miller, Ross. *American Apocalypse: The Great Fire and the Myth of Chicago.* Chicago: University of Chicago Press, 1990.

Sawislak, Karen. *Smoldering City: Chicagoans and the Great Fire, 1871–1874.* Chicago: University of Chicago Press, 1995.

M. M. Quaife/A. E.

See also **Accidents; Chicago; Disasters; Soccer.**

CHICAGO, MILWAUKEE, AND SAINT PAUL RAILWAY COMPANY V. MINNESOTA,

134 U.S. 418 (1890), a case in which substantive due process debuted on the U.S. Supreme Court. In *MUNN V. ILLINOIS* (1877), the Court had refused to overturn rate setting by state legislatures. But thereafter the Court edged ever closer to the idea of due process as a limitation on such state regulatory power, and in this case it finally endorsed the new doctrine.

Justice Samuel Blatchford, writing for a Court split 6–3, struck down a state statute that permitted an administrative agency to set railroad rates without subsequent review by a court. The reasonableness of a railroad rate "is eminently a question for judicial investigation, requiring due process of law for its determination." By depriving a railroad of procedural due process (access to a court to review the reasonableness of rate setting), the state had deprived the owner "of the lawful use of its property, and thus, in substance and effect, of the property itself, without due process of law." Justice Joseph Bradley in dissent contended that the Court had implicitly overruled *Munn*, arguing that rate setting was "preeminently a legislative [function,] involving questions of policy." Substantive due process accounted for some of the Court's worst excesses in the next decades and was abandoned between 1934 and 1937.

BIBLIOGRAPHY

Paul, Arnold M. *Conservative Crisis and the Rule of Law: Attitudes of Bar and Bench, 1887–1895.* Ithaca, N.Y.: Cornell University Press, 1960.

William M. Wiecek

See also **Due Process of Law; Interstate Commerce Laws; Railroad Rate Law.**

CHICAGO RIOTS OF 1919.

During the 1910s Chicago's African American population more than doubled to 109,000. Attracted by better jobs and living conditions, blacks in Chicago expected more than the segregated, overcrowded, crime-ridden neighborhoods of the black belt. Seeking housing in white communities, blacks found themselves unwelcome and sometimes attacked. Competition for jobs and housing increased racial tensions.

But increasingly militant blacks no longer accepted white supremacy and unfair treatment. When on 27 July 1919 Eugene Williams drowned after drifting on a raft into the white section of a Lake Michigan beach, the worst race riot of the violent Red Summer of 1919 erupted. Angry blacks charged stone-throwing whites with murder. After police instead arrested an African American, mobs of blacks struck several parts of the city. The following day white gangs attacked blacks returning home from work, even pulling some from streetcars, and roamed black neighborhoods. African Americans retaliated, and soon innocents of both races were beaten and killed as the riot intensified. Seven days of mayhem produced thirty-eight dead, fifteen whites and twenty-three blacks; 537 injuries; and 1,000 homeless families. On the front lines during the violence, the black-owned *Chicago Defender* provided some of the best print coverage of the riot.

BIBLIOGRAPHY

Doreski, C. K. "Chicago, Race, and the Rhetoric of the 1919 Riot." *Prospects* 18 (1993): 283–309.

Tuttle, William M., Jr. *Race Riot: Chicago in the Red Summer of 1919.* New York: Atheneum, 1970.

Paul J. Wilson

See also **Chicago; Race Relations; Riots.**

CHICAGO SEVEN (also called the Chicago Eight or Chicago Ten), radical activists arrested for conspiring to incite RIOTS at the Democratic National Convention in Chicago, 21–29 August 1968. Ignoring Mayor Richard Daley's warnings to stay away, thousands of antiwar demonstrators descended on Chicago to oppose the Democratic administration's Vietnam policy. On 28 August, skirmishes between protesters and police culminated in a bloody melee on the streets outside the convention center. Eight protesters were charged with conspiracy: Abbie Hoffman, Rennie Davis, John Froines, Tom Hayden, Lee Weiner, David Dellinger, Jerry Rubin, and Bobby Seale. The trial (1969–1970) quickly degenerated into a stage for high drama and political posturing. Prosecutors stressed the defendants' ties with "subversive" groups like STUDENTS FOR A DEMOCRATIC SOCIETY (SDS), the Youth International Party (YIP), and the BLACK PANTHERS. Defense attorney William M. Kunstler countered by calling a series of celebrity witnesses. Judge Julius J. Hoffman's obvious hostility to the defendants provoked low comedy, poetry reading, Hare Krishna chanting, and other forms of defiant behavior from the defendants' table. Bobby Seale, defending himself without counsel, spent three days in court bound and gagged for his frequent outbursts. His case was later declared a mistrial. The jury found five of the other seven defendants guilty of crossing state lines to riot, but these convictions were reversed on appeal. The defendants and their attorneys also faced four- to five-year prison sentences for contempt of court. In 1972, citing Judge Hoffman's procedural errors and bias, the Court of Appeals (Seventh Circuit) overturned most of the contempt findings.

BIBLIOGRAPHY

Danelski, David. "The Chicago Conspiracy Trial." In *Political Trials*. Edited by Theodore L. Becker. Indianapolis, Ind.: Bobbs-Merrill, 1971.

Dellinger, David T. *The Conspiracy Trial*. Edited by Judy Clavir and John Spitzer. Indianapolis, Ind.: Bobbs-Merrill, 1970.

Sloman, Larry. *Steal This Dream: Abbie Hoffman and the Countercultural Revolution in America*. New York: Doubleday, 1998.

Samuel Krislov / A. R.

See also **Democratic Party; Peace Movements; Vietnam War; Youth Movements.**

CHICANOS. *See* **Hispanic Americans.**

CHICKAMAUGA, BATTLE OF (19–20 September 1863). The Army of the Cumberland, under Union General W. S. Rosecrans, maneuvered an inferior Confederate force under General Braxton Bragg out of Chattanooga, TENNESSEE, an important railway center, by threatening it from the west while sending two flanking columns far to the south. When Bragg retreated to the east, Rosecrans pursued until he found that the main Confederate Army had halted directly in his front. In order to unite his scattered corps, he moved northward to concentrate in front of Chattanooga. Bragg attacked on the morning of 19 September in the valley of Chickamauga Creek, about ten miles from Chattanooga. The effective strength was Confederate, 66,000; Union, 58,000.

The fighting began with a series of poorly coordinated attacks in echelon by Confederate divisions; these were met by Union counterattacks. On the second day, the battle was resumed by the Confederate right, threatening the Union communications line with Chattanooga. A needless transfer of troops to the Union left, plus a blundering order which opened a gap in the center, so weakened the right that it was swept from the field by General James Longstreet's attack. Rosecrans and his staff were carried along by the routed soldiers. General George H. Thomas, commanding the Union left, held the army together and after nightfall withdrew into Chattanooga. Rosecrans held Chattanooga until November, when the Confederate siege was broken by reinforcements from the Army of the Potomac under General U. S. Grant.

BIBLIOGRAPHY

Cozzens, Peter. *This Terrible Sound: The Battle of Chickamauga.* Urbana: University of Illinois Press, 1992.

Spruill, Matt, ed. *Guide to the Battle of Chickamauga.* Lawrence: University Press of Kansas, 1993.

Theodora Clarke Smith
Andrew Rieser

See also **Chattanooga Campaign; Civil War; Tennessee, Army of.**

CHICKASAW-CREEK WAR. On 13 February 1793, a Chickasaw national council declared war against the CREEKS, to avenge the murder of two Chickasaw hunters, and the next day Chief Tatholah and forty warriors set out against the Creek towns. Chief Piomingo attributed the murders to Creek resentment of the Chickasaw refusal to join an alliance against the Anglo-Americans. For almost a decade, Creek leaders such as Alexander McGillivray had been seeking support from Spanish Florida to help stem the westward advance of the new United States. Anglo-American settlers in western Georgia and the Cumberland Valley had suffered Creek depredations. Chickasaws who allied themselves with the Americans faced Creek resentment, and in the aftermath of the Creek attacks in 1793, Piomingo and others sought American aid. In a letter to the Americans, Chickasaw chiefs urged, "[L]et us join to let the Creeks know *what war is*." Governor William Blount, of the Southwest Territory, did not join the conflict, but in hopes that a Creek-Chickasaw war would reduce Creek attacks on the frontier, he sent the Chickasaw a large munitions shipment to support their effort.

Much talk, but little fighting, ensued; Spanish officials of Louisiana and West Florida held intertribal hostilities to a minimum as part of their efforts to negotiate a pan-tribal alliance of Creeks, Chickasaws, Choctaws, and Cherokees against the Americans. On 28 October, at Fort Nogales, at the mouth of the Yazoo River, Spain engineered and joined a short-lived treaty of alliance among the southern tribes.

BIBLIOGRAPHY

Champagne, Duane. *Social Order and Political Change: Constitutional Governments among the Cherokee, the Choctaw, the Chickasaw, and the Creek.* Stanford, Calif.: Stanford University Press, 1992.

Elizabeth Howard West/A. R.

See also **Cherokee; Choctaw; Pinckney's Treaty; Warfare, Indian.**

"CHICKEN IN EVERY POT" is a quotation that is perhaps one of the most misassigned in American political history. Variously attributed to each of four presidents serving between 1920 and 1936, it is most often associated with Herbert Hoover. In fact, the phrase has its origins in seventeenth century France; Henry IV reputedly wished that each of his peasants would enjoy "a chicken in his pot every Sunday." Although Hoover never uttered the phrase, the Republican Party did use it in a 1928 campaign advertisement touting a period of "Republican prosperity" that had provided a "chicken in every pot. And a car in every backyard, to boot."

BIBLIOGRAPHY

Mayer, George H. *The Republican Party, 1854–1966.* 2d rev. ed. New York: Oxford University Press, 1967.

Republican Party Campaign Ad. *New York World*, 30 October 1928.

Gordon E. Harvey

See also **Elections, Presidential; Republican Party.**

CHILD ABUSE refers to intentional or unintentional physical, mental, or sexual harm done to a child. Child abuse is much more likely to take place in homes in which other forms of domestic violence occur as well. Despite a close statistical link between domestic violence and child abuse, the American legal system tends to treat the two categories separately, often adjudicating cases from the same household in separate courts. Some think this practice has led to an inadequate understanding of the overall causes and dynamics of child abuse, and interfered with its amelioration.

The treatment of child abuse in law has its origins in Anglo-American common law. Common law tradition held that the male was head of the household and possessed the authority to act as both disciplinarian and pro-

tector of those dependent on him. This would include his wife and children as well as extended kin, servants, apprentices, and slaves. While common law obligated the male to feed, clothe, and shelter his dependents, it also allowed him considerable discretion in controlling their behavior. In the American colonies, the law did define extreme acts of violence or cruelty as crimes, but local community standards were the most important yardstick by which domestic violence was dealt with. Puritan parents in New England, for example, felt a strong sense of duty to discipline their children, whom they believed to be born naturally depraved, in order to save them from eternal damnation. Although Puritan society tolerated a high degree of physicality in parental discipline, the community did draw a line at which it regarded parental behavior as abusive. Those who crossed the line would be brought before the courts.

In the nineteenth century the forces of industrialization and urbanization loosened the community ties that had traditionally served as important regulators of child abuse and neglect. The instability of market capitalism and the dangers posed by accidents and disease in American cities meant that many poor and working-class families raised their children under extremely difficult circumstances. At the same time, larger numbers of child victims now concentrated in cities rendered the problems of child abuse and neglect more visible to the public eye. Many of these children ended up in public almshouses, where living and working conditions were deplorable.

An expanding middle class viewed children less as productive members of the household and more as the objects of their parents' love and affection. While child abuse did occur in middle-class households, reformers working in private charitable organizations began efforts toward ameliorating the problem as they observed it in poor and working-class families. Although the majority of cases brought to their attention constituted child neglect rather than physical abuse, reformers remained remarkably unsympathetic to the social and economic conditions under which these parents labored. Disadvantaged parents commonly lost parental rights when found guilty of neglecting their children. The parents of many institutionalized children labeled as "orphans" were actually alive but unable to provide adequate care for them.

In 1853 the Reverend Charles Loring Brace founded the New York Children's Aid Society. Convinced that the unhealthy moral environment of the city irreparably damaged children and led them to engage in vice and crime, Brace established evening schools, lodging houses, occupational training, and supervised country outings for poor urban children. In 1854 the Children's Aid Society began sending children it deemed to be suffering from neglect and abuse to western states to be placed with farm families. Over the next twenty-five years, more than 50,000 children were sent to the West. Unfortunately, the society did not follow up on the children's care and many encountered additional neglect and abuse in their new households.

Reformers of the Progressive Era (circa 1880–1920) worked to rationalize the provision of social welfare services and sought an increased role for the state in addressing the abuse and neglect of dependent individuals under the doctrine of *parens patriae* (the state as parent). In 1912 the White House sponsored the first Conference on Dependent Children, and later that year the U.S. Children's Bureau was established as the first federal child welfare agency. Child welfare advocates in the Progressive Era viewed the employment of children in dangerous or unsupervised occupations, such as coal mining and hawking newspapers, as a particular kind of mistreatment and worked for state laws to prohibit it.

The increasing social recognition of adolescence as a distinct stage of human development became an important dimension of efforts to address child abuse. Largely influenced by the work of psychologist G. Stanley Hall, reformers extended the chronological boundaries of childhood into the mid-teens and sought laws mandating that children stay in school and out of the workforce. Reformers also worked for the establishment of a juvenile justice system that would allow judges to consider the special psychological needs of adolescents and keep them separated from adult criminals. In 1899, Cook County, Illinois, established the nation's first court expressly dealing with minors. Juvenile courts began to play a central role in adjudicating cases of child abuse and neglect. Over the following decades the number of children removed from their homes and placed into foster care burgeoned. The Great Depression magnified these problems, and in 1934 the U.S. Children's Bureau modified its mission to concentrate more fully on aiding dependents of abusive or inadequate parents.

By the mid-twentieth century, the medical profession began to take a more prominent role in policing child abuse. In 1961, the American Academy of Pediatrics held a conference on "battered child syndrome," and a subsequent issue of the *Journal of the American Medical Association* published guidelines for identifying physical and emotional signs of abuse in patients. States passed new laws requiring health care practitioners to report suspected cases of child abuse to the appropriate authorities. The Child Abuse Prevention and Treatment Act of 1974 gave federal funds to state-level programs and the Victims of Child Abuse Act of 1990 provided federal assistance in the investigation and prosecution of child abuse cases.

Despite the erection of a more elaborate governmental infrastructure for addressing the problem of child abuse, the courts remained reluctant to allow the state to intrude too far into the private relations between parents and children. In 1989, the Supreme Court heard the landmark case *DeShaney v. Winnebago County Department of Social Services.* The case originated in an incident in which a custodial father had beaten his four-year old son so badly the child's brain became severely damaged. Emergency surgery revealed several previous injuries to the child's brain. Wisconsin law defined the father's actions as a crime and he was sentenced to two years in prison. But the boy's noncustodial mother sued the Winnebago County Department of Social Services, arguing that caseworkers had been negligent in failing to intervene to help the child despite repeated reports by hospital staff of suspected abuse. Her claim rested in the Fourteenth Amendment, which holds that no state (or agents of the state) shall "deprive any person of life, liberty, or property, without due process of law; nor deny to any person within its jurisdiction the equal protection of the laws." The Court, however, ruled that the Fourteenth Amendment protects citizens' rights from violations arising from actions taken by the state—not from actions it may fail to take. The boy had not been in the custody of the state, such as in a state juvenile detention center or foster home, when the violence occurred, and therefore, the Court said, no special relationship existed between the child and the state. In other words, children did not enjoy an affirmative right to be protected by the state from violence committed by their custodial parents in the privacy of the home.

Many advocates for victims of domestic violence criticized the ruling, arguing that it privileged the rights of abusive parents over the best interests of children, and worked toward reforming the law. The federal Adoption and Safe Families Act (ASFA) of 1997 established new guidelines for the states that included mandatory termination of a parent's rights to all of his or her children when the parent had murdered, committed a felony assault on, or conspired, aided, or abetted the abuse of any of his or her children. Laws in all fifty states require parents to protect their children from being murdered by another member of the household; failure to do so may result in criminal liability and loss of rights to other of their children. AFSA extended these liabilities to include a parent's failure to protect a child from felony assault. While the act's intent was to promote the best interests of children, critics have noted that this has not necessarily been the result. Prosecutors, for example, have been able to convict mothers who failed to protect their children from violence in the home even though they were also victims of the abuser. Thus, children have been taken from the custody of a parent who did not commit abuse and who could conceivably provide appropriate care after the actual perpetrator was removed from the home.

BIBLIOGRAPHY

Costin, Lela B., Howard Jacob Krager, and David Stoesz. *The Politics of Child Abuse in America.* New York: Oxford University Press, 1996.

Gordon, Linda. *Heroes of Their Own Lives: The Politics and History of Family Violence, Boston, 1880–1960.* New York: Viking, 1988.

Rothman, David J. *The Discovery of the Asylum: Social Order and Disorder in the New Republic.* 2d ed. Boston: Little, Brown, 1990.

Lynne Curry

137

See also **Adolescence; Children's Bureau; Children's Rights; Foster Care; Juvenile Courts; Society for the Prevention of Cruelty to Children.**

CHILD CARE. In modern industrial societies, child care is recognized as an essential social service for women seeking to enter the paid labor force or pursue education or training and, along with paid parental leave, as an essential component of gender equality. Today, the majority of mothers in the United States work outside the home, yet despite decades of advocacy on the part of American children's experts and feminists, there is still no comprehensive, publicly supported system of child care. Instead, provision is divided between the public and private sectors, with the bulk of public services linked to antipoverty "workfare" programs, and provisions vary widely in terms of form, quality, affordability, and accessibility. This "patchwork" system may be explained by the history of American child care, which has its origins in the seventeenth century.

Colonial and Nineteenth-Century Child Care

Both Native American hunter-gatherers and Euro-American farmers and artisans expected women as well as men to engage in productive labor, and both groups devised various methods, such as carrying infants in papooses or placing toddlers in "go-gins," to free adults to care for children while working at other tasks. Notably, neither group considered child care to be exclusively mothers' responsibility, instead distributing it among tribal or clan members (Native Americans), or among parents, older siblings, extended family, and servants (European Americans). Some of the colonies also boasted "dame schools," rudimentary establishments that accepted children as soon as they were weaned.

As industrialization moved productive work from farms and households to factories, it became increasingly difficult for mothers to combine productive and reproductive labor, making them more economically dependent on male breadwinners as they assumed sole responsibility for child care. As this role gained ideological force through concepts such as "Republican motherhood" and the "moral mother," maternal wage earning fell into disrepute, except in times of emergency, that is, when mothers lost their usual source of support. Female reforms sought to facilitate women's work in such instances by creating day nurseries to care for their children. The earliest such institution was probably the House of Industry, founded by the Female Society for the Relief and Employment of the Poor in Philadelphia in 1798. Throughout the nineteenth century, female philanthropists in cities across the nation (with the exception of the South) followed suit, establishing several hundred nurseries by 1900.

With few exceptions, nineteenth-century child care institutions excluded the children of free black mothers, most of whom were wage earners. Slave mothers, however, were compelled to place their children in whatever form of child care their owners devised. Slaveholders on large plantations set up "children's houses" where older slave children or older slaves no longer capable of more strenuous work cared for slave infants, while female slaves, denied the right to care for their own offspring, worked in the fields or became "mammies" to planters' children. After Emancipation, African American women continued to work outside the home in disproportionate numbers, prompting Mary Church Terrell, the founding president of the National Association of Colored Women, to remark that the day nursery was "a charity of which there is an imperative need." Black female reformers like those of Atlanta's Neighborhood Union responded by setting up nurseries and kindergartens for African American children.

By the turn of the century, the need for child care had reached critical proportions for Americans of all races, as increasing numbers of mothers either sought or were financially compelled to work outside the home. To point up the need for more facilities and improve their quality, a group of female reformers set up a "model day nursery" at the 1893 World's Columbian Exhibition in Chicago and then founded a permanent organization, the National Federation of Day Nurseries (NFDN).

Despite being the first national advocate for child care, the NFDN made little headway in gaining popular acceptance of their services, due, in part, to their conservatism. Clinging to a nineteenth-century notion of day nurseries as a response to families in crisis, the NFDN failed to acknowledge the growing trend toward maternal employment. Meanwhile, among policy makers, momentum was shifting toward state-funded mothers' pensions intended to keep women without male breadwinners at home instead of going out to work. But many poor and low-income women did not qualify for pensions, and state funding often dried up, so maternal employment—and the need for child care—persisted. The NFDN, however, eschewed public support for nurseries, preferring to maintain control over their private charities, a decision that left them ill prepared to meet increasing demands. At the same time, day nurseries were coming under fire from reformers who compared them unfavorably to the new kindergartens and nursery schools being started by early childhood educators. But few day nurseries could afford to upgrade their equipment or hire qualified teachers to match those of the nursery schools.

The New Deal to World War II

The child care movement was poorly positioned to take advantage of federal support in the 1930s, when the New Deal administrator Harry Hopkins sought to create a Works Progress Administration (WPA) program that would both address the needs of young children who were "culturally deprived" by the Great Depression and provide jobs for unemployed schoolteachers. Instead, early childhood educators caught Hopkins's attention and took the lead in administering some 1,900 Emergency Nursery Schools. Though the educators did their best to regulate the quality of the schools, to many Americans they carried the stigma of "relief." Nonetheless, they served to legitimize the idea of education for very young children on an unprecedented scale.

The Emergency Nursery Schools were intended to serve the children of the unemployed, but in some instances, they also functioned as child care for wage-earning parents. With the onset of World War II, defense industries expanded, reducing the ranks of the unemployed, and many of the schools were shut down. A handful of federal administrators, aware that maternal employment was on the upswing, fought to convert the remaining schools into child care centers. These met some of the need for services until 1943, when more generous federal funding became available to local communities through the Lanham Act. However, the supply of child care could not keep up with demand. At its height, some 3,000 Lanham Act centers were serving 130,000 children—when an estimated 2 million slots were needed. Mothers who could not find child care devised informal arrangements, sending children to live with relatives, relying on neighbors who worked alternate shifts, or leaving older children to care for themselves—giving rise to the image of the infamous "latchkey" child.

The Postwar Period

Since both the WPA and Lanham Act programs had been presented as emergency measures to address specific national crises, they could not provide the basis for establishing permanent federally sponsored child care in the postwar period. The issue languished until the 1960s and 1970s, when it once again appeared on the public agenda, this time in conjunction with efforts to reform public assistance through a series of amendments to the Social Security Act, which authorized Aid to Families of Dependent Children. Around the same time, Congress also established Head Start, a permanent public program of early childhood education for the poor. Though it proved highly effective, Head Start was not considered child care until the 1990s. Congress did take a first step toward establishing universal child care in 1971, with passage of the Comprehensive Child Development Act, but President Nixon vetoed it with a strong Cold War message that effectively chilled further legislative efforts for the next several decades.

The lack of public provisions notwithstanding, the postwar decades witnessed a significant rise in maternal employment, which in turn prompted the growth of market-based child care services. This trend was aided by several federal measures, including the child care tax deduction passed in 1954 (and converted to a child care tax credit in 1972), as well as a variety of incentives to employers to set up or sponsor services for their employees, beginning in 1962. Market-based services included voluntary or nonprofit centers, commercial services, and small mom-and-pop or family child care enterprises. Quality varied widely and regulation was lax, in part due to the opposition from organized child care entrepreneurs.

Child Care and Welfare Reform

From the 1970s through the 1990s, the link between child care and welfare reform was reinforced by passage of a series of mandatory employment measures that also included child care provisions. The Family Support Act of 1988, which mandated employment or training for most applicants, including mothers of small children, also required states to provide child care; by the mid-1990s, however, the states were serving only about 13 to 15 percent of eligible children. At the same time, efforts to pass more universal legislation continued to meet strong opposition from conservatives like President George H. W. Bush, who believed that middle-class women should remain at home with their children. In 1990, Congress passed the Act for Better Child Care Services (the ABC bill), a compromise that expanded funding for Head Start and provided forms of child care assistance (including the Earned Income Tax Credit). To satisfy conservative calls for devolution to the states, it initiated a new program called the Child Care and Development Block Grant (CCDBG).

The final link between child care and workfare was forged with passage of the Personal Responsibility and Work Opportunity Reconciliation Act (PRWORA) of 1996, legislation that was twice vetoed by President Bill Clinton, not because of its stringent work requirements for poor women, but for having inadequate child care provisions. When PRWORA came up for renewal in 2002, much of the debate turned around the issue of child care and whether proposed funding levels would provide sufficient services so that recipients could meet increasingly stringent work requirements. Among middle- and upper-income families, the demand for child care remains high, with parents relying on private-sector services, babysitting cooperatives, and "nannies," many of whom are undocumented workers. Despite growing concern about the impact of low-quality care on children of all social classes, prospects for universal public child care remain dim, as the division between public and private child care produces a divided constituency that cannot mobilize sufficient political pressure to bring about the necessary legislative changes.

BIBLIOGRAPHY

Michel, Sonya. *Children's Interests / Mothers' Rights: The Shaping of America's Child Care Policy.* New Haven, Conn.: Yale University Press, 1999.

Michel, Sonya, and Rianne Mahon. *Child Care Policy at the Crossroads: Gender and Welfare State Restructuring.* New York: Routledge, 2002.

Rose, Elizabeth. *A Mother's Job: The History of Day Care, 1890–1960.* New York: Oxford University Press, 1999.

Sonya Michel

See also **Head Start; Maternal and Child Health Care; Welfare System.**

CHILD LABOR. Before the twentieth century, child labor was rampant. Knowledge of its extent prior to 1870 is fragmentary because child labor statistics before then are not available, but juvenile employment probably existed in the spinning schools established early in the colonies. As the nineteenth century advanced, child labor became more widespread. The census of 1870 reported the employment of three-quarters of a million children between ten and fifteen years of age. From 1870 to 1910, the number of children reported as gainfully employed continued to increase steadily before the American public took notice of its ill effects.

Early Struggles and Successes

Among the earliest efforts to deal with the problem of child labor in the nineteenth and twentieth centuries were those of organized labor. For example, the Knights of Labor conducted a campaign for child labor legislation in the 1870s and 1880s that resulted in the enactment of many state laws. The American Federation of Labor consistently spoke out against child labor as a cause of downward pressure on wages and campaigned for the "family wage" that would allow for a man to be the sole breadwinner. Nonetheless, during the nineteenth century, working children, although hired for their docility, took part in strikes and occasionally even led their elders in walkouts. The fledgling industrial unions in the early twentieth century organized the youngest workers, and there was even a union of child workers: the Newsboys and Bootblacks' Protective Union, chartered by the Cleveland AFL. The union's purpose was "to secure a fair compensation for our labor, lessen the hours of labor" and "educate the members in the principles of trade unionism so when they develop into manhood they will at all times struggle for the full product of their labor."

As opposition to child labor grew, the campaign against child labor—although an uphill battle—began to score victories. Conditions in the canning industry, the glass industry, anthracite mining, and other industries began to attract considerable attention at the turn of the century. In the South, a threefold rise in number of child laborers during the decade ending in 1900 aroused public sentiment for child labor laws. In the North, insistence on stronger legislation and better enforcement led to the formation of the National Child Labor Committee in 1904. This committee, chartered by Congress in 1907 to promote the welfare of America's working children, investigated conditions in various states and industries and spearheaded the push for state legislation with conspicuous success. The 1920 census reflected a decline in child labor that continued in the 1930s.

Federal Regulation

The backwardness of certain states and the lack of uniformity of state laws led to demands for federal regulation. Early efforts were unsuccessful. In *Hammer v. Dagenhart* (1918) and *Bailey v. Drexel Furniture Company* (1922), the U.S. Supreme Court set aside attempts at congressional regulation. Child labor reformers, nevertheless, began to push for a child labor amendment to the Constitution. In 1924, such an amendment was adopted by Congress and submitted to the states, but by 1950 only twenty-four had ratified it.

The New Deal finally brought significant federal regulation. The Public Contracts Act of 1936 set the minimum age for employment at sixteen for boys and at eighteen for girls in firms supplying goods under federal contract. A year later, the Beet Sugar Act set the minimum age at fourteen for employment in cultivating and harvesting sugar beets and cane. Far more sweeping was the benchmark Fair Labor Standards Act of 1938 (FSLA). For agriculture, it set the minimum working age at fourteen for employment outside of school hours and at sixteen for employment during school hours. For nonagricultural work in interstate commerce, sixteen was the minimum age for employment during school hours, and eighteen for occupations designated hazardous by the secretary of labor. A major amendment to the FSLA in 1948 prohibited children from performing farm work when schools were in session in the district where they resided. There were no other important changes in the FSLA until 1974, when new legislation prohibited work by any child under age twelve on a farm covered by minimum-wage regulations (farms using at least five-hundred days of work in a calendar quarter).

Contemporary Problems

Despite the existence of prohibiting legislation, considerable child labor continues to exist, primarily in agriculture. For the most part, the workers are children of migrant farm workers and the rural poor. Child labor and school-attendance laws are least likely to be enforced on behalf of these children. This lack of enforcement contributes, no doubt, to the fact that the educational attainment of migrant children is still half that of the rest of the population. Beyond agriculture, child labor has emerged, or sometimes reemerged, in a number of areas. Around the turn of the twenty-first century, there have been efforts to relax the minimum-age laws for doing certain kinds of work. The most notable challenge has come from Amish families, who have opened small manufacturing shops in response to the reduced availability of farmland and have sought exemptions on the basis of religious freedom to employ their children in these shops. In addition, the employment of children in sweatshops that produce clothes for major labels has returned to American cities. Also, children and young teenagers selling

developed antiseptic and anesthetic procedures, the use of X rays, and a safer "low" cesarean section that was an improvement over techniques widely used since the 1870s. The move to hospitals also supported the pathological view of childbirth and the increased specialization of physicians.

There was a dramatic parallel shift from midwife to physician attendant in the first three decades of the twentieth century. As late as 1900, half of all the children born in the United States were delivered with the help of a midwife. By 1930, midwife-attended births had dropped to less than 15 percent of all births, and most of these were in the South. Physician-critics of midwifery identified the "midwife problem" as the source of all ills for childbearing women, and published a wave of articles in medical journals and popular periodicals. While public health advocates frequently spoke in their defense, midwives were ultimately in no position, economically or organizationally, to effectively respond to the charges of their critics. Despite the suggestion in national reports issued in the early 1930s that midwives had a consistently better record with maternal mortality, women continued to prefer the hospital to the home because they believed that it offered them a safer and less painful birthing experience.

The use of anesthetics dramatically changed the experience of childbirth and also facilitated widespread efforts in the 1910s to upgrade obstetrical practice and eliminate midwives. Physicians began experimenting with new forms of anesthesia like scopolamine, a drug with amnesiac properties that suppressed a patient's memory of painful contractions and created a state known as "twilight sleep," as well as various forms of spinal anesthetic. Following the publication of an article on scopolamine in *McClure's Magazine* in 1914, a national movement of women who advocated the adoption of twilight sleep methods by American obstetricians saw the use of scopolamine as an opportunity to control their birthing experience. Their strategy ultimately backfired as scopolamine was found to be extremely dangerous to both mother and child. After widespread use until the 1960s, the demand for painless childbirth was ultimately met by physicians, but at the price of many women losing control of the birthing experience by being put to sleep with a variety of drugs that could only be administered under the expertise of hospital attendants.

Scholars have debated the potential consequences of the medicalization of childbirth that followed these developments. Women may have benefited from the technological advances in hospitals. However, they have sacrificed both the ability to make choices for themselves and the supportive environment of home birth in the pursuit of a safer and less painful birthing experience. Improvements in hospital regulations and practices have been credited for the improved safety of birth. Likewise, the prenatal care movement, adoption of sulfonamides, blood transfusions, and X rays, and the use of antibiotics after World War II were also crucial in lowering maternal and infant death rates by the 1940s.

Natural Childbirth and Later Developments

The emergence of the natural childbirth movement of the late 1940s and early 1950s challenged the basis of medicalized childbirth. Grantly Dick-Read's *Childbirth Without Fear: The Principles and Practices of Natural Childbirth*, first published in 1944, opposed the routine use of anesthesia and called for less medical intervention. Marjorie Karmel's *Thank You, Dr. Lamaze: A Mother's Experiences in Painless Childbirth*, which appeared in 1959, also appealed to a growing minority of women who found the scientific approach to childbirth adopted by most hospitals to be lacking in personal satisfaction. In the 1960s and 1970s, feminist health advocates extended this argument by advocating the right of women to control their bodies. The publication of *Our Bodies, Ourselves* by the Boston Women's Health Collective in 1971 provided a political statement urging women to assume greater control over all aspects of their bodies in society, including pregnancy and childbirth. The women's health movement helped to establish collectives across the nation that launched an exhaustive critique of American childbirth practices. During the 1970s, a variety of alternative birthing methods were introduced, including homelike birthing rooms in hospitals, the establishment of freestanding birthing centers, the restoration of birth at home, and renewed interest in midwifery.

The isolation and synthesis of female sex hormones, which led to the development of the birth control pill in the 1950s, also set the stage for modern reproductive technologies like in vitro fertilization by the late 1970s. The implications of new reproductive technologies developed in the 1980s, such as cloning, surrogacy, embryo transfer, and genetic engineering, continue to provide fertile ground for debate. Furthermore, reproductive rights, which include the right to choose procreation, contraception, abortion, and sterilization, also became one of the most politically divisive issues in the late twentieth and early twenty-first centuries. Feminist scholars have shown that these debates have the potential to challenge conventional histories and reshape the culturally constructed meanings of childbirth and reproduction.

BIBLIOGRAPHY

Borst, Charlotte G. *Catching Babies: The Professionalization of Childbirth, 1870–1920.* Cambridge, Mass: Harvard University Press, 1995.

Clarke, Adele E., and Virginia L. Oleson, eds. *Revisioning Women, Health, and Healing: Feminist, Cultural, and Technoscience Perspectives.* New York: Routledge, 1999.

Laqueur, Thomas. *Making Sex: Body and Gender from the Greeks to Freud.* Cambridge, Mass: Harvard University Press, 1990.

Leavitt, Judith Walzer. *Brought to Bed: Childbearing in America, 1750 to 1950.* Oxford, Eng.: Oxford University Press, 1986.

Litoff, Judy Barrett. *The American Midwife Debate: A Sourcebook on Its Modern Origins.* New York: Greenwood Press, 1986.

Wertz, Richard W., and Dorothy C. Wertz. *Lying In: A History of Childbirth in America.* New Haven, Conn.: Yale University Press, 1989.

Eric William Boyle

See also **Maternal and Child Health Care; Medical Profession; Medicine and Surgery; Women's Health.**

CHILDHOOD. Childhood as a historical construct can be defined as a constantly evolving series of steps toward adulthood shaped by a vast array of forces and ideas, ranging from ethnicity to class, from region to religion, and from gender to politics. Historians have tended to focus on two fairly distinct, if imprecise, phases of "growing up": childhood and youth. The former suggests a time of innocence, freedom from responsibility, and vulnerability. The latter includes but is not necessarily restricted to adolescence and is normally characterized as a period of "coming of age," when young people begin taking on the responsibilities and privileges of adulthood. Childhood suggests a period of shared expectations and closeness between parents and children, while youth, at least in the twentieth century, connotes a period of conflict between the generations, as hormonal changes and the new generation's drive for independence spark intense emotions and competition.

Changing Patterns of Childhood

In general terms, the historical arc of childhood in the United States shows several long, gradual, and not necessarily linear shifts. The "typical" free child in the British colonies of seventeenth-century North America belonged to a relatively homogeneous society—with similar values, religious faith, expectations, and opportunities—characterized by rural settlement patterns, informal education, and little contact with institutions outside the family. By the twentieth century, the "typical" child might encounter a bewildering variety of institutions, rules, and choices in a society characterized by wider differences in wealth, increasingly complex contacts with governments at all levels, and greater concentration in cities and suburbs.

Another shift, which began in the middle classes by the mid-nineteenth century but ultimately reached all ethnic and economic groups, was the "extension" of childhood. Although early Americans had distinguished between adults and children in legal terms (certain crimes carried lighter penalties for those under certain ages), on the farms and in the workshops of the British colonies in North America the transition from child to adult could take place as soon as the little available formal schooling was completed and a skill was learned. This gradual extension of childhood—actually, a stretching of adolescence, a term popularized at the turn of the twentieth century by child-psychologist G. Stanley Hall—occurred in several ways. Schooling touched more children for longer periods of time, as states began mandating minimum lengths for school years and cities began to create high schools. (The first high school appeared in Boston in 1821, but even as late as 1940, less than 20 percent of all Americans and 5 percent of African Americans had completed high school. By the 1960s, however, over 90 percent of all youth were in high school.) Lawmakers recognized the lengthening childhood of girls by raising the age of consent, even as the average age at which young women married fell during the nineteenth century from twenty-seven to twenty-two. Reformers in the 1910s and 1920s attempted to strengthen weak nineteenth-century child labor laws, which had generally simply established ten-hour work days for young people; in the 1930s further reforms were incorporated into NEW DEAL programs. The dramatic expansion of colleges and universities after WORLD WAR II added another layer to coming-of-age experiences, and by the 1990s, nearly two-thirds of high-school graduates attended institutions of higher learning, although the percentages for minorities were much lower (11 percent for African Americans and less than 1 percent for Native Americans).

Changes in the health and welfare of children were among the most striking transformations in childhood, especially in the twentieth century. Scientists developed vaccinations for such childhood scourges as diphtheria, smallpox, polio, and measles. Combined with government funding and public school requirements that students be vaccinated, these discoveries dramatically extended the average life expectancy. Not all children shared equally in these developments, however, as infant mortality in poor black families and on Indian reservations remained shockingly above average, even in the early twenty-first century. Prescriptions for "good" child care shifted from an emphasis on discipline among New England Puritans to the more relaxed standards of the child-centered Victorian middle classes to the confident, commonsense approach of the twentieth century's favorite dispenser of child-rearing advice, Dr. Benjamin Spock, whose *COMMON SENSE BOOK OF BABY AND CHILD CARE* first appeared in 1946.

Of course, there were children living in every era of American history who did not fit into the mainstream society of the United States. Native American and African American children, whether slave or free, enemies or wards of the state, were faced, by turns, it seems, with ostracism and hostility or with forced assimilation and overbearing "reformers." Children of immigrants from Ireland in the mid-nineteenth century and from eastern and southern Europe at the turn of the twentieth century encountered similar responses; their lives tended to veer away from the typical lives led by middle-class, native-born, Protestant American children. Immigrant children were crowded into shabby classrooms where teachers demanded rote memorization and forbade them to speak their native languages. SEGREGATION—de jure in the South, de facto in much of the rest of the country—characterized most school systems. Despite the transparent racism of the "separate but equal" philosophy, segregated schools were not equal. Spending for public schools serving black students was often a tenth of the amount spent on white schools, black teachers earned a fraction of their white colleagues' salaries, and black children, especially in the rural South, attended school for fewer days per year than white students. Asian American children were often placed into segregated schools in the West. Hispanic young people found that in some communities they were "white" and in others "colored," which understandably engendered confusion about their legal and social status. Native American children were sometimes forced to attend boarding schools—the most famous of which, the CARLISLE INDIAN SCHOOL in Pennsylvania and Hampton Institute in Virginia, were located half a country away from the students' homes—where they were stripped of traditional ways, given English names, and often subjected to harsh living conditions.

The Common Experiences of American Childhoods

Despite great differences in child-rearing customs, material and ethnic cultures, economic standing, and family size, there were important similarities in the ways that children grew up. For instance, all children were educated to meet the expectations and needs of their communities. Farm boys in New England or Georgia or Ohio were raised to become farmers, girls to perform the chores required of farm wives. The sons and daughters of southern planters were raised to fill their niches in plantation society, even as the children of slaves were educated informally to meet their responsibilities but also to protect their meager sense of self under the crushing burdens of the "peculiar institution." Native American children were taught to be hunters and warriors, wives and mothers, by instructors who were sometimes family members and other times teachers assigned to train large groups of children.

Members of every cultural group raised children to understand their particular traditions, including religious faiths, assumptions about proper use of resources, the importance of family, and appreciation for the larger culture. Each group developed and passed along to the next generation beliefs to sustain them and rituals to remind them of their heritages. Protestants and Catholics from Europe and, later, Latin America, sustained traditions of religious training culminating in first communion, confirmation, and other rites of passage; Jewish adolescents became members of their religious communities through Bar Mitzvahs and Bat Mitzvahs; Native American children participated in equivalent training and ceremonies designed to pass on their own origin myths and spirituality.

Despite the vast differences in cultures among the various ethnic and racial groups in the United States, the relatively steady decline in family size and the idealization of the family and of children—which proceeded at different rates among different groups and in different regions—affected children in a number of ways. For instance, as family size among the white, urban, middle class

dwindled, children became the center of the family's universe. They were given more room—literally and figuratively—and enjoyed greater privacy and opportunities to develop their own interests. Beginning in the mid-nineteenth century, the commercial publishing and toy industries began to take over the play and leisure time of children; nurseries and children's rooms filled with mass-produced toys and with books and magazines published exclusively for children. Although children continued to draw on their imaginations, as the decades passed, the sheer volume of commercially produced toys grew, their prices dropped, and more and more American children could have them. By the 1980s and 1990s, electronic toys, videotaped movies, and computer games, along with the still-burgeoning glut of television programming for children, had deeply altered play patterns; for instance, children tended to stay inside far more than in the past.

Some children and youth took advantage of the environments and the opportunities found in the West and in the cities of the late nineteenth and early twentieth centuries. Children of migrants and of immigrants differed from their parents in that, while the older generation was leaving behind former lives, children were, in effect, starting from scratch. Although they had to work on the farms and ranches of rural America and on the streets and in the sweatshops of the cities, young people managed to shape their lives to the environments in which they lived, which was reflected in their work and play. City streets became playgrounds where organized activities like stickball and more obscure, improvised street games were played, while intersections, theater districts, and saloons provided opportunities to earn money selling newspapers and other consumer items. Such jobs allowed children—mainly boys, but also a few girls—to contribute to the family economy and to establish a very real measure of independence from their parents. Similarly, life on farms and on ranches in the developing West, even as it forced children into heavy responsibilities and grinding labor, offered wide open spaces and a sense of freedom few of their parents could enjoy. Of course, in both of these scenarios, boys tended to enjoy more freedom than girls, who were often needed at home to care for younger siblings or married while still adolescents. The stereotype of the "little mother," a common image in the popular culture of the cities in the late nineteenth and early twentieth centuries, was an equally accurate description of the childhood work performed by rural girls.

Children and Childhood as Social and Political Issues

Even as children in different eras tried to assert themselves and to create their own worlds, a growing number of private and public institutions attempted to extend, improve, and standardize childhood. Motivated by morality, politics, economics, and compassion, reformers and politicians constructed a jungle of laws regulating the lives of children, founded organizations and institutions to train and to protect them, and fashioned a model childhood against which all Americans measured their own efforts to raise and nurture young people.

The middle class that formed in the crucible of nineteenth-century urbanization and industrialization set standards in many facets of American life, including the family. Bolstered by the "domestic ideal," a renewed evangelical religious faith, and a confidence in middle-class American values, the growing middle class established myriad reform movements affecting all aspects of society, including children. Orphanages increasingly replaced extended families; Children's Aid Societies pioneered the "placing out" of needy city children with foster parents living on farms or in small towns. Educational institutions and schoolbooks were designed to instill citizenship and patriotism, create responsible voters, and teach useful vocational skills during the first wave of educational reform early in the nineteenth century.

Children and youth were also the subjects of numerous reforms and social movements in the twentieth century. Settlement houses helped educate, assimilate, and nurture urban children with kindergartens, nurseries, art and other special classes, and rural outings. JUVENILE COURTS, which originated in Chicago in 1899 and quickly spread to other urban areas, separated young offenders from experienced criminals and offered counseling and education rather than incarceration. By the 1910s, child labor reformers began attacking more aggressively than their predecessors the practice of hiring youngsters to work in mines and factories and in the "street trades." The 1930s New Deal included provisions prohibiting the employment of individuals under fourteen years of age and regulating the employment of young people less than eighteen. The modest origins of the U.S. CHILDREN'S BUREAU in 1912 paved the way for greater government advocacy for the health and welfare of children. The civil rights movement of the 1950s and 1960s centered partly on children, as the BROWN V. BOARD OF EDUCATION OF TOPEKA (1954) Supreme Court decision inspired hundreds of individual lawsuits aimed at desegregating the public schools of the South, and, by the 1970s and 1980s, northern school districts. The 1935 Social Security Act included programs like Aid to Dependent Children, which were expanded during the GREAT SOCIETY of the mid-1960s in the form of HEAD START, MEDICAID, school lunch programs, and need-based college scholarships. Finally, late-twentieth-century campaigns to reform welfare obviously affected the children of mothers moved from welfare rolls into the minimum-wage job market, while pupils at public and private schools alike were touched by efforts to improve education through school vouchers and other educational reforms.

The "Discovery of Childhood" and American Children

One of the most controversial elements of the study of children's history is the degree to which children were "miniature adults" in the colonial period, "discovered"

only as family size dwindled and the expanding middle class embraced the concept of the child-centered family. Most historians of American children and youth believe children were always treated as a special class of people, emotionally, politically, and spiritually. Even in the large families of colonial New England or in late-nineteenth-century immigrant ghettos, the high mortality rate did not mean individual children were not cherished.

But Americans' attitudes toward their children have changed from time to time. Because of their necessary labor on the farms and in the shops of early America, children were often considered vital contributors to their families' economies. Public policy regarding poor or orphaned children balanced the cost of maintaining them with the benefits of their labor. For instance, most orphanages, in addition to providing a basic education, also required children to work in the institutions' shops and gardens. Lawsuits and settlements for injuries and deaths of children due to accidents often hinged on the value to parents of the child's future labor, similarly, up through the mid- to late-nineteenth century child-custody cases were normally settled in favor of fathers, at least partly because they were believed to be entitled to the product of their offspring's labor, both girls and boys. The child-nurturing attitudes of the twentieth century, however, recognized the value of children more for their emotional than their economic contributions. Lawsuits and custody settlements came to focus more on the loss of companionship and affection and on the psychological and emotional health of the children and parents than on the youngsters' economic value.

Childhood at the Turn of the Twenty-first Century

Many of the issues that have characterized children's experiences since the colonial period continue to shape their lives nearly four hundred years later. Youth still work, but their jobs tend to be part time and their earnings tend to be their own. For girls, smaller families have eliminated the need for the "little mothers" who had helped maintain immigrant and working-class households generations earlier. The educational attainment and health of minority children, while improving, still lags behind that of white children, with one shocking twist: the most serious health threat facing male, African American teenagers is homicide. Yet, however much the demographics, economics, politics, and ethics of childhood have changed, the basic markers for becoming an adult—completing one's schooling, finding an occupation, marriage—remained the same.

BIBLIOGRAPHY

Berrol, Selma. *Immigrants at School: New York City, 1898–1914.* New York: Arno Press, 1978. The original edition was published in 1967.

Bremner, Robert H., ed. *Children and Youth in America: A Documentary History.* 3 vols. Cambridge: Harvard University Press, 1970–1974.

Calvert, Karin. *Children in the House: The Material Culture of Early Childhood, 1600–1900*. Boston: Northeastern University Press, 1992.

Cremin, Lawrence A. *American Education: The Metropolitan Experience, 1876–1980*. New York: Harper and Row, 1988.

Fass, Paula, and Mary Ann Mason, eds. *Childhood in America*. New York: New York University Press, 2000.

Graff, Harvey. *Conflicting Paths: Growing Up in America*. Cambridge, Mass.: Harvard University Press, 1995.

Hawes, Joseph M., and N. Ray Hiner. *American Childhood: A Research Guide and Historical Handbook*. Westport, Conn.: Greenwood Press, 1985.

Mason, Mary Ann. *From Father's Property to Children's Rights: The History of Child Custody in the United States*. New York: Columbia University Press, 1994.

Nasaw, David. *Children of the City: At Work & At Play*. Garden City, N.J.: Anchor Press, 1985.

Szasz, Margaret. *Education and the American Indian: The Road to Self-Determination Since 1928*. Albuquerque: University of New Mexico Press, 1974.

West, Elliott. *Growing Up in Twentieth-Century America: A History and Reference Guide*. Westport, Conn: Greenwood Press, 1996.

Youcha, Geraldine. *Minding the Children: Child Care in America from Colonial Times to the Present*. New York: Scribner, 1995.

Zelizer, Viviana A. *Pricing the Priceless Child: The Changing Social Value of Children*. New York: Basic Books, 1985; repr. Princeton, N.J.: Princeton University Press, 1994.

James Marten

See also **Child Abuse; Child Care; Child Labor; Education.**

CHILDREN, MISSING.

The phenomenon of missing children gained national attention in 1979 with the highly publicized disappearance of a six-year-old boy named Etan Patz in New York City. Since then the numbers of children reported missing nationally have increased dramatically. The Missing Children's Act of 1982 assisted the collation of nationwide data about missing children. In that year, 100,000 children under the age of eighteen were reported missing; a decade later, the number had risen to 800,000. While the increase might have been partly due to more reporting, experts pointed to other factors, including increased divorce rates, decreased parental supervision, and high numbers of teenage runaways associated with domestic violence and sexual abuse. Although sensational cases of serial killers incited widespread fear, a far more common occurrence involved children taken for a brief period of time, usually by an acquaintance or family member. A 1980s survey indicated that each year 350,000 children were taken by family members, 450,000 ran away, 3,000 were kidnapped and sexually assaulted, and 127,000 were expelled from home by their families. This compared with 200–300 children murdered or abducted by strangers for ransom.

In the 1980s and 1990s most states developed training programs to help police locate missing children, and national clearinghouses offered suggestions to parents and children to ward off abductions. While these techniques have led to the recovery of some missing children, they do not address social, familial, and psychological causes underlying the missing children phenomenon. Most of the children abducted by family members are taken by a parent violating a custody agreement, and 99 percent are eventually returned. Despite the relatively small number of children killed or otherwise never found, these cases command the bulk of media attention and parental fear and often distract attention from the other circumstances and social factors associated with missing children.

BIBLIOGRAPHY

Fass, Paula S. *Kidnapped: Child Abduction in America*. New York: Oxford University Press, 1997.

Tedisco, James N., and Michele A. Paludi. *Missing Children: A Psychological Approach to Understanding the Causes and Consequences of Stranger and Non-Stranger Abduction of Children*. Albany: State University of New York Press, 1996.

Anne C. Weiss/A. R.

See also **Child Abuse; Domestic Violence.**

CHILDREN'S BUREAU.

Signed into law by President William Howard Taft in 1912, during the Progressive Era, the U.S. Children's Bureau (CB) is the oldest federal agency for children and is currently one of six bureaus within the United States Department of Health and Human Services' Administration for Children and Families, Administration on Children, Youth and Families. The Children's Bureau was the brainchild of Lillian D. Wald and Florence Kelley, pioneers in children's rights advocacy. After nine years of efforts and a White House Conference on the Care of Dependent Children, this federal agency was created to investigate and promote the best means for protecting a right to childhood; the first director was Julia Clifford Lathrop, a woman credited with helping to define the role of women in public policy development.

For its first thirty-four years of existence, the bureau was the only agency focused solely on the needs of children. Lathrop and her successors were the primary authors of child welfare policy through 1946, during this time they made significant contributions in raising awareness about the needs of children and families in both urban and rural settings. Their efforts were most evident in the reduction of the nation's maternal and infant mortality rate. The maternal mortality rate dropped from 60.8 deaths per 10,000 live births in 1915 to 15.7 in 1946. The infant mortality rate dropped from 132 deaths per 1,000 live births in 1912 to 33.8 in 1946. The agency was also notable in this time for its studies that recognized race, ethnicity, class, and region as factors in the experiences of children. In 1946, government reorganization transferred the agency to the newly formed Federal Security Agency, and shifted several of its administrative responsibilities to other agencies, thus decreasing the agency's power and status within the federal government.

The bureau did fall short during these first three decades in advocating for children from non-traditional households, including children of working mothers. The agency also failed to recognize and advocate the needs of children who did not come from middle class families, equating a normal home life with middle class ideals. The agency's solution for many struggling families was to place their children in foster homes where they could experience a "normal home life."

Today the bureau is headed by an associate commissioner who advises the Commissioner of the Administration on Children, Youth and Families on matters related to child welfare, including child abuse and neglect, child protective services, family preservation and support, adoption, foster care and independent living. It recommends legislative and budgetary proposals, operational planning system objectives and initiatives, and projects and issue areas for evaluation, research and demonstration activities. With a budget of over four billion dollars, the agency provides grants to states, tribes and communities to operate such services as child protective services, family preservation and support, foster care, adoption, and independent living.

The Children's Bureau has five branches: the Office of Child Abuse and Neglect; the Division of Policy; the Division of Program Implementation; the Division of Data, Research, and Innovation; and the Division of Child Welfare Capacity Building. Through these five branches, the agency works toward the enforcement of the Child Abuse Prevention and Treatment Act (CAPTA), the Children's Justice Act, the Indian Child Welfare Act, and directs the National Center on Child Abuse and Neglect Information Clearinghouse and the National Adoption Information Clearinghouse.

BIBLIOGRAPHY

Children's Bureau, U.S. Department of Health and Human Services, The Administration for Children and Families. Online, http://www.acf.dhhs.gov/programs/cb/index.htm, accessed February 23, 2002.

Levine, Murray, and Adeline Levine. *A Social History of Helping Services: Clinic, Court, School and Community.* New York: Appleton-Century-Crofts, 1970.

Lindenmeyer, Kriste. *"A Right to Childhood": The U.S. Children's Bureau and Child Welfare, 1912–46.* Urbana: University of Chicago Press, 1997.

Mary Anne Hansen

See also **Health and Human Services, Department of; Progressive Movement.**

CHILDREN'S RIGHTS. The legal status of children has evolved over the course of American history, with frequent changes in the balance of rights among the state, parents, and children in response to social and economic transitions. Over time, the state has taken an increasingly active role in protecting and educating children, thereby diminishing the rights of parents. It is fair to say, however, that children's rights as a full-blown independent concept has not developed. Even today there are only pockets of law in which children's rights are considered separate from those of their parents, and these are largely in the areas of reproductive rights and criminal justice.

For the whole of the colonial period and early Republic, Americans viewed children as economic assets whose labor was valuable to their parents and other adults. In this early era, the father as the head of the household had the complete right to the custody and control of his children both during the marriage and in the rare event of divorce. A father could hire out a child for wages or apprentice a child to another family without the mother's consent. Education, vocational training, and moral development were also the father's responsibility. The state took responsibility for children in one of several circumstances: the death of a father or both parents, the incompetence or financial inability of parents to care for or train their children, and the birth of illegitimate children. With these events the two major considerations in determining the fate of the child focused on the labor value of the child and the ability of the adults to properly maintain and supervise the child. Widows often lost their children because they were no longer able to support them. In the era before orphanages and adoption, such children were usually apprenticed or "placed out" to another family, who would support them in exchange for their services. A child born out of wedlock was known as "*filius nullius*" or "child of nobody" and the official in charge of enforcing the town's poor law was authorized to "place out" the child with a family.

Over the course of the nineteenth century, as more emphasis was placed on child nurture and education, various states passed legislation attempting to regulate child labor, largely by requiring a certain amount of schooling for children working in factories. However, such measures were hampered by the presence of loopholes and a lack of effective enforcement machinery. For example, in 1886 the state of New York passed a Factory Act prohibiting factory work by children under the age of thirteen, but appointed only two inspectors to oversee the state's 42,000 factories. The legal concept of "the best interest of the child" was initiated, the first recognition that children had rights independent of their parents. Under this rule, mothers gained favor as the parent better able to handle the emotional and nurturing needs of children of "tender years," and mothers were likely to prevail over fathers in the custody battles following the increasingly common event of divorce. Orphanages were introduced as a more child-centered approach than "placing out" for caring for children whose parents were dead or unable to care for them.

At the beginning of the twentieth century a coalition of civic-minded adults, popularly known as "child-savers," fought for a variety of legal reforms designed to protect children. Efforts were made to enact more effective child labor laws, although these efforts were initially thwarted at the federal level. In *Hammer v. Dagenhart* (1918) the Supreme Court ruled that in its attempt to regulate child labor Congress had exceeded its constitutional authority and violated the rights of the states. The Fair Labor Standards Act of 1938 finally succeeded in prohibiting employment of children under sixteen in industries engaging in interstate commerce. The early reformers were more successful with regard to compulsory school attendance and the establishment of juvenile courts, which handled children who were either neglected by their parents or delinquent in their own behavior. The first such court was established in Chicago in 1899. Government took a decisively more active role, irrevocably reducing parental authority and laying the ground for our modern child welfare and educational structure.

It was not until the civil rights movement of the 1960s that children gained some civil rights of their own, apart from their parents. In 1965 three Quaker schoolchildren were suspended for wearing black armbands in their classroom to protest the Vietnam War. In *Tinker v. Des Moines School District* (1969) the Supreme Court stated that students do not "shed their constitutional rights to freedom of speech or expression at the schoolhouse gate." Yet the Court in the 1970s allowed censorship of school newspapers and gave school authorities wide discretion to search student lockers.

The direction of the Court continued toward limiting student rights. In the early twenty-first century, the Supreme Court gave public school officials much wider authority to test students for drugs, setting the stage for districts to move toward screening everyone who attends school. In *Board of Education v. Lindsay Earls* (2002) the Supreme Court permitted districts to require random tests of any student who takes part in extracurricular activities such as band, chorus, or academic competition. Previously, the Court had upheld mandatory testing of student athletes.

It is in the arena of juvenile justice that courts have most seriously considered rights for children. In 1965, the same year that the Quaker children were protesting the Vietnam War in Des Moines, in Arizona fifteen-year-old Gerald Gault was charged with making an anonymous obscene phone call to an elderly neighbor. Without the benefit of a lawyer or a trial, Gerald was sentenced to incarceration in a boys' correctional institution until age twenty-one. The ensuing landmark Supreme Court decision, *In Re Gault* (1967), later expanded by several subsequent decisions, gave children who were defendants in juvenile court criminal actions nearly all the due process

protections that adult defendants receive in the regular criminal courts, including lawyers and the right against self-incrimination. The rights to a speedy trial, bail, or a jury were still lacking at the close of the twentieth century.

In the 1990s, state legislatures, responding to increased juvenile crime, grew eager to throw juveniles into adult courts at ever-younger ages, and to apply adult punishments to children. In most states a fourteen-year-old can be tried for murder as an adult, and the Supreme Court has declared that a sixteen-year-old can be sentenced to execution (*Thompson v. Oklahoma*, 1988).

While the Supreme Court has been willing to recognize some limited rights for children with regard to schools, courts, and other governmental institutions, it has been reluctant to grant children rights that might interfere with those of their parents. Much of this concern has focused on abortion. Soon after *Roe v. Wade* (1973) the Court conceded that an adult woman's right to abortion extended to adolescent girls as well, but it also carved out a good deal of room for parents' rights. The Court decided that individual states could pass parental consent laws. However, with the ambivalence typical of its earlier decisions on children's rights issues, the Court also held that a girl could bypass her parents by going to a judge. If the judge declared that she was a mature minor, the decision would be hers alone (*Bellotti v. Baird II*, 1979).

A minor's consent to abortion is a contentious issue. States are seriously divided on the issue, and the battles continue. There has, however, been some change on the somewhat less controversial issue of adolescent consent to other sensitive medical procedures, such as the treatment of sexually transmitted diseases and drug and alcohol abuse. In many states, a doctor who cannot give an adolescent an aspirin without parental consent can treat the minor for a venereal disease. On the other hand, in sharp contrast to the adult protections provided children who face possible criminal incarceration, the Supreme Court ruled in *Parham v. JR* (1979) that parents retain the right to commit their minor child to a mental health facility upon the recommendation of a physician with no judicial review. A child "volunteered" by his parents need not be a "danger to self or others"—the adult standard for commitment—but only deemed in need of medical treatment.

In family law, the "child's best interest" is always the standard in determining child custody between biological parents, but in practice the child is rarely granted a representative in judicial proceedings where custody is determined, and the preference of an adolescent child is only one consideration in a long list of factors to be considered in most states. The United Nations has in some ways gone further than the American legal system in expanding and clarifying the rights of the child. The framework of principles articulated in the 1989 U.N. Convention on the Rights of the Child provides that children have a right to a nurturing environment in accordance with their developmental needs; the right to have their voices heard in accordance with their ages; the right to legal representation; and the right to economic and emotional support from their parents and from the state.

BIBLIOGRAPHY

Ladd, Rosalind Ekman. *Children's Rights Re-visioned: Philosophical Readings.* Belmont, Calif.: Wadsworth, 1996.

Mason, Mary Ann. *From Fathers' Property to Children's Rights: A History of Child Custody in America.* New York: Columbia University Press, 1994.

Mnookin, Robert H., and D. Kelly Weisberg. *Child, Family, and State: Problems and Materials on Children and the Law.* 4th ed. Gaithersburg, Md.: Aspen, 2000.

Mary Ann Mason

See also **Child Labor; *In Re Gault*; Society for the Prevention of Cruelty to Children.**

CHILE, RELATIONS WITH. Although the United States began official diplomatic relations with Chile in 1823, the two nations had little contact throughout most of the nineteenth century. Chile looked to Europe for most of its cultural, economic, and military connections. The United States remained a relatively minor trading partner. In the late 1800s, Chile began to assert its claim to power in the Western Hemisphere, and in the War of the Pacific (1879–1883) decisively defeated Peru and Bolivia. In 1891, a minor incident in Valparaíso in which a group of drunken U.S. sailors fought with some Chilean civilians was blown entirely out of proportion, with both nations claiming that their national honor had been sullied.

During most of the twentieth century, Chile remained largely aloof from closer relations with the United States. Although the impact of the two world wars did lead to an increase in American trade and investment in Chile, the United States never dominated the Chilean economy as it did elsewhere in Latin America. Chile continued to follow an independent political and diplomatic course, best evidenced by the fact that, despite intense U.S. pressure, Chile was one of the last Latin American nations to sever diplomatic ties with the Axis during World War II.

Following World War II, U.S. interest in Chile increased. As Cold War battle lines were drawn, the United States began to see Chile as a more and more valuable asset in the struggle against communism. Chile's massive deposits of copper, and smaller but still valuable deposits of iron ore, molybdenum, and nitrates, acquired tremendous importance for the United States. After the rise to power of Fidel Castro in Cuba in 1959, the United States increased its efforts to establish closer relations with all of Latin America. During the 1960s a coalition of the Chilean socialist party, headed by Dr. Salvador Allende, and communist party, steadily gained power. The United States secretly pumped millions of dollars to Allende's opponents in order to forestall his victory in the 1964 Chilean presidential election. In 1970, the United States again resorted to covert efforts to influence the Chilean election, but Allende managed a slim electoral victory. Allende almost immediately affirmed the worst fears of U.S. policymakers by nationalizing many of Chile's most important industries and moving towards closer relations with the Soviet Union and Cuba. The United States reacted by working to isolate Chile economically, and also covertly funded opposition forces plotting against Allende. In 1973, the Chilean military, secretly aided by the United States, toppled Allende, who then reportedly committed suicide. Under the leadership of General Augusto Pinochet, a military dictatorship ruled Chile for the next sixteen years.

BIBLIOGRAPHY

Pike, Fredrick B. *Chile and the United States, 1880–1962: The Emergence of Chile's Social Crisis and the Challenge to United States Diplomacy.* Notre Dame, Ind.: University of Notre Dame Press, 1963.

Sater, William F. *Chile and the United States: Empires in Conflict.* Athens: University of Georgia Press, 1990.

Michael L. Krenn

See also **Latin America, Relations with.**

CHINA, RELATIONS WITH. America has always been interested in China, but rarely has evidenced much understanding of the Middle Kingdom or of the different ways that the two countries viewed political, economic, and social issues over the years. In 1784 at Canton harbor, the empress of China opened trade between the new United States, now excluded from the European mercantilist system of trade, and China. At that time, China was, for the most part, self-sufficient economically, and America had few goods to offer until the expansion of the fur trade in the Pacific Northwest.

Later, in the aftermath of the Opium War (1839–1842) and the British imposition of the so-called unequal treaty system during the late nineteenth century, the United States sought to increase its presence in China. Americans came, as did Europeans, bringing religion (missionaries), drugs (opium largely from Turkey rather than, as did the British, from India), and warriors (naval forces and marines). In 1844, by the terms of the Treaty of Wanghsia, the Qing rulers of China extended most-favored-nation status to the United States.

In the 1840s, the United States settled the Oregon boundary dispute with Great Britain and defeated Mexico, thereby acquiring a long Pacific coastline and several major anchorages. Trade with and interest in China certainly increased, however, the locus of activity shifted eastward. As the British forced open ports north of Canton and as opium continued to devastate South China, many Chinese would emigrate and a goodly number immigrated to North America (the BURLINGAME TREATY of 1868 helped facilitate such immigration), settling eventually in so-called Chinatowns in Vancouver, San Francisco, and elsewhere. Indeed, the Chinese phrase for San Francisco is "jiu jin shan" or "old gold mountain." As the United States began constructing the transcontinental railway and also began mining the great mineral wealth of the West, many of these immigrants found terrible, dangerous work. As the railroad building boom wound down and as the tempo of mining operations changed and became less labor intensive, the periodic cycle of boom and bust turned to depression. Resistance to Chinese emigration increased greatly and violence sometimes resulted. In response, Congress passed the CHINESE EXCLUSION ACT of 1882, suspending Chinese immigration for ten years and declaring Chinese ineligible for naturalization. It was the only time in American history when such drastic immigration legislation was aimed at excluding a single ethnic group.

The pace of China's disintegration accelerated in the aftermath of the SINO-JAPANESE WAR of 1894–1895, and U.S. Secretary of State John Hay produced the famous "Open Door" notes of 1899 and 1900. The western imperialist powers and Japan moved from Britain's model of informal empire that had dominated much of the mid-nineteenth century to grabbing territory and carving up China. While Hay certainly sought to preserve China for U.S. trade, he also was acting to preserve the idea of China and to help improve the image of the United States in China. The decision to use money from the BOXER REBELLION (1900) indemnity to educate Chinese youth also won favor, especially when compared to the actions of European countries and Japan.

The pace of change accelerated in China during the early twentieth century, as the Qing dynasty collapsed, Sun Yat-sen's Guomindang nationalists temporarily were frustrated by Yuan Shih K'ai, a military dictator, and China began a slow devolution into warlordism. Meanwhile, in 1915, as Europe was locked in mortal combat in World War I, the Japanese minister to China delivered the infamous "21 Demands" to Yuan; had Yuan agreed to them, China would have been made virtually a Japanese protectorate. President Woodrow Wilson helped Yuan by pressing Japan to withdraw the demands and the crisis ended.

Sino-American relations suffered following World War I. Modern Chinese nationalism began with the May Fourth Movement on 4 May 1919, when Chinese students in Beijing and other major cities rallied and were joined by townspeople to protest the decision of the major powers to transfer Germany's concession in China to Japan. To China, it was outrageous, while, to President Wilson, it was a price to pay for passage of the Versailles Peace Treaty and to achieve his cherished League of Nations. The Washington Naval Conference (1921–1922) and the various treaties the attending powers signed, promising to respect each other's possessions in the Pacific and calling of an Open Door to China, in the words of historian Akira Iriye, left East Asia in an unstable state. Japan began taking aggressive action—first with the 1928 assas-

sination of Chang Tso-lin, a Manchurian warlord, and then with the Mukden Incident in September 1931 and the takeover of this large and resource rich part of northeastern China. President Herbert Hoover and his secretary of state, Henry Stimson, would not intervene during these beginning years of the Great Depression but they engaged in a kind of moral diplomacy. During the 1930s, as Japan began expanding first into the Chinese provinces adjoining Manchuria, later crossing the Great Wall, and finally engaging in a more general war against the Nationalist government, President Franklin Roosevelt secretly supported the Chinese. Roosevelt ultimately began imposing sanctions on Japan, both to halt its aggression and to force it out of China.

After World War II (1939–1945), the United States became caught up in the Chinese civil war between the Nationalists and the communists, which had begun nearly two decades before. American marines went to North China to help accept the surrender of some 500,000 Japanese troops and found themselves defending communications and transportation as Nationalist leader Jiang Jieshr moved his best troops from southwest China to Manchuria. Communist leader Mao Zedong and his communist guerrillas, however, first won an overwhelming victory in Manchuria and later secured north China, crossed the wide Yangtze River and, in 1949, forced Jiang to flee the mainland for the island redoubt of Taiwan.

Conflict next broke out in Korea in 1950, which soon widened into a fight between the United States and the new and communist People's Republic of China. As the Korean War dragged on until 1953, U.S. Senator Joseph McCarthy began searching for communists in the State Department and other government agencies, while some politicians questioned "who lost China" and a witchhunt began. Thereafter, in the wars breaking out in Indochina, the French received increased support from the United States while the Viet Minh received support from communist China. The Geneva Conference of 1954 brought a temporary halt to the fighting, but it resumed several years later, and President John Kennedy, convinced by the so-called domino theory (that if communists were permitted to take over Vietnam all Asia would eventually fall to communism), expanded the U.S. presence. When President Lyndon Johnson ordered large numbers of troops to South Vietnam beginning in 1964, he did so in part because he believed that the Chinese communist rulers needed to be contained.

In the summer of 1971 President Richard Nixon announced that he would travel to China early in 1972. In February, Nixon flew to Shanghai, then traveled to Beijing and met with both Premier Zhou Enlai and communist leader Mao Zedong. The visit benefited both the United States, which was seeking to balance Soviet expansionism and reduce its involvement in Vietnam, and China, which was concerned about the possibility of a Soviet pre-emptive military strike within its borders.

151

Since Nixon's visit, tens of thousands of Americans have visited China, and many thousands of Chinese have come to the United States to study and to work. Trade has increased, especially if the goods made in China and transshipped through Hong Kong are considered. Nevertheless, great points of stress still exist in the Sino-American relationship. Taiwan remains a source of tension, for Chinese on both sides of the Taiwan Strait believe there is only one China, while the United States continues to support, in a fashion, a separate Republic of China situated on Taiwan. Another source of tension is that China does not always honor patent and copyright regulations and enjoys a huge balance of trade surplus with America while restricting American imports into the mainland. The Chinese crackdown on young people gathered in Tiananmen Square in June 1989 also upset the United States, although China viewed it as an internal matter. In addition, for many years, China sold arms to various groups that threatened the stability around the world and, often, American interests. In the aftermath of 11 September 2001, there appeared to be more concurrence in Sino-American thought on the threat of radical Islamic-based terrorism. The United States is currently the world's preeminent superpower, while China is the emerging power in eastern Asia; the relationship will have to continue to mature and develop.

BIBLIOGRAPHY

Anderson, David L. *Imperialism and Idealism: American Diplomats in China, 1861–1898.* Bloomington: Indiana University Press, 1985.

Cohen, Warren I. *America's Response to China: A History of Sino-American Relations.* 4th ed. New York: Columbia University Press, 2000.

Davis, Elizabeth Van Wie, ed. *Chinese Perspectives on Sino-American Relations, 1950–2000.* Lewiston, N.Y.: Edward Mellen Press, 2000.

Fairbank, John King. *The United States and China.* 4th ed. Cambridge, Mass.: Harvard University Press, 1983.

Foot, Rosemary. *The Practice of Power: U.S. Relations with China since 1949.* New York: Oxford University Press, 1995.

Ross, Robert S., and Jiang Changbin, eds. *Re-examining the Cold War: U.S.–China Diplomacy, 1954–1973.* Cambridge, Mass.: Harvard University Press, 2001.

Van Alstyne, Richard W. *The United States and East Asia.* London: Thames and Hudson, 1973.

Young, Marilyn. *The Rhetoric of Empire: American China Policy, 1895–1901.* Cambridge, Mass.: Harvard University Press, 1968.

Charles M. Dobbs

See also **China, U.S. Armed Forces in; China Trade; Chinese Americans.**

CHINA, U.S. ARMED FORCES IN. The United States maintained a military presence in China throughout the first half of the twentieth century. After the Chinese Revolution of 1911 various treaties and extraterritorial arrangements allowed the U.S. to reinforce its garrisons in China. At this time, the U.S. supported a battalion-sized Marine legation guard at Beijing and an Infantry Regiment at Tianjin. Elements of the U.S. Asiatic Fleet frequented Chinese ports and the Americans established a patrol on the Chang River.

Throughout the 1920s, the U.S. bolstered its garrisons in China. In March 1927, after Jiang Jie-shi marched on Shanghai, the U.S. sent the Third Marine Brigade to help protect the International Settlement. The Fourth Marine Regiment remained at Shanghai while the rest of the brigade marched to Tianjin, where they stayed until January 1929. Sino-Japanese hostilities caused the U.S. to deploy more troops to China in the 1930s. In 1932 the Thirty-first U.S. Infantry Regiment joined the Fourth Marines in Shanghai. The Sixth Marines reinforced the city in 1937. In December 1937, a Japanese air attack sank the U.S. gunboat *Panay* in the Chang. In 1938 the Sixth Marines and the Fifteenth U.S. Infantry departed China. During WORLD WAR II the Fourth Marines left Shanghai for the Philippines in November 1941 and were eventually captured at Corregidor.

In January 1942 Jiang Jie-shi and Lieutenant General Joseph W. Stilwell, his chief of staff, waged war against Japan in the China-Burma-India (CBI) Theater. After the bitter retreat from Burma, Stilwell proposed a thirty-division Chinese Nationalist force for a fresh Burma campaign in the spring of 1943. Jiang was more attracted to the air strategy proposed by Major General Claire L. Chennault. With the entry of the United States into World War II, Chennault took command of the U.S. China Air Task Force. In May 1944 the U.S. military deployed B-29s to Chinese airfields. The Japanese reacted by launching an offensive that overran most of the airfields, and the American military withdrew its B-29s to India. As a result, the CBI was split into two theaters—China and India-Burma—and U.S. commanders sent Lieutenant General Albert C. Wedemeyer to replace Stilwell in China.

China's disappointing contribution to the Allied effort in World War II was in large part the result of Jiang's deliberate policy of conserving his strength to fight the Chinese Communists. With the end of the war, the 55,000-man Third Marine Amphibious Corps arrived in North China to disarm and repatriate the Japanese and to bolster Nationalist forces. Meanwhile, a Soviet army had occupied Manchuria and turned over key ports and cities to the Communists. In January 1946 General George C. Marshall arrived to arbitrate between the Nationalists and Communists. There was a short-lived truce, but by July 1946 it was obvious that Marshall had failed to convince either side to settle their differences peacefully.

The U.S. Marines reduced their occupation force in China until just two battalions were left by the spring of 1949. By then, Mao Ze-dong's Communist forces had defeated the Nationalists. By the end of June the last Amer-

allowed reentry of Chinese who had left the country to visit their families in China. Because Chinese women were few and interracial marriage was illegal at the time, it was almost impossible for most of the Chinese immigrants to have families in the United States. Chinese population declined drastically during the period of exclusion. By 1930 the population had been reduced to 74,954. The 1882 act also made Chinese immigrants "ineligible to citizenship." In the early twentieth century, California and some other western states passed laws to prohibit aliens "ineligible to citizenship" to own land.

Community Organizations and Activities

Living and working in largely segregated ethnic neighborhoods in urban areas, Chinese Americans created many mutual aid networks based on kinship, native places, and common interests. Clan and district associations were two of the most important Chinese immigrant organizations. The clan associations served as the bases for immigration networks. With their own occupational specialties, they assisted members in finding jobs. Both the clan and district associations provided new immigrants with temporary lodging and arbitrated disputes among the members; the district associations also maintained cemeteries and shipped the exhumed remains of the deceased to their home villages for final burial.

Hierarchically above the clan and the district associations was the Chinese Consolidated Benevolent Association (CCBA), known to the American public as the Chinese Six Companies. The CCBA provided leadership for the community. It sponsored many court cases to challenge discriminatory laws. When the Board of Supervisors in San Francisco passed an ordinance to make it impossible for Chinese laundrymen to stay in business, the Chinese took their case to court. In *Yick Wo v. Hopkins* (1886), the court decided that the ordinance was discriminatory in its application and therefore violated the equal-protection clause of the Constitution. In another landmark case, *UNITED STATES v. WONG KIM ARK* (1898), the court ruled that anyone born in the United States was a citizen, and that citizenship by birth could not be taken away, regardless of that person's ethnicity.

Also important is the Chinese American Citizens Alliance (CACA), organized by second-generation Chinese Americans who were born in the United States. In 1930, after several years of CACA's lobbying activities, Congress passed a law that allowed U.S. citizens to bring in their Chinese wives, if the marriage had taken place before 1924. In 1946 this privilege was extended to all citizens.

World War II and Postwar Development

During World War II, about 16,000 Chinese American men and women served in the U.S. military; 214 lost their lives. In addition, thousands of Chinese Americans worked in the nation's defense industries. For the first time in the twentieth century, a large number of Chinese Americans had the opportunity to work outside Chinatowns. In 1943,

as a goodwill gesture to its wartime ally China, the United States repealed the exclusion acts. Although China was given only a token quota of 105 immigrants each year, the repeal changed the status of alien Chinese from "inadmissible" to "admissible" and granted Chinese immigrants the right of naturalization.

The most visible change after the war was the growth of families. After the repeal of the exclusion acts, new immigration regulations became applicable to alien Chinese. The 1945 War Brides Act allowed the admission of alien dependents of World War II veterans without quota limits. A June 1946 act extended this privilege to fiancées and fiancés of war veterans. The Chinese Alien Wives of American Citizens Act of August 1946 further granted admission outside the quota to Chinese wives of American citizens. More than 6,000 Chinese women gained entry between 1945 and 1948. As women constituted the majority of the new immigrants and many families were reunited, the sex ratio of the Chinese American population underwent a significant change. In 1940 there were 2.9 Chinese men for every Chinese woman in the United States (57,389 men versus 20,115 women). By 1960 this ratio was reduced to 1.35 to 1 (135,430 men versus 100,654 women).

The postwar years witnessed a geographical dispersion of the Chinese American population, as more employment opportunities outside Chinatowns became available. But regardless of where they lived, Chinese Americans continued to face the same difficulties as members of an ethnic minority group in the United States.

The Communist victory in the Chinese Civil War in 1949 significantly altered U.S.-China relations and intensified conflict among Chinese American political groups. As the Korean War turned China into an archenemy of the United States, many Chinese Americans lived in fear of political accusations. In the name of investigating Communist subversive activities, the U.S. government launched an all-out effort to break up Chinese immigration networks. The investigation further divided the Chinese American community. When the Justice Department began the "Chinese confession program" in 1956 (it ended in 1966), even family members were pressured to turn against one another.

Post-1965 Immigration and Community

The 1965 Immigration Act established a new quota system. Each country in the Eastern Hemisphere was given the same quota of 20,000 per year. In addition, spouses, minor children under age twenty-one, and parents of U.S. citizens could enter as nonquota immigrants. In the late 1960s and the 1970s, Chinese immigrants came largely from Taiwan, because the United States did not have diplomatic relations with the People's Republic of China until 1979. Between 1979 and 1982, China shared with Taiwan the quota of 20,000 per year. Since 1982 China and Taiwan have each received a quota of 20,000 annually (later increased to 25,620). Hong Kong, a British colony

Chinese Laborers. Thousands of immigrants working for the Central Pacific helped to build the western half of the first transcontinental railroad; some remained, such as these men photographed in the Sierra Nevada in 1880, but the sometimes violent anti-Chinese movement forced many to move on.

until its return to China in 1997, received a quota of 200 from the 1965 Immigration Act. This number increased several times in subsequent years. From 1993 to 1997, Hong Kong received an annual quota of 25,620. With three separate quotas, more Chinese were able to immigrate to the United States than any other ethnic group. Beginning in the late 1970s, a large number of Chinese-ancestry immigrants also entered the United States as refugees from Vietnam. In addition, some immigrants of Chinese ancestry came from other Southeast Asian countries and various Latin American countries. The 1990 census counted 1,645,472 Chinese Americans. Ten years later, Chinese-ancestry population numbered near 2.9 million.

Because so many new immigrants arrived after 1965, a large number of Chinese Americans were foreign born in the year 2000. California had the largest concentration of Chinese Americans, followed by New York, Hawaii, and Texas. Unlike the early Cantonese-speaking immigrants from the rural areas of Guangdong province, the post-1965 immigrants were a diverse group with regional, linguistic, cultural, and socioeconomic differences. Many of them were urban professionals before emigrating. The new immigrants often found that their former education or skills were not marketable in the United States, and many of them had to work for low wages and long hours. A very high percentage of Chinese American women

worked outside the home. New immigrant women often found work in garment industries, restaurants, and domestic services.

Scholars noticed that Chinese American families valued education very highly. Because of the educational achievements of Chinese Americans, and because the U.S. census counted a significantly higher proportion of professionals among the Chinese American population than among the white population, Chinese Americans have been stereotyped as a "model minority" group. According to a number of studies, however, even though a higher percentage of Chinese Americans were professionals, they were underrepresented in executive, supervisory, or decision-making positions, and the percentage of Chinese American families that lived below the poverty line was considerably higher than that of white families.

In addition to historical Chinatowns in San Francisco, Los Angeles, New York, Honolulu, and other large cities, many suburban Chinatowns have flourished in areas with large Chinese American populations. New Chinese American business communities are most visible in the San Francisco Bay area, the Los Angeles area, and the New York–New Jersey area.

BIBLIOGRAPHY

Chen, Yong. *Chinese San Francisco, 1850–1943: A Trans-Pacific Community.* Stanford, Calif.: Stanford University Press, 2000.

Fong, Timothy P. *The First Suburban Chinatown: The Remaking of Monterey Park, California*. Philadelphia: Temple University Press, 1994.

Glick, Clarence E. *Sojourners and Settlers: Chinese Migrants in Hawaii*. Honolulu: University of Hawaii Press, 1980.

Yung, Judy. *Unbound Feet: A Social History of Chinese Women in San Francisco*. Berkeley: University of California Press, 1995.

Zhao, Xiaojian. *Remaking Chinese America: Immigration, Family, and Community, 1940–1965*. New Brunswick, N.J.: Rutgers University Press, 2002.

Xiaojian Zhao

See also **China, Relations with; Transcontinental Railroad, Building of.**

CHINESE EXCLUSION ACT.

Passed in 1882, the Chinese Exclusion Act prohibited the immigration of Chinese laborers for ten years. The law, which repudiated the 1868 Burlingame Treaty promising free immigration between the United States and China, was one in the succession of laws produced by a national anti-Chinese movement. Limited federal intervention began as early as the 1862 regulation of "coolies"; the Page Law of 1875 purported to prevent the entry of "Oriental" prostitutes but precluded the immigration of most Asian women.

Laws following the 1882 exclusion legislation tightened the restrictions. The Scott Act of 1888 excluded all Chinese laborers, even those holding U.S. government certificates assuring their right to return. The original act's ban was extended in 1892 and made permanent in 1902. The government broadened exclusion to other Asians; by 1924, all Asian racial groups were restricted. The 1882 act also foreshadowed other discriminatory legislation, such as the national origins quota laws that discriminated against African and southern and eastern European immigrants from 1921 to 1965.

As America's first race-based immigration restrictions, the anti-Chinese laws caused the decrease of the Chinese-American population from 105,465 in 1880 to 61,639 in 1920. Chinese were again allowed to immigrate in 1943. The last vestiges of the Asian exclusion laws were repealed in 1965, when racial classifications were removed from the law.

BIBLIOGRAPHY

Gyory, Andrew. *Closing the Gate: Race, Politics, and the Chinese Exclusion Act*. Chapel Hill: University of North Carolina Press, 1998.

Hing, Bill Ong. *Making and Remaking Asian America through Immigration Policy, 1850–1990*. Stanford, Calif.: Stanford University Press, 1993.

Gabriel J. Chin
Diana Yoon

See also **Asian Americans; Chinese Americans; Immigration Restriction.**

CHIPPEWA. *See* **Ojibwe.**

CHIROPRACTIC,

coming from a Greek word meaning "done by hand," refers to a method of health care that stresses the relationship between structure and function in the body. Focusing on the spine and nervous system, chiropractic treatment is based on the assumption that disease results from a disturbance between the musculoskeletal and nervous systems. Chiropractors manipulate the spinal column in an effort to restore normal transmission of the nerves. Daniel David Palmer developed the system in 1895. Palmer believed that pinched nerves caused by the misalignment of vertebrae caused most diseases and that these diseases were curable by adjusting the spine into its correct position. Palmer, a former schoolmaster and grocer, opened a practice in Davenport, Iowa, where he combined manipulation and magnetic healing. Religion played an important role in Palmer's philosophy; seeking to restore natural balance and equilibrium, Palmer argued that science served religion to restore a person's natural function.

In 1896 Palmer incorporated Palmer's School of Magnetic Cure; in 1902 he changed the school's name to Palmer Infirmary and Chiropractic Institute. His son, Bartlett Joshua Palmer, took over the school in 1906 and became the charismatic leader chiropractic needed. B. J. Palmer marketed the school intensively and enrollment increased from fifteen in 1905 to more than a thousand by 1921. He also established a printing office for chiropractic literature, opened a radio station, went on lecture tours, and organized the Universal Chiropractors Association.

Although chiropractic gained a good deal of popularity it experienced opposition from the powerful AMERICAN MEDICAL ASSOCIATION (AMA) and the legal system, as well as from within the discipline. Chiropractors split into two groups: the "straights" and the "mixers." The "straights" believed diagnosis and treatment should only be done by manual manipulation, but the "mixers" were willing to use new technologies such as the neurocalometer, a machine that registered heat along the spinal column and was used to find misalignments.

As the popularity of chiropractic grew, the discipline went through a period of educational reform. Early on anyone could be a chiropractor; there was no formal training or background requirement. Eventually chiropractors settled on basic educational and licensing standards. Despite the best efforts of the AMA to discredit chiropractors, including passing a resolution in the early 1960s labeling chiropractic a cult without merit, chiropractic grew and thrived. Chiropractic acquired federal recognition as part of MEDICARE AND MEDICAID in the 1970s.

BIBLIOGRAPHY

Wardwell, Walter I. *Chiropractic: History and Evolution of a New Profession.* St. Louis, Mo.: Mosby Year Book, 1992.

Lisa A. Ennis

See also **Medicine, Alternative; Osteopathy.**

CHISHOLM TRAIL, a cattle trail leading north from TEXAS, across OKLAHOMA, to ABILENE, Kansas. The southern extension of the Chisholm Trail originated near San Antonio, Texas. From there it ran north and a little east to the Red River, which it crossed a few miles from present-day Ringgold, Texas. It continued north across Oklahoma to Caldwell, KANSAS. From Caldwell it ran north and a little east past Wichita to Abilene, Kansas. At the close of the CIVIL WAR, the low price of cattle in Texas and the much higher prices in the North and East encouraged many Texas ranchmen to drive large herds north to market. In 1867 the establishment of a cattle depot and shipping point at Abilene, Kansas, brought many herds there for shipping to market over the southern branch of the Union Pacific Railway. Many of these cattle traveled over the Chisholm Trail, which quickly became the most popular route for driving cattle north from Texas.

After 1871, the Chisholm Trail decreased in significance as Abilene lost its preeminence as a shipping point for Texas cattle. Instead, DODGE CITY, Kansas, became the chief shipping point, and another trail farther west gained paramount importance. In 1880, however, the extension of the Atchison, Topeka, and Santa Fe Railway to Caldwell, Kansas, again made the Chisholm Trail a vital route for driving Texas cattle to the North. It retained this position until the building of additional trunk lines of railway south into Texas caused rail shipments to replace trail driving in bringing Texas cattle north to market.

BIBLIOGRAPHY

Slatta, Richard W. *Cowboys of the Americas.* New Haven, Conn.: Yale University Press, 1990.

Worcester, Donald Emmet. *The Chisholm Trail: High Road of the Cattle Kingdom.* Lincoln: University of Nebraska Press, 1980.

Edward Everett Dale / A. E.

See also **Cattle Drives; Cow Towns; Cowboys; Trail Drivers.**

CHISHOLM V. GEORGIA, 2 Dallas 419 (1793). The heirs of Alexander Chisholm, citizens of South Carolina, sued the state of Georgia to enforce payment of claims against that state. Georgia refused to defend the suit, and the Supreme Court, upholding the right of citizens of one state to sue another state under Article III, Section 2, of the U.S. Constitution, ordered judgment by default against Georgia. No writ of execution was attempted be-cause of threats by the lower house of the Georgia legislature. The Eleventh Amendment ended such actions.

BIBLIOGRAPHY

Corwin, Edward S. *The Commerce Power versus States Rights.* Gloucester, Mass.: P. Smith, 1962.

Orth, John V. *The Judicial Power of the United States: The Eleventh Amendment in American History.* New York: Oxford University Press, 1987.

E. Merton Coulter / A. R.

See also **Constitution of the United States; Georgia; State Sovereignty; States' Rights.**

CHOCTAW. The Choctaws comprise two American Indian tribes whose origins are in central and eastern Mississippi. Their ancestors lived in fortified villages, raised corn, and hunted deer. They first encountered Europeans when Hernando de Soto led his forces from 1539 to 1541 through the Southeast. In the eighteenth century, they traded food and deerskins to British and French traders in exchange for weapons and cloth. Their major public ceremonies were funerals, but otherwise Choctaw religious beliefs were matters of private dreams or visions. They traced descent through the mother's line. The Choctaws settled conflicts between towns or with neighboring tribes on the stickball field, where each team tried to hit a ball of deerskin beyond the other's goal. The game was violent, but its outcome kept peace within the nation. During the American Revolution the Choctaws remained neutral, and they rejected the Shawnee leader Tecumseh's effort to form an alliance against the Americans before the War of 1812. In 1826, to assert their national identity and to show that they were adapting to white civilization, they adopted a written constitution that established a representative form of government. Despite the Choctaws' friendship and signs of adopting American customs, President Andrew Jackson pressed all Indians east of the Mississippi to cede their lands and move west. In 1830, Choctaw leaders signed the Treaty of Dancing Rabbit Creek, and approximately fifteen thousand Choctaws moved to what is now Oklahoma. There they reestablished their constitutional form of government and controlled their own school system. They allied with the Confederacy during the Civil War and afterward were forced to sign new treaties with the United States that ceded parts of their land and allowed railroads to cross their territory. Railroads brought non-Indians to Choctaw lands, and in 1907 the tribal government was dissolved when Oklahoma became a state. Mineral resources, however, remained as communal holdings, and the federal government continued to recognize titular chiefs. Political activism in the 1960s led to a resurgence in tribal identity. At the turn of the twenty-first century, the Choctaw Nation of Oklahoma had over 127,000 members throughout the United States, and the Mississippi Band of Choctaw Indians, des-

Choctaws. This illustration shows two members of the tribe in 1853, when it had long since been resettled, as one of the so-called Five Civilized Tribes, in present-day Oklahoma. LIBRARY OF CONGRESS

cendents of those who resisted removal, numbered over 8,300.

BIBLIOGRAPHY

Debo, Angie. *The Rise and Fall of the Choctaw Republic*. Norman: University of Oklahoma Press, 1934.

Wells, Samuel J., and Roseanna Tubby. *After Removal: The Choctaw in Mississippi*. Jackson: University Press of Mississippi, 1986.

Clara Sue Kidwell

See also **Indian Policy, Colonial; Indian Policy, U.S.; Indian Removal; Indian Territory; Indian Trade and Traders; Indian Treaties; Oklahoma; Tribes: Southeastern;** *and* *vol. 9:* **Head of Choctaw Nation Reaffirms His Tribe's Position; Sleep Not Longer, O Choctaws and Chickasaws, 1811.**

CHOLERA. No epidemic disease to strike the United States has ever been so widely heralded as Asiatic cholera, an enteric disorder associated with crowding and poor sanitary conditions. Long known in the Far East, cholera spread westward in 1817, slowly advanced through Russia and eastern Europe, and reached the Atlantic by 1831. American newspapers, by closely following its destructive path across Europe, helped build a growing sense of public apprehension. In June 1832 Asiatic cholera reached North America and struck simultaneously at Quebec, New York, and Philadelphia. In New York City it killed more than 3,000 persons in July and August. It reached New Orleans in October, creating panic and confusion. Within three weeks 4,340 residents had died. Among America's major cities, only Boston and Charleston escaped this first onslaught. From the coastal cities, the disorder coursed along American waterways and land transportation routes, striking at towns and villages in a seemingly aimless fashion until it reached the western frontier. Minor flare-ups were reported in 1833, after which the disease virtually disappeared for fifteen years.

In December 1848 cholera again appeared in American port cities and, on this occasion, struck down more than 5,000 residents of New York City. From the ports it spread rapidly along rivers, canals, railways, and stagecoach routes, bringing death to even the remotest areas. The major attack of 1848–1849 was followed by a series of sporadic outbreaks that continued for the next six years. In New Orleans, for example, the annual number of deaths attributed to cholera from 1850 to 1855 ranged from 450 to 1,448.

The last major epidemic of cholera first threatened American ports late in 1865 and spread widely through the country. Prompt work by the newly organized Metropolitan Board of Health kept the death toll to about 600 in New York City, but other American towns and cities were not so fortunate. The medical profession, however, had learned that cholera was spread through fecal discharges of its victims and concluded that a mild supportive treatment was far better than the rigorous bleeding, purging, and vomiting of earlier days. More-

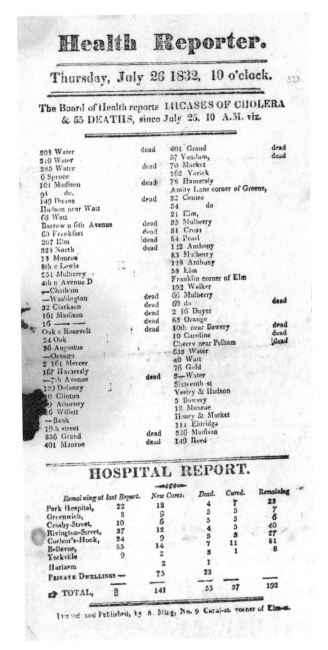

Epidemic: One City, One Day. The New York City Board of Health report issued 26 July 1832 lists (by address and hospital) 141 cases of cholera—and 55 deaths—since 10 A.M. the day before. LIBRARY OF CONGRESS

over, a higher standard of living combined with an emphasis on sanitation helped to reduce both incidence and mortality. Cholera continued to flare up sporadically until 1868, disappeared for five years, and then returned briefly in 1873. In the succeeding years only sporadic cases of cholera were found aboard incoming vessels, leading to newspaper headlines and warning editorials.

BIBLIOGRAPHY

Crosby, Alfred. *Germs, Seeds, and Animals: Studies in Ecological History.* Armonk, N.Y.: Sharpe, 1993.

Duffy, John. *Epidemics in Colonial America.* Baton Rouge: Louisiana State University Press, 1971.

Rosenberg, Charles. *The Cholera Years: The United States in 1832, 1849, and 1866.* Chicago: University of Chicago Press, 1997.

John Duffy / H. S.

See also **Epidemics and Public Health; Influenza; Sanitation, Environmental.**

CHOSIN RESERVOIR. By the end of October 1950, four months after the Korean War began, the U.S. X Corps, composed of the Seventh Infantry Division and the First Marine Division, had nearly reached the Chosin Reservoir, a frozen lake just sixty miles from the Chinese border. General Douglas MacArthur's chief of staff, Major General Edward Almond, commanded X Corps. Almond urged a swift advance, while the commander of the First Marines, General O. P. Smith, preferred to move more cautiously, because he feared an attack by Communist Chinese forces. From 3 to 7 November, marines fought Chinese soldiers of the 124th Division near the icy Chosin Reservoir and forced them to withdraw to the north. Optimists at MacArthur's headquarters concluded that Communist China was unwilling to commit significant forces to Korea. Others, including General Smith, thought the Chinese were likely to spring a trap on the dangerously exposed X Corps.

Nearly three weeks passed without further enemy contact. The First Marine Division occupied positions along the northwestern edge of the Chosin Reservoir. The Seventh Infantry Division had units strung out from the eastern side of the reservoir to a point sixty miles north, nearly reaching the Yalu River on the Chinese border. On November 27, the ten Chinese divisions of the Ninth Army Group, approximately 100,000 soldiers, attacked X Corps along a front of over thirty miles. The marines were reduced to three isolated perimeters but withstood the Chinese onslaught. The exposed Seventh Infantry Division fared less well, as elements of the division were surrounded and overwhelmed while attempting to pull back to join the marines.

On 1 December, the First Marine Division began an orderly fighting withdrawal toward the port of Hungnam, and on 3 December the survivors from the Seventh Infantry Division linked up with the marines. The first elements of X Corps reached Hungnam seven days later, and when the evacuation was complete on 24 December, more than 100,000 American and South Korean troops had been saved. X Corps suffered 705 killed in action, 3,251 wounded in action, and thousands more afflicted with cold weather injuries, as well as 4,779 missing in action. The Chinese may have suffered nearly 72,500 battle and nonbattle casualties in the Chosin Reservoir campaign.

Chosin Reservoir. Marines patrol this part of Korea near the Chinese border, site of the massive Chinese attack beginning in late November 1950. ASSOCIATED PRESS/WORLD WIDE PHOTOS

BIBLIOGRAPHY

Appleman, Roy Edgar. *Escaping the Trap: The U.S. Army X Corps in Northeast Korea, 1950.* College Station: Texas A&M University Press, 1990.

Hastings, Max. *The Korean War.* New York: Simon and Schuster, 1987.

Whelan, Richard. *Drawing the Line: The Korean War, 1950–1953.* Boston: Little, Brown, 1990.

Erik B. Villard

See also **Korean War.**

CHRISTIAN COALITION, a political action and evangelical piety movement based in Washington, D.C., was formed in 1989 by the Reverend Pat Robertson to provide him with a national vehicle for public advocacy. Defeated in the Republican presidential primaries the previous year, Robertson was poised to fill the vacuum among fundamentalist activists caused by the dissolution of the Moral Majority. Ralph Reed, an early executive director, secured wide public exposure for the Christian Coalition through frequent media appearances and by securing it access among prominent politicians. Its subsequent executive director, Roberta Combs, focused on organization and on mobilizing youth activists. The Christian Coalition claimed in 2001 to have nearly two million members nationwide with branches in every state and on many university campuses.

The Christian Coalition was founded on the belief that "people of faith" have a right and a responsibility to effect social, cultural, and political change in their local communities. Its members denounced promiscuity and what they deemed as individualist, feminist, and judicial excesses, and preferred a larger role for independent groups instead of the federal government. Its goals included strengthening "family values" by fighting abortions, pornography, homosexuality, bigotry, and religious persecution, and by endorsing prayer in public places such as schools. Easing the tax burden on married couples and fighting crime by severely punishing culprits while protecting the rights of victims complemented its mission.

Educating, lobbying, and disseminating information through courses, lectures, debate forums, issue voter guides, and scorecards for certain candidates on its issues of concern were the hallmark of the Christian Coalition. Its brochure "From the Pew to the Precinct" emphasized that in order to preserve its tax-exempt status, this movement did not specifically endorse individuals or parties, but the vast majority of its grassroots mobilization supported the Republican Party.

BIBLIOGRAPHY

Harding, Susan Friend. *The Book of Jerry Falwell: Fundamentalist Language and Politics.* Princeton, N.J.: Princeton University Press, 2000.

Itai Sneh

See also **Christianity; Fundamentalism; Moral Majority; Pro-Life Movement; School Prayer.**

CHRISTIAN SCIENCE. See **Church of Christ, Scientist.**

CHRISTIANA FUGITIVE AFFAIR. On 11 September 1851 a battle erupted between members of the black population of Lancaster County, Pennsylvania, and a Maryland slave owner who had come to recapture his four escaped slaves.

On 6 November 1849 four slaves escaped from the Retreat Farm plantation in Baltimore County, Maryland. The plantation, a wheat farm, was owned by Edward Gorsuch. When he received word that his slaves had been found in September 1851, the plantation owner recruited his son and some of the local Christiana authorities to remand the fugitives back to him.

When the attempt was made to recapture the men, who had found refuge in the home of another fugitive slave named William Parker, they resisted. With the support of the local black townspeople (and some of the white) their resistance was successful. Edward Gorsuch was killed in the fray. The fugitives made their way to Canada and remained free.

The skirmish was set in the backdrop of national debate about fugitive slave laws and slavery itself. The free state of Pennsylvania wanted no part of returning the slaves to their Maryland owner and was not obligated to help. The battle heightened this controversy and helped set the stage for the Civil War.

BIBLIOGRAPHY

Slaughter, Thomas P. *Bloody Dawn: The Christiana Riot and Racial Violence in the Antebellum North.* New York: Oxford Press, 1991.

Michael K. Law

See also **Mason-Dixon Line; Slave Insurrections; Union Sentiment in Border States.**

CHRISTIANITY, in its many forms, has been the dominant religion of Europeans and their descendants in North America ever since Columbus. It proved as adaptable to the New World as it had been to the Old, while taking on several new characteristics. The ambiguous and endlessly debated meaning of the Christian Gospels permitted diverse American groups to interpret their conduct and beliefs as Christian: from warriors to pacifists, abolitionists to slave owners, polygamists to ascetics, and from those who saw personal wealth as a sign of godliness to those who understood Christianity to mean the repudiation or radical sharing of wealth.

Colonial Era

The exploration of the Americas in the sixteenth and seventeenth centuries coincided with the Reformation and Europe's religious wars, intensifying and embittering the international contest for possession of these new territories. Spanish, Portuguese, and French settlers were overwhelmingly Catholic. English, Dutch, Swedish, and German settlers were predominantly Protestant. Each group, to the extent that it tried to convert the American Indians, argued the merits of its own brand of Christianity, but few Indians, witnessing the conquerors' behavior, could have been impressed with Jesus's teaching about the blessedness of peacemakers.

Puritans created the British New England colonies in the early 1600s. They believed that the (Anglican) Church of England, despite Henry VIII's separation from Rome, had not been fully reformed or purified of its former Catholic elements. The religious compromises on which Anglicanism was based (the Thirty-nine Articles) offended them because they looked on Catholicism as demonic. The founders of Plymouth Plantation (the "Pilgrim Fathers" of 1620) were separatists, who believed they should separate themselves completely from the Anglicans. The larger group of Massachusetts Bay colonists, ten years later, remained nominally attached to the Anglican Church and regarded their mission as an attempt to establish an ideal Christian commonwealth that would provide an inspiring example to the coreligionists back in England. Neither group had foreseen the way in which American conditions would force adaptations, especially after the first generation, nor had they anticipated that the English civil wars and the Commonwealth that followed (1640–1660) would impose different imperatives on Puritans still in England than on those who had crossed the ocean. We are well informed about the New England Puritans and their reaction to seventeenth-century events because of their exceptional literacy and loquacity. From the works of Increase Mather (1639–1723) and his son Cotton (1663–1728), for example, we can reconstruct a worldview in which every storm, high tide, deformed fetus, or mild winter was a sign of God's "special providence." Theirs was, besides, a world in which devils abounded and witchcraft (notoriously at the Salem witch trials, 1692) seemed to present a real threat to the community.

More southerly colonies, Virginia and the Carolinas, were commercial tobacco ventures whose far less energetic religious life was supervised by the established Church of England. Maryland began as a Catholic commercial venture but its proprietors reverted to Anglicanism in the bitterly anti-Catholic environment of the Glorious Revolution (1688–1689) in the late seventeenth century. The middle colonies of New York, New Jersey, Delaware, and Pennsylvania, by contrast, were more ethnically and religiously diverse almost from the beginning, including Dutch Calvinists, German Lutherans and Moravians, Swedish Baptists, and English Quakers.

All these colonies, along with New England, were subjected to periodic surges of revival enthusiasm that are collectively remembered as the GREAT AWAKENING. The Awakening's exemplary figure was the spellbinding English preacher George Whitefield (1714–1770), who brought an unprecedented drama to American pulpits in the 1740s and 1750s and shocked some divines by preaching outdoors. The theologian Jonathan Edwards (1703–1758) of Northampton, Massachusetts, welcomed the Awakening and tried to square Calvinist orthodoxy with the scientific and cognitive revolutions of Newton and the Enlightenment.

Christianity in the Revolution and Early Republic

By the time of the Revolution (1775–1788), growing numbers of colonists had joined radical Reformation sects, notably the Quakers and Baptists, belonged to ethnically distinct denominations like the Mennonites, or were involved in intradenominational schisms springing from Great Awakening controversies over itinerant preaching and the need for an inspired rather than a learned clergy. The U.S. Constitution's First Amendment specified that there was to be no federally established church and no federal restriction on the free exercise of religion. Some New England states retained established Christian churches after the Revolution—Congregationalism in Massachusetts, for example—but by 1833 all had been severed from the government.

This political separation, however, did not imply any lessening of Christian zeal. To the contrary, the early republic witnessed another immense upsurge of Christian energy and evangelical fervor, with Baptists and Methodists adapting most quickly to a new emotional style, which they carried to the rapidly expanding settlement frontier. Spellbinding preachers like Francis Asbury

(1745–1816) and Charles Grandison Finney (1792–1875) helped inspire the revivals of the "Second Great Awakening" (see AWAKENING, SECOND), and linked citizens' conversions to a range of social reforms, including temperance, sabbatarianism, and (most controversially) the abolition of slavery. Radical abolitionists like William Lloyd Garrison (1805–1879) denounced the Constitution as an un-Christian pact with the devil because it provided for the perpetuation of slavery. John Brown (1800–1859), who tried to stimulate a slave uprising with his raid on Harpers Ferry in 1859, saw himself as a biblical avenger. He anticipated, rightly, that his sacrificial death, like Jesus's crucifixion, would lead to the triumph of the antislavery cause. Christian abolitionists who had prudently declined to join the rising, like Henry Ward Beecher (1813–1887), claimed him as a martyr. Beecher's sister Harriet published *Uncle Tom's Cabin* in 1852, a novel saturated with the sentimental conventions of American Victorian Protestantism; it popularized the idea that abolition was a Christian imperative.

In the South, meanwhile, slaves had adapted African elements to Gospel teachings and developed their own syncretic style of Christianity, well adapted to the emotional idioms of the Second Awakening. Dissatisfied with attending their masters' churches, they enjoyed emotional "ring shout" meetings in remote brush arbors, or met for whispered prayers and preaching in the slave quarters. Slave owners too thought of themselves as justified in their Christianity. Well armed with quotations to show that the Bible's authors had been slaveholders and that Jesus had never condemned the practice, they saw themselves as the guardians of a Christian way of life under threat from a soulless commercial North. The historian Eugene Genovese has shown that on purely biblical grounds they probably had the stronger argument.

The early republic also witnessed the creation of new Christian sects, including the Assemblies of God, the Shakers, the Oneida Perfectionists, and the Mormons. Those with distinctive sexual practices (Shaker celibacy, Oneida "complex marriage," and Mormon polygamy) were vulnerable to persecution by intolerant neighbors who linked the idea of a "Protestant America" to a code of monogamy. The Mormons, the most thriving of all these groups, were founded by an upstate New York farm boy, Joseph Smith (1805–1844), who received a set of golden tablets from an angel. He translated them into the Book of Mormon (1830), which stands beside the Bible as scripture for Mormons, and describes the way in which Jesus conducted a mission in America after his earthly sojourn in the Holy Land. Recurrent persecution, culminating in the assassination of Smith in 1844, led the Mormons under their new leader, Brigham Young (1801–1877), to migrate far beyond the line of settlement to the Great Salt Lake, Utah, in 1846, where their experiments in polygamy persisted until 1890. Polygamy had the virtue of ensuring that the surplus of Mormon women would all have husbands. Mormonism was one of many nine-

teenth- and twentieth-century American churches in which membership (though not leadership) was disproportionately female.

The Mormon migration was just one small part of a much larger westward expansion of the United States in the early and mid–nineteenth century, much of which was accompanied by the rhetoric of MANIFEST DESTINY, according to which God had reserved the whole continent for the Americans. No one felt the sting of manifest destiny more sharply than the Indians. Ever since the colonial era missionaries had struggled to convert them to Christianity and to the Euro-American way of life. These missions were sometimes highly successful, as for example the Baptist mission to the Cherokees led by Evan Jones, which created a written version of their language in the early nineteenth century that facilitated translation of the Bible. The Georgia gold rush of 1829 showed, however, that ambitious settlers and prospectors would not be deterred from overrunning Indians' land merely because they were Christian Indians; their forcible removal along the TRAIL OF TEARS was one of many disgraceful episodes in white-Indian relations. Southwestern and Plains Indians, meanwhile, often incorporated Christian elements into their religious systems. The New Mexican Pueblo peoples, for example, under Spanish domination until 1848, adapted the Catholic cult of the saints to their traditional pantheon; later the Peyote Way, which spread through the Southwest and Midwest, incorporated evangelical Protestant elements.

Further enriching the American Christian landscape, a large Catholic immigration from Ireland, especially after the famine of 1846–1849, tested the limits of older citizens' religious tolerance. It challenged the validity of the widely held concept of a Protestant America that the earlier tiny Catholic minority had scarcely disturbed. A flourishing polemical literature after 1830 argued that Catholics, owing allegiance to a foreign monarch, the pope, could not be proper American citizens—the idea was embodied in the policies of the Know-Nothing political party in the 1850s. Periodic religious riots in the 1830–1860 era and the coolness of civil authorities encouraged the Catholic newcomers to keep Protestants at arm's length. They set about building their own institutions, not just churches but also a separate system of schools, colleges, hospitals, orphanages, and charities, a work that continued far into the twentieth century. The acquisition of Louisiana in 1804, and the acquisition of the vast Southwest after the Mexican-American War (1846–1848), also swelled the U.S. Catholic population.

Soldiers on both sides in the Civil War (1861–1865) went into battle confident that they were doing the will of a Christian God. President Lincoln, and many Union clergy, saw their side's ultimate victory as a sign of divine favor, explaining their heavy losses in the fighting according to the idea that God had scourged them for the sin of tolerating slavery for so long. The defeated Confederates, on the other hand, nourished their cult of the "lost cause" after the war by reminding each other that Jesus's mission on earth had ended in failure and a humiliating death, something similar to their own plight. The slaves, freed first by the Emancipation Proclamation (1863) and then by the Fifteenth Amendment (1865), treated President Abraham Lincoln (1809–1865) as the Great Liberator and compared him to Moses, leading the Children of Israel out of their bondage in Egypt.

Christianity and Industrial Society

Rapid industrialization in the later nineteenth century prompted a searching reevaluation of conventional theological ethics. Fluctuations in the business cycle, leading to periodic surges of urban unemployment, made nonsense of the old rural idea that God dependably rewards sobriety and hard work with prosperity. The theologians Walter Rauschenbusch (1861–1918), George Herron (1862–1925), and Washington Gladden (1836–1918) created the SOCIAL GOSPEL, adapting Christianity to urban industrial life and emphasizing the community's collective responsibility toward its weakest members. Vast numbers of "new immigrants"—Catholics from Poland, Italy, and the Slavic lands; Orthodox Christians from Russia and Greece; and Jews from the Austrian and Russian empires—continued to expand America's religious diversity. They established their own churches and received help from religiously inspired Protestant groups such as the Salvation Army and the settlement house movement.

Meanwhile, Christianity faced an unanticipated intellectual challenge, much of which had been generated from within. Rapid advances in historical-critical study of the Bible and of comparative religion, and the spread of evolutionary biology after Charles Darwin's *Origin of Species* (1859), forced theologians to ask whether the Genesis creation story and other biblical accounts were literally true. These issues led to a fracture in American Protestantism that persisted through the twentieth century, between liberal Protestants who adapted their religious ideas to the new intellectual orthodoxy and fundamentalists who conscientiously refused to do so. In the fundamentalists' view, strongly represented at Princeton Theological Seminary and later popularized by the Democratic politician William Jennings Bryan (1860–1925), the Bible, as God's inspired word, could not be fallible. Anyone who rejected the Genesis story while keeping faith in the Gospels was, they pointed out, making himself rather than the Bible the ultimate judge.

Observers were surprised to note that in the twentieth century American church membership and church attendance rates remained high, indeed increased, at a time when they were declining throughout the rest of the industrialized world. Various theories, all plausible, were advanced to account for this phenomenon: that Americans, being more mobile than Europeans, needed a ready-made community center in each new location, especially as vast and otherwise anonymous suburbs proliferated; that church membership was a permissible way for im-

migrants and their descendants to retain an element of their families' former identity while assimilating in all other respects to American life; even, in the 1940s and 1950s, that the threat of atomic warfare had led to a collective "failure of nerve" and a retreat into supernaturalism. Twentieth-century Christian churches certainly did double as community centers, around which youth clubs, study classes, therapeutic activities, "singles' groups," and sports teams were organized. Members certainly could have nonreligious motives for attendance, but abundant historical and sociological evidence suggests that they had religious motives too.

Christianity and Politics in the Twentieth Century

Christianity remained a dynamic social force, around which intense political controversies swirled. In 1925 the SCOPES TRIAL tested whether fundamentalists could keep evolution from being taught in schools. A high-school biology teacher was convicted of violating a Tennessee state law that prohibited the teaching of evolution, but the public-relations fallout of the case favored evolutionists rather than creationists. In the same year the Supreme Court ruled (in PIERCE V. SOCIETY OF SISTERS) that Catholic and other religious private schools were protected under the Constitution; the legislature of Oregon (then with influential anti-Catholic Ku Klux Klan members) was ruled to have exceeded its authority in requiring all children in the state to attend public schools.

In 1928 a Catholic, Al Smith (1873–1944) of New York, ran as the Democratic candidate for president in a religiously superheated campaign. Southern whites were usually a dependable Democratic block vote, but their "Bible Belt" prejudice against Catholics led them to campaign against him. This defeat was not offset until a second Catholic candidate, John F. Kennedy (1917–1963), was elected in 1960, keeping enough southern white votes to ensure a wafer-thin plurality. After this election, and especially after the popular Kennedy's 1963 assassination, which was treated by parts of the nation as martyrdom, American anti-Catholicism declined rapidly. Kennedy had declined to advocate the federal funding of parochial schools and had refused to criticize the Supreme Court when it found, in a series of cases from 1962 and 1963, that prayer and Bible-reading in public schools violated the Establishment Clause of the First Amendment.

While the Supreme Court appeared to be distancing Christianity from politics, the civil rights movement was bringing them together. A black Baptist minister, Martin Luther King Jr. (1929–1968), led the Montgomery Bus Boycott (1955–1956) and became the preeminent civil rights leader of the 1950s and 1960s. Ever since emancipation, ministers had played a leadership role in the black community, being, usually, its most highly educated members and the men who acted as liaisons between segregated whites and blacks. King, a spellbinding preacher, perfected a style that blended Christian teachings on love, forgiveness, and reconciliation, Old Testament visions of a heaven on earth, and patriotic American rhetoric, the three being beautifully combined in the peroration of his famous "I have a dream" speech from 1963. Like Mohandas "Mahatma" Gandhi, to whom he acknowledged a debt, he knew how to work on the consciences of the dominant group by quoting scriptures they took seriously, interpreting them in such a way as to make them realize their failings as Christians. Religious leaders might disagree about exactly how the movement should proceed—King feuded with black Baptists who did not want the churches politicized, and with whites like the eight ministers whose counsel of patience and self-restraint provoked his "Letter from Birmingham Jail"—but historians of the movement now agree that he was able to stake out, and hold, the religious high ground.

Among the theological influences on King was the work of Reinhold Niebuhr (1892–1971). Born and raised in a German evangelical family in Missouri, Niebuhr was the preeminent American Protestant theologian of the century. Reacting, like many clergy, against the superpatriotic fervor of the First World War years (in which Christian ministers often led the way in bloodcurdling denunciation of the "Huns"), he became in the 1920s an advocate of Christian pacifism. During the 1930s, however, against a background of rising totalitarianism in Europe, he abandoned this position on grounds of its utopianism and naiveté, and bore witness to a maturing grasp of Christian ethics in his masterpiece, *Moral Man and Immoral Society* (1932). His influential journal *Christianity and Crisis*, begun in 1941, voiced the ideas of Christians who believed war against Hitler was religiously justified. He became, in the 1940s and 1950s, influential among statesmen, policy makers, and foreign policy "realists," some of whom detached his ethical insights from their Christian foundations, leading the philosopher Morton White to quip that they were "atheists for Niebuhr." Niebuhr had also helped bring to America, from Germany, the theologian Paul Tillich (1886–1965), who became a second great theological celebrity in the mid-century decades, and Dietrich Bonhoeffer (1906–1945), who worked for a time in the 1930s at Union Seminary, New York, but returned before the war and was later executed for his part in a plot to assassinate Hitler.

To match these Protestant theological celebrities—of whom Niebuhr's brother Richard (1894–1962) was a fourth—the Catholic Church produced its own. The émigré celebrity was the French convert Jacques Maritain (1882–1973), who wrote with brilliant insight on faith and aesthetics, while the homegrown figure was John Courtney Murray (1904–1967), whose essays on religious liberty were embodied in the religious liberty document of the Second Vatican Council (1962–1965). Men like King, the Niebuhr brothers, Maritain, Tillich, and Murray enjoyed almost the same prominence in mid-twentieth-century America that the Mathers had enjoyed in the seventeenth century, Jonathan Edwards in the eighteenth,

and the Beechers in the nineteenth—another sign of the persistence of Christian energy in America.

Ever since the Scopes Monkey Trial the evangelical Protestant churches had retreated from politics, but they had continued to grow, to organize (taking advantage of broadcasting technology), and to generate exceptionally talented individuals of their own. None was to have more lasting importance than Billy Graham (b. 1918), whose revivals became a press sensation in the late 1940s. Graham eschewed the sectarian squabbling that many evangelists relished. Instead he tried to create an irenic mood among all evangelicals while reaching out to liberal Protestants with an emotional message of Christian love, forgiveness, and Jesus as personal savior. He traveled worldwide, befriended every president from 1950 to 2000, and said, perhaps rightly, that more people had seen him and knew who he was than anybody else in the world.

Another skilled evangelical, the Baptist Jerry Falwell (b. 1933) shared many of Graham's skills but brought them directly into politics in a way Graham had avoided. Falwell, convinced that the sexual revolution of the 1960s and 1970s, the feminist movement, the counterculture, and the changing nature of the American family were signs of decadence and sin, catalyzed the MORAL MAJORITY, a pressure group that contributed to the "Reagan Revolution" in the election of 1980. That election was particularly noteworthy as a moment in Christian history not only because of the sudden reappearance of politicized evangelicals but also because the losing candidate, President Jimmy Carter (b. 1924), was himself a self-proclaimed born-again Christian and Baptist Sunday school teacher.

Nearly all America's Christian churches with a liberal inclination participated in a religious protest against nuclear weapons in the 1980s. Nearly all those with a conservative inclination participated in campaigns against legalized abortion. Indeed, as observers noted at the time, both sides in these and other sundering political controversies were strongly represented by Christian advocates. Collectively they demonstrated the extraordinary vitality and diversity of American Christianity into the third millennium.

BIBLIOGRAPHY

Ahlstrom, Sidney E. *A Religious History of the American People.* 2 vols. New Haven, Conn.: Yale University Press, 1972.

Albanese, Catherine L. *America, Religions and Religion.* 2d ed. Belmont, Calif.: Wadsworth, 1992.

Fox, Richard Wightman. *Reinhold Niebuhr: A Biography.* New York: Pantheon Books, 1985.

Garrow, David J. *Bearing the Cross: Martin Luther King, Jr., and the Southern Christian Leadership Conference.* New York: W. Morrow, 1986.

Marsden, George M. *Fundamentalism and American Culture.* New York: Oxford University Press, 1980.

May, Henry F. *Protestant Churches and Industrial America.* 2d ed. New York: Octagon Books, 1977.

Miller, Perry. *The New England Mind.* 2 vols. Boston: Beacon Press, 1961.

Morris, Charles R. *American Catholic: The Saints and Sinners who Built America's Most Powerful Church.* New York: Times Books, 1997.

Noll, Mark. *A History of Christianity in the United States and Canada.* Grand Rapids, Mich.: W. B. Eerdman's, 1992.

Ostling, Richard N., and Joan K. Ostling. *Mormon America: The Power and the Promise.* San Francisco: Harper Collins, 1999.

Raboteau, Albert J. *Slave Religion: The "Invisible Institution" in the Antebellum South.* New York: Oxford University Press, 1978.

Wuthnow, Robert. *The Restructuring of American Religion.* Princeton, N.J.: Princeton University Press, 1988.

Patrick N. Allitt

See also **Baptist Churches; Catholicism; Creationism; Episcopalianism; Evangelicalism and Revivalism; Fundamentalism; Indian Missions; Latter-day Saints, Church of Jesus Christ of; Protestantism; Puritans and Puritanism; Religious Thought and Writings.**

CHRISTMAS. The observance of Christmas in early British North America derived from practices familiar in England, where 25 December was celebrated with a good deal of bawdy revelry. Due to this association, as well as the lack of any biblical sanction for that date, observance of Christmas was opposed by Puritans in England and was banned in the Massachusetts Bay Colony between 1659 and 1681.

In the nineteenth century, Christmas became domesticated, with a shift toward a nuclear family experience of gift giving around a Christmas tree. The tree was popularized by immigrants from Germany, where it had become prominent earlier in the century. Christmas became the principal sales holiday of the year, presided over by Santa Claus, a figure compounded from myth, religious history, and the need for a congenial symbol for the new attitude toward the holiday. He was introduced and promoted by popular literature and illustration, from Clement Moore's "An Account of a Visit from St. Nicholas" (1823) to Thomas Nast's cartoons of the portly character. Charles Dickens toured America in 1867 reading from his enormously popular "A Christmas Carol," which further reinforced the notions that were crystallizing about how Christmas should be celebrated.

The twentieth century saw further merchandising around Christmas, to the point that many religious figures called for "putting Christ back in Christmas." One contentious issue was government sponsorship of symbols of the holiday. In *Lynch v. Donnelly* (1983), the Supreme Court held that the inclusion by the city of Pawtucket, Rhode Island, of the crèche in its Christmas display legitimately celebrated the holiday and its origins because its primary effect was not to advance religion. In *County of Allegheny v. ACLU Greater Pittsburgh Chapter* (1989),

the Court considered two displays, a crèche in the Allegheny County Courthouse and, in a government building some blocks away, a tall Chanukah menorah together with a Christmas tree and a sign stating "Salute to Liberty." The Court ruled that the crèche was unconstitutional because it was not accompanied by seasonal decorations and because "by permitting the display of the crèche in this particular physical setting, the county sends an unmistakable message that it supports and promotes the Christian praise to God that is the crèche's religious message." In contrast, the Christmas tree and the menorah were held not to be religious endorsements, but were to be "understood as conveying the city's secular recognition of different traditions for celebrating the winter-holiday season."

BIBLIOGRAPHY

Horsley, Richard, and James Tracy, eds. *Christmas Unwrapped: Consumerism, Christ, and Culture.* Harrisburg, Pa.: Trinity, 2001.

Nissenbaum, Stephen. *The Battle for Christmas: A Cultural History of America's Most Cherished Holiday.* New York: Knopf, 1996.

Restad, Penne L. *Christmas in America: A History.* New York: Oxford University Press, 1995.

Schmidt, Leigh Eric. *Consumer Rites: The Buying and Selling of American Holidays.* Princeton, N.J.: Princeton University Press, 1995.

James Tracy

See also **Christianity; Holidays and Festivals.**

CHRONIC FATIGUE SYNDROME. As many as one out of four people who consult primary health care providers in the United States complain that they have major problems with fatigue. In the 1980s some researchers claimed that chronic infection with the Epstein-Barr virus, also thought to cause chronic mononucleosis, was the source of such fatigue. Later studies, however, showed chronic infection with the virus in patients who did not demonstrate fatigue symptoms, casting doubt on the virus as the source of the symptoms. Other researchers uncovered evidence of infection with other organisms, along with perturbations in the body's immune system, but could not pinpoint a specific cause of the symptoms. Eventually they labeled disabling fatigue lasting at least six months and of uncertain etiology as chronic fatigue syndrome. Doctors diagnosed the disease more often in women than in men and far less often in the lowest socioeconomic groups.

The media began a public discussion of the syndrome during the late 1980s, followed by the formation of patient support groups. By the late 1990s no consistently effective treatment had been discovered, and medical and lay authorities displayed open public disagreement over the nature and definition of the disease. Patient groups lobbied for recognition of chronic fatigue syndrome as a specific disease, while many physicians were reluctant to create an umbrella term for what they regarded as a set of common symptoms rather than a specific disease.

BIBLIOGRAPHY

Aronowitz, Robert A. "From Myalgic Encephalitis to Yuppie Flu: A History of Chronic Fatigue Syndromes." In *Framing Disease: Studies in Cultural History*. Edited by Charles E. Rosenberg and Janet Golden. New Brunswick, N.J.: Rutgers University Press, 1992.

Duff, Kat. *The Alchemy of Illness*. New York: Pantheon Books, 1993.

Joel D. Howell / c. w.

See also **Medical Profession; Medical Research; Microbiology.**

CHURCH AND STATE, SEPARATION OF.

The First Amendment to the U.S. Constitution, drafted by James Madison, declares that Congress "shall pass no law respecting an establishment of religion, or prohibiting the free exercise thereof." Madison's friend and mentor Thomas Jefferson was proud of his role in drafting and winning assent to Virginia's religious liberty law (1786). In a letter of 1802, he referred to the need for a "high wall of separation" between church and state. Both men considered religious liberty not just a convenient political response to the actual diversity of denominations in the new Republic but as a natural right.

Jefferson's wall metaphor has often been used but it has never been adequate. Everyone stands on one side or the other of a real wall. Citizens of the states, by contrast, often belong to churches too and defy the metaphor by appearing on both sides. Controversy over how to interpret the First Amendment has therefore absorbed immense quantities of time, words, and ink, especially in the years since 1940, when for the first time its religious clauses were extended from the federal to state level.

In the early days of the Republic, despite the First Amendment, several states continued to have "official" established churches. The courts then interpreted the amendment to mean that while Congress could make no laws about religion, the states were free to do so. The actual diversity of religious groups in the states—promoted especially by the fervently democratic mood of the Second Great Awakening—nonetheless encouraged disestablishment. The last established church, Massachusetts Congregationalism, was separated from the state in 1833.

Even so, the idea that the United States was a Protestant country remained widespread. When Horace Mann laid the foundations for the public school system, again in Massachusetts, he took it for granted that the education would be religious and that students would study the King James Bible, which was common to most Protestant churches. Catholic immigration, accelerating after the Irish famine (1845–1850), made this curriculum controversial. The Catholic archbishop of New York, John Hughes, argued that the faith of young Catholics was jeopardized when they studied in public schools and set about creating a parallel parochial school system. At that point, however, the federal judiciary left it to the states to make their own arrangements and most states were emphatic about their Protestant identity and their love of the King James Bible. Only after passage of the Fourteenth Amendment in 1868 did the possibility arise that the Supreme Court could extend the Bill of Rights to the states.

The Court first took an interest in the religion clause of the First Amendment when it adjudicated *Reynolds v. United States* (1879). George Reynolds, a Mormon who was already married, had followed his church's injunction to take a second wife. Most Americans were bitterly critical of Mormon polygamy, and Reynolds was convicted under the bigamy statutes. On appeal, Reynolds claimed he was exercising his First Amendment right under the free exercise clause—but the Court was unimpressed. It answered that Reynolds was free to believe in polygamy but was not free to act on his belief. If he did so, it pointed out, he would in effect be violating the establishment clause by getting an exemption from the bigamy statutes because of his membership in a particular church.

In the twentieth century, cases testing the proper relationship between church and state became more common. Among the first was an Oregon case that the Supreme Court adjudicated in 1925, *Pierce v. Society of Sisters*. The re-formed Ku Klux Klan, powerful in Oregon, where its scapegoat was Catholics rather than African Americans, lobbied the state legislature to pass a law requiring all the state's children to attend public school. The legislation was aimed against Catholic private and parochial schools. Nuns belonging to the Society of Sisters, who ran such schools, sued the state and won their final appeal before the Supreme Court. The justices told Oregon that it was entitled to establish educational standards that all students in the state must fulfill, but that it had no right to forbid children from attending the religious schools their parents had chosen. Justice James Clark McReynolds wrote: "The child is not the mere creature of the state; those who nurture him and direct his destiny have the right, coupled with the high duty, to recognize and prepare him for additional obligations."

Pierce was not a First Amendment case—it was argued under the due process clause of the Fourteenth Amendment. In 1940, however, the Supreme Court for the first time decided that it would review a First Amendment free-exercise case arising in one of the states (*Reynolds* had arisen in the western federal territories). Its 9–0 adjudication of *Cantwell v. Connecticut* (1940) was one of the very few occasions on which the Court has reached a unanimous verdict in a First Amendment case. It overturned the breach-of-peace conviction of a Jehovah's Witness who had distributed anti-Catholic literature and played anti-Catholic gramophone records in a largely Catholic district. Justice Owen Josephus Roberts, writing for the Court, noted that Cantwell may have been pro-

"Church and State—No Union Upon Any Terms." In Thomas Nast's 1871 cartoon, a woman standing between the pillars of a building representing the state rejects the pleas of various religious leaders. LIBRARY OF CONGRESS

voking but "there is no showing that his deportment was noisy, truculent, overbearing, or offensive." His intention had been to interest passersby in his religious views and the First Amendment protected his right to do so.

Cantwell opened the door to Supreme Court adjudication of other First Amendment cases, and they became a regular fixture on its docket from then on. *Pierce* had established the right of religious schools to exist. Many subsequent cases thrashed out the question of whether the state, while permitting children to go to religious schools, was also allowed to contribute to the cost of their education. Religious parents, whose children went to these schools, had a powerful motive to say yes. In their view, after all, they were sparing the state an expense by not availing themselves of the public schools. Was it not discriminatory to make them pay for the public schools through their taxes, then pay again for their own children in the form of tuition fees? In *Everson v. Board of Education* (1947), the Court found, by the narrow vote of 5–4, that states could contribute financially to nonreligious elements of these children's education. In this instance, it could refund the cost of their bus travel to and from school.

Everson was important not only for the substance of its decision but also for its declaration of the general considerations that should govern such cases, all spelled out in Justice Hugo Black's majority decision. He wrote that the First Amendment, as applied to the states through the Fourteenth Amendment, showed that no government "can force nor influence a person to go to or to remain away from church against his will, or force him to profess a belief or disbelief in any religion," and that it could not penalize anyone "for entertaining or professing religious beliefs or disbeliefs, for church attendance or nonattendance."

Numerous subsequent cases refined the constitutional position on schools and had the collective effect of making schools far less religious places than they had been throughout most of the nation's history. In *McCollum v. Board of Education* (1948), the Court ruled that religious teachers could not enter public schools during normal school hours even to give voluntary instruction in each of the religions practiced by the students. In three bitterly contested cases (*Engel v. Vitale*, 1962; *Abington v. Schempp*, 1963; and *Murray v. Curlett*, 1963), it went much further by ruling that public-school children could not recite a

168

nondenominational prayer written by the New York Board of Regents, could not read the Bible or recite the Lord's Prayer, and could not have the Ten Commandments posted in their classrooms. This set of findings overturned laws in nearly every state and brought to a sudden end practices that had been hallowed by a century or more of continuous use. Critics, especially on the political right, demanded the impeachment of Chief Justice Earl Warren, who was already controversial for his judicial activism in other areas. A disgruntled Alabama congressman, mindful of the same chief justice's desegregation decision in *Brown v. Board of Education of Topeka, Kansas* (1954), declared: "First he put Negroes in the classroom—now he's taken God out!"

President John F. Kennedy, the first Catholic to occupy the White House, was in office at the time of these decisions. He had faced electoral opposition in 1960 from Protestant groups that believed his faith made him unfit for the presidency. Kennedy, determined to prove otherwise, had told a meeting of evangelical Protestant ministers in Houston just before the election that he, like all candidates, enjoyed freedom of conscience, that he believed in church-state separation, and that if ever an issue arose in which his religious conscience prevented him from doing his political duty, he would resign, as any president should. Once he was president, he refused to endorse draft constitutional amendments aimed at reversing the controversial school cases and urged citizens to obey the Court's rulings.

In considering these cases it is important to remember that religious groups were well represented among the litigants on both sides. Militant secularism, atheism, and agnosticism were always the preserve of a tiny minority. The American Civil Liberties Union, usually found on the "strict separation" side, counted many ministers, rabbis, and devout members of congregations among its supporters. In the tradition established by Roger Williams more than three centuries earlier and strongly upheld among most Baptist congregations, they feared that entanglement with the state would contaminate their faith. Defenders of school prayer and Bible reading, no less strongly supplied with outspoken clergymen, countered that such contamination was unlikely as long as the religious exercises were voluntary and nondenominational. The important point, in their view, was to underline the godly character of America in its great Cold War confrontation with the Soviet Union and "Godless Communism."

Lemon v. Kurtzman (1971) was among the most important of all the First Amendment school cases, in that it laid down a set of three requirements (the "Lemon test") for judging the constitutionality of laws relating to religious education. The Court has followed the test more or less closely ever since. First, a law must be neutral between religions and between religion and nonreligion. Second, the law's primary intent and impact must be secular; and third, it must not "excessively entangle" the state

with religion. The Lemon test could not resolve all controversies, of course, since "excessive entanglement" was itself open to a wide variety of interpretations.

Public opinion polls showed that the majority of Americans disliked the degree of church–state separation the Court specified, and throughout the 1970s and 1980s state governments looked for ways to reintroduce prayer and religious activities into public schools. The Moral Majority and other evangelical lobbies in the 1980s argued that "secular humanism" was itself a religious position, that it had displaced Christianity in public life, especially in schools, and that it thereby violated the establishment clause. The Court remained skeptical but it did concede, in *Board of Education v. Mergens* (1990), that voluntary religious groups should be allowed to meet on public school property in just the same way as any other student sports team, club, or society.

Religious schools flourished, meanwhile, as ever more parents abandoned the secularized public system. They were heartened by the Court's decision in *Mueller v. Allen* (1983), which upheld the constitutionality of a Minnesota law that gave a $700 state tax exemption to the parents of private school children, whether or not the schools were religious. By the narrowest majority, 5–4, the Court argued that the law, by favoring a broad category of Minnesota's citizens, whatever their beliefs, did not fall afoul of the Lemon test.

Numerous establishment clause cases also arose in nonschool contexts. Depending on the details, the Court sometimes appeared to decide similar cases in opposite ways—further evidence that this was a complex and controverted area of the law. For example, in *Braunfeld v. Braun* (1961), it investigated the dilemma of a furniture-store owner who was forced to close his store on Sundays in accord with Pennsylvania's Sunday closing law. He was an Orthodox Jew, however, and also closed the store on his Sabbath, Saturday, with the result that he lost two business days every week while his Christian competitors lost only one. Was not the Sunday closing law a violation of the establishment clause, based as it was on the Christian tradition of Sunday as Sabbath? The Court said no; it was a matter of national tradition, rather than religious establishment, and as such was defensible.

Two years later the Court appeared to reverse itself but denied that it had done so. In *Sherbert v. Verner* (1963), it examined the plight of a woman who belonged to the Seventh Day Adventists, a Christian group that (as with Judaism) takes Saturday as Sabbath. She was out of work, refused for religious reasons to take a job that compelled her to work on Saturdays, and found, when she applied for unemployment compensation, that she was denied it because she had declined to accept "suitable" job offers. This time the Supreme Court found in her favor, arguing that the state would only have been entitled to withhold her unemployment pay if it had had a "compelling" interest in doing so.

A related pair of cases, several years later, added a few more twists and turns to the labyrinth. The first was *Yoder v. Wisconsin* (1972). The state had passed a law requiring all children to attend schools until they reached the age of sixteen. Amish people in the state wanted to withdraw their children after eighth grade (age fourteen). They feared that the education their children received after that point was likely to draw them away from the Amish community, with its simple, unmechanized farming practices. Their claim for exemption from the state law, in other words, was based on the right to protect their religious free exercise. The Court found in their favor, even though, in doing so, it appeared to grant this one group special treatment because of its religion, which some commentators saw as a violation of the establishment clause.

In the second case, *Employment Division v. Smith* (1990), an Oregon citizen was fired from his job at a drug-rehabilitation clinic after eating peyote, the hallucinogenic fungus used by the Native American church of which he was a member. The drug was illegal in Oregon and the state government had not exempted religious users. When he was denied unemployment pay, Smith sued the state for violating his free-exercise rights. The logic of the *Sherbert* and *Yoder* decisions suggested that he would be upheld, but the Court used the *Reynolds* and *Braunfeld* precedents instead, declaring that Smith was entitled to hold his religious beliefs but that they did not excuse him from obeying generally applicable state laws.

Scholars and justices alike were uneasily aware by 2000 that whatever decision the Court made in a church–state case, it would have a line of precedents at hand to decide one way or the other. Take for example the case of the Christmas crèche owned by the city of Pawtucket, Rhode Island, and placed in the city's public square every December, which the Court might easily have condemned as a violation of the establishment clause. The ACLU and an alliance of ministers sued for its removal in 1980 and won. The city's indignant mayor, Dennis Lynch, appealed all the way to the Supreme Court and finally achieved a reversal of the decision. The Court ruled in *Lynch v. Donnelly* (1984)—at 5–4 another close decision—that the crèche was permissible because it was accompanied by a Santa, various elves, and a brace of plastic reindeer, whose collective effect was to make the display acceptably "traditional" rather than unacceptably "religious."

The sixty-year constitutional struggle over the First Amendment from 1940 to 2000 was largely symbolic; no one seriously believed that any one church was going to be established by law or that any of the citizens' religions were going to be proscribed. No one suffered serious harm from the Court's verdicts. While these cases were argued with so much anguish, few commentators, ironically, paused to observe the fate of twentieth-century Europe's still common established churches. Their lesson was that in the twentieth century establishment was synonymous with religious weakness and indifference, rather than with the tyranny and intolerance it was alleged to imply. While America's disestablished churches drew in nearly half the nation's population every week, the established Church of England, nemesis of the revolutionary generation, could scarcely attract 3 percent of the British people. American experience showed that disestablishment and religious vitality went hand in hand.

BIBLIOGRAPHY

Alley, Robert S, ed. *The Supreme Court on Church and State*. New York: Oxford University Press, 1990.

Eastland, Terry, ed. *Religious Liberty in the Supreme Court: The Cases that Define the Debate over Church and State*. Washington, D.C.: Ethics and Public Policy Center, 1993.

Frankel, Marvin. *Faith and Freedom: Religious Liberty in America*. New York: Hill and Wang, 1994.

Hunter, James D. *Articles of Faith, Articles of Peace: The Religious Liberty Clauses and the American Public Philosophy*. Washington, D.C.: Brookings Institution, 1990.

Kramnick, Isaac, and R. Laurence Moore. *The Godless Constitution: The Case against Religious Correctness*. New York: Norton, 1996.

Levy, Leonard. *The Establishment Clause: Religion and the First Amendment*. 2d rev. ed. Chapel Hill: University of North Carolina Press, 1994.

Menendez, Albert. *The December Wars: Religious Symbols and Ceremonies in the Public Square*. Buffalo, N.Y.: Prometheus, 1993.

Noonan, John T., Jr. *The Believer and the Powers that Are: Cases, History, and Other Data Bearing on the Relation of Religion and Government*. New York: Macmillan, 1987.

Reichley, James. *Religion in American Public Life*. Washington, D.C.: Brookings Institution, 1985.

Patrick N. Allitt

See also **Church of England in the Colonies; Civil Religion; First Amendment; Religious Liberty; *Reynolds v. United States*.**

CHURCH OF CHRIST, SCIENTIST,

is a religious system that emerged in nineteenth-century New England as the region and the nation were transformed by urbanization, industrialization, religious revivalism, and the rising authority of science.

Christian Science was founded by Mary Baker Eddy, born in 1821 in Bow, New Hampshire, and raised as a Congregationalist there. She was also exposed to mesmerism, Spiritualism, and other popular spiritual and healing movements developing in the mid-nineteenth-century Northeast, and was particularly influenced by healing practitioner Phineas P. Quimby, who considered mental error the source of all disease. In 1866, while living in Lynn, Massachusetts, the invalid Eddy experienced a sudden physical healing and religious conversion. Newly empowered, she spent the next several years living in poverty, practicing healing, and developing her religious ideas

Mary Baker Eddy. The founder of Christian Science, which she first described in detail in an 1875 publication.

among the socially dislocated in the industrial cities of New England.

Eddy taught that a universal divine principle was the only reality; that matter, evil, disease, and death were illusory; that Christ's healing method involved a "scientific" application of these truths; and that redemption and healing were available to anyone who became properly attuned with the divine. In 1875, Eddy published *Science and Health with Key to Scriptures*, which outlined her system and a method for discerning the Bible's inner "spiritual sense." Revised by Eddy several times, it became and remains the authoritative text for Christian Science. Eddy's message, emphasizing personal growth and well-being, appealed to Americans—particularly women—experiencing disempowerment and spiritual alienation amid the industrial and urban growth of the late nineteenth century and dissatisfaction with conventional Christianity.

In 1875, Eddy and her followers held their first public service at Eddy's Christian Scientists' Home in Lynn, and four years later, established the Church of Christ (Scientist). In 1881, Eddy moved the church to Boston and founded the Massachusetts Metaphysical College. College trainees, mostly women, spread across the Northeast and Midwest, making Christian Science into a national movement whose members were of increasing wealth and status. In 1886, Eddy established the National Christian Science Association (NCSA). Internal schism, outside cler-

ical criticism, and the emergence of rival movements soon led Eddy to centralize and bureaucratize her church. She dissolved the college in 1889, and in 1892 dismantled the NCSA and established the First Church of Christ, Scientist, in Boston. She appealed to followers nationwide to affiliate their congregations with this "mother church," and appointed a self-perpetuating board of directors to govern it.

Christian Science grew rapidly, especially during its early decades. In 1906 there were 636 congregations with 85,717 members, and by 1936 there were 1,970 congregations with 268,915 members. The church stopped releasing membership statistics, but there were an estimated 475,000 members in the United States by the late 1970s. The church also established a publishing empire, best represented since 1908 by the *Christian Science Monitor*, and continues to spread its message through "reading rooms" nationwide.

Christian Science remains primarily urban and upper middle class in constituency and women continue to predominate its membership. It remains relatively small, beset throughout the twentieth century by legal controversies over members' refusal of conventional medical treatment. But the success of its religion of personal healing sparked the emergence and growth of the New Thought movement and a broader emphasis on healing, counseling, and spiritual wellness in modern American Christianity.

BIBLIOGRAPHY

Gottschalk, Stephen. *The Emergence of Christian Science in American Religious Life*. Berkeley: University of California Press, 1973.

Knee, Stuart E. *Christian Science in the Age of Mary Baker Eddy*. Westport, Conn.: Greenwood, 1994.

Thomas, Robert David. *"With Bleeding Footsteps": Mary Baker Eddy's Path to Religious Leadership*. New York: Knopf, 1994.

Bret E. Carroll

See also **Christianity; Science and Religion, Relations of; Spiritualism; Women in Churches.**

CHURCH OF ENGLAND IN THE COLONIES.

The Church of England, or Anglican Church, first took root in America at Jamestown in 1607. The earliest plans for Virginia envisioned a role for the church, and as soon as the colony was strong enough, it was legally established. All the other southern colonies, except Maryland, were founded under the leadership of churchmen. In time, the Church of England was established in all of them, although not in North Carolina until 1765. Maryland was founded by a Roman Catholic proprietor, George Calvert, and in 1649 its general assembly passed an act protecting freedom of religion; but the Protestant settlers there took control in the Revolution of 1688 and by 1702 had suppressed the open practice of Catholicism and established the Church of England. The Anglican Church dominated the four leading counties of New York. In the other northern colonies Anglicans enjoyed no establishment and depended for support largely upon the English Society for the Propagation of the Gospel in Foreign Parts, founded in 1701.

During the eighteenth century the Church of England advanced in the colonies where it was not established and lost ground in those where it was—a phenomenon that corresponded with the religious awakenings and general breakdown of theological barriers during that century. The American Revolution deprived the church of its establishments in the South and of the aid of the Society for the Propagation of the Gospel in the North and exposed it to some popular opposition. In 1789 the Protestant Episcopal Church broke from the English church and its primate, the archbishop of Canterbury. Although it created a revised version of the *Book of Common Prayer* for use in the United States and set up a native episcopate, the Episcopal Church retained its predecessor's high-church rituals and tradition of apostolic succession.

BIBLIOGRAPHY

Herklots, Hugh G. *The Church of England and the American Episcopal Church*. London: Mowbray, 1966.

W. W. Manross / A. R.

See also **Church and State, Separation of; Episcopalianism; Great Awakening.**

CHURCH OF GOD IN CHRIST. The Church of God in Christ, the largest black Pentecostal denomination in the United States, emerged out of struggles within the black Baptist churches of the American South in the 1890s. Leading figures in its establishment were Charles Harrison Mason and Charles Price Jones, both of whom subscribed to the Wesleyan doctrine of a "second blessing," or sanctification experience following conversion. They also defended slave worship practices, challenging the notion that former slaves should conform to non-African modes of worship and endorsing such practices as the ring shout and the use of dancing and drums in worship. The newly formed "Sanctified Church" became the focus of piety among southern blacks and insisted that they maintain a separate identity through forms of dress, fasting, and rites of passage. Mason was the only early Pentecostal pastor whose church was legally incorporated; this allowed it to perform clerical ordinations, recognized by the civil authorities, of pastors who served other Pentecostal groups throughout the South.

The 1906 Asuza Street Revival in Los Angeles, presided over by the black preacher William J. Seymour, drew the approval of many Pentecostal leaders. Mason sought the baptism of the Holy Spirit at Asuza Street and acquired a new comprehension of the power of speaking in tongues, a gift he soon applied in his public ministry. Debate arose in 1907 between Mason and Charles Jones over the use of speaking in tongues as initial evidence of the baptism of the Holy Spirit, and Mason took about half the ministers and members with him; those who remained with Jones became the Church of Christ (Holiness) U.S.A. The Church of God in Christ quickly built upon its southern constituency, expressing a greater faith in the power of God to transcend human sinfulness than other black denominations. It stressed freedom as the essence of religion and the need for an infusion of the Holy Spirit in order to give power for service. Such power assured individuals and communities of personal security in a region where they lived under oppressive conditions.

Under Mason the Church of God in Christ sought to capture the guiding essence of the Holy Spirit while avoiding the contentiousness of Baptist-style conventions. The instrument for this was the Holy Convocation at Memphis, Tennessee, a combination of annual revival and camp meeting. Held in late November and early December, it consisted of twenty-one days devoted to prayer, Bible teaching, testimonies, and singing. The intention was to preserve, through repetition, the essence of the covenant with God and to inspire listeners with their special status as God's chosen. Following the great migration of African Americans from the rural South to the cities in the early twentieth century, Mason sent out preachers and female missionaries to Texas, Kansas, Missouri, Illinois, Ohio, New York, California, and Michigan. The church experienced phenomenal growth that was aided by the willingness of missionaries to care for children, pray for the sick, and teach homemaking skills.

In 1911 Mason established a Women's Department to make full use of the skills of the church's female members. He welcomed women's free expression of their spiritual gifts, but insisted on the reservation of the offices of pastor and preacher for men; all female leaders remained subordinate to a male. First under Lizzie Roberson and then Lillian Brooks-Coffey, churches were founded and Bible study and prayer groups were organized. They called on women to dress modestly and to respect a pastor's authority. Mother Roberson also succeeded in raising, through her subordinates, the funds needed to open the denomination's first bank account. Ultimately the Women's Department took responsibility for foreign missions to Haiti, Jamaica, the Bahamas, England, and Liberia.

The church experienced a tempestuous transition to a new generation of leaders after Mason's death in 1961. In more recent years, however, it has grown dramatically and become visible to the American public. The church became a leader in ecumenical discussions with nonfundamentalist denominations, and C. H. Mason Seminary, established in 1970, was one of the few Pentecostal seminaries in the nation accredited by the Association of Theological Schools. During the 1970s the church also established military, prison, and hospital ministries. By the early 1990s, the Church of God in Christ, headed by Presiding Bishop Gilbert E. Patterson, had become the fifth largest denomination in the United States, with 5,499,875 members in 1991.

BIBLIOGRAPHY

Clemmons, Ithiel C. *Bishop C. H. Mason and the Roots of the Church of God in Christ.* Bakersfield, Calif.: Pneuma Life, 1996.

Franklin, Robert Michael. "My Soul Says Yes, the Urban Ministry of the Church of God in Christ." In *Churches, Cities and Human Community: Urban Ministry in the United States, 1945–1985.* Edited by Clifford J. Green. Grand Rapids, Mich.: Eeerdmans, 1996.

Paris, Peter. *The Social Teaching of the Black Churches.* Philadelphia: Fortress Press, 1985.

Jeremy Bonner

See also **Pentecostal Churches.**

CIBOLA, an Indian name for the villages of the Zuni in what is now western NEW MEXICO, rumored in the early sixteenth century to be fabulously wealthy. In 1539 the Spanish dispatched an expedition under Friar Marcos de Niza, guided by a Moorish man named Esteban. Esteban went ahead but was killed by the Zuni. De Niza, who had merely glimpsed a Zuni village from a distance, returned to Mexico with an imaginative account of the wealth of the Seven Cities of Cibola. His report inspired a stronger expedition the next year under Francisco Vásquez de Coronado. The name "Cibola" later came to be applied to the entire PUEBLO country and was extended to the GREAT PLAINS.

BIBLIOGRAPHY

Clissold, Stephen. *The Seven Cities of Cibola.* London: Eyre and Spottiswoode, 1961.

Kenneth M. Stewart/A. R.

See also **Conquistadores; Coronado Expeditions; Explorations and Expeditions: Spanish; Southwest; Tribes: Southwestern.**

CIMARRON, PROPOSED TERRITORY OF.

Known as the Public Land Strip, or No Man's Land, the proposed territory of Cimarron took in the area of the present-day Oklahoma Panhandle. Settled by squatters and cattlemen, the territory had no law. To protect squatter claims, settlers started a movement to organize the country into Cimarron Territory. In March 1887 territorial representatives drew up a resolution assuming authority for the territory. The proposal was referred to the committee on territories in Congress. There it remained, without action. The territory became part of Oklahoma, which was admitted to the Union in 1907, and the west-

ernmost county in the Panhandle retained the name "Cimarron."

BIBLIOGRAPHY

Baird, W. David, and Danney Goble. *The Story of Oklahoma.* Norman: University of Oklahoma Press, 1994.

Gibson, Arrell Morgan. *Oklahoma: A History of Five Centuries.* 2d ed. Norman: University of Oklahoma Press, 1981.

Anna Lewis/F. B.

See also **Boomer Movement; Indian Territory.**

CINCINNATI was founded in 1788 and named for the Society of Cincinnati, an organization of revolutionary war officers. When incorporated in 1802, it had only about 750 residents. However, the town went on to become the largest city in Ohio throughout most of the nineteenth century and the largest city in the Midwest before the Civil War. In 1850, Cincinnati boasted 115,436 inhabitants. As the chief port on the Ohio River, it could claim the title of Queen City of the West. Although it produced a wide range of manufactures for the western market, Cincinnati became famous as a meatpacking center, winning the nickname Porkopolis. The city's prosperity attracted thousands of European immigrants, especially Germans, whose breweries, singing societies, and beer gardens became features of Cincinnati life.

With the advent of the railroad age, Cincinnati's location on the Ohio River no longer ensured its preeminence as a commercial center, and other midwestern cities surged ahead of it. Between 1890 and 1900, Cincinnati fell to second rank among Ohio cities as Cleveland surpassed it in population. In 1869, however, Cincinnati won distinction by fielding the nation's first all-professional baseball team. Moreover, through their biennial music festival, Cincinnatians attempted to establish their city as the cultural capital of the Midwest.

During the first half of the twentieth century, Cincinnati continued to grow moderately, consolidating its reputation as a city of stability rather than dynamic change. In the 1920s, good-government reformers secured adoption of a city manager charter, and in succeeding decades Cincinnati won a name for having honest, efficient government. Yet, unable to annex additional territory following World War II, the city's population gradually declined from a high of 503,998 in 1950 to 331,285 in 2000. During the 1940s and 1950s, southern blacks and whites migrated to the city, transforming the once-Germanic Over-the-Rhine neighborhood into a "hillbilly ghetto" and boosting the African American share of the city's population from 12.2 percent in 1940 to 33.8 percent in 1980. Although not a model of dynamism, Cincinnati could boast of a diversified economy that made it relatively recession proof compared with other midwestern cities dependent on motor vehicle and heavy machinery manufacturing. The city prospered as the headquar-

Pike's Opera House. An engraving of one of Cincinnati's cultural symbols from the nineteenth century. CINCINNATI MUSEUM CENTER, DEPARTMENT OF AUDIOVISUAL COLLECTION

ters of Procter and Gamble, and also was headquarters of the Kroger supermarket chain, Federated Department Stores, and banana giant Chiquita Brands.

BIBLIOGRAPHY

Giglierano, Geoffrey J., and Deborah A. Overmyer. *The Bicentennial Guide to Greater Cincinnati: A Portrait of Two Hundred Years.* Cincinnati: Cincinnati Historical Society, 1988.

Silberstein, Iola. *Cincinnati Then and Now.* Cincinnati: Voters Service Educational Fund of the League of Women Voters of the Cincinnati Area, 1982.

Jon C. Teaford

See also **City Manager Plan; German Americans; Miami Purchase; Midwest; Ohio; Ohio River.**

CINCINNATI, SOCIETY OF THE. Organized in May 1783, the Society of the Cincinnati was established by disbanding officers of the American Continental Army. Moved by the bonds of friendship forged during the war years and concerned by the financial plight of many whose pay was in arrears, the officers enthusiastically adopted the suggestion of General Henry Knox for a permanent association. The organization first met at the headquarters of General Friedrich von Steuben at Fishkill, New York, with George Washington as the first president general. The name alluded to Cincinnatus, the Roman general who retired quietly to his farmstead after leading his army to victory. The society established a fund for widows and the indigent and provided for the perpetuation of the organization by making membership hereditary in the eldest male line. There were thirteen state societies and an association in France for the French officers, comprising a union known as the General Society.

The society aroused antagonism, particularly in republican circles, because of its hereditary provisions, its large permanent funds, and its establishment of committees of correspondence for the mutual exchange of information between the member societies. Due to popular suspicion of elitist organizations, the group grew dormant after the French Revolution. About 1900 a revival of interest began that reestablished the dormant societies, enlarged the membership, and procured a headquarters and public museum, Anderson House, in Washington, D.C. In the early 1970s membership numbered about 2,500.

BIBLIOGRAPHY

Resch, John Phillips. *Suffering Soldiers: Revolutionary War Veterans, Moral Sentiment, and Political Culture in the Early Republic.* Amherst: University of Massachusetts Press, 1999.

Wills, Garry. *Cincinnatus: George Washington and the Enlightenment.* Garden City, N.Y.: Doubleday, 1984.

John D. Kilbourne/H. S.

See also **Revolution, American: Military History; Veterans' Organizations.**

CINCINNATI RIOTS.

CINCINNATI RIOTS. In 1883 the criminal courts of Cincinnati, Ohio, sentenced to death only four of the fifty men accused of murder that year, fueling fears that the courts had become corrupt. On the weekend of 28–30 March 1884, mobs repeatedly attacked the jailhouse. After lynching two inmates, the mob stole guns, set fire to the courthouse, looted stores, and waged a bloody battle against a company of state militia, which threw up street barricades where the worst of the fighting ensued. Not until the sixth day were the barricades removed and the streetcar service resumed. At least 45 persons had been killed and 138 injured.

BIBLIOGRAPHY

Gilje, Paul A. *Rioting in America.* Bloomington: Indiana University Press, 1996.

Schweninger, Joseph M. *A Frightful and Shameful Story: The Cincinnati Riot of 1884 and the Search for Order.* Columbus, Ohio, 1996.

Alvin F. Harlow/A. R.

See also **Capital Punishment; Cincinnati; Gilded Age; Riots.**

CINEMA. *See* **Film.**

CIRCUIT RIDERS. Ministerial circuit riding was devised by the English religious dissenter John Wesley. A circuit consisted of numerous places of worship scattered over a relatively large district and served by one or more lay preachers. The original American circuit riders introduced METHODISM into the colonies. Robert Strawbridge, who came to America about 1764, was the first in the long line. Wesley sent eight official lay missionaries to America from 1769 to 1776, and several came on their own. By the end of the American Revolution there were about one hundred circuit riders in the United States, none of whom were ordained. With the formation of the Methodist Episcopal church in 1784, Francis Asbury was chosen bishop, several of the circuit riders were ordained, and the system was widely extended into the trans-Allegheny West.

Circuit riding was peculiarly adaptable to frontier conditions, since one preacher, equipped with horse and saddlebags, could proselytize in a great many communities. In this way the riders kept pace with the advancing settlement, bringing the influence of evangelical PROTESTANTISM to new and unstable communities. Peter Cartwright, active in Kentucky, Tennessee, the Ohio River valley, and Illinois, was the best known of the frontier preachers.

The circuit system largely accounts for the even distribution of Methodism throughout the United States. Other religious bodies partially adopted it, particularly the Cumberland Presbyterians. By spurning religious conventions, preaching to African Americans, and challenging the established churches, these visionary preachers gave voice to a rising egalitarian spirit in American society in the early years of the nineteenth century.

BIBLIOGRAPHY

Hatch, Nathan O. *The Democratization of American Christianity.* New Haven, Conn.: Yale University Press, 1989.

Heyrman, Christine Leigh. *Southern Cross: The Beginnings of the Bible Belt.* New York: Knopf, 1997.

Wallis, Charles L., ed. *Autobiography of Peter Cartwright.* New York: Abingdon Press, 1956.

William W. Sweet/A. R.

See also **African American Religions and Sects; Dissenters; Evangelicalism and Revivalism.**

CIRCUITS, JUDICIAL. Judicial circuits form the largest administrative subunit of the federal judicial system. With the exception of the District of Columbia circuit, each is a multistate unit formed by the federal district court or courts within each state in the circuit. Decisions of the federal district courts are appealable to the U.S. Court of Appeals in the circuit in which the district court resides. The decisions of the Courts of Appeals are subject to review by the U.S. Supreme Court.

Article III, section 1, of the U.S. Constitution establishes the Supreme Court and gives Congress the power to establish "such inferior courts" as it deems necessary. In enacting the Judiciary Act of 1789, Congress created three judicial circuits and established one district court in each state of the Union. Congress then provided for the appointment of district judges, but no circuit judges. The circuit courts were to consist of one district judge and two Supreme Court justices, who were to "ride circuit." As the United States expanded, Congress created new circuits and increased the number of district courts and judges. Circuit court sessions were increasingly difficult to hold, for the burden of travel was too great. In 1869 Congress passed the Circuit Court Act, which created one circuit judge in each circuit, and required the Supreme Court justices to attend circuit court only once every two years. The circuit courts were otherwise to be held by the circuit judge and the district judge, either alone or together.

In the last quarter of the nineteenth century, the United States experienced a tremendous increase in the volume and scope of federal litigation due to the rapid increase of federal lawsuits to settle disputes stemming from the growth of national manufacturing and distribution of goods, as well as litigation produced by the Civil War constitutional amendments and their enforcement legislation. The growing volume of federal litigation caused a severe backlog of cases in the Supreme Court. To ease the workload of the Court and the long delays litigants experienced in waiting for the Court's decisions, in 1890 Congress passed the Evarts Act, which established

Circus Rehearsal. A trainer puts four tigers through their paces in preparation for their performance in the self-proclaimed "Greatest Show on Earth," c. 1920. RINGLING BROS. AND BARNUM & BAILEY

courts of appeals in each of the ten circuits. Final judgments of the district and circuit courts were appealable to them, parties have an absolute right to take an appeal, and their judgments were final except for those cases in which the Supreme Court voted to grant a writ of certiorari and review the decision of the courts of appeals.

Congress created two court of appeals judgeships in each circuit. The new appellate courts were to have panels of three judges—the two court of appeals judges and either a district judge or, on rare occasions, a circuit justice—to decide cases. In 1911 Congress abolished the circuit courts. During the twentieth century Congress created two additional circuits (there are currently eleven plus the U.S. Circuit Court of Appeals for the District of Columbia).

As federal regulation of American society expanded, the courts in the federal circuits became the primary arenas for settling disputes over the nature and scope of permissible governmental intervention in society. The courts of appeals became important policymakers because their judicial decisions are the final decision in all but about 2 percent of the cases, since the U.S. Supreme Court takes and decides only several hundred cases per year from the thousands of circuit courts of appeals cases.

BIBLIOGRAPHY

Frankfurter, Felix, and James M. Landis. *The Business of the Supreme Court: A Study in the Federal Judicial System.* New York: Macmillan, 1928.

Howard, J. Woodford, Jr. *Courts of Appeals in the Federal Judicial System: A Study of the Second, Fifth, and District of Columbia Circuits.* Princeton, N.J.: Princeton University Press, 1981.

Rayman L. Solomon

See also **Supreme Court.**

CIRCUS AND CARNIVAL.

Circuses and carnivals have played important roles in American life and imagination and continue to influence U.S. entertainment and popular culture. Although the two have separate histories, they share common elements, draw upon overlapping industry sectors and audiences, and have influenced one another for over a century.

Circuses and carnivals have European and English antecedents in medieval fairs, menageries, and performances and have been traced back to the Roman Circus Maximus and ancient fertility rites. The first circus to perform within a ring dates from 1770 when Englishman Philip Astley created an equestrian entertainment that expanded to include acrobats and comic acts. Astley's show soon went on the road and inspired competitors.

The idea quickly spread to America, and by 1785 Philadelphia could boast a permanent circus-like event. Scottish equestrian John Bill Ricketts added spectacle and attracted famous patrons such as George Washington. At the same time, traveling menageries featuring exotic animals became popular, beginning with the exhibition of

Getting the Big Top Ready. Horse-drawn circus wagons head toward the Ringling Brothers and Barnum & Bailey's giant tent, 1932. RINGLING BROS. AND BARNUM & BAILEY® THE GREATEST SHOW ON EARTH®

Old Bet, an elephant owned by New York entrepreneur Hachaliah Bailey.

By the middle of the nineteenth century the two forms had combined, with pioneers such as George Bailey, nephew of Hachaliah, exhibiting animals during the day and mounting circus performances at night. The addition of wild animals and handlers such as famed lion tamer Isaac A. Van Amburgh added excitement; in 1871, W. C. Coup introduced a second ring.

The transformation of the circus into a national institution was furthered by legendary showman P. T. Barnum, who joined James A. Bailey in 1880 to form the company that was to become Barnum & Bailey. Barnum's fame rested on his promotional genius and exhibition of human oddities, helping to make the "side show" an indispensable element of the circus.

As America expanded westward, so did the circus, which by the 1880s boasted three rings and was using rail transportation. Between 1870 and 1915 the circus evolved into a big business and established itself as an American icon. In the late nineteenth and early twentieth centuries the annual circus parade, including animals and performers in full regalia, electrified midwestern communities.

In 1917 the Ringling Brothers, siblings from Wisconsin, purchased Barnum & Bailey and rechristened it "The Ringling Brothers and Barnum & Bailey Combined Shows"—or, as it is known to most Americans, "The Greatest Show on Earth." During its heyday, and throughout the twentieth century, Barnum & Bailey recruited some of the most celebrated circus performers in the world, including the great clown Emmett Kelly, the trapeze family known as the Flying Wallendas, and May Wirth, the incomparable equestrian acrobat.

The circus began to slip following World War I, the victim of competing forms of entertainment such as AMUSEMENT PARKS, carnivals, radio, and movies. In 1956 Ringling Brothers passed into the hands of Irvin Feld, an entrepreneur who modernized the show and the business. In the twenty-first century only a few circuses travel in the United States, but the spectacle retains its appeal, especially to children.

Carnivals

The American carnival built on the tradition of the fair and also borrowed from new forms of entertainment that emerged toward the end of the nineteenth century, including the Wild West show, the medicine show, and the circus side show. The crucible of the American carnival, however, was the world exposition or fair, which evolved as a monument to technology and progress from agricultural fairs, trade centers, and "pleasure gardens" of me-

177

dieval and Rennaissance Europe and England. Beginning with London's Crystal Palace in 1851, this phenomenon reached its height with the 1893 World's Columbian Exposition held in Chicago. Millions of Americans experienced the marvels of electrification and the scientific and technological wonders that were showcased in the beaux arts buildings of the "White City."

The exposition also featured the Midway Plaisance, a thoroughfare crowned by the newly invented Ferris wheel and enlivened by purportedly educational displays of near-naked Native Americans and "savages" from Africa and the South Sea Islands. The popular and lucrative midway led away from the exposition proper to more sensational, privately owned concessions pandering "freaks," sex, and rigged games.

The exposition brought together the elements that defined both the American carnival and the stationary amusement park for over 50 years—mechanized rides, freak shows, participatory games, food, and blatant seediness and hokum. In the years following the exposition, showmen such as Frank C. Bostock and Samuel W. Gumpertz reprised its attractions at Coney Island, New York, where three separate entertainment centers coalesced in the first decade of the twentieth century to create the wild, outré modern amusement park.

By 1920 the United States had over 1,500 amusement parks at the edge of cities, and traveling carnivals supplied similar fun to small towns and local fairs. Gradually, however, the raucous industry felt the impact of local regulation, and many of its popular features wilted. The death knell, however, sounded in 1954 with the opening of Disneyland in Anaheim, California. While retaining some of the variety, color, and fantasy of the carnival, Disney and its competitors created an entirely different ambiance of a sanitized, idealized world dramatizing icons and heroes of American culture within the context of American economic and technological power.

The relatively few traveling carnivals that remain have adopted the cultural trappings of the contemporary theme park, writ small. Strates Shows, Inc., for example, a family business organized in 1923, explains the changes this way: "In our technological society, the animals and rare 'freak' shows are a thing of the past, and the famous girl shows have disappeared . . . Strates Shows stays abreast of the market . . . through continued commitment to producing good, wholesome family fun."

BIBLIOGRAPHY

Bogdan, Robert. *Freak Show: Presenting Human Oddities for Amusement and Profit.* Chicago and London: University of Chicago Press, 1988.

Brouws, Jeff, and Bruce Caron. *Inside the Live Reptile Tent: The Twilight World of the Carnival Midway.* San Francisco: Chronicle Books, 2001.

McGowan, Philip. *American Carnival: Seeing and Reading American Culture.* Contributions to American Culture Series, #10. Westport, Conn: Greenwood Press, 2001.

Murray, Marian. *Circus! From Rome to Ringling.* 1956. Reprint, Westport, Conn.: Greenwood Press, 1973.

Wilmeth, Don B. "Circus and Outdoor Entertainment." In *Concise Histories of American Popular Culture.* Contributions to the Study of Popular Culture, #4, edited by M. Thomas Inge. Westport, Conn.: Greenwood Press, 1982.

Perry Frank

See also **County and State Fairs.**

CITIES. *See* **Urbanization.**

CITIZEN KANE, directed by Orson Welles, who also co-wrote the script with Herman J. Mankiewicz and played the film's main character, was released by RKO in 1941. It is widely considered to be the masterpiece of American cinema. A veiled depiction of the publishing industrialist William Randolph Hearst, the film begins at the end of the story with the death of Charles Foster Kane. A reporter is dispatched to investigate Kane's last word, "Rosebud." The film then moves through a series of flashbacks that depict the character's turbulent life.

Citizen Kane. Orson Welles, who co-wrote and directed this landmark film, also stars as the complex American tycoon.
THE KOBAL COLLECTION

The powerful Hearst tried to have the film suppressed, and it enjoyed only limited critical and popular success, receiving nine Oscar nominations but only one award, Best Original Screenplay. By the 1950s, however, *Citizen Kane* began to receive widespread international recognition. It continues to be screened in revivals and film courses, and it has exerted major influence on filmmakers throughout the world. *Kane* is an important film because of its narrative and stylistic complexity. Welles used high-contrast lighting, deep focus, long takes, quick edits, montage sequences, and abrupt changes in sound to heighten the drama and to explicate the psychology of its characters. To achieve the film's remarkable images, Welles and cinematographer Gregg Toland relied on such innovative techniques as optical printers, miniatures, and matte prints. The result is a film with rich subtleties in both story and style.

BIBLIOGRAPHY

Carringer, Robert L. *The Making of* Citizen Kane. Rev. ed. Berkeley: University of California Press, 1996.

Gottesman, Ronald L. *Perspectives on* Citizen Kane. New York: G. K. Hall, 1996.

Daniel Bernardi

See also **Film.**

CITIZENS' ALLIANCES

were agrarian organizations formed first in Kansas and then in the neighboring states of Iowa and Nebraska by townspeople who supported the Farmers' Alliances. When the supreme council of the Southern Alliance met at Ocala, Florida, in December 1890, it recognized the value of such support and assisted in the organization of these groups into the National Citizens' Alliance as a kind of auxiliary. Even more eager than the farmers for third-party action, members of the Citizens' Alliance actively participated in the several conventions that led to the formation of the People's Party, which subsequently absorbed their order.

BIBLIOGRAPHY

Goodwyn, Lawrence. *The Populist Moment: A Short History of the Agrarian Revolt in America.* New York: Oxford University Press, 1978.

McMath, Robert C., Jr. *Populist Vanguard: A History of the Southern Farmers' Alliance.* Chapel Hill: University of North Carolina Press, 1975.

John D. Hicks / A. G.

See also **Agriculture; Conventions, Party Nominating; Cooperatives, Farmers'; Farmers' Alliance; Ocala Platform; Populism.**

CITIZENS BAND (CB) RADIO

is a two-way, low-power radio band for use by the public. The Federal Communications Commission (FCC) first issued CB licenses in 1947. CB operators chat and exchange information on road conditions and the location of police speed traps. Popular among truck drivers, CB came to be identified with the culture of the open road. Operators adopted colorful nicknames ("handles") for use on the air. In the mid-1970s CB radio became a pop-culture phenomenon; by 1977, 20 million were enthusiasts. By the time the FCC ended the licensing requirement for CB operators in 1983, the fad was over. The spread of mobile phones by century's end had cleared the airwaves of all but a core of diehards and emergency personnel.

BIBLIOGRAPHY

Kneitel, Tom. *Tomcat's Big CB Handbook: Everything They Never Told You.* Commack, N.Y.: CRB Research Books, 1988.

James Kates / A. R.

See also **Radio; Telecommunications; Trucking Industry.**

CITIZENSHIP.

The concept of citizenship was at the heart of the Constitution. When Thomas Jefferson wrote in the Declaration of Independence in 1776, "We hold these truths to be self-evident, that all men are created equal, that they are endowed by their Creator with certain unalienable rights, that among these are life, liberty and the pursuit of happiness. That to secure these rights, governments are instituted among men, deriving their just powers from the consent of the governed," he drew upon the writings of the ancient Greeks Solon (circa 640–559 B.C.) and Pericles (490–429 B.C.) who had argued that the state has legitimacy only so far as it governs in the best interest of its citizens.

Jefferson argued that citizens were autonomous beings whose individual needs had value, and he said that governments that interfered with the fulfillment of those needs—"life, liberty and the pursuit of happiness"—were tyrannical and unjust. By "all men," he meant every human being. That Jefferson continued to own slaves shows a profound weakness in his character, but men and women of many ethnic backgrounds understood his words to apply to them, and the ideals of Jefferson were the intellectual foundation upon which many revolutions would follow.

In America, those ideals encouraged abolitionists and suffragettes. When the Constitution was written, its authors were well aware of the ideals that had motivated Americans to fight for their freedom from England. They carefully began the Constitution with a radical, defiant idea. "We the People" is the opening phrase, and it is presented as if it were a decree. In a monarchical society, the monarch would refer to himself or herself as "we," because he or she believed as Louis XIV put it, "I am the state." In a monarchy, power flows down from the top: a person's power stems from his or her relationship to the monarch, and a person has only as many rights and duties as the monarch should choose to give. In "We the People," this is reversed; the power of the new American government is to flow upward, not downward, and the powers of those who govern are to be only as great as the citizens should choose to give.

What constitutes a citizen became a matter of urgent debate because equality and freedom were tied to citizenship. Article I of the Constitution made three references to citizenship, in Sections 2, 3, and 8 (clause 4), governing the House of Representatives, the Senate, and naturalization. Representatives had to have been citizens for seven years and senators for nine years; the U.S. Congress had the power to set the rules for naturalizing citizens. Missing is a definition of citizen, an important point because the representatives in the House were to be apportioned throughout the United States primarily on the basis of population. It was understood that this included free women and children, but did it include slaves? If it did, would the slaves therefore be citizens entitled to the liberties of the Constitution? For the time being, the slaves were not to be counted.

Article II, Section 1 of the Constitution declared that to be president (and therefore vice president, too), a "person" must be "a natural-born citizen" and must have "been fourteen years a resident within the United States." The purpose of this was to make illegal the imposing of a foreign ruler on the nation, but it left in doubt what "natural-born" meant, although it customarily was interpreted to mean born within the borders of the United States or born within the borders of the colonies that became the United States.

It was Article IV that would form the basis of the lawsuit *Dred Scott v. Sandford* that resulted in the infamous Supreme Court ruling of 1857. In Section 2, the constitution declares "the citizens of each State shall be entitled to all privileges and immunities of citizens in the several States." Yet, the matter of who was a citizen was left to the individual state. Thomas Jefferson argued in the vein of Solon that only by being able to vote in the election of leaders is a person truly a citizen, and he argued that being able to vote was both a right and an obligation for every free person; he believed everyone who met the minimum age requirement should be able to vote. John Adams disagreed; he argued that only people who owned property had enough interest in maintaining a just and stable government and that only they should be allowed to vote. This latter idea implied two tiers of citizenship: one with all the rights and responsibilities of citizenship and one with only limited rights and responsibilities that could change by a person's purchasing land. When the Bill of Rights was passed, it was intended to apply to all citizens, landed or not, but many understood the Bill of Rights applied only to property-owning citizens and no others, even foreign nationals who had resided in the United States for many years.

The Matters of Slaves and Women's Citizenship

Jefferson's view slowly supplanted Adams's view, but out of the Constitution emerged at least two explosive dis-

agreements over who merited citizenship. One was over the status of women; the other was over the status of African Americans. After the adoption of the Constitution, there was an erosion of the civil rights of women throughout the country. In those states where women had once been able to hold public office or even vote, women were denied access to polling places. In general, women were held to have rights only through their relationship to husbands or close male kin. This sparked a branching in the abolitionist movement, as women abolitionists tied liberty for slaves to civil rights for women.

In 1857, the Supreme Court heard the appeal of the case of the slave Dred Scott, a slave who had filed suit claiming that when his master took him to a free state while in that state he should be a free man because that state forbade slavery. The court ruled that "negroes of the African race" whose ancestors were "imported into this country, and sold and held as slaves" were not "people" as the word was used in the Constitution, and they could not have citizenship and therefore they did not have even the right to file a lawsuit in the first place. This ruling actually contradicted the idea of "states' rights" as it was understood at the time, but the decision was a political one, not a constitutional one, and was intended to avoid the potential for civil strife between free states and slave states.

President Abraham Lincoln brought to office a view of citizenship born out of his upbringing on the frontier. He saw citizenship as a means for even the poorest Americans to seek redress of wrongs and to have access to education and other sources of social mobility. He summarized this in his Gettysburg Address, in which he said the government of the United States was "of the people, by the people, and for the people." It was his view that the government had no legitimacy beyond what the people gave it, yet in "for the people" he meant that the government was obliged to actively help its people in attaining their civil rights.

His supporters in Congress were called the "Radical Republicans" because they wanted to reshape America's institutions to reflect fully the sovereignty of the individual human being; to them "people" applied to every human being. Thus they sought the abolition of slavery, and most hoped to follow the emancipation of all slaves with the full enfranchisement of women because only by receiving the full protection of the Constitution, including the vote, could women attain a government that represented them; otherwise, according to Lincoln, Jefferson, and even Solon, the government would be tyranny. The Democrats, who had opposed the freeing of slaves, bitterly opposed changing the constitutional status of women.

The Fourteenth Amendment

The Fourteenth Amendment was intended to clarify the nature of American citizenship. For instance, it tried to explain what a "natural-born citizen" was and how to determine it. Its broadest and most important innovation was the assertion of the federal government's authority over every state in all matters pertaining to citizenship. It declared that any citizen of the United States was automatically a citizen in any state in which that person resided, even if that person moved from state to state. It declared that in counting people for representation in the House of Representatives, every human being was to be included except for "Indians not taxed," which meant those Native Americans who retained their native nationality rather than assimilating into American society.

Best known from the amendment is "No State shall make or enforce any law which shall abridge the privileges or immunities of citizens of the United States; nor shall any State deprive any person of life, liberty, or property, without due process of law; nor deny to any person within its jurisdiction the equal protection of the laws." The amendment was ratified 9 July 1868. Hundreds, perhaps thousands, of lawsuits have been filed on the basis of the amendment, but court rulings have had a checkered history. Although the amendment uses the word "person" throughout, women were still denied the right to vote and were denied full protection under the law in business and family dealings. When the issue of segregating African Americans from other Americans first came before the Supreme Court, it ruled that "separate but equal" was not a violation of equal protection under the law.

The Nineteenth Amendment of the Constitution says, "The right of citizens of the United States to vote shall not be denied or abridged by the United States or by any State on account of sex." This was ratified 18 August 1920. If, in light of the Fourteenth Amendment, women were in fact already citizens, this amendment would seem unnecessary, but the earlier amendment had been turned on its head, as if it meant that those states in which women had full citizenship rights did not have the federal rights unless the federal government said so. With the ratification of the Nineteenth Amendment, women, by being able to vote, were to take on the full obligations and rights of citizenship and were no longer to be regarded as half persons, half nonentities.

Some Twentieth-Century Consequences

In 1954, the full effect of the Fourteenth Amendment began to be realized. In the case of *Brown v. the Board of Education*, the Supreme court ruled that separation of people based on race was inherently unequal, a violation of the Fourteenth Amendment. This began a series of rulings in federal courts that redefined citizenship as a human right not to be abrogated by government, resulting in the 1971 ruling in *Rogers v. Bellei* that declared the government could not take citizenship from any American citizen except as allowed by the Fourteenth Amendment (treason) or if the citizen were a naturalized citizen who had lied to gain entry to the United States or gain citizenship. Those people who renounced American citizenship did not have a right to get it back.

BIBLIOGRAPHY

Aleinikoff, Thomas Alexander. *Semblance of Sovereignty: The Constitution, the State, and American Citizenship*. Cambridge, Mass.: Harvard University Press, 2002.

Bates, Stephen. "Reinvigorating Citizenship." *Society* 36, no. 3 (March–April 1999): 80–85.

Clarke, Paul Barry, ed. *Citizenship*. Boulder, Colo.: Pluto Press, 1994.

Denvir, John. *Democracy's Constitution: Claiming the Privileges of American Citizenship*. Urbana: University of Illinois Press, 2001.

Preiss, Byron, and David Osterlund, editors. *The Constitution of the United States of America: The Bicentennial Keepsake Edition*. New York: Bantam Books, 1987.

Shklar, Judith N. *American Citizenship: The Quest for Inclusion*. Cambridge, Mass.: Harvard University Press, 1991.

Smith, Rogers M. *Civic Ideals: Conflicting Visions of Citizenship in U.S. History*. New Haven, Conn.: Yale University Press, 1997.

Kirk H. Beetz

See also **Constitution of the United States; Indian Citizenship; Naturalization; Suffrage; Women, Citizenship of Married;** *and vol. 9:* **President Andrew Johnson's Civil Rights Bill Veto.**

CITRUS INDUSTRY. Citrus trees and shrubs, native to east Asia, were introduced by the Spanish to both Florida and California in the late sixteenth century. The colonial town of St. Augustine, Florida, was said to be full of citrus groves during the eighteenth and early nineteenth centuries, and citrus trees were grown about the missions of southern California during the same period.

In Florida the Spanish traded oranges to Native Americans, which led to the further spread of naturalized orange trees throughout the interior of the peninsula. William Bartram, the naturalist, reported feral oranges along the banks of the St. Johns River in 1773, and by the time the United States completed its acquisition of Florida in 1821, extensive groves of wild trees could be found throughout the forests, especially near the large interior lakes such as Orange, Harris, and Wier. Some of these wild groves were domesticated by American homesteaders; that is, they were cultivated, pruned, and perhaps even fertilized. Small orange groves began to be planted along the central-east coast in the Upper Indian River area, as well as along the St. Johns River during the 1830s.

In 1835 Florida was struck by the most severe freeze on record. Even in coastal St. Augustine the temperature fell to six degrees Fahrenheit, and for three days the temperatures stayed below freezing. Orange trees centuries old were frozen to the roots. A few protected groves survived in the Indian River area, and the intrepid pioneers of northeastern Florida replanted groves throughout the region. The absence of deep-draft, navigable waterways in the interior stymied the growth of agriculture until the coming of the railways to the central peninsula just prior to the Civil War. After the war the South lay in ruins and lacked the ability to make improvements in transportation. Only when northern capital became attracted to the area in the late 1870s and 1880s did the rail lines begin to push southward, opening the peninsula for development. As Henry B. Plant and Henry Flagler brought relatively inexpensive freight transportation to central and southern Florida, the citrus industry began to come into its own. Groves became larger and packinghouses set up operations along the rail lines. The fruit, which had been packed in barrels and cushioned with Spanish moss, now was shipped in nailed, wooden boxes, each fruit wrapped in paper. The packinghouses pasted their distinctive label on the boxes, some of which featured highly decorative artwork depicting idyllic, tropical scenes and other illustrations. These labels have become highly collectible.

Meanwhile in California, citrus remained a minor crop until the late nineteenth century. William Wolfskill obtained orange trees from the Mission San Gabriel in 1841 and planted the first orange grove in Los Angeles, but by 1858 only seven citrus orchards existed in all of California. In 1868 the first shipment of oranges went by boat to San Francisco. California's great distance from the populous regions of the United States severely limited production of perishable products, even with the advent of the transcontinental railways. Yet with the coming of the colony towns to the east of Los Angeles in the 1870s and 1880s, the groundwork was laid for the Citrus Belt located in the foothills of the San Gabriel and San Bernardino Mountains. Several factors were responsible for the boom in California citrus. Some were economic, such as the completion of the Southern Pacific Railroad and the railroad rate wars of the 1880s, and some horticultural, such as the introduction of the Bahia or Washington navel orange from Brazil and a better understanding of the unique growing conditions of the region. In 1881 the first packinghouse was established in Riverside and the following year the first carload of oranges and lemons was shipped to Denver. In 1886 a special orange train on an express schedule was sent to Kansas City.

By 1894 Florida was producing annually over five million boxes of fruit, each weighing ninety pounds. Despite earlier freezes, the industry continued to be located chiefly in the northern part of the peninsula. However, during the winter of 1894–1895, back-to-back freezes virtually destroyed the industry, thus forcing it south into the central part of the state. Not until 1910 did Florida replicate its earlier production.

By far the most significant development in the modern citrus industry was the invention of citrus concentrate. Faced with a crisis resulting from low market prices around 1950, the juice industry was regarded as a Cinderella phenomenon and a godsend to the citrus business. While post–World War II development rapidly diminished the citrus acreage of southern California, Florida plantings increased substantially, reaching over 800,000 acres producing near 200 million boxes by the 1970s. Thus, by the 1960s Florida surpassed California in production, followed by Texas, Arizona, and Louisiana, all relatively small producers.

BIBLIOGRAPHY

Hume, Harold H. *Citrus Fruits and Their Culture.* New York: O. Judd, 1915.

Reuther, Walter et al. *The Citrus Industry.* Vols.1–5. Riverside: University of California at Riverside, 1989.

Ziegler, Louis W., and Herbert S. Wolfe. *Citrus Growing in Florida.* Rev. ed. Gainesville: University Presses of Florida, 1975.

Robert N. Lauriault

See also **California; Florida; Fruit Growing; Osage Orange.**

CITY COUNCILS are the chief legislative bodies of municipalities and have been features of American city government since the colonial era. Although in most colonial municipal corporations the electorate chose the councilors, in Philadelphia, Pennsylvania, and Norfolk and Williamsburg, Virginia, the life-tenure council members filled any vacancies owing to death or resignation. The citizenry had no voice in the selection process. This practice of cooption, however, did not survive the revolutionary era, and from the 1790s on the enfranchised citizenry elected council members in cities throughout the United States.

During the nineteenth century, a growing number of Americans became disenchanted with city councils. Elected by wards, council members represented neighborhood interests and often seemed indifferent to the needs of the city as a whole. Moreover, they reflected the social composition of their wards. Working-class wards elected saloonkeepers, grocers, or livery stable owners who were popular in the neighborhood. To the urban elite, these plebeian councilors hardly seemed worthy of a major voice in city government. Widespread rumors of corruption further damaged the reputations of council members. The city councils were responsible for awarding valuable franchises for streetcar, gas, telephone, and electric services, and thus council members had ample opportunity to secure lucrative bribes. New York City's aldermen were dubbed the "Forty Thieves," and a corrupt pack of Chicago council members were known as the "Gray Wolves."

To curb the power of the socially undistinguished and sometimes corrupt councils, reformers shifted responsibility for an increasing number of functions to independent commissions. Park boards and library commissions, for example, relieved the city councils of responsibility for recreation and reading. In the 1870s, a board of estimate composed primarily of executive officers assumed charge of New York City's finances, thus reducing the city council to a relatively minor element in the government of the nation's largest metropolis. Meanwhile, mayoral authority increased at the expense of the city council. During the nineteenth century, mayors acquired the power to veto council actions. By the end of the century, some city charters no longer required council confirmation of mayoral appointments.

In the early twentieth century, good-government reformers continued to target city councils. The reform ideal was a small, nonpartisan council of seven or nine members elected at large, and an increasing number of city charters provided for such bodies. In 1901, Galveston, Texas, introduced the commission plan that eliminated the city council altogether, substituting a small board of commissioners that exercised all legislative and executive authority. During the first two decades of the twentieth century, hundreds of cities throughout the United States adopted this scheme, but by the 1920s, it had fallen out of fashion, replaced on the reform agenda by the city manager plan. This plan made the city council responsible for determining basic municipal policy, and an expert manager hired by the council was in charge of administration. At the close of the twentieth century, the city manager plan was the most common form of municipal government in the United States.

BIBLIOGRAPHY

Shaw, Frederick. *The History of the New York City Legislature.* New York: Columbia University Press, 1954.

Teaford, Jon C. *The Unheralded Triumph: City Government in America, 1870–1900.* Baltimore: Johns Hopkins University Press, 1984.

Jon C. Teaford

See also **City Manager Plan; Municipal Government; Municipal Reform.**

CITY DIRECTORIES are books introduced in the eighteenth century compiling information on a city's vital statistics, advertising, and residential information. Philadelphia had the first of these directories in 1785 entitled *Macpherson's Directory for the City and Suburbs of Philadelphia*, which created a numbering system to identify all dwellings and properties in the city. Other cities followed, including New York City in 1786, Detroit in 1837, and Chicago in 1844. Published most often through private businesses or cooperatives, the directories helped city officials create a standard system of property identification that did not change until the early twentieth century, when cities created independent systems. Directories paid their expenses by selling advertising space, indicating their orientation towards other businessmen and not necessarily the public at-large. Generally these books were divided into business listings, a register of names in alphabetical order, and then residential information by street address. As the twentieth century progressed, directories began to gather increasingly detailed information about their advertisers and organized that data into specific categories.

Instead of simply providing advertising space, directory publishers expanded into providing marketing and consumer data to businesses. By the late 1960s and early 1970s, the expense of bound volumes led publishers to utilize computers to develop marketing information for particular clients. These companies also moved quickly to take advantage of technological advancements, such as CD-ROMs instead of bound books, and the Internet's ability to provide tailored access and information to clients. Major directory companies today such as Experian, Equifax, infoUSA, and Acxiom deal with information related to direct marketing, telemarketing, sales planning, customer analysis, and credit reference.

BIBLIOGRAPHY

Glaab, Charles N., and Theodore Brown. *A History of Urban America.* New York: Macmillan, 1983.

Matthew L. Daley

CITY MANAGER PLAN, a scheme of government that assigns responsibility for municipal administration to a nonpartisan manager chosen by the city council because of his or her administrative expertise. In 1908, Staunton, Virginia, appointed the first city manager. The figure most responsible for the early promotion of the plan, however, was a wealthy young progressive reformer from New York City, Richard Childs. In 1910, he drafted a model manager charter for Lockport, New York, and embarked on a crusade to spread the gospel of manager rule.

With its emphasis on efficiency and expertise, the plan won an enthusiastic following among Progressive Era Americans. Proponents argued that cities, like business corporations, should be run by professional managers. Like corporate boards of directors, city councils should fix basic policy and hire the manager, but an expert needed to be in charge of the actual operation of the city. In 1913, Dayton, Ohio, became the first major city to adopt the scheme, and the following year, eight managers gathered in Springfield, Ohio, to form the City Managers' Association. In 1915, the National Municipal League incorporated the manager plan in its Model Charter, and, henceforth, good-government reformers and academics acclaimed it the preferred form of municipal rule. By 1923, 251 cities had adopted the plan, and fifteen years later the figure was up to 451.

The American City Bureau of the U.S. Chamber of Commerce joined the National Municipal League and Richard Childs in the promotion of manager rule. Because of the bureau's backing and the plan's supposed resemblance to the operation of a business corporation, manager rule especially appealed to business interests, who in one city after another boosted the reform. Although the nation's largest cities did not embrace the plan, such major municipalities as Cincinnati, Ohio; Kansas City, Missouri; Toledo, Ohio; Dallas, Texas; and San Diego, California, did hire city managers.

183

The reality of manager government, however, did not always conform to the plan's ideal. Many of the early managers were engineers with expertise in the planning and administration of public works, but others were local political figures. For example, the first city manager of Kansas City was a member of Boss Tom Pendergast's corrupt political organization. Moreover, in some cities clashes with council members produced a high turnover rate among managers. According to proponents of the plan, the manager was supposed to administer, and the council was supposed to make policy. But this sharp distinction between administration and policymaking was unrealistic. Managers both formulated and implemented policies, and conflicts with council members resulted. Although the manager was expected to be above the political fray, this often proved impossible.

The plan, however, remained popular, and council members learned to defer to the manager's judgment. During the second half of the twentieth century, hundreds of additional municipalities adopted the manager plan, and by the close of the century, council-manager government had surpassed mayor-council rule as the most common form of municipal organization in the United States.

BIBLIOGRAPHY

Stillman, Richard J., II. *The Rise of the City Manager: A Public Professional in Local Government*. Albuquerque: University of New Mexico Press, 1974.

Stone, Harold A., Don K. Price, and Kathryn H. Stone. *City Manager Government in the United States: A Review after Twenty-five Years*. Chicago: Public Administration Service, 1940.

Jon C. Teaford

See also **Chambers of Commerce; City Councils; Municipal Government.**

"CITY ON A HILL." The term "city on a hill" was initially invoked by English-born Puritan leader John Winthrop. The concept became central to the United States' conception of itself as an exceptional and exemplary nation.

In 1630, aboard the *Arbella* before the ship's departure for the New World, Winthrop recited a sermon to his fellow travelers. Drawing upon Matthew 5:14–15, Winthrop articulated his vision of the prospective Puritan colony in New England as "a city upon a hill": an example to England and the world of a truly godly society. According to historian Perry Miller, Winthrop believed that this religious utopia would be acclaimed and imitated across the Old World, precipitating the Puritans' glorious return to England. This never happened; instead, as settlements like Boston became prosperous, material success and demographic change undermined the religious imperative.

Nonetheless, throughout American history a secularized variation on Winthrop's theme has expressed the United States' more general and ongoing sense of exceptionalism—the nation's sociopolitical separation from, and supposed superiority to, the Old World. During the 1980s, in the aftermath of the Vietnam War, President Ronald Reagan attempted to recover the image of America as "a shining city on a hill."

BIBLIOGRAPHY

Kiewe, Amos, and Davis W. Houck. *A Shining City on a Hill: Ronald Reagan's Economic Rhetoric*. New York: Praeger, 1991.

Morgan, Edmund S. *The Puritan Dilemma: The Story of John Winthrop*. Boston: Little, Brown, 1958.

Winthrop, John. "A Model of Christian Charity." In *The Norton Anthology of American Literature*. Edited by Nina Baym et al. Shorter 5th ed. New York: Norton, 1999.

Martyn Bone

See also **Boston; Massachusetts; Nationalism; Puritans and Puritanism.**

CITY PLANNING. Communities in the United States have planned their development since the early European settlements. City planning has been a profession since the early twentieth century. Its development has been marked by an ongoing contrast or tension between "open-ended" plans intended to encourage and accommodate growth and the less common "closed" plans for towns serving specific limited populations, such as religious utopias, company towns, and exclusive suburbs.

Colonial Squares

The first towns on the Atlantic coast, such as Jamestown, Boston, and New Amsterdam, grew by accretion, rather than systematic design. Yet conscious town planning appeared as early as 1638 with New Haven, Connecticut. Nine large squares were arranged in rows of three, with the central square serving as the town common or green. This tree-shaded community park, preserved as part of the Yale University campus, became a distinctive feature of many colonial New England town plans.

In contrast to the open green of New England towns, the architectural square characterized the courthouse towns of Virginia, which had a smaller green square closely surrounded by private residences, shops, courthouse, and often churches. Versions of these Chesapeake and New England plans reappeared in the nineteenth century as the courthouse square or town square in new communities west of the Appalachians.

William Penn's and Thomas Holme's plan for Philadelphia, laid out in 1682, was a systematic application of the gridiron pattern, with regular blocks and straight streets crossing at right angles. Four public greens, in addition to a central square to serve as a civic center, sought to make Philadelphia a "green country town." Extended from the Delaware to the Schuylkill River, the plan also gave the new settlement room for future growth.

tle Hymn of the Republic," for instance, identifies the will of God with the Civil War aims of the Union army. Similarly, Confederates and Unionists alike used biblical passages to support their views regarding war, slavery, and the condition of the polity.

The civil religion of the United States is not merely religious nationalism. In its theology and rituals, it stresses the importance of freedom, democracy, and basic honesty in public affairs. At its best, it has given the nation a vision of what it may strive to achieve and has contributed to the realization of significant social goals. At its worst, it has been used as a propaganda tool to manipulate public opinion for or against a certain policy or group.

BIBLIOGRAPHY

Bellah, Robert N. *The Broken Covenant: American Civil Religion in Time of Trial.* Chicago: University of Chicago Press, 1992.

Cherry, Conrad. *God's New Israel: Religious Interpretations of American Destiny.* Chapel Hill: University of North Carolina Press, 1998.

Pierard, Richard V., and Robert D. Linder. *Civil Religion and the Presidency.* Grand Rapids, Mich.: Zondervan, 1988.

Woocher, Jonathan S. *Sacred Survival: The Civil Religion of American Jews.* Bloomington: Indiana University Press, 1986.

Glenn T. Miller / s. b.

See also **Evangelicalism and Revivalism; Puritans and Puritanism; Religious Thought and Writings.**

CIVIL RIGHTS ACT OF 1866.

Passed over a presidential veto on 9 April 1866, the law declared all persons born in the United States to be citizens, except for unassimilated Native Americans, and defined and protected citizens' civil rights. The law was part of Congress's attempt to reconstruct the union and eradicate slavery after the Civil War. In 1865 Congress had sent the Thirteenth Amendment, which abolished slavery, to the states for ratification. Under President Andrew Johnson's program for restoring the union, the Southern states were required to ratify the Thirteenth Amendment and abolish slavery in their own states. However, the president set no requirements for the treatment of newly freed slaves. In the South and in many Northern states, free African Americans had not been considered state or national citizens and had been subject to special restrictions of various kinds. In *Scott v. Sandford* (1857)—the DRED SCOTT CASE—the Supreme Court ruled that African Americans were not citizens of the United States. Acting on this view of the law, the Southern state governments reestablished under President Johnson's authority imposed varying restrictions on their black populations.

Although Johnson had been elected with Abraham Lincoln on the UNION PARTY ticket, backed mostly by Republicans, the Republican majority in Congress was unwilling to recognize the restoration of the states created

through his Reconstruction program until the basic civil rights of African Americans were secured. Radical Republicans urged that meeting this goal required the enfranchisement of African American men. More moderate Republicans feared to break with the president on that issue, suspecting that most voters even in the North would back him. Instead, on 13 March 1866 they passed the Civil Rights Act. Overturning the Dred Scott decision and any state law to the contrary, its first section declared that all persons born in the United States, except for Native Americans not subject to taxation (that is, outside state jurisdiction), were citizens of the United States and the states where they lived. It went on to declare that all citizens were entitled to the same basic civil rights as white persons, listing the right to make and enforce contracts, to sue and give evidence, to dispose of property, to get the same protection of the laws, and to be subject to the same punishments. The other sections of the law established stringent provisions for its enforcement, set penalties for its violation, and authorized the transfer of legal proceedings from state courts to federal courts in any state whose courts did not conform to the act's provisions.

President Johnson vetoed the bill on 27 March 1866, signaling his clear break with the leaders of the party that had elected him vice president. However, most Republican voters believed civil rights legislation necessary to protect former slaves, and few followed the president's lead. In June 1866 Congress passed the Fourteenth Amendment, which was ratified by the requisite number of states in 1868. Although developed separately from the Civil Rights Act, its first section established a similar definition of citizenship and a more abstract statement of the rights of citizens and other persons. The Civil Rights Act was repassed as part of the legislation to enforce the amendment. Its provisions are still incorporated in various sections of Title 42 (Public Health and Welfare) of the United States Code.

BIBLIOGRAPHY

Benedict, Michael Les. "Preserving the Constitution: The Conservative Basis of Radical Reconstruction." *Journal of American History* 61 (June 1974): 65–90.

Cox, LaWanda, and John H. Cox. *Politics, Principle, and Prejudice, 1865–1866: Dilemma of Reconstruction America.* New York: Free Press of Glencoe, 1963.

Kaczorowski, Robert J. "The Enforcement Provisions of the Civil Rights Act of 1866: A Legislative History in Light of *Runyon v. McCrary.*" *Yale Law Journal* 98 (January 1989): 565–595.

Zuckert, Michael. "Fundamental Rights, the Supreme Court, and American Constitutionalism: The Lessons of the Civil Rights Act of 1866." In *The Supreme Court and American Constitutionalism.* Edited by Bradford P. Wilson and Ken Masugi. Lanham, Md.: Rowman and Littlefield, 1998.

Michael L. Benedict

See also **Citizenship; Reconstruction;** *and vol. 9:* **President Andrew Johnson's Civil Rights Bill Veto.**

CIVIL RIGHTS ACT OF 1875. Passed 1 March 1875, the law provided that all persons, regardless of race, were entitled to "the full and equal enjoyment" of accommodations of inns, public transportation, theaters, and other amusement places. It provided for either criminal or civil enforcement. If found guilty in a criminal trial, the lawbreaker was punishable by a $500 to $1,000 fine and between thirty days and one year in jail. Alternatively, the victim could file a civil suit for $500 in damages. Another provision barred the disqualification of jurors on account of color in any state or federal court. The Act also made U.S. law enforcement officials criminally and civilly liable if they failed to enforce its provisions.

The equal accommodations provision of the 1875 Civil Rights Act was extremely controversial. It redefined what most Americans had thought to be mere "social rights" as civil rights, to which all were entitled. It also was based on an expansive interpretation of the Civil War constitutional amendments that gave Congress power to enforce rights not just when those rights were impinged on by states but when infringed by individuals as well. It not only barred the total exclusion of African Americans from specified facilities, it seemingly prohibited racially segregated facilities altogether.

African American leaders, former abolitionists, and radical Republicans had pressed for this legislation since 1870, when Massachusetts Republican Senator Charles Sumner proposed an equal accommodations measure as the "crowning work" of Reconstruction. Sumner's proposal required integration not only of inns, transportation, and amusement places, but also of religious institutions, common schools, and legally incorporated cemeteries. However, most Republicans were extremely wary of the measure, fearing the political consequences, especially in the South. Although a truncated version of Sumner's bill passed the Senate in 1872, the House of Representatives never considered it.

Sumner reintroduced the Civil Rights bill in December 1873. Republican opinion remained badly divided. Some southern Republican congressmen supported it in deference to their African American constituents. More conservative southern Republicans warned that it would destroy southern white support not only for the Republican Party but also for the region's struggling public schools. Nonetheless, the Senate passed the bill in May 1874, moved in part by Sumner's death two months earlier. The House passed the bill in March 1875, as a final Reconstruction measure in the lame-duck session of Congress that followed the elections of 1874, in which Republicans lost control of the lower branch in part due to the southern white reaction against the proposal. However, the House stripped the mixed-school provision from the bill, with many Republicans supporting the Democratic motion to do so rather than accept an amendment that would have condoned segregated schools. Recognizing that to insist on mixed schools would now kill the entire bill, radical Republican senators acquiesced to the amended measure.

Despite the potential penalties, the law was only reluctantly enforced by federal officers, leaving most enforcement to private litigants. In 1883 the Supreme Court ruled in the Civil Rights Cases that the law exceeded Congress's constitutional power under the Fourteenth Amendment, because it applied to individual rather than state action. The law was not authorized under the Thirteenth Amendment, which was not limited to state action, because the rights involved were not civil rights, the denial of which would amount to a "badge of servitude." The Court sustained the jury provision in *Ex parte Virginia*, 100 U.S. 339 (1880).

BIBLIOGRAPHY

Franklin, John Hope. "The Enforcement of the Civil Rights Act of 1875." *Prologue: The Journal of the National Archives* 6, no. 4 (winter 1974): 225–235.

McPherson, James M. "Abolitionists and the Civil Rights Act of 1875." *Journal of American History* 52, no. 3 (December 1965): 493–510.

Michael L. Benedict

See also **Reconstruction.**

CIVIL RIGHTS ACT OF 1957, Congress's first civil rights legislation since the end of Reconstruction, established the U.S. Justice Department as a guarantor of the right to vote. The act was a presidential response to the political divisions that followed the Supreme Court's 1954 decision in BROWN V. BOARD OF EDUCATION OF TOPEKA, ending official racial segregation in the public schools.

In 1955, President Dwight D. Eisenhower sought a centrist agenda for civil rights progress. Urged by Attorney General Herbert Brownell, in his 1956 State of the Union message Eisenhower adopted the 1947 recommendations of President Truman's Civil Rights Committee. Brownell introduced legislation on these lines on 11 March 1956, seeking an independent Civil Rights Commission, a Department of Justice civil rights division, and broader authority to enforce civil rights and voters' rights, especially the ability to enforce civil rights injunctions through contempt proceedings.

Congressional politics over the bill pitted southern senators against the administration. Owing to the efforts of House Speaker Sam Rayburn and Senator Lyndon B. Johnson, the bill passed, albeit with compromises including a jury trial requirement for contempt proceedings. The bill passed the House with a vote of 270 to 97 and the Senate 60 to 15. President Eisenhower signed it on 9 September 1957.

The act established the Commission on Civil Rights, a six-member bipartisan commission with the power to "investigate allegations . . . that certain citizens . . . are being deprived of their right to vote" as well as to study other denials of equal protection of the laws. The act forbade any person from interfering with any other person's right to vote, and it empowered the attorney general to prevent such interference through federal injunctions. The act also required appointment of a new assistant attorney general who would oversee a new division of the Justice Department devoted to civil rights enforcement.

The Civil Rights Division was slow to mature. In its first two years it brought only three enforcement proceedings, in Georgia, Alabama, and Louisiana, and none in Mississippi, where voter registration among blacks was only 5 percent. But the division greatly furthered voting rights during the Kennedy administration, under the leadership of Burke Marshall and John Doar. The commission likewise proved to be an effective watchdog, and its reports led not only to a strengthening of the division but also set the stage for further civil rights legislation in the 1960s.

BIBLIOGRAPHY

Doar, John. "The Work of the Civil Rights Division in Enforcing Voting Rights Under the Civil Rights Acts of 1957 and 1960." Florida State University Law Review 25 (1997): 1–18.

Jackson, Donald W., and James W. Riddlesperger Jr. "The Eisenhower Administration and the 1957 Civil Rights Act." In Reexamining the Eisenhower Presidency. Edited by Shirley Anne Warshaw. Westport, Conn.: Greenwood Press, 1993.

Lichtman, Allan. "The Federal Assault Against Voting Discrimination in the Deep South, 1957–1967." Journal of Negro History 54 (1969): 346.

Steve Sheppard

See also **Civil Rights Movement.**

CIVIL RIGHTS ACT OF 1964. Congressional concern for civil rights diminished with the end of Reconstruction and the Supreme Court's 1883 decision in the Civil Rights Cases holding the Civil Rights Act of 1875 unconstitutional. In 1957, Congress, under pressure from the civil rights movement, finally returned to the issue. However, the congressional response was a modest statute creating the Civil Rights Commission with power to investigate civil rights violations but not to enforce civil rights laws and establishing a feeble remedy for voting rights violations. The Civil Rights Act of 1960 slightly strengthened the voting rights provision.

During his campaign for the presidency in 1960, John F. Kennedy drew support from African Americans by promising to support civil rights initiatives. Once elected, Kennedy was reluctant to expend his political resources on civil rights programs he considered less important than other initiatives. Increasing civil rights activism, including sit-ins at food counters that refused service to African Americans, led Kennedy to propose a new civil rights act in May 1963. Kennedy lacked real enthu-

siasm for the proposal, which he saw as a necessary concession to the important constituency of African Americans in the Democratic Party. The bill languished in the House of Representatives until after Kennedy's assassination, when President Lyndon B. Johnson adopted the civil rights proposal as his own, calling it a memorial to Kennedy. Johnson had sponsored the 1957 act as part of his campaign for the Democratic Party's presidential nomination in 1960. Although Johnson was sincerely committed to civil rights, he had not allayed suspicion among liberal Democrats that he lacked such a commitment, and his support for the civil rights bill helped him with that constituency as well.

Johnson demonstrated the depth of his commitment through extensive efforts to secure the act's passage. The act passed the House in February 1964 with overwhelming bipartisan support, but southern senators opposed to the bill mounted the longest filibuster on record to that date. Senate rules required a two-thirds vote to end a filibuster, which meant Johnson had to get the support of a majority of Republicans. He negotiated extensively with Senator Everett Dirksen, the Senate's Republican leader, appealing to Dirksen's patriotism and sense of fairness. Dirksen extracted some small compromises, and with Republican support for Johnson, the filibuster ended. Within two weeks, the statute passed by a vote of 73–27.

The 1964 act had eleven main provisions or titles. Several strengthened the Civil Rights Commission and the voting rights provisions of the 1957 and 1960 acts, including a provision authorizing the U.S. attorney general to sue states that violated voting rights. But the act's other provisions were far more important. They dealt with discrimination in public accommodations and employment and with discrimination by agencies, both public and private, that received federal funds.

Title II

Title II banned racial discrimination in places of public accommodation, which were defined broadly to include almost all of the nation's restaurants, hotels, and theaters. These provisions were directed at the practices the sit-ins had protested, and to that extent they were the center of the act. The Civil Rights Cases (1883) held that the Fourteenth Amendment did not give Congress the power to ban discrimination by private entities. By 1964, many scholars questioned that holding and urged Congress to rely on its power to enforce the Fourteenth Amendment to justify the Civil Rights Act. Concerned about the constitutional question, the administration and Congress relied instead on the congressional power to regulate interstate commerce. The hearings leading up to the statute's enactment included extensive testimony about the extent to which discrimination in hotels and restaurants deterred African Americans from traveling across the country. The Supreme Court, in *Katzenbach v. McClung* (1964) and *Heart of Atlanta Motel v. United States* (1964), had no difficulty upholding the public accommodations provisions against constitutional challenge, relying on expansive notions of congressional power to regulate interstate commerce that had become settled law since the New Deal. Although compliance with Title II was not universal, it was quite widespread, as operators of hotels and restaurants quickly understood that they would not lose money by complying with the law.

Title VII

Title VII of the Civil Rights Act banned discrimination in employment. Representative Howard Smith, a conservative Democrat from Virginia, proposed an amendment that expanded the groups protected against discrimination to include women. A similar proposal had been rattling around Congress for many years. The idea was opposed by many labor unions and some advocates of women's rights, who were concerned that banning discrimination based on sex imperiled laws that they believed protected women against undesirable work situations. Representative Smith, who before 1964 supported banning discrimination based on sex, hoped the amendment would introduce divisions among the act's proponents. His strategy failed, and the final act included a ban on discrimination based on sex.

Lawsuits invoking Title VII were soon filed in large numbers. The Supreme Court's initial interpretations of the act were expansive. The Court, in *Griggs v. Duke Power Company* (1971), held that employers engaged in prohibited discrimination not simply when they deliberately refused to hire African Americans but also when they adopted employment requirements that had a "disparate impact," that is, requirements that were easier for whites to satisfy. The Court's decision made it substantially easier for plaintiffs to show that Title VII had been violated because showing that a practice has a disparate impact is much easier than showing that an employer intentionally discriminated on the basis of race. The Court also allowed cases to proceed when a plaintiff showed no more than that he or she was qualified for the job and that the position remained open after the plaintiff was denied it, such as in *McDonnell Douglas v. Green* (1973). In *United Steelworkers of America v. Weber* (1971), the Court rejected the argument that affirmative action programs adopted voluntarily by employers amounted to racial discrimination.

Later Supreme Court decisions were more restrictive. After the Court held that discrimination based on pregnancy was not discrimination based on sex in *General Electric Company v. Gilbert* (1976), Congress amended the statute to clarify that such discrimination was unlawful. Another amendment expanded the definition of discrimination based on religion to include a requirement that employers accommodate the religious needs of their employees. The Court further restricted Title VII in several decisions in 1989, the most important of which, *Ward's Cove Packing Company, Inc., v. Atonio* (1989), allowed employers to escape liability for employment practices with a disparate impact unless the plaintiffs could show that

the practices did not serve "legitimate employment goals." These decisions again provoked a response in Congress. President George H. W. Bush vetoed the first bill that emerged from Congress, calling it a "quota bill." In Bush's view it gave employers incentives to adopt quotas to avoid being sued. Congressional supporters persisted, and eventually Bush, concerned about the impact of his opposition on his reelection campaign, signed the Civil Rights Act of 1991, which included ambiguous language that seemingly repudiated the *Ward's Cove* decision.

Title VI

Title VI of the Civil Rights Act prohibited discrimination by organizations that receive federal funds. The impact of this provision was immediate and important. Most school districts in the Deep South and many elsewhere in the South had resisted efforts to desegregate in the wake of *Brown v. Board of Education of Topeka* (1954). Attempts to enforce the Court's desegregation rulings required detailed and expensive litigation in each district, and little actual desegregation occurred in the Deep South before 1964. Title VI made a significant difference when coupled with the Elementary and Secondary Education Act of 1965, the nation's first major program of federal aid to local education programs. Proposals for federal aid to education had been obstructed previously when civil rights advocates, led by Representative Adam Clayton Powell Jr., insisted that anyone who received federal funds would be barred from discriminating. These "Powell amendments" prompted southern representatives to vote against federal aid to education. The political forces that led to the adoption of Title VI also meant that southern opposition to federal aid to education could be overcome. The money available to southern school districts through the Elementary and Secondary Education Act of 1965 broke the logjam over desegregation, and the number of school districts in which whites and African Americans attended the same schools rapidly increased.

Federal agencies' interpretations of Title VI paralleled the Court's interpretation of Title VII. Agencies adopted rules that treated as discrimination practices with a disparate impact. In *Alexander v. Choate* (1985), the Supreme Court held that Title VI prohibited only acts that were intentionally discriminatory, not practices with a disparate impact. The Court regularly expressed skepticism about the agency rules, although it did not invalidate them. Instead, in *Alexander v. Sandoval* (2001), the Court held that private parties could not sue to enforce the agencies' disparate-impact regulations. That decision substantially limited the reach of Title VI because the agencies themselves lack the resources to enforce their regulations to a significant extent.

Efforts by courts and presidents to limit the Civil Rights Act of 1964 have been rebuffed regularly. Supplemented by amendments, the act is among the civil rights movement's most enduring legacies.

BIBLIOGRAPHY

Graham, Hugh Davis. *The Civil Rights Era: Origins and Development of National Policy, 1960–1972.* New York: Oxford University Press, 1990.

Stern, Mark. *Calculating Visions: Kennedy, Johnson, and Civil Rights.* New Brunswick, N.J.: Rutgers University Press, 1992.

Whalen, Charles, and Barbara Whalen. *The Longest Debate: A Legislative History of the 1964 Civil Rights Act.* Cabin John, Md.: Seven Locks Press, 1985.

Mark V. Tushnet

See also **Brown v. Board of Education of Topeka**; **Civil Rights Act of 1875**; **Civil Rights Act of 1957**; **Civil Rights Act of 1991**; **Civil Rights Movement**; **General Electric Company v. Gilbert**; **Griggs v. Duke Power Company**; **Ward's Cove Packing Company, Inc., v. Atonio.**

CIVIL RIGHTS ACT OF 1991.

President George H. W. Bush vetoed the proposed Civil Rights Act of 1990, asserting that it would force employers to adopt rigid race- and gender-based hiring and promotion quotas to protect themselves from lawsuits. The act had strong bipartisan support in Congress: cosponsors included Republican senators John C. Danforth, Arlen Specter, and James M. Jeffords. Other Republicans, including the conservative Orrin Hatch of Utah, had helped to shape the bill along lines demanded by President Bush. Sixty-six senators, including eleven Republicans, voted to override the veto, one short of the necessary two-thirds majority. A year later, President Bush signed the Civil Rights Act of 1991, which became law on 21 November 1991.

Congress passed both acts in response to the Supreme Court's decisions in *Ward's Cove Packing Company, Inc. v. Atonio* (1989), *Patterson v. McLean Credit Union* (1989), and four other cases. These decisions reversed nearly two decades of accepted interpretations of existing civil rights statutes, making it more difficult for minorities and women to prove discrimination and harassment in working conditions and in the hiring and dismissal policies of private companies.

Ward's Cove involved a challenge to hiring practices under Title VII of the CIVIL RIGHTS ACT OF 1964. By a five-to-four vote, the Supreme Court ruled that employers need only *offer*, rather than *prove* a business justification for employment practices that had a disproportionate adverse impact on minorities. The decision reversed the precedent in *Griggs v. Duke Power Company* (1971), which required employers to prove they were not discriminating in hiring practices if a plaintiff could show that actual hirings did not reflect racial balance.

Patterson involved a claim of on-the-job racial harassment brought under Title 42, section 1981, of the U.S. Code, a surviving portion of the CIVIL RIGHTS ACT OF 1866. Congress had passed the 1866 act to protect the rights of former slaves; it prohibits discrimination in hiring and guarantees the right to "make and enforce contracts." In *Patterson*, the Court held that Section 1981 "does not apply to conduct which occurs after the formation of a contract and which does not interfere with the right to enforce established contract obligations." In other words, the Court said that the law did not apply to working conditions after hiring and hence did not offer protection from on-the-job discrimination or harassment because of the employee's race or gender.

In adopting the 1991 act, Congress reinstated the earlier interpretations of civil rights law. The Supreme Court clearly understood this to be the intent of the act. In *Landgraf v. USI Film Products* (1994), which interpreted the 1991 act, Justice John Paul Stevens wrote:

> The Civil Rights Act of 1991 is in large part a response to a series of decisions of this Court interpreting the Civil Rights Acts of 1866 and 1964. Section 3(4) expressly identifies as one of the Act's purposes "to respond to recent decisions of the Supreme Court by expanding the scope of relevant civil rights statutes in order to provide adequate protection to victims of discrimination."

In addition to rejecting the Supreme Court's interpretation of the 1964 act, Congress also expanded the scope of remedies available under the 1964 Civil Rights Act. The 1991 act allows plaintiffs to ask for a jury trial and to sue for both compensatory and punitive damages up to a limit of $300,000. Before the 1991 act, employees or potential employees who proved discrimination under Title VII could only recover lost pay and lawyer's fees. Yet, discrimination settlements reached through private suits under state tort law ranged from $235,000 to $1.7 million.

In the 1990 bill vetoed by President Bush, Congress provided for retroactive application to cases then pending before the courts or those dismissed after *Ward's Cove.* Approximately one thousand cases were pending. In the 1991 act, Congress was unclear about retroactivity. Civil rights activists argued that the Court should allow such suits on the ground that the 1991 law reinstated antidiscrimination rules that had existed since adoption of the 1964 Civil Rights Act. After signing the 1991 act, however, President Bush argued that it did not apply to pending cases but only to cases of discrimination that arose after the law. Most federal courts accepted Bush's position, and in *Landgraf v. USI Film Products* and *Rivers v. Roadway Express*, both decided in 1994, the Supreme Court did too. The Court decided both cases by votes of eight to one, the retiring Justice Harry Blackmun dissenting. Justice Stevens wrote the majority opinions.

Although President Bush had labeled the proposed 1990 Civil Rights Act a "quota bill," the 1991 law had nothing to do with quotas. It provided protection for job applicants and workers subject to discrimination or harassment. It gave meaning to the right to enter contracts that was guaranteed to African Americans in the Civil Rights Act of 1866 and to the antidiscrimination provisions of the Civil Rights Act of 1964. It reestablished principles that had been part of civil rights jurisprudence for two decades. In short, the scope of the 1991 act was narrow, returning civil rights law to where it had been before the 1989 rulings of the conservative majority on the Rehnquist Court.

BIBLIOGRAPHY

Karst, Kenneth L. *Law's Promise, Law's Expression: Visions of Power in the Politics of Race, Gender, and Religion.* New Haven, Conn.: Yale University Press, 1993.

Liebold, Peter M., Stephen A. Sola, and Reginald E. Jones. "Civil Rights Act of 1991: Race to the Finish—Civil Rights, Quotas, and Disparate Impact in 1991." *Rutgers Law Review* 45 (1993).

Rotunda, Ronald D. "The Civil Rights Act of 1991: A Brief Introductory Analysis of the Congressional Response to Judicial Interpretation." *Notre Dame Law Review* 68 (1993): 923.

Paul Finkelman / c. p.

See also **Affirmative Action; Civil Rights Movement; Discrimination: Race; Equal Employment Opportunity Commission.**

CIVIL RIGHTS AND LIBERTIES

refer to the various spheres of individual and group freedoms that are deemed to be so fundamental as not to tolerate infringement by government. These include the fundamental political rights, especially the franchise, that offer the citizen the opportunity to participate in the administration of governmental affairs. Since these individual and group freedoms may also be abridged by the action or inaction of private institutions, demand has increased for positive governmental action to promote and encourage their preservation.

Constitutional provisions, statutes, and court decisions have been the principal means of acknowledging the civil rights and liberties of individuals; for those rights to be maximized, their acknowledgment must be accompanied by legislation and judicial enforcement. Any conception of individual rights that does not include this action component may actually be instrumental in limiting the exercise of such rights.

Constitutional Provisions

The U.S. Constitution, drawn up in the summer of 1787, included guarantees of the following civil rights and liberties: habeas corpus (Article I, section 9); no bills of attainder or ex post facto laws (Article I, sections 9 and 10); jury trial (Article III, sections 2 and 3); privileges and immunities (Article IV, section 2), later interpreted to be a guarantee that each state would treat citizens of other states in the same way they treated their own citizens; and no religious test for public office (Article VI, paragraph 3). Four years later ten amendments (the Bill of Rights) were added to the Constitution in response to demands

for more specific restrictions on the national government. The Bill of Rights guarantees certain substantive rights (notably freedom of speech, of the press, of assembly, and of religious worship) and certain procedural rights in both civil and criminal actions (notably a speedy and public trial by an impartial jury). In 1833 (BARRON v. BALTIMORE, 7 Peters 243) the U.S. Supreme Court ruled that these amendments were designed to serve as protections against federal encroachment alone and did not apply to state and local governments. The Supreme Court's position in this case, as stated by Chief Justice John Marshall, was to prevail throughout the nineteenth and early twentieth centuries, despite the efforts of attorneys who argued that the intent of the framers of the Fourteenth Amendment's due process clause (1868) was to extend the protection of the Bill of Rights to the actions of states and localities. From 1925 (*Gitlow v. New York*, 268 U.S. 652) through 1969 (*Benton v. Maryland*, 395 U.S. 784), Supreme Court rulings had the effect of incorporating most of the major provisions of the Bill of Rights into the due process clause of the Fourteenth Amendment, thereby making them applicable to states and localities as well as to the federal government.

Prior to the adoption of the Civil War amendments there had been little effort to invoke federal authority to preserve individual rights. Furthermore, revisionist historians have shown that the generation that framed the first state declarations of rights and the federal Bill of Rights was not as libertarian as is traditionally assumed— the ALIEN AND SEDITION LAWS of 1798 being a case in point. The Thirteenth, Fourteenth, and Fifteenth Amendments and the five general civil rights acts spanning the years 1866–1875 established the bases for a vast expansion of federal authority. Although the Thirteenth abolished slavery and involuntary servitude and the Fifteenth prohibited the abridgment of a citizen's fight to vote because of race, color, or previous condition of servitude, the Fourteenth proved to be of greatest import to the subsequent development of individual rights.

The first sentence of section 1 of the Fourteenth Amendment defines U.S. citizenship: "All persons born or naturalized in the United States and subject to the jurisdiction thereof, are citizens of the United States." This provision overturned the Supreme Court's 1857 decision in the DRED SCOTT CASE (19 Howard 393) and recognized the primacy of national citizenship. (Citizenship was later described by Chief Justice Earl Warren [*Perez v. Brownell*, 356 U.S. 44, 64 (1958)] as "man's basic right, for it is nothing less than the right to have rights.") The remainder of the first section of the amendment prohibits the states from abridging the privileges and immunities of citizens of the United States (which the courts interpreted quite narrowly); depriving any person of life, liberty, or property without due process of law; and denying any person within its jurisdiction the equal protection of the laws.

Judicial Interpretation

The five general civil rights acts of the post–Civil War period were efforts to implement the Civil War amendments. Although Congress was primarily motivated by a concern for the newly freed blacks, these statutes—which provided federal protection of individual rights against interference by either public officials or private individuals—never made specific references to African Americans as such. The last of these nineteenth-century civil rights statutes, the CIVIL RIGHTS ACT OF 1875, was designed to guarantee to blacks equal accommodations with white citizens in all inns, public conveyances, theaters, and other public places. In 1883 the Supreme Court (*Civil Rights Cases*, 109 U.S. 3) concluded that the framers of the Fourteenth Amendment had not intended to enable Congress to prohibit private persons from discriminating against blacks. The Fourteenth Amendment was interpreted as prohibiting discriminatory acts by the states only, and consequently the act was declared void.

The major test of state legislation designed to support the segregation and suppression of blacks came in 1896. In PLESSY V. FERGUSON (163 U.S. 537) the Supreme Court upheld a Louisiana statute requiring separate accommodations for blacks and whites on public carriers, so long as the accommodations were equal. In the years that followed, segregation of the races on the basis of the separate-but-equal doctrine became commonplace throughout the South, and segregation resulting from Jim Crow legislation continued to be pervasive into the mid-twentieth century; in 1947 President Harry S. Truman's Committee on Civil Rights reported that the separate-but-equal doctrine was "one of the outstanding myths of American history, for it is almost always true that while indeed separate, . . . facilities are far from equal."

The separate-but-equal doctrine became deeply entrenched in the field of public education in the South, and it was not until 1938 (MISSOURI EX REL GAINES V. CANADA, 305 U.S. 337) that the Supreme Court began to examine the equality requirement. From then until 1950 the Court, in a series of cases involving graduate school education, held that the separate facilities provided for black students were not equal educationally, but in granting relief to black plaintiffs, the Court did not publicly reexamine the separate-but-equal doctrine. Nevertheless, these decisions paved the way for the Supreme Court's landmark decision of 17 May 1954 (BROWN V. BOARD OF EDUCATION OF TOPEKA, 347 U.S. 483), overturning the *Plessy v. Ferguson* precedent and unanimously holding that the separate-but-equal doctrine had no place in the field of public education. The Court based its decision on the Equal Protection Clause of the Fourteenth Amendment, which prohibited states from denying any person within their jurisdiction the equal protection of the laws. A companion case that year (*Bolling v. Sharpe*, 347 U.S. 497) prohibited segregation in the public schools of the District of Columbia.

A year later, in its implementation decree in the *Brown* case, the Court ordered the desegregation process to be carried out "with all deliberate speed." Massive resistance ensued, most notably in Arkansas and Virginia, and in 1964 (*Griffin v. County School Board of Prince Edward County*, 377 U.S. 218) the Court held that the time for mere "deliberate speed" had run out. Subsequent implementation decrees emphasized the obligation of school districts to terminate dual school systems at once and to operate only unitary schools thereafter. When confronted in 1971 with the question of the scope of a federal district court's ability to order school busing to correct state-enforced racial school segregation, the Supreme Court was unanimous in finding that the district court had not transcended the limits of "reasonableness" in its remedial order concerning busing (*Swann v. Charlotte-Mecklenburg Board of Education*, 402 U.S. 1). After rejecting in 1974 arguments that courts could order metropolitan-wide busing to remedy past discrimination (*Milliken v. Bradley*, 418 U.S. 717), the Supreme Court became increasingly skeptical about the ability of courts to eliminate racially identifiable schools in urban areas.

The Court in *Plessy v. Ferguson* had distinguished between social rights, such as the right to ride on public transportation and the right to education, and civil and political rights, saying that the Constitution protected only the latter. Activist groups such as the NATIONAL ASSOCIATION FOR THE ADVANCEMENT OF COLORED PEOPLE and the AMERICAN CIVIL LIBERTIES UNION would soon argue against that distinction. Eventually the idea of civil rights expanded to include the right against discrimination in employment, in housing, and in all places of public accommodation.

The Civil Rights Movement and New Legislation

The nonviolent civil rights movement, which had its beginning in the Montgomery, Alabama, bus boycott of 1955–1956 led by Martin Luther King Jr., received increasing national attention during the sit-ins and freedom rides of the early 1960s. Mass demonstrations in Birmingham, Alabama, in the spring of 1963, also led by King, further heightened the urgency of African American demands and helped precipitate President John F. Kennedy's civil rights legislative proposals of June 1963. This legislation, including provisions regarding access to public accommodations, use of federal funds without discrimination, and equal employment opportunity, was signed into law on 2 July 1964, during the early months of President Lyndon B. Johnson's administration. It was the most far-reaching civil rights legislation since 1875.

The public accommodations title of the 1964 act, Title II, was similar in substance to the 1875 provisions struck down in the *Civil Rights Cases*; this time the legislation rested upon both the Commerce Clause and the Equal Protection Clause of the Fourteenth Amendment. The Supreme Court in 1964 found the Commerce Clause fully adequate to sustain the public accommodations title

199

(*Heart of Atlanta Motel v. U.S.*, 379 U.S. 241, and *Katzenbach v. McClung*, 379 U.S. 294).

Title VI, which prohibited discrimination in any federally assisted programs, was to prove instrumental in accelerating school desegregation during the Johnson administration. In particular, the passage of the Elementary and Secondary Education Act of 1965 provided funds of sufficient magnitude so that most school districts would be at a serious disadvantage should they lose federal assistance for failing to desegregate. Finally, Title VII created the EQUAL EMPLOYMENT OPPORTUNITY COMMISSION, which struggled for seven years before it was granted enforcement powers—that is, the ability to institute suits in federal courts to enforce U.S. laws against job discrimination.

The VOTING RIGHTS ACT OF 1965 was passed in the aftermath of black-led demonstrations, especially in Selma, Alabama, against discriminatory practices in voter registration in the South. This was the most sweeping voting rights legislation of the century, even though there had been antecedents in the civil rights acts of 1957, 1960, and 1964. The Voting Rights Act of 1970, in addition to being a five-year extension of the 1965 act, included provision for the eighteen-year-old vote in all elections. Before the year was over, the original jurisdiction of the Supreme Court was invoked to test the constitutionality of the new minimum voting age provisions. Although the Court sustained them insofar as they pertained to federal elections, it held that the Fourteenth Amendment's equal protection clause and enforcement clause did not authorize Congress to impose such a requirement in state and local elections. This necessitated the adoption of the Twenty-sixth Amendment, which lowered the minimum voting age to eighteen in all elections.

Of the major civil rights problems confronting the country, housing was the last to be dealt with by Congress. It was not until 1968, shortly after the assassination of King, that Congress—in a new Civil Rights Act—prohibited discrimination in the sale or rental of about 80 percent of the nation's housing, the major exceptions being owner-occupied dwellings with no more than four units and the sale or rental of private homes without the services of a real estate agent.

As the nation's largest minority, blacks have been in the vanguard of efforts to secure individual civil rights. However, the other large minority groups—Indians, Mexican Americans, Puerto Ricans, and Asians—have been victims of the same types of discrimination. Unquestionably, the black revolution has had a salutary effect on the struggles of these minorities to actualize the civil rights guaranteed them by the Constitution. One example is the so-called INDIAN CIVIL RIGHTS ACT, a rider to the Civil Rights Act of 1968. In view of the anomalous position of the tribal governments of American Indians, the legislation was designed to ensure that tribal governments would be bound by the same limitations imposed by the Constitution on the federal and state governments.

Civil Liberties

The term "civil rights" has been associated with claims by racial minorities against racial discrimination. The term "civil liberties" refers to rights to political participation, particularly freedom of expression and in more recent years the right to privacy, held by every citizen. The scope of protection accorded civil liberties was relatively narrow until the 1960s, in part because the Supreme Court defined freedom of expression narrowly and in part because state infringements on civil liberties could not be challenged until the Court held that the Fourteenth Amendment protected people against such infringements. By the late 1960s, however, the Court had developed a robust jurisprudence of civil liberties, insulating speech from punishment unless it threatened immediate social harm, guaranteeing citizens the right to conduct political demonstrations in public places, and protecting the right of privacy in connection with reproductive decisions. Later Court decisions refused to extend these protective doctrines significantly, but the Court's decisions had nurtured a culture of rights that placed political limits on what legislatures could do when addressing concerns that speech caused social harm.

BIBLIOGRAPHY

Abraham, Henry J., and Barbara A. Perry. *Freedom and the Court: Civil Rights and Liberties in the United States.* 7th ed. New York: Oxford University Press, 1998.

Garrow, David J. *Liberty and Sexuality: The Right to Privacy and the Making of* Roe v. Wade. Berkeley: University of California Press, 1998.

Kluger, Richard. *Simple Justice: The History of* Brown v. Board of Education *and Black America's Struggle for Equality.* New York: Knopf, 1975.

To Secure These Rights: The Report of the President's Commission on Civil Rights. Washington, D.C.: United States Government Post Office, 1947.

Urofsky, Melvin I. *A March of Liberty: A Constitutional History of the United States.* New York: Knopf, 1988.

Wilkinson, J. Harvie III. *From Brown to Bakke: The Supreme Court and School Integration, 1954–1978.* New York: Oxford University Press, 1979.

Mark Tushnet
Howard Whitcomb

See also **Bill of Rights in U.S. Constitution; Busing; Civil Rights Act of 1866; Civil Rights Act of 1957; Civil Rights Act of 1964; Civil Rights Act of 1991; Civil Rights Movement; Civil Rights Restoration Act of 1987; Equal Protection of the Law; First Amendment.**

CIVIL RIGHTS MOVEMENT. The civil rights movement comprised efforts of grassroots activists and national leaders to obtain for African Americans the basic rights guaranteed to American citizens in the Constitution, including the rights to due process and "equal protection of the laws" (Fourteenth Amendment) and the right to vote. Although the 1950s and 1960s represent the height of the mass civil rights movement of the twentieth century, activists had sought basic rights for African Americans since before the Civil War.

Civil Rights 1865–1945

Between 1865 and 1870, Congress passed amendments to abolish slavery (Thirteenth Amendment), accord citizenship to African Americans (Fourteenth Amendment), and extend voting rights to black men (Fifteenth Amendment). But the end of Reconstruction in 1877 furthered white opposition to black equality. The oppression of blacks manifested itself most explicitly in southern states in what was known as Jim Crow customs and legislation passed between the 1890s and 1920s to racially segregate public venues, including trains, restaurants, schools, theaters, hospitals, beaches, and cemeteries. Additionally, laws and intimidation tactics prevented blacks from enjoying other rights of citizenship, including the right to vote.

African American activists, and some whites, challenged these injustices through public speaking tours, the black press, and organizations to advocate racial equality. In the 1890s, the journalist Ida B. Wells encouraged blacks to migrate northward to protest unfair hiring practices in the South and the lynching of African American men unjustly accused of assaulting white women. In 1909, Wells, W. E. B. Du Bois, and other activists formed the National Association for the Advancement of Colored People (NAACP), which in subsequent decades became the predominant American organization pursuing equality for blacks through the legal system.

Infringements upon blacks' civil rights did occur in the North and West, although to a lesser extent than in the South. As blacks emigrated from the South to industrial areas during and after World War I, whites in industrial areas, some of them relocated southerners or members of white supremacist groups such as the regenerated Ku Klux Klan, exercised coercion to prevent blacks from competing with whites for jobs and voting. Whites outside the South also practiced segregation and other forms of racial discrimination. Blacks in Chicago, for instance, encountered "white only" signs in businesses and limits on employment, usually being hired only as unskilled laborers. In 1942, James Farmer founded the Congress of Racial Equality (CORE) in Detroit, an interracial organization that sought to desegregate eating establishments, schools, and interstate buses in the 1940s.

World War II invigorated the civil rights movement, galvanizing blacks who during the Great Depression had developed a greater awareness of their potential political influence. During the 1930s many blacks had switched their political affiliation from the Republican Party, "the party of Lincoln" that had freed the slaves, to the Democratic Party, and in 1936 had voted for Franklin Delano Roosevelt to show support for his New Deal programs. The outbreak of war in Europe in 1939 stimulated American industry and the demand for labor. As was the case with World War I, African Americans moved to industrial cities for employment but confronted discrimination in hiring and wages. A. Philip Randolph, president of the Brotherhood of Sleeping Car Porters, informed Roosevelt that 100,000 blacks would march in Washington, D.C., to protest discrimination in defense industries. In June 1941, Roosevelt averted the protest by signing Executive Order 8802, outlawing prejudicial treatment of workers in defense industries and the federal government on the basis of race. Blacks also encountered opportunity along with racism in the armed forces. One million African American men and women served in the military, in segregated units. Blacks in the military and in civilian wartime jobs saw themselves as waging a "double victory" campaign to secure democracy abroad and for themselves in their own country. They emerged from the war with a renewed sense of the rights to equality and freedom in the land that claimed to represent these among the world's nations. During the war, membership in the NAACP swelled tenfold to 500,000.

Conditions for Social Change after World War II

Numerous factors energized the civil rights movement after World War II. In July 1948, President Harry Truman signed Executive Order 9980, barring racial discrimination in the civil service, and Executive Order 9981, mandating "equality of treatment and opportunity for all persons in the armed forces." The postwar economic boom improved job opportunities for blacks, and higher incomes resulted in rising college enrollments for African Americans and increasing donations to civil rights organizations such as the NAACP. The mass media, including fledgling television, publicized civil rights activism. Furthermore, television broadcasts displayed the material prosperity enjoyed by middle-class whites, feeding African Americans' desires for a better standard of living.

International events also influenced the civil rights movement. Observers at home and abroad pointed out that the nation that claimed to represent the ideals of democracy and freedom in the Cold War denied civil rights to a substantial proportion of its own population, provoking Americans of all colors to scrutinize racial discrimination. While opponents of civil rights used red-baiting tactics in their attempts to discredit integrationists, advocates of racial equality contended that racial discrimination in the United States damaged the nation's international image and played into the hands of communist adversaries.

Activists such as W. E. B. Du Bois noted a kinship between the American civil rights movement and decolonization movements in European-controlled countries. In their view, democracy and self-determination for people of color in Africa and Asia paralleled African Americans' struggles for equality. Anti-imperialist movements became for African Americans a metaphor for the civil rights movement in the United States: an effort of a peo-

Rosa Parks. A 1993 photograph of the woman whose refusal to give up her seat on a segregated city bus started the long boycott in Montgomery, Ala.—which brought new energy and leadership to the civil rights movement of the 1950s and 1960s. AP/WIDE WORLD PHOTOS

ple to wrest control of their destinies from a white ruling class.

Turning Points in the 1950s

Landmark judicial decisions and a now famous bus boycott resulted in the civil rights movement gaining unprecedented strength and momentum in southern states in the 1950s. In 1954, with Thurgood Marshall of the NAACP arguing on behalf of the plaintiffs, the Supreme Court ruled in the case of *Brown v. Board of Education of Topeka* that the segregation of public facilities was unconstitutional. In 1955, the Court ordered the desegregation of public schools, though it did not set a deadline for this process. Three years after *Brown*, nearly all southern schools remained segregated. The NAACP decided to push the federal government to enforce the 1955 Supreme Court order to desegregate public schools, focusing on an all-white high school in Little Rock, Arkansas. In September 1957, nine black teenagers enrolled in Central High School. Angry mobs, encouraged by the Arkansas governor Orval Faubus's defiance of the federal government, surrounded and threatened the students. Ultimately, President Dwight Eisenhower reluctantly ordered the National Guard to protect them. The efforts to integrate Central High School made headlines around the world.

In early December 1955, after the arrest of the seamstress and local NAACP secretary Rosa Parks for refusing to move to the back of the bus to accommodate a white passenger, the Montgomery NAACP organized a boycott of the city's buses. The year-long boycott called national attention to the South's Jim Crow practices, achieved the desegregation of Montgomery's public transportation, and established the Reverend Martin Luther King Jr., the young pastor of a local Baptist church, as a renowned spokesman for the civil rights movement.

Dr. King found ideas for a national integrationist movement in philosophy, Christianity, and the example of the nationalist leader Mohandas Gandhi, whose principles of nonviolent civil disobedience shaped a movement that won India's independence from Great Britain in 1948. King and other civil rights activists developed a strategy to oppose racial segregation by nonviolent means, which they believed would win sympathy for their cause and ultimately create a racially integrated society, a peaceful and just "beloved community." The Southern Christian Leadership Conference (SCLC), established in 1957, united black churches, historically a source of inspiration, community support, and activism, to achieve racial integration.

The *Brown* rulings, the success of the Montgomery bus boycott, and the questioning of racism in the country that proclaimed itself the world's leader of freedom and democracy attracted growing numbers of African Americans to the movement. Their magnitude and the movement's momentum gave them the courage to face the vociferous and often violent opposition of those who wished to maintain racial hierarchy.

The 1960s

More challenges to segregation arose in the South during the 1960s. In 1960 four college students initiated a sit-in at a segregated Woolworth's lunch counter in Greensboro, North Carolina, sparking similar acts at public venues across the South. The student sit-ins led to the founding of the Student Nonviolent Coordinating Committee (SNCC), which allowed a younger generation of civil rights activists to develop its own strategies to achieve racial equality. Like SCLC, SNCC advocated nonviolent resistance to racial inequality and trained members in workshops so that they would know how to respond when accosted by adversaries. SNCC and CORE members orchestrated "freedom rides" in 1961 to desegregate interstate public buses and facilities. Black and white freedom riders endured assaults by hostile whites in Alabama. White attacks on blacks in Montgomery prompted Attorney General Robert Kennedy to send 600 federal officers to that city. In September 1961, the Interstate Commerce Commission outlawed the segregation of interstate transportation and facilities such as waiting rooms and restrooms.

Blacks and their white allies communicated their resistance to racial oppression in marches, sit-ins, and

Selma to Montgomery. Martin Luther King Jr. and Coretta King lead a voting rights march into Montgomery, Ala., on the fifth day, 25 March 1965; the first attempt, on 7 March, was called "Bloody Sunday" after police and state troopers attacked the peaceful marchers—which finally prompted action on a federal Voting Rights Act, signed into law on 6 August. BETTMANN ARCHIVE

boycotts that demonstrated their numbers and resolve. African American children became more visible in the movement. In May 1963, they participated in a children's march in Birmingham and, alongside adults, endured police assaults and jail time. The SCLC, NAACP, SNCC, and CORE organized the biggest civil rights march to date in Washington, D.C. On 28 August 1963, 200,000 blacks and 50,000 whites walked from the Washington Monument to the Lincoln Memorial, where they listened to speakers from the various organizations, including Reverend King.

Growing numbers of whites, especially white college students outside the South, expressed their solidarity with blacks. Whites joined African Americans in the sit-ins of 1960, the freedom rides of 1961, and marches in the South. Students for a Democratic Society (SDS), founded in 1961, declared its opposition to racism in its manifesto. Black activists allowed nonblacks to join their organizations to demonstrate multiracial commitment to an integrated society and because the presence of whites attracted greater media attention. White college students from the University of California, Berkeley, for example, participated in civil rights projects in the South during the summer, such as the voter registration project in Mississippi in 1964. In the fall the students returned to their campus, where they educated their peers about civil rights abuses and activism and organized efforts to end racial discrimination in the Bay Area.

As civil rights activists grew bolder, violence against them mounted. Television, which had proliferated in the 1950s, enabled viewers from outside the South to witness mobs pelting blacks with stones, and policemen using clubs, dogs, and fire hoses to subdue peaceable protesters. In 1963, white supremacists bombed a church in Birmingham, killing four African American girls, and the NAACP field director Medgar Evers was murdered in front of his home. At the beginning of SNCC's Freedom Summer drive to register rural black voters in Mississippi in June 1964, three civil rights workers disappeared: two white men, Andrew Goodman and Michael Schwerner of New York, and one black man, James Chaney of Mississippi. In August, the bodies of the three men were found in a swamp. President Lyndon Baines Johnson publicly condemned the evident murder of the civil rights workers. In June 1966, a gunman wounded James Meredith as he

Angela Davis. The professor, Communist Party activist, and advocate of radical African American causes, speaking in Los Angeles in 1970—the year she was briefly a fugitive, accused (but later acquitted) of charges related to a fatal escape attempt by defendants in a California courtroom. AP/WIDE WORLD PHOTOS

marched to Jackson, Mississippi, to encourage other blacks to register to vote.

The civil rights movement culminated in legislation sought by activists for decades. Overcoming opposition from southern politicians, Congress passed the Civil Rights Act of 1964, prohibiting racial discrimination in employment and public facilities, and the Voting Rights Act of 1965, barring states from obstructing African Americans from voting and ensuring federal oversight of registration and voting. Legislating the equal treatment of blacks helped topple Jim Crow and barriers to employment and enfranchised millions. Yet activists were well aware that legislation was not sufficient to eradicate racist attitudes or improve the economic status of African Americans.

The Movement's Ebb

Violence, arrests, and other degradations embittered many black activists who tired of enduring abuse without fighting back. Critics such as the Nation of Islam spokesman Malcolm X denounced the civil rights movement's strategy of nonviolent resistance and its integrationist goals, asserting that blacks were entitled to use violence to defend themselves from attacks, and scorning activists' de-

sire to integrate into a racist white society. Malcolm X argued (though after leaving the Nation of Islam he would alter this position) that blacks must reject integration and instead create separate communities and direct energies toward the economic, spiritual, and cultural development of blacks. The radical ideas of "black power"—the empowerment of African Americans through economic self-reliance, black pride, and, if necessary, militant self-defense—influenced SNCC members such as Stokely Carmichael, who as SNCC chairman (1966–1967) recommended that whites leave the organization so that blacks could take control of their own liberation. SNCC members redirected their attention to economic improvement for blacks and opposition to the Vietnam War. But the subsequent decline in white membership and financial support weakened SNCC, which dissolved by the end of the decade.

Although Martin Luther King remained committed to integration and nonviolence, he too came to see racism as a problem that would take more than desegregation and voting rights to solve, and gave greater attention to the war in Vietnam and to the economic problems of blacks. King publicly announced his opposition to the war as a racist conflict against an Asian people and as example of the institutionalization of racism toward American men of color, who fought and died in disproportionate numbers. In April 1968, as King visited Memphis to support striking garbage workers and launch a Poor People's Campaign, a sniper assassinated him. Riots erupted in over 125 cities around the nation. The murder of King dispirited civil rights supporters, already troubled by previous assaults on activists as well as infighting within and between various civil rights groups.

Voters in the 1968 presidential election were divided on the issue of civil rights. The election of the Republican Richard Nixon to the presidency in 1968, along with the unusually strong showing for the American Independent party candidate George Wallace—a former Democrat, the governor of Alabama, and an unabashed segregationist who in 1963 had vowed to keep African American students out of the University of Alabama—who received 13.5 percent of the popular vote, with support from southern voters as well as northeasterners and midwesterners, represented the limits of change that many white Americans were willing to tolerate. Republican Richard Nixon appealed to white working-class and middle-class voters repelled by riots and protesters, whom mainstream media often portrayed as destructive malcontents. Many white voters also believed that President Johnson's administration had overlooked the Americans whom they considered "respectable" and "hard-working," and whose taxes helped fund Johnson's Great Society programs designed to aid the poor and people of color. Nixon received 43.4 percent of the popular vote, defeating by a .7 percent margin Vice President Hubert Humphrey, who had spoken in support of civil rights and social justice during his campaign. As president, Nixon did advocate school inte-

Jesse Jackson. The prominent, outspoken civil rights leader and political activist starting in the late 1960s, seen here in Oklahoma City after the terrorist bombing in 1995. AP/WIDE WORLD PHOTOS

gration (but not busing children to achieve this) and preferences for minority contractors in the construction industry. The Nixon administration, however, also resisted the program to enforce fair housing and made cuts in civil rights offices in the federal government.

Legacies of the Civil Rights Movement

The civil rights movement's influence has been extensive and enduring. It has inspired movements to promote the rights and equality of women, gays and lesbians, Asian Americans, Indians, Chicanos and Chicanas, and the disabled. Decades after the peak of the civil rights movement, activists for a variety of causes continued to employ strategies such as sit-ins and other forms of civil disobedience popularized by civil rights groups.

The participation of African Americans in local, state, and national politics—as voters and office holders—increased dramatically as a result of the civil rights movement. Between the late 1940s and the mid-1970s—the decades preceding and following the height of the movement—the proportion of southern blacks registered to vote rose from about 10 percent to 63 percent. The number of African American elected officials multiplied from approximately 500 in 1964 to 4,000 by 1980. Presidents became more inclined—and were expected—to appoint African American staff members and judges. White politicians also were more likely to take into account their nonwhite constituents and give greater attention to racial issues.

The civil rights movement transformed American culture and society. Although racism did not disappear, there was far less tolerance for racist attitudes and behavior than before the 1960s. In response to criticisms that educational institutions perpetuated racial biases, educators at all levels, from grade schools to universities, revised curricula to incorporate the histories and cultures of diverse Americans. Educators have found an abundance of materials to draw upon, thanks to the burgeoning scholarship on the nation's many social groups, renewed appreciation of literature by African American authors such as Langston Hughes and Zora Neale Hurston, and more recent works by writers such as Toni Morrison and Alice Walker. Many predominantly white institutions of higher education have made efforts to recruit more non-white students and faculty through programs such as affirmative action, although opponents of this strategy have attempted to eradicate it, contending that it constitutes a form of "reverse discrimination" against whites.

Those who continued to strive for civil rights after the movement's peak years pointed to ongoing problems that they argued reflected the persistence of racism entrenched in institutions and attitudes: poverty, inadequate health care, urban violence, drug addiction, high rates of incarceration for black men and women, police brutality, racial profiling, de facto segregation in inner-city neighborhoods and schools, and nonwhites' difficulties in gaining access to institutions of higher education and professions.

BIBLIOGRAPHY

Branch, Taylor. *Parting the Waters: America in the King Years, 1954–1963.* New York: Simon and Schuster, 1988.

———. *Pillar of Fire: America in the King Years, 1963–1965.* New York: Simon and Schuster, 1998.

Cashman, Sean Dennis. *African-Americans and the Quest for Civil Rights, 1900–1990.* New York: New York University Press, 1991.

Collier-Thomas, Bettye, and V. P. Franklin, eds. *Sisters in the Struggle: African American Women in the Civil Rights–Black Power Movement.* New York: New York University Press, 2001.

Dudziak, Mary L. *Cold War Civil Rights: Race and the Image of American Democracy.* Princeton, N.J.: Princeton University Press, 2000.

Fairclough, Adam. *Better Day Coming: Blacks and Equality, 1890–2000.* New York: Viking, 2001.

Matusow, Allen J. *The Unraveling of America: A History of Liberalism in the 1960s.* New York: Harper Torchbooks, 1984.

Olson, Lynne. *Freedom's Daughters: The Unsung Heroines of the Civil Rights Movement from 1830 to 1970.* New York: Scribners, 2001.

Plummer, Brenda Gayle. *Rising Wind: Black Americans and U.S. Foreign Affairs, 1935–1960.* Chapel Hill: University of North Carolina Press, 1996.

Sitkoff, Harvard. *The Struggle for Black Equality, 1954–1992.* Rev. ed. New York: Hill and Wang, 1993.

———. "Conditions for Social Change." In *A History of Our Time: Readings on Postwar America*. Edited by William H. Chafe and Harvard Sitkoff. 4th ed. New York: Oxford University Press, 1995.

Takaki, Ronald. *Double Victory: A Multicultural History of America in World War II*. Boston: Little, Brown, 2000.

Tushnet, Mark V. *Making Civil Rights Law: Thurgood Marshall and the Supreme Court, 1936–1961*. New York: Oxford University Press, 1994.

Weisbrot, Robert. *Freedom Bound: A History of America's Civil Rights Movement*. New York: Plume, 1991.

Williams, Juan, ed. *Eyes on the Prize: America's Civil Rights Years, 1954–1965*. New York: Viking, 1988.

Donna Alvah

See also **Affirmative Action; *Brown v. Board of Education of Topeka;* Civil Disobedience; Civil Rights Act of 1964; Desegregation; Freedom Riders; Integration; Jim Crow Laws; March on Washington; National Association for the Advancement of Colored People; Reconstruction; Segregation; Southern Christian Leadership Conference; Student Nonviolent Coordinating Committee; Voting Rights Act of 1965; *and vol. 9:* An Interview with Fannie Lou Hamer; The Arrest of Rosa Parks; Student Nonviolent Coordinating Committee Founding Statement.**

CIVIL RIGHTS RESTORATION ACT OF 1987

expanded the coverage of previously enacted federal statutes prohibiting discrimination in employment and other areas. By passing the Restoration Act, Congress overrode a presidential veto and overturned the 1984 Supreme Court decision in *Grove City College v. Bell*. In *Grove City College*, the Court had effectively gutted Title IX of the Education Amendments Act of 1972, and by implication other antidiscrimination statutes, by holding that only those college programs directly receiving federal financial assistance, and not the college as a whole, had an obligation to not discriminate on the basis of sex. The purpose of the Restoration Act was to make clear that when any program or activity of an organization or entity— such as a college, medical center, or private contractor— receives federal funding, the entire organization or entity must comply with laws outlawing discriminatory practices based upon race, religion, color, national origin, gender, age, or disability. Thus, for example, if a college library receives a government grant to enable it to computerize, the entire college is required to comply with all federal civil rights laws. Similarly, a manufacturing company that makes airplane parts for the federal government must practice nondiscrimination in all of its other manufacturing operations as well. The Restoration Act effectively closed a number of significant loopholes in earlier civil rights statutes.

BIBLIOGRAPHY

"The Civil Rights Restoration Act of 1987—A Defeat for Judicial Conservatism." *National Black Law Journal* 12 (Spring 1990): 61–72.

Graham, Hugh Davis. "The Storm Over Grove City College: Civil Rights Regulation, Higher Education, and the Reagan Administration." *History of Education Quarterly* 38, no. 4 (winter 1998): 407–429.

Jack Handler / C. P.

See also **Civil Rights Act of 1964; Civil Rights and Liberties; Civil Rights Movement.**

CIVIL SERVICE,

the term applied to the appointed civilian employees of a governmental unit, as distinct from elected officials and military personnel. Increasingly, most civil service systems in the United States are characterized by a merit system of employment based on technical expertise, as determined by competitive examinations, and on permanent tenure and nonpartisanship. A few positions in the federal civil service and many more in state and local governments are filled by employees who owe their appointments primarily to political considerations. Such employees and the offices that they fill are known as the patronage, and the appointment mechanism is known as the spoils system. Much of the history of the U.S. civil service has had to do with its transformation from a spoils system to a predominantly merit system—a struggle spanning more than a hundred years and still going on in some state and local jurisdictions.

Under President George Washington and his successors through John Quincy Adams, the federal civil service was stable and characterized by relative competence and efficiency. However, the increasingly strong pressures of Jacksonian egalitarian democracy after 1829 rudely adjusted the civil service of the founding fathers, and for more than a half-century the federal, state, and local services were largely governed by a spoils system that gave little or no consideration to competence.

The unprecedented corruption and scandals of the post–Civil War era generated the beginnings of modern civil service reform. An act of 1871 authorized the president to utilize examinations in the appointing process, and President Ulysses S. Grant appointed the first U.S. Civil Service Commission in that year. But Congress refused appropriations; full statutory support for reform waited until 1883 and the passage of the Pendleton Act, which is still the federal government's central civil service law. This act reestablished the Civil Service Commission, created a modern merit system for many offices, and authorized the president to expand this system. Behind the reforms of the late 19th century lay the efforts of the National Civil Service League, supported by public reaction against the corruption of the times. Successive presidents, requiring more and more professional expertise to carry out congressional mandates, continued and consolidated the reform—notably Grover Cleveland, Theodore Roosevelt, and Herbert Hoover. By 1900 the proportion of the federal civil service under the merit system reached nearly 60 percent; by 1930 it had exceeded 80 percent.

The depression period of the 1930s saw both a near doubling of the federal civil service and some renaissance of patronage politics, especially in the administration of work relief. With public and congressional support during his second term, President Franklin D. Roosevelt was empowered to, and did, expand the competitive system to most positions in the new agencies. Moreover, Congress extended a version of the merit system to first-, second-, and third-class postmasters; federal agencies were all required to have personnel offices; the TENNESSEE VALLEY AUTHORITY, under a special merit system statute, commenced to pioneer in government-employee labor relations; and pay- and position-classification systems were improved.

After WORLD WAR II, federal personnel management, which had formerly consisted mainly of administering examinations and policing the patronage, further expanded its functions. The operation of personnel management was largely delegated to well-staffed personnel offices of agencies. Improved pay and fringe benefits, training and executive development, a positive search for first-rate talent, new approaches to performance rating, equal employment opportunity, improved ethical standards, loyalty and security procedures, incentive systems, and special programs for the handicapped were major developments. These developments and a full-scale labor relations system based on a precedent-shattering executive order by President John F. Kennedy in 1962 have characterized the transformation of nineteenth-century merit system notions into public personnel management as advanced as that anywhere in the world. In a federal civil service of 3 million, there are fewer than 15,000 patronage posts of any consequence.

Beginning in the late nineteenth century, civil service reform came also to many state and local governments, although relatively more slowly and less completely. In 1883 New York State adopted the first state civil service act and was followed almost immediately by Massachusetts. By 1940 one-third of the states had comprehensive merit systems; by 1970 two-thirds had them. The reform spread, from the East, through cities as well, after several New York State and Massachusetts cities set up civil service commissions in the 1880s. Chicago followed in 1895. Most metropolitan centers and many of the smaller cities have modern merit systems. A few have systems for police and fire departments only. Most cities act under their own statutes, but in New York, Ohio, and New Jersey, there is general coverage of local jurisdictions by state constitutional or other state legal provision. In one-quarter of the states—notable among which is California—the state personnel agencies may perform technical services for localities on a reimbursement basis. Whereas a bipartisan civil service commission provides administrative leader-

ship in most jurisdictions, the single personnel director is becoming more popular.

The most important twentieth-century developments in civil service have to do with federal-state cooperative personnel arrangements. In part, such arrangements stem from a 1939 amendment to the Social Security Act of 1935, which required the federal government to apply merit system procedures to certain state and local employees paid in whole or in part through grants-in-aid. A considerable number of similar statutes followed, so that by the 1970s perhaps a million state and local positions fell within personnel systems closely monitored by the federal government. Federal supervision was for many years managed by a bureau of the Social Security Administration and later by a division of the Department of Health, Education, and Welfare. The Intergovernment Personnel Act of 1970, signed by President Richard M. Nixon on 5 January 1971, relocated the supervision of grant-in-aid employees within the U.S. Civil Service Commission. But, equally important, this act authorized federal grants-in-aid to state and local governments in support of modern personnel systems within these jurisdictions. The function of handling these grants-in-aid is also with the U.S. Civil Service Commission. Thus, it has become the central personnel agency not only of the federal government but also, in many respects, of the entire intergovernmental system.

In size, the federal civil service has grown from an institution of a few hundred employees in 1789 to nearly 3 million. During major wars the federal civil service has doubled and even quadrupled; its peak occurred in 1945 when civil service employees numbered nearly 4 million. There has been a similar growth in state and local services. The federal civil service saw its greatest continuing expansion between 1930 and 1950; progressive expansion of state and local civil service rosters began in the late 1940s, when state and local governments started on the road to becoming the fastest growing segment of American enterprise, public or private. By the 1970s federal civil employees functioned almost entirely under merit system procedures, as did some 75 percent of those in state and local governments. Civil service reform is therefore nearly an accomplished fact in the United States, but budget cuts in the 1980s and 1990s have created a serious strain on the civil service's efforts to fulfill its duties. Critics of the civil service have described its members as out-of-touch "government bureaucrats" who put their own narrow interests ahead of those of the American people. In an effort to reduce the size of the government, such critics have proposed and implemented significant reductions in the civil service budget. In light of such policies, civil service officers at both the state and federal levels face the challenge of meeting growing obligations with declining resources.

Notwithstanding budget concerns, civil service reform in the United States has produced a uniquely open system, in contrast to the closed career system common to other nations—which one enters only at a relatively early age and remains within for a lifetime, in the manner associated in the United States mainly with a military career. The PENDLETON ACT of 1883 established this original approach, providing that the federal service would be open to persons of any age who could pass job-oriented examinations. Persons may move in and out of public service, from government to private industry and back again, through a process known as lateral entry. It is this openness to anyone who can pass an examination, this constant availability of lateral entry, that has set the tone and character of public service in the United States at all levels. One consequence of U.S. civil service policy has been to provide a notable route for upward mobility, especially for women and blacks. Thus, the U.S. civil service has reflected the open, mobile nature of American society and, in turn, has done much to support it.

BIBLIOGRAPHY

Ingraham, Patricia W. *The State of the Higher Civil Service after Reform: Britain, Canada, and the United States.* Paris: OECD, 1999.

Johnson, Ronald N. *The Federal Civil Service System and the Problem of Bureaucracy: The Economics and Politics of Institutional Change.* Chicago: University of Chicago Press, 1994.

Schultz, David A. *The Politics of Civil Service Reform.* New York: P. Lang, 1998.

Paul P. Van Riper / A. G.

See also **Bureaucracy; Expenditures, Federal; Federal Government; Labor, Department of; Revenue, Public.**

CIVIL WAR. Historians have long debated the causes of the Civil War. They have argued that a split developed between the industrialized North and the agricultural South as both sections vied for control of the nation. Closely related is the belief that the two sections fought over the tariff, which, some have stated, protected Northern manufactures. Others have contended that the war erupted over states' rights. Northerners advocated a more expanded federal government than did Southerners, who held fast to a federal system in which the preponderant power lay with the states. Some have also suggested that politicians in the 1850s failed by their own incompetency to broker a compromise to the sectional controversy during the secession crisis, so that the nation blundered into civil strife.

Each of these explanations has serious shortcomings. The Northern states accounted for two of every three farms in the United States, and Southern staple crop production, especially cotton, provided raw material for many Northern factories. The tariff was not a powerful political issue in the critical decade leading up to the war. Nor did Southerners complain about the import duty when it protected regional interests, such as those of sugar growers. Like their Southern countrymen, many Northerners—perhaps even a majority—believed in states' rights, and

on the surface, the differences of opinion were not sufficient to warrant separation or war. The blundering generation argument assumes that politicians in Washington were unusually incompetent in the 1850s or that there was room to compromise on the vital moral issue of the day: slavery. There is little evidence to substantiate charges of massive political incompetence and the argument plays down the buildup of mistrust that controversies and compromises had generated since the Missouri Crisis four decades earlier. The willingness of so many millions of people to march off to war or endure hardships for their section proves just how deeply people in the North and South felt about the great issues of their day.

Slavery, Secession, and the War's Onset

Slavery lay at the root of the Civil War. The Republican Party dedicated itself to blocking the expansion of the "peculiar institution," and many of its leaders had publicly avowed their desire to see slavery abolished. Southern states had maintained that if a member of the Republican Party were elected president, they would secede. When the voters chose the Republican candidate Abraham Lincoln in 1860, seven slave states voted to leave the union and began to form a Southern confederacy. In their ordinances of secession or justifications, they stated clearly that they dissolved their connection to the United States to protect slavery. As the state of Mississippi argued, "Our position is thoroughly identified with the institution of slavery." Slavery had divided families, religions, institutions, political parties, and finally, the nation itself.

Although the U.S. Constitution did not specifically forbid secession, Lincoln and most Northerners believed that the concept would undercut the linchpin of any democratic republic, respect for the outcome of fair elections. By allowing secession, a group could nullify the expressed wishes of the people acting under constitutional law.

Northerners viewed the union and the Constitution as sacrosanct. It was the basis for the world's great experiment, a democratic republic, a kind of beacon of light for people everywhere. All freedoms derived from the Constitution and the union. For those who had gone before them and for future generations, they had an obligation to preserve that system.

Representatives from the seceding states met during the months of February and March in Montgomery, Alabama, to form a new government, the Confederate States of America. The convention chose Jefferson Davis of Mississippi as provisional president and Alexander Stephens of Georgia as provisional vice president. The constitution itself greatly resembled that of the United States. Major distinctions included a single, six-year term as president, a line-item veto for the president, and a provision stipulating that states could not secede from the country. The most fundamental difference, according to Stephens, rested with the underlying premise: the United States acknowledged the notion that all men were created equal, whereas the Confederate States of America insisted that

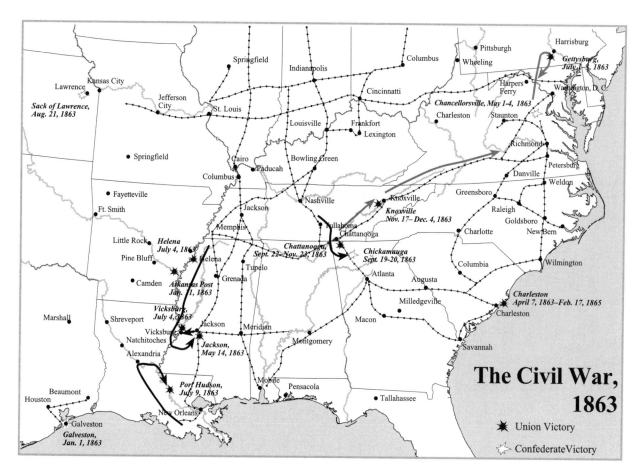

The Civil War, 1863

✴ Union Victory

☆ Confederate Victory

the field. Johnston was wounded and bled to death on the first day of fighting. At Shiloh, Grant's army suffered thirteen thousand casualties, horrifying politicians and civilians alike, and he soon found his reputation damaged and his command responsibilities curtailed.

When his superior, Major General Henry W. Halleck, returned East to become the new general in chief that summer, however, Grant was given a second chance. On 1 May 1862, Union forces began entering New Orleans; opening the entire length of the Mississippi River became a high priority. Grant began the difficult task of securing Vicksburg, Mississippi, a Confederate bastion located high on bluffs that dominated the Mississippi River. After months of toil and failure, including a repulsed assault on the bluffs, Grant finally conceived a way to defeat the Rebels. With Navy help, he shifted his army below the city in April 1863 by marching men along the opposite bank and shuttling them across the river. He then pushed inland toward Jackson, the capital of Mississippi, and turned on Vicksburg. Over the course of several weeks, in perhaps the most brilliant campaign of the war, Grant's forces defeated two Confederate armies in five separate battles and then laid siege to the city. On 4 July 1863, the Vicksburg garrison of nearly thirty thousand men surrendered. Grant had captured his second army, and with news of the fall of Vicksburg, the Confederates at Port Hudson, Louisiana, surrendered, giving the Un-

ion control of the Mississippi River and isolating a large portion of the Confederacy.

After a Union disaster at Chickamauga, Georgia, in September, Grant was brought in to preserve the Federal hold on Chattanooga, Tennessee. With extensive reinforcements and an audacious assault up a steep incline called Missionary Ridge, Grant's command shattered the Rebel positions. The victory drove the Confederates back into Georgia and pushed Grant's star into the ascendancy. In March 1864, Grant was promoted to lieutenant general, commander of all U.S. forces, while his key subordinate, William Tecumseh Sherman, took over in the West.

The Road to Union Victory

To the east, the Union army under Burnside suffered a disastrous repulse at Fredericksburg, Virginia, in December 1862. Again in April and May 1863, the same reinforced army under Major General Joseph Hooker was crushed by a much smaller force under Lee. In the Battle of Chancellorsville, Jackson led a brilliant flanking march that surprised and routed the Union forces, but that night Jackson sustained an accidental mortal wound from his own troops.

With some momentum from the Chancellorsville victory, Lee decided to raid Pennsylvania and perhaps

Brandy Station. The Eighteenth Pennsylvania Cavalry camps at Brandy Station, Va., the site of a daylong battle on 9 June 1863—the largest cavalry engagement of the Civil War, and a rare time when Confederate riders met their match. LIBRARY OF CONGRESS

convince the Northern public that continuation of the war was pointless. His troops marched through Maryland and approached Harrisburg, the capital of Pennsylvania, before pulling back. At a vital crossroad village called Gettysburg, Lee and Hooker's new replacement, Major General George G. Meade, fought the most costly battle of the war. After three days and close to fifty thousand casualties, Lee withdrew back to Virginia, his third-day assault having been repulsed. For the second time, Lee had invaded the Union states and failed.

For the spring campaign of 1864, Grant determined to launch simultaneous offensives to squeeze the outnumbered Confederates. He elected to travel alongside Meade's army in Virginia, while Sherman commanded a group of armies in the West that advanced toward Atlanta. Against Grant, Lee put up a bold defense. His Army of Northern Virginia inflicted unprecedented losses, some sixty thousand, in seven weeks at the Wilderness, Spotsylvania, Cold Harbor, and elsewhere, yet the Yankees kept the initiative. Eventually, Grant was able to lock Lee's army up in a siege around Petersburg. Yet he could not crush Lee's men.

Meanwhile, to the westward, Sherman had more success against the Confederates, led by Joseph E. Johnston. Sherman largely avoided the enormous casualties of the eastern theater, holding and then turning his Rebel opponents. By mid-July, as the Confederates backed up near

Atlanta, President Davis replaced Johnston with the aggressive John Bell Hood. Hood did what Davis expected of him: fight. But in each instance, the Confederates lost. In early September, Sherman forced the Rebel defenders out of Atlanta, a victory that ensured Lincoln's reelection two months later.

By mid-November, Sherman—with three-fifths of his army—began his famous March to the Sea, wrecking railroads, consuming foodstuffs, and proving to the Southern people that their armies could not check these massive Union raids. The other two-fifths of his army served as the core of a large force under Major General George Thomas that crushed the remainder of Hood's army around Nashville, a victory that elevated the importance of Sherman's march all the more.

On water, the Union navy contributed mightily to the ultimate victory. Those original twenty-three active vessels increased to more than 700 thanks to Northern shipbuilding. With this huge fleet, the Federal blockade closed ports or discouraged trading ships, while the wood and ironclad river boats supported land campaigns on the Tennessee, Cumberland, and Mississippi Rivers and also along the coast. In January 1865, the Union sealed the last significant port city, Wilmington, with the fall of Fort Fisher.

That same month, Sherman launched a destructive overland campaign through the Carolinas, once again

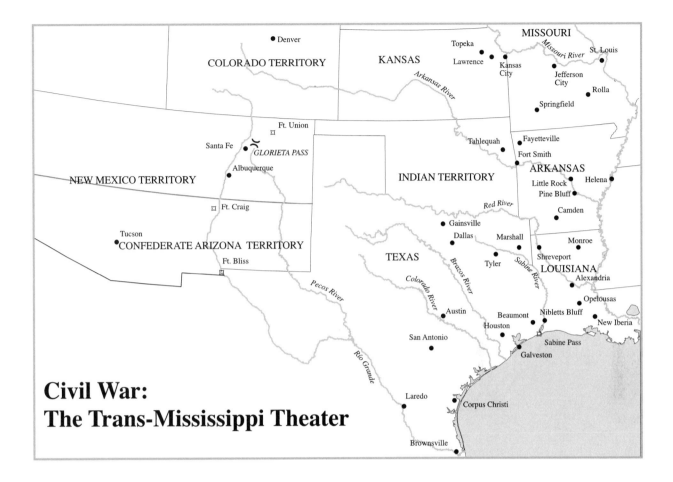

Civil War:
The Trans-Mississippi Theater

wrecking railroads; eating foodstuffs; destroying anything of military value; terrifying civilians; and in the case of South Carolina, burning homes and towns. By late March, the end was in sight. Sherman's army had reached central North Carolina and could be in Virginia in a few weeks. Grant, meanwhile, slowly extended his superior numbers around Lee's flank, severing the railroads that supplied Richmond and Petersburg and penetrating the Confederate rear. His works outflanked, Lee abandoned the Petersburg-Richmond line and took flight westward, hoping to swing around Grant's army and unite with Johnston, who was back in command opposing Sherman. Before Lee could escape, a Union force under Philip Sheridan boxed him in and he surrendered at Appomattox Court House on 9 April 1865. Several weeks later, Johnston surrendered to Sherman near Durham, North Carolina, and all Confederate resistance soon succumbed.

Sustaining the Soldier and Civilian Populations

Approximately 2.25 million served in the Union army, and from 800,000 to 900,000 donned Confederate gray. The Union had over 20,000 African American sailors and almost 180,000 African American soldiers, about 150,000 of whom came from the Confederate States. In the final stages of the war, the Confederacy attempted to create black regiments, with very limited success.

With a large industrial and agricultural base, the Union provided better for its soldiery. After some initial scandals over ostensibly shoddy clothing and shoes and accusations of profiteering on a grand scale, the Northern states churned out vast quantities of food, clothing, weapons, ammunition, and other equipment necessary for war, while providing for its domestic market as well. To offset the labor loss of the up to one million young males who were in service at a given time, women took to the fields and factories and owners adopted more labor-saving machinery. Through hard work, cooperation, technology, and innovation, the Union produced enough food and clothing to provide for those soldiers in the field, the people at home, and in some cases, a number of people in Europe.

To pay for the war, the Union Congress raised the tariff dramatically and passed into law a series of taxes, including the first income tax, under the Internal Revenue Act of 1862. Despite this heavy taxation by the Lincoln administration, much of the war was financed by bond sales and the printing of paper money called greenbacks. The banker Jay Cooke and Secretary of the Treasury Salmon P. Chase convinced the Northern public to buy long-term war bonds. (Cooke's firm alone sold over $1.2 billion worth.) The paper money circulated as legal tender. Still, inflation drove prices up to twice their prewar level,

215

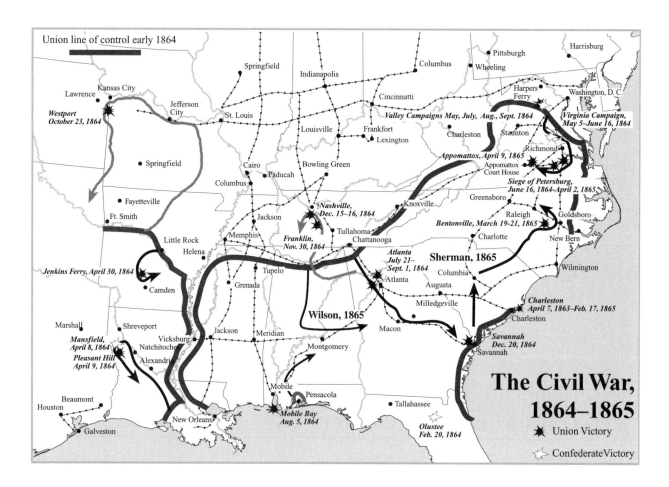

Union line of control early 1864

Westport October 23, 1864

Valley Campaigns May, July, Aug., Sept. 1864

Virginia Campaign, May 5–June 16, 1864

Appomattox, April 9, 1865

Appomattox Court House

Siege of Petersburg, June 16, 1864–April 2, 1865

Nashville, Dec. 15–16, 1864

Bentonville, March 19–21, 1865

Franklin, Nov. 30, 1864

Atlanta July 21– Sept. 1, 1864

Sherman, 1865

Jenkins Ferry, April 30, 1864

Wilson, 1865

Charleston April 7, 1863–Feb. 17, 1865

Mansfield, April 8, 1864

Pleasant Hill April 9, 1864

Savannah Dec. 20, 1864

Mobile Bay Aug. 5, 1864

Olustee Feb. 20, 1864

The Civil War, 1864–1865

✳ Union Victory

✩ Confederate Victory

causing considerable hardship for those on fixed wages and those who did not grow their own food. Families and communal organizations attempted to ease the burden on those with breadwinners in uniform.

Philanthropic organizations also contributed to the well-being of the soldiers. The United States Sanitary Commission was formed to combat the atrocious conditions in Union hospitals. The group promoted cleanliness, better medical care, proper nursing, and a host of other issues to improve care for the sick and injured. The U.S. Christian Commission championed religion through the publication of vast amounts of religious tracts. For those seeking spiritual comfort or for activity-starved soldiers in camp, these readings filled an important void.

The Davis administration lacked the established apparatus to collect taxes, and with the Union blockade, little in the way of import taxes entered the coffers. Congressional laws establishing an income tax, a levy on agricultural products at the source, and a duty on the buying and selling of most basic goods generated more frustration with the government than revenue. The government floated war bonds, which raised a little more than a third of the needed funds. The Confederates generated the remainder by printing money. Early on, the notes circulated reasonably well, but as the fortunes of war declined and the amount of paper money in circulation escalated, its

value plummeted. Late in the war, these paper notes were more a keepsake than a circulating medium.

The Confederate States performed minor miracles in creating a munitions industry, but in other areas, scarcity plagued the armies and the civilian population. Refugees flooded cities, driving up prices and reducing the amount of food crops harvested. Despite an extraordinary agricultural base, southerners devoted too many acres to the production of tobacco and cotton and not enough to food. A congressional resolution and state laws tried to rectify this problem, but they did not succeed satisfactorily. Other basic items, like clothing and shoes, became so rare that only the well-off could afford them. People made do with makeshift footgear, homespun garments, whatever they could. Still, basic shortages damaged morale and resulted in protests and even riots. In one instance, Davis tossed all the money he had in his pockets into a crowd to quell a bread riot.

With limited financial means, huge government expenses, and shortages, inflation rates soared. By the last two years of the war, prices rose so rapidly that many Southern farmers refused to sell their crops and livestock to the Confederate government; the authorized price could not keep up with escalating market prices. In order to feed and supply soldiers, many commissary and quartermaster officials simply impressed the goods or food-

216

Atlanta. The wreckage of General John Bell Hood's twenty-eight-car ammunition train and, beyond the tracks, a factory; during the Confederates' evacuation of Atlanta in 1864, they destroyed whatever they did not have time to take with them. NATIONAL ARCHIVES AND RECORDS ADMINISTRATION

stuffs and provided receipts to the owner. Even though Confederate law authorized these seizures, they alienated many people from the Confederate cause and did little to check inflation. Throughout the war, but especially in the last few months, soldiers and civilians alike suffered severe shortages.

Military Strategy and Administration
Both the Lincoln and the Davis administrations ran their respective war efforts well. For the most part they managed military affairs effectively, appointed fairly competent officers (although both sides suffered through a few dreadful politicians who were appointed as generals), and adopted sensible strategies. Davis was aware of both the demands for protection from all Confederate citizens and the limited resources available to provide it. He therefore attempted to employ what historians have called an "offensive-defensive" strategy. Davis oversaw the creation of large military departments. He had the officers in charge position their major army or armies along the logical invasion routes, and called on them to concentrate their forces to defeat major Union advances. Whenever they had opportunities, Davis encouraged offensives, even raids into Union territories. Those raids would take the war to the enemy, compelling the Northern public to taste the hazards of invasion. He also hoped to draw valuable supplies from the Northern populace. While there was some Confederate guerrilla fighting, the Davis adminis-

tration never embraced it, largely because guerrilla warfare would have exposed their people and property, including slaves, to Federal harassment, destruction, or confiscation.

When both sides optimistically believed the war would be of relatively brief duration, Lincoln embraced Winfield Scott's Anaconda Plan, which called for a blockade, river gunboats to penetrate deep into the Confederacy, and Union armies to slice their way through the rebellious territory. As the war expanded, Lincoln urged his generals to target the Confederate armies as their objectives, not simply Confederate territory. With Rebel military forces crushed, resistance would collapse, Lincoln believed. He skillfully tapped diplomacy to keep European powers and their money out of the conflict, and he used a blockade to cut off supplies to the under-industrialized Confederacy. By proclaiming emancipation, Lincoln won over all advocates of human rights, co-opted those in the North who criticized him for his slowness to embrace the concept, and allowed him to use a weapon that worked doubly, depriving Southerners of a valuable laborers force and putting them to work for the Union cause as soldiers, sailors, teamsters, stevedores, cooks, and farmers. Where Lincoln failed as a strategist was in his belated grasp of the value of Grant and Sherman's raiding strategy. Both generals realized that by marching Union armies directly through the Confederacy, destroying military resources and terrifying Southern people, they could promote the destruction of Rebel armies without suffering the staggering losses of direct military campaigns. Lincoln acquiesced because of his faith in those commanders, a faith that events fully justified, not just in Georgia and the Carolinas but also in Virginia under Philip Sheridan. Those marches destroyed valuable supplies, severed rail connections, damaged Southern morale, and caused mass desertions as soldiers abandoned the army to look after their loved ones.

The greatest administrative failure was in the area of prisons. Neither side prepared adequately for the huge number of captives as both sections assumed that they would exchange or parole prisoners regularly. But two major factors resulted in the breakdown of exchange. The Confederates claimed that many of the prisoners Grant took at Vicksburg were paroled illegally and could therefore return to service without formal exchange. The second revolved around black soldiers. The Confederacy resisted notions of treating them like white soldiers, and refused to exchange them. In response, the trading cartel broke down and prison populations soared beyond anyone's expectations. Lacking adequate preparation, camps quickly became overcrowded. Food, clothing, and housing shortages developed, and sanitary problems escalated as a consequence of these conditions. Over fifty-six thousand men died from the spread of disease as a result of overcrowding and food and clothing shortages in these horrible prison camps.

Confederate and Union Politics

In the political arena, the Confederate Congress exhibited some foresight when it established conscription and passed innovative taxing legislation, but it generally got mired in the inconsequential and failed to address many important issues in a timely way. Congress never passed legislation to flesh out a Supreme Court and other important pieces of legislation died of inertia or petty squabbles. Quite a number of legislators used the halls of Congress as a forum in which to bash Davis, his appointees, and the policies they opposed. Davis's popular election to the presidency in 1861 was unopposed, but administration critics had already begun to complain publicly. The congressional elections of 1863 reflected the public's growing disillusionment. When the second Congress convened in May 1864, clear opponents of Davis fell just short of a majority in both houses. Without organized political parties, however, opposition to the Davis administration splintered. In just one instance did Congress override a presidential veto, and only on a minor postage bill.

Lincoln's relationship with Congress and his own party varied. Early in his administration, with Republicans in the clear majority after secession, Congress passed into law all of the party's important planks for promoting economic growth and opportunity: an increase in the tariff; a homestead bill that offered free western land to anyone agreeing to settle on it; land subsidies for the con-

struction of a transcontinental railroad; and federal land grants to promote agricultural and mechanical colleges. In addition to war legislation, Congress established the first national currency in the Legal Tender Act. Yet the president's relations with Congress and his own party waxed and waned in accordance with progress in the war. The failure of eastern campaigns in 1862, perhaps compounded by an initial backlash to the Emancipation Proclamation, resulted in Republican losses at the polls that year.

Numerous individuals within the Republican Party came to believe that Lincoln was not up to the job of president. They began lobbying to dump him from the 1864 ticket, rallying around John C. Frémont or Salmon Chase. Like so many other people, both men and their supporters underestimated Lincoln's political savvy, and the president outmaneuvered them to secure renomination.

Much has been made about divisions between Lincoln and the more extreme wing in his own party, the Radical Republicans. In fact, Lincoln generally got along with the radical element. His differences with them were often minor policy distinctions, issues of timing or arguments over legislative versus executive power, not necessarily policy objectives.

Many administration critics outside the Republican Party, fueled by wartime failures, huge casualty lists, the draft, emancipation, and civil rights violations, organized into the Peace Democrats. These Copperheads, as supporters of the war called them, made some election gains in 1862, and their leading spokesman, Clement L. Vallandigham, almost won the governorship of Ohio in 1863.

During the difficult days in the summer of 1864, with the armies of both Grant and Sherman apparently bogged down, and Confederate Jubal Early threatening Washington, it appeared to Lincoln that he would not win reelection. The Democratic Party nominated for president the former general George B. McClellan, a pro-war administration critic, on a peace platform. Yet Lincoln stayed the course, and the war issue turned his way when Sheridan defeated Early and Sherman captured Atlanta. With the overwhelming support of Union soldiers, who detested the Copperheads, Lincoln and the Union Party (a coalition of Republicans and pro-war Democrats) swept the 1864 election.

Between his reelection and his assassination at the hands of John Wilkes Booth in April 1865, Lincoln endorsed several important initiatives to help those who had been held in bondage to succeed after the war. He pressed for passage and ratification of the Thirteenth Amendment to the U.S. Constitution, which abolished slavery; encouraged and signed into law the Freedmen's Bureau Bill, which created an organization to assist blacks in the transition from slavery to freedom; and began discussing with close political friends the idea of giving blacks the vote.

Davis and Lincoln As Leaders

Most modern scholars believe that Jefferson Davis did a competent job as Confederate president under extremely adverse circumstances. However, his inability to understand alternative viewpoints and his lack of personal charm served him badly. The distinction of Lincoln, on the other hand, was discernible not in the enactment of laws through his advocacy, nor in the adoption of his ideals as a continuing postwar policy, nor even in his persuasion of Republicans to follow his lead. Rather, the qualities that marked him as a leader were vision, personal tact, fairness toward opponents, popular appeal, dignity and effectiveness in state papers, absence of vindictiveness, and withal a personality that was remembered for its own uniqueness while it was almost canonized as a symbol of the Union cause. Military success, though long delayed, and the dramatic martyrdom of his assassination must also be reckoned as factors in Lincoln's fame. On the Southern side, the myth of the lost cause has diminished the true role of slavery in the war and has elevated the reputation of numerous talented Confederate individuals, most notably Robert E. Lee, Stonewall Jackson, and Jefferson Davis, to extraordinary heights.

The Consequences of the War

The cost of the war was staggering. Some 258,000 Confederates soldiers gave their lives for slavery and an independent nation; more than 360,000 Federals paid the ultimate price for the union. In addition, one-half million sustained wounds in the war and untold thousands permanently damaged their health by contracting wartime illnesses. From a monetary standpoint, the best guess places the cost of the war at $20 billion. The Confederate States alone suffered an estimated $7.4 billion worth of property damage. In fact, so devastated was the Southern economy that it was not until well into the twentieth century that its annual agricultural output reached the 1860 level.

Among the other consequences of the war, the union was established as inviolate. The central government would continue to increase its power at the expense of the states, and the Northern vision of rights, economic opportunity, and industrialization would prevail. For African Americans, in addition to the abolition of slavery forever, the Fourteenth Amendment granted them citizenship. Unfortunately, the court system refused to apply the due process and equal protection clause of that amendment to African Americans, and it was not long before whites regained control in the South and stripped blacks of many of their newfound rights. Southern whites even managed to circumvent the Fifteenth Amendment, which gave African Americans the right to vote. All the while, as Southern whites restored themselves to power and forced blacks into a subordinate position, a Northern public, tired of war and reform, acquiesced. It took another one hundred years for blacks to gain their civil liberties.

BIBLIOGRAPHY

Boritt, Gabor S., ed. *Why the Confederacy Lost.* New York: Oxford University Press, 1992.

Cooper, William C., Jr. *Jefferson Davis, American.* New York: Knopf, 2000.

Davis, William C. *Jefferson Davis: The Man and His Hour.* New York: HarperCollins, 1991.

———. *Look Away!; A History of the Confederate States of America.* New York: Free Press, 2002.

Donald, David Herbert. *Lincoln.* New York: Simon and Schuster, 1995.

———, ed. *Why the North Won the Civil War.* Baton Rouge: Louisiana State University Press, 1960.

Foner, Eric. *Free Soil, Free Labor, Free Men: The Ideology of the Republican Party before the Civil War.* New York: Oxford University Press, 1970.

Gienapp, William E. *The Origins of the Republican Party, 1852–1856.* New York: Oxford University Press, 1987.

Glatthaar, Joseph T. *Forged in Battle: The Civil War Alliance of Black Soldiers and White Officers.* New York: Free Press, 1990.

Hattaway, Herman, and Archer Jones. *How the North Won: A Military History of the Civil War.* Urbana, Ill.: University of Illinois Press, 1983.

McPherson, James M. *Battle Cry of Freedom: The Civil War Era.* New York: Oxford University Press, 1988.

Paludan, Phillip Shaw. *"A People's Contest": The Union and the Civil War, 1861–1865.* New York: Harper and Row, 1988.

Roland, Charles P. *An American Iliad: The Story of the Civil War.* Lexington: University Press of Kentucky, 1991.

Thomas, Emory M. *The Confederate Nation, 1861–1865.* New York: Harper and Row, 1979.

Joseph T. Glatthaar
J.G. Randall

See also **Antietam, Battle of; Appomattox; Army, Confederate; Army, Union; Assassinations, Presidential; Atlanta Campaign; Bull Run, First Battle of; Bull Run, Second Battle of; Chattanooga Campaign; Chickamauga, Battle of; Cold Harbor, Battle of; Confederate States of America; Confiscation Acts; Conscription and Recruitment; Contraband, Slaves as; Copperheads; Donelson, Fort, Capture of; Draft Riots; Emancipation Proclamation; Fredericksburg, Battle of; Freedmen's Bureau; Gettysburg, Battle of; Inflation in the Confederacy; Legal Tender Act; Nashville, Battle of; New Orleans, Capture of; Petersburg, Siege of; Radical Republicans; Richmond Campaigns; Sanitary Commission, United States; Seven Days' Battles; Sherman's March to the Sea; Shiloh, Battle of; Slavery; Spotsylvania Courthouse, Battle of; States' Rights in the Confederacy; Suffrage: African American Suffrage; Union Party; Vicksburg in the Civil War; White House of the Confederacy; Wilderness, Battles of the; *and vol. 9:* Benjamin Butler's Report on Contrabands of War; A Confederate Blockade-Runner; Emancipation Proclamation; Gettysburg Address; Head of Choctow Nation Reaffirms His Tribe's Position; Robert E. Lee's Farewell to His Army; Letter to President Lincoln from Harrison's Landing;**

Letters from Widows to Lincoln Asking for Help; Prisoner at Andersonville; Second Inaugural Address; South Carolina Declaration of Causes of Secession.

CIVIL WAR GENERAL ORDER NO. 100,

a code comprising 157 articles "for the government of armies in the field" according to the "laws and usages of war." By order of Secretary of War Edwin M. Stanton, it was drawn up by Francis Lieber and a special board, and utilized by Union officers. The first code of its kind, it later formed the basis for many codes of military field law and for the conventions of the Hague conferences of 1899 and 1907. Ironically, at the same time that governments began to institute formal codes to regulate military behavior, the practice of targeting civilian populations in wartime became ever more common.

BIBLIOGRAPHY

Lieber, Francis. *Code for the Government of Armies in the Field as Authorized by the Laws and Usages of War on Land.* New York: U.S. War Department, 1863.

Frank Freidel / A. G.

See also **Arrest, Arbitrary, during the Civil War; Contraband of War; Desertion; Military Law; Unconditional Surrender; War Department.**

CIVILIAN CONSERVATION CORPS.

Because of his fervent commitment to preserving natural resources, President Franklin D. Roosevelt made the Civilian Conservation Corps (CCC) the first recovery and relief bill he submitted to Congress. Enacted swiftly on 21 March 1933, the CCC remedy of healthy outdoor work for jobless youth had the highest public approval of any New Deal legislation. Roosevelt even used its appeal to persuade desperate World War I veterans to call off their protest demand for early payment of service bonuses and instead accept enrollment in the CCC as a way to ease their economic plight.

During its nine-year existence the CCC enlisted nearly 3 million single men between the ages of seventeen and twenty-five to work at erosion control, fire prevention, land reclamation, and pest eradication. Concentrating on forest management, the CCC accounted for more than half of all the tree-planting in the United States through the twentieth century. For their service, enrollees received $30 monthly, $25 of which they were required to send home to their families.

Organization of the CCC was shared widely. The Department of Labor selected the men enrolled, the Department of War administered the work camps with army officers, and the Departments of Agriculture and the Interior devised and supervised the projects. Roosevelt chose Robert Fechner as director partly because he had the practical and fiscally cautious qualifications the president favored for such leadership and partly because Fech-

Civilian Conservation Corps. Young men in this extremely popular New Deal program work at an experimental farm in Beltsville, Md., c. 1933. NATIONAL ARCHIVES AND RECORDS ADMINISTRATION

ner's position as vice president of the American Federation of Labor (AFL) allayed union concerns about meager pay and military regimentation.

As with other relief programs, affording aid to all in need faced problems. Camp commanders drawn from a segregated army and Fechner, who was raised in Georgia with conventional southern views, were not inclined to heed the legislative amendment added by the only black member of Congress, Representative Oscar DePriest of Illinois, that "no discrimination shall be made on account of race, color, or creed." Ultimately pressure from the Department of Labor opened the program to blacks. By 1938 the number of blacks reached 11 percent, and by the end of the program over two hundred thousand blacks had served. Less fortunate in finding a place were women, who were excluded altogether in the original act. Only at Eleanor Roosevelt's insistence did eighty-six camps enrolling 8,500 women briefly flourish before Congress eliminated the women's section in 1937.

Camp management included the usual New Deal emphasis on education as the key to rising from disadvantage. Over 100,000 young men who arrived at camps in a woefully weak and deprived state not only rounded into good shape but also learned to read. At a higher level almost 5,000 enrollees completed high school, and another 2,700 earned college degrees.

Roosevelt always believed the CCC was one of the New Deal's best achievements. However, because World War II absorbed the unemployed, the program ended in 1942. Despite later problems with unemployed youth and a damaged environment, general aversion to collective government action prevented any kind of revival of the CCC concept.

BIBLIOGRAPHY

Bernstein, Irving. "Social Programs in Action." In *A Caring Society: The New Deal, the Worker, and the Great Depression*. Boston: Houghton Mifflin, 1985.

Hill, Edwin G. *In the Shadow of the Mountain: The Spirit of the CCC*. Pullman: Washington State University Press, 1990.

Salmond, John A. *The Civilian Conservation Corps, 1933–1942: A New Deal Case Study*. Durham, N.C.: Duke University Press, 1967. The standard survey.

Alan Lawson

See also **Great Depression; New Deal; World War II.**

CIVILIZED TRIBES, FIVE.

Five Civilized Tribes was a collective name used to describe the Chickasaw, Choctaw, Cherokee, Creek, and Seminole Indians during the nineteenth century. The term "civilized" stemmed from the willingness of many of these natives to adopt Christianity and to use the tools of white American culture to preserve their Indian identity. While living in their homelands in the American Southeast, some members of these tribes adopted commercial agriculture and chose to live like their American neighbors. Some established plantations and owned slaves. By 1867, all five tribes had been removed to Indian Territory and were ruled by constitutional governments, which mirrored the political institutions of the United States. These practices continued into the late nineteenth century, as did the tension between those who adopted the majority culture's traditions and those who did not. Those more inclined to white ways were keen on integrating Indian Territory into the national economy, often welcoming white settlers to their homeland and renting out parcels of land to them. By 1890, Indians in the Territory were outnumbered by more than two to one by whites and African Americans. The United States abolished the governments of the Five Tribes in 1898 and admitted Oklahoma to the Union in 1907. In the twentieth century members of these tribes sought to establish unity amongst themselves by defining "Indianness" in terms of blood, not traditional cultural practices.

BIBLIOGRAPHY

Debo, Angie. *And Still the Waters Run: The Betrayal of the Five Civilized Tribes*. Princeton, N.J.: Princeton University Press, 1940.

Perdue, Theda. *Nations Remembered: An Oral History of the Five Civilized Tribes, 1865–1907*. Westport, Conn.: Greenwood Press, 1980.

Nathan Ross Kozuskanich

See also vol. 9: **The Origin of the League of Five Nations.**

CLAIM ASSOCIATIONS

were frontier institutions designed to provide a quasi-legal land system in areas where no land law existed. Settlers who made their homes on land not yet surveyed, or on public land not yet offered at public auction sale, made their improvements with no certainty of continued ownership. Where squatters were fairly numerous, it was natural that they should organize to protect their common interests. Claim associations, or claim clubs, appeared early in the nineteenth century and were found in practically every part of the public land area that received settlers before 1870.

The main features of a claim association were a constitution guaranteeing mutual protection to each claimant of 160 or 320 acres who met the simple requirements for improvements, a "register" who kept a record of all claims and their transfers, and a bidder who represented the group at the public auction sale. The claim associations' registry made it possible to buy and sell claims without the government patent. And the bidder played a key role in the association's efforts to police land auctions and prevent speculators from purchasing member claims and bidding up the price of land.

Early state and territorial law gave legal sanction to many of the practices of the associations, including the registering and transferring of claims. Most important was the Preemption Law of 1841, which legalized squatting upon surveyed lands. It gave the settler the right to "preempt" his claim before the public sale or to purchase the land at the minimum price. The heyday of the associations was in the 1840s and 1850s in Iowa, Kansas, and Nebraska, where practically every township had its protective organization.

BIBLIOGRAPHY

Anderson, George LaVerne. *Essays on the Public Lands: Problems, Legislation, and Administration*. Lawrence, Kan.: Coronado Press, 1971.

Johnson, Hildegard Binder. *Order Upon the Land: The U.S. Rectangular Land Survey and the Upper Mississippi Country*. New York: Oxford University Press, 1976.

White, Richard. *"It's Your Misfortune and None of My Own." A New History of the American West*. Norman: University of Oklahoma Press, 1991.

Paul Wallace Gates/c. p.

See also **Frontier; Public Domain; Western Lands**

CLAIMS, FEDERAL COURT OF,

created by Congress in 1855 under its power to appropriate money to pay the debts of the United States. The court investigated contractual claims against the United States brought before the court by private parties or referred to it by an executive department or by Congress. In 1982, the United States Court of Federal Claims was recreated by the Federal Courts Improvement Act. It retained all the original jurisdiction of the Court of Claims, with the addition of bid protests, vaccine compensation, civil liberties, product liability, and oil spills. Approximately one-quarter of the cases before the court involve tax refund suits.

BIBLIOGRAPHY

Barrow, Deborah J., Gerard S. Gryski, and Gary Zuk. *The Federal Judiciary and Institutional Change.* Ann Arbor: University of Michigan Press, 1996.

Henderson, Dwight F. *Courts for a New Nation.* Washington, D.C.: Public Affairs Press, 1971.

Wheeler, Russell R. *Creating the Federal Judicial System.* Washington, D.C.: Federal Judicial Center, 1994.

P. Orman Ray
Honor Sachs

See also **Constitution of the United States; Federal Agencies.**

CLARK'S NORTHWEST CAMPAIGN.

During the early years of the American Revolution, the British exercised undisputed control over the country northwest of the OHIO RIVER. DETROIT served as the headquarters for the uncounted Native American war parties against colonial settlements south of the Ohio River. George Rogers Clark perceived that KENTUCKY could best be defended by the conquest of Detroit. Too weak to make a frontal attack on Detroit, however, he directed his first blow against the towns of the French in ILLINOIS. Kaskaskia was occupied on 4 July 1778, and the remaining Illinois towns, including Vincennes, were easily persuaded to join the rebel standard. On learning of these developments, Lt. Gov. Henry Hamilton of Detroit prepared a counterstroke. He reclaimed Vincennes on 17 December, but instead of pushing on against Kaskaskia, Hamilton dismissed his Indian allies and settled down for the winter.

Perceiving an opportunity, Clark led his army of 170 men eastward across Illinois to tempt his fate at Vincennes. After thirty-six hours of battle, Hamilton yielded his fort and garrison to the rebel leader on 24 February 1779. Although the conquest of Detroit, Clark's ultimate goal, was never attained, he retained his grip on the southern end of the NORTHWEST TERRITORY until the close of the war. This possession proved an important factor in obtaining the Northwest for the United States in the Definitive Treaty of Peace of 1783.

BIBLIOGRAPHY

Bakeless, John Edwin. *Background to Glory: The Life of George Rogers Clark.* Philadelphia: Lippincott, 1957.

Harrison, Lowell H. *George Rogers Clark and the War in the West.* Lexington: University Press of Kentucky, 1976.

James, James Alton. *The Life of George Rogers Clark.* Chicago: University of Chicago Press, 1928.

Sutton, Robert M. "George Rogers Clark and the Campaign in the West: The Five Major Documents." *Indiana Magazine of History* 76, no. 4 (December 1980): 334–345.

M. M. Quaife / A. R.

See also **Backcountry and Backwoods; Revolution, American: Military History; Revolution, American: Political History; Paris, Treaty of (1783).**

CLASS.

"Class is obviously a difficult word," Raymond Williams wrote in *Keywords: A Vocabulary of Culture and Society* (1976). Class was a difficult word for Williams "both in its range of meanings and its complexity in that particular meaning where it describes social division." As a word in English, class probably first appeared in a Latin form, *classis*, during the sixteenth century. *Classis* was a Roman term for the differences of property among citizens. One mid-seventeenth-century scholar, Williams reports, glossed the term as "an order or distribution of people according to their several Degrees" but restricted the meaning by adding "in Schools (wherein the term is most used)." In 1705 Daniel Defoe remarked, "tis plain the dearness of wages forms our people into more classes than other nations can show." Defoe identified a main force in class formation within early capitalism: the payment of wages for labor. But Defoe referred to an ambiguous plurality of classes, not to a hierarchy based on a division between employers and employed. Class in its modern sense is defined not only by the form of economic subsistence but also by a hierarchical division of labor, privilege, and authority. The formation of classes in America—followed by modern usage of the term "class" to describe them—accelerated in the eighteenth and early nineteenth centuries with the commencement of the Industrial Revolution in the Atlantic basin. It began earlier, however, and occurred in relation to the historical development of race and gender.

The Division of Society into Owning and Working Classes

Long before the word "class" gave a label to the status arrangements within industrial capitalism, the conditions that the term would describe were developing. None were more important than the division between a large and growing population that owned nothing but its labor and a much smaller, profit-driven population that owned productive property, whether land or tools and shops. Where this process began is a source of continuing debate, but one place to look for some of the earlier developments is early modern England. Beginning in the sixteenth century and stretching into the nineteenth century, a series of enclosure acts in England eliminated the traditional feudal rights of peasant communities to hold large pieces of land in common for general use. The termination of these rights made possible the creation of large private, individual holdings for commercial production. The English state simultaneously expanded its power to compel the dispossessed and mobile commoners to labor either in agriculture or the crafts. Commoners either worked in the new system voluntarily or were treated by the state as criminal vagrants and sentenced to workhouses. In North America, where land was much more widely available, workhouses were less common, but both forced and voluntary labor took contractual forms similar to those practiced in England: craft apprenticeships and agricultural indentures.

The indentured agricultural laborer contracted to work for a number of years for a master, or planter, in exchange for the cost of transport to the British North American colonies, not wages. During the late seventeenth century growers in the Chesapeake Bay region, the Carolinas, and the Caribbean shifted exclusively to enslaved African labor. Through the end of slavery, small planters and their families often worked alongside their handful of enslaved laborers and whites continued to do hired agricultural labor. But agricultural labor in commercial production of tobacco, rice, indigo, and cotton became the work of a caste of enslaved workers, distinguishing it from the wage system developing in the crafts. The craft apprentice served a master for a number of years, usually about seven or until maturity, and then became a journeyman who likely earned wages from his master. Journeymen lived with their masters until they married or became skilled enough to complete their own "masterpiece" and open their own shop. The English guilds, which enforced these relationships among craft workers and controlled prices, never crossed the Atlantic. Initially, there were fewer journeymen in craft operations in North America. Masters usually worked for themselves, perhaps with an apprentice or a journeyman. And many of those called masters were really journeymen who simply set up shop for themselves in American cities with few or no craft workers. During the late eighteenth century these masters, like many of their English counterparts, began to enlarge their operations, employing more labor and demanding more from it. These small groups of journeymen who worked together in the shops and lived together in neighborhoods apart from their masters increasingly organized themselves and found cause to strike over wages and hours. Consequently, although master bakers went on strike in New York City in 1741 and master carpenters struck in Savannah, Georgia, in 1746, demanding better prices, it was journeymen carpenters who went on strike in Philadelphia in 1791.

Between 1780 and 1840, the transformation of the craft system into a system of ownership and working classes was perhaps "one of the outstanding triumphs of nineteenth century American capitalism," according to Sean Wilenz (*Chants Democratic: New York City and the Rise of the American Working Class, 1788–1850* [1984]). It was during this period that the changes in labor practices that were detectable in the eighteenth century suddenly seemed to move more rapidly, encompassing a wider demographic. Master craftsmen and shopkeepers had formed a significant—if uncertainly situated—middling class status, or rank, in the commercial cities of British North America from Boston to Savannah. But by 1815 merchant capitalists dominated some of the craft markets, such as textiles and many in this first middle class of small independent producers could no longer maintain themselves. Some masters, in crafts such as silversmithing, possessed significant wealth, but others endured hard labor and seasons of desperate want for themselves and their families. Many master craftsmen became managers working for capitalist

owners who controlled the tools, inventory, and marketing and expected masters to push for the greatest possible productivity for the lowest possible wage. By 1820 New York City had twelve "manufactories" that employed twenty-five or more workers and thirty-five other facilities that employed ten or more workers. Many other masters lost their independence and became wageworkers in these early factories alongside journeymen and apprentices. After about 1820, the rise of stereotyping in printing and sweatshops in clothing and shoes heralded the expansion of mechanized, frenetic, and standardized production.

The emerging class relations of industrialization were broadly impacted by the American Revolution's ideological discourses, which lauded national and individual independence as masculine virtues. Masters who worked crafts that were still not industrialized maintained an independence that could put them in a middling rank, along with small-scale yeoman farmers. This independence was an important source of distinction—or class—and it defined white masculinity while separating it from the status of the enslaved and women, all of whom could not vote and owned little or no property. Even when they organized into citywide craft unions, larger and better organized versions of the eighteenth-century journeymen's combinations, white industrial workers were dependent on insecure employment over which they exercised little control. Class subordination and republican masculinity were contradictory. As both slave labor and wage labor expanded in the early nineteenth century, American workers discovered that "one way to make peace with the latter was to differentiate it sharply from the former," according to David Roediger in *The Wages of Whiteness: Race and the Making of the American Working Class* (1992). African Americans both enslaved and free were stereotyped by all whites as licentious, lazy, and dangerous by nature, fit only for hard labor and dependence on whites. A model of white masculinity defined itself in terms of protecting against blackness and blacks. In nonslave states, white working-class Republican Boys harassed the free black population of the cities, chasing them from public spaces. Whites produced and eagerly attended blackface minstrel productions, which were stereotyped and distorted representations of black culture. In the slave states, whites of all classes, including workers, helped police the enslaved and protect against insurrection.

As the manufactory owners looked less for skill than for cheap, rapid output, they also participated in altering the economic role of women, creating new class cultures, particularly in the cities. In the North, the unpaid labor of women in the household helped fuel early capital accumulation by consuming and using the ever-expanding "labor-saving" devices produced by the industrial sector and reproducing the laboring population. The famous Lowell Mills in Massachusetts, one example of a regional practice, employed farm girls in factory production for fourteen hours a day at a fraction of the wages paid to men. In the larger cities, such as New York, the outwork system, in which women took wage work home, the low wages it paid, and the difficulty for these dispersed women workers to organize helped fuel a new street culture. Juvenile delinquency, attacks against women, and public intoxication all seemed more prevalent after 1820. Middle- and upper-class men sought prostitutes in the working-class neighborhoods. Workingmen had developed a moralistic and paternal attitude toward the street culture and women's labor exploitation. Middle- and upper-class women, claiming an especially moral status as women of "respectable" classes, discovered a public role in moral reform work within the workers' neighborhoods.

Racial Divisions and Rising Worker Consciousness
In the South, where the overwhelming majority of African Americans lived, most of them were enslaved. Slaves were workers, but racism divided them from "the working class," a phrase that, as in the North, carried an often unspoken association to "white." The degree to which the slave South was capitalist and class conscious continues to be a source of debate. Slavery was principally an agricultural labor system with some feudal qualities, but it was also a source of labor for the crafts and industry. In Charleston, South Carolina, artisans employed or owned enslaved African laborers in the eighteenth century. In the antebellum period the Tredgar Iron Works in Richmond, Virginia—the third-largest iron producer in the United States—used slaves for about half of its one-thousand-person labor force. Tredgar's enslaved workers earned wages, mostly for their masters, and worked in every phase of production as founders, colliers, miners, teamsters, and woodchoppers. Slaves were cheap to hire from their masters and could be made to work hard. Racism divided this biracial workforce, making strikes difficult. An unsuccessful strike by white workers at Tredgar in 1847 unsuccessfully demanded the removal of black workers.

Although the Civil War, in a sign of a growing class consciousness, workers formed the first nationwide labor unions and organizations in the United States beginning in the 1860s. In 1877 railroad workers struck after four years of depression in the economy and repeated merciless wage cuts by the railroads, engaging the Pennsylvania militia in a bloody armed confrontation at Pittsburgh and spreading the strike throughout the national rail systems. Another sign of growing class consciousness was the fact that labor organizations grew despite failures such as a massive nationwide strike effort for the eight-hour day in 1886. The Knights of Labor, an early nationwide union, rejected the antebellum model of organizing only skilled white workers and instead organized skilled and unskilled, white and black, reaching possibly one million members, or nearly 10 percent of the American workforce, in 1886. That same year the American Federation of Labor (AFL) was organized by a group of national and regional craft unions. The more massive industrialism became, the more massive the confrontations and workers' organizations became. In 1892 the town of Homestead, Pennsylvania, had only 11,000 residents, but 3,800 of them worked in

its twelve mills. When workers in Andrew Carnegie's Homestead mill went on strike that year after his associate, Henry Clay Frick, announced he would not renew the union's contract and would replace all the workers, virtually the whole town, men and women, joined in active support of the walkout. Frick hired several hundred armed soldiers, and after violent armed confrontations with the strikers and townspeople, he ultimately succeeded in breaking the strike and the union. The Homestead strike and the use of armed force to break it became common during the early twentieth century and underscored the class divisions within American society.

The movement of European, Asian, and Latin American immigrants and African American migrants into U.S. industries during the years between the 1890s and 1940s greatly altered the class system. Millions of immigrant workers labored in Chicago factories and Colorado mines alongside southern-born African Americans who moved North in two great migration waves between 1910 and 1940. Both the men and women of these populations worked in industry. In 1910 nearly one-third of working women still labored in domestic service, but the numbers of women in industrial wage labor were increasing. Ten percent of married women worked for wages in 1920, the year women won the right to vote. Women's total employment reached eleven million before World War II, nearly doubling the female workforce.

These changes in the rapidly expanding industrial workforce stimulated a reformation of the middle class, both outside the corporations and within them. Problems and injustices that were of interest to philanthropic gentlemen and ladies in the British colonial, early national, and antebellum periods—orphan rescue, poor relief, and educational reform—became the concern of new intellectuals. This class not only managed the factories and corporations, but also taught in the expanding universities and colleges, administered the growing state bureaucracies, and founded settlement houses to address the poverty of the largely immigrant and working-class urban population. Their approach to social problems remained moralistic and paternal—teaching immigrant women to be "good mothers," for example—but as in the factories, where managers sought to regulate production through "scientific" discipline and efficiency, reformers adopted "scientific" methods, expanding the study of poverty and creating state welfare programs.

The Great Depression and the administrations of President Franklin D. Roosevelt further institutionalized this new middle, bureaucratic class and removed the barriers of violence and law to union organization that employers and state governments had erected. In addition, the Great Depression delegitimized the capitalist class and its system of private corporate benefit programs. These conditions encouraged not only an expanded welfare state but vigorous union organizing: total American union membership tripled between 1932 and 1939, exceeding eight million. By the end of World War II, as many as one-third of American workers were union members. But the growing Cold War ideological tension between the United States and the Soviet Union following World War II fundamentally altered class politics. After nearly a century, that "spectre" that Marx had declared was "haunting Europe" in 1848 seemed to haunt Americans anew: communism, more as a specter than as an actual mass movement, became enmeshed in American racism and class politics. The Congress of Industrial Organizations (CIO)—later to merge with the AFL—expelled nine unions in 1949 and 1950 because of their refusal to purge communists. The CIO had organized 800,000 southern workers during the war, one-third of them black, but it stagnated under accusations that unions were the leading edge of a communist miscegenation plot to subvert white Christian capitalism. Many workers in the South, North, and West supported the anticommunist campaign. The mainstream of worker consciousness had never been revolutionary; rather it supported the development of a welfare state that protected laborers from the worst vicissitudes of capitalism.

In the later twentieth century, the stall in working-class organization and the relatively higher wages that industrial workers earned, compared to prewar levels, helped spark debate about the reality of class divisions in the United States among the intellectual middle classes. Qualitatively it seemed obvious that class divisions mattered in America: strikes, unions, and police repression of workers all seem to indicate serious class conflict. One Chicago worker in 1940, answering a question about whether there was a working class, expressed a common opinion when he cited class-segregated neighborhoods and social networks:

> Hell, brother, you don't have to look far to know there's a workin' class. We may not say so. But look at what we do. Work. Look at who we run around with and bull with. Workers. Look at where we live. If you can find anybody but workers in my block, I'll eat 'em." (Lizabeth Cohen, *Making a New Deal: Industrial Workers in Chicago, 1919–1939* [1990])

In 1940, however, *Fortune* magazine announced the results of a survey showing that 80 percent of Americans identified themselves as middle class. *Fortune* took the results as evidence that capitalism, "the American way of life," produced general affluence, not class animosities. *Fortune*'s findings were soon challenged by sociologists who found a majority of Americans identified as working class. Ultimately, however, querying Americans on their self placement within the class system offered few solid conclusions. As study after study tested each others' assumptions, methods, and categories and ended with different conclusions, the Left grew skeptical of the objectivity of sociological surveys and the Right grew skeptical of a putatively leftist academy.

Globalization and a New Class Formation

In 1963 the widely influential English historian E. P. Thompson insisted, in *The Making of the English Working Class*, that class was not a fixed social structure or a pos-

session of a fixed set of people, hinting that sociology was looking in the wrong direction. Rather, "class" was simply "something which in fact happens (and can be shown to have happened) in human relationships." With similar logic, two American sociologists argued in the late 1980s that the role of authority and the nature of work have become "central in the capital accumulation process and . . . the exploitation of the working class" (Reeve Vanneman and Lyn Weber Cannon, *The American Perception of Class* [1987]). What defines class is not ownership of property or self-identification, but a person's type of labor and ability to control it. The industrial working class had been defined by hourly and insecure wage labor since its formation in the late eighteenth and early nineteenth centuries. And workers built ever-larger organizations—first in shops, then cities, and finally, nationally—to combat this insecurity and its frequent poverty. As the globalization of industrial capitalism picked up pace in the late twentieth century, North American industrial workers watched their multinational employers move their higher-wage jobs overseas, precipitating a new class formation still unfinished at the end of the century.

The first feature of the new class formation was increased poverty and insecurity, but this "flexibility" and "efficiency" in the workforce—as corporate culture described it—yielded only a moderate degree of new militancy from worker organizations in the United States. During the last decades of the twentieth century, actual poverty—the inability to pay for necessities, such as health care and housing—among low-wage workers deepened. Meanwhile, women and minorities continued to be disproportionately represented among the lowest wage earners. The 1990s poverty rate of 13 percent—which incorporated a short-term decline in poverty among minorities—was misleading because it was calculated on the cost of food. While food prices remained more or less stagnant between the 1960s and 2000, rent and health care costs far outpaced inflation, market wage increases, and governmental adjustments in the minimum wage. Even after modest wage growth for low-wage workers during the 1990s, many American workers lived on 1973 wages at 1999 prices. A disproportionate percentage of the working-class poor were nonwhites and the working class remained divided by race, even after the civil rights movement had run its full course. The southern civil rights movement of the 1950s and 1960s had tended to address race but not class dynamics within the black community. For all its dramatic successes in expanding democracy in the United States, the urban rebellions of the 1960s could be understood as stemming from the failure of the movement to win effective solutions to economic inequalities. The 1992 rebellion in working-class black neighborhoods of Los Angeles, following the acquittal of police officers in the brutal beating of Rodney King, made plain the depth of continuing frustration in the black working class.

A second feature of the new class formation was the official labor movement's efforts to moderate—not revolutionize—globalization and the race and gender disparities and divisions within the American class system. Unions declared a renewed interest in organizing the unorganized, democratic internal governance, international labor coalitions, antiracism and antisexism efforts, and the mobilization of workers to resist globalization on corporate terms. Alongside church, environmental, and student activists, unions supported local anti-sweatshop and living wage campaigns across the country. A Teamsters strike at the United Parcel Service in 1997 seemed to many to announce a newly assertive working class. And the thousands of union members who protested against the World Trade Organization in Seattle in 1999 alongside thousands of students and environmentalists seemed to herald a new activist, militant, mass, and global working-class agenda. The challenge seemed likely to rest in how well the labor movement could address both globalization, with its formation of industrial classes in undeveloped nation-states primarily in the Global South, and the persistent race and gender divisions within the American working class—divisions of wage scales, privileges, and opportunities.

BIBLIOGRAPHY

Boydston, Jeanne. *Home and Work: Housework, Wages, and the Ideology of Labor in the Early Republic.* New York: Oxford University Press, 1990.

Brody, David. *In Labor's Cause: Main Themes on the History of the American Worker.* New York: Oxford University Press, 1993.

Cohen, Lizabeth. *Making a New Deal: Industrial Workers in Chicago, 1919–1939.* Cambridge, U.K.: Cambridge University Press, 1990.

Ehrenreich, Barbara. *Nickle and Dimed: On (Not) Getting by in America.* New York: Metropolitan Books, 2001.

Kelley, Robin D. G. *Race Rebels: Culture, Politics, and the Black Working Class.* New York: Free Press, 1994.

Levine, Bruce et al. *Who Built America? Working People and the Nation's Economy, Politics, Culture, and Society.* Vol. 2: *From the Gilded Age to the Present.* New York: Pantheon Books, 1992.

Marx, Karl. "The Manifesto of the Communist Party." In *The Marx-Engels Reader.* Edited by Robert C. Tucker. 2d ed. New York: Norton, 1978.

Montgomery, David. *Citizen Worker: The Experience of Workers in the United States with Democracy and the Free Market during the Nineteenth Century.* Cambridge, U.K.: Cambridge University Press, 1993.

Morris, Richard B., ed. *A History of the American Worker.* Princeton, N.J.: Princeton University Press, 1976.

Roediger, David. *The Wages of Whiteness: Race and the Making of the American Working Class.* London: Verso, 1991.

Stansell, Christine. *City of Women: Sex and Class in New York, 1789–1860.* New York: Knopf, 1986.

Thompson, E. P. *The Making of the English Working Class.* New York: Vintage Books, 1963.

Vanneman, Reeve, and Lyn Weber Cannon. *The American Perception of Class.* Philadelphia: Temple University Press, 1987.

Wilentz, Sean. *Chants Democratic: New York City and the Rise of the American Working Class, 1788–1850.* New York: Oxford University Press, 1984.

Williams, Raymond. *Keywords: A Vocabulary of Culture and Society.* 1976. Rev. ed. New York: Oxford University Press, 1983.

James O'Neil Spady

See also **American Federation of Labor–Congress of Industrial Organizations; Civil Rights Movement; Discrimination: Race; Gender and Gender Roles; Indentured Servants; Industrial Revolution; Knights of Labor; Race Relations; Slavery; Trade Unions;** *and vol. 9:* **The Theory of the Leisure Class.**

CLASS CONFLICT. Social distinctions have existed in most societies, such as the orders of the European feudal system or the castes of Indian society, but the modern concept of social class emerged during the nineteenth century. In the classic definition of German political economist Karl Marx, societies are divided into classes based on their socioeconomic status, more particularly, those who own capital (factory owners, for example) and those who do not and must rely on wages for subsistence.

Social Classes

In the United States, the high level of social mobility and the high percentage of people owning individual property have sparked a debate over whether there are genuine American social classes at all. Initial immigration came from a relatively narrow social range, mostly craftsmen and peasants from the "middle sort," rich enough to pay for the journey to America but poor enough to have an incentive to do so. Even indentured servants, immigrants placing themselves in voluntary servitude for a period of about five years in exchange for the cost of the trip, gained freedom eventually; furthermore, their number declined after the American Revolution. Only black slaves, disenfranchised and permanently deprived of property ownership, could legitimately be described as a social class.

The peculiar social environment of the frontier, in which opportunities abounded, allowed most white males to experience social mobility, whether upward or downward. The process prevented permanent classes with distinct tastes and ways of life from forming, to the point where the European elite sneered at American nouveaux riches, who had no proper education to match their newfound fortunes. This social hierarchy, based almost solely on wealth acquired by merit, justified the huge income gap that still characterizes American society. A survey reported in the *New York Times* (26 October 1998) found that in 1994, the 30 percent richest Americans commandeered 55.3 percent of the national wealth, a higher percentage than in any similar industrialized country. Still, income inequality gave rise to only limited social unrest.

Faith in Upward Social Mobility

Despite two famous exceptions, the first years of the Republic were relatively conflict free. From 1786 to 1787, Daniel Shays headed a revolt of several hundred men aimed against foreclosures and high taxes. A military failure, Shays's revolt nevertheless convinced the legislature of Massachusetts to pass a law protecting indebted farmers. In 1799, John Fries launched another revolt in Pennsylvania to free from prison citizens who had refused to pay a new property tax. For the first half of the nineteenth century, many Americans believed in the Jeffersonian ideal of a united, peaceful, egalitarian society of yeomen, or small independent farmers.

Many of the captains of industry who rose to prominence after the Civil War had humble origins. Andrew Carnegie, Philip Armour, Gustavus Swift, Daniel Drew, Jay Gould, James Fisk, John D. Rockefeller, Jay Cooke, James J. Hill, and Collis Huntington could legitimately claim that they had gone from rags to riches. William Vanderbilt, Edward Harriman, Henry Villard, and Henry Clay Frick were among the few for whom a more privileged background had served as a stepping-stone. Faith in upward social mobility in the late nineteenth century was best exemplified in the popular novels by Horatio Alger, in which young heroes enrich themselves through honesty, hard work, and—in part—luck.

Many of these entrepreneurs, most prominently steel magnate Andrew Carnegie, the son and grandson of Scottish blue-collar agitators, devoted part of their wealth to philanthropic causes that helped poor people help themselves. (Carnegie funded public libraries, schools, and museums.) The deserving poor, unable to work because of a crippling injury, also received help, but most of the poor, having failed to succeed in an open social environment, were seen as morally deficient. In England, philosopher Herbert Spencer, inspired by the works of Charles Darwin, compared society to a struggle of species, in which superior individuals became rich while the unfit crowded the lower classes. In the United States, sociologist William Graham Sumner, author of *What Social Classes Owe Each Other* (1883), argued that societies, like species, improved through unfettered competition. Hence, he concluded, the state should stay out of class conflicts, as these were essential albeit painful steps in the process of natural selection. This view, known as Social Darwinism, was extremely influential among the rich.

The Elusive Threat of Class Conflict

Throughout the 1870s and 1880s, a wave of farmer unrest known as populism swept the South, the Midwest, and the Great Plains. Populists protested the ever-diminishing prices of agricultural products. This problem was compounded by the deflationary policies followed by the federal government after the Civil War, characterized most notably by the retirement of wartime banknotes (greenbacks) and the maintenance of a gold standard. The populists also loathed the big corporate monopolies that con-trolled grain elevators and set train freight rates. They created farmers' associations such as the Grange, founded 1867, and the Farmers' Alliances, established in the 1870s. They also supported the unsuccessful presidential bids of James B. Weaver (1892) and William Jennings Bryan (1896, 1900, 1908). A rising supply of gold resulted in an inflationary trend and populism declined at the beginning of the twentieth century.

Rapid industrialization made some successful entrepreneurs extremely wealthy at the expense of a class of wage earners, often young women and immigrants, living in dire poverty. This chasm raised the specter of class warfare, which the rise of a militant socialist movement in Europe and the death of William McKinley at the hands of the anarchist Leon F. Czolgosz (1901) made more menacing. Progressives warned that the concentration of economic power stifled upward social mobility, an argument widely disseminated by Upton Sinclair's best-selling novel, *The Jungle* (1906).

On 4 May 1886, police and protesters clashed violently in the Haymarket Riot after the failure of a strike at the McCormick Harvesting Machine Company in Chicago for an eight-hour day. From 11 May to 2 August 1894, a strike originating in the Pullman Palace Car Company near Chicago paralyzed the nation before courts and federal troops stepped in. The Industrial Workers of the World (IWW, or Wobblies), a radical labor union, was formed in Chicago in 1905.

These episodes of class conflict never altered fundamentally the political landscape. Radical candidates enjoyed only rare local successes, while Socialist candidate Eugene Victor Debs trailed far behind in the presidential elections of 1900, 1904, 1908, 1912, and 1920. The IWW faded away during World War I.

The Great Depression, starting in 1929, resulted in renewed hardships for the working class and for farmers, many of whom lost their land in drought-plagued Midwestern states. Yet even this, the greatest economic cataclysm in U.S. history, had limited consequences. During the Great Depression, membership in the Communist Party rose only from 7,000 in 1930 to a peak of about 90,000 in 1939. In 1930, William Green, president of the American Federation of Labor, stated that he opposed unemployment insurance, for it would turn every worker into "a ward of the state."

Inspired by earlier trade unions such as the Knights of Labor (founded 1869), the AFL represented only the elite of the working class, including skilled craftsmen. Yet even the more radical Congress of Industrial Organizations, initiated by United Mineworkers president John L. Lewis in 1935, was hardly a revolutionary organization. The CIO was more confrontational in its tone and more open to blacks and unskilled workers than was the AFL. But despite the rise in union membership and militancy, social legislation—including section 7a of the National Recovery Act (1933) and the Wagner Act (1935), which protected the right of workers to organize—assured that unions would be negotiating partners rather than revolutionary organizations. In 1941, the AFL and the CIO made no-strike pledges for the duration of the war.

The booming postwar economy allowed many blue collars to become middle-class suburban property owners with few reasons to upset the social order. But during the 1960s, liberals argued that a permanently impoverished underclass existed in America, a thesis most famously expounded in Michael Harrington's *The Other America* (1962). President Lyndon B. Johnson launched the Great Society, whose main goals were racial equality and the eradication of poverty. Aside from banning racial discrimination and protecting the right of African Americans to vote, Great Society legislation of the mid-1960s offered the poor free medical care (Medicaid), enhanced educational opportunities (Elementary and Secondary Education Act), early education (Head Start), subsidized housing (Housing and Community Development Act), and urban renewal projects (Community Action Programs). Still, a sharp racial divide continued to exist in America. Considerable racial separation and a high level of African American poverty persisted. In turn, ameliatory measures such as positive discrimination (affirmative action) and busing created a "white backlash" in some segments of America, particularly the working class, whose previous political apathy could be attributed to the belief in a social system based on merit.

There was also a conservative backlash against welfare policies. Public concern about "welfare queens" (a lower class permanently living off welfare) helped conservative candidates such as Ronald Reagan. In his State of the Union Address in 1996, President William Jefferson Clinton declared that "the era of big government is over" and stricter welfare policies instituted during his presidency marked a return to a traditional conception of American society according to which the lower class is a fluid body whose members should escape their social status through merit and work.

BIBLIOGRAPHY

Dawley, Alan. *Struggles for Justice: Social Responsibility and the Liberal State.* Cambridge, Mass.: Harvard University Press, 1991.

Fried, Richard M. *Nightmare in Red: The McCarthy Era in Perspective.* New York: Oxford University Press, 1990.

Matusow, Allen J. *The Unraveling of America: A History of Liberalism in the 1960s.* New York: Harper and Row, 1984.

Newman, Katherine S. *Falling from Grace: Downward Mobility in the Age of Affluence.* Berkeley: University of California Press, 1998.

Philippe R. Girard

See also **American Federation of Labor-Congress of Industrial Organizations; Civil Rights Movement; Class; Farmers' Alliance; Fries' Rebellion; Great Depression; Haymarket Riot; New Deal; Populism; Poverty; Pullman Strike; Shays's Rebellion; Social Darwinism; Strikes; War on Poverty; Welfare System.**

CLAYTON ACT, LABOR PROVISIONS.

By the turn of the twentieth century, the national leadership of the American labor movement had abandoned politics in favor of "pure and simple trade unionism." But the federal courts, wielding the nation's antitrust law, soon drove labor back into national politics. The injunction against the Pullman Railway boycott, upheld by the U.S. Supreme Court in *In Re Debs* (1895), was followed by a series of judicial decrees that used the Sherman Antitrust Act to outlaw strikes and boycotts. Equally ominous were damage suits such as the Danbury Hatters' Case (1908), making trade unionists liable for treble damages for losses occasioned by boycotts. The unanimous Court in that case seemed to condemn not only secondary boycotts, but the very goal of industrywide collective bargaining.

The American Federation of Labor (AFL) campaigned for immunity from the antitrust laws and repeal of the federal courts' equity jurisdiction to issue antistrike and anti-boycott decrees. In 1912 the election of Woodrow Wilson and of a Democratic majority in the House of Representatives combined with the revolt of insurgent Republicans to open the door to reform. When Wilson signed the Clayton Act in 1914, the AFL chief Samuel Gompers hailed its labor provisions as "the Magna Carta" of organized labor.

These provisions included section 6, which declared that labor "is not a commodity or article of commerce" and that "[n]othing contained in the anti-trust laws . . . forbid[s] the existence and operation of labor . . . organizations"; section 20, which proscribed injunctions in labor disputes except where necessary "to prevent irreparable injury to property or to a property right" for which there was no adequate remedy at law and also listed ten "peaceful" and "lawful" labor activities (including strikes and boycotts) that injunctions could not forbid; and sections 21 to 25, which made some procedural reforms in contempt cases arising from injunction suits. In contrast to Gompers's encomiums to the act, other commentators insisted that the statute fell far short of granting labor immunity from antitrust law or of repealing "government by injunction." For example, they noted that a finding of irreparable injury and of no adequate legal remedy were already required under equity doctrine for any injunction. For his part William Howard Taft, president of the American Bar Association at the time, declared that the law did nothing more than state "what would be law without the statute."

Certainly, the language of the act's labor provisions was sufficiently ambiguous to support widely divergent interpretations. That is because it bore the imprint of powerful lobbying by unions and employers alike and of compromise among lawmakers. In effect, Congress largely left the power to define labor's freedom with the courts.

And given the composition of the Supreme Court then, the outcome was fairly predictable. In 1921, the Court held in *Duplex Printing Press Co. v. Deering* that the act had neither legalized peaceful secondary boycotts nor immunized them from injunctions. The tenor of the *Duplex* decision suggests that the Supreme Court believed that the Clayton had merely affirmed what the Court previously had said about labor's rights. Now the Court's chief justice, William Howard Taft authored the opinion in *American Steel Foundries v. Tri-Central Trades Council* (1921), in which he wrote that the act "is merely declaratory of what was the best practice always." Only in the changed legal and political climate of the New Deal would organized labor find relief from "government by injunction" and antitrust liability.

BIBLIOGRAPHY

Ernst, Daniel R. *Lawyers against Labor: From Individual Rights to Corporate Liberalism*. Urbana: University of Illinois Press, 1992.

Kutler, Stanley I. "Labor, the Clayton Act, and the Supreme Court." *Labor History* 3 (1962): 19–38.

William E. Forbath

See also **Danbury Hatters' Case;** *In Re Debs;* **Injunctions, Labor; Labor; Labor Legislation and Administration; Strikes.**

CLAYTON COMPROMISE, on territorial slavery, drafted in 1848 by a bipartisan Senate committee headed by John M. Clayton. This bill excluded slavery from Oregon and prohibited the territorial legislatures of New Mexico and California from acting on slavery. However, in contrast to the absolute ban on slavery in the territories acquired from Mexico proposed in the Wilmot Proviso, the compromise provided for the appeal of all slavery cases from the territorial courts to the Supreme Court. It passed the Senate 27 July 1848, but was tabled in the House of Representatives.

BIBLIOGRAPHY

Potter, David Morris. *The Impending Crisis, 1848–61*. New York: Harper & Row, 1976.

Ranulf Brock, William. *Parties and Political Conscience: American Dilemmas, 1840–50*. Millwood, N.Y.: KTO Press, 1979.

Mary Wilhelmine Williams/ T. M.

See also **Civil War; Compromise of 1850; Guadalupe Hidalgo, Treaty of; Wilmot Proviso.**

CLAYTON-BULWER TREATY, a treaty concluded on 19 April 1850 in Washington, D.C., between Secretary of State John Middleton Clayton (1796–1856) and the British minister plenipotentiary, Sir Henry Lytton Bulwer (1801–1872).

Rivalries between the United States and Great Britain had been sharpening in Central America because of British occupation of the Bay Islands (under the sovereignty of Honduras), their establishment of a protectorate over the Mosquito Indians (on the coast of Honduras and Nicaragua), and the seizure of the mouth of the San Juan River (the most probable end of the future canal) in January 1848.

Until the 1850s, the United States had shown a constant but rather mild interest in building a canal; however, since the discovery of gold in California (1848) and the new territorial acquisitions following the Treaty of Guadalupe Hidalgo (1848), it became urgent to secure a shorter and more convenient access to the Pacific coast. This conjunction of commercial, strategic, and security factors led to a growing interest in the Caribbean and Central America, and in British activities there.

The treaty set out that neither Great Britain nor the United States should have exclusive control over the projected canal, nor colonize any part of Central America, but both would guarantee the protection and neutrality of the canal. The treaty was rather speedily ratified by the Senate (42 to 11), but its wording was so ambiguous that it led to a national uproar and became one of the most unpopular in American history.

The treaty was considered as a betrayal of the Monroe Doctrine; the self-denying pledge was an obstacle to the future and inevitable southward expansion of the United States, and the doctrine was devitalized because Britain was permitted to keep what they had illegally seized. Inversely, the treaty was also considered instrumental in strengthening the Monroe Doctrine nationally and internationally, since Britain had implicitly recognized it by accepting not to expand any further in Central America.

Most historians agree that the treaty was a good compromise between a politically, economically, and culturally dominant world power in Latin America—Britain—and a minor though growing-in-influence regional power. Hence the United States probably obtained then as much as it could from Britain. It was not until Theodore Roosevelt's presidency that the United States did obtain the exclusive right to build and fortify the isthmian canal through the Hay-Pauncefote Treaties (1901).

This treaty can be considered both as laying the foundations for the building of the isthmian canal by the United States at the turn of the twentieth century and as consolidating the Caribbean and Central American regions as priorities for American diplomacy and security.

BIBLIOGRAPHY

Brauer, Kinley J. "The United States and British Imperial Expansion, 1815–1860." *Diplomatic History* 12 (winter 1988): 19–37.

Crawford, Martin. *The Anglo-American Crisis of the Mid-Nineteenth Century*. Athens: University of Georgia Press, 1987.

Travis, Ira Dudley. *The History of the Clayton-Bulwer Treaty*. Ann Arbor, Mich.: The Association, 1900.

Williams, Mary Wilhelmine. *Anglo-American Isthmian Diplomacy, 1815–1915*. Gloucester, Mass.: P. Smith, 1965.

Aissatou Sy-Wonyu

See also **Guadalupe Hidalgo, Treaty of; Hay-Pauncefote Treaties; Monroe Doctrine.**

CLEAN AIR ACT. In 1990, Congress passed substantial amendments to the Clean Air Act of 1970, strengthening the act in a number of ways. Title I imposed new regulations limiting industrial emissions of ozone, carbon monoxide, particulates, nitrogen dioxide, sulfur oxides, and lead. Title II required new emission standards for automobiles and other mobile sources and created a clean-fuel program. Title III substantially limited the emission of hazardous air pollutants, while Title IV established a program to reduce sulfur dioxide emissions from power plants. Title V created an operating permit program for major sources of air pollution that was similar to permit programs found in other major environmental statutes. Title VI implemented the provisions in the Montreal Protocol, an international agreement to halt the destruction of the ozone, by banning the emission of certain chemicals. Finally, Title VII added new enforcement provisions, making it easier to punish violators and substantially increasing both civil and criminal penalties for violations of the act.

Supporters of stronger air pollution controls had fought for over a decade to enact many of these provisions, and they succeeded in 1990 only because of important changes in the political landscape. To begin with, public concern over air pollution had grown due to increased awareness about the effects of acid rain and because of startling revelations about the growing hole in the ozone layer. This concern translated into greater support in Congress and in the administration. In particular, President George H. W. Bush, unlike his predecessor, favored modest strengthening of certain environmental laws, including the Clean Air Act. In the Senate, Democrat George Mitchell of Maine, a clean-air proponent, became majority leader in 1989, replacing Democratic Senator Robert Byrd of West Virginia, who had worked for years to protect the coal mining industry in his state by blocking air pollution legislation. In the House, Democratic Representative Harry Waxman of California used his position as chair of the Subcommittee on Health and the Environment to support the amendments. Meanwhile, environmental organizations united to form the National Clean Air Coalition, effectively counteracting the influence of the industrial lobby's Clean Air Working Group, even though environmentalists played little role in drafting the amendments. Ultimately, the House voted 401–25 in support of the amendments, the Senate passed the amendments 89–10, and President Bush signed the new clean-air legislation into law on 15 November 1990.

During the 1990s, two forces acted to shape the way the act affected American industry and the environment. First, during the mid-1990s, antienvironmental rhetoric and failed legislative attacks by a new, conservative-led Congress intimidated the federal Environmental Protection Agency (EPA) from implementing and enforcing the act as aggressively as the law required. Second, and more generally, the 1990 amendments preserved the clumsy scheme of federalism, whereby the EPA oversaw state implementation plans. In theory, if a state failed to meet the standards set by federal regulation, the EPA had the authority to run the clean-air program within the state. In practice, however, the EPA had neither the resources nor the political support to do this. Despite the strong language of the 1990 amendments, and marked improvements in the national air quality, by the end of the millennium many believed American skies, while cleaner, were not clean enough.

BIBLIOGRAPHY

Bryner, Gary C. *Blue Skies, Green Politics: The Clean Air Act of 1990 and Its Implementation*. 2d ed. Washington, D.C.: Congressional Quarterly Press, 1995.

Reitze, Arnold W. "The Legislative History of U.S. Air Pollution Control." *Houston Law Review* 36 (1999): 696–702.

Shannon C. Petersen

See also **Acid Rain; Air Pollution; Auto Emission Testing and Standards; Environmental Protection Agency.**

CLEAN WATER ACT. The Federal Water Pollution Control Act of 1972, commonly called the Clean Water Act (CWA), filled ninety pages of the *Statutes at Large*. The 1987 amendments to the CWA, officially called the Water Quality Act of 1987, added eighty-two pages. Although the 1987 amendments contributed substantially to the CWA's mass, complexity, and breadth, they did not fundamentally alter the act's scope, except perhaps in the area of nonpoint pollution. The 1987 amendments were the first changes to the CWA since 1977.

The One Hundredth Congress deliberately made the Water Quality Act of 1987 its inaugural piece of legislation. The Ninety-ninth Congress, after much deliberation, had passed essentially identical legislation in 1986, but on 30 January 1987, President Ronald Reagan vetoed that effort. Congress, however, overrode Reagan's veto on 4 February 1987 by a vote of 401 to 26 in the House of Representatives and 86 to 14 in the Senate.

The 1987 amendments built upon the existing framework of the CWA in four important ways. First, the amendments imposed new standards and permitting requirements, including new regulations regarding toxic pollutants and storm water runoff. In addition, the amendments created new protections for national estuaries and for certain aquatic "treasures" such as the Chesapeake Bay and the Great Lakes. Second, the 1987 amendments attempted to better define the federal-state partnership in water pollution control management. Generally, the 1987 amendments preserved significant federal oversight but gave states more flexibility in meeting the act's requirements. For example, the amendments allowed the partial delegation of the CWA's permitting program, the National Pollutant Discharge Elimination System (NPDES), to the states. Third, the 1987 amendments significantly increased the civil and criminal penalties for CWA violations and granted the Environmental Protection Agency and the Army Corps of Engineers substantial new powers to impose administrative penalties. Finally, the 1987 amendments included provisions designed to give regulated industries more guidance as to the requirements of the CWA and allowed industry some relief from the act's strict guidelines when warranted.

The 1987 amendments, however, also included at least one area of water regulation wholly new to the CWA. Until the 1990s, the CWA primarily regulated effluent from pipes and drains, usually attached to or part of industrial plants, manufacturing facilities, or storm water systems. These targets of regulation are so-called "point" sources because the source of the pollution can be pinpointed. The 1987 amendments, however, included a provision, labeled Total Maximum Daily Loads (TMDLs), which arguably allows for the regulation of nonpoint pollution runoff from fields and farms and cities. Based on the ambiguous authority of this provision, throughout the 1990s the EPA gradually increased its regulation of nonpoint pollution. This has meant that since the 1987 amendments the federal government has moved from regulating specific industries to also regulating nonspecific urban, suburban, and agrarian activities.

BIBLIOGRAPHY

Houck, Oliver A. *The Clean Water Act TMDL Program: Law, Policy, and Implementation.* Washington, D.C.: Environmental Law Institute, 2000.

Liebesman, Lawrence R., and Elliott P. Laws. "The Water Quality Act of 1987: A Major Step in Assuring the Quality of the Nation's Waters." *Environmental Law Reporter* 17 (1987): 10311–10312.

Shannon C. Petersen

See also **Environmental Protection Agency; Water Pollution; Water Supply and Conservation.**

CLEARING HOUSE, NEW YORK (NYCH), founded in 1853 when thirty-eight New York City banks organized it as the first bank clearinghouse in the United States. The previous system of Friday settlements had created enormous confusion and danger of loss as runners with bags of currency dashed about the financial district. Even more serious had been the possibility that some bank might accumulate large adverse balances during the week and threaten the stability of the whole group. The

change to daily settlements through the NYCH was so effective a reform that within a few weeks four of the more reckless banks were obliged to close.

The inflexible currency of the mid-nineteenth century and the impotence of the Independent Treasury forced the new clearinghouse to take, sometimes reluctantly, a position of leadership. (The Independent Treasury was established in 1845 to handle its own receipts and payments without utilizing bank services; it was never completely successful in that effort but was not abandoned until 1920.) After the BANKING crisis of 1857 it required its members to hold reserves against their deposits—a device copied by the national banking legislation of 1863 and by the Federal Reserve Act of 1913. Ten times between 1860 and 1914, in order to tide the banks over during a crisis, the NYCH issued loan certificates for use in the settlement of daily balances. It published reports of the condition of member banks and of daily, weekly, and yearly totals of clearings, which served as useful indicators of business conditions when other statistical measures were scarce. Clearings at New York City banks reflected the volume of transactions in the stock market; "outside" clearings of other centers reflected business transactions much more closely than speculative activity.

The NYCH steadily increased the number of its daily clearings and the range of its activities, including clearings of stock certificates, coupons, and foreign trade bills as well as checks of member banks. In the last three decades of the twentieth century, computers became increasingly important in the NYCH's activities. In 1970 it inaugurated its first electronic payments system, called the Clearing House Interbank Payments System (CHIPS), followed by the New York Automated Clearing House (NYACH) in 1975 and the Electronic Payments Network (EPN) in 2000. Despite its great growth in membership, the increasing sophistication of its clearing methods, and the steadily increasing volume of daily clearings into the tens of billions of dollars, the relative importance of the NYCH had declined by the mid-twentieth century as the Federal Reserve banks took over intercity clearing and as the overall national and international economy grew and diversified.

BIBLIOGRAPHY

Garvy, George. *Debits and Clearings Statistics and Their Use.* Rev. ed. Washington, D.C.: Board of Governors of the Federal Reserve System, 1959.

Spahr, Walter Earl. *The Clearing and Collection of Checks.* New York: Bankers Publishing, 1926.

Margaret G. Myers/c. w.

See also **Federal Reserve System.**

CLEARINGHOUSES. The method of clearing—matching offsetting items so that only the balances due after the clearing need to be settled—has been used for centuries by many different kinds of organizations, although by far the most common use of clearing in the United States has been in connection with bank checks.

The pattern for this kind of transaction was set in 1773, when the first London clearinghouse was organized to replace the coffeehouse at which weary bank runners regularly gathered to exchange their batches of checks. American cities copied this example, and by the end of the Civil War there were clearinghouses in New York, Boston, Philadelphia, and Chicago. Others followed as the country expanded westward. In 1900 there were eighty-seven clearinghouses in the United States, and the number reached a peak of 198 in 1920. Small towns with more than one bank either used the facilities of the nearest city clearinghouse or devised an informal local clearing place.

In addition to handling check collections, many of the larger clearinghouses assumed other responsibilities for the BANKING community until the Federal Reserve period: they conducted examinations of their member banks, published reports of their condition, and aided those in difficulty during crises by issuing loan certificates to be used in settling clearing balances. These functions became less important when one state after another, even before the Civil War, began to regulate the banks they had chartered, and the national government, in the National Banking Act of 1863, created the office of comptroller of the currency to regulate banks under national charter. In 1914 the FEDERAL RESERVE SYSTEM took over some of the regulation of all banks that became members of the system.

The establishment of the Federal Reserve system affected check clearing in a number of ways. The twelve Federal Reserve banks handled intercity clearing within their respective districts, leaving intracity checks to local clearinghouses. The time needed for long-distance clearing also decreased. Checks between New York and San Francisco, for example, which had formerly required eight days' travel, were put on a two-day basis, regardless of delays in the actual physical arrival of the checks.

Developments outside the banking system also affected the work of the clearinghouses. Many stock and COMMODITY EXCHANGES cleared the transactions of their members, thus reducing payments made through banks. Greatly increased use of charge accounts and credit cards after World War II reduced the number of transactions by increasing the average size of check payments. Gradual adoption of accounting machinery and computers also altered the nature of clearing.

When American clearinghouses were first organized, their published reports provided important information on the state of the economy, since there were few other available measures of business activity. These figures became less significant after the Federal Reserve banks began in 1918 to collect and publish the monthly totals of "debits to individual accounts." These included all checks drawn, even those exchanged between customers of the same bank and not included in that bank's clearings. The ratio of total clearings to total debits declined steadily. Despite these changes, in the early 2000s the work of the clearinghouses continued to be an essential feature of financial activity.

BIBLIOGRAPHY

Garvy, George. *Debits and Clearings Statistics and Their Use*. Rev. ed. Washington, D.C.: Board of Governors of the Federal Reserve System, 1959.

Spahr, Walter Earl. *The Clearing and Collection of Checks*. New York: Bankers Publishing, 1926.

Margaret G. Myers / c. w.

See also **Clearing House, New York.**

CLERMONT. See **Fulton's Folly.**

CLEVELAND, the largest city in Ohio from 1900 to the 1980s and a leading Great Lakes industrial center during the twentieth century. In 1796, Moses Cleaveland laid out the original plan for the settlement that was to bear his name. The village grew slowly, having only about five hundred residents in 1825. That year, however, the Ohio legislature designated Cleveland the northern terminus of the Ohio and Erie Canal, which linked the Ohio River and Lake Erie. Completed in 1832, the canal transformed Cleveland into a booming commercial center with more than six thousand residents by 1840.

In the early 1850s, the arrival of the railroad ushered in a half century of large-scale industrialization. Cleveland became a major producer of iron and steel and the headquarters of John D. Rockefeller's oil refining empire. Owing in part to the local inventor Charles Brush, the manufacturing of electrical equipment developed as a ma-

Rock and Roll Hall of Fame and Museum. The building, intended as a symbol of Cleveland's return from steady decline, opened in September 1995. GREATER CLEVELAND CONVENTION AND VISITORS BUREAU

jor industry. During the early twentieth century, the motor vehicle industry added thousands of new jobs for Clevelanders.

Attracted largely by employment opportunities, European immigrants flooded the city. Germans predominated through most of the nineteenth century, but by the early twentieth century, eastern Europeans prevailed. Cleveland could boast of the largest Slovak and Slovene settlements in America as well as thousands of Poles, Czechs, and Hungarians.

In the early twentieth century, Cleveland earned a reputation for progressive government as mayors Tom Johnson and Newton Baker battled for municipal ownership of public utilities. By the 1920s, a ring of suburban municipalities was burgeoning around Cleveland, eventually precluding further annexation of territory to the city. Immigration quotas stemmed the tide of European newcomers, although thousands of white and black southerners flocked to Cleveland, especially in the 1940s and 1950s. During the second half of the twentieth century, however, the city's population steadily declined, from 914,808 in 1950 to 478,403 in 2000. New office towers arose in the central business district, but neighborhoods decayed, and after 1970 manufacturing jobs disappeared. In 1966 racial unrest resulted in nationally publicized rioting in the Hough area, and twelve years later the troubled city suffered the humiliation of defaulting on debt payments. Despite loss of population and manufacturing jobs, local boosters in the 1980s and 1990s proclaimed Cleveland's comeback, pointing to the construction of downtown stadiums and such new tourist attractions as the Rock and Roll Hall of Fame and the Great Lakes Science Center.

BIBLIOGRAPHY

Miller, Carol Poh, and Robert Wheeler. *Cleveland: A Concise History, 1796–1990*. Bloomington: Indiana University Press, 1990.

Van Tassel, David D., and John J. Grabowski, eds. *The Encyclopedia of Cleveland History*. Bloomington: Indiana University Press, 1987.

Jon C. Teaford

See also **German Americans; Great Lakes; Midwest; Ohio; Polish Americans.**

CLEVELAND DEMOCRATS.

Members of the Democratic Party who supported the policies and presidential candidacies of Grover Cleveland, primarily during Cleveland's first term (1885–1889), when his reputation as a reformer and his conservative Democratic credentials attracted wide support ranging from southern Bourbons to northern renegade Republican Mugwumps. Cleveland Democrats were conservative reformers holding traditional Democratic views on property rights, low tariffs, states' rights, and minimal government; however, they supported civil service and municipal government reform.

Cleveland's inability to mediate between party factions and his unwillingness to compromise eroded his support. During his second term (1893–1897), his administration revoked the Sherman Silver Purchase Act and used federal troops to put down the 1894 Pullman Strike. Seen as Wall Street lackeys, his supporters were routed at the 1896 Democratic convention by William Jennings Bryan and the SILVER DEMOCRATS.

BIBLIOGRAPHY

Hollingsworth, J. Rogers. *The Whirligig of Politics: Democracy from Cleveland to Bryan*. Chicago: University of Chicago Press, 1963.

McFarland, Gerald W. "The Breakdown of Deadlock: The Cleveland Democracy in Connecticut, 1884–1894," *Historian* 31, no. 3 (May 1969): 381–397.

———. *Mugwumps, Morals, and Politics, 1884–1920*. Amherst: University of Massachusetts Press, 1975.

Welch, Richard E., Jr. *The Presidencies of Grover Cleveland*. Lawrence: University Press of Kansas, 1988.

C. Wyatt Evans

See also **Democratic Party.**

CLIMATE.

The climate of an area, defined as the aggregate of weather conditions over time, is constructed from monthly, seasonal, and annual averages of weather elements, such as temperature and precipitation, combined with statements about the frequency of extreme events, such as droughts or tornadoes. Historically, climate has had important economic implications for agriculture, transportation, and settlement. Climatology, or the scientific study of climate, dates to the mid-nineteenth century and includes such specialties as applied climatology, climate dynamics, and climate change.

The classical heritage related the climate of an area uniquely to its latitude. Climate, from the Greek *klima*, meaning "inclination," was originally thought to depend only on the height of the sun above the horizon, modified in part by special local characteristics. Climate and health have also been closely related throughout history. According to the Hippocratic tradition of ancient Greece, a physician should consider the seasons of the year and what effects each of them produces; the location of a city with respect to winds, waters, terrain, and the rising of the sun; and the particulars of the weather. These were keys to diagnosing and treating diseases in a given location.

The Puzzle of the Early American Climate

Because of its seemingly favorable location in latitudes farther south than most European nations, the New World was expected to have a warm, exotic climate. Initially, colonists and their sponsors envisioned a rich harvest of wine, silk, olive oil, sugar, and spices from their investment. In 1588 the colonial promoter Thomas Harriot pointed out that Virginia was located on the same parallel of latitude as many exotic places, including Persia,

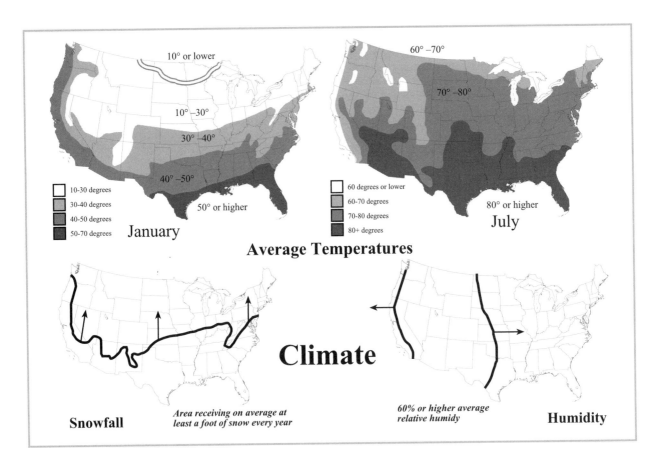

Average Temperatures

January

10° or lower
10°–30°
30°–40°
40°–50°
50° or higher

☐ 10-30 degrees
☐ 30-40 degrees
☐ 40-50 degrees
☐ 50-70 degrees

July

60°–70°
70°–80°
80° or higher

☐ 60 degrees or lower
☐ 60-70 degrees
☐ 70-80 degrees
☐ 80+ degrees

Climate

Snowfall

Area receiving on average at least a foot of snow every year

60% or higher average relative humidy

Humidity

China, and Japan in the East and southern Greece, Italy, and Spain in the West. The reality was much different, however. Early settlers in the Americas found the climate harsher and the storms more frequent and more powerful than in the Old World. In 1644 the Reverend John Campanius of Swedes' Fort, Delaware, wrote of violent winds, unknown in Europe, which tore mighty oaks out of the ground. Another colonist in New Sweden, Thomas Campanius Holm, described rainstorms in which the whole sky was filled with smoke and flames. James MacSparran, a missionary to Rhode Island between 1721 and 1757, warned against immigrating to America because the climate was unhealthy, with excessive heat and cold, sudden changes of weather, unwholesome air, and terrible thunder and lightning.

Because of such reports, many Europeans held considerable disdain for the New World and for its climate, soil, animals, and indigenous peoples. The noted Parisian naturalist Georges-Louis Leclerc de Buffon speculated that, because of the cool and humid climate, the flora and fauna of the New World were degenerate. The celebrated botanist and traveler Pehr Kalm observed, rightly or not, that every life-form had less stamina in the New World. People died younger, women reached menopause earlier, soldiers lacked the vitality of their English counterparts, and even the imported cattle were smaller. He pointed to climatic influences as the probable cause.

Citizens in colonial and early America were quite defensive about these opinions and argued that clearing the forests, draining the swamps, and cultivating the land would improve the climate by changing the temperature and rainfall patterns. No general agreement, however, emerged about the direction or magnitude of the change. The Reverend Cotton Mather wrote in the *Christian Philosopher* (1721) that he believed it was getting warmer. Benjamin Franklin agreed, noting that compared to forested lands, cleared land absorbs more heat and melts snow quicker. In his *Notes on the State of Virginia* (1785), addressed to a European audience, Thomas Jefferson presented an apology for the harsh American climate and an optimistic prognosis for its improvement by human activities. Hugh Williamson of Harvard College spoke for his generation when he wrote in *Observations on the Climate in Different Parts of America* (1811) that settlement would result in a temperate climate and clear atmosphere that would serve as "a proper nursery of genius, learning, industry and the liberal arts." In his mind such changes added up to a continent better suited to white settlers and less suited to aboriginal inhabitants.

Climate Observations and Medical Meteorology

The first comprehensive series of meteorological observations in America, taken by John Lining, a physician in Charleston, were related to his medical concerns. In 1740, Lining collected the intake and outflow of his own body for a period of one year in an effort to understand how the weather affected bodily humors and epidemic diseases. Related efforts by Lionel Chalmers, *An Account of the Weather and Diseases of South Carolina* (1776); William Currie, *An Historical Account of the Climates and Diseases of the United States of America* (1792); and Noah Webster, *A Brief History of Epidemic and Pestilential Diseases* (1799) linked regional health conditions to climate and extreme weather events.

Jefferson and the Reverend James Madison began the first simultaneous comparative meteorological measurements in America in 1778. As president of the American Philosophical Society, Jefferson collected weather journals from around the county. He also directed the Lewis and Clark expedition (1804–1806) to take weather observations along the Missouri River and in the Pacific Northwest. Jefferson was a strong advocate for a national meteorological system and encouraged the federal government to supply observers in each county of each state with accurate instruments. Although such a system was not established in his lifetime, many government agencies soon began collecting and compiling observations. During the War of 1812, the surgeon general of the army, James Tilton, ordered the physicians under his command to "keep a diary of the weather" and to file detailed reports on the effects of the climate on the health of the troops. This was because more soldiers were falling ill in camp than were being injured in military engagements. The U.S. Army Medical Department continued its system of taking meteorological measurements at army posts across the country until 1874, in part to document potential changes in the climate. Other early governmental systems included the General Land Office (1817–1821), interested primarily in settlement west of the Appalachian Mountains, and academies in the state of New York (1825–1850), where students collected climatic and phenological statistics. In the 1850s, the U.S. Navy compiled wind and weather charts for the oceans under the direction of Matthew Fontaine Maury.

Under the direction of Joseph Henry, the Smithsonian Institution served as a national center to advance and coordinate meteorological research. The institution conducted storm studies, experimented with telegraphic weather prediction, and collected climate statistics. It also served as a clearinghouse for cooperative observations taken by the navy, the army topographical engineers, the Patent Office, the Coast Survey, the Department of Agriculture, and the government of Canada. Projects completed with Smithsonian data included *Climatology of the United States* (1857) by Lorin Blodget, *Winds of the Globe* (1875) by James Henry Coffin, and theoretical studies of the general circulation of the Earth's atmosphere by William Ferrel.

In 1858, Ferrel announced a new theory of fluid mechanics that explained both meridional (E-W) and zonal (N-S) wind flows on the rotating Earth. He wrote equations of motion that accounted for most of the observed features of the general circulation: three vertical circulation cells instead of just one traditional "Hadley cell," high-velocity westerly winds in midlatitudes in both hemispheres, easterly trade winds in the tropics, and low pressure with easterly winds near the poles. Later commentators referred to Ferrel's theory as the "principia meteorologica" because of its fundamental implications for subsequent studies of climate dynamics.

In 1870, Congress established the first national weather service and placed it under the auspices of the Army Signal Office. Colonel Albert J. Myer became the first director of a well-funded national storm warning system employing the nation's telegraphy circuits "for the benefit of commerce and agriculture." In addition to providing daily reports of current conditions and "probabilities" for the next day's weather, the Signal Office collected official climate statistics for the nation. By 1891 the U.S. Weather Bureau had been established in the Department of Agriculture, where it remained until 1940, when it was transferred to the Department of Commerce.

Climate Change in the Nineteenth Century

In 1844, Samuel Forry analyzed data gathered from more than sixty army medical officers and concluded (a) climates are stable and no accurate thermometrical observations warrant the conclusion of climatic change, (b) climates can be changed by human activity, but (c) these effects are extremely subordinate to physical geography. Elias Loomis studied the temperature of New Haven, Connecticut, and Charles A. Schott constructed national maps of temperature and rainfall. Neither scientist found evidence that humans were changing the climate. Cleveland Abbe, the chief scientist with the National Weather Service, agreed that the old debates about climate change had finally been settled. In an article entitled "Is Our Climate Changing?" published in *Forum* in February 1889, Abbe defined the climate as "the average about which the temporary conditions permanently oscillate; it assumes and implies permanence."

As the debate over climate change caused by human activities was winding down in the mid-nineteenth century, the discovery that the earth had experienced ice ages produced a plethora of complex but highly speculative theories of climatic change involving astronomical, physical, geological, and paleontological factors. The leading American involved in these discoveries was the prominent glacial geologist T. C. Chamberlin, whose interdisciplinary work on the geological agency of the atmosphere and the effect of carbon dioxide on climate led him to propose a new theory of the formation of the earth and the solar system.

Regional Climates and Identities

Many regions of the United States experience distinctive climatic phenomena. New England, the Appalachian Highlands, and the upper Mississippi Valley have rigorous winters with snow covering the ground, often for several months. The East Coast has a relatively mild climate due to the proximity of the Atlantic Ocean, but these areas are susceptible to land-falling Atlantic hurricanes and

CLIMATE: ANNUAL RAINFALL

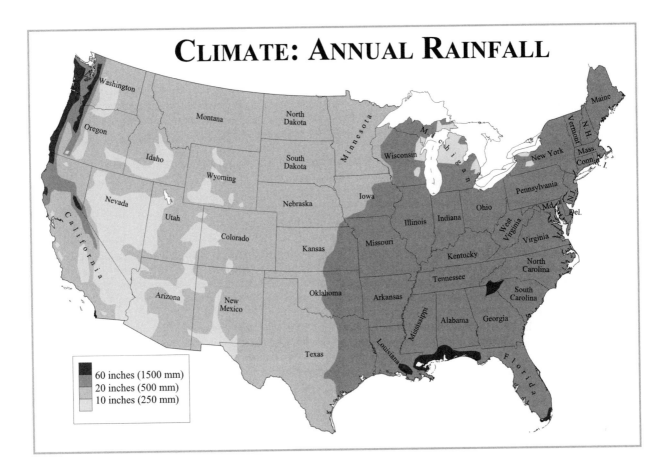

60 inches (1500 mm)
20 inches (500 mm)
10 inches (250 mm)

winter "nor'easters." The Deep South has hot summers and mild winters with high humidity because of the proximity of the warm waters of the Caribbean and the Gulf of Mexico; on average this area has the most thunderstorms. The heartland experiences the most violent tornadoes, while the high Plains have the most hailstorms. Monsoonal flows from Mexico water the desert Southwest, while California is susceptible to drying "Santa Anna" winds that can exacerbate wildfires. As scientists have come to realize, all regions of the country may be affected by the El Niño Southern Oscillation of the Pacific Ocean.

It would be foolish to argue that such climatic differences "determined" social relations in these regions, just as it would be futile to argue that the environment made little or no difference to people's lives. It is more productive to ask how the flux of economic and social activities over time changed human relationships with nature in sometimes subtle but often dramatic ways. Horse-drawn sleighs were traditionally safe, enjoyable, and often productive means of winter transportation, yet the widespread use of the automobile transformed snow from a transportation resource into a hazard. Pioneers facing the onset of winter and the possibility of crop failure due to frosts believed that warmer weather was better weather, while contemporary city dwellers in urban heat islands find the weather unbearably hot. Air conditioning un-

doubtedly stimulated the growth of the Sun Belt, while access to freshwater resources may determine the region's future. In general, social and technological changes and changes in scientific understanding of climate have occurred at much faster rates than have physical changes in the climate system.

Settlers seeking to relocate west of the Appalachian Mountains usually headed due west. They assumed that the climatic zone they were familiar with followed parallels of latitude. Generally, this is not the case, since agricultural hardiness zones gradually slope from northeast to southwest. Thus, for example, settlers from Connecticut established the Western Reserve in Ohio. Further west across the Mississippi River lay the semiarid, treeless prairies that were originally called the "Great American Desert." While farmers on the northern and eastern margins of this area, where annual rainfall totals twenty inches or more, had considerable success, precipitation decreases dramatically to the south and west, attaining true desert conditions in New Mexico and Arizona. The Homestead Act of 1862 encouraged farmers ever westward into marginal lands that were fertile only when it rained. Promoters even resorted to the dubious argument that agriculture somehow increases rainfall, or "rain follows the plow." A succession of drought years could devastate farms, however, as was the case in the decade-long Dust Bowl of the 1930s in the southern Great Plains.

The Keeling Curve

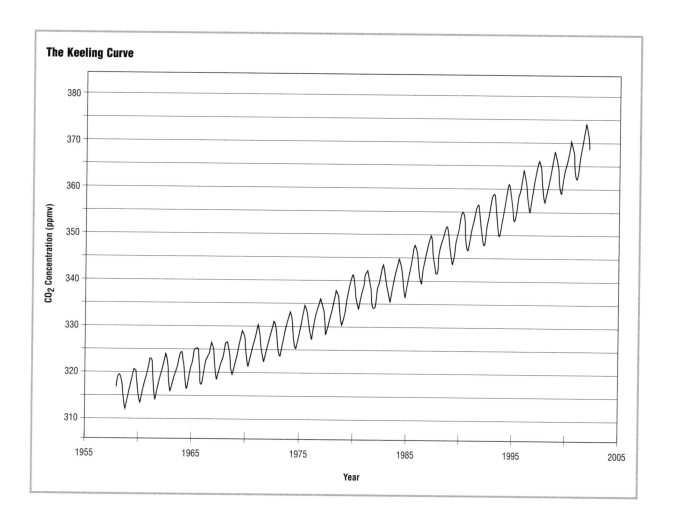

Climate Change in the Twentieth Century

By 1900 most of the chief theories of climate change had been proposed if not yet fully explored: changes in solar output; changes in the earth's orbital geometry; changes in terrestrial geography, including the form and height of continents and the circulation of the oceans; and changes in atmospheric transparency and composition, in part due to human activities. During the International Geophysical Year (1957–1958), Harry Wexler of the U.S. Weather Bureau succeeded in establishing a series of accurate measurements of carbon dioxide. After 1958 these measurements were accurately and faithfully taken at the summit of Mauna Loa volcano in Hawaii by Charles David Keeling. Subsequently, many more international baseline stations have been established. The Keeling curve, the famous saw-toothed curve of rising carbon dioxide concentrations, became the environmental icon of the twentieth century.

In the 1950s, Gilbert Plass developed a computer model of infrared radiative transfer in support of his research on carbon dioxide and climate. Several years later, in the interest of national security, a climate model known as Nile Blue was developed by the Advanced Research Projects Administration (ARPA) in the Department of Defense. It was hoped that this model could be used to test the sensitivity of the climate to major perturbations, including Soviet tinkering or a major environmental war. In 1967, Syukuro Manabe and Richard T. Wetherald developed a computerized climate model that included the effects of both radiation and convection to calculate temperature as a function of latitude. It predicted a mean warming of 2.3 degrees Celsius for a doubling of carbon dioxide. Two years later, Manabe and Kirk Bryan added basic oceanic features to the model.

The rise of the environmental movement in the early 1970s generated interest in global environmental problems, including climate change. In 1971, when some meteorologists were looking into the possibility of a widespread global cooling, a report from the Study of Man's Impact on Climate conducted at the Massachusetts Institute of Technology returned the focus to carbon dioxide emissions, calling them the largest single anthropogenic change that may influence the climate in the foreseeable future. During this period, anthropogenic effects on climate were called "inadvertent" climate modification. Several other regional and global pollution issues also emerged in the 1970s, including acid deposition and possible damage to the stratosphere by ozone-depleting chemicals and by the exhaust gases of a fleet of supersonic transport planes.

In the 1980s, scientists debated the possibility of a "nuclear winter" caused by an all-out nuclear exchange. Discovery of depleted levels of ozone over Antarctica in 1985 led to the international Montreal Protocol on Substances that Deplete the Ozone Layer, signed in 1987. In 1988 the scientist James Hansen of the National Aeronautics and Space Administration announced to Congress and the world, "Global warming has begun." He went on to report that, at least to his satisfaction, he had seen the "signal" in the climate noise and that the earth was destined for global warming, perhaps in the form of a runaway greenhouse effect. Hansen later revised his remarks, but his statement remained the starting point of widespread concerns over global warming. That same year the Intergovernmental Panel on Climate Change was formed as a joint program of the United Nations Environmental Program, the World Meteorological Organization, and the International Congress of Scientific Unions. It has a mandate to prepare regular assessments of what is known and what should be done about anthropogenic climate change.

The 1992 United Nations Conference on Environment and Development (the Earth Summit) in Rio de Janeiro produced the Framework Convention on Climate Change (FCCC), which calls for a stabilization of atmospheric carbon dioxide concentrations at a level that would prevent human-induced changes in the global climate. The 1997 Kyoto Protocol, calling for legally binding greenhouse gas emission targets for all developed countries, remained a contentious issue in the early twenty-first century. These conventions and protocols represent geopolitical interventions in the climate system. Many more policies were initiated. Economics also began to play a role, as taxes and incentives were put in place to reduce unwanted emissions. Meanwhile, green social engineers attempted to convince the general public to live sustainably, while "geoengineers" hold in reserve massive technical fixes for the climate system. Notably, health issues related to possible climate change returned as policy issues.

Conclusion

The climate issues that puzzled colonists and early Americans were eventually resolved by government-supported scientists who compiled climate statistics for the continent. Changes in human-climate relations were typically caused not by climate change but by people migrating to new regions or by changes in social relations or technology. An older medical geography of "airs, waters, and places" was replaced by the germ theory of disease. Yet as Americans gained control of their microclimatic environments through irrigation, central heating, and air conditioning, they began to lose control of the damage they inflicted on the environment, for example, by excessive burning of fossil fuels. In the second half of the twentieth

century, new reasons for climate apprehension emerged in the form of local, regional, and global threats to the atmosphere and to human health. By the dawn of the twenty-first century, the social aspects of the climate had grown to encompass scientific, economic, governmental, and diplomatic initiatives regarding the health and future of the planet.

BIBLIOGRAPHY

Fleming, James Rodger. *Meteorology in America, 1800–1870.* Baltimore: Johns Hopkins University Press, 1990.

———. *Historical Perspectives on Climate Change and Culture.* New York: Oxford University Press, 1998.

Fleming, James Rodger, ed. *Historical Essays on Meteorology, 1919–1995.* Boston: American Meteorological Society, 1996.

Kupperman, Karen Ordahl. "The Puzzle of the American Climate in the Early Colonial Period." *American Historical Review* 87 (1982): 1262–1289.

Ludlum, David M. *The American Weather Book.* Boston: Houghton Mifflin, 1982.

Mergen, Bernard. *Snow in America.* Washington, D.C.: Smithsonian Institution Press, 1997.

Meyer, William B. *Americans and Their Weather.* New York: Oxford University Press, 2000.

James Fleming

See also **Acid Rain; Global Warming; Meteorology; Ozone Depletion; Weather Service, National.**

CLINICAL RESEARCH, the controlled use of humans in medical experiments, dates from the Greek physician Galen (c. 129–199), the founder of experimental medicine. Clinical research in the United States, however, rose in importance in the late nineteenth century following European advances in MEDICAL RESEARCH. In 1884, disease investigators in the United States formed the American Clinical and Climatological Association, and in 1909, medical experimenters established the American Society of Clinical Investigation, which promoted correlation of clinical research with medical practice. For much of the twentieth century clinical researchers investigated the safety and effectiveness of diagnosis, prevention, and treatment of human diseases and disorders. Usually, but not always, basic laboratory research and animal experimentation preceded human testing.

In the twentieth century, clinical research increased with the expansion of military medical research, the growth of academic medical science, the rise of pharmaceutical companies, and the establishment of private research clinics. As a result of the 1906 Pure Food and Drug Act and its subsequent amendments, new drugs underwent clinical testing prior to widespread use by physicians. The importance of clinical research grew significantly after the establishment of the National Institute of Health (NIH) in 1930 and NIH expansion to multiple institutes after World War II. By then, the Public Health Service, which included the FOOD AND DRUG ADMINISTRATION and the NIH, was probably the most generous supporter of clinical research in the country. In 1953, the NIH opened the largest clinical research center in the nation in Bethesda, Maryland.

Following World War II, the Nuremberg Code, drawn up after revelations of brutal experiments on humans by the Nazis, exerted significant influence on clinical researchers in the United States. The code limited the degree of risk in clinical research to a level that would not exceed that determined by the humanitarian importance of the problem to be solved by the experiment. Subsequently, many institutions used the code as ethical guidance. In 1962, Congress enacted the first federal law regulating human medical experimentation. After learning that thalidomide had caused the birth of deformed babies in Europe, the legislators amended the Food and Drug Act to require that patients be informed that they were being given experimental drugs not fully licensed by the federal government.

Later in the century, clinical research came under fire because of revelations about the federal government's neglect of women, minorities, and the elderly in clinical trials; radiation experiments on humans, especially those lacking informed consent; and charges of fraud. Congress responded in 1993 by passing the NIH Health Revitalization Act to correct the imbalance of women and minorities in clinical research. Subsequently the NIH launched the largest clinical health trial in the history of the United States by selecting 63,000 women for a nine-year trial to determine the effects of certain regimens on preventing cancers, osteoporosis, and coronary heart disease. Congress and the executive branch also investigated charges of impropriety in conducting potentially harmful radiation exposure experiments on humans and allegations of fraud.

Despite the controversies, the nation has benefited from clinical research. Trials in the 1970s showed that lowering blood cholesterol diminished chances of heart disease in men. In the 1980s, clinical research saved patients with soft tissue sarcomas of the limbs from amputations by demonstrating the effectiveness of radiation therapy and chemotherapy combinations. And in the late 1980s, clinical tests indicated that azidothymidine (AZT), an antiviral drug, could slow down the development of AIDS in some patients.

BIBLIOGRAPHY

Annas, George J., and Michael A. Grodin, eds. *The Nazi Doctors and the Nuremberg Code: Human Rights in Human Experimentation.* New York: Oxford University Press, 1995.

Grady, Christine. *The Search for an AIDS Vaccine: Ethical Issues in the Development and Testing of a Preventive HIV Vaccine.* Bloomington: Indiana University Press, 1995.

Marks, Harry M. *The Progress of Experiment: Science and Therapeutic Reform in the United States, 1900–1990.* New York: Cambridge University Press, 1997.

Mastroianni, Anna C., Ruth R. Faden, and Daniel Federman, eds. *Women and Health Research: Ethical and Legal Issues of Including Women in Clinical Studies.* 2 vols. Washington, D.C.: National Academy Press, 1994.

McNeill, Paul M. *The Ethics and Politics of Human Experimentation.* New York: Cambridge University Press, 1993.

Ruth Roy Harris / C. P.

See also **Acquired Immune Deficiency Syndrome; Chemotherapy; Epidemics and Public Health; Medicine and Surgery; National Institutes of Health; Pharmaceutical Industry; Pure Food and Drug Movement.**

CLINTON IMPEACHMENT. *See* **Impeachment Trial of Bill Clinton.**

CLINTON SCANDALS. When President Bill Clinton took office in January 1993, he hoped to legislate a reform agenda. Having received only 43 percent of the popular vote in 1992 and facing difficult policy choices regarding such matters as the deficit, he also carried with him a history that was not easily put to rest. Rumors abounded during the 1992 campaign about his past philandering and his apparent draft dodging, but he overcame those liabilities and won his party's presidential nomination and the election that followed.

But one story that surfaced in 1992 had staying power even after Clinton became president. The story concerned a land deal and a failed savings and loan bank in Arkansas and involved Clinton and his wife Hillary Rodham Clinton. A complicated story known as Whitewater, it seemed to imply shady doings by the two when Bill Clinton was governor of Arkansas and Hillary Clinton was the bank's lawyer. Although no evidence was ever adduced to convict them of illegal behavior, the Whitewater affair placed their probity and character under serious scrutiny by both Congress and an independent counsel, whose appointment by the Justice Department later had serious consequences for the Clinton presidency.

Spreading the cloud of scandal more deeply over Clinton, Paula Corbin Jones in 1994 filed a civil lawsuit charging Clinton with sexual impropriety when he was still governor of Arkansas. But before her case went trial in late 1997, a money scandal directly related to the high costs of funding Clinton's reelection campaign of 1996 enveloped the administration. The concerns revolved around the flow of illegal money into the campaign coffers of the National Democratic Committee from Indonesian and Chinese sources. In addition questions arose over the constant flow of people into the White House for kaffeeklatsches and sleepovers who paid substantially for their close proximity to the president. Among the participants in this money-driven environment at the White House was an individual with shady political connections.

Not rising to the level of scandal but viewed by some as scandalous was Clinton's decision to take from the State Department and give to the Commerce Department the authority to decide whether shipments of sensitive satellite technology to China should be given a green light. Unlike the Defense Department and the State Department, which questioned such sales, the Commerce Department was prepared to give the shipments the green light. The president of the Loral Corporation, who was the most generous financial contributor to the Democratic Party in 1996 and whose company manufactured sensitive satellite equipment and sold it to China, benefited from Clinton's move.

The historic scandal of Clinton's presidency was his affair with the White House intern Monica Lewinsky, which threatened to capsize his presidency. By denying a sexual relationship with Lewinsky in the Jones civil trial, Clinton not only gave perjured testimony but possibly obstructed justice as well. As a result the Office of the Independent Counsel (OIC), headed by Kenneth Starr, submitted a report to the House of Representatives stating that Clinton may have committed impeachable acts as a result of his testimony and action in the context of the Jones civil trial.

Clinton's behavior as outlined in the Starr report angered and shamed many Americans, but a majority did not favor his impeachment, believing he was doing a good job as president. In the majority opinion, his affair with Lewinsky was purely a private matter and did not impinge on his duties. Thus it did not merit consideration either as a high crime or as a misdemeanor. Conservative Republicans, on the other hand, were eager to see Clinton removed from office. They were convinced that as a result of his behavior he had sullied the office and had embarrassed the country at home and around the world. Such were the views of both sides as the House of Representatives, driven by partisan political considerations and passionately held convictions, voted to impeach President Clinton on several counts. He thus became the first elected president in American history to be so indicted.

Responding to public opinion, which overwhelmingly opposed the action taken by the House, the Senate refused to convict Clinton of the charges. Clearly in this case he also was helped by the strong economy, which protected him during the Senate trial, but he was seriously tarnished by the affair. A majority of Americans no longer respected him as a person, even though they still admired his political skills and generally approved of his public policy initiatives. Clinton's behavior became an issue in the context of the 2000 presidential election, which surely hurt Vice President Al Gore's bid for the White House.

Although Clinton avoided a conviction in the Senate, he had reason to fear that after he left office the OIC would prosecute him for lying to the court in the Jones case. So Clinton made a deal with the OIC and issued a statement admitting his culpability, at which point the prospect of further legal action against him was dropped.

That arrangement notwithstanding, Clinton was unable to shake the stench of scandal even as he departed from office on 20 January 2001. On that day he pardoned Marc Rich, a billionaire fugitive and commodities dealer who owed the American government $48 million in back taxes. Clinton also commuted the sentence of Carlos Vignali, the notorious head of a Los Angeles cocaine ring, who was serving a fifteen-year prison sentence. Clinton's actions produced a storm of protest from Democrats and Republicans alike, who were outraged at what many believed was a clear abuse of the president's pardoning power. Thus if scandal or rumor of scandal accompanied Clinton's move into the White House, those controversial last-minute pardons of Rich and Vignali provided a scandalous backdrop to his departure from the presidency.

BIBLIOGRAPHY

Berman, William C. *From the Center to the Edge: The Politics and Policies of the Clinton Presidency.* Lanham, Md.: Rowman and Littlefield, 2001.

Posner, Richard A. *An Affair of State: The Investigation, Impeachment, and Trial of President Clinton.* Cambridge, Mass.: Harvard University Press, 1999.

William C. Berman

See also **Clinton v. Jones; Impeachment Trial of Bill Clinton; Special Prosecutors;** *and vol. 9:* **Clinton's Rose Garden Statement.**

CLINTON V. JONES, 520 U.S. 681 (1997). In May 1991 Paula Corbin Jones, an Arkansas state employee, was brought to a hotel room in Little Rock, Arkansas, where, she alleged, Governor Bill Clinton made "abhorrent" sexual advances to her. Having rejected his advances, she later claimed that her refusal resulted in discrimination against her in her work. Consequently, she filed suit in a federal district court seeking to recover damages from him even while he was serving as the president of the United States.

Clinton requested that the federal judge in Little Rock dismiss the pending civil trial on grounds of presidential immunity. The judge refused, ruling that such a trial would be stayed only until his presidency had ended. Clinton then appealed the judge's decision to the United States Court of Appeals for the Eighth Circuit, which in turn ruled that he lacked immunity and that the case could go to trial.

Subsequently, Clinton asked the United States Supreme Court to delay proceedings until he had left office. On 27 May 1997 the Court, in the case of *Clinton v. Jones,* let stand the decision of the Federal Court of Appeals for the Eighth Circuit, denying Clinton immunity in a civil suit not related to his office. As a result of the Court's action, the Jones case went to trial, during which Clinton gave perjured testimony about his affair with Monica Lewinsky. His testimony later provided the grounds for his impeachment by the House of Representatives.

BIBLIOGRAPHY

Posner, Richard A. *An Affair of State: The Investigation, Impeachment, and Trial of President Clinton*. Cambridge, Mass.: Harvard University Press, 1999.

William C. Berman

See also **Impeachment Trial of Bill Clinton.**

CLIPPER SHIPS, long, narrow wooden vessels with lofty canvas sails, reigned as the world's fastest oceangoing ships from about 1843 to 1868. The word "clipper" might have originated from "clip," meaning to run swiftly. Tea from China quickly lost its flavor in the hold of a ship, and about 1843 the clippers began quicker delivery of that commodity. The discovery of gold in California provided another incentive for speed. After carrying their cargoes of gold prospectors and merchandise around Cape Horn to California, the ships would either return to Atlantic ports for another such cargo or would cross the Pacific Ocean to China and be loaded with tea, silk, and spices.

Clippers were more dependable than earlier ships. They strained less in a heavy sea and crossed belts of calm better than low-rigged vessels. The swift schooners built at Baltimore during the War of 1812 were known as Baltimore clippers, but the first real clipper was the *Ann McKim*, built there in 1832. Beginning about 1850 the California clippers increased rapidly in size, ranging from 1,500 to 2,000 tons register. The *Stag-Hound*, built in 1850, was the pioneer clipper of this type. The *Flying Cloud*, built in Boston in 1851, sailed to San Francisco in eighty-nine days; the *Andrew Jackson* and the *Flying Fish* achieved similar feats. It was more than a quarter of a century before the steamship was able to break the speed records of the fastest clippers. After the Civil War, American SHIPBUILDING for overseas carrying trade declined. Although a few more clipper ships were built, the steamships gradually replaced them.

BIBLIOGRAPHY

Cutler, Carl C. *Greyhounds of the Sea: The Story of the American Clipper Ship*. 3d ed. Annapolis, Md.: Naval Institute Press, 1984. The original edition was published New York: Halcyon House, 1930.

Howe, Octavius T., and Frederick C. Matthews. *American Clipper Ships, 1833–1858*. New York: Dover, 1986.

Charles Garrett Vannest/A. R.

See also **China Trade; Coasting Trade; Shipping, Ocean; Trade, Foreign.**

CLOCK AND WATCH INDUSTRY. The history of American clock- and watchmaking is a microcosm of the early history of American manufacturing. It includes the story of a tremendously talented line of artisans and of the training that passed from one to the other. Their ingenuity led to the spread of the "American system" of production—a forerunner of mass production. Finally, large-scale production of clocks and watches depended on the development of an elaborate system of distribution, through which the clocks and watches produced in such large quantities were distributed to urban and rural Americans.

The first clockmaker of record in America was Thomas Nash, an early settler of New Haven in 1638. Throughout the seventeenth century, eight-day striking clocks with brass movements, similar to those made in England, were produced by craft methods in several towns and villages in Connecticut. The wooden clock was not made in America until the eighteenth century, although it was known to exist in Europe in the seventeenth century, probably originating in Germany or Holland. By 1745 Benjamin Cheney of East Hartford was producing wooden clocks, and there is some evidence that these clocks were being made as early as 1715 near New Haven. Cheney was not the only maker of wooden clocks during the second half of the eighteenth century, but he was the most successful. Benjamin Willard, founder of the Willard Clock dynasty of Massachusetts, was apprenticed to Cheney.

The main line of descent of the American clock industry derives from Thomas Hatland, who emigrated from England in 1773 and opened a shop in Norwich, Connecticut. A clock- and watchmaker employing traditional craft methods, he was the first prominent European in that trade to settle in Connecticut. Hatland trained a substantial number of talented clockmakers, the most famous of whom was Daniel Burnap, who established his own business in East Windsor about 1780. Together Hatland and Burnap were the forerunners of the modern, industrial era of clockmaking. This distinction derives from the fact that Eli Terry, the first to systematize clock production on a basis similar to that of interchangeable parts manufacture, was apprenticed to Daniel Burnap in 1786. It was most probably under Burnap's tutelage that Terry, who is recognized as the outstanding Connecticut clockmaker of the nineteenth century as well as the originator of clockmaking by machinery, was introduced to the concept of volume production as opposed to the customary practice of production to order.

Leaving Burnap's shop, Terry commenced business at Plymouth, Connecticut, in 1794. Shortly after 1800 he began to produce wooden clocks in quantity and in 1808 contracted with the Porter brothers of Waterbury for the production of 4,000 wooden clock movements at $4 each. Production in such quantities was unheard of up to that time, and the contract price contrasted sharply with the more usual $25 average price for movements. About 1814 Terry designed and manufactured the thirty-hour wooden shelf clock, hundreds of thousands of which were produced until his retirement in 1833.

Seth Thomas and Chauncey Jerome, both of whom worked for Eli Terry, greatly elaborated the system of factory production and carried the clock industry into its distinctly modern phase. Jerome worked for Terry for a year or two after 1816. Then he engaged in itinerant clockmaking and moved to Bristol in 1821. In 1825 Jerome designed the bronze looking-glass clock, which was an instant commercial success. Even though Joseph Ives of Bristol must be given credit for the pioneer development of the cheap American brass clock, which evolved from his work around 1815, it was Chauncey Jerome who, in 1838, developed the commercial possibilities of the thirty-hour rolled-brass movement. By 1842 Jerome was exporting brass clocks in large quantities to England. By 1855 almost all common clocks in America were brass, the four largest firms producing 400,000 rolled-brass movements in that year. Virtually every major firm in existence at the end of the nineteenth century could trace its descent from these early Connecticut-based establishments.

Watchmaking helped establish and carry forward a new standard of accuracy in American metalworking. Until World War I, nearly all watches produced in the United States were pocket watches, and for much of this time they were luxury goods. Although watches were probably made in America before the Revolution, the earliest production of watches in some volume is accorded to Thomas Haftand of Norwich, Connecticut. Between 1809 and 1817 Luther Goddard of Shrewsbury, Massachusetts, produced about 500 movements. Goddard learned the art of clockmaking from his cousin Simon Willard, son of Benjamin Willard; and thus this line of mechanical influence can be traced from Benjamin Cheney. Between 1836 and 1841 James and Henry Pitkin of East Hartford, Connecticut, made perhaps 800 movements, using the most elaborate tools known in America up to that time. Shortly before 1850 Aaron Dennison and Edward Howard made plans to manufacture watches on a volume basis, using a system of interchangeable parts, some of the parts being held to an accuracy of 1/10,000 of an inch. Dennison had learned clockmaking in Maine and watchmaking in Boston. Howard had been apprenticed to Aaron Willard Jr. for five years commencing in 1829—again in the Cheney line of descent. Other men who contributed prominently to the watchmaking industry throughout the balance of the nineteenth century were Ambrose Webster, Charles Mosley, Edward Marsh, and Charles Vander Woerd.

Dennison and Howard's attempts to use interchangeable parts in watch manufacture resulted in the formation of Dennison, Howard, and Davis, the firm that was the predecessor of the American Watch Company, later the Waltham Watch Company. When it was formed in 1850, the Waltham Watch Company was the only firm manufacturing watches in the United States, and it maintained a virtual monopoly on watch production through the 1870s. Although the factory used machinery, it depended on workers' abilities to manipulate and adapt very complicated technology. Owners offered generous wages and benefits, a clean working environment, and promises of promotion to retain and recruit the highly skilled labor force they needed. New watchmaking firms were established in the years just preceding and following the Civil War, and Waltham employees were in high demand by companies in Chicago, Providence, Springfield, Massachussetts, and Springfield, Illinois. All American watchmaking firms can trace their lineage either through the Waltham Watch Company prior to 1885 or through personnel associated with that firm. The watchmaking business expanded in the 1890s, when many firms began marketing cheaper "dollar watches." Just as Eli Terry had made clocks into an affordable item for many Americans, now watches were something that many people could see themselves owning. These watches did not use the jeweled parts that had been part of older and more expensive watches. Rather, a punch press was used to stamp highly standardized and cheaper parts out of sheets of metal. Simultaneously, railroads issued new requirements for the watches worn by their employees. Because reliable timekeeping was so essential to the scheduling and operation of railroads, the watches worn by employees had to be of very high quality; these watches represented the opposite end of the spectrum of "dollar watches." Firms developed ever more sophisticated techniques to produce ever more precise watches. Watches gained an even bigger market when American firms began producing wristwatches. First developed in Switzerland and marketed as women's watches, wristwatches were distributed to soldiers in World War I, and they quickly became popular items for both men and women.

The American watch industry declined considerably in the interwar years, the result of overexpansion and the high costs of specialized machinery. Only seven firms survived the 1930s, and the industry continued to contract in subsequent decades. While many Americans continue to wear watches, these are often manufactured overseas.

BIBLIOGRAPHY

Gitelman, H. M. "The Labor Force at Waltham Watch during the Civil War Era." *Journal of Economic History* 25 (June 1965).

Hounshell, David A. *From the American System to Mass Production, 1800–1932.* Baltimore: Johns Hopkins University Press, 1984.

Jaffee, David. "Peddlers of Progress and the Transformation of the Rural North, 1760–1860." *Journal of American History* 78 (September 1991).

Murphy, John Joseph. "Entrepreneurship in the Establishment of the American Clock Company." *Journal of Economic History* 26 (June 1966).

Paul Uselding/T. D.

See also **Automation; Industries, Colonial; Mass Production.**

CLOSED SHOP refers to a union security clause in labor-management contracts that stipulates that all persons who are to be employed must be members of a specified union as a precondition for such employment.

The closed shop was a dominant feature of early unionism in the United States, a natural outgrowth of the guild features of craft organization of work. The focus of the guild was on the maintenance of the quality of output through strict enforcement of APPRENTICESHIP standards. Many early unions stipulated that employers could hire only fully certified journeymen and would be subject to penalty if they failed to do so. Craft members, moreover, were subject to fines if caught working with persons not members of the union. The strong fraternal character of early unions helped buttress such arrangements, which seemed justified (at least to members) by the attention they gave to sustaining the quality of work by preserving the integrity of craft skills. Such arrangements also boosted wages by restricting the size of the pool of available workers. Although seldom made contractually explicit, closed shop arrangements were pervasive throughout the early twentieth century and were a source of considerable controversy and conflict.

In 1935, the NATIONAL LABOR RELATIONS ACT legislated a major intrusion of public policy into collective bargaining in an effort to reduce the widespread industrial conflict. Major provisions, which the newly created National Labor Relations Board (NLRB) was to implement, were aimed at reducing strikes over union recognition. Appropriate bargaining units were to be defined by the board; a secret-ballot vote was then to be taken under board supervision in the matter of union representation. A union gaining more than half of that vote was to be certified by the board as the exclusive bargaining agent for that unit. The employer was then obligated to bargain in good faith with that union, and the union was obligated to equally represent all persons in the bargaining unit, whether members or not.

There were obvious advantages to the union movement in shifting the locus of decision making about union recognition from the economic to the political arena. In securing the right to exclusive representation for at least a year following certification, the union had the opportunity to extend its influence over the bargaining unit. One logical extension of such recognition was to strengthen the union's membership base and its revenue flow. Rather than overtly pursuing an exclusionary policy involving a closed shop with a union that limited membership, most unions preferred to adopt an inclusionary posture. They negotiated union security clauses to expand rather than to restrict membership. The ultimate result was a growth in closed shop arrangements.

However, the closed shop arrangement could be used against the worker as well as against the employer. Expulsion from the union meant loss of job rights, and there were several reasons why a union might expel a member. A worker might be expelled for refusing to adhere to the production ceilings established for piece-rate operations. The union might undertake selective retaliation against dissidents within the union political structure. Or, retaliation might follow a member's support of another union

vying for representation rights in the shop. In brief, with a closed shop, the union was no longer a private fraternal organization. It controlled the job. It was a dispenser of bread.

Initial assaults against union exclusionary policies took the form of conspiracy charges—that the monopolistic privileges accruing to union members increased product prices, reduced production, curtailed employment, and diminished wages in nonunion industries because of the additional flow of labor squeezed out of "protected" sectors. The 1947 TAFT-HARTLEY ACT amendments to the National Labor Relations Act were designed to remedy these ills by banning the closed shop. The public policy behind Taft-Hartley, as well as the 1959 Landrum-Griffin amendments to the National Labor Relations Act, was to restrict traditional union control over the point of ingress into the labor market. Obeisance to the union movement was not to be a requisite for favored treatment in pay or promotions within the plant. The economic status of the worker was to reflect the bilateral influences of both employer and union, not the unilateral discretion of the union. Nonmembers and members were to be treated as persons with undifferentiated status in the distribution of collective-bargaining gains. Controversy diminished during the late twentieth century as unions adhered to a new doctrine: employers have the "freedom" to hire nonunion employees, just as workers have the freedom to refuse to work with nonunion employees.

Also affected by public policy and union stance were alternative forms of union security, to be sharply distinguished from the closed shop. A *favored union clause*, now illegal, is one in which the employer openly identifies his partiality to a union and encourages membership in that organization. An *agency shop* allows the union to collect agency fees or service fees from workers, while not requiring the formality of membership. These fees cover union expenses associated with collective bargaining, and are justified by the union's obligation to bargain for all employees in the bargaining unit regardless of union affiliation. A 1980 amendment to the National Labor Relations Act provides that workers with religious objections cannot be fired for failing to pay service fees to a union.

Another form of union security is the *union-shop agreement*. Union-shop agreements formerly specified that workers in a union were to maintain membership affiliation as a condition of employment, with escape periods typically provided during the term of the contract. The National Labor Relations Act still permits contract provisions that require employees to join the union within thirty days of hire. However, in 1985 the Supreme Court held that contracts may not limit a worker's ability to resign from the union. Union-shop agreements can no longer require maintenance of union membership. In addition, several states have also enacted RIGHT-TO-WORK LAWS that prohibit union-shop agreements altogether.

In short, changes in labor law and its judicial interpretation over the course of the twentieth century have undermined the ability of unions to bargain for contract provisions that enhance their security and their ability to discipline members.

BIBLIOGRAPHY

Commons, John R., et al. *History of Labour in the United States.* 4 vols. See especially Volume 1, Part 6. New York: Macmillan, 1946. The original edition was published in 1918.

Hanson, Charles Goring, Sheila Jackson, and Douglas Miller. *The Closed Shop: A Comparative Study in Public Policy and Trade Union Security in Britain, the USA, and West Germany.* New York: St. Martin's Press, 1981.

Harris, Howell John. *Bloodless Victories: The Rise and Fall of the Open Shop in the Philadelphia Metal Trades, 1890–1940.* Cambridge, U.K.: Cambridge University Press, 2000.

Rustin, Bayard. *"Right to Work" Laws; A Trap for America's Minorities.* New York: A. Phillip Randolph Institute, 1967.

Schiller, Reuel E. "From Group Rights to Individual Liberties: Post-War Labor Law, Liberalism, and the Waning of Union Strength." *Berkeley Journal of Employment and Labor Law* 20, no. 1 (1999): 1.

Sultan, Paul E. *Right-to-Work Laws: Study in Conflict.* Los Angeles: Institute of Industrial Relations, University of California, 1958.

Paul E. Sultan / c. p.

See also **Labor; Labor Legislation and Administration.**

CLOTHING AND FASHION.

Though often used interchangeably, there are distinct and important differences between clothing, fashion, and style. The term *clothing* first appeared in the thirteenth century and refers to garments in general. *Fashion* and *style* are fourteenth-century words. Style describes the form of something, while fashion refers to prevailing styles during a particular time. All clothing can be described in terms of the style of specific features, such as a mandarin collar or a gathered sleeve, and if the style is currently popular, it is considered fashionable. Garment styles periodically recur, though usually in slightly different forms. Coco Chanel, the famous French designer, once said that anyone who claimed originality had no knowledge of history.

The Colonies

Colonization of America began in the late 1500s with the Spanish in Florida, followed by the French in Acadia and the English in Jamestown, Virginia, and Massachusetts. The Dutch, Swedes, and Germans would have settlements by 1683. All of these groups brought their native garb with them. As in Europe, clothing for the wealthy was elaborate and made of fine fabrics. Men set the fashions, and women and children followed them. Humbler folk wore less complicated clothing of a more serviceable nature. The colonies were not meant to be self-supporting and were seen as a good source of exports from the mother countries. Attitudes toward attire would develop largely based on whether an area was settled by adventurers or those seeking religious freedom. Clothing was important and often passed on from one generation to the next upon death. Few garments survived in their original form, having been recut to fit a different figure or to reflect a newer fashion.

As they became established, wealthy southern planters tended to keep up with court fashions by importing clothes made in England. Their wives and daughters wore silk, velvet, brocade, and satin gowns when in town. Clothing on the plantations was more utilitarian, with men wearing working clothes of breeches and jerkins made of canvas or a rough fabric called frieze, coarse wool hose, and leather shoes, and women wearing simple gowns over homespun petticoats and usually an apron. Masters clothed their laborers and servants. Some planters maintained a store on site with various goods, while others relied on itinerant peddlers for fashion news, supplies, and gossip.

Sumptuary laws were enacted mid-seventeenth century in Massachusetts by conservative Pilgrims who felt that too much money was being spent on clothing. They tried to regulate the length and width of sleeves, as well as prohibiting the use of silk (except for hoods or scarves), silver, gold, lace, and ribbons of gold or silver. Goods in defiance were confiscated and exported. Officials thought a person's clothing should accurately reflect their social prestige and rank, and they put many violators of the sumptuary laws on trial. It was possible, however, to have charges dropped if one could prove sufficient financial status.

By the late seventeenth century, William and Mary were on the English throne. Relations with the colonies were good and nearly every ship brought luxuries. Fashion was less than a year behind England. Dolls dressed in the latest styles arrived in London from Paris once a month, and were regularly sent on to America where dressmakers would create interpretations for colonial women. Children were dressed in styles very similar to their parents.

Not all people followed trends, however. Though financially sound, the Quakers recommended their members abstain from rich colors and use soft gray, dull drab, sage greens, and somber browns. They made their clothes the same shapes as court clothes, minus the showy trims, and used beautiful and costly cloth.

The first half of the eighteenth century was prosperous and comfortable. Fashion was conspicuous among the rich, with merchant ships from China and the Indies supplying silk, tissues, and embroidered gauzes. Small patches were worn not only as beauty marks, but also as a sign of political sway: a patch on the left side of the face supported the Whigs, while the right side indicated a Tory. Fans were an important accessory as well, enabling an elaborate method of nonverbal communication.

The Revolution

As political difficulties with England escalated, the fashionable looked toward France for style. As early as 1768,

New England ladies agreed to use local manufacturers and to boycott English items. They abandoned heavy black mourning clothes, a frequent import, and abstained from eating lamb so more sheep would grow to maturity and produce more American wool, thereby undermining one of England's primary exports. Tradesmen adopted sturdy leather clothing for work. Men and women discarded all imported goods and wore domestic homespun. After Bunker Hill, only Tories continued to import English fashion. During the war, officers had greatcoats made out of Dutch blankets, and the Minutemen wore whatever they had, usually homespun or leather hunting shirts, leather breeches, and buckskin shoes. A few regiments had uniforms, but there was no regularity. Official papers list a resolution that 13,000 coats would be provided for noncommissioned officers and soldiers of the Massachusetts forces. After Independence, George Washington was inaugurated in a domestic homespun suit.

The United States of America
Though now free of English rule, the new country still looked to Europe for style. The stiff brocades and rustling silks of late eighteenth-century France gave way to simpler styles as the Terror consumed Paris. It would be decidedly unhealthy to appear too aristocratic there, and this fashion change migrated across the Atlantic. People stopped the 100-year-old practice of powdering their hair, and adopted closer fitting garments. For men, the tails were cut away from coat fronts and became longer in back. Vests, called waistcoats, were low in front and worn over ruffled shirts. Women wore dresses of thin, fine Indian cottons with narrow skirts, waistlines very high under the bust, long tight sleeves, and bare shoulders with a muslin or gauze piece tucked in the front when at home. A long scarf thrown around the shoulders and cascading to the ground in front was worn outside. The Empire style had the advantage of actually being comfortable for women and children, though rather lightweight for colder regions. Fur muffs provided some warmth.

As early as 1785, fashion magazines were sent regularly from London and Paris. These included colored plates of the latest styles, serial stories, poetry and literary reviews. By 1800, they had replaced the fashion dolls. Following the English and French format, Philadelphian Louis Godey began publication of his *Lady's Book* in 1830.

The Beginnings of Industry
Within a few years, technology would increase cloth production far beyond prior abilities.

The 1794 patent of the cotton gin increased cotton processing from one pound per day to fifty pounds per day per person. Slavery, which had begun to die out, was revived as a source of labor for the now profitable crop. Samuel Slater arrived in America with the ability to both build and operate English spinning machinery. He opened the first successful water-powered mill in Rhode Island in 1793, establishing a blueprint for mills that would be cop-

ied throughout New England. In 1813, Francis Cabot Lowell collaborated with inventor Paul Moody to create an efficient power loom that could keep pace with the abundant supply of cotton and wool yarn. Fashion was relatively simple under Thomas Jefferson's terms of office, 1801–1809, partly due to French styles, but partly because of Jefferson's own views. Dolly Madison was welcomed as a breath of fresh air in 1809 when clothing became more festive. Though still following France more closely than England, the new States could not help but be influenced by the lavish extravagance of the Regency period (1810–1819). With more fabric readily available, dresses became fuller, the waistline descended to a more natural position, and decoration replaced simplicity. A domestic lace machine based on an English model was developed in 1823, and purportedly produced good quality lace.

Sleeves became so large between 1825 and 1835 that they required as much cloth as a skirt. Skirts were ankle length, full and gathered into a band at the natural waist. With the fullness of the skirt and the size of the sleeves, waistlines appeared impossibly small. As the Industrial Revolution produced more cloth, fashionable garments required increasing amounts. Famous and influential people impacted fashion. Queen Victoria's 1840 wedding gown started a trend for lace, and Madame Pompadour, an investor in the East India Company, started the craze for Indian Paisley shawls.

Mid-Nineteenth Century
As increasing numbers of immigrants arrived in America, the population headed west in search of land and opportunity. The discovery of gold in California in 1848 sparked a rush of miners and prospectors seeking fortune. Though unable to sell his heavy canvas for tents in the mild climate, Levi Straus made them into rugged work pants and started a style that continues through present day. Meanwhile, the 1853 marriage of the French Princess Eugenie inspired fashion to even greater extravagance. Now the French Empress, she was a great lover of clothing with a large and elegant wardrobe. Skirts became so full that layers of petticoats were necessary to support them. In 1854, Charles Worth, the famous French couturier, invented the hoop skirt, a petticoat with wire bands slipped through casings at descending intervals that allowed great expanse with very little weight. The device took only two years to appear in Philadelphia. Unfortunately, the sheer scale of the skirts made it difficult for women to enter and exit carriages and to pass by others wearing equally large skirts. There are numerous incidents reported of women who unknowingly brushed too close to fireplaces and caught fire, resulting in injury and even death.

Hair was worn parted in the middle with long curls coming down the sides over the ears. The mid-century woman thus looked almost like a hand bell, with a narrow top and a very full bottom. She appeared stationary and unapproachable, surrounded by her clothing. In contrast,

Women's Fashion. This photograph by Frances Benjamin Johnston shows what young women in Massachusetts were wearing in 1902. LIBRARY OF CONGRESS

men of the period were adopting increasingly understated attire. As fortunes were made, the newly wealthy allowed their wives and children to reflect their success, while the men themselves wore what would eventually become the business suit.

Children's clothing followed that of their parents. Those lower on the financial rung actually enjoyed more comfortable attire. Offspring from more prominent families were dressed according to their station. All children wore dresses until age three or four, when boys were given short pants. Little girls wore hoops like their mothers. At about age ten, a boy received long trousers as a rite of passage from childhood. There was no similar recognition for girls as they passed into young womanhood.

Civil War

Conflict over slavery and states' rights set the North and South at odds. The ensuing Civil War interrupted life for the entire country, and ultimately devastated the South. At the beginning of the conflict, Southern ladies continued to dress stylishly to keep up their courage, but fashion was discarded as the war progressed. Military uniforms for both sides were produced quickly using the sewing machine, which had been invented by Elias Howe and Isaac Singer in the 1840s. After the war, it was largely used to produce prison uniforms and garments for stevedores until the turn of the twentieth century.

Expansion

In 1869, the rail lines coming from the East and the West finally converged in Utah, and the grueling journey that once took months over dusty plains and high mountains was reduced to about six days. Communication and the transportation of goods became a relatively simple matter. The pace of life picked up and fashion reflected the new speed. Hoop skirts were eventually abandoned, and by 1870, skirts were swept back and fastened into a bustle. Hair also was pulled to the back, giving a woman the appearance of moving briskly forward, even when standing still. As manufacturing increased, a dazzling array of goods could be had. Previously, money was tied to land and inherited, but now industry made fortunes. The new rich seemed compelled to exhibit their social status by dressing as conspicuously as possible in very elaborate, highly decorated garments with tiny waists accomplished by tight corsets. In an effort to reduce the deleterious effects of undergarments, worn even when pregnant, a dress reform movement appeared in the 1880s. A health corset was designed, featuring a straight piece down the front, rather than pushing into the stomach. The movement also decried the practice of dressing children as miniature adults. It proposed that the young be allowed to wear soft fabrics and loose garments.

By 1890, 30 percent of Americans lived in towns with populations greater than 8,000. New York boasted more than 1.5 million residents, and Chicago and Philadelphia each had over 1 million. The country was slowly changing from a group of rural settlements to a series of thriving urban cities. Portrayed by the artist Charles Dana Gibson, and dubbed the Gibson Girl, a new idea of womanhood was emerging. Often employed as a shop assistant, typist, or governess, she was strong, self-confident, and independent. Her participation in sports, especially bicycling, gave her a newfound freedom from chaperones. Her dress of choice was a tailor-made suit that consisted of a long skirt, a matching fitted jacket, and a shirtwaist blouse. Many of the blouses were made at home, but by 1909, 600 sewing shops employing 30,000 workers were manufacturing blouses in America. Standard sizing became a necessity, as these garments were sold in stores and through catalogues. The success and convenience of purchasing simple garments that did not require elaborate fitting encouraged more people to buy "off the rack" or "ready to wear." Sweatshops continued to spring up to meet the demand, often taking advantage of new immigrants who came from Europe with sewing skills. Many settled in New York, making it the center of American garment manufacture. The twentieth century would see clothing change from a custom-made, one-of-a-kind business, to an automated, mass manufactured industry.

Labor Unions

In 1900, the International Ladies Garment Workers Union (ILGWU) was formed to protest low pay, fifteen-hour days, lack of benefits, and unsafe working conditions. In 1909, 20,000 shirtwaist workers staged the first strike in the industry. Mostly women and children, many of the workers were beaten or fired; however, they did win a small pay raise and a reduction of the workweek to fifty-two hours. A second strike occurred in 1910, when 50,000 mostly male cloakmakers walked out. They won uniform wages across that industry, a shorter week, and paid holidays. The ILGWU membership swelled. Tragedy struck in 1911 when a fire broke out at the Triangle Shirtwaist factory. Doors were locked, exits blocked and 146 mostly female garment workers perished in the blaze. The government was finally prompted to take action and establish regulatory control over the industry.

World War I to World War II

The onset of World War I took many American men overseas, and women had no choice but to step in and run family businesses and keep the country going. Clothing became practical and functional. When the war was over and the men returned, young women in particular were loath to give up their freedoms. Many adopted a boyish look by cutting their hair, flattening their bosoms, and dropping their waistlines to the hip. Called the flapper, this woman wanted control of her own life and equal rights. By downplaying her feminine curves, she challenged notions of weakness and dependence. The horror of the war sent an entire generation in search of a means to forget, but unfortunately the stock market crash of 1929 ended the party. Many people were financially ruined in the crash, and clothing became serious, conservative, and grown-up. Any display of extravagance was considered to be in poor taste, so clothing was understated except on private estates, where Paris still largely dictated fashion. For the average person, life was somewhat grim; escape, however, could be found cheaply at the movies. Hollywood starlets became icons of fashionable dress, and were much admired and copied.

As the Depression began to lift, fashionable clothing became attainable again. Manufacturers and department-store buyers sailed to France so often that the transatlantic ship the *Normandie* was nicknamed "the Seventh Avenue shuttle." French designs were either purchased or copied from memory. Once home, the styles were produced in several qualities of fabrics with varying degrees of sophistication. Thus, manufacture made fashion available to most strata of society.

During World War II, women once again stepped into the workplace. They adopted trousers and accepted the shortages of nearly everything, as all materials were applied to the war effort. Restrictions were placed on the amount and type of fabric that could be used for apparel. Once Paris fell to the Germans, America was stylistically on her own. Known as the "Mother of American Fashion," Claire McCardell was instrumental in creating the uniquely American style. Using humble fabrics and keeping the average income in mind, McCardell designed a variety of clever, comfortable, affordable clothing. While several prestigious designers came to America during the war years, McCardell was the one who best understood the emerging American lifestyle.

The Rising Middle Class

Post-war affluence allowed a large middle class to emerge. As men climbed the corporate ladder, appropriate attire was required. The gray business suit became a standard, while a variety of magazines helped the wives make proper choices in everything from clothing to breakfast cereal. Between 1946 and 1964, 72 million children were born. Known as the baby boomers, they scorned conformity and chafed against the confines of their parents' narrow lifestyle. Their resulting rebellion was noticeable in their rejection of fashion. Long hair, vintage clothing, and worn jeans became the uniform of youth in the 1960s.

American Independence

Once broken free of the dictates of Paris and the restrictions of a rigid society, American fashion became a vast commercial enterprise. Though still considered the center of fashion, Parisian influence declined as the trend toward youthful clothing swept the globe. Americans realized that they were fully capable of producing garments that appealed to their own sensibilities and lifestyles. In the last three decades of the twentieth century, American designers continued to look around the world for inspiration. But the world began to look to the United States as well, where garments of all styles and qualities were available to nearly every budget. With an enormous industry and vast manufacturing capabilities, Americans have developed a casual style of dress that is recognizable world over.

BIBLIOGRAPHY

Earle, Alice Morse. *Two Centuries of Costume in America, 1620–1820.* Rutland, Vermont: Charles E. Tuttle Company, 1971.

McClellan, Elisabeth. *Historic Dress in America 1607–1870.* New York: Arno Press, 1977.

Milbank, Caroline R. *New York Fashion: The Evolution of American Style.* New York: Abrams, 1989.

Murray, Maggie Pexton. *Changing Styles in Fashion: Who, What, Why.* New York: Fairchild, 1989.

Watson, Linda. *Vogue: Twentieth-Century Fashion: From Haute Couture to Street Style.* London: Carleton Books, 2000.

Christina Lindholm

See also **Bloomers; Flapper.**

CLOTHING INDUSTRY. Throughout the eighteenth century, clothing manufacture—from the raising of the raw materials, through the spinning and weaving, to the sewing—was largely a household industry in the United States. In the colonial period fine imported textiles, including clothing and bed and table linens, were costly items. Tailoring shops, particularly in the larger cities, produced up-to-date, custom-made clothing for the well-to-do. But in the average family all stages of clothing manufacture were carried on in the home, where women and children made plain, durable clothes of wool or linsey-woolsey, a wool and linen or cotton mixture. The preliminary stages of spinning and weaving were eliminated from home work after the 1830s, when American manufacture of textiles became an established industry. Machine-made cloth was sold to rural householders through country stores and traveling drummers.

The ready-to-wear industry made a tentative beginning in the men's branch of the trade in the late eighteenth century with the establishment of slop shops, which sold rough clothing to sailors in port cities. Custom tailors also began to make up some clothing in slack times to keep their workers busy. The first recorded clothing factory was located in New York City in 1831. Early haberdashery stores, such as Brooks Brothers, sold both custom- and ready-made clothing at midcentury. But the output of ready-made clothing was inconsequential in quantity compared to the amount of clothing made at home. Much of the ready-made clothing was of a cheap grade and was sold in the West or in the South for use by settlers and slaves. Because of its regular shipping connections with southern states, New York City rapidly became the center of the ready-to-wear trade with the South, and some clothing of good quality was sold there.

The Civil War demand for uniforms provided an impetus for increased production that coincided with the widespread adoption of the sewing machine in clothing manufacture. This demand led to the introduction of standardized sizes. In the same period, women's clothing, especially cloaks and capes, began to be ready-made, and many women found employment in the women's wear branch of the industry. Use of the sewing machine, patented in 1846 by Elias Howe and further perfected by Isaac Singer, marked a major technical change in the industry from hand to machine labor. Sewing machines, powered at first by foot treadles and later in the century by electricity, vastly increased the output of ready-made clothing.

In many ways the characteristics of the sewing machine determined the structure of the clothing industry up to the present. Its low cost, portability, and simplicity promoted a decentralized industry based on unskilled labor, piecework, and low capital investment. Since sewing machines cost relatively little—$50 for some models in 1858—and could be set up anywhere, the industry was remarkably easy to enter. Especially in the men's wear trade, there were some large, integrated firms—known as inside shops—that controlled all stages of manufacture on their own premises. But since adding more machines to a shop introduced few economies of scale, a manufacturer's greatest cost was the labor involved in making clothes. Consequently, most production was carried on by small, marginal firms known as outside shops.

Contractors organized the actual production in the outside shops. With as little as $50 for a deposit, a contractor could obtain precut cloth from a manufacturer. Work was then subdivided among individuals (often recent immigrants) who did the sewing in their own homes. Tasks were highly specialized. Workers usually worked on only one part of a garment, the sewing of a coat, for example, being broken into as many as 150 operations. Sometimes the task system was used, in which a team of workers was jointly responsible for finishing a number of garments. The system was fragmented, decentralized, and fraught with constant competition among contractors and workers. It also produced relatively cheap, ready-made clothing. In 1899 ladies' cloth jackets made under these conditions cost as little as $5, while ladies' tailored suits sold for from $8.50 to $100.

This pervasively marginal operation was the basis of the infamous sweatshop in the needle trades. With thousands of small contractors competing against one another in selling finished clothes, workers at the turn of the century had to work long hours for low pay—as little as $10.99 for a week of 16-hour days in 1895—to retain their jobs. In addition, clothing workers' earnings were highly seasonal; workers might be laid off for four to five months of the year. Also, because laborers often worked at home, contractors shifted many of the overhead costs of production to them: laborers usually had to buy or rent their own machines; furnish thread; replace spoiled cloth; and

Clothing Factory. Women seated at long tables work in the sewing room of a shirt factory in Troy, N.Y., c. 1907. LIBRARY OF CONGRESS

provide their own heat, light, and working space. These were all expensive supplies, and many garment workers labored without adequate heat, ventilation, light, or sanitation. Sometimes whole families ate and slept in the same room where clothing manufacture was carried out. In 1896 and 1897 New York State's new factory legislation banned families' living and working in the same quarters, but workers were still crowded together in empty tenement rooms and lofts. In 1911 in New York City, 145 workers, mostly young girls, were burned to death in the Triangle Shirt Waist Factory fire because their tenement factory lacked adequate fire escapes.

Decentralized production, low wages, and cutthroat competition continued to dominate the clothing industry in the 1920s as production shifted outside of urban centers. Submanufacturers and jobbers (sometimes called stock houses) became important links in the chain of production. While full manufacturers owned their own cloth and sold directly to retailers, submanufacturers bought cloth from jobbing firms and could sell finished orders only through these firms. Stock houses pressured submanufacturers to lower their costs. Since these submanufacturers were not covered by union contracts, they lowered costs by lowering wages. These conditions exacerbated the competitiveness and fragmentation of the

industry, while increased competition in fashion aggravated the irregularity of work.

Large-scale industrial unions brought some measure of regularity to the garment industry. In 1910 workers struck at the Hart, Shaffner, and Marx factory in Chicago. Strikers won an agreement in 1911 to arbitration of future disputes, which resulted in a wage increase, a 54-hour week, and a preferential union shop. Other men's wear branches of the industry were organized by the newly formed Amalgamated Clothing Workers of America. The women's wear branch of the industry was organized by the International Ladies Garment Workers Union (ILGWU). Members of the ILGWU participated in two massive strikes in 1909, resulting in the first collective settlement by clothing firm owners.

Throughout the post–World War I period and the depression of the 1930s, the unions acted as an important force in stabilizing the competitiveness and fragmentation of the industry. They sought agreements that outlawed submanufacturing and contracting and made the primary manufacturer responsible for working conditions and wage scales. In addition, they fought piece rates and tried to ensure a full year's work, or at least the spreading of available work during dull seasons. In 1937 they finally achieved industry-wide collective bargaining, an important step toward rationalizing the industry.

Statistics on the growth of the ready-made clothing industry throughout the twentieth century attest to its increased importance in the economy. From 1899 to 1948 capital invested in the clothing industry increased from $541 million to $2 billion, while the workforce employed in the apparel and accessory trades increased from 225,000 in 1900 to 824,000 in 1950. By 1929 clothing constituted the third-largest category of expenditure in the average family budget. After World War II the increased income of the American consumer and the new self-confidence of American designers created a market for new kinds of clothing, especially sportswear. By 1957 Americans were spending over $25 billion a year on clothing of all types, a figure almost eight times as large as the amount spent on all private education and almost double that spent on purchases of autos in the same year.

Although clothing remained an important aspect of families' expenditures, American firms lost ground in subsequent decades. The once flourishing U.S. garment industry floundered in the 1970s, 1980s, and 1990s, threatening virtually to disappear. Employment began declining in the mid-1970s, and the industry lost a quarter of its workers. In the period 1989–1993 exports of garments ran between $2.3 billion and $5.5 billion, but imports ranged from $25.3 billion to $35.5 billion, with four countries—China, Hong Kong, South Korea, and Taiwan—accounting for nearly half of the imports. Despite a precipitous drop in wages for U.S. garment industry workers, to an average hourly wage in 1993 of $7.06, the United States seemingly could not compete. The industry is labor intensive: Production workers make up 84 percent of employees, compared to 68 percent for all U.S. manufacturing positions. The downward trend led to illegal sewing operations and a return to sweatshop conditions, primarily among nonregistered aliens (some children) willing to work at below minimum wage.

International trade agreements exacerbated the decline. The North American Free Trade Agreement, the General Agreement on Tariffs and Trade, and the World Trade Organization worked to lower tarriffs and phase out quotas on imported goods, thus further opening the American market to cheaper imported textiles and increasing the pressure on American manufacturers to lower wages. Despite overall industry weakness, in February 1995 the ILGWU and the Amalgamated Clothing and Textile Workers Union merged to form the Union of Needletrades, Industrial and Textile Employees, thereby increasing the clout of the combined 355,000 members. In addition, retail buyers in the United States became increasingly sensitive to the need for quick responses from wholesalers. In a trend-sensitive business, retailers want to restock empty racks quickly, respond to fads, control inventory, and maintain quality. Some buyers began shifting from foreign to U.S. garments to reduce the time from order to delivery.

BIBLIOGRAPHY

Argersinger, Jo Anne. *Making the Amalgamated: Gender, Ethnicity, and Class in the Baltimore Clothing Industry, 1899–1939*. Baltimore: Johns Hopkins University Press, 1999.

Gamber, Wendy. *The Female Economy: The Millinery and Dressmaking Trades, 1860–1930*. Urbana: University of Illinois Press, 1997.

Glenn, Susan A. *Daughters of the Shtetl: Life and Labor in the Immigrant Generation*. Ithaca, N.Y.: Cornell University Press, 1990.

Green, Nancy L. *Ready-to-Wear and Ready-to-Work: A Century of Industry and Immigrants in Paris and New York*. Durham, N.C.: Duke University Press, 1997.

Wolman, Leo, ed. *The Clothing Workers of Chicago: 1910–1922*. Chicago: The Chicago Joint Board, Amalgamated Clothing Workers of America, 1922.

Polly Anne Earl
Brent Schondelmeyer / T. D.

See also **Amalgamated Clothing Workers of America; Clothing; International Ladies Garment Workers Union; Piecework; Sweatshop.**

CLOTURE is a procedure used by the United States Senate to end a filibuster or prolonged debate and reach a final vote on the pending motion, bill, amendment, or conference report. Unlimited debate in the Senate was curtailed by the addition of cloture under Senate Rule 22, adopted in 1917. To invoke cloture, a senator must file a motion signed by at least sixteen members. Once the cloture motion is filed, only germane amendments may be offered and may only be introduced by the next legislative day.

The Senate later modified the cloture procedure to reduce the number of votes required to end debate for most matters to 60 percent of the entire Senate. Postcloture debate was reduced to 100 hours in 1979 and then to 30 hours in 1986. Proposed changes to Senate rules still require a two-thirds supermajority vote to invoke cloture. In the period since 1975, more than 300 cloture votes have been taken, with debate successfully ended 40 percent of the time. Use of the cloture procedure reduces the effectiveness of impassioned minority viewpoints, allowing a supermajority to move forward on controversial agenda items.

BIBLIOGRAPHY

Binder, Sarah A., and Steven S. Smith. *Politics or Principle?: Filibustering in the United States Senate*. Washington, D.C.: Brookings Institution Press, 1997.

Congressional Quarterly, *Guide to the Congress of the United States*. Washington, D.C.: Congressional Quarterly Service, 1971.

Brian D. Posler

See also **Filibuster, Congressional.**

CLUBS, EXCLUSIONARY. Exclusionary clubs are voluntary associations whose new members are selected by the existing members for conviviality. Exclusionary clubs often exercise the right of private segregation based on gender, race, religion, ethnicity, or ancestry. The earliest known private supper club was the South River Club of Annapolis, Maryland, established around 1700. In the 1830s many private supper clubs consciously emulated the new British men's clubs of London by selecting members for their social esteem. These included New York City's Union Club (1836), Boston's Temple Club (1829), and the Philadelphia Club (1834). Their new clubhouses contained meeting rooms, restaurants, gaming facilities, and residential quarters for members. Intraclub rivalries, quarrels, and discriminations encouraged new clubs. New York City's Union Club spawned nine additional exclusionary men's clubs over such matters as ancestry, as in the case of the Knickerbocker Club (1871), and politics, as with the Union League Club (1863). The latter formed namesake clubs in Chicago and San Francisco with reciprocal memberships.

After the Civil War, city clubs formed country clubs. The Country Club (1882) in Brookline, Massachusetts, was the first to admit members' families to full participation. By 1900 over one thousand private country clubs provided outdoor social sports to members. Women formed their own exclusionary clubs. Architect Stanford White designed the New York City Colony Club for women in 1907. Boston's Chilton Club (1910) and Philadelphia's Acorn Club (1889) catered to socially esteemed women of those cities. In 1895 New York City listed fifty-six exclusive clubs; in 1951 the number was up to sixty-eight. The U.S. Supreme Court officially ended private segregation with its decision in *New York State Club Assn. v. City of New York* (1988). Up-and-coming politicians began dropping their membership in exclusionary private clubs—as associate attorney general–designate Webster Hubbell did in 1993—to avoid unfavorable publicity.

BIBLIOGRAPHY

Mayo, James. *The American Country Club: Its Origins and Development.* New Brunswick, N.J.: Rutgers University Press, 1998.

Bill Olbrich

See also **Social Register.**

COAL is a major source of energy in the United States. It formed as the legacy of trees and plants that grew in primeval swamps and forests. For millions of years, the debris of these jungles accumulated in shallow water or in boggy soil, decayed, and was converted into peat bogs. The mountain-building era subjected these bogs to extreme pressures as well as to the internal heat of the earth. The combination of these factors transformed the peat into coal. Coal has the same chemical composition as diamonds and is sometimes referred to as "black diamonds."

Strip Mining. Surface operations in Pennsylvania, which remains a major source of the nation's coal. PHOTO RESEARCHERS, INC.

The conversion of peat into coal is estimated by geologists to have taken hundreds of thousands of years.

Bituminous coal is the most abundant type of coal in the United States and the one most commonly used for power generation, heating, and industrial purposes. Nearly all eastern bituminous coals have "coking" properties. Coking is a heating process that breaks down coal, leaving the relatively pure carbon needed for metallurgy. Many western bituminous coals are noncoking, or "free burning." Bituminous coals used in the coking process are heated in a sealed oven. After the volatile liquids and gases have been driven off, the coke, a porous, dull-gray mass, remains. The by-products driven off during the carbonization process, consisting of gases, light oils, and tar, have many important uses in the chemical industry.

The only source for anthracite coal, which is a clean-burning coal with little volatile matter, is northeastern PENNSYLVANIA, although history records small deposits in Rhode Island during the early nineteenth century. Anthracite production peaked during 1917, when 100 million tons were produced and nearly 150,000 miners toiled to reach that tonnage. Another peak was reached in 1944 when 64 million tons were produced with a workforce of 78,000 men. After that time, the consumption of anthracite coal declined; by 1973 only 6,000 men were employed in the industry. Similar statistics for the bituminous coal industry record the first peak in production in 1918, when 550 million tons were mined with a labor force of 615,000. The maximum production by the industry occurred in 1947, when 630 million tons were produced with a labor force of 420,000 miners. In 1974 approximately 590 million tons of coal were produced with a labor force of only 125,000 miners.

The coal-producing areas of the United States are divided into six large provinces: the Eastern province, the Interior province, the Gulf province, the Northern Plains province, the Rocky Mountain province, and the Pacific Coast province. Coal mining activity migrated westward from its eighteenth-century beginnings in the Eastern province, and significant production was reported from the Interior province during the 1830s. By the late 1850s the Pacific Coast province was producing significant amounts of coal, as was the Gulf province in the late 1860s. The Rocky Mountain province began producing well into the mid-1870s and the Northern Plains province in the late 1870s.

The Eastern, or Appalachian, field, after its modest beginning as a small mine along the Monongahela River opposite Fort Pitt (now PITTSBURGH, Pennsylvania), in 1760, became the most important source of bituminous coal for the nation. Beginning in western Pennsylvania, it extends southwesterly into Alabama and contains large mining operations in the states of Pennsylvania, Ohio, West Virginia, Kentucky, Tennessee, Virginia, and Alabama. Pennsylvania was for many years the largest producer of coal in the province, but after 1946 it was superseded by West Virginia. The Eastern province was responsible for approximately two-thirds of the total coal produced in the United States in the mid-1970s.

West of the Appalachian field is the Interior province, which is subdivided into eastern and western portions. The eastern portion includes deposits through most of Illinois, western Indiana, and western Kentucky; the western portion covers deposits in Iowa, Missouri, eastern Kansas, Oklahoma, and Arkansas. Two isolated fields included in the Interior province are in Texas and central Michigan.

The Eastern and Interior provinces have always furnished most of the coal produced in the United States and contain the largest reserves of coking coals. The coalfields found in the other provinces contain the largest percentage of reserves on a tonnage basis but consist mainly of subbituminous coals and lignites. With lower-grade coals and locations remote from major consuming industries, they have not been extensively developed, although development is assured in the ever-pressing need for additional energy supplies.

Coal Miners. Despite mechanization of underground operations, miners such as these still perform dangerous, backbreaking work.

Scientists evaluate a region's coal supply by measuring its reserves and resources. Reserves are the amount of coal that is commercially accessible and can be readily mined. Resources are the total amount of coal in a region, whether or not it is accessible. In 2002, the total U.S. estimated recoverable coal reserves was some 274 billion short tons, while U.S. coal production for 2001 was approximately 1.1 billion short tons. The U.S. Geological Survey estimated in 1997 that the identified resources of U.S. coal were some 1,731 billion short tons. With improved technological innovations and increased efficiency in mining methods, these reserves and resources could be greatly extended.

Coal is mined by two principal methods, underground and surface operations, and both practices are widely used in the United States. Coal seams within two hundred feet of the earth's surface are generally more adaptable to surface mining methods, although attention must also be paid to the content and thickness of the overburden (rock and other material) on the coal seam and to the thickness of the seam. Strip mining is often used to mine surface coal. In this method, huge earth-moving machines strip away areas of vegetation, and explosives shatter sedimentary rock to access underlying coal deposits. Area and contour mining methods allow for strip mining of hilly areas, as machines move away landscape and slice large cuts into a hillside to access coal. Giant augers that bore into hillsides and throw out buried coal are also used on rough terrain. In the late 1990s, coal mining companies started using global positioning system (GPS) and satellite technology to track mines and machinery and increase their efficiency.

Mechanization of underground mining operations received its greatest impetus with the introduction of Joy loading machines in the early 1920s. Earlier attempts to introduce machinery to the industry proved unsuccessful except for the first successful undercutting machine, introduced in 1877. The introduction of rubber-tired haulage units in 1936 gave further impetus to mechanization, and during the late 1940s total mechanization of underground operations was becoming a reality. Mechanization of mining operations increased significantly after World War II, with a trend toward larger capacity machinery and the elimination of many laborious manual operations. Improved underground machinery has led to continuous mining. U.S. coal production rose rapidly during the nineteenth century, from an annual production in 1800 of approximately 120,000 tons to approximately 265 million tons by 1900. The average output per man per day exceeded twenty tons, a significant increase over the five-ton average prior to extensive mechanization.

The U.S. coal industry has been subjected to labor unrest, loss of important markets, and most importantly, has exposed workers to tremendous dangers. Underground coal miners were constantly exposed to dangerous gases such as explosive methane and poisonous carbon monoxide. After a mine explosion in the 1800s, miners took to releasing a canary into mine shafts to test for poisonous gases before entering. If the canary did not return, miners improved ventilation systems down the shaft. The coal dust produced in the blasts and hauling was also extremely flammable and harmful to miners' lungs. Prolonged inhalation of coal dusts produces pneumoconiosis, or black lung disease, as well as a number of other problems, such as heart disease, emphysema, and cancer. Mining protests and labor activism in the 1900s brought about much reform in mining conditions.

The environmental impact of recovering coal increased concern over mining methods during the late twentieth century. Strip mining destroys large areas of vegetation and habitat, leaving them exposed to erosion. The waste products of strip mining create acid drainage that combines with oxygen in water and air to create sulfuric acid, polluting water and contaminating soil. Burning coal produces greenhouse gases that trap heat in the earth's atmosphere and lead to GLOBAL WARMING. Sulfur dioxide emissions combine with water and oxygen in air to form ACID RAIN. Since the U.S. CLEAN AIR ACT passed in 1970, and was revised in 1990, industries that burn coal are required to reduce emissions of carbon dioxide and sulfur to safer levels. Coal mining companies are required to submit detailed reports of mining plans to ensure minimal destruction of the environment. In 1986 the U.S. government and private industry began working together through the Clean Coal Technology Program to find cleaner, more efficient methods of mining coal and using its energy.

BIBLIOGRAPHY

Blatz, Perry K. *Democratic Miners: Work and Labor Relations in the Anthracite Coal Industry, 1875–1925.* Albany: State University of New York Press, 1994.

Bowman, John R. *Capitalist Collective Action: Competition, Cooperation, and Conflict in the Coal Industry.* New York: Cambridge University Press, 1989.

Dix, Keith. *What's a Coal Miner to Do?: The Mechanization of Coal Mining.* Pittsburg, Pa.: University of Pittsburg Press, 1988.

Fishback, Price V. *Soft Coal, Hard Choices: The Economic Welfare of Bituminous Coal Miners, 1890–1930.* New York: Oxford University Press, 1992.

Seltzer, Curtis. *Fire in the Hole: Miners and Managers in the American Coal Industry.* Lexington: University Press of Kentucky, 1985.

J. H. Hoffman / H. S.

See also **Air Pollution; Anthracite Strike; Appalachia; Coal Mining and Organized Labor; Conservation; Energy Industry.**

COAL MINING AND ORGANIZED LABOR.

One fourth of all known COAL reserves in the world are located in the United States. Anthracite (hard coal) mining is concentrated in five counties of east central Pennsylvania, and various bituminous coals (soft, volatile coals) are mined in Pennsylvania, Ohio, the Virginias, Indiana, Illinois, Kentucky, Alabama, and, to a lesser extent, Maryland, Missouri, Tennessee, Colorado, Utah, and Alaska.

From the Civil War to 1950, coal was the nation's chief source of fuel. Its decline began after World War I when other fossil fuels began to displace coal. Following World War II, rapid substitution of competing fuels, swift mechanization of underground mining, and massive strip mining accelerated the decline in production and employment. Contributing more than 90 percent of the country's thermal energy in 1880 and 53 percent in 1940, coal furnished barely 23 percent in 1970. Employment in bituminous mines fell from the 1923 peak of 704,000 workers to less than 140,000 in 1970. Anthracite employment fell from its peak of 179,000 in 1914 to fewer than 7,000 in 1970. Obviously these contractions profoundly affected the industry and its workers.

Always dirty and exceedingly dangerous, coal mining has been historically an industry plagued by instabilities of production, consumption, and price. The existence of many dispersed production units, ranging from a host of small marginal mines to the great captive mines (those owned by and producing coal for the steel and railroad companies), have either engendered or threatened cutthroat competition. They also have made private, as well as governmental supervision, inspection, and regulation extremely difficult, although from the industry's earliest days operators and workers alike have generally conceded the necessity of many types of regulation.

Early Unionization and Its Obstacles

Unionization of mine LABOR began in the 1840s. It was variously a response to fraternal impulses among workers, unhealthy and dangerous working conditions, unsatisfac-

Health Hazards. In this 1961 photograph by Larry Rubenstein, coal miners at a rally in Washington, D.C., carry signs such as "Coal dust kills coal miners." © UPI/CORBIS-BETTMANN

tory wages, truck payments (payment in goods), abuses by company towns and privatized police, the introduction of scab labor, blacklisting and yellow dog contracts, and seasonal and chronic unemployment. Unionization was complicated by the presence of thousands of immigrant workers in the pits; by the use of slave and, later, convict labor in mines; by ethnic, cultural, racial, and linguistic barriers among and between foreign and native-born workers and the general public; by the isolation of miners from one another; by their relative immobility; and by dual unionism and organizational mistakes.

Since January 1890, miners have been chiefly represented by the UMWA, an industrial union that was founded by bituminous miners from Pennsylvania, Ohio, Indiana, and Michigan but quickly encompassed anthracite miners also. Creation of the UMWA was preceded by half a century of abortive unionization. Prominent among the early unions were the Bates Union of 1848; the American Miners' Association, formed by Illinois and Missouri miners in 1861; John Siney's famed Workingmens' Benevolent Association, which in the 1870s sustained the Long Strike and battled the Reading Railroad;

the Miners' and Laborers' Benevolent Association of the 1870s, also led by Siney; and the Knights of Labor, which, in company with the National Federation of Miners and Mine Laborers, carried unionism into the 1880s. Of these early unions, nearly all were led by English, Irish, Scottish, Welsh, and occasionally Polish or Hungarian immigrants. Nearly all, contrary to myth, were moderate and conciliatory, favoring arbitration over strikes. Although all of these unions were short-lived, all contributed to educating mine workers about their condition and their rights.

Employers' reactions to mine unionism varied. Sometimes they tried to undermine unions by associating them with subversive or violent movements, as in the anthracite fields in the mid-1870s, when unions were invidiously associated with MOLLY MAGUIRES or, as in the efforts to unionize southern fields in the 1930s and 1940s, when they were associated with communism. Sometimes employers have resorted to armed repression, although evictions, lockouts, and strikebreaking have been more common reactions. On the other hand, employers have often recognized the conservative influences of mine unions and tacitly accepted and often cooperated with them to help stabilize the industry and discipline labor.

Government reactions to mine unionism have also varied. The use of local police, state militias, or federal troops against unions was common in the nineteenth century, becoming rarer after the militia violence against miners killed twenty men, women, and children in 1914 at Ludlow, Colorado. The Wilson administration invoked the aid of the courts to forestall a coal strike in 1919, and injunctions against union activities were frequent in the 1920s.

Rise of the UMWA: Better Conditions for Mine Workers

The UMWA rose to power under two of the most famous and conservative unionists of their generations. John Mitchell led the union through the great coal strike of 1902, winning national notoriety for his 150,000 followers, as well as shorter hours and better wages. He also fended off challenges from rebel movements such as the INDUSTRIAL WORKERS OF THE WORLD (IWW). John L. Lewis led the union from 1920 to 1960. During the first Truman administration, Federal District Judge T. Alan Goldsborough heavily fined both the UNITED MINE WORKERS OF AMERICA (UMWA) and Lewis for noncompliance with federal policy. In the 1920s, Lewis dealt with factional battles among union officials as union membership dwindled from its all-time peak of 425,700 to 150,000. Membership recovered after passage of the National Industrial Recovery Act of 1933, and the UMWA went on to become the driving force behind the creation of the Committee for Industrial Organization (CIO) in 1935 (which in 1938 became the Congress of Industrial Organizations) and to help organize workers in other mass-production industries, such as steel and automobiles.

Miners' Strike. Speakers from the United Mine Workers of America address a crowd in Harlan, Ky., during a 1939 strike by coal miners in that area. © UPI/CORBIS-BETTMANN

Since the 1930s, despite President Franklin D. Roosevelt's legal bouts with the UMWA and his threat to use troops to mine coal during World War II, government has generally moved positively to regulate the coal-mining industry and its labor through the Norris–LaGuardia Act of 1932, the National Industrial Recovery Act of 1933, the Guffey Coal Acts of 1935 and 1940, wage stabilization measures, the TAFT-HARTLEY ACT of 1947, the Federal Coal Mine Health and Safety Act of 1969, and supervision of union elections.

During the last quarter of the twentieth century, coal experienced a resurgence. Rising prices and tightening supplies of oil and natural gas, as well as the failure of nuclear power to fulfill its promise, led to increased use of coal. By the end of the century, coal was furnishing more than 32 percent of the country's thermal energy and generating more than half of the nation's electric power. Employment, on the other hand, continued to decline as operations became more efficient and machines handled more of the work. By 2000, total employment in coal mines had fallen to about 87,500. More than half of these miners were members of the UMWA, and as a result of union wage agreements in the industry, they were among the highest-paid industrial workers in the country. Better

yet, even though mining continued to be a dangerous occupation, the number of injury-producing accidents declined over the last quarter of the century in part as a result of the Coal Mine Health and Safety Act of 1969. Years of union agitation and negotiation vastly improved labor's circumstances in the coal-mining industry in important respects (working conditions, wages, pensions, medical benefits, and other welfare programs) over the conditions prevalent until World War II, despite the diminished importance of the coal industry and the reduced mine payrolls.

BIBLIOGRAPHY

Blatz, Perry K. *Democratic Miners: Work and Labor Relations in the Anthracite Coal Industry, 1875–1925.* Albany: State University of New York Press, 1994.

Corbin, David Alan. *Life, Work, and Rebellion in the Coal Fields: The Southern West Virginia Miners, 1880–1922.* Urbana: University of Illinois Press, 1981.

Dubofsky, Melvyn. *We Shall Be All: A History of the Industrial Workers of the World.* Chicago: Quadrangle Books, 1969.

Fox, Maier Bryan. *United We Stand: The United Mine Workers of America, 1890–1990.* Washington, D.C.: United Mine Workers of America, 1990.

Lewis, Ronald L. *Black Coal Miners in America: Race, Class, and Community Conflict, 1780–1980.* Lexington: University Press of Kentucky, 1987.

Long, Priscilla. *Where the Sun Never Shines: A History of America's Bloody Coal Industry.* New York: Paragon House, 1989.

Montgomery, David. *The Fall of the House of Labor: The Workplace, the State, and American Labor Activism, 1865–1925.* New York: Cambridge University Press, 1987.

C. K. Yearley / c. p.

See also **American Federation of Labor–Congress of Industrial Organizations; Colorado Coal Strikes; Cripple Creek Mining Boom; Cripple Creek Strikes; Injunctions, Labor; Labor Legislation and Administration; Strikes.**

COALITION OF LABOR UNION WOMEN

(CLUW). Over three thousand women from fifty-eight unions formed the Coalition of Labor Union Women in Chicago on 23 March 1974. The coalition was founded by Olga M. Madar, the first woman to be international vice president of the United Auto Workers, and by Addie Wyatt of the United Food and Commercial Workers. Madar served as president of CLUW from 1974 to 1977. The emergence of the CLUW in 1974 was related to three developments—the growing women's movement, employment laws prohibiting discrimination against women, and the growing number of women in the workforce.

CLUW is open only to members of labor unions. Its structure is similar to that of international unions, with policies made at the national level and carried out at the local level. The major objective of the organization is to make unions more responsive to women workers. More specifically, the goals are to organize women workers, to encourage women to participate politically at every level, to work for affirmative action in the workplace, and to increase women's role in their unions. Toward these ends, women are encouraged to become more knowledgeable about laws, labor contracts, and collective bargaining.

CLUW members worked to change the policy of the AFL-CIO on the EQUAL RIGHTS AMENDMENT. Not only did the organization support the amendment, but it also vowed to work for ratification. Other issues that CLUW championed in its early years were full employment, childcare, job safety, and enforcement of equal pay laws.

In 1979, the coalition established the CLUW Center for Education and Research, which provides the knowledge base for advocacy. More recently, CLUW has taken up the cause of domestic violence affecting the workplace. Union stewards are trained to recognize domestic violence and deal with both victims and abusers. CLUW has also lobbied for the reform of Social Security with a view to establishing equity for women workers.

One of the most important results of the formation of CLUW was to give women leadership experience. With this experience, they were able to attain leadership roles in their local unions and bring women's issues to the negotiating table. After founding CLUW, Addie Wyatt went on to become the first woman vice president of the Amalgamated Meat Cutters Union. During the 1980s, many women became leaders in their unions. For example, in 1980, Joyce Miller, CLUW president from 1977 to 1993, became the first woman elected to the Executive Council of the AFL-CIO.

From 1974 on, women joined the workforce in record numbers and by 1999 comprised 46 percent of the total workforce. In the 1990s, women were the majority of new union members. Throughout its existence, CLUW has kept up the drumbeat for organizing the unorganized, and though it cannot claim responsibility for the phenomenal growth in women union members, it did help set the agenda. Presently there are 20,000 members of CLUW.

BIBLIOGRAPHY

Fix, Janet L. "New Face of Labor: Female Workers Make up the Bulk of New Recruits and a Growing Number of the Union's Leaders." *Detroit Free Press,* 24 March 2001.

Kenneally, James J. *Women and American Trade Unions.* Montreal, St. Albans, Vt.: Eden Press Women's Publications, 1981.

Bonnie Ford

See also **Labor; Trade Unions; Women in Public Life, Business, and Professions; Women's Rights Movement.**

COAST AND GEODETIC SURVEY.

The Coast and Geodetic Survey was born in 1807 when Congress, on the initiative of President Thomas Jefferson, passed a law authorizing "a survey to be taken of the coasts of the United States." The Survey, originally called the Coast Survey, was—for the first time in the history of the new nation—"to designate the islands and shoals, with the roads and places of anchorage, within twenty leagues of any part of the shores of the United States. . . ." The Survey, using new scientific methods, would be responsible for producing accurate charts of these features and would also identify other key characteristics of what can roughly be defined as the coastal zones of the United States. As the nation grew, new areas such as Florida, Texas, the Pacific Coast, and Alaska were added to the Survey's growing mission.

Historians agree that the Coast Survey led American science away from the older descriptive methods to the modern methods of statistical analysis and the prediction of future states of natural phenomena based on mathematical modeling. Virtually all branches of science, including the social and biological sciences, have adapted similar methodologies and similar techniques in their quest for scientific truth. (National Oceanic and Atmospheric Administration, "Comments on the Archive of the Coast and Geodetic Survey," 1991).

The survey was placed under the jurisdiction of the Treasury Department but its gestation and evolution were complicated and politicized from the outset. A Swiss immigrant to the United States, the geodesist and mathematician Ferdinand Rudolph Hassler, was selected to head the Survey. He left for Europe in 1811 to secure the necessary scientific books, instruments, and knowledgeable expertise necessary for conducting a massive, complex, and accurate survey of the coastal areas of the United States. None of these necessities was available in America at that time. Hassler remained in Europe until 1815 and it was not until 1816 that Congress appropriated the funds for the survey. Hassler was officially made superintendent of the survey in 1816. However, in 1818 Congress changed the law and specified that only military and naval officers could be employed in the survey, neither of which Hassler was. The instruments and management of the project were turned over to the Navy Department.

In 1832 Congress reactivated the original 1807 legislation placing the Survey in the Treasury Department, and Hassler was again appointed superintendent. The tensions between military and civilian control of the Survey continued. In 1834 the Survey was again transferred to the Department of the Navy, but after repeated protests from Hassler it was once more returned to the jurisdiction of the Treasury Department in 1836. Further efforts to move the Survey to naval jurisdiction continued until 1882.

After the death of Hassler in 1843, Alexander Dallas Bache, a great-grandson of Benjamin Franklin, took over as superintendent of the Coast Survey. Bache built on the strong foundation that had been created, and is credited with developing the Survey into the first real scientific organization in the federal government. He became a leader in the American Association for the Advancement of Science and was a founding member of the National Academy of Sciences.

The scope and flair of the Survey is captured in the following description taken from an analysis of its annual reports:

> The Survey was continental in scope, tying together east and west coasts by an invisible transcontinental network of triangles while leading American commerce by means of precise nautical charting surveys into the ports of our Atlantic, Gulf, and Pacific shores. Storms, mountains, dust, mud, deserts, wild beasts, heat and cold; all were the companions of the Coast Surveyors. They engaged in a great physical adventure that is little known and little understood. Beyond the romance of the Coast Surveyors, there was an enduring intellectual adventure as the field men and the office force of the Coast Survey engaged in a fascinating quest for the ultimate limits of accuracy of scientific measurement. They were seekers of scientific "truth." No effort was too great or hardship too onerous to overcome in this quest. The perseverance and fortitude of the field men was matched by the office force of mathematicians, physicists, geodesists, astronomers, instrument-makers, draftsmen, engravers, and pressmen. These men and women (the Coast Sur-

vey hired women professionals as early as 1845) helped push back the limits of astronomic measures, designed new and more accurate observational instruments for sea and land surveying, developed new techniques for the mathematical analysis of the mountains of data obtained by the field parties, and further refined techniques of error analysis and mitigation. (National Oceanic and Atmospheric Administration, "Comments on the Archive of the Coast and Geodetic Survey," 1991)

In 1878 the program was officially renamed the Coast and Geodetic Survey. In 1903 it was transferred to the Department of Commerce and Labor and it remained in Commerce after Labor became a separate cabinet department in 1913. In 1920 the title "superintendent" was changed to "director."

In 1965 the Coast and Geodetic Survey became part of the Environmental Science Services Administration (ESSA), which also incorporated the Weather Bureau and the National Bureau of Standards' Central Radio Propagation Laboratory. When the National Oceanic and Atmospheric Administration (NOAA) was created in 1970 as a new entity within the Department of Commerce, ESSA and thus the Survey became part of NOAA.

The Survey is considered to have been one of the major birthplaces of modern American science, including many disciplines not generally associated with geodesy and hydrology. Its creation is a cornerstone of the rapid growth of science and technology and of the development of natural resources for commercial use in the United States.

BIBLIOGRAPHY

Dracup, Joseph F. *The United States Horizontal Control Network, 1816–1976.* Rockville, Md.: National Oceanic and Atmospheric Administration, n.d.

National Oceanic and Atmospheric Administration. "Comments on the Archive of the Coast and Geodetic Survey." Available at http://www.lib.noaa.gov.

National Oceanic and Atmospheric Administration. "Functions of the Coast Survey and the Coast and Geodetic Survey." Updated February 17, 2000. Available at http://www.lib.noaa.gov.

U.S. Department Commerce. *U.S. Coast and Geodetic Survey: 150 Years of Service, 1807–1957.* Washington, D.C., 1957.

Wright, A. Joseph, and Elliot B. Roberts. *The Coast and Geodetic Survey, 1807–1957: 150 Years of History.* Washington, D.C.: U.S. Department of Commerce, 1957.

Steffen W. Schmidt

See also **Geological Survey, U.S.**

COAST GUARD, U.S., one of the armed forces of the United States and the principal federal agency for marine safety and maritime law enforcement. It operates under the Department of Transportation except when serving as a part of the navy.

U.S. Coast Guard. A recruiting poster from World War II. NATIONAL ARCHIVES AND RECORDS ADMINISTRATION

Congress established the Coast Guard's parent service, the U.S. Revenue Marine (later the Revenue Cutter Service), on 4 August 1790, on the advice of Alexander Hamilton, then the secretary of the treasury. The act authorized the secretary of the treasury to construct and operate ten small cutters to ensure the collection of customs duties on imports imposed by the Revenue Act of 1789. Hamilton insisted that revenue-cutter officers be given military rank to "attach them to their duty by a nicer sense of honor." Administrative responsibility initially resided with the Treasury Department.

The cutter service soon became better known for its expertise and daring in aiding ships and seamen in distress than for safeguarding the revenue. At the time of the Quasi War with France, there being no other U.S. naval force, Congress on 1 July 1797 authorized the president to allow cutters "to defend the seacoast and to repel any hostility to their vessels and commerce"—in effect, to oppose the whole French fleet and the French privateersmen then threatening U.S. trade. The service soon distinguished itself as a fighting force. After the establishment of the navy (1798), Congress decreed that the cutters "cooperate with the Navy . . . whenever the President shall so direct," a mandate subsequently confirmed and broadened by other acts. Since then, except for the brief imbroglio with Tripoli (1801–1805), cutters and cutter men have sailed with the navy against all armed enemies of the United States.

Other areas of law enforcement and marine safety led Congress to establish several other, essentially unifunctional agencies. The first, the Lighthouse Service, launched by an act of 7 August 1789, tacitly acknowledged federal responsibility for maintaining lighthouses, buoys, and related navigation aids. In 1832, explosions destroyed 14 percent of all American STEAMBOATS, prompting Congress, by an act of 7 July 1838, to create the Steamboat Inspection Service (later the Bureau of Marine Inspection and Navigation) to regulate the construction, equipping, manning, and inspection of vessels in the interest of safety. Meanwhile, such hazardous areas as Cape Cod and North Carolina's Outer Banks became veritable graveyards for ships and seamen of all nations. Private lifesaving efforts, however commendable, were unequal to the task presented by hundreds of disasters along thousands of miles of coast. Eventually recognizing the need, Congress, by an act of 3 March 1847, authorized the secretary of the treasury to equip lighthouses for rendering aid to shipwrecked persons. Subsequent legislation soon formally established the Life-Saving Service, a chain of lifeboats stationed along the coasts.

Successive efforts to rationalize the federal structure and to centralize responsibilities along functional lines led eventually to the amalgamation of all these agencies around the Revenue Cutter Service as nucleus. The first merger (28 January 1915) combined the Life-Saving Service with the Revenue Cutter Service to form the U.S. Coast Guard, thus centralizing federal marine search-and-rescue activities into one agency. In 1939, President Franklin D. Roosevelt transferred the Lighthouse Service to the Coast Guard, broadening the latter's direct concern with the prevention of disasters. An act of 22 June 1936 clarified the Coast Guard's general responsibility for the enforcement of all applicable U.S. laws on the high seas and waters of the United States, and in 1942 the transfer to the

Coast Guard of the Bureau of Marine Inspection and Navigation's marine safety duties gave the Coast Guard specific responsibility for the enforcement of navigation laws. On 1 April 1967, in a sweeping reorganization, Congress relocated the Coast Guard itself from the Treasury Department to the Department of Transportation, newly organized to exercise federal responsibilities in all transportation fields.

During American military operations in Vietnam, Coast Guard cutters and patrol craft served with the U.S. Navy's Seventh Fleet, providing gunfire support aimed at sea and shore targets, interdicting enemy replenishment by sea, and engaging in a variety of civic actions. Other Coast Guard units engaged for the most part in normal peacetime duties.

The modern Coast Guard performs a multitude of varied duties, including providing search-and-rescue operations for vessels in distress; maintaining "ocean stations" along most-traveled routes to furnish meteorological data to the National Weather Service, collect oceanographic data, and provide navigation aids; maintaining military readiness in time of war or when the president directs; enforcing U.S. laws on the high seas and waters under U.S. jurisdiction; enforcing U.S. laws dealing with the safety of small boats and their occupants; providing lighthouses, buoys, and other aids to safe navigation; providing icebreaking services in support of American commerce and the national defense; ensuring the security of U.S. ports and ships therein; conducting surveys, research, and special air-sea patrols in support of national oceanographic policies; and maintaining a program of research and development for improving Coast Guard capabilities and effectiveness.

The Coast Guard is headed by a commandant, an officer with the rank of admiral, whose headquarters are in Washington, D.C. Major field commands include the Atlantic and Pacific areas, with five districts each, and two inland districts. The U.S. Coast Guard Academy, at New London, Connecticut, offers a four-year academic and professional course to cadets selected by nationwide competitive examinations. On graduation a cadet is awarded a B.S. degree (engineering) and a commission as ensign in the career-officer corps. Intermediate ranks ranging up to admiral correspond to those of the navy.

BIBLIOGRAPHY

Coast Guard, United States. *Record of Movements: Vessels of the United States Coast Guard, 1790–December 31, 1933.* Washington, D.C.: Department of Transportation, 1989. The original edition was published in 1935.

Evans, Stephen H. *The United States Coast Guard, 1790–1915: A Definitive History.* Annapolis, Md.: United States Naval Institute, 1949.

Fighting Ships of the U.S. Coast Guard in World War II. Canoga Park, Calif.: Challenge Publications, 1986.

Kaplan, H. R., and James F. Hunt. *This Is the Coast Guard.* Cambridge, Md.: Cornell Maritime Press, 1972.

Stephen H. Evans / c. w.

See also **Hamilton's Economic Policies; Oceanographic Survey; Transportation, Department of; Weather Service, National.**

COASTING TRADE. From the beginning of British settlement in North America until after 1850, shipping along the coasts was the principal means of transportation and communication between sections of the new country. In the colonial period it served to distribute European imports as well as to exchange local products. Colonial coasting trade was reserved to British and American vessels by the Navigation Acts of 1651 and 1660. The policy was continued after the formation of the federal Union. A prohibitive tax was placed on foreign built and foreign owned ships in 1789, followed by their complete exclusion from coastwise competition under the NAVIGATION ACT OF 1817.

From 1800 until the Civil War, the SCHOONER was the typical American coasting vessel. After 1865 steamers and barges towed by steamers were used increasingly, until by 1920 the sailing vessel had largely disappeared.

With the growing diversity of sectional production and the expansion of intersectional trade, coastwise shipping grew from 68,607 tons in 1789 to 516,979 tons in 1830 to 2.6 million tons in 1860. Manufactured goods of the Northeast were exchanged for the cotton and tobacco of the South, while the surplus agricultural products of the Mississippi Valley came to the Atlantic coast by way of New Orleans, LOUISIANA. Following the completion of railroad trunk lines along the coast and across the Appalachian Mountains after 1850, passengers, merchandise, and commodities of value traveled increasingly by rail, while such bulk cargoes as coal, lumber, ice, iron, steel, and oil were shipped by sea. After 1865 the tonnage engaged in coastal shipping continued to increase (4.3 million tons in 1900, 10 million tons in 1935) but not with the rapidity of rail and motor transportation. The late 1800s witnessed bitter struggles between ship and railroad operators, which were characterized by rate wars, followed by agreements and growing control of coast-to-coast trade by the railroads.

BIBLIOGRAPHY

Shepherd, James F., and Gary M. Walton. *Shipping, Maritime Trade, and the Economic Development of Colonial North America.* Cambridge, U.K.: University of Cambridge Press, 1972.

John Haskell Kemble / A. R.

See also **Clipper Ships; Colonial Commerce; *Gibbons v. Ogden*; Industries, Colonial; Pacific Fur Company.**

COASTWISE STEAMSHIP LINES. American steamers made coastwise voyages as early as 1809, but the first regular lines were placed in operation in the sheltered waters of Long Island Sound and between Boston and the coast of Maine about 1825. Local services were established in the Gulf of Mexico by Charles Morgan in 1835, while the United States Mail Steamship Company opened a regular line from New York to Charleston, South Carolina; Havana, Cuba; New Orleans, Louisiana; and the Isthmus of Panama in 1848. In 1849 the Pacific Mail Steamship Company pioneered the route from Panama to San Francisco and Oregon. Steamships played a crucial role in the CIVIL WAR, helping the Union to blockade Southern ports and to keep its own supply lines open.

Prior to 1860 the railroads served chiefly as feeders for the steamship lines, but after the Civil War they offered serious competition. Although the coastwise lines remained active, they were forced to consolidate (Eastern Steamship Company, Atlantic, Gulf and West Indies Steamship Company), and in some cases the railroads gained control of the steamships, as when the Southern Pacific Railroad acquired the Morgan line (1885). Increasing competition from railroads, motor buses, and trucks, mounting operating costs, and labor difficulties resulted in the withdrawal of a considerable part of the coastwise steamship service from the Atlantic and virtually all from the Pacific Coast south of Alaska by 1937.

BIBLIOGRAPHY

Dayton, Fred Erving. *Steamboat Days*. New York: Tudor, 1939.

Pedraja, René De La. *The Rise and Decline of U.S. Merchant Shipping in the Twentieth Century*. New York: Twayne, 1992.

Taylor, William Leonhard. *A Productive Monopoly; The Effect of Railroad Control on New England Coastal Steamship Lines, 1870–1916*. Providence, R.I.: Brown University Press, 1970.

John Haskell Kemble / T. D.

See also **Great Lakes Steamships; Steamboats; Transportation and Travel.**

COCA-COLA. The soft drink Coca-Cola was invented by the Atlanta pharmacist and patent medicine maker John S. Pemberton in 1886. Its name, suggested by an employee, Frank Robinson, derived from its two principal drug ingredients, the Peruvian coca leaf (cocaine) and the West African kola nut (caffeine). Coca-Cola was originally sold as a "nerve tonic" to cure the then-popular supposed disease of neurasthenia, and its promoters claimed it treated headaches and hangovers as well. The sugary syrup, mixed with carbonated water, was also sold as a "delicious and refreshing" soda fountain drink.

Pemberton died penniless in 1888, but a fellow Atlanta pharmacist, Asa G. Candler, with the assistance of Frank Robinson, made Coca-Cola a national soda fountain success by the end of the century, gradually abandoning patent medicine claims. The current Coca-Cola

Coca-Cola. An early advertisement, claiming that the beverage appeals to "All Classes, Ages and Sexes" and puts "vim and go into tired brains and bodies." © BETTMANN/CORBIS

Company was incorporated in 1892. Candler saw no future in bottling the drink and gave the bottling rights to Benjamin Thomas and Joseph Whitehead, two Chattanooga lawyers, in 1899. Thomas and Whitehead parlayed the contract into a successful bottling franchise system that truly democratized the drink. In 1903, under considerable social pressure, Candler removed the cocaine from Coca-Cola. In 1919 his children sold the business for $25 million to a syndicate of bankers headed by the Atlanta businessman Ernest Woodruff. Plagued by high sugar prices, Woodruff unsuccessfully attempted to abrogate the perpetual bottling contract. In 1923, his son Robert W. Woodruff took over the presidency of the troubled company and made Coca-Cola, popularly called "Coke," a symbol of the American way of life through ubiquitous, effective advertising. The patriarchal Woodruff passed on every major company decision until his death in 1985 at the age of ninety-five.

During World War II, Coca-Cola was deemed an essential morale booster for American troops overseas, and Coke employees established bottling plants behind the lines, thus positioning the company for swift global expansion in the postwar world. In France and elsewhere during the early 1950s, communists spread rumors that Coke destroyed health and virility, but efforts to halt the soft drink's international expansion failed.

Beginning in the depression era, Pepsi-Cola arose as a fierce competitor, offering more drink for a nickel. Coke finally matched Pepsi ounce for ounce and offered Sprite, Fanta, and other drinks from the 1960s onward. In the 1980s and 1990s, the aggressive chief executive officer Roberto Goizueta revolutionized the company, giving the revered Coke name to Diet Coke and in 1985 changing the flavor of Coca-Cola in the New Coke disaster. Ironically, this marketing blunder reinvigorated sales of Classic Coca-Cola when the company brought it back after a three-month hiatus. Following brief forays into diversification, notably in Columbia Pictures, Goizueta refocused the company solely on soft drinks. Under his leadership the share price shot up. Following Goizueta's death in 1997, the company entered a difficult period during which its stock declined.

Although the "cola wars" continued into the twenty-first century, Coca-Cola remained the world's preeminent soft drink. The world's most widely distributed product at that time, "Coca-Cola" was reputedly the second best-known word on Earth after "okay." The history of Coca-Cola provides a case study in modern image marketing, in which a fizzy soft drink, mostly sugar water, assumed massive symbolic weight for both critics and advocates.

BIBLIOGRAPHY

Allen, Frederick. *Secret Formula*. New York: HarperBusiness, 1994.

Greising, David. *I'd Like the World to Buy a Coke: The Life and Leadership of Roberto Goizueta*. New York: Wiley, 1998.

Oliver, Thomas. *The Real Coke, the Real Story*. New York: Random House, 1986.

Pendergrast, Mark. *For God, Country, and Coca-Cola*. 2d ed. New York: Basic Books, 2000.

Mark Pendergrast

See also **Soda Fountains; Soft Drink Industry.**

COD FISHERIES of North America lie off the coasts of New England, Newfoundland, and Labrador. The earliest explorers to the northeastern coast of North America noted the abundant presence of the cod. John Cabot spoke of it, and in 1602 Bartholomew Gosnold gave CAPE COD its name because of the great quantity of the fish in its waters. The earliest fishermen came from Spain and France, attracted by the lure of the bank fisheries off the Newfoundland coast. In the sixteenth century, Englishmen made frequent fishing voyages to the Grand Banks.

Captain John Smith's successful fishing venture in 1614 off the New England coast helped to establish the popularity of that region. Within a few years, colonists had established fishing colonies in Massachusetts (Cape Ann) and Maine (Monhegan Island and Pemaquid). Massachusetts Bay colonists in particular engaged in cod fishing from an early date. Within less than forty years after its settlement, Boston was a busy trade center for fish.

England often exasperated the colonies by failing in treaties with France to accord a proper interest to the fisheries. In treaties from that of St. Germain (1632) to Ryswick (1697), the French fisheries benefited. British colonists were particularly bitter in 1697 when England returned Acadia to France. The Treaty of Utrecht (1713) awarded Newfoundland and Nova Scotia (Acadia) to England, but France retained the island of Cape Breton and some fishing privileges.

The final defeat of France in the great colonial struggle with England, concluded by the Treaty of Paris (1763), left France with only the fishing islands of St. Pierre and Miquelon and restricted fishing privileges. The New England cod fisheries expected to benefit by the triumph, but new discontent appeared when the British Parliament passed the Sugar Act of 1764. Its enforcement threatened to ruin the profitable trade with the French West Indies that depended on the exchange of the poorer grade of cod for sugar and molasses, which the North Americans then manufactured into rum. Like the Molasses Act of 1733 this proved ineffective, largely because of smuggling.

Cod fishing suffered severely during the American Revolution, but when the United States secured extensive fishing privileges from England in the preliminary Treaty of Paris (1782), expectations for revival soared. The contraction of the market in Catholic Europe and the immediate exclusion of Americans from trade with the British West Indies, however, delayed recovery. Fishing bounties began to be paid in 1789 but did not become a real aid to the fisheries until considerably later.

The Peace of Ghent (1814) did not provide for the continuance of the fishing privileges that Americans had been enjoying in British colonial waters. The Convention of 1818 attempted to settle the fisheries question, but it continued to be a sore spot in British-American relations until the award of the Hague Tribunal of Arbitration in 1910.

After the War of 1812 the cod and mackerel fisheries entered a long period of expansion. The European market for salt codfish declined, but the expanding domestic market more than offset this loss. The Erie Canal provided access to the Mississippi Valley, and introduction of the use of ice for preservation opened new domestic markets for fresh fish. Tariffs from 1816 to 1846 on imported fish greatly helped New England fishermen to control the home market.

After the Civil War the cod lost its distinction as the principal food fish of the American seas. From about 1885 the cod fisheries began to decline, not only in relation to other American fisheries but also in the amount of tonnage employed. Such cities as Boston and Gloucester, Massachusetts, and Portland, Maine, continued to serve as centers for an industry whose importance in American history is symbolized by Massachusetts' use of the "sacred codfish" as its emblem. By the end of the twentieth century, however, overfishing, international competition, and declining demand had taken a toll on the American cod industry, whose annual landings averaged 4,100 tons between 1981 and 1997.

BIBLIOGRAPHY

Judah, Charles Burnet, Jr. *The North American Fisheries and British Policy to 1713.* Urbana: University of Illinois, 1933.

Kurlansky, Mark. *Cod: A Biography of the Fish That Changed the World.* New York: Walker, 1997.

Morison, Samuel Eliot. *Maritime History of Massachusetts, 1783–1860.* Boston: Houghton Mifflin, 1941.

F. Hardee Allen / c. w.

See also **Ghent, Treaty of; Paris, Treaty of (1783); Sugar Acts; West Indies, British and French.**

CODE, U.S. The *United States Code* is a large, multivolume consolidation and codification of the general and permanent laws of the United States. The volumes are arranged into fifty titles according to subject matter. The *Code* does not contain regulations issued by federal agencies, decisions of the federal courts, laws enacted by state or local governments, or treaties.

Before 1926 federal statutory law was extremely difficult to research. Federal statutes enacted before 1875 appeared in one volume, *Revised Statutes of the United States* (1875), but this volume contained inaccuracies. Laws adopted after 1875 were published periodically in chronological order in volumes of the *United States Statutes at Large* without subject matter organization or a cumulative index. In 1926, Congress approved the publication of the *Code*, bringing together all valid federal laws in one publication arranged by subject matter.

After publication, however, the *Code* was never submitted to Congress in its entirety to be enacted into positive law. A statute's text appearing in the *Code* therefore was considered only prima facie evidence of the law. The authoritative source for the text of federal laws was still the *United States Statutes at Large.* Congress responded to this peculiarity by creating the Office of the Law Revision Counsel, charged with revising the *Code* and with submitting individual titles to Congress for enactment into positive law. By the beginning of the twenty-first century, less than half of the titles had been revised and enacted into law. The text of titles enacted into positive law is legal evidence of the law contained in those titles; other titles of the *Code* remain as prima facie evidence only.

Each title of the *Code* is divided into chapters that in turn are divided into sections. Citations to the *Code* indicate the title and section numbers and the year of publication, for example, 42 U.S.C. § 1983 (1996). The *Code* is published anew every six years, and cumulative supplements are issued during the intervening years.

BIBLIOGRAPHY

Cohen, Morris, Robert C. Berring, and Kent C. Olson. *How to Find the Law.* St. Paul, Minn.: West, 1989.

Jacobstein, J. Myron, Roy M. Mersky, and Donald J. Dunn. *Fundamentals of Legal Research.* 7th ed. New York: Foundation Press, 1998.

U.S. House of Representatives, Office of the Law Revision Counsel. http://uscode.house.gov/uscode.htm.

Kent Greenfield

See also **Congress, United States.**

CODE BREAKING. *See* **Cryptology.**

CODE NAPOLÉON. Among the most important postrevolutionary reforms in France was the unification and simplification of the French laws, prepared under Napoleon Bonaparte's direction and promulgated in 1804 as the French civil code, commonly called the Code Napoléon. It served as the model for the digest of the civil laws of Orleans Territory, promulgated in 1808 and commonly called the Old Louisiana Code, which, revised and amended in 1825, 1870, and 1974 as the civil code of LOUISIANA, remains today the basic law of the state of Louisiana. Louisiana is unique among the states in that its legal system is based on Roman civil law, not common law.

BIBLIOGRAPHY

Drago, George. *Jefferson's Louisiana: Politics and the Clash of Legal Traditions.* Cambridge, Mass.: Harvard University Press, 1975.

Haas, Edward F., ed. *Louisiana's Legal Heritage.* Pensacola, Fla.: Perdido Bay Press, 1983.

Walter Prichard / t. m.

See also **Common Law; Orleans, Territory of; State Constitutions.**

CODE NOIR, also known as Black Code, is the name commonly applied to the Edict Concerning the Negro Slaves in Louisiana, issued by Louis XV in March 1724, and promulgated in the colony by the colonial governor, Jean Baptiste Le Moyne, Sieur de Bienville, on 10 September 1724. A number of slaves had been brought to the colony during the administrations of Antoine Crozat and John Law, and a definition of their legal status had become desirable. The Code Noir, consisting of fifty-four articles, fixed the legal status of slaves and imposed certain specific obligations and prohibitions upon their masters. It prescribed in detail regulations concerning holidays, marriage, religious instruction, burial, clothing and subsistence, punishment, and manumission of slaves. It also defined the legal position and proper conduct of freed or free blacks in the colony. Article I of the code, rather curiously, decreed expulsion of Jews from the colony. Article III prohibited the exercise of any religious creed other than Roman Catholicism and Article IV decreed confiscation of slaves placed under the direction or supervision of any person not a Catholic. The essential provisions of the code remained in force in Louisiana until 1803, and many of them were embodied in later American Black Codes. By the late antebellum period "black codes" governed slave life throughout the southern states. Although the codes varied somewhat from state to state, all granted wide powers to slave owners. The black codes ceased functioning only with the abolition of SLAVERY in 1865.

BIBLIOGRAPHY

Berlin, Ira. *Many Thousands Gone: The First Two Centuries of Slavery in North America.* Cambridge, Mass.: Harvard University Press, 1998.

Johnson, Walter. *Soul by Soul: Life Inside the Antebellum Slave Market.* Cambridge, Mass.: Harvard University Press, 1999.

Wilson, Theodore B. *The Black Codes of the South.* Tuscaloosa: University of Alabama Press, 1965.

Walter Prichard/A. G.

See also **Black Laws; Code Napoléon; Colonial Assemblies; Mason-Dixon Line.**

CODES OF FAIR COMPETITION. Passed amidst spiraling deflation and unemployment, the National Industrial Recovery Act of 16 June 1933 set sweeping guidelines—including production restrictions, minimum wages, and working conditions—to limit competition and foster a spirit of teamwork among industry rivals. Industry representatives helped draft the standards, which were enforced by the NATIONAL RECOVERY ADMINISTRATION (NRA). In exchange for their cooperation, compliant corporations received exemption from antitrust prosecution. Some trade associations used the "fair competition" codes to restrict legitimate competition, however, and after repeated legal challenges, the Supreme Court declared the NRA unconstitutional in 1935.

BIBLIOGRAPHY

Brand, Donald R. *Corporatism and the Rule of Law.* Ithaca, N.Y.: Cornell University Press, 1988.

Hawley, Ellis W. *The New Deal and the Problem of Monopoly.* Princeton, N.J.: Princeton University Press, 1966.

Romasco, Albert U. *The Politics of Recovery.* New York: Oxford University Press, 1983.

Myron W. Watkins/A. R.

See also **Antitrust Laws; Government Regulation of Business.**

COEDUCATION, the practice of educating male and female students in the same institution, is the dominant mode at all levels of EDUCATION in the United States. The custom began in the colonial period, when New En-

gland colonies legally obligated parents to teach reading and writing to boys and at least reading to girls. While much of this education took place in the home, many towns also funded primary schools. Elsewhere, subscription schools were open to male and female students whose parents contributed to the schools' operating costs. Female education expanded after the American Revolution, when the ideology of republican womanhood supported elite women's arguments that educated wives and mothers were essential to an enlightened citizenry. By the early nineteenth century, a few chartered academies admitted girls on an equal basis with boys; others allowed girls restricted use of their facilities. Although coeducational secondary schools had appeared by the 1840s, people generally maintained that girls (as well as most boys) required no education beyond elementary school. Paradoxically, rising female attendance necessitated more elementary school teachers, which eventually opened up educational opportunities for women.

Oberlin College (founded in Ohio, 1833) provided the first model of coeducational college education. Other small religious colleges adopted coeducation for financial reasons. In 1855 the University of Iowa became the first public institution to establish coeducation, followed by state universities in Wisconsin (1865), Kansas (1869), and Minnesota (1869). Both private and public schools frequently denied women full use of facilities or unrestricted attendance in classes. Several prestigious universities resisted coeducation, opting instead for coordinate colleges like Harvard and Radcliffe. Most of these institutions adopted full coeducation by the mid-1970s. In the 1990s, women seeking admission to The Citadel and Virginia Military Institute, the only remaining public men's colleges, forced the courts to consider whether excluding women from universities promotes harmful and archaic stereotypes about men and women. Conversely, some single-sex colleges see coeducation as restricting freedom of choice and threatening their existence.

Although coeducation prevailed in the early 2000s, some asserted that it has had mixed results for precollegiate boys and girls. By the early 1990s, the AMERICAN ASSOCIATION OF UNIVERSITY WOMEN reported that girls did not receive the same quality or quantity of education as boys because male students demanded more disciplinary attention from their teachers. By 1994 some school districts had established single-sex math and science classes for girls to improve their performance on standardized tests. Studies in the late 1990s found that boys, whose emotional development often lags behind that of girls, can also benefit from a single-sex environment.

BIBLIOGRAPHY

Howe, Florence. *Myths of Coeducation: Selected Essays, 1964–1983.* Bloomington: Indiana University Press, 1984.

Kaestle, Carl F. *Pillars of the Republic: Common Schools and American Society, 1780–1860.* New York: Hill and Wang, 1983.

Solomon, Barbara Miller. *In the Company of Educated Women: A History of Women and Higher Education in America.* New Haven, Conn.: Yale University Press, 1985.

Tyack, David, and Elisabeth Hansot. *Learning Together: A History of Coeducation in American Schools.* New Haven, Conn.: Yale University Press, 1990.

Myrna W. Merron/s. b.

See also **Education, Higher: Colleges and Universities; Education, Higher: Women's Colleges; Schools, Single-Sex; Women's Educational Equity Act; Women's Studies.**

COERCIVE ACTS, also known as the Intolerable Acts, were a series of four measures passed by the British Parliament in 1774, partly to retaliate for such incidents as the Boston Tea Party but also to implement a more vigorous policy in the American colonies. The Boston Port Act, enacted in response to the Tea Party, closed the harbor to all shipping until the town had compensated the East India Company for the destruction of its tea and assured the king of its future loyalty. The Massachusetts Government Act deprived Massachusetts of its charter and the right to choose its own magistrates. The Act for the Impartial Administration of Justice provided that English colonial officials indicted for murder in Massachusetts should be tried in England. Finally, the Quartering Act allowed the housing of troops in any town in Massachusetts.

BIBLIOGRAPHY

Middlekauff, Robert. *The Glorious Cause: The American Revolution, 1763–1789.* New York: Oxford University Press, 1982.

Thomas, Peter D. G. *Tea Party to Independence: The Third Phase of the American Revolution, 1773–1776.* New York: Oxford University Press, 1991.

Frank J. Klingberg/s. b.

See also **Colonial Policy, British; Parliament, British; Revolution, American: Political History; Taxation.**

COEUR D'ALENE RIOTS, in the lead and silver mines of northern Idaho, erupted throughout the 1890s, beginning in 1892. Relations between mine owners and mine workers had become increasingly hostile, due to mine owners' indifference to the extreme danger and poor working conditions the miners endured. In 1892, miners struck for union recognition. The mine owners responded with armed guards and nonunion workers, and to quell the resulting melee, Governor Frank Steunenberg sent in state and federal troops. The defeat of the strikers marked a larger pattern in America: political power was shifting from the local to the state level, and corporations increasingly drew on state troops to crush labor unrest.

BIBLIOGRAPHY

Hart, Patricia, and Ivar Nelson. *Mining Town: The Photographic Record of T.N. Barnard and Nellie Stockbridge from the Coeur d'Alenes.* Seattle: University of Washington Press, 1984.

Lukas, Anthony J. *Big Trouble: Murder in a Small Western Town Sets Off a Struggle for the Soul of America.* New York: Simon and Schuster, 1997.

Stoll, William T. *Silver Strike: The True Story of Silver Mining in the Coeur d'Alenes.* Moscow: University of Idaho Press, 1991.

Cornelius James Brosnan
Dorothea Browder

See also **Injunctions, Labor; Lead Industry; Mining Towns; Silver Prospecting and Mining; Strikes; Western Federation of Miners.**

COFFEE. The coffee plant attracted human interest and consumption as early as 800 A.D. in the Kaffe region of Ethiopia. By the fifteenth century the plant was cultivated in Yemen and a beverage made from its beans was sold in Arabian coffeehouses. Constantinople's first coffeehouses had opened by the middle of the sixteenth century. The beverage spread eastward to India and via Mocha on the Arabian Peninsula back to Holland. Venice had a coffeehouse by 1645. The students of Oxford soon follow suit, discovering by 1650 the academic advantages of a beverage that sharpens the wits. Before 1800 much of Europe had coffeehouses and also had witnessed governmental attempts to close them as sources of sedition. Those same governments soon taxed rather than prohibited coffee consumption. Coffeehouses became social and business centers where merchants and shippers gathered to exchange information and make deals. By the late 1660s coffee consumption had spread to North America; New York City's first coffeehouse, The King's Arms, opened in 1696.

Arab coffee cultivators and merchants attempted to monopolize the trade by preventing export of the coffee plant, but by the seventeenth century, the Dutch had acquired coffee plants that they planted in Ceylon. Other Europeans planted coffee in East Asian and, later, Latin American colonies. In the early twenty-first century, milder arabica beans are grown primarily in Latin American and the Caribbean, while more bitter robusta beans come primarily from African and Asian producing countries. Green coffee beans are among the highest-value commodities legally traded in today's world. The Green Coffee Association of New York City formed in 1923 to encourage standard contracts. Much of the product is traded on the Coffee, Sugar, and Cocoa Exchange, now a subset of the New York Board of Trade, and on the London, Tokyo and Brazilian commodity exchanges.

New processing techniques eased preparation of the beverage in the field during the U.S. Civil War. Military demand again hastened easy preparation when Maxwell Coffee developed an instant beverage in 1941, building on Swiss producer Nestle's Nescafe, which that the company had created for Brazilian growers in 1938. In modern production, the exported green beans are precisely roasted and blended in importing countries to produce the flavor that consumers desire; because oxidation causes bitter flavor, the processed coffee must be used quickly or packaged carefully.

Price inelasticity of demand for coffee leads to sharp price fluctuations. To counter these fluctuations, producing countries established the International Coffee Association in 1963 primarily to control price through export quotas; price stability, however, has not been achieved.

With economies of scale in production and distribution, a few firms and their brands dominated U.S. and world production of roasted coffee in the second half of the twentieth century. These companies have distributed their brands primarily through grocery stores. Per capita consumption has fallen in traditional coffee markets, but is rising in such nontraditional markets as Japan and, more recently, China and South Korea; there, as in Great Britain, instant coffee is making inroads into the tea market. In the 1970s specialty coffee producers began to challenge the preeminence in traditional markets of the multinationals and have constituted the most rapidly growing segment of the coffee market in mature economies. These specialty forms of coffee, sold primarily through coffeehouses and gourmet shops, are relatively expensive, differentiated blends processed on a smaller scale. This development echoes the early days of coffee consumption; an increasingly affluent middle class is willing to spend on luxury beverages consumed in inviting shops.

BIBLIOGRAPHY

Commodity Research Bureau. *The CRB Commodity Yearbook 2001.* New York: Wiley, 2001.

Dicum, Gregory, and Nina Luttinger. *The Coffee Book: Anatomy of an Industry from the Crop to the Last Drop.* New York: New Press, 1999.

Paige, Jeffry, *Coffee and Power: Revolution and the Rise of Democracy in Central America.* Cambridge, Mass.: Harvard University Press, 1997.

Ann Harper Fender

COHENS V. VIRGINIA,

6 Wheaton 264 (1821). The Cohens had been convicted of selling lottery tickets in Virginia, a practice prohibited by state law but allowed under federal law in the District of Columbia. On appeal to the United States Supreme Court, the state asserted its legal sovereignty and denied the federal court's right of review. Invoking the doctrine of national supremacy, Chief Justice John Marshall upheld its appellate jurisdiction over state court judgments in cases where the conviction violated some right under the Constitution or federal laws. This was one of Chief Justice John Marshall's most influential opinions, establishing national authority over the states.

BIBLIOGRAPHY

Hall, Kermit L. *The Supreme Court and Judicial Review in American History.* Washington, D.C.: American Historical Association, 1985.

Luce, W. Ray. *Cohens v. Virginia (1821): The Supreme Court and State Rights.* New York: Garland, 1990.

Charles Fairman / A. R.

See also **Constitution of the United States; Judicial Review; Judiciary; Lotteries;** *McCulloch v. Maryland; Osborn v. Bank of the United States;* **Supreme Court.**

COINAGE. *See* **Currency and Coinage.**

COIN'S FINANCIAL SCHOOL.

Written by W. H. ("Coin") Harvey in 1894 to generate support for bimetallism among people suffering from the prevailing hard times. The book showed prominent bankers, editors, and other gold monometallists as asking and taking instruction from "Coin, the smooth little financier." Through graphic illustrations, homily allusions, glib arguments, and the use of prominent names, the narrative obtained wide credence as a portrayal of actual occurrences. Printed in cheap paper editions, it circulated very widely among farmers, debtors, and other distressed classes, preparing many minds to receive William Jennings Bryan's free-silver arguments.

BIBLIOGRAPHY

Nichols, Jeannette. "Bryan's Benefactor: Coin Harvey and His World." *Ohio Historical Quarterly* 67, no. 4 (1958): 299–325.

Riter, Gretchen. *Goldbugs and Greenbacks: The Antimonopoly Tradition and the Politics of Finance in America.* New York: Cambridge University Press, 1997.

Jeannette P. Nichols / C. P.

See also **Bimetallism; Crime of 1873; Financial Panics; Free Silver; Pamphleteering; Populism.**

COINTELPRO (FBI).

In 1956 the Federal Bureau of Investigation launched a formal counterintelligence program against the Communist Party of the United States. Eleven more programs opened in the next decade, targeting an array of groups and causes: Groups Seeking Independence for Puerto Rico, White Hate Groups (such as the Ku Klux Klan), Black Nationalist Hate Groups (such as the Black Panther Party), New Left, Cointelpro-Espionage, Cuban Matters, Hoodwink (to cause disputes between the American Communist Party and the Mafia), Mexican Communist Party Matters, Socialist Workers Party, Special Operations (Nationalities Intelligence), and Yugoslav (Violence-Prone Yugoslav Emigrés to the United States). The program aimed at the New Left was compromised in 1972 by anti–Vietnam War activists who broke into an FBI office and mailed a number of "liberated" files to Congress and the media. That security breach led the FBI to terminate all twelve programs.

J. Edgar Hoover and other FBI officials created COINTELPRO unilaterally. Goals were nearly identical in every case: "to expose, disrupt, misdirect, discredit, or otherwise neutralize." Specific Black Hate operations, for example, ranged from petty harassments to a carefully orchestrated police raid that ended in the murder of the Chicago Black Panther leader Fred Hampton. The FBI informant who helped with that raid's logistics received a cash reward. Martin Luther King Jr. was another COINTELPRO target in this category, and that fact has helped keep alive several of the sensational if largely baseless conspiracy theories surrounding his assassination. Regardless, the counterintelligence programs were not what one would normally expect to see in a democracy.

BIBLIOGRAPHY

Churchill, Ward, and Jim Vander Wail. *The COINTELPRO Papers*. Boston: South End Press, 1991.

O'Reilly, Kenneth. *"Racial Matters": The FBI's Secret File on Black America, 1960–1972*. New York: Free Press, 1979.

U.S. Department of Justice. Federal Bureau of Investigation. *COINTELPRO Files: The Counterintelligence Program of the FBI*. 30 reels. Microfilm ed. Wilmington, Del.: Scholarly Resources, 1978.

Kenneth O'Reilly

See also **Federal Bureau of Investigation.**

COLD HARBOR, BATTLE OF

COLD HARBOR, BATTLE OF (3 June 1864). Following failures to smash and outflank Gen. Robert E. Lee at Spotsylvania, Gen. U. S. Grant on 20 May directed the Army of the Potomac southeast on a turning movement, sideslipping toward Richmond until the Confederates stood on a six-mile front without reserves, their right on the Chickahominy, their center at Cold Harbor, Virginia. On 3 June Grant ordered a direct drive, 60,000 men on 4,000 yards' frontage. The assault against well-entrenched lines cost 5,600 Union casualties and failed completely. Grant held Lee in position until 12 June, then resumed sideslipping and, crossing the James River, threatened Richmond through Petersburg.

BIBLIOGRAPHY

Baltz, Louis J. *The Battle of Cold Harbor*. Lynchburg, Va.: H. E. Howard, 1994.

Trudeau, Noah A. *Bloody Roads South: The Wilderness to Cold Harbor*. Boston: Little, Brown, 1989.

Elbridge Colby / A. R.

See also **Civil War; Petersburg, Siege of; Richmond Campaigns; Spotsylvania Courthouse, Battle of; Wilderness, Battles of the.**

COLD NUCLEAR FUSION, an intensely disputed and largely discredited method for generating thermonuclear fusion at room temperature conditions. In nuclear fusion hydrogen atoms merge to form one helium atom, releasing energy. In its conventional form, such as that occurring within stars and hydrogen bombs, nuclear fusion requires high pressure and temperature, which force the atoms together. Proponents of cold nuclear fusion maintain that certain catalysts can coax hydrogen atoms to fuse without extreme pressure or heat. One form of cold nuclear fusion, known as muon-catalyzed cold fusion and first suggested in the 1940s, is undisputed. The process, in which a subatomic particle known as a muon captures two hydrogen atoms and forces them to fuse, has been demonstrated in the laboratory but appears not to be feasible as an energy source. The controversial form of cold nuclear fusion was first heard of in March 1989, when two University of Utah chemists, Martin Fleischmann and B. Stanley Pons, reported that they had produced fusion in a test tube at room temperature by running an electrical current through heavy water, a type of water in which the hydrogen atoms are of the isotope deuterium. They claimed that the current drove the deuterium atoms into a palladium rod in the water, forcing the atoms to pack closely enough to fuse. This announcement raised a furor in the scientific community. After other researchers failed to obtain similar results with the technique, a consensus emerged that the Utah scientists had used a flawed apparatus and misinterpreted the data from the experiment. A small but vocal minority of researchers continued to pursue variations on the approach.

BIBLIOGRAPHY

Huizenga, John R. *Cold Fusion: The Scientific Fiasco of the Century*. Rochester, N.Y.: University of Rochester Press, 1992.

Mallove, Eugene F. *Fire From Ice: Searching for the Truth behind the Cold Fusion Furor*. New York: Wiley, 1991.

Vincent Kiernan / A. R.

See also **Physics: Nuclear Physics; Scientific Fraud.**

COLD WAR. In December 1991, Mikhail Gorbachev resigned as president of the Soviet Union, signaling the end not only of communist rule in that country but also of the Cold War. Just a few years earlier, no one could have imagined the dramatic changes that were to occur in the world from 1989 to 1991. While the Cold War in the 1980s was not at its coldest point ever, it was still going strong. Yet, through the leadership of Mikhail Gorbachev, Ronald Reagan, and George H. W. Bush, the Cold War came to an end and a new era in world history began.

The Cold War remained an ominous cloud over the world from the end of World War II to the early 1990s. Although every country in the world experienced different events and issues during this time, few escaped the influence of the Cold War. Historians may disagree as to exactly when the Cold War began, who should be blamed for its start, and why it lasted so long, but they all accept that it started soon after World War II and left an indelible imprint on the world.

Roots of the Conflict

The Cold War began when the World War II alliance between the United States, Soviet Union, and Great Britain fell apart in the face of misunderstandings, mistrust, and at times, deliberate actions. To begin to understand the collapse of this wartime partnership, one must recognize that the alliance had been anything but natural. Prior to 1941, the United States and other Western powers looked upon the Soviet Union with tremendous mistrust, and the feelings were mutual. This animosity originated with the communist seizure of power in Russia in 1917 and the resulting disagreements between the Western powers—including the United States, Great Britain, and France—and the new regime. For example, when Russia signed a peace treaty with Germany in 1918, ending its involvement in World War I as an ally of the Western powers, tensions were raised with these countries. Soon thereafter, the intervention of these same allies in support of noncommunist forces during the Russian civil war poisoned the Russians' view of the West.

Relations did not improve much before the start of World War II. Communist leader Vladimir Lenin changed the name of Russia to the Union of Soviet Socialist Republics (or Soviet Union) in the early 1920s and began the process of consolidating communist control, which continued after 1925 under Joseph Stalin, but the United States refused to recognize the legitimacy of the Soviet government until 1933. Even after this recognition, relations did not improve substantially as the world drifted toward a new war. As the Western powers and the Soviet Union attempted to deal with the rise of Adolf Hitler and the Nazi Party in Germany, they struggled without success to find a common policy. The result was that each country looked out for its own interests, and in August 1939 the Soviet Union signed a nonaggression pact with Germany. In the pact, both countries pledged their neutrality in wars the other might wage and agreed to divide Poland between them. This pact and the conquest of Poland by Germany and the Soviet Union in September 1939 shocked and angered the Western powers.

These feelings of mistrust did not ease until June 1941, when Germany invaded the Soviet Union in violation of their nonaggression pact. With the Soviet Union now clearly in need of assistance against the seemingly unstoppable Nazi machine, an uneasy alliance developed. The United States, although still not officially in the war, immediately began to send aid to the Soviet Union. After Japan attacked Pearl Harbor on 7 December 1941 and the United States entered the war, the alliance took a fuller form. For the next three and a half years, the Western powers and the Soviet Union put aside most of their differences to wage war against their common foe.

While the war encouraged greater cooperation, the differences between the two sides never went away. Although they shared a common goal, cooperation remained limited, and generally speaking, the two sides fought separate wars. The Russians suffered the most as they fought the Germans on the Eastern Front, while the British, Americans, and other allies battled the Axis powers in North Africa, Italy, and eventually western Europe. After Germany collapsed in May 1945 and Japan surrendered in September, the one truly unifying feature for the alliance, a common enemy, ended. Very quickly in 1945, the limited level of cooperation that had been reached in the war fell victim to mutual incriminations, mistrust, and differing views of what constituted world security.

The beginning of the collapse of the Grand Alliance could already be seen before the final bombs dropped on Germany and Japan. At meetings in 1943 and 1944, the Allied powers sought agreements concerning the structure of the postwar world. The United States, which had emerged as the dominant Western power in the war, championed an international system built on democratic principles and the capitalist economic system. The Soviet Union saw these ideas as the antithesis of communism and desired more than anything to maintain its security by creating a buffer zone between itself and a potentially resurgent Germany. The result was the development of a bipolar world divided between those nations that generally supported the United States and its policies and those countries that supported the Soviet Union. Ultimately this bipolar world would grow more complex as nations like China, France, India, and others asserted a degree of independence from either so-called superpower.

Many of the problems in the immediate postwar years resulted from different interpretations of agreements reached during the war itself. At the YALTA CONFERENCE in February 1945 the Allied powers agreed to the establishment of the United Nations, the temporary division and occupation of Germany, and basic policies involving eastern European countries. All of these decisions precipitated disagreements between the United States and Soviet Union after the war. The structure of voting in the United Nations ensured contention; no plan was established describing how Germany would eventually be reunited, and the question of what constituted free elections in the eastern European countries was left undefined. Not surprisingly, the mistrust that preceded World War II quickly resurfaced.

Postwar Years

In 1945 and 1946, disagreements between the Western powers and the Soviet Union arose over many issues, including the end of U.S. LEND-LEASE aid, elections in eastern European countries, and the withdrawal of Allied forces from Iran. Whatever the disagreement, each side perceived the other as acting in a threatening manner. Simply put, neither side could overcome the mistrust that had already existed for almost thirty years. For example,

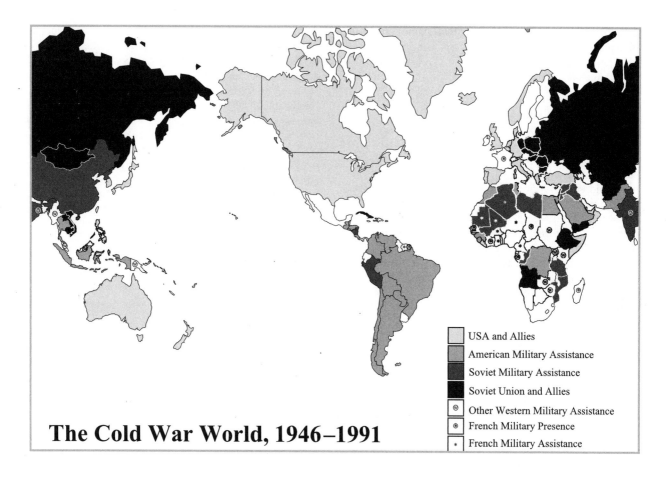

The Cold War World, 1946–1991

	USA and Allies
	American Military Assistance
	Soviet Military Assistance
	Soviet Union and Allies
⊛	Other Western Military Assistance
⊛	French Military Presence
*	French Military Assistance

Soviet leaders did allow elections in the eastern European countries that from their perspective met the promises in the Yalta accords. The United States and other Western powers did not agree with this assessment, since they believed elections that involved a limited number of candidates and generally guaranteed communist dominance were patently undemocratic. While Western leaders assumed the communists were simply trying to expand their power, the Soviet Union saw control over the eastern European countries as essential in providing a buffer zone against a future German resurgence.

Although there were efforts to maintain a semblance of cooperation until 1947, U.S. President Harry S. Truman's initiation of the TRUMAN DOCTRINE in March of that year clearly marked the end of the alliance. In many ways, the Truman Doctrine marked the formal acceptance of the strategy that would dominate U.S. thinking throughout the Cold War—containment. First articulated by George F. Kennan in 1946, the strategy called for the United States to contain communism within its current areas of control. The continuity of the strategy of containment can be seen in following examples where the United States actively tried to stop the spread of communism: the KOREAN WAR from 1950 to 1953, the VIETNAM WAR in the 1960s and 1970s, and the GRENADA INVASION in 1983. While there were other national security issues that the United States had to deal with in the sec-

ond half of the twentieth century, the idea of containing communism was never too far removed.

The passage of the Truman Doctrine, the development of the MARSHALL PLAN in 1948, and the creation of the NORTH ATLANTIC TREATY ORGANIZATION (NATO) in 1949 formed the foundation for U.S. efforts in waging the Cold War. Besides representing the broad theme of containing the spread of communism, the Truman Doctrine specifically called for aid to Greece and Turkey to combat communist influences. The United States established the Marshall Plan to provide funds for rebuilding western Europe after the devastation of World War II. American leaders saw a rebuilt Europe as a bulwark against communism as well as a valuable trading partner. The creation of NATO grew out of concerns that only through collective security could Western countries resist Soviet expansion.

The Soviet Union followed similar paths in cementing its control of eastern European countries by taking steps to integrate their economies with its own. It also provided limited funds and supplies to groups attempting to facilitate the rise of communism in different areas of the world, such as China, North Korea, and Vietnam. Furthermore, it created the Warsaw Pact in 1955 to counter NATO. From the Soviet perspective, these actions were needed not only to preserve communism at home but also to reduce the danger of enemies arising on its borders.

The acceleration of the divisions between the United States and the Soviet Union in the late 1940s led to several crises and at times open confrontations. One of the legacies of the Yalta Conference was the division of Germany and Berlin into four occupation zones with France, Great Britain, the United States, and the Soviet Union controlling one zone each. The French, British, and Americans gradually consolidated their zones into West Germany and West Berlin, while the Soviet Union established a separate East Germany. The location of West Berlin in the center of East Germany sparked several crises including the Soviet blockade of West Berlin in 1948, the BERLIN AIRLIFT to circumvent it over the next year, and finally the construction of the BERLIN WALL in 1961 to completely separate West Berlin from East Germany.

After the 1948–1949 Berlin crisis came to an end, other events occurred pointing to the growing dangers of the Cold War. The Soviet test of an atomic bomb and the triumph of communism in China in the fall of 1949 seemed to indicate that the Soviet Union was indeed winning the Cold War. Even more important, especially in terms of the American military, the Korean War began in June 1950 when communist forces from North Korea attacked South Korea. Under the auspices of the United Nations, the United States and almost fifty other countries intervened to save South Korea. For three years the war raged, costing the lives of several million Korean and Chinese as well as almost 37,000 Americans.

1950s and 1960s

During this period there was not much improvement in relations, as little common ground could be found to begin discussions. Even worse, the 1950s witnessed the acceleration of the arms race as the superpowers introduced new delivery and weapons systems—intercontinental ballistic missiles, submarine-launched ballistic missiles, and long-range bombers—that both countries would rely upon throughout the Cold War. By the end of the decade, both countries were quickly obtaining the capability of destroying each other.

The late 1950s and early 1960s revealed the growing complexity of the Cold War as well as the dangers of a confrontation. In the mid to late 1950s, the United States became involved in two separate disputes between Communist China and Taiwan over the islands of Quemoy and Matsu. While the crises did not lead to a war, the countries went to the brink before pulling back. A more dangerous situation arose when the Soviet Union began constructing nuclear missile sites in Cuba in the summer of 1962, precipitating the CUBAN MISSILE CRISIS, which brought the world closer to a nuclear war than ever before. For a week at the end of October, the world waited for an end to the crisis. Fortunately, the two countries did reach an agreement ending the standoff.

The decade after the Cuban Missile Crisis witnessed the Cold War expanding into new areas. While the United States continued to try to contain the Soviet Union in Europe and also to beat the Russians to the moon, the main concern of the 1960s and early 1970s was the Vietnam War. Since 1945, the United States had kept a careful eye on events in Vietnam. Although opposed to colonization, the United States found it necessary to aid France in Vietnam in order to preserve French support in the Cold War. The collapse of French efforts in 1954 led to more direct American involvement in preserving a noncommunist government in what became South Vietnam. Starting in 1965, the United States began a major military commitment that lasted until 1973. In the name of containing communism, 58,000 Americans died in Vietnam.

While the United States struggled with the Vietnam War, the Soviet Union experienced its own share of problems. In 1964, Soviet Premier Nikita Khrushchev lost a power struggle in the Kremlin with Leonid Brezhnev, a hard-liner in the Communist Party, and was forced into retirement. Under Brezhnev's leadership in the late 1960s, the Soviet Union expanded its military arsenal, experienced open hostilities with China, and cracked down on opposition to communism in eastern Europe by intervening militarily in Czechoslovakia. The dynamics of the Cold War had definitely changed by 1970, as neither superpower could any longer afford to focus its attention solely on the other.

1970–1991

The changes in the world in the late 1960s actually facilitated a thaw in the Cold War. Both the United States and the Soviet Union had begun to realize the futility of their ongoing feud and the need to work toward a better relationship. In 1972, President Richard M. Nixon took important steps by making historic visits to both China and the Soviet Union. These visits led to improved American relations with both countries and the signing of the Strategic Arms Limitation Treaty and the Anti-Ballistic Missile Treaty. While these treaties had only a limited impact, they signaled a thaw in the Cold War known as détente. Furthermore, there were increased efforts at cooperation in the form of cultural exchanges and economic transactions. Unfortunately these improvements proved relatively short-lived as tensions increased again in the late 1970s.

Relations between the United States and the Soviet Union reached new lows after the Soviets invaded Afghanistan in 1979. Responding to this action, the United States led a boycott of the 1980 Summer Olympics in Moscow and withdrew its support for a new arms-control treaty. Additionally, after being elected in 1980, Ronald Reagan initiated a massive military buildup and showed a greater willingness to confront communism. Calling the Soviet Union an "evil empire," he provided aid to anticommunist forces in Latin America and ordered the invasion of Grenada in 1983 to prevent the establishment of a communist government there.

As the United States became more assertive in the 1980s, the Soviet Union entered a period of decline. Its invasion of Afghanistan proved a debacle as Soviet forces struggled there until 1988 without success. Their difficulties in Afghanistan paled in comparison to other problems the Soviet leadership faced. By the early 1980s, Brezhnev was old and ineffective and the country was nearly bankrupt. After his death in 1982, the Soviet Union struggled until 1985 to find a new leader who could help the country out of its economic doldrums. It seemed to find that leader in Mikhail Gorbachev, who was younger than previous Soviet leaders, independent of the hardliners in the Communist Party, and willing to seek reform. However, no one, including Gorbachev, realized how bad the situation was. In essence the Soviet Union was dying from inefficiency and corruption. Although Gorbachev set out to modernize and reform the Soviet Union without abandoning the basic tenets of communism, he actually unleashed the forces of change that ultimately would lead to his downfall and the collapse of the Soviet Union.

In the realm of foreign policy, Gorbachev recognized that the Soviet Union could no longer afford the arms race. With this in mind he initiated talks with the United States, where he found a surprisingly receptive president. Despite his rhetoric, Reagan was horrified by the prospects of a nuclear war. Even before Gorbachev made his initiatives, Reagan was already thinking along similar lines. Although difficult negotiations had to occur, the two leaders reached a significant agreement in 1987 eliminating all intermediate-range nuclear missiles. This agreement led to more talks between Gorbachev and Reagan's successor, George H. W. Bush, that reduced tensions even further.

While making efforts to improve relations with the United States, Gorbachev also encouraged internal reforms in Soviet society and in eastern Europe. As he struggled to reform communism at home, Gorbachev made clear to the eastern European countries that they could also make changes without fear of Soviet intervention. Little did he know that this freedom would spark the revolutions of 1989 that saw the overthrow of communist regimes throughout eastern Europe and the rise of opponents in the Soviet Union who wanted even more reform than he could deliver. After an abortive coup by communist hard-liners in August 1991 and the dissolution of the Soviet Union into separate states, Gorbachev resigned in December, effectively ending both communist rule in Russia and the Cold War.

The end of the Cold War represented a dramatic turn in the world's history. For almost fifty years, the two superpowers and their various allies waged an undeclared war. Although historians will continue to debate different issues related to the Cold War, all would agree that few events in the world between 1945 and 1991 can be completely understood outside its context.

BIBLIOGRAPHY

Ambrose, Stephen E., and Douglas Brinkley. *Rise to Globalism: American Foreign Policy Since 1938*. 8th rev. ed. New York: Penguin, 1997.

Cohen, Warren I. *The Cambridge History of American Foreign Relations: America in the Age of Soviet Power, 1945–1991*. New York: Cambridge University Press, 1993.

Fischer, Beth A. *The Reagan Reversal: Foreign Policy and the End of the Cold War*. Columbia: University of Missouri Press, 2000.

Gaddis, John L. *We Now Know: Rethinking Cold War History*. New York: Oxford University Press, 1997.

Judge, Edward H., and John W. Langdon. *A Hard and Bitter Peace: A Global History of the Cold War*. Upper Saddle River, N.J.: Prentice Hall, 1996.

LaFeber, Walter. *America, Russia, and the Cold War, 1945–2000*. 9th ed. Boston: McGraw-Hill, 2002.

Leffler, Melvyn P. *A Preponderance of Power: National Security, the Truman Administration, and the Cold War*. Stanford University Press, 1992.

———. "The Cold War: What Do 'We Now Know'?" American Historical Review 104 (1999): 501–524.

Levering, Ralph, et al. *Debating the Origins of the Cold War: American and Russian Perspectives*. New York: Rowman and Littlefield, 2002.

Whitfield, Stephen. *The Culture of the Cold War*. 2d ed. Baltimore: Johns Hopkins University Press, 1996.

David L. Snead

See also **Arms Race and Disarmament; Russia, Relations with;** *and vol. 9:* **American Diplomacy.**

***COLE* BOMBING.** On 12 October 2000, two terrorists detonated a powerful bomb in a small boat next to the guided missile destroyer U.S.S. *Cole* while it was docked in the harbor at Aden, Yemen. The *Cole* had entered the port a few hours earlier to refuel. The blast blew a large hole into the side of the *Cole*, flooding the engine room and destroying several compartments. Seventeen U.S. sailors were killed and over thirty others were injured.

Suspicion soon focused on the Al Qaeda terrorist network led by Osama bin Laden. Scores of individuals were detained for questioning. The investigation revealed that a sophisticated and well-funded organization had planned and executed the attack on the *Cole*. The conspiracy had also planned to attack other U.S. targets in the Middle East. Several suspects were eventually arrested in Yemen. Despite a cooperative arrangement between U.S. and Yemeni investigators, the Yemeni government refused to extradite the suspects to the United States for prosecution.

In December 2000, the *Cole* was transported to the United States for major repairs. In April 2002, it returned to active duty at a cost of $250 million. An onboard memorial commemorates the victims of the attack.

BIBLIOGRAPHY

Bergen, Peter L. *Holy War, Inc.: Inside the Secret World of Osama bin Laden.* New York: Simon and Schuster, 2001.

Eisman, Dale. "Cole Investigation Update: Case Marches Toward Justice." *Virginian-Pilot* (Norfolk, Virginia), 22 April 2002.

William J. Aceves

See also **Terrorism.**

COLLECTING.

Americans are voracious collectors. They collect anything and everything. While probably not as popular as stamps, American collections include coins, baseball cards, comic books, and Beanie Babies.

The First American Collectors

Rev. William Bentley of Salem, Massachusetts, may have become the first documented American collector when he purchased a William and Mary period settee in 1819 for the sole purpose of owning a piece of furniture of an earlier American time. More than a score of years earlier, in 1793, the Massachusetts Historical Society became the first public institution to receive a decorative arts bequest, a chair "of antique fashion" by a resident of Salem. Within a decade several historical and colonial societies had been founded in New England. These were the beginnings of what would become a national interest in squirreling away its past in public and private collections.

Because of the great interest in historical events and individuals, various objects such as furniture, silver, pewter, clothing were preserved and kept in public view as reminders. The librarian of the American Antiquarian Society, Samuel F. Haven, reported in 1842 that "old pictures, old furniture, old plate, and even old books, which have heretofore suffered neglect, and enjoyed but a musty reputation, as uncongenial to the go-ahead habits of our people, are now sought with eagerness as necessary adjuncts of style and the most cherished ornaments of the drawing room." At the time, collecting was an enlightened amateur affair. There were no antique dealers or guidebooks to identifying antiques.

During much the same time, cultured Americans could read freshly written accounts about the newest science and archaeology, learn to discern between Greek and Roman sculpture, develop a profound interest in Gothic architecture and the medieval life it represented, or study the roots of the Renaissance as they were being uncovered in Florence, Rome, and elsewhere. Americans even went to England or Europe to live and to collect. Collections helped determine aesthetic preferences and influenced the direction deemed proper for contemporary art production. In the 1850s, they also influenced preservationists, such as Cummings E. Davis of Concord, Massachusetts, who gathered what he could find of local colonial relics. His accumulation eventually formed key components of the Concord Antiquarian Society collection. By

Exhibition Site for Collections. This poster advertises coverage by *Harper's Weekly* of the two years of work preparing for the 1893 World's Columbian Exposition in Chicago. © CORBIS

the 1850s, a broad public awareness of national history led to the preservation of such relics as "Old Ironsides," or Mount Vernon.

The Influence of Collectors

As the nation began to anticipate its centennial celebration in 1876, a few furniture dealers began to sell antiques in Boston and New York, and public interest in antiques began to grow with exhibitions focused on American decorative arts. In Boston, The Bunker Hill Centennial Exhibition featured furniture, pewter, and ceramics from the collection of Maj. Ben Perley Poore of Newburyport, Massachusetts, one of the nation's most prominent collectors of colonial objects. Books published in 1877, such as *The House Beautiful* by Clarence Cook and *Pottery and Porcelain* by William C. Prime, helped feed public interest in antiques. When Irving Lyon began collecting furniture in Hartford, Connecticut, in 1877, his focus sparked several of his Hartford friends to do the same, and eventually led to his publishing *The Colonial Furniture of New England* in 1891, the first book devoted to the subject. The expanding number of collectors led to more books and articles on American decorative arts. In 1892, Alice Morse Earle's *China Collecting in America* became the first scholarly work on ceramics in America. In 1896, Theodore S.

Art Collections on Exhibit. Italian paintings and sculpture are displayed in a room of the Fine Arts Building at the World's Columbia Exposition in Chicago, 1893. © CORBIS

Woolsey, a Yale professor and silver collector, wrote the first article on the collecting of American silver for the popular *Harper's New Monthly Magazine.*

The Chicago World's Columbian Exposition (1893) devoted much space and ink to collecting. The Fine Arts Building was devoted almost exclusively to paintings and sculpture from American and Europe, while Connecticut, Massachusetts, Rhode Island, and New York exhibited their colonial furniture tradition.

When William H. Crim auctioned his important decorative arts collection in 1903, he set a new trend in dispersing collections. The following year, Charles L. Pendleton began another tradition when he bequeathed his collection of furniture, silver, ceramics, and paintings to the Rhode Island School of Design. In 1909, the New York Metropolitan Museum of Art held an exhibition in conjunction with the Hudson-Fulton Celebration. Several collectors participated, and after the show, Eugene Bolles sold his extensive furniture collection to the Museum. The exhibition had also provided an opportunity to establish the Walpole Society, the first American organization devoted to collecting.

Starting just after 1900, Henry Francis Du Pont of Winterthur, Delaware, began to amass an extensive collection of American decorative arts. In 1951, it became the Winterthur Museum. About the same time, Ima Hogg's American collection, second only to Du Pont's, went public in her house museum, Bayou Bend, in Houston.

As if birthing twins, the same cities that saw the genesis of colonial arts collecting also saw the gathering of oriental art objects, as a result of growing trade with the Far East. As early as 1800, the Peabody Museum in Salem, Massachusetts, had materials brought from India, China, and Japan to the East India Marine Society and the Essex Institute. An early leader of Japanese art collecting in America was Ernest Fenellosa, a great scholar of oriental art at Harvard and the Fine Arts Academy of Tokyo. His collection, dating from the 1880s and 1890s, is in the Boston Museum of Fine Arts. In 1923, Charles Lang Freer's outstanding oriental collection moved into its own museum, the Freer Gallery of Art at the Smithsonian Institution in Washington, D.C. In addition to an astounding array of oriental art, Freer had bought some one hundred paintings and a thousand prints from James Abbot McNeill Whistler. But it was Freer's acquisition of the whole *Harmony in Blue and Gold: The Peacock Room* that focused that aspect of his collecting.

In 1804, Thomas Jefferson owned several works of questionable authority; the painter John Trumbull exhibited his small collection at the Park Theater in New York; and the Gallery of the Pennsylvania Academy of the Fine Arts opened. Nevertheless, Americans did not enter the world of seriously collecting paintings until the second half of the nineteenth century. A rarity among collectors, the pioneer collector J. J. Jarves (1818–1888) lived in Florence for about thirty years after 1851. His collection of 119 works was deposited at Yale Art School in New Haven in 1867. Isabella Stewart Gardner commuted between America and Europe, acquiring works on the advice of Charles Eliot Norton, a Harvard professor of fine art. Her collection—arranged the way she had lived with it at Fenway Court in Boston—was opened to the public after she died in 1924. Norton also influenced Bernard Berenson, who, after his graduation from Harvard in 1887, moved to Florence and, from there, asserted an enormous influence as a connoisseur and collector in his villa "I Tatti."

In general, it was only after 1900 that the magnates of American industry and finance—Henry Walter, Andrew Mellon, Samuel H. Kress, J. Pierpont Morgan, Benjamin Altman, Henry Clay Frick, and Joseph E. Widener—began to accumulate extraordinary collections that became available to the public from the 1920s to 1950s. The great dealer, Sir Joseph Duveen, who began his activities in 1886, aided several of these collectors.

Aiming at the serious collector, in 1846, Michael Knoedler set up business in New York as a representative of the French gallery Goupil. Since 1857, the firm has been known as Knoedler's. In 1879, Mary Cassatt and Mrs. Henry O. Havemeyer met and their friendship helped influence several collectors. Two Paris dealers, Paul Durand-Ruel and Ambroise Vollard, also helped. In 1886, Durand-Ruel organized an exhibition of over three hundred impressionists in New York, where he opened a branch of his Paris gallery three years later. In Chicago, another friend of Mary Cassatt, Mrs. Potter Palmer, showed impressionist paintings in her home during the Chicago World's Columbian Exposition. At about the same time, Martin A. Ryerson, a trustee of the Art Institute of Chicago, exhibited his taste with sixteen paintings by Monet, five by Renoir, and five by Redon.

In 1898, Miss Etta Cone bought several paintings by Theodore Robinson. This led her and her sister Claribel into the still exotic and generally unaccepted world of contemporary art. In their Baltimore home, they eventually gathered some three thousand objects from around the world . At about the same time Dr. Albert C. Barnes was beginning his pursuit of contemporary works, particularly paintings by Cézanne and Renoir.

Twentieth-Century Collectors

From 1911 to his death in 1924, John Quinn, a New York lawyer, acquired a hoard of some two thousand paintings, prints, drawings, and sculptures, representing more than 150 contemporary artists. Duncan Phillips in Washington, D.C., opened his collection to the public in 1921, becoming the first permanent museum of modern art in America.

The early 1950s saw a flowering of art collecting across the United States. In Chicago, Edward and Lindy Bergman, Joseph and Jory Shapiro, Ruth and Leonard Horwich, and Morton and Rose Neumann created complete artistic environments to live in, focusing on Surrealism, outsider art, and Chicago contemporary. They were followed in the 1960s by Dennis Adrian, Lolli Thurm, Roger Brown, and Larry and Evelyn Aronson, who focused almost exclusively on Chicago's own artists, including the Harry Who and the Chicago Imagists.

By the early 1960s, America became the world's center of collecting through the emergence of many American collectors of international significance, such as Dominique de Menil, whose sweeping collection is in Houston, Texas.

BIBLIOGRAPHY

Richardson, Brenda. *Dr. Claribel & Miss Etta: The Cone Collection of the Baltimore Museum of Art.* Baltimore, Md.: Baltimore Museum of Art, 1985.

Taylor, Joshua. *The Fine Arts in America.* Chicago: University of Chicago Press, 1979.

Zilczer, Judith. *"The Noble Buyer": John Quinn, Patron of the Avant-Garde.* Washington, D.C.: Smithsonian Institution Press, 1978.

Rolf Achilles

COLLECTIVE BARGAINING is a process of negotiated rule-making between a group of unionized workers and the management of one or more firms. In theory the system is one of voluntary accommodation between two private parties, but in reality much supporting legislation, and its vigorous enforcement, is essential to the health of this system. Some form of collective bargaining has existed since the late nineteenth century, but this practice proved routine—albeit for only one-quarter to one-third of all American workers—only during the middle decades of the twentieth century.

Collective Bargaining in the Late Nineteenth and Early Twentieth Centuries

The phrase "collective bargaining" was coined by British labor reformers Sidney and Beatrice Webb in the 1890s, but by that time, forms of collective accommodation between unionized workers and employers were already common in the United States. In the printing crafts, metal trades, commercial construction, and coal mining, as well as among skilled railroad personnel, practices known as "arbitration," "conciliation," "conferring," "trade agreements," and union "legislation" governed the relationship between organized workers and their collectively associated employers. These systems were unstable—and in the *Lochner v. New York* judicial era, legally suspect—but where unions had the power they were able to "legislate" a work, wage, or hour standard and then use the strike weapon to impose it on as many industry shops and firms as possible. Thus, in the years before World War I (1914–1918), collectively bargained work rules were of far less consequence than employer recognition of trade unionism itself. The latter was often bitterly resisted, but when accepted, it implied employer accommodation to a preexisting set of union standards.

Advocates of collective bargaining in the early decades of the twentieth century thought it essential for three reasons. First and foremost, a system of peaceful and routine bargaining would go a long way—or so it was thought—toward the elimination of the industrial strife and violence that had been such an alarming feature of American industrialization. Since the railroads were both a vital service and the scene of some of the most dramatic strike battles, Congress enacted the first laws facilitating collective bargaining in this industry. The Railway Labor Act of 1926 sanctioned the power and bargaining role of the powerful railroad brotherhoods, in return for which they accepted a legal regime that made strikes virtually illegal.

Second, collective bargaining stood for "industrial democracy," an idea that flourished during the Progressive Era and the early years of the New Deal. There could be no "political democracy," Supreme Court Justice Louis Brandeis told the U.S. Industrial Commission in 1915, without an "industrial democracy," giving workers an actual participation in the governance of the firms for which they worked. And Harvard's Sumner Slichter, the dean of American labor economists after World War I, defined collective bargaining as a procedure "introducing civil rights into industry, that is, of requiring that management be conducted by rule rather than by arbitrary decision." Thus, quasi-judicial grievance and arbitration systems, pioneered in the needle trades, would pacify and democratize day-to-day industrial life. Such grievance procedures became an essential, prominent feature of all collective bargaining contracts negotiated in the years after 1940.

And finally, collective bargaining promised to make American capitalism work, especially during the crisis of the Great Depression, when "underconsumption," unemployment, and regional wage inequalities generated a vicious downward spiral. "If the wages of mill workers in the South should be raised to the point where workers could buy shoes," asserted Frances Perkins, President Franklin D. Roosevelt's Secretary of Labor, "that would be a social revolution." Thus collective bargaining in the New Deal era was designed to increase mass purchasing power, eliminate the southern wage differential, and equalize wages within each industry, thereby curbing the cutthroat competition that so many reformers—and some businessmen—sought to regulate.

In 1932, even before Roosevelt came to power, Congress passed the Norris-LaGuardia Act, which strengthened the unions by curbing antistrike injunctions and proscribing some employer antiunion tactics. Three years later the National Labor Relations Act, sponsored by New York Senator Robert Wagner, put the federal government even more forcefully in support of a policy "encouraging the practice and procedure of collective bargaining." The 1935 Wagner Act did so by eliminating company-sponsored unions, banning a series of unfair employer labor practices, protecting union organizing rights, and establishing a National Labor Relations Board (NLRB) empowered to determine union jurisdictions and certify unions, often after holding an on-site election to determine the will of employees. The Wagner Act defined as an "unfair labor practice" employer failure to bargain with duly designated employee representatives.

Collective Bargaining's Heyday

The heyday of collective bargaining lasted from 1937, when the affiliates of the new Committee for Industrial Organizations negotiated first contracts with General Motors and U.S. Steel, until the 1970s and early 1980s when union density plunged, management hostility increased, and government indifference robbed the system of its internal vitality and pattern-setting potency. Four elements characterized collective bargaining during this half-century heyday. First, unionism grew rapidly during the 1930s and 1940s, when millions of heretofore marginalized workers—many of them immigrants (or the sons and daughters of immigrants) or African American migrants—took advantage of NLRB and War Labor Board policies to achieve the industrial citizenship promised by New Deal proponents of an American industrial democracy. Union membership grew from 3 million to 15 million in the twenty years after 1933, reaching about one-third of the nonfarm workforce in the early 1950s. In mature, unionized industries, like auto, steel, and rail transport, more than 90 percent of all workers were covered by collective bargaining contracts. Thereafter, union density slowly declined, even as 3 million public employees were recruited to union ranks in the 1960s and 1970s.

Second, collective bargaining did not generate the industrial peace promised by its proponents. Strikes were large and frequent, not only in the 1930s, but in the next three decades as well. Except in the South, corporations did not try to break the unions, but they were quite willing to "take a strike" in order to test union willpower before and during collective bargaining negotiations. Except for 1919, a year of near-revolutionary expectations, all of the largest and longest strikes in American history took place between 1945 and 1973, the mature years of institutionalized collective bargaining. Strikes became less frequent and more predictable as the standard term of the collective bargaining contract grew from one or two years in the 1940s to three or five years in the 1960s and 1970s.

Third, collective bargaining did raise and equalize wages across a wide spectrum of America's working population. Real wages doubled between 1940 and 1973. Economists debate the extent to which the unions themselves were responsible for this achievement, because these were also years of enormous productivity growth and Keynesian fiscal stimulus. But collective bargaining exerted a continuous upward pressure within almost all of the nation's key industries, thereby tempering the regional, racial, and skill differentials that had long divided the working population. Uniform, company-wide wage standards were essential in order to reinforce a sense of solidarity within the workforce and deprive managers of an incentive to shift work to low-paid regions, factories, or departments. Beginning in 1948, many unions negotiated contracts that linked wages to the government's cost-of-living index. Additional annual pay awards assured steady growth in real income. In its most fully developed form, "pattern bargaining" made wages and benefits more equitable across a range of industries, first in steel, autos, and rubber, and later in meatpacking, electrical products, long-distance trucking, the airlines, and metropolitan construction work. Between the 1940s and the 1960s, wages in the packinghouse industry tracked those in steel, while nonunion white-collar salaries and benefits in unionized heavy industry were invariably boosted after labor and management negotiated a new contract.

Fourth, during these years the scope of collective bargaining expanded from wages, hours, and working conditions to encompass a set of fringe benefits that included pensions, supplemental unemployment insurance, health care, longer vacations, and a variety of employment guarantees. This development was unique to the United States, largely because of the underdeveloped character of the American welfare state. Thus, the growth of a privately negotiated welfare system began in the late 1940s when it became clear that President Harry S. Truman's Fair Deal was incapable of either bolstering Social Security or enacting national health insurance. In 1949 and 1950, big unions like the United Steelworkers and the United Automobile Workers negotiated pension and health insurance benefit packages that later spread to other industry sectors, some nonunion. By the mid-1970s about two-thirds of all American workers held some kind of company-paid health insurance, and about half were covered by an employer-paid pension.

The Eclipse of Collective Bargaining

In the years after 1980, the collective bargaining system became increasingly marginal to the wage standards of American workers and to the shape of the political economy. It was weakened from within and battered from without. Since the 1940s, when Congress passed the TAFT-HARTLEY ACT over President Truman's veto, the legal and administrative regime had become more hostile toward unionism and collective bargaining. Taft-Hartley effectively ghettoized private-sector unionism within a Northeastern–Upper Midwest–Pacific Coast blue-collar archipelago. Foremen, managers, and professionals were deprived of NLRB protections, and the president was empowered to suspend strikes for an eighty-day "cooling-off" period. In the South and the mountain West, Taft-Hartley enabled conservative state legislators to pass "right-to-work" laws that made organizing more difficult. Subsequent judicial rulings enabled employers to intimidate workers participating in union certification elections, and in 1964, the Supreme Court declared outside the scope of collective bargaining those issues, such as production planning and investment decisions, that "lie at the core of entrepreneurial control."

After the onset of the 1973–1974 recession, globalized competition in the world economy added greatly to these political and legal difficulties. Collective bargaining works best in fully organized, oligopolistic industries, where wages and working conditions are uniform among competing firms. The emergence of an internationally competitive market in steel, electrical products, automobiles, apparel, and other products enhanced unilateral management efforts to set wage- and work-rule standards. Employers did this in two ways: by moving production and services to the American South or to low-wage nations, or by "concession bargaining" with a unionized workforce. President Ronald Reagan's 1981 destruction of the Professional Air Traffic Controller's Organization signaled that government policy had turned hostile to unionism, while a simultaneous series of dramatic wage and workforce reductions at the hard-pressed Chrysler Corporation opened the door to a management offensive at hundreds of unionized firms.

With wages and fringe benefits now back in competitive play, management's resistance to unionism hardened, as did its hostility to long-established norms generated by a half-century of collective bargaining. Through the 1980s and 1990s, it was once again routine for a strike to end with the destruction of the trade union that called it. Ballooning health care costs generated a bitter set of bargaining disputes, and pattern bargaining was eliminated in former bastions like steel, trucking, electrical products, and coal mining. Corporations deployed the most sophisticated legal and psychological tools to persuade workers to eschew unionism, and where the NLRB did certify a union election victory, more than half of all negotiations failed to secure a first contract. By 2002, union density had plunged to less than 14 percent.

Collective bargaining is still practiced in the twenty-first century, but among many of its union advocates it is no longer the most hopeful road toward either high wages or an updated industrial democracy. Key service-sector trade unions have sought to fulfill these goals through a set of increasingly political initiatives. In the janitorial, hotel, and health care sectors of the economy, firm-centered collective bargaining has been linked, and in some cases subordinated, to political and social mobilizations designed to advance the well-being of all workers, regardless of their union status.

BIBLIOGRAPHY

Bronfenbrenner, Kate, et al. *Organizing to Win: New Research on Union Strategies.* Ithaca, N.Y.: ILR Press, 1998.

Dubofsky, Melvin. *The State and Labor in Modern America.* Chapel Hill: University of North Carolina Press, 1994.

Fraser, Steven. *Labor Will Rule: Sidney Hillman and the Rise of American Labor.* New York: Free Press, 1991.

Freeman, Joshua. *Working-Class New York: Life and Labor Since World War II.* New York: The New Press, 2000.

Freeman, Richard, and James Medoff. *What Do Unions Do?* New York: Basic Books, 1984.

Harris, Howell John. *The Right to Manage: Industrial Relations Policies of American Business in the 1940s.* Madison: University of Wisconsin Press, 1982.

Lichtenstein, Nelson. *Walter Reuther: The Most Dangerous Man in Detroit.* Urbana: University of Illinois Press, 1997.

———. *State of the Union: A Century of American Labor.* Princeton, N.J.: Princeton University Press, 2002.

Lichtenstein, Nelson, and Howell John Harris. *Industrial Democracy in America: The Ambiguous Promise.* New York: Cambridge University Press, 1993.

Montgomery, David. *The Fall of the House of Labor: The Workplace, the State, and American Labor Activism, 1865–1925.* New York: Cambridge University Press, 1987.

Moody, Kim. *Workers in a Lean World: Unions in the International Economy.* New York: Verso, 1997.

Nissen, Bruce, ed. *U.S. Labor Relations, 1945–1989: Accommodation and Conflict.* New York: Garland Publishing, 1990.

O'Brien, Ruth. *Workers' Paradox: The Republican Origins of New Deal Labor Policy, 1886–1935.* Chapel Hill: University of North Carolina Press, 1998.

Stebenne, David. *Arthur Goldberg: New Deal Liberal.* New York: Oxford University Press, 1996.

Nelson Lichtenstein

See also **Air Traffic Controllers Strike; National Labor Relations Act; Strikes; Trade Unions; Wages and Hours of Labor, Regulation of.**

COLLECTOR V. DAY, 11 Wallace 113 (1871). Between 1864 and 1867, Congress passed revenue acts taxing the income of "every person residing in the United States." Day, a probate judge in Barnstable County, Massachusetts, paid the tax under protest and sued to recover on grounds that it was inappropriate for the federal government to tax his judicial salary. By an 8 to 1 vote, the Supreme Court agreed with Day. The Court did not, as is sometimes claimed, invalidate the federal tax. An unintended result of *Collector v. Day* was a miasma of tax exemptions for state and federal employees. The Court repudiated the principle of intergovernmental exemption in the case of *Graves v. New York* (1939).

BIBLIOGRAPHY
Fairman, Charles. *Reconstruction and Reunion, 1864–88*. New York: Macmillan, 1971.

Alvin F. Harlow
R. Volney Riser

See also **Taxation.**

COLLEGE ATHLETICS. Colonial American colleges adhered to a strict policy of in loco parentis, which encouraged administrators and professors, acting in the place of parents, to take charge of the moral as well as the academic growth of students. This authoritarian approach to education severely constrained campus life, and students gradually developed extracurricular activities, including literary societies, fraternities, and sports, to channel their energies.

The first campus athletic events grew out of hazing rituals pitting sophomores against freshmen in often violent wrestling or football contests (which at first looked more like soccer than modern American football), but when students started to identify more with their school than their class, they initiated competition with rival colleges. The first intercollegiate sporting event took place in 1852, when a railroad official inspired by the English Cambridge-Oxford rivalry sponsored a crew race between Harvard and Yale, two schools that dominated college athletics for the rest of the nineteenth century.

The race established a pattern of commercialism that many modern observers mistakenly consider a recent trend in college sports. Though schools claimed (and still claim) to follow the ideals of amateurism, they very quickly turned to professionalism in practice. Many of the first intercollegiate sporting events were organized by promoters who paid athletes with perks and prizes. In addition, as early as the 1860s, the desire to win led a number of college teams to hire professional coaches and aggressively recruit student athletes without regard for their academic qualifications.

Throughout the nineteenth century, four sports—crew, baseball, football, and track and field—dominated college athletics. The most popular sporting events of the period were the 1870s regattas and the New York Thanksgiving Day football games of the 1890s, each of which drew between thirty and forty thousand spectators. Professional baseball and Olympic track and field eventually diminished the popularity of their college predecessors.

But football and basketball did not achieve professional popularity until the 1940s, and they became (and remain) the two big-time college sports. The NCAA basketball tournament, known as March Madness, and the college football bowl games epitomize modern college athletics.

Institutionalization

College sports were for several decades controlled by students, not administrators. Occasionally, the faculty or the president would assert their power—for example, by refusing permission for weekday away games—but students organized practices, drew up schedules, and raised money for equipment and travel. Soon, however, college athletics became centralized and institutionalized. Students themselves took the first step in limiting their autonomy by hiring professional coaches to do a job once filled by student captains. They were willing to submit to outside authority if it meant victory. At Yale, alumnus Walter Camp ran every aspect of the football program from the 1880s to 1911, and his teams won eleven national championships.

Though students formed the first governing bodies, such as the Rowing Association of American Colleges and the American College Baseball Association, administrators got involved in athletic programming when they started to suspect that sports interfered with their academic and moral interests. Harvard, Yale, and Princeton formed faculty athletic committees in the early 1880s, and most schools quickly followed suit. Simultaneously, alumni associations who believed sports enhanced the reputation of their alma maters pushed for greater rationalization of athletics. In the 1890s, the Dartmouth College Board of Trustees took over a struggling athletic program, and with better funding and organization it thrived.

Finally, the 1880s and 1890s also saw several movements for interinstitutional control of athletics, led by administrators worried that athletic abuses were tarnishing the image of higher education. In 1895 leading Midwestern schools organized the first athletic conference, the powerful Big Ten. Three years later, leading eastern colleges met unsuccessfully to straighten out the mess of eligibility rules, which had grown so lax that many teams fielded players with no affiliation to the sponsoring college. The most important decision on intercollegiate organization came in 1905, in the aftermath of a heated controversy about brutality in football. Many schools considered banning the sport, especially after a Union College player died from injuries sustained in a pile-up, but finally they decided to create what became the National Collegiate Athletic Association. In the early 2000s, the NCAA, a colossal and well-funded bureaucracy of athletic directors, had more than 1,000 member institutions.

Women and Title IX

Though women played college sports for much of the twentieth century, the generally held conviction that competition was unfeminine kept their contests mostly informal until the 1960s and 1970s. When a number of

College Athletics. Senda Berenson *(in the long skirt)*, called the "Mother of Women's Basketball," tosses up a basketball to students during practice at Smith College, 1904; other than at women's colleges, however, college sports for women were generally limited before Title IX legislation in 1972.

previously all-male schools decided to accept women, they also began to field women's teams. More importantly, however, Title IX of the Education Amendments of 1972 outlawed sex discrimination in higher education, which in practice meant that schools had to provide equal facilities and coaching staffs for women athletes and, more controversially, that they had to strive for a ratio of female to male athletes roughly equal to the ratio of women to men in the student body as a whole. Many critics of Title IX argued that in practice it required cuts in athletic programs for men (departments could not afford to expand, so they contracted), but after it went into effect, women's sports exploded in popularity.

The Association for Intercollegiate Athletics for Women (AIAW), formed in 1971, was the first successful governing body for women's college sports. It tended to approach athletics with a less competitive attitude than the NCAA. For instance, the AIAW invited all teams, not just winners, to participate in national championships. In 1980, however, the NCAA decided to offer its own women's championships, and the AIAW shut down two years later. Under the leadership of the NCAA, women's college sports steadily if slowly gained mainstream acceptance, but some women argue that the NCAA squeezed the unique qualities out of women's athletics, turning it into the men's version writ small.

Crisis

Since the 1980s, critics have been claiming that college athletics in its present form is inconsistent with the values of higher education. They argue that athletic programs (which, contrary to popular opinion, almost always run at a deficit) siphon off millions of dollars that should go to a wider range of student activities, that gambling and lucrative licensing and television contracts taint the educational missions of nonprofit and public institutions, and that student athletes often fail to meet academic standards and are unable to get a proper education because their sports require all their time and effort. On the other side, defenders respond that sports teaches students skills they cannot learn in a classroom and that it helps create a sense of community pride on campus.

These problems are not new. In 1939 the president of the University of Chicago abolished its very successful football program on the grounds that the point of education was to make the curriculum "rational and intelligible," not to provide extracurricular escapes from it. Another serious controversy erupted in 1951, when seven leading college basketball teams, including the City College of New York national champions, were implicated in a point-shaving scandal (gamblers paid them not to cover the spread).

Concerns about the corrupting influence of money in college sports prompted the NCAA to regularize athletic scholarships in 1956, but the eight schools that had formed the Ivy League in 1954 refused to accept the new rules. In 1985 the NCAA forced the Southern Methodist University football team to disband for a year (the so-called death penalty) because boosters had paid players $60,000. The next year, the NCAA instituted Proposition 48, later Proposition 16, which established minimum academic requirements for incoming student athletes.

Despite the rule changes and strict sanctions, many observers saw college athletics getting worse, not better. The influential book *The Game of Life*, published in 2001, analyzed a huge amount of data to argue that athletes had a distinct admissions advantage over other applicants, did worse than nonathletes in the classroom, and tended to create their own athlete culture that had little to do with the rest of campus life. In addition, almost all schools lost money on sports, and athletic success did not translate into alumni giving. In short, the book made the case that college sports were becoming increasingly segregated from both the day-to-day lives of most students and psychic identity of colleges. Even so, reformers were unlikely to remake college sports in the near future. Regardless of possible incommensurability of big-time athletics and higher education, intercollegiate sports are an extremely lucrative and popular part of the sports industry in general.

BIBLIOGRAPHY

Rosen, Charles. *Scandals of '51: How the Gamblers Almost Killed College Basketball*. New York: Hold, Rinehart, and Winston, 1978.

Shulman, James L., and William G. Bowen. *The Game of Life: College Sports and Educational Values*. Princeton, N.J.: Princeton University Press, 2001.

Smith, Ronald A. *Sports and Freedom: The Rise of Big-Time College Athletics*. New York: Oxford University Press, 1988.

Sperber, Murray. *College Sports Inc.: The Athletic Department vs. the University*. New York: Holt, 1990.

Watterson, John Sayle. *College Football: History, Spectacle, Controversy*. Baltimore, Md.: Johns Hopkins University Press, 2000.

Welch, Paula. *Silver Era, Golden Moments: A Celebration of Ivy League Women's Athletics*. Lanham, Md.: Madison, 1999.

Jeremy Derfner

See also **National Collegiate Athletic Association.**

COLOMBIA, RELATIONS WITH. *See* Latin America, Relations with; Panama Canal.

COLONIAL ADMINISTRATION, SPANISH.

Spanish colonial institutions in the Americas evolved over decades and in various locales. In contrast to the English colonies, where religious, royal, and proprietary colonies existed concurrently, under Spanish colonial administration, proprietary, missionary, and royal colonies existed in consecutive stages. Many aspects of the colonial administration were derived from experience in the Reconquest of Spain, but even more of its workings stemmed from the experience of conquest and colonization in the New World itself.

The initial model for colonization was similar to that for the English proprietary colonies. Hernán Cortes was the first *adelantado* in the New World; Juan de Oñate was the first to hold that office in what became the United States. Oñate negotiated a contract with the king for certain rights and offices. The monarchy realized the disadvantages of this type of colony. Within less than a generation the model was changed to a civil government, consisting of appointed and elected officials and ideally supplemented by the mission and presidio (fort).

Levels of Government

The highest body of the civil government in the Americas was the Council of the Indies. Although this body ideally included men with experience in the Americas, it never went there. Officially formed in 1524, the council was an outgrowth of the Council of Castile. The Council of the Indies drafted and issued American laws, served as the appellate court for civil cases arising in the American colonies, and exercised the power of royal nomination for American religious and secular offices. The Crown appointed the members of the council, who served at royal discretion.

In the New World, the highest-ranking royal representatives were the viceroys (assistant kings), deputies of the Crown who ruled in the monarch's name. Both the Crown and the Council of the Indies appointed these officials, all of whom were *peninsulares*, or Spaniards born in Spain. Although the law specified the term of a viceroy, these officials served at the discretion of the Crown and answered to the Council of the Indies. The viceroys governed large areas of land and were responsible for preserving Spanish control of their colonies, implementing royal orders and polices, maintaining and fostering the Catholic faith, and defending the population. Although the viceroy did not directly approve further exploration, his opinion carried great weight and his nominees were usually given preference.

Initially, there were two viceroyalties and several subordinate *audiencias*. The first viceroyalty was in Mexico (New Spain), created in 1535 with its capital at Mexico City. The second was Peru (New Castile), established in 1542 with its capital at Lima. The first viceroy of New Spain—constituting what later became the nation of Mexico and the western United States—was Antonio de Mendoza.

Judicial and advisory bodies known as *audiencias* assisted the viceroys. *Audiencias* were the appellate courts of their area, being subordinate judicially to the Council of the Indies. They also assumed full viceregal powers when the viceroy was absent or incapacitated. *Audiencias* differed from one another both in size and in power and their operation at any given time depended on local circumstances. Their members ordinarily served longer terms than viceroys and as corporate entities the *audiencias* provided administrative continuity.

Local government varied according to time and place. In seventeenth-century New Mexico, for example, the model was relatively simple. The *gobernador* (governor) ruled the northern province of New Mexico—the Rio Arriba, with its seat in Santa Fe—while the lieutenant governor administered the southern portion, the Rio Abajo. Except for Santa Fe and its environs, there were in later times subordinate *jurisdicciones* (districts) where an *alcalde mayor* governed.

Ideally, the *alcalde mayor* headed a *cabildo* (town council), which served an important and broad role in the political life of the community. Four *regidores* (councilmen), who initially were elected by the citizens of the villa (town), made up the *cabildo*; the *alcalde mayor* presided over the *cabildo*. The *cabildo* members appointed two *alcaldes ordinarios* (municipal magistrates) as well as an *alguacil* (bailiff), notary, and *alférez real* (royal standard bearer). In addition to executive and military roles, the *alcalde mayor* exercised judicial powers. Community governments, however, became weaker as the Spanish Empire itself declined. *Regidores* secured their posts through appointment, and as a result, town councils became self-perpetuating. The Crown reduced the powers of the *cabildo*. A strong *cabildo* and popular political participation survived only in marginal areas, at a distance from the capital, and through neglect. By 1700 very little remained of the municipal autonomy that was traditional in the earlier Hispanic world. In smaller towns without an *alcalde mayor*, the *cabildo* performed administrative functions on its own. In New Mexico during most of the colonial period, only the *cabildo* in Santa Fe operated. Even this body ceased to function from the 1740s at the latest until the first decade of the nineteenth century. During this time local government was almost exclusively the domain of the *alcalde mayor* and his assistants.

Law and the New World

Spain had an extensive body of laws dealing with the administration of the New World. They originally were issued as the *New Laws* (1573) but then were recompiled in 1681 as the *New Laws of the Indies*. The *Instrucciones* of 1786 not only recompiled some of the laws but also instituted a major reorganization of New World government into *intendencias*, or military administrative units. The reorganization occurred because of an increased need for defense against both Native Americans and European invaders. Some offices, such as the *regidores* and *alcalde mayors*, ceased to exist at this time.

Although there was a law for almost every situation, Spanish colonies were often known for their noncompliance with the laws of the empire. In fact, the principle of *obedzago pero no cumplo* (I obey, but I do not comply) embodied this ambiguity that led over the decades to conflicting regulations, local discretion in enforcing the laws, and ultimately to paralysis of action and proliferation of paperwork. This paralysis, followed by the chaos of the Mexican period (1821–1846), made the U.S. military takeover of what would become the southern United States easier.

BIBLIOGRAPHY

Bourne, Edward Gaylord. *Spain in America, 1450–1580.* New York: Barnes and Noble, 1962.

Gibson, Charles. *Spain in America.* New York: Harper and Row, 1966.

Simmons, Marc. *Spanish Government in New Mexico.* Albuquerque: University of New Mexico Press, 1990.

Stefanie Beninato

See also **Spanish Borderlands**.

COLONIAL AGENT. Anglo-American agents worked in several capacities in the seventeenth and eighteenth centuries. Colonial merchants and commercial enterprises hired agents to represent them in London. British ministries assigned diplomatic agents on missions to other nations, including colonial governments. Agents served specifically as liaisons to crown colonies. Others, stationed in London, more generally attended to the interests of each of the British colonies in North America. These agents, perhaps the most historically visible (including Benjamin Franklin, who served as an agent of Pennsylvania in England from 1757 to 1762), represented their colonies as paid lobbyists. Though never officially members of the imperial government, agents were essential to colonial administration. By the end of the seventeenth century, colonists and the crown recognized the necessity of maintaining a permanent presence in England.

English officials relied heavily on colonial spokesmen, the best means of communication with an extensive and far-flung empire. Though many agents were colonials, many were Englishmen (some of whom never actually journeyed to the colonies) who had special interests in America. Agents forwarded documents, drafted and presented petitions, shepherded colonial legislation through the proper channels, and settled land disputes, among numerous other duties. They appeared before the Privy Council, met with the royal cabinet members, and consulted with the Board of Trade and other governmental branches. Over the course of the eighteenth century, however, in the face of the increasingly factional nature of British politics, attempts by the crown to control all aspects of colonial government, and rising recalcitrance on the part of the colonies, it became more difficult for agents to function effectively as lobbyists.

BIBLIOGRAPHY

Kammen, Michael G. *A Rope of Sand: The Colonial Agents, British Politics, and the American Revolution.* Ithaca, N.Y.: Cornell University Press, 1968.

Leslie J. Lindenauer

COLONIAL ASSEMBLIES had their beginnings in the Virginia HOUSE OF BURGESSES, which Governor George Yeardley convened in 1619. After the Sandys-Southampton group gained control of the Virginia Company, they initiated a new policy that provided for a unicameral assembly composed of the governor, his council, and two burgesses to represent each town, plantation, and hundred. Subsequently, the counties, along with certain priveleged towns and cities, comprised the units of representation. In the latter part of the seventeenth century the elected representatives separated from the parent assembly, creating a bicameral legislature. From the start, the Virginia assembly claimed and exercised the right to initiate legislation, and under Governor John Harvey asserted the right to control taxation. After Governor Sir William Berkeley's withdrawal from public life in 1652 the House of Burgesses exercised great authority with little outside interference except for the limitations the Navigation Act of 1651 placed on commerce. When Berkeley returned to power in 1662, he failed to call elections and retained the old assembly until BACON'S REBELLION in 1676. Due to popular resentment of his attempt to control the legislature, the assembly reverted to its representative character after Bacon's Rebellion.

As in Virginia, other southern colonies witnessed fluctuation in the balance of power between colonial assemblies, colonists, and proprietors or royal governors. Upon coming into possession of his Maryland proprietary, Cecilius Calvert, 2d Baron Baltimore, called an assembly of freemen. He attempted to establish the principle that the proprietor alone might initiate legislation, and sent over drafts of a series of measures. The assembly rejected them, claiming sole powers of initiation, and passed a number of bills framed by its own members. Although Baltimore rejected these, claiming they violated his rights, he finally acknowledged the assembly's competence to initiate laws. He insisted, however, that the legislature submit all measures to him for acceptance or rejection. In seventeenth-century Carolina, the divergent aims of the proprietors and settlers confused legislative processes. The settlers were determined to uphold the binding nature of the so-called Concessions and Agreement of 1665, which provided for a popularly elected assembly of freeholders. In opposition to this, the proprietors attempted to enforce the feudal Fundamental Constitutions with its complicated lawmaking machinery designed to guarantee proprietarial control of legislation. As in Maryland, the proprietors (and later the royal governors) of Carolina had to compromise with the assemblies in order to govern effectively.

In New England colonial assemblies enjoyed considerable power. Plymouth set up a popular assembly consisting of all qualified freemen, which evolved into a bicameral body as the colony incorporated out-settlements. In Massachusetts Bay, Governor John Winthrop and his supporters attempted to concentrate legislative authority in the Court of Assistants, limiting the General Court to the activities of a court of election. This effort failed because the town deputies demanded that the colonial government observe the provisions of the royal charter, which called for a legislative body. After experimenting with a primary assembly of all freemen that featured proxy voting, a representative bicameral system evolved there as in Plymouth. The Massachusetts General Court was uniquely powerful among other colonial assemblies. As in most colonies, the lower house was popularly elected. The members of the lower house, in turn, elected the members of the council, or the upper house. In other colonies, the colonial governor performed this task, and the Massachusetts assembly's popular power became a bone of contention between Massachusetts and the British government in the 1770s. In Rhode Island, the towns were empowered to initiate legislation that they referred to the assembly. Conversely, the assembly would refer measures to the towns for their approval or disapproval. The system was ineffective, however, and the charter of 1663 gave the assembly a dominating role in all matters of government. Connecticut, under its Fundamental Orders of 1639, had a General Court that served as both a representative body and, upon sitting as a court of election, a primary assembly. The latter feature continued under the charter of 1662, although in the mid-eighteenth century it disappeared in favor of local election of colonial officials. As in Rhode Island, the Connecticut assembly was the real center of governmental authority and throughout the colonial period enjoyed great freedom from outside interference.

The powers that colonial assemblies exercised in the Middle Colonies varied widely. The Duke of York ruled NEW YORK for many years without the aid of any popularly elected body, much to the dissatisfaction of the English-speaking population. When Governor Edmund Andros retired to England in 1680, the settlers refused to pay imposts, which made it necessary for the Duke of York either to send an army to subdue the people, or to grant an assembly. He chose the latter course, sending Thomas Dongan as governor, but the laws passed by the deputies were never ratified, and James II forbade future assemblies upon ascending the throne. In 1684 he withdrew the Massachusetts charter and joined the NEW ENGLAND COLONIES with New York, East Jersey, and West Jersey under the auspices of the DOMINION OF NEW ENGLAND, in which lawmaking powers were centered not in the colonial assemblies, but in the appointed Dominion council. The Dominion collapsed with the conclusion of the Glorious Revolution in 1689, and the ascension of William and Mary initiated a period in which the royal government interfered little with colonial affairs. In contrast, PENNSYLVANIA had a popularly elected assembly from its founding. In this colony, tensions emerged between the Quaker-dominated assembly and the increasingly diverse population. Particularly, western inhabitants objected to the Quakers' pacifist policies, which impeded the founding and funding of a colonial militia that might protect frontier residents against attacks by American Indians. As white settlers extended their claims in western Pennsylvania, thereby intensifying conflicts with Indian groups who occupied that territory, they increasingly resented the Quaker assembly that refused to provide military support.

Tensions between the colonial assemblies, colonial governors, and the colonists themselves emerged throughout Anglo-America in the mid-eighteenth century. In Massachusetts Bay, contentious issues included appropriations for a permanent establishment and construction of forts, as well as the control of the office of speaker of the house of representatives. In New York and in New Jersey, as the result of Lord Cornbury's controversial administration, the assemblies gained new powers over financial disbursements and administration. In Pennsylvania, the French and Indian War ignited controversies over the issue of paper money, and the assembly's authority to tax proprietary lands. When Parliament threatened in 1756 to compel all officeholders in Pennsylvania to take the required oaths (which violated Quaker tenets), many Quakers resigned in protest and a non-Quaker majority controlled the assembly for the first time. Conflicts with the governors, as a rule, left the assemblies in a strongly entrenched position, in spite of the continued control of colonial legislation on the part of the Privy Council.

With the approach of the Revolution, divisions between assemblies and governors in all of the colonies widened except in the two corporate colonies (Connecticut and Rhode Island). The degrees of friction varied, however, from the violent manifestations in Massachusetts Bay to the relatively friendly relations between Governor John Penn and the Pennsylvania assembly.

BIBLIOGRAPHY

Bailyn, Bernard. *The Ideological Origins of the American Revolution.* Cambridge, Mass.: Harvard University Press, 1992.

Bonomi, Patricia U. *The Lord Cornbury Scandal: The Politics of Reputation in British America.* Chapel Hill: University of North Carolina Press, 1998.

Lockridge, Kenneth A. *Settlement and Unsettlement in Early America: The Crisis of Political Legitimacy before the Revolution.* Cambridge, U.K.: Cambridge University Press, 1981.

Lovejoy, David S. *The Glorious Revolution in America.* Middletown, Conn.: Wesleyan University Press, 1987.

Morgan, Edmund S. *Inventing the People: The Rise of Popular Sovereignty in England and America.* New York: Norton, 1988.

Lawrence Henry Gipson/Shelby Balik

See also **Carolina, Fundamental Constitutions of; Colonial Councils; Colonial Settlements; Duke of York's Proprietary; General Court, Colonial.**

COLONIAL CHARTERS were empowered when the king gave a grant of exclusive powers for the governance of land to proprietors or a settlement company. The charters defined the relationship of the colony to the mother country, free from involvement from the Crown. For the trading companies, charters vested the powers of government in the company in England. The officers would determine the administration, laws, and ordinances for the colony, but only as conforming to the laws of England. Proprietary charters gave governing authority to the proprietor, who determined the form of government, chose the officers, and made laws, subject to the advice and consent of the freemen. All colonial charters guaranteed to the colonists the vague rights and privileges of Englishmen, which would later cause trouble during the revolutionary era. In the second half of the seventeenth century, the Crown looked upon charters as obstacles to colonial control, substituting the royal province for corporations and proprietary governments.

The Massachusetts and Virginia charters were given to business corporations. Regular meetings of company officers and stockholders were the only governmental institutions required. The Virginia charter, issued in 1606, was revoked upon bankruptcy of the Virginia Company of London in 1624. The second colonial charter was granted to Massachusetts in 1629. In 1684, the Chancery Court in England voided the charter and changed it to a royal colony. Charles II placed Massachusetts under the Dominion of New England in 1685. After William III came to the throne, he issued Massachusetts Bay a new liberal charter in 1691.

Charles II granted Connecticut its charter in 1662 with the right of self-government. When James II ascended the throne in 1685, he tried to revoke the Connecticut charter and sent Sir Edmund Andros to receive it for the Crown. Joseph Wadsworth stole the charter and hid it in a hollow oak tree, the "charter oak," until James was overthrown. Connecticut temporarily lost the right of self-government under the Dominion of New England in 1687, but it was reinstated in 1689. The last charter by Charles II was issued to Rhode Island in 1663. Connecticut and Rhode Island attained colonial charters as already established colonies that allowed them to elect their own governors.

As a result of political upheavals, most colonies surrendered their charters to the Crown by 1763 and became royal colonies. By 1776, Maryland, Delaware, and Pennsylvania remained proprietary colonies under a charter, Connecticut and Rhode Island continued as corporation colonies under charters, and Massachusetts was governed as a royal province while operating under a charter.

BIBLIOGRAPHY

Bridenbaugh, Carl. *Early Americans.* New York: Oxford University Press, 1981.

Ernst, Joseph Albert. *The Forming of a Nation, 1607–1781.* New York: Random House, 1970.

Middleton, Richard. *Colonial America: A History, 1585–1776.* Cambridge, Mass.: Blackwell, 1996.

Ubbelohde, Carl. *The American Colonies and the British Empire, 1607–1763.* New York: Crowell, 1968.

Michelle M. Mormul

See also **Colonial Policy, British; Dominion of New England; Royal Colonies;** *and vol. 9:* **Charter to Sir Walter Raleigh; The Mayflower Compact, November 11, 1620.**

COLONIAL COMMERCE. From the earliest American settlements, colonial commerce was the province of diverse groups of settlers. Puritans in Boston, Pilgrims at Plymouth Plantation, Quakers in Philadelphia, Dutch in New Amsterdam (New York City), and Scots in the Chesapeake were all part of the colonial American merchant establishment. As early as 1621, the famed "triangular trade" underpinned that commerce and laid the groundwork for American prosperity. North American merchants could not sell enough directly to England to pay for the English goods they needed, so they eventually traded tobacco, foodstuffs, and even slaves to obtain the sugar, molasses, and rum English merchants craved for the manufactures (tools, textiles, and weapons, for the most part) that the burgeoning North American colonies required.

Colonial Traders

While the British settlers in all their diversity came to dominate colonial commerce, the Dutch, who arrived early in New Amsterdam, helped pioneer that triangular trade. Dutch colonists began arriving in numbers as early as 1624 and dominated not only what became New York City but also the Hudson River valley as well. Dutch patrons along the Hudson were closely involved with the Dutch East India Company merchants on Manhattan Island, the latter forming the vital center of the commerce that ever after dominated the economic life of New York. Dutch New York was already a major American colonial merchant outpost when the English conquered it in 1664.

Already by that date Parliament and the British Board of Trade were establishing the ground rules for exploiting England's growing colonial empire in the New World. Beginning in 1663 the Navigation Acts defined the limits imposed on colonial commerce. They succeeded in constantly reminding American merchants, tradespeople, and artisans of the profit-squelching restrictions and second-class status under which American trade operated. They failed through lack of enforcement to actually improve British trade profits and did not hamper American economic growth. The acts altogether were thus a disaster for the mother country. They strained ties to the colonies, especially among the zealous Puritan merchants in Massachusetts Bay, even as they failed to reign in colonial commerce. The acts rankled symbolically, however, especially among the Puritan merchant elite in New England. On paper, the high (but largely uncollected) taxes and the list of goods that could not be traded (they were anyway) still remained a constant reminder to merchants of their second-class national status.

So even as the American colonies prospered, the perception grew in the seventeenth and eighteenth centuries that parliamentary restrictions were choking colonial economic growth. The reality was that major American port cities grew and prospered. Ultimately 80 percent of the American population in the thirteen colonies lived, worked, and farmed along the Atlantic seaboard. Urban commercial centers in Newport, Rhode Island; Boston; New York City; Philadelphia; and Charleston became thriving trade-oriented metropolises, with satellite port cities flourishing as well: New London, Connecticut; Wilmington, Delaware; Norfolk, Virginia; and Savannah, Georgia, among them.

These cities and towns were dominated by the merchant elite made well-to-do, even rich, by Britain's domination of world trade, restrictions notwithstanding. But this gentry, particularly in political centers like Boston and New York City, chafed under perceived British restrictions imposed by Parliament and the Board of Trade. It should be remembered as well that the laboring classes in the port cities, from the cartmen, who carried the goods to the skilled artisans on the docks, to the more proletarian seamen, who comprised the crews on colonial American bottoms, made their livings at trade. All depended utterly on the health and profitability of the triangular trade, and their politics, separated though the groups were by class distinctions, reflected their common economic realities. So it was that when in 1764 the British government actually moved rigorously to enforce the old Navigation Acts, it found strong resistance among all classes in all thirteen colonies.

Conflicts

The resurgence of British control over the culturally and politically independent colonists in North America coincided with the end of the French and Indian War (1754–1763) (variously called the Seven Years' War and the Great War for Empire) in 1763. British victory once and for all ended the French threat to wrest at least part of North America from English rule. It was no longer necessary, in the British government's view, to placate the thirteen colonies to keep them from the grasp of the French (never, except in Canada, a cultural or national possibility anyway). But the point was that French economic penetration of North America had always been a threat in the wilderness West, and the Seven Years' War effectively put a lid on that possibility. It was now time for the colonies to pay their own way, to put their treasures in the hands of the Crown for the sake of all the empire as England saw it. To this end the Crown determined to enforce the Navigation Acts, some dating back a century. To a large degree, seen in this way, the American Revolution (1775–1783) was about commerce as much as anything else. Capitalist free-enterprise notions

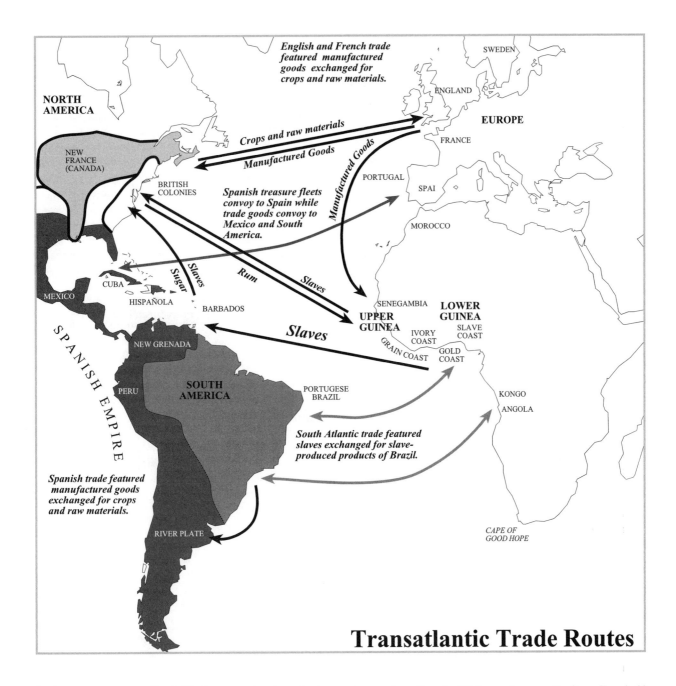

English and French trade featured manufactured goods exchanged for crops and raw materials.

NORTH AMERICA

EUROPE

SWEDEN

ENGLAND

NEW FRANCE (CANADA)

FRANCE

Crops and raw materials

Manufactured Goods

BRITISH COLONIES

PORTUGAL

SPAI

Spanish treasure fleets convoy to Spain while trade goods convoy to Mexico and South America.

Manufactured Goods

MOROCCO

Slaves

Sugar

Rum

Slaves

MEXICO

CUBA

HISPAÑOLA

BARBADOS

Slaves

SENEGAMBIA

UPPER GUINEA

LOWER GUINEA

SLAVE COAST

IVORY COAST

GRAIN COAST

GOLD COAST

S P A N I S H   E M P I R E

NEW GRENADA

SOUTH AMERICA

PERU

PORTUGESE BRAZIL

KONGO

ANGOLA

South Atlantic trade featured slaves exchanged for slave-produced products of Brazil.

Spanish trade featured manufactured goods exchanged for crops and raw materials.

RIVER PLATE

CAPE OF GOOD HOPE

Transatlantic Trade Routes

had over a century and a half taken root in the colonies as they had in the mother country. To a large extent that commitment to trade and profit permeated the ranks of the underclass artisan, mechanics, tradespeople, and yeoman farmers alike. Perhaps only laborers on the farms and seamen on the docks did not wholly buy into this commerce-based worldview.

In any event, all economic and social classes played their parts in the events leading up to the American Revolution. And these events started out as commerce-based grievances. The goals were to free commerce from the stultifying repressions of the Crown, the Board of Trade, and Parliament. The Sugar Act of 1764 claimed only to resurrect the unenforced Molasses Act of 1733 and—a

generation after the Molasses Act—to finally collect half the duties prescribed in the old law, which was levied on the rich trade among the West Indies, the British Isles, and the thirteen American colonies. Enforcement of the 1733 law was seen correctly in the colonies as a new enforcement that would cut colonial profits and wages, however. British arrogance ran up against American nationalism over the question of who controlled American commerce and who gleaned the profits of trade. Commercial questions morphed into political questions of who controlled the colonies, what were the colonists' responsibilities to the Crown, and to what extent did political rights under Magna Carta and Parliament accrue to the former English subjects who became Americans in the New World.

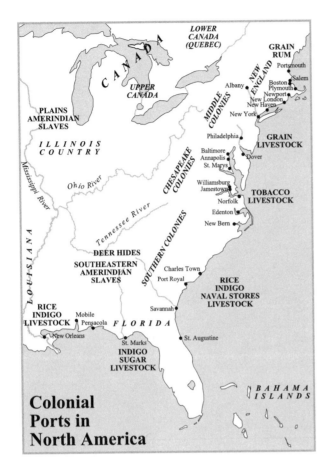

Colonial Ports in North America

with the extreme economic pressure of effective boycotts of British imports. The merchant-dominated Continental Association joined with the working-class Sons of Liberty, first in Boston and New York City and soon along the entire Tidewater, stretching from Massachusetts to Georgia, to provide an economic response to perceived coercion. Loyalists in America argued as strongly that boycotts threatened profits as they denounced the long-term effects of political instability inherent in denunciations of the Crown's authority.

The century and a half of colonial commercial growth and the reality of increasing independence from effective British control created both a politically independent population spread over all classes in the colonies and a political ideology that increasingly articulated a capitalist free-enterprise ethos. The astoundingly radical Declaration of Independence of 1776 is both a ringing declaration of human rights, individual liberties, and political freedom and a reaffirmation of capitalism based on free commerce. Commitment to "Life" and "Liberty" was conjoined with the "Pursuit of Happiness," a euphemism for "Property" as John Locke originally expressed it. To this end it should be remembered that the American elite that drafted this world-changing document pledged not only its "Lives" and "Sacred Honor" but its merchant-driven "Fortunes" as well.

BIBLIOGRAPHY

Bruchey, Stuart. *The Roots of American Economic Growth, 1607–1861*. New York: Harper and Row, 1965.

Rakove, Jack N. *The Beginnings of National Politics: An Interpretive History of the Continental Congress*. New York: Knopf, 1979.

Carl E. Prince

See also **Colonial Policy, British; Colonial Society;** *and vol. 9:* **The Continental Association.**

These momentous questions of free trade, colonial commercial profitability, and actual political independence within the empire or without played out in the streets of the port cities of North America, particularly in Boston and New York City. The familiar milestones along the path to independence all had as overt causation questions involving taxation and trade that also became in the eyes of the colonists questions of human rights, individual liberties, and free enterprise.

The responses to the Sugar Act of 1764, the Stamp Act of 1765, the Townshend Duties of 1767, and the Intolerable Acts of 1774 all formed around grievances that raised these issues. Commerce-based capitalist control blended completely with the most basic, articulated demands for individual liberties and republican values in the maturation of the American Revolution. By 1774, commerce-driven protests were couched in the rhetoric of American independence rooted in the political freedom from the oppressions of the Crown, Parliament, and the Board of Trade. The British responded in kind, understanding all too well that commercial profit in the colonies was closely linked to the Enlightenment-driven high rhetoric of political rights. The Intolerable Acts of 1774 not only quartered British troops in American port cities and suspended the fractious Lower House of the Massachusetts legislature, but they closed Boston port as well. The First Continental Congress of 1774–1775 responded

COLONIAL COUNCILS existed in all colonies. They comprised the upper house of the legislature and, with the governor, formed a supreme court of appeals in civil cases. The council was also an executive and administrative body for the governor and approved and implemented executive acts. Charters and instructions to the royal governor specified councils' duties, although their specific roles evolved over time. In royal colonies the crown appointed the council, in proprietary colonies the proprietor did so, and in charter colonies councils were elected. In the royal and proprietary colonies, council members served during good behavior and could be removed only by the crown or proprietors. Councils varied in size, ranging from ten to thirty.

BIBLIOGRAPHY

Daniels, Bruce C., ed. *Power and Status: Officeholding in Colonial America*. Middletown, Conn.: Wesleyan University Press, 1986.

Katz, Stanley N., and John M. Murrin. *Colonial America*. New York: Knopf, 1983.

O. M. Dickerson / s. b.

See also **Colonial Assemblies; Colonial Charters; General Court, Colonial.**

COLONIAL DAMES OF AMERICA.

The National Society of the Colonial Dames of America was founded in 1891 in Philadelphia to promote interest in colonial history. Eligibility is determined by descent from certain categories of civil servants in the colonies who served on or before 6 July 1776. The NSCDA provides scholarships, publishes books, and preserves paintings, manuscripts, and buildings of historic importance. In 2000, the NSCDA received an award from the National Trust for its preservation of the ninety-five historic properties it owns or maintains. In 2001, the organization had fifteen thousand members. There are two other societies with the words "colonial dames" in their titles that have lineage as the criterion for membership: Colonial Dames of America, founded in 1890, and the National Society, Colonial Dames XVII Century, founded in 1915.

BIBLIOGRAPHY

"Colonial Dames Win National Preservation Award." National Trust for Historic Preservation. Available from http://www.nationaltrust.org.

Lamar, Clarinda Huntingdon. *A History of the National Society of the Colonial Dames of America, from 1891 to 1933*. Atlanta, Ga.: Walter W. Brown, 1934.

Bonnie Ford

See also **Daughters of the American Revolution; Preservation Movement.**

COLONIAL POLICY, BRITISH.

English colonial policy, which became "British" with the union of England and Scotland in 1707, promoted domestic industry, foreign trade, fisheries, and shipping by planting colonial settlements in the New World and exploiting its resources through such commercial companies as the Hudson's Bay Company and the South Sea Company. The colonial policy began with the sixteenth-century patents to Sir Humphrey Gilbert and Sir Walter Raleigh. In 1606 patents were granted to the London and Plymouth Companies of Virginia, and a settlement policy of direct Crown control was established. In 1609 this was modified by a charter issued to the Virginia Company substituting indirect for direct control and providing for a definite and extensive grant of land. This new policy led to the creation of the Council for New England in 1620. Direct control reappeared in 1624, when the political powers of the Virginia Company were withdrawn and Virginia became the first of the royal colonies under a system of government that included a governor appointed by the king and a co-lonial assembly. In 1629, however, the corporate colony of Massachusetts Bay was granted a charter that permitted the transfer of the government of the company to the New World. In 1632 the first proprietary colony of Maryland was established with the granting of wide powers to the Baltimore family. Thus three types of colonial government, royal, corporate, and proprietary, appeared.

Three types of British colonies existed in America. The first were plantation colonies in the Caribbean and the South Atlantic seaboard. These included Jamaica, Barbados, Virginia, the Carolinas, and Georgia, which produced sugar, tobacco, rice, and indigo. A second group, the Middle Colonies of Maryland, Delaware, New Jersey, Pennsylvania, and New York, produced wheat and timber. The third group consisted of the New England colonies of Connecticut, Massachusetts, Rhode Island, New Hampshire, and Maine, whose economy rested on trade in rum and slaves and on shipbuilding.

The king directed colonial policy until the outbreak of the first English civil war, when the Long Parliament assumed control, acting mainly through a special commission or council provided for by the Ordinance of 1643. This ordinance gave its president, the earl of Warwick, the title of governor in chief and lord high admiral of all the English colonies in America. Between 1645 and 1651 Parliament enacted regulations for strict control of colonial commerce in favor of English shipping and manufactures. The Restoration did not reverse this parliamentary interference with the colonies but added a series of measures, beginning with the Navigation Act of 1660 and culminating in the Act of 1696. During the Commonwealth period Oliver Cromwell introduced a temporary departure in colonial policy in 1654 with his plan called the Western Design, whose purpose was the acquisition of Spanish colonies in the New World and settlement of them by English colonists.

The growing importance of the colonies led to various experiments in their supervision, such as the Laud Commission appointed by Charles I and the various councils of Charles II. The experiments ended with the transference in 1675 of this function to the Lords of Trade, a committee of the Privy Council, which continued to function until 1696, when William III established the Lords Commissioners for Trade and Plantations, a body that survived until after the American Revolution.

Colonial policy in the eighteenth century tried to reduce the corporate and proprietary colonies to royal colonies, which largely succeeded. In addition the policy increased restrictions upon colonial enterprise with such acts as the Woolen Act of 1699, the White Pine Acts, the Hat Act of 1732, the Sugar Acts of 1733 and 1764, and the Iron Act of 1750.

From 1754 until 1763 the English and the French contested for the fur trade in the Ohio Valley. After a faltering start, when General Edward Braddock was routed by a force of French and Indians before Fort Duquesne on the site of the present city of Pittsburgh, Pennsylvania, the English gained the military initiative under the political leadership of the Elder Pitt (William Pitt). Jeffrey Amherst captured Louisbourg. In 1759 General James Wolfe defeated the Marquis Montcalm on the Plains of Abraham under the walls of the fortress of Quebec, and the war was all but over.

In 1764 the cost of governing the colonies was £350,000 a year, while colonial trade brought at least £2 million into Great Britain. Yet the Seven Years' War had created a war debt of £130 million. British landowners, who controlled Parliament, already paid a tax of 20 percent, and they refused to pay more. Prime Minister George Grenville estimated the average English taxpayer paid an annual tax of 26 shillings, while a British subject living in Massachusetts paid one shilling a year and the average Virginian only 5 pence. Grenville argued that, since the colonials had gained the most from the FRENCH AND INDIAN WAR, they should do their part in paying off the war debt.

Since Great Britain did not want to pay for more Indian wars, Parliament passed the Proclamation Act of 1763, which forbade the colonists from moving west of the Appalachian Mountains. The colonists had fought the French primarily to gain control of the western lands, and they were angered over these restrictions, which were difficult to enforce.

In 1764 Britain passed the Sugar Act, the first of several revenue measures passed to try to reduce Britain's war debts. The tax on molasses, used to make rum, a valuable commodity in the slave trade, prior to the 1764 act was 6 pence a pound. American merchants felt that this tax was so high that they were morally justified in ignoring it and paying a bribe of a penny or two to customs agents. If they were arrested, they could usually count on local juries to acquit them. The Sugar Act struck at both of these problems. It reformed and enlarged the customs service, slashed the tax to 3 pence a pound, and set up a new system of courts that would try customs violators without juries. The colonists protested by boycotting British imports. Britain responded to this pressure by reducing the tax in 1766 to a penny a barrel.

In 1765 Parliament passed the STAMP ACT, which required that legal documents, newspapers, pamphlets, playing cards, and handbills be taxed. A stamp was affixed to the taxed object to show that the tax had been paid. This act caused an uproar in the colonies. Local Sons of Liberty groups were formed to protest the act and to enforce a boycott of British goods.

In October 1765 thirty-seven delegates from nine colonies assembled in New York City to oppose the Stamp Act. This STAMP ACT CONGRESS was the first time representatives of most of the colonists met together. The legal question was whether or not Parliament, a legislative body to which the colonists elected no members, had the right to impose taxes on the colonists. The colonists maintained that under custom and the British constitution only their own elected COLONIAL ASSEMBLIES could do so. This was expressed in the slogan "no taxation without representation." The colonists asserted the claim that they could not be taxed without their consent and that colonial legislatures held taxation powers equivalent to those of Parliament. Representatives to the colonial legislatures and local councils were elected by propertied citizens on a district basis, but leaders of Parliament argued that every English subject was "virtually" represented in the English Parliament. They contended that even though a member of Parliament was elected from a specific geographic district, he legally represented the interests of the citizens of the empire at large. Actually the interests of unrepresented constituents were of small concern to members elected by the tenth of the English adult male population that voted for Parliament, and the colonials regarded this doctrine of virtual representation sophistry.

Parliament repealed the Stamp Act in 1766 in response to colonial pressure, but at the same time it passed the Declaratory Act, which reaffirmed parliamentary supremacy. In 1767 the chancellor of the exchequer, Charles Townshend, imposed duties on paper, paint, lead, glass, and tea imported into the colonies. Colonial objections and boycotts caused trade to fall off by 50 percent, which made Parliament back down. The TOWNSHEND ACTS were repealed in 1770 except for a 3-pence tax on tea. For the next three years no new taxes or duties were imposed on the colonies, and the protests subsided.

However, large numbers of British soldiers were stationed in the colonies, and tension developed between them and the colonists. On 5 March 1770 a Boston crowd began heckling and throwing snowballs at a group of British soldiers. The soldiers panicked and fired into the crowd, killing five people. This "BOSTON MASSACRE" motivated the colonists to form committees of correspondence to keep each other informed about events throughout the colonies. In 1772 a group of colonists boarded the British customs vessel *Gaspee* after it had run aground, seriously wounded the ship's captain, then burned the ship.

In 1773 Parliament granted the British East India Company a monopoly on tea. This monopoly was not intended to hurt or tax American merchants but to help the financially strapped East India Company. The act allowed the East India Company to handle both the shipping and the sale of its tea, which prior to the act had been sold by the company at public auction. This act would lower the price of tea, but competing merchants like John Hancock would be stripped of an important source of revenue. The colonists feared that other British companies might gain similar privileges at their expense.

The colonists responded to the tea monopoly with a tea boycott. On 16 December 1773 about 150 Bostonians disguised as Indians climbed aboard three British merchant ships loaded with tea that had been waiting in Boston Harbor for the opportunity to unload their cargo. In less than three hours 342 chests of tea were thrown overboard. Parliament retaliated in 1774 with the Coercive Acts, which the colonials called the INTOLERABLE ACTS. These acts (1) closed the port of Boston until the destroyed tea was paid for, (2) suspended self-government in Massachusetts, (3) allowed trials of colonists to be moved to other colonies or to Britain, and (4) allowed soldiers to be quartered in private homes. Britain hoped the Coercive Acts would isolate Massachusetts and set an example. Instead the Coercive Acts united the colonies.

In response to the Intolerable Acts the First Continental Congress met in September 1774 and agreed to a boycott of English goods. In response to the BOSTON TEA PARTY and the colonial boycott, Britain moved more soldiers to the colonies. In 1775 seven hundred soldiers of the British army marched out of Boston to arrest the colonial leaders Samuel Adams and John Hancock and to capture colonial military supplies in the towns of Lexington and Concord, Massachusetts. The colonists called up their militia to resist the British. When the British arrived at Lexington early in the morning of 19 April, seventy "minutemen" were there to meet them. Someone fired a shot, and during several volleys eight colonials were killed. The British then marched to Concord, where a larger group of Americans opened fire on them. Surprised and alarmed by the extent of the resistance, the British retreated to Boston and were fired upon most of the way. The British lost 73 dead, 174 wounded, and 26 missing, 20 percent of the British soldiers. American losses were 49 dead and 39 wounded. The War for Independence had begun.

The American colonies declared their independence on 4 July 1776. The Declaration of Independence, drafted by Thomas Jefferson, was based on the natural rights ideas of European political philosophers, especially the English philosopher John Locke, and was derived from many of the reforms proposed during the two English civil wars but not fully adopted in Britain. Many of the questions raised by the Americans and the American Revolution brought amelioration of British colonial policy elsewhere in the British Empire after 1783.

BIBLIOGRAPHY

Gipson, Lawrence Henry. *The British Empire before the American Revolution.* New York: Knopf, 1939–1970.

Rose, J. Holland, A. P. Newton, and E. A. Benians, eds. *Cambridge History of the British Empire.* Vol. 1. New York: Macmillan, 1929–.

Jon Roland

See also **Continental Congress;** *and vol. 9:* **Stamp Act; The Writ of Assistance, 1762; Townshend Revenue Act.**

COLONIAL SETTLEMENTS.

In the sixteenth century, England sought to emulate other European powers by establishing colonies in the New World. The goal of the colonists and their supporters was to increase England's territorial hegemony and to enrich themselves. Little gold or silver was found in England's North American colonies, but colonists who came to America for a variety of reasons nonetheless accomplished that goal.

Chesapeake Colonies

The first attempts at settlement of North America occurred on Roanoke Island in 1585, under the sponsorship of Sir Walter Raleigh. England claimed North American territory on the basis of the 1497 and 1498 voyages of John Cabot. The Roanoke colony was also to serve as a base from which the English could launch attacks on Spanish vessels as they sailed for European waters. The initial colony and two subsequent attempts failed.

The Virginia Company, a joint stock company composed of London and Plymouth merchants, undertook the next attempt at English colonization. Issued a charter in 1606 by James I, three ships carrying 144 adventurers, soldiers, and fortune hunters were sent in 1607 to establish a colony on the James River in Virginia. The Jamestown settlers were unable to find large stores of precious metals but the colony prevailed, despite an appallingly high death rate. Virginia prospered with the introduction of tobacco cultivation in 1612 and the establishment of private land ownership in 1616. Large plantations were needed for tobacco, which quickly damaged the soil. The need for more territory and population growth led to two major Indian attacks, with 347 colonists killed in 1622 and 500 killed in 1644. As a result of the first attack, the Virginia Company lost its charter and Virginia became the first royal colony, with the governor and council appointed by the Crown and a popularly elected assembly. Tobacco also necessitated a large labor force, and the demand for labor was met by both English indentured servants and African slaves. The population reached 50,000 by the end of the seventeenth century.

Maryland was established by George Calvert, Lord Baltimore, as a refuge for Roman Catholics, who suffered persecution in England, with a charter issued by Charles I in 1632. Following the death of his father, Cecilius Calvert sent some 200 colonists to establish the colony in 1634. Like Virginia, Maryland's prosperity rested on tobacco cultivation, with labor supplied by black slaves and white servants. The colony also produced wheat, fruits, and vegetables. Baltimore attracted settlers by promising 100 acres to every adult man and woman, 50 acres to every child, and granting over sixty manors of 2,000 acres to those who qualified. The population reached 32,000 by 1700. Although a Catholic refuge, Maryland included a substantial number of Protestants, and it was Protestants who seized control of the government during the English civil wars. The Calvert family regained control of the colony with the 1660 restoration of Charles II to the throne.

New England

While Virginia was settled primarily by fortune hunters, the first settlements in New England, like those in Mary-

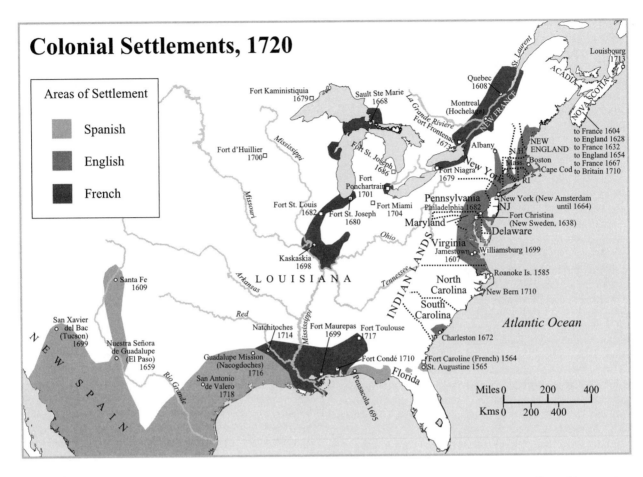

Colonial Settlements, 1720

Areas of Settlement

- Spanish
- English
- French

land, were prompted by religious reasons. The Church of England persecuted a group of extreme Puritans called Separatists. After fleeing their homeland in 1608 and settling unsuccessfully in the Netherlands, the Separatists returned to England and decided to establish a colony in North America. A small group of 102 colonists, 35 of whom were Puritans, sailed for an area just north of Virginia but instead landed much further north on Cape Cod, which they reached on 9 November 1620. They soon proceeded to Plymouth, where they arrived December 16. Most wintered on the ships but the death toll was high, with approximately half the colonists dying before spring. The Wampanoag Indians put up no resistance to the small invasion since their own ranks had been seriously depleted by disease brought by earlier European explorers. The Separatists created a representative government, with only church members who were worth £20 eligible to vote or hold public office. The colony of Plymouth remained separate from Massachusetts until 1691.

Puritans also settled Massachusetts for religious reasons. Charles I granted a charter in 1629 to the New England Company, which promptly changed its name to the Massachusetts Bay Company. A group of a thousand Puritans, led by the attorney John Winthrop, sailed in fifteen ships for New England to form a utopian society in Massachusetts. The Puritans took their charter with them rather than leaving it in London, as was customary, per-

mitting Massachusetts to become virtually a self-governing commonwealth. The English monarchs spent the next several decades in efforts to recall the colony's charter. The government established in Massachusetts was not precisely a theocracy, since ministers did not hold public office, but voting and the holding of public office were restricted to church members, and the church was supported by the state, which also punished heresy. A law code based not on English common law but on the Bible was soon adopted. By 1700, nine years after Massachusetts received a new charter and was united with Plymouth, its population was 80,000.

Minister Roger Williams, forced out of England because of his Puritan beliefs, established Rhode Island only a few years after his 1631 arrival in Massachusetts. Williams was too radical for the Massachusetts Puritans, rejecting the authority of the English king and advocating both a complete separation of church and state and religious toleration. Williams further questioned the right of the English king to grant land in America. Forced out of Massachusetts, Williams founded the colony of Rhode Island, which received a charter from Parliament in 1644 that allowed it to establish a liberal government permitting religious toleration and granting the vote to all free adult white males. Population remained small, with only 4,000 at the end of the seventeenth century.

Minister Thomas Hooker established the colony of Connecticut in 1636, while New Haven, established in 1638 by Theophilus Eaton and the Reverend John Davenport, was separate from Connecticut until 1662. By 1700, the population of Connecticut reached 30,000. New Hampshire originated as the private estate of John Mason, who sold it to the Crown, while Maine was the property of Sir Fernando Gorges. To provide for defense, the United Colonies of New England was formed in 1643. The union included Massachusetts, Connecticut, Plymouth, and New Haven, but not Rhode Island, considered too radical by the other New England colonies. The economy of all the New England colonies was largely based on subsistence farming, the fur trade, fishing, and naval stores.

New York and New Jersey

The residents of the Chesapeake and New England colonies enjoyed a somewhat homogenous society in terms of ethnicity and religion, but this was not the case in New York and New Jersey, where settlers were culturally diverse. European settlement of this area followed Henry Hudson's voyage of exploration in 1609. Sailing for the Dutch East India Company, Hudson's report of the excellence of furs in the area caused the company to establish a trading post at Fort Orange, site of present-day Albany. The Dutch West India Company, formed in 1621, established a community at the tip of Manhattan Island, called New Amsterdam. The New Netherland territory was vast and effectively separated the New England and Chesapeake colonies. The territory included parts of Maine, New Hampshire, the islands from Cape Cod to Cape May except for Block Island, the western half of Connecticut to the Connecticut River, New York, New Jersey, Pennsylvania, and Delaware. To increase the small population of only 10,000 the West India Company drew colonists from several European countries who practiced several different religions.

New Netherland's small population made it relatively easy for the English to seize the province from the Dutch in 1664. King Charles II promptly gave the territory to his brother, James, duke of York. The duke established a nonrepresentative, authoritarian government in the province, with an appointed governor and council. New York's growth was slow compared to that of Massachusetts, reaching only 30,000 in 1700, partly because English governors established a manorial system. Colonists preferred owning their own land in nearby colonies to becoming tenants on a New York manor lord's estate.

Owing favors to two courtiers, John Lord Berkeley and Sir George Carteret, James paid them off by giving them part of the conquered territory. Carteret named the territory New Jersey, in honor of his island home. James claimed he gave away only the soil in New Jersey, not the rights of governance. The new proprietors, who had split the territory into separate colonies of East New Jersey and West New Jersey, disagreed. Several years of strife ensued as New York governors tried to exert authority over New Jersey. This strife, coupled with insecure land titles and multiple proprietors, eventually led New Jersey residents to request that the province be made a royal colony. The request was granted and East and West New Jersey united as a royal colony in 1702, by which time the population had reached 15,000. Like New York, New Jersey's economy was based primarily on the fur trade and the export of wheat and other agricultural products such as pitch and tar, wood products, and horses.

Southern Colonies

Charles II further expanded the empire in 1663, when he granted a charter to eight proprietors for the territory that would comprise North Carolina, South Carolina, and Georgia. Settlement in North Carolina was sparse throughout the seventeenth century, with only about 5,000 settlers by 1700, its growth and development slowed because it did not have a good harbor. North Carolina was settled mostly by freed indentured servants and poor whites who lived on small subsistence farms. The fur trade and the production of naval stores bolstered the economy. Originally part of South Carolina, it became a separate colony in 1712.

South Carolina had an excellent harbor at Charles Town, which developed into a cultured and sophisticated city. Its white settlers were mostly displaced planters from the West Indies, who acquired vast estates. The colony attracted about 7,000 colonists by 1700, and its economy boomed with the introduction of rice cultivation, followed in the eighteenth century by the cultivation of indigo. Like tobacco, rice required a large labor force, resulting in a black majority in the colony by 1720.

Georgia's development began in the eighteenth century when James Edward Oglethorpe, who was interested in establishing a haven for European Protestants, promoted its settlement. George II granted a charter in 1732, and Georgia became a Crown colony in 1751. A decade later, the population had reached 9,000.

Pennsylvania

Another vast territory settled for religious reasons was developed after 1681, when Charles II granted William Penn Jr. a charter for Pennsylvania. A convert to the Quaker faith, Penn led Quakers to the Pennsylvania area shortly thereafter, the colony becoming a refuge not only for Quakers but for other persecuted religious minorities, reaching a population of 20,000 by 1700. Known for his equitable treatment of the indigenous Indians, Penn quickly established good relations with them. The territory was briefly taken away from Penn following the 1688 Glorious Revolution but returned to him by 1696. It remained in the hands of William Penn's descendants until the American Revolution.

While settled for a variety of reasons, the plantations endured and prospered to form part of the first British Empire. In 1607, the only English settlement on the

North American mainland was in Jamestown, Virginia. In 1763, by the terms of the Treaty of Paris that concluded the French and Indian War, the English acquired Florida from the Spanish and Canada from the French. The line of English colonies stretched in an unbroken chain down the entire eastern seaboard of North America and to the west as far as the Mississippi River.

BIBLIOGRAPHY

Bremer, Francis J. *The Puritan Experiment: New England Society from Bradford to Edwards.* Rev. ed. Hanover, N.H.: University Press of New England, 1995.

Calloway, Colin G. *New Worlds for All: Indians, Europeans, and the Remaking of Early America.* Baltimore: Johns Hopkins University Press, 1997.

Delbanco, Andrew. *The Puritan Ordeal.* Cambridge, Mass.: Harvard University Press, 1989.

Kulikoff, Allan. *Tobacco and Slaves: The Development of Southern Cultures in the Chesapeake, 1680–1800.* Chapel Hill: University of North Carolina Press, 1986.

Matson, Cathy. *Merchants and Empire: Trading in Colonial New York.* Baltimore: Johns Hopkins University Press, 1998.

Morgan, Edmund S. *American Slavery, American Freedom: The Ordeal of Colonial Virginia.* New York: Norton, 1975.

Rountree, Helen C. *The Powhatan Indians of Virginia: Their Traditional Culture.* Norman: University of Oklahoma Press, 1989.

Webb, Stephen Saunders. *1676: The End of American Independence.* New York: Knopf, 1984.

Mary Lou Lustig

See also **Chesapeake Colonies; Massachusetts Bay Colony; New England Confederation; New Haven Colony; New Netherland; New York Colony; Plymouth Colony; Puritans and Puritanism; Virginia Company of London;** *and vol. 9:* **Starving in Virginia, 1607–1610.**

COLONIAL SHIPS, which brought the first European settlers to the New World, were very small. Sir Humphrey Gilbert's vessel, on which he lost his life, was a ten-ton ship. Christopher Newport's three ships, in which the first Virginians came to America, were of 100, 40, and 20 tons. The *MAYFLOWER* was a 180-ton ship, its keel length 64 feet, beam width 26 feet, and depth from beam to keel 11 feet, while the full length was 90 feet. The *Dove* and the *Ark*, which carried Lord Baltimore's company to Maryland, were of 50 and 400 tons, respectively.

Passengers spent weeks or months crossing the Atlantic on these vessels. One ship made the journey in four weeks, but the Pilgrims' voyage took ten. The first Virginians and Lord Baltimore's party were at sea four months, and some Germans did not reach America until six months aboard ship. Because of this delay, food and water supplies were soon wretched. Scurvy generally incapacitated one-tenth of those on board. It was only when lemons and oranges were found to prevent scurvy that this condition improved. Overcrowding, smallpox, sea-sickness, fevers, dysentery, and mouth diseases added their quota to the misery and suffering of the transatlantic voyage.

Small vessels were soon being made in the colonies, often in the forests, from where they were rolled on logs to the water's edge. By 1676, 730 ships had been built in Massachusetts alone, and hundreds more had been built in other New England colonies.

BIBLIOGRAPHY

Millar, John F. *American Ships of the Colonial and Revolutionary Periods.* New York: Norton, 1978.

Charles B. Swaney/A. R.

See also **Industries, Colonial; Schooner; Shipbuilding.**

COLONIAL SOCIETY. The basis of American society has always been the individual and political rights and ideals of freedom and equality that most Americans today take for granted. Many of these rights were won, either by design, chance, or circumstance, during the period when the thirteen colonies that formed the United States were under British control. The revolutionary generation, who numbered about 2 million, wanted to retain the best of the English system while rejecting the worst. To a certain degree they were successful. English concepts of freedom and liberty established in the colonial era were retained, but with a peculiarly American flavor.

The People

The character of American society was determined in part by the immigrants themselves. Most settlers who chose to come to America were termed the "middling sort," or what we would call today "middle class," since neither the very wealthy nor the very poor emigrated. Hence there was no hereditary aristocracy in colonial America, and the accumulation of wealth alone was usually considered sufficient to elevate a person to the ranks of the elite. Colonists were largely farmers, artisans, merchants, fishermen, or craftspeople. Others were adventurers or fortune hunters, who, after finding there were no precious metals to be had along the eastern seaboard, turned to other employments. Many came as indentured servants, spending a certain number of years working to pay off the cost of their voyage to the New World. Others were convicted felons, who were neither wanted nor willingly tolerated in the provinces. All European immigrants found economic opportunity here that did not exist at home, and in time some amassed large fortunes.

The distinctiveness of American society was also caused by a racial, ethnic, and religious diversity that was rare in Europe. America was not an uninhabited wilderness but was settled by indigenous Indian tribes upon whom early settlers often depended for food. These tribes were pushed aside or exterminated when they resisted the sale of their land to white settlers. Nevertheless, the very presence of Indians and the frontier, a moving line where Indian and white society met, forced adaptations on Europeans as they struggled to cope with an environment entirely different from that of Europe.

The development of American society was also influenced by the presence of African slaves, with the first slaves imported in 1619. Slavery was unknown in England but was quickly accepted in England's colonies. A large workforce was particularly necessary in the southern tobacco- and rice-producing colonies. Planters turned to slave labor as the pool of Englishmen who were willing to indenture themselves decreased. Slaves were preferred to white indentured servants because they and their offspring served for life. Racism was not particularly prevalent in the early seventeenth century but increased by the end of the century, when, by law, slavery in all colonies was lifelong, inherited through the mother, and not changed by conversion to Christianity. Unrest followed restrictive legislation, leading to several slave rebellions that were ruthlessly suppressed. These, in turn, brought even harsher slave codes and heightened racism.

Despite a largely rural population, colonial cities grew rapidly. These cities were dirty and crowded, and people suffered from frequent epidemics of yellow fever, smallpox, typhoid, typhus, and dysentery. Living conditions for the poor in both urban and rural areas were squalid. Life itself was brutal, with public executions in which the condemned were burned alive or hanged, drawn, and quartered, or broken on the wheel.

Legal Rights

Colonists worked to establish basic rights for themselves and their offspring. Among these rights was representative government, which was quickly adopted in every colony except New York, which did not have a representative assembly until 1691. The Puritan New England colonies also followed English tradition in creating representative government, but they refused to accept English common law in the seventeenth century. As they pointed out, common law developed in an older, settled society and had no application in a frontier environment. Instead, they enacted entire sections of the Bible into law and resisted English practices or laws until forced to accept both in 1686 under the Dominion of New England government. Most other colonies readily accepted English common law, with some resistance coming from New York, where the Dutch civil law tradition persisted for some time.

Women in New York were particularly affected by the transition from civil to common law, which, after the 1664 English conquest, gave women far fewer legal rights than they enjoyed under Dutch law. Under English law, married women had no legal existence except through their husbands, even losing control of their dowry. In all the colonies, marriage was usually by choice, but parents' consent was necessary. If widowed, a woman was entitled to one-third of her deceased husband's estate, and if she remarried she could negotiate a prenuptial agreement to protect her late husband's property for herself and her children from the previous marriage. Remarriage was usually rapid because single parents, particularly in a frontier environment, could not maintain a household and raise children without the help of a partner. Among Puritans until 1686, marriage was a civil contract that carried specific obligations for husband and wife. If these obligations were not met, then it was possible to obtain a divorce. This was less possible in other colonies, where an assembly act was necessary for a divorce. The European double standard was evident in America, as it was much easier for a man to obtain a divorce from an adulterous spouse than it was for a woman to obtain a divorce for the same reason.

Women in seventeenth-century America were notorious for their outspoken involvement in political controversies such as Bacon's Rebellion and the Leisler Rebellion. This changed somewhat by the 1760s, when women apologized for offering their opinions on current affairs. During the course of a married woman's reproductive years, she would probably be pregnant five to nine times, with death in childbirth a distinct threat, particularly in the seventeenth century. The child mortality rate was also high but improved by the eighteenth century, when life expectancy was about fifty years, exceeding that of people born in England.

Education and Religion

Colonial society valued education, but its benefits were not offered equally and varied by geographic location. Some southern schools were established for the children of farmers, while wealthy planters hired tutors for their children. Education for the lower orders of society was more readily available in most New England colonies, where any town with a hundred families had to provide a grammar school. The male children of well-to-do families learned Latin and Greek, a necessity for the college bound, but girls' education usually ended after primary school since they were not accepted in colleges. In New Netherland and New York, both the Dutch Reformed Church and the English Society for the Propagation of the Gospel made provision for the education of poor children. Higher education was particularly important to the Puritans, who established Harvard College in 1636 and Yale in 1701. In Virginia, the College of William and Mary was founded in 1691.

Religious toleration originated in the colonial era, forced on Americans by circumstance rather than conviction. While most English colonies were ethnically and religiously homogenous in the seventeenth century, with mostly Anglicans in Virginia and the Carolinas, mostly English Catholics and Puritans in Maryland, and a majority of English Puritans, or Congregationalists, in New England, exceptions existed. New York was unique among England's colonies because its settlers were drawn from many parts of Europe and represented numerous religions. In the eighteenth century, the ethnic and religious diversity that would become the rule in the nineteenth and twentieth centuries was increased in all colonies with the influx of large number of Scots, Scots-Irish, French Huguenots, German Lutherans, and Irish immigrants. In the largely Protestant English colonies, public worship for Catholics and Jews was permitted in only three colonies: Rhode Island, Pennsylvania, and Maryland. The Church of England was established only in Virginia and South Carolina, although some futile efforts were made to establish it elsewhere. The pluralistic religious beliefs of the middle colonies was one of the many factors that eventually led to the separation of church and state under the Constitution.

Religion, which prompted the settlement of the New England and Maryland colonies, continued to be important in the eighteenth century, sparking a major religious revival called the Great Awakening. The Great Awakening followed the triumphal 1739–1740 tour through the colonies of the English minister George Whitefield, when scores of people claimed to have experienced a religious conversion. While church membership increased and interest in religion ran high during this period, the Awakening also split congregations into Old and New Lights, or those who continued to favor an educated ministry and those who favored the ministry of untrained laymen. The Awakening thus had the unintended effect of splitting American religious society into different factions, leading to the proliferation of sects. By 1776, the Congregational church had the largest membership, with over a half million members, followed by the Quakers and Presbyterians, with Baptists and Methodists starting to win converts. The Great Awakening also led to the establishment of the College of New Jersey (Princeton) in 1746, the College of Philadelphia (University of Pennsylvania) in 1740, the College of Rhode Island (Brown) in 1764, Dartmouth in 1769, King's College (Columbia) in 1754, and Queen's College (Rutgers) in 1766.

Newspapers and Leisure Pursuits

Americans of all educational levels insisted on being well informed on public issues. A growing literacy rate kept pace with the demand for information, which was met in part by newspapers. The first colonial paper, the *Boston News-Letter*, was established in 1704, followed in 1719 by the *Boston Gazette*. Soon every colonial city had its own newspaper, which informed and politicized the lower and middling sort, reprinted foreign news and essays written by British opposition leaders, carried local advertisements, published political satire, reported on crimes and runaway slaves and servants, and in the case of the *New-York Weekly Journal*, carried the first political cartoons. The cartoons in the *Journal* attacked an unpopular governor, William Cosby, who had the printer of the paper, John Peter Zenger, arrested and charged with seditious libel. An account of the trial written by the attorney James Alexander was widely circulated in England and the colonies and eventually helped to establish the legal principle that truth was a defense against libel. A love of knowledge

was accompanied by a commitment to leisure pursuits. Attending religious services provided, in addition to spiritual solace, a chance to exchange local news. For relaxation, the elite in colonial society often conducted scientific experiments. David Rittenhouse of Philadelphia designed and made an orrery to illustrate the workings of the solar system, while John Bartram named and bred different species of plants. Other people relaxed from daily demands by playing ball and by betting on horse racing, cock fighting, dog fights, wrestling matches, and bear baiting. Colonists also played cards and dice, sang, danced, and played musical instruments, the wealthy holding recitals in their homes. All classes drank, with a per capita consumption of over seven gallons of liquor a year. The upper classes favored imported wines and brandy while the lower orders drank home-brewed beer, hard cider, and rum. In Virginia and Maryland, people attended theatrical performances of Shakespeare's plays and those of other playwrights.

Civil Unrest

By the mid-eighteenth century, differences between the elite and lower classes pointed to a less egalitarian society. For the first time, cities were forced to provide food and shelter for the poor, while the wealthy built large houses and filled them with expensive imported furniture. The poor resented these ostentatious displays of wealth and made their displeasure evident in prerevolutionary riots, with urban crowds frequently demolishing the homes of the wealthy while protesting British measures.

The rejection of royal rule that followed civil unrest was sparked in part by a growing sense that American society was different from English society. English examples of government and individual rights were adopted but modified for the American condition. On the other hand, conditions peculiar to America led to the adoption of religious toleration and the separation of church and state, while the frontier experience brought a greater individualism than that fostered by European society. The roots of racism and violence also spring from this period. For better or worse, the patterns of American society that affect us today were colonial in origin.

BIBLIOGRAPHY

Breen, T. H., and Stehen Innes. *"Myne Owne Ground": Race and Freedom on Virginia's Eastern Shore, 1640–1676.* New York and Oxford: Oxford University Press, 1980.

Brown, Kathleen M. *Good Wives, Nasty Wenches, and Anxious Patriarchs: Gender, Race, and Power in Colonial Virginia.* Chapel Hill: University of North Carolina Press, 1996.

Hoffer, Peter Charles. *The Brave New World: A History of Early America.* New York: Houghton Mifflin, 2000.

Jennings, Francis. *Empire of Fortune: Crown, Colonies, and Tribes in the Seven Years War in America.* New York: Norton, 1988.

Maier, Pauline. *From Resistance to Revolution, Colonial Radicals and the Development of American Opposition to Britain.* New York: Knopf, 1972.

Morgan, Edmund S. *American Slavery, American Freedom: The Ordeal of Colonial Virginia*. New York: Norton, 1975.

Nash, Gary B. *Red, White and Black: The Peoples of Early North America*. 4th ed. Upper Saddle River, N.J.: Prentice Hall, 2000.

Wallace, Anthony F. C. *Jefferson and the Indians: The Tragic Fate of the First Americans*. Cambridge, Mass.: Belknap, 1999.

Mary Lou Lustig

See also **Bacon's Rebellion; Colonial Settlements; Common Law; Great Awakening; Leisler Rebellion; Puritans and Puritanism; Slavery;** *and vol. 9:* **Massachusetts School Law; Untitled Poem.**

COLONIAL WARS.

For most of the seventeenth century, English settlements in North America were largely insulated from the wars waged by their mother country. The first few generations of immigrants experienced their share of armed violence, but this bloodshed was limited mainly to conflicts with neighboring Indian tribes. The colonists' relative isolation from the turbulent currents of European politics, however, came to an end in the 1680s. Over the next seven decades, the colonies were drawn into a series of four wars pitting England and assorted allies against a shifting coalition of adversaries led by France. All of the wars, save for the last, originated in Europe, sparked by disputes over territorial or dynastic issues. Once hostilities commenced on the continent, the conflagration quickly spread to the overseas possessions of the warring powers. Even when triggered by events on the other side of the Atlantic, though, the North American component of these conflicts was always more than just a byproduct of the struggle for supremacy being played out in Europe. English, French, and Spanish colonials, as well as different groups of Indians, all took up arms to advance their own interests, whether it was to expand their access to land, resources, or trade, or simply to preserve what they already had. Reflecting the dual character of the contests, each war acquired two names: one as it came to be called in the English colonies, and the other as it was known in Europe.

King William's War/War of the League of Augsburg (1689–1697)

The first colonial war set the pattern for the three that followed. The war aims of English settlers were fueled first and foremost by concerns for their own security. Colonial authorities viewed the presence of a hostile French colony in Canada—and a Catholic one at that—as a serious threat to English settlements throughout New York and New England. Fears of French aggression were magnified by France's alliance with the Algonquian tribes in Canada, and the Abenaki Indians who inhabited the New England borderlands. The danger was driven home during the first year of the war when mixed forces of Canadians and Indians burned Schenectady, New York, and several villages on the New England coast. Confronted by the twin specters of "popery" and "savagery," the English resolved to drive the French out of North America completely. The plan of conquest devised by colonial leaders entailed a two-pronged attack on their foes. One prong would advance northward from Albany and seize Montreal, while the second would sail up the St. Lawrence River and take Quebec by seaborne assault. Possession of these two places would give the English a stranglehold on the St. Lawrence, thus isolating the French outposts in the interior. To assist with the overland thrust from New York, the English enlisted the support of the powerful Five Nations of the Iroquois Confederacy, whose homeland stretched across upper New York. The Iroquois and the French had a long history of hostilities going back to the start of the century, and, in fact, were already fighting again at the time King William's War broke out. Consequently, Iroquois warriors were willing partners in the campaign to dismantle France's North American empire.

New France, however, did not fall in King William's War. Although English settlers outnumbered the French by a ratio of twenty to one or more, colonial leaders never managed to capitalize on their enormous manpower advantage. The colonies south of New York simply sat out the war as bystanders. The metropolitan government in London also declined to furnish assistance in the form of regular soldiers or warships. Left to their own devices, colonial authorities in New York and New England carried on as best they could, but they lacked the resources, organizational experience, and military skills to execute their ambitious double offensive. The joint Iroquois-English expedition that marched on Montreal in 1690 dissolved before it even reached the southern end of Lake Champlain. The other arm of the pincer fared only slightly better. Departing from Boston, a small armada of vessels under the command of wealthy New Englander Sir William Phips managed to plant 2,200 men outside of Quebec in the fall of 1690. But Phips's army was too weak to storm the citadel, and so the men retreated to their ships and sailed back to Boston.

The failed English offensive of 1690 aside, most of the military activity in King William's War consisted of raids, counter-raids, and ambushes—a kind of warfare that the French labeled *la petite guerre*. In the mid-1690s, the governor-general of New France, Louis de Buade de Frontenac, also launched a series of large-scale incursions into Iroquois territory. The purpose of these assaults was to punish the Five Nations and drive a wedge between them and their English allies. The strategy worked. In 1701, the exhausted Iroquois sued for peace with the French, and pledged to remain neutral in future Anglo-French conflicts. This agreement represented a major coup for the French. Although no territory changed hands as a result of King William's War, the northern English colonies emerged from the struggle in a weaker strategic position than the one they had started out in.

Queen Anne's War/War of Spanish Succession (1702–1713) and King George's War/War of Austrian Succession (1740–1748)

The arena of conflict broadened considerably in the next two wars, as the British colonists found themselves fighting against both the Spanish in the South and the French in the North. For all intents and purposes, though, each theater of combat remained distinct from the other. In the case of King George's War, the Anglo-Spanish phase actually amounted to a separate struggle that the British called the War of Jenkins's Ear, in reference to an English sea captain who had his ear lopped off by Spanish authorities. That conflict started in 1739, and was all but over by the time the British commenced fighting with the French up north in 1744.

The rivalry between the Spanish and the English had created a combustible situation in the South long before the two countries were officially at war with one another. In the 1680s and 1690s, English traders from Carolina seeking deerskins and slaves staged periodic raids on Indians living in mission settlements in Spanish Florida. When Queen Anne's War began, Carolinians leaped at the chance to plunder their neighbors again and assert their claims to the disputed stretch of land between Charleston and St. Augustine. The colonists were joined by large numbers of friendly Indians, most notably the Creeks, who marshaled close to one thousand warriors for a massive raid on Spanish territory. The combined Carolinian-Indian onslaught laid waste to the chain of missions that Franciscan priests had established across northern Florida in the seventeenth century. The Spanish defeat was not total, for they managed to hold onto their fortified posts at St. Augustine and Pensacola; but most of the countryside in between was left a smoking, depopulated ruin.

In the War of Jenkins's Ear, colonial leaders in the South set out to finish what their predecessors had started. The creation of the colony of Georgia in 1732 provided the British with a more advanced base from which to stage an attack on Florida. In 1740, James Oglethorpe, an ex-British officer and one of the founders of Georgia, initiated operations against St. Augustine at the head of an army that included several hundred Carolina and Georgia militiamen, an equally large contingent of Creek and Cherokee warriors, and a regiment of regulars, all supported by a squadron of Royal Navy frigates. This impressive military assemblage, however, failed to overwhelm the Castillo de San Marcos, the massive stone fort that guarded the approaches to St. Augustine. Two years later, the Spanish struck back and invaded Georgia, but were also repelled. Following this flurry of offensive activity, the war in the South settled into an uneasy stalemate.

In the North, Queen Anne's War and King George's War unfolded in a fashion similar to the first Anglo-French confrontation. Lacking the military strength to subdue the British colonies by direct assault, the French resorted to their traditional strategy of frontier raiding.

The strategic effect of these hit-and-run attacks was limited, but they kept the outlying areas of New England in a state of alarm, and forced the provincial assemblies to divert men and money to the protection of the frontier. British colonials responded to these raids almost exactly as they had in 1690: by plotting to dismember New France through a dual attack on Montreal and Quebec. Assistance from the colonies below New York was again lacking, but toward the end of Queen Anne's War, the British government consented, for the first time, to commit substantial forces to a joint campaign against New France. The scheme misfired, however, as the Royal Navy squadron that was supposed to rendezvous with the New England militia at Boston in 1709 never materialized. Two years later, the colonists and the British tried again—with even worse results. On this occasion, the Royal Navy did show up in Boston with a fleet of sixty-four sail and more than five thousand troops. Yet the entire enterprise turned into a fiasco when several ships ran aground in the fog while ascending the St. Lawrence, leading to heavy loss of life and the hasty cancellation of the expedition. More disappointment awaited New Englanders during King George's War, when the British ministry in 1746 reneged on its promise to provide ships and regulars for an assault on Quebec.

The British still came away from Queen Anne's War with something to show for their efforts. British forces chipped away at the extremities of France's North American empire, gaining possession of Acadia, Newfoundland, and trading posts along the shores of Hudson Bay. But the failure of the joint ventures of 1709 and 1711 produced bitter feelings between the colonists and British officials. During King George's War, Anglo-American efforts to cooperate were somewhat more successful. In 1745, a New England expeditionary force accompanied by a Royal Navy squadron pulled off a stunning achievement, capturing the great French fortress and privateering base at Louisbourg on Cape Breton Island. Yet much of the goodwill generated by the victory evaporated the following year when the British backed out of their agreement to participate in the planned attack on Quebec. Colonial disillusionment with the mother country became complete when, in the 1748 treaty that ended the war, the British handed Louisbourg back to the French.

The French and Indian War/Seven Years' War (1754–1763)

The lengthy contest for dominion over the eastern part of North America came to a climax in the fourth colonial war. Unlike its predecessors, this war started in America and then expanded, eventually becoming global in scope. The immediate cause of hostilities was the clash of imperial interests in the Ohio valley. Both the French and Expansionist-minded colonists in Virginia claimed this area for themselves, and in the early 1750s, each side took steps to fortify the disputed territory. Mounting tensions in the region erupted into open warfare when seven hundred French soldiers, Canadian militia, and Indians in the

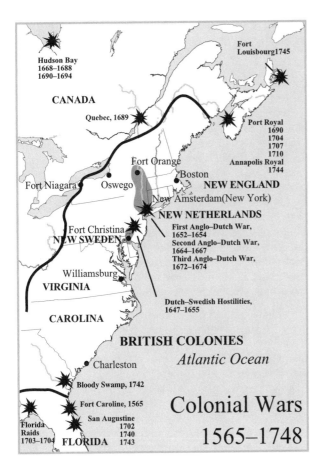

Hudson Bay
1668–1688
1690–1694

Fort
Louisbourg1745

CANADA

Quebec, 1689

Port Royal
1690
1704
1707
1710
Annapolis Royal
1744

Fort Orange

Fort Niagara   Oswego   Boston   NEW ENGLAND

New Amsterdam(New York)

NEW NETHERLANDS

First Anglo–Dutch War,
1652–1654
Second Anglo–Dutch War,
1664–1667
Third Anglo–Dutch War,
1672–1674

Fort Christina
NEW SWEDEN

Williamsburg
VIRGINIA

Dutch–Swedish Hostilities,
1647–1655

CAROLINA

BRITISH COLONIES
Atlantic Ocean

Charleston

Bloody Swamp, 1742

Fort Caroline, 1565

San Augustine
1702
1740
1743

Florida
Raids
1703–1704   FLORIDA

Colonial Wars
1565–1748

portion of its war expenses. Colonial leaders responded enthusiastically to his offer. For the 1758 campaign, Massachusetts alone raised seven thousand volunteers. More than twenty thousand British redcoats were also on hand to spearhead the assault against the French.

Compared to all of the false starts and misadventures in the past, the multi-phase offensive launched by Pitt in 1758 proceeded like clockwork. Louisbourg fell to the British that year, as did key French posts on Lake Ontario and the Ohio River. In 1759, Major General James Wolfe and some 4,500 regulars fought a pitched battle just outside of Quebec against a French force of roughly equal size led by General Louis-Joseph de Montcalm. Both generals lost their lives in the celebrated engagement, but the French abandoned the field, enabling the British to occupy Quebec. As news of the British victories spread across the Great Lakes and down into the Ohio country, France's network of Indian alliances began to crumble. The coup de grâce was finally delivered in 1760, when no less than three British and provincial armies converged on Montreal, prompting the badly outnumbered French defenders to capitulate without a fight.

The Treaty of Paris in 1763 formalized what the sweeping British successes on the battlefield had already decided. The French accepted the enormity of their defeat and surrendered their entire North American empire, ceding the territory east of the Mississippi to the British, and leaving the rest to Spain in a separate treaty. The British also gained Spanish Florida as part of the settlement. At this point, the British triumph seemed complete; but Anglo-American euphoria was destined to be short-lived. With the acquisition of these vast new domains, the British were also forced to confront the question of how to govern their much-expanded empire. British efforts to solve this problem of imperial administration would lead, in the space of only about a dozen years, to further conflict and even more profound changes in the geopolitical landscape of North America.

spring of 1754 overwhelmed an expedition of three hundred Virginia volunteers commanded by George Washington. Initially, the war went badly for the British for many of the same reasons their military endeavors had miscarried in the past: faulty planning and logistics, weak leadership, and a lack of colonial unity. But the appointment in 1756 of John Campbell, earl of Loudoun, to oversee military operations in North America created its own set of problems. Loudoun's imperious mannerisms and abrasive personality made him a poor choice for the post, and he ended up alienating many of the provincial leaders whose support he needed most. Meanwhile, the French had devoted the interval between the end of the last war and the start of the next to shoring up relations with the Delaware, Shawnee, and other western tribes. Once hostilities commenced, Indian war parties wreaked havoc on the frontier regions of Pennsylvania and Virginia.

Anglo-American military fortunes reached their lowest point with the loss of Fort William Henry at the foot of Lake George in 1757. However, they rebounded dramatically when the brilliant British statesmen William Pitt took control of the war effort. Besides removing Loudoun, Pitt redirected Britain's strategic attention away from Europe and focused most of the country's military energies on winning the war in North America. He also initiated a new policy with respect to the provincial governments, promising to reimburse each colony for a large

BIBLIOGRAPHY

Anderson, Fred. *A People's Army: Massachusetts Soldiers and Society in the Seven Years' War.* New York: Norton, 1985.

———. *Crucible of War: The Seven Years' War and the Fate of British Empire in North America, 1754–1766.* New York: Knopf, 2000.

Eccles, W. J. *The French in North America: 1500–1783.* East Lansing: Michigan State University Press, 1998.

Leach, Douglas Edward. *Arms for Empire: A Military History of the British Colonies in North America, 1607–1763.* New York: Macmillan, 1973.

Marshall, P.J., ed. *The Oxford History of the British Empire, Volume II: The Eighteenth Century.* Oxford: Oxford University Press, 1998.

Steele, Ian K. *Warpaths: Invasions of North America.* New York: Oxford University Press, 1994.

Weber, David J. *The Spanish Frontier in North America.* New Haven: Yale University Press, 1992.

White, Richard. *The Middle Ground: Indians, Empires, and Republics in the Great Lakes Region, 1650–1815.* Cambridge, U.K.: Cambridge University Press, 1991.

Jeff Seiken

See also **French and Indian War; King George's War; King William's War.**

COLONIZATION MOVEMENT.

The Colonization Movement sprang from the American antebellum reform period as an attempt to alleviate racial problems by sending all or part of the African American population to settlements in either Africa or Central America. While the movement was never a true reformist threat to Southern slavery, proponents nonetheless considered it successful because it proved that African Americans could support and govern themselves in a free land.

Antecedents of the movement stretch back as far as the American Revolution. In 1776, some enlightenment thinkers, chief among them Thomas Jefferson, envisioned a plan that would remove African Americans from North America. As President, Jefferson would later propose moving Native Americans to an "Indian Territory" carved out of the Louisiana Purchase. His thoughts and actions reflect a widespread theory of the time that free mixed races could not live and work close to each other. In the 1850s, southern slaveholders would use that same argument against abolitionists.

In 1789, the Free African Society of Newport (Connecticut) was formed to promote relocations, but organized efforts did not begin in earnest until after the War of 1812. In 1815, Paul Cuffe, a well-to-do free African American ship owner in New England, paid for the passage of thirty-eight other free African Americans to the British colony of Sierra Leone on the African Coast, which British abolitionists had founded and the British government had controlled since 1808. In December 1816, with Cuffe as a consultant, the American Colonization Society was formed with the express purpose of transporting free African Americans out of the United States. The Society attracted many well-known Americans, including Henry Clay, who was then speaker of the House of Representatives; President James Monroe; and Supreme Court Chief Justice John Marshall. While the Society initially concentrated on transporting free African Americans, it would later scheme to buy the freedom of slaves and relocate them as well.

The American Colonization Society received monetary backing from the private donations of members, from both Northern and Southern state governments (many of which passed bills for colonization allocations) and the federal government, which was then actively fighting illegal slave importation. By virtue of the Constitution, slave importation into the United States ended in 1808, but smuggling continued. The U.S. Navy patrolled the Gulf of Mexico and the Caribbean Sea to halt smugglers, and in 1819 Congress authorized patrols along

Awaiting Resettlement. African American families, en route to Liberia from Arkansas, gather at Mount Olivet Baptist Church in New York, c. 1880. © CORBIS

the African coast. Those patrols rescued many enslaved Africans and returned them to the free colony of Sierra Leone.

Colonization Society leader Bushrod Washington, a Supreme Court justice, soon asked Monroe for help in founding a colony similar to Sierra Leone that could be a haven for free African Americans. By executive action, Monroe authorized naval patrol ships to carry colonization emissaries who would negotiate for a free region. The ships would also carry supplies for a settlement. Poor climate, geography, and disease scuttled early settlement attempts, but in 1821 Navy Lieutenant Robert F. Stockton negotiated for title to Cape Mesurado on the coast of Africa at the mouth of the St. Paul River. Settlers called the initial city Monrovia in honor of President Monroe's efforts on their behalf. Monrovia ultimately became the capital of Liberia, a 600-square-mile region that formally declared its independence in 1847. Liberians established their government with a declaration of independence and a constitution, both based on the United States' models.

The colonization movement received varied degrees of support. Abolitionists believed that the existence of a free African American nation would encourage Southerners to release their slaves. Slaveholders never did, of course, as they had built their economic system around slave labor. After 1830, many Northern reformers shifted their support from colonization to more aggressive abolition. Southern individuals and state governments that supported colonization did so because they saw local communities of free African Americans as a threat to slavery. Even American Colonization Society members may have lent their organization a backhanded type of support. Many may have supported (or at least not opposed) racially prejudiced local and state laws that, by comparison, made Liberia look appealing. Many free African Americans themselves opposed colonization, and in 1817, some 3,000 of them met in Philadelphia to denounce the American Colonization Society as a hindrance to personal liberty, and as a group that would ultimately strengthen southern slavery. Martin Delany, an African American physician, criticized the operation of the Society, and in 1859 he led his own expedition to the Niger Valley where he signed a settlement treaty. But, like many Society members, Delany agreed that the chance of whites and free African Americans living peacefully together in the United States seemed hopeless.

The Civil War (1861–1865) ended American slavery with immediate emancipation. Interestingly, in the first year of the war President Abraham Lincoln clung to a colonization plan in Central America as a possible way to end the conflict. Lincoln never endorsed Liberia as a possible alternative for free African Americans.

The American Colonization Society, seeing that emancipation and Reconstruction did little to improve life for freedmen, remained effectively in existence until 1899. Throughout its existence, the Society had helped more than 15,350 African Americans emigrate to Liberia at a cost of $2.75 million. In the 1920s, at the height of the Harlem Renaissance and post–World War I civil rights agitation, African American leader Marcus Garvey advocated a new colonization movement called "Back-to-Africa," but it met with little success.

BIBLIOGRAPHY

Bracey, John H. Jr., August Meier, and Elliott Rudwick, eds. *Black Nationalism in America*. Indianapolis, Ind.: Bobbs-Merrill, 1970.

Fehrenbacher, Don E. *The Slaveholding Republic: An Account of the United States Government's Relations to Slavery*. New York: Oxford University Press, 2001.

Foner, Eric. *Politics and Ideology in the Age of the Civil War*. New York: Oxford University Press, 1980.

McCardell, John. *The Idea of a Southern Nation: Southern Nationalists and Southern Nationalism, 1830–1860*. New York: Norton, 1979.

Meier, August and Elliott Rudwick. *From Plantation to Ghetto*. New York: Hill and Wang, 1970.

Nevins, Allan. *Ordeal of the Union*. New York: Scribner, 1947.

Staudenraus, P. J. *The African Colonization Movement, 1816–1865*. New York: Columbia University Press, 1961.

R. Steven Jones

See also **Africa, Relations with; African Americans; Reconstruction; Slavery.**

COLORADO. Archaeological evidence reveals that humans have lived in the area that is now Colorado for over 10,000 years. In the aftermath of the last ice age, over 6,000 years ago, humans adapted to the main geographical regions of Colorado: the high plains of the east; the Rocky Mountains that cross the state from north to south; and the western plateaus and mesas. Rock paintings, remains of campsites, and other evidence reveal the social complexity of successive cultures of peoples who lived primarily through hunting and foraging, and later, agriculture. By the beginning of the Common Era, groups developed trading networks that skirted the Rocky Mountains south to New Mexico. The Ancestral Pueblans, also known as the Anasazi, built spectacular villages in southwestern Colorado. Mesa Verde, one of the best-known sites, was inhabited between 600 and 1200 A.D. By 1500, many Native American groups lived in Colorado. The Ute lived in the mountains and western plains, while the Apache, Navajo, Comanche, Cheyenne, and Arapaho occupied the eastern plains.

The Spanish claimed Colorado as part of the province of New Mexico, but because it was at the northernmost edge of the empire, the Spanish presence was intermittent until the 1700s. However, the Spanish influence was profound. They brought with them the horse, which Native Americans adopted throughout the 1600s and 1700s, greatly affecting the social and economic base of their societies.

Over the centuries, the Spanish defended their claim to Colorado from the Ute and Comanche, the French, and the Americans. After the 1803 Louisiana Purchase, the U.S. government dispatched expeditions to survey its new territory. In 1805, Lieutenant Zebulon Pike led an expedition into the area and described the mountain now known as Pike's Peak. The Spanish captured Pike in 1806 and did not release him until the following year. In 1819 the U.S. and Spanish governments negotiated an international boundary that ran along the Arkansas River.

Mexico gained independence from Spain in 1821. The new government encouraged trade with the United States, and the Santa Fe Trail, from Missouri to New Mexico, became an important route. Trinidad, Colorado, developed on the basis of this trade. In the 1830s and 1840s, the Mexican government gave away land grants in its New Mexico province to elite residents, with the expectation that the grantees would encourage settlement by farmers. One of the first towns the farmers established was San Luis, in present-day Colorado. During the next several decades, Spanish-speaking farmers created towns throughout southern Colorado based on the patterns they had known in New Mexico. These farmers irrigated their crops, a technique that later settlers would adopt.

At the beginning of the nineteenth century, trappers became an important presence in the region. These men sold beaver pelts to European and American markets via the New Mexico-Missouri trade route. The trappers traveled along the Rocky Mountains' rivers, lived and worked among Native Americans and Mexicans, and often married into these groups. Native American and Mexican women gave their husbands access to trade networks and social acceptance. In Colorado, settlements such as Bent's Fort, Fort Vasquez, and Fort Lupton became centers for trade and social interaction in this multiethnic enterprise. By the 1840s, however, the trappers had nearly wiped out the beaver. Some trappers became full-time traders and established new settlements, the most famous of which was El Pueblo (present-day Pueblo), which was founded in 1842.

The 1846–1848 war between Mexico and the United States ended in the Treaty of Guadalupe Hidalgo (1848). This treaty required Mexico to surrender huge portions of its land to the United States; southern Colorado was part of the cession. The United States was slow to organize this territory, and present-day Colorado was variously considered part of Texas and the territories of Utah, New Mexico, Nebraska, and Kansas. The impetus for the organization of the Colorado territory was the discovery of gold.

Gold-Rush Colorado

From the time of the first Spanish explorers, many people hoped to find gold in Colorado, but it was not until 1858 that this hope was realized. The 1859 gold rush brought over 100,000 prospectors, merchants, and speculators to the region. Even after the initial claim dwindled, more discoveries of gold continued to bring settlers to the Rocky Mountains.

The confluence of the South Platte River and Cherry Creek became the headquarters for the rush, bypassing the region's older towns. Two groups established towns on either side of Cherry Creek—Auraria and Denver City—each hoping that its town would become the dominant city. Denver won this contest and absorbed Auraria. Denver emerged as the transportation, business, and cultural hub of the region.

The Plains tribes—the Cheyenne and the Arapaho—were alarmed by the flood of settlers traveling through, and building cities on, land they considered theirs. Unlike the fur traders, these settlers had no interest in striking alliances with Native Americans. The tribes did not have a unified response to the settlers. Some, such as the Arapaho chief Little Raven, and the Cheyenne chief Black Kettle, advocated peacefully accommodating the newcomers, while others, especially members of Cheyenne warrior societies, argued for war. In the 1851 Fort Laramie Treaty, the Cheyenne and Arapaho agreed to restrict themselves to the land between the South Platte and Arkansas Rivers. Ten years later, the 1861 Fort Wise Treaty forced these groups to cede their claims to the foothills.

On 28 February 1861, the U.S. government organized the Territory of Colorado. (Colorado City and Golden served as the territory's capital, before Denver was declared the capital in 1867.) The territory was immediately thrown into the Civil War (1861–1865). Although the territory's residents included Southern sympathizers, radical and moderate abolitionists, and former slaves, the territory aligned itself with the Union cause. Troops from the Colorado Territory defeated General Henry S. Sibley's Confederates in the 1862 battle of Glorieta Pass, in New Mexico.

Another notorious military action was waged against the Cheyenne and the Arapaho. During 1864, the tensions between the Plains tribes and the settlers steadily escalated. Black Kettle led a group of his Cheyenne and Arapaho followers to their winter camp near Sand Creek, in southeastern Colorado Territory, after having declared his peaceful intentions to the military authorities. An American flag and a white flag flew over the camp, which largely consisted of the elderly, women, and children. The First and Third Colorado Volunteers, under the leadership of Colonel John Chivington, attacked this settlement on 29 November 1864. The soldiers killed over 150 people, wounded scores of others, and mutilated the dead. The Sand Creek Massacre began a cycle of violence between whites and Native Americans throughout the territory. In 1867, many of the Cheyenne and Arapaho agreed to the Medicine Lodge Treaty, which required them to relocate to Indian Territory.

Colorado in the Nineteenth Century

Colorado became a state on 1 August 1876. Due to the expansion of the railroads across the plains and into the mountains, and the subsequent increase in economic linkages, the state's population quickly grew. In 1870 there were 40,000 people in the Colorado Territory; by 1880, the population had increased to over 194,000.

Colorado's settlers demanded that the Ute, who occupied most of the western plateaus, cede their land. In 1879, several Northern Ute at the White River Agency rose up against the Indian agent and killed him, along with eleven other white men. Outraged Coloradoans called for the expulsion of the Ute. In March 1881, in Washington, D.C., the federal government concluded a treaty with the Ute that required the tribe's various bands to live in reservations in Utah or Colorado. Prospectors and farmers quickly swarmed into the land vacated by the Ute.

Farming, ranching, and mining formed the pillars of nineteenth-century Colorado's economy. Politicians and business leaders were preoccupied with encouraging economic development and growth. However, the state's economy proved to be vulnerable to violent fluctuations—a boom-and-bust cycle.

Colorado's early farmers grew grains, but by the early twentieth century sugar beets and potatoes had also become important crops. Farmers in western Colorado were known for their fruit orchards. Many farmers had to irrigate their fields, and the reliance on irrigation sparked off arguments between Colorado and its neighbors over water rights that still continue today.

Colorado was home to numerous, often short-lived, agricultural colonies. Some, such as Greeley, had utopian origins. Members of ethnic or religious groups also organized colonies. For example, in 1882 Jewish emigrants from Poland and Russia lived in a colony in Cotopaxi. One of the last colonies was the African American settlement of Dearfield, established in 1910–1911.

Livestock ranching was an important sector of the economy. By the 1880s, cattle ranchers had large establishments along the South Platte and Arkansas Rivers. Cattle ranching later spread to western Colorado. From the 1880s to the 1920s, cattle ranchers and sheepherders repeatedly clashed over land in northwest Colorado. Access to public land for grazing also became a longstanding conflict between Colorado and the federal government.

In the nineteenth century, mining was a mainstay of the economy. Some settlements, such as Leadville and Georgetown, developed into full-fledged towns, while scores of mining camps faded when the vein of ore was exhausted. Mining activities altered the land: hills were deforested and many streams became polluted.

Smelting gold, silver, and other metals was an important component of the mining industry. This process gradually moved from the mining towns to large cities such as Pueblo and Denver. Pueblo was also a steel town and the home of Colorado Fuel and Iron, an enormous company that was eventually owned by the industrialist John D. Rockefeller.

Companies developed the coalfields in northern and southern Colorado and established "company towns" for their workers. The coal towns were racially and ethnically diverse. Whites, African Americans, and Hispanics worked alongside immigrants from Asia and central and eastern Europe.

The mining industries were the site of labor conflicts from the 1880s to the 1920s. During the nineteenth century, miners demanded better safety and working conditions, but the state was reluctant to enforce such measures. This situation led to many workers joining unions. Many gold and silver miners joined the Western Federation of Miners, while the United Mine Workers made progress on the coalfields. The strikes were often long and occasionally violent, such as the 1903–1904 strike by gold miners in Cripple Creek. From 1913 to 1914, coal miners striked in southern Colorado for greater health and safety regulations, recognition of their union, and an increase in wages. On 20 April 1914, at Ludlow, the National Guard attacked a tent colony, and the subsequent fire killed two women and eleven children.

Colorado in the Twentieth Century

Colorado began the century as a leader in some national reform movements. In 1893, women in Colorado received the right to vote. The state enacted prohibition of alcohol in 1916, long before the rest of the country. Colorado became home to two national parks at the beginning of the twentieth century. Mesa Verde became a national park in 1906; Rocky Mountain National Park was dedicated in 1915.

World War I (1914–1918) was a stimulus for Colorado's economy. The demand for crops such as sugar beets and wheat, and metals—molybdenum, vanadium, and tungsten—led to an economic boom. The bust came after the war, when prices for metals and agricultural commodities plummeted.

After the war, Colorado politics took a turn to the right. The state was consumed by a "Red Scare" over feared Communist and Socialist influence. During the 1920s, the Ku Klux Klan emerged as a powerful statewide organization, widely disseminating its hate-based politics. The Klan dominated politics in Denver and held weekly cross burnings. Klan members and sympathizers controlled the lower house of the state legislature. Although the Klan's influence faded somewhat after the mid-1920s, local and state governments took little initiative in protecting the civil rights of political, racial, or ethnic minorities.

Colorado was ill equipped to deal with the economic disaster of the Great Depression. Prices dropped even lower for minerals and agriculture, and between 1933 and 1938, many of the farms of eastern Colorado were stripped bare by the Dust Bowl's winds. Displaced farmers and workers received very little aid from city and state governments that had only minimal provisions for the unemployed and needy. President Franklin Roosevelt's New Deal programs helped fill this gap. For example, one New

Deal program, the Works Progress Administration, became one of the state's largest employers, and by 1942 had completed over 5,000 projects in Colorado.

World War II had a wide-ranging impact on Colorado. After the attack on Pearl Harbor, President Roosevelt ordered the detention of Japanese Americans living on the Pacific coast and in Arizona. A detention camp, Amache, was located in southeast Colorado. However, Colorado's governor resisted demands to intern Japanese American Coloradoans and allowed Japanese Americans from other parts of the country to settle in the state. Many military bases and facilities, such as Camp Hale, home of the Tenth Mountain Division, were located in the state. War industries boomed. Even the mining sector revived with the demand for uranium.

During the Cold War, industries involved in defense, aerospace, and high technology research moved into the state. The federal government also located many facilities in the state, including the new Air Force Academy, in Colorado Springs. This inflow of industry, commerce, and population, however, was concentrated among the Front Range cities.

Many of Colorado's oldest economic sectors were in steep decline by the 1970s. Sugar beet processors closed their operations. Mining was greatly diminished and concentrated on coal and molybdenum. In the 1970s, the Exxon Corporation developed facilities in northwest Colorado for processing oil shale into oil. When Exxon abruptly abandoned the project on 2 May 1982, the resulting crash had statewide ramifications.

Since the 1970s, Colorado's service industries have become an increasingly important part of the economy. For example, the tourism and recreation sectors have developed from the spas and campgrounds of the early twentieth century to the ski resort industry, which emerged after World War II.

During the last quarter of the twentieth century, Colorado wrestled with controversial issues, such as desegregation, environmental policy, the size of government, and nuclear energy. The issue of civil rights for African Americans, Native Americans, Hispanics, and gays and lesbians repeatedly surfaced during this time. Longstanding issues, including water policy, land use, and growth, remain vexing. Colorado's natural beauty and opportunities continue to attract immigrants from around the country and the world. According to the 1990 census, less than half of the population was born in the state. Over 82 percent of Colorado's 4.4 million people live in urban areas, and most of the population is concentrated on the Front Range. As the state enters the twenty-first century, it faces challenges and opportunities that are both grounded in its history and common to all of the United States.

BIBLIOGRAPHY

Abbot, Carl, Stephen J. Leonard, and David McComb. *Colorado: A History of the Centennial State*. 3d ed. Niwot: University Press of Colorado, 1994.

Deutsch, Sarah. *No Separate Refuge: Culture, Class, and Gender on an Anglo-Hispanic Frontier in the American Southwest, 1880–1940*. New York: Oxford University Press, 1987.

Jameson, Elizabeth. *All That Glitters: Class, Conflict, and Community in Cripple Creek*. Urbana: University of Illinois Press, 1998.

Taylor, Quintard. *In Search of the Racial Frontier: African Americans in the American West, 1528–1990*. New York: W.W. Norton, 1998.

Ubbelohde, Carl, Maxine Benson, and Duane A. Smith. *A Colorado History*. 8th ed. Boulder, Colo.: Pruett Publishing Company, 2001.

West, Elliot. *The Contested Plains: Indians, Goldseekers, and the Rush to Colorado*. Lawrence: The University Press of Kansas, 1998.

Wyckoff, William. *Creating Colorado: The Making of a Western American Landscape, 1860–1940*. New Haven, Conn.: Yale University Press, 1999.

Modupe G. Labode

COLORADO COAL STRIKES of 1903–1904 and 1913–1914 in Trinidad, Colo., were the result of the refusal of mine operators to recognize the right of workers to unionize and to hear demands by the miners for higher pay; more healthful working conditions; and the right to live, trade, and seek medical attention wherever they pleased. The last demand grew out of the maintenance of "closed" camps and towns by the Colorado Fuel and Iron Company, the Gould-Rockefeller–controlled operating company, where none but company stores were permitted and which only company-approved persons could enter.

The first strike involved ten thousand workers and began on 9 November 1903, following the mine operator's refusal to confer with representatives of the United Mine Workers. Those in the northern field returned to work on 27 November; the other strikers returned to work in June 1904 after the state militia withdrew from the area and without having won any material advantages.

The second strike was in response to the mine operator's open-shop drive led by the Colorado Fuel and Iron Company. It began on 23 September 1913 and involved a mixed reign of terror and civil war of several months' duration in the area between Walsenburg and Trinidad. The LUDLOW MASSACRE of 20 April 1914, in which the state militia killed fourteen men, women, and children, was the most tragic event of the strike. Federal troops entered the area in May 1914 and restored order. Thereafter, strikers returned to work under more satisfactory working conditions. The state enacted legislation to prevent similar occurrences in the future, and the Colorado Fuel and Iron Company adopted a more constructive labor policy.

BIBLIOGRAPHY

Gitelman, Howard M. *Legacy of the Ludlow Massacre: A Chapter in American Industrial Relations*. Philadelphia: University of Pennsylvania Press, 1988.

McGovern, George S., and Leonard F. Guttridge. *The Great Coalfield War*. Boston: Houghton Mifflin, 1972.

Suggs, George G. *Colorado's War on Militant Unionism: James H. Peabody and the Western Federation of Miners*. Norman: University of Oklahoma Press, 1991. The original edition was published Detroit: Wayne State University Press, 1972.

George L. Anderson / c. p.

See also **Coal Mining and Organized Labor; Strikes; United Mine Workers of America; Western Federation of Miners.**

COLORADO RIVER EXPLORATIONS.

The Spanish explorer Francisco de Ulloa unwittingly reached the mouth of the Colorado River, in the Gulf of California, in 1539, but it was not until the following year that Hernando de Alarcón braved the fierce tidal bore of the river's mouth and proceeded upstream in boats drawn by tow ropes. Though Alarcón did not meet with Francisco Vásquez de Coronado's overland expedition, two of Coronado's officers, Melchior Díaz and García López de Cárdenas, did reach the Colorado that same year. Indeed, Cárdenas is generally credited as being the first European to see the GRAND CANYON.

The Colorado River was given its name by FRANCISCAN missionaries, who were the predominant explorers of the next two centuries. The name came from the river's red tinge during the spring melt. While missionaries traveled the Colorado frequently during this period, their missions were more concerned with converting souls than they were in contributing to the geographical knowledge of the region. One exception among the Franciscans was Silvestre Vélez de Escalante, who explored the river in the 1770s.

American trappers and fur traders were the next group of Europeans to take interest in the Colorado. William H. Ashley organized the American fur trade in the ROCKY MOUNTAINS and hired Jedidiah Smith, who discovered the beaver-rich Green River. Ashley himself descended the Green River—conducting the first navigation of the river—in 1825 in bullboats and provided the first authentic information regarding the upper Colorado, painting "Ashley, 1825" on a huge rock at Ashley Falls.

Whereas the early Spanish adventurers had explored the Colorado from its mouth and headed northward, the American trappers had explored the river's northern tributaries, discovering and charting the geographies of the Green River and its junction with the Colorado. The greatest explorer of the Colorado connected the two ends of the river in exploring the last unmapped part of the continental United States. John Wesley Powell, the intrepid, one-armed leader of the Colorado River Exploring Expedition, embarked on his first—and historically more significant—trip through the Grand Canyon in 1869, departing from up the Green River in western Wyoming in May. After a dangerous 900-mile journey, in which three men deserted, the party concluded its voyage at the mouth of the Virgin River, in southeastern Nevada on 29 August. Powell's subsequent expeditions were scientifically more productive than the first, and enriched by the participation of the scientific artist of such eminent geologists as Grove Karl Gilbert and Clarence Dutton as well as the archaeologist William H. Holmes. Their collaboration was instrumental in the formulation of the basic principles of structural geology. As well as the geography and geology of the Colorado River, Powell was also intensely interested in the ethnology of the region and devoted considerable time to this study. As a result of the success of the second expedition, Powell was appointed director of the Survey of the Rocky Mountain Region in 1877. In 1881 he was made bureau chief of the new U.S. Geological Survey, a position he held until 1894. *The Exploration of the Colorado River of the West* (1875) and *The Geology of the Eastern Portion of the Uinta Mountains* (1876) are among Powell's important publications from his Colorado River explorations.

While Powell might have closed the book on discovery-oriented explorations of the Colorado, the river has been explored extensively throughout the twentieth century. The damming of Glen Canyon in the 1950s required considerable analysis of sites, while recent talk of dam removal has also prompted further investigation of the river's ecology.

BIBLIOGRAPHY

Pyne, Stephen J. *How the Canyon Became Grand: A Short History*. New York: Viking Press, 1998.

Stegner, Wallace. *Beyond the Hundredth Meridian: John Wesley Powell and the Second Opening of the West*. Lincoln: University of Nebraska Press, 1982.

Worster, Donald. *A River Running West: The Life of John Wesley Powell*. Oxford: Oxford University Press, 2001.

Michael Egan

See also **Explorations and Expeditions: U.S.; Fur Trade and Trapping.**

COLORED NATIONAL LABOR UNION.

The Colored National Labor Union (CNLU) was a post–Civil War attempt by African American laborers to achieve collective representation. Before the war, free blacks had had some success at labor organization. Societal and workplace changes after the war, however, focused more attention on labor unions than ever before. Railroads and heavy industries boomed and slavery ended, freeing all African Americans. While the practicalities of their economic situation kept most freedmen in the South for another generation, some faced white opposition when they sought industrial or skilled jobs.

White laborers began to organize for more control over their workplace, and African Americans tried the same. After unsuccessfully asking the National Labor Union to integrate them, in 1869, 214 African American delegates created the Colored National Labor Union, with Isaac Myers as its president. Myers, a lifelong free African American and a skilled ship caulker, had organized fellow black shipyard workers into a successful cooperative after their employer fired them. That cooperative had ultimately purchased its own shipyard. Under Myers's leadership, the CNLU unsuccessfully petitioned Congress to subdivide southern public lands and give African Americans their own acreage. The CNLU was egalitarian, accepting men and women, skilled and unskilled workers, and industrial and agricultural workers. In 1872, famed civil rights leader Frederick Douglass became head of the CNLU, aligning it more with the Republican party. The CNLU ceased to exist as an independent entity after it adopted the ideas of other African American labor groups.

While some largely white labor groups, such as the KNIGHTS OF LABOR, accepted black members, others, like the AMERICAN RAILWAY UNION, rejected them. Although African American workers proved vital to the industrial home front during World War I, it was not until another major war loomed in 1940 that the federal government supported them with the creation of the Fair Employment Practices Commission.

BIBLIOGRAPHY

Aguiar, Marian. *Labor Unions in the United States.* Available from http//www.africana.com.

Berry, Mary Frances and John W. Blassingame. *Long Memory: The Black Experience in America.* New York: Oxford University Press, 1982.

Brooks, Thomas R. *Toil and Trouble: A History of American Labor.* New York: Dell, 1971.

Cassedy, James Gilbert. "African Americans and the American Labor Movement." In *Prologue: Quarterly of the National Archives and Records Administration,* vol. 29, no. 2 (1997). Available from http://www.archives.gov/publications/prologue/summer_1997_american_labor_movement.html.

"Isaac Myers." *The African American Resource Center.* Available at http://www.genealogyforum.rootsweb.com/gfaol/resource/AfricanAm/Myers.htm.

Taylor, Paul F. *The ABC-CLIO Companion to the American Labor Movement.* Santa Barbara, Calif.: ABC-CLIO, 1993.

R. Steven Jones

See also **African Americans; Labor.**

COLT SIX-SHOOTER. The first practical "revolving pistol" was invented by Samuel Colt and first manufactured in 1836. Its innovations included a cylinder that came in line with the rifled barrel by pulling the hammer back to full cock. The pistol proved its worth during the Seminole Wars and the Texas border conflicts. The first government orders for heavy revolvers of .44 caliber came in January 1847. Many of the 554,283 powder-and-ball revolvers manufactured at Colt's Hartford, Connecticut, factory between 1856 and 1865 were used by both sides during the Civil War. Colt six-shooters, popular with rangers and cattlemen as well as troops, played a prominent part in the conquest and settlement of the West.

BIBLIOGRAPHY

Edward, William B. *The Story of Colt's Revolver.* Harrisburg, Pa.: Stackpole Books, 1953.

Samuel M. Stone / A. R.

See also **Munitions; Texas Rangers; West, American.**

"COLUMBIA." By the 1690s the term "Columbia" had come into use to refer to the New World discovered by Christopher Columbus. During the early eighteenth century, the word spread through colonial culture as a name for places and things and in poetry, songs, and political discourse. In the 1760s, as colonists began to resist British power, the term evolved into an image and symbol of distinct American identity. Columbia appeared in art and illustrations as a female classical deity, in a white gown and accompanied by American icons: a liberty pole, the flag, an eagle, thirteen stars, or the dates 1776 and 1789, and often beside George Washington. Columbia symbolized liberty, progress, republican values, and female republican virtue.

"Hail, Columbia" served as the nation's first anthem. Commissioned by actor Gilbert Fox to compose a patriotic song for an upcoming performance, Joseph Hopkinson penned lyrics to the tune of the federalist song, "The President's March." Amid partisan division over the British-French conflict in Europe, Hopkinson's words, like the image of Columbia herself, emphasized American independence, unity, and separation from European affairs. The song premiered 25 April 1798. Its instant popularity helped to quiet partisan tensions and calls for America's entry into the European war.

BIBLIOGRAPHY

Schlereth, Thomas J. "Columbia, Columbus, and Columbianism." *Journal of American History* 79 (Dec. 1992): 937–968.

James Tejani

COLUMBIA, BURNING OF. Gen. William Tecumseh Sherman's Union army reached Columbia, South Carolina, on 17 February 1865, on its famous march through the Carolinas. That night, one-third of the city burned to the ground. Sherman claimed that the fire started initially from bales of cotton ignited by evacuating Confederates under Gen. Wade Hampton. Whatever the fire's origins, Columbia's civilian authorities, demoralized and scattered by the invasion, were unable to bring the blaze under control. Union soldiers spread the flames and plundered the city, wreaking vengeance on the capital of the first state to secede. In his memoirs Sherman dismissed the notion that he should have confined his men to camp to prevent the conflagration.

BIBLIOGRAPHY

Glatthaar, Joseph T. *The March to the Sea and Beyond.* New York: New York University Press, 1985.

Lucas, Marion B. *Sherman and the Burning of Columbia.* College Station: Texas A&M University Press, 1976.

Royster, Charles. *The Destructive War.* New York: Knopf, 1991.

D. D. Wallace / A. R.

See also **Civil War; Sherman's March to the Sea.**

COLUMBIA RIVER EXPLORATION AND SETTLEMENT.

For nearly two centuries before Europeans first saw the Columbia River, geographers eagerly theorized that a Great River of the West penetrated deep into the center of the North American continent. A number of speculative maps variously located this river between forty-two and fifty degrees north latitude and connected it to the mythical Northwest Passage, thus making it part of a navigable water route between the Pacific and Atlantic Oceans. No easy water route across the continent existed, but the belief that whoever claimed this river would control the commerce of North America eventually proved correct.

The Columbia was first described and mapped during a period of intense imperial interest in the North Pacific, when Europeans and Americans sought to establish commercial and territorial claims in the region. Spanish captain Bruno Hezeta first observed a large estuary in 1775 near forty-six degrees latitude, where the Columbia meets the Pacific, and his report soon attracted the attention of English, Russian, French, and American interests. Hezeta's claim that he had seen the mouth of a great river, and not a large bay, was eventually confirmed on 11 May 1792, when an American trader, Captain Robert Gray, sailed across the river's treacherous bar and into the fresh waters of the Columbia, which he named in honor of his ship, the *Columbia Rediviva.* Under the direction of British captain George Vancouver, Lieutenant William Broughton sailed more than one hundred miles up the Columbia in October 1792 and produced the first detailed map of the lower river. The American explorers Meriwether Lewis and William Clark described the Columbia from its confluence with the Snake River to the Pacific in 1805 and 1806, and six years later the North West Company fur trader David Thompson mapped the entire twelve-hundred-mile river from its source in the Canadian Rockies.

Jointly claimed by Great Britain and the United States, the Columbia River basin became an important arena for the international fur trade. Strongly influenced by established Native markets and distribution networks along the Columbia, the trade all but collapsed in the 1830s due to overexploitation by the Hudson's Bay Company. Weakened by disease and increasingly unable to control the terms of their encounters with outsiders, Native communities were quickly displaced by the thousands of overland migrants who poured across the Oregon Trail in the 1840s. While this new settlement depended on the advice of ex-trappers turned guides, who provided detailed information on interior waterways, it also benefited from the work of Lieutenant Charles Wilkes and the U.S. Exploring Expedition, which mapped the Columbia Basin in 1841.

The presence of so many new arrivals from the United States not only replaced the fur trade economy with one based on agriculture, fishing, lumber, and mining, but also transformed the jointly administered territory into an exclusively American province. Basing its claims on the explorations of Gray and Lewis and Clark, the United States negotiated a treaty with Great Britain in 1846 that divided the Columbia River at the forty-ninth parallel. All lands to the south became part of United States, eventually forming the states of Oregon, Washington, Idaho, and part of Montana.

BIBLIOGRAPHY

Allen, John L. "The Canadian Fur Trade and the Exploration of Western North America, 1797–1851." In *North American Exploration.* Edited by John Logan Allen. Vol. 3: *A Continent Comprehended.* Lincoln: University of Nebraska Press, 1997.

Gibson, James R. "The Exploration of the Pacific Coast." In *North American Exploration.* Edited by John Logan Allen. Vol. 2: *A Continent Defined.* Lincoln: University of Nebraska Press, 1997.

Meinig, D. W. *The Great Columbia Plain: A Historical Geography, 1805–1910.* Seattle: University of Washington Press, 1968. Reissued in 1995 with a forward by William Cronon and new preface from the author.

Mark David Spence

See also **Columbia River Treaty; Exploration of America, Early; Explorations and Expeditions: British, Spanish, U.S.; Geological Survey, U.S.; Geophysical Explorations; Lewis and Clark Expedition; Oregon Trail; Oregon Treaty of 1846; Vancouver Explorations; Western Exploration.**

COLUMBIA RIVER TREATY,

a waterpower and water storage agreement between the United States and Canada to run for sixty years, signed in Washington, D.C., on 17 January 1961 and ratified by both nations. Under the terms of the treaty, the United States completed construction of the Libby Dam on the Kootenay branch of the Columbia River (northern Montana), and Canada built dams at Arrow Lake, Duncan Lake, Lower Bonnington, and Mica Creek in British Columbia. Waterpower and water storage developments supply HYDRO-ELECTRIC POWER to the states of Washington, Oregon, Idaho, and Montana and also to the provinces of British Columbia and Alberta.

BIBLIOGRAPHY

Craig, Gerald M. *The United States and Canada.* Cambridge, Mass.: Harvard University Press, 1968.

Martin, Lawrence. *The Presidents and the Prime Ministers: Washington and Ottawa Face to Face: The Myth of Bilateral Bliss, 1867–1982.* Toronto and Garden City, N.Y.: Doubleday, 1982.

Thomas Robson Hay / A. G.

See also **Canada, Relations with; Canadian-American Waterways; Treaties with Foreign Nations.**

COLUMBIA UNIVERSITY is the oldest, richest, and most famous of all institutions of higher education in the New York metropolitan region and a member of the prestigious Ivy League. As King's College, it received a royal charter on 31 October 1754 from George II of England "to promote liberal education" and to "prevent the growth of republican principles which prevail already too much in the colonies." But the college would produce a crop of American rebels, including John Jay, Alexander Hamilton, Robert Livingston, and Gouverneur Morris. In 1760, it moved to a three-acre site near the Hudson River in lower Manhattan on land donated by Trinity Church. In 1770, its School of Medicine awarded the first M.D. degrees in what would become the United States.

Between 1776 and 1783, when New York City was the headquarters for British military operations in the American Revolution, King's College suspended all classes and its building became a military hospital. The college reopened in 1784 as Columbia, using a word that had recently been coined by patriotic poets. In 1813, the School of Medicine merged with the College of Physicians and Surgeons.

Having remained a small institution until the mid-nineteenth century, Columbia began a period of expansion during the administration of Charles King. In 1857, it moved to a site at Forty-seventh Street and Park Avenue; it established a School of Law in 1858 and a School of Mines (later the School of Engineering) in 1864. During the presidency of Frederick A. P. Barnard, the college became one of America's first major universities. The Graduate School of Arts and Sciences began operating in 1880, the School of Architecture in 1881, the School of Library Service in 1887, the School of Nursing in 1892, and the School of Social Work in 1898. And before the turn of the century, both Barnard College, one of the original Seven Sisters and the first private college in the city to award liberal arts degrees to women, and Teachers College, which was to become the preeminent training ground for educational professionals in the United States, became semi-independent affiliates of Columbia. In 1896, the institution declared itself a university, and in 1897, it formally moved to Morningside Heights on the Upper West Side of Manhattan. The centerpiece of the new rectangular campus became Low Memorial Library, a classical Roman building with Grecian detail. Other buildings were designed in the Italian Renaissance style by McKim, Mead and White.

During the first half of the twentieth century, and especially during the presidency of Nicholas Murray Butler, Columbia became one of the world's largest and most prominent universities. The Graduate School of Journalism began in 1912, the Graduate School of Business in 1916, the School of Dentistry in 1917, and the School of Public Health in 1921. Seven years later, the new Columbia-Presbyterian Medical Center in Manhattan's Washington Heights became the first institution in the world to unite physician training, medical research, and patient care in a single giant complex. Meanwhile, Columbia College launched its famous compulsory Contemporary Civilization survey for undergraduates in 1919. The influential course traced the development of Western thought and made the study of original masterworks the foundation of Columbia's core curriculum.

During the twentieth century, more than sixty persons affiliated with Columbia won the Nobel Prize, including Harold C. Urey in chemistry, I. I. Rabi and Polykarp Kusch in physics, André Cournand and Dickinson Richards in medicine, and William Vickrey in economics. The students were similarly distinguished and included such persons as Franklin Delano Roosevelt, Lou Gehrig, Paul Robeson, Lionel Trilling, Benjamin Spock, Jack Kerouac, Virginia Apgar, and Ruth Bader Ginsburg.

In the spring of 1968, the Columbia campus became a battleground when students occupied five buildings to protest the proposed construction of a university gymnasium in a nearby park and to fight against institutional involvement in the military-industrial complex. After five days of relative standoff, President Grayson Kirk asked the New York Police Department to clear over a thousand protestors from university buildings. The ensuing chaos injured eighty-nine persons and led to 712 arrests. A positive consequence was the creation of the University Senate, a deliberative body with representation from the administration, faculty, alumni, staff, and student body. A negative consequence was the temporary shattering of a long tradition of peaceful debate.

After a difficult financial period during the 1970s, Columbia returned to strength under the administration of Michael Sovern. He instituted a renewal program that included the creation of 120 endowed professorships. In 1983, Columbia College admitted women for the first time (Barnard College continued to admit women only) and applications from both male and female students soon increased markedly. In 1993, George Rupp became Columbia's eighteenth chief executive officer. His administration was characterized by a doubling of Columbia's applicant pool and unprecedented success at fund-raising. By the early years of the twenty-first century, the university had enrolled more than twenty-thousand full-time students; with its affiliates Barnard College and Teachers College, the total stood at about twenty-seven thousand. It included sixteen schools, dozens of distinguished academic departments, and more than seventy venues for specialized research. Columbia College, however, continued to have the smallest undergraduate enrollment in the Ivy League at four thousand. Lee Bollinger became the nineteenth president of Columbia University on 1 July 2002.

BIBLIOGRAPHY

A Brief History of Columbia. Available online at: http://www .columbia.edu/cu/aboutcolumbia/history.html.

Kenneth T. Jackson

See also **Education, Higher: Colleges and Universities, Women's Colleges; Ivy League; Seven Sisters Colleges.**

COLUMBINE SCHOOL MASSACRE. On 20 April 1999, in one of the deadliest school shootings in national history, two students at Columbine High School in Littleton, Jefferson County, Colorado, killed twelve fellow students and a teacher and injured twenty-three others before committing suicide. Eric Harris, age eighteen, and Dylan Klebold, age seventeen, used homemade bombs, two sawed-off twelve-gauge shotguns, a nine-millimeter semiautomatic rifle, and a nine-millimeter semiautomatic pistol in a siege that began shortly after 11 A.M. Mark Manes and Phillip Duran were convicted of securing weapons for the shooting, while Robyn Anderson, who also allegedly supplied one of the weapons, was not convicted of any crimes. Harris and Klebold, reportedly influenced by neo-Nazi dogma, were said to have targeted athletes and minority students for revenge against social exclusion they said they had experienced at the school of 1,870 students. While school violence in the nation had been in decline after the 1993–1994 academic year, the massacre occurred at the end of an apparent epidemic of shootings in the late 1990s.

Nine civil suits were filed against Sheriff John P. Stone and the Jefferson County Sheriff's Department for various acts of negligence, including failing to act on indications of the coming violence. In November 2001, all but one of the suits were dismissed in federal court. The judge ruled that while possibly negligent, officials were protected by governmental immunity unless their actions were "willful and wanton." The only case allowed to move forward involved a teacher who bled to death while waiting to be rescued. The Harris and Klebold families, Manes, and Duran also faced several wrongful death suits, one of which was settled in April 2001 for $2.53 million to be shared by more than thirty families of victims. Lawsuits were also filed against school officials and the Tanner Gun Show, where Anderson bought her gun when she was eighteen years old. Watched by millions of Americans on live television, Columbine prompted a national debate on access to guns, school security, violence on television and in computer games, and child psychology. While several states, including Colorado, passed stricter gun control

Grieving. A group of students from Columbine High School in Littleton, Colorado, gather near a memorial to their fallen classmates to gain support from each other during their time of tragedy. © AP/WIDE WORLD PHOTOS

laws in the aftermath of Columbine, gun control continues to be contentiously debated in the nation's legislatures.

BIBLIOGRAPHY

Aronson, Elliot. *Nobody Left to Hate: Teaching Compassion After Columbine.* New York: W. H. Freeman, 2000.

Janofsky, Michael. "Year Later, Columbine Is Learning to Cope While Still Searching for Answers." *New York Times* (17 April 2000): A12.

———. "$2.53 Million Deal Ends Some Columbine Lawsuits." *New York Times* (20 April 2001): A10.

Verhovek, Sam Howe. "15 Bodies Are Removed from School in Colorado." *New York Times* (22 April 1999): A1.

Eric S. Yellin

COLUMBUS, OHIO, is the capital and most populous city of Ohio. It was laid out on the high east bank of the Scioto River in 1812 expressly to serve as the capital and was named for the great Italian explorer. Ohio's leg-

Columbus, Ohio. National Guard troops arrive outside the Statehouse to put down a streetcar strike in July 1910. LIBRARY OF CONGRESS

islature chose the site owing to its central location in the state and because Columbus's promoters offered to donate land and construction money for the state house and penitentiary. During the course of the nineteenth century, Columbus garnered virtually all of the state's institutions, including the schools for the blind and deaf; the "lunatic asylum"; the "asylum for idiots"; and the land-grant college, Ohio State University. Completed in 1831, a feeder canal linked Columbus with the Ohio and Erie Canal. Two years later, the National Road reached the city, providing access to the East. These transportation advantages spurred Columbus's growth, and in 1850 it was the second largest city in the state with almost eighteen thousand inhabitants.

During the 1850s and 1860s, the construction of numerous rail lines further enhanced Columbus's commercial fortunes. Owing to its proximity to the coalfields of southeastern Ohio, Columbus became a major coal shipping center. During the late nineteenth century, the city's industrial sector expanded, and Columbus won recognition as a leader in the manufacturing of buggies and carriages and as the home of numerous foundries and machine shops. Meanwhile, Columbus attracted thousands of German immigrants, although at the close of the nineteenth century, the foreign born constituted less than 10 percent of the city's population, a figure far below that of most midwestern industrial cities.

The city continued to grow at a steady pace, yet in 1930 its population of 290,564 earned it only fourth rank among Ohio cities, behind Cleveland, Cincinnati, and Toledo. During the half century following World War II, however, it pulled ahead of its rivals, and by the mid-1980s was the state's largest city. In 2000, its population reached 711,470. Unlike Cleveland and Cincinnati, Columbus was able to annex vast tracts of new territory, its area more than tripling during the 1950s and 1960s. Thus, it acquired thousands of new residents and escaped encirclement by suburban municipalities. Columbus was not as dependent on heavy industry as many rust belt cities and was spared the worst effects of the late-twentieth-century decline in midwestern manufacturing. State gov-

ernment was the city's chief employer, and as long as the state of Ohio survived, the city's economic future remained secure.

BIBLIOGRAPHY

Cole, Charles C., Jr. *A Fragile Capital: Identity and the Early Years of Columbus, Ohio.* Columbus: Ohio State University Press, 2001.

Hunker, Henry L. *Columbus, Ohio: A Personal Geography.* Columbus: Ohio State University Press, 2000.

Jon C. Teaford

See also **Midwest; Ohio.**

COLUMBUS QUINCENTENARY (1992). Marking the 500th anniversary of the arrival of Christopher Columbus in the land that would become known as the Americas, the Columbus Quincentenary was a problematic commemoration. Major events took place, including a summer Olympics dedicated to Columbus in Barcelona, Spain; the Universal Exposition (Expo '92) in Seville, Spain; and the AmeriFlora exposition in Columbus, Ohio, the largest flower show in the western hemisphere. Nevertheless, attendance at some of these events was disappointing, media attention was sparse, and financial goals were not met. In the United States, the Christopher Columbus Quincentenary Jubilee Commission, established in 1984, was intended to "plan, encourage, coordinate, and conduct the commemoration of the voyages of Christopher Columbus," but the Commission was ineffective due to financial mismanagement and poor leadership. Planned events, including a reprise of the 1893 World's Columbian Exposition, were either curtailed or canceled. One frequently cited reason for lackluster or failed events was the worldwide recession and the United States' federal budget deficit. Another major factor was scholars' and indigenous peoples' resistance to celebrating an event they believed had brought conquest, colonization, disease, and environmental exploitation to the Americas. One positive outcome of the commemoration's failure, however, was that uncritical treatments of Columbus and his achievements were replaced by the efforts of teachers, academics, museum professionals, and cultural organizations to explore, debate, and teach the significance of the event within the larger context of the meaning, documentation, and interpretation of the past. The Library of Congress published *Keys to the Encounter*, a resource guide for researching the "age of discovery." The Smithsonian Institution's "Seeds of Change" exhibit explored the dietary, environmental, and cultural impact of Columbus's encounter with the Americas, and public libraries in fifty states and three territories exhibited a traveling version of this exhibit. A seven-part PBS series, "In Search of Columbus," gave a scholarly and relatively balanced view of the encounter.

BIBLIOGRAPHY

Vorsey, Louis de. *Keys to the Encounter: A Library of Congress Resource Guide for the Study of the Age of Discovery*. Washington, D.C.: Library of Congress, 1992.

Herman, Viola J., and Carolyn Margolis. *Seeds of Change: A Quincentennial Commemoration*. Washington: Smithsonian Institution Press, 1991.

Royal, Robert. *1492 And All That: Political Manipulations of History*. Washington, D.C.: Ethics and Public Policy Center, 1992.

Sale, Kirkpatrick. *The Conquest of Paradise: Christopher Columbus and the Columbia Legacy*. New York: Knopf, 1990.

Summerhill, Stephen J., and John Alexander Williams. *Sinking Columbus: Contested History, Cultural Politics, and Mythmaking during the Quincentenary*. Gainesville: University Press of Florida, 2000.

Kirkpatrick Sale
Christine Whittington

See also **Exploration of America, Early; Explorations and Expeditions: Spanish.**

Comanche. This photograph by W. S. Soule shows a few of these Southern Plains Indians outside their tipis in 1873. LIBRARY OF CONGRESS

COMANCHE. Indians were the dominant military and economic power on the Southern Plains for the eighteenth and most of the nineteenth centuries. They controlled the flow of goods, particularly horses and horse gear, from Spanish New Mexico to the Plains.

Based on linguistic evidence, speakers of Eastern SHOSHONE (including the Comanches and the Wind River Shoshone of Wyoming) probably diverged from other Shoshone speakers about A.D. 1500. This provides a date for their movement onto the northwestern Plains. While some turned north, confronting the Algonkian-speaking BLACKFEET, who ultimately pushed them back (so that they became the Wind River Shoshone), others turned south in about 1700. The latter confronted UTE, who named them *komanci* (my adversary), or Southern Ute, who called them *kumanchi* (other, or stranger). The "tribal" category "Comanche" did not comprise a single political entity. Rather, there were multiple political organizations in time and space, derived from a common cultural model but based on differing political and domestic economic resources.

Perhaps the best way to understand the Comanche social and political structure is to start at the bottom. While nuclear families might, for whatever reason, choose to live separately for a while, the normal Comanche residential pattern consisted of groups of related extended families. Those families formed the local, or residential, band. The bands were focused around a core extended family, whose leader was the group's chief. Whereas the local residential band was structured on kinship, the widest Comanche social structure—the division—was of local group, or bands, linked into political networks; in historic times in New Mexico, and apparently briefly in Texas, the divisional principal chief was "elected" from amongst the constituent local band chiefs.

Four economic bases can be identified: hunting, warfare and raids, trade, and, in the pre-reservation period of Euro-American interaction, political gifts. Items produced in any one of these areas could be translated into others: for instance, items produced in hunting (such as products of the buffalo), raiding (material booty as well as captives), and the political gifts from Euro-Americans were all translated into trade items with others.

There is no way to know the pre-contact Comanche population. Early reports ranged upwards to 20,000, but none of those making these early reports had accurate personal knowledge of the Comanches as a whole. Again, while certainly there were devastating epidemics, there are no unambiguous contemporary accounts. The earliest "census" was in 1879, counting 1,479 persons. The low point occurred in 1904, with just 1,399 Comanches reported. In 1999, the Comanche tribe reported a total population of approximately 10,000.

The Comanches were one of the typical Plains tribes. They shared the pattern of horse-mounted buffalo hunting, the tipi and travois, and religion focusing on personal spiritual power.

A number of Comanche leaders became prominent in inter-tribal, and international affairs. As remembered by a dozen Comanche consultants in 1933, the greatest of pre-reservation leaders was the Yamparika Ten Bears. He participated in a number of treaty councils between 1853 and 1868 and traveled to Washington twice. After Ten Bears, historically the most important Comanche leader was Quanah Parker, the son of a captive white woman from Texas and a Comanche man. In the later reservation period Quanah was the Comanche "principal" chief. While Quanah was important in shaping internal Comanche events, he was also important as a proselytizer of the new peyote, or Native American Church.

Relations with the Spaniards of New Mexico and Texas for most of the eighteenth century alternated between hostility and periods of peaceful trading. In 1785 in Texas and 1786 in New Mexico, strong leaders arranged relatively permanent peace treaties, which lasted until the collapse of the Spanish Empire in 1821. Mexico attempted to continue the policies of Spain with treaties in 1823 and 1826, but the new government did not have the resources to maintain either major trade or political gifts. Meanwhile, the United States was trying to lure the Comanches from their Spanish alliances by providing gifts to Comanche visitors at Natchitoches, Louisiana. With the opening of the SANTA FE TRAIL, parts of which went right through Comanche territory, American policy became one of trying to keep the Comanches away from the trail, by treaty if possible, by military force if not.

Treaties or other agreements between the United States and the Comanches were signed in 1835, 1846, 1853, 1861, 1865, and 1867. Several treaties were negotiated with the Confederate States in 1861. But as with the Spanish and Mexican treaties, all of these agreements involved only a portion of the Comanches. The last treaty—Medicine Lodge Creek, signed in 1867—created a reservation in southwestern Indian Territory, but it was not until 1875 that all Comanches were forced to live there permanently. The reservation was allotted and dissolved in 1901. A few Comanche are alleged to have participated in the GHOST DANCE of 1890, but apparently there is no direct evidence for it. At the same time, a number of Comanches became active participants in the new NATIVE AMERICAN CHURCH.

By the twentieth century, many Comanches had become active participants in the general economy. While many original reservation allotments remain in Indian hands, relatively few Indians actually work their land; most is leased to non-Indians.

A number of Comanches served in the armed forces in World War I. In 1939, a group of Comanches fluent in their native language was recruited to act as Code Talkers. They served in Europe, landing at Normandy on D DAY.

BIBLIOGRAPHY

Foster, Morris W. *Being Comanche: A Social History of an American Indian Community.* Tucson: University of Arizona Press, 1991.

Kavanagh, Thomas W. *Comanche Political History: An Ethnohistorical Perspective, 1706–1875.* Lincoln: University of Nebraska Press, 1996.

Thomas Kavanagh

See also **Tribes: Great Plains.**

COMICS are a series of drawings, usually arranged horizontally on the page of a newspaper, a magazine, or a book, that read as a narrative. The drawings carry the story, but words may appear to enhance the narration. Text, when included, often relies on the use of conversation to convey information and on onomatopoeic sounds, such as Wham! Pow! Slam!, to complement the action. *The Yellow Kid* (1895) was among the first to regularly employ text within the narrative frame by writing words on the shirt of "the Kid." Since the late nineteenth century, comics have usually featured a regular cast of characters, and contain either a complete story or a series of episodes.

Modern comics have several forms: the single-frame story, in which one picture conveys the entire tale, relies heavily on familiar characterization and sequence of spatial relationships within the frame; the gag strip, made up of three or four pictures with a joke in the last frame, such as *Sad Sack* (1942); the serial strip, which shows a new piece of the story every day or once a week, such as *Terry and the Pirates* (created in 1934 by Milton Caniff); and the comic book, in which complete stories are contained within the pages, the first of which, *Funnies on Parade*, was published by Procter and Gamble in 1933 and sold for ten cents. By the late 1940s, more than 50 million copies of comic books were sold a month. The first comic strips were syndicated in 1914, and any small-town newspaper could purchase them. By the mid-twentieth century, Chic Young's *Blondie* was the most highly syndicated comic strip in the world, and Mort Walker's *Beetle Bailey*, which displayed an American irreverence to military authority, was syndicated in more than fifty countries.

The modern comic emerged from three forms of visual art: mural arts, humorous cartoons, and the photographic arts. As an art form of social commentary, the modern comic strips are also a direct outgrowth of the nineteenth-century humorous cartoon, which was often a political or social comment. Thomas Rowlandson (1757–1827) pioneered political cartooning with the creation of a regular character, Dr. Syntax. George Cruikshank (1792–1878) introduced dialogue within the frame, usually included in balloons. The narrative sequences of William Hogarth (1697–1764) translated caricature into an art form and showed the sequence of narrative pictures featuring a regular cast. For portrayal of action, comics are indebted to Eadweard Muybridge's "Study of the Body in Motion," a series of photographs of a galloping horse, which became the foundation for the creative depiction of basic elements of action. Other historians credit the Swiss artist Rodolphe Töppfer (1799–1846) with the first awareness of the expressive qualities of line that allow a wide range of exaggerated facial expression in his collection of picture stories, *Histoires en estampes* (1846).

Changes in technology furthered the development of the comic. The invention of photoengraving in 1873 made newspaper illustration relatively inexpensive. In addition, the size of the reading public grew, and at the turn of the

(1915) in 1948. Gary Trudeau's *Doonesbury* (1970) depicted campus unrest of the 1960s and 1970s, and Trudeau won a Pulitzer Prize for his work in 1975. Berkley Breathed created a satirical comic, *Bloom County*, for which he won a Pulitzer Prize in 1987.

BIBLIOGRAPHY

Aldridge, George Perry, and Alan Aldridge, eds. *The Penguin Book of Comics: A Slight History*. Baltimore: Penguin, 1967.

Boxer, Sarah. "When Fun Isn't Funny: Evolution of Pop Gore." *New York Times* (1 May 1999).

Gagnier, S. Richard. "A Hunger for Heroes." *School Library Journal* 43, no. 9 (1997): 143.

Marschall, Rick. "100 Years of the Funnies." *American History* 30, no. 4 (1995): 34.

O'Sullivan, Judith. *The Art of the Comic Strip*. College Park: University of Maryland Department of Art, 1971.

Silverman, Francine. "Tracing the History of America's First Comic Character." *Editor & Publisher* 127, no. 48 (1994): 16–19.

Springhall, John. "Horror Comics: The Nasties of the 1950s." *History Today* 44, no. 7 (1994): 10–13.

Ruth A. Kittner

See also **Literature: Popular Literature; Newspapers.**

Jerry Siegel. The cocreator, with Joe Shuster, of Superman— the exceptionally influential star of comic books, comic strips, movies, and television for more than sixty years. AP/WIDE WORLD PHOTOS

nineteenth century, a wide range of comics became a staple in American life. In 1892, James Guilford Swinnerton's strip for the *San Francisco Examiner* was among the first to include continuing characters in a daily newspaper. In 1893, Joseph Pulitzer's *New York World* published its first full-page color comic, and in that same year the *New York Recorder* also featured a color page of comics. By the early 1900s, regular strips were appearing in the newspapers of major cities throughout the United States. Comics could be original or adaptations of literary works: in 1929, Harold Foster adapted Edgar Rice Burrough's 1914 *Tarzan of the Apes* for distribution by the Metropolitan Newspaper Service.

Not everyone viewed the comics benignly. Frederic Wertham's *The Seduction of the Innocent* (1954) maintained that comics exercised a bad influence on young people and led to an increase in juvenile delinquency. This attack led to the creation of the Comics Code Authority in 1955 and the Newspaper Comics Council, in an effort to police the content of comic books and strips.

As an instrument of popular culture drawing on the fine and literary arts, comics have successfully reflected social frustrations, like their eighteenth and nineteenth century predecessors. Rube Goldberg's *The Inventions of Professor Lucifer Gorgonzola Butts* (1914) described revolt against the tyranny of machines, and Goldberg received a Pulitzer Prize for *Professor Lucifer* and for *Boob McNutt*

COMMANDER IN CHIEF OF BRITISH FORCES in North America was a position of high importance in the last half of the eighteenth century. Horatio Sharpe (1754), Edward Braddock (1755), William Shirley (1755–1756), John Campbell, Earl of Loudoun (1756–1757), James Abercrombie (1758), Jeffrey Amherst (1758–1763), and Thomas Gage (1763–1775) all held it; Sir William Howe (1775–1778), Sir Henry Clinton (1778–1782), and Sir Guy Carleton (1782–1783) each held it with more limited control. Appointed by the crown and supervised directly by the British ministry, commanders supervised the American military and its financial expenditures, an astonishing scope of responsibility and power.

BIBLIOGRAPHY

Carter, Clarence, ed. *The Correspondence of General Thomas Gage*. New Haven, Conn.: Yale University Press, 1931.

Alfred P. James / c. w.

See also **Colonial Policy, British; Revolution, American: Diplomatic Aspects, Military History, Political History.**

COMMERCE, COURT OF, created by act of Congress, 18 June 1910, intended to provide a specialized tribunal for the increasingly complex volume of trade litigation. It consisted of five judges appointed by the president for five-year terms. Its jurisdiction covered all civil suits arising under the Interstate Commerce Act, the ELKINS ACT, and the Interstate Commerce Commission. Early on, the court appeared unduly solicitous for railroad interests and inclined to hamper effective regulation by the Interstate Commerce Commission. A strong congressional minority opposed its creation in 1910. When one of its members, Judge Robert W. Archbald, was impeached, convicted of corruption, and removed from the bench in 1913, the demand became so imperative that Congress dissolved the court on 22 October 1913.

BIBLIOGRAPHY

Berk, Gerald. *Alternative Tracks: The Constitution of American Industrial Order, 1965–1917*. Baltimore: Johns Hopkins University Press, 1994.

Kolko, Gabriel. *Railroads and Regulation, 1877–1916*. Princeton, N.J.: Princeton University Press, 1965.

Thomas, William G. *Lawyering for the Railroad: Business, Law, and Power in the New South*. Baton Rouge: Louisiana State University Press, 1999.

W. A. Robinson / H. S.

See also **Commerce Clause; Interstate Commerce Commission; Interstate Commerce Laws.**

COMMERCE, DEPARTMENT OF,

or DOC, was created by an act of Congress in 1913. The secretary of commerce, who heads the department of that name, is appointed by the president with the advice and consent of the Senate and is a member of the president's cabinet. Among those who have served as Commerce secretary are such well-known personalities as Herbert Hoover, Harry Hopkins, Henry Wallace, Averell Harriman, Elliot Richardson, and Ron Brown.

The role of the Commerce Department to promote trade and U.S. economic and technological advancement has evolved and grown as the needs of the national economy have changed. The DOC took on the role of promoting tourism starting in the 1960s, and in the late twentieth century drastically improved its statistical information on the economy as a resource for commerce, reflecting the increasingly complicated and sophisticated needs of a global economy. With the growing emphasis on diversity and issues pertaining to women and minorities, the DOC stepped up its activities on behalf of those groups. It also greatly expanded its role in promoting foreign trade.

BIBLIOGRAPHY

Friedman, Thomas L. *The Lexus and the Olive Tree*. New York: Farrar, Straus, Giroux, 1999.

Nash, George H. *The Life of Herbert Hoover*. New York: Norton, 1983.

Sherwood, Robert E. *Roosevelt and Hopkins: An Intimate History*. New York: Harper, 1950.

Guy B. Hathorn / A. G.

See also **Cabinet; Debt and Investment, Foreign; Free Trade; Gold Exchange; Interstate Trade Barriers; Labor, Department of; Laissez–Faire.**

COMMERCE CLAUSE.

The judicial history of the commerce clause of the U.S. Constitution (Article I, section 8, paragraph 3) can be divided into three eras: the first 150 years after the Constitution went into effect in 1789; the 1937–1995 period; and 1995 and beyond. *Gibbons v. Ogden* (1824) defined the first era. In that case, Chief Justice John Marshall wrote for the Supreme Court that commerce encompassed "every species of commercial intercourse" and that if Congress had legislated in the area, federal power was plenary. Such breadth did not make the unimplemented power exclusive, however, and it was ultimately the Court, under Chief Justice Roger B. Taney, that resolved the issue of the extent of state power in the absence of federal legislation. After several indecisive attempts, Justice Benjamin R. Curtis (*Cooley v. Board of Wardens of Port of Philadelphia* [1851]) set forth a "selective exclusiveness" formula, holding that when Congress was silent, the states might act, unless the specific subject required "uniform national control." The ruling left the clause itself the most important basis for judicial review in limitation of state power prior to ratification of the Fourteenth Amendment (1868). Of the approximately 1,400 cases that reached the Supreme Court under the clause before 1900, the overwhelming proportion found the Court curbing state legislation for invading an area proper to federal commerce concern. A classic example was the case of *Wabash, St. Louis, and Pacific Railway Company v. Illinois* (1886), denying the right of a state to regulate that part of an interstate railroad journey that was entirely within its borders on the ground that Congress's power was exclusive. Congress responded with the Interstate Commerce Act of 1887, granting the federal government positive supervisory power over the railroads. Congressional extension of such authority limited the ability of the courts to negate it by interpretation (until after 1900), and commerce power in the transportation field was mostly nominal.

Positive federal use of the clause grew rapidly from the 1890s on. The Sherman Antitrust Act (1890) found constitutional justification in the clause, as it seemed to afford broad federal authority to prohibit combinations in restraint of trade and general market monopolization. The Court, however, relying on a distinction between production and distribution, held the statute inapplicable to a sugar monopoly that had acquired nearly complete control over the manufacture of refined sugar (*United States v. E. C. Knight Company* [1895]). "Commerce succeeds to manufacture, and is not part of it," stated Chief Justice Melville W. Fuller: "Commerce among the states does not begin until goods commence their final movement from the state of their origin to that of their destination." Over the next forty years, the Court applied the same restrictive principle to the control of mining, fishing, farming, oil production, and the generation of hydroelectric power. Similarly, the Court, in *E. C. Knight*, evolved another restrictive formula, the "direct effect" doctrine, which again ensured legal limits on federal use of the clause: only if a local activity directly affected interstate commerce was federal control valid.

Regulation-minded progressive leaders of the early twentieth century sought to evoke judicial rulings that would expand the sweep of the clause. In *Swift v. United States* (1905), Justice Oliver Wendell Holmes Jr. responded. "Commerce among the States is not a technical legal conception, but a practical one, drawn from the course of business," he argued, setting forth a "stream of commerce" concept according to which the purchase of cattle, while a local process, became a federally regulatable one when it was part of an interstate commercial transaction. In the *Minnesota Rate Cases* (1913) and the *Shreveport Rate Case* (1914), the Court went further. In the former, Justice Charles Evans Hughes made clear that "direct" regulation of foreign or interstate commerce by the states was out of the question. In the latter, he took the next step, stating that "wherever interstate and intrastate activities are so related that the government of the one involves the control of the other, it is Congress, and not the States that is entitled to prescribe the final and dominant rule." But the social reform climate of the Progressive Era also intervened to affect expansion of the commerce power. When the Court sought to extend application of the Sherman Antitrust Act to labor organizations (*Loewe v. Lawlor* [1908]), Congress acted to retract such coverage in the Clayton Antitrust Act (1914).

The Progressives sought to use the clause in another novel way. In the effort to evolve a national police power, the clause was made the basis for legislation prohibiting lottery tickets, impure food and drugs, adulterated meat, transportation of women across state lines for immoral purposes, and, ultimately, child labor. The Court generally sustained such use, holding that Congress could validly close the channels of interstate commerce to items that were dangerous or otherwise objectionable. The Court made an exception with regard to child labor and returned to limiting federal power. In this case, the Court drew a much-criticized distinction between prohibiting the use of the facilities of interstate commerce to harmful goods, on the one hand, and using the commerce clause to get at the conditions under which goods entering that commerce were produced, on the other (*Hammer v. Dagenhart* [1918]).

The 1920s found similar interpretive strands continued. The movement of stolen cars (and ultimately interstate shipment of stolen goods in general) was prohibited (*Brooks v. United States* [1925]). And whereas child-labor restrictions were again overthrown, federal authority was further extended in other areas through the widening of the "stream of commerce" concept to the regulation of the business of commission men and of livestock in the nation's stockyards. It became possible to regulate not only the "stream" but the "throat" through which commerce flowed (*Stafford v. Wallace* [1922]). In *Railroad Commission of Wisconsin v. Chicago, Burlington and Quincy Railroad Company* (1922), federal altering of intrastate rail rates was affirmed, the Court holding that the nation could not exercise complete effective control over interstate commerce without incidental regulation of intrastate commerce.

On this broad judicial view of the clause, New Dealers of the early 1930s based the National Industrial Recovery Act (1933) and other broad measures, such as the Bituminous Coal Act (1935). Judicial response to these acts was not only hostile but entailed a sharp return to older formulas—especially the "production-distribution" and "direct effect" distinctions of the 1895 *E. C. Knight* case (*Schechter Poultry Corporation v. United States* [1935]). Charging that the Court had returned the country to a "horse-and-buggy" definition of interstate commerce, Franklin D. Roosevelt—especially after that body persisted in its narrow views on commerce (*Carter v. Carter Coal Company* [1936])—tried to "pack" the Court in hopes of inducing it to embrace broad commerce precedents. The success he achieved was notable. Starting with *National Labor Relations Board v. Jones and Laughlin Steel Corporation* in 1937, the Court not only rejected the whole battery of narrow commerce formulas (a process it extended in *United States v. Darby Lumber Company* [1941]) but also validated the clause as the principal constitutional base for later New Deal programs, authorizing broad federal control of labor relations, wages and hours, agriculture, business, and navigable streams. In 1946, Justice Frank Murphy stated: "The federal commerce power is as broad as the economic needs of the nation" (*North American Company v. Securities and Exchange Commission*). The 1960s demonstrated that it was also as broad as the social needs of the nation. In the Civil Rights Act of 1964, Congress banned racial discrimination in all public accommodations. The constitutional foundations for the statute were the commerce clause and the equal protection clause of the Fourteenth Amendment. In *Heart of Atlanta Motel, Inc. v. United States* (1964), the Supreme Court found the commerce clause alone fully adequate to support the statute.

United States v. Lopez (1995) signaled that a more conservative Supreme Court may be ready to usher in a new era of commerce clause jurisprudence. In *Lopez*, the Court, in an opinion written by Chief Justice William H. Rehnquist, declared unconstitutional a 1990 congressional statute that had made it a federal crime to possess a gun on school property. The chief justice emphasized "first principles" and federalism and concluded that the possession of a gun in a local school zone was not an economic activity that might, through repetition elsewhere, "substantially affect" interstate commerce. Rather, he argued, the statute in question was an attempt by Congress to exercise a nonexistent national police power over a subject—criminal law—that was primarily of state and local concern. Significantly, *Lopez* marked only the second occasion since 1937 that the Court had held that Congress had exceeded its authority under the commerce clause, and the other occasion—*National League of Cities v. Usery* (1976)—had been overruled less than a decade after it had been decided (*Garcia v. San Antonio Metro Transit Authority* [1985]).

The conservative Court's reluctance to permit Congress to exercise broad legislative authority under the commerce clause was again in evidence at the dawn of the twenty-first century. In *United States v. Morrison* (2000), the Court, in another opinion by Chief Justice Rehnquist, struck down the federal Violence Against Women Act on the ground that Congress lacked authority under the commerce clause to enact it because it did not involve economic or interstate activity. Importantly, though, both *Lopez* and *Morrison* were five-to-four decisions, so the final chapter on Congress's authority under the commerce clause has yet to be written.

BIBLIOGRAPHY

Benson, Paul R., Jr. *The Supreme Court and the Commerce Clause, 1937–1970.* New York: Dunellen, 1970.

Epstein, Richard. "Constitutional Faith and the Commerce Clause." *Notre Dame Law Review* 71 no. 2 (January 1996): 167–193.

Frankfurter, Felix. *The Commerce Clause under Marshall, Taney, and Waite.* Chapel Hill: University of North Carolina Press, 1937.

Ramaswamy, M. *The Commerce Clause in the Constitution of the United States.* New York: Longman's Green, 1948.

Scott D. Gerber
Paul L. Murphy

See also **Carter v. Carter Coal Company**; **Constitution of the United States**; *Cooley v. Board of Wardens of Port of Philadelphia*; *Gibbons v. Ogden*; **Interstate Commerce Laws**; *National Labor Relations Board v. Jones and Laughlin Steel Corporation*; *Schechter Poultry Corporation v. United States*; **Sherman Antitrust Act**; **Shreveport Rate Case**; *Stafford v. Wallace*; *United States v. E. C. Knight Company*.

COMMISSION GOVERNMENT.

Commission government is a form of municipal government that vests all legislative and executive authority in a small board of commissioners. Elected at large, each commissioner is responsible for the administration of one branch of municipal business, such as public safety, public works, and finance.

The scheme arose out of a natural disaster in Galveston, Texas. In September 1900 a hurricane and tidal surge devastated the island city, and as an emergency measure Texas's governor appointed five leading citizens to oversee the prostrate community. The following year a permanent five-person elected commission took charge and became a model for other cities. In 1905 nearby

Houston adopted commission rule, as did Dallas and Fort Worth two years later. By the close of 1914, 383 cities were in the commission fold, including such major municipalities as Des Moines, Memphis, New Orleans, Jersey City, and St. Paul. Appealing especially to business leaders, the commission plan seemed to maximize accountability by concentrating authority in a small board and to offer more efficient government with less participation by plebeian ward politicians.

After 1914, however, reformers turned from the commission plan to city manager rule. Elected commissioners did not necessarily have the expertise to administer city services, and under the commission plan there was no single, dominant figure capable of providing unified direction to city government. By vesting executive authority in a single expert administrator, the manager plan avoided these shortcomings. At the close of the twentieth century, the overwhelming majority of cities had rejected commission rule, including most that had once employed it. Responses from 4,555 municipalities to a 1996 survey showed only 66 cities with commission government.

BIBLIOGRAPHY

Rice, Bradley R. *Progressive Cities: The Commission Government Movement in America, 1901–1920.* Austin: University of Texas Press, 1977.

Woodruff, Clinton Rogers, ed. *City Government by Commission.* New York: Appleton, 1911.

Jon C. Teaford

See also **Municipal Government; Municipal Reform.**

COMMISSION MERCHANTS AND FACTORS.

The factor or commission merchant was one of the significant figures in the early commercial life of the country. These merchants were responsible for all facets of exchange and took responsibility for transporting and disposing of goods themselves, as well as providing credit to their customers.

The factorage system was known through the colonial and early national periods but was of most importance from 1815 to 1860. During these years cotton, tobacco, sugar, and rice from southern plantations were sent to urban centers in the Northeast and in Europe. Southern planters then purchased manufactured goods and supplies from these cities. Commission merchants advanced money to planters and manufacturers; in return, the products of farm and factory were consigned to them for sale. The planter and manufacturer were thus freed from the expense and trouble of selling and could devote their time, capital, and energy to the production of goods.

Frequently, however, the proceeds of the sales did not equal the sum advanced by the merchant, leaving the planter or manufacturer in debt. Southern planters especially resented that their trade and credit went through northern merchants. Consequently, there were numerous attempts by southerners to bypass northern commission merchants and build up direct trade connections between Europe and the southern ports. All of these attempts failed, and only the development of the commodity exchanges, the tremendous increase of industrial capital, and the improved methods of transportation and communication ended the dominant position of the commission merchant in American economy.

BIBLIOGRAPHY

Porter, Glenn, and Harold Livesay. *Merchants and Manufacturers.* Baltimore: Johns Hopkins University Press, 1971.

Woodman, Harold D. *King Cotton and His Retainers: Financing and Marketing the Cotton Crop of the South, 1800–1925.* Columbia: University of South Carolina Press, 1990.

T. P. Govan/T. D.

See also **Credit; Hardware Trade; Trade, Foreign.**

COMMITTEE OF INSPECTION.

The Committee of Inspection was the most radical and intrusive of the organizations within the New York network of revolutionary-era committees of correspondence. It poked into the efforts of elite merchants to evade colonial boycotts. Led by radical Whigs Alexander McDougall and Isaac Sears, the committee was particularly active in discouraging merchants from paying the tea tax of 1773 and in protesting the INTOLERABLE ACTS of the following year. A large proportion of its members were working-class artisans and mechanics and not averse to crowd action. While groups in other colonies assumed similar functions, only in New York City was the term "Committee of Inspection" employed.

BIBLIOGRAPHY

Gilje, Paul A. *The Road to Mobocracy: Popular Disorder in New York City, 1763–1834.* Chapel Hill: University of North Carolina Press, 1987.

Carl E. Prince

See also **Committees of Correspondence.**

COMMITTEE ON PUBLIC INFORMATION,

set up by executive order of President Woodrow Wilson, 14 April 1917. Formally it consisted of the secretaries of state, war, and the navy, with the journalist George Creel as civilian chairman. The committee was responsible for uniting American support behind the WORLD WAR I effort. Creel, handling most of the work, plus a far-flung organization abroad and at home, presented the war issues with pamphlets, films, cables, posters, and speakers (known as Four-Minute Men). The committee's sophisticated use of propaganda became a model for future government efforts to shape mass opinion.

BIBLIOGRAPHY

Creel, George. *How We Advertised America.* New York: Arno, 1972.

Gary, Brett. *The Nervous Liberals: Propaganda Anxieties from World War I to the Cold War.* New York: Columbia University Press, 1999.

Vaughn, Stephen. *Holding Fast the Inner Lines: Democracy, Nationalism, and the Committee on Public Information.* Chapel Hill: University of North Carolina Press, 1980.

Wiegand, Wayne A. *An Active Instrument for Propaganda: The American Public Library During World War I.* New York: Greenwood, 1989.

Guy Stanton Ford/A. G.

See also **Conscription and Recruitment; Mobilization; Propaganda; War Department.**

COMMITTEE ON THE CONDUCT OF THE WAR.

Established on 10 December 1861, this joint committee of the House and Senate was empowered to examine all aspects of the war, with authority to subpoena witnesses and papers. In 1864 its jurisdiction was expanded to include investigation of war contracts and expenditures. The committee consisted of five Republicans and two Democrats, with RADICAL REPUBLICANS in the majority. A total of eleven senators and representatives served over the committee's life of three and a half years. Its most important Republican members were its Radical chairman Benjamin F. Wade, senator from Ohio, who attended nearly all of its 272 meetings and wrote nearly all of the committee's reports; the Michigan senator Zechariah Chandler; and the Indiana representative George W. Julian. The Democratic senator Andrew Johnson of Tennessee and the Democratic New York representative Moses F. Odell were also active.

Created because congressional Republicans believed the Lincoln administration was too timid in its war policies, the committee pressured the administration into appointing military commanders who advocated aggressive measures against the South. Its members uncovered corruption and mismanagement, but they also engaged in partisan warfare against generals whom they saw as too sympathetic to Southerners and too accommodating of slavery. Publicizing Southern atrocities and the maltreatment of Union prisoners of war, the committee rallied Northern support for the struggle. However, the committee members had little knowledge of tactics or strategy. They saw delays and defeats as the result of pro-Southern sympathies, often loading the witness list to support the conclusions they had already reached. Investigating aspects of campaigns of every leading commander but Ulysses S. Grant, they were easily used by officers to shift the blame for defeats and mistakes from themselves to others. This problem was exacerbated by the committee's loose procedures, which welcomed hearsay testimony, permitted badgering and leading questions, and denied that the Fifth Amendment's protection against self-incrimination applied to its investigations. The committee's leaders were suspicious of officers trained at West Point and were partial to amateurs who shared Radical Republican political commitments. As a result the committee fostered resentment among military professionals, dissension among commanders and subordinates, suspicion between military officers and civilians, and pressure on commanders to act prematurely and even rashly. On some occasions the committee's bitter attacks on military officers led to real acts of injustice.

President Abraham Lincoln cooperated with the committee, although he must have resented its tendency to demean his acumen, to blame him for defeats and misadventures, and to pressure him to make dubious military appointments. However, Lincoln also understood that the committee's criticism of his generals, especially George B. McClellan, provided political cover for his decisions to replace them. Persistently pressing for a radical antislavery policy toward the South, the committee tried to influence Reconstruction near the close of the war. Its members unsuccessfully urged Lincoln to acquiesce in the Radical Wade-Davis Reconstruction Bill. Fearing that Lincoln was sacrificing the rights of African Americans, the committee took testimony designed to undermine his efforts to reestablish loyal government in Louisiana. However, with the surrender of the Confederate armies, the committee lost its influence and adjourned for the last time on 22 May 1865. When Congress created a new Joint Committee on Reconstruction in December 1866, not one of the members of the Committee on the Conduct of the War was appointed a member.

BIBLIOGRAPHY

Doyle, Elisabeth Joan. "The Conduct of the War, 1861." In *Congress Investigates: A Documented History, 1792–1974*. Edited by Arthur M. Schlesinger Jr. and Roger Bruns. New York: Chelsea House, 1975.

Tap, Bruce. *Over Lincoln's Shoulder: The Committee on the Conduct of the War*. Lawrence: University Press of Kansas, 1998.

Michael L. Benedict

See also **Civil War.**

COMMITTEES OF CORRESPONDENCE

COMMITTEES OF CORRESPONDENCE were used in eighteenth-century America to maintain contact among institutions and communities. The Massachusetts Assembly established such a committee to deal specifically with the problem of British policy as early as 1764. In 1771 the Boston Town Meeting appointed a committee to rouse fervor elsewhere in Massachusetts. The committee was the idea of Samuel Adams. Relations with Britain were quiescent at the time, but Adams believed Britain's seeming retreat in 1770 by its repeal of four of the five Townshend taxes had only been tactical and that colonials needed to be prepared for another crisis.

Initially the Bostonians met skepticism. Some towns believed the goal was a boycott of British trade for the sake of selling off Boston's own surplus goods. But the committees of Boston and four other towns agreed in November 1773 to resist the importation of East India tea. By mid-1774 a network of committees spanned Massachusetts.

Outside Massachusetts committees developed more slowly. Virginia's House of Burgesses proposed in March 1773 that colonial assemblies appoint committees to exchange information when each house was not sitting. New York City's Committee of Fifty-One was not elected until 19 May 1774, when a tumultuous public meeting debated the punishment Britain imposed on Boston and Massachusetts for the Tea Party. The young aristocrat Gouverneur Morris wrote as he watched that "the mob begin to think and to reason," and he likened its members to "poor reptiles." In Tryon County, on New York's western frontier, a committee also gathered, but its members were self-appointed and they met secretly. The local grandee Sir John Johnson opposed the American movement, and he had support from both his tenants and Mohawk Indians. When Sir John chanced upon a public meeting to elect a militia captain, he broke it up, flailing his horsewhip.

Both Morris, who did become a patriot, and Johnson, who remained a Loyalist, understood the fundamental issue. These committees marked the beginning of the destruction of established political institutions and the creation of a countergovernment. The very act of sending out express riders like Paul Revere challenged the monopoly of the Crown's official post office and insinuated that postmasters could not be trusted with sensitive messages. The separate riders became an organized Constitutional Post in May 1774.

Whether their members were elected or self-appointed, the committees that towns and communities appointed from 1771 onward signified a new stage in American resistance. They recognized the need for organization both within the separate colonies and across provincial lines. After the Tea Party they helped to establish the point that Boston and Massachusetts needed support. They brought new faces into political affairs. Perhaps most important, they posed the problem of what was to be done, since it was clear that exchanging information was bound to lead to some form of direct action.

BIBLIOGRAPHY

Ammerman, David. *In the Common Cause: American Response to the Coercive Acts of 1774*. New York: Norton, 1975.

Brown, Richard D. *Revolutionary Politics in Massachusetts: The Boston Committee of Correspondence and the Towns, 1772–1774*. Cambridge, Mass.: Harvard University Press, 1970.

Countryman, Edward. *A People in Revolution: The American Revolution and Political Society in New York, 1760–1790*. Baltimore: Johns Hopkins University Press, 1981.

Maier, Pauline. *From Resistance to Revolution: Colonial Radicals and the Development of American Opposition to Britain, 1765–1776.* New York: Knopf, 1972.

Ryerson, Richard Alan. *The Revolution Is Now Begun: The Radical Committees of Philadelphia, 1765–1776.* Philadelphia: University of Pennsylvania Press, 1978.

Edward Countryman

See also **Revolution, American; Revolutionary Committees.**

COMMITTEES OF SAFETY formed the bridge between the colonial political order, in which institutions ultimately derived authority from the Crown, and the American republican order, in which the fount of power was "the People." John Adams wrote in *Thoughts on Government* (1776) of the need to "glide insensibly" from the old order into the new. But these committees were profoundly revolutionary and deeply disruptive.

The committee movement went through three phases. In the first phase informal and locally created committees of correspondence exchanged information. The second saw committees of observation enforcing the Continental Association, which was the boycott of British commerce ordered by the First Continental Congress in September 1774. In the third phase committees of safety assumed full governmental powers while the institutions of the old order collapsed.

In Massachusetts the whole process was completed by the autumn of 1774. Rather than submit to the Massachusetts Government Act, towns resolved not to permit the Crown courts to open for business. The closures were without violence, but the townsmen who met the judges were armed and drawn up into militia companies. From then until the Commonwealth adopted a constitution in 1780, town- and county-level power was in the hands of committees chosen by town meetings. The massive turnout of militia to confront the retreating British regular soldiers after the firefights at Lexington and Concord on 19 April 1775 grew directly from committeemen's success in organizing townspeople for conflict.

Elsewhere development was slower. Although the association called for committees of inspection "in every city, county, and town," those committees appeared mostly in major ports like New York City and in lesser commercial centers like Albany. Non–New Englanders did not form governing committees until late April and early May 1775, when express riders brought the news of war in Massachusetts. Popular meetings elected the new committees, which were considerably larger and much more widespread than their predecessors. Both for that reason and because elections were frequent, the committees brought many previous outsiders into the center of affairs. Once they formed committees of safety, rebellious Americans found themselves in a situation of "dual power," with two sets of institutions that were vying for power.

Initially the committeemen of Albany, New York, were hesitant to move into the city council chamber. But as the committeemen took on more and more governmental functions, the old mayoralty, common council, and courts faded. Writ large, the Albany story could be told in many places. When Congress called in May 1776 for the extinction of royal government, little actually remained. Committees were meeting both the ordinary tasks of regular government and the extraordinary tasks of revolution and war.

Supposedly the authority of the committees ended when new state constitutions took effect. In practice the transition to constitutional government took time. New York's constitution described the committees as "temporary expedients," but committees of safety still met months after the constitution was proclaimed. Committees reappeared in the northern states in 1779 in response to an economic crisis brought about by drastic inflation. Gliding "insensibly" was not how the old order yielded to the new.

BIBLIOGRAPHY

Bushman, Richard L. *King and People in Provincial Massachusetts.* Chapel Hill: University of North Carolina Press, 1985.

Countryman, Edward. *A People in Revolution: The American Revolution and Political Society in New York, 1760–1790.* Baltimore: Johns Hopkins University Press, 1981.

Fischer, David Hackett. *Paul Revere's Ride.* New York: Oxford University Press, 1994.

Holton, Woody. *Forced Founders: Indians, Debtors, Slaves, and the Making of the American Revolution in Virginia.* Chapel Hill: University of North Carolina Press, 1999.

Ryerson, Richard Alan. *The Revolution Is Now Begun: The Radical Committees of Philadelphia, 1765–1776.* Philadelphia: University of Pennsylvania Press, 1978.

Edward Countryman

See also **Revolution, American; Revolutionary Committees.**

COMMODITIES EXCHANGE ACT, enacted in 1936, set forth a regulatory framework governing futures trading of agricultural commodities on organized exchanges. Futures contracts involve an agreement for delivery of an amount of goods at a specified future time for an agreed price. The 1936 Act expanded upon a previous 1922 legislation and sought to facilitate honest and fair practices and to restrain fraud, excessive speculation, and manipulation in commodity exchanges. Under the 1936 law, Congress established the Commodity Exchange Commission and delegated day-to-day regulatory duties to the secretary of Agriculture. The secretary, in turn, established the Commodity Exchange Administration to undertake these regulatory responsibilities. Substantial amendments in 1974 transferred regulatory authority to a newly created, five-member Commodity Futures Trading Commission. Since federal oversight of futures began in the 1920s, regulation has expanded beyond traditional futures contracts in agricultural products to futures in many other markets, such as energy commodities, government securities, and foreign currencies.

BIBLIOGRAPHY

Campbell, Donald A. "Trading in Futures under the Commodity Exchange Act." *George Washington Law Review* 26 (1958): 215–254.

Markham, Jerry W. *The History of Commodity Futures Trading and Its Regulation.* New York: Praeger, 1987.

Stassen, John H. "The Commodity Exchange Act in Perspective: A Short and Not-So-Reverent History of Futures Trading Legislation in the United States." *Washington and Lee Law Review* 39, no. 3 (summer 1982): 825–843.

Elizabeth Lee Thompson

See also **Exchanges.**

COMMODITY EXCHANGES. The enormous expansion of markets after 1850 required the formation of organizations that could handle exchanges of commodities on a large scale. The buyers and sellers of commodities in every city and market of large commercial importance formed boards of trade, also known as chambers of commerce. In 1848, buyers and sellers of commodities organized the Chicago Board of Trade. The New York Produce Exchange was organized two years later. By 1854 the Merchants Exchange of Saint Louis had the characteristics of a modern exchange. In 1870 the New York Cotton Exchange came into existence, while the New York Coffee Exchange was organized in 1882.

BIBLIOGRAPHY

Ferris, William G. *The Grain Traders: The Story of the Chicago Board of Trade.* East Lansing: Michigan State University Press, 1988.

Lurie, Jonathan. *The Chicago Board of Trade, 1859–1905: The Dynamics of Self-Regulation.* Urbana: University of Illinois Press, 1979.

Fred M. Jones / A. E.

See also **Clearinghouses; Commodities Exchange Act; Exchanges; Grain Futures Act; Pit.**

COMMON LAW. In 1765, in the first volume of his *Commentaries on the Laws of England,* William Blackstone explained that the law had two main parts: the statute law and the common law. The common law consisted of the general customs of the realm. It was often called an unwritten law because the common-law principles could not be found in any one place, but rather in the decisions of judges in thousands of individual cases. Those customs, built up over the generations by judicial decisions and cataloged by scholars, represented (supposedly) the wisdom of the ages. Blackstone thought such a law was entitled to respect precisely because it represented practices

stretching as far back as the human mind could recall. Such immemorial usage testified that the common law was correct. He was so proud of the common law that he called it "the perfection of reason."

Blackstone defined the common law in static terms, which made change difficult. Judges had to follow the precedent of the unwritten common law unless it was patently absurd or unjust—a high standard to meet. Thus many believe, with Francis Bacon, that judges are expounders and not makers of the common law. The common law in Blackstone's England was a body of principles arcane and difficult to understand, for sometimes the rationale underlying rules had been obscured by the mists of time. Nevertheless, it was also based on reason. That obscure but still rational law was difficult to challenge.

The Common Law after the Revolution

By the time of the American Revolution, however, an alternative understanding of the nature of the common law was emerging. Through the study of legal history, introduced by Matthew Hale's *History of the Common Law* (1713), both English and American lawyers began to understand that the common law evolved and that the law seemed to support a growing emphasis on liberty. An increasing historical consciousness led to views like that expressed by the scientist Joseph Priestley, who emigrated from England to America shortly after the Revolution: "Many things in the present state of the law are unintelligible without the knowledge of the history and progress of it." At the same time, the law became more complex to accommodate increases in commerce. So, faced with a rapidly expanding body of law and a sense that the law had changed in the past, American judges began to think of the common law as an evolving, rather than a static, body of principles. They spoke favorably of recrafting the common law to bring it into line with American values.

That recrafting took place along many fronts, including changing the rules for distribution of property at death. Where English rules gave preference to the eldest male child, Americans distributed property more equally to children (and grandchildren) at death. Across areas from property to contract to tort law, judges reexamined English precedent to see whether it fit American needs. Often those judges spoke about their desire to promote economic growth—for example, by limiting liability of corporations for harm they caused to neighbors—and at other times of the need to promote morality. The law was made more humane to provide at least minimal protection to families from creditors, to wives from abusive or prodigal husbands, and even (on rare occasions) to tenants from landlords. The decisions frequently were phrased in terms of expediency and, in rare instances, in terms of humanity. The Supreme Court Justice Joseph Story wrote in the 1830s about the common law as a mixture of ancient tradition and modern, commercial needs.

Even as conservative judges were acknowledging their ability to remake the law to bring it into line with

American views of economy and society, they were careful to portray the common law as evolving slowly. They needed to guard against the image that the common law might effect rapid change, for they needed to preserve the law's majesty. Few maintained the fiction of Blackstone's era that the law had been the same from time immemorial, but many continued to believe that judges had little power in remaking the law. The dominant view of the early nineteenth century was that judges were expounders of the common law and only had the power to make incremental changes.

Questioning the Common Law

Many outside the legal system saw the issue differently, however. Those outsiders saw the common law not as the perfection of reason but as the perfection of nonsense. In speeches and newspapers, outsiders to the legal system—usually adherents of the Democratic Party—attacked the common law as the creation of judges, who were making law to protect property against democracy. These debates occurred at a time when judges were using common-law doctrines to outlaw union organizing, to require the return of fugitive slaves, and to protect merchants and creditors at the expense of consumers and debtors. The critics of the common law ridiculed it as an arbitrary collection of abstruse rules. William Sampson's attack was among the most vitriolic. He thought Americans "had still one pagan idol to which they daily offered up much smokey incense. They called it by the mystical and cabalistic name of Common Law." Some principles were ancient, others recent, but in all instances, the common law sat "cross-legged and motionless upon its antique altar, for no use or purpose but to be praised and worshiped by ignorant and superstitious votaries." Many Americans agreed with Ralph Waldo Emerson's call in his 1836 book *Nature* for "our own works and laws and worship."

Related to that attack on the common law was a movement to limit the power of judges. Around 1810 the United States Supreme Court prohibited the creation of "common law" crimes; after that, in order to be prosecuted for crime in federal court, the accused had to be charged with violating a law passed by Congress rather than a rule created by a judge. A related drive for codification of other laws would have similarly limited judges' power to make new rules in such areas as contract, torts, property, and court procedure. The codification movement had two parts. The more radical branch, advocated by people like Thomas Jefferson and Sampson, sought to limit judges' discretion; a less radical branch, advocated by moderates and conservatives like Timothy Walker and Hugh Legaré, sought merely to clarify the law that judges applied.

Following the Civil War, the common law was increasingly seen as the creation of its history, and the trend toward decisions that facilitated economic growth seems to have continued. Proponents of the law and economics movement argued toward the end of the twentieth century that judges after the Civil War produced a common law that promoted efficient use of resources; they claimed that judges have long been concerned with creating economically efficient common-law rules. Oliver Wendell Holmes's 1881 book *The Common Law* was an important part of the postwar recognition that law evolved and that it was the product of historical events, rather than simply the result of reason. Holmes's book, focusing on experience rather than logic, is often seen as the legal analog to Charles Darwin's *Origin of Species*, focusing on biological processes rather than divine ones.

Holmes helped popularize the understanding that law evolves, but it was left to the legal realists of the early twentieth century, who linked that insight with a systematic critique of the rules that judges announced, to show that judges' own attitudes were central to making the law. Justice Benjamin N. Cardozo's 1921 book *The Nature of the Judicial Process* acknowledged that judges ought to look to their surrounding society, as well as precedent, for guidance in deciding cases. He engaged in the heresy of treating the "judge as legislator." That view of the common law reached its height in what the U.S. district judge Joseph Hutcheson called the judicial "hunch"—the belief that judges decided cases based on instinct rather than on precedent. Similarly, Karl Llewellyn expressed "rule skepticism," which debunked the priority of rules in judges' decision making. He focused on the importance of the sentiments of judges, lawyers, and the community in deciding cases. The U.S. district judge Jerome Frank took that a step further with his skepticism toward both law and facts. Frank's *Law and the Modern Mind* (1930), which offered a psychoanalytic interpretation of judges, ridiculed Americans' attachment to what he viewed as the myth that law could be certain. He argued that judges decided cases according to their own personal prejudices and foibles.

Interpretations since World War II

After World War II there was a growing interest in the use of the common law as a tool for social reform. While some academics spoke of the legal process school—the belief that there were methods of common-law and statutory interpretation that were independent of politics—other academics and jurists on both ends of the political spectrum urged judges to use their common-law power to remake the law. Where once judges had wielded the law to limit corporate liability, some began to expand tort law to make it easier for injured parties to recover in areas from hazardous working conditions to dangerous drugs to professional malpractice. Related developments in contract law relieved consumers with little bargaining power from unfair bargains, and changes in landlord-tenant law gave tenants more power. Meanwhile, judges from the right of the political spectrum, particularly after 1980, became increasingly concerned with considerations of economic efficiency. In areas from antitrust to environmental regulation and contracts, judges drew insights from economics to reshape the common law, such as the idea that sometimes monopolies are beneficial to consumers because they reduce costs.

In modern America, the common law continued to be the product of generations of judicial decision, but at the beginning of the twenty-first century it was understood to be the product of judge-made innovations. However, a more static conception of the common law has been reemerging in the United States Supreme Court. In several late-twentieth-century lines of cases, the Supreme Court limited the power of the courts to reinterpret the law. In 1993 in *Lucas v. South Carolina Coastal Commission*, the Court concluded that the state of South Carolina must recognize the traditional property rights of an owner of coastal property, primarily the right to build along the coast. A South Carolina court could not depart from the long-established precedent that property owners had a right to build along the shore. Then, in 1997 in *City of Boerne v. Flores*, the Supreme Court rejected the argument that Congress had the power to make its own findings about what constituted violations of constitutional rights. It thereby protected the right of courts to be the arbiter of what constituted violations of constitutional rights. Together those lines of decisions suggest that the Supreme Court was protecting courts' power under the common law while limiting the ability of judges to alter that law.

Yet every day, as has happened for centuries, judges grapple with new facts and struggle to apply precedent. These judges are using the common-law system, which affords them the power to apply old precedent to new cases and to remake old precedent when necessary.

BIBLIOGRAPHY

Brophy, Alfred L. "Reason and Sentiment: The Moral Worlds and Modes of Reasoning of Antebellum Jurists." *Boston University Law Review* 79 (December 1999): 1161–1213.

Holmes, Oliver Wendell. "The Path of the Law." *Harvard Law Review* 10 (1897): 457–478.

Horwitz, Morton J. *The Transformation of American Law, 1780–1860.* New York: Oxford University Press, 1992.

Hutcheson, Joseph C. "The Judgment Intuitive: The Function of the 'Hunch' in Judicial Decision." *Cornell Law Quarterly* 14 (1929): 274–288.

Karsten, Peter. *Heart versus Head: Judge-Made Law in Nineteenth-Century America.* Chapel Hill: University of North Carolina Press, 1997.

LaPiana, William P. *Logic and Experience: The Origin of Modern American Legal Education.* New York: Oxford University Press, 1994.

Llewellyn, Karl. "A Realistic Jurisprudence—The Next Step." *Columbia Law Review* 30 (1930): 431–465.

Posner, Richard. "A Theory of Negligence." *Journal of Legal Studies* 1 (1972): 29–96.

Sampson, William. *Sampson's Discourse, and Correspondence with Various Learned Jurists, upon the History of the Law.* Washington, D.C.: Gales and Seaton, 1826.

Story, Joseph. "Common Law." In *Encyclopaedia Americana.* Edited by Francis Lieber. Volume 3. Philadelphia: Carey, Lea and Carey, 1829.

Walker, James M. *The Theory of the Common Law.* Boston: Little, Brown, 1852.

Alfred L. Brophy

See also **Boerne v. Flores.**

COMMON MARKET. *See* **European Community.**

"COMMON SENSE," influential revolutionary pamphlet by Thomas Paine, published in Philadelphia, January 1776. Paine stressed the logic of America's independence, emphasizing the defects of Britain's monarchy and the economic costs of participating in Britain's repeated European wars. Reconciliation with Britain, Paine wrote, would constitute "madness and folly." "Common Sense" avoided abstract philosophy, favoring instead the ordinary language of artisans and biblical examples to support Paine's arguments. The "plain truth" (Paine's original title for the tract) he espoused found a broad readership; around 100,000 copies circulated in 1776 alone, and the pamphlet stirred politicians and ordinary citizens to embrace American independence.

BIBLIOGRAPHY

Conway, Moncure Daniel. *The Writings of Thomas Paine.* 4 vols. New York: B. Franklin, 1969.

Foner, Eric. *Tom Paine and Revolutionary America.* London and New York: Oxford University Press, 1976.

Sally E. Hadden

See also **Independence; Revolution, American: Political History;** *and vol. 9:* **Common Sense.**

COMMON SENSE BOOK OF BABY AND CHILD CARE. Written during World War II by pediatrician Dr. Benjamin Spock and his first wife, Jane Cheney Spock, *The Common Sense Book of Baby and Child Care* (1946, and six subsequent editions) became the most widely read child-rearing manual of the twentieth century. It offered anxious, middle-class mothers precise and accessible advice and a new, more flexible approach to discipline, derived from the educational theory of John Dewey and the psychology of Sigmund Freud. What Reverend Norman Vincent Peale labeled "permissive" child-rearing came under attack in the late 1960s for producing a generation of spoiled radicals. In the 1970s feminists attacked the book for content oppressive to women.

BIBLIOGRAPHY

Spock, Benjamin, M.D., and Mary Morgan. *Spock on Spock: A Memoir of Growing Up with the Century.* New York: Pantheon Books, 1989.

Weiss, Nancy Pottishman. "Mother, The Invention of Necessity: Dr. Benjamin Spock's Baby and Child Care." *American Quarterly* 29 (winter 1977): 519–546.

Zuckerman, Michael. "Dr. Spock: The Confidence Man." In *The Family in History*. Edited by Charles E. Rosenberg. Philadelphia: University of Pennsylvania Press, 1975.

William Graebner

See also **Childhood; Family.**

COMMONWEALTH V. HUNT, 45 Mass. 111, 4 Met. (1842). In 1842 Chief Justice Lemuel Shaw of the Massachusetts Supreme Judicial Court ruled that a combination of workers to protect their interests by peaceable collective action was not an indictable criminal conspiracy. The decision has long been understood by many labor and legal historians as a pro-labor departure from the harsh criminal conspiracy doctrine of the early nineteenth century. Actually, the decision had little impact on case law, which generally treated labor organizations as criminal conspiracies until the Norris-La Guardia Act (1932) and the Wagner Act (1935) recognized labor's right to organize and bargain collectively.

BIBLIOGRAPHY

Levy, Leonard Williams. *The Law of the Commonwealth and Chief Justice Shaw*. Cambridge, Mass.: Harvard University Press, 1957.

Nelles, Walter. "*Commonwealth v. Hunt*." *Columbia Law Review* 32 (November 1932): 1128–1269.

Tomlins, Christopher L. *Law, Labor, and Ideology in the Early American Republic*. New York: Cambridge University Press, 1993.

David Park

See also **Norris-La Guardia Act.**

COMMUNES. *See* **Utopian Communities.**

COMMUNICATION SATELLITES. Artificial communication satellites can relay television, radio, and telephone communication between any two places on the globe and from space to other objects in space or on earth. The military, commercial companies, and amateurs from over twenty nations have hundreds of communication satellites orbiting the earth. This has been accomplished in a mere forty-five years.

The origin of artificial communications satellites began over a century ago with Guglielmo Marconi's electric waves transmission in 1896. The possibilities for satellites improved gradually with advances in short wave communication and radar in the 1930s, and with the possibilities of rocket flight after Robert H. Goddard's rocket demonstration in the 1920s. In 1945, British scientist and science fiction author Arthur C. Clarke published an article in which he predicted the launching of orbital rockets that would relay radio signals to earth. At last, on 4 October 1957, the Soviet Union launched *Sputnik I*, the first artificial satellite. Clarke's seemingly far-fetched prediction had come true in about ten years. It took over fifty years from the early possibilities to the first satellite, but the next forty-five years saw tremendous and rapid technical advancement and proliferation of worldwide satellite communication.

Early Communication Satellites

The United States entered the Space Age when it launched the *Explorer 1* satellite in January 1958. At the end of 1958, an Atlas B rocket launched a SCORE communications satellite, which contained two radio receivers, two transmitters, and two tape recorders. It broadcast a taped Christmas greeting from President Dwight D. Eisenhower. Then, in August 1960, the National Aeronautics and Space Administration (NASA) launched *Echo 1*, a giant, ten-story Mylar balloon reflector that relayed voice signals. It was so bright it could be seen by the naked eye. *Echo 1* launched the American satellite communication era.

At that time, there were two principal viewpoints toward satellite relay. One side favored the Echo passive satellite system, artificial "moons" that would reflect electromagnetic energy. The other view favored active satellites, which would carry their own equipment for reception and transmission. *Courier 1B*, launched in October 1960 shortly after *Echo 1*, was the first active transmitter and used solar cells and not chemical batteries for power. *Telstar 1*, the first commercial satellite, was built by AT&T and launched by NASA in 1962. It provided direct television transmission between the United States and Japan and Europe and proved the superiority of active satellite communication, as well as the capability of commercial satellites (COMSATS) to provide multichannel, wideband transmission.

Satellites receive signals from a ground station, amplify them, and then transmit them at a different frequency to another station. Most ground stations have huge antennas to receive transmissions. Smaller antennas than used in years past have been placed closer to the user, such as on top of a building. By using frequencies allocated solely to a satellite, rather than going through the earth microwave stations, communications are much faster. This allows for teleconferencing and for computer-to-computer communications.

International Communications

In 1962, President John F. Kennedy signed legislation to create the Communications Satellite Corporation to represent the United States in a worldwide satellite system. In 1964, under United Nations auspices, the International Telecommunications Satellite Consortium (Intelsat) was formed. From then on, communication satellites had synchronous, high-altitude, elliptical orbits, which improved communications. The *Intelsat1* (Early Bird) was launched in 1965 for transatlantic communication service. It could transmit 240 simultaneous telephone calls or one color television channel between North America and Europe.

GPS Satellite. An artist's rendering of a U.S. Air Force Navstar Global Positioning System Block IIF satellite, built by Rockwell International Corporation to collect navigational data for both military and civilian uses. AP/WIDE WORLD PHOTOS

By 1970, the *Intelsat* 4s provided 4,000 voice circuits each; by 1990, each satellite could carry over 24,000 circuits. As of 2002, there were 19 Intelsats in orbit, as well as many other competing satellite communications systems in the United States and Europe. Intelsats can communicate with each other and with other satellite systems as well. For instance, Intelsats and the Russian satellites provide the hotline between Washington, D.C., and Moscow.

Development in communication satellites systems results from many sources. The first ham, or amateur, radio satellites were launched in 1961. By 1991, thirty-nine amateur communications satellites had been launched, many sent free as ballast on government rockets. As of 2002, there were six countries that owned their own communications satellites for domestic telephone service and some twenty-four countries that leased from the Intelsat systems for domestic service. Commercial satellites have been developed by some twenty countries and provide many communications services. Television programs can be transmitted internationally by beaming off satellites. Satellites also relay programs to cable television systems and homes equipped with dish antennas, until recently only a possibility for sophisticated military use.

New Technology

One new technique of the 1990s is called frequency reuse, which expands the capabilities of satellites in several ways. It allows satellites to communicate with a number of ground stations using the same frequency. The beam widths can be adjusted to cover different-sized areas—from as large as the United States to as small as a single small state. Additionally, two stations far enough apart can receive different messages transmitted on the same frequency. Also, satellite antennas have been designed

to transmit several beams of different sizes in different directions.

The satellite communications systems of NASA, called Tracking and Data Relay Satellites (TDRS), which began in 1983, provide links between space shuttles and ground control. By 1990 one TDRS satellite could relay all the data in a twenty-four volume encyclopedia in five seconds. The new TDRS converts solar energy to electricity and uses antennas to transmit up to 300 million bits of information per second per radio channel. The latest versions allow communication between spacecrafts, between a shuttle and a space station, or with the Hubble Space Telescope.

There is also now a mobile telecommunications network which provides data digital links and telephone and fax communication between ships or with airplanes on international flights. Ships can also use two satellites at two different locations for navigation purposes. Laser beams, operating in the blue-green wavelength which penetrates water, have been used for communication between satellites and submarines.

In the early 2000s, developments in satellites use networks of small satellites in low earth orbit (1,200 miles or less above the earth) to provide global telephone communications. The special telephones used allow access to regular telephone networks from anywhere on the globe, creating a true "global village."

BIBLIOGRAPHY

Curtis, Anthony R. ed. *Space Almanac.* Houston: Gulf Publishing Co., 1992.

McGraw Hill Encyclopedia of Space. West Germany: Editions Rombaldi, 1967.

Diane Nagel Palmer

COMMUNICATIONS INDUSTRY in the United States is best understood as a rapidly changing industrial sector that is engaged in the production and distribution of content designed to inform and entertain. When characterized more generally as the "core copyright industries," this industry is estimated to have contributed more than $457 billion to the U.S. economy in 1999.

Background

Traditional distinctions between sectors of this industry have become blurred through a process of convergence enabled by the production, storage, and transmission of more and more information goods and services in digital form. While primarily technological, this process of convergence also includes an accelerating trend toward integration and consolidation within the industry through mergers and acquisitions. Changes in regulatory philosophy that began to take shape in the late 1960s have also broken down the distinctions between organizations primarily engaged in the production of information and those that specialize in its distribution and sale.

Characterization of the communications industry in the United States is challenged further by a process of globalization that has been marked by dramatic growth in the size and scope of transnational media corporations. This growth has been enabled by reduction of regulatory barriers to foreign ownership and participation in domestic communications markets. Although direct investment and participation in the domestic market by foreign firms is relatively small, exports from this industry exceeded those of all other industrial sectors, including motor vehicles in 1999.

The history of the communications industry in the United States has been marked by the emergence and maturation of its component sectors at different points in time. Economists and historians of technology have attempted to associate the emergence of different technological systems with specific changes in social and economic relationships in society. James Beniger's important book *The Control Revolution* (1986) goes a long way toward describing the ways in which chains of innovation move through organizations specializing in production, distribution, and consumption management in responses to crises in each sphere of economic activity. The characterization of the United States as an "information economy" reflects the centrality of this industry to the economy as a whole, although the production of information goods for the consumer market has been secondary to the production of information for business and industry.

Communications media are now best defined in terms of their technological forms, rather than by their content. The emergence of print-based media—newspapers, magazines, and books—predates the birth of the United States as an independent nation. While printing technology has changed considerably since then, the fundamental character of text and graphic representation has not. The motion picture industry has also been transformed marginally by the addition of sound, color, and increasingly sophisticated special effects, but its thematic core has remained essentially the same. It has been transformed more substantially, however, by the development of alternative means of distribution. Broadcast, cable, and satellite television systems have extended the reach of the Hollywood production centers at the same time that videotape and DVD technology have made it easier for consumers to access this content in accordance with their individual schedules, tastes, and preferences. Similarly, the music industry has been transformed by advances in production and distribution technology as well as by devices designed for the convenience of household consumers.

Since the late twentieth century, the Internet has represented potentially the most dramatic influence on the character of the communications industry. Its initial impact centered on text-based news and information segments of the industry. This narrow focus reflects limitations on the amount of information, or bandwidth, that

can be transmitted over the telecommunications network and displayed on computer screens. Improvements in the capacity of digital media systems to process, capture, store, and distribute information are said to follow "Moore's law" (named for Gordon Moore, cofounder of Intel), and double approximately every eighteen months. However, changes in the fundamental character of the audiovisual content accessed through the Internet will depend upon more widely distributed access to broadband, or high-capacity telecommunications systems.

Perhaps the most important challenge facing the communications industry is the development of appropriate business plans and a regulatory regime that will ensure that an expanded technological capacity is put to its most socially and economically productive use. Adjustments in the regulations governing the management of intellectual property will be necessary to ensure that sufficient incentives can be provided as rewards to support effort and creativity, and at the same time that prices offered to consumers will make these goods and services attractive. Conflicts between the commercial interests of intellectual-property owners and the privacy interests of consumers are expected to move to the center stage of regulatory policy debates. The impact of these policy struggles will vary across the different sectors of the communications industry, in part reflecting their distinct histories of development.

Newspapers

As one of the oldest sectors of the communications industry in the United States, the newspaper business has reached maturity, and in terms of circulation it has actually begun to decline in relation to its potential market. The high point in daily circulation was reached in 1990 at around 62.3 million, although this plateau had essentially been established by 1970. Despite this decline in circulation, the industry remains highly profitable, with a median return on revenues that was exceeded only by pharmaceuticals in 1997. The income of the industry is derived primarily from advertising, and because of newspapers' access to a highly desirable group of consumers, they are still able to claim approximately one-fifth of total advertising revenues. It is primarily through the elimination of direct competition that firms within the industry have been able to maintain such high profits from advertising and circulation. The proportion of cities in the United States with directly competing daily newspapers declined from nearly 40 percent in 1923 to less than 2 percent by 1985. This proportion continues to fall.

Television and Radio

Television and radio broadcasting are the principal alternatives to newspapers for advertisers hoping to reach desirable targets. With nearly 98 percent of U.S. households having access to television, broadcasters have increased their share of advertising revenues. At the same time, however, firms in the industry have had to divide those revenues among an expanded network of claimants. The number of television signals available to the average household increased in critical stages, beginning with the emergence of successful independent UHF stations. The number of these stations tripled during the 1980s, and they provided a basis for the establishment of additional networks such as Fox, introduced in 1987. A more powerful challenge came from the distribution of imported signals from other markets by CATV (cable) systems. This expansion continued with an increasing supply of original programming from cable networks. The distribution of theatrical motion pictures, and later original programming, by Home Box Office (HBO) in 1975 marked a critical takeoff point for the cable industry. By the year 2000 there were more than 175 basic television networks being delivered via satellite to cable systems.

Additional competition for traditional broadcasters emerged with the spread of satellite direct broadcasting services (DBS) such as DirecTV. While approximately 67 percent of television households had cable service in 2000, satellite distribution nearly tripled between 1995 and 2000, moving from 3.3 million to 9.6 million households. By the turn of the century, almost all television households had access to more than thirty different channels.

With so many sources of content for consumers to view through their television screens, it is not surprising that the average number of hours of television usage has increased steadily over the years, from 6 hours and 43 minutes per day in 1980–1981 to 7 hours and 24 minutes per day in 1999–2000. However, the share of television viewers' attention captured by the three major networks (ABC, CBS, and NBC) slipped from 84 percent in 1980–1981 to 41 percent in 1999–2000.

Broadcast and cable television networks split in excess of $20 billion in advertising revenues in 1997–1998. However, unlike newspapers and broadcasters, cable and satellite distributors derive most of their revenue from subscription and carriage fees rather than from advertising. Although cable and satellite distribution technology was initially a resource that increased the revenue of broadcast networks, each of these distribution technologies supported the development of powerful competitors once the new firms won the right to distribute information and entertainment directly to the consumer.

Although radio broadcasters, such as the Westinghouse station KDKA in Pittsburgh, initially used music, drama, and informational programming in the 1920s as "loss leaders" that they hoped would stimulate demand for receivers, they eventually developed highly specialized programming to capture the attention of desirable listeners throughout the day. Radio's adoption of a specialized, magazine-like approach to programming was in response to the competition for general-interest audiences that television represented for both media after it emerged in the 1950s. The greater fidelity of its signals made the FM band a natural home for specialized musical formats, while sports, news, and all-talk formats were concentrated on the AM band.

Today nearly two-thirds of radio listening takes place outside the home. Of the more than 600 million radios in use in the United States in 2000, nearly 25 percent were in automobiles, and some 30 percent of radio listening took place there. There are, however, many other opportunities for radio listening throughout the day. Lightweight portable radios have even become essential gear for joggers and others who fit exercise into their busy schedules.

With so many opportunities to reach desirable consumers, the radio industry as a whole remains profitable, although independent stations have continued to struggle. Unlike newspapers, however, the number of radio stations has increased somewhat dramatically following decisions by the Federal Communications Commission to liberalize its multiple station and cross-media ownership regulations in the 1980s. This process of consolidation accelerated following the passage of the Telecommunications Act of 1996.

Recorded Music

Just as the motion picture industry had established a close working relationship with the broadcast-, cable-, and satellite-distributed television industry, radio broadcasters evolved a mutually beneficial relationship with the recorded music industry. With the total retail value of music shipments exceeding $12.7 billion in 2000, and with recorded music becoming the dominant source of content broadcast by the nation's radio stations, the demand for recorded music is generated to a large degree through the unpaid advertising that music programming provides.

The music industry in the United States is highly concentrated, with five global corporations controlling nearly 90 percent of the industry's revenue. While firms based in the United States no longer dominate the industry, the domestic market continues to be the largest in the world. The fortunes of the music industry have changed several times in response to improvements in consumer technology. The introduction of compact discs in the 1980s marked a dramatic expansion in the market for recorded music. However, at the turn of the century, the introduction of digital compression techniques (MP3) and the sharing of music over the Internet through services such as Napster were seen by many in the industry as a threat to its survival. The fact that in 2001 more than 20 million music lovers used Napster or one of its imitators to download near-perfect copies of their favorite performers' music without compensation to the copyright holders was enough to mobilize a powerful, and initially successful, legal challenge to the practice.

Book Publishing

Like the music industry, book publishing depends primarily upon circulation, or sales to consumers, rather than advertising revenue. While newspaper circulation has declined, and the number of daily papers has shrunk rather dramatically, book publishing is a thriving industry with an increasing number of publishers. Book sales in the United States in 1998 topped $23 billion, with estimates of the number of new titles published each year exceeding 60,000. The nature of the industry is difficult to describe in part because it is composed of quite distinct submarkets or specialties, which include professional and educational books as well as mass-market paperbacks. The book publishing industry is more competitive than many other segments of the communications industry, and it is especially noteworthy that two of the most dominant firms in the domestic industry in 2001 were foreign owned, and Bertlesmann AG, a German firm, headed the list of major publishers.

Some concerns were expressed in 2000 about the consequences that a changing population profile would have for the publishing industry. The same decline in readership that threatened the survival of the newspaper industry seemed likely to affect the demand for mass-market paperbacks, although other segments of the publishing industry seemed poised for continued growth.

Motion Pictures

Theatrical motion pictures are part of another communications industry that depends on circulation, rather than advertising, for its revenue. These movies have continued to capture a substantial share of recreational dollars in North America. From modest beginnings as a novel amusement called the nickelodeon, introduced in the United States around 1896, motion pictures have remained at the core of the entertainment industry in the United States. Domestic box-office receipts exceeded $7.6 billion in the United States and Canada in 2000, rising sharply after a plateau had been established at around $5 billion in 1993. The number of theatrical films released in the United States has varied from year to year, reflecting the state of the economy and the nature of competition. A high point was reached in the 1950s with the release of 483 films, but only 248 were released in 1960, and output dropped to a low of 233 in 1980. The industry later climbed to a new peak of 510 films in 1997. The number of screens in the United States increased steadily from around 17,500 in 1980 to nearly 37,400 in 2000.

The financial success of the motion picture industry is no longer dependent, however, upon revenue from movie theaters. Videotape and DVD distribution has become a reliable source of revenue as well. The number of homes with VCRs increased at a spectacular rate, from 27 percent in 1985 to 70 percent by 1990, and it leveled out at around 85 percent of households by 1998. This installed base of VCRs and a network of video distributors provides consumers with the opportunity to rent or purchase cassettes. The number of cassettes sold for the rental market in the United States grew from 15.2 million in 1985 to in excess of 78 million by 2000. The number of DVD players in U.S. households in 2000 was estimated at around 14 million, and the number of movies and music

video titles available in that format was expected to exceed 8,500 by the end of the year.

Online Communications

Developments in computers and telecommunications networks have enabled still other firms in the United States to create a vibrant market in remote access to information goods and services. An online information industry emerged in the 1960s to supply businesses with scientific and technical information. Traditional database publishers like Reed Elsevier and Thomson Corporation earned upwards of 30 percent of their revenue from electronic publishing by 1998. The firms that created the online information industry in the 1980s were joined in the 1990s by a new group of information providers. These newcomers included Internet portal services such as America Online (AOL) and the Microsoft Network (MSN).

A market for consumer-oriented data services could not develop, however, until there was a substantial installed base of personal computers equipped with modems. The number of U.S. households with computers increased from approximately 34 million in 1994 to approximately 57 million by 2000. Although the Internet was not capable of delivering competitive video programming at the end of the twentieth century, the percentage of households with access to the Internet from home was expected to exceed 50 percent by 2002.

One measure of the Internet's growth is the number of computers with a standardized network address (or host). The number of hosts around the world grew from 213 in 1981 to more than 110 million in 2001. The most spectacular growth in Internet hosts occurred following the introduction of a graphical Web browser (Mosaic) in 1993. With the development of the World Wide Web and the subsequent commercialization of the Internet, the "gift economy" that had characterized the computer-based network when it served the scientific and technical community was replaced by a "new economy" oriented toward information entrepreneurs.

As the number of informational resources available through the World Wide Web increased exponentially, several indexing and searching services emerged to help users find the information they were seeking. Firms like Yahoo, Excite, and Infoseek struggled to survive in a business environment that was still being defined. By 1999 advertising revenues captured by Internet publishers were only a fraction of the total spent on advertising that year. The most optimistic projections for online advertising in the United States were that it would capture 3.2 percent of advertising expenditures by 2002.

The acquisition of the traditional media conglomerate Time Warner by the Internet newcomer AOL, which was announced in 2000, marked the beginning of the Internet era in the U.S. communications industry. Although the early days of 2001 were marked by a spectacular failure of many Internet businesses, the development of online marketers and distributors of information commodities, such as Amazon.com, represented an important change in the ways in which consumers might acquire information and entertainment in the future. Although the company had not yet realized a profit, Amazon.com increased its sales from $16 million in 1996 to $610 million by 1998, primarily on the basis of sales of books, CDs, and videotapes.

Conclusion

The future of the communications industry will continue to be shaped by innovations in technology, adjustments in regulatory policy and social norms, and, more critically, the continued elaboration of demand for information goods and services. Although the structural character of the industry will surely change, there is little doubt that its economic importance will grow in the coming years.

BIBLIOGRAPHY

Baldwin, Thomas F., D. Stevens McVoy, and Charles Steinfield. *Convergence: Integrating Media, Information, and Communication.* Thousand Oaks, Calif.: Sage, 1996.

Beniger, James. *The Control Revolution.* Cambridge, Mass.: Harvard University Press, 1986.

Compaine, Benjamin M., and Douglas Gomery. *Who Owns the Media?* 3d ed. Mahwah, N.J.: Lawrence Erlbaum, 2000.

Computer Science and Telecommunications Board, National Research Council. *The Digital Dilemma: Intellectual Property in the Information Age.* Washington, D.C.: National Academy Press, 2000.

Croteau, David, and William Hoynes. *The Business of Media: Corporate Media and the Public Interest.* Thousand Oaks, Calif.: Pine Forge Press, 2001.

McChesney, Robert W. *Rich Media, Poor Democracy.* Urbana: University of Illinois Press, 1999.

Neuman, W. Russell. *The Future of the Mass Audience.* New York: Cambridge University Press, 1991.

Owen, Bruce M. *The Internet Challenge to Television.* Cambridge, Mass.: MIT Press, 1999.

Preston, Paschal. *Reshaping Communications.* Thousand Oaks, Calif.: Sage, 2001.

Schiller, Dan. *Digital Capitalism.* Cambridge, Mass.: MIT Press, 1999.

Straubhaar, Joseph, and Robert LaRose. *Media Now: Communications Media in the Information Age.* 3d ed. Belmont, Calif.: Wadsworth, 2002.

Oscar H. Gandy Jr.

See also **Computers and Computer Industry; Internet; Music Industry; Publishing Industry; Radio; Television: Programming and Influence.**

COMMUNICATIONS WORKERS OF AMERICA (CWA) began as an employee association in the Bell System just after the end of World War I. At the start of the twenty-first century, it was the largest U.S. communications and media union, made up of some 1,200 charter local unions representing more than 700,000 members, who work in telecommunications, general manufacturing, electronics, gas and electric utilities, and other fields. As of 2000, the CWA had successfully negotiated more than 2,000 collective bargaining agreements granting its members higher wages, benefits, better working conditions, and training and educational programs with child- and family-care provisions. Some of the leading employers of CWA members are: American Telephone and Telegraph (AT&T), the Regional Bell telephone companies, General Telephone and Electric, General Electric, Disney, the Canadian Broadcasting Corporation, the state of New Jersey, and leading newspapers. The CWA's broad organizing success in fields beyond the U.S. telephone industry helped make it one of the most visible and effective industrial unions in the history of American labor.

Company Union Roots

From 1878 to 1895, the U.S. telephone industry remained virtually free of union activity, thanks to the vigorous anti-union stance of the Bell System, the largest U.S. telephone company, which was owned and operated by AT&T. Despite some early organization drives by the International Brotherhood of Electrical Workers (IBEW) and other affiliates of the American Federation of Labor (AFL), American telephone workers remained largely nonunion.

The growing dominance of U.S. telephony by AT&T and the Bell System emerged by the time of America's entry into World War I. In 1917, Bell's employee ranks swelled to over 199,000, while those of smaller (non-Bell) telephone companies rose to only 46,000. Corporate control of the industry was temporarily ceded when a strike by the IBEW in November 1917 prompted the federal government to take control of American telephony to ensure continuous service and to maintain the secrecy of wartime communications. After the war, the IBEW leadership resumed its union activities, but refused to provide full union membership to women telephone operators.

In 1919 the IBEW struck again with some 25,000 Bell employees, at the time about 9 percent of the industry's 278,000 workers. The strike was short-lived, however, as many workers stayed on the job. After the strike, most workers were compelled to join Bell's new company unions under the threat of losing their seniority and pension rights. These organizations were patterned after similar company union structures established by Western Union Telegraph, Standard Oil of New Jersey, and U.S. Steel. (A 1935 Department of Labor study later found that most company unions drafted employee labor agreements without consulting workers and they rarely led to the substantive improvement of wages, benefits, or working conditions.)

New Deal Changes

With the passage of the National Industrial Recovery Act in 1933, trade unions became legal in the vast majority of U.S. industries. Four years later, company unions were made illegal with the Supreme Court's affirmation of the Wagner Act in 1937. Acting with the overwhelming support of management, who wished to preserve as much control as possible, telephone workers that same year formed the National Federation of Telephone Workers (NFTW), a confederation of former company unions. While the new NFTW constitution continued to provide local autonomy for Bell telephone workers and generous pension rights, the confederation arrangement also served as a barrier to national unionization because it tended to favor the former company union leadership. Management continued to play a strong role in the NFTW by providing work-release time and other financial incentives. The Bell System's main objective through this period was to comply with federal law and, at the same time, ensure that telephone workers did not join forces with unions affiliated with the AFL or the more militant Congress of Industrial Organizations (CIO).

After 1941, organization drives by the IBEW, and the CIO-affiliated American Communications Association (ACA) and United Electrical, Radio, and Machine Workers of America (UE), were not successful against the NFTW. From 1939 to 1945, NFTW membership almost quadrupled (from 45,000 to 170,000).

NFTW Becomes CWA

After World War II, telephone workers, under the direction of NFTW president Joseph Beirne, moved to counter the centralized power of the Bell System by building a national union. The growing militancy of the NFTW—made more extreme with wartime deprivations and a newer, younger, and lower-paid workforce—led to a strike threat in 1946. Although the strike never materialized, the threat substantially helped to raise telephone workers' wages.

One year later, the union did strike over the issue of industry-wide bargaining, which the Bell System (and parent AT&T) historically opposed. While the NFTW lost the 1947 strike, the work stoppage helped to bring telephone workers together in an unprecedented manner. The rank and file argued for a reorganization of NFTW bylaws to create a national union of telephone workers (the Communication Workers of America), rather than a series of autonomous local chapters. Seeking to block the new CWA formation, the CIO created the Telephone Workers' Organizing Committee (TWOC), as a means to attract some of the more militant CWA factions. When faced with the prospect of joining the AFL-affiliated IBEW, the CWA merged with the TWOC and became the CIO's fourth largest union in 1949.

CWA president Beirne's success in winning large wage increases and system-wide bargaining from the Bell System also helped the union to become influential in national and local Democratic politics as the CWA fought for wider social and economic reforms. In 1950, CWA membership was 180,000 workers, which grew to 260,000 in 1960. Two decades later, CWA membership was more than 500,000. The CWA's ranks continued to swell with new members in telephone and other communication industries as it focused on the rapid convergence of media technologies in the workplace. At the start of the twenty-first century, the CWA was one of the most politically active and powerful U.S. industrial labor unions.

BIBLIOGRAPHY

Bahr, Morton. *From the Telegraph to the Internet: A 60 Year History of the CWA.* Washington, D.C.: National Press Books, 1998.

Fink, Gary, ed. *Labor Unions.* Westport, Conn.: Greenwood Press, 1977.

Palladino, Grace. *Dreams of Dignity, Workers of Vision: A History of the International Brotherhood of Electrical Workers.* Washington, D.C.: International Brotherhood of Electrical Workers, 1991.

Schacht, John. *The Making of Telephone Unionism, 1920–1947.* New Brunswick, N.J.: Rutgers University Press, 1985.

Dennis W. Mazzocco

See also **AT&T; Communications Industry; Trade Unions.**

COMMUNIST PARTY, UNITED STATES OF AMERICA,

was formed in 1919 when the left wing of the Socialist Party became convinced that the Bolsheviks in Russia had discovered a swift road to socialism. One left faction attended the Socialist Party's convention in Chicago in hopes of seizing control. When that failed, they walked out and on 31 August founded the Communist Labor Party (CLP), led by John Reed and Benjamin Gitlow. The CLP thundered that it had "only one demand: the establishment of the Dictatorship of the Proletariat," and sent Reed to Russia to win support from the Communist International (Comintern). Another faction met on 1 September, also in Chicago, and founded the Communist Party of America (CPA), announcing that "Communism does not propose to 'capture' the bourgeoisie parliamentary state, but to conquer and destroy it." Led by Charles Ruthenberg, the CPA sent Louis Fraina to Russia to seek Comintern endorsement. The CPA's membership was about 24,000, organized largely in immigrant federations whose members spoke little English. The CLP's membership was about 10,000 and also largely immigrant. Meanwhile, U.S. attorney general A. Mitchell Palmer launched a series of raids to round up alien radicals. His chief targets were syndicalist and anarchist groups, but the Palmer raids netted many communists and about a thousand were deported, with more leaving voluntarily. State governments also prosecuted citizens who were communists, and New York jailed the CLP's Gitlow and the CPA's Ruthenberg. Both parties

Communist Protest. Labor agitation, such as this demonstration in 1930, gained the Communist Party public attention even as it was becoming rigidly Stalinist. LIBRARY OF CONGRESS

went underground, losing more than half of their members in the process.

Unity, Stalinization, and a Revolutionary Program

The Comintern ordered a merger, but the two parties were unable to agree on terms. In May 1920, a minority CPA faction merged with the CLP to form the United Communist Party. Comintern representatives forced the remaining part of the CPA into a merger in May 1921 that created a single Communist Party of America. The Comintern also provided this new, united CPA with secret subsidies that allowed it to establish a daily newspaper, numerous foreign-language newspapers, and a large staff of organizers. Sections of the syndicalist Industrial Workers of the World shifted to the Communist Party, and the movement gained a labor arm when William Foster brought his Trade Union Educational League into the movement. After government attacks ceased, the Comintern ordered formation of an aboveground arm, which was done in December 1921 with the creation of the Workers Party of America. The CPA remained underground until dissolved in 1923. In 1925, the Workers Party became the Workers (Communist) Party of Amer-

ica, which in 1929 was renamed the Communist Party, United States of America (CPUSA).

Throughout the 1920s the party remained small, inconsequential, and beset by internal factionalism, with Comintern representatives stepping in to pick leaders, guide policy, and impose unity. In early 1929, the CPUSA expelled James Cannon and his supporters when Cannon became an adherent of Leon Trotsky, the Bolshevik leader who had lost out to Joseph Stalin. Later that year, the Comintern expelled Jay Lovestone and Benjamin Gitlow—then the party's chief figures—along with scores of veteran CPUSA militants for being followers of Nikolai Bukharin, another rival to Stalin.

By the early 1930s, the CPUSA had become thoroughly Stalinized, internal factionalism had ended, and Earl Browder had become the party's leader. In response to the Great Depression, the CPUSA offered the abolition of capitalism and Soviet rule. William Foster, its presidential candidate in 1932, promised in *Toward Soviet America* (1932) that when communists came to power "all the capitalist parties—Republican, Democratic, Progressive, Socialist, etc.—will be liquidated. . . . The press, the motion picture, the radio, the theatre, will be taken over by the government" (pp. 275, 317). Foster received 102,991 votes, less than 1 percent of the vote. After the election, communists denounced Franklin Roosevelt's New Deal as "social fascist." The party's agitation for unemployment relief and its leading role in several dramatic strikes brought attention to it, but by 1934 membership was still only 26,000.

The Popular Front

In 1935 the Comintern proclaimed a Popular Front policy that downplayed revolution and emphasized alliances with reformers and other leftists against the common menace of fascism. Embracing this stance with the slogan "Communism is twentieth-century Americanism," the CPUSA shifted to support of Roosevelt and sought a cooperative role on the left of the broad New Deal coalition. Communists achieved a limited but nonetheless significant presence in mainstream politics through their participation in New York's American Labor Party, the Minnesota Farmer-Labor Party, the End Poverty in California movement, the Wisconsin Farmer-Labor Progressive Federation, and the Washington [state] Commonwealth Federation. Two members of Congress, Representatives John Bernard (1937–1938) of Minnesota's Farmer-Labor Party and Hugh De Lacy (1945–1946), a Washington State Democrat, became secret members. Two open communists won election to the New York City Council.

Communists also took leading although usually secret roles in numerous liberal-left advocacy groups such as the American League for Peace and Democracy, National Negro Congress, American Writers Union, and American Youth Congress. Communists had no role in founding the Congress of Industrial Organizations (CIO), but in 1936, after secret negotiations, CIO leaders hired more than fifty communist organizers and brought into the CIO several small communist-led unions. Working from this base, by the end of World War II, communists led eighteen CIO affiliates that represented 1,370,000 workers, a quarter of the CIO's total. CPUSA membership also grew, reaching 66,000 members in 1939. At the party's origins, most members had been impoverished working-class immigrants, predominately of Russian origin. In the mid-1920s, Finnish immigrants were briefly the largest group in the party. By the mid-1930s, the majority of communists were native-born, while college-educated professionals were a growing proportion of the party's membership and Jews were the largest single ethnic group. Communists championed black rights and devoted significant resources to organizing African Americans, but black membership remained small. Throughout all of its history a large share of the party's members lived in the New York City area.

The Nazi-Soviet Pact, World War II, and a Postwar Reversal

The CPUSA supported the Nazi-Soviet Pact of August 1939 without reservations, and shifted from avid support for Roosevelt's foreign policies to savage rejection. Communists opposed Roosevelt's reelection in 1940 and organized the American Peace Mobilization to agitate against President Roosevelt's policy of providing American military and economic aid to nations fighting Nazi Germany. CPUSA abandonment of the antifascist cause prompted most liberals to turn against cooperation with communists. In reaction to CPUSA support for the Nazi-Soviet Pact, the Roosevelt administration imprisoned communist chief Earl Browder for passport fraud. To avoid threatened U.S. government regulation, the CPUSA dropped formal affiliation with the Communist International in 1940.

The Nazi attack on the USSR in June 1941 prompted the CPUSA to resurrect its Popular Front tactics, embrace Roosevelt's policies, and reach out for liberal allies. As a gesture to the Soviet alliance, President Roosevelt in 1942 released Browder from prison. Believing that the Soviet-American wartime alliance would continue after the war, Browder decided that the Popular Front stance was a permanent strategy. In mid-1944, the CPUSA dissolved and reconstituted itself as the Communist Political Association. Revolution and socialism were consigned to the distant future and communists presented themselves as the militant left of the New Deal and the Democratic Party. In April 1945, however, Moscow signaled that Browder's views were unacceptable. In July, the Communist Political Association called an emergency convention, dissolved itself, and reestablished the CPUSA. Browder was expelled and two Moscow loyalists, William Foster and Eugene Dennis, became the party's leaders. The reconstituted CPUSA shifted from cooperation with mainstream liberals to demanding support for a foreign policy congenial with Stalin's postwar goals.

Party Headquarters. A 1934 photograph of the Communist Party's national headquarters, on Thirteenth Street, just south of Union Square, in New York City. © CORBIS

Cold War Anticommunism

The development of the Cold War put the communists in opposition to President Harry Truman's anti-Soviet policies. Evidence of communist cooperation with Soviet espionage led Truman to create a loyalty program that excluded communists from government employment and to imprison CPUSA leaders under sedition sections of the Smith Act. In 1948, communists committed their cadre to the presidential campaign of Henry Wallace and the new Progressive Party. Truman's reelection and Wallace's poor showing destroyed the CPUSA's influence among liberals and led to the expulsion of communists from the CIO. During the Korean War, in which U.S. troops fought communist soldiers, anticommunism became a highly popular cause among both Republicans and Democrats, and Congress passed a number of anticommunist laws. Although the CPUSA was never outlawed and continued to function openly, these factors combined to reduce the party's membership to twelve thousand by the mid-1950s, as well as bring about its political isolation.

Another blow came in 1956, when Soviet leader Nikita Khrushchev confirmed that Joseph Stalin had committed monstrous crimes during the purges of the 1930s. This was quickly followed by evidence that Stalin's purges of the early 1950s also included an anti-Semitic element, and then by Soviet crushing of the popular revolution against communist rule in Hungary. These events devastated communist morale and the party fell into turmoil as reformers called for independence from Soviet control. Moscow loyalists had carried the day by 1958, but by that time the party's membership had plummeted to three thousand.

The Vietnam War, Gorbachev, and the Post–Cold War Era

Gus Hall became party chief in 1959 and insisted on rigid loyalty to Moscow and ideologically orthodox Marxism-Leninism. The CPUSA slowly regained members, aided by the Vietnam War backlash against anticommunism and by those veterans of the New Left of the 1960s and 1970s who were seeking a new vehicle for radicalism. It was also aided by continued secret Soviet subsidies that reached $3 million a year in 1988. Although it regained a minor role in liberal-left politics in California and New York, membership by the late 1980s did not exceed ten thousand. Soviet leader Mikhail Gorbachev's democratizing of Soviet communism appalled Hall, and he supported the abortive 1991 coup by Soviet hard-liners. This sparked revolt against Hall by CPUSA reformers, but at a late 1991 convention Hall retained control and the reformers left the party. Loss of Soviet subsidies also caused a severe cutback in the party's activities: its daily newspaper became a weekly, several of its specialized journals ceased publication entirely, and its staff was drastically reduced in size. By the time of Hall's retirement in 2000, membership had dropped below two thousand.

BIBLIOGRAPHY

Draper, Theodore. *The Roots of American Communism.* New York: Octagon Books, 1977.

———. *American Communism and Soviet Russia: The Formative Period.* New York: Vintage Books, 1986.

Foster, William Z. *Toward Soviet America.* New York: International Publishers, 1932.

Isserman, Maurice. *Which Side Were You On? The American Communist Party during the Second World War.* Middletown, Conn.: Wesleyan University Press, 1982.

Klehr, Harvey. *The Heyday of American Communism: The Depression Decade.* New York: Basic Books, 1984.

Klehr, Harvey, and John Earl Haynes. *The American Communist Movement: Storming Heaven Itself.* New York: Twayne, 1992.

Klehr, Harvey, John Earl Haynes, and Kyrill M. Anderson. *The Soviet World of American Communism.* New Haven, Conn.: Yale University Press, 1998.

Klehr, Harvey, John Earl Haynes, and Fridrikh Igorevich Firsov. *The Secret World of American Communism.* New Haven, Conn.: Yale University Press, 1995.

Starobin, Joseph R. *American Communism in Crisis, 1943–1957.* Cambridge, Mass.: Harvard University Press, 1972.

John Earl Haynes

See also **Abraham Lincoln Brigade; Anticommunism; Hiss Case; McCarthyism; Palmer Raids; Radicals and Rad-** icalism; **Russia, Relations with; Socialist Party of America.**

COMMUNITY ACTION PROGRAM. Probably the most controversial feature of President Lyndon B. Johnson's WAR ON POVERTY, the Community Action Program, initiated under the Economic Opportunity Act of 1964, attempted to fight poverty on a local level through a massive infusion of federal funds. Despite large local variations, community action programs shared certain characteristics: nonprofit corporation status; local governing boards; heterogeneous staffs composed of professional social workers, academics, and paraprofessionals; and collective funding from many sources, including foundations and local governmental agencies as well as federal agencies. Similar approaches had been tried before, but what made the new community action programs unique and controversial was, first, the massive size of federal sponsorship; second, the speed with which programs came into being; and third, the statutory requirement that all community action programs structure board and staff decision making to include local residents.

The Economic Opportunity Act was signed into law in August 1964, and the initiative passed for a time from the federal government to the localities. Besides bringing the existence of poverty to public attention, community action programs soon generated strong adverse criticisms of the "social service establishment" for regulating the poor while maintaining them at or near subsistence levels. In some areas criticism soon led to protest demonstrations, class-action lawsuits against state and federal agencies, and demands that poor people be granted representation on all agencies that dealt with problems of poverty. Congress soon passed legislative revisions that earmarked funds for less controversial and more controllable programs, such as Project Head Start. After 1967, community action programs rapidly declined, and the reform energies that had previously gone into community action shifted to advocacy and social action movements independent of federal sponsorship. The administration of Richard M. Nixon further curtailed community action programs and substituted proposals for a largely automated national program of income maintenance.

BIBLIOGRAPHY

Moynihan, Daniel P. *Maximum Feasible Misunderstanding.* New York: Free Press, 1969.

Patterson, James T. *America's Struggle against Poverty, 1900–1985.* Cambridge, Mass.: Harvard University Press, 1986.

Daniel Knapp / A. G.

See also **Great Society; Poverty; Social Work.**

COMPACT DISCS (CDs) are small, thin, plastic discs twelve centimeters in diameter that contain a metallized surface that holds optically recorded digital information, such as sound, images (still and motion), and computer programs. Data is recorded by creating microscopic pits along a single track on the metallized surface; playback incorporates a red laser beam reflected onto the surface that measures the pits and translates them into binary information. A standard CD can hold between 74 and 82 minutes of audio, or approximately 780 million bytes of data. CDs are nearly unaffected by the number of times they are played. The disc's durable surface tolerates fingerprints and small scratches, making it an ideal solution for optically storing and preserving digital information.

Development of the CD to replace vinyl records began in the 1970s with Royal Philips Electronics of the Netherlands and Sony Corporation of Japan. Philips produced the optical storage technologies, while Sony pioneered error correction circuitry. The result was a set of industry standards established in the late 1970s for the CD's physical and logical characteristics, which among other things, ensured compatibility among discs and players from diverse manufacturers. This standard, known as the Compact Disc Digital Audio system, was in place in the early 1980s, and in 1983, the compact disc and the first CD players were introduced to consumers.

As standards evolved, so did the uses for CDs. Changes in recording techniques allowed for specialized uses such as the CD-Read-Only Memory (CD-ROM) for use in computers, CD-Interactive (CD-I), a stand-alone audio and video hardware system designed for audio and visual data, and the Video-CD (VCD) for high-quality video playback. The rewriteable CD (CD-RW) standard, created in 1996, enabled nearly anyone with a home computer and a CD-RW drive to record music, data, and video on a compact disc.

The future remains bright for the compact disc. The Digital Versatile Disc (DVD) standard has increased storage capacities to nearly five gigabytes (4.7GB) of information, or twenty-eight times that of its CD-ROM cousin, and DVD-Video has pushed VHS videotapes from store shelves as the preferred format for popular movies. Upcoming innovations in manufacturing processes, such as the improved pinpoint light-focusing ability of the blue-violet laser beam and higher transfer rates of players and recorders, will see DVD storage capacities climb to nearly thirty gigabytes of data on one shiny disc.

BIBLIOGRAPHY

Armstrong, Elizabeth. "DVD Lasers: Why Blue Beats Red." *Wired* (June 2002): 50.

Pohlmann, Ken C. *Principles of Digital Audio.* 4th ed. New York: McGraw-Hill, 2000.

Michael Regoli

See also **Digital Technology.**

COMPANY OF ONE HUNDRED ASSOCIATES,

a privileged corporation established by Cardinal Riche-

lieu in 1627 to colonize New France (Canada), was also known as the Company of New France. The company's charter required it to send colonists to Canada until 1643, to provide for colonists for the first three years, and thereafter to furnish them enough cleared land for their support. In return, the company exercised political power over the colony, seigneurial control of the land, and enjoyed a monopoly of all trade except the whale and cod fisheries. Since the company focused on trade at the expense of colonization, New France failed to prosper, and France revoked the charter in 1663.

BIBLIOGRAPHY

Eccles, W. J. *The French in North America.* Markham, Ontario, Canada: Fitzhenry & Whiteside, 1998.

McCusker, John J., and Kenneth Morgan. *The Early Modern Atlantic Economy.* New York: Cambridge University Press, 2000.

Mary Borgias Palm S.N.D./S. B.

See also **Cod Fisheries; French Frontier Forts; Fur Trade and Trapping; New France.**

COMPARABLE WORTH is a concept introduced in the 1970s to circumvent the effects of job segregation practices. Its premise is that men and women holding different jobs should be similarly compensated if the jobs require comparable skills, training, effort, and responsibility. For example, a company should provide the same compensation to a male truck driver as to a female nurse if worker qualifications, the complexity of the jobs, and the value of the two jobs to the company are comparable.

Fueling the emergence of the comparable worth or pay equity movement were studies revealing that on average, working women earned sixty cents for every dollar earned by men, a pay gap that had not changed substantially for several decades. Pay equity advocates attributed most of this earnings differential to the sex-segregation of the workforce. Women dominated such lower-paying occupations as nursing, retail sales, and clerical services. Sex stereotyping discouraged or restricted women from entering many higher-paying, tradionally male occupations, and the consequent overcrowding in the low-paying positions further depressed wages. In addition, employers undervalued women's work. To rank jobs and assign wage rates, they often used job evaluation systems that contained discriminatory features or relied upon community wage rates, which were in part a product of the discriminatory practices of other employers.

Advocates argued that, by raising the pay for traditionally female occupations, comparable worth would improve the economic situation of many women and their families and would decrease the sex-segregation of the workforce, as men would follow the higher wage rates into traditionally female jobs. Opponents of comparable worth argued that the wage gap reflected factors other than discrimination and that widespread implementation of comparable worth principles would disrupt the economy of the United States.

Employers were able to apply differential wage scales to women because prevailing interpretations of the law through the 1960s and 1970s required equal pay only when men and women performed the same job. In the 1980s federal courts found little merit in suits that would broaden the reach of the Equal Pay Act of 1963 and Title VII of the CIVIL RIGHTS ACT OF 1964 by forcing employers to apply comparable worth principles to compensation. The courts held that pay disparities between sexes are a product of supply and demand rather than of intentional employer discrimination.

Comparable worth advocates have had more success in the legislatures than in court. In 1973 the state of Washington became the first state to conduct a study of its own workforce to test for unequal compensation rates between sex-segregated jobs. In 1983 Minnesota became one of the first states to pass legislation to adjust the wages of all of its employees to provide equal pay for comparable work. By 1987 only four states had undertaken no comparable-worth action—data collection, creation of a task force, job evaluation studies, or salary adjustments—at all, while twenty states were implementing pay equity plans based on comparable worth principles.

BIBLIOGRAPHY

Aaron, Henry, and Cameran M. Lougy. *The Comparable Worth Controversy.* Washington, D.C.: Brookings Institution, 1986.

Mezey, Susan Gluck. *In Pursuit of Equality: Women, Public Policy, and the Federal Courts.* New York: St. Martin's Press, 1992.

Nelson, Robert, and William P. Bridges. *Legalizing Gender Inequality: Courts, Markets, and Unequal Pay for Women in America.* New York: Cambridge University Press, 1999.

Treiman, Donald, and Heidi Hartmann, eds. *Women, Work, and Wages: Equal Pay for Jobs of Equal Value.* Washington, D.C.: National Academy Press, 1981.

Irwin N. Gertzog
Cynthia R. Poe

See also **Equal Pay Act.**

COMPREHENSIVE EMPLOYMENT AND TRAINING ACT

(CETA) was enacted by Congress in 1973 to consolidate a number of existing federal job-training programs to help unemployed, underemployed, and disadvantaged individuals. Prior to CETA, federal job training was fragmented and complex, with numerous programs targeting specific groups, such as disadvantaged youths, unemployed older adults, or welfare recipients. Services overlapped, but because administration of each program was distinct, coordination was difficult.

CETA replaced this fragmented situation with federal government block grants providing funds to state and local governments, "prime sponsors," who were responsible for identifying training needs and delivering the

training following federal guidelines. Services funded via CETA included on-the-job training, classroom training, and public service employment. Public service employment was a program of federally subsidized jobs and was the most controversial aspect of CETA.

While CETA was enacted to counter the earlier problems with myriad, category-specific programs, a number of later additions to CETA added specific programs and target groups. Frustration with this trend, questions about program effectiveness, and controversy over public service employment led to CETA's replacement with the 1982 passage of the Job Training Partnership Act (JTPA). JTPA furthered the decentralization of federal job training to the state and local levels.

BIBLIOGRAPHY

Franklin, Grace A., and Randall B. Ripley. *CETA: Politics and Policy, 1973–1982.* Knoxville: University of Tennessee Press, 1984.

Grubb, W. Norton. *Learning to Work: The Case for Reintegrating Job Training and Education.* New York: Russell Sage Foundation, 1996.

Orr, Larry L., et al. *Does Training for the Disadvantaged Work? Evidence from the National JTPA Study.* Washington, D.C.: Urban Institute Press, 1996.

John Budd

See also **Employment Service, U.S.**

COMPROMISE OF 1790,

a supposed bargain arranged by Secretary of the Treasury Alexander Hamilton, Congressman James Madison, and Secretary of State Thomas Jefferson in June 1790. In return for Hamilton's agreement to provide the congressional votes necessary to locate the national capital on the Potomac River, Jefferson and Madison promised to round up sufficient support to assure enactment of Hamilton's plan for assumption of the Revolutionary War debts of the states by the federal government. In order to secure sufficient votes, a further concession by Hamilton involving direct payments to those states with little or no debt proved necessary.

BIBLIOGRAPHY

Bowling, Kenneth R. *The Creation of Washington, D.C.: The Idea and Location of the American Capital.* Fairfax, Va.: George Mason University Press, 1991.

Cooke, Jacob E. "The Compromise of 1790." *William and Mary Quarterly* 27 (October 1970): 523–545.

Risjord, Norman K. "The Compromise of 1790: New Evidence on the Dinner Table Bargain." *William and Mary Quarterly* 33 (April 1976): 309–314.

Jacob E. Cooke / T. M.

See also **Debts, State; Hamilton's Economic Policies; Washington, D.C.**

COMPROMISE OF 1850, a designation commonly given to five statutes enacted in September 1850, following a bitter controversy between the representatives of the North and South. The controversy reached a fever pitch during the weeks following the assembling of Congress in December 1849, when the election of a speaker under the customary majority rule was prevented by the unwillingness of the Free Soil members, who held the balance of power, to be drawn into an arrangement with either of the two major parties. In the course of the prolonged balloting, criminations and recriminations passed between the hotheaded spokesmen of the two sections. Pointing to indications that the principle of the WILMOT PROVISO might be enacted into law and receive the signature of President Zachary Taylor, southerners insisted as a matter of right upon the recognition of the Calhoun doctrine, which stated that under the Constitution all the territories should be deemed open to SLAVERY. There was talk of secession unless this principle was recognized in fact or as a basis for some adjustment. Plans were underway for the discussion of a satisfactory southern program at a southern convention called to meet at Nashville in June.

In the face of increasing sectional strife Henry Clay returned to the U.S. Senate in 1849 and on 29 January 1850 suggested a series of resolutions intended to provide the basis for the prompt adjustment of the main questions at issue between the two sections. His resolutions were shortly referred to a select committee of thirteen, of which he was made chairman. Its report (8 May), which covered the ground of Clay's resolutions, recommended an "OMNIBUS BILL" providing for the admission of California under its free state constitution, for territorial governments for Utah and New Mexico silent on slavery, and for the settlement of the boundary dispute between Texas and the United States. It also recommended a bill for the abolition of the slave trade in the District of Columbia and an amendment to the fugitive slave law.

The hope of compromise was tied up with the fate of the omnibus bill. Clay rallied to his support the outstanding Union men, including Daniel Webster, Lewis Cass, Henry S. Foote, and Stephen A. Douglas; the latter became the active force in the promotion of the necessary legislation. President Taylor wanted the admission of California but no action on New Mexico and Utah until they should be ready to become states; he was, therefore, a formidable obstacle to the plans of the compromisers until his death on 9 July. Even the active support of the bill by his successor, Millard Fillmore, did not offset the fact that the idea of compromise "united the opponents instead of securing the friends" of each proposition.

Compromise as such had clearly failed; the ground that it had contemplated was covered in five statutes each formerly included as sections of the proposed omnibus bill. The act establishing a territorial government for Utah (9 September) contained the important POPULAR SOVEREIGNTY clause providing that any state or states formed out of this territory should be admitted with or without slavery as their constitutions should prescribe. Popular sovereignty deftly removed slavery as an obstacle to congressional organization of these territories, but it did not remove the divisive issue of slavery in the territories from the national political scene. An identical clause was appended to the New Mexico territorial act (9 September), which also resolved the conflict between Texas and the federal government over the Santa Fe region by a cession, with compensation to Texas, to the newly created territory. On the same date, the act admitting California under its constitution—prohibiting slavery in the new state—was approved. The FUGITIVE SLAVE ACT of 18 September 1850, which amended the original statute of 12 February 1793, provided for the appointment of special commissioners to supplement the regular courts empowered after a summary hearing to issue a certificate of arrest of a fugitive "from labor," which authorized the claimant to seize and return the fugitive (with a fee of ten dollars when the certificate was issued and of only five dollars when denied); in no trial or hearing was the testimony of the alleged fugitive to be admitted as evidence nor was a fugitive claiming to be a freeman to have the right of trial by jury; federal marshals and deputy marshals were made liable for the full value of fugitives who escaped their custody and were empowered to call to their aid any bystanders, or *posse comitatus*; and any person willfully hindering the arrest of a fugitive or aiding in his rescue or escape was subject to heavy fine and imprisonment, as well as to heavy civil damages. The Act Abolishing the Slave Trade in the District of Columbia was approved on 20 September.

These statutes were presented to the country as a series of compromise measures. They did not, however, magically calm the sectional storm. In the North there was widespread denunciation of the iniquitous features of the Fugitive Slave Act and deliberate declaration that its enforcement would never be tolerated. At the same time the conservative forces organized a series of Union meetings and pleaded the obligations of the North to pacify the South. In the latter section the other four enactments precipitated one of the most serious disunion crises the country had ever faced. In Georgia, Mississippi, and South Carolina the Southern Rights, or secession, forces were checkmated only by the most strenuous efforts of the Union or Constitutional Union elements. Both sides foreswore old party labels and fought under their new banners to win control over the official state conventions that were ordered. The Southern Rights forces lost in the first test fight in Georgia (see GEORGIA PLATFORM) and had to carry this moral handicap in the remaining contests. It was not until the elections of 1852 that the country at large made clear its (albeit temporary) acquiescence in what at length became known by the oversimple label the Compromise of 1850.

BIBLIOGRAPHY
Freehling, William W. *The Road to Disunion.* New York: Oxford University Press, 1990.

Hamilton, Holman. *Prologue to Conflict: The Crisis and Compromise of 1850.* Lexington: University of Kentucky Press, 1964.

Holt, Michael F. *The Political Crisis of the 1850s.* New York: Norton, 1983.

Potter, David Morris. *The Impending Crisis, 1848–1861.* Edited and completed by Don E. Fehrenbacher. New York: Harper and Row, 1976.

Remini, Robert V. *Henry Clay: Statesman for the Union.* New York: Norton, 1991.

Arthur C. Cole / T. M.

See also **Conscience Whigs; Missouri Compromise; Nashville Convention;** *and vol. 9:* **The Crime Against Kansas.**

COMPROMISE OF 1890.

In 1890 three bills vied for attention in the U.S. Senate. In order to break the legislative gridlock, the Republican majority reached a compromise that allowed for the passage of the Sherman Silver Purchase Act and the McKinley Tariff Act. Perhaps most importantly, the Republicans withdrew their support for the Federal Elections Bill, thereby signaling the end of the Republican commitment to African American suffrage.

The Tariff Act, sponsored by William McKinley of Ohio and supported by northern industrial interests, established the highest protective tariff in U.S. history by raising rates an average of 49.5 percent. It also gave the president much greater authority to conduct foreign trade by allowing him to hold trade conventions, negotiate reciprocity agreements, and build a federal bureaucracy to deal with the intricacies of global trade.

The Sherman Silver Act was sponsored by Senator John Sherman of Ohio, and supported by silver interests and western Republicans. It was a means of appealing to western farmers in return for their support of the McKinley Tariff. The act, by including silver in federal coinage, was intended to bring a higher price for that product, which would trigger inflation and bring higher farm prices and better terms for debtors. Republicans in the West hoped that these results would stem the flow of farmers into the nascent Populist Party.

The Federal Elections Bill, sponsored by Massachusetts senator Henry Cabot Lodge, and derisively called a Force Bill by its southern opponents, was an attempt to establish federal supervision of congressional elections. The bill would have applied to the entire country, but it was aimed primarily at congressional districts in the South that had begun to deny African Americans the right to vote. The bill would have backed up the Fifteenth Amendment by protecting African Americans against disfranchisement. The primary feature of the bill would have made the federal circuit courts the monitor of election procedures and returns, rather than state governors and state election boards.

The compromise that saw passage of the Tariff Act and Silver Act in return for the withdrawal of support for the Elections Bill highlighted the perceived threat of the populism. More importantly, it demonstrated the ascendancy of economic issues and business interests within the Republican Party and the end of its traditional commitment to African American suffrage. Further, it showed the apathy of those in the West and the North to the issue of civil rights for African Americans.

The defeat of the Elections Bill had severe consequences for African Americans in the South as disfranchisement become more systematic in the period after 1890. The denial of a political voice for African Americans accelerated the construction of the social, cultural, political, and economic system of segregation known as Jim Crow. Not until passage of the voting rights acts of 1957, 1960, and 1965 and the Constitutional Amendment of 1964 outlawing the poll tax would Congress and the states adopt measures to fulfill finally the promises of the Fifteenth Amendment.

BIBLIOGRAPHY

Perman, Michael. *Struggle for Mastery: Disfranchisement in the South, 1888–1908.* Chapel Hill: University of North Carolina Press, 2001.

Welch, Richard E., Jr. "The Federal Elections Bill of 1890: Postscripts and Prelude." *Journal of American History* 52 (1965): 511–526.

Steve Hageman

See also **Farmers' Alliance; Reconstruction; Sherman Silver Purchase Act; Tariff.**

COMPTROLLER GENERAL OF THE UNITED STATES,

the head of the General Accounting Office (GAO), which was created by the Budget and Accounting Act of 10 June 1921. The comptroller general is appointed by the president with the advice and consent of the Senate for a fifteen-year term and is subject to removal only by a joint resolution of Congress for specified causes or by impeachment. The comptroller general directs an independent agency in the legislative branch that was formed to assist Congress in providing legislative control over the receipt, disbursement, and application of public funds through a postaudit function. A power of the comptroller general that has sometimes been controversial is the function of "settling" accounts. In practice this amounts to passing upon the legality of expenditures by governmental agencies; if such expenditures are not in accordance with the law as interpreted by the comptroller general, they may be disallowed. Thus, in essence, a preaudit function has evolved.

The 1921 law vested the GAO with all of the powers of the six auditors and the comptroller of the Treasury, as set forth in the Dockery Act of 1894 and in other statutes extending back to the original Treasury Act of 1789. The law also broadened the government's audit activities and established new responsibilities for reporting to Congress. Although the GAO continues to audit government financial records, it now also evaluates the overall efficiency of government programs and aids Congress in its legislative oversight duties.

BIBLIOGRAPHY

Mansfield, Harvey C. *The Comptroller General: A Study in the Law and Practice of Financial Administration.* New Haven, Conn.: Yale University Press, 1939.

Mosher, Frederick C. *The GAO: The Quest for Accountability in American Government.* Boulder, Colo.: Westview Press, 1979.

Trask, Roger R. *Defender of the Public Interest: The General Accounting Office, 1921–1966.* Washington, D.C.: U.S. General Accounting Office, 1996.

Guy B. Hathorn / A. G.

See also **Expenditures, Federal; General Accounting Office; Office of Management and Budget.**

COMPTROLLER OF THE CURRENCY.

The National Currency Act of 1863 created a system of federally chartered national banks and the Office of the Comptroller of the Currency, a bureau of the Treasury Department, to administer the new banking system. The legislation aided the Union's financing of the Civil War by enabling national banks to issue a new paper currency, national bank notes, backed by purchases of U.S. government bonds. The Comptroller held the bonds, and if a bank failed, the Comptroller liquidated them and reimbursed the bank's note holders. This policy was a major step toward a safer and more uniform national paper currency, replacing the diverse bank notes issued by hundreds of state-chartered banks.

A revised National Bank Act of 1864 authorized the Comptroller of the Currency to hire a staff of examiners to supervise and inspect national banks. The Comptroller also received authority to regulate national bank lending and investment activities. Fifteen decades later, at the start of the twenty-first century, these remained among the Comptroller's chief functions. Other functions later conferred on the office include approving or denying applications for new charters, branches, and changes in bank capitalization, as well as the power to act against banks engaging in unsound practices, including removing bank officers and directors.

From the 1860s to the 1920s, comptrollers interpreted their legislative mandate narrowly, in particular holding that the law did not permit national banks to open branches. This interpretation, together with laxer state banking laws and regulations, led to a revival of state-chartered banking. The United States became a country with a "dual banking system" of federal and state-chartered banks. At the peak of U.S. bank numbers in the early 1920s, there were more than thirty thousand commercial banks, of which only eight thousand, with about half of U.S. bank assets, were under the Comptroller's supervision.

The devastating bank failures of the Great Depression ushered in a period of strict banking regulation that lasted until the 1980s. For much of this period, comptrollers along with other banking regulators acted to prevent bank failures by restricting new entry and banking competition. Few banks failed in these decades, but strict regulation caused banking to lose financial-system market share to non-bank financial intermediaries and the securities markets.

Starting in the 1960s, several comptrollers worked to expand the powers of national banks and free them from what they regarded as excessively strict regulation. This expansion led to regulatory conflicts with the Federal Reserve System, which, in addition to executing monetary policy, also supervises banks. Congress supported the Federal Reserve more than the Comptroller in many of these conflicts, but the Comptroller's continuing advocacy of deregulation for national banks influenced the Federal Reserve to move in the same direction.

Deregulation and bank consolidations brought major changes to U.S. banking at the end of the twentieth century. In 2001, the Comptroller supervised some 2,200 national banks in a system of 8,200 commercial banks, with the national banks accounting for about 55 percent of the assets of U.S. banks.

BIBLIOGRAPHY

Robertson, Ross M. *The Comptroller and Bank Supervision: A Historical Appraisal.* Washington, D.C.: Office of the Comptroller of the Currency, 1995.

White, Eugene N. *The Comptroller and the Transformation of American Banking, 1960–1990.* Washington, D.C.: Comptroller of the Currency, 1992.

Richard Sylla

See also **Banking: Overview; Federal Reserve System; Treasury, Department of the.**

COMPUTERS AND COMPUTER INDUSTRY.

The electronic digital computer is the herald of the Information Age. Just as technologies developed in earlier ages liberated people from physical toil, computers have liberated people from the more tedious kinds of mental toil—and have revolutionized the transfer of information. The banking, insurance, and travel industries, to name a few, are vastly quicker and more responsive than they were a half-century ago. The computer industry employs hundreds of thousands directly, but many millions of people outside the industry use computers as an important tool in their jobs.

Calculating devices such as the abacus have existed for thousands of years. The distinctive feature of modern

Early IBM Computer. Howard Aiken in 1944 presents his Mark I, the first completely automatic calculator, to Harvard University, where the U.S. Navy put it to use during World War II. © CORBIS

computers is that they are digital, operating on digits of 1s and 0s according to specified instructions. Computers are therefore programmable. A programmer can create complex behavior undreamed of by the computer maker, just as a novelist can use a typewriter to create new works of art.

The "Difference Engine" of English mathematician Charles Babbage (1792–1871) was an ancestor of the computer. Babbage proposed it as a calculating machine to improve the accuracy of celestial tables used in navigation. Human error introduced wrong numbers into these tables, costing lives at sea. To further limit the effects of human error, Babbage wanted to automate the whole process of entering numbers and combining results, so that complex formulas could be automated, or "programmed." To this end he designed the Analytical Engine with two parts: one part read and interpreted coded instructions from punch cards, and the other performed arithmetic. Babbage kept altering his designs, and the English government withdrew its support in frustration. Yet most of the elements of modern digital computers were present in Babbage's plans.

Although Babbage's concepts were essentially neglected for more than a hundred years, other developments took place. In 1886 William Burroughs built the first commercially successful adding machine. In 1936

Cambridge mathematician Alan Turing described a theoretical machine that manipulated symbols on a tape. By implication, computers were not limited to number crunching. Given specific, clear instructions, they could manipulate any kind of data. During World War II, Turing designed a working mechanical device (the Turing Bombe) that broke the German Enigma code and demonstrated the power of Turing's ideas.

The First Electronic Computers

Two factors spurred development of computers in the mid-twentieth century. One was the war effort, which needed quick calculation of ballistic paths. The other was electronics, which made it possible to use wires and vacuum tubes to simulate logical operations. Engineers could replace Babbage's slow interactions of levers and gears with particles whose speed approached that of light.

During World War II the U.S. Army funded development of a digital computer, planning to use it for military calculations. On 14 February 1946 J. Presper Eckert and John Mauchly unveiled the first electronic digital computer at the University of Pennsylvania. They called their machine the Electronic Numerical Integrator and Computer (ENIAC). ENIAC required 1,800 square feet and 18,000 vacuum tubes. The use of vacuum tubes made it unreliable, for their combined heat often caused one or

UNIVAC. Two men work at a 1950s model of a computer—still huge, slow, and expensive. © CORBIS

more to malfunction. Each month operators had to replace 2,000 tubes. Yet for all its limitations, ENIAC proved useful for its time. It performed a then-impressive 5,000 additions and 360 multiplications per second.

Improvements soon followed. Hungarian-born scientist John von Neumann (1903–1957) suggested the idea of storing programs in memory alongside data. This freed a user from having to reprogram a computer every time it was used for a different purpose. (Consider that when you run a personal computer, you can run different programs with the click of a button.) So significant was this advance that computer scientists sometimes refer to modern computers as "von Neumann processors."

Although Eckert and Mauchly's invention changed the world, they never reaped the financial rewards that others did. They left the University of Pennsylvania in 1946 to form the Eckert-Mauchly Computer Corporation. But production of computers required capital, and shortly afterward they sold their firm to the Remington Rand Corporation. Joining Rand as engineers, they produced the Universal Automatic Computer (UNIVAC) in 1951. The first model was installed at the U.S. Bureau of the Census.

From the start UNIVAC was intended for general commercial use. But throughout the 1940s and 1950s computers remained expensive, and commercial acceptance came slowly. By 1957 only forty-six UNIVAC machines were in use. The high cost of computing power can be seen by looking at a late-model UNIVAC. This machine offered a 1.3 megahertz processor, half a megabyte of RAM (Random-Access Memory), and a 100 megabyte hard drive—all representing a fraction of the power available by the early 2000s for less than $1,000. In 1968 this UNIVAC model could be had for $1.6 million.

Data storage became important, especially for commercial uses, and devices such as magnetic tape and drums

came into use. Meanwhile, new programming languages were developed. FORTRAN (FORmula TRANslation) and COBOL (COmmon Business Oriented Language) facilitated easier, faster writing of scientific and business applications, replacing much of the work being done with machine code.

The Rise of IBM

In contrast to Rand's commercial difficulties with the UNIVAC, International Business Machines (IBM) succeeded so well in the 1950s and 1960s that for a time it became synonymous with the computer industry itself. A merger in 1911 formed the company as the Calculating-Tabulating-Recording Company, and later Thomas J. Watson Sr. took over the company, renamed it, and expanded the product line, overseeing production of its first computers. The field was a natural one for the company to expand into, because it already made tabulating machines that used punch cards.

As much as any technical innovation, IBM's army of salesmen and its marketing expertise contributed to its success. Beyond selling machines, IBM sold a reputation for service and support. At the time a computer was not a commodity but a major investment, and IBM's size and solidity reassured customers. This strategy served the company well up until the era of personal computing. Spurred on by the Korean War, IBM developed the 700 series to meet the needs of the Defense Department. Meanwhile, IBM's lower-cost 650 series and 1400 series brought commercial success, selling 1,800 and 12,000 units respectively.

During the late 1950s Thomas J. Watson Jr. succeeded his father as chairman and decided to invest $10 billion in a new line of computers, the 360 series. For the time, this was an astounding sum of money. Watson's gamble was the most expensive development ever attempted in any private industry. It amounted to betting the company. The investment paid off. For several decades the 360 series (and its successor, the 370 series) secured IBM's dominance in the field of large computers—now called "mainframes"—and demand mushroomed. Around the world computers began to take over tasks previously relegated to roomfuls of clerks: compiling statistics, retrieving data, calculating actuarial tables, and printing company payrolls.

From Mainframe to Minicomputer

The growing acceptance of computers in the corporate world was aided by further developments in applied physics. In 1948 physicists at Bell Laboratories (including controversial Nobel Prize-winner William Shockley) invented the transistor; this is a device that enables a small current to control another, potentially larger current. By placing different kinds of transistors together, engineers can simulate logical operations such as AND, OR, and NOT. Transistors can therefore act as building blocks for digital processors, just as vacuum tubes once did.

Transistors offered many advantages over vacuum tubes. Because they produced almost no heat, they could be placed close together; this made miniaturization possible, in turn reducing the distance that electrons had to travel. Transistors improved speed, power, and reliability—all while lowering cost.

Individual transistors began to replace the use of vacuum tubes in the 1950s. But that was a small change compared with what followed. The 1960s saw the development of integrated circuits, combining many transistors on a small rectangle (or "chip") of silicon. As of the early 2000s, a silicon chip, not much bigger than a postage stamp, could contain more than 20 million transistors.

The availability of greater computing power at much lower cost led to fragmentation of the market. At one end better mainframes were developed to take advantage of greater computing power. At the other end new, cheaper lines of computers made computing accessible to smaller organizations, and prices fell dramatically.

This smaller type of computer was dubbed the "minicomputer." In some ways the name is misleading because, although smaller than a mainframe, a minicomputer is larger than a personal computer. (Personal computers were at first called "microcomputers.") There is no absolute dividing line between mainframes and minis; the distinction is partly subjective. Generally, a machine is a "mainframe" if it is among the larger and more powerful computers that the technology of the day can produce. Minicomputers are smaller and more affordable.

The field of minicomputers became the focus of a company founded in 1960 named Digital Equipment Corporation (DEC). The company produced the PDP (Program Data Processor) line of computers and, later, the VAX (Virtual Address eXtension) line. These enjoyed particularly wide use at universities. DEC revolutionized the business by pioneering the concept of time-sharing, first developed at the Massachusetts Institute of Technology.

Traditionally, only one program ran on a computer at a time. Users had to submit programs in punch-card form to a system administrator. The results might be returned the next day. Time-sharing, in contrast, switches control of the computer between multiple users several times a second. (During each switch the computer saves the work of the previous user and restores the work of the next.) In this setup each user communicates with the computer by means of a monitor and a keyboard, and each user has the illusion that he or she is the only one. This was a major step toward personal computing.

The Arrival of the Personal Computer

The development of better integrated circuits led ultimately to the placement of a complete central processing unit (CPU) onto a single chip. In the early 1970s the California-based Intel Corporation was the first to produce such a chip, dubbed the "microprocessor." A personal computer uses one microprocessor, along with other chips to control memory and peripheral devices. Mainframe and minicomputers can run many microprocessors in parallel.

The first commercially available personal computer was the Altair, announced in 1974. The customer received a kit requiring hours of difficult assembly. Programming the finished machine was just as complex. Still, for $397 a hobbyist could claim to have a working computer. William Henry "Bill" Gates III and Paul Allen formed Microsoft in 1975 to sell a usable BASIC (Beginner's All-purpose Symbolic Instruction Code) language for the Altair, making it easy to program.

In 1977 Steven P. Jobs and Stephen G. Wozniak founded Apple Computer, which produced a more successful product, the Apple II. Unlike the Altair, the Apple II included a keyboard and a monitor, came assembled, and could do useful work. At first Jobs and Wozniak assembled computers out of a garage, but they soon became multimillionaires. The success of Apple proved the commercial viability of personal computing. Other companies, such as Commodore and Tandy, soon announced personal computers of their own.

In 1981 IBM stepped into the fray with its own personal computer, dubbed "the PC." IBM realized it was coming late to the market and needed to get a product out fast. To this end it set up an independent division in Boca Raton, Florida, which met its deadlines by using off-the-shelf parts and an operating system from Microsoft.

IBM chose a different strategy from Apple, which had a closed system: users had to buy parts from Apple, and opening the system box voided the warranty. (The system box is the heart of a personal computer, containing all the important parts except for the monitor, keyboard, printer, and external devices.) IBM adopted an open architecture, leaving users and equipment manufacturers free to open the system box and make modifications. This contributed to the PC's success. Although the first models were limited, they could always be upgraded. And everyone wanted the IBM label.

The company made one other fateful decision. It did not buy Microsoft's MS-DOS operating system outright but rented a license, paying a fee for each computer sold. IBM let Microsoft keep the rights to license the system to others, never foreseeing the extent to which other companies would capitalize on the PC's success by developing low-cost "clones." To build a clone, a manufacturer needed only to purchase the Intel processor, emulate the PC's low-level behavior, and lease Microsoft's operating system. After a few years, Microsoft and Intel became the true designers of the PC environment (or "platform"), deciding what features would go into the next version of MS-DOS.

During the 1980s two designs—the Apple Macintosh and the PC—drove out the competition. The PC's advantage, in addition to open architecture, was that thou-

Steven P. Jobs. The cofounder of Apple Computer, in a 1992 photograph. ARCHIVE PHOTOS, INC.

sands of programmers wrote software for it; soon it had a huge base of programs and users. Apple stayed competitive by introducing the Macintosh in 1984; it was the first affordable graphical user interface (GUI) system (after a flirtation with the more expensive Lisa, named for Jobs's daughter).

The concept of a GUI was developed by Xerox in the late 1970s, although Apple for a time claimed ownership (a claim rejected during Apple's lawsuit against Microsoft, which ended in 1994). A GUI replaced the use of cryptic command names with menus, icons, and a pointing device called a "mouse." Microsoft saw the potential of such systems. But while the Macintosh's graphical features were built into its Read-Only Memory (ROM), Microsoft had to produce a system loaded from disk, like ordinary software. It also had to fit this system into the more limited memory of a PC. In 1986 Microsoft released its GUI system, called Windows. At first it was clumsy compared with the Macintosh and was not widely accepted. But eventually a better interface and improvements in PC hardware made Windows a success. In 1995 Microsoft celebrated by releasing its Windows 95 with great fanfare. In the early 2000s approximately 90 percent of personal computers were PCs running Microsoft Windows.

Changes Wrought by the Internet

Just as personal computers had allowed Microsoft to displace IBM, many observers felt that a new technology might allow even newer companies to displace Microsoft. This technology was the Internet, originally sponsored by the Department of Defense in the late 1960s as the ARPANET. The purpose of this system was to enable military communication after a nuclear attack. In the early

1990s the World Wide Web was launched to share information not just between government agencies, but also universities, nonprofit organizations, and private companies (the last designated by the ".com" suffix), among others. As a "hypertext" system, the Web supported links functioning as automated cross-references. The Internet provided the infrastructure for the World Wide Web, as well as for sending and receiving electronic mail (E-mail) and for downloading files.

Much information accumulated on the Web, but none of it was available to ordinary users. This changed in 1993, when University of Illinois student Marc Andreessen developed the Mosaic browser. The university retained ownership of Mosaic, but Andreessen formed Netscape Communications with Jim Clark in 1994 and produced an even better browser, called Navigator. (Netscape was originally named "Mosaic Communications" but changed its name when it was unable to acquire rights to the Mosaic browser.) Within three years Netscape grew to a size that it had taken Microsoft its first eleven years to attain. This success helped initiate the "dot com" boom of the 1990s. In 1998 America Online (AOL) acquired Netscape Communications.

The Internet opened up new areas for computing. Previously, millions of people purchased computers but used them mainly for word processing and possibly balancing their checkbooks. As they signed up for Internet service providers such as AOL and MSN (Microsoft Network), people found that features such as E-mail, news, and stock quotes made computers more useful than ever. They could also use the Web to do research and buy products.

Several companies, including Netscape, AOL, and Sun Microsystems, a maker of minicomputers, saw in the Internet an opportunity to change the industry. Microsoft had defined the single-user PC environment, but operations on a single computer were no longer as important as information shared between computers. Sun Microsystems developed a new programming language, Java, to take advantage of this fact. Java used a system of universal codes understood by different computers (each with its own interpreter). Because the underlying machine was no longer important, went the theory, Java itself would become the defining architecture rather than Windows.

Microsoft responded by embracing the Internet. Products such as Microsoft Word incorporated Web access into their design. More controversial was Microsoft's inclusion of its own Web browser (Explorer) into Windows itself. Critics contended that this undercut Netscape's browser by essentially distributing Explorer for free. The charge contributed to the antitrust case against Microsoft, which alleged that Microsoft took advantage of its monopolistic power due to Windows' success. In January 2000 Judge Thomas Penfield Jackson issued a decision to split the company. An appellate panel overturned this penalty in summer 2001, citing bias of the judge as revealed in published interviews.

Other Developments

In the mid-1960s Intel cofounder Gordon Moore predicted that for a given size of silicon chip, the amount of computing power would double every twelve to eighteen months. By the early 2000s this law continued to hold. New possibilities included moving from solid-state transistors to optical storage, using photons as the bearers of information. Meanwhile, as Internet subscribers moved from standard modems to digital subscriber lines (DSL), access times for the Web decreased by a factor of more than a hundred. The trend was toward the general merging of television, radio, and computers.

But technical advances brought new risks as well. As more people began to use electronic mail and the Web on a daily basis, the world became more vulnerable to computer viruses and worms: programs that attach themselves to applications, make copies of themselves, and then use the Internet to infect other computers. Computer security increasingly became an issue for individuals, government, and corporations.

While the Internet changed computing at the low end, advances continued at the high end, where mainframes evolved into supercomputers. In 1964 Seymour Cray built the CDC 6000 with parallel processing. This remained the most powerful computer in the world for years. He went on to start Cray Research, specializing in ever-more-powerful computers with important uses in research, mathematics, and space exploration.

A landmark demonstration of supercomputer power occurred in 1996, involving the Deep Thought computer program (named for a godlike computer in Douglas Adams's novel *The Hitchhiker's Guide to the Galaxy*). Able to examine 100 million positions a second, Deep Thought won a chess game against world champion Gary Kasparov. To some this was a demonstration that computers were finally "smarter" than the most intelligent humans. But the demonstration was incomplete; computers have always handled logical calculations better than people. Far more mysterious realms of human consciousness—emotion, creativity, and the ability to write good poetry—remain unconquered. For all their progress, computers remain the servants of the human race, not the masters.

BIBLIOGRAPHY

Carroll, Paul. *Big Blues: The Unmaking of IBM.* New York: Crown, 1993.

Deutschman, Allan. *The Second Coming of Steve Jobs.* New York: Broadway, 2000. A fascinating account of what happened to Jobs after leaving Apple, including his role in 3-D computer animation.

Downing, Douglas A., Michael A. Covington, and Melody Mauldin Covington. *Dictionary of Computer and Internet Terms.* 7th ed. New York: Barron's, 2000. A compact book with a wealth of explanations on all areas of computing.

Hodges, Andrew. *Alan Turing: The Enigma.* New York: Simon and Schuster, 1983. The story of Turing's remarkable life.

Ichbiah, Daniel, and Susan L. Knepper. *The Making of Microsoft.* Rocklin, Calif.: Prima, 1991. One of the first accounts of Microsoft's early years, it remains an interesting account of one of the world's most successful companies.

Kaye, Barbara K., and Norman J. Medoff. *The World Wide Web: A Mass Communication Perspective.* Mountain View, Calif.: Mayfield, 1998. A straightforward guide to basics of the Web and the Internet.

McCartney, Scott. *ENIAC: The Triumph and Tragedies of the World's First Computer.* New York: Walker, 1999.

Segaller, Stephen. *Nerds 2.0.1: A Brief History of the Internet.* New York: TV Books, 1998. The history of the Internet from its beginnings through the start-ups of the 1990s.

Wallace, James, and Jim Erickson. *Hard Drive: Bill Gates and the Making of the Microsoft Empire.* New York: Wiley, 1992. Contains in-depth portraits of some of the leading players in the business.

Brian Overland

See also **Internet; Microsoft; Silicon Valley.**

COMSTOCK LODE, one of the richest deposits of precious ores ever discovered, located in Virginia City, Nevada. Between 1859 and 1979, these mines produced more than $500 million in silver and gold, creating great fortunes for San Francisco–based investors. This lode, especially the Big Bonanza mine, made Virginia City one of the most influential political, financial, and social hubs in the West.

Enormous amounts of technology helped build the city around the lode. Water was imported to the city through pipes, tunnels, and flumes made in San Francisco to fit around mountains and cross valleys. To extract the silver from the rock, the old Mexican patio method was first used; later, the amalgamating process was employed for the reduction of the ore.

BIBLIOGRAPHY

Goldman, Marion S. *Gold Diggers and Silver Miners: Prostitution and Social Life on the Comstock Lode.* Ann Arbor: University of Michigan Press, 1981.

James, Ronald M. *The Roar and the Silence: A History of Virginia City and the Comstock Lode.* Reno: University of Nevada Press, 1998.

James, Ronald M., and C. Elizabeth Raymond, eds. *Comstock Women: The Making of a Mining Community.* Reno: University of Nevada Press, 1998.

Smith, Grant H. *The History of the Comstock Lode, 1850–1997.* Reno: Nevada Bureau of Mines and Geology, 1998.

Effie Mona Mack / H. S.

See also **Boomtowns; Gold Mines and Mining; Mining Towns; Nevada; Silver Prospecting and Mining.**

CONCILIATION AND MEDIATION, LABOR, is the settlement of industrial disputes either by direct conference between the employers and employees involved, or by joint boards representing them, without the assistance of outside agencies. Mediation refers to the informal intervention of an outside agent to bring the disputants together for the purpose of settling their controversy amicably. The terms "conciliation" and "mediation," however, are often used interchangeably. Both procedures presume voluntary compliance. In the United States, the Federal Mediation and Conciliation Service, an independent body formed in 1947, provides most effective mediation and conciliation work. Federal statutes and numerous state statutes provide machinery for conciliation and mediation.

BIBLIOGRAPHY

Stern, James L., and Joyce M. Najita, ed. *Labor Arbitration under Fire.* Ithaca, N.Y.: Cornell University Press, 1997.

Gordon S. Watkins / A. E.

See also **Arbitration; Federal Agencies; Labor; Railroad Mediation Acts; Strikes.**

CONCILIATION COURTS, DOMESTIC.

Conciliation, or mediation, is an informal process whereby a third person tries to help the parties to a controversy reach an agreement to settle their dispute. Conciliation should not to be confused with arbitration, which is the process whereby the parties agree to refer the matter to a third party and abide by its decision. Just prior to the Civil War, six states added provisions to their constitutions authorizing their legislatures to establish conciliation tribunals.

However, no use of this power was made until the second decade of the twentieth century when, in an effort to provide a mechanism allowing small businessmen and laborers to go to court to resolve matters involving small amounts of money, states and cities instituted several judicial reforms, including the creation of conciliation courts. The emergence of these courts, also known as small claims courts or small debtors' courts, is linked to the rise of a system of municipal courts with wide powers over their own organization and procedure. In 1913, the Cleveland Municipal Court became the first court to make conciliation an important part of its procedure. In 1921, North Dakota adopted the first statewide conciliation act. By 1923, five states and twelve cities had small claims systems.

In the early 2000s, small claims courts continued to provide an informal and expeditious process for resolving disputes involving small amounts of money. In addition, the conciliation process was used by parties in a wide variety of types of disputes, especially those involving domestic and labor matters.

BIBLIOGRAPHY

Spurrier, Robert L., Jr. *Inexpensive Justice: Self-Representation in the Small Claims Court.* Port Washington, N.Y.: Kennikat Press, 1980.

Yngvesson, Barbara Y., and Patricia H. Hennessey. "Small Claims, Complex Disputes: A Review of the Small Claims Literature." *Law and Society Review* 9 (1975): 219–274.

Francis R. Aumann / C. P.

See also **Arbitration; Judiciary.**

CONESTOGA WAGON

is one of the most distinctively American vehicles. Originating among the Pennsylvania Dutch, it first came into general use on the overland routes across the Alleghenies just after the American Revolution. The Conestoga wagon was huge and heavily built, with broad wheels suited to dirt roads and a bed higher at either end of the wagon than in the middle. Its canvas-covered top presaged the PRAIRIE SCHOONER of a later day. Four to six horses drew it, with the driver usually riding wheelhorses. Sometimes the wagons moved in solitary grandeur but more frequently in long caravans.

BIBLIOGRAPHY

Gardner, Mark L. *Wagons for the Santa Fe Trade: Wheeled Vehicles and Their Makers, 1822–1880.* Albuquerque: University of New Mexico Press, 2000.

Charles H. Ambler / A. E.

See also **Covered Wagon; Transportation and Travel; Wagon Trains; Wagoners of the Alleghenies.**

CONEY ISLAND. See **Amusement Parks.**

CONFEDERATE AGENTS

refers to the diplomats who represented the Confederacy during the CIVIL WAR. Confederate President Jefferson Davis sent agents to Mexico, Canada, France, Britain, and many other nations around the world. The agents purchased supplies, bought ships, secured loans, and propagandized on behalf of the Confederacy. Many Southern states and even some Southern railroads sent their own agents to represent their interests in foreign markets. A multiplicity of cotton agents—state, Confederate, and army—brought such confusion that the Confederate government ultimately centralized agent activity into two departments, one for the Lower South and one for the Trans-Mississippi region.

BIBLIOGRAPHY

Crook, David P. *The North, the South, and the Powers: 1861–1865.* New York: Wiley, 1974.

Owsley, Frank Lawrence. *King Cotton Diplomacy: Foreign Relations of the Confederate States of America.* Chicago: University of Chicago Press, 1959.

Ella Lonn / A. G.

See also **Confederate States of America; Lower South; Mason-Dixon Line; Seal of the Confederate States of America.**

CONFEDERATE EXPATRIATES IN BRAZIL.

Perhaps half of the eight to ten thousand southerners who emigrated after the Civil War went to Brazil, whose Emperor Pedro II had issued a call for experienced farmers. They came from all over the South (a few came from the North as well) and represented all socioeconomic levels, but the largest groups were landowners from Alabama, Texas, and South Carolina. They put careful preparations into their journey, forming associations and sending ahead emissaries to select land for settlement. Many of them settled in the São Paulo state and founded the town of Americana a few kilometers from the town of Santa Bárbara. The climate and soil of this region was most like that of their native southern states, and the pecans and peaches they introduced thrived, as did the American varieties of corn and cotton they brought with them. Most of the expatriate farmers did not purchase slaves in Brazil, where slavery remained legal until 1888, because, except on plantations, slave labor was economically inefficient. Confederate families also settled in the states of Bahia, Espírito Santo, Pará, Rio de Janeiro, and Santa Catarina. Some, especially those in Americana, prospered, but most only got by. The Confederates suffered from tropical insects and diseases, a lack of capital, and homesickness for friends and relatives. Although a few hundred remained, most returned to the United States after some years.

BIBLIOGRAPHY

Holloway, Thomas H. *Immigrants on the Land.* Chapel Hill: University of North Carolina Press, 1980.

Lesser, Jeffrey. *Welcoming the Undesirables.* Berkeley: University of California Press, 1995.

Robert M. Levine

See also **Expatriation.**

CONFEDERATE STATES OF AMERICA,

a breakaway slaveholding republic founded in February 1861 after the secession from the Union of the lower South states. It originally comprised seven states (South Carolina, Mississippi, Alabama, Florida, Georgia, Louisiana, and Texas) but gained four additional members from the upper South (Virginia, Arkansas, Tennessee, and North Carolina) in the wake of President Abraham Lincoln's decision to force the seceded states back into the Union after the attack on Fort Sumter in April. The overall population of the Confederate States in 1861 was approximately 9 million, of whom 3.5 million were African American slaves.

Founding

Delegates from the lower South states met in convention in early February in Montgomery, Alabama, to write a new constitution. They quickly agreed on a provisional document, and under its authority elected Jefferson Davis of Mississippi and Alexander H. Stephens of Georgia as president and vice president, respectively. On 11 March 1861, delegates unanimously adopted a permanent constitution for the Confederate States. Most of the new constitution's provisions were identical to those of its federal counterpart, but some changes reflected the new republic's states-rights origins and distinctive society. There was no general welfare clause; Confederate funding of internal improvements was prohibited and protective tariffs banned; and the Confederate president was to serve a single six-year term. The constitution forbade the passage of any law undermining the holding of slaves—the Confederacy's founders avoided the euphemisms of their federal forefathers—but delegates rejected a reopening of the foreign slave trade, which many radicals had been advocating. The convention also rejected proposals to incorporate into the constitution the right of secession. In general, Confederate founding represented the defeat of "fire-eating" radicalism and a reassertion of the conservative political authority of the South's planter class.

Organization and Mobilization

For the first year of the Confederacy's existence, members of its constitutional convention also served as members of the provisional congress. In May 1861, the congress voted—over President Davis's veto—to move the Confederate capital from Montgomery to Richmond, Virginia. The switch was made possible by Virginia's ratification of secession on 23 May and dictated by Richmond's location, size, and commercial and industrial capacity; among other things, Richmond was the site of the Tredegar Iron Works, the largest facility of its kind in the South. Military mobilization began almost as soon as political organization, and throughout 1861 and early 1862, the congress passed numerous acts designed to stimulate and regulate recruitment. This legislation produced a bewildering situation in which volunteers could enter the Confederate army either directly or as members of state militias and could serve for terms that ranged from six months to three years. The number of those willing to serve during the first few months of the war far exceeded the quantity of available arms, thereby limiting the army's capabilities. By the end of 1861, however, enthusiasm for volunteering had begun to decline, and the imminent expiry of the twelve-month recruits' term of service caused the Confederate congress on 16 April 1862 to enact the first conscription law in American history. The law required three years of service from men aged eighteen to thirty-five. The upper age limit was extended to forty-five on 27 September 1862. Finally, on 17 February 1864, the congress required military service from all able-bodied men aged seventeen to fifty, with those under eighteen and over forty-five being reserved for state defense. One of the most contentious aspects of Confederate conscription was the policy of exemption, first defined in April 1862 to include Confederate and state officials and a range of occupations such as telegraph operators, transportation workers, and ministers of religion. On 11 October 1862, the list was considerably expanded to bring in industrial workers and, most controversially, to exempt from military service men responsible for overseeing twenty slaves or more. Widespread abuses prompted congress in the February 1864 act to end industrial exemptions. Conscripts could also avoid Confederate service by hiring substitutes, a policy that encouraged corruption and, like exemption, aroused resentment from those who charged that it discriminated against the poorer classes. As a result, substitution was abolished in December 1863. In total, an estimated 900,000 men served in the Confederate armed forces, or just under half the number of their federal opponents.

Government and Politics

The Confederate government was closely modeled on that of the federal Union. The most conspicuous differences were the single, six-year terms for the president and vice president, and the failure to establish a Confederate supreme court, provision for which had been made in the new constitution. In November 1861, Jefferson Davis and Alexander Stephens were elected president and vice president under the permanent constitution. As provisional president, Davis had selected his cabinet initially upon the basis of state representation. Filling the most important positions were Robert Toombs of Georgia as secretary of state, Christopher G. Memminger of South Carolina as secretary of the treasury, and Leroy P. Walker of Alabama as secretary of war. Anxious to pursue his military and political ambitions, Toombs resigned in July 1861 and was replaced by Robert M. T. Hunter of Virginia, the first of many cabinet changes that Davis was forced to make. In total, the Confederacy had four secretaries of state, five attorney generals, two secretaries of the treasury, and six secretaries of war. Probably the most able cabinet member was Judah P. Benjamin of Louisiana, whose prominent role in the Davis administration aroused resentment because of his Jewish background. Benjamin served the Confederacy between 1861 and 1865 as attorney general, secretary of war, and secretary of state.

The Confederate congress sat as a provisional unicameral body during the republic's first year and was replaced by a permanent senate and house in February 1862. The congress's contribution to Confederate governance was undermined by its high turnover of personnel: only about 10 percent of members served continuously from 1861 to 1865, with many of the South's planter-politicians preferring to serve in the army rather than the legislature. Overseeing the senate was the vice president Alexander Stephens, who emerged as one of Davis's most passionate critics. Political opposition to Davis was apparent from early in the war, but it intensified after the congressional elections of 1863, which, despite their low turnout, represented a judgment on the Confederate government's conduct of the war, indeed on the Confederacy itself. The second Confederate congress, which convened in May 1864, saw a significant rise in the number of antiadministration members. Despite constant disagreement, however, the Confederate president in the main kept control of policymaking and was generally sup-

We, the people of the Confederate States, each State acting in its sovereign and independent character, in order to form a more permanent federal government, establish justice, insure domestic tranquillity, and secure the blessings of liberty to ourselves and our posterity—invoking the favour and guidance of Almighty God—do ordain and establish this Constitution for the Confederate States of America.

—Preamble to the Constitution of the Confederate States

SOURCE: Reprinted from James D. Richardson, *The Messages and Papers of Jefferson Davis and the Confederacy,* 2 vols. New York, 1983.

ported by the legislature on important issues. Jefferson Davis exercised his veto power thirty-nine times, and on every occasion except one—a bill to allow free postage on soldiers' newspapers—Congress upheld his action. As defeat in the war approached in early 1865, the legislature, led by the volatile senator Louis Wigfall of Texas, sought to assert its authority over the president by insisting on changes to the civil and military administration. The demands included the resignation of the cabinet, which Davis resisted even while accepting the departure of James A. Seddon, the secretary of war, and the granting of extra power to the general-in-chief, Robert E. Lee, to which the president acceded.

By far, the Confederacy's most significant departure from previous American practice was the absence of a two-party system. Secession and Confederate founding in many respects had been a reaction against party politics, which Davis and other leaders, reverting to an earlier ideology, regarded as corrupting and antipathetic to their vision of southern unity. But political opposition to the Davis government could not be stilled, and, from the outset, serious differences arose over major aspects of wartime policy, including conscription and impressment. In the absence of political parties, opposition was fragmented, individualistic, and often highly personal in tone. Much of the public opposition to the Davis administration came from governors, who were anxious to protect state prerogatives against the encroachments of Confederate nationalism, and by far the most persistent of the gubernatorial critics was Governor Joseph E. Brown of Georgia, who viewed the policy of conscription as destructive of both states' rights and popular liberty. Although states' rights opposition may have helped undermine public confidence in Davis's conduct of the war, it failed to deflect the president, whose actions were endorsed by Congress and, crucially, by state supreme courts that invariably found the conscription legislation to be constitutional.

Foreign Relations

A number of factors, including widespread contemporary belief in free trade and the legitimacy of secession, caused southern leaders to expect European and especially British support. Nonetheless, the Confederate States used the power of "King Cotton" to try to ensure that support. Cotton accounted for approximately three-quarters of American exports to Britain during the late 1850s, and an estimated 20 percent of the British population earned its livelihood directly or indirectly from the manufacture of cotton products. If cotton was withheld, southerners insisted, Britain and France would be forced to intervene and, at the very least, formally recognize the independence of the Confederate States. Ironically, the strategy backfired, partly as a result of the South's own success as a producer: in 1861, cotton stocks in British warehouses had never been greater, obviating any immediate need for action by the textile industry. As part of the Confederate strategy to gain recognition, diplomats urged European governments to accept that the federal blockade of southern ports was illegal, a "paper" blockade, but were unable to explain why, if that was the case, the South itself was avoiding sending raw cotton to Europe.

The first Confederate commission to Europe—William L. Yancey, A. Dudley Mann, and Pierre A. Rost—failed to capitalize on the opportunities arising from Britain and France's neutrality proclamations of, respectively, May and June 1861. In November, two new envoys, James M. Mason and John A. Slidell, were appointed. Seized by the Union navy from the British steamship *Trent*, Mason and Slidell were eventually released and arrived in Europe in January 1862. Throughout 1862 and 1863, Mason and Slidell continued to press the British and French governments on the recognition issue but without success. Their diplomatic effort was assisted by a propaganda campaign spearheaded by the Swiss-born Henry Hotze, who in May 1862 established *The Index*, a weekly newspaper published in London. In the second half of that year, both the British and French governments considered mediation proposals but the former was unprepared to act without significant evidence of Confederate military progress and the latter would not act without Britain. The onset of Lincoln's emancipation policy in 1862 also changed the debate about the nature of the American conflict, rendering it more difficult for Britain and France to consider action on behalf of a slaveholding republic.

The following summer, 1863, southern diplomatic spirits briefly revived when the British parliament debated a motion for Confederate recognition proposed by John A. Roebuck, who had privately discussed intervention with the French emperor. However, Roebuck's initiative collapsed after failing to gain the support of either the British government or Tory opposition. Military setbacks at Gettysburg and Vicksburg in July 1863 further frustrated southern attempts to persuade skeptical Europeans about the need for intervention, and after the withdrawal of Roebuck's motion, Confederate diplomacy in Europe was in retreat. Particularly significant was the British government's change of policy over Confederate warships being built in Britain. In July 1862, the *Alabama* had escaped from the Laird shipyards near Liverpool to begin a destructive career against Union commerce, but the following year the government accepted the U.S. argument that permitting the construction of such vessels violated British neutrality. By 1863, anti-British feeling in the Confederacy was running high, and in October, following several months of incidents, the Davis cabinet unanimously agreed to the expulsion of all British consuls in the South. Confederate relations with France, which invaded Mexico in 1863, proved more productive, particularly on the commercial front, though again failed to achieve the desired aim of recognition. In early 1865, the Confederacy played its final diplomatic card when it dispatched Duncan F. Kenner of Louisiana to Europe with an offer to emancipate the slaves in exchange for recognition. The mission predictably proved a failure, as by this time both Britain and France were convinced of the Confederacy's imminent defeat.

Economy and Society

An agricultural society overwhelmingly geared to the production of staple crops, the Confederate States of America was seriously deficient in the economic resources necessary to fight a protracted war for independence. Southern industrial capacity was dwarfed by that of the federal states, which on the eve of the conflict had produced approximately 90 percent of the nation's manufactured goods. Broadly self-sufficient in food production, the South lacked an adequate transportation system, with its railroads in particular comparing poorly in mileage and quality to those of the industrializing North. During the war, the Confederate government through its various War and Navy Department supply bureaus made great strides toward remedying its industrial shortfall, and by 1863 the South had begun to meet its military-industrial needs. Driving the development in state-sponsored manufacturing was the Pennsylvania-born ordnance chief, General Josiah Gorgas. His overall contribution to the Confederate war effort was immense; without his energy and organizational genius, the southern republic's armed forces would have proved even less capable of resisting its far better equipped and resourced northern rival.

Financing the war also proved a problem for a society that traditionally was not persuaded by the merits of taxation. Initially, the Confederacy raised funds through a variety of bonds, loans, and taxes; the latter included an export tariff of one-eighth cent a pound on raw cotton. In August 1861, under the provisional constitution, the Confederate congress passed a direct tax on all property, including slaves. The measure largely proved ineffective as the majority of the states, who had been encouraged to assume responsibility for the tax, chose to raise the money by borrowing rather than by direct imposition on the people. Over the next two years, debate raged about the expediency and constitutionality of direct taxation. Finally, on 24 April 1863, the Confederate congress passed into law a comprehensive bill whose provisions included occupational and license taxes, a graduated income tax, and a tax-in-kind on agricultural products, including livestock. The 1863 act was resented by many sections of society, including hard-pressed farmers; it proved costly and difficult to enforce, and evasion was widespread. In total, the Confederacy raised only about a twentieth of its revenue from taxation. Overwhelmingly, the war was financed through loans, both Confederate and state-issued, and by the printing of a constant supply of redeemable treasury notes. The Confederacy's currency never became legal tender, however, and the number of notes in circulation soon far outstripped need, fueling inflation. In early 1863 the government also sought to harness its most valuable agricultural commodity by negotiating a cotton-backed loan of $15 million with the French financiers, Erlanger and Company, but the initiative proved a failure as military defeats gradually undermined the Confederacy's international credit.

Inflation was economically and socially corrosive and helped to undermine the confidence of ordinary southerners in the Confederacy. By 1863, many families were experiencing severe hardship. Although Confederate supply never entirely failed, numerous factors, including labor depletions, the crumbling transportation system, and the tightening of the Union blockade, left communities bereft of food and other essential items. In 1863, "bread" riots broke out in many southern towns and cities. The largest incident occurred in April, when female-led demonstrators, fueled by anger over military impressment of food supplies, attacked stores in the capital, Richmond, and were only dispersed after the arrival of President Jefferson Davis. Such localized unrest, however, reflected a broader pattern of social disaffection. As the screws of war tightened, class resentments between small farmers and planters intensified. Many nonslaveholders came to believe that the conflict was no longer being fought in their interest, and they pointed to the Confederate policies of exemption, substitution, and impressment as evidence of a "rich man's war, poor man's fight." By 1864 the disillusionment of many ordinary people was being reflected in increased levels of desertion from the army and in the growth of disaffected areas in states such as Alabama, Georgia, and North Carolina. While many southerners continued to support the Confederate war effort, their patriotism now focused on General Robert E. Lee's Army of Northern Virginia rather than the government in Richmond.

The greatest breakdown occurred in black-white relations. Despite their public confidence in slave loyalty, owners could not afford to relax their guard as the war made deep incursions into the South's economic and social life. Fears of insurrection were common from the beginning of the conflict. Although no large-scale black uprisings occurred between 1861 and 1865, the Confederacy's African American population rarely failed to dem-

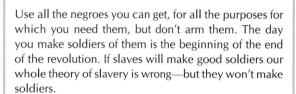

Use all the negroes you can get, for all the purposes for which you need them, but don't arm them. The day you make soldiers of them is the beginning of the end of the revolution. If slaves will make good soldiers our whole theory of slavery is wrong—but they won't make soldiers.

—Howell Cobb to James A. Seddon, 8 January 1865

SOURCE: From Vol. 3 of *War of the Rebellion: Official Records of the Union and Confederate Armies,* Series IV. 130 vols. Washington, D.C., 1888–1901.

onstrate its preference for freedom over slavery when the chance arose. As federal troops approached, masters were often forced to move their slaves into the interior. This movement, known as "refugeeing," helped loosen the bonds of slavery as familiar plantation routines were abandoned. Slave discipline was also undermined by the Confederate government's impressment of black labor for service on military defenses and other installations, and by rapid wartime urbanization that drew large numbers of rural slaves into towns and cities where white supervision was harder to maintain. In areas penetrated by the Union army, disruption of the plantation system was extensive. From early in the war, refugees from slavery sought sanctuary in the camps of the northern invaders. In 1862, the Union began to accept black troops into its armed forces; after Lincoln's emancipation proclamation of 1 January 1863 increasing numbers of slaves escaped from the South to enlist in the struggle against their former masters. Of the 180,000 Africans Americans who fought in the Union army, approximately three-quarters had been slaves. In late 1864, faced with an acute manpower shortage, the Davis government began to contemplate arming the South's slaves. Although the proposal aroused virulent opposition from all sections, in March 1865 the Confederate congress passed a bill providing for the enlistment of black troops while at the same time rejecting the guarantee of emancipation. However, the war ended before the legislation could be implemented.

Defeat

The surrender of General Robert E. Lee's Army of Northern Virginia at Appomattox Courthouse on 9 April 1865 effectively ended the Confederate States of America's bid for independent nationhood. Members of the Davis government, including the president, had evacuated Richmond on 2 April, fleeing south, but lingering hopes of continuing the struggle were soon quashed when the Confederacy's other main surviving force, General Joseph E. Johnston's Army of Tennessee, capitulated on 26 April near Durham Station, North Carolina. Davis himself was captured at Irwinville, Georgia, on 10 May.

The collapse of the Confederate States resulted from a military defeat in which the superior human and material resources of the Union proved decisive. Other factors that contributed to the South's final inability to resist federal power include the lack of political unity, the failure of King Cotton diplomacy, and popular demoralization. Postwar southern ideology insisted that the Confederacy had been united in its opposition to the North. In truth, large numbers of southerners, black and white, had failed consistently to support the bid for independence and in many cases had actively resisted it.

BIBLIOGRAPHY

Beringer, Richard E., Herman Hattaway, Archer Jones, and William N. Still Jr. *Why the South Lost the Civil War.* Athens: University of Georgia Press, 1986.

Coulter, E. Merton. *The Confederate States of America 1861–1865.* Baton Rouge: Louisiana State University Press, 1950.

Durden, Robert F. *The Gray and the Black: The Confederate Debate on Emancipation.* Baton Rouge: Louisiana State University Press, 1972.

Eaton, Clement. *A History of the Southern Confederacy.* New York: Macmillan, 1954.

Escott, Paul D. *After Secession: Jefferson Davis and the Failure of Confederate Nationalism.* Baton Rouge: Louisiana State University Press, 1978.

Faust, Drew Gilpin. *The Creation of Confederate Nationalism: Ideology and Identity in the Civil War South.* Baton Rouge: Louisiana State University Press, 1988.

Freehling, William W. *The South versus the South: How Anti-Confederate Southerners Shaped the Course of the Civil War.* New York: Oxford University Press, 2001.

Gallagher, Gary W. *The Confederate War.* Cambridge, Mass.: Harvard University Press, 1997.

Hubbard, Charles M. *The Burden of Confederate Diplomacy.* Knoxville: University of Tennessee Press, 1998.

Mohr, Clarence. *On the Threshold of Freedom: Masters and Slaves in Civil War Georgia.* Athens: University of Georgia Press, 1986.

Neely, Mark E., Jr. *Southern Rights: Political Prisoners and the Myth of Confederate Constitutionalism.* Charlottesville: University Press of Virginia, 1999.

Owsley, Frank L. *King Cotton Diplomacy: Foreign Relations of the Confederate States of America.* Chicago: University of Chicago Press, 1931, 1936, 1959.

Rable, George C. *The Confederate Republic: A Revolution against Politics.* Chapel Hill: University of North Carolina Press, 1994.

Ramsdell, Charles W. *Behind the Lines in the Southern Confederacy.* Baton Rouge: Louisiana State University Press, 1944.

Roland, Charles P. *The Confederacy.* Chicago: University of Chicago Press, 1960.

Thomas, Emory M. *The Confederate Nation, 1861–1865.* New York: Harper and Row, 1979.

Todd, Richard C. *Confederate Finance.* Athens: University of Georgia Press, 1954.

Vandiver, Frank E. *Ploughshares into Swords: Josiah Gorgas and Confederate Ordnance.* Austin: University of Texas Press, 1952.

Wiley, Bell I. *Southern Negroes, 1861–1865.* New Haven, Conn.: Yale University Press, 1938. Reprinted in 1953 and 1974.

Woodward, C. Vann, ed. *Mary Chesnut's Civil War.* New Haven, Conn.: Yale University Press, 1981.

Yearns, Wilfred B. *The Confederate Congress.* Athens: University of Georgia Press, 1960.

Martin Crawford

See also **Antislavery; Appomattox; Army, Confederate; Blockade Runners, Confederate; Civil War; Emancipation Movement; Impressment, Confederate; Inflation in the Confederacy; King Cotton; Navy, Confederate; Slavery.**

CONFEDERATION. The era 1781–1789 takes its name from the Articles of Confederation, the first constitution of the new United States, ratified by the Second Continental Congress on 1 March 1781. This decade has sometimes been described as an era in which America experienced disastrously weak government under an inept Confederation Congress, an unstable economy that brought the nation to the brink of depression, and a society torn by violence and class conflict; in sum, a decade when the new republic threatened to unravel completely.

On the surface things did look bleak. But overt problems notwithstanding, the new nation made great strides in important ways. While national leadership was wanting during the Confederation period, there remained a strong center of political stability in most states. Both within the Confederation Congress and without, a healthy debate continued in the wake of the Revolution between Federalists, who pressed for a strong central government, and Antifederalists, who stressed preservation of individual liberties protected by strong state sovereignty. This political division culminated in the Constitutional Convention of 1787, the elections that followed of the first constitutional government, and the promulgation of the Bill of Rights in the form of the first ten amendments to the Constitution.

The 1780s also saw a rebirth of American merchant trade as the Confederation Congress established diplomatic relations and forged commercial ties with continental Europe and its Caribbean colonies. Agriculture benefited from the start of a dynamic westward expansion into the Ohio Valley, and with passage of the Northwest Ordinance of 1787, the Confederation Congress established the framework for further westward movement through its organization of the NORTHWEST TERRITORY, thus providing the blueprint for systematic transition from territory to statehood down to the present. The ordinance did more: it prohibited slavery in the new territory, which marked the first time any federal action was taken restricting the advance of the "peculiar institution," a vital precedent often invoked in the next century.

Overall, though, this progress was masked by political conflict—not only between Federalists and Antifederalists but between tidewater merchant interests and western agrarians—and by economic instability brought on by the lack of a national currency and the confusion generated by a muddle of state currencies. These problems were mostly a continuation of conflicts dating back to early in the colonial period, problems the Confederation Congress was too weak to cope with.

Political and Social Unrest

The currency mess created by thirteen fully sovereign states working at cross purposes was a problem that symbolized for ordinary people and legislators alike the need to somehow modify and weaken state sovereignty without sacrificing individual liberties in the process. The economic dislocation caused by the absence of federal authority, and the growing rift between large and small states over a host of economic and trade issues, drove the desire to reform the Articles that characterized much of the politics of the decade. This problem played out as well within many states. A tidewater/piedmont (eastern seaboard versus backcountry) schism in many states played powerfully into the economic instability of the era. In New Jersey, North Carolina, Rhode Island, and Massachusetts, for example, violence erupted as paper-money factions (usually debtor farmers and unskilled labor) fought a virtual class war against tidewater merchants, lawyers, and the landowning elite in an attempt to address the crisis that an absence of usable currency created for farmers and wage workers.

SHAYS'S REBELLION, on the western frontier of Massachusetts in the heart of the Berkshire Mountains, was the worst of these confrontations. In 1786 frontier farmers in Stockbridge took the law into their own hands, in what quickly became a symbol across the nation of widespread class-oriented social unrest. The rebels, led by former Continental army captain Daniel Shays, were suppressed by eastern Massachusetts militia driven by well-to-do merchants from the eastern seaboard of the state. This social unrest, repeated elsewhere n America, generated enormous support in the new nation for a revision of the Articles of Confederation. In 1787 a convention initially called only to reform the Articles matured into a full-blown movement to scrap it and start anew in developing a workable government framework for the infant republic.

The Constitutional Convention

The debates at the Constitutional Convention of 1787 encapsulated the experience of the Confederation era. It was as if the decade formed a period of trial and error as Americans, divided politically into Federalist and Antifederalist camps, moved toward a resolution that preserved both the order that a stable nation required to function in a world of nations and the liberty uniquely espoused by the founders, hard won in the Revolutionary War. The Constitution was very much a product of both the conflicts and successes of the Confederation. The Constitution embodied the enduring principles of representative government so central to the ideology and content of the Articles, and it uniformly incorporated all the legislative, diplomatic, and expansionist successes of the 1780s. More than anything else, it accommodated Antifederalist demands that state sovereignty be preserved even as the federal government was imbued with a new sovereign power of its own. The key notion that sovereignty could be divided was a revolutionary republican idea born entirely of the Confederation experience. Fears of executive autocracy and restoration of the monarchy experienced by colonial America were assuaged by severe checks on presidential power. Representative self-government as a basic operating principle was vested in a House of Representatives that looked very much like the old Confederation Congress. Elite fears of mob rule, with Shays's Rebellion and its like elsewhere in the 1780s, were met by the creation of the U.S. Senate as an upper house (building on a colonial model), and power over the military vested in the president. These were accommodations made possible only by the reality of experience endured in the decade beginning at the end of the American Revolution.

These accommodations framed by the Constitution of 1787 were tested in the final chapter of the Confederation era, the ratifying election campaigns in the states in 1788. In these separate polls each state was asked to elect delegates to a ratifying convention that would establish the Constitution drafted the year before as the law of the land. All the issues raised by the experiences of the 1780s, as well as the ideological conflicts between Federalists and Antifederalists, were played out in these ratifying elections, as the Confederation era drew to a close.

The nine states needed to ratify the Constitution were co-opted by the promises made by the victorious Federalist delegates to the ratifying conventions, who promised a Bill of Rights to meet Antifederalist fears of tyrannical authority vested in a strong central government. Critical as were the issues of that decade, tumultuous as were the politics, uneven as the economy turned out to be, the Confederation era of the 1780s stands as the gateway to the permanent establishment of the democratic republic most Americans wanted at the time of the American Revolution.

BIBLIOGRAPHY

Borden, Morton. *The Antifederalist Papers.* East Lansing: Michigan State University Press, 1965.

Jensen, Merrill. *The New Nation: A History of the United States During the Confederation, 1781–1789.* New York: Knopf, 1950.

Jenson, Merrill, and Robert A. Becker. *The Documentary History of the First Federal Elections, 1788–1790.* Madison: University of Wisconsin Press, 1976–1989.

Kenyon, Cecelia M., ed. *The Antifederalists.* Boston: Northeastern University Press, 1966.

Carl E. Prince

See also **Antifederalists; Articles of Confederation; Bill of Rights in U.S. Constitution; Constitution of the United States; Continental Congress;** *Federalist Papers;* **Federalist Party.**

CONFIRMATION BY THE SENATE,

the constitutional requirement that appointments by the president be made "by and with the Advice and Consent of the Senate" (Article II, Section 2). Although Congress may by statute waive this requirement in the case of low-level appointments, by 1975 there were 319 office titles the holders of which required confirmation by the Senate. Confirmation by the Senate is by majority vote, and in some cases it is generally given as a matter of course. During the late twentieth century, however, Senate confirmations became the arena for bitter partisan battles, particularly in regard to appointments to the Supreme Court and to cabinet or subcabinet positions. For example, the Senate's rejection of Robert Bork's nomination to the Supreme Court in 1987 set off a series of confirmation battles in the late 1980s and throughout the 1990s.

The necessity of obtaining Senate approval operates, on the whole, as a considerable check on presidential power. It is the principal basis for the practice of senatorial patronage and for the twin practice of senatorial courtesy, in accordance with which the Senate will ordinarily refuse to confirm appointments not recommended and therefore opposed by the senators of the appointee's home state.

BIBLIOGRAPHY

Matthews, Christopher. *Hardball: How Politics Is Played, Told by One Who Knows the Game.* New York: Simon and Schuster, 1999. Originally published in 1988.

Smith, Hedrick. *The Power Game: How Washington Works.* New York: Random House, 1988.

Vieira, Norman, and Leonard Gross. *Supreme Court Appointments: Judge Bork and the Politicization of Senate Confirmations.* Carbondale: Southern Illinois University Press, 1998.

Clarence A. Berdahl / A. G.

See also **Ambassadors; Cabinet.**

CONFISCATION ACTS.

On 6 August 1861, early in the Civil War, Congress passed the First Confiscation Act, which was designed to confiscate property used to aid the Confederacy—primarily slaves—and thereby weaken the insurrection. Proposed by Senator Lyman Trumbull, a Republican from Illinois, the act reflected concern over the fugitive slaves entering Union lines, anger at a Confederate law to confiscate Northerners' debts, and a desire to punish Confederates. However, the act failed to free any slaves or confiscate much property.

Interest in a stronger confiscation measure increased by late 1861. Many in the North wanted a more vigorous attack upon the Confederacy, its leaders, and slavery. In December Trumbull proposed the Second Confiscation Act, which became law in July 1862 following lengthy debates, many compromises, and the lack of military success. This act authorized the president to confiscate and sell the property of six classes of Confederate supporters. Advocates claimed it would help finance the Union's war effort, punish the leading traitors, abolish slavery, and begin the reconstruction of the South. Opponents, including Lincoln, believed the law was too punitive. Fearing a presidential veto, Congress agreed to a resolution prohibiting the confiscation of property beyond the life of the owner. Lincoln said this prevented the law from being a bill of attainder, which is prohibited in the Constitution's first article. Many supporters believed this compromise was unwarranted and predicted that it would obstruct the distribution of confiscated property to ex-slaves and poor whites, thereby preventing a real reconstruction of the South.

Lincoln and Attorney General Bates of Missouri implemented the Second Confiscation Act conservatively. It too was a complicated, difficult law to administer because prosecutions could occur only in areas secure enough for the courts to function. In the end, the Second Confiscation Act realized little revenue for the North and had very little impact upon the South, despite the fears of many. Radicals, who had lost enthusiasm for confiscation as the war progressed, bore much of the responsibility for its failure. Lincoln and Johnson also pardoned many under the act's authority, which allowed former rebels to regain their confiscated land soon after the war ended.

BIBLIOGRAPHY

Belz, Herman. *Abraham Lincoln, Constitutionalism, and Equal Rights in the Civil War Era.* New York: Fordham University Press, 1998.

Belz, Herman. *A New Birth of Freedom: The Republican Party and Freedmen's Rights, 1861–1866.* New York: Fordham University Press, 2000.

Lucie, Patricia Allan. *Freedom and Federalism: Congress and the Courts 1861–1866.* New York: Garland Publishing, 1986.

Randall, James G. *Constitutional Problems Under Lincoln.* Revised Edition. Urbana, Ill.: University of Illinois Press, 1964.

John Syrett

See also **Civil War; Reconstruction; Slavery.**

CONFISCATION OF PROPERTY

has occurred in the United States during wartime, ever since the revolutionary war. As a means of financing hostilities against England, the Continental Congress declared in 1776 that the property of LOYALISTS was subject to seizure. By the end of 1781, every state had passed a confiscation act, and Loyalists had lost property worth millions of pounds. Article V of the Definitive Treaty of Peace (1783) provided that Congress would urge the states to compensate former owners whose property had been seized, but only South Carolina responded to this plea. With the United States itself refusing to provide compensation, the British Parliament ultimately indemnified a large number of Loyalists in an amount exceeding £3 million.

During the Civil War, both the North and the South confiscated property. The Confederacy's scheme, adopted in 1861, required all northern debts to be paid to the government in return for bonds. Designed essentially to produce revenue, it was not successful. The North's use of confiscation, culminating in the EMANCIPATION PROCLAMATION, effective 1 January 1863, was directed primarily toward the liberation of slaves. The slaveholders' losses incurred because of freed slaves has been estimated at $2 billion. The total value of confiscated nonhuman property, though greater in the South than in the North, was not large by modern standards, and some property was returned after the war.

World War I and World War II witnessed a revival of property seizure as an instrument of policy. Departing from its general policy of not disturbing alien-owned property in time of war, Congress enacted the Trading with the Enemy Act on 6 October 1917. This statute created the Office of Alien Property Custodian, which took over and operated in trust about $700 million of enemy-owned or enemy-controlled property. After the war, Congress decided to return most of this property, and in 1935 the office was abolished. Under the above statutory scheme, property had not actually been confiscated but merely "frozen" for return or other use upon termination of hostilities.

A similar approach was taken during World War II, when Congress amended the original Trading with the Enemy Act and reestablished the Office of the Alien Property Custodian. Enemy property worth millions of dollars was frozen once again. After the war, Congress enacted the War Claims acts of 1948 and 1962, under which German and Japanese property held in trust by the United States was vested and used to satisfy in part the war claims of U.S. citizens. Using the former enemy property in this fashion did not constitute confiscation, since it was done pursuant to the Potsdam Agreement of 1945 and the Paris Reparation Agreement of 1946, with respect to Germany, and pursuant to the Treaty of Peace of 8 September 1951, with respect to Japan.

During the postwar period, the United States continued the policy of freezing rather than vesting alien property in the absence of special agreement. Title V of the International Claims Settlement Act of 1949 (as amended on 16 October 1964) allowed certain claims of U.S. citizens against Cuba. It contained provisions for vesting Cuban assets that the United States had frozen previously in retaliation for Cuba's confiscation of more than $1.8 billion of American-owned property in Cuba. Congress amended the act again on 19 October 1965, deleting the vesting provisions and thereby preserving the policy of the United

States against taking foreign property without adequate compensation. To support U.S. national security and foreign policy goals since 1962, the Office of Foreign Assets Control has frozen—but has not vested—foreign assets of various countries, organizations supporting terrorism, and international traffickers in narcotics.

BIBLIOGRAPHY

Domke, Martin. *The Control of Alien Property: Supplement to Trading with the Enemy in World War II.* New York: Central Book, 1947.

Hyman, Harold M. *A More Perfect Union: The Impact of the Civil War and Reconstruction on the Constitution.* Boston: Houghton Mifflin, 1975.

Lucie, Patricia M. L. "Confiscation: Constitutional Crossroads." *Civil War History* 32, no. 4 (Dec. 1977): 307–321.

Martin, W. F., and J. R. Clark. *American Policy Relative to Alien Property.* Washington, D.C.: GPO, 1926.

Norton, Mary Beth. *The British-Americans: The Loyalist Exiles in England, 1774–1789.* Boston: Little, Brown, 1972.

Randall, J. G. *The Civil War and Reconstruction.* 2d rev. ed. Boston: Little, Brown, 1973.

Schwab, John Christopher. *The Confederate States of America 1861–1865: A Financial and Industrial History of the South during the Civil War.* New York: B. Franklin, 1968.

Van Tyne, Claude Halstead. *The Loyalists in the American Revolution.* New York: B. Franklin, 1970.

Richard B. Lillich

See also **Property.**

CONGLOMERATES are corporations consisting of a number of different companies operating in diversified fields. In geology circles, the analogous definition of conglomerate is something consisting of loosely cemented heterogeneous material. Conglomerates in business are organizations built on the acquisition of firms that are usually in a type of business indirectly related, if at all, to the acquiring company's other corporate divisions. The parent company is what holds these loosely related companies together.

Although conglomerates existed before World War II, they became increasingly popular during the late 1950s and early 1960s. One reason for the adoption of the conglomerate strategy was that such entities could make acquisitions and grow yet maintain immunity from the antitrust prosecution that companies making acquisitions in the same line of business often found themselves facing. Thus, businesses that were constrained within their own industry were able to freely expand into different markets. In addition, of particular importance at the time was that the conglomerate strategy allowed firms heavily engaged in defense contracts to diversify and reduce the risks associated with overspecialization.

One of the best examples of conglomeration and its focus on diversification was Textron Incorporated. After early beginnings as a parachute and textiles manufacturer, Textron, which was headed by Royal Little, began to acquire unrelated companies in an effort to expand profits and experience beneficial tax treatments. This diversification became so wide reaching that Textron began to acquire companies whose products ranged from cement to helicopters; by 1963, Textron was no longer even in the textile business.

Some experts believe that the techniques used by conglomerates to achieve the astounding growth for which they were noted was a direct violation of sound corporate operating principles. Conglomerates exercised few, if any, limits on diversification, often purchased less than 10 percent of their acquisitions, operated with complex capital structures, and exhibited high debt-to-earnings ratios. This loose-cement method often meant that a conglomerate's stock price could fall as quickly as it rose. In addition, conglomerate corporations often paid debt securities, such as bonds, debentures, and preferred shares, for the companies they acquired. This was derisively referred to as "funny money" because the payment did not represent ownership in the acquiring company, and the company being acquired would surrender outright ownership although in return it would receive nothing more than evidence of the acquirer's indebtedness.

Litton was one of the first conglomerates to take advantage of this acquisition technique. It was not, however, the originator of this corporate form. Before Litton came companies like U. S. Hoffman, Penn-Dixie Industries, Merritt, Chapman & Scott, and Aeronca, Incorporated. Each of these conglomerates started out small, made a series of acquisitions, and quickly became top stock market performers. They all failed, however, because they either purchased poorly performing companies, failed to add any substantial businesses, squeezed the worth from their acquisitions, or used slick accounting methods to appear stable.

Although the exact origins of conglomerates are unclear, Litton seems to be the model that lit the fuse on the conglomerate explosion of the late 1950s and early 1960s. The company, which was created and led by Charles "Tex" Thornton, began in 1953 by purchasing three privately held companies with $3 million in combined sales. For the next fifty-seven straight quarters, a period spanning fourteen years, the company reported increases in quarter-to-quarter earnings per share. In 1968, sales reached an astounding $168 billion before the earnings record and the company collapsed. The company's stock price dropped from a high of 120 3/8 in 1967 to 8 1/2 in 1973—a 93 percent decline. Despite its failure, which Litton blamed on management problems, the company's earnings record encouraged dozens of new firms to take on the conglomerate form.

While efficient management helped many conglomerates improve the performance of acquired companies, others were seemingly more interested in earning profits from securities. Acquiring companies for stocks and bonds and later selling off portions of the acquired companies generated profits and funds for expansion. James J. Ling of Ling-Temco-Vought (LTV) used this method of building conglomerates to achieve remarkable success. By selling off portions of acquired companies and using the money to expand, Ling took his company from the 204th largest industrial organization in America to the 14th spot in just four years. He would eventually step down as chairman, however, after the government mounted serious antitrust challenges and LTV began to suffer substantial losses, including a $10.59 per share loss in 1968.

Business went well for conglomerates until 1969, when antitrust indictments challenged some of them and business began to slow. In 1969 and 1970, ten national investigations, including studies by the Federal Trade Commission, Securities and Exchange Commission, and Department of Justice, began to explore the conglomerate culture. This increased scrutiny, along with the publication of stories detailing securities manipulations of certain conglomerate promoters, began to greatly affect their ability to continue doing business in the same way. As the economy began to slow in the early 1970s, the managers of some conglomerates were proved to have been far less efficient than they had claimed. Nearly a quarter of the conglomerates doing big business in the 1960s failed to make it beyond the 1970s. But while most conglomerates survived the recession of the early 1970s, they were no longer regarded with the enthusiasm they had enjoyed for over a decade.

The trend at the end of the twentieth century was for conglomerates to move from being large, unfocused behemoths to firms that created organizations focused on core capabilities. This means more companies began to avoid acquisitions that clashed with their business mix and focused on acquiring companies with related synergies. This, of course, is in direct opposition to the mindset of the conglomerate boom, when market focus and business streamlining were, at best, secondary concerns.

BIBLIOGRAPHY

Bagley, Edward R. *Beyond the Conglomerates: The Impact of the Supercorporation on the Future of Life and Business.* New York: AMACOM, 1975.

Matsusaka, John G. "Takeover Motives During the Conglomerate Merger Wave." *Rand Journal of Economics* 24, no. 3 (1993): 357–379.

Sobel, Robert. *The Rise and Fall of the Conglomerate Kings.* New York: Stein and Day, 1984.

Winslow, John F. *Conglomerates Unlimited: The Failure of Regulation.* Bloomington: Indiana University Press, 1973.

James T. Scott

CONGREGATIONALISM. Congregationalist Churches trace their ancestry to the Non-Separating Puritans who originally settled the New England colonies. The first century of their existence was a stormy period in which the New England churches searched for principles of church order that would be adequate to the new American situation. The first systematic exposition of those principles was the CAMBRIDGE PLATFORM (1648), which accepted the Calvinist Westminster Confession of Faith as a doctrinal standard and affirmed that the policy of New England was to admit to the sacraments only those "visible saints" who could relate a conversion experience. This system left unanswered the question of whether or not the children of believing nonmembers could be baptized. After considerable controversy, the HALFWAY COVENANT, which allowed for two types of church affiliation—including both those who could and those who could not relate a conversion experience—was adopted by a synod in 1662 to resolve the issue. By the turn of the century, the churches were clearly moving toward a general "established" church pattern.

The Great Awakening (1733–1746) was a period of crisis for the Congregational way. On the one hand, the evangelical wing of the church wished to return to the earlier ideal of a converted church of "visible saints." On the other hand, the liberal wing of the church, which was moving in a more latitudinarian direction, was offended by the emotionalism and lack of clarity of the evangelicals. The more extreme evangelicals withdrew from the state church system to establish their own separate churches, and many Boston-area liberals accelerated their movement toward Unitarianism. Some Congregational churches even disbanded after the Revolutionary War.

In the early nineteenth century, a number of New England Congregationalists moved west and spread their gospel with missionary zeal. Under the Plan of Union (1801) and the Accommodation Plan (1808), Congregationalists and Presbyterians agreed to share the responsibility for the evangelization of the West. Thirteen frontier colleges, including Beloit (1846), Grinnell (1846), and Carleton (1866), trace their roots to the Congregationalists' efforts in the Midwest. In addition, Rev. Horace Bushnell and others cultivated ties with German Evangelical churches, paving the way for a twentieth-century merger of these organizations. The Congregationalist-Presbyterian arrangement gradually disintegrated as Presbyterians became disturbed over the liberal drift of the so-called New England theology, and, by 1837, the two sects had separated.

The early part of the nineteenth century also saw the splitting off of the Unitarian churches, which were located primarily in the area around Boston. But Congregational parishes continued to thrive among the older, more static communities of New England. Along with the FEDERALIST PARTY, many Congregational clergy opposed the War of 1812. A number of prominent Congregationalist women, such as Emma Willard, Catherine Beecher, and Harriet Beecher Stowe, took leading roles in promoting public school reform and opposing slavery. During the second half of the nineteenth century, Congregationalism continued its movement in a more liberal direction. The denomination was one of the leading ecclesiastical opponents of slavery in the 1850s; never very popular in the South, Congregationalism did not suffer the institutional division that plagued many other Protestant denominations in the years preceding the CIVIL WAR. After the war, Congregationalism was deeply affected by the Social Gospel. Congregationalists working through the American Missionary Association tended to the educational needs of free blacks in the South. In the North, Rev. Josiah Strong, Rev. Washington Gladden, and Jane Addams all brought attention to the problems of industrialization and refocused attention from individual salvation to social and political reform. A national council was formed in 1871 to provide some denominational coordination among Congregationalists, and, in 1913, a liberal confession of faith was adopted at Kansas City.

The twentieth century saw Congregationalism taking a position of leadership in the ecumenical movement. In 1931 Congregationalists merged with the Christian Churches (a group founded by frontier evangelicals in 1794) to become the Congregational Christian Churches. In the 1940s this denomination began negotiations to merge with two churches deeply rooted in the German Diaspora in North America: the Evangelical Synod of North America—strongest in the Midwest, and the Reformed church—German religious separatists that had broken their ties with Europe in the 1790s and had only just united to form their organization in 1934. The union of Yankee and German did not occur without debate and controversy. The Congregational Christians wanted to preserve local control over church operations. On the other hand, the Evangelical and REFORMED CHURCHES believed that congregations should be made accountable to one another and were less concerned about centralizing authority. After ten drafts for an agreement of union and a federal lawsuit, the Evangelical and Reformed churches were merged with the Congregational Christian Churches at the Uniting General Synod in Cleveland, Ohio, on 25 June 1957, creating the United Church of Christ (UCC).

The UCC was a standard-bearer of liberal Protestantism in the twentieth century. Men and women like the UCC minister Andrew Young, later a U.S. congressman and United Nations ambassador, were active in the struggle for black equality during the CIVIL RIGHTS MOVEMENT of the 1960s. In 1972 a UCC church in San Francisco ordained one of the first openly gay men to a Christian ministry. Changing regional demographics and the revitalized evangelical movement reduced the UCC's membership in the 1980s and 1990s. In 1973 the UCC claimed 1,895,016 members; by 2002 the number had dropped to 1,359,105. Like other mainline Protestant denominations, the UCC has embraced growing Hispanic and immigrant communities in the hopes of growing its membership.

The UCC is the largest church in the Congregational family. However, not all Congregational churches were content with the new body. In 2002 the somewhat liberal Congregational Christian Churches (continuing Congregational) had 70,000 members, down from 110,000 in 1973. By contrast, the Conservative Congregational Christian Conference, which opposed abortion rights and believed homosexuality to be a sin, had grown from 19,000 members in 1973 to 40,000 members in 2002. The Unitarian Universalist Association should be considered a member of the Congregational family. The Unitarians withdrew from orthodox Congregationalism in the early nineteenth century under the leadership of such eminent pastors as William Ellery Channing. Initially, the group stressed the unity of God, the revelation by Christ but not His divinity, a nonsubstitutionary doctrine of the atonement, and each human's ethical duties to his or her neighbor. The rise of transcendentalism in the 1830s further liberalized the movement, and the Unitarians have been moving progressively away from distinctively Christian affirmations since that time. Unitarians now stress an intellectual humanism rooted in the values of all religions.

Although John Murray gathered the first Universalist church in Gloucester, Massachusetts, in 1779, the greatest influence on American Universalism was Hosea Ballou, who stated the classical Universalist position in his *Treatise on Atonement* (1805). According to Ballou, Christ's death is to be regarded as effecting salvation for all men. Ballou also moved Universalism in a more Unitarian direction; in 1803, the denomination accepted a statement of faith in harmony with his views. In 1961 the Unitarians and the Universalists formally merged in the Unitarian Universalist Association, which in 2002 had approximately 156,000 members.

BIBLIOGRAPHY

Atkins, Gaius, G., and Frederick Louis Fagley, *History of American Congregationalism*. Boston: Pilgrim Press, 1942.

Chrystal, William G. *A Father's Mantle: The Legacy of Gustav Niebuhr*. New York: Pilgrim Press, 1982.

Gunnemann, Louis H. *The Shaping of the United Church of Christ: An Essay in the History of American Christianity*. Cleveland, Ohio: United Church Press, 1999.

Robinson, David. *The Unitarians and the Universalists*. Westport, Conn.: Greenwood Press, 1985.

Von Rohr, John. *The Shaping of American Congregationalism, 1620–1957*. Cleveland, Ohio: Pilgrim Press, 1992.

Youngs, J. William T. *The Congregationalists*. Westport, Conn: Praeger, 1998.

Glenn T. Miller/A. R.

See also **Evangelicalism, and Revivalism; Great Awakening; Latitudinarians; Puritans and Puritanism; Social Gospel; United Church of Christ.**

CONGRESS, UNITED STATES. The principal institution of representative democracy in the United States, Congress is defined in the first and longest article of the Constitution. The Constitution vests all legislative power in the Senate and House of Representatives, requiring them to assemble at least once every year. The length of each Congress is two years, normally divided between a first and second session. The Constitution enumerates a list of congressional powers that include taxation, borrowing and coining money, regulation of foreign and interstate commerce, establishment of post offices and post roads, creating a court system, raising and supporting military forces, and declaring war. It further authorizes Congress to make all laws "necessary and proper" for exercising those powers.

Following American independence, the first national government under the Articles of Confederation (1781–1789) consisted of a unicameral Congress, in which each state had one vote. That Congress lacked the power to tax or to regulate commerce, nor could it compel the states to comply with its actions. Economic decline and civil unrest encouraged the states to send delegates in 1787 to a Constitutional Convention to devise a more effective central government. Seeking to make the government more powerful without allowing it to grow autocratic, they divided authority among executive, legislative, and judicial branches and further split the Congress into two houses. Through this system of checks and balances they prevented any single branch from gaining absolute power.

The Constitutional Convention deadlocked over the issue of representation in Congress. The Virginia Plan, supported by the larger states, would have set membership in both houses of Congress according to the size of a state's population. The New Jersey Plan, offered by the smaller states, would have preserved the equality of the states in congressional voting. A special committee then devised the CONNECTICUT COMPROMISE, or Great Compromise, which apportioned the House by population and gave all states, regardless of size, two senators. The Constitution further stipulated (in Article 5) that no state could lose its equal vote in the Senate without its consent.

During the public debate over the Constitution's ratification, opponents objected to the absence of a Bill of Rights. As a remedy, the First Congress proposed the first ten amendments to the Constitution, which among other things prohibited Congress from making any laws regarding freedom of religion, freedom of speech, freedom of the press, or the right to assemble peacefully and to petition the government (First Amendment). Powers not delegated to the national government were reserved to the states (Tenth Amendment).

House and Senate

When the new government commenced in 1789, members of the House of Representatives were the only federal officials people directly elected by the people. The Electoral College elected the president, while state legislatures chose senators. Representatives had to be twenty-five years or older, residents of their states, and citizens for at least seven years. Members of the House stood for election every two years. In the case of vacancies special elections would be held, since no one could be appointed to the House. The House elected a Speaker, who was initially a neutral presiding officer, although over time that position evolved into a powerful party leader. The larger size of the House (which began at sixty-five members and rose to 435) encouraged the development of rules to limit the time for debate, expedite business, and allow the majority party to exert its will.

With all House seats contested biannually, the framers of the Constitution expected that body to reflect the prevailing political mood. As a "necessary fence" against the "fickleness and passion" of public opinion, they assigned senators six-year terms, with only one-third of the Senate seats contested in any general election. Since two-thirds of the senators remained through each election, the Senate defined itself as a "continuing body" that did not need to readopt its rules at the start of each new Congress. Senators had to be at least thirty years of age, residents of their states, and citizens for nine years. Elected by state legislatures, senators were envisioned as "ambassadors" of their states. As a smaller body, the Senate was expected to perfect legislation originating in the House and to serve as an advisory council to the president. The Constitution gave the Senate sole authority to advise and consent on treaties and nominations.

While the "upper house" in most parliamentary governments steadily lost power to the "lower house," the U.S. Senate remained equal with the House of Representatives. This was due in part to the MISSOURI COMPROMISE of 1820, which provided that the admission of each state permitting slavery would be balanced by the admission of a state that prohibited slavery. With the North and South equally divided in the Senate on this emotional issue, such leading members of the House as Henry Clay, Daniel Webster, and John C. Calhoun gravitated to the Senate, where debate centered in the tumultuous decades prior to the Civil War. Early in the twentieth century, when European reformers stripped upper houses of the power of the purse and of most of their ability to block legislation, Progressive reformers in the United States instead trusted the will of the people. The Seventeenth Amendment (1913) provided for direct election of senators, although reformers were deeply disappointed when voters reelected every incumbent senator running in 1914. The Senate survived the reform era with all of its powers intact and with the bonds between senators and citizens strengthened by the ballot.

Visiting Congress in 1831, Alexis de Tocqueville contrasted the boisterous, "vulgar demeanor" of the House with the sedate decorum and elegant orations of the Senate. He assumed that the Senate drew a better class of legislators; however, Thomas Hart Benton, who represented Missouri in both bodies, pointed out that most senators had previously served in the House. The different ethos of the two bodies reflected their contrasting

sizes and rules of procedure. Since the Constitution authorized each house to set its own rules and elect its own officers, the rules and procedures of the two houses evolved differently. The larger House debates under specific rules that determine how many amendments to a bill may be considered and for how long. It can further expedite business by suspending the regular order and operating as a Committee of the Whole, a legislative strategy that the smaller Senate does not employ. The Senate allows for "unlimited debate" and generally does not restrict the number of amendments that senators may offer or require those amendments to be germane to the bill. Senate leaders can seek unanimous consent agreements to establish parameters for floor debates, but the objection of a single senator can prevent adoption of such agreements. The extreme version of unlimited debate is the FILIBUSTER. Taken from the Dutch word for pirate, filibusters use extensive speeches and other delaying tactics to hold the floor and prevent the majority from calling for a vote.

Apportionment also accounted for differences between the Senate and the House. By the end of the twentieth century, California, with a population of more than 30 million, elected fifty-two members of the House, while Wyoming, with less than 500,000 residents, had one representative. Yet California and Wyoming each had two senators. Since a majority of the senators represent a minority of the population, the Senate does not operate as a "majoritarian" body. Senate rules and procedures require a supermajority of three-fifths of the senators to vote cloture and cut off filibuster, and they tolerate "holds" by individual senators that can delay votes on bills and nominations.

The Constitution does not require Congress to conduct its business in public. When the First Congress convened in 1789, representatives, who would face voters again in two years, immediately threw open their doors to the public and the press. The first Senate chamber, by contrast, had no public gallery. Senators conducted all business in closed sessions for five years. Even after admitting the public to its legislative debates, the Senate debated and voted on executive business—treaties and nominations—in closed session until 1929. The trend toward legislative openness continued with the enactment of "sunshine" rules in the 1970s that required committees to conduct most business in public view. The Constitution also required each house of Congress to publish a journal of its proceedings. The journals consist of minutes and recorded votes. The verbatim accounts of speeches and floor debates that appear daily in the *Congressional Record*, however, evolved from notes recorded and published by various newspapers. Congress eventually hired its own reporters of debate and since 1873 has published the *Congressional Record*. Congress also publishes most of the hearings and reports of its committees and the text of all bills and resolutions.

351

Congressional Leadership

While the Constitution provided for a Speaker of the House and made the vice president the presiding officer of the Senate, it made no mention of political parties or majority and minority leaders. When members of Congress divided into parties, they established party caucuses or conferences that made committee assignments and steering committees that decided the order of legislative business. The larger House began electing party floor leadership by the mid-nineteenth century. The Senate resisted formally designated leadership until the 1920s. Senate rules and precedents give party leaders few specific powers. The Senate Majority Leader controls the Senate calendar, determining what bills to call up for debate and in what order. Party leaders also have the right of "first recognition," meaning that the presiding officer will call on them before other senators. Otherwise, as Lyndon B. Johnson observed, a majority leader's chief power is the "power of persuasion."

To handle specific legislative tasks, the House and Senate at first elected a stream of ad hoc committees. By 1816 the need for sustained expertise on the myriad of legislative issues caused them to establish standing committees. House and Senate rules set the jurisdictions of these committees and the number of committees on which members could serve. The party conferences appoint members to the standing committees, where they advance via seniority to chairmanships. By the late nineteenth century, the committee chairs had amassed such power over the legislative agendas that they were called "barons." Chairmen could bottle up legislation, refusing to allow bills they opposed to be reported to the floor. Changes in the rules during the 1970s diminished that power and gave other committee members greater voice in matters of staff and agenda. The most influential committees have traditionally been the House Ways and Means Committee and the Senate Finance Committee, which raise revenue through tariffs and taxation, and the House and Senate Appropriations Committees, which authorize all federal funding. Through its "power of the purse" Congress exerts its greatest influence over the executive branch, which can spend nothing without congressional approval.

Congressional committees conduct oversight hearings over the activities of executive agencies and investigate corruption, mismanagement, scandal, and sedition. Congressional investigations date back to 1792, when the House inquired into a military defeat in the Northwest Territory. Other major investigations reviewed the CRÉDIT MOBILIER scandal (1872), TEAPOT DOME (1923–1924), the Army-McCarthy hearings (1954), WATERGATE (1973–1974), and IRAN-CONTRA (1987). Most investigations targeted government agencies and officials, but in *McGrain v. Daugherty* (1927) the Supreme Court ruled that even private citizens could be subpoenaed to testify before congressional committees. *Sinclair v. United States* (1929) further recognized Congress's right to investigate, whether or not it led to the enactment of any new laws. But the anticommunist investigations of the 1940s and 1950s raised questions about the abuse of witnesses. In *Watkins v. United States* (1957) the Supreme Court found the investigative powers of Congress subject to the limitations imposed by the Bill of Rights. Successful congressional investigations have required persistence, diligence, sharp questioning, and the ability to focus media attention on the issues under investigation.

Since 1800 Congress has met in the U.S. Capitol Building in Washington, D.C. Starting as a small sandstone structure that housed the Senate, House, Supreme Court, and Library of Congress, the Capitol expanded along with the nation. The admission of new states to the union required the construction of massive wings on the Capitol in the 1850s to accommodate larger chambers, and the increased space permitted congressional committees to hire their first clerks. Construction of the first House and Senate office buildings in 1906 and 1909 made room for members to hire personal staffs. Staff sizes remained small until the Legislative Reorganization Act of 1946 established professional staffs for committees and authorized members to hire administrative assistants. The rapid expansion of both legislative business and staff required construction of a complex of House and Senate office buildings and other support networks on Capitol Hill. Congress's ability to hire its own staff reduced its reliance on the expertise of cabinet agencies, especially after legislators grew suspicious of the executive branch during the Vietnam War and the Watergate scandal. Congress eventually amassed the largest legislative staff in the world. Many new members of Congress now come to office with previous experience on the staff.

An Open Branch of Government

Under the "speech and debate" provision of the Constitution (Article 1, Section 6), members of Congress may not be prevented from attending a session or be subject to prosecution for libel or slander regarding anything that they say in Congress. But each house of Congress has the power to punish its own members for disorderly behavior. The House and Senate find it painful to discipline colleagues and would prefer for the voters to judge members' ethics. However, pressure from the press and public, as well as internal outrage, have periodically required Congress to censure or expel some of its members. The House or Senate may censure a member by a simple majority vote. Although censure carries no specific punishment, it is still a severe rebuke in a collegial body. Censured members rarely win reelection. Expulsion requires a two-thirds vote and is generally reserved for cases of treason or for conviction of a crime. The House, by a majority vote, may vote to impeach presidents, judges, and other federal officials. The Senate then sits as a court (with the chief justice of the Supreme Court presiding at presidential impeachment trials) and may remove that official from office by a two-thirds vote. Presidential impeachment trials of

Andrew Johnson in 1868 and Bill Clinton in 1999 both resulted in acquittal.

Congress has long operated as the most open branch of government, inviting the public to view its proceedings and establishing press galleries for the media. The Senate authorized the first press gallery in 1841, sixty years before the White House opened a press room. By 1880 both the House and Senate had turned over control of the press galleries to Standing Committees of Correspondents, which reporters themselves elect and which judge applications for press accreditation. Resistance from newspaper correspondents to admitting reporters for other media led Congress to establish separate press galleries for radio and television, periodical press, and press photographers. Congress has regularly employed the newest means of communication to maintain contact with its constituents. The first telegraphic news emanated from the Capitol in 1844. Committee hearings have been broadcast on radio and television, and since 1979 and 1986 the House and Senate respectively have permitted gavel-to-gavel TV coverage of their floor proceedings on C-SPAN (the Cable-Satellite Public Affairs Network).

Despite these efforts to accommodate the press, presidents have tended to overshadow Congress in attracting media attention. The Cold War vastly increased presidential power and prestige, sharply reducing congressional influence over foreign policy. The adoption of a bipartisan foreign policy and the idea that "politics stops at the water's edge" further ceded authority to presidents, who sent troops into combat without requesting formal declarations of war. Presidents argued that they were better equipped to make decisions about war and peace than were "535 secretaries of state" in Congress. The Vietnam War disrupted bipartisan foreign policy, and the rise of an "imperial presidency" that could impound appropriated funds and ignore public protests over military escalations led Congress to reassert itself. Over presidential vetoes Congress passed the WAR POWERS ACT (1973) and Congressional Budget and Impoundment Act (1974).

At the same time the Senate also increased its scrutiny of presidential nominations. While senators have rejected only a tiny percentage of all cabinet nominations, believing that presidents deserve their own advisers, they have voted down a higher percentage of Supreme Court nominations, due to the justices' lifetime appointments and the independence of the judiciary. Some have argued that the Senate should restrict itself to examining a nominee's personal integrity and competence, but some nominees have been rejected because of political differences between the president and the Senate majority, as well as because of ideology, personal character, and offensive behavior. If senators from the nominee's home state object to the nomination, other senators generally support them out of "senatorial courtesy," a system that gives senators leverage over the appointment of judges, U.S. attorneys, federal marshals, and other positions in their states.

To enact legislation, both the House and Senate must pass a bill in the same language. If they produce different versions of the bill, they appoint a conference committee to reach a compromise. Each house must then pass the conference report "up or down," with no further amendments. If the president vetoes the bill, Congress may override that veto by a two-thirds vote in each house. Since 1803 the Supreme Court has claimed the right of judicial review and has declared various acts of Congress unconstitutional. These checks and balances mean that only a fraction of the many bills introduced in each session of Congress will ever become law. A bill will often require many years to make its way successfully to enactment. As cumbersome and frustrating as the process has seemed to activist presidents and reformers of all ideological hues, it reflects the original division of powers that the framers of the Constitution devised. Voters have regularly reinforced those divisions by electing presidents and congressional majorities from different parties, increasing the likeliness of legislative gridlock.

An institution of many contradictions, Congress has sought to balance local interests with national needs. Its members work for consensus legislation, but their individual success depends as much upon maintaining their relations with voters in their districts and states as upon their accomplishments in Washington. As a result, the conflicting demands of lawmaking and representation have often resulted in a low public opinion of the legislative branch as a whole but a high reelection rate of individual members.

BIBLIOGRAPHY

Baker, Richard A. *The Senate of the United States: A Bicentennial History.* Malabar, Fla.: Krieger, 1988.

Binder, Sarah A., and Steven S. Smith. *Politics or Principle? Filibustering in the United States Senate.* Washington, D.C.: Brookings Institution, 1997.

Currie, James T. *The United States House of Representatives.* Malabar, Fla.: Krieger, 1988.

Davidson, Roger H., and Walter J. Oleszek. *Congress and Its Members.* 7th ed. Washington, D.C.: CQ Press, 2000.

Fisher, Louis. *The Politics of Shared Power: Congress and the Executive.* 4th ed. College Station: Texas A&M Press, 1998.

Ornstein, Norman J., Thomas E. Mann, and Michael J. Malbin. *Vital Statistics on Congress.* Washington, D.C.: American Enterprise Institute, 2000.

Peters, Ronald M., Jr. *The American Speakership: The Office in Historical Perspective.* 2d ed. Baltimore: Johns Hopkins University Press, 1997.

Ritchie, Donald A. *The Congress of the United States: A Student Companion.* New York: Oxford University Press, 2001.

Donald A. Ritchie

See also **Checks and Balances; Confirmation by the Senate; Constitution of the United States; District, Congressional; Federal Government; Proportional Representation; Representation; Rules of the House; Separation of**

Congress of Racial Equality. Members of CORE picket outside a Woolworth store in Harlem on 13 February 1960 to protest the discount chain's discrimination against African Americans at its stores' lunch counters in North Carolina—a policy that ended as a result of northern boycotts of the stores and southern sit-ins at the lunch counters. © BETTMANN/CORBIS

Powers; Steering Committees; Two-Party System; *and* vol. 9: **Congress Debates the Fourteenth Amendment.**

CONGRESS OF INDUSTRIAL ORGANIZATIONS. *See* American Federation of Labor–Congress of Industrial Organizations.

CONGRESS OF RACIAL EQUALITY. Founded

in 1942 in Chicago, the Congress of Racial Equality (CORE) was originally an interracial group seeking to use Gandhian tactics of nonviolent direct action in the struggle for racial equality. During the 1940s, it organized sit-ins and pickets to protest segregation in public accommodations and had success in integrating public facilities in the North. In 1947, CORE organized the "Journey of Reconciliation," the precusor to its later "Freedom Rides." Eight black and eight white men traveled together throughout the upper South to test the 1946 SUPREME COURT ruling that segregation on buses in interstate travel was unconstitutional. The men were beaten in some towns, and three ended up working on a chain gang in North Carolina after convictions under local segregation laws. But the journey was not a failure; it garnered national publicity and kicked off CORE's long campaign against discrimination in interstate travel.

Despite the success of its early efforts, CORE remained a minor organization until the southern black college student sit-ins of 1960, for which CORE officials provided guidance. The organization became nationally famous a year later with its Freedom Rides. In December 1960, the Supreme Court extended its earlier decision banning segregation on interstate buses with a ruling that prohibited segregation in the waiting rooms and restaurants serving interstate bus passengers. CORE decided to test compliance with the decision by once again sending interracial teams on buses throughout the Deep South. The freedom riders' dramatic challenge to southern segregation and the violent response ultimately led to the ending of segregation on interstate bus routes.

By the end of 1961, CORE had 53 chapters throughout the United States. For the next four years, it played a major role in the African American protest movement, North and South. CORE participated in President Kennedy's Voter Education Project. It was part of the 1963 Birmingham campaign that included the CORE-SNCC (Student Nonviolent Coordinating Committee) Freedom Walk in honor of a white postal carrier who had been assassinated as he walked across Alabama wearing signboards urging an end to segregation. CORE also cosponsored the 1963 MARCH ON WASHINGTON. Along with SNCC and the NAACP, it organized the Mississippi

Freedom Summer project in 1964. And it organized rent strikes, school boycotts, and demonstrations against police brutality in cities outside of the South.

By the middle of the 1960s, however, CORE was losing members and, in the minds of some, relevancy. In 1966, Floyd McKissick replaced James Farmer as National Director of the organization. McKissick endorsed "BLACK POWER" and moved the organization away from its original commitment to interracialism and nonviolent direct action. Current National Director Roy Innis replaced McKissick in 1968. Innis focused CORE's efforts on black economic development and community self-determination. Innis has become one of the country's leading black conservatives, a philosophical position indicated by his support of the nominations of Robert Bork and Clarence Thomas to the U.S. Supreme Court. By the end of the twentieth century, CORE had a membership of around 100,000.

BIBLIOGRAPHY

Bell, Inge Powell. *CORE and the Strategy of Nonviolence*. New York: Random House, 1968.

Branch, Taylor. *Parting the Waters: America in the King Years 1954–63*. New York: Simon and Schuster, 1988.

Farmer, James. *Freedom,When?* New York: Random House, 1965.

Meier, August, and Elliott Rudwick. *CORE: A Study in the Civil Rights Movement, 1942–1968*. New York: Oxford University Press, 1973.

Powledge, Fred. *Free At Last?: The Civil Rights Movement and the People Who Made It*. Boston: Little, Brown, 1991.

Sitkoff, Harvard. *The Struggle for Black Equality, 1954–1980*. New York: Hill and Wang, 1981.

August Meier
Cynthia R. Poe

See also **Black Nationalism; Civil Rights Movement; Freedom Riders; National Association for the Advancement of Colored People; Student Nonviolent Coordinating Committee; Suffrage: African American Suffrage.**

CONGRESSIONAL RECORD, a daily, unofficial publication of the proceedings of the sessions of Congress. The Senate and House journals contain the official records. The *Record* prints not only the daily actions of each chamber but also a checked stenographic record of all remarks and formal debate. Congress has published this daily account of legislative action and opinion since 1873, before which three separate series of reports served a similar function. These three reports, *Annals of Congress* (1789–1824), *Register of Debates* (1824–1837), and *Congressional Globe* (1834–1873), were privately inspired and privately published with a consequently questionable accuracy.

BIBLIOGRAPHY

Amer, Mildred. *The Congressional Record: Content, History, and Issues*. Washington, D.C.: 1993.

George C. Robinson / c. w.

See also **Congress, United States.**

CONNECTICUT
Geography
The state of Connecticut covers 5,006 square miles (the third smallest of America's states) and is located in the northeastern United States, with New York along its western border, Massachusetts to the north, Rhode Island to the east, and the Long Island Sound along its southern coast. Across Long Island Sound is Long Island, part of which once belonged to Connecticut but was ceded to New York. In exchange for Long Island, Connecticut was able to keep its southwestern handle, which jutted into New York and in which the cities of Greenwich, Stamford, and Norwalk are found. This was no simple process. The first agreement in 1664 fell apart because of very bad surveying of the borders. In 1683, commissioners from New York and Connecticut again tried to settle their border dispute, agreeing to trade Connecticut's territory on Long Island for the panhandle, but Connecticut backed out because the borders were again badly drawn, costing it several towns. In 1684, the commissioners finally agreed on the trade of territory and on borders, but their governments continued to bicker over who had what territory.

In 1700, King William III of England confirmed the 1684 agreement as binding, but Connecticut and New York continued to bicker. In 1718, New York tried to restart the whole process, but Connecticut essentially ignored them; New York then declared itself satisfied with the 1684 agreement; in 1723, Connecticut appointed new commissioners to negotiate with New York's commissioners, which appointed new commissioners in 1725, and a new survey was begun but ran out of funding before it was complete. In 1731, it all began again, this time with

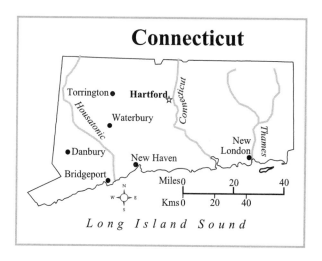

a complete survey, and then both sides decided to go with the 1684 agreement. Arguments over the border continued almost incessantly, although the trade of the panhandle for Connecticut's Long Island territory was considered official. In 1855, Connecticut restarted official inquiries because markers for the 1684 agreement's border had disappeared and the state's government thought it had been denied northern lands that should belong to it. Commissioners of New York and Connecticut redid the border survey in January 1856, trying to settle where an area called the "Oblong" was located, but the commissioners could not agree on what the survey had found. In 1859, new commissioners met in September in Port Chester, but did not agree on a border. In 1860, New York independently marked the border from the panhandle to Massachusetts as it saw fit. Connecticut complained about this until new commissioners were appointed by both states in 1878, who met in 1878 and 1879, finally agreeing on 5 December 1879 that the 1860 New York line was acceptable where it matched the 1731 line, about which there was still uncertainty because of lost markers. Eventually, both state legislatures ratified the 1860 (based on the 1731) border, and in 1881, the United States Congress confirmed the border. This did stop the states from continuing to bicker over the details for seemingly endless decades thereafter.

Connecticut is shaped in large part like a rectangle and its borders look as though they were planned, but in fact Connecticut owes its shape to about 150 years of wrangling with its neighbors from about 1633 to statehood in 1776.

Connecticut is split north to south by the Connecticut River, which enters the state from Massachusetts to the north near the town of Enfield, flows south to Middletown, then shifts to a southeasterly direction, eventually flowing into Long Island Sound at the town of Old Saybrook. The Connecticut River is shallow at its mouth, limiting accessibility to ships, but the river itself has served as a highway for people since before the coming of European settlers. The Mohawks probably used it to raid Connecticut tribes just before English colonists arrived in Massachusetts.

Temperatures in Connecticut usually vary from July highs in the low 70s to January highs in the mid-20s. However, severe heat occasionally occurs, with 105 the record high on 22 July 1929 at Waterbury, and lows can be very low indeed, with 32 below zero being the record low, set on 16 February 1943 at Falls Village. Annually, rain and snow combine for about forty-eight inches of precipitation.

The banks of the Connecticut River have been appealing to farmers for their nutrient rich, smooth soil, although during the industrialization of the state, the adjacent land was turned over to mills and other factories that used the flowing water to generate power and to dump waste. The rest of Connecticut's soil is very rocky, and although farmers cleared native forests to create huge tracts of farmland, the rocky terrain makes agriculture a difficult proposition.

Geographers customarily divide Connecticut into four parts: the eastern hill country, the Connecticut River Valley, the western hill country, and the southern coast. Some geographers suggest that the southwestern handle be considered a separate region of Connecticut because of its dense population, starting with the city of Danbury in the north to Stratford in the southeast to Greenwich in the southwest.

The Connecticut River valley has been the center of commerce and political power since colonial times because the river made a good trade route and so the first colonial settlements were established near it. Rivers attracted population elsewhere in Connecticut, although to a lesser extent. The western hill country has always been less populated than other parts of Connecticut, although the city of Waterbury is located on the Naugatuck River. The eastern hill country is most heavily populated along the southern part of the Thames River, where the towns of Norwich and Ledyard are located. Much of the northern part of the eastern hill country has remained heavily forested since prehistoric times.

The Connecticut coast is sometimes referred to as the Gold Coast of Connecticut because of its many seaports and its attractive beaches. Since the late 1600s, Connecticut's ports have been a source of international trade, with Yankee traders sailing far and wide in search of markets and goods. The Connecticut River valley has been a rich source of manufactured goods since the early 1700s and many of them were shipped overseas.

Prehistory

Connecticut was covered by a glacier 11,000 years ago. When this glacier retreated, it scoured the land, leaving many indentations that became lakes and pools that total 146 square miles. A great forest grew after the retreat of the glacier; it became dense with several different species of trees and home to abundant wildlife.

There may be no way to tell when human beings first entered the region of Connecticut because some may have been there before or during the last ice age; if so, the glacier would have obliterated their remains as it retreated. It is likely that at least three waves of culturally diverse Native American groups passed through Connecticut as they explored the North American coastline. It is also possible that none of these groups were the direct ancestors of the Native Americans that colonists found when they began exploring the Connecticut River.

The Narragansetts were in eastern Connecticut and Rhode Island. It was a large, politically savvy, and well-organized tribe. In southeastern Connecticut were the Mohegans, and to their west the Pequots. The Mohegans and the Pequots were of the same cultural stock, but they were enemies at the time Europeans arrived. It is possible that a dispute over a sachem, a political leader similar to a chief, led to hostilities between the two tribes.

By 1630, the Pequots and Mohegans were drifting apart in their social organization. The Mohegans had a loose tribal organization in which individual villages looked after their own affairs and tended to be small and far apart. Each village had its own sachem, who selected an overall leader for negotiations with other tribes or for leading the Mohegans into war. The Pequots were more centrally organized, living in large stockades. In the early 1600s, the Mohegans stretched from southern Rhode Island into New York, but the Pequots migrated from the Hudson River valley into western Connecticut to the Connecticut River, displacing the Mohegans west of the river. Both the Mohegans and the Pequots were primarily farmers.

The Sequins (sometimes called the River People or Quinnipiacs) were also farmers who lived along the Connecticut River and had probably been in Connecticut longer than any other group of Native Americans. In addition to farming, the Sequins traded with the Narragansetts and other tribes that lived to the north in what is now Massachusetts. The Sequins gave Connecticut its name, because they called the river Quinnipiac (variously translated as "long tidal river," "long river," and "land along the long river"). The word "Quinnipiac" was transliterated into "Connecticut."

In the early 1600s, the Pequots and Mohegans stopped fighting one another when a new, bigger problem arose as the Mohawk tribe began raiding the tribes in Connecticut. The Mohawks were part of the Iroquoian Five Nations, a well-organized federation of powerful tribes. Their attacks on other Native Americans resulted in burned villages, lost crops, and dead villagers, including children. The Mohawks also captured people for slaves. It was at this time that the English began colonizing Connecticut.

Colonial Era

In 1614, Dutch explorer Adrian Block was shipwrecked on the New England coast. He and his sailors built another ship, but because it was too small for a sea voyage, Block decided to explore the coast. When he found the mouth of the Connecticut River, he sailed into it, eventually meeting the Sequins, who were friendly and willing to trade goods with the sailors.

Windsor, the first English colony in Connecticut, was established in 1633. It was intended to be a trading outpost. Wethersfield was established in 1634 and was populated by farmers and traders. In 1635, Thomas Hooker led about one hundred of his followers from Newtown, Massachusetts, to Hartford. Hooker and his followers were fleeing the oppressive Puritan colonies to the north, and hoped to create a freer society. In 1638 Hooker said, "The foundation of authority is laid, firstly, in the free consent of the people." On 14 January 1639, the Fundamental Orders—based on Hooker's ideas about freedom—were adopted. They were a set of rules that limited the scope of the government. Although not fully a constitution, the Fundamental Orders have earned Connecticut the nickname "the Constitution State."

The Pequot War was fought in 1637. The Pequots had always been hostile to the colonists and had killed explorers and traders, and during that year they tried to form alliances with the Narragansetts and other tribes to wage war against the colonists. Meanwhile, the Mohegans and Sequins had been friendly with immigrants from Massachusetts, encouraging their settlement to form a buffer between them and their more violent enemies. The efforts of the Pequots were alarming enough so that the colonists and Mohegans formed an alliance and attacked them. A force of about one hundred colonists and seventy Mohegans twice defeated the Pequots in battle, burning their largest stockade and nearly wiping them out

In 1665, the various villages established by colonists were united into the Connecticut colony. During the 1600s, large areas of forest were cleared to make way for farming. Farming on rocky soil, however, was very difficult, and by the 1720s Connecticut's people were leaving their farms for work in mills and factories. In 1702, Abraham Pierson established a "collegiate school" at Killingworth (later called Clinton). In 1716 the college moved to New Haven; in 1718, it was named Yale College after Elihu Yale, a merchant who donated a small fortune to it.

In 1765, the Sons of Liberty was founded in Connecticut. The organization was at first intended to resist the Stamp Act of 1765 that taxed newspapers and other publications, but as dissatisfaction with Britain's treatment of its colonies grew, it became a resistance organization. By 1776, the only large community of pro-royalists, or Tories, was in Connecticut's southwestern region; otherwise, Connecticut almost entirely backed revolt against Britain. When war broke out, Connecticut contributed several thousand soldiers to the Continental army. No major battles were fought in Connecticut, but it was invaded four times, with British troops burning towns and killing civilians. In 1781, the British army captured about eighty American soldiers at Fort Griswold and massacred all of them.

Statehood

At the close of the American Revolution, in 1783, there was confusion among the states about matters such as trade, currency, and taxes. Connecticut enjoyed success as a manufacturing state and "Yankee peddlers" carried and sold Connecticut manufactured goods and imports in the other states. Connecticut itself had a decentralized government, with most political power resting in small communities. Only rich, landed men could vote. When the Constitutional Convention was held in Philadelphia to determine the future of the United States, Connecticut resisted the creation of a strong central government, but it was outvoted. The convention stalled on the type of legislature the new American government should have; one based on population would favor the states with bigger populations. Connecticut delegate Roger Sherman presented the Connecticut Compromise, which proposed dividing the legislature into two parts: one elected by population, the other elected on the basis of two senators from each state regardless of population, thus ensuring a degree of security for small states. This approach having been adopted, Connecticut in 1788 became the fifth state to ratify the new Constitution.

In 1818, Connecticut overhauled its Fundamental Orders, expanding the right to vote beyond landed men and providing a stronger central state government. This constitution would govern Connecticut until 1965. The 1818 constitution gave the state's cities, towns, and villages one or two representatives each to the state's assembly, regardless of population. The state capitol moved between New Haven and Hartford for nearly sixty years. In 1964, the United States Supreme Court ruled Connecticut's constitution unconstitutional, and at a state constitutional convention, legislators created a constitution providing for one man-one vote representation.

During the 1840s, Connecticut received a large number of Irish immigrants who were integrated into the state's manufacturing economy. By the beginning of the Civil War, Connecticut was a major arms manufacturing center that contributed many weapons to the Union army. The state had been a hotbed of antislavery sentiment in the antebellum years, and during the war, it contributed more troops, mostly volunteers, to the Union cause than any state except Massachusetts. In 1875, Hartford was chosen as the permanent home of state government and the capitol building there was finished in 1880. Influxes of immigrants arrived from eastern Europe and Italy, with Italian Americans becoming the largest ethnic group in the state.

The era from 1880 to the Great Depression was one of expansion and social change. In 1865, the were 500,000 people living in Connecticut; by 1900, there were 1,000,000. In 1870, the gross state product was $160,000,000; in 1900, the gross state product was $300,000,000. Immigrants from Europe were drawn to Connecticut because of jobs in mills and the small arms industry. In 1917, a submarine base was established in Groton, and the manufacturing of submarines became one of the state's biggest employers. Nuclear submarines were still made there at the turn of the twenty-first century.

While this growth was underway, Connecticut farms were failing, with farm families abandoning their homes for jobs in the city. The western countryside of Connecticut looked desolate, with old roads passing by empty homes and overgrown farmland. Yet, in about 1900, Connecticut began to attract artists who enjoyed the privacy of Connecticut country life and wealthy New Yorkers and Bostonians who could pick up large swaths of land cheaply and turn them into estates. With the advent of the automobile, much of rural Connecticut became bedroom communities for people who worked in New York or Massachusetts and then commuted in their cars to homes away from the noise of the city.

Modern Era

During the Great Depression of the 1930s, Connecticut suffered along with the rest of the nation. About one-fourth of the state's workers were unemployed and the areas of highest industrialization, especially in cities, were decaying. At this time, service industries such as insurance were becoming more important. During World War II, Connecticut's economy boomed as money for weapons poured in. The state was also a major manufacturer of submarines and aircraft engines. In 1954, the first nuclear submarine, the *Nautilus*, was launched at the shipyards in Groton.

A great disparity of wealth between the inner cities and the suburbs of Connecticut began during the 1980s and became acute in the 1970s as the state's middle class abandoned the central cities for the more secure and beautiful countryside.

Although African Americans made up only about 8 percent of the state's population, they were densely packed into cities. In 1967, a ferocious race riot in Hartford was followed by another in Bridgeport, the state's second and third largest cities—inspired by high unemployment among African Americans and a perception that African American needs were being neglected by the state and city governments. Afterward, efforts were made to revitalize city centers by making them tourist attractions and tourism became one of Connecticut's major sources of income.

During the 1990s the state's population declined, although many immigrants arrived from Southeast Asia. By the twenty-first century, the population was approximately 3.2 million people, the twenty-seventh largest state population in the United States. About 84 percent of the population was European American (exclusive of Hispanics), 8 percent African American, 6.5 percent Hispanic American, and 1.5 percent Asian American. Most of the population was centered in the cities, with agriculture accounting for only one percent of the state's revenue by 2001. Insurance and banking were the biggest employers, with employment in defense-related industries shrinking after the end of the Cold War. Even so, Connecticut was a major manufacturer of helicopters, aircraft engines, high technology electronics, and weapons. Growth in the financial and tourist industries in the 1990s began to change the state's economy, with people working in Connecticut while living in New York or Massachusetts. The per capita income in Connecticut is the highest of any state ($31,816 in 2000).

Much of the remaining original forest of Connecticut is in the northwest, but the forest has reasserted itself in many regions that had been cleared of trees by the 1800s. About one third of the state is covered by forest and the numerous state parks have become important attractions for campers and hikers, while the old towns have become attractions for tourists. The few descendants of the Pequots and Mohegans began operating casinos on their lands in the 1980s and 1990s, attracting tourists and pumping over $100 million in taxes annually to the state government.

BIBLIOGRAPHY

Allen, Thomas B. "Connecticut." *National Geographic* (February 1994): 64–93.

Brown, Barbara W., and James M. Rose. *Black Roots in Southeastern Connecticut, 1650–1900.* New London, Conn.: New London County Historical Society, 2001.

Dalin, David G., and Jonathan Rosenbaum. *Making a Life, Building a Community: A History of the Jews of Hartford.* New York: Holmes and Meier, 1997.

Dayton, Cornelia Hughes. *Women before the Bar: Gender, Law, and Society in Connecticut, 1639–1789.* Chapel Hill: University of North Carolina Press, 1995.

Dugas, Rene L., Sr. *Taftville, Connecticut, and the Industrial Revolution: The French Canadians in New England.* 2d ed. New London, Conn.: Rene L. Dugas, 2001.

Eisler, Kim Isaac. *Revenge of the Pequots: How a Small American Tribe Created the World's Most Profitable Casino.* New York: Simon and Schuster, 2001.

Grant, Ellsworth S. *Miracle of Connecticut.* Hartford: Connecticut Historical Society, 1997.

Grasso, Christopher. *A Speaking Aristocracy: Transforming Public Discourse in Eighteenth-Century Connecticut.* Chapel Hill: Published for the Omohundro Institute of Early American History and Culture by the University of North Carolina Press, 1999.

Hamblin, Charles P. *Connecticut Yankees at Gettysburg.* Edited by Walter L. Powell. Kent, Ohio: Kent State University Press, 1993.

Holbrook, Jay Mack. *Connecticut Colonists: Windsor 1635–1703.* Oxford, Mass.: Holbrook Research Institute, 1986.

Jones, Keith Marshal, III. *Farms of Farmingville: A Two-Century History of Twenty-Three Ridgefield, Connecticut, Farmhouses and the People Who Gave Them Life.* Ridgefield: Connecticut Colonel Publishing, 2001.

Klein, Woody. *Westport, Connecticut: The Story of a New England Town's Rise to Prominence.* Westport, Conn.: Greenwood, 2000.

Larkin, Susan G. *The Cos Cob Art Colony: Impressionists on the Connecticut Shore.* New Haven, Conn.: Yale University Press, 2001.

Mann, Bruce H. *Neighbors and Strangers: Law and Community in Early Connecticut.* Chapel Hill: University of North Carolina Press, 1987.

Philie, William L. *Change and Tradition: New Haven, Connecticut, 1780–1830.* New York: Garland, 1990.

Selesky, Harold E. *War and Society in Colonial Connecticut.* New Haven, Conn.: Yale University Press, 1990.

Siskind, Janet. *Rum and Axes: The Rise of a Connecticut Merchant Family, 1795–1850.* Ithaca, N.Y.: Cornell University Press, 2002.

Thomas, Peter A. *In the Maelstrom of Change: The Indian Trade and Cultural Process in the Middle Connecticut River Valley, 1635–1665.* New York: Garland, 1991.

Weaver, Glenn. *Jonathan Trumbull, Connecticut's Merchant Magistrate: 1710–1785.* Hartford: Connecticut Historical Society, 1997.

Wills, Charles A. *A Historical Album of Connecticut.* Brookfield, Conn.: Millbrook Press, 1995.

Kirk H. Beetz

See also **Pequot War; Riots; Sons of Liberty (American Revolution); Suburbanization; Tribes: Northeastern; Yale University.**

CONNECTICUT COMPROMISE, which was based on a proposal by jurist and politician Roger Sherman of CONNECTICUT, resolved an impasse in the Constitutional Convention of 1787 between large and small states over the apportionment of representation in the proposed senate. The larger states supported the Virginia Plan, which would create a bicameral legislature in which "the rights of suffrage . . . ought to be proportioned to the Quotas of contributions, or to the number of free inhabitants." Anticipating greater burdens from the centralization of power in a new national government, these states demanded a commensurate share of control. The small states, jealous of their welfare, refused to be moved from their demand for equality in a unicameral house. This was the fundamental problem of balance in a federation of states differing so greatly in size.

On 11 June, Sherman offered a compromise: two houses, one with equal representation for all states and the other with proportional representation based on population. The convention delegates adopted amendments to this proposal that required bills raising revenue to originate in the House of Representatives. The amendments also based representation in the House on total white population and three-fifths of the black population. Sherman's proposal was adopted in its amended form; this agreement has since been known as the Connecticut, or Great, Compromise.

BIBLIOGRAPHY

Collier, Christopher, and James L. Collier. *Decision in Philadelphia: The Constitutional Convention of 1787.* New York: Random House, 1986.

Farrand, Max, ed. *The Records of the Federal Convention of 1787.* Rev. ed., 4 vols. New Haven, Conn.: Yale University Press, 1937. The original edition was published in 3 vols., 1911.

Rakove, Jack N. *Original Meanings: Politics and Ideas in the Making of the Constitution.* New York: Knopf, 1996.

Rossiter, Clinton. *1787: The Grand Convention.* New York: Macmillan, 1966.

Theodore M. Whitfield/c. p.

CONNOLLY'S PLOT. In 1775 John Connolly, a Loyalist officer who had lived at Fort Pitt (Pittsburgh) for some years and knew the frontier situation, proposed to John Murray, Lord Dunmore, that Connolly should enroll a force of British troops and Indians at Detroit, capture Fort Pitt, march on Winchester, Virginia, and join Lord Dunmore in putting down the rebellion in Virginia. Dunmore and British general Thomas Gage both voiced support for the plan, whereupon Connolly set out for Detroit. George Washington had been warned, however, and sent word to the Maryland Committee of Safety. Connolly was captured on 20 November 1775 at Hagerstown, Maryland, and imprisoned in Philadelphia. Had it been successful, the plot might have caused western Indians to attack the frontier two years before they actually did.

BIBLIOGRAPHY

Burton, Clarence Monroe. "John Connolly, a Tory of the Revolution." *American Antiquarian Society Proceedings* 20 (1911).

Nelson, William H. *The American Tory.* 1961. Reprint, Boston: Northeastern University Press, 1992.

Thwaites, R. G., and Louise P. Kellogg. *The Revolution on the Upper Ohio, 1775–1777.* 1908. Reprint, Salem, Mass.: Higginson Book Company, 1997.

Louise Phelps Kellogg / T. D.

See also **Dunmore's War; Indians in the Revolution; Loyalists.**

CONQUISTADORES. Spain authorized military expeditions by *conquistadores* (conquerors) in the Americas. The conquistadores were armies typically numbering a thousand soldiers, but the term denotes primarily the intrepid leaders of these expeditions. Driven by an insatiable booty mentality reminiscent of medieval crusaders, they expected to secure entitlement, land, power, and tributes during the Spanish *entrada* (entrance) of the sixteenth century.

As the Spanish penetrated the American mainland, fantastic stories of Cíbola, Gran Quivira, El Dorado, fountains of youth, and amazon women fired their imaginations. Hernán Cortés in 1519 vanquished the Aztecs of Tenochtitlán with the assistance of rival Natives. Juan Ponce de León, who sailed around Florida in 1513, was encouraged by Cortés's triumph to undertake a return expedition to the peninsula in 1521. He died from wounds received in a fight with the Calusas. To the south, the conquest of the Incas by Francisco Pizarro in 1532 revivified the visions of grandeur.

In 1528, Pánfilo de Narváez surveyed the Gulf Coast from Florida to Texas, but Apalachee archers and a tempest brought the mission to an end. Four castaways, including Álvar Núñez Cabeza de Vaca, Alonso del Castillo, Andrés Dorantes, and the black slave Esteban, survived and managed to reach Galveston Island. They traveled among the Natives until 1536, when Spanish slave hunters found them in the province of Sinaloa, Mexico. In 1539, their observations became entangled with the claims of the Franciscan Fray Marcos de Niza regarding the treasures of Cíbola to intensify the allure of the "northern mystery."

Further expeditions pushed the frontiers of the Spanish empire from Georgia to New Mexico. In 1539, Hernando de Soto, a seasoned veteran of the Incan conquest, maneuvered nine ships and more than six hundred soldiers on a journey in search of another Cuzco. After landing in Florida, De Soto and his companions literally fought their way through the woodlands. They crossed the Mississippi River about twenty-five miles below Memphis and advanced into Arkansas and Oklahoma. However, De Soto died from an illness in 1542. His men left his body at the river before returning to New Spain empty-handed. Francisco Vásquez de Coronado in 1540 commanded an army that crossed the Rio Grande and attacked the Pueblo Indians. Coronado dispatched several reconnaissance parties, and after a two-year quest that ended in the midcontinent grasslands, he conceded that there were no golden cities in North America. In 1598 the last conquistadore, Juan de Oñate, directed a colonization venture into Pueblo lands, thus initiating a new phase of mission building and permanent occupation.

From the Andes Mountains to the Grand Canyon, the conquistadores unleashed a catastrophe of a magnitude unknown before the sixteenth century. Although the Spanish Orders for New Discoveries in 1573 curbed the atrocities, the explorers left behind smallpox, malaria, measles, and sexually transmitted diseases. Their discoveries unveiled the physical and cultural geography of Native America, but their presence turned the New World upside down.

BIBLIOGRAPHY

Stannard, David E. *American Holocaust: Columbus and the Conquest of the New World.* New York: Oxford University Press, 1992.

Thomas, Hugh. *Who's Who of the Conquistadors.* London: Cassell, 2000.

Weber, David J. *The Spanish Frontier in North America.* New Haven, Conn.: Yale University Press, 1992.

Wood, Michael. *Conquistadors.* Berkeley: University of California Press, 2000.

Brad D. Lookingbill

See also **Coronado Expeditions; Explorations and Expeditions: Spanish; Oñate, Juan de, Explorations and Settlements of; Western Exploration.**

CONSCIENCE WHIGS. A New England–based, Massachusetts-centered faction of the Whig party, the Conscience Whigs opposed the annexation of Texas and the Mexican War because they feared the extension of slavery to new territories would endanger the republic. In Massachusetts, young, politically ambitious Conscience

Whigs defined themselves in opposition to Old Line or Cotton Whigs, who wished to downplay the slavery issue in order to preserve both sectional harmony and the lucrative cotton trade with the southern states. Beginning in 1846 bitter debates over the WILMOT PROVISO gradually split the national Whig party and divided northern Whig state parties. Conscience Whigs consistently attacked slavery as immoral and argued that antislavery principles were more important than party loyalty. By the summer of 1848 numerous Conscience Whigs, including Charles Francis Adams and Charles Sumner of Massachusetts, had bolted their old party to help form the national Free Soil Party. Cotton Whigs embraced the COMPROMISE OF 1850 and declared the slavery issue dead, but former Conscience Whigs continued to charge that New England's Whig businessmen supported the economic interests of southern slaveholders. Over Cotton Whig protests, in spring 1851 the Massachusetts legislature sent Sumner to the United States Senate, where he subsequently helped lead Free Soil, and after 1854, Republican Party antislavery efforts.

BIBLIOGRAPHY

Brauer, Kinley J. *Cotton versus Conscience: Massachusetts Whig Politics and Southwestern Expansion, 1843–1848.* Lexington: University of Kentucky Press, 1967.

Formisano, Ronald P. *The Transformation of Political Culture: Massachusetts Parties, 1790s–1840s.* New York: Oxford University Press, 1983.

O'Connor, Thomas H. *Lords of the Loom: The Cotton Whigs and the Coming Of the Civil War.* New York: Scribner's, 1968.

Julienne L. Wood

See also **Free Soil Party; Whig Party.**

CONSCIENTIOUS OBJECTORS.

Unlike draft resisters or evaders, conscientious objectors make no secret of their desire not to participate in military service. Their objections rest on publicly stated and defended principles. Never a large number, conscientious objectors have always been more important as a symbol, especially during unpopular wars like Vietnam.

Conscientious objection has traditionally been closely related to pacifist religious groups. As early as 1661, the colony of Massachusetts made provisions for exempting men from military service on religious grounds. In 1790 a measure to guarantee the right of conscientious objection in the Bill of Rights passed the House but failed to pass in the Senate despite the support of James Madison. The Quakers received a group exemption in Pennsylvania in 1701 from William Penn. Other groups such as the Mennonites and the Dunkards (who ironically had a church badly damaged at the 1862 Civil War Battle of Antietam) received similar exemptions. During the Civil War, both sides allowed for conscientious objection if the objector could provide a substitute or pay a fine. In this manner, conscientious objectors differed little from anyone else trying to evade service. Despite their legal protection, conscientious objectors inevitably became objects of scorn and targets of charges of treason.

The Selective Service Act of 1917 recognized conscientious objectors and did not require them to bear arms. Men who belonged to historically pacifistic religious groups had guaranteed access to conscientious objector status. Nevertheless, the act authorized President Woodrow Wilson to conscript conscientious objectors for noncombatant service. Many men refused even this service, and the federal government tried 450 men for refusal to serve. Some received prison terms as long as twenty-five years, though nearly all received amnesty in 1919. Almost 4,000 men accepted the government's offer of noncombatant service, often in labor camps whose arduous routines resembled those of prison work gangs. Despite the active opposition of some groups to American entry into World War I, conscientious objectors amounted to just .0023 percent of all men required to register.

The numbers were also quite small in World War II, with conscientious objectors comprising just .0029 percent of all men required to register. Recognition of conscientious objector status became a hallmark of liberal ideology. None of the Axis powers recognized conscientious objection, nor did the Soviet Union. The United States and Great Britain, on the other hand, widened their definitions to include, in the United States, men with "religious training and belief" that compelled them to avoid military service. A connection with religion thus remained, but was broadened to encompass men who were not members of traditionally pacifistic religious groups like the Quakers.

Two court cases attempted to broaden the justification of conscientious objection beyond solely religious grounds to social, political, and intellectual grounds. In both cases (*United States v. Kauten*, 1943, and *Berman v. United States*, 1946), the courts disallowed nonreligious grounds for conscientious objection. As in World War I, most conscientious objectors served in work camps that resembled the Department of Corrections more than the Department of the Army. Only 6 percent of the nation's 100,000 conscientious objectors served any time in prison.

New draft legislation passed in 1948 specifically allowed for conscientious objection. In the same year, the Central Committee for Conscientious Objectors was founded, supplementing the National Interreligious Service Board for Conscientious Objectors, which had been founded in 1940. Between 1948 and 1965, the work camp model of alternate service disappeared in favor of service in hospitals or mental institutions. The number of conscientious objectors grew in proportion to those drafted but remained low. Fewer than 35,000 men declared conscientious objector status between 1948 and 1965.

In 1965 the Supreme Court heard the landmark conscientious objection case of *United States v. Seeger*. The two defendants claimed religious exemption but were not members of traditional pacifist religious groups and had no religious training as required under the 1948 legislation. One defendant professed that he believed in a "supreme reality" while the other asserted belief in "a universal reality." The court ruled that an individual's understanding of his own religious beliefs must be considered when determining conscientious objector status. The case greatly expanded the religious basis for conscientious objection to incorporate "people with general theistic belief systems" whether or not they had any formal religious training. The Court also included for the first time "nontraditional variances" of pacifist religious expression such as Judaism, Islam, and Buddhism.

The unpopularity of the Vietnam War increased both the number and the visibility of conscientious objectors. Between 1965 and 1970 more than 170,000 registrants applied for conscientious objector status. The *Seeger* ruling did not have a wide impact on conscientious objection because local draft boards were free to interpret the ruling as they saw fit. The most celebrated case was that of boxer Muhammad Ali, who in 1966 claimed that military service was inconsistent with his conversion to Islam. Ali should have been covered under *Seeger*, but his local draft board found his beliefs to be insincere and sentenced him to five years in prison. He remained free on bond until his case was overturned in 1971, but hundreds of Muslims (especially black Muslims) went to jail because courts refused to accept their religion as the basis for conscientious objection.

Men seeking conscientious objection status during the Vietnam era were helped by lawyers who specialized in getting the exemptions. Many men saw conscientious objection in the Vietnam period less as a principled stand on religious grounds than as a legal way out of service. Good draft lawyers were well within the financial reach of most men from middle-class families, and they could at least tie up the conscription system with paperwork for months or even years. Most were successful in gaining conscientious objector status for their clients, who were normally ordered to perform an alternative service of two years of low-paying work in the public sector in a location beyond commuting distance from home. In reality, draft boards were so overwhelmed by their responsibilities that supervision of conscientious objectors was minimal.

Many men genuinely objected to the war in Vietnam on moral, but not religious, grounds. No law covered their beliefs until *Welsh v. United States* (1970). In that ruling, the Supreme Court held that a man could claim conscientious objector status based on the "depth and fervency" of his beliefs, even if they were not religious in character. Welsh himself had declared that his objection to Vietnam was based on historical and sociological grounds.

During the Gulf War of 1990–1991, a new problem arose as more than 2,000 men and women already in uniform claimed conscientious objection. Previously, the vast majority of cases revolved around the desire to avoid military service. These cases involved men and women already in the service who desired to avoid a combat theater. Since they had voluntarily enlisted (conscription having ended in 1973), they could not claim that military service was inconsistent with deeply held beliefs. The army chose to reassign or release most conscientious objectors, but the Marine Corps imprisoned fifty. As previously, the numbers remained small, but conscientious objectors maintained a visibility far beyond their size as America wrestled with the question of how to exempt those whose beliefs clash with their legal obligations to serve.

BIBLIOGRAPHY

Baskir, Lawrence M., and William A. Strauss. *Chance and Circumstance: The Draft, the War, and the Vietnam Generation.* New York: Vintage, 1978.

Frazer, Heather, and John O'Sullivan. *We Have Just Begun to Fight: An Oral History of Conscientious Objectors in Civilian Public Service During World War II.* New York: Twayne, 1996.

Goossen, Rachel Waltner. *Women Against the Good War: Conscientious Objection and Gender on the American Home Front 1941–1947.* Chapel Hill: University of North Carolina Press, 1997.

Moskos, Charles, and John Whiteclay Chambers II, eds. *The New Conscientious Objection: From Sacred to Secular Resistance.* New York: Oxford University Press, 1993.

Schlissel, Lillian, ed. *Conscience in America: A Documentary History of Conscientious Objection in America, 1757–1967.* New York: Dutton, 1968.

Michael S. Neiberg

See also **Pacifism.**

CONSCRIPTION AND RECRUITMENT.

The U.S. armed services fills most of its manpower needs either through draft or recruitment. The draft is the selection of some of the male population for compulsory military service. It is a peculiarly American concept, distinct from the European practice of conscription, which involves the regularized training of the entire male population, generation after generation. But since the reorganization of the armed forces for peacetime service in 1787, the U.S. armed services have depended for the greatest number of their troops on recruitment by voluntary enlistment. Throughout the history of the armed services, the number of recruits at any given time has varied greatly.

The practices of universal military training and of compulsory military service in time of emergency were established in the United States under the legal systems of all the colonial powers. But universal military training did not remain in practice for very long in the new nation. The colonies used compulsory militia laws sporadically during the Revolution both for local defense and for support of the Continental army. Individual colonies conducted selection of eligibles, often by use of a lottery, yet draftees could avoid service in the Continental force by

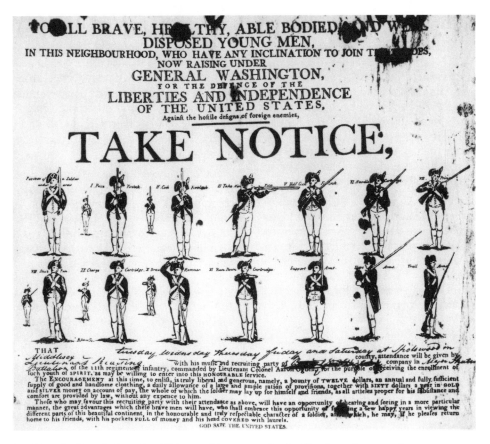

Looking for Revolutionaries. This recruiting poster for the Continental army seeks young men to help General George Washington, "for the defence of the liberties and independence of the United States, against the hostile designs of foreign enemies." LIBRARY OF CONGRESS

hiring a substitute or by direct payment of a fee. The new states wrote compulsory universal-militia service into their constitutions, and the concept remains a force in the majority of state codes to the present day. Additionally, the CONSTITUTION OF THE UNITED STATES provides for the training of state militias under standards to be prescribed by Congress. The Militia Act of 8 May 1792 provided a broad organizational structure for the militia but contained no means of enforcing a program of training. The inadequacies of that legislation and the disappearance of any continuing military threat in the more populous eastern states led to disintegration of the old universal-militia concept.

From the end of the Revolution until 1863, American military manpower procurement for the regular services was based almost entirely on volunteers. Although the able-bodied manpower of the states was still enrolled in the militia and reported more or less regularly, the only viable units of the militia were also composed entirely of volunteers. During the MEXICAN-AMERICAN WAR (1846–1848), the United States also mustered companies of Texas Rangers, the law enforcement body of the Republic of Texas, into the federal service for scouting, patrol, and raiding missions.

During the Civil War, the armies of both the Union and the Confederacy were organized on the same basis—a mass of state volunteer militia units organized around a nucleus of regulars from the prewar U.S. Army. The initial surge of enthusiasm for war on both sides wore off in the bloody campaigns of 1861 and 1862. Thereafter, the states sought to keep their original regiments up to strength and to create new units by resorting to the Revolutionary War formula of compulsion and bounties. Once again, those selected in the state lotteries could avoid service by hiring a substitute or by payment of a fee. Union recruitment involved, in many instances, paying recruits a sum of money for joining, a bounty. This practice was ineffective, because many people collected the money and then paid others only a small portion of it to take their places on the rolls.

When neither voluntary enlistment nor the erratic pattern of state compulsory service produced the manpower needed, both the North and the South resorted to a federal draft. The southern Congress enacted a draft in 1862. The U.S. Congress passed a militia law that same year and implemented a draft the next year through the Enrollment Act of 1863. The army administered the Union's Civil War draft through presidential quotas assigned to each congressional district. Voluntary enlistments were credited against the district quotas, with selection of the remainder by lot. The federal system continued to authorize hiring substitutes or paying fees in lieu of service. Resentment against the gross economic discrimination of the state system flared into open violence when those inequities were continued and expanded under the federal draft. Bitter opposition to the draft continued through the rest of the war. Only about 6 percent of the Union army was a direct product of the draft. The indirect pressures, notably through operation of the substitution and bounty systems, produced a substantially larger total of enlistments.

From the end of the Civil War until 1903, military manpower procurement reverted to the prewar voluntary system. During the SPANISH-AMERICAN WAR the army met its manpower needs by individual voluntary enlistments and by accepting entire units from the state volunteer militias as "U.S. Volunteers." The best-known volunteer force was Theodore Roosevelt's Rough Riders. The standing navy carried out most of the fighting and the decisive battles of the war.

Between 1903 and 1916, Congress enacted a number of changes in American military policy that helped lay the foundation for an army that, once mobilized, could be supported only by a federal draft. It brought the state volunteer militia—by now known as the National Guard—under greater federal control. It also created a federal military reserve under the direct control of the War and Navy departments. The idea behind these changes was that over a prolonged period of mobilization, the infusion of draft-produced replacements and the products of the then newly established Reserve Officer Training Corps would gradually eliminate the distinctions between units originally identified with the regular army, the National Guard, and the "national army" formed subsequent to mobilization. These changes would produce a much different force from the aggregation of state militias envisaged by the framers of the Constitution.

Organization of an effective army general staff as part of the pre–World War I reforms helped to make possible a thorough review of the mistakes of the Civil War draft and the development of plans for a more efficient and a more equitable system. These plans had scarcely been formulated when they were ordered into effect by the Selective Service Act of 1917. The army general staff developed manpower requirements and apportioned them as state quotas. A lottery determined the order of induction. And local civilian boards organized under federally appointed state directors and operating under uniform federal regulations, rather than soldiers as was the case during the Civil War, administered selection and enrollment. Civilians also established the categories of deferment and acted on appeals. The act outlawed the hiring of substitutes and the payment of bounties.

Despite the relatively short duration of American participation in WORLD WAR I, the diffusion of drafted men throughout all units of the army was well under way at the time of the armistice. Of approximately 4 million men under arms, over half were draftees. The Supreme Court held that the World War I draft was constitutional (*Arver v. United States* [1918]). And in general, the public accepted the new Selective Service program as fair and reasonable. But opposition to any continuing program of compulsory service in peacetime continued to be overwhelming, and the several proposals to continue the program got nowhere.

Twenty years later, the fall of France and the worsening of U.S. relations with Japan prompted Congress to enact the nation's first peacetime draft—the Selective Training and Service Act of 1940. This act incorporated all the principal features of the World War I model. The impact of the WORLD WAR II draft was pervasive. Over 10 million men were inducted, representing the most extensive mobilization of the nation's manpower in its history. Draftees were assigned to all the armed services, including the U.S. Navy and Marine Corps—services that had previously maintained themselves by voluntary recruitment even in time of war. By 1946 the armed forces were a homogeneous instrument of federal power. That power represented a blend of all the traditional elements of American military strength, both state and federal, but the influence of the federal draft was at once dominant and indispensable.

With the exception of one year (March 1947 to March 1948), the draft was in continuous operation from 1940 to early January 1973. The administrative machinery established during World War II was modified but never dismantled. From 1940 until 1967, the Selective Service System was geared to the requirements of total war and total mobilization. Therein lay the seeds of political turmoil. The system's reputation for fairness had been built upon the near total use of the nation's manpower during the two world wars. The military manpower requirements of the Korean and Vietnam conflicts were much smaller. Requirements during the intervals of international tension between those wars were even more limited. Successive administrations chose to deal with this problem by liberalizing deferments, thereby reducing the pool of eligibles to the size needed.

By the end of the 1960s, the pool of those eligible for the draft came to consist largely of young men who had not chosen to marry and to father a child in their teens, who were not successfully enrolled in a college or university, who had not enlisted in the National Guard or reserve forces, and who, upon graduation from college, had not taken jobs in teaching or in one of the other exempted occupations. So long as this system resulted only in a period of active service with little or no personal risk, its obvious inequities were tolerated or ignored. But, as the manpower requirements of the VIETNAM WAR and the personal risks of service increased, the consequences of the deferment policies could no longer be accepted. A significant percentage of draftees were poor and black. By 1967, Martin Luther King and the leaders of the STUDENT

NONVIOLENT COORDINATING COMMITTEE supported resistance to the draft. The initial response by the successive administrations of presidents Lyndon B. Johnson and Richard M. Nixon was a return to the lottery as a substitute for some of the most obviously discriminatory deferments. The counterresponse was an escalation of protest and resistence.

On 27 January 1973 the Nixon administration ended the draft but maintained the Selective Service System in a standby, or "zero draft," status. The manpower requirements of the active and reserve forces were met by large increases in pay and related incentives and expanded job training opportunities. In 1972 the navy offered training in fifteen occupational categories and had sixty-six schools and courses. The air force offered four major fields of study and guaranteed the availability of assignments in any field in which the recruit qualified on the aptitude exams. An army recruit in the 1970s could also choose from among four specialized fields of study. The army also devised a new recruiting slogan to replace the World War I legend "Uncle Same Wants You!" The new slogan—"Today's Army Wants to Join You"—was designed to avoid the impersonality of the old-style recruitment as well as the feeling of authority, which many young people found objectionable.

Beginning with the decline in inductions in 1972, the National Guard and reserve forces experienced great difficulty in maintaining strength. Even when total authorizations were met, imbalances existed between units, and the quality of the recruits was subject to frequent criticism. Critics in Congress and elsewhere claimed that an outbreak of violence and sabotage aboard ships of the U.S. Navy in 1972 reflected a reduction in moral and mental standards in order to meet recruiting goals. They also alleged that in order to create an appearance of success, the authorized manpower of the army was being adjusted steadily downward to conform to the number of recruits available. After local draft boards were dismantled in 1973, the diversion of cadres from training to recruiting duties further weakend unit performance. And critics charged that reliance on economic incentives to generate volunteers was the old Civil War substitution system in a new and vastly more expensive form.

With the all-volunteer force plagued by inadequate numbers and disproportionate representation of minorities, the administration of President Jimmy Carter reinstituted compulsory draft registration for eighteen-year-old males in 1980, partly as a political response to the Soviet invasion of Afghanistan. In *Rostker v. Goldberg* (1981) the Supreme Court held that the registration of only men and not women was constitutional because women could not be assigned to combat duty. About 9 percent of those men required to register failed to do so. President Ronald Reagan, who had campaigned against the draft as an unnecessary infringement on individual liberty, nonetheless continued compulsory registration and prosecuted those who refused to register. Congress subsequently tied registration to federal education benefits.

Reagan relied on higher pay to increase enlistments. Some observers, however, urged a return to the draft to ensure that the armed forces were socially representative and to overcome the isolation of the military from society. Opponents continued to characterize the draft as undemocratic, expensive, and unprofessional. Furthermore, the GENERAL ACCOUNTING OFFICE reported that the all-volunteer force cost much less than conscript forces. The end of the COLD WAR temporarily muted the debate, but it reemerged at the end of the twentieth century in calls for a period of mandatory national service for young adults either in the military or through a civilian service organization such as the PEACE CORPS. The successes of the all-volunteer force in the Gulf War of 1991 and in the Afghanistan War of 2002 did not necessarily settle the question of how armed forces should be raised in a post–Cold War era.

BIBLIOGRAPHY

Bernstein, Iver. *The New York City Draft Riots: Their Significance for American Society and Politics in the Age of the Civil War.* New York: Oxford University Press, 1989.

Cohen, Eliot A. *Citizens and Soldiers: The Dilemmas of Military Service.* Ithaca, N.Y.: Cornell University Press, 1985.

Dunnigan, James F., and Raymond Macedonia. *Getting It Right: American Military Reforms After Vietnam to the Persian Gulf and Beyond.* New York: Morrow, 1993.

Flynn, George Q. *The Draft 1940–1973.* Lawrence: University Press of Kansas, 1993.

Keene, Jennifer D. *Doughboys, the Great War, and the Remaking of America.* Baltimore: Johns Hopkins University Press, 2001.

Moore, Albert Burton. *Conscription and Conflict in the Confederacy.* Columbia: University of South Carolina Press, 1996.

Murdock, Eugene Converse. *One Million Men: The Civil War Draft in the North.* Madison: State Historical Society of Wisconsin, 1971.

Segal, David R. *Recruiting for Uncle Sam: Citizenship and Military Manpower Policy.* Lawrence: University Press of Kansas, 1989.

Small, Melvin, and William D. Hoover, eds. *Give Peace a Chance: Exploring the Vietnam Antiwar Movement. Essays from the Charles DeBenedetti Memorial Conference.* Syracuse, N.Y.: Syracuse University Press, 1992.

J. Garry Clifford
William V. Kennedy
Loring D. Wilson/c. p.

See also **Civil War; Military Service and Minorities: African Americans; Militias; Minutemen; National Guard; Persian Gulf War of 1991; Reserve Officers' Training Corps (ROTC); Rough Riders; Substitutes, Civil War; Texas Rangers; Volunteer Army; Women in Military Service;** *and vol. 9:* **Pardon for Vietnam Draft Evaders.**

CONSERVATION is the term coined by the forester Gifford Pinchot in 1907 to describe the philosophy that the environment must be managed to assure adequate supplies of natural resources for present and future generations. Several other definitions of conservation exist, and an examination of the evolution of the conservation movement in the United States may help elucidate how and why the term has come to have different meanings for different people at different times.

Utilitarian Conservationism

Throughout most of American history, the prevailing attitude toward the natural environment was that it was something to be subdued and used for the good of humankind. This exploitative ethos was grounded partly in the Judeo-Christian tradition that gave humans "dominion . . . over every living thing." The perception that the continent was endowed with limitless natural resources and the dogma of free enterprise with the concomitant view that private property was sacrosanct and beyond the scope of government regulation also encouraged exploitation. Accordingly, as the nation expanded westward, hunters, loggers, miners, ranchers, and settlers heedlessly laid waste to the country's wildlife, forests, minerals, grasslands, and soil in the name of progress, civilization, and manifest destiny.

By the mid-nineteenth century, a few scattered individuals foresaw the dangers of such practices. In 1832, for example, the artist George Catlin warned in *North American Indians* that the American wilderness eventually would vanish unless subject to formal preservation, and he consequently proposed setting aside a large area of the West as a national park where Indians and wildlife could survive. In the following decade, the transcendentalist Henry David Thoreau castigated his fellow citizens for prizing only the material potential of the landscape and urged preservation of portions of the countryside in their pristine states. In 1864, the geographer George Perkins Marsh traced in *Man and Nature* the disastrous consequences of deforestation in terms of flooding, soil erosion, and degradation of the water supply and implored society to take responsibility for its actions. In 1878, the geographer John Wesley Powell issued his *Report on the Lands of the Arid Region of the United States*, in which he advised settlement of the West in a planned manner that took account of the constraints of the environment. In 1872, Congress established Yellowstone National Park, the country's and the world's first national park, to protect the area's unique geysers and geological formations.

But the creation of Yellowstone National Park was an anomaly, and farsighted people like Catlin, Marsh, and Powell were lone voices crying in the rapidly diminishing wilderness. Not until the late nineteenth century, when it was no longer possible to ignore the evidence that the country's natural resources were not in fact limitless, did those voices turn into a chorus. It is not insignificant that this occurred at the same time that the accelerated settlement of the West led the Census Bureau to proclaim the closing of the frontier in 1890. In addition, in this era the burgeoning cities were vacuuming their hinterlands of resources, the increased pace of industrialization was depleting the nation's raw materials, the ownership of resources was concentrating in fewer and fewer hands, a newly imperialistic United States required ever greater material holdings to stoke its military and economic engines, and the rising rate of immigration seemed to increase competition for assets. It accordingly dawned on forward-looking policymakers that what was left of the public domain would have to be administered in a more thoughtful and planned manner if future generations were to avail themselves of nature's bounty.

Conserving wildlife. Persons whose work or avocation brought them in contact with wildlife were among the first to manifest a conservationist ethic. Ornithologists, mammalogists, foresters, and sportspeople became increasingly concerned that North America's game animals were dwindling in number drastically. The numbers were decreasing because the advancing tide of settlement caused widespread habitat destruction and also because it was in the immediate financial interest of many Americans, for example, farmers, tanners, milliners, furriers, and market hunters, to kill as many wild animals as possible. As a result, several species of North American game had been exterminated by the beginning of the twentieth century, and the outlook was bleak for a number of other animals.

In 1887, Theodore Roosevelt founded and became first president of the exclusive Boone and Crockett Club, with membership limited to an elite core of one hundred big-game hunters. Roosevelt's most important successors as president of the club were George Bird Grinnell, a famous ethnologist and the influential editor of the nation's foremost periodical for sportspeople, *Forest and Stream*; and Madison Grant, an amateur anthropologist and the powerful chairman of the New York Zoological Society. Aristocratic sportspeople like Roosevelt, Grinnell, and Grant accepted that those in a position of power and prominence were obligated to husband the nation's resources for the benefit of their less-enlightened compatriots. They set about convincing their fellow sportspeople that, if big-game hunting were to survive beyond the nineteenth century, they would have to lobby for restrictive game laws. Consequently, the Boone and Crockett Club was transformed from an association of gentleman hunters into one of the seminal conservation organizations in the United States. To implement its agenda, the club's members cultivated key legislators, entertained important newspaper editors, submitted articles to influential journals, and appeared frequently before congressional committees. Within a few years, a number of other organizations devoted to conservation joined the Boone and Crockett Club on the national scene, and together they racked up a number of legislative victories for wildlife protection. Many species that had been headed toward extinction at the beginning of the twentieth century were relatively common by the end of the century.

But the legislative successes of the conservationists and the proliferating number of organizations devoted to wildlife protection did not ensure the popularity of the conservation movement at the dawn of the twentieth century. The vast majority of the American people still looked upon conservationists as effete "sentimentalists" and aristocratic "busybodies" who threatened the right of average Americans, especially the hard-working hunters, trappers, loggers, ranchers, and miners of the West, to benefit from the country's public resources. Conservationists countered that, aside from any sob sister concern about wild animals, the true economic interests of most westerners lay in preserving rather than using the wildlife and resources of their region. In the long term, far more people could make far more money in guiding, lodging, rafting, and outfitting than in market hunting, clear-cutting, and strip mining. But the conservationists were few in number; not until the 1920s did the conservation organization the Izaak Walton League attract a mass membership. Conservationists were still part of a narrow-gauged effort that had succeeded so far precisely because it was composed of a small but well-connected elite with ready access to the corridors of power in Washington, D.C., and certain state capitals.

Fortuitously for the perpetuation of the conservation movement, the founder of the Boone and Crockett Club ascended to the U.S. presidency in 1901. During his tenure in office, President Roosevelt vigorously espoused conservation and transformed the previously esoteric philosophy into a popular movement. In addition to making wildlife protection an important priority of the federal government, Roosevelt also raised the public's consciousness about the need to conserve the nation's forests and to protect its water resources.

Conserving forests and water. From its inception, the federal government had pursued an energetic policy of transferring into private hands the vast quantities of land, known as the "public domain," it had obtained as a result of the nation's westward expansion. A variety of disposal laws encouraged land speculators, railroad magnates, cattle kings, mining interests, timber syndicates, and others to lease, purchase, develop, or otherwise acquire "usable" areas of the public domain. Toward the end of the nineteenth century, however, conservationists began urging the government to "withdraw" areas of particular value from the operation of the disposal laws so they could be permanently protected under the control of the federal government. The creation of Yellowstone National Park provided the model for the practice of withdrawing discrete areas from the public domain to preserve unique qualities. The next major step in this process was the Forest Reserve Act of 1891, which authorized the president to protect areas covered wholly or in part by trees. The creation by executive order of such forest reserves, which became known as the national forests, would put those

lands beyond the reach of the loggers who were decimating the nation's timberland to meet Americans' unquenchable demand for wood to build their homes and for fuel to run their steamboats, locomotives, and factories. Presidents Benjamin Harrison and Grover Cleveland proceeded to set aside 38 million acres of public land as forest reserves, all in the western part of the country, as the East had long since been denuded of its old-growth forests.

The forest reserves were supported by a number of groups, including wildlife organizations, who appreciated that forests provide habitat for fauna; hydrologists, who understood that forests protect watersheds and temper flooding; and agronomists, who realized that trees block the wind and prevent soil erosion. But the forest reserves were extremely unpopular in the West, where the average citizen, remarked Roosevelt, had always had but one thought about a tree—to cut it down. Westerners bitterly resented the federal "lock up" of public lands and grew increasingly angry over the magnitude of presidential withdrawals. Politicians, including President William McKinley, noted the level of the westerners' enmity and began listening attentively to their demand that the forest reserves be restored to public sale.

When Roosevelt became president, he was fully determined not just to retain but to expand the nation's forest reserves. He and his close friend Pinchot, the head of the U.S. Forest Service, worked together to create many new forest reserves, and by the time Roosevelt left office in 1909, he had quadrupled the extent of the national forests to 172 million acres. But Pinchot correctly feared that future presidents might be less sympathetic to forest conservation than Roosevelt. He understood that, if the reserves were to be protected in perpetuity, the opposition of the West would have to be taken into consideration. Accordingly, he explained to suspicious westerners that the federal government had no intention of locking up the forests forever. Rather, he and Roosevelt simply sought to replace wasteful, short-term exploitation by selfish lumber barons with efficient, long-term management by the federal government. In Pinchot's vision, forests, if protected properly and harvested judiciously, could be renewable resources that would last forever. Just as the Boone and Crockett Club wanted to save animals now so they could be hunted later, so Pinchot's Forest Service wanted to conserve trees now so they could be harvested later.

For Pinchot, conserving forests was a matter of both fiscal prudence and fealty to the tenets of democracy. "The natural resources," Pinchot declared, "must be developed and preserved for the benefit of the many, and not merely for the profit of a few. Conservation means the greatest good to the greatest number for the longest time" (*Breaking New Ground*, pp. 46–48). He furthermore pointed out that forests, if wisely managed, not only would return crops of timber but also would accommodate land for grazing and, most importantly, protect watersheds that could be used for irrigation. Thus, forest reserves would benefit local, that is, western, residents most of all and were not just a pet cause of effete tree lovers. To drive home the point, Pinchot changed the name of the forest reserves to "national forests." The former term implied that the trees were being reserved from the nation's use, while the latter implied they were being conserved for the nation's use. "The object of our forest policy," repeated Pinchot, "is not to preserve the forests because they are beautiful. . . . The forests are to be used by man. Every other consideration comes secondary" (Hays, *Conservation*, p. 42). It was not at all illogical therefore that in 1905 the national forests were removed from the jurisdiction of the Interior Department and placed under the control of the Department of Agriculture. "Forestry," explained Pinchot, "is tree farming" (*Breaking New Ground*, p. 31).

Pinchot's defense of the national forests provided the manifesto of the nascent conservation movement, which sought to "conserve" the resources of the nation in the present to ensure a supply in the future. Pinchot's philosophy fit well the tenor of the times, for conservationism mirrored the progressives' enthrallment with scientific management, rational use of resources, and long-term planning by the federal government. This helps explain why the public so rapidly embraced the concept of conservation during the Roosevelt administration and why the public eagerly agreed with the president that it was not just wildlife and trees that needed to be conserved. Water, for example, was now seen as a resource worthy of conservation, and Congress passed the Newlands Reclamation Act (1902) to fund water reclamation projects in arid western states. In 1907, the government created the Inland Waterways Commission to oversee multiple-purpose river development, including irrigation, navigation, flood control, and power creation.

In addition, President Roosevelt set aside millions of acres of coal, phosphate, and other mineral reserves to prevent private exploitation, and he kept the momentum going by hosting the historic White House Governor's Conference on Conservation in 1908 to persuade state governments and corporations of the importance of conservation. The Governor's Conference led in turn to the creation of conservation commissions in forty-one states, and it also appointed the National Conservation Commission, chaired by Pinchot, to inventory the nation's resources as a guide to future policy decisions.

Aesthetic Preservationism
President Roosevelt accepted the utilitarian rationale for conserving trees. "These [forest] reserves," he stated unequivocally, "are created purely for economic purposes" ("Wilderness Reserves," p. 23). He reminded Congress that "forest protection is not an end in itself: it is a means to increase and sustain the resources of our country and the industries which depend on them. The preservation of our forests is an imperative business necessity" (Pinchot, *Breaking New Ground*, p. 190).

But in conserving trees, Roosevelt was also motivated by a sentimental consideration, his genuine love of nature. While his first priority was utilitarian, he also wished to have some forested areas remain in their natural conditions, untouched by the ax of the logger, no matter how "inefficient" such a policy would be. "In addition . . . to the economic use of the wilderness," he wrote, "it is wise here and there to keep selected portions of it . . . in a state of nature . . . for the sake of preserving all its beauties and wonders unspoiled by greedy and shortsighted vandalism" ("Wilderness Reserves," pp. 23–24).

Roosevelt's conflicting motives for expanding the national forests highlight the fact that in the early twentieth century the growing conservation movement was actually fed by two different streams. On one side were the utilitarian conservationists, epitomized by Pinchot, who were interested in conserving the nation's resources so they could continue to be used by future generations. On the other side, led by John Muir, who in 1892 founded the Sierra Club, were the aesthetic preservationists, who were interested in preserving nature for its scenic values and who lobbied for the creation of inviolate sanctuaries, for example, national parks and wildlife refuges, where fauna and flora could be preserved in their pristine states, safe from the encroachments of modern civilization. Muir and his followers disdained the utilitarians for seeing only the material, as opposed to the spiritual, benefits of nature and were aghast that the Forest Service encouraged lumbering, grazing, and mining in wilderness areas. As far as the preservationists were concerned, the only way the nation's forests should be exploited by humans was as sites for recreation and contemplation.

The preservationists were part of the long American tradition in which citizens responded to the ravages of urbanization and industrialization with a romantic yearning to "get back to nature." And certainly at the beginning of the twentieth century, the aesthetic and recreational charms of the outdoors were ever more inviting to the increasing proportion of the population that was living in urban areas and evincing disgust at the congestion, corruption, pollution, and inequalities of the cities.

While the popular mind viewed both the Pinchotian conservationists and the Muirian preservationists as part of the conservation movement, a large gulf existed between those who looked at a forest and saw, in Pinchot's words, "a manufacturing plant for the production of wood" (O'Brien, "Environmentalism as a Mass Movement," p. 9) and those who looked at a forest and saw an inviolate temple of nature. To be sure, some persons, like Roosevelt, appreciated the arguments of both the conservationists and the preservationists. But the two sides were generally hostile toward each other, and their philosophical differences became starkly evident during the protracted battle between 1901 and 1913 over whether or not to construct a dam in the isolated Hetch Hetchy Valley

Conservationist, Preservationist. President Theodore Roosevelt (*left*) and John Muir at Glacier Point in Yosemite Valley, which they visited in 1903 and again in 1906, after Muir convinced Roosevelt to have the valley added to Yosemite National Park. © CORBIS

Despite their defeat at Hetch Hetchy, the preservationist wing of the conservation movement won a number of victories in the early twentieth century. In 1903, for example, they convinced President Roosevelt to create the first national wildlife refuge at Pelican Island, Florida, and Roosevelt created more than fifty national wildlife refuges during his administration. In addition, preservationists persuaded Congress to enact the Antiquities Act of 1906, which authorized the president to protect areas of scientific or historical interest by designating them "national monuments." The Roosevelt administration created sixteen national monuments, including Devils Tower, Muir Woods, and Natural Bridges. Congress also created many new national parks during this period, including Sequoia and Yosemite in 1890; Mount Rainier in 1899; Crater Lake in 1902; Wind Cave in 1903; Mesa Verde in 1906; Glacier in 1910; Rocky Mountain in 1915; Lassen Volcanic in 1916; Denali in 1917; Grand Canyon and Zion in 1919; Hot Springs in 1921; Shenandoah in 1926; Bryce Canyon in 1928; Acadia and Grand Teton in 1929; Carlsbad Caverns and Great Smoky Mountains in 1930; and Isle Royale in 1931. To administer this greatly expanded system, the National Park Service was formed in 1916 with an institutional philosophy of aesthetic preservationism that counterbalanced the utilitarian policies of the Forest Service.

Finally, in one of their more notable accomplishments, the preservationists saved the California redwood trees, the tallest and among the oldest living things on Earth. The Save-the-Redwoods League, formed in 1917, raised millions of dollars to purchase groves of trees from the loggers and converted them into the thirty-seven California State Redwood Parks, where they are protected forever. All of the efforts, from saving roosting pelicans to protecting giant trees, represented aesthetic preservationism at its purest, for conservationists were saving scenery—impractical, intangible, nonutilitarian scenery.

Wildlife Management

The conservation movement lost some of its public momentum in the 1910s and 1920s in part due to the departure of Roosevelt from the White House in 1909, the dismissal of Pinchot by President William Howard Taft in 1910 in the wake of the BALLINGER-PINCHOT CONTROVERSY, the involvement of the United States in World War I, the enthronement of big business during the Roaring Twenties, and the expenditure of effort on internecine clashes between the utilitarian conservationists and the aesthetic preservationists. While conservation experts continued to work unobtrusively on such prosaic and utilitarian projects as resource surveys, management systems, forest fire protection, flood control projects, mineral leasing programs, and soil erosion research, the crusading spirit of the Progressive Era waned, and conservation faded from the public's consciousness.

But out in the field significant developments were taking place. By the late 1910s, ominous hints indicated

in Yosemite National Park. Pinchot weighed in in favor of building the dam, which would create a water reservoir for San Francisco. He did so both as a conservationist and as a progressive advocate of public utilities. After all, James D. Phelan, the reform mayor of San Francisco who sought to protect his constituents from the monopolistic practices of the privately owned Spring Valley Water Company, which specialized in poor service, high prices, and unsafe water, wanted the dam built. Furthermore, the residents of San Francisco had approved the dam in a 1908 referendum by an overwhelming 7–1 margin. But Muir and his preservationist allies, especially Robert Underwood Johnson, the editor of *Century*, were incredulous that anyone could even think of destroying the priceless beauty of the Hetch Hetchy Valley, and they fought for years to prevent construction of the dam. The difference between the two sides was summarized by Mayor Phelan when he accused Muir of engaging in "aesthetic quibbling" while "the 400,000 people of San Francisco are suffering from bad water" (Fox, *John Muir and His Legacy*, p. 141). Muir and the preservationists thus found themselves in the uncomfortable position of opposing the legitimate needs of "the people." In 1913, Congress finally approved construction of the dam, whereupon the Hetch Hetchy Valley disappeared under the waters.

that the preservationists may have been too successful for their own good. The problem was that the populations of some of the species of animals they had saved in wildlife refuges were expanding so rapidly that the animals were actually beginning to exhaust their food supplies and perish from starvation. As the President's Committee on Outdoor Recreation explained in 1927, "Over-protection, paradoxical as it may seem, defeats its end, and under its stimulus certain types of game animals multiply beyond their means of subsistence and cruel starvation ensues" (Cameron, *The Bureau of Biological Survey*, p. 192).

One of the most famous examples of this took place in the Grand Canyon National Game Preserve on Arizona's Kaibab Plateau. President Roosevelt had created the million-acre refuge in 1906 to protect the three thousand endangered Rocky Mountain mule deer on the plateau. Hunting was prohibited in the area except by agents of the Forest Service, who went after the main predators of the deer—wolves, mountain lions, bobcats, and coyotes—with a vengeance. Within a few years the protected mule deer had managed to double their numbers, and the Grand Canyon National Game Preserve was hailed as a great success. But with no natural enemies, the Kaibab deer herd kept right on growing. Between 1906 and 1924, the herd increased from 3,000 to perhaps as many as 100,000 animals, far beyond the carrying capacity of the range. After the herd depleted its natural food supplies, malnutrition, disease, and starvation wreaked havoc with the deer herd, which plummeted to a few thousand gaunt animals.

Tragedies like the one on the Kaibab Plateau were repeated in many places throughout the continent where a favored species had been granted protection, and preservationists began to understand that simply placing animals in a refuge and passively hoping for the best was not always in the best interests of the animals. They realized that wildlife populations needed to be actively managed to ensure their healthy survival.

The strongest proponent of a more dynamic approach to wildlife conservation in the 1920s was Aldo Leopold, the nation's first professor of wildlife management at the University of Wisconsin and the author of the seminal monograph on the subject, *Game Management* (1933). Leopold, whose *A Sand County Almanac* (1949) joined the works of Thoreau and Muir as the founding texts of the environmental movement of the 1960s, believed that all species, including *Homo sapiens*, exist in a symbiotic interdependence. His theories prefigured the modern science of ecology, defined as "the study of the interrelationships of organisms to one another and to the environment," and his words were echoed later by proponents of the "Gaia hypothesis." Leopold preached the need for humans to appreciate "the indivisibility of the earth—its soil, mountains, rivers, forests, climate, plants and animals—and respect it collectively" (Chase, *In a Dark Wood*, p. 45). He understood that a region's flora and fauna subsist in an intricate web of interdependencies

and that to single out one species, such as the Kaibab deer, for protection at the expense of others is to disrupt a natural equilibrium that had been eons in the making. In a development emblematic of the evolution of conservationism from a movement staffed by upper-class amateurs to one composed of middle-class professionals, Leopold called for a new generation of scientifically trained experts conversant in population dynamics and the operation of food chains to become involved in game management. He taught that wildlife officials could institute a number of practices to maintain the balance of what became known as the "ecosystem," such as practicing selective castration, conducting breeding programs, and allowing predators and even licensed hunters to cull dangerously expanding populations.

Ironically, preservationists had devoted years to convincing the public and Congress of the need for inviolate wildlife refuges, and as a result most Americans were revolted by the idea of predators and hunters being allowed to kill supposedly protected animals in refuges and national parks. But according to the theories of wildlife management, understandable but misplaced sympathy for the fate of the individual animal must not be allowed to override concern for the welfare of the herd as a whole. Just as foresters cut down a diseased tree that threatens the overall health of the forest, so game officials should cull an individual animal that endangers the survival of the herd. These theories slowly won acceptance among wildlife professionals. In the early 1940s, for example, the National Park Service finally overrode public sentiment and began killing a certain number of its game animals every year to maintain the wildlife population at its optimum level.

Eugenics. The philosophy of wildlife management was in tune with other political and social developments of the time. In the first few decades of the twentieth century, for example, the Progressives and their New Deal heirs tried to regulate not only big business but also the political system, public utilities, working conditions, and public health, and now even the wild animals of the forests were going to be managed scientifically. Through expert analysis and intelligent planning, the most fundamental processes of nature were going to be controlled.

In this context, it is notable that the eugenics movement became popular in the United States at the same time that the tenets of wildlife management were formulated. Eugenics was an effort to improve the nation's "germ plasm" by discouraging the propagation of "unfit" humans and encouraging the "fittest" members of society to breed more prolifically. Eugenicists were particularly anxious to preserve the blond-haired, blue-eyed "Nordic" race, whose survival, they feared, was threatened by the unprecedented influx and high birthrate of non-Nordic immigrants from southern and eastern Europe. Thus, conservationists and eugenicists both were interested in managing and regulating breeding to protect the noblest endangered species of the United States, whether they were bison, redwoods, or the "master race" of human beings.

It is not an accident that many of the leading conservationists, most notably Madison Grant, were also eugenicists. In the 1920s, conservationists like Grant, who was the guiding force behind the Bronx Zoo in New York, the Save-the-Redwoods League, and the American Bison Society, saw that the protected animals on their wildlife refuges were dangerously increasing in number, and they adopted the techniques of wildlife management to control them. At the same time, eugenicists like Grant warned that the "inferior" races in the United States were dangerously increasing in number and exhorted the public to accept the techniques of eugenics to control them. In essence, Grant simply applied the concepts he developed in wildlife management to the human population. Thus, Grant led the fight to pass the immigration restriction legislation of the 1920s, successfully lobbied legislatures to enact antimiscegenation laws, and influenced many states to implement coercive sterilization statutes under which thousands of Americans deemed "unworthy" were sterilized in the 1930s. The connection between such measures and the conservation movement was made explicit by the eugenicist Ellsworth Huntington when he declared: "The germ plasm is the nation's most precious natural resource. Eugenics is thus an integral component in the conservation of our natural resources" (*Tomorrow's Children*, p. 9).

Interestingly, conservationism and eugenics again crossed paths after World War II. At that time, conservationists began to fear that overpopulation and industrial poisons were wreaking havoc with the environment, while eugenicists worried that the population explosion in the Third World and the mutative effects of atomic radiation threatened the purity of the germ plasm. Thus, both movements jointly embraced family planning and environmentalism in the 1950s.

Conservation during Depression and Prosperity

The New Deal. Conservation usually is viewed as an indulgence of affluent societies, as only they can afford the luxury of reserving from immediate consumption a portion of their resources. But during the Great Depression, when the public accepted the necessity of dynamic federal action on behalf of the public welfare, the United States entered its second notable period of conservationism. Like his cousin Theodore Roosevelt, Franklin Delano Roosevelt was an ardent conservationist, and he took advantage of the economic emergency to launch government programs that conserved the country's natural resources at the same time that they provided a living wage to its human resources.

During the first hundred days in 1933, Congress created two of the most famous conservation agencies, the Tennessee Valley Authority, which rehabilitated the natural landscape and improved the standard of living of an entire region of the country, and the Civilian Conservation Corps, which sent out 2.5 million young men to dig reservoirs, stock lakes, maintain fire trails, work on erosion control, plant more than 2 billion trees, and undertake a host of other conservation projects. A number of other New Deal agencies, including the Public Works Administration (PWA) under Harold Ickes and the Works Progress Administration (WPA) under Harry Hopkins, spent billions of dollars on hundreds of projects, many of which were related to conservation. In addition, Franklin D. Roosevelt designated more than 2 million acres of federal land as national monuments, including Death Valley, Joshua Tree, and White Sands, and created several new national parks, including Everglades in 1934, Big Bend in 1935, Olympic in 1938, and Kings Canyon in 1940.

The federal government also took a number of steps to deal with the dust bowl, which ravaged western farmlands in the early 1930s thanks to poor agricultural practices, disastrous overgrazing, and a series of dry years. The Soil Erosion Service, established in 1933, and then the Soil Conservation Service, established in 1935 under Hugh Hammond Bennett, aided landowners in soil and water conservation. The Taylor Grazing Act of 1934 halted overgrazing on public lands, the Bankhead-Jones Farm Tenancy Act of 1937 provided for reforestation of abandoned or submarginal farmland, and the Shelterbelt Program planted more than 18,000 miles of tree belts on the Plains to break up the wind, to provide shade for livestock, and to retain moisture in the soil.

As with the rest of the New Deal, Roosevelt's conservation program suffered from little coordination, frequent redundancies, and even blatant inconsistencies. Nevertheless, Roosevelt initiated an unprecedented level of federal involvement in the natural environment, and as a result, the conservation movement became linked with liberalism and the Democratic Party, an association that lasted through the rest of the century.

The 1950s and the wilderness movement. Conservation was put on hold during World War II, but during the 1950s, the movement reemerged and gained momentum. This was mainly due to the noticeably worsening state of the environment. The country's growing population and booming economy, featuring tremendous growth in the automobile, plastics, petroleum, and chemical industries, put increased stress on the nation's finite resources and led to highly visible and noxious forms of pollution. The public was increasingly cognizant that water was unfit to drink, food was laced with chemical additives, milk was contaminated with radioactive fallout, and cities were choked by poisonous air. A number of well-publicized episodes helped heighten awareness of the environmental crisis. For example, in 1948 in Donora, Pennsylvania, thousands of residents became ill, and twenty died from severe air pollution. As a result air, water, and noise pollution were no longer proudly pointed to as signs of modernization but were decried as disfiguring to the landscape and dangerous to public health. The fear arose that the list of species whose survival was endangered might have to include *Homo sapiens*.

That the Republican Party, now far removed from its Theodore Roosevelt days, returned to power in the 1950s did not help the environment, but it did help the conservation movement. The Dwight D. Eisenhower administration threatened to reverse the gains of previous decades by cutting funding of federal conservation agencies and opening protected areas to military use. Eisenhower also appointed a wealthy automobile dealer named Douglas "Giveaway" McKay, whose sole qualification for office was a large campaign contribution to the Republican Party, as secretary of the interior. McKay promptly opened national wildlife refuges to gas and oil leasing.

With the state of the environment deteriorating and the government showing no interest in stemming the tide, the public turned to private conservation organizations to take up the slack. All the major conservation groups experienced healthy growth in the 1950s, as they broadened their membership bases, increased their budgets, hired professional staffs, expanded their range of activities, and cooperated with each other to push the conservation agenda. The movement's resurgence was exemplified by the broad-based and successful fight from 1950 to 1955 to save Dinosaur National Monument from being drowned by the proposed $417 million Echo Park Dam.

In addition, in the 1950s the conservation mosaic added a new element, the wilderness preservation movement. Americans had historically viewed wilderness areas, whether swamplands, forests, prairies, or deserts, as wasted areas with no value until they had been drained, cut, cultivated, or irrigated. But in the increasingly crowded postwar world, undeveloped areas became valuable precisely because they had been left in their natural states. Where wildlife and forest groups heretofore had dominated conservationism, wilderness organizations joined them on the front lines. Among those leading the charge were the Nature Conservancy, formed in 1951, which sought to preserve biological diversity by purchasing tracts of threatened wilderness, and the Wilderness Society founded in 1935 by Robert Marshall, Aldo Leopold, and Robert Sterling Yard, which lobbied the government to protect primitive areas from contamination by civilization. The wilderness forces shared a bond with the earlier efforts by the aesthetic preservationists to preserve the scenery of the United States. Their differences were that scenery is meant to be seen, whereas wilderness should ideally exist unseen so it can remain untouched and unspoiled by humans. The wilderness movement's efforts were rewarded with the passage of the Wilderness Act of 1964, which established the National Wilderness Preservation System.

The resurgence of the conservation movement in the 1950s laid the groundwork for its evolution into the mass movement of the 1960s and the 1970s known as environmentalism. By then, the forebears of the environmentalists, utilitarian conservationists, aesthetic preservationists,

wildlife managers, and wilderness preservationists, had already established a formidable and enduring legacy, witnessed by the fact that at the beginning of the twenty-first century, the United States included 55 national parks of 83 million acres, 75 national monuments of 4 million acres, 177 national forests and grasslands of 192 million acres, 530 national wildlife refuges covering 93 million acres, and over 700 national wilderness areas of 104 million acres, where fauna, flora, water, scenery, and other natural resources survived as living embodiments of the philosophy of conservation.

BIBLIOGRAPHY

Cameron, Jenks. *The Bureau of Biological Survey: Its History, Activities, and Organization*. Baltimore, Md.: Johns Hopkins Press, 1929.

Chase, Alston. *In a Dark Wood: The Fight over Forests and the Rising Tyranny of Ecology*. Boston and New York: Houghton Mifflin, 1995.

Fox, Stephen. *John Muir and His Legacy: The American Conservation Movement*. Boston: Little, Brown, 1981.

Hays, Samuel P. *Conservation and the Gospel of Efficiency: The Progressive Conservation Movement, 1890–1920*. Cambridge, Mass.: Harvard University Press, 1959.

Huntington, Ellsworth. *Tomorrow's Children: The Goal of Eugenics*. New York: Wiley, 1935.

Leopold, Aldo. *A Sand County Almanac, and Sketches Here and There*. New York: Oxford University Press, 1949.

Nash, Roderick Frazier, ed. *American Environmentalism: Readings in Conservation History*. New York: McGraw-Hill, 1990.

O'Brien, Jim. "Environmentalism as a Mass Movement: Historical Notes." *Radical America* 17, no. 2–3 (March–June 1983): 7–27.

Pinchot, Gifford. *Breaking New Ground*. New York: Harcourt, Brace, 1947.

Reiger, John F. *American Sportsmen and the Origins of Conservation*. Rev. ed. Norman: University of Oklahoma Press, 1986.

Roosevelt, Theodore. "Wilderness Reserves." In *American Big Game in Its Haunts*. Edited by George Bird Grinnell. New York: Forest and Stream Publishing, 1904.

Trefethen, James B. *An American Crusade for Wildlife*. New York: Winchester Press, 1975.

Jonathan P. Spiro

See also **Environmental Movement; Forest Service; Forestry; National Park System; New Deal; Wildlife Preservation; Yellowstone National Park.**

CONSERVATION BIOLOGY, an interdisciplinary, mission-oriented science with the goal of alleviating the extinction crisis and fostering biological diversity. Conservation biologists include researchers and managers from fields as varied as ecology, genetics, evolution, biogeography, wildlife biology, forestry, captive species breeding, and restoration ecology. Scientists hope that by studying why species become extinct, they can improve the management of natural areas and endangered species in ways that will prevent further extinctions.

The groundwork for the modern field of conservation biology was laid in the early 1900s with the development of the fields of fisheries, forestry, and wildlife management, along with the first modern formulation of a land ethic, generally credited to Aldo Leopold. Tremendous theoretical progress in community ecology and biogeography during the 1960s and 1970s established a scientific foundation for conservation. At the same time, growing evidence of the massive extinction of species was raising concern within the biological community. Experts estimated that as many as a quarter of all surviving species could be doomed to extinction by the year 2025 if current trends continued. As many as 20,000 species could be lost or doomed every year, most of them unknown to Western science, and virtually all of them victims of human activity.

According to Harvard professor E. O. Wilson, a leader in the field, the current rate of extinction (the number of species lost each year) is between 1,000 and 10,000 times greater than the estimated rate of extinction before the evolution of humans. A species may be vulnerable to extinction for many reasons. Small populations can be wiped out by random local events, social dysfunction, or genetic deterioration. Species that cannot disperse well or that reproduce slowly are in danger. Those exploited by humans are particularly vulnerable because harvesting may drive populations too low, either inadvertently or intentionally. Species dependent on a threatened habitat will suffer the fate of that habitat. Species with large home ranges, such as elk, caribou, bears, and wolves, are also vulnerable because it is difficult for conservationists to protect a land area large enough to support a viable population. (A viable population has a 95 percent probability or better of surviving for more than 100 years.)

From its inception, two core goals of conservation biology have been to preserve functioning samples of all global ecosystems in their natural range and to maintain viable populations of all native species within those ecosystems. Part of the challenge to conservation biologists has been to use scientific principles to select and manage wildlife reserves that meet these two goals. Historically, most parks and other protected areas were chosen for aesthetic or recreational value or because they appeared to have no desirable extractable resources. Conservation biologists now help to choose and redesign protected areas to foster biological diversity.

In practice, this has meant developing a few rules for designing refuges. First, large areas are preferable to small ones because larger areas are more likely to support species with extensive home ranges, and the larger area provides more of a buffer between the refuge and human activities on surrounding lands. Natural disturbances, such as fires and floods, are also less likely to cause extinctions when species can move away from the disturbance yet still remain on protected lands. This is particularly important

because some ecosystems require periodic disturbances to maintain their integrity. Some tree species in Yellowstone National Park, for example, require fire to establish seedlings and regenerate the forest. Conversely, periodic fires help maintain midwestern prairie ecosystems where most tree species are not well-adapted to fire. Second, protected zones should have few roads, because they encourage increased human activities, such as logging, trampling, hunting, and dumping, which may be detrimental to native flora and fauna, and because even the mere presence of roads themselves can affect the suitability of an ecosystem for certain species, especially certain birds. Third, protected zones should be close together and connected. Linkages increase the effective size of protected areas by permitting seasonal movements or migrations, dispersal to prevent inbreeding or to recolonize other sites, and long-distance range shifts in response to climate change.

Because of the sweeping ecological change that has already occurred, in addition to preventing further extinctions, many conservation biologists argue that attempts must be made to restore threatened and endangered ecosystems, populations, and species. Restoration ecology has been the subject of considerable controversy. Questions central to the debate include whether current levels of scientific knowledge and technology make restoration feasible, how scientists can measure the successes and failures of restoration projects, whether preservation is more cost-effective than restoration, and whether it is appropriate to remove preservationist constraints on one site, thus allowing rapid environmental change, on the promise that another site will be restored to a former habitat, a process often fraught with problems, delays, and unforeseen expenses.

While these issues remain unresolved, majority opinions within the world of conservation biology have emerged. First, preservation is generally more cost-effective than restoration. Second, because ecological change and damage are ongoing, restoration projects must be attempted despite failures. Third, it is unwise to allow the possibility of restoration to support the continued expansion of ecologically destructive practices. Fourth, measurement of restoration must include scrutiny of ecosystem function over the long term.

At the start of the twenty-first century, the Society for Conservation Biology (SCB), one of the most prominent organizations in the field of conservation biology, brought together a wide range of interested people, including resource managers, public and private conservation workers, and students and educators from around the world to study—and take action to solve—the problems associated with protecting biological diversity. Because the goals and purposes of conservation biology are political in addition to scientific, research in the field typically is linked to an explicit ecological agenda. Michael Soule, a cofounder of SCB, described conservation biology as a "crisis discipline," in which it is sometimes necessary to make tactical decisions without information. He proposes that in crisis disciplines "the risks of nonaction may be greater than the risks of inappropriate action."

BIBLIOGRAPHY

Ehrlich, Paul R., and Anne H. Ehrlich. *Extinction*. New York: Random House, 1981.

Noss, Reed F. "The Wildlands Project Land Conservation Strategy." *Wild Earth* (1993): 10–25.

Soule, Michael E. *Conservation Biology*. Washington, D.C.: Island Press, 2001.

Susan J. Cooper / c. w.

See also **Conservation; Endangered Species; Marine Sanctuaries; Species, Introduced; Wildlife Preservation.**

CONSERVATISM.

A national political and intellectual movement of self-described conservatives began to congeal in the middle of the twentieth century, primarily as a reaction to the creation of the New Deal welfare state, but also in response to the alleged erosion of traditional values and the American failure to win a quick victory in the Cold War. Among the factions within this movement, traditionalists typically stressed the virtues of order, local custom, and natural law; libertarians promoted limited government, laissez-faire economics, and individual autonomy; and militant cold warriors sought primarily to combat communism. Despite these internal differences, by 1960, conservatives had formulated a coherent critique of liberalism and built a network of political activists. In 1964, they mobilized to win the Republican presidential nomination for Senator Barry Goldwater and, subsequently, remained a major political force.

Although this late twentieth-century movement stands out in its size and success, from the outset, American life was influenced by men and women who, by some plausible standard, can be considered conservatives. Modern conservative thinkers sought to legitimate their own worldviews by discovering precursors in the eighteenth, nineteenth, and early twentieth centuries. Liberals responded that conservatives were merely stringing together an incongruous list of heroes for a nation whose history was, in a broad sense, liberal. Conservatives themselves often acknowledged the dilemma. Disagreeing among themselves about the essential features of modern conservatism, they offer differing evaluations of plausible precursors. Thus, any account of a conservative "tradition" is inherently problematical.

Early American Conservatives

Few modern conservatives honor the Loyalists, whose commitment to order led them to oppose the American Revolution. Rather, Edmund Burke, a British Whig who supported the cause of independence but despised the French Revolution, is typically cited as the intellectual founder of American (or Anglo-American) conservatism. The Constitution wins praise from modern traditionalists

for protecting private property and limiting democracy, and its foremost authors are rightly credited with skepticism about human perfectibility. In the late eighteenth century, however, a charter that established a republic and barred religious tests for office hardly looked conservative. Moreover, skeptical of the strong central government latent in the Constitution, libertarians sometimes hail the Antifederalist defense of local prerogatives and insistence on a Bill of Rights.

While a handful of libertarians look back favorably on Thomas Jefferson, most modern conservatives scorn his optimistic view of human nature and enthusiasm for the French Revolution. They find the leaders of the Federalist Party, which rose and fell in competition with the Jeffersonian Republicans, much more appealing. Certainly, the Federalists valued hierarchy, order, and religious fidelity more than equality, democracy, and tolerance. Yet the party was by no means unambiguously conservative by modern standards. Alexander Hamilton's economic program sanctioned federal intervention, not laissez-faire, to foster capitalist development. John Marshall's jurisprudence grudgingly yielded to legislative expressions of the popular will. Furthermore, the second generation of Federalist politicians tried to save the party in the 1810s by muting their public critique of democracy.

Equally problematical is the relationship between modern conservatism and the Whig Party, which rose and fell in competition with the Jacksonian Democrats. Especially in New England, the Whigs were more likely to value decorum, orthodox Christianity, and deference to authority. The party insisted that it was preserving the moderate democracy of the nation's founders against the usurpation of power by "King Andrew" Jackson. Prominent Whigs, including Daniel Webster, even called themselves conservatives. Yet the Whig record falls short of the modern libertarian or traditionalist ideal. The party not only advocated federal appropriations for "internal improvements," but also pioneered flamboyant electoral politics in the "hard cider" campaign of 1840.

The Civil War and Conservative Politics

The antebellum South produced a distinctive intellectual conservatism in which a critique of unfettered democracy, federal power, and bourgeois individualism was increasingly tied to a defense of slavery. In the writings of James Thornwell, William Trescott, and George Fitzhugh, the slave South remained within the mainstream of Christian civilization, while the free North was capitulating to "ultraism" in the form of infidelity, socialism, and women's rights. At the same time, John C. Calhoun adapted the founders' republican ideas to protect southern interests. According to Calhoun's doctrine of the "concurrent majority," the two foremost factions in the United States—the slave states and the free states—had a right to protect their basic interests. Accordingly, the Constitution should be amended to provide for two presidents, one from each section and both armed with the veto.

Defeat of the South in the Civil War facilitated the rise of what the political scientist Clinton Rossiter called "laissez-faire conservatism." The leading ideologist of this persuasion, William Graham Sumner, adapted social Darwinism to the American scene. Not only did the fittest survive to acquire great wealth, Sumner contended, but the concentration of wealth in the hands of a competent few also maximized its productive (hence, moral) use. In a democracy, the less fit majority tried to capture the state in order to redistribute or redirect wealth. But no government could administer wealth as wisely as the industrialists and entrepreneurs who created it.

Not only did the dour, secular Sumner decline to think of himself as a conservative, but he also recognized that laissez-faire conservatives fell short of his limited government ideal. The Federalist and Whig belief in social stewardship did steadily erode with the disappearance of those parties. Yet late nineteenth-century Republicans in particular advocated both protective tariffs and federal expenditures for internal improvements. In order to strike down popular legislation that impinged on property rights, laissez-faire conservatives increased the power of at least one branch of the federal government: the judiciary. Similarly, it is ironic that the hundreds of vetoes cast by conservative Democrat Grover Cleveland in order to limit regulations and expenditures actually enhanced the power of the presidency.

What is usually called the Progressive movement has been particularly perplexing to modern conservatives—and with good reason. As libertarians lament, Theodore Roosevelt, Woodrow Wilson, and others who rode the bipartisan tide of reform created the regulatory state. Traditionalists regret that they also rallied "the people" against so-called special interests. Yet progressive Republicans and Democrats were sufficiently nationalistic in their social views and restrained in economics to preclude the creation of an explicitly conservative party. Furthermore, seeking to limit the influence of "unfit" ethnic and racial minorities, many Progressive reformers supported less democratic forms of municipal government and the disfranchisement of African Americans.

The New Deal and the New Conservatives

World War I, the subsequent red scare, and the cultural conflicts of the 1920s combined to move the political center of gravity in a more conservative direction. The major party presidential nominees were more skeptical of the regulatory state than Roosevelt or Wilson had been. Social critics and social scientists assailed the excesses of mass democracy. Organizing to protect their ways of life, diverse cultural conservatives promoted "100 percent Americanism," defended Prohibition, campaigned against the teaching of evolution in public schools, and expanded the Ku Klux Klan into the largest nativist organization in American history.

Culturally, conservative literature and criticism flourished, too. During the nineteenth century, James Fenimore Cooper, Nathaniel Hawthorne, Herman Melville, and many lesser writers affirmed tradition, order, and authority rather than economic development and democracy. Their post–World War I counterparts included the irreverent pundit H. L. Mencken, the "new humanists" Irving Babbitt and Paul Elmer More, and the Nashville Agrarians.

The Great Depression and the New Deal finally produced a clear and durable left-center-right political spectrum. Proponents of the welfare state, in calling themselves liberals, typically supported the Democratic Party and followed Franklin D. Roosevelt. Opponents complained that Roosevelt had stolen that honorable label to camouflage his socialism, but they nonetheless came to call themselves conservatives. Conservative attacks mixed laissez-faire conservatism with venerable fears of federal control and corruption. Few defended laissez-faire more zealously than the former Democrats who led the anti-New Deal Liberty League. Although the question of federal intervention in the economy was central to sorting out the political spectrum, conservatives also thought that Roosevelt's Jewish, Catholic, and cosmopolitan followers fell short of being 100 percent Americans, as did his activist wife, Eleanor. Starting in 1937, southern Democrats—incensed by the New Deal's mild concessions to African Americans and Roosevelt's attempt to expand the Supreme Court—joined northern Republicans in an informal conservative congressional coalition to fight further expansion of the welfare state.

A distinct far right crystallized during the 1930s. Senator Huey Long, Father Charles Coughlin, and lesser activists agreed with conservatives like former President Herbert Hoover and Senator Robert Taft that the New Deal was bureaucratic, corrupt, and un-American. But far right activists not only placed a higher priority on revitalizing (as opposed to conserving) what they considered to be the American way of life, but sometimes also favored economic redistribution. Most of them rooted their politics in theologically conservative versions of Christianity, and many embraced anti-Semitic conspiracy theories. To liberals and radicals, this far right looked like an American fascism.

World War II and the Cold War heightened fears of disorder and subversion, energized a religious revival, and strengthened the congressional conservative coalition. Leaders of the modern conservative movement that began to coalesce in this hospitable environment ranged from irresponsible demagogues like Senator Joseph McCarthy to impressive thinkers like the traditionalist Richard Weaver and the libertarian economist Milton Friedman. No intellectual was more important than William F. Buckley Jr., who provided a forum in *National Review* magazine for attacking what he called President Dwight Eisenhower's "dime store New Deal." In 1960, Buckley took the lead in founding the Young Americans for Freedom, which became a base for the Goldwater campaign. While warding off liberal charges of "extremism," the modern conservative movement set its own boundaries to the right by repudiating anti-Semites, the John Birch Society's conspiracy theories, and segregationist presidential candidate George Wallace. Staunch conservatives typically opposed civil rights legislation as a violation of states rights and local custom. Equally important, the residual fear of military intervention abroad that had marked Robert Taft and Herbert Hoover subsided as conservatives demanded victory in the Cold War.

The political polarization of the 1960s and early 1970s strengthened conservatism. Racial conflict, secularization, liberalizing sexual mores, and the stalemated war in Vietnam War alienated many moderate Democrats, especially white southerners and working-class Catholics. Richard Nixon and Gerald Ford drew these groups into the Republican Party, even as many conservatives denounced both presidents for compromising with congressional liberals and the Soviet Union. During the late 1970s, Democrats also lost support within two other constituencies. Jewish "neoconservative" intellectuals thought Jimmy Carter too hard on Israel and too soft on the Soviet Union. Theologically conservative Protestants discovered that this "born again" Baptist president was more liberal than they had thought. Such fundamentalists and evangelicals formed the bulwark of the New Christian Right. The leading organization of this kind, the MORAL MAJORITY, was led by the Baptist minister Jerry Falwell.

The election of President Ronald Reagan in 1980 brought significant change to modern conservatism. The Republicans were now clearly the more conservative major party. Yet Reagan's conservatism was more complicated than Goldwater's two decades earlier. While Reagan denounced big government, promoted tax cuts, and undermined labor unions, his administration ran record deficits and only slightly diminished the welfare state. He celebrated religious faith in general but gave scant support to New Christian Right efforts to ban abortion or restore prayer to public schools. A large military buildup and strident anticommunist rhetoric were intended to weaken the Soviet Union. Ultimately, however, Reagan accepted a version of détente as a means to end the Cold War.

Post–Cold War Conservative Identity

Post–Cold War conservatism was marked by a loss of focus, internecine disputes, and false starts. The New Christian Right leader Pat Robertson ran an ineffective race for the Republican presidential nomination in 1988. Conservative Pat Buchanan challenged President George H. W. Bush's renomination in 1992, primarily because Bush had agreed to a tax increase. Bush's defeat by Bill Clinton, a supporter of affirmative action, gay rights, and abortion, brought temporary unity to conservative ranks. In 1994, assailing Clinton's advocacy of national health insurance as well his cultural liberalism, Republicans under the leadership of Representative Newt Gingrich won control of both houses of Congress for the first time in forty years.

During 1998–1999, conservatives spearheaded the unsuccessful effort to remove Clinton from office for lying under oath about his sex life. Adapting old arguments, traditionalists and New Christian Right clergy presented Clinton as a symbol of corrupt cultural relativism in general and the moral decline of the 1960s in particular.

This campaign not only dissipated energy on the right, but also revealed many conservatives as self-righteous and hypocritical. George W. Bush won the presidency in 2000 by advocating a practical and ecumenical conservatism that welcomed women, blacks, and Hispanics to the cause. Aside from a few traditionalist intellectuals and the staunchest fundamentalist Christians, there was no coherent conservative movement to Bush's right.

BIBLIOGRAPHY

Allitt, Patrick. *Catholic Intellectuals and Conservative Politics in America, 1950–1985.* Ithaca, N.Y.: Cornell University Press, 1993.

Brennan, Mary C. *Turning Right in the Sixties: The Conservative Capture of the GOP.* Chapel Hill: University of North Carolina Press, 1995.

Buckley, William F., Jr., ed. *American Conservative Thought in the Twentieth Century.* Indianapolis, Ind.: Bobbs-Merrill, 1970.

Dillard, Angela D. *Guess Who's Coming to Dinner Now? Multicultural Conservatism in America.* New York: New York University Press, 2001.

Doenecke, Justus D. *Not to the Swift: The Old Isolationists in the Cold War Era.* Lewisburg, Pa.: Bucknell University Press, 1979.

Genovese, Eugene D. *The Southern Tradition: The Achievement and Limitations of an American Conservatism.* Cambridge, Mass.: Harvard University Press, 1994.

Hodgson, Godfrey. *The World Turned Right Side Up: A History of the Conservative Ascendancy in America.* Boston: Houghton Mifflin, 1996.

Kirk, Russell. *The Conservative Mind: From Burke to Eliot.* 7th rev. ed. Chicago: Regnery, 1986.

Lora, Ronald. *Conservative Minds in America.* Chicago: Rand McNally, 1971.

Nash, George H. *The Conservative Intellectual Movement in America since 1945.* New York: Basic Books, 1976.

Patterson, James T. *Congressional Conservatism and the New Deal: The Growth of the Conservative Coalition in Congress, 1933–1939.* Lexington: University of Kentucky Press, 1967.

Rossiter, Clinton L. *Conservatism in America: The Thankless Persuasion.* 2d rev. ed. New York: Vintage, 1962.

Leo R. Ribuffo

See also **Liberalism; Republican Party; Whig Party;** *and vol. 9:* **The New Right: We're Ready to Lead.**

CONSPIRACIES ACTS OF 1861 AND 1862, attempts to suppress antiwar activities in the North during the Civil War. One statute (31 July 1861) provided for a fine and imprisonment for those who conspired by threats, intimidation, or force to obstruct or overthrow the government. The act of 17 July 1862 (also known as the Confiscation Act) identified antiwar activity as treason and softened the death penalty for treason to the alternative of death or imprisonment and fine. Prosecutions under these acts were less effective than arbitrary arrests and confiscations.

BIBLIOGRAPHY

Hyman, Harold M. *A More Perfect Union: The Impact of the Civil War and Reconstruction on the Constitution.* New York: Knopf, 1973.

Klement, Frank L. *Dark Lanterns: Secret Political Societies, Conspiracies, and Treason Trials in the Civil War.* Baton Rouge: Louisiana State University Press, 1984.

Martin P. Claussen/T. M.

See also **Arrest, Arbitrary, During the Civil War; Confiscation Acts; Copperheads; Treason.**

CONSPIRACY. A conspiracy is an agreement between two or more persons to commit an illegal act or to achieve a legal objective through illegal means. The essence of a conspiracy is the agreement; and the perceived harm is the increased danger from concerted action. An overt act in furtherance of the agreement is sometimes required by statute to complete a conspiracy, but the purpose of this requirement is merely to demonstrate an active agreement. Conspiracy may be prosecuted as a crime or as a civil cause of action. The presence of conspiracy expands the rules of evidence and procedure.

The crime of conspiracy originated as a series of statutes in fourteenth-century England prohibiting agreements to support false accusations in legal proceedings. Very soon thereafter, liability for an illegal agreement was also found for "confederacies" to evade taxes, commit treason, cheat, or evade just price, wage, and guild regulations. By the beginning of the eighteenth century, confederacy and conspiracy merged into the common law crime of conspiracy as it is now understood. Whether or not a criminal conspiracy was alleged or proved, a party who suffered harm as a result of a conspiracy could bring a civil suit in law or equity. In the United States, early conspiracy cases in the state courts included claims that workers unlawfully conspired to raise wages by concerted action.

Federal courts did not recognize common law crimes against the United States, and early efforts to prosecute conspiracies proved difficult. For example, Aaron Burr was acquitted of treason in 1807 despite recruiting an army in order to secure the secession of Louisiana. Burr was not shown to have personally participated in conduct considered "levying war" as charged in his indictment, but only in procuring and advising "levying war." Conspiracy to commit treason was not treason except by operation of the common law. On the other hand, John Mitchell was convicted of treason in 1795 for participation in the Whiskey Rebellion. Although Mitchell had not actually carried arms against the United States, he was present and participated in the insurrection, and was held responsible for all acts performed in its course. The Sedition Act of 1798 made a conspiracy "with intent to oppose any measure or measures of the government . . . or to impede the operation of any law" a crime, but it expired in 1801.

The general federal conspiracy statute, Title 18 *U.S. Code* Section 371, originally enacted in 1867, made it a crime to conspire to commit an offense against the United States, or to defraud the United States in any manner. The prototypical political conspiracy, Watergate, was a conspiracy to commit an offense (obstruct justice) by "covering up" the burglary of the Democratic Party's 1972 presidential campaign headquarters. Conspiracy "to defraud" has been interpreted broadly to include any conduct that "impaired or obstructed the lawful function of any government agency." In *United States v. Dennis* (1966), the Supreme Court found sufficient an indictment that charged labor leaders with conspiracy to defraud the National Labor Relations Board by falsely claiming to have resigned from the Communist Party, even though requiring noncommunist affidavits was unconstitutional. In addition to the general conspiracy statute, there are more than twenty specific prohibitions against conspiracy attached to substantive offenses in the *United States Code.*

Conspiracy cases have substantial procedural advantages for prosecutors and are among the most frequently charged federal crimes. Conspiracy is a separate offense from the substantive crime that it intends, enabling multiple prosecutions for the same conduct without double jeopardy attaching. Conspiracy can exist where the substantive crime cannot be proved, and even where its commission is impossible. All coconspirators can be charged together in one indictment, and crimes pertaining solely to individual conspirators are often included in the indictment despite prejudice to codefendants. All coconspirators are responsible for all conduct engaged in by any coconspirator during the course of the conspiracy, and the statute of limitations on the conspiracy runs from the last act of any of the coconspirators. The statements of coconspirators during the course of the conspiracy are not "hearsay" and may be admitted into evidence against all coconspirators.

The influence of federal criminal law enforcement increased dramatically in the last half of the twentieth century because of the threat of international criminal conspiracies. The Kefauver Committee's investigation into organized crime in 1950 and 1951 spurred the enactment in 1970 of the Racketeer Influenced and Corrupt Organization Act (RICO) and the organization of the Department of Justice's Strike Force Against Organized Crime. The Comprehensive Drug Abuse Prevention and Control Act of 1970 created a comprehensive regulatory and law enforcement apparatus based on a conspiracy model of crime. These initiatives were responsible for extending federal criminal jurisdiction to legitimate business enterprises and traditional state court crimes.

Popular belief in vast unsubstantiated conspiracies is a recurring theme in American history. For example, the Red Scare of 1919 and 1920 (thirty-six bombs simultaneously mailed to prominent citizens) instigated a nationwide search for a Bolshevik conspiracy. Similarly, Senator Joseph McCarthy's 1950 allegation that communists had infiltrated the State Department precipitated wholesale investigations unjustifiably stigmatizing many individuals and organizations. Conspiracy theories can persist in the absence of credible supporting evidence. For example, many people believe that the 1963 assassination of President John Kennedy was the act of a broad conspiracy despite extensive investigation and the Warren Commission's contrary conclusion.

BIBLIOGRAPHY

Bassano, Joseph J. *Conspiracy.* Vol. 16 of *American Jurisprudence.* 2d ed. Rochester, N.Y.: Lawyers Co-operative Publishing, 1998.

Davis, Beth Allison, and Josh Vitullo. "Federal Criminal Conspiracy." *American Criminal Law Review* 38 (2001): 777–817. An annual survey of the state of the law.

Fenster, Mark. *Conspiracy Theories: Secrecy and Power in American Culture.* Minneapolis: University of Minnesota Press, 1999.

Forkosch, Morris D. "The Doctrine of Criminal Conspiracy and Its Modern Application to Labor." *Texas Law Review* 40 (1962): 303–338, 473–508.

Goldstein, Abraham S. "Conspiracy to Defraud the United States." *Yale Law Journal* 68 (1959): 405–463.

Selz, Shirley A. "Conspiracy Law in Theory and in Practice: Federal Conspiracy Prosecutions in Chicago." *American Journal of Criminal Law* 5 (1977): 35–71.

M. Susan Murnane

See also **Alien and Sedition Laws; Crime; Justice, Department of; Racketeer Influenced and Corrupt Organization Act; Warren Commission; Watergate; Whiskey Rebellion.**

CONSTITUTION, an American forty-four-gun frigate authorized by Congress on 27 March 1794. She was designed by Joshua Humphreys, built in Edmund Hartt's shipyard, Boston, and launched 21 October 1797. In the naval war with France she served as Commodore Silas Talbot's flagship, and in the Tripolitan War as the flagship of Commodore Edward Preble, participating in five attacks on Tripoli from 25 July to 4 September 1804. The *Constitution* was victorious in several notable single-ship engagements in the WAR OF 1812. During the fight with the British frigate *Guerrière* on 19 August 1812, a seaman gave her the nickname "Old Ironsides" when, seeing a shot rebound from her hull, he shouted, "Huzza, her sides are made of iron." While cruising off South America four months later, Commodore William Bainbridge on the *Constitution* sighted the British *Java.* After a battle of about two hours, the British ship surrendered. On 20 February 1815, the *Constitution* met the British frigate *Cyane* and the sloop-of-war *Levant* some two hundred miles northeast of the Madeira Islands and forced both ships to surrender.

Ordered broken up in 1830 by the Department of the Navy, the *Constitution* was retained in deference to public sentiment aroused by Oliver Wendell Holmes's poem "Old Ironsides." She was rebuilt in 1833 and served as a training ship at Portsmouth, Va., from 1860 to 1865. She underwent a partial rebuilding during the 1870s and was restored in 1925 and again during the 1970s and the 1990s. From her berth next to the USS *Constitution* Museum in Boston's Charlestown Navy Yard, the still unbeaten *Constitution* once again sailed under her own power to mark her bicentennial in 1997, reminding Americans of their rich naval history.

BIBLIOGRAPHY

Hollis, Ira N. *The Frigate Constitution: The Central Figure of the Navy under Sail.* Boston: Houghton Mifflin, 1900.

Horgan, Thomas P. *Old Ironsides: The Story of USS Constitution.* Boston: Burdette, 1963.

Louis H. Bollander / A. R.

See also **Barbary Wars; Navy, United States; Warships.**

CONSTITUTION OF THE UNITED STATES.

The Constitution, which has served since 1789 as the basic frame of government of the republic of the United States, was the work of a constitutional convention that sat at Philadelphia from late May 1787 until mid-September of that year. The convention had been called into being as the culminating event of a lengthy campaign for constitutional reform staged by a number of nationalistic political leaders, above all James Madison and Alexander Hamilton, both of whom had long been convinced that the ARTICLES OF CONFEDERATION were hopelessly deficient as a frame of government. By 1786, the growing somnolence of the Confederation Congress, the manifest incompetence of the Confederation government in foreign affairs, and the obvious state of national bankruptcy, together with the sense of panic and dismay occasioned by SHAYS'S REBELLION in Massachusetts, had at long last spurred the states into concerted action.

The Virginia legislature issued an invitation to its sister states to meet in convention in Philadelphia in May 1787. As one after another of the other states responded, the Confederation Congress reluctantly joined in the call.

Twelve states in all sent delegates to the convention at Philadelphia. Rhode Island alone, then in the grip of a paper-money faction fearful of federal monetary reform, boycotted the meeting. In all, the twelve participating states appointed seventy-four delegates, of whom fifty-five actually put in an appearance. Of these, some fifteen or twenty men were responsible for virtually all of the convention's work; the contribution of the others was inconsequential.

Dominating the convention's proceedings from the beginning was a group of delegates intent upon the creation of a genuinely national government possessed of powers adequate to promote the security, financial stability, commercial prosperity, and general well-being of all of the states. Prominent among them were George Washington, whom the delegates chose as their presiding officer; James Madison, whose leadership in the convention would one day earn him the well-deserved title of "Father of the Constitution"; James Wilson, congressman and legal scholar from Pennsylvania; Gouverneur Morris, a brilliant and conservative aristocrat of New York background, also present as a Pennsylvania delegate; Rufus King, a highly respected veteran congressman from Massachusetts; and Charles Cotesworth Pinckney and John Rutledge of South Carolina, representatives of that state's rice-planter aristocracy. In the nationalist camp also were the aged, garrulous, but vastly prestigious Benjamin Franklin of Pennsylvania; the pretentious but somewhat lightweight Edmund Randolph of Virginia; and Alexander Hamilton, whose extremist beliefs in centralized aristocratic government together with his inability to control the STATES' RIGHTS majority in the New York delegation cast a shadow on his convention role.

The nationalists also could command on most occasions the support of a group of moderate delegates who accepted the necessity for strong central government but were willing to compromise substantially with the convention's states' rights bloc when that proved necessary. Prominent among these men were Elbridge Gerry of Massachusetts, Oliver Ellsworth and Roger Sherman of Connecticut, and Abraham Baldwin of Georgia.

A small, but significant, bloc of states' rights delegates was firmly opposed to the creation of a sovereign national government. Its leaders included William Paterson of New Jersey, the author of the New Jersey Plan; John Dickinson from Delaware; Gunning Bedford of Maryland; and John Lansing and Robert Yates of New York. These men recognized the necessity for constitutional reform but believed strongly that a confederation type of government ought to be retained and that by granting the Congress certain additional powers—above all the power to tax and to regulate commerce—the Articles of Confederation could be converted into an adequate frame of government.

Voting in the convention was by state, each state having one vote. On most occasions, the nationalist bloc controlled the votes of Massachusetts, Pennsylvania, Virginia, and the two Carolinas; on several critical decisions they proved able to muster the votes of Connecticut and Georgia as well. The states' rights party, by contrast, could count upon the votes of New York, New Jersey, Maryland, and Delaware, and occasionally Connecticut and Georgia. (New Hampshire was not yet represented in the convention.) Thus, the nationalist bloc in general controlled

the convention. However, the states' rights delegates held one trump card—their implicit threat to break up the convention if they did not obtain certain concessions deemed by them to be fundamental to their cause.

The nationalist faction demonstrated its power at the very outset of the proceedings. Following organization for business, Edmund Randolph rose and in the name of his state presented what has since become known as the Virginia Plan—a proposal for a thoroughly nationalistic frame of government. Without debate the convention accepted the fifteen resolutions of the Virginia Plan as the basis for its further deliberations. The outstanding characteristic of this plan was its provision for a government that would exercise its authority directly upon individuals, in contrast to the Confederation government's dependence upon the states as agents to effect its will. The plan thus called for a genuinely national government rather than one based upon state sovereignty. The Virginia Plan's nationalism was also apparent in the broad sweep of legislative power it granted to Congress: to legislate in all cases in which the states were severally "incompetent." An ill-conceived provision would have empowered Congress to use force against any state derelict in its obligations to the Union, a procedure the nationalists soon recognized as unwise and unnecessary in a genuinely national government that would no longer use the states as agents to effect its will.

For the rest, the Virginia Plan provided for a two-house legislature, the lower house to be elected by the people of the several states and the upper to be elected by the lower out of nominations submitted by the state legislatures. A separately constituted executive officer was to be elected by Congress for an unspecified term and to be ineligible for reelection. There was also provision for a national judiciary, a portion of which, sitting with the executive, was to constitute a "council of revision," with an absolute veto over all legislation.

All this added up to a proposal to junk the Articles of Confederation outright, and to erect a powerful new national government, federal only in that it would still leave to the states a separate if unspecified area of sovereignty. Although several states' rights–oriented delegates objected that this would commit the convention to the establishment of an all-powerful central government, the Randolph-Morris resolution carried almost unanimously, Connecticut alone voting opposition.

The most serious conflict between the nationalist and states' rights factions came over the composition of the legislature. Here the nationalists, after intermittent debate lasting some seven weeks, were eventually forced to compromise, although without vital damage to the principle of nationalism. Madison, Wilson, Morris, and their fellow nationalists began the debate with the demand that both houses of Congress be apportioned according to representation and that the lower house, at least, be elected directly by the people of the several states. Only on the mode of election of the upper house did they show a disposition to compromise: here the convention early accepted unanimously a recommendation by Dickinson that senators be elected by state legislatures. But the states' rights faction, with some support from the moderates, early made it clear that they would accept nothing less than state equality in at least one house. In mid-June, to emphasize their point, they introduced the so-called New Jersey Plan, which called for a one-chamber legislature based upon state equality—that is, a continuation of the Confederation Congress. The New Jersey Plan met prompt defeat, but the impasse remained.

The ultimate solution was found in the so-called Great Compromise, reported early in July by a special Committee of Eleven, one delegate from each state. This provided that the lower house of Congress be apportioned according to population, that each state have one vote in the upper house, but that all bills for raising revenue originate in the lower house. A further resolution, offered by Elbridge Gerry, provided that senators were to vote as individuals and not as state delegations. After two weeks of further debate, the nationalists yielded and accepted the compromise.

The debate on the executive proved to be protracted and difficult, but it too yielded what amounted ultimately to a victory for a strong national government. The nationalists were determined to have a powerful, independently constituted executive, and to this end they soon decided that the provision in the Virginia Plan for election of the president by Congress was altogether unsatisfactory. But for a long time no adequate alternative appeared. Direct popular election, early proposed by Wilson, was rejected as too democratic; choice of the president by state legislatures conceded too much to states' rights.

At length, after protracted debate marked by vacillation and uncertainty rather than bitter dispute, the delegates accepted another idea originally advanced by Wilson: choice of the president by electors chosen by the several states. In early September, a second Committee of Eleven brought in a plan to allot to each state a number of electors equal to its whole number of senators and representatives. Each state was to be allowed to choose its representatives as it wished—thus reserving a role for the states but opening the door for eventual choice of electors by popular vote. The electors, assembled in their separate states, were to vote by ballot for two candidates for president. The candidate receiving the highest total vote among all the states, if this were a majority of the electors, was to be declared elected president, while that candidate receiving the second highest number of votes, if that were also a majority of the electors, was to be declared elected vice president. If no candidate received a majority, the Senate was to elect the president from the five leading candidates. The convention altered the committee proposal only to provide for election of the president by the House of Representatives, voting by states, instead of by the Senate, should no candidate receive an electoral ma-

jority. The Senate, in the amended plan, was to elect the vice president.

In practice, the convention's solution to the problem of electing the president was to prove a victory for the proponents of a strong president, for nationalism, and—in the long run—for democracy. The rise of political parties resulted in a situation in which the ELECTORAL COLLEGE, rather than the Congress, commonly chose the president—only one election, that of 1824, being settled in the House of Representatives for want of an electoral college majority for any candidate. The requirement for an electoral college majority also was to prove a powerful factor in encouraging intersectional political parties and the reconciliation of sectional differences, again an important element in the development of American nationalism. Finally, the fact that the finished Constitution allowed the states to choose their electors in any manner they wished opened the way, after 1789, for the selection of electors by direct popular election—a mode of election every state in the Union except South Carolina was to adopt by 1832. Adaptability of the Constitution to the growth of political democracy was to be a major factor in the new charter's remarkable durability.

Equally nationalistic in its long-range implications was the convention's resort to the judiciary to solve the difficult problem of guaranteeing federal sovereignty and national supremacy against incursion by the states. The convention early rejected coercion of derelict states as inconsistent with the prospective government's sovereign character. State coercion, the nationalists had come to realize, implied state sovereignty. A little later the delegates abandoned congressional disallowance of state legislation as also involving a wrong principle; exercise of a veto over unconstitutional legislation, they had concluded, was properly a judicial, rather than a legislative, function.

Quite surprisingly, the states' rights–oriented New Jersey Plan supplied the final solution. This plan carried a clause declaring the Constitution, treaties, and laws of the national government to be the "supreme law of the respective states" and binding the state courts to enforce them as such, anything in their own constitutions and laws to the contrary notwithstanding. Following rejection of the congressional veto, the convention adopted the supremacy clause from the New Jersey Plan, at the same time altering its language to make the federal Constitution, treaties, and acts of Congress "the supreme law of the land."

Incorporation of the supremacy clause in the new Constitution was a tremendous victory in disguise for the nationalist cause. On the surface the clause made an agency of the states—the state courts—the final judge of the limits of both federal and state sovereignty, which explains why the states' rights faction acceded so readily to its adoption. But the convention, meanwhile, had also provided for the establishment of a national judiciary, with a SUPREME COURT and such lower courts as Congress should determine upon, and had vested in the federal courts jurisdiction over all cases arising under the Constitution, treaties, and laws of the United States. By implication, as the nationalists were shortly to realize, this gave the federal judiciary appellate power to review state court decisions involving federal constitutional questions. This in turn meant that the Supreme Court of the United States would possess the ultimate power to settle questions involving the respective spheres of state and federal sovereignty. The JUDICIARY ACT OF 1789, virtually an extension of the Constitution itself, was to write into federal law this system of appeals from state to federal courts on constitutional questions. And the Supreme Court in *MARTIN V. HUNTER'S LESSEE* (1816) and *COHENS V. VIRGINIA* (1821) was to confirm the constitutionality of the Supreme Court's role as the final arbiter of the constitutional system.

Meanwhile, in a concession to the states' rights party, the convention had quietly dropped the sweeping delegation to Congress of power to legislate in all cases in which the states were severally "incompetent" and had resorted instead to a specific enumeration of the powers of Congress, as the Articles of Confederation provided. The new Constitution's enumeration, however, was far more impressive than that in the articles. In addition to the familiar authority to legislate upon matters of war, foreign affairs, the post office, currency, Indian affairs, and the like, Congress was also to possess the all-important powers of taxation and regulation of foreign and interstate commerce, as well as authority to enact naturalization, bankruptcy, and patent and copyright laws. Further, the convention in its final draft incorporated an important clause giving Congress the power to enact "necessary and proper" legislation in fulfillment of its delegated powers, and it accepted a vaguely drafted "general welfare clause" that, with the "necessary and proper" provisions, was to serve in the twentieth century as the basis for a tremendous expansion of federal power.

In mid-September 1787 the convention put its various resolutions and decisions into a finished draft and submitted the Constitution to the states for approval. The convention had provided for ratification of the Constitution by conventions in the several states, stipulating that ratification by any nine states would be sufficient to put the Constitution into effect. This mode of ratification gravely violated the provision in the Articles of Confederation for ratification of constitutional amendments by unanimous action of the several state legislatures; but it also gave the Constitution a reasonable chance for adoption, which it otherwise would not have had.

In fact, the Federalists, as the proponents of ratification of the Constitution soon became known, in the next ten months carried every state but two, failing only in Rhode Island and North Carolina. There were several reasons behind their impressive victory. Most important, the Federalists had a positive and imaginative remedy to offer for the country's grave constitutional ills. Their opponents, the Antifederalists, although they opposed the Constitution as a dangerous instrument of potential tyranny, could offer no constructive proposal of their own.

Very influential was the fact that most of the young republic's illustrious public figures—Washington, Franklin, Hamilton, Madison, Jay, Rutledge, King, Pinckney, and Wilson among them—favored ratification. It was a galaxy that quite outshone Antifederalists Patrick Henry, Richard Henry Lee, George Mason, and the vacillating Sam Adams. Such was his immense prestige that Washington's voice alone may well have been decisive in the ratification debate.

The distribution of delegates in the state ratifying conventions also helped the Federalist cause. Delegates to these bodies were in every instance elected from the existing districts of the various state legislatures, most of which had for many years been gerrymandered in favor of the tidewater regions. But it was precisely in these districts that the people generally were most keenly aware of the deficiencies of the Confederation government and that support for ratification was strongest.

The Federalists also won impressive early victories in several less populous states, where public sentiment was heavily influenced by the Constitution's provision for state equality in the Senate. Delaware and New Jersey, which ratified in December; Georgia and Connecticut, which ratified in January; and Maryland, which ratified in April, fell into this category. This initial ratification surge proved to be very favorable psychologically to the Federalist cause.

The Federalists' political strategy also was far superior to that of their opponents. In Pennsylvania, where public sentiment strongly favored ratification, the Federalists first defeated an attempt in the legislature to block the quorum necessary for a convention call. Under Wilson's masterful leadership, the Federalists in December then drove the Constitution through to ratification in the state convention. In South Carolina, the Federalists effectively thwarted an Antifederalist attempt to defeat a convention call. They controlled the subsequent convention without difficulty.

Federalist strategy was most impressive in Massachusetts, Virginia, and New York. In each instance, initial prospects for ratification had been dubious. In Massachusetts, where Antifederalist feeling was exacerbated by bitter memories of Shays's Rebellion, the Federalists first won over John Hancock and Sam Adams with hints of high national office. They then converted a number of marginal Antifederalists by freely accepting a variety of proposals for a federal bill of rights. Ratification followed in February by the narrow vote of 187 to 168. The Virginia convention, which assembled in June, witnessed a spectacular debate between Patrick Henry and Madison, in which the quiet and scholarly Madison used carefully reasoned analysis of the Constitution to refute Henry's impassioned assault. Again, ready Federalist acceptance of proposals for a bill of rights helped carry the day. The Federalists triumphed on the ratification vote (89 to 79).

381

In New York, over two-thirds of the delegates to the June convention were declared Antifederalists, and the state's powerful landed aristocracy also opposed ratification, mainly because of the Constitution's potential impact on New York's revenue system. But the Constitution's supporters earlier had softened public opinion somewhat with a series of newspaper articles by Hamilton, Madison, and Jay, published eventually under the title of *The Federalist*, which still stands as one of the most brilliant analyses of the Constitution ever written. News that both New Hampshire and Virginia, the ninth and tenth states to ratify, had lately acted favorably and that the Constitution would in any event go into operation badly damaged Antifederalist morale. Again, conciliatory Federalist acceptance of proposed amendments, together with their support for a meaningless resolution calling for a second federal convention, proved decisive. On the final vote the Constitution was ratified (30 to 27).

The Rhode Island legislature, still controlled by hostile paper-money advocates, had refused even to call a convention. In the essentially frontier state of North Carolina, where public sentiment heavily opposed ratification, the state convention, meeting in July, was dominated by Antifederalists. This body finally adjourned without any formal vote on ratification. At length, in November 1789, a second North Carolina convention, convening several months after the new government had gone into operation, ratified the Constitution without incident. In Rhode Island, a Federalist faction captured control of the state legislature in the spring of 1790. The new assembly promptly called a convention, which ratified the Constitution in May (34 to 32).

Both the drafting and ratification of the Constitution were triumphs for the framers' Enlightenment philosophy: faith in the essentially rational character of man and society, and belief in man's ability to define and solve social and political problems adequately. Indeed the Constitution itself is perhaps best understood as an Enlightenment document, embodying as it does in its preamble the objectives of justice, order, liberty, and the general welfare, and with its explicit and implicit commitments to the ideals of limited government, civil liberties, separation of church and state, the confinement of military power, and an open society.

The Constitution has sometimes been interpreted either as an antidemocratic document—as contrasted with the Declaration of Independence with its profession of faith in universal human equality—or as no more than an instrument of selfish class interests. Both views are superficial and essentially erroneous. The Constitution was adopted by a process far more democratic than was the Declaration of Independence, which was promulgated without any popular validation or consent whatever. At the time of its adoption, the Constitution also was by far the most popular and democratically oriented frame of national government in the world. It provided for a republican government when all others, with a few minor exceptions, were monarchical. Furthermore, in its provisions for a popularly based legislative house and for a president and Senate indirectly subject to democratic processes, in its sharp limitation upon the power of government to punish for treason, and in its general concern for limited government and civil liberties, it went a great deal further in the direction of modern democracy than any other national government then in existence. Moreover, the Constitution's open-ended character, which later made it possible to adapt its provisions to the steady growth of political democracy, was no accident. It expressed instead the self-conscious belief of the framers in the idea of flexibility and growth in government, rather than stifling rigidity.

Nor was the Constitution, viewed in the large, a product of selfish and exclusive class interests. In 1913 the historian Charles A. Beard published *An Economic Interpretation of the Constitution of the United States*, in which he asserted that the Constitution was the work of an economic elite whose wealth was concentrated in paper: land speculators, bondholders, moneyed merchants and lawyers, and the like. The Constitution, Beard asserted, reflected the interests of this class. In support of his argument, he pointed to the Constitution's provisions banning states from issuing paper money or impairing the obligations of contracts, guaranteeing the national government control over money and credit, and guaranteeing the national debt. But careful research in the 1950s and 1960s has shown that the framers as a group were not especially involved in bondholding and speculative operations and that they were drawn as much from planter, agrarian, and nonspeculative mercantile and legal interests as from any moneyed elite. The Constitution did indeed reflect the special concern of men of property, learning, position, and community standing for stable, well-ordered government. This was hardly narrow selfishness; rather it constituted enlightened patriotism.

BIBLIOGRAPHY

Beard, Charles A. *An Economic Interpretation of the Constitution of the United States.* New York: Macmillan, 1961.

Bowen, Catherine Drinker. *Miracle at Philadelphia: The Story of the Constitutional Convention.* Boston: Little, Brown, 1966.

Kenyon, Cecelia. *The Anti-Federalists.* Boston: Northeastern University Press, 1985.

Main, Jackson Turner. *The Anti-Federalists: Critics of the Constitution, 1781–1788.* Chapel Hill: University of North Carolina Press, 1961.

McDonald, Forrest. *We the People: The Economic Origins of the Constitution.* Chicago: University of Chicago Press, 1958.

Rakove, Jack N. *Original Meanings: Politics and Ideas in the Making of the Constitution.* New York: Knopf, 1996.

Rossiter, Clinton L. *1787: The Grand Convention.* New York: Norton, 1987.

Wood, Gordon S. *The Creation of the American Republic, 1776–1787.* Chapel Hill: University of North Carolina Press, 1969.

Alfred H. Kelly / A. G.

See also **Annapolis Convention; Bill of Rights in U.S. Constitution; Civil Rights and Liberties; Colonial Assemblies; Commerce Clause; Connecticut Compromise; Enumerated Powers; "Federalist Papers"; First Amendment; General Welfare Clause; Inherent Powers; Petition, Right of; Rights of Englishmen; Search and Seizure, Unreasonable; Separation of Powers; War and the Constitution;** *and vol. 9:* **Congress Debates the Fourteenth Amendment; Constitution of the United States; The Call for Amendments.**

CONSTITUTIONAL UNION PARTY.

Late in 1859, with growing dissatisfaction in the southern states over excessive protective tariffs and failures to enforce fugitive slave laws, old-line Whigs and members of the American (Know-Nothing) Party, alarmed at excesses of partisanship and sectionalism and fearing secession, formed a new party under the leadership of Kentucky Senator John J. Crittenden. Meeting in convention on 9 May 1860 in Baltimore, delegates chose John Bell of Tennessee and Edward Everett of Massachusetts as candidates for president and vice president. Affection for the Union was reflected in the meager platform, which disregarded sectional issues and sought to rally moderate men to support "the Constitution, the Union and the Laws." Bell trailed the Republican candidate, Abraham Lincoln, and the two Democratic nominees, Stephen A. Douglas and John C. Breckinridge. He obtained 591,658 popular votes (12.6 percent of the total) and carried the states of Virginia, Kentucky, and Tennessee with their thirty-nine electoral votes. The party thereby temporarily disrupted the secession movement, and perhaps contributed later to keeping Kentucky in the Union. In the ensuing months, party leaders called for reconciliation of the sections through compromise, but without success. With the coming of the Civil War, the party dissolved.

BIBLIOGRAPHY

Rhodes, James F. *History of the United States from the Compromise of 1850 to the Final Restoration of Home Rule at the South in 1877.* Reprint of the 1892–1919 edition. Port Washington, N.Y.: Kennikat Press, 1967.

Allen E. Ragan
Jon Roland

See also **Political Parties; Secession.**

CONSUMER PROTECTION.

Legislative protection of the consumer dates back to the codes of antiquity. On the North American continent, provisions protecting consumers were incorporated into the earliest colonial codes. The 1648 *Laws and Liberties of Massachusetts,* for example, regulated the price of bread and butter, set standards for barrels and staves, and provided for inspections of commercial enterprises to ensure compliance with these regulations. A century and a half later, the architects of the new nation gave the federal government the power to promote consumer protection by granting Congress the Constitutional authority to "regulate Comerce . . . among the several States," and to "coin Money, regulate the Value thereof, . . . and fix the Standard of Weights and Measures."

Just as the economy underwent a transformation in the nineteenth century, so too did the amount and nature of consumer protection. In colonial agrarian communities, the buyer was effectively shielded by his knowledge of products and often by strong community sanctions against fraudulent practices. Rapid population growth, the rise of urban centers, and industrialization with its specialization and division of labor undermined these traditional protections. As a consequence, during the early nineteenth century, state and local authorities passed a deluge of economic restrictions. They enacted laws controlling the manufacture and sale of a wide range of products including chocolate, clapboards, firewood, fish, flaxseed, gunpowder, hops, nails, oils, sandals, shingles, shoes, and wood. They expanded the number of trades for which one needed a license. And they passed laws dealing with public markets, sale of unwholesome provisions, monopolies, frauds, usury, and weights and measures.

One feature of this early regulatory regime was that authority was local and diffuse. Legislatures did not create agencies to protect consumers, but rather gave this responsibility to an array of local and public officials—including mayors, justices of the peace, inspectors, weighers, cullers, surveyors, measurers, and gaugers. In the late nineteenth century, however, social and economic changes led to a centralization of regulatory authority and new mechanisms for protecting consumers. By the early twentieth century, a movement to create state commissions to regulate electric and gas utilities was sweeping across the country. During this same period, federal intervention in the economy became directed at stabilizing industries wracked by competition, while at the same time protecting consumers. Following journalistic exposés of the sale of unsanitary meats and the peddling of worthless patent medicines, Congress passed the Meat Inspection Act and the Pure Food and Drug Act in 1906. That same year, it expanded the powers of the Interstate Commerce Commission to include railroad rate-setting. And in 1914, Congress established the Federal Trade Commission to monitor false and misleading advertising.

Much of this late-nineteenth- and early-twentieth-century consumer legislation was ineffective because of narrow court interpretations and inadequate enforcement. Furthermore, the business community often helped draft the legislation and favored regulatory strategies that ameliorated only the worst effects of competition and that did not offer the most comprehensive or effective protection to consumers. Out of this milieu emerged a consumer movement directed at the proliferation of rival, often exaggerated product claims and dubious business practices. The advertising industry responded by creating the National Better Business Bureau in 1925 in an effort at self-policing. The Bureau was to monitor the integrity of national advertising, but it had to rely on voluntary codes of conduct since it had no enforcement powers. Private consumer education groups and club-women pushed for more protective legislation and published "guinea pig" books, which warned against product quackery. This agitation lead to the creation of Consumers Research in 1928, a private nonprofit organization designed to substitute the publication of laboratory test results for partisan advertising claims. Consumers Research was soon to be overshadowed by a rival nonprofit testing organization, Consumers Union, formed in 1936. The latter had by the beginning of the twenty-first century, a subscription roster of over four million for its magazine *Consumer Reports.*

These early consumer testing efforts greatly accelerated the growth of consumer legislation, including amendments that strengthened the Food and Drug Act and the Federal Trade Commission law and laws that mandated and supported consumer protection efforts in the Department of Agriculture, the Department of Transportation, and a host of other federal, state, and local governmental agencies. In 1961, President John F. Kennedy formed the Consumer Advisory Council. Lyndon B. Johnson established the position of special assistant on consumer affairs and the President's Committee on Consumer Interests.

These new executive branch offices reflected the emergence of the modern consumer movement. And the man most responsible for the modern consumer movement was Ralph Nader. Nader can claim credit for some of the nation's most important federal consumer protection laws, including the National Traffic and Motor Vehicle Safety Act (1966), the Freedom of Information Act (1966), and the Consumer Product Safety Act (1972). Perhaps Nader's greatest success was improved auto safety. His 1965 book, *Unsafe at Any Speed*, exposed the safety mishaps and design flaws of U.S. automobiles and spurred safety and design changes in the auto industry leading to such innovations as seat belts, air bags, and antilock brakes. Traffic deaths in the United States fell from roughly 55,000 in the early 1970s to 47,000 in 1990 due to Nader's efforts as well as such other factors as the raising of the drinking age to twenty-one in most states.

Nader extended and institutionalized his effort by using the almost half-million dollars he received from General Motors to settle an invasion of privacy lawsuit in the 1960s to fund a network of dozens of consumer groups. These organizations became training grounds for political activists and lawyers. Some of Nader's Raiders eventually went into private law practice where they continued to sue businesses on behalf of injured consumers and workers, helping to generate an increase in tort lawsuits in the 1970s and 1980s. Many of these lawsuits addressed real wrongs. Thousands of women were part of the class-action suits brought against the manufacturers of tampons causing toxic shock syndrome, a form of poisoning that killed or permanently injured the women. The lawsuit won millions of dollars in damages for women around the country and forced tampon manufacturers to alter their products. Lawsuits also recovered damages for victims of the Ford Pinto, an automobile that, because of a design flaw, tended to explode and burn when struck from behind. Businesses claimed, however, that many lawsuits were filed on much less justifiable grounds, clogging the courts and leading to outlandish jury verdicts, particularly when juries awarded punitive damages designed to punish defendants for their actions rather than compensate plaintiffs.

Nader did not work alone. The Consumer Federation of America formed national, state, and local consumer organizations in the 1960s and 1970s to assist in the handling of buyers' complaints, to lobby for legislation, and to introduce consumer education into the schools. Other organizations emerged, such as the Center for Science in the Public Interest, to support research and advocacy. And consumer testing organizations similar to the Consumers Union sprang up abroad and became federated in an International Organization of Consumers Unions founded in The Hague in 1960 to afford an international technical interchange.

As the modern consumer movement matured during the late 1970s and into the 1980s and 1990s, it found itself both enjoying the successes of trying to improve product safety and consumer awareness but also battling strong political and business attempts to curb or eliminate the movement's power. The consumer movement's successes included such important safety measures as the standard use of seat belts and air bags in cars and trucks sold in the United States. Consumers could also learn about the nutritional level of the packaged foods they bought, once the federal government, under prodding of the consumer movement, forced foodmakers to include such labeling on products. The movement also showed success on the anti-smoking front, with many public and private places across the country banning smoking. In addition, it forced regulatory agencies to recognize that their mission is not centrally that of assisting business but of helping to provide honest and fair dealing in the marketplace.

To others, however, the movement's maturity strangled the nation and business with regulations, increased costs for consumers, employed too many nonproductive lawyers, and added to the individual and collective sense of aggrievement that permeated much of American society during the late twentieth century. As conservatives reasserted their power—first with Ronald Reagan's two terms as president during the 1980s, then with the Republican sweep of the 1994 congressional elections—many of the political and bureaucratic gains of the consumer movement came under attack. Taking their cue from the 1994 campaign document known as the "Contract with America," congressional Republicans introduced legislation the following year to curb or repeal such legislation as the Clean Water (1967) and Clean Air (1970) acts, which they deemed harmful to business. They continued efforts begun in the 1980s to restrict punitive damages. They sought to severely restrict the ability of stockholders to sue a company while also making it more difficult to sue a company for product liability. And they moved to repeal some of the nation's banking and bankruptcy laws that benefited consumers. Although some of these efforts were successful, the strength of the consumer movement and the deep public support for its fundamental aims ensured strong resistance to any serious threats to the laws and regulatory apparatus that provides protection to consumers.

BIBLIOGRAPHY

Goodwin, Lorine Swainston. *The Pure Food, Drink, and Drug Crusaders, 1879–1914.* Jefferson, N.C.: McFarland, 1999.

Holsworth, Robert D. *Public Interest Liberalism and the Crisis of Affluence: Reflections on Nader, Environmentalism, and the Politics of a Sustainable Society.* Boston: G.K. Hall, 1980.

McCraw, Thomas K. *Prophets of Regulation.* Cambridge, Mass.: Belknap Press of Harvard University Press, 1984.

Mayer, Robert N. *The Consumer Movement: Guardians of the Marketplace.* Boston: Twayne Publishers, 1989.

Nader, Ralph. *Crashing the Party: Taking on the Corporate Government in an Age of Surrender.* New York: Thomas Dunne Books/St. Martin's Press, 2001.

Novak, William J. *The People's Welfare: Law and Regulation in Nineteenth-Century America.* Chapel Hill: University of North Carolina Press, 1996.

Silber, Norman Isaac. *Test and Protest: The Influence of Consumers Union.* New York: Holmes & Meier, 1983.

Thomas G. Gress
Colston E. Warne/ c. p.

See also **Accidents; Automobile Safety; Bankruptcy Laws; Consumers Leagues; Federal Trade Commission; Food and Drug Administration; Licenses to Trade; Meat Inspection Laws; Nader's Raiders; Product Tampering; Pure Food and Drug Movement; Toxic Shock Syndrome;** *Unsafe at Any Speed.*

CONSUMER PURCHASING POWER.

Consumer purchasing power measures the value in money for which consumers may purchase goods or services. Tied to the Consumer Price Index, or the Cost of Living Index as it is also known in the United States, consumer purchasing power indicates the degree to which inflation affects consumers' ability to buy. As a general rule, if income rises at the same rate as inflation, consumers can maintain their present standard of living. If, however, income rises faster than the rate of inflation, the standard of living will improve. By the same token, if inflation rises faster than income, even if wages and salaries also increase, then the standard of living will decline as consumers, although receiving more money in their paychecks, find their income inadequate to counteract rising prices.

Consumer purchasing power is determined by the Consumer Price Index, which surveys changes in the prices of goods and services over a period of months or years. First published in 1921 and prepared monthly from data compiled by the Bureau of the Census for the Bureau of Labor Statistics, the Consumer Price Index indicates a rise or fall in the price of four hundred select items ranging from groceries to housing. Even small changes in the price of the commodities listed on the Consumer Price Index provide the best estimate of consumer purchasing power.

Between 1922 and 1928, just after the federal government began to publish monthly reports on the cost of living and consumer purchasing power, per capita income in the United States climbed approximately 30 percent and real wages rose by an average of 22 percent. Consumer purchasing power had rarely been stronger as America became the first country in the history of the world to experience mass affluence. Yet mounting consumer debt severely restricted consumer purchasing power, a development that contributed to the onset of the Great Depression in the 1930s. The massive unemployment that accompanied the depression naturally limited consumer purchasing power even further.

To control inflation and bolster consumer purchasing power during World War II, President Franklin D. Roosevelt instituted the Office of Price Administration to fix prices on thousands on nonagricultural goods. This mechanism worked effectively in wartime, but when price controls lapsed in June of 1946, Americans experienced the worst inflation in their history, and with it a marked decline in consumer purchasing power. The price of agricultural commodities, for example, rose 14 percent in one month and 30 percent before the end of the year, which sent food prices soaring.

Despite the economic problems that beset the immediate postwar years, the increased productivity of agriculture and industry brought unprecedented affluence to the vast majority of Americans. Expendable income rose from $57 in 1950 to $80 in 1959, while consumer debt had increased 800 percent by 1957, enabling Americans to purchase everything from household appliances and television sets to sporting equipment and swimming pools—all unimaginable luxuries only a generation earlier. Strong consumer purchasing power, combined with stable prices and a minuscule inflation rate, made goods and services relatively less expensive. There had never been a better time to be a consumer.

This period of affluence ended in the early 1970s, when rising inflation, skyrocketing energy costs, and growing unemployment wreaked havoc on the American economy. Presidents Richard Nixon, Gerald Ford, and Jimmy Carter each imposed limits on wage and price increases, but to no avail. The economy continued to falter, and consumer purchasing power diminished. To rejuvenate the economy, Ronald Reagan, who became President in 1981, proposed to reduce taxes, balance the federal budget, curtail government spending on social programs, and withdraw regulations on business. Together these measures constituted what Reagan's economic advisors called "supply-side" economics. The initial results of the so-called Reagan Revolution were unsettling: stock prices tumbled, unemployment climbed to 10.8 percent, and the federal deficit reached $195 billion. It was only in 1982, when Reagan abandoned "supply-side" dogma and persuaded the Federal Reserve to expand the money supply and lower interest rates in an effort to improve consumer purchasing power, that the economy began to show signs of recovery.

By July 1990 the economic boom of the 1980s had run its course and the economy again gradually sank into recession. Given the sluggish performance of the economy during the late 1980s and early 1990s, few could have predicted the remarkable developments of the later 1990s. The emergence of the Internet and the evolution of the global economy generated unprecedented economic prosperity in the United States that lifted consumer purchasing power to new heights. Stock values escalated while inflation receded and unemployment fell. As a result, consumer confidence rose and consumer spending accelerated. At the end of 2000, however, economic growth had slowed, though sustained consumer spending prevented the downturn from worsening.

BIBLIOGRAPHY

Bruchey, Stuart. *The Wealth of a Nation: An Economic History of the United States.* New York: Harper and Row, 1988.

Chandler, Lester V. *Inflation in the United States, 1940–1948.* New York: Harper, 1951.

Galbraith, John Kenneth. *The Affluent Society.* Boston: Houghton Mifflin, 1958.

Leuchtenburg, William E. *The Perils of Prosperity, 1914–1932.* Chicago: University of Chicago Press, 1993.

Port, Otis. "Customers Move into the Driver's Seat." *Business Week,* 4 October 1999, 103–106.

Mark G. Malvasi

See also **Consumer Protection; Consumerism; Consumers Leagues; Installment Buying, Selling, and Financing.**

CONSUMERISM describes the shift in American culture from a producer-oriented society in the nineteenth century to a "consumerist" society in the twentieth century. Changes in domestic demographics and advances in industrialization, manufacturing, transportation, and communication all contributed to the change. Consumerism also contributed greatly to the liberal thrust of the Progressive Era and spawned a long-running trend of consumer advocacy and consumer protection legislation.

Early History of American Consumerism

From the colonial era until the late nineteenth century, the United States was a producer-oriented nation. Simply, most Americans produced what they needed, generating only what their immediate families or villages could use. Farmers—sometimes inaccurately called "subsistence

farmers"—grew a variety of crops and vegetables on small acreages, stored what their families could use, and peddled whatever surplus there might be in the nearest town. The raising of livestock usually centered on one or two family dairy cows and some swine and fowl for slaughter. Few large commercial herds existed.

In villages and towns, artisans produced durable goods—such as furniture, clothing, tools, and firearms—but on a piece-by-piece basis. No mass production existed, and while artisans strove for uniformity, every chair, musket, or watch had to be handmade.

Of course, exceptions existed. In New England, American shipbuilders, exploiting an abundance of timber, made ships and boats that, through the British mercantile system, ultimately serviced much of Europe and the New World. In the South, where open fields were plentiful and lent themselves to plantations, agrarians created world markets for tobacco, rice, sugar, indigo, and later, cotton. None other than George Washington created a seaboard market for fish that his slaves and workers seined out of the Potomac River. But in the main, most Americans produced only what they could use or sell close by, and bought only what their neighbors had to offer. The market was one of scarcity.

The producer-oriented dynamic gave Americans an advantage as they sparred with England over issues of taxation and representation prior to the American Revolution. As Parliament levied tax after tax on goods that British merchants sold to American buyers, the Yankees protested with a "nonconsumption" movement, choosing not to buy taxed goods but instead to make them at home. American women, who had to fill the gaps nonconsumption left by spinning thread and making extra candles or garments, proved to be the backbone of the movement.

In the early days of the republic, however, some American leaders urged a broadening of the American economy. Alexander Hamilton, President Washington's secretary of the Treasury, and most members of the New England–based Federalist Party believed that for the United States to become fiscally sound it needed to sell products to the rest of the world. Hamilton's "Report on Manufactures" (1791) advocated larger, consumer-oriented businesses that could carve niches in world markets. External trade, of course, was Hamilton's impetus, but the mechanisms that Americans would create to achieve larger world markets would also change domestic buying.

Hamilton's stance caused the rise of the first American party system. Believing that agrarian, producer-oriented independence was essential for a strong republic and democracy, Thomas Jefferson and his followers in the Democratic-Republican Party opposed Hamilton's bid to strengthen business. Ultimately, Americans would balance both ideas for more than a century.

Improvements in Manufacturing

One of the key elements in the development of a consumerist nation would be uniformity and speed in manufacturing. By 1798, thanks to the brainchild of Eli Whitney, that element was taking hold. Whitney, best known for creating the cotton gin (which made southern cotton profitable and renewed southern dependence on slavery), also developed the idea of interchangeable parts. Whitney realized that artisans could speed their work and double, perhaps triple, their output if they did not have to handcraft every part of whatever they built. For instance, why hand make every lock mechanism for a musket? Instead, create a machine that could uniformly stamp or mold each lock, trigger, pan, and so on. The benefits would be manifold: artisans or manufacturers could more rapidly turn out individual pieces; prices for the pieces would drop, making them more accessible to consumers; and the items would become more durable. Instead of requiring a whole new item if a component part broke, the owner could simply get a cheap replacement part.

Manufacturing soon adopted the idea of interchangeable parts. One of the first to do so was textile mills and clothing makers. With sewing machines now cheaper to operate, the entrepreneur Francis Cabot Lowell saw an opportunity. He collected hundreds of sewing machines into a manufactory at Waltham, Massachusetts, between 1812 and 1814, and then he sought seamstresses to operate them. Lowell encouraged young women to leave their family farms and live in dormitories he built at Waltham. They would work during the day, and they could attend Lowell-sponsored education classes by night. At Waltham, Lowell created a "company town," and he encouraged one of the first farm-to-city migrations in the nation's history. Other manufacturers followed suit, and a cycle began: Americans gradually began leaving family farms to work at industrial, née urban, centers, quickly making cheaper goods that other Americans could afford.

Transport and Territorial Expansion

Another factor also stimulated growth: American expansion and transportation. Even before the American Revolution, Americans were taking territory west of the Appalachian Mountains. With American victory in the Revolution, the nation had control of the land south of the Great Lakes and west to the Mississippi River. Settlers quickly spread into those regions. Open acreages were conducive to commercial agriculture, but the agrarians discovered that it was difficult to get their produce back over the Appalachians to eastern markets. The quickest route was to float goods down the Ohio River, onto the Mississippi River, and out the Gulf of Mexico, around Spanish Florida, and up the Atlantic coast to New York. Such a trip was cumbersome and fraught with the potential for financial loss.

The arrival of steamships (whose engines could be efficiently built with interchangeable parts) revolutionized market shipping. Now boat captains could go upriver instead of only downriver. And if rivers did not exist from one place to a convenient market, Americans simply created a waterway with the advent of the "Canal Era."

Americans hesitated little to mold the land to their needs. They built canals from city to city throughout the East and in some portions of the South. The most famous was the Erie Canal. Completed in 1825, it connected the Great Lakes with the Hudson River in New York, and the Atlantic Ocean. Thus, the American West was connected with the sea.

Steam-powered locomotives and railroads, however, soon supplanted the canals. Canals were prone to stagnation in summer months. Also, towing animals often fell in them and drowned; and sediment deposits forced frequent dredging. Railroads had none of those problems—one could simply lay down some tracks and run a locomotive over them. By the 1840s, most areas of the Northeast and North were becoming linked to the west by rails. In short, manufacturing and transportation were coming together to make products cheaper and more accessible to Americans.

Railroads continued to boom for the next two decades, and in 1862, during the Civil War, the United States Congress passed the Pacific Railroad Act that authorized a transcontinental railroad to link the East with the far West. That same year, Congress passed the Homestead Act, which promised settlers free land in the West for simply occupying and improving the land. Both measures did much to help the United States utilize the land it had claimed by treaty and war in the early nineteenth century.

They also did much to speed consumerism. Railroads made more money carrying freight than they did carrying passengers. With the first transcontinental railroad completed in 1869 and others soon to follow, railroad managers realized that for the western lines to remain profitable they had to find a way to carry goods to the settlers in the West and their produce or manufactured items back to the East. That certainly would not work if the settlers remained in a producer-oriented, subsistence cycle.

Gradually railroad agents and grain brokers convinced western farmers that the open expanses of the West were ideal for commercial farming. That is, the farmers could concentrate vast acreages in one or two crops, ship the produce to the East, and use their profits to buy supplies and other food that the railroads shipped in from the East.

Railroads did the same for livestock. In 1866, Texans and other southerners looking for opportunities after the Civil War began rounding up wild longhorn cattle in south Texas and driving them to northern markets. Instead of driving them all the way to Chicago, however, the first drivers took herds to a railhead at Sedalia, Missouri. Later they drove cattle to more westerly railheads at Kansas towns like Abilene, Caldwell, and Dodge City. The expanding rail network then took the cattle to stockyards, most notably in Chicago but later, as railroads spread across the South, in Fort Worth as well.

Technology and Consumerism

A postwar boom in technology sped the transportation of goods. With a device called a steam brake, George Westinghouse invented a safer, easier way to stop trains; also, advances in telegraphy made it easier for railroad headquarters to coordinate schedules. After inventor Alexander Graham Bell perfected a telephone in 1879, railroads could do the same thing by voice. Refrigerated cars enabled railroads to carry perishable goods safely across the country. Railroads themselves became more durable. American industrialist Andrew Carnegie imported from Great Britain the "Bessemer Process" for making steel. Stronger than iron, steel was perfect for rails and the running gear on locomotives and cars. It made Carnegie millions of dollars, and it provided another step in the dominance of rail transportation.

The same technological boom affected other areas of the economy. Industrial workplaces boomed. Plants made steel, locomotives, rail cars, trolleys, wagons, textiles, clothing, furniture, and new electrified appliances such as the first American refrigerators and washing machines. Inventor Thomas Alva Edison's electric light bulb made it possible for industrial employees to work before sunrise and after sunset, the traditional agrarian limits of work. Industrial areas became centralized, largely in the Northeast and North, and created urban centers as they grew. After financial panics—the early-day equivalent of depressions—in 1837, 1857, and 1873, more and more farmers and farm families gave up on the vagaries of weather, drought, and crops to move to cities and take steady, if grueling, work in industry. As those new industrial workers gave up traditional reliance on the land, they became dependent on the growing commercial and transportation system. Cities and urban areas grew around industrial centers; grocery and general stores, drugstores, doctors' offices, and municipal water, gas, and electrical supply grew to support the industrial workers and their families.

At the same time, industry created more efficient ways for the decreasing number of American farmers to feed more and more people. Implements such as Cyrus McCormick's reaper, an early combine, quickly facilitated crop harvests. Augers sped planting; steel plows made short work of cultivation.

A New Society

Most historians point to 1880 as the start of the American consumerist movement, not because of any one event, but because by that year the essential elements of a consumerist society were in place. Industrial centers supported agricultural regions; agricultural regions fed industrial centers. People in both consumed what the other produced. Service industries sprang up around both. And in the middle, rapid communication and transportation linked the two.

The social transformation was not easy, and it bore heavily on those at the bottom arc of the cycle—the workers, both industrial and agricultural. On the farms, growers soon felt enslaved by the railroads. They were bound to pay whatever freight rate the railroads demanded, and there was little competition to mitigate those rates. If upstart railroads started competing against older lines, the more established company would start a rate war, slashing its rates until the new company went out of business. Then the older company would raise prices even higher simply because it could. Railroads might also alter schedules to remote areas, forcing farmers to store their grain—at exorbitant prices—in railroad-owned storage silos. It did not take long for growers to realize that grain brokers, who sold their grain in eastern markets, were making more off the crops than the farmers were.

In the industrial workplace, employees faced long hours—often twelve or more per day—in sweaty, dangerous conditions. Pay was low, and employees had little recourse against employers, who protected their own pocketbooks rather than their workers. Industry owners felt no obligation to recompense employers injured on the job or the families of workers killed in workplace accidents.

Urban centers that grew around the industrial centers also attracted foreign immigrants, many fleeing famine and political unrest in Europe. Political "boss machines"—usually corrupt systems for maintaining order in the chaotic urban areas—found ways to fit immigrants into the complex cities, usually by giving them jobs in exchange for votes on election day. Nevertheless, cities became crowded, polluted, infested, and malignant. Yet the cities thrived, as the rest of the nation, now consumerist, devoured their products.

As production soared, businessmen had to continually create markets. They did so with mass advertising. Newspapers and magazines began carrying ads for everything from corsets to constipation remedies. As homes gradually became electrified, industrialists advertised electrical products such as irons, washing machines (essentially the same old wash tub with electric rollers fitted to it), and home-permanent devices for women, something that, when in use, made the user look like an electrified Medusa.

Coca-Cola, based in Atlanta, Georgia, and Dr. Pepper, from Waco, Texas, entered the American vernacular through advertising. So did patent medicines like Lydia E. Pinkham's elixir for all women's problems. Buyers would later rebel when they discovered that most patent medicines contained 20 percent or more of opiates and alcohol.

Consumer Protection Movements

As consumers began to feel more trapped by the new consumerist system, they appealed to the government for help. Thus, consumerism led directly to the Progressive Era, much of which was aimed at consumer advocacy and protection. In fact, the three main epochs of American liberalism—the 1900s, 1930s, and 1960s—all contain significant consumer protection movements.

Midwestern and Western farmers were the first to push for significant consumer protection from the mighty railroads. Banding together in the late 1870s as the Patrons of Husbandry—more popularly known as the Grangers—they sought government intervention into the malevolent rate practices of the railroads. That farmers would ever seek such intervention from the government was in itself a watershed, for Americans had traditionally wanted a laissez-faire government, one that handled foreign relations, wars, the coinage of money, and tariffs but kept its nose out of the affairs of private individuals and businesses.

The efforts of the Grangers coalesced into the Populist Party in the 1880s and bore fruit in 1887 when Populists convinced Congress to pass the Interstate Commerce Act. The act created the Interstate Commerce Commission, designed to watch over the practices of the railroads. It was the first such interventionist act in American history.

By the elections of 1896, the mainstream Democratic Party had co-opted the Populist platform, and populism itself melded into a new era known as progressivism. Like populism, progressivism sought consumer protections, but also protections for the industrial, urban working classes that fueled consumerism. Progressivism would ultimately see a variety of acts strengthen the Interstate Commerce Act: eight-hour workdays established, fire safety mandated in workplaces, child labor abolished, and monopolies attacked.

One of the biggest breaks for consumers came in the administration of President Theodore Roosevelt (1901–1909) when Congress passed legislation to guard the purity of prepared foods and drugs. Consumer advocates had known for some time that packing companies used additives such as formaldehyde and other chemicals to preserve food, and Congress considered bills in 1892 and 1902 to protect buyers from harmful ingredients. Republicans, many of whom had interests in or connections to meatpacking, defeated the measures.

By 1906, however, the political climate was changing. Muckrakers—journalists who used often-sensational investigative reporting to expose graft, corruption, and wrongdoing in a variety of business arenas—began targeting food preparation. One of them, Upton Sinclair, a socialist who was attempting to expose the plight of immigrants in American cities, inadvertently added fuel to the consumer advocacy groups when he published *The Jungle* in 1906.

Some of the characters in *The Jungle* worked in a Chicago meatpacking plant. In his narrative, Sinclair detailed how rats, rat poison, rat feces, and even human body parts often got mixed in with processed meats and marketed to the public. Sickened, the public, advocacy groups, and Roosevelt himself pressured Congress to once again take up a pure food act. In fact, the Senate had passed a new bill just as Sinclair's book appeared. The public clamor and the weight of the American Medical Association prompted the House to also pass the Pure Food and Drug Act, 1906.

The act mandated a system of government inspections on meat processed at packing plants. In an age when Americans still had a large measure of faith in the government, a federal stamp on a side of beef meant it had passed inspection.

As the name implies, the act also sought to safeguard the purity of drug preparations. With no mandated ingredient labeling, "pharmaceutical" companies—often purveyors of quack patent remedies—were free to market preparations for both adults and children containing large quantities of alcohol and opiates. Government inspections after passage of the act largely curtailed such practices.

After a brief detour to supply Allied and American armies in World War I, American industry and agriculture once again sped consumerism in the 1920s. New products—and their concomitant advertising—deluged American buyers. Henry Ford had long since revolutionized automobile manufacturing (all manufacturing, really) with his assembly-line process. Essentially, instead of one team of workers building a car from the ground up, car parts on an assembly line passed by workers who performed one or two specialized tasks. The streamlined process made cars cheaper, but Ford went one better. He made it possible for people to buy cars "on time," or on credit, by making affordable monthly payments.

Ready access to automobiles created a new type of consumerist culture—the car culture. Americans took to the roads, prompting state and local governments to begin paving projects. Motor courts, the forerunners of motels, sprang up to accommodate travelers. Motor courts featured individual bungalows clustered around an office and offered well-appointed bedrooms, bathrooms, and kitchenettes. Automobiles, of course, needed refueling, and oil companies placed filling stations at strategic points along major roadways. Filling station advertising and billboards championed the highest octane in their gasoline; the cleanest restrooms—a must for urgent travelers; and the quickest service. Oil companies also issued some of the first credit cards to speed motorists on their way.

Roadsides offered new advertising space to merchants. They hawked everything from soft drinks to headache powders on large billboards erected to catch motorists' attention. The most popular of the advertisements, Burma-Shave signs, peddled shave cream with serialized rhyming signs, all ending with the distinctive Burma-Shave logo.

Advertisements and American Consumers

Advertising perhaps preyed on emotion and basic human need as a way to create markets. As the car culture took hold and enabled suburbia to spread, many young housewives and mothers found themselves increasingly isolated from traditional family connections. Advertising stepped up to fill the void, with ad copy that offered thinly veiled familial wisdom: whole grain cereals were the key to health in children; clean bathrooms were the key to social acceptance; mouthwashes and toothpastes the key to sexual appeal. Such advertising barraged women from newspapers, magazines like *Good Housekeeping* and *Ladies' Home Journal*, and the newer medium of radio.

Economic historian Don Slater has said that the 1920s marked an ideological milestone in the progression of consumerism. Mass advertising of new products heralded them as the key to modernity, and consumers embraced the idea. Advertising implied that "consumerism itself [was] the shining path to modernity: [it] incited [the] public to modernize themselves, modernize their homes, their means of transport." Indeed, Slater sees in the consumerism of the 1920s a "double face," one which shows mainstream middle America embracing consumerism as a path toward security and contentment and a radical youth/flapper culture embracing it as a license for pleasure. For whatever sector, sociologists would argue that 1920s consumerism pointed both groups away from the carnage of World War I.

Late in the decade, however, some consumer advocates voiced concern that advertising was unfairly targeting human fears in order to sell goods, and manifestly lying by saying that new, health-related products had undergone scientific testing and carried the approval of the medical community. In 1927, authors Stuart Chase and F. J. Schlink published *Your Money's Worth: A Study in the Waste of the Consumer's Dollar.* The authors charged that producers were fleecing consumers and, as in the case of some cosmetics containing harmful chemicals, endangering their health.

Consumers' clubs and research groups began to spring up, and state university extension home economists began to champion the rights of consumers. They also attempted to educate consumers on how to make better purchasing decisions.

The Great Depression and Consumerism

The stock market crash of October 1929 and the advent of the Great Depression shifted the American economy from one of plenty to one of scarcity once again. Across the nation, unemployment averaged more than 30 percent. In some urban areas, where industry fed consumerism, it reached nearly 50 percent.

All but the most financially insulated of Americans once again had to save what little money they had. Those lucky enough to remain in a job often found themselves "underemployed," meaning that their wages were significantly less than before the depression began. However, depression-era Americans were subtly different than their pre-consumerist forefathers. While the latter had never dreamed of a consumerist culture (and may well have seen it as wretchedly excessive had they done so), the former had tasted it and wanted to remain consumers as best they could. What had been necessity in the 1920s became luxury in the 1930s, but Americans still consumed.

One of the biggest consumer goods in the 1930s was entertainment. It makes sense: faced with financial crisis or unrelenting poverty at home, Americans sought escape when they could. A few extra cents now and then bought a ticket into a theater where people could watch newsreels, cartoons, a serial, teasers, and a feature. Indeed, the 1930s were Hollywood's "Golden Age." Movies were cheap to make and relied on writing and acting rather than special effects. Studios could crank out "B" movies in less than a week; "A" movies took a little longer. Such actors as Clark Gable, Humphrey Bogart, John Wayne, Bette Davis, and Katharine Hepburn became stars in the 1930s, and moviegoers saw in their situations a way out of their own troubles. Stan Laurel and Oliver Hardy and the Marx Brothers made classic comedies that poked fun at authorities—symbolic of the same authorities who had steered the country into depression.

If they could not make it to the theater, Americans consumed entertainment in other forms. Pulp novels, long a reading staple, continued to thrive, as did comic books. The 1930s saw the origin of two classic American superheroes—Superman and Batman—who fought crime and injustice, again metaphors for the trouble in which the United States found itself. And, for cheaper fare, Americans could simply turn on a radio. Radio offered music, concerts ranging from local bluegrass and religious groups to the Metropolitan Opera; dramas in the form of serials and "soap operas," so named because soap manufacturers sponsored them; and comedy with George Burns and Gracie Allen, Bob Hope, and Jack Benny weekly bringing riotous laughter into homes.

In government, President Franklin D. Roosevelt ushered in the New Deal, a program of deficit spending designed to get Americans back on their feet. In 1938, after five years of wrangling, Congress passed new legislation that increased the oversight power of the Food and Drug Administration to protect consumers, and also strengthened the hand of the Federal Trade Commission, which watched over advertising practices.

World War II Brings Change

The depression gave way to World War II, and while defense spending brought the nation out of the depression and erased unemployment, the war years saw Americans still living in an economy of scarcity. The government rationed perishable goods and food staples, gasoline, and durable goods such as tires and shoes to Americans; the American industrial and agricultural machines had to supply American and Allied soldiers first if they were to defeat global tyranny. In the automobile industry, the 1942 model year was the last for a while; automakers retooled to make army jeeps, tanks, helmets, and a host of other military items.

With millions of men in the armed services, women went to work as they had never done before. In manufacturing plants they built bombers and tanks and aircraft carriers; in business they assumed traditionally male clerk and secretarial roles; at home they managed family finances. With men getting government pay and women at work, some families found themselves, for the first time ever, with two paychecks. They were poised, at war's end, to resume consumerism with a vengeance.

After a brief recession in 1946 as the nation reconverted to a peacetime economy, consumerism boomed in 1947. Holding tidy nest eggs, couples began buying homes, often in expanding suburbs. They replaced worn-out automobiles. They began having the children who would become the baby boomers, the most consumer-oriented generation the world had yet seen.

The 1950s ushered in an era of consumerism that has rolled on virtually unopposed to the present. Americans purchased homes, cars (sometimes two), television sets, new home furnishings, modern refrigerators, clothes for work and their newfound leisure time, barbeque grills, lawn mowers—the list is endless. They continued to consume entertainment as movies continued to boom. Movies also touched off ancillary consumer purchases. When Disney Studios produced a largely fictitious but popular series about Davy Crockett starring Fess Parker, seemingly every boy in America had to have a Disney-marketed coonskin cap like Parker wore in the films.

The recording industry boomed as kids bought up millions of 45-rpm records to play on compact record players in their bedrooms. The crooning styles of Bing Crosby in the 1930s and Frank Sinatra in the 1940s had now given way to the rock 'n' roll beat of Elvis Presley, Chuck Berry, Jerry Lee Lewis, and Bill Haley and the Comets.

But television was beginning to revolutionize entertainment as well. Comedies such as *I Love Lucy* and *Love That Bob* and westerns like *Gunsmoke* and *Maverick* ran weekly. All carried corporate sponsors, and series stars frequently hawked merchandise in both televised commercials and coordinated print ads.

Situation comedies—the first sitcoms—like *Leave It to Beaver*, *Father Knows Best*, and *Ozzie and Harriet* promoted an idealistic, family-centered American lifestyle. Through set design, product placement, and costuming, they also subtly suggested how American homes should look and how people should dress. Consumerism continued to roll as Americans sought to achieve the televised ideal.

Sociologists consider 1950s consumerism as an attempt to achieve contentment and security in a complicated world. The United States had won World War II, defeating the most nefarious enemies the modern world had yet seen—totalitarian Germany and Japan—yet in the 1950s it faced new, ominous threats: an aggressive Soviet Union and nuclear weapons. The United States was a reluctant superpower. Pledged to halt the spread of communism, the country, so recently victorious, looked impotent as China became communist in 1949; as communist aggressors touched off the Korean War in 1950; and

as Red-baiter Senator Joseph McCarthy imagined communists at high levels of American government. Faced with such uncertainties and perceived threats, a new washing machine, a roomy sedan, and a clean toilet spelled homogeneity, continuity, and security for many Americans.

A Liberated Consumerism

The 1960s brought a liberated consumerism. Sexually free with the advent of birth control pills in 1960, and encouraged by such books as Betty Friedan's *The Feminine Mystique* (1963) to drop the June Cleaver wardrobe and attitudes of the 1950s, women sought new and different avenues for their lives. They also became fresh targets for advertisers. Commercials encouraged free lifestyles with portable hair curlers and blow dryers. Women were shown that they need not be tied to motherly chores like cooking with the appearance of such baby boom staples as toaster pastries and instant puddings; they need not dress like their mothers and grandmothers, either, as bell-bottom pants, hip-huggers, and flower-print shirts set a breezy, liberated style for the era. Marketing reminded women that to be any less was to be "square"; yet the double face of marketing continued to chide women for having a less-than-spotless kitchen floor or mirrors that did not sparkle.

Advertising also continued to prey on the male psyche as well. Men needed to drink, smoke, and dress like James Bond. Family sedans were passé: instead, muscle cars like the Pontiac GTO and Oldsmobile 442 were the way to go. Better yet, get into sporty pony cars like the Ford Mustang, Chevrolet Camaro, and Pontiac Firebird. If you could afford it, the Chevrolet Corvette was the ultimate expression of male virility on the road, as Martin Milner and George Maharis had proved in the popular television drama *Route 66*.

Consumer protection took an upswing in 1962 when President John F. Kennedy introduced his Consumer Bill of Rights. Kennedy said that all consumers have a right to safety, the right to be informed about products, the right to choose, and the right to be heard. His platform set the stage for new investigative hearings into the safety of products ranging from over-the-counter medicines to cosmetics.

Undoubtedly the most influential consumer advocate of the age was Ralph Nader. In 1965 he published *Unsafe at Any Speed*, an investigation of the automobile industry, charging that car manufacturers gave little concern to motorist safety in the design of their cars. Nader's attack ultimately led to more convenient seat belts in all cars and side turn indicator lights beginning with the 1968 model year. His crusade also spelled the end of the rear-engine Chevrolet Corvair. Deemed patently unsafe, the Corvair's last model year was 1969.

Consumer advocacy brought a "truth-in-packaging" bill from Congress in 1966. In the 1960s, Congress also mandated that cigarette packages carry the now-famous surgeon general's warning about tobacco and cancer. And, in 1970, Congress forced an end to televised cigarette commercials.

Technology Impacts Consumerism

Technology has increasingly impacted consumerism. Compact computers designed to help astronauts fly to the moon in the 1960s became the basis for the first handheld calculators of the 1970s. Both are the forerunners of today's personal computers and Macs. The obsolescence curve of computer equipment ensures a continually fresh curve of computer consumers.

The appearance of videocassette recording technology in the late 1970s gave American television viewers more latitude in their viewing habits. No longer were they slaves to television schedules; they could record one program while watching another. Videocassette recorders also gave rise to the entirely new video rental industry, in the 1980s. As the new millennium began, digitally recorded movie discs—DVDs—were pushing videocassettes aside.

In music, the rapid public acceptance of compact discs—CDs—in 1986 made vinyl records obsolete. Suddenly a new market opened up, as millions of baby-boom rock 'n' rollers strove to replace their vinyl record collections with new digital ones.

And, since the early 1980s, computers increasingly have assisted the systems in automobiles, from engine function to climate control. Not only have computers improved engine performance and fuel efficiency, they have also done away with the "shade-tree mechanic." No longer can a car buff effectively tune his car on a weekend afternoon; consumers need trained computer techs to do the job.

The shift from a producer-oriented culture to consumerism in the nineteenth century was gradual. With the marked exception of the depression and World War II, consumerism in the twentieth century became a way of life for Americans.

BIBLIOGRAPHY

Aaker, David A., and George S. Day, eds. *Consumerism: Search for the Consumer Interest.* New York: The Free Press, 1974.

Fox, Richard Wightman, and T. J. Jackson Lears, eds. *The Culture of Consumption: Critical Essays in American History, 1880–1980.* New York: Pantheon Books, 1983.

Lee, Martyn J., ed. *The Consumer Society Reader.* Malden, Mass.: Blackwell Publishers, 2000.

Van Doren, Charles, ed. *Webster's American Biographies.* Springfield, Mass.: Merriam-Webster, 1984.

R. Steven Jones

See also **Advertising.**

CONSUMERS LEAGUES

CONSUMERS LEAGUES are voluntary organizations dedicated to securing good working conditions in factories and industry and to promoting the manufacture of safe consumer goods. In 1888 shirtmaker Leonora O'Reilly asked middle-class activist Josephine Shaw Lowell to work with the New York Working Women's Society to enlist middle-class women to help secure better working conditions for women. Two years later the women circulated a "White List" identifying retail stores that treated their employees fairly and asking women to shop only at those stores. In 1890 women formally organized the Consumers' League of New York, with Lowell as its president. An 1898 meeting of representatives of leagues from seven states produced the National Consumers' League (NCL), which in 1899 hired the noted reformer Florence Kelley as its general secretary. Under Kelley's leadership, NCL membership grew quickly: in 1901 there were thirty leagues in eleven states; in 1906 there were sixty-three leagues in twenty states; and by 1913 the NCL had 30,000 members.

From 1899 through the 1930s leagues worked to eliminate goods that were produced under conditions Kelley termed "injurious to human life and health." Leagues demanded maximum-hours and minimum-wage laws and under the leadership of Lucy Mason and Mary Dublin Keyserling the NCL helped enact the Fair Labor Standards Act of 1938. In the 1970s Keyserling brought the NCL into the pro–Equal Rights Amendment coalition. At the end of the twentieth century the NCL was investigating Internet fraud and leading a national antisweatshop taskforce.

BIBLIOGRAPHY

Storrs, Landon R. Y. *Civilizing Capitalism: The National Consumers' League, Women's Activism, and Labor Standards in the New Deal Era.* Chapel Hill: University of North Carolina Press, 2000.

Maureen Flanagan

See also **Fair Labor Standards Act; Minimum-Wage Legislation.**

CONTEMPT OF CONGRESS

CONTEMPT OF CONGRESS. The investigative power of Congress and its role as policymaker would be hindered without the ability to compel testimony and documents from witnesses. Just as a failure to comply with a court order can subject individuals to a charge of contempt of court, the failure to comply with a congressional order can lead to a charge of contempt of Congress. In 1982, Environmental Protection Agency administrator Anne M. Gorsuch refused to provide documents subpoenaed by the House Committee on Energy and Commerce regarding Superfund enforcement. The committee passed a resolution citing Gorsuch for contempt, and the resolution passed the full House. Had Gorsuch continued to withhold the documents, the referral to the U.S. Attorney for prosecution could have resulted in a sentence of one year in prison and a fine of $1,000.

The procedures and penalties for contempt of Congress are set by statute, 2 U.S.C. 192. While the Constitution does not explicitly provide for the congressional contempt power, the Supreme Court held in *Anderson v. Dunn* (1821) that such power is implicit in Congress's function as a legislature. Congress may cite individuals for contempt for failing to appear before Congress, refusing to provide testimony or documents to Congress, or bribing or libeling a member of Congress. There are, however, some limitations on Congress' power. The Supreme Court established in a series of cases surrounding McCarthyism that a congressional committee may only investigate areas in which it is empowered to legislate and may only issue contempt citations in areas where the committee exercises jurisdiction.

Congress has long used contempt citations as a political tool. The very first contempt citation by the Senate involved the attempted silencing of William Duane, editor of the Democratic-Republican newspaper the *Aurora*. Duane had published an article in the last term of Federalist president John Adams, giving the full text of a bill to establish a Federalist-dominated committee to review Electoral College ballots in the election of 1800 and incorrectly asserting that the bill had been passed by the full Senate. After initially submitting to congressional authority, Duane went into hiding after being cited for contempt. Upon the election of a new Antifederalist-dominated Congress and the government's move to Washington, D.C., Duane resurfaced in Philadelphia and returned to publishing his newspaper. In recent history, congressional committees have often brought contempt charges against high-level executive officers, only to have the full House or Senate reject the charges. Among these contempt citations was a charge in 1998 by the Republican-dominated House Government Reform and Oversight Committee against Attorney General Janet Reno for failing to appoint an independent counsel to investigate alleged campaign finance improprieties of the Clinton-Gore 1996 campaign.

BIBLIOGRAPHY

Goldfarb, Ronald L. *The Contempt Power.* New York: Columbia University Press, 1963.

Donald A. Downs
Martin J. Sweet

See also **Congress, United States.**

CONTINENTAL CONGRESS, the central governing body of the American colonies prior to and during the American Revolution and also the first government of the United States until the establishment of the U.S. Constitution in 1789. The Continental Congress followed in the steps of earlier, brief colony-wide gatherings to discuss shared issues of importance, as the Albany Congress of 1754 and the Stamp Act Congress of 1765 had done. In Philadelphia, delegates from twelve colonies (Georgia did not participate) gathered from 5 September to 26 October 1774 to discuss possible responses to British actions that threatened their rights. In particular, they sought the repeal of Parliament's measures—commonly called the Coercive or Intolerable Acts—directed at Massachusetts following the Boston Tea Party of 1773.

The First Continental Congress

At the 1774 gathering, later known as the First Continental Congress, colonial representatives considered the best means by which to gain redress of their grievances. They called for a boycott on the purchase or consumption of British goods (a strategy that had worked well in the 1760s during protests against the Stamp Act and the Townshend Duties) and a ban on the sale of colonial goods to England, which collectively became known as the Continental Association. Economic threats had been effective previously, and public sentiment strongly supported the Association at local levels. The delegates in Congress also prepared a petition to send to King George III of England, asking that the Coercive Acts be repealed, and arranged for a second congress to convene in May 1775 if Parliament did not withdraw the detested laws.

In October 1774 Congress also adopted a "Declaration of Rights and Grievances" that outlined members' views on the correct constitutional relationship between mother country and colonies. In argument and style, the Declaration mimicked the greatest English charters of rights, Magna Carta (1215) and the English Bill of Rights (1689), claiming that settlers who originally emigrated from England "by no means forfeited, surrendered, or lost any of those rights" and that the "foundation of English liberty, and of all free government, is a right in the people to participate in their legislative council"—a right colonists did not enjoy by direct representation in Parliament. The Declaration asserted the immemorial right of subjects to "assemble, consider of their grievances, and petition the King" and claimed that "keeping a Standing army in these colonies, in times of peace . . . is against the law." Every representative rejected Parliament's claims of absolute legislative supremacy over the colonies, but on other points delegates forged compromises. The suggestion from Virginia's Patrick Henry and Richard Henry Lee that the colonies raise a militia for home defense in case England decided to retaliate was dropped from the Declaration. The positions outlined in Congress's petition to King George and the Declaration of Rights assumed that Britain would take the first step toward compromise by withdrawing the offensive laws, and many representatives appeared convinced at this time that some sort of reconciliation remained possible with England.

The Second Continental Congress

Parliament did not remove the objectionable laws, and delegates from all thirteen colonies met in Philadelphia in May 1775 to consider their options. This gathering, known as the Second Continental Congress, faced greater difficulties, for reconciliation now seemed even more remote: armed conflict between British troops and American militiamen had occurred the preceding month at Lexington and Concord, Massachusetts. Rebel troops now gathered outside of Boston, where the British army had retreated, and Congress moved to support the patriots, assumed authority over the provincial militiamen, and at the same time named George Washington commander in chief of continental military forces (15 June 1775). For the next six years Congress guided the course of the war, dispatched ambassadors to seek alliances and financial support, and functioned as the de facto national government. Just as the Committees of Correspondence and Safety or provincial assemblies had already done—assuming control of local and state government affairs with no charter or grant of authority at first, other than the people's tacit consent—Congress took over the day-to-day business of governing Americans on a national level, while representing American interests in international relations as well.

Governing was one thing; independence was another. Nearly a year passed after the events of Lexington and Concord and military conflict with Britain before Congress abandoned hope of reconciliation and moved toward independence. Congress's most well known actions occurred 2 July 1776, when Congress voted in favor of independence from Britain, and on 4 July 1776, when it formally adopted Thomas Jefferson's Declaration of Independence.

Military men would have voted for independence much sooner than Congress did. The rapport between Congress and its Continental Army and officers was never strong, in part because Congress—weakly funded and heavily dependent on French foreign aid—could not provide the army with sufficient material goods or munitions to prosecute the war effort fully. Soldiers and commanders alike thought that it was Congress's intent to "starve the army at pleasure" through denying it much needed supplies. The army's inability to stop the British from advancing forced Congress to relocate repeatedly, from Philadelphia (1775–1776) to Baltimore (1776–1777), then back to Philadelphia, Lancaster, and York Pennsylvania (all in 1777), and finally back to Philadelphia (1778–1781) before the war's end. Congress's peripatetic movement, combined with its repeated turnover in personnel, meant that its actions often seemed slow or ill-informed to outsiders. The prestige of Congress was never very high, and many politicians appointed to Congress stayed only briefly before returning to their home states and local political affairs.

The Articles of Confederation

After declaring independence, Congress next moved to create a permanent government structure that could coordinate the new states' national activities. Using a plan drafted by Congress member John Dickinson and his committee of thirteen, Congress adopted confederation as its preferred style of government. Given that state governments already existed and had local support, it is doubtful Congress could have successfully recommended the creation of a strong national government with sweeping powers. Yet even a weak confederated government

was not welcomed wholeheartedly. Congress delayed and bickered over the plan from 1776 to 1777, attempting to reconcile competing views from large and small states on methods of representation, overlapping western land claims to undeveloped territory, and the means by which the new government would be funded. Ultimately, the Articles of Confederation resolved many of these issues by relying on past practices—as the Continental Congress had permitted each state a single vote, so too the new Articles Congress would allocate each state one vote. Indeed, the very structure of the Articles government drew its inspiration from the Continental Congress, having only a unicameral legislature and no executive or judiciary to conduct business, and continuing to depend on states to fund Congress through requisition requests, rather than direct taxation. It took nearly four years, from November 1777 to March 1781, for all thirteen states to ratify the proposed Articles of Confederation. Once ratified, Congress became the country's legitimate government until it was replaced by the U.S. Constitution.

Foreign Relations and Peacemaking

Shortly after war with Britain broke out, Congress dispatched diplomats to seek foreign aid. Although Russia, Spain, and the Netherlands offered no assistance, England's traditional enemy France gave help to the new nation. At first covertly, then openly after America's victory at the Battle of Saratoga, France extended the Continental Congress military support, a sweeping alliance, and the first recognition of America's independence by another nation. Congress sent its most experienced diplomat, Benjamin Franklin, to strengthen relations with France during this critical period. After the defeat of the British at Yorktown in 1781, Congress instructed Franklin and the rest of its peacemaking delegation (including John Jay and John Adams) to coordinate all their efforts with the French when arranging peace with Britain. Franklin determined that it would be best to ignore Congress's directions, and secretly negotiated a preliminary peace with Britain that served America's interests first, gaining the new country large western land concessions from England. Like all governments in the eighteenth century, Congress often had to rely on the initiative of its soldiers and diplomats in the field—the slow movement of information in this age limited the direct authority that a government could wield over its agents.

Peace brought an end to Congress's wartime problems, but created others. Discord between the sovereign states and the inherent weakness of the Articles structure now revealed Congress's difficult position in the confederacy. Without a direct source of revenues, it could not readily repay the nation's foreign debt, and without a permanent militia it could not protect itself from domestic disturbances when men like Daniel Shays launched armed protests. All major decisions, according to the Articles, required unanimity among the thirteen states, slowing any progress the new government might make. Finally, in 1787, another group of politicians met in Philadelphia to consider how to revise the Articles of Confederation. Their proposed plan framed a stronger national government, in which Congress would be only one of three branches. Once ratified in 1789, the Constitution replaced the old Continental Congress with a bicameral legislature of nearly the same name.

BIBLIOGRAPHY

Continental Congress. *Journals of the Continental Congress, 1774–1789.* Edited by Worthington Chauncey Ford et al. 34 vols. New York: Johnson Reprint Corp., 1968.

Continental Congress. *Papers of the Continental Congress, 1774–1789.* 204 microform reels. Washington: National Archives and Records Service, 1959–.

Henderson, H. James. *Party Politics in the Continental Congress.* New York: McGraw-Hill, 1974.

Rakove, Jack. *The Beginnings of National Politics: An Interpretive History of the Continental Congress.* New York: Knopf, 1979.

Sally E. Hadden

See also **Assemblies, Colonial; Coercive Acts; Committees of Safety; Confederation; Intolerable Acts; Provincial Congresses;** *and vol. 9:* **Address of the Continental Congress to Inhabitants of Canada; Declaration and Resolves of the First Continental Congress; Declaration of Independence.**

CONTRA AID.

As President James Earl Carter prepared to leave office in 1980, his administration began funneling money to Nicaraguan dissidents in Honduras who planned to interdict the flow of arms from the Sandinistas (who had overthrown the Somoza family dictatorship after more than forty years of rule) to leftist rebels in El Salvador. Soon after taking office in January 1980, President Ronald Reagan approved National Security Decision Directive 17, which increased aid to these dissidents, a small army of anti-Sandinista guerrillas that became known as the contras.

Over the next nine years the contra numbers grew to nearly twelve thousand soldiers. Working from bases in Costa Rica and Honduras, they attacked military and civilian targets in Nicaragua. Initially the stated goal of the contras was the interdiction of arms and containment of the Sandinista threat, but some American policymakers focused on the force as a possible alternative to the Sandinista government. Despite millions of dollars of assistance, the contras gained little support in Nicaragua. The presence of many former members of the regime of Anastasio Somoza—the president of Nicaragua from 1967–1972 and 1974–1979—among the contras undermined efforts by the Reagan administration to portray the organization as a group of freedom fighters.

Ultimately, U.S. congressional efforts to limit contra funding under the Boland Amendments caused a constitutional crisis in the Iran-contra affair. Oliver North and other National Security Council members circumvented congressional restrictions on aid to the contras with funds secured from arms sales to Iran. A significant scandal followed, limiting the ability of the Reagan administration to assist the contras. Furthermore, President Oscar Arias Sánchez of Costa Rica helped negotiate an end to the fighting in Central America. By 1990 most of the contras had laid down their arms. That same year, the Sandinistas lost power in an election to Violeta Barrios de Chamorro. One of the last Cold War struggles ended with the transfer of power from the Sandinistas to her government.

BIBLIOGRAPHY

Kagan, Robert. *A Twilight Struggle: American Power and Nicaragua, 1977–1990.* New York: Free Press, 1996.

LeoGrande, William M. *Our Own Backyard: The United States in Central America, 1977–1992.* Chapel Hill: University of North Carolina Press, 1998.

Kyle Longley

See also **Iran-Contra Affair; Nicaragua, Relations with;** *and vol. 9:* **Report on the Iran-Contra Affair.**

CONTRABAND, SLAVES AS,

the Union policy during the Civil War that, prior to the implementation of the EMANCIPATION PROCLAMATION, applied to slaves of disloyal Southerners who came under the jurisdiction of Northern military authorities. Major General Benjamin Butler initiated this policy in May 1861, after three Virginia slaves escaped from labor on Confederate fortifications and arrived within his command at Fortress Monroe. By designating them "contrabands of war," Butler finessed the 1850 Fugitive Slave Act. His action justified employing them and the many slaves who subsequently came within his lines as labor and, later, while he was in command of the occupation of New Orleans, in active service for the Union military. The U.S. Congress applied Butler's approach to the entire Confederacy in the First Confiscation Act of 6 August 1861 and in a new article of war adopted in March 1862 that prohibited the military from returning to their owners slaves who had arrived from beyond Union lines. However, even after Abraham Lincoln's emancipation policy went into effect, the Fugitive Slave Act, which was not repealed by Congress until 28 June 1864, still applied to escaped slaves of loyal citizens within areas exempt from the Emancipation Proclamation. This created a fluid situation in places such as western Virginia and southern Louisiana, where officers were expected to differentiate between slaves and contrabands. As the conflict lengthened, Union authorities increasingly treated even the slaves of loyal owners as contrabands.

Although some African Americans objected to being called contrabands, the term became a popular label for all former slaves who fell under the auspices of the federal military in the South. Private citizens in Cincinnati, for example, formed the Contraband Relief Association. When General Ulysses S. Grant faced the problem of caring for multitudes of destitute blacks during his Tennessee and Mississippi campaign, he appointed the chaplain John Eaton to assume charge of the contrabands. Eaton and other superintendents of contrabands established contraband camps throughout the occupied South, where blacks were given help but often were subjected to abuse. Many contrabands labored for the Union army, and thousands of male contrabands were either impressed or enticed into Union military service. Federal authorities also arranged for large numbers of contrabands to work for minimal wages on confiscated or abandoned plantations, generally under the supervision of white lessees.

During the war's early stages, the contraband policy provided Northern authorities with a rationale for withholding African American labor from the Southern cause that was not so flagrantly emancipationist as to provoke still-loyal slave states into leaving the Union. But by denying white Southerners' claims to blacks as property, it also helped prepare public opinion in the North and the border South for the likelihood of slavery's eventual abolition.

BIBLIOGRAPHY

Gerteis, Louis S. *From Contraband to Freedman: Federal Policy toward Southern Blacks, 1861–1865.* Westport, Conn.: Greenwood Press, 1973.

Jordan, Ervin L., Jr. *Black Confederates and Afro-Yankees in Civil War Virginia.* Charlottesville: University Press of Virginia, 1995.

Walker, Cam. "Corinth: The Story of a Contraband Camp." *Civil War History* 20, no. 1 (March 1974): 5–22.

Robert E. May

See also **Civil War; Fugitive Slave Acts; Slavery;** and vol. 9: **Benjamin Butter's Report on Contrabands of War.**

CONTRABAND OF WAR, a term in international law that refers to a belligerent's right to prevent an enemy from receiving goods of value in waging war and to seize and condemn any cargo shipped by a neutral nation to a warring power, usually on the high seas. The term has been important in United States military history since the late eighteenth century. In the 1790s Britain and France tried to limit sea imports to and from each other and arbitrarily seized hundreds of American ships for contraband violations. Consequently, the U.S. Navy waged an unofficial war on France between 1798 and 1800 to defend its right to transport noncontraband cargoes. During the Civil War, U.S. cruisers captured British ships transporting goods to the Confederacy and seized their cargo, whether it was contraband or not. The U.S. Supreme Court later upheld the seizure of these blockade-running, British-owned ships. The Court's decision did little to ease tensions between the British and Americans. In 1872 the Geneva Tribunal met to arbitrate a dispute between the two nations over damages perpetrated by British-built Confederate warships on Union shipping. The tribunal held that, under international law, a neutral country must

accept responsibility for any citizens who ship contraband to a belligerent nation, and Britain agreed to pay the United States $15.5 million in damages. (See ALABAMA CLAIMS.) Contraband continued to be a significant legal issue throughout the twentieth century.

During World War I Great Britain imposed broad categories of contraband on neutral shipping and virtually ended American trade with Germany. The Germans' desperate attempt to break the British blockade through unrestricted submarine warfare hastened American entry into the war. The issue of contraband also shaped the course of World War II. On 21 May 1941, when a German submarine torpedoed an American merchant ship allegedly carrying goods to British South Africa, the two nations began fighting an undeclared war in the Atlantic. In November 1941 Congress took a step toward entering the war on the side of the Allies when it partially repealed the Neutrality Act of 1939 and permitted American merchants to carry any cargo, including contraband, through war zones to and from Great Britain. Since merchant ships were privately owned and operated, this decision allowed the United States to provision Britain without technically abrogating international restrictions on contraband.

After World War II the 1949 Geneva Convention tried to alter the rules of contraband and called for free passage of medical supplies and religious objects, as well as food, clothing, and tonics for children and maternity cases. Yet, meticulous observance of the law of contraband remained almost impossible in the Cold War. During the Yom Kippur War of 1973, for example, the Soviet Union transported supplies to Egypt and Syria, while the United States shipped arms to Israel. Under international law, Arab forces had a legal right to stop American aircraft carrying goods to Israel, while the Israeli army had the same right to intercept Soviet ships loaded with contraband. The realities of a geopolitical world transformed by long-range missiles and airpower, however, prevented either side from stopping American or Soviet contraband shipments.

BIBLIOGRAPHY

Hickey, Donald R. *The War of 1812.* Urbana: University of Illinois Press, 1990.

Kaufman, Burton I. *The Arab Middle East and the United States.* New York: Twayne, 1996.

LaFeber, Walter. *The American Age.* New York: Norton, 1994.

Pyke, Harold Reason. *Contraband and the War.* London: Oxford University Press, H. Milford, 1915.

Eric J. Morser
Paul B. Ryan

See also **Blockade; International Law; Navy, United States; Neutral Rights; Neutrality.**

CONTRACEPTION. See **Birth Control.**

CONTRACT CLAUSE. Article I, Section 10, of the U.S. CONSTITUTION provides that no state shall pass any law "impairing the Obligation of Contracts." Broad interpretation of this clause by the Supreme Court under Chief Justice John Marshall made it the basic constitutional instrument for the protection of private property in the nineteenth century—a primary link between law and economic growth and a basic source of national authority over the states. The framers and ratifiers of the Constitution paid little attention to this clause, and what they said about it at the constitutional and ratifying conventions suggests that the clause was intended to supplement the prohibition in Article I, Section 10, against state-issued paper money. More important, the clause was thought to embrace only private contracts. Even interpreting the clause in this limited sense, the Court was able to impose controls on state bankruptcy, insolvency, and laws that threatened to undermine the reliability of private contracts or redistribute wealth. Two basic principles guided judicial interpretation in this area, both designed to protect property rights: (1) state laws touching private contracts must be prospective (OGDEN V. SAUNDERS [1827]); and (2) such laws may alter only the remedy and not the substance of the contract (STURGES V. CROWNINSHIELD [1819] and Ogden v. Saunders).

By extending the clause beyond the intent of the framers to embrace public contracts—an interpretation begun on the circuit level in the 1790s and completed by the Marshall Court in FLETCHER V. PECK (1810) and Dartmouth College v. Woodward (1819)—the Court gained jurisdiction over state land grants and tax exemptions, municipal bonds, and agreements between the state and its political subunits. Especially crucial in shaping national economic development was the Dartmouth College decision, which held that a corporate charter was a contract, the terms of which constituted a property right that the state could not subsequently impair. Over the course of the nineteenth century, the Court limited this protection for private property in four ways: (1) by the state's power to take property by eminent domain; (2) by the right of the state to explicitly reserve the power to amend or rescind a charter; (3) by the inability of charter rights to pass by implication (Charles River Bridge v. Warren Bridge [1837]); and (4) by the state's inability to contract away its POLICE POWER (Stone v. Mississippi [1880]). Despite these limits, the overall impact of judicial interpretation of the clause was to hold the state to its promises, thus providing the rational and stable environment essential to corporate growth.

The judicial exegesis of the contract clause reflected nineteenth-century American emphasis on economic individualism and free enterprise. During the twentieth century, the contract clause lost its central place in U.S. constitutional law. Beginning in the 1890s, the more flexible due process clause of the Fourteenth Amendment progressively replaced the contract clause as the constitutional bulwark of property. More important, the complexities of urban, technological society necessitated legislative modification of absolute property rights. In the early 2000s, the Court would uphold regulations if the state could demonstrate that the impairment of contract was a "reasonable and necessary" means of achieving an important public benefit. (United States Trust v. New Jersey [1977]). The contract clause had not disappeared as a source of limitation on state economic legislation, but it was no longer the dynamic legal force it had been in the nineteenth century.

BIBLIOGRAPHY

Buckley, Francis H., ed. The Fall and Rise of Freedom of Contract. Durham, N.C.: Duke University Press, 1999.

Ely, James W., Jr. Property Rights in American History from the Colonial Era to the Present. Vol. 4, The Contract Clause in American History. New York: Garland, 1997.

Scheiber, Harry N., ed. The State and Freedom of Contract. Stanford, Calif.: Stanford University Press, 1998.

Wright, Benjamin F. The Contract Clause of the Constitution. Cambridge, Mass.: Harvard University Press, 1938.

Kent Newmyer/c. p.

See also **Charles River Bridge Case; Charters, Municipal; Dartmouth College Case; Land Speculation; Minnesota Moratorium Case.**

CONTRACT LABOR, FOREIGN. During the Civil War (1861–1865), immigration went into a sharp decline, creating, among other things, a shortage of industrial labor. As a result, in 1864, the Union government adopted a contract labor law—the Act to Encourage Immigration. The law provided for the creation of the United States Emigration Office and companies such as American Emigrant Company, which sought to provide both skilled and unskilled foreign labor from Europe to U.S. companies suffering shortages. The contracts exchanged labor for prepaid passage to the United States. Yet because it was difficult to prevent workers from breaking their contracts, the American Emigrant Company and others never succeeded in attracting more than a few thousand workers.

The contract labor law was repealed in 1868, ending government involvement in recruiting foreign laborers. However, companies like the Six Companies continued to recruit. Unlike the American Emigrant Company, their focus was on bringing unskilled laborers from China to the railroad and mining industries. Yet this too had limited success. Racist sentiments rose against such immigrants, and labor unions organized around the issue that such workers were being brought in as strikebreakers. Stating that contract labor violated the free labor system, organizations such as the KNIGHTS OF LABOR pushed for the passage of the Foran Act in 1885, which prohibited the contract labor system. The law did exempt actors, artists, lecturers, singers, and domestic servants, as well as skilled labor required for new industries. Enforcement and revision of the Act became an ongoing issue for labor organizations. The AMERICAN FEDERATION OF LABOR successfully sought updates to the Foran Act in 1891, 1903, 1907, and 1910.

BIBLIOGRAPHY

Erickson, Charlotte. *American Industry and the European Immigrant, 1860–1885.* Cambridge, Mass.: Harvard University Press, 1957.

Parmet, Robert D. *Labor and Immigration in Industrial America.* Boston: Twayne Publishers, 1981.

Peck, Gunther. *Reinventing Free Labor: Padrones and Immigrant Workers in the North American West, 1880–1930.* Cambridge, U.K.: Cambridge University Press, 2000.

Margaret Keady

See also **Immigration.**

CONTRACT WITH AMERICA.

The Contract with America, a ten-point legislative program spearheaded by Newt Gingrich, the minority leader in the U.S. House of Representatives, served as a Republican blueprint for reform entering into the 1994 midterm election season. Candidates who signed the Contract agreed to support a balanced-budget amendment, welfare reform, and congressional term limits, among other items. Implementation of the provisions of the Contract became the rallying cry of the new Republican majority in the House in the spring of 1995. The work to enact the Contract resulted in modest legislative victories and pushed congressional politics in a more conservative direction. However, congressional Democrats successfully worked to block passage of most of the Contract's initiatives, thereby blunting its impact as a major issue in the 1996 federal elections. The polarized, partisan atmosphere created by fights over the Contract set the context for the impeachment of President Bill Clinton in 1998.

BIBLIOGRAPHY

Balz, Dan, and Ronald Brownstein. *Storming the Gates: Protest Politics and the Republican Revival.* Boston: Little, Brown and Company, 1996.

Richard M. Flanagan

CONVENTION OF 1800

tacitly detached the United States from its alliance with France at the price of American claims for damages resulting from French actions against U.S. commerce since the beginnings of the French revolutionary wars. The convention ended a naval war between the two countries that had developed from France's resentment over John JAY's TREATY (1794) with England. American attempts to seek rapprochement in 1797 led to the insulting XYZ AFFAIR, in which the French foreign minister, Charles Maurice de Talleyrand-Périgord, refused to receive the American commissioners until they paid bribes. The unexpected militance of the American response prompted the French to reopen negotiations.

President John Adams sent another mission to secure indemnities for spoliations and an annulment of the alliance. After more than a year of negotiations, the final French terms posed problems for the commissioners: if the alliance was terminated, so would American claims be—indemnities would be considered only if the treaties were still in force. The commissioners agreed to defer both indemnities and treaties, a deferment that in effect meant abandonment of both. The convention thus ended the Quasi-War between France and the United States with mutual restoration of captured naval vessels and liberalization of the treatment of American ships in French ports.

BIBLIOGRAPHY

Blumenthal, Henry. *France and the United States: Their Diplomatic Relation, 1789–1914.* Chapel Hill: University of North Carolina Press, 1970.

DeConde, Alexander. *The Quasi-War: The Politics and Diplomacy of the Undeclared War with France, 1797–1801.* New York: Scribner, 1966.

Lawrence S. Kaplan / A. G.

See also **France, Quasi-War with; France, Relations with; Treaties with Foreign Nations.**

CONVENTION OF 1818 WITH ENGLAND,

a treaty signed in London in October and ratified in Washington, D.C., the following January. The convention gave U.S. citizens the right to fish on limited portions of the Canadian maritimes; established the Northwest boundary from the Lake of the Woods west to the Rocky Mountains along the forty-ninth parallel; stipulated that territory west of the Rockies claimed by either nation should be open equally to both for ten years; and referred U.S. claims to indemnification for slaves seized by British forces during the American Revolution to arbitration by a friendly sovereign. The convention failed to resolve the Oregon boundary issue.

BIBLIOGRAPHY

Bemis, Samuel Flagg. *John Quincy Adams and the Foundations of American Foreign Policy.* New York: Knopf, 1949.

Bourne, Kenneth. *Britain and the Balance of Power in North America, 1815–1908.* Berkeley: University of California Press, 1967.

Philip Coolidge Brooks / A. G.

See also **Aroostook War; Canada, Relations with; Great Britain, Relations with; Oregon Treaty of 1846; Treaties with Foreign Nations.**

CONVENTION ON THE ELIMINATION OF ALL FORMS OF DISCRIMINATION AGAINST WOMEN.

The First World Conference on Women sponsored by the United Nations in Mexico City in 1975 called for a treaty for women's rights. The General Assembly of the United Nations adopted the Convention on the Elimination of All Forms of Discrimination Against Women (CEDAW) on 18 December 1979, and it became effective on 3 September 1981.

The convention, which consists of a preamble and thirty articles, defines and condemns discrimination against women in the areas of politics, law, employment, education, health care, commercial transactions, domestic relations, and reproduction. It also requires signers to take action against traffic in women.

As of May 2001 there were 168 signatories to the convention. Signers made a commitment to take positive action to end discrimination against women. They send in a country report at least every four years, which is reviewed by the UN Committee on the Elimination of Discrimination Against Women. In 1999 the General Assembly adopted an optional protocol by which the committee may also consider violations of women's rights if the petitioners have exhausted all remedies available to them in their home countries. The committee may also initiate inquiries into grave violations of women's rights. Both of these procedures may only be invoked when member states have signed both the convention and the protocol.

The United States was active in the drafting of CEDAW and signed the treaty on 17 July 1980, but the Senate did not ratify it. On 8 March 1999 Senator Jesse Helms, chair of the Senate Committee on Foreign Relations, expressed his opposition to CEDAW. By 2002 the United States was the only industrialized country that had not ratified the treaty.

BIBLIOGRAPHY

Askin, Kelly D., and Dorean M. Koenig, eds. *Women and International Human Rights Law.* Ardsley, N.Y.: Transnational, 1999.

Bonnie L. Ford

See also **United Nations; Women's Rights Movement: The Twentieth Century.**

CONVENTIONS, PARTY NOMINATING,

take place at the state and national levels to nominate party candidates, and shape party strategies. Part carnival, part revival, and part business meeting, these colorful conclaves have been both the stuff of political legend and forums for serious debate. Great battles have broken out in these quintessentially American institutions over particular policies and specific candidates, as well as over broader tensions between democratic and elite rule, between substance and style, between leading and following the people.

First Conventions

Originally, state legislators and party bosses nominated party candidates. Nationally, from 1800 to 1824, the Democratic-Republicans nominated presidential and vice-

presidential nominees with a congressional caucus. On 26 September 1831 the populist, suspicious, Anti-Masonic Party convened in Baltimore the first national convention ever, and nominated William Wirt of Maryland to run for president. In December 1831 delegates from eighteen states met, also in Baltimore, to nominate Henry Clay as the standard bearer of the National Republican Party. In May 1832 three hundred Democratic-Republicans met to renominate Andrew Jackson as president, and to nominate Martin Van Buren for vice president. The delegates adopted a rule that nominees must be nominated by two-thirds of the delegates. This Democratic National Convention has convened quadrennially since 1832—and the "two-thirds" rule handcuffed Democrats until 1936, granting a minority virtual veto power over nominees. The Republican Party has met regularly since 1856.

Until the spread of primaries in the second half of the twentieth century, state conventions nominated state candidates as well as delegates to the national conventions. The national conventions were high points in the American political calendar. Party activists from all over the United States met at sites that became legendary, such as Chicago's Wigwam or New York's Madison Square Garden. The credentials committee would finalize the delegates and alternates, and often adjudicate delicate intrastate delegate disputes. The permanent organization committee would settle on the convention leadership. The rules committee would update the procedures for decision-making and nominating. And the platform or resolutions committee would draft a party manifesto.

As the committee work progressed, excitement would mount. A keynote address would set the tone for the convention. Floor fights could break out over seating particular delegations or over controversial platform planks. The delegates would present their credentials, and the florid nominating speeches would begin. Often advancing states' "favorite sons," these speeches made every Democrat a Jackson, a Jefferson, a Washington, every Republican a Lincoln, a Jefferson, and a Washington, and every politician a statesman.

The nominations would commence in a sea of red, white, and blue bunting, amid a chorus of huzzahs for favored candidates, and for particular states. Conventions became famous for the great pageantry and oratorical excess with which "the great state" of Louisiana or Arkansas or Texas or Rhode Island could be hailed.

Nineteenth-Century Conventions: Volatile, Unpredictable, Exciting

At these conventions "dark horses" could emerge, as did James Knox Polk, selected on the ninth ballot at the Democratic National Convention in 1844. Often, the actual nomination came as a surprise because nominees were not necessarily in attendance. The nominee's Acceptance Letters became hasty but quite crucial marriage contracts between suitors who had already publicly announced their betrothal.

The unpredictability and the high stakes made for some volatile conventions—and some classic political drama. In 1848 rival delegations from New York clashed over the slavery issue at the Democratic convention. The "Hunkers," who "hankered after spoils," wanted to placate Southerners; the Barnburners, who were "radical enough to burn down the barn to get rid of the rats," supported the Wilmot Proviso, which challenged the extension of slavery into the territories ceded after the Mexican war. Democrats tried to split the difference, and give each faction half of New York's delegate total. Both sides rejected the compromise and no New York delegation was seated. Twelve years later, in 1860, the Democratic party splintered over the slavery issue at the party's convention in Charleston, South Carolina—and two Democrats ended up running for president, former Vice President John C. Breckinridge, and "the Little Giant," Senator Stephen A. Douglas of Illinois.

Slavery equally stymied the Democrats' opponents. In 1852 the Whig Party only settled on a candidate on the fifty-third ballot. General Winfield Scott could not unite the party and the Whigs soon collapsed. The new Republican Party, while firm in its opposition to slavery, also had trouble choosing a nominee. In 1860 the convention bypassed such an obvious choice as New York Governor William Henry Seward, turning instead on the third ballot to an Illinoisian who had served in the Congress only one term before losing, Abraham Lincoln. "My name is new in the field, and I suppose I am not the first choice of a very great many," Lincoln wrote to a supporter explaining his convention strategy in 1860. "Our policy, then, is to give no offense to others—to leave them in a mood to come to us if they shall be compelled to give up their first love."

Even as the Republicans came to dominate national politics, they were often divided. In 1872 "Mugwump" Liberal Republican reformers, disgusted with the growing corruption in the party, bolted and joined the Democrats, albeit temporarily and unsuccessfully. Eight years later, another "dark horse," James A. Garfield, emerged on the thirty-sixth ballot, and was paired with a more loyalist party "Stalwart" vice-presidential nominee, Chester A. Arthur.

In 1912 the Republican Party split once again over the elites' power in the party. Former president Theodore Roosevelt tried to capture the nomination by winning primaries against his handpicked successor, President William Howard Taft. "We stand at Armageddon, and we battle for the Lord," Roosevelt told a frenzied crowd of supporters the night before the Republican convention. Roosevelt had the passion and the people, but Taft had the votes. Most delegates remained beholden to the bosses. Taft won, and Roosevelt stormed out of the convention hall—and toward his run on the Progressive ticket for president.

The Democrats' great, post–Civil War division emerged over the free silver issue. In 1896 an obscure Congressman from Omaha, Nebraska, gave a thunderous speech. William Jennings Bryan's "Cross of Gold" oration catapulted him to the nomination and led to a fusion of sorts between the silverite Populists and the Democrats, even as it shattered the Democratic Party with a brutal battle over the currency plank in the platform.

On this, and so many issues, the Democratic Party was also polarized regionally. The 1832 "two-thirds" rule disproportionately favored southerners with their segregationist agenda, even as northern immigrants were streaming into the party. These tensions—and the rule—set the stage for the longest and arguably most divisive of conventions in the Democrats' long and contentious history. In 1924 John W. Davis of West Virginia secured the nomination of a battered and divided party on the one-hundred-third ballot.

During this time, even as they were more active, candidates did not address the conventions. Only in 1932, trying to demonstrate that his administration would offer a New Deal to the America people, Franklin D. Roosevelt refused to stand on ceremony. Dispensing with the ritualized notification ceremony, Roosevelt chartered a plane and went to Chicago. His dramatic acceptance speech inspired the delegates and, thanks to the magic of radio, the American people. In using the convention as a dramatic stage setting, Franklin D. Roosevelt ushered in the future. Increasingly, the balance of power in conventions shifted from parties to candidates, the function of conventions shifted from decision-making to ratification—and many began to wonder about the importance of these once-essential gatherings.

The Conventions Upstaged

The spread of primaries upstaged the conventions. The democratic initiative that allowed more and more people to choose their party's nominees spread throughout the twentieth century. In 1932 only a handful of states relied on primaries. By 1960 John F. Kennedy's successful campaign strategy used visible victories in critical primaries to build momentum. Since 1952 nominees have been selected on the first ballot. At the 1968 Democratic Convention in Chicago, although a majority of Democratic primary voters had chosen one antiwar candidate or another, delegates nevertheless defeated an antiwar resolution. The resulting soul-searching, exacerbated by the ugly riots in the streets of Chicago, led to a series of creative attempts to make the convention as representative of the American people as possible.

As the Democrats struck the McGovern-Fraser commission, followed by others, to fiddle with the formulas of delegate selection, television also transformed the conventions. Traditional political conventions were too colorful, too chaotic, too unruly for television. Conventions became more sanitized and more elaborately choreographed, precisely at the point when primaries allowed nominees to know their status months in advance. By the early 2000s there was a vigorous debate over the value of conventions, and the networks had dramatically curtailed their coverage. Many considered the conventions made-for-television pseudoevents, long and tedious advertisements for one party or another. Still, with the drama of nominating the vice-presidential candidate, with the great pageantry of the nominee's acceptance speech, with the diversity of thousands of delegates assembled from across the United States, conventions remained grand exercises in participatory democracy, and classic—and very revealing—American political institutions.

BIBLIOGRAPHY

Beck, Paul Allen, and Frank J. Sorauf. *Party Politics in America.* 7th ed. New York: HarperCollins, 1992.

Polakoff, Keith I. *Political Parties in American History.* New York: Wiley, 1981.

Polsby, Nelson W., and Aaron Wildavsky. *Presidential Elections: Contemporary Strategies of American Electoral Politics.* 8th ed. New York: Free Press, 1991.

Reichley, A. James. *The Life of the Parties: A History of American Political Parties.* New York: Free Press, 1992.

Troy, Gil. *See How They Ran: The Changing Role of the Presidential Candidate.* Cambridge, Mass.: Harvard University Press, 1991, 1996.

Gil Troy

See also **Caucuses, Congressional; Free Silver; Platform, Party; Political Parties; Taft-Roosevelt Split.**

CONVICT LABOR SYSTEMS. In 1718 the British government decided that "transportation," the banishing of convicts to work in the colonies, created a more effective deterrent to recidivism than the standard punishments of whipping and branding. This change in policy was favored because of high demand for labor in the colonies, and because facilities for long-term imprisonment were lacking. Between 1718 and 1775, approximately 50,000 British convicts were sentenced to long-term labor contracts, transported to America, and sold to private employers. They represented a quarter of all British and half of all English arrivals to British North America in this period. Most were convicted of some form of property crime, including horse and sheep stealing. While transported convicts were predominantly English and male, approximately 13 to 23 percent were Irish and 10 to 15 percent were female.

Convict transportees were given one of three possible sentences—namely seven years, fourteen years, or a lifetime of banishment—that became the length of their labor contracts. Among those transported, 74 percent had seven-year sentences, 24 percent had fourteen-year sentences, and 2 percent had life sentences. Once convicts had served their sentences (contracts), they were free to return to Britain or to stay in America. The number who eventually returned to Britain is unknown. Convicts caught returning to Britain before completing their sentences were hanged.

To minimize the cost of transportation, the British government channeled convicts through the existing trans-atlantic market for voluntary servant labor, which served those who wanted to emigrate but lacked sufficient cash to pay the cost of passage. Emigrants could secure passage to the colonies of their choice by negotiating long-term labor (servant) contracts that they would fulfill in America as payment for their passage. The typical voluntary servant negotiated a four-year contract. By contrast, British courts fixed the length of convict labor contracts and turned the convicts over to private shippers who would transport and dispose of the convicts for profit in the colonies chosen by the shippers. The typical convict was sentenced to a seven-year contract. Colonists mockingly referred to arriving convicts as "His Majesty's seven-year passengers."

Shippers carried both voluntary and convict servants, and upon arrival auctioned both to the private employers who bid the highest. The monies received defrayed the shippers' transportation expenses. By law, shippers had to show employers the conviction papers that stated each convict's sentence and crime. While convicts sold for higher prices than voluntary servants, on average for 11 versus 8.5 pounds sterling, in most cases profits from shipping convicts did not exceed what was earned shipping other immigrants. The higher sale price was matched by the higher costs involved in chaining convicts during shipment and paying delivery fees to county jailers in England, who played one shipper off another. The British government subsidized one shipper in the London market and he was the only one to realize excess profits on transporting convicts—at least before factoring in the cost of political bribes.

The vast majority of convicts were landed in Virginia and Maryland, and were employed in agriculture or at iron forges, often alongside slaves and other servants. Post-auction, with the exception of having a longer contract, convicts were largely indistinguishable from voluntary servants. A convict lived in the employer's house and ate at the employer's table. Criminal conviction, however, carried a stigma for which employers demanded compensation, in the form of price discounts received from shippers in the convict auction relative to what was paid to shippers for comparable voluntary servant labor. Per year of labor, the typical convict sold for a 21 percent discount, and convicts guilty of crimes that signaled greater destructive potential or professional criminality, for example arsonists or receivers of stolen goods, sold for even greater discounts. Convicts also ran away from their employers more often than did voluntary servants, at a rate of 16 versus 6 percent.

Convict sentences were not rigidly tied to particular crimes. For example, highway robbers received either seven-year, fourteen-year, or life sentences (38, 50, and 12 percent, respectively). Per given crime, a fourteen-year versus a seven-year sentence signaled the British courts' perception of the severity of the harm inflicted by, and

Convict Labor. Convicts are no longer sent from abroad to work here, but American inmates have often been sentenced to hard labor, as on this project in the Third Mississippi River District, Vicksburg, Miss., in May 1922. NATIONAL ARCHIVES AND RECORDS ADMINISTRATION

the incorrigibility of, the convict. American employers responded to this information by demanding greater discounts. Per year of labor, convicts sentenced to fourteen years and to life, as opposed to seven years, for the same crime, sold for an additional 48 and 68 percent discount, respectively. Employers also paid premiums or received discounts for certain convict attributes. For example, convicts who were significantly taller than average sold for a 20 percent premium, and female convicts who had venereal disease (8 percent of the females) sold for 19 percent less than females without disease.

While individual colonies tried to legally prevent convict labor from being imported, the British government disallowed such laws. However, with independence, the United States legally stopped convict importation. The resulting penal crisis in Britain was solved by shifting convict transportation to Australia in 1788. Australia eventually received more than three times as many convicts as colonial America.

BIBLIOGRAPHY

Coldham, Peter Wilson. *Emigrants in Chains: A Social History of Forced Emigration to the Americas of Felons, Destitute Children, Political and Religious Non-Conformists, Vagabonds, Beggars, and Other Undesirables, 1607–1776.* Baltimore: Genealogical Publishing, 1992.

Ekirch, A. Roger. *Bound for America: The Transportation of British Convicts to the Colonies, 1718–1775.* New York: Oxford University Press, 1987.

Grubb, Farley. "The Transatlantic Market for British Convict Labor." *Journal of Economic History* 60, no. 1 (March 2000): 94–122.

———. "The Market Evaluation of Criminality: Evidence from the Auction of British Convict Labor in America, 1767–1775." *American Economic Review* 91, no. 1 (March 2001): 295–304.

Smith, Abbot Emerson. *Colonists in Bondage: White Servitude and Convict Labor in America, 1607–1776.* Baltimore: Genealogical Publishing, 2000.

Farley Grubb

See also **Indentured Servants.**

CONVOYS. Employed from classical antiquity for the secure passage of land and seaborne commerce, as well as for passage of migrant peoples and fighting forces through hostile regions, convoys proved of signal importance during the European penetration of Africa, the Orient, and the Americas. The maritime convoy system of medieval England, which emerged early in the thirteenth century, afforded the model, providing armed escort vessels for both the cross-Channel wool trade and troop transports bound for beleaguered Calais and Bordeaux.

Early in the conquest of America, Spain employed close escorts and support forces to safeguard its homeward-bound treasure galleons. It established a compulsory convoy system in 1543, enabling the merchants of Seville to dispatch a *flota* ("fleet") of thirty to ninety merchantmen twice annually to the West Indies, thereby frustrating repeated attacks by British and French freebooters. The Armada of 1588 itself represented a classic prefiguration of the modern troop convoy.

Subsequent English overseas expansion rested not only on mercantile enterprise, an emergent Royal Navy, and deliberate nurture of the colonial system through the NAVIGATION ACTS, but also on resolute enforcement of

Convoy Duty. Crew members aboard the U.S. Coast Guard cutter USS *Spencer,* part of a World War II convoy, watch as one of their depth charges sinks the German submarine *U-175* in the North Atlantic southwest of Ireland on 17 April 1943. LIBRARY OF CONGRESS

the convoy acts, dating from 1650, that regulated the organization of convoys and required the arming of merchantmen. Throughout its conflict with France from 1674 to 1815, England refined—notably in the Compulsory Convoy Act of 1798—the complex operation of its ocean and coastal convoy systems. During the American Quasi-War with France (1798–1800), U.S. frigates escorted British convoys in the Caribbean; less than fifteen years later those frigates, abetted by privateers, attacked British transatlantic convoys with but limited success.

With the establishment of the Pax Britannica, the vital role of convoys rapidly diminished. Notwithstanding the virtual disintegration of the American merchant marine during the CIVIL WAR, the British Admiralty in 1872 acquiesced in abolishing the Compulsory Convoy Act, relying thereafter on naval patrol of threatened sea routes. That policy proved disastrously ineffective during WORLD WAR I against commerce-raiding German U-boats. Not until May 1917, when shipping losses threatened Britain with imminent starvation and U.S. escort vessels became available, did the Admiralty reinstitute convoys. The vast shipping control system that developed, with its complex intelligence apparatus, decisively reduced losses of merchant ships bound for Britain and safeguarded the massive American troop movements to France.

Allied convoy systems during WORLD WAR II achieved worldwide dimensions, owing to the phenomenal range of Germany's commerce-raiding effort, which included a substantial Luftwaffe threat in the North Sea, the Arctic, and the Mediterranean. The Allies virtually eliminated Germany's surface raiders during 1943, but German U-boats, operating singly or in "wolf packs" of fifty or more submarines, extended "tonnage warfare" strategy from the North Atlantic to the Caribbean, the South Atlantic, and ultimately the Indian Ocean. Allied experience indicated both the suicidal impracticality of independent mer-

chantman sailings and the striking economy of large convoy formations, particularly as land and carrier-based air cover, pinpoint location of individual stalkers by radar and high-frequency direction finders, and evasive convoy-routing procedures increasingly hampered U-boat reconnaissance patrolling.

With the advent of nuclear weaponry, the wide dispersion of convoyed shipping, and the employment of aerial transports, as during the BERLIN AIRLIFT (1948–1949), became characteristic elements of modern convoy operations.

BIBLIOGRAPHY

Marcus, Geoffrey J. *A Naval History of England: The Formative Centuries.* London: Longmans, 1961.

Morison, Samuel Eliot. *The History of United States Naval Operations in World War II.* Boston: Little, Brown, 1947.

Roskill, Stephen W. *The War at Sea: 1939–1945.* London: H. M. Stationery Office, 1954.

United States, Department of the Army. *Military Convoy Operations in the Continental United States.* Washington, D.C.: Headquarters, Dept. of the Army, 1981.

Philip K. Lundeberg/C. W.

See also **Merchantmen, Armed; Shipping, Ocean; Submarines; World War I, Navy in; World War II, Navy in.**

CONWAY CABAL, the name applied to the NEW ENGLAND coterie in the CONTINENTAL CONGRESS and its efforts (1777–1778) to regain control of the army and the Revolution. The name comes from Major General Thomas Conway's letter to Horatio Gates, proposing to replace Washington with Gates as leader of the military campaigns. More generally, members opposed the alliance with France and resented Congress and Washington's authority. The plan backfired, however. When the plots were exposed, Washington received renewed public support that overwhelmed the conspirators both in Congress and in the army. Conway resigned from the army and was replaced by Gen. Friedrich von Steuben.

BIBLIOGRAPHY

Brookhiser, Richard. *Founding Father: Rediscovering George Washington.* New York: Free Press, 1996.

Mintz, Max M. *The Generals of Saratoga: John Burgoyne and Horatio Gates.* New Haven, Conn.: Yale University Press, 1990.

John C. Fitzpatrick/T. D.

See also **Revolution, American: Military History; War and Ordnance, Board of.**

COOK, JAMES, EXPLORATIONS OF. Captain James Cook (1728–1779), a British explorer, navigator, and navy commander, is best known for his contributions to the geography of the Pacific Ocean, which he explored on three voyages between 1768 and 1779. His first voyage

Captain James Cook. A portrait of the prominent British explorer, whose voyages throughout the Pacific Ocean took him, among other places, along the coast of the Pacific Northwest and then to the Hawaiian Islands, where he was killed in 1779. LIBRARY OF CONGRESS

in the *Endeavour* (1768–1771), sponsored by the Royal Society, had three objectives, namely to observe the transit of Venus (the planet Venus's passing between the earth and Sun in 1769) from Tahiti, the discovery of the unknown southern continent (Terra Australis Incognita), and the annexation of new lands for the British Empire. During this voyage, Cook charted more than 5,000 miles of coastline in the Pacific, proved the insularity of New Zealand, added the eastern coast of Australia to the map, and claimed New Zealand and eastern Australia for Britain. Although he did not discover the southern continent, his voyages delimited the region in which this continent could be found.

Cook resumed the search for the southern continent on his second voyage (1772–1775) in the *Resolution* and *Adventurer*, sponsored by the British Admiralty. On 17 January 1773, his expedition became the first to cross the Antarctic Circle. His second voyage proved that the southern continent as conceived in the eighteenth century did not exist. He further discovered many new islands in the Pacific (including the Hood and Palliser groups); charted new coastlines such as the New Hebrides, the northeast coast of New Caledonia, and Norfolk Island; and sug-

gested the existence of the Antarctic continent, which was not proven until the nineteenth century.

Cook's third and final voyage (1776–1779) brought him from retirement, on the request of the British Admiralty, to search for a northwest passage from the North Atlantic Ocean to the Pacific. Cook directed the search from the Pacific side in the *Resolution* and *Discovery*. After numerous stops in the South Pacific, Cook entered the North Pacific in December 1777, and from March through August 1778, he charted the North American coastline from Oregon to the Bering Strait. Prince William Sound in present-day Alaska was examined in the fruitless hope that it might provide a passage, while investigations of river systems in the area proved equally unsuccessful. Cook concluded that the North American continent extended farther west than expected, and continued to explore the coast as far as Cape Prince of Wales (the most westerly point of the continent). At seventy degrees north latitude, ice prevented further advance to the north, and Cook was forced to abandon his search and returned south. On the return journey, Cook, along with four fellow marines, met his death on 14 February 1779 at the hands of the indigenous people of Hawaii. Charles Clarke took over command of the voyage that returned safely to Britain in 1780. Cook's discoveries and surveys made important contributions to nineteenth-century geography, led to the emergence of the North Pacific maritime fur trade and the North Atlantic cod industry, and further enabled Britain to extend its political control over Canada, New Zealand, and Australia.

BIBLIOGRAPHY

Baker, J. N. L. *A History of Geographical Discovery and Exploration.* London: George G. Harrap, 1931.

Beaglehole, John Cawte, ed. *The Journals of Captain James Cook on His Voyages of Discovery.* Reprint. 3 vols. Rochester, N.Y.: Boydell Press, 1999.

Phia Steyn

See also **Explorations and Expeditions: British.**

COOKE, JAY, AND COMPANY, a private investment bank, established in Philadelphia in 1861. Jay Cooke learned the banking trade from E. W. Clark and Company, a domestic exchange and investment house. Early in the CIVIL WAR, the Treasury's campaign to raise money for the war effort through the sale of U.S. loans stalled. Cooke was appointed special agent to sell U.S. Treasury bonds known as "five-twenties." His well-organized firm advertised the bonds directly to the people. By 1865 Jay Cooke and Company was regarded as the leading American banking house. But peace brought serious difficulties. In search of more government work, Cooke forged a close relationship with Secretary of the Treasury Hugh McCulloch. Political and rival-banker opposition, and the failure of early refunding bills in Congress, prevented the Treasury from giving them much work.

With no government business, Cooke, like other bankers, turned to railroad finance. First he sold minor issues, and in 1869 he undertook to finance the Northern Pacific. Railways were built from Lake Superior to the Mississippi and Missouri rivers. But Jay Cooke and Company failed in 1873 because of heavy advances to the railroads.

Jay Cooke and Company's financial savvy proved invaluable to the Union war effort. The company demonstrated the effectiveness of aggressive investment selling; it introduced the use of the underwriting syndicate for large loans; and, by its failure, it revealed the risk bankers run in assuming great financial responsibilities without adequate supports and controls. Finally, by making the transition from banker to master planner on a national scale, the firm exemplified the rising power of large corporations and financial conglomerates in the late nineteenth century.

BIBLIOGRAPHY

Harnsberger, John L. *Jay Cooke and Minnesota: The Formative Years of the Northern Pacific Railroad.* New York: Arno Press, 1981.

Oberholtzer, Ellis P. *Jay Cooke: Financier of the Civil War.* New York: B. Franklin, 1970.

Henrietta M. Larson / A. R.

See also **Greenbacks; National Bank Notes; Ten-Forties; War Costs.**

COOKERY. *See* **Food and Cuisines.**

COOLEY V. BOARD OF WARDENS OF PORT OF PHILADELPHIA, 12 Howard 299 (1852). In the case of *Gibbons v. Ogden* (9 Wheaton 1 [1824]), Chief Justice John Marshall intimated that the commerce clause of the Constitution gave Congress exclusive power over interstate and foreign commerce. But subsequent Courts fell into confusion over the question. In the *Cooley* case, Associate Justice Benjamin R. Curtis resolved much of the uncertainty by distinguishing interstate commerce, which demanded uniform congressional regulation, from local concerns (such as control of pilotage in various ports), where states remained free to act during the silence of Congress. The Cooley case conclusively established the SUPREME COURT as arbiter of federal and state conflict over commerce.

BIBLIOGRAPHY

Benson, Paul R., Jr. *The Supreme Court and the Commerce Clause.* New York: Dunellen, 1970.

Frankfurter, Felix. *The Commerce Clause under Marshall, Taney and White.* Chapel Hill: University of North Carolina Press, 1937.

Charles Fairman / A. R.

See also **Brown v. Maryland; Commerce Clause; Constitution of the United States; Enumerated Powers; Interstate Commerce Laws; License Cases; Trade, Domestic.**

COOPER UNION FOR THE ADVANCEMENT OF SCIENCE AND ART. Opened in 1859 as a multipurpose civic institution by the philanthropist Peter Cooper, the Cooper Union for the Advancement of Science and Art has housed a number of schools, museums, and organizations. Its original plan included the largest free public reading room in New York City, as well as the incorporation of the existing New York Female School of Design, night schools of science and art, and several scientific and natural history exhibits. Cooper was most proud of his plan for the Great Hall, modeled on Boston's Lowell Institute, which hosted many important public occasions, including Abraham Lincoln's "Right Makes Might" speech in 1860. A radical Unitarian, Peter Cooper mandated that all of the institution's educational functions were to be free of any exclusion on the basis of religion, race, or the ability to pay.

Over time Cooper Union relinquished some of its roles to other public and private agencies, though it started the Museum for the Arts of Decoration (now the Cooper-Hewitt Museum, part of the Smithsonian Institution) and, in 1901, a day program in technical science that became what is now its School of Engineering and Science. Between 1898 and 1934 most of the public programs were organized by the People's Institute. The Cooper Union remains a full scholarship college offering undergraduate degrees in art, architecture, and engineering, as well as providing a continuing education program and public events in its Great Hall.

Cooper Union. The building in lower Manhattan, home of various evening classes and exhibits, in which Abraham Lincoln delivered his famous first speech in the East, "Right Makes Right," on his way to the presidency. © BETTMANN/CORBIS

BIBLIOGRAPHY
Krasnick, Phyllis D. "Peter Cooper and the Cooper Union for the Advancement of Science and Art." Ph.D. diss., New York University, 1985.

Peter Buckley

See also **Education, Higher: Colleges and Universities.**

COOPERATIVES, CONSUMERS'.

Cooperatives (co-ops) for consumers are groups of people who band together in order to create a service, or to save money through volume buying. Consumer co-ops may be a utility company such as telephone, electricity, or cable services, an insurance cooperative, a housing cooperative, or other types.

Formal cooperatives have certain common traits. Each member has one vote no matter how many stocks they own—one criterion that sets a cooperative apart from a corporation. Members can purchase commodities or services at reduced rates because volume buyers pay less. When there is money left after co-op expenses are paid at the end of the year, members receive the net proceeds. If a cooperative is new and has start-up expenses, or a disaster strikes and it takes unexpected capital to keep the systems running, or the board of directors makes poor decisions, dividends may not be paid to members. If a co-op fails, its members are not financially obligated for more than the value they initially invested.

In 1844 the Rochdale Equitable Pioneers Society, a food buyers' co-op, began in England. The Society started with twenty-eight men who decided to pool their money in order to buy foods in quantity, thus achieving wholesale buying power. This co-op was a model for other food cooperatives throughout the world, including the American colonies. Present day health food stores most closely resemble the Rochdale cooperative.

Food, however, is not the only commodity handled in a consumer co-op; clothing, bookstores, and housing are among the other possibilities. Most cooperatives require people to join and only allow members to participate, but co-ops that do not require memberships also exist, and they encourage individuals to buy shares. Shareholders generally commit to volunteering in the cooperative to keep the costs down for the products.

The physical layout of the retail and service or production areas are often more open to the clientele in a co-op, which makes members feel that they are part of the business. In a cooperative that does repairs, such as a bicycle shop, tools are available to be loaned to members and classes are held to teach repair techniques. The co-op thus helps to increase people's independence while at the same time underscoring the value of helping each other.

There are also co-ops for group health coverage and other insurance. The first fire insurance company was founded in 1736, in Charlestown, Massachusetts. However, a huge fire devastated the town and the company then closed. Benjamin Franklin met with more success when he promoted his plan for house fire insurance by organizing the Philadelphia Contributorship in 1752. This company was the first successful mutual insurer in the American colonies. He said mutual insurance was a matter in which "every man might help another, without any disservice to himself," and this principle continues to guide companies that join together to form insurance cooperatives. There are also consumer-owned insurance co-ops that offer group health care. Health Maintenance Organizations (HMOs) are co-ops, and hospitals and clinics create co-ops for purchasing supplies. As in other co-ops, they can buy more items for their money when they buy in quantity.

Rural electric co-ops brought lights and power to rural areas of the United States. Rural co-ops operate over 50 percent of the distribution lines for electricity, and in 2002 they provided electricity for 26 million people. Telephone company co-ops also continue to be an integral part of modern life, especially in rural areas, though some urban areas have begun to establish co-ops as well in order to get away from monopolies.

Housing co-ops are somewhat different in the way they are organized and operated. In a condominium, residents own their individual housing units. However, in a housing co-op corporation, title to the dwelling is held by the corporation instead of individuals. Yet, the philosophy of a co-op is upheld in that the individuals have input into how the housing unit is operated. Since such a co-op does not exist to make a profit, but only to provide housing for owner-residents, costs are usually lower for these residents. Housing co-ops have a board of directors and membership meetings. Frequently they hire a manager to oversee the day-to-day work, and the manager answers to the board. In fact, most co-ops operate within this same framework, since individual members do not have the time or the expertise to conduct daily business within the co-op.

BIBLIOGRAPHY
Buford, James A., Jr. *When the Lights Came On: A History of Pioneer Rural Electric Cooperative.* Montgomery, Ala.: River City, 2000.

Shapiro, Sylvia. *The Co-op Bible: Everything You Need to Know about Co-ops and Condos: Getting in, Staying in, Surviving, Thriving.* New York: St. Martin's, 1998.

Peggy Sanders

See also **Cooperatives, Farmers'; Cooperatives, Tobacco; Health Maintenance Organizations.**

COOPERATIVES, FARMERS'.

A cooperative is a group of people getting together and agreeing to sell or buy items in larger amounts than an individual would normally sell or buy. The larger amounts allow for better prices due to volume purchased.

A farmers' cooperative generally must meet four major criteria: members must be agricultural or aquacultural (raising of plants or animals in or near water) producers; no matter how much stock a member owns or how much capital a member has invested, each member has one vote; business can be conducted with nonmembers (such as in a store open to the public), business done with nonmembers cannot exceed the dollar value of business done with members; and the cooperative must divide any patronage benefits among its members. (Different states may have some differences in these requirements.)

The one member, one vote of a cooperative sets it apart from a corporation in which the number of votes depends upon the number of shares owned. A corporation is expected to make money for its investors, while a cooperative is designed to save money for its members.

Farmers' cooperatives have evolved into three main kinds: marketing, purchasing, and service. The cooperative theory of higher volume equals higher prices for selling and lower prices for buying holds true for all three types. Marketing is of commodities that the farmers produce and wish to sell such as grains, fruits and vegetables, and dairy products; purchasing concerns itself with buying products used by the farmers, including fertilizer, chemicals, and seed. Service cooperatives provide various services, for example, a cooperative that sells tires or fertilizer comes to a farm to do on-site repair for tractor tires, or brings to the farm the machinery (and workers) to apply the fertilizer.

The first statistics on cooperatives, compiled in the early 1860s, showed thirty-five cooperative cheese factories in the United States. One of those included a cooperative formed by dairy farmers in 1810 at Goshen, Connecticut. These farmers milked cows, separated the cream from the milk, made cheese and butter, and sold their products. They worked individually or together, as the process dictated, to negotiate better prices. Selling their dairy products was the primary goal of this cooperative.

From 1913 to 1915 the Office of Markets and Rural Organization, a subdivision of the United States Department of Agriculture (USDA), did a nationwide survey of cooperatives. The findings were of 5,424 cooperatives with a business volume (sales and purchases) of approximately $636 million annually. By 1919, when the Bureau of Census did a survey that broke down purchases and sales by cooperatives, it found tremendous increases. Sales alone by 511,383 farmers were about $722 million; purchases made by 329,449 farmers were another $85 million. Surveys over the years have shown continual growth of cooperatives.

Beginning in 1916, the National Milk Producers' Federation pressed Congress to pass legislation to support cooperatives; in 1922, the National Council of Farmer Cooperatives Marketing Association was formed. By 1925 the American Institute of Cooperation, which advocated for education about cooperatives, had been organized. Agricultural colleges and land grant universities, which were affiliated with the USDA, began to pay more attention to cooperatives in education classes, courses of study, and research. Today many of these cooperative groups form the National Council of Farmer Cooperatives (NCFC.)

Afoul of Antitrust?

The question of whether cooperatives infringed on antitrust laws arose while the cooperatives were establishing themselves. In response, Congress passed the CAPPER-VOLSTEAD ACT in 1922; this act gave farmers the right to form cooperatives without violating antitrust statutes. In 1926, Congress passed a law requiring the secretary of agriculture to create a Division of Cooperative Marketing under the USDA's Bureau of Agricultural Economics. This division assisted rural residents in organizing new cooperatives and in improving cooperatives already operating.

National Grange

A very early co-op was the National Grange, principally founded by Oliver Hudson Kelly of Massachusetts. Sent by President Andrew Johnson to assess the agricultural conditions in the South after the Civil War, Kelly was disturbed by what he saw and heard; he decided that he might be able to help these farmers help themselves. With six other men, Kelly started the National Grange in 1867, with himself as chief recruiter. By 1874, his efforts had garnered 268,368 members (this number is so precise because 1874 was the first year the Grange collected dues). The next year membership jumped to 858,050 as state Granges sprang up throughout the nation. Members' goals included working, buying, and selling together. The theory of the Grange was to eliminate the middleman in conducting business, which would, in turn, lower prices for purchases. Farmers, rallying to improve their financial conditions, embraced this theory. They recruited their neighbors and Grange membership increased markedly in a short time.

However, the National Grange grew too fast and the organization imploded and collapsed. By the mid-1880s membership had fallen to under 100,000. The Grange, however, was not a failure. Because it attempted to eliminate the middleman (who took a large sum for services), and because the Grange considered the railroads to be middlemen, the Grange took on the railroads. Granges were successful in getting many state legislatures to pass laws creating state railroad commissions to oversee and regulate railroads. Lower freight rates were one outcome of these new laws. In the early years of the twenty-first century, the National Grange still had chapters in thirty-seven states.

Cooperatives are strictly regulated by law. A manager runs the day-to-day operation; a board of directors oversees the cooperative and makes the larger decisions, in consultation with the manager. Members are urged to be involved and may attend an annual meeting of the full membership at which time directors are elected and other major business is discussed.

BIBLIOGRAPHY

Cobia, David. *Cooperatives in Agriculture.* Englewood Cliffs, N.J.: Prentice Hall, 1989.

Keillor, Stephen J. *Cooperative Commonwealth: Co-ops in Rural Minnesota, 1859–1939.* St. Paul: Minnesota Historical Society, 2000.

Woeste, Victoria Saker. *The Farmer's Benevolent Trust: Law and Agricultural Cooperatives in Industrial America, 1865–1945.* Chapel Hill: University of North Carolina Press, 1998.

Peggy Sanders

See also **Agriculture, Department of; Granger Movement.**

COOPERATIVES, TOBACCO. The Grangers formed associations for the marketing of tobacco after the Civil War, but the American Society of Equity was the first organized group to make a major effort to control tobacco prices early in the twentieth century. This effort, characterized by "night riders" who tried to force individual growers to market their tobacco exclusively through pools to boost its price, generated more violence than cooperation and failed in its objective.

In 1921, after a drastic fall in the price of tobacco made many growers desperate, Aaron Sapiro, a California lawyer, began to promote strong centralized tobacco-marketing associations in several of the major producing areas. To maintain tight control over the tobacco crop, these organizations employed ironclad five-year membership contracts that bound individual producers to market their crops exclusively through the association. The Supreme Court upheld the legality of these contracts in its landmark decision on the Bingham Cooperative Marketing Act of 1922 (*Liberty Warehouse Company v. Burley Tobacco Growers Cooperative Marketing Association,* 276 U.S. 71 [1928]). The Supreme Court victory gave commodity marketing associations the appearance of success for a few years, but in 1925 internal weaknesses and the difficulties inherent in attempting to maintain monopoly control led to their collapse.

After World War II a number of tobacco cooperatives successfully performed marketing functions for their members; many maintained auction warehouses or performed marketing or related services. The principal function of the most important tobacco associations, however, was to facilitate the administration of the federal government's mandatory price support program for tobacco. From 1969 to 1970, for example, twenty-eight tobacco-marketing associations served more than 300,000 members and had a sales volume of about $337 million.

Since Congress passed the No-Net-Cost Tobacco Program Act in 1982, the federal tobacco program has guaranteed minimum prices on tobacco to American tobacco growers in exchange for strict limits on production.

The act requires that the system operate at no cost to federal taxpayers. (The program cost the federal government approximately $700 million between its inception in the 1930s and 1982.)

Based on the 1982 law, the Commodity Credit Corporation (CCC), a federal funding agency, extends loans to tobacco cooperatives in years when supply exceeds demand. This allows the cooperatives to purchase tobacco passed over at auction at a fixed minimum price, preventing sharp drops in the market price of tobacco. The cooperatives then process and store the tobacco until they can sell it at a profit, which they use to repay CCC loans plus interest.

BIBLIOGRAPHY

Knapp, Joseph G. *The Rise of American Cooperative Enterprise, 1620–1920.* Danville, Ill.: Interstate Printers and Publishers, 1969.

———. *The Advance of American Cooperative Enterprise, 1920–1945.* Danville, Ill.: Interstate Printers and Publishers, 1973.

Joseph G. Knapp / c. w.

See also **Agricultural Price Support; American Tobacco Case; Tobacco Industry.**

COPPAGE V. KANSAS, 236 U.S. 1 (1915). By 1915 thirteen states had enacted laws prohibiting an employer from requiring its workers to sign contracts not to affiliate with unions. In *Coppage v. Kansas* the Supreme Court overturned these pro-union laws by invoking the freedom-of-contract doctrine of the Fourteenth Amendment. The court also reaffirmed the right of employees to sell their labor on their own terms, holding that the ruling in *Adair v. United States* (1908)—that employers could discharge workers because of their affiliation with unions—illegally implied the right to insist upon nonunion pledges as a condition of employment.

BIBLIOGRAPHY

Forbath, William E. *Law and the Shaping of the American Labor Movement.* Cambridge, Mass.: Harvard University Press, 1991.

Tomlins, Christopher L. *The State and the Unions: Labor Relations, the Law, and the Organized Labor Movement in America, 1880–1960.* New York: Cambridge University Press, 1985.

Royal E. Montgomery / a. r.

See also **Contract Clause; Labor; Right-to-Work Laws; Strikes; Yellow-Dog Contract.**

COPPER INDUSTRY. Archaeological evidence found in pits on the Upper Peninsula of Michigan and on Isle Royal in Lake Superior reveals that copper mining and the making and use of copper implements and weapons in North America were carried on during a prehis-

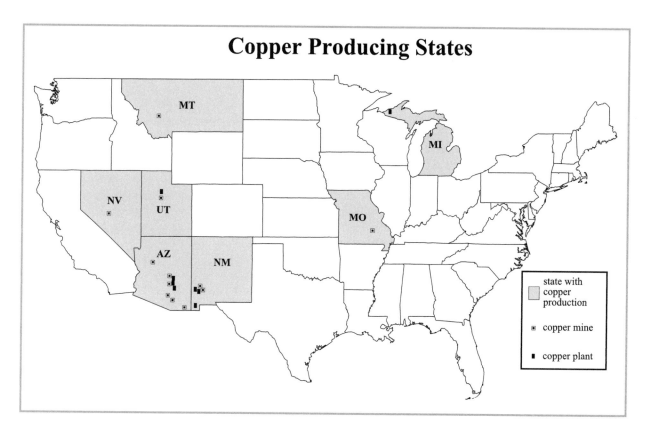

Copper Producing States

toric period extending from about 5,000 to 1,000 B.C. Vast copper mining pits remained that indicated extensive production. Copper production revived in the United States with the discovery of a vein of copper ore at Simsbury, Connecticut, in 1705. In 1709 copper production began from this ore, followed later by the discovery and development of other deposits in the colonies. English colonial law forbade smelting in the colonies, and so most of the ore was shipped to England. Small amounts of ore were smelted in the colonies, however, in spite of the prohibition.

It was not until exploitation of the rich ore deposits of the Upper Peninsula of Michigan in the early 1850s that copper production in the United States exceeded a few hundred tons per year. In 1842 the Chippewa Indians ceded all claims to thirty thousand square miles of the Upper Peninsula. In 1843 the copper rush began as thousands came to the peninsula to try their luck in the mines. The Keweenaw Peninsula, in Lake Superior, rapidly filled with copper mining boom towns, and several important harbors opened. Copper was shipped on Lake Superior to the St. Mary's River Canal at Sault Ste. Marie until the Soo Locks opened in 1855. The opening of the locks, combined with the advent of the railroad, increased both productivity and immigration to the area. In 1849, miners discovered massive deposits of copper buried deep in the earth at the Cliff Mine area near Eagle Harbor, Michigan. Unlike surface copper, which prehistoric glaciers had scattered across the countryside, the Cliff Mine area boasted rich veins of ore. Rapid developments in copper

mining technology produced equipment capable of hoisting massive amounts of metal from deep mine shafts.

Production of Michigan copper increased from 728 tons in 1850 to more than 30,000 tons in 1880. In the early 1850s the U.S. copper industry was dominated by the Calumet and Hecla Mining Company in Michigan, which was producing one-half of the domestic output from ore that ran as high as 20 percent copper. All the Michigan copper, known as Lake Copper, was marketed by Calumet and Hecla through a pooling agreement known as the Lake Pool. The preeminence of Michigan in copper mining was considered unassailable, particularly by those who financed the Lake development.

Despite Michigan's apparent monopoly, competition from the western states mounted. The first discovery of copper in Montana was at Butte in 1866 in the Parrot mine, which was then being mined for silver. The area became famous for copper production in the early 1880s from the output of the Anaconda mine. Later, the ANACONDA COPPER Mining Company gained control of most of the mining properties in the Butte area. During this same period, exploitation of the southwestern oxidized silver-copper deposits also began. In ARIZONA the operations of two mines, the Bisbee and the Copper Queen, merged in 1885, forming the basis for the great copper mining operations in Arizona. In the 1970s, the Arizona mines accounted for about one-half of the domestic production of primary copper.

In the 1860s the emerging electrical industry created a new demand for metals from which to make conductors. Copper proved to work best as an electrical conductor. The potential size of the electrical industry as a market was apparently not recognized, and the competition for a supposedly limited market between the western producers and the Lake Pool headed by Calumet and Hecla became critical. Prices were slashed, and by 1886 copper sold for ten cents per pound, compared with the average selling price of twenty cents per pound during the previous ten years. The price war scarcely checked western production, and the increasing production of Butte copper surpassed the Lake Pool total Michigan output by 1888. By 1900 the Michigan mines had reached maturity, and mining there became too expensive an endeavor. This shifted the focus of the copper industry to the West.

Advances in technology had considerable impact on the U.S. copper industry. Introduction of the Bessemer steel converter for smelting copper in the late 1880s made it possible to treat many lower-grade ores. The beginning of open-pit mining in 1907 permitted profitable exploitation of the huge bodies of low-grade disseminated copper sulfide ores in the Southwest. The flotation process introduced into the copper concentrators between 1913 and 1916 drove the tenor of profitable ore even lower. Since the standard blast furnace-converter process was not suitable for smelting the fine-grain flotation concentrate, the blast furnace was replaced by the open-hearth steel-making furnace to smelt roasted concentrates. Later, after the Phelps Dodge Company demonstrated that unroasted concentrates could be smelted, many companies eliminated the roasting step.

WORLD WAR I provided tremendous impetus to the domestic copper industry. The United States became the copper clearinghouse for the Western Hemisphere and for the world. With increasing worldwide demand, South American and African deposits were developed and brought into production, largely with U.S. capital. World War II brought the copper industry to all-time high production records. Refining output soared to 1.5 million tons annually, and the United States firmly established dominance in copper production. Even so, the nation's needs outstripped domestic production, and by 1970, imports accounted for about 17 percent of the domestic supply.

Following WORLD WAR II, hydrometallurgy grew as a commercial method of extracting copper in the United States. Dissolution and precipitation—collectively referred to as leaching—were used extensively for treating copperbearing mine waste and for processing oxide ores. The copper precipitates produced by this method, which accounted for less than 5 percent of the total domestic copper produced in 1945, accounted for about 12 percent in 1970.

The processing of copper ores supplies a host of byproducts important to the economy, including lead, zinc, gold, silver, molybdenum, palladium, and platinum. Production of copper from the porphyry deposits in the western United States provides the only domestic source of the metal rhenium. Another important by-product is sulfuric acid, made from the stack gases at copper smelters. In 1970 about 600,000 tons of this acid were produced from this source. The production of acid and other sulfurous products, whether marketable or not, increased dramatically in the late twentieth century as smelter operators strived to meet new and stringent air-pollution regulations, which severely restricted the amount of sulfur dioxide that could be discharged into the atmosphere. Pollution abatement at smelters is costly and will force the industry to adopt new smelting technologies.

In 1974 U.S. consumption of refined copper was 2.3 million tons—of which 1.6 million tons were produced domestically—and an additional 0.8 million tons of copper were consumed as scrap in production of alloys, chemicals, and other products. By 1991 the United States produced almost 18 percent of the world copper production of some 8.8 million metric tons. By the early 2000s the largest copper ore producing states were Arizona, Utah, and New Mexico.

Because copper is so malleable and has high electrical conductivity properties, the largest use of copper is in electrical applications, which consume about one-half of the supply. Copper is extremely ductile and can be drawn into wires with diameters as small as .025 mm. It is widely used in outdoor power cables and in household wiring, as well as in signaling devices, electromagnets, and communications equipment. Copper wires are commonly used in the manufacture of electric motors, power generators, motor-generator sets, electrical controls, and related apparatuses, which require the use of copper for best performance.

BIBLIOGRAPHY

Finn, Janet L. *Tracing the Veins: Of Copper, Culture, and Community from Butte to Chuquicamata.* Berkeley: University of California Press, 1998.

Hildebrand, George Herbert, and Garth L. Mangum. *Capital and Labor in American Copper, 1845–1990: Linkages between Product and Labor Markets.* Cambridge, Mass.: Harvard University Press, 1992.

Hyde, Charles K. *Copper for America.* Tucson: University of Arizona Press, 1998.

Lankton, Larry D. *Beyond the Boundaries: Life and Landscape at the Lake Superior Copper Mines, 1840–1875.* New York: Oxford University Press, 1997.

Thurner, Arthur W. *Strangers and Sojourners: A History of Michigan's Keweenaw Peninsula.* Detroit, Mich.: Wayne State University Press, 1994.

James T. Dunham / H. S.

See also **Air Pollution; Electricity and Electronics; Electrification, Household; Mining Towns.**

COPPERHEADS. Originally, a label used about 1840 in Luzerne County, Pennsylvania, to designate the Democratic followers of Andrew Beaumont who opposed the Democratic faction led by Hendrick B. Wright. On 20 July 1861, the term "Copperhead" appeared in the *New York Tribune* and within a year was widely employed to describe pejoratively both Democrats sympathetic to the South and all Democrats opposed to the war policy of President Abraham Lincoln. Literally, the word denotes a poisonous snake. Strongest in Ohio, Indiana, and Illinois, the Copperheads, sometimes known as Butternuts or Peace Democrats, particularly objected to the EMANCIPATION PROCLAMATION because they completely rejected the idea of black equality and feared an influx of freed blacks into the northern states. Having fled Europe to avoid mandatory military service, some German-American and Irish-American Democrats vigorously objected to the military draft and engaged in antidraft riots in several northern cities, notably in New York City (see NEW YORK CITY DRAFT RIOTS).

Generally branded by Republicans as traitorous, most Copperheads defined themselves as a patriotic, loyal opposition that advocated a union restored by negotiation rather than war. They denounced military arrests, conscription, emancipation, and other controversial war measures as unconstitutional attacks by a tyrannical president on the civil liberties of American citizens. Copperhead leaders included Clement L. Vallandigham of Ohio, Alexander Long of Cincinnati, Fernando Wood of New York, and Benjamin G. Harris of Maryland. Prominent newspapers supporting the Copperheads were the *Columbus Crisis* (Ohio), the *Cincinnati Enquirer*, and the *Chicago Times*.

Harassed by Union supporters and the military, Copperheads created secret societies. The KNIGHTS OF THE GOLDEN CIRCLE borrowed the name and ritual of a southern rights organization. By 1863, this organization was known as the Order of American Knights. In May 1863, the military arrest and court martial of Vallandigham for alleged disloyal statements embarrassed the Lincoln administration. Although they condemned Lincoln's policies, Copperheads, in July 1863, demonstrated their lack of sympathy for the Confederates by joining unionists in defending Indiana and Ohio during Confederate Colonel John Hunt Morgan's raid.

In 1864, Vallandigham, then supreme commander of the Copperhead Order of SONS OF LIBERTY, counseled his supporters against treason and violence. In that year, however, extremists of his order were charged with plotting the formation of a "Northwestern Confederacy," and planning the release of Confederate prisoners at Camp Douglas near Chicago and elsewhere. The plot was uncovered before any overt acts took place, and members of the Sons of Liberty were tried for treason before a military court in Indiana. Three of those tried, including the Democratic politician Lambdin Milligan, were condemned to death. In its landmark decision in EX PARTE MILLIGAN,

the Supreme Court declared that the men should have been tried in Indiana's civil courts and freed them.

By 1864 Democrats hoped to elect a new president. Copperheads were able to control the party's national platform, including a plank written by Vallandigham pronouncing the war a failure and demanding peace on the basis of a restored federal union. Democratic presidential candidate George McClellan, however, rejected this plank. Crucial Union battle victories and Lincoln's reelection helped discredit the Copperheads. After the war Democrats at the national, state, and local levels gradually overcame recurrent Republican charges that their party had supported the South, secession, and treason.

BIBLIOGRAPHY

Klement, Frank L. *The Copperheads in the Middle West*. Chicago: University of Chicago Press, 1960.

———. *Dark Lanterns: Secret Political Societies, Conspiracies, and Treason Trials in the Civil War*. Baton Rouge: Louisiana State University Press, 1984.

Neely, Mark E., Jr. *The Fate of Liberty: Abraham Lincoln and Civil Liberties*. New York: Oxford University Press, 1991.

Silbey, Joel H. *A Respectable Minority: The Democratic Party in the Civil War Era, 1860–1868*. New York: Norton, 1977.

Charles H. Coleman
Julienne L. Wood

See also **Civil War; Secret Societies; Treason.**

COPYRIGHT protects works of authorship; such works include not only books but music, paintings, sculptures, maps, architectural works, compilations of information, and computer programs, to name just a few. The exclusive rights that presently comprise copyright are the rights to reproduce the work, transmit it, publicly perform it, display it, and create derivative works based on it.

Article 1, section 8 of the U.S. Constitution authorizes Congress to secure "for limited Times to Authors . . . the exclusive Right to their . . . Writings." Congress acted quickly after ratification of the Constitution to implement its power, passing the first copyright statute in 1790. That first statute protected books, maps, and charts for a fourteen-year term, plus a similar renewal term. The formal prerequisites to obtaining protection were substantial, including registering the work with a federal court and publishing newspaper notices of that registration record. Originally, federal law protected published works, and state laws protected unpublished works. The past two hundred years have been marked by four developments in copyright protection: the progressive broadening of the class of works entitled to protection (presently including computer software and sound recordings); the lengthening of the term of protection (now the life of the author plus seventy years); the near elimination of the formalities required to preserve copyright; and the extension of federal law to unpublished works and consequent extinguishment of most state protection.

The 1790 statute was substantially revised in 1831, 1870, and 1909. After 1909 the term was twenty-eight years, with a renewal of twenty-eight years; the scope included photographs, music, and the graphic arts; and one claimed a federal copyright by publishing the work with a suitably placed copyright notice. Registration was a prerequisite to enforcing the copyright. The development of new technologies placed pressure on the 1909 act. Efforts begun in 1957 culminated, after years of struggle between contending interests, in the major revision of 1976. The continuing pace of change in technology and the globalization of the economy for information-based products led to more than thirty more amendments by 2000. The most significant were the Berne Convention Implementation Act of 1988, designed to facilitate U.S. adherence to an international copyright agreement, and the Digital Millennium Copyright Act, passed in 1998 to enhance copyright in the digital environment.

The statute now comprises eight chapters of Title 17 of the *U.S. Code*. However, many questions concerning a work are governed by the law in effect when the work was created or published; this means the copyright status of a work created in 1940 may turn on the rules in effect in 1940. Although copyright law is a matter of substantial complexity (the current law is about eight times longer than the 1909 law), a few observations can illuminate its core precepts.

First, in 1879 in *Baker v. Selden*, the Supreme Court established the principle (now found in Title 17, Section 102 of the *U.S. Code*), that copyright extends only to the expression of an idea and not to the idea itself. Thus, the owner of copyright in a book describing a system of bookkeeping was not permitted to control the system itself—only the author's particular way of explaining the system.

Second, the threshold qualitative requirement for protection is originality, which exists if the author has exercised a modest degree of creativity and judgment in creating the work. A 1991 Supreme Court decision, *Feist Publications, Inc. v. Rural Telephone Service Company*, established that the compilation of telephone numbers and names in a white-pages phone directory lacked the attribute of originality and so was not copyrightable. Originality is a substantially lower standard than the nonobviousness requirement for patent protection.

Third, the present law provides that copyright attaches as soon as a work is embodied in a tangible medium of expression with the authority of the owner. Thus, a songwriter obtains a copyright in a song when making an audio tape, or written draft of it; no government application is involved.

Fourth, the law provides that, notwithstanding the presence of copyrightable subject matter and an apparent violation of an exclusive right, a use may be privileged under the doctrine of fair use. The fair-use doctrine involves consideration of factors that, taken together, focus on whether the accused damaged the copyright owner. Many, many cases explore the boundaries of this privilege.

Copyright has grown more and more important with the development of the information economy. The value of trade in books, music, motion pictures, television, computer software, and databases is enormous—$280 billion of the U.S. gross domestic product in 1996. Copyright has become a major practice area for lawyers and the law that gives value to the assets of many companies large and small.

BIBLIOGRAPHY

Chisum, Donald S., and Michael A. Jacobs. *Understanding Intellectual Property Law*. New York: Matthew Bender, 1992.

Halpern, Sheldon W., Craig Allen Nard, and Kenneth L. Port. *Fundamentals of United States Intellectual Property Law: Copyright, Patent, and Trademark*. The Hague, Netherlands: Kluwer Law International, 1999.

John A. Kidwell

See also **Intellectual Property; Patents and U.S. Patent Office; Trademarks.**

CORAL SEA, BATTLE OF THE

CORAL SEA, BATTLE OF THE (7–8 May 1942). As part of its WORLD WAR II plan to isolate Australia, Japan sought to capture Port Moresby, in southeastern New Guinea. In early May 1942 an invasion force of three carriers under Rear Adm. Sadamichi Kajioka moved into the Coral Sea, east of New Guinea. American intelligence had broken the Japanese code, however; and a task force under Rear Adm. Frank J. Fletcher, including the carriers *Lexington* and *Yorktown*, was in position to intercept.

On the morning of 7 May, Japanese planes sank an American oiler and an American destroyer in an attack on what they thought was the main body of Fletcher's task force. American fliers, meanwhile, sank the *Shoho*. When the Japanese finally did go after Fletcher's force, they failed to locate it in the growing darkness and lost a score of planes in the effort. The next morning Fletcher's pilots missed the *Zuikaku* in a rainsquall but seriously damaged the *Shokaku*. The Japanese sank the *Lexington* but suffered heavy plane losses. Deprived of air cover, Kajioka called off the Port Moresby invasion.

The Battle of the Coral Sea, history's first carrier battle, was tactically a draw: the Americans lost more ships, and the Japanese, more planes. But it was an American strategic victory. Not only was Port Moresby saved, but both surviving Japanese carriers had been put out of action—the *Shokaku* for repairs and the *Zuikaku* in order to replenish its aircraft. Neither could take part in the great battle of Midway, in June, whereas the *Yorktown* was repaired in time to participate.

BIBLIOGRAPHY

Hoyt, Edwin P. *Blue Skies and Blood: The Battle of the Coral Sea*. New York: Jove, 1975.

Corn. Cultivation near Tulsa, Okla., of what has long been one of the nation's most important—and versatile—crops. LIBRARY OF CONGRESS

Lundstrom, John B. *The First South Pacific Campaign: Pacific Fleet Strategy, December 1941–June 1942.* Annapolis, Md.: Naval Institute Press, 1976.

Morison, Samuel Eliot. *History of United States Naval Operations in World War II.* Vol. 4. Boston: Little, Brown, 1949.

Stanley L. Falk / A. R.

See also **Aircraft Carriers and Naval Aircraft; Bismarck Sea, Battle of; Midway, Battle of; World War II, Navy in.**

CORN. Although the exact origins of Indian corn, or maize, are unknown, American Indians probably first grew it in prehistoric times in Peru, Bolivia, or the highlands of Mexico. By the time Europeans arrived in the New World, Indians on both American continents grew a variety of corn types, including sweet corn and popcorn. Indians helped secure the survival of the Jamestown and Plymouth settlements by supplying them with corn, and later taught English settlers to grow their own in hills fertilized with fish. Corn proved itself an ideal frontier crop. The grain could be eaten green, or parched and ground into meal to make cornbread or johnnycakes. It also made an excellent feed for hogs, cattle, and poultry. Finally, any surplus corn could be distilled into whiskey, either for home consumption or for sale.

In areas north of Virginia, settlers found a variety of corn known as flint, an early maturing type that continued to be grown well into the nineteenth century. This corn, usually yellow in color, kept well because of the hardness of its kernels. Farther south, white gourdseed corn dominated. The soft-kerneled gourdseed matured later and produced a heavier yield than the northern flint variety. Prior to the CIVIL WAR, corn was the South's most widely grown agricultural product, exceeding even cotton as the region's most valuable crop.

Although haphazard mixing of these two varieties undoubtedly occurred from time to time, the first record of their conscious mixing came in 1812. John Lorain of Philipsburg, Pennsylvania, demonstrated that particular mixtures of gourdseed and flint varieties yielded much greater harvests while retaining many of flint's desirable qualities. The varieties resulting from the work of Lorain and others were known as "dents." One famous variety, Robert Reid's yellow dent, came into being in 1847, largely by accident. The previous year, Reid had planted in Illinois a light reddish-colored variety that he had brought with him from Ohio; when a poor stand resulted, Reid used a small early, yellow variety, probably a flint, to replant the missing hills. The Reid family then developed the resulting successful mixture into a yellow dent that later came to dominate the CORN BELT.

Even as the yellow dents were making the American corn belt one of the most productive agricultural areas in the world, research workers were developing hybrids to replace them. Drawing first upon the theories of Charles

Darwin and then upon those of Gregor Mendel, a number of American researchers published studies showing how corn could be bred for certain characteristics, including high yield. They included William James Beal of Michigan State College (1876), George Shull of Princeton University, and Edward M. East (1908), H. K. Hayes (1912), and Donald F. Jones (1919, working with East) of the Connecticut Agricultural Experiment Station. In 1926 the Pioneer Hi-Bred Corn Company offered hybrid-corn seed for sale on a continuing commercial basis, and thereafter more and more companies competed to provide the new hybrid seeds. As farmers adopted the new hybrids, corn yields increased at a spectacular rate, and by the end of WORLD WAR II, the hybrids dominated American corn growing. From 1910 to 1919 the average acre yielded 26 bushels of corn; by 1971 it was 87 bushels. Yield increased to 118 bushels per acre in 1990 and to about 140 bushels per acre in 2000.

Corn spred throughout the world from the Americas. Just prior to WORLD WAR I, the United States produced two-thirds of the world supply—about one-half of the national total originating in Nebraska, Iowa, Missouri, Illinois, Indiana, and Ohio. Mexico, Hungary, Argentina, Rumania, and Italy were the next leading nations in corn production. The production of corn as a food crop on a worldwide basis expanded greatly after 1950. The Rockefeller Foundation made a particular effort in an experimental center in Mexico to develop improved hybrids and methods for worldwide production, with emphasis on the tropics and subtropics. By 1973 the United States produced only one-half of the world total (143,344,000 metric tons), followed by the People's Republic of China (25,000,000), Brazil (15,200,000), and the Soviet Union (13,440,000).

Of the nearly 80 million acres of corn harvested annually in the United States, 86 percent is used for grain and the remainder for forage and silage. About 40 percent of the grain is fed to hogs, 25 percent to other livestock, and 15 percent to poultry. About 10 percent of the grain is exported, and the remaining 10 percent is industrially processed. Processed corn contributes to the manufacture of many products, including breakfast foods, corn meal, flour, and grits, as well as cornstarch, corn syrup, corn sugar, corn oil, and alcohol. Alcohol, lactic acid, and acetone are in turn used in the manufacture of hundreds of different products.

Since 1933, federal agricultural legislation has attempted to adjust production to demand and to ensure fair prices to farmers, affecting both the size and the value of the country's annual harvest.

BIBLIOGRAPHY

Mangelsdorf, Paul C. *Corn: Its Origin, Evolution, and Improvement.* Cambridge, Mass.: Harvard University Press, 1974.

Wallace Henry A., and William L. Brown. *Corn and Its Early Fathers.* Ames: Iowa State University Press, 1988.

Weatherwax, Paul. *Indian Corn in Old America.* New York: Macmillan, 1954.

Wayne D. Rasmussen / c. w.

See also **Agriculture; Cereal Grains.**

CORN BELT is the uniquely fertile region of the "prairie triangle" in the upper MISSISSIPPI VALLEY, stretching from Ohio to Nebraska, in which farmers since the mid-nineteenth century have specialized in the corn crop. In 2002, Iowa, Illinois, Indiana, and Ohio together were responsible for almost half of American corn production. Corn-belt farming emphasizes a judicious combination of producing corn both for the market and for fattening swine and beef steers. Since 1960, SOYBEANS have rivaled corn as the leading cash crop. Cultivating domestic grasses and small grains such as OATS and winter wheat and dairying are other important agricultural activities in the corn belt.

BIBLIOGRAPHY

Cayton, Andrew R. L., and Susan E. Gray, eds. *The American Midwest: Essays on Regional History.* Bloomington: Indiana University Press, 2001.

Corn. A close-up of this crucial crop, photographed by Theodor Horydczak. LIBRARY OF CONGRESS

Hudson, John C. *Making the Corn Belt: A Geographical History of Middle-Western Agriculture.* Bloomington: Indiana University Press, 1994.

Robert P. Swierenga/A. E.

See also **Agriculture; Cereal Grains; Corn; Dairy Industry.**

CORN BORER, EUROPEAN.

Introduced through southern European broom corn into the United States about 1910, the European corn borer spread into nearly every major corn-growing area of the country, causing an estimated loss of 313,819,000 bushels of corn in 1949. The insect also attacks nearly all herbaceous plants large enough for its larvae to enter. Extensive research by entomologists in the state and federal governments, stimulated by the appropriation of $10 million, began in 1922. Although as of 2002 the insect still caused considerable damage, the introduction of inbred corn lines and hybrids resistant to the borers, the development of controls involving the use of insecticides, and the introduction of parasites had materially reduced annual losses.

BIBLIOGRAPHY

Baker, W. A., W. G. Bradley, and C. A. Clark, *Biological Control of the European Corn Borer in the United States.* Washington, D.C.: 1949.

Brindley, T. A., and F. F. Dicke, "Significant Developments in European Corn Borer Research," *Annual Review of Entomology* 8 (1963): 155–176.

Tom A. Brindley/c. w.

See also **Entomology; Grasshoppers; Insecticides and Herbicides.**

CORNELL UNIVERSITY

had its origin in the desire of Ezra Cornell, a millionaire telegraph contractor and member of the New York state legislature, to establish an institution of higher learning where practical education could be obtained by all who sought it. When the Morrill Land Grant Act was passed in 1862, he foresaw that the 990,000 acres in the form of land scrip to which New York State was entitled might be made to provide a large endowment for a university: at the rate the public lands were passing into private ownership, especially the white pinelands of the Lake states, an investment in them would be sure to return a high capital gain in a few years. With the aid of Andrew D. White, a wealthy Syracusan and a fellow member of Cornell's in the state legislature, the state granted a charter for Cornell University in 1865. In 1868 the university opened for instruction on the hill overlooking Cayuga Lake in Ithaca. White, who was Cornell's first president, departed from the founder's ideas of a university and designed Cornell along the lines of Oxford and Yale; and Henry W. Sage, a millionaire lumberman and chairman of the board of the new institution, made a spectacular success of the investment in Wisconsin pinelands that Ezra Cornell had acquired with the scrip. The university's endowment in 1890 then surpassed the endowments of all but one or two other American universities.

Unlike Michigan State University and the University of Illinois, other land grant institutions, Cornell started as a private institution for which no public appropriations were made, with the exception of the initial granting of land scrip. In fact, the teaching of agricultural science, which the Morrill Act intended to foster, limped along at the new institution until the late 1880s, when the federal government made appropriations for research and teaching agricultural science under the Hatch Act of 1887 and the second Morrill Act of 1890. In 1893 NEW YORK STATE, encouraged by the remarkable success of Liberty Hyde Bailey in making agricultural science useful to the average farmer and by the shrewd lobbying of Jacob Gould Schurman, Cornell's president from 1892 to 1920, began appropriating funds to Cornell for agriculture, and in 1895 it provided for the financial basis for the Veterinary College. Later came the College of Home Economics and the School of Industrial and Labor Relations, making four state schools on the Cornell campus. The School of Nutrition is also partly state funded. The colleges of Engineering, Arts and Sciences, Medicine, and Architecture; the schools of Hotel, Business, Public Administration, and Nursing; and the Law and the graduate schools have always been entirely private, although since 1961 the federal government has made funds available for research and buildings for many of these schools. Cornell University thus developed into a hybrid institution, partly private and partly public—both a member of the Ivy League and a partner of the State University of New York.

Cornell, White, and Sage were early advocates of coeducation, and Cornell University admitted women beginning in 1872, although Sage College for Women was not completed until 1875. From the outset the university's stand in behalf of secular education, when sectarian influences were still strong in higher education, brought upon its trustees, White, and the faculty frequent attacks for their putative godlessness. Among the innovations of the university may be cited the elective system, which was in operation at Cornell from the very first, well before it was introduced at Harvard. The Hotel School and the School of Industrial and Labor Relations became the models for similar institutions elsewhere. They, like all the Cornell schools, greatly broadened the offering of courses of instruction available to students, who were encouraged to cross-register.

At the end of the twentieth century, Cornell had a total enrollment of nearly 20,000 students, including more than 13,600 undergraduates and more than 5,600 graduate students in Ithaca, along with nearly 700 students in the university's two medical graduate/professional schools in New York City. The student body balanced almost evenly between men and women, and minority students made up more than a quarter of the undergraduate population.

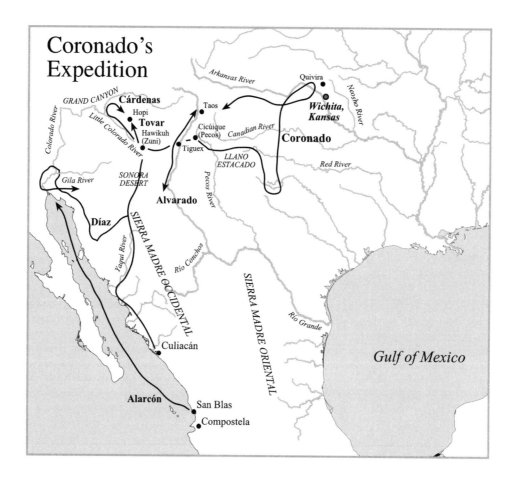

Coronado's
Expedition

BIBLIOGRAPHY

Bishop, Morris. *A History of Cornell.* Ithaca, N.Y.: Cornell University Press, 1962.

Gates, Paul Wallace. *The Wisconsin Pine Lands of Cornell University: A Study in Land Policy and Absentee Ownership.* Ithaca, N.Y.: Cornell University Press, 1943.

Parsons, Kermit Carlyle. *The Cornell Campus: A History of Its Planning and Development.* Ithaca, N.Y.: Cornell University Press, 1968.

Paul W. Gates/A. R.

See also **Coeducation Movement; Education, Higher: Colleges and Universities; Hatch Act; Ivy League; Land Grants for Education; Lumber Industry; Morrill Act.**

CORONADO EXPEDITIONS. From 1540 to 1542, Francisco Vásquez de Coronado, the governor of Nueva Galicia, commanded an *entrada* (entrance) licensed by the Spanish Crown. Funded by Viceroy Antonio de Mendoza and the governor's wealthy wife, Beatriz de Estrada, the expeditions explored the mysterious country north of the Rio Grande. The thirty-year-old conquistador donned a plumed helmet and gilded armor as he marched his army away from Compostela, Mexico, on 22 February 1540. The rank and file included 336 Spaniards, more than 800 Tlaxcalan warriors, and 6 Franciscans.

The Franciscan Fray Marcos de Niza vowed to guide them to "the greatest and best discoveries," particularly the seven golden cities Native informants called Cíbola. They reached the Zuni pueblo of Hawikuh on 7 July. The Zunis attempted to ambush Coronado's party, but the guns and steel swords of the army overwhelmed them. However, the village of stone and adobe hardly matched the Spanish expectations for splendid wealth.

Resolved to continue his search for fortune, Coronado in 1541 dispatched expeditions in all directions. Don Pedro de Tovar led one scouting party across the Painted Desert and eventually encountered the Hopis. García López de Cárdenas reconnoitered to the Colorado River and observed the Grand Canyon near Moran Point. To support Coronado's expeditions, the viceroy ordered three ships commanded by Hernando de Alarcón up the western coast of New Spain. Alarcón, who failed to make contact with any of Coronado's other parties, investigated the banks of the Colorado River before returning home. Coronado sent Hernando de Alvarado beyond the "sky city" of Acoma into Tiguex, where he encountered the modest dwellings of the Tiwas. The Spanish pushed on to Cicuye and dubbed one unusual captive from Pecos "El Turco" because his Apache headdress reminded them of the Turks in Europe. El Turco told them of Gran Quivira, a rich land to the east. Buoyed by the tale, Coronado camped for the winter at Alcanfor.

In April 1541, Coronado followed El Turco, his new guide, through the Llano Estacado. He took a small detachment of thirty mounted men along the great bend of the Arkansas River to the mud huts of the Wichitas, where the Spaniards became convinced of El Turco's duplicity. Before the Spanish garroted him, El Turco admitted he had exaggerated to rid his homeland of their presence. Finally disillusioned, Coronado followed his compass to the Rio Grande for the winter and departed for Mexico City the following spring.

Although they discovered little of interest to the booty seekers of the age, the Coronado expeditions extended Spanish influence in the New World. The reconnaissance, coupled with the near simultaneous wanderings of Hernando de Soto, inaugurated the conquest of the North American borderlands.

BIBLIOGRAPHY

Bolton, Herbert E. *Coronado: Knight of Pueblos and Plains.* Albuquerque: University of New Mexico Press, 1990.

Castañeda de Nájera, Pedro de. *The Journey of Coronado, 1540–1542.* Translated and edited by George Parker Winship. Golden, Colo.: Fulcrum Publishers, 1990.

Weber, David J. *The Spanish Frontier in North America.* New Haven, Conn.: Yale University Press, 1992.

Brad D. Lookingbill

See also **Conquistadores; Exploration of America, Early; Explorations and Expeditions: Spanish; Western Exploration.**

CORPORATIONS. A corporation is an independent entity: it exists separately from its owners, the shareholders. Most corporations are businesses for profit that raise capital for corporate activities by selling shares of stock, which represent ownership and are transferable. There are also charitable, cooperative, municipal, and religious corporations, all of which have distinctive features. A corporation's shareholders elect the board of directors that hires the corporation's officers, who run the day-to-day business. For many purposes, the corporation is treated as if it were a person. The corporation can sue or be sued, enter into legally binding agreements, and own property.

One important element of the corporate form is that it allows for limited liability. The liability of individual shareholders is limited to the amount they actually invested, even if the corporation runs up large debts. However, there are extreme cases in which shareholders can be held liable for the acts of a corporation—a situation called "piercing the corporate veil." American courts have developed several criteria in determining whether or not to pierce the corporate veil. One factor the courts consider is whether the corporate action involves a contract or personal injury–type action, in which case the person affected normally has no choice but to deal with the corporation. The courts may also hold shareholders liable

for corporate actions when the shareholders are involved in fraud or some other wrongdoing, such as siphoning off company profits. This occurs most often in closely held corporations, with very few shareholders and in which the majority shareholder plays a substantial role in company management. Other occasions on which courts have held shareholders liable are when the corporation was knowingly undercapitalized and when it failed to follow normal corporate formalities, such as issuing stock or keeping corporate meeting minutes.

One benefit that corporations provide is that they are freely transferable, with ownership interests in the corporation represented by shares that can be sold quickly and easily, without many limitations.

Origins of the Modern Corporation

The modern corporate form is a combination of two historical types of companies: the joint-stock company, actually a partnership between shareholders, and the traditional corporations that had originally been developed for medieval guilds, municipalities, monasteries, and universities in England. The first American corporations were monopolies chartered by the English Crown in the sixteenth century, with the intent of pursuing profit in the New World. Before the American Revolution, the London and Plymouth companies, Massachusetts Bay Company, and Hudson's Bay Company played a large role in establishing and supporting the European colonies. The royal charter of these companies allowed them to control governmental functions like customs regulation and terms of trade, as well as the formulation of foreign policy within their jurisdictions.

In the eighteenth century, corporations' exercise of essential government functions was curtailed and courts began to hold that the trade monopolies excluded fair competition from other incorporated companies. However, since companies who were incorporated at that time could lawfully compete with the monopolies, a great deal of economic activity was organized by single proprietors or partnerships under existing contract and property common law.

State Control of Incorporation

After 1776, the power to grant incorporation moved from the Crown to individual state legislatures. The interstate commerce clause in the U.S. Constitution granted incorporators the freedom to incorporate in one state without limiting their ability to transact business in other states. States eventually began to compete, liberalizing their laws to attract more requests for incorporation.

At first states passed a special act for each incorporation, but in 1811 New York enacted a general incorporation law that enabled the secretary of state to grant charters. The general incorporating statute enacted by New York was of limited application. The Connecticut incorporating act of 1837 was broader and more flexible, and New Jersey went on to create an incorporating act in

1875 that included a number of the provisions businesses had long sought from other states. But the privileges granted by corporate charters remained insufficient to facilitate the centralization of manufacturing that some businesses desired. In response, New Jersey enacted laws greatly liberalizing its 1875 act.

In the Dartmouth College Case of 1819 (*Trustees of Dartmouth College v. Woodward*), the Supreme Court held that an incorporation charter was a binding contract between a state and a corporation. Thus, the charter could not be altered without the corporation's consent. Since that decision, however, few perpetual charters have been granted and states have specifically reserved the right to alter or annul incorporation charters.

Individuals wishing to incorporate a business, or incorporators, must file an official document—called the articles of incorporation—with the secretary of state and pay a filing fee. The articles of incorporation must contain the corporation's name, a purposes clause, and form of capitalization (the number of shares the company plans to issue). Until the late 1880s, corporations were created for very limited and well-defined purposes, and the articles of incorporation would explain their corporate structure in great detail. In addition, the incorporators were forced to prove to the legislature that the corporation would serve a public purpose, should the state grant them the right to incorporate. In the twentieth century, though, corporations were allowed to provide a very broad purpose, and most companies used the phrase "to engage in any lawful business" or something similar.

The state in which a company incorporates is important, since the law of that state will control most matters, including acquisitions, mergers, and powers of the board of directors. At the end of the twentieth century, many businesses chose to incorporate in Delaware because of the state's extensive history of corporate formation and its finely tuned statutes and accompanying case law.

Growth of Corporations

The U.S. Constitution gives Congress the power to regulate commerce between the states and with foreign nations, a power that Congress used to charter national banks and transcontinental railroads in the nineteenth century. Congress has used its power solely to regulate state-chartered corporations through various federal rules, including extensive antitrust laws, rather than engaging in federal incorporation.

The end of the nineteenth century saw an unprecedented expansion and dominance of the corporate form. Large companies like the Standard Oil Company and United States Steel began to exercise monopolistic powers in their respective markets. Public concern over the abuses exercised by these behemoth corporations led to antitrust legislation, laws restricting business practices considered unfair or monopolistic and aimed at preserving competition. In 1890, Congress enacted the Sherman Antitrust Act to prevent interference with interstate trade and to promote a freely competitive market.

Between 1875 and 1893, the New Jersey legislature enacted a series of statutes intended to liberalize its 1875 incorporation laws. Previous legislation designated the geographical region in which a corporation incorporated in New Jersey could hold property and do business. In 1887, the state amended the law to allow foreign corporations to own real estate in New Jersey. Five years later, the state removed all restrictions on companies incorporated in New Jersey that were doing business outside the state. While earlier laws had restricted growth in other ways, the new revised laws greatly facilitated corporate growth and mergers. The revisions granted corporations the power to merge, increase amounts of capital stock, exchange newly issued stock for property, and purchase stock in other corporations.

In 1895 the Supreme Court declared that the federal government did not have the power to prevent a state-chartered corporation from acquiring control of manufacturing plants producing 98 percent of the refined sugar in the nation (*United States v. E. C. Knight Company*). Combined with the liberal incorporation laws of New Jersey, corporate combinations that would have otherwise been considered restraints on trade were declared legal. A relatively few large corporations now controlled American industry, and with the simultaneous relative decline of agriculture, the American economy shifted from one organized primarily around small businesses to an industrial nation.

Antitrust Measures

In 1903 Congress reacted to the movement toward mergers and oligopolies by creating the Antitrust Division of the Department of Justice. The government also established the Bureau of Corporations, with the mission of investigating and publicizing the control of industries by corporations.

Largely based on the work of the Bureau of Corporations, the Supreme Court ordered both the Standard Oil Company and American Tobacco Company to be dissolved in 1911. Woodrow Wilson became governor of New Jersey that same year, and began mounting an effort to return to a more restrictive approach to incorporations. In response, companies began leaving New Jersey and incorporating in Delaware, which had liberal statutes very much like those of New Jersey prior to the restrictive measures. When New Jersey later amended its statutes to undo the Wilson-era reforms, many of the corporations that had moved to Delaware could find no reason to move back.

In 1914 Congress passed the Clayton Antitrust Act to supplement the Sherman Act. This new federal law included specific provisions prohibiting the contract tying, exclusive dealing contracts, mergers, interlocking directorates, and price discrimination that tended to lessen competition or create a monopoly. But in 1920, in the

United States Steel case, the Supreme Court sanctioned a corporate structure in which one company controlled about half of the steel industry. Thirty years later, the federal government again strengthened the law on corporate mergers and acquisitions with the creation of the Celler-Kefauver Act.

The federal government continued strengthening corporate regulations with the creation of the Securities Exchange Act, regulating the use of manipulative or deceptive methods in the purchase or sale of securities (the stocks, bonds, notes, convertible debentures, warrants, or other documents that represent a share in a corporation). The Act's original intent was to prevent company insiders from making false statements about a company's health, so that they could buy shares of stock at lower prices. It was not until later in the century that the practice of receiving inside information to buy and sell stocks for the largest gain became common.

Despite the original requirement for corporations to serve the public interest, the public's confidence in corporations began to wane in the 1960s. Labor unions and collective bargaining grew in response to public wariness around corporations. In the 1960s and 1970s, the power of corporations over the lives of consumers also elicited the growth of public interest law firms, class-action suits, and organized political and educational activities by groups of consumers and environmentalists.

The Rise of Conglomerates

Eventually, another form of corporation would emerge. Conglomerates are corporations that consist of a number of different companies operating in diversified fields, often only indirectly (or not at all) related to other corporate divisions. Conglomerates became increasingly popular during the late 1950s and early 1960s because such entities could make acquisitions and grow, yet maintain immunity from the antitrust prosecution that companies faced when making acquisitions in the same line of business. Thus businesses that were constrained within their own industry were able to freely expand into different markets.

Some of the traditionally powerful American corporations began to lose their influence in the late 1960s. The government continued strengthening its antitrust efforts, launching attacks on various conglomerates that misstated earnings. The federal government turned its attacks on IBM in 1969 and AT&T in 1974. In addition, the increasing ease of travel for business contributed to a global economy with increased market competition. As industry internationalized, American business transformed. Competition for American dollars moved from a national to a multinational stage. In fact, almost all of the largest American corporations at the beginning of the twenty-first century operated in world markets directly or through subsidiary corporations.

Modern Corporations

By the 1970s, a handful of communications media, education, research and development, computing machines, and financial and real estate companies accounted for as much as 40 percent of the country's gross national product. Microsoft, a developer of personal computer software systems and applications, was formed in 1975. The corporation moved to the front of the software market in the 1980s when its operating system became the standard for personal computers across the country. By 1993, its newest operating system release was selling more than one million copies per month. Three years later, its net income topped $2.1 billion, and it could be argued that Microsoft is the corporation that had the largest impact on American history in the twentieth century. However, the company faced charges of unfair competition and a Department of Justice investigation in 1994. In 1996, the Department of Justice reopened its investigation and, following a 30-month trial, found the corporation guilty of antitrust violations and ordered its breakup. An appeals court overturned the breakup order, but found the company guilty of trying to maintain a monopoly.

Enron Corporation, formed from the merger of natural gas pipeline companies Houston Natural Gas and InterNorth, was exposed for inflating profits in 2001. A Wall Street Journal report disclosed that Enron took a $1.2 billion charge against shareholder equity. Shortly thereafter, Enron announced that it had overstated earnings by almost $600 million, dating back four years. The Department of Justice opened a criminal investigation and found that the company actually inflated profits by $1 billion. The government also indicted Enron's accounting firm, Arthur Andersen LLP, for obstructing justice, based on evidence that the company inappropriately shredded documents related to the Enron bankruptcy.

Not long after Enron's questionable accounting practices were revealed, WorldCom, Incorporated, disclosed that it had hidden $1.2 billion in losses by failing to report $3.85 billion in expenses. The Securities and Exchange Commission (SEC) charged the long-distance telephone and data services company with fraud. The company's cofounder and chief executive officer resigned amid an SEC investigation that included questions about $366 million in personal loans from the company. Shares of WorldCom, which had flown to $64 in 1999, dropped to $.09 by July of 2002. Under the weight of both $30 billion in debt and the federal investigations, the company filed for bankruptcy, becoming the nation's largest company to ever declare insolvency.

In July 2002, as the American public voiced concern around corporations and their apparent disdain for the public interest, the U.S. stock market tumbled and the government again pledged to investigate corporate activities. The SEC began investigations of Qwest Communications International, Inc., Global Crossing Ltd., and other corporations. As more scandals of spurious accounting practices emerged across the country, some experts marveled at the irony that the increased competition resulting from antitrust legislation may have encouraged certain companies to cross the line of legality in order to remain viable.

BIBLIOGRAPHY

Beatty, Jack, ed. *Colossus: How the Corporation Changed America.* New York: Broadway, 2001.

Kaysen, Carl. *The American Corporation Today.* New York: Oxford University Press, 1996.

Sobel, Robert. *The Age of Giant Corporations: A Microeconomic History of American Business, 1914–1992.* Westport, Conn.: Praeger, 1993.

Soderquist, Larry D., et al. *Corporations and Other Business Organizations: Cases, Materials, Problems.* 4th ed. Charlottesville, Va.: Michie, 1997.

James T. Scott

CORRUPT BARGAIN.

CORRUPT BARGAIN. When the 1824 election ended without any candidate receiving a majority in the electoral college, the House of Representatives awarded the election to John Quincy Adams. Andrew Jackson's outraged supporters claimed that a corrupt bargain had been struck whereby Henry Clay supported Adams in the House vote in return for the office of secretary of state.

BIBLIOGRAPHY

Nagel, Paul. *John Quincy Adams: A Public Life, a Private Life.* New York: Knopf, 1997.

Remini, Robert V. *Andrew Jackson and the Course of American Freedom, 1822–1832.* New York: Harper and Row, 1981.

Erik McKinley Eriksson / A. G.

See also **Elections, Presidential; Electoral College.**

CORRUPTION, POLITICAL.

CORRUPTION, POLITICAL. Three major areas of political corruption are worth noting. First, bribery is clearly an example. Second, some people claim that certain government practices such as patronage, while legal, might be suspect. This definition sets a very high standard for political propriety. The conflict-of-interest definition—use of public office for personal gain, usually money—is a third aspect of political corruption. This is an ethical issue dealing with the premise that power corrupts and absolute power corrupts absolutely. Corruption, therefore, is a catchall expression for illegal as well as ethically questionable behaviors. Ironically, the very nature of federalism contributed to the potential for corruption. Since power corrupts, the challenge is to require accountability at all levels of government and to create virtuous and ethical citizens.

History of Political Corruption

From the beginnings of European settlement to the American Revolution, the colonies witnessed some out-rageous instances of corruption. Royal governors and corporate placemen used their official positions to enrich themselves in every possible way. Many of them considered this a privilege of their offices. The growing discontent with British rule in the eighteenth century contributed to the later American definition of conflict of interest, while the idea of natural rights contributed to the notion of a public interest and welfare.

Land, a large source of wealth in the colonies, contributed to schemes and speculation and bribery of both local and royal politicians. Legal and illegal struggles over land added to the colonial desire for independence. Later, of course, this struggle would be expressed as honest graft (inside information about future land use), bribing over zoning ordinations, and tax abatement, a legal but highly unethical policy.

Officials were not the only ones to skirt the law in the American colonies. Colonial merchants and rebels, in their opposition to the Acts of Trade and Navigation, ignored tariff duties and mercantile regulations. Arguing against taxation without representation, these groups simply circumvented the navigation laws, since they did not express "the will of the people."

Politics and the American Revolution shaped this constant argument over corruption. Americans, with their New World innocence and historical exceptionalism, sought a society free of "European" contamination. The goal of classical republicanism became the American Revolution's political discourse. The taming of corruption (through the separation of powers and checks and balances) was a major feature of the federal Constitution of 1787. The founders were seriously worried about the baleful efforts of corruption on the republic's future. They had reason to be concerned.

But by the early nineteenth century, the political culture had changed. Commercial republicanism considered the marketplace to be fair and just and replaced classical republicanism, with its virtuous polis. America was moving west and becoming urban and industrial. Alexis de Tocqueville observed that "democratic" corruption had replaced "aristocratic" corruption. With the rise of the common man, with the American emphasis on rugged individualism, with every man having his price, the opportunities for boodle were vast. Despite the founders' efforts to restrict corruption in government, the truth was that governmental contracts at all levels provided major possibilities for official malfeasance. From corrupt agents in the Bureau of Indian Affairs to colorful scandals of the Ulysses S. Grant era such as the CRÉDIT MOBILIER, the "salary grab" act, and the WHISKEY RING, the times were alive with spoilsmen. Even at the height of the Civil War President Abraham Lincoln worried about the War Department under Simon Cameron's guidance, replacing him in 1862 with Edwin M. Stanton. The disputed election of 1876, in which Rutherford B. Hayes lost the popular vote but won the presidency with one more electoral vote than Samuel Tilden, was the jewel of electoral political corruption in the nineteenth century, unrivaled until the presidential election of 2000. In the latter the issue was not just that George W. Bush won the election but how it was conducted in Florida and other states, damaging the public trust by allowing that the election of the president of the United States was only "politics."

The local governmental agencies often outperformed their federal counterparts when it came to corruption. Tammany Hall in New York City and similar organizations created political machines that ran on illegal contributions from businesses and other interest groups. Until about 1945 the urban political machine was a standard feature of politics, but the growth of the suburbs and other factors limited its power after that point.

Reform

The history of political corruption is also the history of reform. Starting with the Pendleton Act of 1883, which created a federal civil service, the excesses of patronage were checked. (To be sure, the desire for a governmental appointment still shaped party discipline and organization for many individuals.) By the beginning of the twentieth century the issue of political contributions to candidates was legislatively resolved. The direct election of U.S. senators provided a limited solution, and the Tillman Act of 1907 stopped banks and corporations from contributing to federal elections. Three years later, a federal law required congressional candidates and their organizations to report contributions and expenditures. But the laws have loopholes, as the post-Watergate years demonstrated: SOFT MONEY, POLITICAL ACTION COMMITTEES, and so forth.

The problem is that reform legislation in the area of political corruption occurs after a particular event or situation has already happened. Various interests can find a way through the new law. However, some improvement can be noted. As a result of the TEAPOT DOME affair and other corrupt behavior in President Warren G. Harding's administration, political contributions were more closely regulated in 1925. The Federal Regulation of Lobbying Act of 1946 was an advance; however, both Harry S. Truman's and Dwight D. Eisenhower's presidencies were plagued by questionable behavior regarding lobbyists.

While the Grant-era corruptions highlighted the nineteenth century, the Watergate affair (1972–1974) was the defining moment for political corruption in the twentieth century. Before that scandal the 1964 probe of Robert G. "Bobby" Baker, a secretary to the Senate Democratic Majority Leader, revealed a simple case of influence peddling and kickbacks to Baker, a self-styled wheeler-dealer. The legislative results were the Select Committees on Standards and Conduct for members of Congress and, by 1971, the Federal Election Campaign Act. Reacting to the widespread corruption of WATERGATE, Congress passed the Foreign Corrupt Practices Act (1977), which disallowed gifts to foreign officials by American companies, and the Ethics in Government Act (1978), which

created the position of independent counsel to investigate charges of governmental misconduct. The office of the independent counsel kept very busy during Ronald Reagan's and Bill Clinton's presidencies, although it produced mixed results.

Meanwhile, the KOREAGATE scandal of 1976–1978, the ABSCAM scandal of 1978–1980, and the "Wedtech" affair of 1986 all dealt with the old-fashioned practices of kickbacks and the use of one's public office for private financial gain. Undoubtedly such incidents will continue in the twenty-first century, but their prosecution could be hampered by several Supreme Court decisions during the 1970s and 1980s. In *Buckley v. Valeo* (1976), *First National Bank of Boston v. Bellotti* (1978), and *Federal Election Commission v. National Conservative Political Action Committee* (1985), the Court ruled that earlier laws and regulations regarding campaign contributions violated the right of free speech guaranteed under the First Amendment. *McNally v. United States* (1987) greatly limited the use of mail-fraud statutes in charging local and state officials with corruption.

BIBLIOGRAPHY

ABC-Clio. *Crime and Punishment in America: A Historical Bibliography.* Santa Barbara, Calif.: ABC-Clio Information Services, 1984. Many excellent citations.

Amick, George. *The American Way of Graft.* Princeton, N.J.: Center for Analysis of Public Issues, 1976. An examination of institutional corruption at the state and local level.

Eisenstadt, Abraham S., Arj Hoogenboom, and Hans Trefousse, eds. *Before Watergate: Problems of Corruption in American Society.* Brooklyn, N.Y.: Brooklyn College Press, 1978. Solid historical essays.

Drew, Elizabeth. *The Corruption of American Politics: What Went Wrong and Why.* Woodstock, N.Y.: Overlook, 2000. A depressing narrative of the Clinton presidency and election finance reform.

Noonan, John T., Jr. *Bribes.* New York: Macmillan, 1984. A massive history of corruption from biblical times to the date of publication.

Summers, Mark W. *The Plundering Generation: Corruption and the Crisis of the Union, 1849–1861.* New York: Oxford University Press, 1987. A historical example showing that corruption and the perception of it have significant consequences.

Donald K. Pickens

See also **Lobbies; Pendleton Act; Political Action Committees; Political Scandals.**

COSA NOSTRA. *See* **Crime, Organized.**

COSMETIC SURGERY, like reconstructive surgery, has its roots in plastic surgery (coming from the Greek word "plastikos," meaning to form or mold), which is the repair, restoration, or improvement of lost, injured, or misshapen body parts. Records of plastic surgery are found as early as 800 B.C. Unlike reconstructive surgery, cosmetic surgery is performed solely for reasons of enhancing appearance. Most consider the sixteenth-century Italian Gasparo Tagliacozzi the father of plastic surgery. Tagliacozzi was a pioneer in nasal reconstruction, often repairing damage from a brawl or duel. Another pioneer was Charles C. Miller, considered the father of modern plastic surgery. Operating in the early twentieth century, Miller published numerous works on improving a person's appearance. Plastic surgery remained a small and obscure area of medicine until World War I. Trench warfare caused facial wounds so frequent and severe that special groups of doctors were formed to deal with facial injuries. Among the volunteer doctors were two Americans, Varaztad Kazanjian and Vilray Blair, who were instrumental in developing new techniques and sharing their knowledge after the war. By 1921, plastic surgeons holding both medical and dental degrees organized into the American Association of Oral and Plastic Surgeons; in 1941 the name was changed to the American Association of Plastic Surgeons. The American Society of Plastic and Reconstructive Surgeons was formed in 1931, followed by the American Board of Plastic Surgery in 1937.

BIBLIOGRAPHY

Haiken, Elizabeth. *Venus Envy: The History of Cosmetic Surgery.* Baltimore: Johns Hopkins University Press, 1997.

Lisa A. Ennis

See also **Medicine and Surgery; Medicine, Military.**

COST OF LIVING. The cost of living is the monetary cost of maintaining a particular standard of living; its fluctuations are closely tied to rates of inflation and deflation. To estimate the cost of living, such items as food, clothing, rent, fuel, and miscellaneous items such as recreation, transportation, and medical services are considered. The cost of living is usually measured by calculating the average cost of a number of these particular goods and services; the average cost is then used as an index for a given cluster of consumables.

Measuring changes in the cost of living is essential to determine fixed-income payments, such as welfare and social security, family allowances, tax exemptions, and the minimum wage; it is also an important factor in wage negotiations. Because the supply and demand of certain products are subject to change, it becomes difficult to make precise cost-of-living comparisons and adjustments.

Determining the Cost of Living

The cost of living is determined by the amount of money needed to buy the goods and services necessary to maintain a specific standard of living. In 1890, the Bureau of Labor Statistics made the first attempt to gather data on the cost of living in the United States, introducing the cost-of-living index. In 1944 the government changed the

name of its measurement from the "cost-of-living index" to the "consumer price index" (CPI), when a presidential committee made a comprehensive study and concluded that the cost-of-living index did not reflect all changes in living costs. Using the CPI, the government can keep track of even incremental changes in retail prices. These changes are then compared to prices in a previously selected base year, which shows the percentage increase or decrease in the cost of living over time. In addition to changes over time, these studies also consider regional differences in the cost of living. The CPI is based on data collected in eighty-seven urban areas throughout the country and from about 23,000 retail and service establishments. Data on rents are collected from about 50,000 landlords or tenants. The CPI also compiles price quotes per month in twenty-three selected areas on approximately 304 commodities and services. It is revised periodically, with short-run comparisons tending to be more accurate than long-run comparisons.

Changes in prices are of major importance to many segments of the population. For workers earning the minimum wage or retired persons living on a fixed income, a rise or decline in living costs partly determines the standard of living that they can achieve and maintain. Price changes also may affect the purchasing power of a person's income. Social security benefits and pensions are also closely tied in with the CPI and may be changed accordingly, through a cost-of-living adjustment. Other legal forms of compensation, such as the property settlement and alimony in a divorce, may also be adjusted periodically to accommodate changes in the index.

The CPI provides a gauge to determine the degree to which inflation and deflation affect the average consumer. However, in times of double-digit inflation, the CPI may exaggerate the rate of inflation the average consumer experiences.

Since its inception the cost-of-living index has been steadily improved in both coverage and accuracy. Revisions in the index are based on comprehensive studies of consumer expenditures to determine "the kind, qualities, and amounts of all goods and services bought by each consumer unit." The patterns of consumer spending determine the relative importance given to each item in the index.

The Cost of Living in American History

During the colonial era, wage earners suffered declines in real income when commodity prices fluctuated in nearly every colony. The inflation that accompanied the Revolutionary War also undoubtedly hurt workers, especially in the eastern seaboard cities, although no detailed statistical study has ever been done on the subject. After the war, prices during the 1790s began another sharp rise; in response, American workers went on some of the first labor strikes in American history. Between 1789 and 1850, there is little evidence of any continuous urban retail price quotations. However, from 1850 on, existing records show that the American standard of living rose at an increasing rate over the long run, increasing on average 1.67 percent after 1850.

During the twentieth century, specifically during the period between 1913 and 1975, the cost of living in the United States increased steadily, though not to the same extent it rose in other parts of the world. The CPI saw its first substantial increase during World War I, rising to a peak of 203 percent change from the base year by 1920. At this time, the cost of living had so far outrun increases in wages that the annual number of labor strikes grew from 1,204 to 3,630 between 1914 and 1919. After 1920, the index remained at about 175 percent for a decade. The index then dipped to 131 in 1933 and recovered slowly to 142 by 1940.

During World War II, the federal government attempted to place a firm lid on the cost of living. Yet, the CPI inched upward to 182 by 1945. Since wage controls were comparatively flexible and employment was brisk, the vast majority of civilians enjoyed a notable increase in real income, an unusual occurrence during wartime. The actual cost of living increased somewhat more than the index showed, due to such factors as ceiling-price violations and the black markets that emerged to trade in scarce commodities. Although some economists dispute the accuracy of the figures for this period, the cost of living was still well below what it would have been had market forces been allowed to operate unrestricted.

The CPI spurted upward in 1946, and continued in that direction until it had reached 243 by 1950. After 1950, the CPI drifted gradually but steadily upward, with slight declines occurring during recessions. By 1960, it had attained 299, which was low compared to its 1965 level of 319, its 1972 level of 428, and its 1974 level of 525. In the 1970s, America faced new problems: a combination of inflation, recession, and unemployment to which economists gave the inelegant label "stagflation." Swollen federal deficits, largely the result of expenses incurred in the Korean and Vietnam Wars, had aggravated the problem throughout the 1950s and 1960s. Although some economists believed that a moderate amount of inflation was of no concern or consequence, the presidential administrations from Harry Truman to Jimmy Carter tried to contain inflation. In the meantime, more incomes, especially fixed incomes such as federal old-age pensions, were being protected by what were known as escalator clauses. Modeled after labor contract clauses, the escalator clause makes sure that income is automatically adjusted every three to six months to compensate for changes in the CPI.

With inflation at 10 percent by 1978, President Carter established the Council on Wage and Price Stability. The Council was to set pay-increase standards of 7 percent a year, as well as standards to limit price increases. Unfortunately, the council was generally ineffective in trying to control inflation and rising costs, due largely to the energy crisis. By 1981, President Ronald Reagan had abolished the council when studies showed that workers and companies were unwilling to moderate wage or price increases, as these measures did not appear able to stop inflation.

The Quest for Accuracy

Measuring changes in the cost of living can be difficult. Critics of the CPI believe that the index overstates the actual rise in prices because the manner in which the CPI is calculated is flawed. These same critics also point to what they believe to be weaknesses in the current system, such as the failure of the CPI to reflect improvements that have taken place, the inability of the index to add new items and subtract old ones quickly enough, delays in showing the effects of new methods of distribution on prices, particularly with reference to the rapid growth of discount houses and grocery store chains, and finally the dependence of the index on prices from the base period. This last factor has resulted in overestimations of living costs. The problems with the CPI measurements have often clouded economic realities. During the late 1970s and early 1980s, for instance, interest rates and the cost of new homes were factored into CPI housing costs. However, as critics pointed out, few people buy more than one house a year. Although increases in mortgage rates affect the overall price of a home, they do not affect homeowners who are already paying off a mortgage. Based on this calculation, the CPI was overstating the reported inflation rate by at least 2 to 3 percentage points.

The Boskin Commission

By the mid-1990s, some economists were questioning whether the use of the CPI to determine the cost of living was warranted. In early December 1996, the Boskin Commission, made up of a panel of five academics, stated what they believed to be the distorting effects of the CPI. The council, named after its head, the former chairman of the Council of Economic Advisors, Michael Boskin, announced one of the most extraordinary statistical discoveries in American economic history: CPI projections were off by as much as 30 percent. The magnitude of this error, the panel concluded, had cost American taxpayers billions of dollars and distorted numerous economic decisions.

According to the commission, these flaws were the result of faulty procedures used by the Bureau of Labor Statistics, which had in effect elevated the federal budget by more than a trillion dollars. The commission also stated that if corrections were to be made to the CPI, they would save the government, and incidentally the American people, more than a trillion dollars over the next decade.

According to the commission, the CPI should not be considered a cost-of-living index, even though everyone regards it as the barometer of changes in the cost of living. According to the commission, for instance, if the CPI rises 3.5 percent, then labor contracts would follow with automatic wage increases of 3.5 percent to cover the increase in the cost of living. Social security payments and government pensions are also automatically increased to reflect rising costs. Other things such as legal contracts and rents trigger similar automatic increases.

The commission found, however, that the design of the CPI prevents it from representing accurate changes in the cost of living. There are three reasons for the discrepancies. First, the CPI did not account for what the commission called the "Substitution Bias" by which American consumers adapt their consumption patterns to avoid those goods which have increased the most in price. This failure causes the CPI to exaggerate the rate of inflation. The second factor the CPI failed to take into consideration is the "New Goods Bias." The CPI does not adequately account for the impact of new goods, such as cell phones, DVD players, and high-definition television sets, on consumer prices. The third factor that the CPI ignores is the "Quality Change Bias." Simply put, many of the goods Americans buy are better than those they could purchase in the past. Automobiles are safer and more efficient. Electronics are more sophisticated and more durable. Recognition of these improvements rarely finds its way into the CPI; and if it does, it is usually only as an increase in price, not as an offset to the cost of living. As a result, economists account for improvements in a product's quality as well as increases in its price.

The Boskin Committee has determined that if the defects in the CPI remain uncorrected, they will cause government figures to continue to exaggerate the rate of inflation by as much as a 30 percent a year. When the CPI calculates inflation as 3.6 percent, for example, it is, according to the Boskin committee, really only at 2.5 percent. If unaltered, the current mechanism for gauging the cost of living in the United States will make the possibility of accuracy even more remote.

BIBLIOGRAPHY

Baker, Dean. "The Boskin Commission after One Year." *Challenge* 41/2 (March-April 1998): 6–12.

Brown, Clair. *American Standards of Living 1918–1988*. New York: Blackwell Publishers, 1994.

Forbes, Steve. "Poison Proposal," *Forbes* 159/11 (June 2, 1997): 27.

Glickman, Lawrence B. *A Living Wage: American Workers and the Making of Consumer Society*. Ithaca: Cornell University Press, 1997.

Marcoot, John L. "Revision of Consumer Price Index is now under way." *Monthly Labor Review* 108 (April 1985): 27–39.

Marcoot, John L., and Richard C. Bahr. "The Revised Consumer Price Index: Changes in Definitions and Availability." *Monthly Labor Review* 109 (July 1986): 15–23.

Wykoff, Frank C. "The Hubbell of Economics: The CPI Is Off by One-Third." *The Quill* 85/2 (March 1997): 39–43.

Meg Greene Malvasi

See also **Economic Indicators; Inflation; Standards of Living.**

COST-OF-LIVING ADJUSTMENT. The Cost-of-Living Adjustment (COLA) is an adjustment of wages or benefits designed to offset changes in the cost of living. It is often measured by the Consumer Price Index (CPI), reported monthly by the Bureau of Labor Statistics, and usually varies at a percentage at or near the average INFLATION rate. In the case of pensions, COLA begins when the pension starts. In some pension plans, the monthly pension benefit remains at a fixed amount; with COLA-adjusted pensions, the monthly pension benefit grows each year. The dramatic increase in the rate of inflation during the 1970s led to the widespread use of cost-of-living adjustments in wage agreements, real estate leases, and such government benefits as SOCIAL SECURITY. To compensate for inflation, Congress periodically adjusted and increased social security benefits, but by 1975 had begun to make the adjustments on an annual basis. However, in recent years, labor unions have traded cost-of-living adjustment clauses for other forms of compensation. Various explanations have been offered for the erosion of COLA coverage in union contracts, including reduced inflationary uncertainty, diminished union power, and structural shifts in the economy away from manufacturing. The federal government in recent years has also tried to reduce COLAs in social security, but has met with fierce resistance.

BIBLIOGRAPHY

Johnson, Richard W. "A Not-So-Unkind Cut—Social Security COLAs." *Christian Science Monitor*, 29 March 1999, 11.

Ragan, James F., Jr., and Bernt Bratsberg. "Un-COLA: Why Have Cost-of-Living Clauses Disappeared from Union Contracts and Will They Return?" *Southern Economic Journal* 67, no. 2 (October 2000): 304–324.

Meg Greene Malvasi

See also **Trade Unions.**

COTTON. Although grown in the South since the founding of Jamestown in 1607, cotton did not become a cash crop during the colonial period, and most domestic production was consumed locally in domestic manufacture. By the late eighteenth century, revolutionary inventions in the English textile industry began the process that would transform the American South into the "cotton kingdom." John Kay's flying shuttle (patented 1733) and James Hargreaves's spinning jenny (patented 1770) speeded up weaving and spinning processes, and when these innovations were adapted first to water power and then to steam power, English textile production soared. Cotton imports into England increased fiftyfold in the second half of the eighteenth century, but rising prices indicated that the cotton supply was failing to meet the spiraling demand of Lancashire's mills. When trade with England reopened after the Revolution (1783), American planters in the coastal areas of South Carolina and Georgia found a lucrative market for their long-staple, black-seed cotton. Further inland, only the short-staple (or uplands) variety would grow; and because its green seeds stuck so tenaciously to the staple, they had to be picked out by hand, a time-consuming process that even prevailing high prices could not support.

This all changed in 1793 when Eli Whitney invented his cotton gin, a device that quickly and cheaply separated the seeds from the staple. The new invention allowed Georgia and South Carolina planters to expand exponentially their production of the now-profitable short-staple cotton. Exports increased from 500,000 pounds in 1793 to 18 million pounds by 1800 and more than 90 million pounds a decade later. The cotton belt in Georgia and South Carolina rapidly expanded westward as farmers and planters pushed into the virgin lands in south-central Alabama; into the rich delta lands in Mississippi, northern Louisiana, Arkansas, and Tennessee; and into western Texas. In 1860, the United States produced more than 2 billion pounds (4.5 million bales) of cotton, almost 80 percent of which came from the states of Georgia, Alabama, Mississippi, and Louisiana. About 75 percent of this crop was exported, mainly to England where American cotton enjoyed a near monopoly.

Southerners proclaimed that "cotton was king," and indeed the evidence seemed to support this view. Cotton attracted millions of settlers into the Southwest; southern demand for foodstuffs helped bring population into the Old Northwest; eastern merchants found some of their best customers in the cotton belt; New England textile manufacturers and workers relied for their well-being on the South's chief export; and in the last three antebellum decades, cotton provided well over half the nation's exports.

Many small farmers grew cotton, but the most efficient and extensive producers were planters with gangs of slave labor. Planting began in early spring; slaves spent the long hot days of summer thinning the plants and chopping out menacing weeds; picking started in late August and continued for several months. Planters then ginned, pressed, and baled their cotton on the plantation before shipping it to market—usually New Orleans, Charleston, Savannah, or Mobile—typically consigning it to factors who sold it to representatives of American and European mills. Factors purchased supplies and other goods for their clients and then, after deducting expenses and commissions, remitted the net proceeds of the crop to the planter.

The CIVIL WAR proved the limits of king cotton's power. The Union blockade separated the South from its markets and sources of supply; and the British, despite the so-called cotton famine, neither recognized the South nor attempted to break the blockade. The war left most cotton farmers destitute, their fields and equipment in neglect or ruin, and their black labor force free. Gradually the South returned to cotton but under a greatly altered system of production and marketing. Land was rented out in small parcels, usually under the sharecropping system by which the tenant, in return for the right to use the land

Confiscated Cotton. African Americans on Port Royal Island, S.C., in 1862 prepare the cotton they have picked to be ginned and auctioned off in the North. After a battle in November 1861, the Union held this enclave deep in the Confederacy, using it as a supply base for ships blockading the South and later as a refuge for escaped slaves. LIBRARY OF CONGRESS

and some equipment, shared his crop with the landlord according to a fixed contract. For his supplies, food, and clothing, the sharecropper turned to a local storekeeper (called the "furnishing merchant"), who furnished goods on credit in return for a crop lien that gave him first call on the sharecropper's proceeds from the growing crop. At first recently freed slaves made up the vast majority of tenants, but in time more and more farmers themselves lost their land and became tenants. In 1880, 36 percent of cotton farmers were tenants; in 1920 this figure had risen to almost 50 percent; and in 1935 it had risen to over 60 percent. By the turn of the century, more whites than blacks were tenants.

Meanwhile, cotton production increased. Within a decade after the end of the Civil War, the prewar high of 4.5 million bales was equaled, and the output continued to grow, reaching 10 million bales by 1900 and 16 million bales on the eve of WORLD WAR I. Acreage devoted to cotton increased from fewer than 8 million acres in 1869 to 25 million in 1900 and more than 35 million in 1914.

By this time there were signs of serious trouble in the southern cotton belt. Declining prices and production inefficiencies brought poverty and hardship to millions of cotton growers, a condition worsened by the boll weevil infestation that entered Texas in 1892 and gradually spread north and east, reaching Georgia and South Carolina in 1922. The United States lost its complete domination of the raw cotton markets as countries such as In-

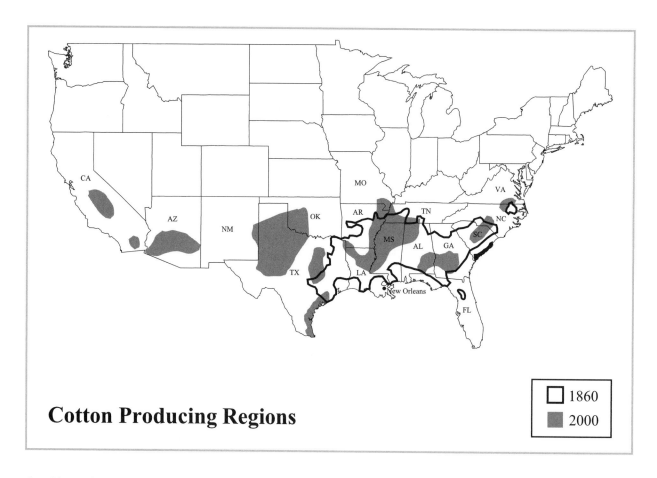

Cotton Producing Regions

1860
2000

dia, China, the Soviet Union, and Brazil increased their production. Rich, irrigated lands in the western states of California, Arizona, and New Mexico were shifted to cotton production; and these areas—free from the uncertainties of weather, the boll weevil, and weed infestation—offered disastrous competition to the older cotton areas. With the GREAT DEPRESSION, cotton prices dropped still lower and conditions reached crisis proportions.

Once again change came to the cotton belt. Cotton acreage, which had reached a high of almost 45 million in 1925, dropped to half that total in the immediate post–World War II years and continued to drop, reaching about 11 million in 1971. Production also declined but at a much slower rate. While acreage devoted to cotton dropped 75 percent from the mid-1920s to 1972, production decreased only about 30 percent, from 16 million to 11 million bales. As marginal lands shifted away from cotton, production on better lands became mechanized and more efficient with the introduction of tractors, plows, weeders, and automatic pickers. Sharecroppers fled the cotton fields or were driven away by the introduction of machinery; output per man-hour on the mechanized cotton farms increased nine times between 1940 and 1973. The eastern cotton states became minor producers as the cotton belt shifted west. In 1970, Texas was the largest producer, followed by Mississippi, California, and Arkansas; and Arizona grew more cotton than did Alabama, Georgia, and the Carolinas.

Although the United States remained the world's leading cotton producer in 1970, its onetime near monopoly was gone. By the early 1960s its share of world production had dropped to less than 30 percent, and by 1971, to 19 percent. Moreover, cotton growers, despite increasing efficiency and ample government price supports, apprehensively faced a new threat in the increasing popularity of man-made fibers. Per capita consumption of cotton in the United States fell from 30 pounds in 1950 to less than 19 pounds in 1970, while per capita consumption of artificial fibers rose from 10 pounds to 32 pounds during the same period. Despite these threats to the continued vitality of the industry, the United States recovered its position somewhat in the 1980s and 1990s, accounting for 25 to 30 percent of the world trade in raw cotton by 2000. Although China passed America to become the world's leading producer, the United States remained the world's largest exporter of the fiber, which despite its decline, still contributed over $25 billion annually in goods and services to the American economy at the end of the century.

Cotton Manufacturing

The processing of raw cotton by modern methods begins with the breaking of compressed bales (average weight 478 pounds). Bale breakers, openers, and pickers loosen and blend the tufts of cotton and remove impurities. Carding engines complete the cleaning process, eliminate short

Cotton Gins. Laborers in Dahomey, Miss., in the 1890s operate the machines that separate cotton fiber from seeds and unwanted materials. LIBRARY OF CONGRESS

and broken fibers, and separate and align those remaining into soft, ropelike "slivers." To obtain high-quality yarn, combers process fine (thin) cotton into slivers, removing as much as 20 percent of the shorter fibers. Drawing frames begin the process of attenuating and twisting the slivers and enhance their regularity by drawing them between rollers and arranging them in parallel rows. A series of machines collectively known as "speed frames" conclude the preparation of cotton for the spinning frames, principally by further drawing out and twisting the material into a rope called "roving" and adding strength to the fibers by making them cling to each other more closely. In the spinning stage, frames equipped with ring spindles draw and twist the fibers into yarn while winding them on a bobbin. The process is continuous, with drawing, twisting, and winding taking place simultaneously. During the preparatory and spinning processes cotton suffers a loss in weight of 9–12 percent. In comparison, man-made filament fibers spun into yarn on cotton textile machinery incur a negligible loss. Approximately two-thirds of man-made fibers come from chemical producers already processed as filament yarn.

Machines then process cotton yarns into fabrics by knitting, tufting, and weaving. Knitting consists essentially of interlacing a single strand of yarn into a series of interlocking loops. Modern knitting mills produce literally hundreds of items of cotton and cotton-blended apparel. They also convert considerable quantities of cotton yarn into a variety of tufted products on tufting machines

and consume them in various nonwoven constructions, in which machines bond fibers together with adhesives. Manufacturers continue to channel the greatest proportion of cotton yarn into broadloom weaving, where additional preparation is required depending on whether it is destined to be warp (longitudinal) or weft (transverse) yarn. Weaving, conducted on high-speed automatic looms, involves the interlacing of yarn at right angles so as to form a fabric.

Upon leaving the weave shed, most unbleached gray goods undergo one of many finishing treatments. Initially, the fabric passes in succession through a series of scouring, washing, and bleaching units before being dyed and printed. Textile engineers have developed a wide range of mechanical and chemical processes to render the fabric more useful and fashionable. Mechanical processes can stiffen, glaze, and improve the texture of the cloth. Chemistry can also provide additional strength, such as fire retardance and abrasion and wind resistance, or it can impart various qualities desirable in apparel, such as permanent press, crease resistance, and shrinkage control, as well as a silklike sheen and the puckering quality of seersucker.

Industry Changes

The breakdown of major end-uses for all fibers reflects the eroding role of cotton in the American textile industry from the mid-1960s to the end of the twentieth century. Between 1968 and 1973, for example, cotton's percentage of total poundage in apparel dropped from 45 to 33 percent; in home furnishings, from 45 to 29 percent; in other consumer-type products, from 45 to 29 percent; and in industrial uses, from 32 to 21 percent. Aggregate cotton consumption by U.S. mills in 1973 amounted to 3,641,700,000 pounds (29.2 percent of total fiber consumption) compared to 3,773,600,000 pounds consumed in 1970 (39.5 percent of total fiber consumption).

During the 1960s the American textile industry became increasingly multifiber. The versatility of modern textile technology permitted the processing of cotton, cotton-synthetic blends, and various man-made fibers without requiring a change in machinery layout. In addition, both capital and labor requirements fell as faster and larger-capacity equipment reduced both the number of machines and the number of operatives and maintenance workers needed for a given output. A small number of large, multiplant firms thus account for a high proportion of capital expenditures for plant and equipment as well as for most textile research. During the 1958–1970 period, capital expenditures for the textile industry as a whole increased at an 11.3 percent annual rate. For knit fabric mills the annual rate was 23 percent; for cotton broadloom weaving establishments, on the other hand, the rate was only 3.7 percent per annum.

The new textile technology flourished primarily in the sprawling, single-story structures dotting the southeastern United States, where large pools of white and black female labor are readily available in hundreds of small communities. At the same time, the trend toward technological modernization has hastened the obsolescence of the aged, multistory mills that predominated in New England. By 1970 three-fourths of cotton textile employment was concentrated in the Southeast. Blue-collar occupations—primarily semi-skilled machine tending—constituted 85 percent of textile employment, a smaller share of jobs going to professional, research, clerical, and sales personnel than in most manufacturing industries. Women workers made up more than 65 percent of the employees in knitting mills but only 25 percent of the employees in textile-finishing establishments.

Although cotton manufacturing remains more fragmented and highly competitive than most industries, a trend toward fewer and larger firms is taking place; numerous mergers and acquisitions were effected during the 1960s, and many small mills shut down. By 1970, the four largest establishments making cotton broadwoven fabric accounted for 33 percent of total industry value of shipments (compared with 13 percent in 1947), while the eight largest firms accounted for 50 percent of the value of broadwoven shipments (compared to 22 percent in 1947). In the 1980s and 1990s, pressures on the textile industry increased as expanded foreign production cut into the U.S. industry's export profits. Then, in the late 1990s, a 40 percent decline in the average worth of Asian currencies, coupled with a 25 to 30 percent decline in the price of Asian yarn and fabric exports, sent the American industry into a crisis. In 1996 alone over 100 U.S. textile mills closed, taking over 60,000 jobs with them. The industry responded by pressuring the national government to help it open new overseas markets and by turning to newer, more efficient production technologies to reduce production costs.

BIBLIOGRAPHY

Gray, Lewis C. *History of Agriculture in the Southern United States to 1860.* Gloucester, Mass.: Peter Smith, 1958.

Holley, Donald. *The Second Great Emancipation: The Mechanical Cotton Picker, Black Migration, and How They Shaped the Modern South.* Fayetteville: University of Arkansas Press, 2000.

Kane, Nancy F. *Textiles in Transition: Technology, Wages, and Industry Relocation in the U.S. Textile Industry, 1880–1930.* New York: Greenwood Press, 1988.

Woodman, Harold D. *King Cotton and His Retainers.* Lexington: University of Kentucky Press, 1968.

Jack Blicksilver / c. w.

See also **Boll Weevil; Irrigation; King Cotton; Sharecroppers; Slave Trade; Slavery; Textiles.**

COTTON GIN, the implement or machine used to pull the cotton fibers from the seed. Each fiber grows from the seed like hairs from the head. There are two basic types—the black-seed cotton, from which the fibers pull away rather easily, and the green-seed cotton, from which it is difficult to free the fibers. North American colonists commonly used the roller gin, adapted from the "churka" of India, with which cotton fibers were pulled from the seed by hand-turned rollers. These implements could be used only to gin the Sea Island cotton, a black-seed type; the rollers crushed the green seeds and stained the fiber. But in the ever increasing inland acreage, only green-seed cotton could be grown, and this had to be ginned by hand.

In 1792 Eli Whitney, a Yale graduate then tutoring at an estate near Savannah, Georgia, found that many planters were interested in increasing their cotton production but were frustrated by the inefficiency of having to manually remove the seeds before the fiber could be baled for shipment. In a letter to his father (11 September 1793), Whitney wrote that if a machine "could be invented which would clean the Cotton with expedition, it would be a great thing both to the Country and to the inventor." In the same letter he boasted that his invention would "do more than fifty men with the old machines." Although the reference to "old machines" has been interpreted by some authors to mean the roller gins, it may not; there are unproven claims that Whitney had seen machines similar to his prior to his invention. Nevertheless, Eli Whitney was granted a patent on 14 March 1794 for a "new and useful improvement in the mode of Ginning Cotton." His machine used spiked teeth set into a wooden cylinder to pull the cotton fibers through the slots in a metal breastplate; the slots were too small to allow the seeds to pass through. A second cylinder with brushes freed the fibers from the teeth. Court cases involving competing patents for gins with sawtoothed cylinders were found in Whitney's favor; the saw pattern would eventually be preferred as the more efficient system of gin design.

Whitney and his partner, Phineas Miller, kept the cotton gin under their immediate control by selling ginning services, not machines. When a fire in their New Haven manufacturing shop delayed a shipment of gins, southern blacksmiths began making their own versions of the easily copied machine. After years of court suits, several southern states finally paid Whitney. He received almost $100,000 for the patent rights—a relatively modest amount for a patent that would increase cotton production in America from 3,000 bales in 1790 to more than 2 million bales by 1850. By 1836 cotton comprised two-thirds of all American exports. Patented improvements in the mechanization of the earlier roller gin began in the 1830s, and improvements in the saw gin continued throughout the nineteenth century, although the basic principle remained the same.

BIBLIOGRAPHY

Britton, Karen G. *Bale O'Cotton: The Mechanical Art of Cotton Ginning.* College Station: Texas A&M University Press, 1992.

Nevins, Allan, and Jeannette Mirskey. *The World of Eli Whitney.* New York: MacMillan, 1952.

Grace R. Cooper / A. R.

See also **Agricultural Machinery; King Cotton.**

COTTON KINGDOM refers to the cotton-producing region of the southern United States up until the Civil War. As white settlers from Virginia and the Carolinas forced the original Native American inhabitants farther and farther west, they moved in and established plantations. The section remained indelibly tied to and controlled by plantation agriculture. From the Atlantic coast to Texas, tobacco, rice, and sugar were staple crops from 1800 to the 1860s. It was cotton production, however, that controlled life in the region.

The predominant feature of the Cotton Kingdom was the employment of slave labor. The societal structure of the area in the antebellum era was built around slavery. The vast majority of the population of the southern United States at this time, slaves, freedmen, and farmers without slaves, were ruled by a disproportionate minority of less than 2,000 large landowners (those who owned more than one hundred slaves).

Because of the isolation and self-containment of the plantation system, coupled with a small population with limited resources, social services were practically nonexistent. This meant that social life, community services, education, and government rested in the hands of the large landholders. The only other outlet for community life was the church.

The notion of mass production of cotton in the South, and slavery with it, was dying out prior to the turn of the nineteenth century due to slow and unprofitable methods employed by the farmers. In 1793 that changed with the invention of Eli Whitney's cotton gin. The gin made mass cotton production in the South feasible and helped to institutionalize slavery in the region. The Louisiana Purchase and the annexation of Texas as a slave state helped to expand the Cotton Kingdom. Politically, cotton became the foundation of southern control of the Democratic Party.

The period from the mid-1830s to the election of 1860 saw the rise of a strong U.S. federal government, disunion with international importers of cotton, and increased support of abolition. The Civil War brought victory for abolition and utter destruction of the land in the region.

With the end of the Civil War on 9 April 1865, cotton was no longer the backbone of southern politics, but it remained the largest crop and source of income. Both prosperity and population dropped after the Civil War and continued to decline until an upsurge in the 1960s. Since then, the southern United States has replaced cotton with industry.

BIBLIOGRAPHY

Branford, Robert E. *Cotton Kingdom of the New South.* Cambridge, Mass.: Harvard University Press, 1967.

Dodd, William E. *The Cotton Kingdom.* Washington, D.C.: Ross and Perry, 2002. The original edition was published in 1926.

Michael K. Law

See also **Civil War; Slavery; South, the: The Antebellum South.**

COTTON MONEY, certificates issued by banks on baled cotton, generally used in commercial and financial operations by planters in the Old South. When secession demoralized the cotton exchanges, growers called on the Confederate government to issue cotton money. MISSISSIPPI, the only state to comply, issued $5 million in treasury notes to be advanced on 1861 cotton stored and pledged for delivery by owners. Although planters clamored for additional issues of cotton money, the legislature refused to issue notes on cotton raised after 1861. Before the cotton money was repudiated in 1869 as part of the Confederate debt, more than half of it had been redeemed.

BIBLIOGRAPHY

Ball, Douglas B. *Financial Failure and Confederate Defeat.* Urbana: University of Illinois Press, 1991.

Johnson, Ludwell H. *Red River Campaign: Politics and Cotton in the Civil War.* Baltimore: Johns Hopkins University Press, 1958.

John K. Bettersworth / A. R.

See also **Confederate States of America; Currency and Coinage; Money; Tithes, Southern Agricultural; Tobacco as Money.**

COUNCIL FOR NEW ENGLAND,

the name of the Plymouth branch of the Virginia Company after its members reorganized and incorporated under a new charter in 1620. This charter vested the council with the right to settle and govern colonies along the Atlantic coast between Long Island to the Bay of Fundy, as well as with monopolistic trade and fishing rights in that territory. In many respects the council appeared to be a trading company, but its members, who were nobles and landed gentry rather than merchants, were more interested in developing the land than in trade. They pursued their objectives by granting much of the region to council members as fiefs and manors organized pursuant to English land law. They gave the rest of the land to other individuals or groups along with rights of local self-government, although these recipients remained subject to the authority of the council's governor general.

Sir Ferdinando Gorges, president of the council, was the dominating figure throughout its history, but his agents in New England enjoyed limited success. From time to time the council tried to reorganize so as to invigorate the enterprise, and they considered exchanging their charter for one that better represented the landed interests of its members. Nothing came of these attempts, and the enterprise failed. Eventually, New England was colonized not through the efforts of this council, but through the unexpected success of two small grants to nonmembers: the PILGRIMS who settled on Cape Cod in 1620 and the Puritans who settled in Massachusetts Bay in 1629. These migrants altered the character of settlement in New England by replacing the council's conception of a single aristocratic and Anglican province with a patchwork of small, independent, middling Puritan and separatist colonies.

The Massachusetts Bay grant was particularly significant in that the grantees' powers of self-government derived not from the council, but directly from the king. Thus, the council could not maintain unchallenged authority in directing New England's growth. The council attempted to annul the MASSACHUSETTS charter by surrendering its "grand patent" and asking the king to regrant the whole region in partitions to preselected council members. The process of negotiating the transfer would enable the new proprietors to confirm or cancel previous grants, including the Massachusetts Bay patent. In 1635 the council therefore surrendered its charter and designated eight members who would receive land by royal charters. The proprietors initiated proceedings against the Massachusetts Bay Company, and Gorges was appointed governor-general of New England to preserve the administrative unity of the region. But the English Civil War interrupted this vigorous campaign. Only one charter, that of Maine to Gorges, made its way through the seals, and the action against Massachusetts Bay came to naught. On the other hand, twenty years of civil war and Puritan governance in England gave the Puritans in New England the opportunity to strengthen their foothold and develop the region into a number of little colonies more or less centering around Massachusetts.

BIBLIOGRAPHY

Clark, Charles E. *The Eastern Frontier: The Settlement of Northern New England, 1610–1763.* New York: Knopf, 1970.

Cooke, Jacob Ernest, et al., eds. *Encyclopedia of the North American Colonies.* New York: Scribners, 1993.

Labaree, Benjamin W. *Colonial Massachusetts.* Millwood, N.Y.: KTO, 1979.

Morison, Samuel Eliot. *Builders of the Bay Colony.* Boston: Houghton Mifflin, 1958.

Viola F. Barnes / S. B.

See also **Colonial Settlements; Massachusetts Bay Colony; Plymouth Colony; Plymouth, Virginia Company of; Puritans and Puritanism; Separatists, Puritan.**

COUNCIL OF ECONOMIC ADVISORS.

Congress established the Council of Economic Advisors to the President (CEA) as part of the Employment Act of 1946, which committed the federal government to maintaining "maximum employment, production, and purchasing power" in the economy. The creation of the CEA was meant to bring the science of economics to bear on the political process of making policy. It also reflected both the increased responsibility that the federal government assumed for the health of the economy during the depression and World War II (1939–1945) and the increasing administrative capacities of the executive branch, a trend that began during the Progressive Era but accelerated during the 1930s and 1940s.

The CEA consists of three members, each of whom the president nominates and the Senate confirms. From 1946 to the 2000s all but three CEA members have had academic experience, and from 1953 to the 2000s all have been economists. Commensurate with the CEA's advisory, rather than operational, role, Congress provided for a small professional staff, which has numbered between fifteen and twenty-five, expecting the CEA to draw on statistical and data collection services available elsewhere in the executive branch or from consultants for its information needs. There has been high turnover among CEA members and staff, often coinciding with changes in administration.

Though Congress did not specify its exact role, the CEA soon emerged as a body that was responsible for providing the president with practical and relevant economic advice. The Employment Act charged it with the production of an economic report for delivery to the Joint Economic Committee in the Congress, which the 1946 act created. The president, at his discretion, adds his comments to the report, which constitutes his economic policy statement. The committee holds hearings and reports its findings and recommendations to Congress as a whole. CEA members, however, have become active in national and intragovernmental debates on a number of topics, including productivity, capital formation, and industrial competitiveness. Thus, from its inception as an advisory group that was concerned with macroeconomic issues, the CEA has become increasingly involved in microeconomic issues and has functioned as a source of economic advice, broadly conceived. Reflecting the position of the economics profession generally, there has been much greater agreement among CEA members regarding microeconomic issues than macroeconomic ones.

Together with the Treasury Department and the Office of Management and Budget (OMB), the CEA has responsibility for advising the president on fiscal policy. The heads of these agencies form a group known as the Troika, which analyzes economic conditions and makes recommendations. Historically, the secretary of the Treasury heads the group. The prestige and influence of the CEA peaked during the 1960s. During the 1980s and 1990s, Treasury, OMB, and other officials have increased their influence relative to the CEA.

The effectiveness of the CEA has been a function of the president's desire to consult it. President Harry S. Truman did not see the CEA as a useful source of information and policy advice. His successor, Dwight D. Eisenhower, however, relied heavily on the CEA for the formulation of domestic economic policy. Indeed, Eisenhower reorganized the CEA, elevating the chairman to its operating chief. Under chairmen Arthur F. Burns (1953–1956) and Raymond J. Saulnier (1956–1961), the CEA emerged as a respected and integral contributor to policymaking within the executive branch. Under Walter Heller (1961–1964), the CEA established its credibility in a number of economic fields by providing analyses and arguments that the president and other officials found to be convincing. By the 1980s, the CEA was performing five functions for the president, in addition its initial brief of preparing the annual economic report of the president. These were: forecasting economic conditions; educating the president on the capacity of economic thinking to inform policymaking; vetting departmental and agency proposals within the executive branch for their consistency with presidential policies; advocating the president's policies before Congress, interest groups, and the public; and defending presidential policies on technical grounds.

Because Presidents John F. Kennedy and Lyndon B. Johnson relied heavily on the CEA to guide their decisions, economists had unprecedented influence over economic policymaking during the 1960s. Both presidents routinely referred cabinet secretaries and the heads of

other agencies to the CEA to vet their policy proposals, even when the expertise of the latter did not extend to the field of policy under discussion. Thus, for instance, Johnson asked Wilbur Cohen, his secretary of health, education, and welfare, if he had reviewed the Medicare bill with the CEA. In contrast to the economic advisors of the Eisenhower administration, the CEA during the 1960s strongly recommended economic growth over stability, even if it meant sacrificing the balanced budgets cherished by President Eisenhower and his advisors. The CEA, adhering to "domesticated" KEYNESIANISM—as Herbert Stein, CEA chairman from 1972 to 1974, phrased it— persuaded President Kennedy of the need for an income tax cut to enable real economic output to reach its potential, which supposedly held the key to reducing unemployment. When inflation became a concern after 1965, as a high employment economy became an overheated one, the CEA advised President Johnson on the need for an income tax surcharge to pay for federal government spending associated with the Great Society and the Vietnam War. The CEA also took on the role of policy advocate, engaging business and labor leaders directly in the interest of controlling wages and prices on a voluntary basis. Through adopting an adversarial role, however, the CEA suffered some diminishment of its reputation. Moreover, this direct engagement with business distracted the CEA's attention away from the macroeconomic sources of rising prices.

The relative influence of the CEA on policy development fell during the Richard M. Nixon administration. The Troika, for instance, operated through a liaison in the White House, rather than directly through the president. Further, reorganization of the White House in July 1970 shifted the primacy of domestic economic policy away from the CEA, toward the Treasury Department. The role of the CEA chairman as the chief spokesperson for the administration likewise diminished, as the Treasury secretary played the leading role in communicating policy to Congress and the nation. The CEA continued to participate in the most important committees that had responsibility for making policy, and CEA members continued to analyze key economic issues. However, presidents after Nixon on did not rely on the CEA for policy development to the extent that Kennedy and Johnson did. Under President Ronald Reagan, the reputation of the CEA declined, as Reagan's first two CEA chairmen resigned. Both Murray Weidenbaum (1981–1982) and Martin Feldstein (1982–1984) differed with other top officials on the administration's supply-side approach to economic policy. During the George H. W. Bush administration, the influence of the CEA declined further, in relation to other advisors, who were closer to the president personally.

The academic economists that comprised most of the appointees to the CEA recognized that their usefulness depended on their ability to provide politically relevant and realistic advice. While the CEA might attempt to educate the president on the need to take a course of action, its advice has ultimately had to comport with the course that the president and his closest advisors have charted. CEA recommendations therefore have reflected political realities as much as, or more than, economic theories. During the 1970s, for instance, inflation emerged as a major domestic policy concern. As part of its response, the Nixon administration adopted mandatory wage and price controls, which proved to be no more than a politically acceptable panacea. At the same time, Alan Greenspan, who served as CEA chairman from 1974 to 1977, was an ardent advocate of both limited government and market-based policy solutions. He was critical of intervention in the form of progressive income taxes, corporate subsidies, antitrust and consumer protection laws, and so forth. He therefore rejected wage and price controls as a solution to inflation and believed that restrictive monetary policy and balanced budgets held the key to containing inflation. With the Federal Reserve in control of the former, Greenspan initially focused on budget cutting to achieve the latter. With the economy in recession during the second half of 1974, however, Greenspan conceded the need for a tax cut in the face of pressure from Congress, even though it assured that a large budget deficit would occur and promised to aggravate inflation. Greenspan made this concession even though he opposed addressing long-term economic problems with short-term fixes that introduced uncertainty into policymaking, which tended to diminish capital formation and other economic activities on the part the private sector.

The CEA, of course, is not infallible. Its faulty prediction of a recession in 1962, for instance, raised questions among members of Congress regarding the quality of the advice that President Kennedy was receiving from his experts. In another instance, the CEA backed the Treasury Department in refusing to sanction expansionary fiscal policy during 1959 when the economy showed signs of slipping back into recession. In not advocating a full employment policy, the CEA's decision contributed to the economy falling back into recession during 1960. At this time, the CEA was concerned above all with controlling inflation, as was the rest of the Eisenhower administration. On the whole, however, the CEA's record of advising the president has ensured that its members have played an important, if not decisive, role in the making of economic policy.

At the same time, the participation of professional economists in the policymaking process has politicized the social science of economics. The public and members of Congress tend to view the positions that CEA economists adopt as partisan ones. Since the media have privileged CEA economic points of view above others, the CEA has served to link economic argument to the agendas of political parties. Indeed, the record of CEA appointments around the turn of the twenty-first century has suggested that presidents explicitly value policy orientation over professional reputation as the decisive selection criteria. The impossibility of separating politics and economics in practice means, of course, that the goal of the creators of the Employment Act of 1946—that economists inform policymaking in a nonpartisan manner—cannot be realized ideally.

BIBLIOGRAPHY

Flash, Edward S., Jr. *Economic Advice and Presidential Leadership: The Council of Economic Advisers.* New York: Columbia University Press, 1965.

Frendreis, John P., and Raymond Tatalovich. *The Modern Presidency and Economic Policy.* Itasca, Ill.: F. E. Peacock, 1994.

Hargrove, Erwin C., and Samuel A. Morley, eds. *The President and the Council of Economic Advisers: Interviews with CEA Chairmen.* Boulder, Colo.: Westview, 1984.

Norton, Hugh S. *The Employment Act and the Council of Economic Advisers, 1946–1976.* Columbia: University of South Carolina Press, 1977.

Stein, Herbert. *The Fiscal Revolution in America.* Chicago: University of Chicago Press, 1969.

———. *Presidential Economics: The Making of Economic Policy from Roosevelt to Clinton.* 3d. rev. ed. Washington, D.C.: American Enterprise Institute for Public Policy Research, 1994.

———. "The Fiscal Revolution in America, Part II: 1964–1994." In *Funding the American State, 1941–1995: The Rise and Fall of the Era of Easy Finance.* Edited by W. Elliot Brownlee. Washington, D.C.: Woodrow Wilson Center Press and New York: Cambridge University Press, 1996. See pp. 184–286.

Michael R. Adamson

See also **Economics; Employment Act of 1946; Office of Management and Budget; Treasury, Department of the.**

COUNCIL OF NATIONAL DEFENSE was six cabinet members and an unpaid civilian advisory committee, created by Congress on 29 August 1916, to investigate the concentration and utilization of national resources in wartime. On paper it thus became America's first decisive step toward becoming a nation-in-arms. Actually, organization was not completed until March 1917, and lack of appropriations after 1920 limited its experience to the war period itself. As the parent body of the WAR INDUSTRIES BOARD it enjoyed early influence, but it gradually lost ground to more authoritative agencies. Its major importance was as an instrument for the mobilization of civilian forces.

BIBLIOGRAPHY

Leuchtenburg, William E. *The Perils of Prosperity, 1914–32.* Chicago: University of Chicago Press, 1958.

Wayne Grover/c. w.

See also **Preparedness; World War I; World War I, Economic Mobilization for.**

COUNCIL OF REVISION, NEW YORK. This council, part of the checks and balances in the first New York State constitution of 1777, was established to veto unconstitutional legislation. It was composed of the chancellor, the judges of the state supreme court or any two of them, and the governor. It was apparently the inspiration for the proposal for a similar body in the U.S. Constitution made by James Madison at the Philadelphia Constitutional Convention, although that proposal was rejected. The New York Council of Revision was abolished by the constitution of 1821 because the veto power of the governor was thought sufficient.

BIBLIOGRAPHY
Street, Alfred B. *The Council of Revision of the State of New York.* Albany, N.Y.: W. Gould, 1859.

Jon Roland

See also **New York; State Constitutions.**

COUNTERCULTURE. A stratum of American and western European culture that began in the mid-1960s. Its adherents, mostly white, young, and middle class, adopted a lifestyle that embraced personal freedom while rejecting the ethics of capitalism, conformity, and repressive sexual mores. The mainstream media sometimes referred to members of the counterculture as "hippies," "freaks," or "flower children."

The counterculture was no more a "culture" than the diverse antiwar movement was a "movement." Rather, the term was applied by social critics attempting to characterize the widespread rebellion of many western youths against the values and behaviors espoused by their parents. However, many young people adopted certain counterculture trappings, such as those involving music, fashion, slang, or recreational drugs, without necessarily abandoning their middle-class mores. Various factors nurtured the counterculture, including the postwar growth of the American middle class (whose "materialism" the counterculture disdained), wide availability of "the pill" for reliable contraception (thus reducing one risk of sexual experimentation), the increasing popularity of hallucinogenic drugs like LSD (which encouraged introspection and alienation from "straight" culture), and the Vietnam War (which convinced many young people that America had lost its soul).

The counterculture's deepest roots lay in the "Beat Generation" of the 1950s, a relatively small group of nonconformist intellectuals who chafed under the rigid orthodoxy of the era. Beat writers like Jack Kerouac, William S. Burroughs, and Allen Ginsberg espoused unconventional behavior and individual rebellion, often fueled by espresso, marijuana, and mescaline.

Just as New York City's Greenwich Village became identified with the "beatniks," the Haight-Ashbury district of San Francisco developed into a mecca for the

Counterculture. Hippies enjoy music in the Haight-Ashbury district of San Francisco in April 1967, just before the "Summer of Love." © CORBIS

counterculture. A poor area of the city, its cheap rentals attracted many who valued community over luxury. In time the "Haight's" reputation drew still more youths curious about the emerging lifestyle. Some left the urban areas behind to form rural communes loosely modeled on utopian communities of the past, but few of these proved to be self-sustaining.

BIBLIOGRAPHY
Gitlin, Todd. *The Sixties: Years of Hope, Days of Rage.* New York: Bantam Books, 1993.

Miller, Timothy. *The Hippies and American Values.* Knoxville: University of Tennessee Press, 1991.

J. Justin Gustainis

See also **Beat Generation; Hippies.**

COUNTERFEITING. To counterfeit means to imitate with intent to defraud. Most counterfeit paper money can be classified in one of three categories: (1) notes that imitate legitimate notes; (2) alterations of legitimate notes, including notes raised from a lower to a higher denomination; and (3) spurious notes—that is, notes representing obligations of fictional institutions. Counterfeit notes of the period prior to the CIVIL WAR had to be distinguished not only from ordinary legal tender, but also from legitimate paper money circulating at a discount because it represented obligations of broken or failed banks. (Such notes were legal and worth whatever fraction of their face value the liquidated assets of the bank would permit.)

The circulation of both counterfeit notes and valid, but discounted, notes of commercial banks gave rise to the publication of pamphlets known as *Bank Note Reporters* and *Counterfeit Detectors*, published at any interval from semiweekly to annually by money brokers in centers of financial activity. These pamphlets gave up-to-date information on the validity and value of notes currently in use, and were used by anyone who dealt in large amounts of nonlocal currency. After the effective end of state bank-note issues in 1867, the *Bank Note Reporters* became unnecessary because all bank-note and government-issued currency thenceforth circulated at par.

Counterfeiting is, of course, a crime, and for a long time many countries punished it with death. If, after a counterfeit note is passed the first time, it remains undetected, it becomes a part of the monetary system. At a time of full employment of resources it acts as a tax on the general public in favor of the counterfeiter. It raises prices by the percentage that the value of the counterfeit note bears to the total stock of money in the economy. If numbers of resources are unemployed, counterfeit notes have the effect of stimulating spending and, ultimately, reducing unemployment. Thus, at a time of less than full employment, the counterfeiter might be considered a public benefactor. Of course, counterfeit notes have never entered the monetary system in sufficient volume to make these general effects operable.

At least one case is recorded in which a responsible government legalized existing counterfeit issues—an action taken by the CONFEDERATE STATES OF AMERICA during the Civil War. In an effort to spare the possibly innocent individual detected with a counterfeit note, the Confederate government legalized the acceptance of bogus notes late in the war. Indeed, the government had little choice. Because of the poor quality and multiplicity of issues of reputable Confederate notes, and also because of the masses of counterfeits in circulation—many originating in the North—hardly anyone could tell the difference between real and fake money. Frequently the counterfeit notes were of better quality.

Counterfeiting in the twenty-first century is a minor part of total crime. The techniques, skills, and machinery required for effective counterfeiting are very costly and pay off well enough when used in legitimate enterprise with much less risk.

BIBLIOGRAPHY

Benner, Judith. *Fraudulent Finance: Counterfeiting and the Confederate States, 1861–1865.* Hillsboro, Tex.: Hill Junior College Press, 1970.

Dillistin, William H. *Bank Note Reporters and Counterfeit Detectors, 1826–1866.* New York: American Numismatic Society, 1949.

Johnson, David R. *Illegal Tender: Counterfeiting and the Secret Service in Nineteenth-Century America.* Washington, D.C.: Smithsonian Institution Press, 1995.

Richard H. Timberlake Jr. / c. w.

See also **Banking; Banking: Bank Failures; Currency and Coinage; Mints, Private; Money; National Bank Notes.**

COUNTRY STORE. Beginning in the colonial period, country (or general) stores served as a source of goods for people far removed from the urban markets of the Atlantic seaboard. They also, however, played a critical intermediary role in fostering and promoting exchange relationships among the mostly farm households located in the isolated interior of the young nation. Indeed, as agricultural settlement pushed westward in the early nineteenth century, enterprising frontier merchants represented a vanguard of the so-called American "market revolution."

Many owners of country stores started as itinerant peddlers, only establishing permanent locations once they had accumulated capital (two thousand to five thousand dollars' worth of inventory could suffice) and found an advantageous crossroads (many towns took their names after store owners). It was a precarious existence, however. Most rural merchants found it necessary either to barter their wares for produce or to sell on credit to their cash-starved farm clientele. Annual buying expeditions to the wholesale and auction houses of northeastern cities, especially New York, could take longer than six weeks and were fraught with difficulties. More successful store owners might stake their kinfolk in nearby branch operations or move from a wooden to a brick building in a budding town; the less successful simply went out of business, often pulling up stakes and seeking their fortunes elsewhere.

Country stores assumed particular significance in the economy of the post–Civil War South. In the regional system of sharecropping and widespread tenant farming that characterized postbellum cotton production, the number of stores grew tremendously. The rural "furnishing" merchant played a pivotal role as a provider of seasonal credit, annually provisioning families with supplies, often at exorbitant rates of interest. Underpinning this credit was the crop lien, an agreement by which the merchant established a legal claim to future crop proceeds. For more than half a century, the lien system placed the merchant at the center of class conflict in the region—attacked on the one hand by planter-landlords who contested the priority of their claims on the crop and on the other hand, and, more importantly, by small farmers

Country Store. Walker Evans's 1936 photograph shows people holding watermelons at a roadside stand near Birmingham, Ala.
GETTY IMAGES

whose independence was threatened by debt at a time of declining world prices for cotton. Although the isolated market of the southern country store has led some to condemn its operations as a "territorial monopoly," in fact rural merchants were themselves hard-pressed, not only by local competition but also by creditors, absconding debtors, and the same fickle cotton market they shared with their critics.

The expansion of the railroad network in the late nineteenth century, especially in the Midwest, meant that buying trips became more frequent and convenient, and if they purchased their stock from the growing number of traveling salesmen and "drummers" (wholesalers' agents), store owners never had to leave home at all. By the early twentieth century, however, the emergent national system of retail distribution (mail-order houses; chain, department, and specialty stores; brand-name products) and its associated urban and transportation infrastructure began to render general stores economically

superfluous, although a few persist even now, mostly as "convenience stores." To this day, few institutions can evoke folk nostalgia among old-timers as much as the country store, a sentiment that helps confirm its importance alongside school, church, and courthouse as a focal point of community life in rural and small-town America.

BIBLIOGRAPHY

Cronon, William. *Nature's Metropolis: Chicago and the Great West.* New York: Norton, 1991. Scattered throughout this ambitious account of midwestern development are keen descriptions and insights regarding the key role of country retailers in facilitating nineteenth-century "commodity flows."

Marler, Scott. "Merchants in the Transition to a New South: Central Louisiana, 1840–1880." *Louisiana History* 42, no. 2 (Spring 2001): 165–192.

Ransom, Roger L., and Richard Sutch. *One Kind of Freedom: The Economic Consequences of Emancipation.* 2d rev. ed. Cam-

THE COUNTRY STORE AS SOCIAL INSTITUTION

What one eminent historian wrote of the southern country store holds no less true for most rural and small-town retailers elsewhere in the United States:

> The country store in a way was far more symbolic of the southern way of rural life than were other institutions. Even the church and the school were administered as much from the store as from their own buildings. The storekeeper was all things to his community. He served as school trustee, deacon or steward, railway agent, fertilizer salesman, social adviser, character reference, politician, lodge master, and general community "obliger." His store was the hub of the local universe. It was market place, banking and credit source, recreational center, public forum, and news exchange. There were few aspects of farm life . . . which were uninfluenced by the country store.

SOURCE: From Thomas D. Clark, *Pills, Petticoats, and Plows: The Southern Country Store* (New York: Bobbs Merrill, 1944; repr., with a foreword by John D. W. Guice, Norman: University of Oklahoma Press, 1989, pp. x–xi).

bridge and New York: Cambridge University Press, 2001. Originators of the disputed "territorial monopoly" thesis, their work is based on painstaking archival research.

Scott P. Marler

See also **Peddlers; Retailing Industry.**

COUNTY AND STATE FAIRS.

Originally set up on major trade routes, county and state fairs began as a venue where people could display their crafts and skills, and sell or trade produce or other items. The fairs combined socialization and amusement, but offered a more serious side of learning and selling.

America's first fairs were promoted by King George II in 1745 in Trenton Township, New Jersey, for the buying and selling of livestock and other products. The fairs, held in April and October, continued for five years until they were banned by the legislature. (Begun again in 1858, fairs were only held on a sporadic basis and in various locations within Trenton Township. After the Inter-State Fair Association was formed in 1888, land was purchased in Trenton to establish a permanent home for the Inter-State Fair.)

In 1798, the descendents of the Umberfield family, the first settlers in the town of Burton, Ohio, held what they called a "jollification," later known as a fair. Twenty-five years later the "jollification" was taken up by Geauga

County, Ohio, farmers when they joined together in 1823 to form the Geauga County Agricultural and Manufacturing Society. The members organized a county fair to show the progress in agricultural products and farm-related labor saving tools and machines. Individuals brought produce from their harvests to show and share.

As activities and exhibits began to reflect wider interests and were no longer limited strictly to agricultural-related endeavors, more people attended fairs. The backbone of the fairs—competitions between gardeners, cooks, quilters, and seamstresses—has always remained a big draw to the fair events. Other competitions included livestock, crops, rodeos, cornhusking by hand, and pie eating contests. Prizes were given for the best exhibits and to event winners.

Horse races were early attractions. Then came Pawnee Bill's Wild West Show, which began in 1888, and others like it. In the late 1800s and early 1900s, as transportation styles changed, hot-air balloons were exhibited with parachutists jumping from them as an added attraction. The introduction of the automobile during the same period soon brought car racing to fairs. Carnivals—including merry-go-rounds powered by live horses—became a fair mainstay. County fairs are smaller than state fairs and generally have one or more permanent structures such as exhibit halls, grandstands, cattle barns, and stables. County fairs are usually held for two to four days and are run by volunteers. A state fair lasts at least a week and can go on for as long as a month. Although many volunteers are used for state fairs, the overall management is in the hands of either a state fair board or a private company.

BIBLIOGRAPHY

Marling, Karal Ann. *Blue Ribbon: A Social and Pictorial History of the Minnesota State Fair.* St. Paul: Minnesota Historical Society, 1990.

Perl, Lila. *America Goes to the Fair: All About State and County Fairs in the USA.* New York: Morrow, 1974.

Peggy Sanders

See also **Circus and Carnival.**

COUNTY GOVERNMENT.

County governments in the United States function as local administrative arms within the states. In the early 2000s the National Association of Counties recognized 3,066 U.S. counties. All states except Connecticut and Rhode Island have functioning county governments. Alaska and Louisiana call their equivalent political units boroughs and parishes respectively. Originally counties were placed so that a county seat would be no more than a day's journey for everyone within the county borders. However, contemporary U.S. counties share no equivalence in either geographic size or population. Arlington County, Virginia, is 67 square kilometers while the North Slope Borough of

Kentucky State Fair, Louisville. County and state fairs—normally held once a year, often in late summer—were originally held as gatherings where merchants could sell their goods and where local residents could enter their crops or livestock in agricultural competitions. Since the early eighteenth century, such fairs have evolved to include carnival rides and games, horse races, concerts, and much more, in addition to the original sales and competitions. LIBRARY OF CONGRESS

Alaska is 227,559 square kilometers. Loving County, Texas, has 140 residents while Los Angeles County, California, has 9.2 million residents. County governments perform essential administrative functions such as registering voters, supervising elections, keeping records, providing police protection, and administrating health and welfare services.

Origins and Early History
American county governments are historically rooted in the English shire. Shires were governmental units created in the ninth century by the kingdom of England to serve as local administrative arms of the crown. The shires were renamed "counties" after the Norman Conquest in 1066, but retained their function. Government in the English county operated under a plural executive. The shire-reeve, or "sheriff" shared power with the justices of the peace.

The American colonies incorporated the county as a form of local government. The first colonial counties were established in Virginia in 1634. Eight counties served as administrative districts for the commonwealth. The colonial governor appointed multiple officials to a county court that governed the counties. The sheriff and several justices of the peace shared executive power. The other colonies established county governments shortly after Virginia. The counties in the southern colonies modeled themselves on Virginia, while northern colonies developed differently. These colonies did adopt a plural form of county governance, but the county had reduced

responsibilities due to the predominance of already existing towns and cities. New York and New Jersey even went so far as to establish city and town officials as representatives on the county boards of supervisors. Northern counties were the first to elect rather than appoint county officials.

After American independence, counties simply became administrative arms of the states rather than the crown. Executive power remained diffused and the North-South distinctions in the scope of county responsibility also remained. The "middle" states and the new northwestern states created counties that were hybrids of the northern and southern models. Counties were the first form of local government in these states, yet these states lacked a landed aristocracy. The most influential case of this type is Pennsylvania, which in 1682 established three county commissions with commissioners elected "at large" by the citizens of each county. Like the southern colonies, Pennsylvania established counties as the predominant form of local government. Like the northern colonies, the local officials were elected by the citizenry rather than selected by and from the landed elite. This Pennsylvania model of county government spread to western states such as Ohio, Michigan, Wisconsin, and Illinois. By the 1830s most states had established elected county boards.

Functions
The U.S. Constitution makes no mention of local government. Unlike the states, which enjoy a federal governing relationship enshrined in the constitution, counties

437

are part of a unitary governing relationship within the various states. The U.S. Constitution established a federal system whereby governmental power was divided between the national government and the states. The unitary system that controls local government vests all power in the state governments. Counties exist merely as agents of the states and enjoy only those powers expressly given to them by the state government. The relationship is best summarized in the 1845 U.S. Supreme Court case *State of Maryland v. Baltimore and Ohio Railroad.* The court held that "counties are nothing more than certain portions of the territory into which the state is divided for the more convenient exercise of powers of government."

For most of U.S. history the core function of county government was to fulfill the administrative mandates of their respective states. This included "housekeeping" functions such as assessing and collecting property taxes, registering voters and administering elections, providing law enforcement, prosecuting criminals, administering a jail, recording deeds and other legal records, maintaining roads, keeping vital statistics, and controlling communicable diseases.

Urbanization (and suburbanization) brought to highly populated counties additional government functions such as the administration of mass transportation, airports, water supply and sewage disposal, hospitals, building and housing codes, public housing, stadiums, recreation and cultural programs, libraries, and consumer protection. Counties have also played a major administrative role in welfare programs such as Temporary Assistance for Needy Families (TANF) and Medicaid, and in state mandated environmental programs. The number of functional roles that a county government assumes is highly dependent on the population of the county. While nearly all counties assume the traditional "housekeeping" roles identified earlier, only the counties with populations over one million tend to assume all of the roles identified above.

The growing functional role of county governments has not been met with increased autonomy or legislative power. The functions that county governments assume are highly determined by what the states mandate. County governments rarely legislate general ordinances in the way that city councils do. Instead, the county government's legislative power is usually limited to zoning issues and building regulations.

Governmental Structure and Reform

Although county governments have a variety of organizational structures, most have a similar core of officials. The county sheriff heads police protection, serves warrants from the county courts, and runs the county jail. The coroner runs the county morgue and oversees medical investigations. The county attorney prosecutes people suspected of crimes and provides legal counsel to the county. The clerk of the court registers and keeps legal records. The county treasurer collects and disburses county funds. The election commissioner oversees voter regis-

tration and elections. Until the early twentieth century most officials derived compensation primarily from the fees and fines that the county government collected. This "fee system" of compensation was established in and protected by many state constitutions. The fee system yielded to a salary system in the Progressive Era of the 1900s under charges that fee-based compensation led to rampant corruption.

The commission has historically been the predominant governing structure at the county level. The average county commission has three to five members, although the numbers range from just one to over one hundred. There is no chief executive officer on the commission. The commission shares administrative responsibility among the many members and other elected officials such as the sheriff and treasurer. The commission form of government still served as the organizational basis for 61 percent of U.S. counties in the early 2000s.

A Progressive Era reform movement sought to alter the commission structure by adding a professional executive. Iredell County, North Carolina, was the first county government to adopt a council-administrator organizational form. In the early 2000s, 26 percent of U.S. counties operated under this organizational form, in which an elected county council creates policy and an appointed professional administrator carries out this policy.

A much smaller percentage of U.S. counties (thirteen percent) elect an executive. This system has separate elected legislative and executive branches of government. The executive is the formal head and spokesperson of the county, prepares the budget, hires and fires department heads, administers the policies enacted by the council and often has veto power over legislation.

Finally, less than one percent of U.S. counties have merged with cities. Denver, Philadelphia, and San Francisco are simultaneously cities and counties. The first such consolidation was New Orleans and Orleans Parish, Louisiana, in 1805. Philadelphia, San Francisco, and New York were also consolidated in the nineteenth century. Many more mergers have been proposed than have been approved by the voters. In the twentieth century local voters rejected roughly eighty percent of merger proposals.

The reform with the most potential for serious change in county government is not structural, but constitutional. "Home rule" reforms to state constitutions allow counties to create and revise their own charters. Under this system counties could potentially exercise a high degree of discretionary authority. Home rule can be thought of as a shift from a unitary to a limited federal system within a state. For counties, this shift means moving from a government that simply enforces state laws, to a government that passes laws of its own. Progressive Era reformers pushed for home rule provisions and found some success. The first home rule charter was adopted by Los Angeles County, California, in 1913. By the early 2000s more than half of the U.S. states had some provision for county home rule. These provisions range from simply structural home rule (the ability of a county to determine its system of government) to functional home rule, which allows counties to undertake any function unless it is prohibited by state law. The local public has been reluctant to adopt home rule. Less than three percent of U.S. counties have actually created and approved their own charters.

BIBLIOGRAPHY

Berman, David R., ed. *County Governments in an Era of Change*. Westport, Conn.: Greenwood, 1993.

Coppa, Frank J. *County Government: A Guide to Efficient and Accountable Government*. Westport, Conn.: Praeger, 2000.

Jeffrey, Blake B., Tanis B. Salant, and Alan L. Boroshok. *County Government Structure*. Washington, D.C.: National Association of Counties, 1989.

National Association of Counties. Home page at http://www.naco.org.

Stephens, G. Ross, and Nelson Wikstrom. *Metropolitan Government and Governance: Theoretical Perspectives, Empirical Analysis, and the Future*. New York: Oxford University Press, 2000.

Daniel John Sherman

See also **Commission Government; Home Rule; Local Government; Metropolitan Government.**

COURIER SERVICES are companies that transport and deliver documents, packages, and larger shipments of products, although traditionally they specialized in the rapid delivery of such items as legal documents that required signatures. They provide services to companies and individuals who need rapid service, accountability, and tracking that regular mail does not accommodate. Major courier services that performed these functions in the early 2000s included commercial delivery services, the U.S. Postal Service, and bicycle messenger services.

Courier services began during the late nineteenth and early twentieth centuries, with small companies in a handful of cities across the United States. When few homes had telephones, personal messages had to be carried by hand. Some early companies provided delivery of luggage and other packages. With the rise of large retail and department stores in the early twentieth century, package delivery services became even more popular. The scale of such services grew over the next several decades. Although fuel and rubber shortages during WORLD WAR II caused a decline in the courier industry, the use of air freight by courier services after the war allowed for wider markets.

Courier services became multifaceted and competitive after 1970 because of the increasingly far-flung nature of business operations in the international economy, the popularity of mail-order retailing, and rising postal rates. Courier services overlapped other forms of transport,

such as trucking, and the differences became less distinct. Commercial delivery services, once a supplement to the U.S. Postal Service, competed with the government-operated mail system. The Postal Service responded with greater emphasis on its overnight Express Mail delivery and two-day Priority Mail service.

The growth and diversification of the delivery industry raised regulatory issues. Companies that delivered by plane or truck were often governed by separate laws regarding rates and other aspects of their operations. In the late 1980s the document delivery business faced new competition with the development of fax machines and ELECTRONIC MAIL. The need for physical delivery of some items remained, however, and the delivery industry was bolstered by the continuing growth of the global marketplace. Some delivery companies began to branch out and offer new services to their clients. These included "logistics," or support, services to help clients increase efficiency by electronically tracking materials used in manufacturing and assisting with processing sales orders and shipments.

Among the oldest and largest U.S. private delivery companies is United Parcel Service (UPS), founded in Seattle, Washington, as the American Messenger Company in 1907. Originally a local parcel delivery service for department stores, UPS expanded and established a large network to ship and deliver packages. In the early 2000s, UPS was the largest carrier for e-commerce, shipping online purchases to customers worldwide. In 1999, UPS shareholders voted to make 10 percent of the company stock available to the public. Another major company, Federal Express, founded by entrepreneur Frederick W. Smith in the early 1970s, pioneered large-scale overnight delivery by air, using its own fleet of planes and a central terminal (originally in Memphis, Tenn.) to sort and reroute items.

Both the large commercial courier services and the U.S. Postal Service have increased the speed of national and international package delivery due to the advent of wide-body airplanes that can carry an increased amount of freight. Yet, bicycle messenger services provide an invaluable and timeless service for small-scale, local delivery. Bike messengers were used as early as the late nineteenth century for rapid delivery of Western Union telegrams and government documents. During the 1980s bicycle messenger services became a particularly popular way to deliver items quickly within cities. Their numbers declined slightly with the advent of fax machines and e-mail, but in the early twenty-first century their services remained important links between businesses in large cities like New York and Washington, D.C., as well as in smaller cities throughout the world.

BIBLIOGRAPHY

Haldi, John, and Joseph F. Johnston, Jr. *Postal Monopoly: An Assessment of the Private Express Statutes*. Washington, D.C.:

American Enterprise Institute for Public Policy Research, 1974.

Moroney, Rita L. *History of the U.S. Postal Service, 1775–1982.* Washington, D.C.: The Service, 1983.

Side, W. Hampton. "Bicycle Messengers Bite the Dust." *New Republic* (21 December 1992): 16–19.

John Townes/H. S.

See also **Mail-Order Houses; Postal Service, U.S.; Office Technology; Western Union Telegraph Company.**

COURT PACKING. *See* **Supreme Court Packing Bills.**

COURTS-MARTIAL are the oldest system of justice in the United States, dating to the Continental Congress's decision in 1789 to continue the British system. One of America's most famous courts-martial, that of Benedict Arnold for using troops for his own personal gain, even predates that decision by ten years. The modern legal basis of courts-martial is the Uniform Code of Military Justice (UCMJ), adopted in 1950, and the Manual for Courts-Martial issued in the following year. Although the UCMJ is normally considered to be stricter than civilian laws, in a court-martial the defendant has the right to choose trial by a judge or by a jury of peers at equivalent or higher rank. Enlisted defendants also have the right to a jury that is constituted of at least one-third enlisted personnel.

There are three levels of court-martial: the summary court-martial, which can impose penalties of up to one month in prison; the special court-martial, which can impose penalties of up to six months; and the general court-martial, reserved for the most serious offenses, which can impose any penalty, including death. Since World War II, courts-martial have come to look more like civil trials. Professionally trained military lawyers, who must be qualified to try cases before a state's highest court, must be present at all general courts-martial. Review procedures have also been modified to come more into line with civilian practices. Many of these reforms were enacted to protect the rights of enlisted personnel. Since 1950, commanders can no longer impose confinements of more than one week without calling a court-martial.

Several courts-martial have become American causes célèbres. The court-martial of William (Billy) Mitchell in 1925 was a national media event. Mitchell, a brigadier general in the Army Air Corps, was tried for his outspoken criticism of the senior military leadership's alleged negligence in developing airpower. Although he was found guilty by his peers and resigned from the army, his trial highlighted the problems of entrenched bureaucracy and the army's failure to fully understand the new technology of aviation.

The court-martial of Lieutenant William Calley in 1970–1971 also became a national media event. Calley was charged with three counts of premeditated murder in the My Lai massacre of 1968, in which as many as four hundred Vietnamese civilians were killed. After a court-martial that lasted four months, Calley was found guilty and sentenced to life at hard labor. His commanding officer, Captain Ernest Medina, was acquitted of involuntary manslaughter (failure to exercise proper control over his men engaged in unlawful homicide) due to a mistake by the military judge. The Calley trial was the most carefully followed court-martial in American history.

These famous cases were, of course, exceptions. The majority of courts-martial deal with the day-to-day jurisprudence of military communities. Over time, they have lost many of the features that distinguished them from civilian trials and today they are broadly similar to civilian counterparts.

BIBLIOGRAPHY

Byrne, Edward. *Military Law: A Handbook for the Navy and Marine Corps.* Annapolis, Md.: Naval Institute Press, 1981.

DiMona, Joseph. *Great Court-Martial Cases.* New York: Grossett and Dunlap, 1972.

Michael S. Neiberg

See also **Military Law; Uniform Code of Military Justice.**

COUTUME DE PARIS, French customary feudal law, was administered in the courts of French colonial Canada and LOUISIANA, frequently supplemented by royal edicts and provincial ordinances. Under British rule (after 1763) the military commandants administered the *coutumes* and retained French civil law until 1792, although the Quebec Act (1774) introduced the English criminal code. The system continued in a modified form after the American occupation of Illinois country, and the laws of the NORTHWEST TERRITORY guaranteed to the French inhabitants existing *coutumes* in family relations and inheritance practices. In Louisiana, the *coutumes* remained in force until 1769, when Alexander O'Reilly, an Irish soldier in the Spanish army, imposed Spanish law.

BIBLIOGRAPHY

Conrad, Glenn R., ed. *The French Experience in Louisiana.* Lafayette: University of Southwestern Louisiana Press, 1995.

Eccles, W. J. *The French in North America, 1500–1783.* Markham, Ont.: Fitzhenry and Whiteside, 1998.

Raymond C. Werner/s. B.

See also **Colonial Policy, British; French and Indian War.**

COVENANT, CHURCH, the formal and public act of mutual engagement that, according to the theory of the New England clergy, must be entered into by the

Emigrants Attacked by the Comanches. Pioneers move their covered wagons into a defensive circle in this engraving by Captain Seth Eastman, published in 1857 in Henry Rowe Schoolcraft's multivolume study of Indian tribes. © CORBIS

founders of a particular church before the church could be considered legitimate. All New England churches were established upon such an agreement, and later recruits subscribed to the covenant; at times of revival, the covenant was often unanimously "renewed." The clergy of New England wrote more voluminously in defense of it than on any other single subject. Their argument contained the seeds of principles later transplanted to the realm of political theory, particularly the assertion that no society can have power over a man until he has voluntarily and explicitly contracted to accept its regulations.

BIBLIOGRAPHY

Foster, Stephen. *The Long Argument: English Puritanism and the Shaping of New England Culture, 1570–1700.* Chapel Hill: University of North Carolina Press, 1991.

Perry Miller / A. R.

See also **Meetinghouse.**

COVERED WAGON, the means of transcontinental transportation used for two centuries of American history. The covered wagon was fundamentally a wagon box with a framework of hoop-shaped slats over which a canvas tent was stretched to make a "covered" wagon. Each wagon was drawn by several teams of horses, mules, or oxen. Many were boat shaped with oarlocks so they might be floated over streams, the animals swimming across.

Although derived from the Conestoga wagons built in Lancaster, Pa., in the early eighteenth century, the covered wagon used by emigrants on the Oregon and California trails differed in size, design, and purpose. Conestoga wagons were primarily designed to haul heavy goods for trade along the eastern coast, while smaller covered wagons were the vehicle of choice for emigrant groups headed to western destinations.

Emigrants using covered wagons assembled at such points west of the Missouri River as Independence, Mo., and Council Grove, Kans., and organized into caravans—called WAGON TRAINS—for companionship and protection. Emigrants usually took between four and six months to make the two-thousand-mile trek that lay between the Missouri and the Pacific Ocean. Although the threat of Indian attack was small, emigrants would often draw their wagons into a circle to serve as a corral for their animals and post sentinels to guard against livestock raids. Covered wagons remain in museums, including the CONESTOGA WAGON original at Pittsburgh, Pa., and Ezra Meeker's PRAIRIE SCHOONER at Tacoma, Wash.

BIBLIOGRAPHY

Dunbar, Seymour. *History of Travel in America.* Indianapolis, Ind.: Bobbs-Merrill, 1915.

Winther, Oscar Osborn. *The Transportation Frontier: Trans-Mississippi West, 1865–1890.* New York: Holt, Rinehart and Winston, 1964.

Keith Clark / F. B.

See also **Oregon Trail; Transportation and Travel.**

COW TOWNS. A by-product of the dramatic growth of the cattle business in the latter part of the nineteenth century, cow towns flourished from 1867 until the 1890s when railroads ended the necessity for long cattle drives. The first of what became the stereotypical cow town was Abilene, Kansas. A small rural community that consisted of a dozen log huts, most with dirt roofs, Abilene provided what ranchers needed: acres of undeveloped fields of tall grass crossed by streams of water and a rail line to Chicago's meatpacking plants. By the 1870s, cattle drives resulted in dozens of other cow towns joining Abilene in replacing log huts with saloons, gambling rooms, and whorehouses to entice the cowboys. Although the number of gunshots fired in cow towns was far fewer then Hollywood portrayed, the violence did create conflict between the merchants and the cowboys and revealed a class conflict that characterized much of the developing West. Many of the merchants and landowners were from the North and Republican Party members, while the cowboys tended to be ex-Confederates who supported the Democratic Party. Before this class conflict could be played out, however, the era of the cow town was over. The railroad provided a more profitable means to transport beef. The cow town would continue but only in dime novels and on movie screens.

BIBLIOGRAPHY

Brown, Richard Maxwell. "Violence." In *The Oxford History of the American West.* Edited by Clyde A. Milner II, Carol A. O'Connor, and Martha A. Sandweiss. New York: Oxford University Press, 1994.

White, Richard. *"It's Your Misfortune and None of My Own": A History of the American West.* Norman: University of Oklahoma Press, 1991.

David O'Donald Cullen

See also **Abilene Trail.**

COWBOY SONGS.

> What keeps the herd from running,
> And stampede far and wide?
> The cowboy's long, low whistle
> And singing by their side.

Between 1870 and 1890, probably 10 million semiwild longhorn cattle traveled from Texas to Kansas and other northern markets. A group of cowboys rode with each herd of from 2,000 to 5,000 cattle to push them up the trail by day and to night-herd them after dark. Any unusual noise after the cattle were asleep might send them into a wild and destructive stampede. To drown those disturbing noises, the cowboys came to croon or yodel to the cattle. From these cattle calls grew some of the trail songs descriptive of cowboy life. So long as the cattle could hear a familiar voice crooning some cattle lullaby, they had no fear of the howl of a wolf, the scream of a panther, or any of the other sudden noises of the night. Thus what the men sometimes called "dogie" songs soothed the cattle to sleep quietly. The singing of these lonely young buckaroos as they rode around the sleeping longhorns was good economics, and the conditions were ideal for creating ballads: the night, the shimmering stars, the unending prairies, and brave young hearts adventuring. Cowboys sang because they were lonely and because singing helped them in their work. They sang around the campfire and in the cow town saloons to amuse themselves. They sang the old ballads along with the sentimental songs of TIN PAN ALLEY, and they made up new songs and adapted old ones that told about themselves and their work in their own lingo.

> Whoopee-ti-yi-yo, git along little dogies,
> It's your misfortune and none of my own;
> Whoopee-ti-yi-yo, git along little dogies,
> For you know Wyoming will be your new home.

A sudden rainstorm at night found all the cowboys riding round and round the milling circle of frightened cattle. Sometimes the lightning would play among the crowded animals so that myriad balls of fire would jump from tip of horn to tip of horn.

> I've been where the lightning, the lightning, tangled
>   in my eyes;
> The cattle I could scarcely hold.
> I think I heard my boss man say,
> "I want all brave-hearted men who ain't afraid to die
> To whoop up the cattle from morning till night
> 'Way up on the Kansas line."

Such stirring descriptive passages paint a revealing picture of the open-range days.

More than 200 cowboy songs have survived. Many of the tunes are borrowed. Enough of them seem genuine to claim a place for cowboy songs as a unique ballad product of the American southwest.

Jack Thorpe of New Mexico published locally a small pamphlet collection of cowboy songs without music in 1907. John A. Lomax's *Cowboy Songs and Other Frontier Ballads*, published in 1911, was the first printing of cowboy music. The radio and the motion picture both gave cowboy songs a tremendous vogue. "Home on the Range" has been a favorite since 1933, and its authorship provoked a suit for half a million dollars, which the court dismissed.

BIBLIOGRAPHY

Carlson, Paul H., ed. *The Cowboy Way: An Exploration of History and Culture.* Lubbock: Texas Tech University Press, 2000.

Clayton, Lawrence, Jim Hoy, and Jerald Underwood. *Vaqueros, Cowboys, and Buckaroos.* Austin: University of Texas Press, 2001.

Lee, Katie. *Ten Thousand Goddam Cattle: A History of the American Cowboy in Song, Story, and Verse.* Albuquerque: University of New Mexico, 2001.

Slatta, Richard W. *Cowboys of the Americas.* New Haven, Conn.: Yale University Press, 1990.

John A. Lomax/A. E.

See also **Cattle; Cattle Drives; Country and Western Music; Stampedes; Trail Drivers.**

COWBOYS.

COWBOYS. The heirs of ancient pastoral traditions, cowboys have worked as mounted herders on the cattle ranges of the American West for more than three centuries. They first rose to national prominence as an occupational group, however, with the rapid expansion of the western range cattle industry during the second half of the nineteenth century. Cowboy life attracted young, unmarried men, most of them in their late teens and early twenties, from a variety of social and ethnic backgrounds. Whatever their age and upbringing, cowboys, sometimes called "cowhands," "cowpunchers," or "buckaroos," pursued a demanding and sometimes dangerous occupation that required stamina, athleticism, and a specialized knowledge of horses and cattle.

At roundup time cowhands lived undomiciled for months at a time gathering, sorting, branding, and driving cattle. They typically worked in crews consisting of ten or twelve men under the command of a range boss and supported a cook and a chuck wagon, which carried the outfit's food and bedrolls. Each cowboy maintained a string of a half-dozen or more horses, which he changed periodically throughout the work day. Despite toiling long hours, often under difficult conditions, for wages that in the 1880s ranged from $25 to $30 per month, cowboys were self-reliant, fiercely independent, and rarely organized labor unions or engaged in strikes.

Skilled ropers and riders, American cowboys employed tools and techniques perfected by Spanish vaqueros (cowboys) in Mexico and the southwestern United States. They snared livestock with ropes made of rawhide or Manila hemp and rode heavy stock saddles equipped with a horn, which served as a snubbing posts while roping. Cowboys also adopted a distinctive, often colorful style of dress that reflected the requirements of the job, the local work environment, and personal taste. Most wore wide-brimmed hats to protect their head from sun and weather, tall-topped boots with underslung heels to help secure their feet in the saddle stirrups, and spurs, sometimes embellished with silver, to motivate their horses. In brush-infested regions they also donned leather leggings, called chaps, shorthand for the Spanish term *chaparejos*. Most ranchers, however, banned the wearing of firearms along with drinking and gambling.

During the era of the open range, cowboy work was seasonal, lasting from spring until fall. Ranchers laid off most of their cowboys during the winter months, retaining only a few to keep track of their herds and watch for cattle thieves, many of whom were out-of-work ranch hands. Driving cattle to railhead markets usually fell to separate crews of professional drovers hired by independent contractors.

By the mid-1880s, the open range style of cattle ranching had given way to more organized methods. The

Bill Pickett. The best known of the many cowboys, ranch hands, and rodeo performers who were African American (contrary to the common image in legends, novels, and movies) and the first black elected to the Rodeo Hall of Fame—though not until 1971, nearly forty years after his death. © UPI/CORBIS-BETTMANN

advent of barbed wire fences, which divided the range into ever smaller pastures, allowed the separation and upgrading of cattle herds, reduced the number of hands needed to tend them, and changed cowboy life and work forever. In the new order, cowboys were often called upon to cut hay, fix windmills, and build fences as well as ride the range. Married cowboys became more common as twentieth-century advances in transportation and communication and denser settlement patterns mitigated rural isolation. The eventual introduction of motor vehicles and horse trailers which, along with better roads, allowed cowboys to return to their homes and families after each day's work, gradually eliminated chuck wagon–based roundups.

Amid the inexorable economic and social changes that swept away the open range and the unfettered lifestyle of the horseback cowboy, there emerged a more enduring cowboy of legend. By the turn of the twentieth century, literature, art, and popular culture had rescued cowboys from historical anonymity and negative stereotypes and replaced them with a rugged, chivalrous hero. The writings of such authors as Theodore Roosevelt, Owen Wister, and Zane Grey; the art of Frederic Remington and Charles M. Russell; and the theatrics of Buffalo Bill's Wild West show, shaped and polished the image of the cowboy hero, whose independence, individualism, bravery, and common sense became the ideal of American masculinity. Later, motion picture and television portrayals by such actors as William S. Hart, Tom Mix, John Wayne, Gary Cooper, Gene Autry, and Roy Rogers, further defined and reinforced the model, as did countless novels and short stories. The sport of rodeo also played a part in establishing the cowboy's heroic image, while dude ranches offered western tourists the chance to vicariously participate by dressing in western style clothing, riding horses, herding cattle, and imagining the open range. Meanwhile, shrewd merchants and advertisers capitalized on the universal appeal of cowboy imagery to sell a vast array products from cologne to cigarettes.

BIBLIOGRAPHY

Dary, David. *Cowboy Culture: A Saga of Five Centuries.* New York: Knopf, 1981.

Price, B. Byron. *Cowboys of the American West.* San Diego, Calif.: Thunder Bay Books, 1996.

Rollins, Philip Ashton. *The Cowboy: An Unconventional History of Civilization on the Old-Time Cattle Range.* New York: Scribners, 1936.

Savage, William W., Jr. *The Cowboy Hero.* Norman: University of Oklahoma Press, 1979.

Savage, William W., Jr., ed. *Cowboy Life: Reconstructing an American Myth.* Norman: University of Oklahoma Press, 1975.

B. Byron Price

See also **Barbed Wire; Cattle Drives; Individualism; Remington and Indian and Western Images; Rodeos; Westerns; Wild West Show.**

COWBOYS AND SKINNERS, bands of guerrillas and irregular cavalry who operated chiefly in the "Neutral Ground" of Westchester County, New York, during the American Revolution. The "Cowboys" were the Westchester Light Horse Battalion, a Loyalist provincial corps of the British army, commanded by Col. James de Lancey. The battalion was an irregular unit of the British army from 1777 until the end of the war, taking part in some of the principal battles.

The "Skinners," named after Gen. Cortland Skinner's Brigade of New Jersey Volunteers, had no regular organization and did not consistently serve either the Americans or the British. They attacked and robbed local civilians from 1778 to 1783 and sold their plunder to both sides. They were also sometimes employed by the British or Americans as scouts and spies.

BIBLIOGRAPHY

Kim, Sung Bok. "The Limits of Politicization in the American Revolution: The Experience of Westchester County, New York," *Journal of American History* 80 (December 1993): 868–889.

E. Irvine Haines / T. D.

See also **Loyalists; Revolution, American: Military History.**

COWPENS, BATTLE OF (17 January 1781), one of the most brilliant American victories in the Revolution. In December 1780, Gen. Nathanael Greene, commander of the American army in the South, sent Gen. Daniel Morgan with 600 men to threaten the British post at Ninety-Six, South Carolina. Lord Charles Cornwallis sent Col. Banastre Tarleton against Morgan while he himself marched northward, thereby hoping to get between the two wings of the American army. Morgan, reinforced with several hundred more men, marched northward rapidly with Tarleton's army in pursuit. On 17 January, Morgan took position on the slope of a hill at Cowpens, South Carolina (formerly a cattle roundup center) and arranged his army in three lines. Morgan had 940 men, Tarleton 1,150. As the British approached, the first two lines of Morgan's army, as they had been instructed, fired and fell back. The British thought they had won an easy victory and advanced in disorder, only to be met by a deadly fire and bayonet attack from a third line of troops from Maryland, Virginia, and Georgia. At the same time the cavalry struck them on the right flank and the re-formed militia on the left. Finding themselves surrounded they surrendered. The British losses were 600 prisoners and over 200 killed and wounded; the American losses were 72 killed and wounded. On 4 March 1929, the one-acre battleground was designated a national battlefield site.

BIBLIOGRAPHY

Fleming, Thomas. "The Cowpens." *The Quarterly Journal of Military History* 1, no. 4 (1989): 56–67.

Higginbotham, Don. *Daniel Morgan, Revolutionary Rifleman.* Chapel Hill: University of North Carolina Press, 1961.

Treacy, M. F. *Prelude to Yorktown.* Chapel Hill: University of North Carolina Press, 1963.

Hugh T. Lefler / A. R.

See also **Eutaw Springs, Battle of; Revolution, American: Military History; Southern Campaigns.**

COXEY'S ARMY. During the depression following the panic of 1893, businessman and reformer Jacob Coxey of Massillon, Ohio, and his California associate Carl Browne designed a publicity march on Washington to support bills that would create new jobs. Coxey led a march of the unemployed, followed by reporters, from Ohio to the capitol, demanding large issues of legal-tender currency and money for roads and public improvements. Coxey left Massillon on Easter Sunday, 1894, with about five hundred men and arrived in Washington in time for a great demonstration on MAY DAY. His parade was cheered by an enormous crowd, but when he tried to speak from the Capitol steps he was arrested, fined, and sent to jail for carrying banners and walking on the grass on the Capitol grounds.

Other "industrial armies" formed by the unemployed on the Pacific coast and elsewhere decided to join Coxey in Washington. When the railroads refused to give them free rides on freight trains, they hijacked the trains. When local authorities were unable or unwilling to suppress them, federal judges filed injunctions against them. These were enforced by U.S. marshals or the army, setting precedents for the government's action against the Pullman strikers in July. About twelve hundred from Coxey's Army encamped in Washington until the District of Columbia finally paid their way home.

The Coxeyites, also known as Commonwealers or Industrials, demanded measures that were mainly Populist, and they were generally supported by the Populists and organized LABOR. Although they failed in their objectives, they were significant as symptoms of the economic unrest of the period and as an unusual type of Populist propaganda.

BIBLIOGRAPHY

McMurry, Donald Le Crone. *Coxey's Army: A Study of the Industrial Army Movement of 1894.* Seattle: University of Washington Press, 1968. The original edition was published Boston: Little, Brown, 1929.

Schwantes, Carlos A. *Coxey's Army: An American Odyssey.* Lincoln: University of Nebraska Press, 1985.

Vincent, Henry. *The Story of the Commonweal.* New York: Arno Press, 1969.

Donald L. McMurry / H. S.

See also **Financial Panics; Populism.**

COYOTE (*Canis latrans*) is a wild dog species, smaller than WOLVES but larger than foxes. The subject of many Native American creation tales and myths, coyotes came under attack during the twentieth century. Livestock ranchers, aided by government bounty hunters, used poison, traps, and aerial hunting to kill 428,849 coyotes in 1988 and an estimated 20 million during the entire century. Nevertheless, coyotes have expanded their numbers and domain from the trans-Mississippi west to every state except Hawaii because they are omnivorous, adaptable, and freed from competitors and predators by those same hunters. Coyotes demonstrate that humans often cannot control nature as they wish.

BIBLIOGRAPHY

Ryden, Hope. *God's Dog: A Celebration of the North American Coyote.* New York: Lyons and Burford, 1989.

David C. Hsiung

See also **Indian Oral Literature; Livestock Industry.**

CRAIG V. BOREN, 429 U.S. 190 (1976), established the constitutional test for laws that discriminate on account of gender. In 1958, Oklahoma enacted a law allowing women to purchase beer containing 3.2 percent alcohol at age eighteen, while men could not do so until they reached twenty-one years of age. In 1972 Craig, a man under twenty-one years of age, and Whitener, a woman operating a bar, challenged the law in the U.S. District Court for the Western District of Oklahoma, arguing that it constituted "invidious discrimination against males eighteen to twenty years of age," thus violating the equal protection clause of the Fourteenth Amendment. The District Court upheld Oklahoma's law, triggering a Supreme Court appeal.

Previously, gender distinctions were judged by a "rational basis test," which asked whether legislative bodies had reason to believe that sex discrimination in certain instances served the public interest. But in *Reed v. Reed* (1971), the Court broke with a century-long trend in Fourteenth Amendment interpretation, invalidating a Utah law that discriminated on account of sex, because it found that "rational basis" was not enough to sustain the discrimination. The Reed opinion appeared to signal a shift toward the application of the "strict scrutiny" test for racial classifications to gender classifications. *Frontiero v. Richardson* (1973) revisited the issues presented by *Reed v. Reed*, but did not clarify whether "strict scrutiny" would apply to gender discriminations. In *Craig v. Boren* the Court finally established which test would apply in gender classifications.

Oklahoma argued that the statute improved public safety, pointing to statistical evidence showing that men were slightly more likely to commit alcohol-related traffic offenses than women. The District Court, citing *Reed v. Reed*, had found that Oklahoma's statistical evidence endorsed the gender distinction, supporting the statutory goal of increased traffic safety. The Supreme Court disagreed, finding that evidence to be exceptionally thin, and offered "only a weak answer to the equal protection question presented here." Justice William Brennan, writing for the 7 to 2 Court majority, emphasized that evidence used to defend discriminations would have to be compelling. Striking down Oklahoma's statute, Brennan stated that the "relationship between gender and traffic safety becomes far too tenuous to satisfy *Reed v. Reed's* requirement that the gender-based difference be substantially related to achievement of the statutory objective." *Craig v. Boren* established that the Court would apply neither "rational basis" nor "strict scrutiny" tests, relying instead on

445

"heightened" or "intermediate" scrutiny of gender-based discriminations.

R. Volney Riser

See also **Discrimination: Sex.**

CRAIG V. STATE OF MISSOURI, 4 Peters 410 (1830). The Missouri legislature, in 1821, established an office for issuing paper MONEY that would be loaned to debt-burdened MISSOURI farmers. When Hiram Craig defaulted on his loan, a suit was brought in the circuit court of Chariton County to force payment. This court and the Missouri Supreme Court decided that Craig must pay. In an opinion rendered by Chief Justice John Marshall, the U.S. Supreme Court reversed the decision, ruling that the loan-office certificates were unconstitutional because they were bills of credit emitted by a state in violation of Article I, Section 10 of the Constitution.

BIBLIOGRAPHY

Albert J. Beveridge. *The Life of John Marshall.* Holmes Beach, Fla.: Gaunt, 1997.

W. J. Hamilton / A. R.

See also **Bank of the Unites States; Banking: State Banks; Bills of Credit; Constitution of the United States.**

CREATIONISM, the belief that life on Earth is the product of a divine act rather than organic evolution, has had a strong and persistent presence in American culture. From the first responses to Charles Darwin's theory of evolution in the 1860s through vigorous curriculum debates at the end of the twentieth century, American voices have been raised in defense of biblical accounts of the history of life. Indeed, prior to the publication of Darwin's *Origin of Species* in 1859, America's leading naturalist, Louis Agassiz, had articulated a scientifically sophisticated creationism—a position he continued to defend until his death in 1873, using it to point out flaws in Darwin's theory. In response to Darwin's work, many American scientists sought to retain a place for divine intervention in the history of life, even if they—like renowned botanist Asa Gray—considered themselves evolutionists. While American naturalists were embracing some form of organic evolution, conservative American theologians criticized the theory for its inconsistency with scriptural accounts.

As organic evolution became a generally accepted scientific principle and an element in school curricula in the early years of the twentieth century, American Christianity was experiencing the rise of fundamentalism. These two cultural developments collided dramatically in the 1920s as fundamentalist-led movements in twenty states sought to outlaw the teaching of evolution in public schools. Although their challenges to evolutionary theory were rooted in its incompatibility with a literal interpretation of the Bible, Christian critics also made opportunistic use of criticisms raised about the scientific merits of Darwin's theory. The conflict between supporters of evolutionary theory and the theory's fundamentalist opponents reached a high point in 1925, when a Tennessee high school teacher, John Thomas Scopes, confessed to violating that state's new law forbidding the teaching of evolution. The courtroom clash between defense attorney Clarence Darrow and Williams Jennings Bryan ended badly for the creationist movement, despite their guilty verdict, as Bryan—elderly and poorly prepared—failed to present a coherent challenge to the evolutionists.

The creationist movement, as it was now known, received less publicity during the four decades following the SCOPES TRIAL. Nevertheless, a strong constituency opposed to evolution remained among American Christians, especially conservative fundamentalists and evangelicals. For the first time, a significant number of individuals with advanced scientific training became active in the movement. This gave the creationists a more effective voice in criticizing evolutionary theory for its scientific flaws as they organized groups such as the Creation Research Society (founded in 1963). Increasingly, the debate between creationists and evolutionists used the language, credentials, and style of science.

The goal of scientific creationism, as the movement came to be known in the 1970s, differed from that of earlier creationist movements. Rather than trying to outlaw the teaching of evolution, scientific creationists argued for equal curriculum time. By working to demonstrate that evolution and creationism were two competing, legitimate scientific theories, they portrayed the exclusion of creationism from textbooks and classrooms as an act of prejudice rather than a defensible exclusion of religion from scientific education. This tactic brought significant victories. More than twenty state legislatures considered balanced treatment laws, and several passed them. While most of these legal victories were quickly reversed, the debate's impact on textbooks, teachers, and local school boards was subtle and long-lived. Particularly in the South and Midwest, where fundamentalist Christianity had the greatest influence, the argument for a balanced science curriculum swayed classroom content away from the rigorous teaching of evolutionary theory. The universal condemnation of scientific creationism by accepted scientific authorities was labeled intolerance by the creationists.

By the end of the twentieth century, the American-based creationist movement had inspired similar movements in a number of other countries. While evolutionary theory retained the full confidence of practicing scientists, the wider public remained more skeptical, with sizable fractions of the population around the country professing not to accept evolution. Clearly, the persistence of the creationist movement helped this belief survive well beyond the community of fundamentalist Christians.

BIBLIOGRAPHY
Godfrey, Laurie R., ed. *Scientists Confront Creationism.* New York: Norton, 1983.

Numbers, Ronald L. *The Creationists: The Evolution of Scientific Creationism.* Berkeley: University of California Press, 1993.

———. *Darwinism Comes to America.* Cambridge, Mass.: Harvard University Press, 1998.

Ruse, Michael, ed. *But Is It Science? The Philosophical Question in the Creation/Evolution Controversy.* Amherst, N.Y.: Prometheus, 1996.

Loren Butler Feffer

See also **Evolutionism; Fundamentalism.**

CREDIBILITY GAP. Term used to criticize a public figure or institution by suggesting that there exists a "gap" between official claims and the public's perceptions. In short, the term alleges that the people do not believe what they are being told.

The phrase first appeared in 1965 newspaper stories concerning the policies of President Lyndon Johnson. Several accounts claimed that Johnson had frequently been duplicitous in announcing one policy and then enacting another. The most politically damaging example involved the 1968 Tet Offensive in Vietnam, which caught the U.S. military completely by surprise after Johnson had spent months predicting imminent victory.

BIBLIOGRAPHY
Gardner, Lloyd C. *Pay Any Price: Lyndon Johnson and the Wars for Vietnam.* Chicago: I. R. Dee, 1995.

Turner, Kathleen J. *Lyndon Johnson's Dual War: Vietnam and the Press.* Chicago: University of Chicago Press, 1985.

J. Justin Gustainis

See also **Vietnam War.**

CREDIT. There are two primary types of credit: producer credit and consumer credit. Producer credit is extended to businesses; consumer credit is extended to individuals. Credit can be extended long term or short term. Long-term credit generally has a maturity of one year or more.

Businesses seek credit to finance operations or to purchase long-lived assets such as machinery or real estate. A strict accounting may not precede the credit contract, yet businesses are presumed to take profit maximization concerns into account when deciding to borrow.

Individuals seek credit for parallel reasons, although the terminology differs. Businesses finance operations; individuals finance household expenses. Businesses purchase long-lived assets such as machinery or real estate; individuals purchase durable goods or homes. Whereas businesses consider the bottom line, individuals borrow for more complex reasons.

The most important distinction between producer credit and consumer credit is the role of credit in generating the funds with which the debt is repaid. Businesses borrow to produce and sell a product, and thus generate the revenue with which the loan is repaid. Families borrow in order to buy products, not to generate family income. This distinction mattered to lenders, especially in the nineteenth and early twentieth centuries. Lenders, particularly bankers, were unwilling to extend credit to individuals to buy consumer goods unless the product would "pay for itself": pianos could be used to give piano lessons and sewing machines could be used to take in sewing, and credit was readily available for families buying these products.

Credit extended to producers or consumers is typically—but not always—a loan. What is and is not a loan is primarily a legal distinction. Most credit—but not all—is secured by a real or financial asset. If the debtor breaches the contract that is secured by property, the creditor (lender) can claim or repossess the property.

Producer Credit

In the United States, the demand for producer credit probably dates back to the day of first settlement. Because the economy had little transportation or manufacturing, demand for producer credit was largely mercantile and agricultural. There were, however, few institutional arrangements that extended credit. What credit existed was usually extended directly by individuals or by merchants.

Borrowers were frequently located long distances from creditors, and often planned to use their borrowings for activities about which the potential creditors had little knowledge. The long physical distances tended to preclude many transactions. The difficulty in evaluating a project's creditworthiness limited credit availability even more. Search, information gathering, and administration are, however, all subject to increasing returns to scale, so that average costs can be substantially reduced if these activities are centralized; moreover, risk is reduced if the benefits of insurance are obtained by the introduction of some institution between lender and borrower.

In 1781, the BANK OF NORTH AMERICA was chartered in Philadelphia. Commercial banks were soon opened in the other Northeast cities. By 1810 there were 88 banks, and by 1930, 30,000. Early banks were largely devoted to supplying the credit needs of the mercantile community. They lent the savings of stockholders and a few depositors, and also issued bank notes in exchange for commercial IOUs (commercial paper). Banks continue to function in much the same way today. After 1865, however, the creation of demand deposits (checking accounts) largely replaced bank note issue as the means of extending credit.

In the nineteenth century, local banks dominated the short-term credit market in the North and West. In the South, credit was provided by a combination of merchants and people in the cotton industry (supported at times by northern banks). Legal restrictions prevented the

To convey the general attitude of society toward consumer credit, Clyde Phelps wove together several quotes from articles published in popular and professional journals between 1926 and 1928.

The use of credit, and particularly the installment type, by consumers was characterized as "an economic sin," as "enervating to character because it leads straight to serfdom," as setting "utterly false standards of living," causing judgment to become "hopelessly distorted," and tending to "break down credit morale." It was attacked as "marking the breakdown of traditional habits of thrift," as tending to "weaken the moral fiber of the Nation," and as dangerous to the economy of the United States. It was accused of "breaking down character and resistance to temptations, to extravagance, and to living beyond one's means, breeding dishonesty," causing "many young people to get their first experience of being deadbeats through yielding to temptations that are placed before them," and "creating a new type of criminal or causing professional deadbeats to shift to this new and highly lucrative opportunity."

SOURCE: Clyde William Phelps, *The Role of the Sales Finance Companies in the American Economy.* Baltimore: Commercial Credit Company, 1952, pp. 39–40.

establishment of national banks. Local banks mobilized credit within regions, but there were few mechanisms to move credit between regions. Demand for finance was high in the South and West but supply was greatest in the East. Commercial paper houses such as Goldman Sachs emerged to facilitate interregional flow of funds. These institutions began operating in the East in the 1840s. They moved into the Midwest in the early 1870s and to the Pacific coast by the turn of the century. Commercial paper houses bought commercial paper from banks in high-interest regions and sold it to banks in lower-interest areas.

Demand for long-term credit increased in the 1820s, 1830s, and 1840s as canal building dominated transportation firms, factory production emerged in manufacturing firms, and new technology transformed agriculture. Existing commercial banks and new industrial banks such as the Morris Canal and Banking Company were initially able to meet the increased demand for credit. But the loan defaults during the panic of 1837 and depression of 1839–1842 convinced some bankers that long-term loans were unsafe, and commercial banks began to shy away from extending long-term producer credit.

Other institutions emerged as major suppliers of long-term credit. The first savings bank had opened its doors in 1816. The idea spread rapidly; by 1825, most Northeast cities had at least one savings bank. Savings banks were the most important suppliers of long-term credit from the late 1830s until the end of the century. The Bank for Savings of New York City, established in the early 1800s to serve the working poor, made a substantial contribution to the financing of the Erie Canal. The Provident Institution for Savings in Boston was instrumental in financing the New England textile industry. Savings banks, however, held primarily the meager savings of the poor and were never important outside the Northeast.

In the East, Midwest, and South, life insurance companies provided long-term producer credit. Life insurance business first grew substantially in the 1840s, but its fastest growth came after 1870 with the establishment of tontine and industrial insurance. Life insurance companies passed savings banks in importance in the early years of the twentieth century.

As transportation, manufacturing, and government demand for credit increased in the nineteenth century, formal capital markets developed to facilitate the extension of producer credit. The New York Stock Exchange was formally organized in 1817. Local markets soon emerged in eastern seaboard cities such as Boston and Philadelphia. By the 1830s, there were local markets as far inland as St. Louis. Improvements in communication and the financial advantages enjoyed by New York led to centralization of securities exchanges in New York City. The exchanges initially dealt only in public issues but began dealing in transportation securities in the early nineteenth century and in public utilities shortly thereafter. By the end of the nineteenth century, they were handling a substantial volume of manufacturing securities. By 1914, the market was mobilizing credit for all branches of American activity except agriculture. Although the system suffered a temporary setback after the crash of 1929, it rebounded during World War II (1939–1945) and remains an important route for the extension of long-term producer credit.

Consumer Credit

Consumer credit allows individuals to buy goods and services they may not otherwise be able to pay for. The use of credit by individuals is as old as commerce itself. The forms of consumer credit have evolved over time.

Until the late nineteenth century, most consumer credit was extended directly by merchants and service providers, or by pawnbrokers. Store credit, also known as merchant or service credit, was extended by doctors, funeral parlors, grocers, dry-goods merchants, and others. Unexpected expenses, unexpected declines in income, a seasonal pattern to income, or a lack of currency in the community led individuals to use store credit. There was usually no collateral; only the family's promise to repay typically secured the credit.

Pawnbrokers, known colloquially as "loan sharks," extended money loans particularly to working-class families. This "small lending" was also extended by small loan

paid themselves outrageous profits. A cynic might say that the first construction site was at the U.S. Treasury.

Within six years Representative Oakes Ames (R-Mass.), a major shareholder, lent money to congressional colleagues to purchase shares at par, half of the market value. He used this stock where it produced the most good. Ames distributed funds to fifteen House members, including several key committee chairmen; six senators; and Vice President Schuyler Colfax. In 1869 a perfunctory Justice Department investigation of Ames's sale of the shares found nothing irregular. Three years later, an unhappy promoter, H. S. McComb, released letters from Ames that provided damaging details about the scheme.

On the eve of the 1872 election the *New York Sun* exposed the relationship. A later investigation revealed that Ames and others had taken more than $23 million, intended for a congressionally approved permanent endowment for construction, for their personal use, including sharing the stolen funds with congressional members. After the election, during a lame-duck session, Speaker of the House James G. Blaine (R-Maine), who had prior knowledge of the situation, set up an investigative committee that recommended Ames be expelled. The House only voted for censure—not for conflict of interest but for bribing House members. The web of corruption was wide. Schuyler Colfax, the lame-duck vice president; the new Vice President Henry Wilson; and Representative James A. Garfield (R-Ohio) were implicated and tarnished. Garfield recovered from the scandal and was eventually elected president of the United States. Representative James Brooks (D-N.Y.) was censured. Other members escaped punishment.

Blaine, however, paid a price. In the atmosphere of moral outrage following public exposure of the scandal, he defeated the censure charge, but it cost him the Republican nomination for president in 1876. In 1884, as the Republican presidential candidate, Blaine lost a close election to the Democratic challenger, Grover Cleveland. The "Mulligan Letters," written by Blaine to a railroad contractor with whom he had questionable financial dealings (one containing the famous injunction to "Burn this letter"), significantly contributed to his defeat. In addition to the literary results of Mark Twain and Charles Dudley Warner's *The Gilded Age* (1873) and Henry Adams's *Democracy* (1880), the Crédit Mobilier scandal gave Grover Cleveland his political reputation as an active opponent of governmental corruption.

The larger historical significance of the Crédit Mobilier scandal was what it revealed about the political culture. It illustrated the famous distinction by the Tammany Hall politician George Washington Plunkitt between dishonest graft—theft or bribery—and honest graft, or taking economic advantage of inside governmental information. Ames's distribution of shares was classified as bribery, but the men receiving those favors were not considered as having received a corrupting gift. Only the provider of the bribe was guilty of wrongdoing. No code

regarding official misconduct was forthcoming, and ad hoc judgments became the norm. Between 1873 and 1968 only one senator was mildly censured for having a lobbyist on his payroll, in 1929. The record of Congress in this area has been better codified since 1968, despite some mild judgments.

BIBLIOGRAPHY

Bain, David Haward. *Empire Express: Building the First Transcontinental Railroad.* New York: Viking, 1999. Richly detailed account of the scandal.

Crawford, Jay Boyd. *The Crédit Mobilier of America; Its Origin and History, Its Work of Constructing the Union Pacific, and the Relation of Members of Congress Therewith.* Boston: C. W. Calkins, 1880. A pioneer account and still one of the best sources for understanding the corrupt incident.

Huneke, William F. *The Heavy Hand: The Government and the Union Pacific, 1862–1898.* New York: Garland, 1985. A bit revisionist in emphasis.

Donald K. Pickens

See also **Mulligan Letters; Political Scandals.**

CREDIT UNIONS. The first 190 credit unions in the United States, organized between 1909 and 1921, differed from other depository institutions in the following ways: (1) officers were volunteers; (2) members were skilled artisans and thus had a common occupational bond; (3) the purpose was to help members accumulate capital so that they could set up their own businesses; and (4) they were democratic. Deposits took the form of dividend-paying share accounts. Regardless of the amount deposited, each of the 72,310 members of the first credit unions had only one vote in the elections of the committees that decided on loans and investments.

Credit unions did not have any full-time, professional staff until the National Extension Bureau was established in 1921, then reorganized as the Credit Union National Association (CUNA) in 1934. Arguing that employees with home mortgages and consumer installment credit are less susceptible to "bolshevism" and other forms of radicalism (for example, labor unions), the Extension Bureau staff lobbied the nation's leading industrialists to subsidize credit unions (for example, with free office space). Consequently, by the time of the 1929 stock market crash, an additional 784 credit unions were organized for 192,598 new members. However, this growth came at a price: not only had the purpose of credit unions changed but the common bond among members had changed too. Now members simply shared the same employer.

Without government intervention, mortgage defaults during the GREAT DEPRESSION would have bankrupted the credit unions. Largely through the Federal Credit Union Act of 1934, the government established the National Credit Union Association to regulate the credit unions and serve as their lender of last resort. It exempted the credit unions from taxes and subsidized their expansion among government employees. And the government imposed interest rate ceilings on commercial bank deposits that were lower than what credit unions offered for deposits. As a result, credit unions mushroomed in the postwar period, to a peak 22,533 in 1976. Largest by far was the Navy's credit union, with $568 million of the total credit union assets of $45 billion (the $45 billion itself being about 5 percent of total commercial-bank assets at the time).

However, the rapid postwar growth of credit unions came at the expense of actively discriminating against the poor and others without steady employment. Having thus abandoned their progressive roots, the credit unions became vulnerable to attacks by commercial banks. By emphasizing the word "union" in their name, the American Bankers Association argued that credit unions contributed to the spread of socialism in America. In response to the banks' lobbying, sections that rendered credit unions largely indistinguishable from other depository institutions were put into the Interest Rate Control Act of 1977, the Depository Institutions Deregulation and Monetary Control Act of 1980, and the Garn–St. Germain Act of 1982.

In particular, the elimination of interest rate ceilings that favored credit unions at the expense of commercial banks caused a hemorraging of deposits from, and thus a major consolidation of, credit unions under the auspices of CUNA. As a result, individual credit unions became little more than branch offices of CUNA. While individual credit unions still collect deposits and originate loans, these loans are now pooled by CUNA for issuing mortgage-backed and other types of securities. CUNA's asset managers invest the excess funds of the credit unions. CUNA also uses the individual credit unions as branches for offering stock brokerage services, money market accounts, ATMs, electronic fund transfers, credit cards, IRA and Keogh retirement accounts, and even some commercial loans.

Nonetheless, many progressives see the democratic origins of credit unions as a potential model for keeping local money in the local economy. They thus envision a role for credit unions in strategies for sustainable development that could displace the current tendency toward corporate-led globalization. There is a precedent for this progressive vision of credit unions. In the 1960s, 672 credit unions were established in poor urban areas. The OFFICE OF ECONOMIC OPPORTUNITY subsidized 245 of them, so that they could lend money for food and rent.

BIBLIOGRAPHY

Moody, J. Carroll and Gilbert Fite. *The Credit Union Movement.* Lincoln: University of Nebraska Press, 1971.

Pearce, Douglas. "Recent Developments in the Credit Union Industry." In *Contemporary Developments in Financial Institutions and Markets.* Edited by Thomas Havrilesky and Robert Schweitzer. Arlington Heights, Ill.: Harlan Davidson, 1984.

Edwin Dickens

See also **Banking**.

CREE. The Crees are a tribe with a long history in the United States and Canada. Their current territory ranges from the eastern shores of James Bay, down through northern Ontario, across the Prairie Provinces of Canada to the Rocky Mountains, north to the Northwest Territories, and south to the states of Montana and the Dakotas.

Traditionally the Crees were adept at selecting from other cultures those things they saw as useful while ignoring the rest. This trait was especially evident during the fur trade, when they were known as middlemen. The Crees' trade practices in Prince Rupert's Land involved holding the prime locations around Hudson Bay Company posts. The trade goods they received were paid for with furs that came from other Crees in the northwest. The Crees near the posts would use the goods for a time and then pass them on to other Crees. Eventually, these used goods, especially firearms, would be traded to other tribes, such as the Blackfeet, for horses. In turn, the Blackfeet would use the guns to protect themselves from other warlike tribes and, in the process, protect the Crees from

Cree. A Cree inductee (*left*) into the U.S. Army in 1952 sits with another soldier waiting to have his braided hair shorn at Fort Lewis, Wash. LIBRARY OF CONGRESS

these same people. Using trade goods to arm a buffer tribe between themselves and their enemies is a good example of the Crees' astute use of an economic power in the political arena.

In the modern era, the Crees have been major players in the political activities of Aboriginal people in Canada. They successfully negotiated a modern treaty in the James Bay area (1975) and are often found as political leaders in tribal organizations. Despite their history of economic and political astuteness, many Crees are located on isolated reserves and suffer from extreme poverty. Land claims and other claims for past mismanagement and abuse are now seen as the basis for re-creating the Crees' economic system. From their historic leader Big Bear in the 1880s and his dream of a collective of tribes living in western Canada to the Crees' modern political leaders, the object remains the same: the establishment and protection of a self-reliant nation of Crees.

BIBLIOGRAPHY

Mandelbaum, David G. *The Plains Cree: An Ethnographic, Historical, and Comparative Study.* Regina, Saskatchewan: Canadian Plains Research Centre, University of Regina, 1979. Originally published in 1940, it is one of the best sources for Cree cultural practice in the Plains area. Despite its age, there is no other work currently available that describes in such detail the Crees' spiritual, cultural, and social activity, with attention to specific practice and its development in the latter part of the nineteenth century and the early twentieth century.

Milloy, John S. *The Plains Cree: Trade, Diplomacy, and War, 1790–1870.* Winnipeg: University of Manitoba Press, 1990. A telling description of the Crees' use of fur trade economics for their political requirements. The descriptions of why and how the Plains Crees used trade as a political tool should be required reading for anyone who assumes that First Nations were unable to manage the fur trade for their own purposes.

Richardson, Boyce. *Strangers Devour the Land.* Vancouver, British Columbia: Douglas and McIntyre, 1991. One of the better descriptions of a modern treaty-making process and the Crees' determination not to be disadvantaged by hydroelectric development. Combined with the two texts mentioned above, this work should provide the reader with an excellent overview of the reality of the Crees, historically and in the modern era.

Fred Shore

See also **Fur Trade and Trapping; Tribes: Great Plains.**

CREEK. The Creek Nation is centered in Muskogee, Oklahoma, but its early history rests in the Southeast. In the sixteenth century, long before a Creek people existed, Old World diseases, especially smallpox, decimated Natives in the Southeast, destroying towns and forcing survivors into refugee communities. By the end of the 1600s, some of these survivors, scattered in thirty to forty towns along Georgia and Alabama rivers, joined together in an

Chitto Harjo (Crazy Snake). A 1903 photograph of the leader of a Creek resistance movement that unsuccessfully fought the U.S. dissolution of the Creek Nation. LIBRARY OF CONGRESS

alliance. Their residents, numbering about ten thousand, spoke a number of languages, including Muskogee, Alabama, and Hitchiti. But despite their varying ethnic origins, they presented a united front to Spanish, French, and English colonists. South Carolina colonists were soon calling these allied peoples "Creeks," a shorthand for Indians living on Ochese Creek in Georgia.

In the late seventeenth century, the Creeks established an active trade with French, Spanish, and English colonists. The Creeks traded Indian slaves and deerskins in exchange for textiles, kettles, and guns. The slave trade declined after the Yamasee War of 1715, when South Carolina determined that the risk of enslaving Indians was too great. The deerskin trade continued to flourish, however, especially after English colonists established the Georgia colony in 1733. In the 1750s, Savannah exported over sixty thousand skins annually. In Creek towns the profits of the trade, including cloth, kettles, guns, and rum, eased the labor of Creeks but also introduced new conflicts among men and women and rich and poor.

By 1800, the deer population had plummeted, and white Americans began seeking Creek lands rather than Creek deerskins. Under compulsion, Creeks ceded vast amounts of territory. At the same time, U.S. Indian agents pressured them to adopt American economic and religious practices. Grassroots resistance to these changes built until a civil conflict known as the Red Stick War erupted within the tribe in 1813. U.S. troops led by Andrew Jackson soon entered the fray on the side of the friendly Creek leadership. The rebels were defeated, and the Creek Nation lay in ruins. Removal followed swiftly, despite Creek resistance. In 1832, the Creeks agreed to cede their remaining southeastern lands, and U.S. troops hastened the process by rounding them up at gunpoint in the Creek War of 1836.

By 1837, more than 23,000 Creeks had left their southeastern homelands for Indian Territory (now Oklahoma), where they suffered terrible floods, droughts, and epidemics. The population fell almost by half to 14,000 in the space of twenty years. Yet some Creeks fared well, particularly plantation owners who exploited slave labor. The Civil War dealt yet another blow to the Creeks. It freed roughly 2,000 slaves held in the Creek Nation but devastated the land, destroying crops, buildings, and equipment. Although Creeks rebuilt their nation, at the end of the nineteenth century the Curtis Act (1898) dissolved the Creek Nation. Despite resistance organized in 1900 by Chitto Harjo, or Crazy Snake, the United States divided Creek lands into individual allotments and unilaterally dissolved the Creek government.

The Creeks lost millions of acres of land, and their government nearly ceased functioning until 1971. In that year, the Creek Nation elected a principal chief for the first time since 1899. In 2001, the revitalized Creek Nation counted more than 50,000 citizens.

BIBLIOGRAPHY

Debo, Angie. *The Road to Disappearance. A History of the Creek Indians.* Norman: University of Oklahoma, 1941.

Green, Michael D. *The Politics of Indian Removal: Creek Government and Society in Crisis.* Lincoln: University of Nebraska Press, 1982.

Saunt, Claudio. *A New Order of Things: Property, Power, and the Transformation of the Creek Indians, 1733–1816.* New York: Cambridge University Press, 1999.

Claudio Saunt

See also **Georgia; Indian Removal; Trail of Tears; Tribes: Southeastern.**

CREEK WAR (1813–1814), also known as the Red Stick War, began as a civil war between those who accepted and those who rejected the U.S. policies of acculturation. The CREEKS were feeling increased pressure from the white land seekers of the expanding United States, and during the half century preceding the war they were increasingly divided over how best to cope with the intrusions. Benjamin Hawkins, agent to the Creeks just before the turn of the nineteenth century, had administered a program of "civilization" that promoted the planting of cotton and other cash crops, the acquisition of private property, and even the purchase of African slaves.

The policy appealed to many Creeks of mixed white-Indian ancestry but aroused the opposition of more traditional members, who opposed the abandonment of sacred traditions and the distribution of communal lands among individual Creeks. A strong opposition to the proposed changes developed among the Upper Creeks of central Alabama, influenced in 1813 by a visit from the Shawnee chief Tecumseh, who preached nativism, anti-Americanism, and resistance to further encroachments by the whites. The Upper Creeks, known as the Red Sticks, were hostile, while the Lower Creeks, or White Sticks, remained loyal to the United States. Numerous prophets fanned religious fervor among the Red Sticks, inciting them to civil war.

On 30 August 1813, the Red Sticks sacked and burned an American stockade, Fort Mims, on the Alabama River, killing more than 350 Americans and Indians and bringing American troops into the conflict. Retaliatory forces assembled in Tennessee, Georgia, and Mississippi, but the principal attack came from Tennessee militiamen under General Andrew Jackson, aided by Cherokees and White Stick Creeks. Jackson vigorously pursued a campaign against the Red Sticks, sacking the Indian village of Talishatchee on 3 November and on 9 November crushing a Creek force at Talladega. With a force of Georgians and White Stick Creeks, General John Floyd on 29 November attacked the Creek village of Auttosee on the Tallapoosa River, burning the village and killing two hundred Creeks. At the battle of Econochaca in northern Alabama on 23 December, Mississippi volunteers burned the village of the Red Stick leader William Weatherford (Red Eagle).

On 27 March 1814, Jackson almost wiped out the Red Stick forces at the Horseshoe Bend of the Tallapoosa River in eastern Alabama, killing an estimated 850 to 900 warriors and making prisoners of some 500 women and children. This defeat effectively broke the power of the Red Sticks, many of whom fled to join the Seminoles in Florida, while others went into hiding. Ironically, the White Sticks, despite having aided Jackson in the war, were compelled to sign the Treaty of Fort Jackson (9 August 1814), under the terms of which they were forced to cede to the United States more than 20 million acres in the present states of Georgia and Alabama. These land cessions only increased white demand for the Creeks' southeastern lands, and these demands ended only when Creeks were removed to INDIAN TERRITORY (NOW OKLAHOMA) in 1835 and 1836.

BIBLIOGRAPHY

Martin, Joel. *Sacred Revolt: The Muskogees' Struggle for a New World.* Boston: Beacon Press, 1991.

Nunez, Theron A., Jr. "Creek Nativism and the Creek War of 1813–14." *Ethnohistory* 5 (Winter 1958): 17–41; (Spring): 131–175; (Summer): 292–301.

offenders; anyone who commits three offenses of any kind may be sentenced to an extraordinarily long period behind bars.

Long terms of incarceration have significant effects throughout the system of American law. State courts send far more convicts to state prisons than existing institutions can accommodate. The crowding that ensues makes prison life, already harsh, more oppressive. Even before the flood of new prisoners in the 1980s, federal courts had held the poor conditions found in many state prisons to constitute cruel and unusual punishment in violation of the Constitution. Those courts ordered prison officials to make numerous adjustments and to eliminate crowding. With the subsequent flow of prisoners increasing so dramatically, most states have responded by constructing more penal facilities. New prisons, in turn, are little more than human warehouses confining prisoners for ever-increasing periods of time at the least possible cost.

Treating juveniles as adults. The prosecution of juveniles as adults began in earnest in the 1990s. Previously, under juvenile justice codes adopted earlier in the twentieth century, persons under a certain age (typically eighteen) were formally regarded as unable to commit a serious criminal offense. They might engage in conduct that would be criminal if committed by an adult, but because of their immaturity (and thus their diminished culpability) they were treated differently. Young people were typically held to appear before special juvenile courts, which adjudicated them to be delinquent and, on that basis, specified remedial programs thought to be appropriate. In some instances, juveniles were sent to reformatories for vocational training; more often, they were channeled into some form of community supervision and counseling. In the 1990s, however, the extreme violence of which juveniles proved to be capable prompted many states to subject at least some of them to ordinary criminal charges, trial in ordinary criminal courts, and, if convicted, punishment of the ordinary (enhanced) kind.

The treatment of juveniles as adults also has important effects on the system as a whole. Tens of thousands of teenagers have received lengthy sentences, ostensibly to be served in one of the prisons designed to confine adults. Most penal authorities recognize that young offenders cannot easily be mixed with older convicts and have established special units for teenagers within larger institutions. Yet the length of the sentences imposed on young prisoners guarantees that they will eventually be assimilated into the adult prisoner population.

Expansion of the federal role. The idea that crime is a serious problem has led to the (quite different) idea that it is a national problem as well. Congress has responded by extending federal criminal jurisdiction on a host of fronts. In most instances Congress continues to base federal criminal statutes on its authority to regulate commerce among the states. Yet modern enactments dramatically extend that authority to activities with little demon-strable connection to interstate commerce. Toward the end of the twentieth century Congress enacted federal criminal legislation in virtually every session. Examples include the Omnibus Crime Control and Safe Streets Act of 1968, the Organized Crime Control Act of 1970, the Comprehensive Drug Abuse Prevention and Control Act of 1984, the Anti-Drug Abuse Acts of 1968 and 1988, the Crime Control Act of 1990, the Violent Crime Control and Law Enforcement Act of 1994, and the Anti-Terrorism and Effective Death Penalty Act of 1996. Those statutes did not consolidate federal crimes in a coherent code but rather added numerous freestanding offenses to the sprawling body of federal law. By the year 2000 there were more than three thousand separate federal offenses. By the beginning of the twenty-first century, not only were more activities considered federal crimes than ever, but those crimes, like their state counterparts, typically carried extremely long prison sentences as well.

The federalization of American criminal law has significance for a variety of other governmental agencies and functions. Certainly the growth of federal crimes demands a consequent growth in federal law enforcement agencies and personnel: the Federal Bureau of Investigation (FBI), the United States Marshal Service, the Drug Enforcement Agency (DEA), and related organizations. For the first time in its history, the United States has commissioned a powerful central police force. The introduction of federal criminal law into spheres of local affairs also creates conflicts with state authorities. In many instances, suspects can be charged with violating a federal criminal statute, a similar state statute, or both. That overlap demands cooperation between federal and state law enforcement officials that was unnecessary before the 1990s. Federal criminal cases dominate the dockets of federal trial courts, forcing other judicial business to be postponed. The courts, in turn, sentence large numbers of convicts to lengthy terms of imprisonment at federal penal facilities that have no room for them. Thus the federal government, like many states, has launched a major prison-building campaign. Where once the Federal Bureau of Prisons operated only a few federal prisons like Leavenworth and Alcatraz, in 2002 the Bureau controlled 102 institutions.

Regulating corporate behavior. The use of criminal law as a means of regulating corporate behavior is a twentieth-century innovation. So-called white-collar crime, committed by comparatively wealthy people holding positions of trust, has substantial historical footing in American law. In many cases individual perpetrators commit familiar offenses for their own benefit: offenses like embezzlement, tax evasion, and fraud. In other cases, however, corporate officers and employees implicate their companies in criminal offenses like restraints of trade, unlawful manipulations of stocks and bonds, and violations of environmental protection statutes. Corporate crime thrives in the complexities of the modern technological economy and is characteristically difficult to detect and prosecute. The demand for effective enforcement has prompted the federal government to bring its considerable resources to bear on the problem. Congress has enacted a variety of statutes to contend with white-collar and corporate crime, most prominently the Racketeer Influenced and Corrupt Organization Act of 1970.

Individuals convicted of white-collar offenses are sentenced to some form of incarceration at about the same rate that street criminals are sentenced to prison. However, the terms for white-collar criminals are substantially shorter, measured in months rather than years. Of course, corporations cannot be given prison sentences for their crimes (though the individuals who act for corporations certainly can be). Accordingly, corporations are typically fined or subjected to some other form of economic penalty. Some academics contend that it is a mistake to subject corporations to criminal liability at all, because "civil" fines can achieve the same objective: the creation of economic disincentives to behave in a socially disadvantageous way.

Addressing drug problems. The policy of making it a crime to possess, manufacture, or sell hallucinogenic and addictive drugs has contributed significantly to the developing nature of American criminal law. By some accounts the criminalization of drugs increases the price that drug dealers can charge for their product and thus increases the resulting profits. Those high profits, in turn, perversely foster the very behavior that antidrug laws are meant to discourage. Certainly drug dealing has developed into a massive industry, stretching from source points both in this country and in foreign nations (principally South American states) through manufacturing facilities to "retail" sales on the streets. One-third of all state criminal prosecutions are for drug-related offenses, and one-fourth of the inmates serving terms in state prisons are there for possessing or selling drugs. A disproportionate number of those prisoners are young African Americans from inner-city areas.

The criminalization of drugs is also intimately linked with the expanding role of the federal government in crime control. Early in the twentieth century Congress enacted numerous federal criminal statutes regarding drugs, among them the Harrison Narcotic Drug Act of 1914, the Marijuana Tax Act of 1937, and the Opium Poppy Control Act of 1942. Subsequently, the growth of the drug industry, with its many international connections, prompted Congress to expand the federal "war on drugs" to much larger dimensions. The Comprehensive Drug Abuse Prevention and Control Act of 1970 organized federal criminal drug laws, and the Anti-Drug Abuse Act of 1986 established mandatory minimum prison sentences for many violators. Between 1980 and 1990, when the general rate of criminal prosecutions in the federal courts rose by 69 percent, the rate of federal prosecutions for drug offenses rose by 300 percent. Drug cases in 2000 accounted for nearly half the criminal trials in federal court. The federal government's commitment

to antidrug laws generated a corresponding expansion in the federal bureaucracy. The DEA was established in 1973 to take primary responsibility for federal enforcement efforts. Not only the DEA and the FBI but many other agencies (including the Immigration and Naturalization Service, the navy, and the Coast Guard) are also engaged in interdicting the drug trade in this country, in foreign nations, and on the high seas.

All these features of modern criminal law have evoked intense controversy. With the exception of the prosecution of corporate crime, the practical consequence of each development has been the long-term imprisonment of a large and increasing population of Americans, a disproportionate number of whom are young, poor people of color. There is no discounting the profound social (and moral) implications of a system that incarcerates so many of its dispossessed members. Nevertheless, public concerns about crime, particularly violent crime, continue to drive American policy toward more (and more punitive) uses of criminal sanctions.

BIBLIOGRAPHY

Blumstein, Alfred, and Joel Wallman, eds. *The Crime Drop in America.* Cambridge, U.K.: Cambridge University Press, 2000.

Friedman, Lawrence M. *Crime and Punishment in American History.* New York: Basic Books, 1993.

Geis, Gilbert, and Robert F. Meier, comps. *White-Collar Crime: Offenses in Business and the Professions.* New York: Free Press, 1977.

Gray, James P. *Why Our Drug Laws Have Failed and What We Can Do About It: A Judicial Indictment of the War on Drugs.* Philadelphia: Temple University, 2001.

Robinson, Paul H., and John M. Darley. *Justice, Liability, and Blame: Community Views and the Criminal Law.* Boulder, Colo.: Westview, 1995.

Silberman, Charles E. *Criminal Violence, Criminal Justice.* New York: Random House, 1978.

U.S. Department of Justice. Bureau of Justice Statistics. *Report to the Nation on Crime and Justice.* 2d ed. 2 vols. Washington, D.C.: Justice Statistics Clearinghouse, 1988.

Zimring, Franklin E., and Gordon Hawkins. *Crime Is Not the Problem: Lethal Violence in America.* New York: Oxford University, 1997.

Larry Yackle

See also **Abortion; Drug Trafficking, Illegal; Federal Bureau of Investigation; Justice, Department of; Juvenile Courts; Mann Act; Prohibition; Salem Witch Trials; Sherman Antitrust Act; Volstead Act.**

CRIME, ORGANIZED. Organized crime is a term that has been used selectively in the twentieth century to identify particular criminal coalitions, often ethnically based, that others wished to define as dangerous criminal conspiracies. The criminals identified to be part of "organized crime" have seldom possessed the hierarchical structure or the power ascribed to them. Yet, labeling them as "organized crime" often influenced popular attitudes and the policies of law enforcement. A history of organized crime, then, includes both a history of criminal structures and of the selective use of the term.

From the 1860s into the twentieth century, certain types of gambling received increased coordination in many cities. During and after the Civil War, policy gambling—a type of illegal lottery—became widely popular. Fans could bet on the numbers in bars, barber shops, newspaper kiosks, and similar retail outlets. Concurrently, entrepreneurs backed the local retailers, so that the retailer retained a fixed percent of each bet while the backer(s) paid off when bettors won. By the 1880s, as betting on horse racing also became popular, off-track bookmaking was coordinated much like policy, with bets placed in local bars and other hangouts for men, while bookmakers backed the local sellers. As a result, especially by the 1890s, policy and bookmaking syndicates enjoyed the support of bettors, local businessmen, and the politicians who sought their votes.

Outside the South, the Irish were heavily involved in the policy and bookmaking syndicates. Among the earliest and most famous was John Morrissey. After winning a disputed boxing match in September 1853, many recognized him as the American champion until October 1857, when after a successful title defense, he retired. He used his fame to open gambling houses in New York City and during the Civil War put together a major syndicate to back the rising policy gambling in the city. In Saratoga Springs, New York, during the summer racing season, he also operated perhaps the finest casino in the world and found time to serve two terms in the state legislature and two terms in the U.S. Congress. However, criminal entrepreneurs like Morrissey emerged too early to be labeled organized crime.

The term "organized crime" was first used in the 1920s, perhaps from John Landesco's *Organized Crime in Chicago*, a book-length section of the Illinois Crime Survey, published by the Illinois Association for Criminal Justice (1929). But the concept of powerful bootlegging gangs was popularized by newspaper stories and by movies about Al Capone (and other bootleggers). They were key factors in ascribing to the often decentralized and independent bootleggers a mythical power. In the same decade, activities such as labor and business racketeering were also called "organized crime," capturing the fears of elite businessmen and lawyers that the urban underworld was becoming organized bureaucratically like legitimate businesses. A fear that some criminal activities were now more dangerous because more organized continued as an undercurrent among some criminal justice professionals and academics through the 1930s and 1940s.

From the 1950s into the 1970s, the danger from "organized crime" was reinforced by identifying it with a belief that an Italian American "mafia" exercised nationwide domination of crime. In 1950 and 1951, the idea received popular dissemination when the Senate Special Committee to Investigate Organized Crime (popularly known as the Kefauver Committee after its chair, Senator Estes Kefauver of Tennessee) held televised hearings, which were America's first big TV event. Listeners were fascinated as the Committee moved from city to city and allowed the public to hear various alleged crime kingpins respond to the grilling by the staff and members of the committee. Perhaps the high point was the testimony of Frank Costello. In eight days during March 1951, he refused to allow his face on camera, but the audience could hear his gravelly voice and watch his clasping hands as he responded defiantly, evasively, or honestly to the committee.

In 1967, the President's Commission on Law Enforcement and Administration of Justice published a report on organized crime, based chiefly upon FBI wiretaps. The report claimed that twenty-four cartels, consisting solely of Italian Americans, cooperated across the nation in the coordination of gambling, loansharking, and drugs. Combating this menace became a central focus of law enforcement. The U.S. Justice Department established Organized Crime Task Forces in many cities where Italian Americans were active in criminal activities. States and cities cooperated. The news media reported the investigations in detail, while novels and movies such as *The Godfather* (1972) provided the public with vivid and exaggerated images of the power of such men. The focus of federal, state, and local prosecutions on Italian Americans, combined with media attention, increased the idea of the power of such groups, while obscuring and ignoring the complexity and diverse roots of criminal activities.

In the 1970s, with the launching of the "war on drugs," drug trafficking gradually began to supplant the "mafia" as the focus for law enforcement and media attention. It became clear that a so-called mafia could not explain the extensive drug trafficking that provided marijuana, LSD, cocaine, and heroin to a diversity of users. The term "organized crime" was extended to foreign drug "cartels" or to powerful and profitable domestic drug organizations. Again, the effect was to simplify a complex system but also to externalize America's drug problem by suggesting that powerful foreign organizations were at fault. More recently, the expansion of international banking and trade, combined with the management of the international economy by computers, has expanded the term "organized crime" to encompass money laundering, banking and credit card fraud, and other criminal activities embedded in the new economy. After the destruction of the World Trade Center buildings by Middle Eastern hijackers on 11 September 2001, terrorism was added to other transnational crimes as part of international "organized crime."

The term "organized crime," introduced in the 1920s, has been applied to a diversity of criminal activities, generally ethnically based. The effect has often been to simplify an understanding of complex and loosely coordinated activities, to suggest that the activities constitute a foreign danger to the United States, and to exaggerate the power of those engaged in the activities labeled "organized crime."

BIBLIOGRAPHY

Fox, Stephen. *Blood and Power: Organized Crime in Twentieth-Century America.* New York: Morrow, 1989.

Haller, Mark H. "Ethnic Crime: The Organized Underworld of Early Twentieth-Century Chicago." In *Ethnic Chicago: A Multicultural Portrait.* Edited by Melvin G. Holli and Peter d'A. Jones. Chapter 19. Rev. ed. Grand Rapids, Mich.: W. B. Eerdmans Publishing, 1984.

————. "Bootleggers as Businessmen: From City Slums to City Builders." In *Law, Alcohol, and Order: Perspectives on National Prohibition.* Chapter 9. Westport, Conn.: Greenwood Press, 1985.

Lacey, Robert. *Little Man: Meyer Lansky and the Gangster Life.* New York: Century, 1991.

Reuter, Peter. *Disorganized Crime: The Economics of the Visible Hand.* Cambridge, Mass.: MIT Press, 1984.

Mark Haller

See also **Bootlegging; Drug Trafficking, Illegal; Organized Crime Control Act; Tweed Ring.**

CRIME OF 1873

CRIME OF 1873 refers to the omission of the standard silver dollar from the coinage law of 12 February 1873. The sixty-seven sections of the law constituted a virtual codification of the then extant laws relating to the mints and coinage. Section seventeen of the act provided that "no coins, either gold, silver or minor coinage shall hereafter be issued from the mint other than of the denominations, standards, and weights herein set forth." Section fifteen listed the denominations of silver coins the mint would issue, but did not list the standard silver dollar. The omission of the silver dollar from this list became, for more than two decades after 1876, the Crime of 1873.

The movement for the free coinage of silver began about 1876, when decreased use of silver as a monetary metal and increased production caused the price of silver to decline. The leaders of the movement defended the bimetallic standard and charged that the demonetization of silver was the result of a conspiracy entered into by British and American financial interests to secure in a surreptitious manner the adoption of the gold standard in the United States. The "silverites" clung tenaciously to the plot theory in spite of the fact that the act of 1873 was simply a legal recognition of the existing fact that the silver dollar had not been in circulation for decades. In addition, the act had been considered in five sessions of Congress and discussed frequently by Treasury officials. Nevertheless, for two decades millions of people thought that a crime had been committed and voted their convictions at every opportunity.

BIBLIOGRAPHY

Nugent, Walter T. *Money and American Society, 1865–1880.* New York: Free Press, 1968.

Riter, Gretchen. *Goldbugs and Greenbacks: The Antimonopoly Tradition and the Politics of Finance in America.* New York: Cambridge University Press, 1997.

Weinstein, Allen. *Prelude to Populism: Origins of the Silver Issue, 1867–1878.* New Haven, Conn.: Yale University Press, 1970.

George L. Anderson/ c. p.

See also **Bimetallism;** *Coin's Financial School;* **Free Silver; Money; Populism; Silver Legislation; Trade Dollar.**

CRIPPLE CREEK MINING BOOM

CRIPPLE CREEK MINING BOOM began in the early 1890s southwest of Pikes Peak in COLORADO, on a former cattle ranch. Robert Womack, a cowboy who prospected occasionally, discovered a promising vein of gold in January 1891. Spring brought many PROSPECTORS. On 4 July, W. S. Stratton staked the Independence claim that was to bring him wealth and preeminence as a mine operator. The gap between the mines' wealthy investors and its poorly paid miners, along with an influx of new workers in 1893, led to serious strikes in 1894 and 1904. The district's gold output reached $50 million in 1900 and thereafter declined. The Cripple Creek mines closed in the early 1960s.

BIBLIOGRAPHY

Neuschatz, Michael. *The Golden Sword: The Coming of Capitalism to the Colorado Mining Frontier.* New York: Greenwood Press, 1986.

Rodman, Paul W. *Mining Frontiers of the Far West, 1848–1880.* New York: Holt, Rinehart and Winston, 1963.

LeRoy R. Hafen/ f. b.

See also **Boomtowns; Gold Mines and Mining; Mining Towns.**

CRIPPLE CREEK STRIKES

CRIPPLE CREEK STRIKES. The mine workers of Cripple Creek, Colo., went on strike in August 1893 to prevent the lengthening of their working day. Their success led to a period of rapid unionization of miners and organization of mine operators. The miners went on strike again in January 1894 and, despite some violence, won a substantial victory. A subsequent period of peace ended with the strike of 1903–1904. The strike was a sympathetic one, designed to force the reduction-mill operators in Colorado City to consent to unionization of their employees. The mine owners defeated the well-organized, well-financed, and politically powerful unions. The strike is remembered for the loss of life, destruction of property, abuse of state militia power, and the practical elimination of unions in the mining district.

BIBLIOGRAPHY

Dubofsky, Melvyn. *We Shall Be All: A History of the Industrial Workers of the World.* Chicago: Quadrangle Books, 1969.

Langdon, Emma Florence. *The Cripple Creek Strike: A History of Industrial Wars in Colorado.* New York: Arno Press, 1969. The original edition was published Denver, Colo.: Great Western Publishing, 1904–1905.

Rastall, Benjamin McKie. *The Labor History of the Cripple Creek District.* Madison: University of Wisconsin, 1908.

George L. Anderson / C. P.

See also **Coal Mining and Organized Labor; Colorado; Colorado Coal Strikes; Strikes; Western Federation of Miners.**

CRITTENDEN COMPROMISE, the most promising of several attempts to resolve issues dividing the North and the South following Abraham Lincoln's election as president in November 1860. The Kentucky senator John J. Crittenden presented his compromise in the U.S. Senate on 18 December 1860 as a comprehensive package of six unchangeable constitutional amendments and four congressional resolutions. He introduced it on 22 December to a special Senate Committee of Thirteen on the sectional crisis, of which he was a member. Crittenden's first amendment proposed settling the territorial dispute by extending the Missouri Compromise line of 36 degrees 30 minutes across the remaining U.S. territory, applying it to land "hereafter acquired," and requiring that the U.S. government guarantee slavery in territory below the line. Other amendments addressed southern grievances by, among other things, restricting the ability of Congress to interfere with slavery in the District of Columbia or on federal property (for example, forts) within the slave states, requiring congressional compensation to slave owners encountering interference when trying to recover escaped slaves, and precluding amendment of the Constitution's three-fifths clause. The more sectionally balanced resolutions included a call for Congress to alter provisions in the 1850 Fugitive Slave Act deemed offensive by northerners.

The plan generated substantial public enthusiasm, especially in mid-Atlantic cities and the border slave states. But unanimous Republican opposition blocked the measure in committee and doomed it when on 2 March 1861 it came up for a belated vote in the full Senate. Republicans, many of them taking their cue from Lincoln, objected especially to the hereafter clause, fearing it might prompt southern initiatives to gain tropical lands for slavery's expansion, and the requirement that U.S. authorities actively protect slavery below 36 degrees 30 minutes.

BIBLIOGRAPHY

Knupfer, Peter B. *The Union as It Is: Constitutional Unionism and Sectional Compromise, 1787–1861.* Chapel Hill: University of North Carolina Press, 1991.

Potter, David M. *Lincoln and His Party in the Secession Crisis.* New Haven, Conn.: Yale University Press, 1942.

Robert E. May

See also **Antislavery; Missouri Compromise; Slavery.**

CROATIA. *See* **Yugoslavia, Relations with.**

"CROSS OF GOLD" SPEECH. William Jennings Bryan delivered his powerful words, "You shall not press down upon the brow of labor this crown of thorns, you shall not crucify mankind upon a cross of gold," on 8 July 1896 at the Democratic National Convention in Chicago. His pro-agrarian rhetoric appealed to the free-silver delegates from primarily rural areas, which suffered after the panic of 1893. Bryan, a Nebraskan, castigated the moneyed interests who espoused a single gold standard, which helped trade but harmed the lower classes. His carefully planned performance secured Bryan the nomination of both the Democrats and the Populists in 1896, but the Republican candidate William McKinley subsequently defeated Bryan.

BIBLIOGRAPHY

Cherny, Robert W. *A Righteous Cause: The Life of William Jennings Bryan.* Norman: University of Oklahoma Press, 1994.

Itai Sneh

See also **Free Silver; Gold Democrats; Gold Standard; Populism; Silver Democrats.**

William Jennings Bryan. The three-time Democratic candidate for president *(center)*, whose first nomination followed his electrifying speech at the 1896 convention. LIBRARY OF CONGRESS

Crow Drummer. Crows often helped the U.S. military against the Lakota and other tribes that had moved into Crow territory in Montana and Wyoming. DEPARTMENT OF ANTHROPOLOGY, SMITHSONIAN INSTITUTION

CROW.

The Crow Indians of Montana call themselves *Apsáalooke*, or "Children of the Large-Beaked Bird." This term was erroneously translated as "Crow" by early European traders and has since been their English name. The ancestors of the Crows were affiliated with the Hidatsa of the upper Missouri River. In the late 1400s they migrated westward, coming to control southeastern Montana and northeastern Wyoming. Historically, the Crows were nomadic hunters and warriors who lived in tipis, traveled in search of game, primarily buffalo, and fought intertribal battles over honors and horses.

The Crows were divided into three political bands: the Mountain Crows, who lived along the Yellowstone River; the River Crows, who occupied the territory north of the Yellowstone River; and the Kicked in the Bellies, who moved about the Bighorn Basin of Wyoming.

By the 1700s the Crows were important middlemen in an intertribal trade network. To the east they traded horses and products of the hunt with the Hidatsa and Mandan for agricultural goods and European trade items, especially the gun. To the west they traded with the Shoshones and Nez Perce for horses, decorative shells, and edible roots.

In the mid-1800s, other native groups, especially the Lakotas and their allies, had moved into Crow territory. In response, the Crows often assisted the U.S. military against a common enemy and to maintain control of their land. With the Fort Laramie Treaty of 1868, the Crows gradually came under the control of the federal government.

Their present reservation is a mere 2.2 million acres, compared to the 38 million acres they once controlled. In 2000 their population was slightly more then 10,000 individuals, with most living on or near the reservation. Contemporary Crow people have accepted some Euro-American practices and beliefs, but they continue to utilize their native language and culture.

BIBLIOGRAPHY

Frey, Rodney. *The World of the Crow Indians: As Driftwood Lodges.* Norman: University of Oklahoma Press, 1987.

Hoxie, Frederick E. *Parading Through History: The Making of the Crow Nation in America, 1805–1935.* New York: Cambridge University Press, 1995.

Lowie, Robert Harry. *The Crow Indians.* Lincoln: University of Nebraska Press, 1983.

McCleary, Timothy P. *The Stars We Know: Crow Indian Astronomy and Lifeways.* Prospect Heights, Ill.: Waveland Press, 1997.

Medicine Crow, Joseph. *From the Heart of the Crow Country: The Crow Indians' Own Stories.* New York: Orion Books, 1992.

Timothy P. McCleary

See also **Laramie, Fort, Treaty of; Tribes: Great Plains;** *and* vol. 9: **Fort Laramie Treaty of 1851.**

CROWN HEIGHTS RIOTS.

Despite living side by side, Hasidic Jews, African Americans, and people from the Caribbean in Crown Heights, Brooklyn, New York, rarely socialized before 1991. The groups occupied separate cultural worlds, and a climate of mutual suspicion and tension prevailed. On 19 August 1991, after a Jewish driver tragically killed a young black child, Gavin Cato, anti-Semitic violence erupted, and African Americans attacked Jews, Jewish property, and city police. Later that evening a mob of about fifteen African Americans shouting "Kill the Jew" attacked Yankel Rosenbaum, a native of Australia. Bearded and wearing a yarmulke, Rosenbaum was beaten and stabbed, but before he bled to death he identified his assassin as sixteen-year-old Lemrick Nelson. Three more days of rioting ensued.

Nelson was acquitted of murder in a state court in 1992, and he later celebrated his acquittal with some of the jurors. In 1994 the federal government charged Nelson and Charles Price, who was accused of inciting the attack, with violating Rosenbaum's civil rights. Convicted as an adult, an unrepentant Nelson received 235 months in prison, while Price received 260 months. New York City then settled a lawsuit by several Crown Heights residents for $1.1 million.

The official state report on the riots criticized New York City Mayor David Dinkins for his inaction during the riots; Dinkins later lost his 1993 reelection bid to Rudolph Giuliani. Community leaders, a community mediation center, and numerous community groups subsequently sponsored integrated activities in efforts to reduce cultural divisions in Crown Heights.

BIBLIOGRAPHY

Conaway, Carol B. "Crown Heights: Politics and Press Coverage of the Race War That Wasn't." *Polity* 32 (Fall 1999): 93–118.

Loewenstein, Andrea Freud. "Confronting Stereotypes: *Maus* in Crown Heights." *College English* 60 (April 1998): 396–420.

Paul J. Wilson

See also **New York City; Race Relations; Riots.**

CRYPTOLOGY, the technology of making and breaking codes and ciphers, has furnished America with excellent protection for its transmitted documents and with its best intelligence.

Revolution to World War I

James Lovell, a member of the Continental Congress who may be considered America's first cryptanalyst, solved British cryptograms for the rebels. One of them enabled Washington to alert the French admiral Comte de Grasse to blockade Yorktown, which then surrendered. Edgar Allan Poe popularized cryptology in 1843 with his story "The Gold Bug." During the Civil War, the Union utilized a word-transposition cipher; the South, a letter-substitution. The State Department printed its first cable code in 1867. In 1878, the *New York Tribune* solved and published encrypted telegrams showing that Democrats had bought electoral votes for Samuel J. Tilden in 1876. Though the Republican candidate, Rutherford B. Hayes, had nevertheless won the presidency, the disclosures helped lead to Republican gains in the midterm elections and to a Republican president, James A. Garfield, in 1880.

Code Breaking

Though some army officers investigated cryptology, the United States had no official cryptanalytic bureau until World War I. U.S. involvement in the war came about in part through codebreaking: Britain had cryptanalyzed a German offer to Mexico to make joint war on the United States; five weeks after newspapers headlined this, Congress declared war on Germany. In the spring of 1917, the Army's Military Intelligence Section established a codebreaking agency, called MI-8, placing a charismatic former State Department code clerk, Herbert O. Yardley, in charge. One of its solutions convicted a German spy. The American Expeditionary Forces had its own code-breaking unit, G.2 A.6, to solve German front-line codes, and its own Code Compilation Section, which printed and distributed new codes every few weeks. In 1919, MI-8 evolved into the joint Army-State Cipher Bureau under Yardley. During the Washington naval disarmament conference of 1921–1922, it solved Japanese diplomatic messages that helped America compel Tokyo to accept the equivalent of a battleship-and-a-half less than it wanted. America, Japan, and other nations saved millions that would otherwise have been spent on warships.

In 1929, Secretary of State Henry L. Stimson withdrew the Bureau's funds, on the ground that "gentlemen do not read each other's mail." Yardley, jobless in the Depression, awoke America to the importance of cryptology in his best-selling *The American Black Chamber* (1931). His bureau's work was assumed by the army's tiny Signal Intelligence Service (SIS) under the brilliant cryptologist William F. Friedman. During World War I, Friedman, at the Riverbank Laboratories, a think tank near Chicago, had broken new paths for cryptanalysis; soon after he joined the War Department as a civilian employee in 1921, he reconstructed the locations and starting positions of the rotors in a cipher machine. His work placed the United States at the forefront of world cryptology. Beginning in 1931, he expanded the SIS, hiring mathematicians first. By 1940, a team under the cryptanalyst Frank B. Rowlett had reconstructed the chief Japanese diplomatic cipher machine, which the Americans called purple. These solutions could not prevent Pearl Harbor because no messages saying anything like "We will attack Pearl Harbor" were ever transmitted; the Japanese diplomats themselves were not told of the attack. Later in the war, however, the solutions of the radiograms of the Japanese ambassador in Berlin, enciphered in purple, provided the Allies with what Army Chief of Staff General George C. Marshall called "our main basis of information regarding Hitler's intentions in Europe." One revealed details of Hitler's Atlantic Wall defenses.

The U.S. Navy's OP-20-G, established in 1924 under Lieutenant Laurence F. Safford, solved Japanese naval codes. This work flowered when the solutions of its branch in Hawaii made possible the American victory at Midway in 1942, the midair shootdown of Admiral Isoroku Yamamoto in 1943, and the sinking of Japanese freighters throughout the Pacific war, strangling Japan. Its headquarters in Washington cooperated with the British code breaking agency, the Government Code and Cypher School, at Bletchley Park, northwest of London, to solve U-boat messages encrypted in the Enigma rotor cipher machine. This enabled Allied convoys to dodge wolf packs and so help win the Battle of the Atlantic. Teams of American cryptanalysts and tabulating machine engineers went to the British agency to cooperate in solving German Enigma and other cipher systems, shortening the land war in Europe. No other source of information—not spies, aerial photographs, or prisoner interrogations—provided such trustworthy, high-level, voluminous, detailed, and prompt intelligence as code breaking.

At the San Francisco conference of 1945, which created the United Nations, the United States used information from code breaking to get its way on important matters, such as its desire, despite French opposition, for

467

a veto procedure in the Security Council. In the 1940s, the United States began solving Soviet spy messages. Disclosed in 1995, these solutions, codenamed venona, showed that the Soviet Union had conducted massive espionage in America, including espionage related to nuclear armament.

Code Making

Dramatic though code breaking is, more important than getting other people's secrets is keeping one's own. America has excelled in this as well. The first law specifying the duties of the Post Office, 20 February 1792 made it a crime for its employees to open mail, thus protecting privacy before European countries did. Thomas Jefferson invented an ingenious cipher system but filed and forgot it; the U.S. Army adopted an independent invention of it in 1922 that was used until World War II. In 1917, an engineer at the American Telephone & Telegraph Company, Gilbert S. Vernam, devised the first online cipher machine. Based on a teletypewriter, it electromechanically added the on-off impulses of the plain-text message to those of a key tape and transmitted the resultant ciphertext. This mechanism, the first binary device in cryptology, was perfected by Major Joseph O. Mauborgne, who, by making the key tape random and prohibiting more than a single use of it, created the only theoretically unbreakable cipher, the one-time tape. Also in 1917, an amateur inventor, Edward H. Hebern of California, devised the first rotor cipher machine before three Europeans independently had the same idea. In the 1930s, Rowlett and Friedman irregularized the turning of rotors. Their cipher machine, the sigaba, armored U.S. Army and Navy communications against the technology of the time; none of its messages were broken by Axis powers. During World War II, Navajos in the Marine Corps translated English-language orders into their language for walkie-talkie transmission; the Japanese never understood them. In 1943, AT&T engineers built a radiotelephone scrambler, sigsaly, that used a one-time key and proved invulnerable to German eavesdropping. Another AT&T employee, Claude E. Shannon, the conceiver of information theory, provided cryptology with a theoretical underpinning in his article "Communication Theory of Secrecy Systems," published in 1949.

In 1976, the National Institute of Standards and Technology promulgated a Data Encryption Standard so computers could intercommunicate securely; it was replaced on 26 May 2002 by the Advanced Encryption Standard. Also in 1976, an electrical engineering student, Whitfield Diffie, aided by Professor Martin Hellman, both of Stanford University, devised the most important advance in cryptography since the invention of cryptography itself: public-key cryptography. This permitted people to communicate in secret without prearrangement and ultimately opened the way to online ELECTRONIC COMMERCE.

BIBLIOGRAPHY

Alvarez, David. *Secret Messages: Codebreaking and American Diplomacy, 1930–1945.* Lawrence: University Press of Kansas, 2000.

Haynes, John Earl, and Harvey Klehr. *VENONA: Decoding Soviet Espionage in America.* New Haven, Conn.: Yale University Press, 1999.

Kahn, David. *The Codebreakers: The Story of Secret Writing.* 2nd ed. New York: Scribner, 1996.

Rosenheim, Shawn James. *The Cryptographic Imagination: Secret Writing from Edgar Poe to the Internet.* Baltimore: Johns Hopkins University Press, 1997. A literary essay.

Rowlett, Frank B. *The Story of Magic: Memoirs of an American Cryptologic Pioneer.* Laguna Hills, Calif.: Aegean Park Press, 1998.

Schlesinger, Stephen. "Cryptanalysis for Peacetime: Codebreaking and the Birth and Structure of the United Nations." *Cryptologia* 19 (July 1995): 217–235.

David Kahn

See also **Intelligence, Military and Strategic.**

CRYSTAL PALACE EXHIBITION (1853), officially known as the Exhibition of the Industry of All Nations, was held in New York City in 1853. It was the first international exposition held in the United States. Inspired by and imitating London's Crystal Palace exhibition of 1851, a group of New York civic and business leaders, led by Horace Greeley, raised the necessary funds to stage the exhibition; to provide a place for the exhibition grounds, the city leased them Reservoir Square (now Bryant Park). The glass-and-iron structure that housed the exhibition became known as the "Crystal Palace." It was built in the form of a Greek cross and contained almost 250,000 square feet of floor space. Almost half of the 4,854 exhibitors came from twenty-three foreign nations. The opening, set for 1 May 1853, was delayed until 14 July because so many of the exhibits were not ready; many did not open until September. This "Iliad of the Nineteenth Century" cost $640,000 and despite popular interest in the exhibition incurred a deficit of $300,000. It closed on 1 December; efforts to revive it came to naught. The Crystal Palace was itself destroyed by fire on 5 October 1858.

BIBLIOGRAPHY

Findling, John E., ed. *Historical Dictionary of World's Fairs and Expositions, 1851–1988.* New York: Greenwood Press, 1990.

Frank Monaghan / c. w.

See also **World's Fairs.**

CUBA, RELATIONS WITH. As early as the late eighteenth century, the United States and Cuba became inextricably tied. When the Spanish Crown opened its empire to trade in 1778, American merchants made Ha-

Crystal Palace of New York. A depiction of the large glass-and-iron structure housing the first international exposition in the United States, 1853. LIBRARY OF CONGRESS

vana and other Cuban ports major places of business and continued doing so until near the end of Spanish rule.

U.S. Acquisition Efforts

In the mid-nineteenth century Americans focused their attention on Cuba. Cuba retained slavery, and its agro-export economy strongly resembled that of the American South. Discontented with Spanish rule, Cuban exiles in New York City, New Orleans, and other cities made speeches, published newspapers, and lobbied Congress for Cuba's annexation to the United States. Allied with sympathetic Americans—and especially southerners, who saw the acquisition of Cuba, as well as countries in Central America, as essential to the survival of slavery in the United States—the movement gained strength in the 1850s.

In response to the clamor the federal government tried to buy the island from the Spanish on several occasions. In 1848 President James Polk offered Madrid $100 million for it, but Spain immediately rejected the bid. After purchase attempts had failed some Americans planned to seize it. The most serious was General Narciso López, a Venezuelan-born adventurer who adopted Cuba as his homeland. In August 1851 he and five hundred men—including William Crittenden, son of President James Buchanan's attorney general—boarded ships for Cuba. The Spanish killed or executed the men, including Crittenden and López.

The United States continued its efforts to purchase Cuba in the 1850s. President Franklin Pierce instructed the U.S. minister to Spain, Pierre Soulé, to offer Madrid

$130 million for the island. When rebuffed, Soulé conducted talks with other American ministers, and they agreed in the Ostend Manifesto of 1854 that if Spain refused to sell the island, then the United States could justify seizing it. Although neither Washington nor Madrid officially recognized the statement, it sparked fierce debates. However, tensions subsided temporarily as attention was diverted to the American Civil War.

The Cuban Struggle for Independence

After the Civil War the United States faced a major crisis over Cuba. In October 1868 a group of Cubans declared independence and asked Washington to annex the island. However, U.S. leaders hesitated. For ten years the Cubans fought for independence. Much to their consternation, Washington officially supported continued Spanish rule, although it pressured Madrid to make reforms. In 1878 the insurrection ended when the Spanish implemented reforms, including the abolition of slavery and amnesty for the rebels.

A small minority of Cubans, including José Martí, refused to surrender. For nearly two decades he called for Cuban independence and the establishment of a democratic and egalitarian society through his writing and oratory. Finally, in 1895, Martí and General Máximo Gómez rallied Cubans and declared independence.

Most Americans enthusiastically supported the Cuban independence movement. American attention heightened as the fighting escalated, catching U.S. investors and businessmen between the warring factions. Additional problems evolved when the Spanish commander, General

469

Valeriano Weyler y Nicolau, began herding Cuban civilians into concentration camps. In response American journalists and their editors stirred up public anger against the Spanish.

In 1897 President William McKinley told Congress that the United States must avoid intervention if possible. However, Washington sent the USS *Maine* to Havana to protect American citizens. Tensions heightened in February 1898 with the publication by a New York City newspaper of a private letter in which Enrique Dupuy de Lôme, the Spanish minister to Washington, injudiciously called McKinley a weak leader. This insult infuriated Americans. Less than a week later, an explosion wracked the *Maine*. The ship sank quickly, sealing the fates of 260 American sailors.

The Spanish American War
With the general public clamoring for retribution, McKinley sent Madrid an ultimatum demanding significant concessions on Cuban policy. The Spanish refusal to meet all of McKinley's demands ended diplomatic efforts. Rebuffed, McKinley went to Congress and asked for a declaration of war. On 20 April Congress passed a four-part resolution supporting him. The fourth section, the Teller Amendment, was the most controversial because it rejected any American claim to Cuban territory. Congress formally declared war on 25 April.

Dubbed "a splendid little war" by future Secretary of State John Hay, the conflict went well for the United States. The war on land and sea ended quickly in July. U.S. troops and Cuban irregulars captured Santiago, and the U.S. Navy destroyed the Spanish fleet as it fled the area. U.S. troops also took Puerto Rico, losing only three men. On 12 August an armistice was signed. On 1 October Spanish and American diplomats went to the bargaining table in Paris. After more than two months of negotiations they signed a peace treaty on 10 December 1898 calling for the withdrawal of Spanish troops from Cuba and permitting U.S. occupation. In addition, the treaty ceded Guam, the Philippines, and Puerto Rico to the United States.

The Platt Amendment, Batista, and the Cuban Revolution
The fate of Cuba remained in limbo for several years until it was defined by U.S. policymakers in the Platt Amendment. Drafted in 1901, the amendment effectively gave the United States control over a nominally independent Cuba. It prohibited the Cuban government from entering into treaties with foreign nations that impaired Cuba's independence, provided for U.S. military bases on the island, and conceded Washington the right to intervene in Cuban affairs to preserve stability. For more than thirty years, the Platt Amendment remained in place.

During the era of the Platt Amendment the threat of intervention, and actual occupation from 1906 to 1909, kept Cuba's political parties from defying Washington. In

1933, however, President Franklin D. Roosevelt faced a major challenge when Cubans revolted against their authoritarian president Gerardo Machado. Following a short-lived democratic experiment, army sergeant Fulgencio Batista seized control. In 1934 Washington abrogated the Platt Amendment, passed favorable tariff concessions, and provided loans to the government. Batista and his cronies would rule for twenty years, providing the United States and its businessmen with a very favorable climate in Cuba.

Problems resurfaced in the early 1950s as Batista faced a determined enemy, Fidel Castro. As a young man in 1953, Castro led a failed attack on the Moncada Barracks in Santiago. Jailed for two years, he wrote a manifesto that outlined his desire to restore constitutional government and create a more egalitarian society. After his release he began a three-year guerrilla war. Over time he gained a strong following among those tired of Batista's corruption and of foreign control of the economy.

The administration of President Dwight D. Eisenhower apprehensively watched the revolution unfold, fearful of losing a strong anticommunist ally in Batista. As early as 1955, FBI director J. Edgar Hoover reported that Castro and his followers could threaten U.S. security. In October 1955 FBI agents arrested and interrogated Castro when he visited New Jersey. They ultimately released him, and he returned home to fight.

Early Deterioration of Relations and the Bay of Pigs
On 1 January 1959 Castro emerged victorious as Batista fled into exile. Castro immediately implemented controversial programs, including cutting the electric prices of the U.S.-dominated Cuban Electric Company. In March the Cuban government nationalized that American-owned subsidiary of the International Telephone and Telegraph Corporation. Finally, it promulgated the Agrarian Reform Law in May 1959, which expropriated estates larger than one thousand acres and distributed them to small private owners and cooperatives.

By early 1960 relations between Havana and Washington had deteriorated further. Castro increased his level of anti-Americanism, denouncing the use by Cuban exiles of Florida's airfields to drop propaganda and allegedly some bombs on Cuba. The gulf widened when in February, Castro welcomed the Soviet first deputy premier Anastas Mikoyan to open a trade exhibition in Havana. Soon after, the Cubans signed an agreement with Moscow to exchange sugar for industrial products.

The final break began in March 1960 when Eisenhower approved a plan, eventually code-named Project Zapata, that allowed the CIA to recruit and train Cuban exiles to overthrow Castro. As the Eisenhower administration prepared to leave office, the United States terminated diplomatic relations with Cuba on 3 January 1961.

President John F. Kennedy continued Eisenhower's policies. On the morning of 17 April 1961, Cuban exiles landed at Playa Girón, the Bay of Pigs. Problems immediately developed with the landing, and the expected arrival of internal Cuban dissidents to aid the invasion never developed. Instead, Castro's regular army routed the exiles. Kennedy ultimately admitted American complicity and negotiated the release of the captured men in exchange for American agricultural supplies.

In retaliation for the defeat in Cuba, Kennedy ordered Operation Mongoose, under which General Edward Lansdale headed a group that coordinated attacks on sugar mills, bridges, and oil refineries in Cuba. At the same time, it tried to assassinate Castro, planning at least eight different attempts between 1961 and 1965.

The Cuban Missile Crisis

President Kennedy and his brother, Attorney General Robert Kennedy, sought no accommodation or negotiation with Cuba, and in turn Castro adopted all measures necessary to protect his revolution. One of Castro's responses was to seek more Soviet assistance. In the summer of 1962 the Soviets began stationing missiles in Cuba. On 14 October, two U-2 reconnaissance planes on a routine mission photographed the missile sites. In response President Kennedy organized a group of his advisers into Ex-Comm (Executive Committee of the National Security Council) and asked for policy options. Former Secretary of State Dean Acheson and others recommended air strikes to destroy the missiles, while the Joint Chiefs of Staff pushed for a full-scale invasion of Cuba. Meanwhile, a group led by Robert Kennedy pressed for a naval blockade, or "quarantine," of Cuba.

After much argument, the president decided on a quarantine. Soon American ships were deployed around Cuba to stop approaching Soviet ships. Kennedy then took a dramatic step and made a national television address on 22 October denouncing the Soviets and calling for Soviet leader Nikita Khrushchev to remove the missiles.

In the end the Soviets chose a prudent course. On 26 October, Moscow proposed to remove the missiles in return for a U.S. promise not to invade Cuba. Khrushchev also asked for the elimination of U.S. Jupiter missiles in Turkey. After some tense moments Washington agreed. Soviet ships carrying more missiles to Cuba turned back on 28 October. Over Castro's vigorous objections, the Soviets removed the missiles already in Cuba. The Cuban Missile Crisis had taken the world closer to the point of nuclear conflict than at any other time during the Cold War.

The Johnson and Nixon Administrations

The preoccupation with Cuba continued into the administration of President Lyndon Johnson, which intervened in the Dominican Republic in 1965 to prevent another Cuba. Johnson's successor, Richard Nixon, had an even stronger preoccupation with Castro. When Nixon took office, he ordered the CIA to increase efforts to sabotage

Flight from Cuba. Refugees hoping to be accepted into the United States are transferred from the Coast Guard cutter *Baranof* to a U.S. Navy warship. AP/WIDE WORLD PHOTOS

Cuba and renewed attempts to organize anti-Castro elements.

In September 1970 a fresh crisis developed. Intelligence agents presented National Security Adviser Henry Kissinger with U-2 photographs showing construction of a submarine base at the harbor of Cienfuegos. Nixon moved prudently. Meeting privately with the Soviet ambassador Anatoly Dobrynin, Nixon emphasized that he viewed the base with great concern. Without consulting Castro, the Soviets responded that they would respect the 1962 agreement about offensive missiles. In early October Nixon sent a note to Dobrynin stating that the United States would not allow nuclear-missile-carrying submarines to station in Cuba. The Soviet submarines continued visiting the island, although no ballistic-missile-carrying vessels made port calls.

President Carter and a Failed Rapprochement

When President Jimmy Carter took over in 1977, he and his advisers tried altering U.S. policy toward Cuba. His secretary of state, Cyrus Vance, had convinced the president that the boycott in place since the early 1960s had been ineffective and that negotiation could prevent misunderstanding and confrontation. Once in office Carter moved quickly. Early in 1977 the administration removed most restrictions on travel to Cuba and suspended spy flights over Cuban territory. In May the two nations agreed to establish "interest sections" in third-party embassies in Washington and Havana.

The efforts at a rapprochement lasted only a short time. In February 1978 the Carter administration began complaining about the presence of Cuban troops in Africa. President Carter stated that the withdrawal of those forces from the region would be required before any normalization of relations between the United States and

Cuba. The reported discovery of a Soviet combat brigade in Cuba in 1979 set off another diplomatic controversy that increased Washington's focus on Cuban activities in Central America and the Caribbean. By 1980 the Carter administration had returned to the old policies of isolation and containment.

As relations chilled, Washington increasingly denounced Castro's human rights record. In response Castro suddenly invited Cuban Americans to Mariel to pick up their relatives. A mass exodus of 125,000 Cubans began. Painted into a corner, Carter accepted them at first but over time restricted the flow. In a final insult Castro emptied his jails and mental hospitals and put the people on ships bound for Florida. When U.S. officials discovered this, the Mariel boatlift ended.

The Perpetuation of Hard-Line U.S. Policies

During the administration of President Ronald Reagan, relations between the two countries remained tense. Cuban assistance to the Sandinistas and other revolutionary forces in Latin America ensured further distance. In 1983 Cuban workers fought U.S. troops on the island of Grenada. The virulently anticommunist Reagan and his advisers made no significant efforts to end the two-decade-long policy of embargo and isolation.

Despite the end of the Cold War, relations between the United States and Cuba remained uneasy into the 1990s, although Castro began making concessions. By 1992 he had withdrawn his troops from overseas, announced that Cuba would provide no additional assistance to revolutionary movements, and initiated some free market reforms. Nevertheless, the administration of President George H. W. Bush responded by signing the Cuban Democracy Act of 1992, strengthening the trade embargo and punishing companies investing in Cuba. This act required open elections, constitutional reforms, and free markets before improved relations could occur.

After his election President Bill Clinton perpetuated U.S. policy, following the precedents established by his eight predecessors. The result was more flight from the devastated Cuban economy, now in disarray without Soviet subsidies. Thousands of refugees, including Castro's daughter and granddaughter, fled the country. A crisis developed when Cubans began hijacking boats to flee, leading Castro to plan for allowing 35,000 refugees to leave. Clinton responded quickly and negotiated with Havana to increase legal immigration in return for Cuban prohibition on illegal immigrants. Washington also announced it would immediately return all future illegal refugees to Cuba.

Problems resurfaced in February 1996. A Cuban exile group, Brothers to the Rescue, flew over Havana and dropped propaganda leaflets. Ultimately, Cuban MIGs shot down two planes, killing four people. A political outcry arose. Secretary of State Madeleine Albright called the act cowardly, and Senator Jesse Helms (R-N.C.) and Representative Dan Burton (R-Ind.) pushed through a law allowing U.S. citizens to sue foreign businesses using confiscated Cuban lands and barred the easing of sanctions until democratic elections occurred.

Many complained that the Helms-Burton law made it easier for Castro to control dissent by allowing him to continue blaming the United States for his economic failures. Ultimately, the Clinton administration suspended parts of the act because the European Union complained that it violated rules of the World Trade Organization. By 1999 the Clinton administration had eased other restrictions by allowing more American flights to Cuba, permitting Cuban Americans to send a modest sum of $1,200 per year to their families in Cuba, and easing restrictions on the transfer of food and medicine through nongovernmental agencies. Still, the rhetoric remained strident. The Elían GONZÁLEZ episode in 2000, when fishermen rescued a Cuban boy at sea who had been attempting to escape the country with his mother, sparked an international confrontation. Cuban American relatives in Florida tried to prevent the boy's father in Cuba from gaining custody, but ultimately the Justice Department extracted him and returned him home. Relations appeared unlikely to thaw with the election of President George W. Bush because of the prominence of the Cuban American constituency in a state important to him and his brother, Florida Governor Jeb Bush.

BIBLIOGRAPHY

Benjamin, Jules R. *The United States and the Origins of the Cuban Revolution: An Empire of Liberty in an Age of National Liberation.* Princeton, N.J.: Princeton University Press, 1990.

Foner, Philip S. *The Spanish-Cuban-American War and the Birth of American Imperialism, 1895–1902.* New York: Monthly Review Press, 1972.

Gellman, Irwin. *Roosevelt and Batista: Good Neighbor Diplomacy in Cuba, 1933–1945.* Albuquerque: University of New Mexico Press, 1973.

Hernández, José M. *Cuba and the United States: Intervention and Militarism, 1868–1933.* Austin: University of Texas Press, 1993.

Morley, Morris H. *Imperial State and Revolution: The United States and Cuba, 1952–1986.* New York: Cambridge University Press, 1987.

Offner, John L. *An Unwanted War: The Diplomacy of the United States and Spain over Cuba, 1895–1898.* Chapel Hill: University of North Carolina Press, 1992.

Paterson, Thomas G. *Contesting Castro: The United States and the Triumph of the Cuban Revolution.* New York: Oxford University Press, 1994.

Pérez, Louis A., Jr. *Cuba under the Platt Amendment, 1902–1934.* Pittsburgh, Pa.: University of Pittsburgh Press, 1986.

———. *Cuba and the United States: Ties of Singular Intimacy.* 2d ed. Athens: University of Georgia Press, 1997.

———. *The War of 1898: The United States and Cuba in History and Historiography.* Chapel Hill: University of North Carolina Press, 1998.

Welch, Richard E., Jr. *Response to Revolution: The United States and the Cuban Revolution, 1959–1961.* Chapel Hill: University of North Carolina Press, 1985.

Kyle Longley

See also **Bay of Pigs Invasion; Central Intelligence Agency; Mariel Boatlift; Ostend Manifesto; Platt Amendment; Spanish-American War; Teller Amendment;** *and vol. 9:* **The Monroe Doctrine and the Roosevelt Corollary.**

CUBAN AMERICANS began forming communities in the United States in the late nineteenth century. In the 1860s, cigar manufacturers began moving their shops to Florida to avoid political turmoil in Cuba, and workers followed. Struggling to end Spanish colonialism in Cuba, political exiles organized clubs and expeditions. By 1870, more than 1,000 Cubans lived in Key West. Communities also emerged in New York City, Philadelphia, Boston, Tampa, Jacksonville, and New Orleans. Migration continued, responding largely to political and economic changes in Cuba. With the 1959 Cuban Revolution, migration increased dramatically, and was shaped by the Cold War. Cuba instituted socialist reforms, while the United States defined its refugee policy based on anticommunism. American welcomed Cubans as refugees fleeing communism.

Cubans came in three major "waves" of migration. From 1959 to 1962, more than 215,000 Cubans arrived. Hoping to overthrow Castro and return to Cuba, some 1,300 exiles, with support from the Central Intelligence Agency, invaded Cuba at the Bay of Pigs in 1961. The invasion failed. During the 1962 Cuban Missile Crisis, the United States pledged not to intervene militarily in Cuba in exchange for the Soviet removal of missiles there.

From 1965 to 1973 more than 300,000 Cubans arrived, as the U.S. and Cuban governments permitted those with relatives in the United States to come via an organized airlift. In 1980 migration was rapid, and less controlled. The Cuban government opened the port of Mariel, and Cuban Americans rushed there by boat to retrieve relatives and friends. Another 125,000 Cubans came. Between waves, close to 100,000 Cubans arrived through third countries or through the Florida Keys by boat.

Cuba's upper classes dominated the first wave and constituted a significant proportion of the second wave. Described as "golden exiles," the first arrivals were political and military supporters of the former dictator Fulgencio Batista, those most threatened by Cuba's redistribution policies, and professionals. Although the second wave was less homogenous, it was the third wave that more closely resembled Cuba's population. This migration was more socio-economically diverse and included a higher proportion of blacks and mulattoes. The migrants, however, were overwhelmingly male (70 percent), younger

Cuban Americans. In this 1997 photograph by Alan Diaz, a rally in Miami features crosses, representing loved ones who died in Cuba, and American and Cuban flags. AP/WIDE WORLD PHOTOS

by an average of about ten years, and included a significant number of gay men. The new arrivals were less welcome by the United States and the Cuban American community. Perceiving Cuba as dumping their "undesirables" in the United States, the U.S. media labeled them as "criminals." Yet authorities released half of the 1980 immigrants to sponsors in Miami. Of the others, held in military camps, an estimated 16 percent had been jailed in Cuba, some as convicted felons but many for participating in the black market or refusing military service.

U.S. government programs eased Cubans' settlement. The 1961 Cuban Refugee Program provided unprecedented and comprehensive assistance, with emergency relief checks, food distribution, medical care, education, job training, and loans. The 1966 Cuban Adjustment Act facilitated the transition from refugees to permanent residents by cutting red tape and allowing permanent residency regardless of how they had entered the country. With education and skills, as well as federal and private loans, early arrivals created an economic enclave in Miami that provided jobs to later arrivals. Cuban women entered the work force in much higher proportions than they had in Cuba. Their employment was facilitated by the enclave's garment industry jobs and by three-generation households, where grandmothers provided childcare. The resettlement program sought to disperse Cubans beyond Dade County, Florida, where the overwhelming majority lived. Communities emerged in Union City and West New York, New Jersey; New York City; and San Juan, Puerto Rico.

As more Cuban Americans became naturalized citizens and registered to vote, they became a force in Florida politics. By the mid-1980s, Cuban-born mayors represented Miami, Hialeah, West Miami, and several small municipalities in Dade County, and ten Cuban Americans served in the state legislature. In national politics, the Cuban American National Foundation, founded in 1981 and based in Washington, D.C., voiced anti-Castro views and sought to influence U.S. policy toward Cuba. During the 1970s activists, and especially the younger generation, challenged the vehemently anti-Castro stance that dominated the Cuban American community. As they advocated an open "dialogue" with the Cuban government, family visits, and the release of political prisoners, some in the Cuban American community responded with violence.

Cuban migration is still shaped by U.S.-Cuba relations. A 1984 agreement between the two governments stipulated the admission of up to 20,000 Cubans per year. Yet during the late 1980s and early 1990s, the United States admitted an average of just 2,500 per year. As pressures mounted, Cubans tried to reach U.S. shores. In 1994, American authorities intercepted 36,791 rafters. The exodus slowed when Cuba agreed to seize rafters, and the United States agreed to issue at least 20,000 immigrant visas per year. U.S. policies toward Cubans shifted. Rafters already in the United States were detained for more than eight months before being admitted. In 1995 U.S. policy became to return rafters to Cuba. Although Cubans would ostensibly be treated like other migrants, in reality political context still shaped U.S. responses. By the 2000 census, 1,242,685 Cuban Americans lived in the United States, constituting 3.5 percent of the Latino population. Most, 67 percent, lived in Florida, especially Miami, Hialeah, and Tampa.

BIBLIOGRAPHY

García, María Cristina. *Havana USA: Cuban Exiles and Cuban Americans in South Florida, 1959–1994.* Berkeley: University of California Press, 1996.

Herrera, Andrea O'Reilly, ed. *ReMembering Cuba: Legacy of a Diaspora.* Austin: University of Texas Press, 2001.

Portes, Alejandro and Alex Stepick. *City on the Edge: The Transformation of Miami.* Berkeley: University of California Press, 1993.

Carmen Teresa Whalen

See also **Bay of Pigs Invasion.**

CUBAN MISSILE CRISIS. Often regarded as the most dangerous crisis of the nuclear age, the Cuban missile crisis of October 1962 was a culmination of several Cold War tensions that had been building for some time. As a result of Cuban leader Fidel Castro's turn toward Soviet-style communism in the early 1960s and the failed U.S.-sponsored Bay of Pigs invasion of April 1961, U.S.-Cuban relations were openly hostile by 1962. In April and May 1962, the Soviet premier Nikita Khrushchev decided to deploy Soviet nuclear missiles in Cuba, just ninety miles from Florida. In an agreement with Castro, the weapons would be shipped and installed secretly, so that

when they were operational, the West would be presented with a fait accompli.

During August and September 1962, U.S. intelligence found evidence of increasing Soviet military aid arriving in Cuba, including advanced surface-to-air missile installations, IL-28 Beagle nuclear-capable bombers, and several thousand Soviet "technicians." Refugee reports also suggested that Soviet ballistic missiles were on the island. Although U.S. intelligence could not confirm these reports, critics of President John F. Kennedy's administration used them in political attacks during the lead-up to the November congressional elections. In response, in September, Kennedy publicly warned that if weapons designed for offensive use were detected in Cuba, "the gravest consequences would arise."

On 14 October, a U-2 aerial reconnaissance flight over Cuba returned photographs of long, canvas-covered objects. As American photo analysts pored over the photos during the next twenty-four hours and compared their findings to their catalogs of known Soviet weaponry, it became clear that the Soviets were installing medium-range ballistic missiles (MRBMs) and launch pads in Cuba, where they would be within easy striking distance of much of the mainland United States.

Having just dealt with the civil rights riots at the University of Mississippi, the Kennedy administration again found itself confronted with a crisis. The president was informed of the discovery on the morning of 16 October and immediately convened a White House meeting of his top national security advisers, a body that later became officially known as the Executive Committee of the National Security Council, or ExComm. Kennedy decided not to confront the Soviets until he and the ExComm could consider and prepare courses of action. During this series of top secret meetings, several courses of action were considered, ranging from direct military strikes on the missile sites, a full-scale invasion of Cuba, a quid pro quo removal of American Jupiter missiles in Turkey, and a blockade of the island. Acutely aware that miscalculation by either side could spark nuclear war, Kennedy settled upon a blockade of Cuba in tandem with an ultimatum to the Soviets to remove the missiles, both to be announced during a special national broadcast on television during the evening of 22 October. In that broadcast, Kennedy declared that a naval quarantine of Cuba would go into effect on the morning of 24 October and would not be lifted until all offensive weapons had been removed. He also announced that he had ordered increased surveillance of Cuba and, ominously, that he had directed the armed forces "to prepare for any eventualities."

On 24 October, as U.S. strategic nuclear forces were placed on DEFCON 2, the highest alert status below actual nuclear war, the world waited anxiously for the Soviet response to the quarantine. Despite some tense moments, the deadline ultimately passed without serious incident, as several Soviet-chartered ships either changed course or stopped short of the quarantine line. On 25 October, the

Cuban Missile Crisis. This U.S. aerial reconnaissance photograph shows launch pads and related equipment at the Mariel Port Facility in Cuba, 4 November 1962. © CORBIS

U.S. ambassador to the United Nations, Adlai E. Stevenson, famously confronted his Soviet counterpart, Valerian Zorin, with photographic evidence and said he would "wait until hell freezes over" for a Soviet explanation. At U.S. insistence, the Organization of the American States officially condemned the Soviet-Cuban action and thereby formalized Cuba's hemispheric isolation.

Over the next few days, U.S. intelligence reported that not only were the MRBMs nearing operational status, but there were also intermediate-range ballistic missiles (IRBMs) and tactical nuclear weapons on the island. While U.S. forces continued to mobilize, a series of letters between Kennedy and Khrushchev was supplemented by several secret unofficial channels, the most notable of which was Attorney General Robert F. Kennedy's secret meetings with Anatoly Dobrynin, the Soviet ambassador to the United States, and Georgi Bolshakov, the intelligence chief at the Soviet embassy.

On Saturday, 27 October, the crisis was at its peak. During the afternoon, reports came in of an American U-2 being shot down over Cuba by a surface-to-air missile. As tension mounted, the Joint Chiefs of Staff reported that they were ready to launch an invasion of Cuba within twenty-four hours. In communications on 27 and 28 October, Khrushchev formally capitulated by agreeing to dismantle the missiles and ship them back to the Soviet Union. In turn, Kennedy publicly announced that he had pledged to provide a noninvasion guarantee to Cuba conditional on the offensive weapons being removed and the implementation of effective international verification. Secretly, he also agreed to remove the American Jupiter missiles from Turkey.

Although the crisis had been largely defused peacefully, it was not over. Castro refused to allow UN inspectors onto Cuban sovereign territory, and Khrushchev ini-

tially refused to accept that the Soviet IL-28 Beagle bombers were offensive weapons. Intensive discussions through the United Nations finally led to Khrushchev agreeing on 20 November to remove the bombers in exchange for a lifting of the naval quarantine.

For many, the crisis demonstrated the dangers of the nuclear age. Subsequently, a telephone hotline was established linking the White House and the Kremlin and efforts were intensified to secure arms control agreements and détente.

BIBLIOGRAPHY

Fursenko, Aleksandr, and Timothy Naftali. *One Hell of a Gamble: Khrushchev, Castro, and Kennedy, 1958–1964.* New York: Norton, 1997.

Garthoff, Raymond L. *Reflections on the Cuban Missile Crisis.* Rev. ed. Washington, D.C.: Brookings Institution, 1989.

May, Ernest, and Philip Zelikow, eds. *The Kennedy Tapes: Inside the White House during the Cuban Missile Crisis.* Concise ed. New York, Norton, 2002.

David G. Coleman

See also **Bay of Pigs Invasion; Cold War; Russia, Relations with.**

CUBISM. The term "cubism" was first used by the French critic Louis Vauxcelles in his review of a 1908 exhibition of paintings by Georges Braque. Cubist artists abandoned academically correct representation, which approximated the actual appearance of objects. Instead, the Cubists represented objects from multiple points of view and forms were reduced to basic geometric configurations. In theory, the Cubists justified their experiments as a search to uncover the essential structure of an object and its relation to other parts of a composition. Cubist painters such as Pablo Picasso, Georges Braque, and Juan Gris were profoundly affected by the art of Paul Cézanne, who maintained that natural forms could be reduced to simple geometric figures such as the cube, the sphere, and the cylinder. The Cubists also admired the art of so-called primitive cultures such as those of Africa and Egypt. Cubism made a decisive break with the centuries-old Western tradition of illusionistic representation, and in so doing initiated a revolution in the visual arts that all subsequent painters dealt with in some way.

A few American painters were exposed to cubism early on—notably Max Weber, who worked in Paris from 1905 until 1909, when he returned to New York City. Weber certainly knew such cubist artists as Picasso and in New York City during the winter of 1910–1911 Weber adopted cubist theory to American subject matter in canvases such as his *Rush Hour, New York* (1915). Weber's urban subjects combine his interest in cubism with the Italian avant-garde futurist artists' concern for dynamic movement and nature in flux. Weber's interest in cubist-futurist experiments lasted only a few years, but had a profound impact on John Marin and Joseph Stella, both active in New York City. Marin's *The Woolworth Building* (1912) and Stella's *Brooklyn Bridge* (1917) illustrate how lessons from both the French and Italian avant-gardes could be used to express the hectic pace of big city America. Cubist painting in France after World War I was increasingly concerned with creating compositions from areas of flat, often bright colors. Artists such as Stuart Davis, who encountered cubism at the 1913 Armory Show, owed their subsequent highly individual development to their early study of cubist work.

Still other expatriate American artists such as Morgan Russell, Stanton MacDonald-Wright, and Patrick Henry Bruce formed a movement that they called synchronism, which combined cubist analysis of form with a colorful palette inspired by the work of contemporary French artists such as Robert Delaunay. By the mid-1920s, the importance of cubism for American artists was in decline, but the movement was the stepping-off point for the subsequent development of American abstract art.

BIBLIOGRAPHY

Golding, John. *Cubism: A History and an Analysis, 1907–1914.* London; Boston: Faber and Faber, 1988.

Rubin, William. *Picasso and Braque: Pioneering Cubism.* New York: Museum of Modern Art, 1989.

Victor Carlson

See also **Armory Show; Art: Painting.**

CULPEPER'S REBELLION (1677–1679). Beginning in 1677 the thinly populated county of Albemarle, claimed by both Virginia and Carolina and suffering drought and political fears of a coastal aristocracy, broke out in rebellion against the colonial government. Led by John Culpeper, who may have been the brother of Frances Culpeper Stephens Berkeley, wife of the Virginia governor, the rebels aimed to prevent the acting governor Thomas Miller and his hated deputy Thomas Eastchurch from collecting the tobacco duty, a financial burden the rebels believed prevented northern merchants from buying their crops. Seizing the men who supported the proprietors' government of Carolina, the rebels elected a rival assembly and chose a government with Culpeper as customs agent and John Jenkins as military general. This new government tried Miller for treasonous words in an obviously manipulated trial decided by a jury of known smugglers.

Putting down the rebellion was delayed by BACON'S REBELLION in Virginia, the Davis-Pate rebellion in Maryland, and the death of Eastchurch as he returned to Albemarle to restore order. After two years of rebel government Culpeper went to England to plead the rebels' case before the king and his council. But Miller, who had escaped custody, met Culpeper there and charged him with treason. With the support of the earl of Shaftesbury, a proprietor of Carolina, Culpeper was found not guilty of treason since he acted on the orders of a properly elected assembly, albeit a rebellious one. Problems in Albemarle County, particularly with Virginia's claims of authority, continued until 1689, when the governor of Albemarle was made a deputy of the Carolina governor. The rebellion was largely the fault of the proprietors, who had little control of the outlying counties and their administration and who were unwilling to draw royal attention to problems, fearing a quo warranto investigation by the Crown.

BIBLIOGRAPHY

Rankin, Hugh. *Upheaval in Albemarle: The Story of Culpeper's Rebellion, 1675–1689.* Raleigh, N.C.: Carolina Charter Tercentenary Commission, 1962.

———. *Rebel of Albemarle: The Story of George Durant.* Edited by Jack P. Hailman. Madison, Wis.: J. P. Hailman, 1981.

Margaret Sankey

See also **Albemarle Settlements; North Carolina; Tobacco Industry.**

CULTS. Scholars and religious leaders, as well as the public, often have debated the defining characteristics of religious groups known as cults. Many Christian leaders, disturbed by the increase in such groups, label almost all variations from mainstream religion as cults, contending that they have a disruptive effect on society and on their followers. Others divide religious movements into three categories: churches, sects, and cults. All agree that churches represent mainstream religious authority. Mainstream religious leaders disagree on the characteristics of sects and cults. Some contend that sects represent a variation of Western religions and that cults adopt belief systems from non-Western sources. Others argue that all religious movements, Western or non-Western, begin as cults and, as they grow in popularity and power, evolve into sects and, finally, churches. Using this second argument, one could identify the Seventh-Day Adventists, the Mormons, and the Christian Scientists as groups that successfully shed their cult status and acknowledge UTOPIAN COMMUNITIES like Oneida, Amana, New Harmony, and the Shakers as religious groups that failed to survive as churches. Basically, the categorization of religious alternatives as cults rests on the extent to which they challenge mainstream religious institutions.

Historically, the United States has seen a variety of religious movements. Since the earliest years of European colonization, tension has existed between members of churches and adherents of smaller and less empowered religious beliefs. The nation's ensurance of disestablishment (that the state would not designate a particular religious group as favored by civil authorities) and the FIRST AMENDMENT guarantee of religious freedom allowed a number of alternative religious groups to take root and flourish in the United States. Indeed, the same national guidelines that allowed nontraditional religious groups to establish themselves in the United States also created a climate favorable to religious expression and may account for the generally religious character of most Americans. Religious groups identified as cults proliferated during the twentieth century. Decline of religious authority, increase in contact between people of diverse backgrounds, and development of mass communication allowed cult leaders to gain personal followings through newspapers and other periodicals, radio, television, and computerized mailing lists. Cults appeared in all regions of the United States, often in areas receiving an influx of migrants. In the early 1900s the West Coast, a region experiencing massive immigration, became known for religious experimentation. Mainstream religious denominations were not well established there, and migrants formed groups with beliefs reflecting their new lives. Cults often arose from groups virtually excluded from mainstream denominations and even from society at large, such as people of color, women, the young, and the poor. Marginalized, they found strength through religious alternatives. Cults also appealed to people seeking to restore their physical and mental health, having found little hope from mainstream religion.

One of the first mass cults was Father Divine's Peace Mission Movement. An African American minister who taught the power of positive thinking and encouraged his disciples to recognize him as God, Father Divine built a national and international following beginning in the 1930s and lasting through the 1950s. Known for elaborate ceremonies that often consisted of extravagant banquets, he attracted much attention. Other African American religious leaders, such as Daddy Grace, founder of the United House of Prayer for All People, and Guy W. Ballard, leader of the I AM, came to national prominence during these same years.

Cults increased tremendously in the 1960s and 1970s. In this era of rebellion and reform, many people were inspired to question authority. A variety of faiths appeared, with Eastern mysticism gaining much popularity. Probably the most notable new group was the International Society for Krishna Consciousness (ISKCON), better known as the Hare Krishnas. A. C. Bhaktivedanta Swami Prabhupada had established the ISKCON in India and brought it to the United States in 1965, when he began proselytizing in New York City's Tompkins Square Park and attracted followers associated with the hippie movement. He opened a temple and commenced publication of *Back to Godhead*, devoted to yoga, meditation, and vegetarianism. A resurgence of interest in Christianity in the 1970s led to the Jesus People movement, which sponsored Bible studies and revivals. Several of its groups established communes. Out of this cult came the Family of Love, better known as the Children of God. A highly controversial group, the Children of God borrowed features from the Christian holiness movement. The cult was accused of recruiting by brainwashing and through a tech-

Charles Manson. His cultlike "family" of mostly female followers, inspired in part by messages perceived to be found in Beatles songs, killed seven people in two outbursts of violence in August 1969. All but one woman, the star prosecution witness, ended up serving life sentences in prison. AP/WIDE WORLD PHOTOS

nique known as flirty fishing, which involved securing converts through sexual favors.

Of all groups to gain prominence during this era, the Unification Church, founded by the Reverend Sun Myung Moon, proved the most controversial. Oriented toward fundamentalist Christianity and politically conservative, the Unification Church supervised the lives and activities of followers and focused on preparing the world for God's kingdom on earth. On joining the church, single members practiced celibacy and devoted themselves to missionary work. At the end of their initiation, church leaders paired members with suitable mates and married them in mass ceremonies. Throughout the 1970s and into the 1980s, the Unification Church recruited on college campuses and gained a foothold in publishing through ownership of the *Washington Times*, while building a large portfolio of business investments. Reverend Moon alarmed many members of mainstream churches through the authority he exerted and his claim of being the Lord of the Second Advent, a role analogous to Christ.

An anticult movement developed during this time, targeting so-called destructive cults. According to anticultists, destructive cults exhibited three characteristics: demand for unquestioning acceptance of a leader, recruitment through brainwashing, and maintenance of secrecy.

Anticultists received enormous attention in the mid-1960s with the publication of *The Kingdom of the Cults* by an Evangelical Christian author, Walter Martin. The book underwent thirty-six printings between 1965 and 1985 and was still in print in 2001. It heightened concerns about the possible use of brainwashing in cults.

The anticult movement developed methods of deprogramming, designed to reorient cult members toward mainstream spirituality, but in many ways the methods of deprogrammers resembled the tactics of the supposed programmers. In the 1970s there were frequent reports of families who hired deprogrammers to kidnap their children from a cult, take them to secluded places, and spend days, sometimes weeks, breaking down their acceptance of cult teachings.

The rise of the anticult movement in the United States led to tensions and sometimes even violence. One of the most alarming incidents occurred in Guyana, South America, where the San Francisco cult minister Jim Jones had relocated his Peoples Temple in the hope of establishing an interracial religious commune and farming cooperative. In November 1978, shortly after U.S. Congressman Leo Ryan and four members of his party were killed by Jones's cult members, Jones presided over a suicide ceremony in which his followers drank cyanide.

Academics who study groups targeted by anticultists prefer the term "new religious movement," to the term "cult" and criticize anticultists for jeopardizing religious freedom in the United States. They emphasize that destructive cults are rare, that few cult members are coerced into joining, and that most cult followers leave groups of their own accord.

Incidents at the close of the twentieth century again increased fears of cult activity. Concern over the dangers presented by cults that stockpiled arms achieved national prominence in 1993 when a clash occurred between federal authorities and the Branch Davidians, a Bible-based cult led by a former rock musician named David Koresh, who claimed to be a messiah. Another armed cult, the Church Universal and Triumphant, led by Elizabeth Clare Prophet, received attention for its activities and ownership of bomb shelters in Paradise Valley, Montana. The group's presence generated a great deal of hostility from the local population. In March 1997, members of the Heaven's Gate cult engaged in a mass suicide, believing their souls would enter higher beings in a spaceship traveling behind the comet Hale-Bopp. The group, led by Marshall Herff Applewhite, used the Internet to recruit members and supported itself by designing World Wide Web sites. Its use of contemporary technology led many anticultists to fear the potential reach of the Internet as the millennium approached, but nothing on the scale of the Heaven's Gate suicides occurred in the United States between 1997 and 2001.

BIBLIOGRAPHY

Bromley, David G., and Anson D. Shupe, Jr. *Strange Gods: The Great American Cult Scare.* Boston: Beacon Press, 1981.

Melton, J. Gordon. *Encyclopedic Handbook of Cults in America.* Rev. and updated ed. Religious Information Systems Series, vol. 7. New York: Garland, 1992.

Melton, J. Gordon, and Robert L. Moore. *The Cult Experience: Responding to the New Religious Pluralism.* New York: Pilgrim Press, 1982.

Washington, Joseph R., Jr. *Black Sects and Cults: The Power Axis in an Ethnic Ethic.* Garden City, N.Y.: Doubleday Anchor, 1973.

Jill Watts / F. B.

See also **African American Religions and Sects; Jonestown Massacre; Nativist Movements (American Indian Revival Movements); Religion and Religious Affiliation; Waco Siege.**

CULTURAL LITERACY refers to the concept that citizens in a democracy should possess a common body of knowledge that allows them to communicate effectively, govern themselves, and share in their society's rewards. E. D. Hirsch Jr., a literary scholar, popularized the term in the best-selling book *Cultural Literacy: What Every American Needs to Know* in 1987. He argued that to participate fully in society, a person needs more than basic literacy, that is, the ability to read and write. Hirsch opposed the long-accepted view of educator John Dewey, who argued for a child-centered pedagogy that stressed experiential learning. Rather, Hirsch maintained that early education should focus on content and that all students, not just a bright few, could achieve cultural literacy. Hirsch offered in his book 5,000 terms that he thought culturally literate Americans should recognize. The list included dates ("1776"), historical persons ("Brown, John"), titles of historic documents ("Letter from a Birmingham Jail"), figures of speech ("nose to the grindstone"), and terms from science ("DNA"). Hirsch maintained that American children had to inherit this cultural knowledge if they were to share in the intellectual and economic rewards of a complex civilization. The argument drew initial support from officials in President Ronald Reagan's administration, and educational policy-makers in the 1980s and 1990s increasingly supported uniform educational standards. Critics feared that Hirsch's cultural literacy list was simplistic, that it presumed a uniform Eurocentric culture, and that it failed to reflect the nation's diversity of race and ethnicity. Hirsch answered his critics and greatly expanded his list in *The Dictionary of Cultural Literacy*, published in 1988 and revised in 1993 and written with Joseph F. Kett and James Trefil. The book sold more than 1 million copies.

BIBLIOGRAPHY

Hirsch, E. D. Jr. *Cultural Literacy: What Every American Needs to Know.* Boston: Houghton Mifflin, 1987.

Moses, Wilson Jeremiah. *Afrotopia: The Roots of African American Popular History.* New York: Cambridge University Press, 1998.

James Kates / s. b.

See also **Curriculum; Education; Education, Department of.**

CUMBERLAND, ARMY OF THE,

originally the Army of the Ohio, commanded by Gen. D. C. Buell, but renamed when Gen. W. S. Rosecrans took command on 30 October 1862. Gen. George H. Thomas succeeded Rosecrans on 16 October 1863. Operating mainly in Kentucky, Tennessee, and Georgia, the Army of the Cumberland played an important part in the battles of Mill Springs, Shiloh, Perryville, Stone's River, Chickamauga, Chattanooga, Lookout Mountain, and Missionary Ridge, as well as in Gen. William Tecumseh Sherman's Atlanta campaign—in the latter numbering 60,773 men. It comprised regiments chiefly from Ohio, Indiana, Illinois, Michigan, Minnesota, and Wisconsin.

BIBLIOGRAPHY

McPherson, James. *Battle Cry of Freedom.* New York: Ballantine Books, 1989.

W. N. C. S. Carlton / c. w.

See also **Atlanta Campaign; Chickamauga, Battle of; Civil War; Lookout Mountain, Battle of; Shiloh, Battle of.**

CUMBERLAND GAP,

one of the clearest passes through the Cumberland Mountains in the Appalachian Range, lies where Kentucky, Tennessee, and Virginia meet. First used to connect the vast system of trails used by the Indians to the game-rich country of Kentucky, the pass became, by the nineteenth century, one of the most significant gateways for white hunters. Dr. Thomas Walker named the gap in 1750 when he and his party went through it while speculating for the Loyal Land Company. In 1775, Daniel Boone and his party marked out the WILDERNESS ROAD through the Gap to the Kentucky River for the Transylvania Company, which facilitated both settlers and commerce through the mountains.

Cumberland Gap was a strategic point during the CIVIL WAR. The Confederates occupied it very early, but retired in June 1862 to strengthen their hold on Chattanooga. Soon thereafter Gen. George W. Morgan, who had been trying to dislodge Gen. Kirby Smith, then in command there, fortified his position and from it distributed supplies to East Tennessee until after Smith's victory at Richmond on 30 August 1862, when the Confederates occupied the pass again. Gen. Braxton Bragg retreated through the defile after his defeat at Perryville in October 1862, but Union forces did not retake it until September 1863. They retained possession until the end of the war.

The Southern and the Louisville and Nashville Railroads reached the pass in 1889 and 1890, respectively, and today a major highway also uses the gateway.

BIBLIOGRAPHY

Chinn, George Morgan. *Kentucky Settlement and Statehood, 1750–1800.* Frankfort: Kentucky Historical Society, 1975.

Faragher, John Mack. *Daniel Boone: The Life and Legend of an American Pioneer.* New York: Holt, 1992.

Friend, Craig Thompson, ed. *The Buzzel about Kentuck: Settling the Promised Land.* Lexington: University Press of Kentucky, 1999.

Jonathan T. Dorris / h. s.

See also **Appalachia; Perryville, Battle of.**

CUMBERLAND RIVER,

which flows through southern Kentucky and northern Tennessee, was named by Dr. Thomas Walker in 1750. Near it, Walker's exploring party built the first-known cabin in Kentucky and spent the winter of 1750–51. The Wilderness Road crossed the river a short distance from Cumberland Gap, and many early adventurers and settlers in Kentucky and Tennessee followed the river to their destinations. Among the earliest were the Long Hunters (so called because they were absent from home for long periods) in 1769 and the settler parties of John Donelson and James Robertson in 1779 and 1780. In 1780, 300 bushels of corn grown at Boonesborough were shipped in pirogues via the Kentucky, Ohio, and Cumberland Rivers to the fort where Nashville now stands.

BIBLIOGRAPHY

Arnow, Harriette Louisa Simpson. *Seedtime on the Cumberland.* New York: McMillan, 1960.

McCague, James. *The Cumberland.* New York: Holt, Rinehart and Winston, 1973.

Jonathan T. Dorris / h. s.

See also **Land Companies; Wilderness Road.**

CUMBERLAND ROAD,

also known as the National Road, was the first national road in the United States. It had tremendous influence of the development of the Ohio River Valley and the NORTHWEST TERRITORY. Congress passed enabling acts in 1802 and 1803 before Ohio's admission into the Union that set aside 5 percent of the net proceeds of the public lands sold by Congress within Ohio for building a national road to and through the state of Ohio. In March 1806, Congress authorized the accumulated funds for the marketing and construction of a road from Cumberland, Maryland, through Wheeling, Virginia, to Ohio.

The construction of the road began in 1811, and by 1818 the U.S. mail was running over the 130 miles to

Wheeling, now in West Virginia. Immediately the popularity of the road was tremendous, and stagecoach, carriage, and livestock traffic proved that maintenance costs would be high. Congress soon voted money for repairs and, in March of 1825, appropriated funds for extending the road from Wheeling to Zanesville, Ohio, following the first road built in Ohio, Zane's Trace.

The road reached Columbus in 1833, but by this time, canals were eclipsing roads for federal interest and investment. The road reached its terminus in Vandalia, Illinois, through private aid, and control of the road was turned over to the states through which it passed.

BIBLIOGRAPHY

Ierley, Merritt. *Traveling the National Road: Across the Centuries on America's First Highway.* Woodstock, N.Y.: Overlook Press, 1990.

Jordon, Phillip Dillon. *The National Road.* Indianapolis, Ind.: Bobbs-Merrill Co., 1948.

Raitz, Karl B., ed. *The National Road.* Baltimore: Johns Hopkins University Press, 1996.

Francis Phelps Weisenburger / H. S.

See also **Ohio; Ohio River; Ohio Valley; Roads.**

CUMBERLAND SETTLEMENTS. The immense domain acquired from the CHEROKEE by the Transylvania Company in March 1775 by the Treaty of Sycamore Shoals covered lands on the CUMBERLAND RIVER and below. Until the state line between VIRGINIA and NORTH CAROLINA was extended in 1779–1780, the status of the country around French Lick was uncertain. Richard Henderson, leader of the Transylvania Company, engaged James Robertson to lead a party to French Lick, later the site of Nashborough (Nashville), to found a settlement. For himself, Henderson accepted appointment as one of North Carolina's commissioners to survey and mark the Virginia–North Carolina line westward. Robertson and a small party set out from Holston and Watauga on 6 February 1779 for French Lick, where they built cabins and planted corn to make bread for the main body of immigrants who were to arrive in the fall. The new residents settled in villages nestled around several crude forts. In April 1780, Henderson, who had finished his survey of the state line and concluded that the region was in North Carolina, organized a government in French Lick under articles drafted by him, known as the Cumberland Compact. This instrument embodied agreements between the Transylvania Company and the settlers respecting lands to be acquired from the company. The legislature of North Carolina, in 1783, declared the Transylvania purchase void but provided for Henderson and his associates a consolation grant of 200,000 acres of land on Clinch and Powell Rivers.

BIBLIOGRAPHY

Cayton, Andrew R. L. *The Frontier Republic: Ideology and Politics in the Ohio Country, 1780–1825* Kent, Ohio: Kent State University Press, 1986.

Nobles, Gregory H. "Breaking into the Backcountry: New Approaches to the Early American Frontier, 1750–1800." *William and Mary Quarterly* 46 (October 1989): 641–670.

Samuel C. Williams / A. R.

See also **Indian Treaties, Colonial; Land Companies; Land Grants: Overview.**

CUMMINGS V. MISSOURI, 4 Wallace 277 (1866). Acting against the interests of congressional Republicans, the U.S. Supreme Court invalidated a provision in the Missouri constitution of 1865 that required public and corporation officers, attorneys, teachers, and clergymen, as a qualification of entering the duties of their office, to take an oath that they had never given aid to the rebellious Confederate states or expressed sympathy with the secessionist cause. The requirement, ruled the Court, violated the federal constitutional prohibition of bills of attainder—legislative acts that allow an individual or group to be singled out and punished without a trial.

BIBLIOGRAPHY

Belz, Herman. *Abraham Lincoln, Constitutionalism, and Equal Rights in the Civil War Era.* New York: Fordham University Press, 1998.

Cox, LaWanda C. Fenlason, and John H. Cox, *Politics, Principle, and Prejudice, 1865–1866; Dilemma of Reconstruction America.* New York: Free Press of Glencoe, 1963.

P. Orman Ray
Andrew C. Rieser

See also **Ex Parte McCardle; Ironclad Oath; Loyalty Oaths.**

CURRENCY AND COINAGE. Until WORLD WAR II, coinage was thought to have played a great role in U.S. economic history through its relations to money supply and monetary policy. Colonial coin shortages, the uncertain coinage policies of the early nineteenth century, and the bimetallist controversies of the late nineteenth century are standard features of older histories. Studies in the last half of the twentieth century, however, made it apparent that coinage has been a rather passive institution in American affairs. The denominations, metallic content, and volume of U.S. coins have done little either to retard or to advance U.S. economic development. Apart from occasional financial crises, the coinage system has generally accomplished well enough what has been demanded of it.

In the colonial period, it is true, the lack of an adequate volume of coins was certainly irritating. Unlike the Spaniards, the English denied their American colonies the right to possess local mints. Massachusetts coined "pine tree shillings" from 1652 to 1684, but no other colony managed to strike more than a small number of coins. Colonists in less-prosperous areas used wampum, tobacco, beaver skins, and other forms of commodity money. Elsewhere the lack of an adequate amount of English specie was compensated by French, Dutch, Portuguese, and above all Spanish coins, all of which were allowed legal-tender privileges by the English authorities. For large transactions the colonists could use bills of credit and other forms of paper currency. One could even say that the English monopoly of coinage in colonial America proved a blessing in disguise, since when independence was won, none of the states possessed a vested interest in a state minting operation.

The term "dollar" has European origins. It comes from the English corruption of the German word "thaler," the term for the widely circulated silver coin from the Joachimsthal silver-mining center, which was located in what is now the Czech Republic. The English and their colonists applied the term indiscriminately to thalers, to French silver "dollars" (écus), and to the Spanish "pieces (pesos) of eight," or eight reals. In keeping accounts, colonists and colonial governments reckoned usually in pounds, shillings, and pence; but the most common coins were probably the real (nominally a sixpence, but usually rated at seven or eight pence) and the eight-real piece, or "dollar." Because the sixpence and the real carried the slang name "bit," the two-real piece, or quarter of a dollar, was sometimes called "two bits."

The present U.S. coinage system was established, at least in outline, by the Coinage Act of 2 April 1792. By this act the dollar was fixed at about the same weight of silver as the Spanish peso. In true Enlightenment fashion, and perhaps also as a symbol of independence from the European system of pounds, shillings, and pence in England and livres, sous, and deniers in France (signified by the symbols £, s., and d.), the American statesmen Robert Morris, Thomas Jefferson, and Alexander Hamilton decided on a decimal system of relations among the coins—the world's first. For accounting purposes they divided the dollar into one hundred "cents" (a new term) and also into half-dollars; quarter-dollars; "dismes," or dimes (the term, like "cent," shows the French influence); and half-dismes. The actual coins were to be of silver, except for the copper cents and half-dismes. In addition, gold coins would serve as multiples of the dollar, as in "eagles," or ten-dollar pieces; half-eagles; and quarter-eagles. But the gold-silver ratio that was chosen, 1 to 15, meant that a satisfactory bimetallic system was exceedingly difficult to maintain. At this rate, gold was heavily undervalued, and therefore it was either sent out of the country, hoarded, or consumed in industry. Not enough was brought to the new Philadelphia mint to satisfy the country's needs for large-denomination coins.

Silver available for coinage, too, was decidedly rare during the first half of the nineteenth century. The United States produced only a tiny trickle of precious metal; consequently, U.S. bullion supplies usually failed to meet transaction requirements. Hoping to encourage gold coinage, the government in 1834 changed the mint ratio to 1 to 16; thus, it was silver's turn to be undervalued. However, while the shortage of specie undoubtedly worsened the Panic of 1837, on the whole, it seems to have been more an annoyance than a severe impediment to the conduct of business. Foreign silver continued to fill the gap for both large and small denominations. The bountiful note issues of state banks took up the currency slack.

It was not until 1850 that the government decided to make improvements to its small change. By this time, the outpouring of California gold was driving up the price of silver so rapidly that there was a severe decline in the already insufficient amount of silver coinage. With some misgivings, Congress in 1851 authorized the first bullion (mixed silver and copper) coin, a three-cent piece. The coin was an immediate success, and few seemed bothered by its "subsidiary" character—that is, by the fact that there was slightly less than three cents' worth of silver and copper in the coin. Encouraged by the public's obvious willingness to accept slightly "debased" coins, in 1853 Congress ruled that all the other silver coins (except the dollar) also be turned into subsidiary coins. Almost overnight, the U.S. need for foreign coins vanished as the new pieces poured out of the mint. Since foreign coins were no longer needed, keeping accounts in pounds, shillings, and pence finally ended. This reform also virtually wiped out a thriving business in counterfeiting the small change.

In 1856 the United States made its first experiment with coinage made from nickel: the "flying eagle" one-cent piece. It was called a nickel until a five-cent piece of the same metal appeared ten years later, when the term was transferred to the coin of larger denomination. Meanwhile, the gold production of California and Australia made it easier to supply the country with coins of large denomination, including "double eagles" ($20). And the mints, with improved, more powerful machinery, were able to meet higher demands. By the beginning of the CIVIL WAR, therefore, the technical problems—if not the political and economic problems—of providing an expanding nation with a satisfactory coinage system had been solved. The government had gone a long way toward its goal of making as many transactions as possible based on specie or specie-backed paper currency. The war brought severe coinage shortages, gaps that had to be filled by "shinplasters" (fractional paper notes), but these substitutes were gradually driven out of circulation during the 1870s.

Coinage after the Civil War has little proper history of its own. As the use of notes increased, the volume of coinage, as a fraction of total paper and metal currency, shrank from about 50 percent in 1860 to about 15 percent in 1960. The many coinage "reforms" of the era reflected mainly the changing political fortunes of competing gold, silver, nickel, and copper interests or the support given to

Populist leaders, who believed that "free coinage" of silver would greatly augment the total money supply and would therefore hold up general prices and wages during severe depressions. The Bland-Allison Act of 1878, the Sherman Act of 1890, and the Silver Purchase Act of 1934 all attempted to force more silver into circulation by requiring the government to buy set amounts of silver each year and to strike at least some silver dollars from this bullion. Silver dollars had not been struck at all between 1806 and 1836 and only in small amounts until the 1870s. But they came to be struck again and in enormous volumes: $22.5 million in 1878 and $38 million in 1890.

Apart from some regions in the West, however, silver dollars never became popular and were regarded mainly as objects of only numismatic interest. Besides, in spite of being called standard money in law, silver dollars were just as much "token" or "fiduciary" coins as their fractions. In 1939, for example, the bullion value of a silver dollar was only thirty cents. A large fraction was not even circulated; it remained in bags in vaults and thus benefited no one but the silver-mine operators.

The lack of American concern over the silver content of coins was highlighted when, in 1964 and 1965, part-silver half-dollars, quarters, and dimes were withdrawn and replaced by nickel-clad copper coins. The Bank Holding Company Act Amendments of 1970 brought about the withdrawal of silver from the dollar and its replacement with copper and nickel alloy. This closing episode in the centuries-old drama of government-fiat coins versus "sound money" caused hardly a ripple.

The only coinage issue to spark extensive debate after 1970 was the introduction of a one-dollar coin. Because coins have a longer life span than paper currency, they require less-frequent replacement. Congress introduced one-dollar coins in 1979 with the Susan B. Anthony dollar and again in 2000, when the Sacagawea dollar entered circulation. Most Americans avoided Susan B. Anthony coins, however, finding them too similar in shape and appearance to quarters and preferring the ease of using paper dollars. Some experts feared the new Sacagawea dollar would suffer the same fate as the Susan B. Anthony dollar. By the end of 2001, however, the U.S. Mint reported that the Sacagawea dollar had gained popular support among Americans and that some 700 million of the coins were minted in its first year of circulation, seven times as many as initially projected.

BIBLIOGRAPHY

Carothers Neil. *Fractional Money: A History of the Small Coins and Fractional Paper Currency of the United States.* New York: Wiley, 1930.

Hepburn, A. Barton. *History of Coinage and Currency in the United States and the Perennial Contest for Sound Money.* New York: Macmillan, 1903.

Schwartz, Anna Jacobson. *Money in Historical Perspective.* Chicago: University of Chicago Press, 1987.

Schwarz, Ted. *A History of United States Coinage.* San Diego, Calif.: A. S. Barnes; London: Tantivy Press, 1980.

Wilson, Thomas F. *The Power "To Coin" Money: The Exercise of Monetary Powers by the Congress.* Armonk, N.Y.: M. E. Sharpe, 1992.

Martin Wolfe / A. R.

See also **Bimetallism; Cotton Money; Financial Panics; Free Silver; Gold Standard; Hard Money; Legal Tender; Mint, Federal; Mints, Private; Money; Pieces of Eight; Pine Tree Shilling; Specie Payments, Suspension and Resumption of; Tobacco as Money.**

CURRICULUM in most countries emanates from the national government, but in the United States control of public school curriculum resides with the states, and in practice much of the responsibility for developing curriculum is delegated to local school districts. In an official sense, then, in the United States it is not possible to speak of a national curriculum. If diversity with respect to what is taught is an obvious fact of life in American schools, however, it is possible to discern an American curriculum.

Perhaps the greatest influence on curriculum is a sense of what is appropriate to teach, which in the United States has traditionally been drawn from the Western intellectual tradition, which means such subjects as mathematics, history, English language and literature, and science. Such traditional subjects are often supplemented by subjects that reflect national concerns. For example, the United States is unique in including driver education in the high school curriculum. Other subjects that reflect national concerns, such as sexually transmitted diseases, race relations, alcoholism, drug abuse, and unwanted pregnancies, frequently find their way into the curriculum of U.S. schools. In fact, this sheer breadth of courses has often been a source of considerable controversy, with some critics charging that schools are undertaking responsibilities they cannot successfully address or are offering courses that in some sense intrude on the responsibilities of other social institutions such as the family.

A second major influence on the American curriculum has been the programs of the U.S. Department of Education, which usually originate in congressional legislation. Federal aid to education in the mid-1990s is about 10 percent of national public school costs, but the way in which such aid is distributed—with specific stipulations regarding how school systems can spend the money and frequent requirements that states match federal dollars, thus effectively multiplying the amount of money spent on federal programs—frequently has a large effect on the curriculum of schools. Perhaps the most visible example is the prominence of vocational education. Since passage of the SMITH-HUGHES ACT of 1917, the federal government has supported vocational education and home economics. In 1958 the National Defense Education Act provided millions of dollars for mathematics, science, and foreign languages. Although many of

The Mississippi in Time of Peace. A popular 1865 lithograph by Currier and Ives, the companion to the company's *The Mississippi in Time of War,* also from the year the Civil War came to an end.

the curriculum reform projects supported by that legislation achieved a certain measure of success, the effects on the American curriculum were not as long-lived as in the case of vocational education. Apart from these nationalizing tendencies, the curriculum is also subject to political influence in communities as well as state departments of education.

The 1960s saw a new wave of progressive education in the United States, and in general curricula opened in response to issues raised in the civil rights and women's movements. Then, in the 1970s, a "back to basics" movement gained momentum, with many states adopting minimum competency tests in reading, writing, and mathematics. These and other standardized tests gained increasing importance over the next three decades, spurred by the federal government's increased role in education, its attempts to gauge the success of its investment, and its goal of holding school systems accountable by requiring that they report scores publicly. In the mid-1980s, the issue of a shared national core curriculum became heated following the formation of the Core Knowledge Foundation by E. D. Hirsch, eventually leading the state governors to adopt, in 1988, the National Education Goals. Stressing math and science, Goals 2000 established shared standards in the different subject areas, provoking numerous controversies about what they should (and should not) include.

BIBLIOGRAPHY

Hirsch, E. D., Jr. *Cultural Literacy: What Every American Needs to Know.* Boston: Houghton Mifflin, 1987.

———. *The Schools We Need and Why We Don't Have Them.* New York: Doubleday, 1996.

Kliebard, Herbert M. *The Struggle for the American Curriculum, 1893–1958.* Boston: Routledge & Kegan Paul, 1987.

Marshall, J. Dan, James T. Sears, and William H. Schubert. *Turning Points in Curriculum: A Contemporary American Memoir.* Upper Saddle River, N.J.: Merrill, 2000.

Herbert M. Kliebard/c. w.

See also **Education; Education, Higher: Colleges and Universities; Multiculturalism; Pluralism.**

CURRIER AND IVES became America's most famous lithographers by perfecting the process of printing with treated stone in the mid-1800s. Currier and Ives prints, widely known and collected in their day, became the ideal art for a democracy, mass produced and affordable, but still of high quality. Over their many years in business Currier and Ives, and the many artists who worked for them, depicted both the mundane and the historic in over 7,000 different prints. Still reproduced today on calendars and cards, the prints have long represented an idealistic vision of the nineteenth century, with an emphasis on distinctly American scenes, both cultural and natural. While the firm produced lithographs of tragic current events, such as fires and war, collectors have paid more attention to their many sentimental representations of everyday life, such as sporting events and westward pioneering.

Nathaniel Currier began his printing career as an apprentice in Boston as a very young man. By 1835, having relocated to New York City, Currier had opened his own business, first in a Wall Street office and later moving to his famous Nassau Street shop. Currier's business included publishing, printing, and engravings, but by the time James M. Ives joined the firm in 1852 Currier had already established a reputation for his popular lithographs. Ives came to the firm first as a bookkeeper, but his responsibilities expanded and in 1857 his name was added to that of the firm. Nathaniel's brother Charles also worked with the firm, in an informal arrangement, and contributed to the business primarily through his invention of a new crayon used to treat the stones before printing.

Currier's first great success came with an 1840 print entitled, "Awful Conflagration of the Steam Boat 'Lexington' in Long Island Sound." This timely print was distributed with news of the tragic event, first in New York and then around the country. Its extremely wide distribution insured interest in future Currier works, and helped inaugurate a new era of pictorial journalism. "Rush stock" prints of newsworthy events became an important part of the business, but "stock prints," of city views, baseball games, horse racing, sailing ships, and home-life scenes, among many other everyday portraits, remained the primary topics of the lithographs. Numerous Currier and Ives prints depicted America's natural scenery, especially in tourist areas such as the White Mountains and the Catskills, providing remembrances for tourists or visual access for those who could not afford to travel. While Currier and Ives prints came in different sizes and carried different prices, the firm became most famous for its colored lithographs. Printed first, then hand colored by women working in the Currier and Ives factory, these prints became both beautiful and affordable popular art.

After Nathaniel Currier retired in 1880 his son Edward ran the firm with Ives. By 1907 both families were out of the business, which folded shortly thereafter. Although the lithographs never lost their appeal, and indeed gained in value after the firm closed, improvements in photography doomed lithography as the chief means of illustrating everyday life.

BIBLIOGRAPHY

Baragwanath, Albert K. *Currier and Ives*. New York: Abbeville Press, 1980.

Le Beau, Bryan F. *Currier and Ives: America Imagined*. Washington, D.C.: Smithsonian Institution Press, 2001.

David Stradling

See also **Printmaking.**

CUSHING'S TREATY (3 July 1844), also known as the Treaty of Wanghia, marked the opening of political relations between the United States and China and, through establishment of the most-favored-nation doctrine in matters of commerce, secured for Americans the trading privileges won by England as a result of the Opium War. It introduced the principle of extraterritoriality in the relations between China and the West. Provision was made that citizens of the United States accused of committing any crime in China should be tried only by their own consul under American law and that disputes between American citizens in China should be regulated by their own government.

BIBLIOGRAPHY

Cohen, Warren I. *America's Response to China: A History of Sino-American Relations*. 4th ed. New York: Columbia University Press, 2000.

Hunt, Michael H. *The Making of a Special Relationship: The United States and China to 1914*. New York: Columbia University Press, 1983.

Foster Rhea Dulles/A. G.

See also **China, Relations with; China Trade; Extraterritoriality, Right of; Treaties with Foreign Nations.**

CUSTER DIED FOR YOUR SINS appeared in 1969 with the subtitle *An Indian Manifesto*. On the one hand, it represented a continuation of Indian writing evaluating Indian-White relations going back at least to George Copway in the early nineteenth century. On the other hand, the book was the defining document marking the relationship of NATIVE AMERICANS to the CIVIL RIGHTS MOVEMENT. *Custer* was the first major publication of Vine Deloria Jr., the scion of a distinguished Sioux family that included his grandfather Philip, his father Vine Sr. and his aunt Ella. *Custer* and a series of later books that included *We Talk, You Listen: New Tribes, New Turf* (1970), *God Is Red* (1973), and *Behind the Trail of Broken Treaties: An Indian Declaration of Independence* (1974), defined Deloria as the most prominent Indian public intellectual of his time.

Custer argued fervently against the federal policy of termination, advocating self-determination and the upholding of treaties. The book exposed callousness and hypocrisy on the part of white specialists such as anthropologists, government bureaucrats and the missionaries who ministered to Indian people. *Custer* also argued that the agendas put forth by the African American leadership of the civil rights movement were not appropriate for Native Americans.

BIBLIOGRAPHY

Biolsi, Thomas, and Larry J. Zimmerman, eds. *Indians and Anthropologists: Vine Deloria Jr. and the Critique of Anthropology*. Tucson: University of Arizona Press, 1997.

Deloria, Vine, Jr. *Custer Died for Your Sins: An Indian Manifesto*. With a new preface by the author. Norman: University of Oklahoma Press, 1988.

Gary Bevington

See also Literature: Native American Literature; Race Relations.

CUSTOMS SERVICE, U.S.

From its inception on 31 July 1789 the Customs Service has been responsible for oversight of all imports into the country. It has always collected tariff revenues and is charged with preventing smuggling; at its inception it oversaw the Coast Guard and America's lighthouses. In the early nineteenth century for a time it was responsible as well for enforcing the 1807 embargo on Britain, and it administered immigration until well after the Civil War. In the twentieth century, Customs has at different times enforced Prohibition laws, been charged with interdiction of the illegal traffic in drugs, and prevented the importation of pornography. At its origin it generated 2 million dollars in annual revenue for the financially pressed new nation, an amount that would reach 18 billion dollars two centuries later.

The American Board of Customs Commissioners in the English Customs Service was actively involved in the American Revolution. In 1767 that American presence was introduced as part of the enforcement apparatus of the Townshend Acts. Unwelcome in Boston, the English and American customs officers were the chief victims of the Boston Tea Party in 1773. Customs confrontations with John Hancock in that port city resulted in the earliest organized American response that culminated in the American Revolution. By the mid-1770s, American customs inspectors under English oversight supervised America's ports, large and small, and usually sided with the revolutionaries. Weak central government in the 1780s left customs enforcement in the hands of the states, a situation that changed under the auspices of the Constitution. The newly constituted U.S. Customs Service was politicized from its inception. In the 1790s the Federalist Treasury secretary Alexander Hamilton made sure that most of the more than 500 customs officers he appointed to serve in all the Atlantic ports were Federalists, many of them veterans of the Continental Army as well.

The die was cast. For much of the nineteenth century the service was tied to whichever political party was in power. Inevitably, even as it continued to effectively enforce the tariff laws and collect huge amounts of revenue, its politicization opened the door to corruption. On the one hand, in the age of Andrew Jackson, it became the vehicle Jackson used to suppress South Carolina's nullification of the Tariff Act of 1828, forcing that state to comply with federal law in 1832. On the other hand, using Customs as a major source of time-honored patronage resulted in the first of many major scandals, this one in the New York customhouse. Successive collectors Samuel Swartout, in 1838, and Jesse Hoyt, in 1841, took their embezzled federal funds and fled to England to avoid prosecution. But even the patronage system that fed corruption in American ports had its silver lining. It provided safe havens with little work for major American writers like the historian George Bancroft and the novelists Herman Melville and Nathaniel Hawthorne, among many others. In the latter instance, one need only read the opening chapter ("The Custom House") of *The Scarlet Letter* to perceive the significant support role the Customs Service played in encouraging American belles lettres.

The Civil War was played out in microcosm in the Customs Service. Southern federal customs officers switched allegiances openly or in secret. In border states and captured Southern ports chaos reigned as federal employees followed their political bents. Treasury Secretary Howell Cobb dispatched Charles Cooper, his top Customs investigator, to sort out the personnel in these ports, only to learn a year later that Cooper was doing the same thing for the Confederacy as its chief Customs investigator. The war did not stem the flow of graft.

The most striking fact of the Gilded Age in terms of the service was that the New York Customs collector Chester A. Arthur became president of the United States in 1881. As Chet Arthur the spoilsman he seemed not to have been on the take, but he did not do much either to prevent other customs officers from accepting bribes. As president, though, Arthur's intimate knowledge of corruption caused him to champion civil service reform. Because his efforts were met with a stone wall of opposition, he was not really successful, but his exposure of the Customs Service to public scrutiny did some cosmetic good and opened the door to real change two decades later. When another New Yorker, Theodore Roosevelt, succeeded to the presidency after the assassination of William McKinley in 1901, real Progressive Era civil service reform followed, particularly in the Customs Service.

So the twentieth century ushered in a dramatically improved U.S. Customs Service. Its revenue collection shot upward, its responsibilities increased, and it grew from 8,800 employees in the 1880s to 20,000 in 2002. Customs handled espionage scares and terrorist activity in World War I; it enforced Prohibition (with little thanks from anyone) in the 1920s and early 1930s; it expanded its oversight to airports as well as seaports in the years just before and after World War II; and it dealt with artistic fraud from overseas sources with increasing sophistication as the century progressed.

Most importantly, as drug traffic increased after the 1950s and involved smuggling from every corner of the world (Mexico, Colombia, the Bahamas, Thailand, and Afghanistan, to name only the most prominent sources), the Customs Service has taken major responsibility to interdict the flow. It has had only indifferent success. The problem remains larger than the mechanisms of enforcement can cope with. Search and seizure laws, as always, must correctly be tempered by the limits imposed by the Constitution and Bill of Rights. Customs rectitude of a much higher order in the twentieth century than the nineteenth notwithstanding, the government has had to expand its enforcement efforts beyond the Customs Service to include the Drug Enforcement Agency and the appointment of a cabinet-level "drug czar" who is not part of Customs. The United States Customs Service nevertheless remains central to federal government operations, carrying out its traditional and ongoing responsibilities to enforce tariff and trade laws, collect the revenue, and prevent more traditional kinds of smuggling.

BIBLIOGRAPHY

Prince, Carl E., and Mollie Keller. *The U.S. Customs Service: A Bicentennial History.* Washington D.C.: U.S. Government Printing Office, 1989.

Carl E. Prince

See also **Boston Tea Party; Drug Trafficking, Illegal; Townshend Acts.**

CYBERNETICS.

In a groundbreaking book in 1948 the mathematician Norbert Wiener described cybernetics as "the science of control and communication in the animal and the machine." Wiener derived the term from the Greek word *kybernetes* (steersman). Wiener became interested in the topic of cybernetics during WORLD WAR II while working with a colleague, Julian Bigelow, on improving the accuracy of a radar-guided antiaircraft gun. For several years, cybernetics greatly influenced research on ARTIFICIAL INTELLIGENCE. Cybernetics centers on feedback mechanisms, or methods by which information on the state of an organism or machine is fed back into the organism or machine in order to direct further changes. A biological example of feedback is the way in which warm-blooded animals automatically regulate their temperatures, keeping them within a narrow range of acceptable values by using a variety of mechanisms that lose or retain heat.

By the early 2000s, cybernetics—often known as systems science—comprised a wide range of interdisciplinary research interests and applied sciences that extended well beyond Wiener's original scope of inquiry, encompassing research in such varied realms as neural networks, chaos theory, artificial intelligence, dynamical systems, and the study of other complex, adaptive systems. The field gained its unity by emphasizing the connectedness and interactions of the diverse parts of a system, in contrast to the more traditional analytic approach that focused on comprehending systems by breaking them down into their component parts.

BIBLIOGRAPHY

Wiener, Norbert. *Cybernetics: or, Control and Communication in the Animal and the Machine.* 2nd ed. Cambridge, Mass.: M.I.T. Press, 1961.

———. *The Human Use of Human Beings: Cybernetics and Society.* New York: Avon Books, 1967. The original edition was published Boston: Houghton Mifflin, 1950.

Vincent Kiernan / c. w.

See also **Automation.**

CYBORGS.

A cybernetic organism, or cyborg, is the melding of man and machine and ranges in scope from creating computers that have human attributes, such as independent thinking or the ability to learn, to the artificial heart, pacemaker, and a variety of synthetic implants. Cyborg advocates hypothesize that in the future mankind will use science and technology to transform into a virtually immortal being—still human, but with machine parts that perfect natural organs, muscle fiber, and bone.

In modern society, cyborgs have taken on a new meaning, particularly as computers have become more powerful and ubiquitous. While religious and ethical questions about cyborgs remain, people no longer fear machines that outthink, outperform, and are physically more powerful than humans. Science fiction, movies, and television shows portraying the cyborg-driven future have not only dispelled fear, but actually set expectations for further advances in providing computers with human attributes and vice versa for the betterment of both.

Since machines, such as pacemakers and kidney dialysis units, keep people alive, many argue that the world is already a cyborg community. Given the pace of technological development, there is little doubt that the human/cyborg melding will proceed.

BIBLIOGRAPHY

Gray, Chris Hables, ed. *The Cyborg Handbook.* New York: Routledge, 1996.

———. *Cyborg Citizen: Politics in the Posthuman Age.* New York: Routledge, 2001.

Messina, Lynn, ed. *Biotechnology.* New York: H.W. Wilson, 2000.

Rorvik, David M. *As Man Becomes Machine: The Evolution of the Cyborg.* Garden City, New York: Doubleday, 1971.

Bob Batchelor

See also **Computers and Computer Industry; Transplants and Organ Donation.**

CYCLOTRON,

a machine for accelerating charged nuclear particles, commonly protons, so that they may be used to probe the nuclei of target atoms. Such "atom smashers" are considered the microscopes of nuclear physics.

In the nineteenth century, some physicists still labored under the theory—really, the dream of alchemists for centuries—that elements could be made to transmute into other elements through chemical processes. In 1902, Ernest Rutherford and Frederick Soddy explained the new phenomenon of radioactivity as a "transformation" of one element into another, occurring spontaneously in nature; and in 1919, Rutherford succeeded in deliberately causing transmutations by bombarding light elements with the alpha particles emitted from naturally decaying radioelements. Since very few of the projectile alpha particles collided with nuclei of the target atoms, the number of

Cyclotron. Nobel Prize winner Ernest O. Lawrence leans against an "atom smasher." © CORBIS

transmutations was relatively small. Therefore, scientists sought new ways to increase the number of projectile particles and to accelerate them to higher energies. The copious production of charged particles was the easier task; the high-voltage engineering required for acceleration proved far more difficult.

Scientists tried a number of different approaches to the acceleration problem, including a voltage multiplier circuit (Sir John Douglas Cockcroft and Ernest Walton) and an electrostatic generator (Robert J. Van de Graaff), both linear accelerators. In 1930, University of California at Berkeley physicist Ernest O. Lawrence, with the help of one of his students, M. Stanley Livingston, designed and constructed the first of many magnetic resonance accelerators. Lawrence's accelerator operated at voltages much lower than other machines, yet imparted as much or more energy to its projectiles. Lawrence won the 1939 Nobel Prize for Physics for his work on the cyclotron. During WORLD WAR II he headed a unit of the MANHATTAN PROJECT that worked to perfect the process of separating uranium-235 for the atomic bomb.

These cyclotrons, destined to be the chief tool of nuclear physics, worked on the principle that charged particles, accelerated across a voltage gap, travel in a circular path under the influence of a magnetic field. If confined to a hollow disk-shaped chamber built in two D-shaped halves (called "D's") and if subjected to a radio-frequency voltage alternation as the particle passes from one half to the other, the particle receives two accelerations per cycle and travels at higher velocities in ever-larger circles. The beam of rapidly moving particles may then be deflected onto a target, producing observable nuclear reactions.

The D's of Lawrence's first cyclotron were only about 4 inches in diameter. Subsequent models of 9, 11, 27, 37, and 60 inches followed, with a new model built almost every other year. These larger machines surpassed an early goal of one million electron volts projectile energy; many different types of atoms were split; and scores of new radioisotopes were identified, including the first transuranium elements.

Higher energies, suitable for the production of mesons, were impossible with the fixed-frequency cyclotrons, because the projectiles would experience a relativistic mass increase at the required velocities, destroying the resonant operating condition. After World War II scientists overcame this handicap with a new generation of accelerators that use a variable-frequency voltage alternation that exactly balances the mass-velocity change. The synchrocyclotron was the largest machine to use a single magnet.

This postwar synchrocyclotron became the foundation for a government-funded national accelerator. Work on a four-mile-long circular machine in Weston, Illinois, thirty miles west of Chicago, was completed in 1971. Project leader Robert O. Wilson envisioned a series of magnets to boost particle speeds, and he insisted on allowing for space in the tunnel of the main ring for the addition of a second magnet system. When the main ring was about to operate in 1971 he described his idea of a "doubler" that would take the protons from the magnetic ring and inject them into a new ring of super-conducting magnets and double their energy. Physicists working at the laboratory, which in 1974 was named the Fermi National Laboratory for physicist Enrico Fermi, solved the technical problems of building the doubler. The principal Fermilab accelerator subsequently became known as the Tevatron (one TeV is a trillion electron volts). In 1994 the Tevatron revealed the existence of the so-called top quark, the last of twelve subatomic building blocks of all matter.

BIBLIOGRAPHY

Livingston, Milton Stanley. *Particle Accelerators: A Brief History.* Cambridge, Mass.: Harvard University Press, 1969.

Mladenovic, Milorad. *The Defining Years in Nuclear Physics, 1932–1960s.* Bristol, Pa.: Institute of Physics, 1998.

Riordan, Michael. *The Hunting of the Quark: A True Story of Modern Physics.* New York: Simon and Schuster, 1987.

Wilson, Robert R., and Raphael Littauer. *Accelerators: Machines of Nuclear Physics.* Garden City, N.Y.: Anchor Books, 1960.

Lawrence Badash / A. R.

See also **Physics: Overview; Physics: High-Energy Physics; Physics: Nuclear Physics; Superconducting Super Collider.**

DAGUERREOTYPE. *See* **Art: Photography; Photographic Industry.**

DAIRY INDUSTRY. In the early seventeenth century, the first English and Dutch colonists brought cattle with them. Despite the rigors of the environment, cattle proliferated in all the settled areas. Although shelter and feed were in short supply and native grasses were not satisfactory for haymaking, pasture was usually adequate through the summer months. Settlers initially substituted wild marsh hay, straw, and corn fodder for winter feed but later brought over from Europe better pasture grasses and tame hays. The cattle came primarily from England and Holland. There were no specific dairy breeds, and the unimproved stock soon lost weight and shape through poor management and interbreeding. Only in New England, where animals grazed under the care of a town cowherd, was there much supervision. There the townspeople even exercised some control over breeding through communal choice of sires. Elsewhere the cattle, usually identified through earmarks or brands, mostly fended for themselves. Almost every farm and most town households kept one or two cows. Women and children customarily milked the animals, except in winter when the cows dried up. They also manufactured the butter and cheese. Before 1700 some producers regularly exported dairy goods from New England.

By the mid-eighteenth century some areas, such as the Narragansett district, the lower Hudson Valley, and the counties around Philadelphia, had earned reputations for producing prime butter or cheese. Exports had stimulated better management even before the American Revolution, at which time dairies of a dozen or more cows were no longer uncommon. Between 1790 and 1805, cheese exports exceeded one million pounds annually, and by 1812, New York butter wagons regularly traveled as far south as Charleston, South Carolina. In the early 1820s, some Ohio cultivators were peddling cheese and butter in small towns along the Ohio River from Wheeling to Louisville. The dairy, nevertheless, remained a seasonal and a household undertaking, a by-product of "general" farming, until the mid-nineteenth century.

Commercial growth was rapid from the late 1820s. In 1840 dairy manufactures, valued at $33.8 million, took place in all thirty states. New York (31 percent), Pennsylvania (9.4 percent), and Massachusetts (7.1 percent) were the largest producers, but relative to population, Vermont and New Hampshire were the most specialized. Outside the northeastern United States, only Ohio and Virginia were large producers. By 1860 American butter output had greatly increased, notably in Vermont, New York, Pennsylvania, and Ohio, and Illinois was a sizable newcomer to the industry. Cheese output, heavily concentrated in Vermont, New York, and Ohio, lagged after 1850. New York produced a quarter of the nation's butter and almost half the cheese in 1860. It also contributed the greater part of cheese exports, which had doubled between 1845 and 1850 to about 15 percent of the national output.

New York remained the heart of "America's dairyland" until Wisconsin displaced it in the opening decades of the twentieth century. For all the increased output, dairying only became a specialty in areas in which declining grain yields and western competition had undermined the economic basis of the wheat culture. Generally, farmers resisted the more exacting routine of a balanced dairy husbandry, and developments after 1840 brought little improvement in farm management, except as more grass and livestock arrested the depletion of the soil. Although Yankee dairy pundits had long recognized Ayrshires and Jerseys to be superior milkers, most herds were still made up of "native" or "scrub" cattle, the progeny of innumerable crosses upon the old colonial stock. Lewis F. Allen's first *American Herd Book* (1846) registered Shorthorns, and even in the late 1950s, Charles L. Flint of Massachusetts attributed increases in milk yields to better buildings and more ample feed, not to "improvements in the dairy quality of the stock."

Meanwhile, the perishable nature of milk had limited the city milk trade, the most profitable branch of dairying. City dwellers could get good, bad, and indifferent butter or cheese at corresponding prices, but fresh milk from farm-fed cattle was only available locally in season. Most big-city milk supplies were watered, adulterated, expensive, and more lethal than city water. In spite of the exposés of reformers, beginning with those of Robert M. Hartley in New York City after 1838, many city herds still ate brewery swill and distillery mash in the 1850s. Between 1856 and 1861, Massachusetts outlawed adulteration and slop feeding and instituted nominal inspection. New York and five other states followed suit in the decade after 1862, but until local milk trains, put into operation around Boston and New York City in the early 1840s, had supplanted barges, wagons, and slop-milk systems, little progress could occur.

Gail Borden began to make patented condensed milk in 1859, and within a few years, the unsweetened variety constituted a third of New York City's milk supply. In 1870 Xerxes A. Willard of the American Dairyman's Association hailed it as the solution to New York City's milk problem. Condenseries offered a powerful price incentive for pure milk deliveries, but federal hygiene reports traced 325 outbreaks of typhoid, diphtheria, and scarlet fever to contaminated milk between 1865 and 1895. Dr. Harvey D. Thatcher's sanitary dairy bottle, patented in 1884, and Dr. Henry L. Coit's medically "certified milk," introduced in 1894, eased the problem, but the real solution, pasteurization, was a product of the laboratory, not of technology or regulation.

Demonstrated by a New York philanthropist, Nathan Strauss, in 1893, pasteurized milk became mandatory in a few cities before World War I. Because of opposition from milk producers and sections of the medical profession, the requirement was perfunctory before the 1920s, by which time milk from tuberculin-tested herds was also coming on the market. Finally, between 1924 and 1927, the U.S. Public Health Service developed a model uniform sanitary regulation for voluntary adoption by state and municipal authorities.

A more radical change in the dairy industry began with the shift from farm to factory cheesemaking. Whereas buttermaking was simply a mechanical process of churning gravity-separated cream, cheese-making was a complex chemical process involving precise coagulation, working, and curing of curd into digestible cheese. Few men or women were masters of the art, which explained the unreliability of much farm cheese. The factory enabled expert cheesemakers to process milk gathered from numerous herds into a superior standard article. The factory system of cheese-making, inaugurated by Jesse Williams of Oneida County, N.Y., in 1851, spread during the Civil War decade. Annual output soared to 172 million pounds by 1880, the most notable increase coming in Wisconsin, which already ranked third after New York and Ohio. By 1876 exports of cheddar-type American cheese regularly absorbed half the nation's greatly expanded output. Under leadership of the Wisconsin Dairyman's Association and William D. Hoard, publisher of *Hoard's Dairyman*, the most prestigious dairy trade paper, Wisconsin became the banner cheese state by 1905 with 1,518 factories.

No such rapid revolution occurred in buttermaking. In 1861 Alanson Slaughter of Orange County, New York, established the first butter factory, or "creamery," but farm production of butter increased until about 1900. Creamery output, notably in Iowa, Illinois, Wisconsin,

and Pennsylvania, did not accelerate before the 1880s, when over 3,000 refrigerator cars were already in service between Chicago and eastern terminals. The premium in buttermaking was on scale rather than skill, and both the relative simplicity and the size of creamery operations fostered mechanization and cooperative enterprise. In 1878 Dr. Carl G. DeLaval of Sweden patented a continuous centrifugal cream separator, which proved much more efficient than gravity methods. Furthermore, after 1885 he also marketed small hand separators for use on farms, where the farmer could feed skim milk to hogs. Since most farmers were slow to appreciate the feed value of whey, butter dairying in conjunction with corn-hog raising gained a financial edge over cheese. Nevertheless, it was cheese factory patronage or nothing in the northern areas, where cool summers and a short growing season limited the corn crop in the days before silage and hybrid corn. The early dairy plants were mostly private ventures or partnerships. Many were "mutual benefit associations," some were Granger-type cooperatives, and a few were corporations. Cooperative ownership was common around 1900 in the newer creamery districts of Wisconsin, Iowa, and Minnesota, and cooperatives increased in number and shares of output thereafter. By 1944, however, cheese cooperatives were down a third from the late 1920s, and their output share had fallen from 32 to 16 percent. There were still 1,164 butter cooperatives in 1944: more than twice the number making cheese and five times the number processing evaporated and dried milk.

All dairy producers benefited from a cheap, practical butterfat test perfected by the Wisconsin chemist Stephen M. Babcock in 1890. The test measured the fat content of milk and furnished a more objective and equitable basis for payments to farmers by processing plants and city dealers. Babcock and his associates also did the basic research on milk enzymes that culminated after 1903 in the more efficient "cold curing" of cheese. These laboratory triumphs, combined with the growth of domestic cheese consumption, helped dairying recover from the loss of the British market that had followed the export of much substandard "skim" and "filled" cheese. Export volume fell by 75 percent between 1881 and 1896. States appointed dairy and food commissions to police the industry, and the promotional energies of dairy producers' associations shifted to lobbying actions to secure tariff protection (1894) and curbs and taxes on oleomargarine. After 1886 federal laws prevented mislabeled or inferior oleo from inundating butter markets, but more wholesome vegetable oleo subsequently made steady inroads on butter sales. By 1950, when Congress repealed the discriminatory Oleomargarine Act of 1902, margarine output was rapidly overtaking that of butter.

Advances in dairy husbandry began in the 1880s with the practice of feeding the animals ensilage, such as unripened corn, clover, and alfalfa. Farmers preserved the green feed in closed pits or tower structures called silos. Silage feeding lengthened the milking season up to 10 weeks, which allowed manufacturing plants to stay open throughout the year. Adaptation of German scientific feeding principles resulted in a balanced dairy ration that combined the nutritive components of various feeds in the proportions required by a cow's flow of milk. The Babcock test helped farmers cull their low-fat producers. Beginning with the rivalries of breed associations in the 1880s, emphasis shifted to raising milk output through official cow testing, extension activity on the part of the agricultural colleges, cooperative herd improvement associations, and disease-eradication and sire-proving programs. Purebred Holstein-Friesians, Jerseys, Guernseys, Ayrshires, Brown Swiss, and, from the 1930s, Red Danish all proved to be excellent dairy cattle, while the dual-purpose breeds, such as Devons, Shorthorns, and Red Polls, lost ground on specialized dairy farms. These farms adopted milking machines in the 1920s and installed cooling equipment later.

Average annual yield per cow climbed from 3,050 pounds of milk in 1890 to 4,508 in 1950, 9,609 in 1970, and 18,204 in 2000. The greatest relative increases occurred on farms with fifty or more cows in new dairy states, such as Florida, Arizona, and California. In 1993 California replaced Wisconsin as the nation's top dairy state and currently produces one-third more milk annually than Wisconsin does. The number of milk cows reached 25.8 million in 1944 but fell to 12.4 million by 1970 and to 9.2 million by 2000. Between 1950 and 1970, the numbers of farms reporting milk cows fell by 80 percent, and thousands of small dairy farmers went out of business. This trend has continued into the twenty-first century as large-scale producers replace small, family-run operations. Nevertheless, milk products, worth more than $21 billion in 2000, were second only to sales of cattle and calves in cash value to American farmers, and that income included the culling of some dairy cattle. In 1997 the dairy was the largest single source of farm income in six states and second largest in five others.

Small-scale dairy manufacturing also went into eclipse. When insulated cars and trucks led to much larger milksheds at processing plants, high-volume plants began to achieve the substantially lower unit costs hitherto enjoyed only by condenseries and "centralizer" creameries. As average size of output increased, however, the number of plants declined, especially since the 1930s. By 1945 over 100 large "flexible" plants already made multiple products, most frequently evaporated milk, butter, and cheese, as cost and price relationships changed.

Concentration in marketing agencies complemented structural changes in farming and manufacture. The mid-nineteenth-century method of consigning products to distant wholesalers on a commission basis gave way to price bargaining on local product exchanges. After 1900 producers grew suspicious of the auction prices and weekly quotations announced by regional boards of trade or call-boards, such as those in Elgin, Illinois, and Plymouth, Wisconsin, which provided the basis for contracts be-

Milk. A capped bottle, c. 1920, not long before pasteurized—and safe—milk began to be common. LIBRARY OF CONGRESS

tween buyers and sellers. Some producers formed marketing cooperatives. Distribution channels narrowed in the 1920s when packinghouses such as Armour and Swift and huge corporations such as Borden and National Dairy Products increased their purchases and began to absorb the functions and profit margins of independent dealers, jobbers, and brokers. About 1930 grocery chains such as the Atlantic and Pacific Tea Company and Safeway still bought from independents, although, for a period, some chains had tried manufacture on their own account. The nationally advertised brands and packaged items of Fairmont and Beatrice creameries and the Kraft and Phoenix ("processed") cheese companies became part of the cultural environment.

Producers still complained about middlemen's profits, and many still thought that cooperatives were the way to eliminate intermediaries. These cooperatives took on a greater role in distribution and price bargaining. Sales of four of the largest cooperatives, Land O' Lakes, Dairymen's League, Challenge, and Pure Milk Association, increased 162 percent between 1931 and 1949, but the incentives to large-scale concentration affected cooperatives no less than corporations. From 1950 to 1968, their numbers fell by 43 percent to 1,100. By 1970 there were only 971 dairy cooperatives in the United States, and that number decreased even further to only 264 in 1990. At the same time, the annual net business volume per co-

TABLE

Per Capita Consumption of Dairy Products

	(pounds milk equivalent)								
	1910	1920	1930	1940	1950	1960	1970	1980	1990
All Dairy Products	752	729	813	821	740	653	562	575	577
Fluid Milk and Cream	323	356	347	343	348	321	260	390	400

operative rose. It is noteworthy that the growth of big business in the manufacture and marketing of dairy products accelerated after the depression of the 1930s, when dairy interests first became the beneficiaries of federal marketing, purchase, and price-stabilization programs.

Meanwhile, although consumers may not be sovereign, they are not altogether without power. Despite efforts by industry lobbies and compliant federal administrations to administer dairy prices and moderate competition from substitutes, consumers have shown a growing preference for margarine, coffee whiteners, whipped toppings, vegetable-fat-filled milk, and nondairy beverages over dairy-based articles. A health- and weight-conscious public has been reducing its overall per capita intake of dairy manufactures and fluid milk (see table), notwithstanding the dietary value of milk minerals and vitamins. The relative fat and cholesterol content, as well as the forms and prices, of different dairy products has affected decisions to reduce purchases of butter, cream, and evaporated milk and to increase consumption of low-fat milks, yogurt, processed and Italian-style cheese, and nonfat dry milk solids. Between the 1950s and 1998, the average American per capita consumption of milk fell 35 percent while the consumption of cheese rose by over three and a half times. Ice cream is an exception, although among all frozen products, ice milk, sherbet, and nondairy mellorine have gained ground. Thus, the large and complex dairy industry manifests a continuing division of labor, in which larger farms confine their efforts to raw milk production, highly capitalized corporate and cooperative organizations process and distribute milk off the farms, and supermarkets and food stores increasingly retail dairy products to final customers in standard paper or plastic containers. Mid-twentieth-century changes in milk production and in the structure of manufacturing and marketing agencies are a response to rising costs of production, health and sanitary regulations, and changes in demand for dairy products.

BIBLIOGRAPHY

Cochrane, Willard Wesley. *The Development of American Agriculture: A Historical Analysis.* Minneapolis: University of Minnesota Press, 1993.

Gough, Robert. *Farming the Cutover: A Social History of Northern Wisconsin, 1900–1940.* Lawrence: University Press of Kansas, 1997.

Hurt, Douglas R. *American Agriculture: A Brief History.* Ames: Iowa State University, 1994.

Jensen, Joan M. *Loosening the Bonds: Mid-Atlantic Farm Women, 1750–1850.* New Haven, Conn.: Yale University Press, 1986.

McMurry, Sally Ann. *Transforming Rural Life: Dairying Families and Agricultural Change, 1820–1885.* Baltimore: Johns Hopkins University Press, 1995.

Okun, Mitchell. *Fair Play in the Marketplace: The First Battle for Pure Food and Drugs.* Dekalb: Northern Illinois University Press, 1986.

Eric E. Lampard / A. E.

See also **Agriculture; Cattle; Food and Cuisines; Food and Drug Administration; Genetic Engineering; Pure Food and Drug Movement; Wisconsin.**

DAKOTA. *See* **Sioux.**

DAKOTA EXPEDITIONS OF SIBLEY AND SULLY (1863–1865). In 1863, during the American CIVIL WAR, Major General John Pope ordered Union general Henry Hastings Sibley to march from Camp Pope near Fort Ridgely, Minnesota, against the Dakota (Sioux) Indians, who had taken part in hostilities of 1862 in MINNESOTA. He was to drive them west toward the MISSOURI RIVER, and General Alfred Sully was ordered to proceed up the Missouri and intercept the Dakotas before they could cross to the western side of the river. Sibley set out on 16 June and established his field base at Camp Atcheson, North Dakota. He defeated the Dakotas in three battles: at Big Mound, Kidder County, on 24 July; at Dead Buffalo Lake on 26 July; and at Stony Lake on 28 July. Retreating Dakota fighters held back Sibley's army until their families crossed to safety on the western side of the Missouri.

Sibley established his camp at the mouth of Apple Creek, near present-day Bismarck, North Dakota. On 1 August he began his return march by way of Camp Atcheson to Fort Abercrombie, which he reached on 23 August. Meanwhile, Sully established headquarters at Sioux City, Iowa, and set up a base camp at Fort Pierre, South Dakota. On 13 August he left the fort for a quick march northward. On 3 September he fought a battle near White Stone Hill, North Dakota; the Dakota camp was dispersed and their supplies destroyed. Sully took prisoners and returned to his winter quarters at Sioux City.

Sully conducted the next two summer campaigns. In the summer of 1864 his army proceeded up the Missouri River from Sioux City, accompanied by two steamboats that carried his supplies to the rendezvous point at the site of the new army post at Fort Rice, North Dakota. Leaving a part of his force to construct the fort, he marched northwest to the Dakota camp located in the Killdeer Mountains. There a battle was fought on 28 July, and the Dakotas were defeated and scattered. The following summer, Sully's force moved up the Missouri River to Fort Rice and marched north of Devils Lake. On 2 August he set out for the Mouse (Souris) River and from there marched southwest to Fort Berthold. There he met the famous Jesuit missionary Father Pierre Jean De Smet. Sully's force returned to Fort Rice on 8 September and went into winter quarters at Sioux Falls, South Dakota.

BIBLIOGRAPHY

Jones, Robert Huhn. *The Civil War in the Northwest: Nebraska, Wisconsin, Iowa, Minnesota, and the Dakotas.* Norman: University of Oklahoma Press, 1960.

O. G. Libby / A. R.

See also **Indian Policy, U.S., 1830–1900; Indians in the Civil War; Sioux; Sioux Uprising in Minnesota.**

DAKOTA TERRITORY. The Dakota Territory corresponded to the present states of North Dakota, South Dakota, and much of Wyoming and Montana. The first trading post in this region was built by Jean Baptiste Truteau in Charles Mix County, South Dakota, in 1794. The most famous trading post on the MISSOURI RIVER was Fort Union, built at the mouth of the Yellowstone River in 1829. The Dakotas were mostly populated by the SIOUX, or Dakota Indians, who resisted violently to protect their rights to the region after the discovery of gold in the BLACK HILLS region of South Dakota led to an influx of white settlers and aggressive claims to the region by the United States government.

The United States reorganized its territorial claims to this region often. It all fell within the vast Missouri Territory created in 1812, part of which was added to Michigan Territory in 1834. In 1836, 1838, and 1849, Dakota became part of Wisconsin, Iowa, and Minnesota Territories, respectively. From 1834, the western part of the later Dakota Territory was designated INDIAN COUNTRY, and, in 1854, became part of Nebraska Territory. Dakota Territory, created by Congress in 1861, included lands west of present-day Minnesota and almost all of Nebraska Territory north of the forty-third parallel to the Missouri River. Montana Territory was cut off from Dakota Territory in 1864. When Wyoming Territory was created in 1868, Dakota Territory was reduced to the region comprising the two Dakotas of today, with a capital at Bismarck. In 1889, the territory was divided into the existing states of NORTH DAKOTA and SOUTH DAKOTA.

BIBLIOGRAPHY

Barbour, Barton H. *Fort Union and the Upper Missouri Fur Trade.* Norman: University of Oklahoma Press, 2001.

Lamar, Howard. *Dakota Territory, 1861–1889: A Study of Frontier Politics.* New Haven, Conn: Yale University Press, 1956.

O. G. Libby / H. S.

Dalkon Shield Protest. Dressed in black and wearing paper cutouts of this intrauterine device, Karen Hicks *(left)*, president of the Dalkon Shield Information Network, and Fran Cleary carry signs outside the federal courthouse in Richmond, Va., 1987. © BETTMANN/CORBIS

DALKON SHIELD. Hugh Davis, a Johns Hopkins University gynecologist, created the Dalkon Shield intrauterine device (IUD) in 1967 and 1968. A dime-sized plastic triangle, with five fins on each lower side (to prevent expulsion from the uterus) and a string hanging from its bottom corner (for removal), it resembled a police badge or shield. Marketed between 1971 and 1974 as a revolutionary advance in birth control technology, the A. H. Robins Corporation sold more than 2.2 million units in the United States and another 1.5 million abroad. During the next decade, doctors and lawyers traced eighteen deaths and over 200,000 illnesses to the device.

By the spring of 1974, A. H. Robins had received more than 400 complaints. Women often fainted from the pain of insertion. Many experienced cramping, bleeding, and infections that resulted in hysterectomies or sterility. Women who conceived despite wearing the device suffered a 60 percent miscarriage rate, often coupled with life-threatening blood infections. The remaining pregnancies resulted in premature births and severe birth defects.

A. H. Robins lost its first lawsuit in 1975, and the shield's defects came to light. The manufacturers claimed the device prevented 98.9 percent of pregnancies (much higher than other IUDs and comparable to the birth control pill) when they knew that its failure rate was actually 5.3 percent. The shield's fins predisposed it to becoming embedded in, and sometimes perforating, the uterine wall. The string transmitted bacteria from the vagina into the uterus, promoting infection. Company documents proved that corporate officers hid these problems to protect profits. This malfeasance, along with many physicians' insensitivity to women's suffering, made the Dalkon Shield synonymous with sexism, malpractice, and corporate irresponsibility. Protests against the shield helped fuel the women's health movement, and resulted in federal legislation regulating medical devices.

After paying more than $485.6 million in settlement and legal costs, A. H. Robins declared bankruptcy in 1986. A $2.5 billion trust fund settled claims from another 325,000 women. Until his death in 1996, Davis maintained that the shield never caused an injury. Subsequently, other intrauterine devices remained a controversial form of birth control.

BIBLIOGRAPHY

Hawkins, Mary F. *Unshielded: The Human Cost of the Dalkon Shield.* Toronto: University of Toronto Press, 1997.

Mintz, Morton. *At Any Cost: Corporate Greed, Women, and the Dalkon Shield.* New York: Pantheon, 1985.

Tone, Andrea. *Devices and Desires: A History of Contraceptives in America.* New York: Hill and Wang, 2001.

Gregory Michael Dorr

See also **Birth Control; Childbirth and Reproduction; Medicine and Surgery.**

DALLAS is the second-largest municipality in Texas (2000 population 1,188,580), though the Dallas–Fort Worth "Metroplex" is the state's largest urban area.

Dallas. A street scene in the bustling city, c. 1920, shortly before the heyday of the oil industry in the region. LIBRARY OF CONGRESS

The city was established in 1841 as a trading post near an easy crossing of the Trinity River, as the Republic of Texas was encouraging settlers to populate the area. After Texas joined the Union in 1845, Dallas was named the county seat. A nearby French utopian settlement called La Réunion founded in 1855 disbanded within a few years, but some of the colony's tradesmen and artisans settled in Dallas, distinguishing the young town (incorporated in 1856) from similar agricultural trade centers across North Texas.

Some pioneer settlers had been recruited from Ohio and the Old Northwest, but many more came from the American South. City residents voted heavily in favor of state secession in 1861, and the city became a commissary post for the Confederate army.

A subsidy of cash and land persuaded the Houston and Texas Central Railroad to divert its planned north-south route through the town in 1872. The Texas and Pacific line from St. Louis made the town a rail crossroads the next year, and, more importantly, the railroad ended there for four years before being extended to Fort Worth. By that time, merchants and industrial concerns had established Dallas as the regional capital. By 1890, it was the largest city in Texas, with 38,000 residents.

As the plantation system declined in the Old South, the rich blackland prairie surrounding Dallas became the nation's premier cotton-growing region, and Dallas the market center for this commodity. The city was designated in 1914 for a Federal Reserve Bank. Discovery of oil in nearby East Texas in 1930 spurred further growth, and the willingness of Dallas banks to lend money secured by oilfield reserves made the city the financial capital of the region. Petroleum companies established their headquarters in Dallas, though no oil is produced in the metropolitan area. Dallas also achieved a reputation as a fashion center, home of the Neiman Marcus department store.

The growing city absorbed several adjacent municipalities, most notably (in 1903) Oak Cliff, across the Trinity River. A mayor-commission form of government was adopted in 1907, and for decades that system's apolitical efficiency was prized by civic leaders. A 1911 city plan calling for river levees, new bridges, parks, and boulevards was largely accomplished after a 1920 update, testimony to civic aspirations. Making the Trinity River navigable has been discussed from the city's founding to the present day, but only a few boats have ever managed to reach the city. Instead, the river became notorious for springtime floods. A huge inundation in 1908 prompted construction of levees, completed in 1931, to protect the business district.

The city's business community cemented its booster reputation by having Dallas—a city that hadn't even existed during the Texas Revolution—chosen for the 1936 Texas Centennial Exposition. The Art Deco exposition buildings built at Fair Park remain as the site of the annual State Fair, and expositions and trade shows became an

Dallas Skyline. A cowboy keeps an eye on a herd of cattle grazing near the booming city, 1945.
LIBRARY OF CONGRESS

important part of the economy, with the Dallas Market Center eventually becoming the world's largest wholesale merchandise mart. Having organized to build the Centennial Exposition, city business leaders came to dominate local politics. Unions were strongly discouraged as the city became more industrial, and for sixty years the city's mayors were in practice selected by the downtown business establishment's Citizen Charter Association.

World War II defense plants brought the aviation industry to the area, and manufacturing employment grew rapidly in postwar decades. Apparel firms were attracted by the nonunion labor force, and the city also became a major headquarters center for insurance firms. Electronics firms such as Texas Instruments prospered in the 1970s and 1980s, spawning and attracting other high-tech firms. A bold move to create a huge regional airport (opened in 1974) between Dallas and Fort Worth paid off, attracting both distribution facilities and corporate headquarters to the region.

The city's reputation for conservatism became the subject of much civic soul-searching in the wake of President John F. Kennedy's 1963 assassination in downtown Dallas. Racial integration of downtown stores and public facilities was accomplished quietly in the 1960s, but forced busing for school integration spurred white flight from Dallas into adjacent suburbs in the 1970s. Forced to adopt single-member districts, the city council became more demographically representative in the 1970s and 1980s, but also more confrontational, highlighting dis-

parities between well-off, booming North Dallas and the poorer underdeveloped areas of South and West Dallas.

Office and retail development followed the suburban dispersion, diminishing downtown Dallas's role as the region's hub. In the 1990s, a light-rail system centered on downtown Dallas opened with hopes that it could refocus regional patterns. Areas near downtown have recently attracted new residential projects while the West End entertainment area and Arts Center ensure downtown's place as the region's cultural center.

BIBLIOGRAPHY

Greene, A. C. *Dallas, USA.* Austin: Texas Monthly Press, 1984.

Hazel, Michael V. *Dallas: A History of "Big D."* Austin: Texas State Historical Association, 1997.

Hill, Patricia Evridge. *Dallas: The Making of a Modern City.* Austin: University of Texas Press, 1996.

Dennis McClendon

See also **Cotton; Midcontinent Oil Region; Oil Fields.**

DAME SCHOOL, a type of school transplanted to some of the American colonies from England, usually conducted by a woman in her home. Young children of the neighborhood were taught the alphabet, the HORN-BOOK, elements of reading, and moral and religious subjects. In New England, such schools prepared boys for admission to the town schools, which would not receive them until they could "stand up and read words of two syllables and keep their places." The "dame school" prefigured women's central role in the public school system and the professionalization of EDUCATION in the nineteenth century.

BIBLIOGRAPHY

Monaghan, E. Jennifer. "Literacy Instruction and Gender in Colonial New England." *American Quarterly* 40 (March 1988): 18–41.

Sugg, Redding S. *Motherteacher: The Feminization of American Education.* Charlottesville: University Press of Virginia, 1978.

Edgar W. Knight / A. R.

See also **Colonial Society; Women in Public Life, Business, and Professions.**

"DAMN THE TORPEDOES," a reply by Union Adm. David Glasgow Farragut to a warning of the dangerous proximity of submerged torpedoes (now called mines) at the critical juncture of the Battle of Mobile Bay (5 August 1864). As the Union fleet approached the harbor entrance, which was known to be nearly closed by mines, the monitor *Tecumseh* struck a mine and immediately sank. The following ships closed into a disordered group while heavy cross fire from the Confederate fleet and forts threatened them with early defeat. Farragut, in the flagship *Hartford*, took the lead, signaling the fleet to follow, and steamed safely through the mine fields into the harbor.

BIBLIOGRAPHY

Knox, Dudley W. *A History of the United States Navy.* New York: Putnam, 1948.

Dudley W. Knox / C. W.

See also **Armored Ships; Ironclad Warships; Mobile Bay, Battle of.**

DAMS. *See* **Hydroelectric Power.**

DANBURY HATTERS' CASE. The Danbury Hatters' Case was the popular name for *Loewe v. Lawlor*, 208 U.S. 274 (1908), the first U.S. Supreme Court case to find that the Sherman Antitrust Act applied to organized labor. The decision dealt a crippling blow to consumer boycotts organized by the nation's labor movement. *Loewe* originated in the efforts of the United Hatters of North America to unionize a hat company in Danbury, Connecticut. Most of the nation's hat manufacturers had made their peace with the union. Dietrich Loewe, however, was among the minority of proprietors who refused to unionize, preferring to undersell competitors by paying sub-

standard wages. The union responded with a strike and a boycott, the latter backed by the American Federation of Labor (AFL).

When the boycott prompted a drop in orders, Loewe brought suit for treble damages under the Sherman Act against individual union members at his plant. The federal trial court dismissed the suit, holding that the union was not a combination under the antitrust law and that the boycott was not a conspiracy in restraint of interstate commerce. The Supreme Court, however, ruled in a 9 to 0 decision that the act covered union activities and that a boycott conducted across state lines was a conspiracy in restraint of interstate commerce, even though the restraint was remote and indirect. The ruling deprived workers of an important organizing tool, and led the AFL to lobby for reform of the antitrust laws. The sought-for reform seemingly came with the Clayton Act of 1914; however, its labor provisions were ambiguous, and unions won exemption from antitrust litigation only in the late 1930s.

BIBLIOGRAPHY

Ernst, Daniel R. *Lawyers against Labor: From Individual Rights to Corporate Liberalism.* 1992.

William E. Forbath

See also **Clayton Act, Labor Provisions; Sherman Antitrust Act; Trade Unions.**

DANCE. The history of American dance is as varied as the numerous dance forms that compose it. Dominated by competing senses of athleticism and grace, the American dance form came of age during the twentieth century, perfecting a combination of European and African roots. In colonial America dancing was popular wherever religious sanctions did not prevent freedom of expression. Primarily primitive in nature, colonial American dance reflected the juxtaposition of numerous immigrant groups and Native American tribes. Nevertheless, it was a blending of traditional western European and western African dance forms that provided the backbone of American dance in the twenty-first century. This amalgamation began at the end of the colonial era and continued slowly until the end of the nineteenth century with the dawning of the jazz era.

From the mid-eighteenth century to the latter part of the nineteenth century, American dance progressed from minuets and country-dances to cotillions and quadrilles. These dances were almost ritualized; they required grace and knowledge of the complex steps. Regional or country-dances, such as the Irish step dances, the Scotch-Irish jigs, or German reels, reflected the cosmopolitan nature of American dance. Incorporated into this category were the various African dance forms, such as the religious ring shout, funeral and processional strut dances, and seasonal dances. Thus, American dance combined old-world technique with new environmental and social trends to create a new hybrid of dance and music.

Perhaps the best example of this hybridization is the "jig," a step dance that was popular first in Europe, and then in America. This foot-stomping dance extended beyond class boundaries and, when combined with the African step dances, became the precursor to the twentieth-century American dance form, tap. This hybridization became the hallmark of American dance, combining a sort of individualism and improvisation that was distinctly American.

Incorporating this distinctly American style was the first "ballet" style dance. Using techniques similar to pantomime, this ballet was presented in 1735 by Henry Holt, a British dancing instructor who had opened a dancing school in 1734 in Charleston, South Carolina. The first classical performers in America were English, French, and Italian touring companies, which presented operas, operettas, and pantomimes. Dancing also made its way into circuses and variety shows, where the first notable American dancer, John Durang, made his debut. As a blackface comic, he combined comedy, acting, acrobatics, and rope dancing—again, a uniquely American style. Durang began his career in Philadelphia with the Old American Company, one of the earliest theatrical touring groups. His popularity paved the way for the joint debut in Philadelphia of two American ballerinas, Augusta Maywood, who danced primarily in Europe, and Mary Ann Lee, who danced the first American *Giselle* in Boston in 1846. However, these dancers were exceptions, as European dancers dominated the American scene in the nineteenth century.

Theatrical dancing, including ballet, pageantry, and melodrama, peaked in 1866 with the production at Niblo's Gardens in New York of *The Black Crook*, which became a fixture on the American stage for the remainder of the nineteenth century. Prior to this performance, William Henry Lane, whose stage name was Master Juba, was the only black singer-dancer to perform in white minstrel shows. The ingenuity of his improvised dance steps created a sense of interaction between dancer and audience, and his footwork originated the form known as tap dance.

The cakewalk, a black American social dance, became the first indigenous African American dance fad to spread to Europe. The cakewalk presumably began around 1850 on the plantations of the South, and its high-kneed strut was meant to parody the solemn decorum of the white masters as they promenaded in the formal marches that opened their balls. The white masters, apparently oblivious to the actual meaning, encouraged the development of this dance form.

Dance became more of a public affair in the mid-nineteenth century. In the early 1800s the popularity of the waltz, an import from Europe, and round dancing, including the polka, quadrille, and mazurka brought by new waves of eastern European immigrants, reflected the new public representation of dance. More public ball-

Merce Cunningham. The longtime dancer-choreographer *(center)*, who formed his own company in 1950, is framed by other dancers as they perform *Trackers*, his first work created (in 1991) using a computer. © JOHAN ELBERS 1997

rooms were built, and dances became egalitarian events, in contrast to the smaller, more private parties of the preceding century, which had demanded a sort of ballroom etiquette. Dance manuals published in the late nineteenth century devoted less space to ballroom etiquette, and more information to the images detailing the actual dance technique itself.

At the turn of the century a rash of "animal" dances became popular. Dances like the Turkey Trot, the Kangaroo Hop, and the Grizzly Bear continued the trend in couple dances by incorporating gestures and steps from African animal dances. All body appendages could be used; elbows would flap, and heads bob, as the dancers hopped around the dance floor like bunnies. The Charleston, which had originated in black neighborhoods around 1910, made it to the white stage in *Runnin' Wild* in 1922. This dance craze represented a complete break from all European elements. With its African American dance elements, including the flying kicks, shimmying shoulders, and swaying hips, the Charleston made a star overseas of its protégé, Josephine Baker.

The turn of the century also inaugurated an entirely new form of dancing: the expressive or interpretive dance, known as modern dance. With the popularity of such dances as the cakewalk or the Charleston, intensity of expression became extremely important in the world of American dance. Perhaps the best-known proponent of interpretive dance was Isadora Duncan. Born in 1877 in San Francisco, California, Duncan tried the commercial stage but found it restrictive and uncreative. In 1903 in Berlin she delivered a speech entitled "The Dance of the

497

Alvin Ailey. This dancer-choreographer's numerous enduring works, created for his multiracial American Dance Theater and other companies, often reflect jazz and African dance elements. LIBRARY OF CONGRESS

Future," in which she argued, "the dance of the future will have to become again a high religious art as it was with the Greeks. For art which is not religious is not art, is mere merchandise." When she returned to the United States, she went where no other solo dancer had dared to go; by dancing to the music of Ludwig van Beethoven, Frédéric Chopin, and Pyotr Ilich Tchaikovsky, she transformed the public arena of the stage. Her performances were poorly received by dance critics, who questioned her physical interpretation of symphonic music, as well as her simplistic approach to costumery. Duncan sponsored many young American dancers, and trained them in her expressive, "naturalistic" style of dancing. Her uninhibited approach to art set the foundation for the success of modern dance in America.

Similarly, the uninhibited dance style of Ruth St. Denis, originally a vaudeville dancer, ignited the imagination of her followers. She became very interested in the dance of eastern cultures and, inspired by an image of the goddess Isis in an advertisement for Egyptian Deities cigarettes, created her own unique form of dance. She began her career as a solo artist in 1905 with the dance "Radha," the story of the mortal maiden loved by the god Krishna. Like Duncan, she never felt she would receive the attention she craved in the United States, so she moved to Europe, where she built her reputation as an exotic dancer with a classical style. She returned to the United States, where she began to work with Edwin Meyers "Ted" Shawn, a stage dancer who later became her husband. Together they founded the Denishawn Company, which soon dominated the modern dance arena.

One of the protégés of the Denishawn Company, Martha Graham became one of the most influential figures of the first half of the twentieth century. She learned to discard the strict choreography and footwork that had restricted her desire for innovation. She formed her own company in 1925; her programs featured exotic solos, and her dances attempted to draw attention to the plight of the human condition. She worked closely with Louis Horst, a major figure on the American dance scene in the 1920s, 1930s, and 1940s, who encouraged her to work with contemporary composers rather than with eighteenth- and nineteenth-century music, as had previously been done. By 1930 Martha Graham had identified a method of breathing and relaxation she called "contraction and release," in which the movement originated in the tension of a contracted muscle and continued in the flow of energy released from the body as the muscle relaxed. This method gave Graham's dancers an angular look, one completely incongruous with the smooth dance styles of her predecessors. Before her death in 1991, she was often accused of making dance an "ugly" art form, but she ignited an interest in freedom of expression.

With the 1916 arrival in New York of Serge Diaghilev's Ballets Russes, ballet actually began to be taken seriously in the United States. However, it was not until the Russian dancer George Balanchine and the American Lincoln Kirstein formed the New York City Ballet in 1948 that American ballet became a recognized and valid entity. Initially based in New York's City Center, it moved to the New York State Theater at the Lincoln Center for the Performing Arts in 1964. Balanchine extended the range and symbolism of American ballet; by infusing traditional and classical steps with contemporary techniques and energy he created a uniquely American ballet. While the New York City Ballet attempted a return to neoclassicism, reveling in its simplicity, dancers Lucia Chase and Richard Pleasant in 1940 formed the beginnings of a company that incorporated a variety of choreographic techniques. The Ballet Theatre, which became the American Ballet Theatre in 1957, provided a stage for such works as Agnes de Mille's *Fall River Legend* and Antony Tudor's *Romeo and*

Juliet, as well as for classic works of the nineteenth century such as *Giselle* and *Swan Lake*. The main focus of the American Ballet Theatre was to provide a forum for both classical and contemporary works.

Concurrently, in the post–World War II era, another group of dancers focused on choreography that emphasized idiosyncrasy and physicality, a formula that became the modern dance of the twentieth and twenty-first centuries. Acting independently, these were modern dance choreographers such as Martha Graham, Merce Cunningham, Alvin Ailey, Glen Tetley, and José Limón. Cunningham in particular began to use chance devices to structure the movement and program the timing of movement of the performing space, which gave the dance stage a new set of possibilities. Alvin Ailey created his own touring troupe in 1958, when the idea of a modern dance company, and specifically a black modern dance company, was practically inconceivable. At the time, Broadway theaters were not hospitable to the concept of modern dance, nor were modern dance companies stable enterprises. However, Ailey encouraged the enjoyment of dance as a vibrant form of theater, and his company's style focused entirely on physicality. His dancers seemed to slide across the stage with an emphasis on ecstasy. Ailey noted that he wanted to create a black folkloric company that would combine bawdy humor, earthy emotion, and honesty with the intense physicality of pelvic thrusts and long body-lines.

New dance forms are continually evolving, particularly in terms of self-expression, thanks in part to the groundbreaking work of Martha Graham, George Balanchine, Jerome Robbins, and their contemporaries. For example, choreographer Mark Morris attempted to challenge preconceived notions, just as did his predecessors. He is perhaps best known for his 1988 work, *L'Allegro, il penseroso ed il moderato*, set to the Handel score. He also continued in the tradition established by Martha Graham of combining well-known composers and musicians with choreographers, working with cellist Yo-Yo Ma and composer Lou Harrison. Modern dance seeks a social context, and even ballroom dancing, which has evolved as a sport in its own right, incorporates the dances popular in the nineteenth century, such as the waltz, foxtrot, and quick-step, with a contemporary pulse.

In the latter part of the twentieth century and at the beginning of the twenty-first century, dance acquired a sense of athleticism and was touted for its health benefits. Dancing in clubs only increased in popularity with American youth; movements are centered in pelvic rotations, swiveling hips, bobbing heads, and stomping and sliding feet. Popularized by the syncretic choreography of "boy bands" such as the Backstreet Boys and 'N Sync, popular dance was very much infused with the musical performance. The focus was as much on the music as on the choreography. Similarly, Oriental dance (commonly known as "belly dancing"), square dancing, Latin rhythms such as the merengue and samba, and such popular forms as

Twyla Tharp. The dancer-choreographer, who has alternated between her own dance companies and work for American Ballet Theatre, Paul Taylor, and others, performs one of her dances based on songs sung by Frank Sinatra. © BEATRIZ SCHILLER 1997

jazz and tap, each focus on the combination of "feeling the music" and the choreography itself. Many popular films, including *Dance with Me* or *Center Stage*, also prompted an obsession with dance in modern culture. Dance in America is closely synonymous with everyday life, and is inspired by social and cultural issues.

BIBLIOGRAPHY

Carbonneau, Suzanne. "Dance at the Close of the Century." *USIA Electronic Journal* 3, no. 1 (1998).

Cohen, Selma Jeanne. *Dance as a Theatre Art: Source Readings in Dance History from 1581 to the Present.* New York: Harper and Row, 1976.

Garafola, Lynn. *Diaghilev's Ballets Russes.* New York: Oxford University Press, 1989.

Mazo, Joseph. "Ailey and Company." *Horizon* 27, no. 6 (1984): 18–24.

Parks, Gary. "Critical Mass: Vintage Reviews: A Look at the Dance World through Seventy Years of *Dance Magazine* Reviews." *Dance Magazine* 71, no. 6 (June 1997): 14–35.

Riis, Thomas L. *Just before Jazz: Black Musical Theater in New York, 1890 to 1915.* Washington, D.C.: Smithsonian Institution Press, 1989.

Thorpe, Edward. *Black Dance.* Woodstock, N.Y.: Overlook Press, 1990.

Jennifer Harrison

See also **Alvin Ailey American Dance Company; American Ballet Theatre; Ballet; Discos; Martha Graham Dance Company; New York City Ballet.**

DANCE, INDIAN. North American Indian Dance is not a single entity—the several hundred indigenous nations of the United States and Canada each have their own distinct traditions. The Apache Crown Dance, Tewa Buffalo Dance, Kiowa Black Leg Society dances, and Yupik Bladder Feast are as different from each other as classical ballet is from hip-hop. Some dances are strictly ceremonial and an essential part of spiritual practices, while others are more social, but all honor the sacredness of the dance circle.

People organize and participate in seasonal dances; feast days and fiestas; life-cycle, agricultural, healing, and honoring ceremonies; family and clan events; special tribal religious ceremonies; and medicine rites. These occasions ensure the continuation of ancient lifeways, honor deities and members of the community, celebrate family and friends, and affirm Indian identities. Dances, along with music, oratory, poetry, drama, and visual arts, are symbolic manifestations of spiritual power—reaffirmations of relatedness. The dances of American Indian peoples are embodiments of indigenous values: a vital means of cultural survival in response to difficult historical circumstances. They are powerful expressions of survival.

Traditional Dance. Dwight White Buffalo, a Cheyenne, performs in traditional costume for the American Indian Dance Theatre. HANAY GEIOGAMAH

During the colonization of indigenous North America, Christian missionaries, government agents, and Western educational systems tried to suppress American Indian practices, notably performances of music and dancing. For colonizers, the dancing Indian body signified the antithesis of all things "civilized." Indigenous ceremonies were viewed as time-consuming pagan practices that ran counter to the Christian work ethic and undermined the "civilizing" goals of assimilation. Native dancing intertwined with spiritual practices became a punishable offence, subject to a series of prohibitions by the late nineteenth-century federal government. Many Native American communities hid their ceremonies, holding their dances in conjunction with Anglo celebrations such as the Fourth of July and Thanksgiving. In 1934, when the Indian Reorganization Act signaled the end of forced assimilation, the U.S. government lifted its ban, and dance activities resumed in the context of changing reservation life. Despite considerable losses of ceremonial knowledge in many communities, indigenous music and dance performance were subsequently embraced openly, publicly celebrated, and accompanied by substantial revitalization.

Traditional practices are not static. They incorporate a historical continuum subject to innovation over time. Some events grow out of older practices and spread to new contexts, for example, the annual summer sun dances of the Plains tribes are ceremonial and social complexes of sacrifice, thanksgiving, and renewal that were widely disseminated across the Plains region in the eighteenth and nineteenth centuries, with marked variations in form. During a period of revitalization in the 1980s, communities whose sun dance ceremonies had ceased turned to neighboring tribes, as well as anthropological records, for assistance with re-creation.

The most public ceremonial and social dance complex is the POWWOW. The word derives from a Narraganset (Algonquian) term for curing ceremonies and was used by European settlers to refer to any Indian gathering. The contemporary powwow originated in the warrior societies of the Omaha, Kansa, Ponca, and Pawnee tribes of the Plains. The "Omaha dance" (also known as the Crow Belt Dance, Hot Dance, Grass Dance, and War Dance) spread through intertribal contact. As warrior societies declined at the end of the nineteenth century, events became more social, allowing women and children to take active parts. Since World War II the specific styles of competitive powwow dancing, singing, and regalia have diffused throughout rural and urban Indian communities. Modern powwows are intertribal celebrations of family, community, nation, and Native identity. In addition to competitive dancing for cash prizes, powwows incorporate occasions for honoring relatives and other individuals through naming ceremonies and giveaways of blankets, star quilts, and other household goods. Northern Plains powwows differ slightly from those on the southern plains, each tribe adding its own traditions, styles of dress, and dancing.

custody at Fortress Monroe, Virginia. He remained in custody until 14 May 1867, when he was released on a $100,000 bond. The editor of the *New York Tribune* Horace Greeley, the former abolitionist Gerrit Smith, and the business tycoon Cornelius Vanderbilt were among the prominent Northerners who posted the bond. Charges relating to the assassination were never substantiated. The United States government brought indictments for treason against Davis in Richmond, Virginia, the former Confederate capital, on the grounds that it was the place where the crime of treason was committed.

Salmon P. Chase, the chief justice of the United States Supreme Court, was the justice assigned to try cases in the federal district courts of Virginia. The trial of Davis was initially delayed because of Chase's refusal to hear cases until military rule ended in Virginia. Once the courts were restored, the government asked for and received several delays in the proceedings. All the while, Davis eagerly sought a trial and refused all considerations of pardon. The impeachment proceedings against Andrew Johnson, which were held from March to May in 1868, and the constitutional requirement that Chase preside over those proceedings, further delayed Davis's trial.

In early December 1868 the government was prepared to go forward on an indictment for treason issued in March 1868 under a 1790 law that carried a mandatory penalty of death by execution upon conviction. Prior to the commencement of the trial, Chase suggested to Davis's attorneys that they request dismissal of the charges based on section 3 of the Fourteenth Amendment, which provided for a disqualification from office for those who had taken an oath to support the Constitution and then supported the Confederacy. If this prohibition was found by the court to be a penalty, it would bar further prosecution on the basis of double jeopardy. At the start of the trial the motion was made and argued by counsel.

Chase and the local federal district judge, John C. Underwood, disagreed on the question, and the matter was referred to the U.S. Supreme Court for a final decision. On 25 December 1868, President Andrew Johnson issued a general amnesty proclamation for most Confederates. The Supreme Court dismissed the case against Davis on 26 February 1869, and lawyers for Davis were advised that a *nolle prosequi* (no further proceedings) was entered. A trial of Davis would have raised the ultimate legal question of the Civil War: Was secession treason?

BIBLIOGRAPHY

Blackford, Charles M. "The Trials and Trial of Jefferson Davis." *Southern Historical Society Papers* 29 (1901): 45–81.

Bradley, Chester. "Was Jefferson Davis Disguised As a Woman When Captured?" *Journal of Mississippi History* vol. 36 (Aug. 1974): 243–268.

Fairman, Charles. *Reconstruction and Reunion 1864–88.* Part I. New York: Macmillan, 1971.

Hagan, Horace Henry. "United States vs. Jefferson Davis." *Sewanee Review* 25 (1917): 220–225.

LEGENDS SURROUNDING THE ARREST OF JEFFERSON DAVIS

Jefferson Davis was arrested by Lieutenant-Colonel Benjamin Pritchard of the Fourth Michigan Cavalry in Irwinville, Georgia, on 10 May 1865. An official report of the capture was given to Secretary of War Edwin M. Stanton on 14 May 1865. This report asserts that Davis was wearing women's clothing at the time of his arrest. A *New York Times* account of 15 May 1865 states that Davis hastily put on one of Mrs. Davis's dresses and started to run for the woods when he was overtaken by his captors. The Northern press delighted in depicting the fallen Southern president in this unheroic disguise. The famous showman P. T. Barnum presented depictions of Davis fleeing in women's clothing to his circus audiences, thereby perpetuating this version of events.

Generations of scholars have debated the accuracy of these accounts. Davis consistently denied the allegations, going to great lengths to attempt to dispel the speculation and attacks on his masculinity. Eyewitness accounts and the statements of Davis and his wife, Varina, reveal a more accurate account of the events: Upon learning of the arrival of the federal troops, Davis emerged from his tent wearing a water-repellent cloak, or raglan, with wide, loose sleeves. This type of garment was commonly worn by both men and women, and Davis may have mistakenly picked up his wife's cloak. As he exited the tent, Varina threw her black shawl around his shoulders due to the inclement weather. When Davis was confronted by the Federal troops a few feet away from the tent, he threw off both the raglan and the shawl.

Nichols, Roy F. "United States vs. Jefferson Davis, 1865–1869." *American Historical Review* 31 (1926): 266–284.

Watson, David K. "The Trial of Jefferson Davis: An Interesting Constitutional Question." *Yale Law Journal* 24 (1915): 669–676.

C. Ellen Connally

See also **Treason.**

DAVIS-JOHNSTON CONTROVERSY, the factional differences between Confederacy president Jefferson Davis and his friends on the one hand, and Gen. J. E. Johnston and his partisans on the other. Disagreements included (1) the relative ranking of general officers after the First Battle of Bull Run; (2) transfer of command of the Army of Northern Virginia from Johnston to Robert

E. Lee in the spring of 1862; (3) Johnston's assignment to command the forces in Tennessee, where he served in the winter of 1862–1863; (4) the unsuccessful defense of Vicksburg in the summer of 1863; and (5) Johnston's relief by Gen. J. B. Hood during the Atlanta campaign in the summer of 1864 and his restoration nearly a year later, after Hood had wrecked his army (see HOOD'S TENNESSEE CAMPAIGN) and the Confederacy was near collapse. For many years the arguments and accusations between the Davis and Johnston factions echoed savagely throughout the South, contributing to the violent anti-Davis sentiment of the winter of 1864–1865.

BIBLIOGRAPHY

James, A. P. "General Joseph Eggleston Johnston, Storm Center of the Confederate Army."*Mississippi Valley Historical Review.* (1927).

Symonds, Craig L. *Joseph E. Johnston: A Civil War Biography.* New York: Norton, 1992.

Woodworth, Steven E. *No Band of Brothers: Problems in the Rebel High Command.* Columbia: University of Missouri Press, 1999.

Thomas Robson Hay / T. D.

See also **Atlanta Campaign; Tennessee, Army of (Confederate).**

DAWES COMMISSION.

The commission helped pave the way for the creation of the state of Oklahoma from what had been Indian Territory. Commonly called the Commission to the Five Civilized Tribes, it was appointed by President Grover Cleveland in 1893 to negotiate with the Cherokees, Creeks, Choctaws, Chickasaws, and Seminoles. The object was to induce these Indians, to whom the Dawes General Allotment Act did not apply, to take their lands "in severalty" (that is, to convert lands to individual ownership), abolish their tribal governments, and come under state and federal laws. The original commission consisted of Henry L. Dawes, Archibald S. McKennon, and Meredith H. Kidd. Despite some resistance, including that led by the Creek Chitto Harjo, or Crazy Snake, the commission secured the necessary agreements with the tribes, made up tribal rolls, classified the tribal lands, and allotted to all citizens their rightful share of the common property. Its work being finished, the commission was abolished by law on 1 July 1905.

BIBLIOGRAPHY

Debo, Angie. *And Still the Waters Run: The Betrayal of the Five Civilized Tribes.* 1940. Reprint, Princeton, N.J.: Princeton University Press, 1968.

Perdue, Theda. *Nations Remembered: An Oral History of the Five Civilized Tribes, 1865–1907.* Westport, Conn.: Greenwood Press, 1980.

Wickett, Murray R. *Contested Territory: Whites, Native Americans, and African Americans in Oklahoma, 1865–1907.* Baton Rouge: Louisiana State University Press, 2000.

Frank Rzeczkowski

See also **Dawes General Allotment Act.**

DAWES GENERAL ALLOTMENT ACT.

Named after its chief sponsor, Republican Senator Henry Dawes of Massachusetts, the Dawes Act of 1887 represented an attempt to speed the assimilation of Native Americans into U.S. society. The act proposed to break up tribal communities, which were seen as impediments to the civilizing process, and redistribute communal lands to individual Indians. In the view of reformers and government supporters of the policy, distributing lands "in severalty" (that is, to each member) would promote individual initiative and enable Indians to become self-supporting. The act provided for the issuing of 160 acres of land to each head of household, 80 acres to each single adult and orphan under the age of eighteen, and 40 acres to each minor child. The act also stipulated that the government would hold allotted lands in trust for twenty-five years, thereby preventing them from being taxed or sold and protecting the allottee's interests. At the end of this period the allottee would receive a fee-simple patent to the land. After a reservation had been allotted surplus land would be purchased by the government and sold to homesteaders.

Although conceived primarily by eastern reformers, the Dawes Act also responded to the land hunger of western states and settlers. Indian tribes resisted the new law, but the government applied pressure to numerous tribes to accept its principles. Between 1887 and 1934 the government allotted 118 out of 213 reservations. During this period the Indian estate shrank from 138 million acres to 52 million acres through the cession of surplus land and the alienation of land after the end of the trust period.

Overall, the act failed to convert Indians into self-sufficient farmers. On many reservations allotments proved too small to be commercially viable, and heirship proceedings following the deaths of the original allottees often left Indians with scattered and fragmented landholdings. Ironically, the act also failed to destroy tribal communities on most reservations. After its failures were documented by the Meriam Report, issued by the Department of the Interior in 1928, the Dawes Act was finally repudiated as federal Indian policy by the Indian Reorganization Act, passed by Congress in 1934.

BIBLIOGRAPHY

Hoxie, Frederick E. *The Final Promise: The Campaign to Assimilate the Indians, 1880–1920.* Lincoln: University of Nebraska Press, 1984.

McDonnell, Janet A. *The Dispossession of the American Indian, 1887–1934.* Bloomington: Indiana University Press, 1991.

Frank Rzeczkowski

See also **Indian Land Cessions; Indian Reorganization Act.**

DAWES PLAN, which was adopted in August 1924, resulted from Germany's failure to pay its World War I reparations. Germany began defaulting on its payments in January 1923 as a consequence of its refusing to raise taxes and allowing spiraling inflation to destroy the value of the mark. Beginning in January 1924, a group of business experts headed by the Chicago banker Charles G. Dawes devised a system for currency stabilization and payment reductions. Under the Dawes Plan, American and British bankers provided loans to enable Germany to expand production and make reparations payments to the Allies; these payments rose gradually until 1929, when the Young Plan again reduced the final amount owed. But with the onset of the Great Depression, Germany ceased reparations payments, and in 1932 the Allies canceled them altogether. Germany transferred a total of 16.8 billion marks to the Allies while receiving 44.7 billion in speculative mark purchases and loans, resulting in investors paying "reverse reparations."

BIBLIOGRAPHY

Kent, Bruce. *The Spoils of War: The Politics, Economics, and Diplomacy of Reparations, 1918–1932.* Oxford: Clarendon Press, 1989.

McNeil, William C. *American Money and the Weimar Republic: Economics and Politics on the Eve of the Great Depression.* New York: Columbia University Press, 1986.

Parrini, Carl P. *Heir to Empire: United States Economic Diplomacy, 1916–1923.* Pittsburgh, Pa.: University of Pittsburgh Press, 1969.

Schuker, Stephen A. *American "Reparations" to Germany, 1919–33: Implications for the Third-World Debt Crisis.* Princeton, N.J.: Princeton University Press, 1988.

Trachtenberg, Marc. *Reparation in World Politics: France and European Economic Diplomacy, 1916–1923.* New York: Columbia University Press, 1980.

James I. Matray

See also **Young Plan.**

DAY CARE. *See* **Child Care.**

DAYLIGHT SAVING TIME. Traditionally, Americans adjusted their hours to fit changes in daylight. Farmers, as well as railroads, steamship lines, shops, and factories changed their hours of operation seasonally. These seasonal schedules declined after American railroads implemented standard time zones in 1883. In 1907, an English builder and golfer named William Willett proposed the basic outline of what became daylight saving time. His plan found ready ears in the United States.

American commercial interests began pushing for "more daylight," especially the burgeoning leisure time industry. An hour of light after work meant bigger crowds at ball games, amusement parks, and department stores. Commercial interests seized on the fact that in 1916, some European nations adopted "fast time" to promote efficiency and save fuel. The U.S. Senate began investigating daylight saving time that year, hearing testimony from the "National Daylight Saving Convention," a lobbying group of businessmen, chambers of commerce, and trade organizations. In 1917, these groups tied daylight saving to patriotism, efficiency, and economy, urging, "mobilize an extra hour of daylight and help win the war." Although no savings of fuel was ever demonstrated, in March 1918 Congress passed a bill to "save daylight and provide a standard time." Besides establishing a period of summer daylight saving, the bill made standard time zones into national law.

Daylight saving met with considerable skepticism, primarily from those on the borders of existing time zones, and workers who rose extremely early. On the western edge of the eastern zone, adopting daylight saving put clocks nearly two hours ahead of the daylight. Farmers in those regions resisted daylight saving because it forced them to start too early in the morning. Labor organizations, including the American Federation of Labor, also resented rising in deeper darkness so middle-class businessmen might play golf after work. Additional objections called the measure absurd, like robbing Peter to pay Paul, while a minority detested changes to "God's time." Some businesses, particularly the movie industry, lost sales under daylight saving.

Repealed in 1919, daylight saving remained in use by local option until the Uniform Time Act of 1966 made daylight saving national law. During World War II, year-round daylight saving prevailed, and in 1974 President Richard Nixon, reacting to the first energy crisis, set the clocks ahead for fifteen months. In 1986, lobbied by the makers of sporting goods, charcoal grills, and insect repellants, Congress established calendar dates in early April and late October for daylight saving.

BIBLIOGRAPHY

Bartky, Ian, and Elizabeth Harrison. "Standard and Daylight Saving Time." *Scientific American* 240 (May 1979): 46–53.

O'Malley, Michael. *Keeping Watch: A History of American Time.* New York: Viking, 1990.

Michael O'Malley

D DAY. The term "D Day" indicates the beginning of an attack or other military operation when the specific date has yet to be selected or secrecy is required. "H Hour" is similarly used to designate the time of the attack.

D Day. Soldiers pack a U.S. Coast Guard landing barge headed for the beach at Normandy.
NATIONAL ARCHIVES AND RECORDS ADMINISTRATION

The "D" and "H" are derived from the first letters of "day" and "hour." There is one D Day and H Hour for all units participating in an operation. Plus and minus signs are used to indicate the number of days or hours that precede or follow the specific operation. Thus, D − 5 means five days before D Day and H + 2 means two hours after H Hour.

Planning for operations can begin months before the anticipated time of the operation. The use of D Day minus "X number of days" signifies the date by which certain actions, such as planning or the training of units, must be complete. At the appropriate time an order is published giving a specific date for D Day.

The U.S. Army first used the term on 7 September 1918, when it issued First Army Field Order Number 9: "The First Army will attack at H Hour on D Day with the object of forcing the evacuation of the St. Mihiel Salient." The term is most commonly associated with the invasion of Normandy on 6 June 1944.

Frank R. Shirer

See also **Normandy Invasion.**

DE SOTO. *See* **Soto, Hernando de, Explorations of.**

DEAF IN AMERICA. An estimated 28.8 million people comprise the American deaf community. Deaf culture has traditionally centered around residential schools for the deaf, where language, primarily American Sign Language (ASL), conveys culture. Values and self-identity are passed from peer to peer, rather than through families. The history of the deaf community stems largely from the educational experiences of generations of deaf Americans.

In early eighteenth-century America, deaf education consisted of private tutoring or schooling in Europe. European schools used either the oral method, utilizing speech, lip-reading, and written language to stimulate learning, or the manual method, which relied on signs and writing. In 1815, educator and reformer Thomas Hopkins Gallaudet visited the Royal Institute for the Deaf in Paris where he met a deaf teacher, Laurent Clerc. Returning to the United States in 1817, they founded the American Asylum for the Deaf in Hartford, Connecticut. This school communicated in a mixture of French Sign Language and indigenous signs, which the deaf gradually synthesized to form ASL.

As a result of early nineteenth-century educational reforms and growth, many states established their own schools, most utilizing ASL. While many educators and deaf citizens supported manualism, others, including Samuel Gridley Howe and Horace Mann, advocated oralism.

Few early schools incorporated articulation and speech training into their curricula, but by the late nineteenth century, numerous schools were promoting oralism, including the prominent Clarke School in Northampton, Massachusetts.

While the average American achieved, at best, an elementary-level education, many deaf students graduated from their institutions ready to enter numerous trades, with some achieving white-collar status. Yet they continued to socialize largely with their fellow deaf, and lived near a sizeable deaf population or near the schools. Journalists Edmund Booth and Laura Redden Searing and architect Olof Hansen were part of a burgeoning deaf middle class in the second half of the nineteenth century.

In 1857 Gallaudet's son, Edward Miner Gallaudet, became superintendent of the Columbia Institution for the Deaf and Dumb in Washington, D.C. In 1864, Abraham Lincoln chartered that institution as the National Deaf-Mute College, later renamed Gallaudet University. At the close of the Civil War, most states operated at least one school for the deaf, and a college existed in Washington, D.C. But the educational conflict between proponents of oralism and manualism heightened after 1865. Social Darwinism, cultural imperialism, and the rise of scientific "answers," including eugenics, led to the gradual displacement of ASL by oralism. Edward Miner Gallaudet and Alexander Graham Bell, respectively, personified the debate between manualism and oralism. In 1880 an international congress on deaf education in Milan, Italy, endorsed oralism. The conference influenced American educators, and by the early 1900s, most state schools had opted for voiced speech in education and communication.

Deaf Americans experienced a nadir during the first half of the twentieth century, as did blacks and other minorities. Undereducated and underemployed, many deaf people existed on the fringes of society. The reemergence of the deaf community and ASL began during World War II, when many companies hired deaf employees in the absence of hearing males. In the 1960s, civil rights and other social movements sparked changes within the deaf community.

In the early 1970s, ASL and signed systems reemerged in deaf education. In succeeding decades, schools and colleges began to offer classes in ASL and deaf culture. Theater, television, and movies increasingly showcased the deaf community and ASL. A burgeoning civil rights movement among the deaf and other disabled groups instigated changes in education and employment, most notably with the passage of the Americans with Disabilities Act in 1990. Protests included the successful Deaf President Now! movement at Gallaudet University in 1988.

New laws, cultural consciousness, and technological advances continue to reshape both deafness and the deaf. Where once most deaf people hid their language and culture and worked in marginal jobs, ASL at the end of the twentieth century was taught nationwide. A deaf middle class continues to make strides and awareness of deafness and other disabilities contributes to a multicultural society.

BIBLIOGRAPHY

Benderly, Beryl Lieff. *Dancing without Music: Deafness in America.* New York: Anchor Press, 1980.

Buchanan, Robert. *Illusions of Equality: Deaf Americans in School and Factory, 1850–1950.* Washington, D.C.: Gallaudet University Press, 1999.

Van Cleve, John Vickrey, and Barry A. Crouch. *A Place of Their Own: Creating the Deaf Community in America.* Washington, D.C.: Gallaudet University Press, 1989.

David S. Evans

See also **Americans with Disabilities Act; Gallaudet University; Sign Language, American.**

DEARBORN, FORT.

Chicago, long recognized as a center of control for the region between Lake Michigan and the Mississippi River, proved vital to U.S. military supremacy in the Ohio and Mississippi Valleys. As part of a the campaign to oust the British and their Indian allies from the northwestern territories, an army led by Gen. Anthony Wayne forced twelve Native American tribes to sign the GREENVILLE TREATY in August 1795. The treaty exacted the cession of a tract six miles square at CHICAGO to serve as the site for a future fort, established in 1803 and named after secretary of war Gen. Henry Dearborn. With the outbreak of the WAR OF 1812, the troops and civilians stationed at Fort Dearborn and led by Capt. Nathan Heald were massacred by Native Americans on 15 August while evacuating to Fort Wayne, and the fort was abandoned.

On 4 July 1816, troops reoccupied Chicago and built a second Fort Dearborn. From 1823 until 1832, the fort was alternately abandoned and then garrisoned when new Indian trouble flared. Occupied periods included 1828 to support the government's campaign against the WINNEBAGO Indians, and 1832 at the outbreak of the BLACK HAWK WAR. The development of modern Chicago began in 1833. By 1836, the original Native American occupants of Chicago had been defeated, relocated, or killed, and Fort Dearborn was again, and finally, evacuated. Its military reservation was transformed into Grant Park, the front door to the Chicago Loop.

BIBLIOGRAPHY

Cronon, William. *Nature's Metropolis: Chicago and the Great West.* New York: Norton, 1991.

Quaife, Milo M. *Chicago and the Old Northwest, 1673–1835: A Study of the Evolution of the Northwestern Frontier, Together with a History of Fort Dearborn.* Chicago: University of Chicago Press, 1913.

M. M. Quaife/A. R.

See also **Army Posts; Illinois; Indian Land Cessions; Indian Policy, U.S., 1775–1830; Indian Treaties.**

DEARBORN WAGON,

a light, four-wheeled vehicle with a top and sometimes side curtains, usually pulled by one horse. Long-standing tradition, dating back to 1821, attributes its design to General Henry Dearborn. It usually had one seat but sometimes as many as two or three, and they often rested on wooden springs. The station wagon of its day, from 1819 to 1850 it was in almost universal use in the United States by truck farmers, peddlers, emigrants, and people traveling for pleasure. Those who traveled by it appreciated its respectable appearance and affordability.

BIBLIOGRAPHY

Taylor, George Rogers. *The Transportation Revolution, 1815–1860*. New York: Rinehart, 1951.

Stanley R. Pillsbury / A. E.

See also **Transportation and Travel; Wagon Manufacture.**

DEATH AND DYING.

In the last 400 years, life expectancies in America have increased, the leading causes of death have changed, and twentieth-century technology has spawned the invention of antibiotics, vaccines, organ transplants, cloning, and genetic engineering. But in seventeenth-century America, death was a terrifying and uncontrollable reality. Half of the original Pilgrims who landed at Plymouth died in the first winter of 1620–1621. Puritan tradition taught that death was a release from the world but juxtaposed this comfort with a fear of God's punishment for earthly sin.

Life in the colonies was made more precarious by infectious diseases, fevers, intestinal worms, spoiled food, and tainted water supplies. One in ten children died before the age of one, and forty percent of children did not reach adulthood. Epidemics (such as diphtheria, influenza, pneumonia, and smallpox), diseases, and accidents were the primary causes of adult deaths, together with frontier Indian wars. Death was so common, and Puritan beliefs so encompassing, that early colonists had no elaborate rituals for the dying or the dead. Funerals were simple; sermons focused on sin and the judgment of God rather than the individual. Bodies were wrapped in cloth (known as winding sheets) or a shroud for burial, and vigils were limited. Wood markers were used to mark graves and listed little more than a person's name. Images on markers were forbidden, and the focus was on preparing the soul to be judged, not on remembrance.

Eighteenth-century America treated death with more elaborate ritual, even though death continued to be a constant, if not more controllable, companion. One in seven children died in childhood, and life expectancies were limited by sweeping epidemics. Urban areas along the coast developed primitive sanitation systems and attracted physicians wishing to set up practice. But the general lack of medical advances (bleeding patients and applying herbal remedies were the mainstays of medical care), limited sanitation practices, poor food preservation, and military casualties during the Revolutionary War limited natural life spans. After the spiritual revivals of the 1730s and 1740s (known as the GREAT AWAKENING), colonists viewed death as a spiritual transition rather than a fearful judgment of God. American society embraced European traditions such as tolling the bell to announce deaths and publishing invitations to funerals. Bodies were laid out for vigil, allowing friends and family time to gather. Trinkets such as gloves or rings were offered to funeral participants in memory of the dead. The act of dying and the treatment of death had evolved into a more individualized and elaborate event. Care for the dying and the dead attended to the physical process of death while showing concern for the soul. Bodies were washed and wrapped (using a cloth shroud similar to a nightgown) to preserve them for visitation and were sometimes placed in icehouses or cellars to keep preserved until the funeral could take place. Stonemasons began producing permanent gravestones; the vivid symbols of skulls, the face of Medusa, and urns were carved on stones, as were epitaphs. By the end of the eighteenth century, an aesthetic of simplicity engaged the newly independent United States, and elaborate mourning rituals and funerals fell out of fashion. Death again became a simpler process, now focused on reunion with God and family in heaven. The gentler symbols of cherubs and mourning angels became popular.

The nineteenth century brought a period of expansion and abundance, followed by the INDUSTRIAL REVOLUTION. Medical advances remained limited until late in the century, and death rates remained high compared with twentieth-century standards. The child death rate remained high, and by 1850, one in sixty-six children died in childhood. Less than ten percent of all adults living in 1860 arrived at adulthood with both parents living and all siblings surviving. At the beginning of the nineteenth century, the average woman gave birth to seven children during her lifetime—a phenomenon that reflected the expectation that children would die from childhood diseases. As medical care, housing, and food preservation improved, birth rates decreased to an average of 3.5 children in 1900. As westward expansion distributed the population throughout the Deep South and the Midwest, Americans experienced a variety of climates and harsh living conditions. Frontier towns such as Detroit and St. Louis had open sewage lanes running through their main streets, and professional medical care was limited in rural areas. INFLUENZA and scarlet fever epidemics plagued the North, and MALARIA and YELLOW FEVER epidemics spread through the South throughout the century, killing thousands at a time. The Civil War (1861–1865) brought the greatest carnage, resulting in an estimated 618,000 deaths by combat, disease, and imprisonment by 1865. This did not include the 472,000 wounded or the numerous civilian deaths caused by disease, malnutrition, and natural causes. It was generally believed in the nineteenth century that diseases were caused by bad air, vapors, and stagnant marshes. Physicians recommended little more for patients than limited bathing, a light diet, and fresh air. Bloodletting and narcotics such as opium powders were used as well, and medicinal concoctions, often laced with lead or mercury, were given as tonics. As a result, the sick often died from the remedies or became invalids. Dying had become such a natural topic of discussion that manuals and books of consolation on preparing the sick for death or coping with loss became popular.

The American middle class emerged in the 1830s, bringing with it a desire to be accepted by the affluent, which required that it follow the appropriate fashions, rituals, and etiquette of genteel society. Many etiquette and household manuals included a section on caring for invalids, laying out the dead, dressing in mourning, preparing a funeral, and decorating the home for mourning. Americans were highly influenced by English and French customs and adapted them to suit American society. Mourning, rather than the dead themselves, became the focus. Once a death had occurred, the body was laid out, washed, and dressed in a shroud or in formal attire. The hair was dressed, and locks were sometimes cut and saved for later use in hair jewelry, hair wreaths, or other memorials. The body was laid out for vigil in a coffin or on a bed in the family home. Concern for the preservation of the body became much more important to Americans, and the process of embalming bodies (removing the bodily fluids and replacing them with preservative chemicals) became common by the time the Civil War began. Wood, metal, and iron coffins were common throughout the nineteenth century, and floral wreaths and arrangements were placed on graves. The funeral industry had begun: cabinetmakers built coffins, liveries arranged or provided hearses and carriages, and professions such as "layers out of the dead" could be found in city directories. (Undertakers were known in England in the 1840s, but the first undertakers in the United States did not establish themselves until the 1870s.) Death was considered a gentle deliverance and was not feared as it had been by the early colonists. Private graveyards gave way to commercially designed cemeteries, where the dead could rest and the living could visit in a pastoral setting. Gravestones evolved into monuments and works of art, rife with symbolism such as weeping willows and hands pointing toward heaven. Epitaphs included more personal information, poems, and phrases such as "at rest" or "going home." Mourning was a feminine responsibility. Women wore black garb trimmed with crape, and veils to hide their faces; they also removed themselves from social activities. Photography brought a peculiar innovation to nineteenth-century death rites. For the first time, Americans could have photos of family members to remember them by. A culture of postmortem photography began in the 1840s and continued through the 1930s. Photos of the dead, of the family in mourning, and of funeral flowers and mementos became an option for mourning memorials.

The twentieth century brought gradual and sweeping changes in the way Americans dealt with death and dying. World War I led to the demise of the visual mourning so important to the Victorians. The emerging garment industry could not keep up with deaths caused by extensive European battles and the mass mourning that ensued. Mourning rituals that demanded special clothing and the mourner's removal from society became archaic luxuries. World War II furthered this trend, as women stepped out of the home and into factories to support the war effort. By 1970, most Americans were not wearing black for funerals and were not using any sign of visual mourning, such as black wreaths, crape, and memorials, in their homes.

The twentieth century also brought great strides in medical care, hygiene, and the extension of life. Vaccines, antibiotics, antiviral drugs, improved water and sewage systems, better food preservation, and food enhancements have allowed Americans to live healthier and longer lives. In 1900 the average life span was 47.5 years; by the end of the century, the average life span had increased to 76.5—a thirty-year increase in 100 years. Cultural focus has shifted to the "cult of youth"; death has become secondary, and for many Americans, the approach to death emphasizes the physical rather than the spiritual. This shift toward a focus on life has taken death outside the home and into hospitals, nursing homes, hospices, assisted living facilities, and funeral homes. This trend began when nursing homes and assisted living facilities were created to provide better medical care for the sick and the elderly. Responsibility for medical care was transferred from the family to corporations and government. Removal of the elderly from the family caused the focus on youth to grow, and the discussion of death and mourning became almost taboo. In the last years of the twentieth century, however, a growing elderly population increased compassion for the dying. Patients' rights, living wills, EUTHANASIA, and ASSISTED SUICIDE have all become important concerns for Americans.

In modern America, bodies are no longer laid out in the home but taken to a morgue and then transferred to a funeral home, which carries out arrangements requested by the family. Family members do not participate in the process of washing and laying out the body, although they may still keep vigil through visitation at a local house of worship or funeral parlor. The funeral industry provides comprehensive services that include transportation and preparation of the body, caskets or cremation, visitation of the body, printing of memorial cards, transportation for the family, and the actual burial and service at the cemetery. Preservation of the body continues to be important in U.S. culture, though cremation is becoming more accepted. Cremation (burning of the body at a high temperature to reduce it to ashes) has been practiced since the Stone Age (circa 3000 B.C.). Cremation was common in pagan societies, but the early Christians associated it with paganism and rejected it. In 1873, crematoriums were reintroduced in Europe and were gaining acceptance by the 1880s. Americans did not openly accept cremation until about 1980, as funeral and burial costs have risen, and cremation remains one of the cheapest methods of disposal. Ashes are disposed of by burial or scattering or are kept in the home. Most Americans still prefer traditional burial, and preparation of the body includes embalming and dressing the corpse in favorite clothing. Unique to this century is the desire to make the body look lifelike by using cosmetics on the face and hands and dressing the hair. The second half of the century has also brought experiments with mummification, cryonics (freezing), and even sending bodies into space to preserve them. Preparation of the body is followed by display and visitation in a funeral home or house of worship, a funeral service, and interment at a cemetery or memorial garden. Persons who have chosen cremation are given a traditional funeral or memorial service after the family has had time to mourn. Visual presentations of mourning are limited to flowers, a memorial card, a hearse, and a procession with cars. Services in the late twentieth century have become very individualized and include favorite music, the display of scrapbooks and pictures, the deceased's favorite objects, or participation by clubs to which the deceased belonged. The funeral has become a celebration and remembrance of life rather than a mourning of death.

Since the late twentieth century, Americans have had many new death-related issues to contend with and choices to make. In the 1990s the leading causes of deaths in America were heart disease, cancer, and stroke. Since 1981, Americans have also had to contend with ACQUIRED IMMUNE DEFICIENCY SYNDROME (AIDS), a deadly epidemic that has killed over thirty-six million people worldwide since its discovery. Technology in the twentieth century expanded the frontiers of science and pushed the ethics of medicine to the brink. Organ transplants, CHEMOTHERAPY, and other medical advances have improved the length and quality of life, and stem cell research, cloning, and GENETIC ENGINEERING are taking Americans into unknown realms of medical options.

BIBLIOGRAPHY

Ariès, Philippe. *The Hour of Our Death*. New York: Knopf, 1981.

Callahan, Maggie, and Patricia Kelley. *Final Gifts: Understanding the Special Awareness, Needs, and Communications of the Dying.* New York: Bantam Doubleday Dell, 1997.

Coffin, Margaret M. *Death in Early America: The History and Folklore of Customs and Superstitions of Early Medicine, Funerals, Burial, and Mourning*. Nashville, Tenn.: Nelson, 1976.

Curl, James Stevens. *The Victorian Celebration of Death*. Phoenix Mill, U.K.: Sutton, 2000.

Halttunen, Karen. *Confidence Men and Painted Women: A Study of Middle-Class Culture in America, 1830–1870*. New Haven, Conn.: Yale University Press, 1982.

Jones, Barbara. *Design for Death*. Indianapolis, Ind.: Bobbs-Merrill, 1967.

Kübler-Ross, Elisabeth. *On Death and Dying*. New York: Scribners, 1997.

Mitford, Jessica. *The American Way of Death Revisited*. New York: Vintage, 2000.

Prothero, Stephen R. *Purified by Fire: A History of Cremation in America*. Berkeley: University of California Press, 2001.

Reich, Warren T., ed. *The Encyclopedia of Bioethics*. New York: Macmillan, 1995.

Karen Rae Mehaffey

See also **Bioethics; Cemeteries; Epidemics and Public Health; Funerary Traditions.**

DEATH OF A SALESMAN, THE. Commentators on the American stage often single out Arthur Miller as the nation's premier playwright; *Death of a Salesman*, written in 1948 and first produced in 1949, is Miller's masterpiece. Willy Loman, the play's tragic protagonist, resembles the many real-life salesmen Miller knew while coming of age in depression-era Brooklyn, New York, men who, according to Miller, "forever imagin[ed] triumphs in a world that either ignores them or denies their presence altogether." *Salesman's* riveting New York production combined the talents of the director Elia Kazan, the set designer Jo Mielziner, and Lee J. Cobb as Loman. Running for 742 performances, it won the prestigious New York Drama Critics' Circle Award and a Pulitzer Prize.

The dramatic force of Miller's play derives in part from expressionistic techniques he used to portray Loman's psychological anguish and guilt-ridden fantasy life. Throughout the play, sudden changes in lighting, blocking, and sound interrupt the main action and announce the beginning of dreamlike memory sequences, in which past events and the contents of Loman's mind are gradually revealed on stage. In addition to Loman's inner life, Miller focuses on the troubled bond between father and son. Biff, Willy's older son, struggles to secure his father's love even as he resists Willy's flawed ideals and unrealistic expectations.

In the end, it is Biff who comes closest to understanding Willy's tragic flaw: "He had the wrong dreams," Biff says, after his father's suicide. If destructive and misguided, Willy Loman's dreams were nevertheless American dreams—the pursuit of freedom, commercial success, affection, respect. *Salesman* is therefore more than a moving portrait of one man's self-delusion and exhaustion. It is a complex presentation of American aspirations and universally felt dilemmas of existence. *Salesman* has been performed to audiences around the world. In 1983, Miller famously directed an all-Chinese cast in a Beijing production of the play.

In the decade and a half after 1776, Americans sometimes referred to the Declaration as the "instrument of our Independence," as if it, and not Congress's less familiar resolutions of 2 July, had ended America's subservience to Britain. Otherwise, the document was all but forgotten until the 1790s, when it emerged from obscurity not as a revolutionary manifesto—by then Independence was old news—but a statement affirming human equality and the existence of "unalienable rights."

The document's celebrants were at first members of the Jeffersonian Republican Party. But as its fiftieth anniversary approached after the War of 1812, the Declaration became a national icon, though one soon embroiled in controversy. As antislavery advocates enlisted the Declaration in their cause, Southern defenders of slavery and their northern allies vociferously denied that "all men" are "created equal" and have "unalienable rights." The Declaration's assertions, they said, applied at best to white men only, and should have been omitted from a document that was meant only to separate America from Britain.

On the opposite side stood a set of men, shaped in the patriotic culture of the 1820s, who later found a home in the Republican Party and whose most eloquent spokesman was Abraham Lincoln. The equality in the Declaration, they said, never implied that men were equal in intellect or strength or appearance. It consisted, they said, in men's equal possession of rights. Had the Declaration's purpose been confined to independence, it would be only "an interesting memorial of the dead past" with no practical use in later times. As a testament to personal rights, however, the Declaration was, and was always meant to be, a document of continuing significance. It set up, Lincoln said, "a standard maxim for free society" that was to be enforced "as fast as circumstances should permit," gradually extending its influence and "augmenting the happiness and value of life to all people of all colors everywhere" (Springfield, 26 June 1857). Members of the Republican Party finally added the principles of the Declaration of Independence, as they understood them, to the Constitution by enacting the Thirteenth Amendment, which ended slavery, and, following Lincoln's death, the Fourteenth Amendment, which precluded the states from depriving "any person of life, liberty, or property, without due process of law."

Today Americans revere the Declaration of Independence less as "the instrument of our Independence" than a statement of rights. They remember only those opening phrases of its second paragraph that speak of equality and of unalienable rights to life, liberty, and the pursuit of happiness. Even the engraving on the Jefferson Memorial in Washington, D.C., cuts off Jefferson's carefully constructed long sentence in the middle, ending with the assertion "that to these rights governments are instituted among men." The right of revolution, the original point of the sentence, was edited out, transforming a revolutionary manifesto into an assertion of the rights that established governments must protect, much like a bill of rights. Not only the members of the drafting committee and other delegates to the Second Continental Congress edited the Declaration of Independence, but also generations of later Americans. They gave it a function with which Jefferson would not perhaps have disagreed, but that remains nonetheless different from that of the document as he understood it.

BIBLIOGRAPHY

Boyd, Julian P. *The Declaration of Independence: The Evolution of the Text.* Reprint, Charlottesville, N.C.: International Center for Jefferson Studies at Monticello, 1999.

——, ed. *The Papers of Thomas Jefferson.* vol. 1. Princeton, N.J.: Princeton University Press, 1950.

Hazelton, John H. *The Declaration of Independence: Its History.* Reprint, New York: Da Capo Press, 1970.

Larson, Carlton F. W. "The Declaration of Independence: A 225th Anniversary Re-Interpretation," *Washington Law Review,* LXXVI (2001): 701–787.

Lucas, Stephen E. "The Rhetorical Ancestry of the Declaration of Independence," *Rhetoric and Public Affairs,* I (1998): 143–184.

Maier, Pauline, *American Scripture: Making the Declaration of Independence.* New York: Knopf, 1997.

Pauline Maier

See also **Independence; Jeffersonian Democracy; Revolution, American;** *and vol. 9:* **Declaration of Independence.**

DECLARATION OF RIGHTS.

The Declaration of Rights on 14 October 1774, promulgated by the First Continental Congress, was an obvious precursor of the Declaration of Independence of 4 July 1776 in both language and content. It should be noted that fifteen years later, its very title as well as its content informed the first stirrings of the French Revolution (1787–1799). With the example of the American Revolution (1775–1783) in mind, the First Estates General issued its own Declaration of the Rights of Man and of the Citizen in 1789.

The American declaration marked a significant escalation in the expression of colonial grievances. First, it was put together by a national entity, revolutionary in itself, representing as it did twelve of the thirteen colonies. Second, it articulated for the first time a specific historic linkage to escalating events, citing violations of colonial rights during the Stamp Act Crisis of 1765, the blanket affirmation of total British sovereignty embodied in the Townshend Duties and the ensuing Declaratory Act of 1767, and the Coercive Acts applied to Massachusetts in general and Boston Port in particular in 1774. Finally, the language of the Declaration of Rights boldly asserted America's higher sovereign authority rooted in Natural Law as expressed in the Enlightenment discourse of the seventeenth and eighteenth centuries.

Specifically, the declaration was the first American revolutionary document to articulate the right to "life, liberty and property," the most common American expression of Natural Law. The declaration went even further. It challenged English authority by claiming that the colonists were Englishmen and Englishwomen, asserting "all the rights, liberties and immunities of free natural born subjects, within the realm of England." Directly confronting the Coercive Acts of 1774 and the creation of an autocratically appointed upper house and the suspension of the local judiciary in the Bay Colony, the Declaration of Rights proclaimed both the "right in the people to participate in their legislative councils" and "the privilege of being tried by their peers of their vicinage [locality]."

If it sounded as if the members of the Congress wanted it both ways, they did. They wanted both their rights as Englishmen and the liberty of establishing their own government. The Declaration of Rights then was a radical document, the most revolutionary expression of American rights yet articulated. It both reflected and engendered a growing sense of national purpose and, as such, in 1774 moved America significantly closer to independence.

Ironically, the inspiration for the American Declaration of Rights may have come from the English Parliament of 1689. At the end of the Glorious Revolution (1688), English representatives forced on William III their own Declaration of Rights forbidding the Crown to suspend any parliamentary act, granting to Parliament the sole right to tax, and again, tellingly, guaranteeing protection of the law to every English subject. All of these elements were in evidence in 1774 in the New World. What went around came around.

The American Declaration of Rights was a milestone in the process of eroding royal authority. Crown prerogatives, even given the limitations placed on them by parliamentary encroachment over five hundred years, were rooted in the idea of king as father figure, the paternal, wise, and beneficent ruler who presided in mystical bond with his subjects. The declaration specifically rejected "the exercise of legislative power in several colonies by the King." This official assault on the Crown, who was characterized as not wise and beneficent after all, was reinforced by the steady barrage of propaganda coming out of Massachusetts Bay and Philadelphia. John Dickinson, John Adams, and Samuel Adams particularly undermined royal authority among colonists. They defined Loyalists directly as those loyal to the king.

Samuel Adams, one of the delegates representing Massachusetts at the First Continental Congress, was already deemed a radical in 1774, and he was joined by John Adams in telling the Bay Colony's story of the events following the Boston Tea Party in 1773. By every measure, John Adams had been a moderate until then, not advocating independence in his influential writings prior to 1774. But his endorsement of the Declaration of Rights at the Congress marked the movement of moderates generally and John Adams specifically to the radical camp that espoused independence as the only way to secure American liberties. The 1774 declaration then was a key moment in the maturation of the American Revolution, as it articulated a growing and perhaps by then irreversible estrangement between the mother country and its rebellious colonies.

BIBLIOGRAPHY

Namier, Louis Bernstein. *England in the Age of the American Revolution.* New York: St. Martin's, 1962.

Rakove, Jack N. *The Beginnings of National Politics: An Interpretive History of the Continental Congress.* New York: Knopf, 1979.

Carl E. Prince

See also **Coercive Acts; Continental Congress.**

DECLARATION OF SENTIMENTS

DECLARATION OF SENTIMENTS was presented to the first women's rights convention held in Seneca Falls, New York, in 1848. Modeled on the Declaration of Independence, it articulated the rights of women, listed types of discrimination women faced in the mid-1800s, and offered solutions. Elizabeth Cady Stanton and Lucretia Coffin Mott were among those who wrote the document.

Such efforts were not without precedent. In Revolutionary France in 1791, Olympe de Gouges wrote the Declaration of the Rights of Woman and Citizen in response to the National Assembly's adoption of the Declaration of the Rights of Man and Citizen. Gouges's treatise focused on women's role in the state and devoted considerable attention to the needs of mothers who lacked independent income and legal standing. Gouges was guillotined for her support of the French monarchy and her public feminist principles.

As with the French example, the Declaration of Sentiments utilized much of the language of the original with the intention of pointing out both its familiarity and its supposed inclusion of all. The declaration begins: "When, in the course of human events," a "portion of the family of man" finds it necessary to assume a new position, it must explain its course of action. It continues: "We hold these truths to be self-evident: that all men and women are created equal." The document lists men's "oppressions" against women, which include monopolizing almost all "profitable employments;" keeping woman subordinate in church and state; and working to destroy their confidence in their own powers. Resolutions to overcome these realities proposed providing full information concerning laws controlling women's lives and ending different standards for manners and morality in men and women. Sixty-eight women and thirty-two men signed the document, which remained a force in the women's movement of the nineteenth century.

BIBLIOGRAPHY

Anderson, Bonnie S. *Joyous Greetings: The First International Women's Movement, 1830–1860.* Oxford: Oxford University Press, 2000.

Buhle, Mari Jo, and Paul Buhle, eds. *The Concise History of Woman Suffrage: Selections from the Classic Work of Stanton, Anthony, Gage, and Harper.* Urbana: University of Illinois Press, 1978.

Stanton, Elizabeth Cady, Susan B. Anthony, and Matilda Joslyn Gage, eds. *History of Woman Suffrage.* Six vols. New York: Source Books, 1970.

Hilda L. Smith

See also **Suffrage: Woman's Suffrage; Women's Rights Movement: The Nineteenth Century;** *and vol. 9:* **The Seneca Falls Declaration of Rights and Sentiments.**

DECLARATORY ACT, 1766. The first defining fact of the Declaratory Act of 1766 was that it followed hard on the heels of Parliament's repeal of the detested STAMP ACT of 1765, England's first major retreat in the face of colonial American resistance. The Declaratory Act, in mid-March, affirmed England's right "to bind the colonies . . . in all cases," whether it be the right to tax, enforcement of all parliamentary laws, or crown prerogatives over its colonies in general; all were subject always to British sovereignty. In basking in their immediate political victory, Americans lost sight of the significance of the Declaratory Act. It was almost a word-for-word reprise of the 1719 Irish Declaratory Act that delivered Ireland into disastrous bondage to the crown. The same was meant to be the fate of America as well.

The second defining fact, often overlooked by historians, was that it established once and for all the British Customs Service on the ground in America. Whitehall, at Parliament's behest, sent to the American colonies experienced British customs supervisors who acted as the American Board of Customs Commissioners. These Englishmen—centered on Boston at first, then other ports in New England, then the middle colonies and the South—supervised the rapid spread of customs enforcement to all major and most minor American ports. Within a year after the Declaratory Act, trade laws were enforced with a vengeance for the first time in American waters. The duties imposed by the TOWNSHEND ACTS of 1767, under the broad mandate cast by the Declaratory Act and sustained by columns of British redcoats in Boston, were collected eventually in American harbors large and small.

As always, with armed foreign troops standing by, Boston was the place where enforcement met the most resistance. "Tidesmen" were now sent aboard vessels before unloading could begin. The seizure of two of John Hancock's vessels for smuggling violations in early 1768 touched off an organized colonial resistance. Boston's SONS OF LIBERTY confronted the customs commissioners. With the power of the Declaratory Act in place, the customs commissioners did what Whitehall would not and used armed troops to repress organized rioting; the Bos-

TON MASSACRE in March 1770 was the defining moment in the new round of violence and repression. While Parliament may have wavered, the military, customs, and civil authorities on the scene in Boston did not.

Whitehall responded with characteristic lack of resolve and repealed the Townshend duties, with the exception of the tax on tea. The customs commissioners, relying on the intent of the Declaratory Act, resolved to enforce that levy. The collection of the tea tax rankled the now-organized colonials, and the inevitable denouement came in the form of the BOSTON TEA PARTY in December 1773. While the Sons of Liberty's action in Boston Harbor was the overt event, the looming blanket terms of repression found in the Declaratory Act remained the proximate cause of mounting opposition in America, as demonstrated a few months later in the American revolutionaries' militant reaction to the INTOLERABLE ACTS.

The harsh terms of the Declaratory Act, affirming as it did "Parliament's right as the sovereign legislature" to rule the American colonies without limit, made the Intolerable Acts' passage in London virtually inevitable. In retrospect, the die was cast, and the American Revolution in the spring of 1774 moved inexorably forward.

BIBLIOGRAPHY

Namier, Louis B. *England in the Age of the American Revolution.* 2d ed. New York: St. Martin's Press, 1962. The original edition was published in 1930.

Prince, Carl E., and Mollie Keller. *The U.S. Customs Service: A Bicentennial History.* Washington, D.C.: U.S. Government Printing Office, 1989.

Rakove, Jack N. *The Beginnings of National Politics: An Interpretive History of the Continental Congress.* New York: Knopf, 1979; Baltimore: Johns Hopkins University Press, 1982.

Carl E. Prince

See also **Revolution, American: Political History.**

DECORATIONS, MILITARY

Medal of Honor

The highest American decoration for valor is the Medal of Honor. In separate army, navy, and air force versions, the president awards it in the name of Congress to a member of the armed forces conspicuously displaying gallantry and intrepidity at the risk of life, above and beyond the call of duty, while engaged in armed conflict. The navy medal may be awarded for noncombatant heroism such as lifesaving. On rare occasions the Medal of Honor has been awarded to individuals in peacetime. The medal has also been awarded to the American Unknown Soldiers and, by special legislation, to the Unknown Soldiers of U.S. allies in World War I.

The medal dates from December 1861, when Congress approved the creation of a Navy Medal of Honor for enlisted personnel; thus it is America's oldest badge of honor in continuous use. Congress authorized an Army

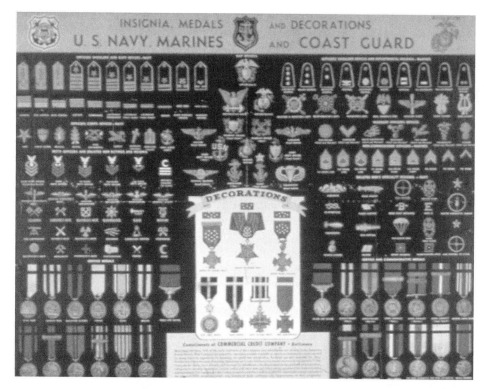

Military Decorations. A World War II display of insignias, medals, and decorations of the U.S. Navy, Marine Corps, and Coast Guard. NATIONAL ARCHIVES AND RECORDS ADMINISTRATION

Medal of Honor in July 1862; legislation in March 1863 extended the medal to army officers and made the award retroactive to the start of the Civil War for all army personnel. Provisions to award the Navy Medal of Honor to navy and Marine Corps officers came in 1915, and the air force received authority to award the medal in 1949. In 1963, members of the Coast Guard (formerly eligible for the medal from the navy) received the same eligibility as members of the other services.

Distinguished Service, Navy, and Air Force Crosses
Ranking next below the Medal of Honor, the Distinguished Service Cross was established for the army on 2 June 1918; the Navy Cross for the navy on 4 February 1919; and the Air Force Cross for the air force on 6 July 1960 (whose members had been eligible for the Distinguished Service Cross). The award is made to armed forces members who distinguish themselves by extraordinary heroism while engaged in action against an enemy of the United States; while engaged in military operations involving conflict with a foreign opponent; or while serving with friendly foreign forces in an armed conflict against an opposing armed force.

Distinguished Service Medal
The secretary of each branch of the armed services awards the Distinguished Service Medal to those who distinguish themselves in any capacity by exceptionally meritorious

service in any duty of great responsibility. Congress authorized the army version on 6 July 1918, making it retroactive to 6 April 1917. The first recipients were the Allied Army commanders.

Members of the air force received this version until 6 July 1960, when Congress authorized their own distinctive award; Congress authorized the navy version, also awarded to Marine Corps personnel, on 4 February 1919, making it retroactive to 6 April 1917. The Coast Guard medal was authorized in 1951 for peacetime service, when that service is not under navy control.

Silver Star
Congress first authorized the Silver Star for all services on 9 July 1918, for gallantry in action as cited in published orders issued by the headquarters of a general officer. Since the award was made retroactive, many individuals "cited in orders" back to the Spanish-American War received the citation star. The Silver Star is the third highest award for combat heroism and ranks fourth in overall precedence.

Legion of Merit
Congress created the Legion of Merit, which ranks just below the Silver Star, on 20 July 1942, retroactive to 8 September 1939, when President Franklin D. Roosevelt proclaimed a state of emergency before World War II. It is awarded to members of the American armed forces and

526

of friendly foreign nations who "have distinguished themselves by exceptionally meritorious conduct in the performance of outstanding services." It is the only U.S. decoration with specific degrees of rank.

Distinguished Flying Cross

First authorized by Congress on 2 July 1926, and amended by executive order on 8 January 1938, the Distinguished Flying Cross was made retroactive to 11 November 1918, for heroism or extraordinary achievement while participating in aerial flight. The first awards were made to Capt. Charles A. Lindbergh for his transatlantic solo flight (1927) and to Commander Richard E. Byrd (1926) for his North Pole flight. Both also received special awards of the Medal of Honor. Amelia Earhart is the only civilian recipient. The criteria for the award are the same for all services.

Soldier's Medal

The Soldier's Medal is a non-combat award given to any person who, while serving in any capacity with the army, displays heroism not involving actual conflict with an enemy after 2 July 1926. It is a highly respected sign of personal bravery usually indicating risk of life. On 6 July 1960, Congress authorized the equivalent Airman's Medal.

Navy and Marine Corps Medal

Authorized by Congress on 7 August 1942, the Navy and Marine Corps Medal parallels the Soldier's Medal and is awarded to any person who, while serving in any capacity with the navy or the Marine Corps, displays heroism not involving actual conflict with an enemy after 6 December 1941. Persons to whom the secretary of the navy, before 7 August 1942, awarded a letter of commendation for heroism may also win this medal, regardless of the date of the act of heroism. President John F. Kennedy won this award as the commander of PT 109 in World War II.

Bronze Star Medal

First authorized in 1944, the regulations covering the Bronze Star have undergone numerous revisions. It may be awarded by the secretary of a military department, or by the secretary of transportation with regard to the Coast Guard when it is not operating as a service in the navy, to anyone who, while serving in any capacity in or with the army, navy, air force, Marine Corps, or Coast Guard after 6 December 1941, performs heroic or meritorious achievement not involving aerial flight during military operations. It can also be awarded to all personnel authorized the Combat Infantry Badge or Combat Medical Badge between 7 December 1941 and 2 September 1945.

Air Medal

Established on 11 May 1942, the Air Medal is given to any person who, while serving with the armed forces subsequent to 8 September 1939, performs meritorious achievement while participating in aerial flight.

Purple Heart, Order of the

Established by George Washington on 7 August 1782, for meritorious service and extraordinary fidelity, the Order of the Purple Heart is America's oldest military decoration. After the Revolution it fell into disuse until the War Department reestablished it in 1932 to recognize a "singularly meritorious act," including wounds received in action, retroactive to 5 April 1917. Since 1942, when the Legion of Merit was established, the Purple Heart has been awarded to members of the armed forces and, in some cases, civilians, for wounds and other specific injuries received in action.

BIBLIOGRAPHY

Kerrigan, Evans E. *American War Medals and Decorations.* New York: Viking Press, 1964.

John E. Jessup Jr.
Warren Stark / C. W.

See also **Air Force, United States; Army, United States; Coast Guard, U.S.; Marine Corps, United States; Navy, United States.**

DEERFIELD MASSACRE. In the early morning of 29 February 1704, a force of 50 French soldiers and 200 Indian allies from Canada, under the command of Major Hertel de Rouville, climbed up high snow drifts over the unguarded stockade at Deerfield, Massachusetts, one of New England's most northwestern settlements. The invaders quickly overcame the sleeping inhabitants, encountering no effective resistance except at the Stebbins house, where seven men and four or five women with their children successfully held off attackers until militia from neighboring Hadley arrived. Of the 300 inhabitants, about 50 were killed, 137 escaped, and 111 were taken captive. During the harrowing journey to Canada, 17 of the captives died from exposure or at the hands of their captors. As one of the opening engagements of Queen Anne's War (known in Europe as the War of Spanish Succession)—the second in a series of wars between France and England between 1689 and 1763—the stunning victory left New Englanders in dread fear of the French and their Indian allies, who appeared capable of attacking from Canada in almost any weather. After prolonged negotiations lasting several years, 60 of the captives were allowed to return home; some, however, preferred to remain in Canada.

BIBLIOGRAPHY

Demos, John. *The Unredeemed Captive: A Family Story from Early America.* New York: Knopf, 1994.

Melvoin, Richard I. *New England Outpost: War and Society in Colonial Deerfield.* New York: Norton, 1988.

Phillip M. Brown / J. H.

See also **Captivity Narratives; Colonial Wars.**

DEFENSE, DEPARTMENT OF (DOD), established by the National Security Act (1947), was initially named the National Military Establishment (NME). Including cabinet departments of the army, navy, and air force, the JOINT CHIEFS OF STAFF, and several other defense agencies, the NME replaced the War and Navy departments. President Harry S. Truman, understanding the need for interservice coordination and the security threats posed by the Soviet Union, had urged creation of the new national security system, which included the Central Intelligence Agency and the NATIONAL SECURITY COUNCIL.

James V. Forrestal, the first secretary of defense (1947–1949), had a difficult task—molding a workable organization, dealing with squabbling among the services over roles and missions, and developing a viable defense budget. In addition, he had to deal with the Soviet takeover of Czechoslovakia, the Berlin blockade and airlift, and the Sinai War between Arabs and Israelis. Creation of the Marshall Plan (1948) and the NORTH ATLANTIC TREATY ORGANIZATION (NATO, 1949) also challenged the DOD. In 1949, based on Forrestal's proposals, the NME became the Department of Defense; the army, navy, and air force became departments without cabinet status; and the secretary of defense's control over these departments was broadened.

Forrestal's successor, Louis A. Johnson (1949–1950), took some of the blame for initial U.S. military reverses in the Korean War, which began in June 1950. He also had trouble with the services over roles and missions and military funding. In September 1950, General George C. Marshall replaced him as secretary. By this time, the United States had begun to carry out NSC-68, a document emphasizing Soviet aggressiveness and urging increased production of atomic weapons, enlargement of the military budget, expansion of the services, and broadened military and economic assistance to allies. War costs caused the defense budget to increase from $13.5 billion to $48 billion for the fiscal year (which then began in July) 1951. Marshall supported Truman's 1951 decision to dismiss General Douglas MacArthur, the Far East commander who challenged the president's policy against expanding the Korean military action into Communist China. His successor, Robert A. Lovett (1951–1953), carried on his policies.

President Dwight D. Eisenhower (1953–1961) gave personal attention to defense, and three men served as secretary of defense under him—Charles E. Wilson (1953–1957), Neil H. McElroy (1957–1959), and Thomas S. Gates, Jr. (1959–1961). Eisenhower's New Look policy assumed that any major war would be nuclear, with weapons to be delivered by strategic air forces (massive retaliation), expanded continental defense, modernization of reserve units, and thereby smaller conventional forces. This approach, Eisenhower believed, would make possible defense budget cuts. Secretary Wilson carried out this policy in the face of severe criticism from within the army and the public. To some observers, the New Look ruled out limited or nonnuclear war. McElroy and Gates promoted deployment in Europe of intermediate-range ballistic missiles to offset the intercontinental-range missiles (ICBMs) deployed by the Soviet Union. The United States began development of the Minuteman ICBM in underground silos in the United States as a deterrent and for use after an attack. Charges against Eisenhower that the Soviet Union was ahead of the United States in missile development played a role in the 1960 presidential campaign but turned out to be unfounded.

President John F. Kennedy appointed Robert S. McNamara, president of the Ford Motor Company and an advocate of systems analysis in defense decision making, as secretary of defense in 1961. McNamara's civilian "whiz kids" played an important role in his controversial decisions on weapon systems by which he cancelled the B-70 bomber but carried forward the F-111 aircraft. McNamara supported Kennedy's flexible response policy, including maintaining strategic arms to deter nuclear attacks against the United States. Kennedy disavowed massive retaliation, which he thought narrowed U.S. choices to "inglorious retreat or unlimited retaliation." Conventional forces again became important, and this, along with the military buildup necessitated by involvement in Vietnam after 1964, led to a significant force expansion. McNamara's relations with the services gradually deteriorated, both because of this effort to centralize authority in the Office of the Secretary of Defense and decisions the services considered detrimental to their interests. In addition to two crises involving Cuba—the Bay of Pigs invasion (1961) and the missile crisis (1962)—there was the war in Vietnam, McNamara's biggest problem. The secretary supported President Lyndon B. Johnson's increased military personnel in Vietnam (from 17,000 in 1963 to 550,000 in 1968). Gradually, however, McNamara changed his mind, as the dollar and human cost of the conflict rose. When he and his department became targets of a massive antiwar movement, the disillusioned secretary resigned in February 1968. His successor, Clark M. Clifford (1968–1969), persuaded Johnson to halt troop increases and stop the bombing in North Vietnam. By the time Johnson left office in January 1969, the United States had begun to negotiate with North Vietnam.

Melvin R. Laird (1969–1973), President Richard M. Nixon's first secretary of defense, developed the policy of Vietnamization, shifting the military burden to South Vietnam. U.S. forces in Vietnam declined from a peak of 543,400 under Johnson to 24,200 at the end of 1972. Secret negotiations by Nixon and Henry Kissinger led to a belated settlement of the VIETNAM WAR in January 1973. In September 1971, Laird also ended the controversial military draft. He retired in January 1973. His successor, Elliot L. Richardson, served only four months before becoming attorney general. Secretary of Defense James R. Schlesinger (1973–1975) believed it necessary to maintain a strategic nuclear capacity essentially equivalent to that of the Soviet Union. He adopted a partial counterforce policy—attack only military targets and avoid cities in the hope that the Soviet Union would follow suit. Schlesinger vociferously argued for larger defense budgets, and President Gerald R. Ford disagreed and dismissed him in late 1975, but his successor, Donald H. Rumsfeld (1975–1977, and again for President George W. Bush, 2001–), continued Schlesinger's policies, including advocacy of increased budgets.

The Democrats, the party of President Jimmy Carter (1977–1981), argued for decreased defense spending, and Carter did cut the defense budget for fiscal year 1978. Heavy criticism from Republicans, combined with crises in Afghanistan (the Soviet invasion in 1979) and Iran (the fall of the shah and the taking of American hostages in 1979), caused Carter to begin a defense buildup. Secretary of Defense Harold Brown (1977–1981) pursued a policy of essential equivalence in nuclear capacity with the Soviet Union. He worked to upgrade the strategic triad of long-range bombers, ICBMs, and submarine-launched ballistic missiles (SLBMs). He pushed members of the North Atlantic Treaty Organization to increase defense spending and emphasized arms control, which moved ahead with the Strategic Arms Limitation Treaty of 1979 (SALT II).

Under President Ronald Reagan (1981–1989) and Secretary of Defense Caspar W. Weinberger (1981–1987), the DOD's budget increased to $300 billion, strengthening the U.S. strategic position, which Reagan believed had fallen behind the Soviet Union. Strategic bomber modernization (B-1B bombers), production of the MX ICBM, and development of a new SLBM (Trident II) and a stealth (radar-evading) aircraft were central to Reagan's defense program. Weinberger obtained large budget increases, but gradually Congress became less willing to approve increases. Secretary of Defense Frank C. Carlucci (1987–1989) was less pressing on the budget but carried on the Reagan policies. The president used force to achieve U.S. objectives—he expelled a Marxist dictator from Grenada (1983) and arranged for the bombing of Libya (1986), suspected of international TERRORISM. He also warmed to arms control, however, agreeing to the 1987 Intermediate-range Nuclear Forces Treaty with the Soviet Union and talks on limiting longer-range weapons.

Reagan's successor, George H. W. Bush, and his secretary of defense, Richard B. Cheney (1989–1993), also used force. The United States invaded Panama in 1989 to oust a leader hostile to the United States, and after Iraq's dictator, Saddam Hussein, invaded neighboring Kuwait in August 1990, Bush sent 500,000 troops to Saudi Arabia. In the Gulf War of 1991, the United States and its United Nations allies drove Iraqi forces from Kuwait. Meanwhile, pressure increased to cut defense spending, stimulated in part by a serious national budget deficit, the end of the COLD WAR, and the dissolution of the Soviet Union. Bush and his successor, President Bill Clinton, had to devise a new policy to respond to the collapse of the nation's main adversary. The DOD decided to close many

military bases, slow or cancel production of some weapon systems, and reduce troops stationed overseas, especially in Europe. The military services began to decline from a total of more than two million service personnel in the 1980s to a stated goal of about 1.4 million in the late 1990s. President Clinton pledged a military force large enough to protect the nation's interests. He and Secretaries of Defense Les Aspin (1993–1994), William J. Perry (1994–1997), and William S. Cohen (1997–2001) proceeded with a process of downsizing the military services and their budgets. By 2001, the active duty forces of the U.S. had been reduced to 1.37 million, with 1.28 million ready on stand-by reserve, and about 670,000 civilian employees.

Donald H. Rumsfeld, Secretary of Defense for Ronald Reagan, returned to the office in 2001 with the administration of George W. Bush. The terrorist attacks of 11 September 2001 and subsequent military campaign against terrorist forces in Afganistan completed the DOD's break from Cold War approaches to national security. In the early 2000s, the DOD focused on creating a smaller, more mobile and technologically advanced army, one capable of countering "asymmetical threats"—that is, opponents employing nontraditional strategies, such as guerilla warfare or terrorism, to gain an advantage against conventional military power—at short notice in the remotest corners of the globe.

BIBLIOGRAPHY

Blechman, Barry M., et al. *The American Military in the Twenty-First Century.* New York: St. Martin's Press, 1993.

Cole, Alice C., et al., eds. *The Department of Defense: Documents on Establishment and Organization, 1944–1978.* Washington, D.C.: Office of the Secretary of Defense, Historical Office, 1978.

Gaddis, John Lewis. *Strategies of Containment: A Critical Appraisal of Postwar American National Security Policy.* New York: Oxford University Press, 1982.

Hammond, Paul Y. *Organizing for Defense: The American Military Establishment in the Twentieth Century.* Princeton, N.J.: Princeton University Press, 1961.

Preston, Thomas. *The President and His Inner Circle: Leadership Style and the Advisory Process in Foreign Affairs.* New York: Columbia University Press, 2001.

Rearden, Steven L. *History of the Office of the Secretary of Defense, Vol. 1: The Formative Years, 1947–1950.* Washington, D.C.: Office of the Secretary of Defense, Historical Office, 1984.

Trask, Roger R. *The Department of Defense, 1947–1997: Organization and Leaders.* Washington, D.C.: Office of the Secretary of Defense, Historical Office, 1997.

Roger R. Trask / A. R.

See also **Arms Race and Disarmament; Military-Industrial Complex; Persian Gulf War; War Costs; World War II.**

DEFENSE, NATIONAL. As in most countries, in the United States "national defense" is usually officially construed as the pursuit of all national interests by military means. Because of its location between two oceans, the weakness of its immediate neighbors, and the fortuitous presence of the Royal Navy during the nineteenth century, the United States seldom had to "defend" itself in any literal sense. Not until the advent of long-range nuclear weapons in the mid-twentieth century did the United States face a serious threat to its survival. The terrorist attacks on New York and Washington, D.C., in September 2001 introduced a new challenge to American "national defense," one without precedent in the nation's history.

In 1789 the new U.S. Constitution gave the federal government powers to provide for the common defense, balanced by state control of the militia and the right of the citizenry to bear arms. The Congress was empowered to levy taxes, declare war, raise armies, and provide for a navy. The president was named commander in chief of the army and navy and in 1795 received authority to call out the militia to execute the laws, suppress insurrection, and repel invasion. The Militia Act of 1792 established the principle of universal obligation to military service for all free white male citizens between the ages of 18 and 45.

From a strength of 750 men at the time of George Washington's inauguration, the regular army (established in 1775) grew to about 9,000 on the eve of the WAR OF 1812. The Marine Corps was also founded in 1775. The navy, reestablished formally in 1798, gained valuable experience in the undeclared Quasi-War with France (1798–1800) over neutral maritime rights and in later operations against Tripolitan corsairs. President Thomas Jefferson (1801–1808) cut back both the army and the navy, relying for defense mainly on the militia and harbor fortifications supplemented by gunboats. His administration did see the founding of the U.S. Military Academy at WEST POINT (1802) and the acquisition of the vast Louisiana Territory (1803).

The War of 1812, fought with Great Britain over the issue of neutral maritime rights, demonstrated the inadequacy of a national defense based on militia and maritime commerce raiding. The British, although absorbed in the struggle with Napoleon until 1814, were able to defend Canada successfully, sweep the tiny American navy from the seas, and penetrate the Atlantic and Gulf coast defenses at several points.

During the century after 1815 the United States poured its energies into economic growth, territorial expansion, and domestic politics. Thanks mainly to British concurrence and sea power, the hemispheric hegemony rashly proclaimed by the MONROE DOCTRINE in 1823 met no serious challenge. Up to the MEXICAN-AMERICAN WAR (1846–1848) the army's normal strength hovered around 6,000, mostly scattered along the advancing frontier and engaged in sporadic clashes with the Indians. The navy's few frigates and sloops watched for slave traders and showed the flag. Still committed to the militia tradition, Congress in 1821 rejected Secretary of War John C. Cal-

houn's plan for a professional peacetime army that could be expanded rapidly in an emergency.

In both regular services, meanwhile, a new professionalism was emerging, nurtured both at West Point and at the Naval Academy, established at Annapolis in 1845. The war with Mexico growing out of the annexation of Texas was fought largely with the regulars and volunteer forces raised by the states. Victory brought annexation of most of the remaining areas west of the Mississippi.

The CIVIL WAR (1861–1865) remains the costliest war, in relative human and material terms, in American history. Its demands far exceeded the meager capabilities of the existing military system. Only a handful of regular officers proved equal to the test of higher command, and the tiny regular army remained mostly on the western frontier. Both sides resorted to conscription, mainly as a spur to volunteering. Militia, as such, served only as state local defense forces. By the end of the war, the Confederate government was attempting to control or operate such essential activities as munitions production and blockade-running, anticipating the rigors of twentieth-century "total" war.

After 1865 the army went back to protecting the frontier against Indian raids, and the navy returned to patrolling distant stations. Until the 1890s the army's strength remained in the neighborhood of 25,000, with a strong cavalry component to combat the Plains Indians. In the 1880s the seacoast fortifications were modernized, and the navy began belatedly to replace its wooden sailing ships and smooth-bore guns with modern vessels and armament. By 1898 it had a powerful fleet built around five battleships.

The war with Spain (1898–1899) was a response to U.S. expansionist pressures. Victory, won with relative ease, gave the United States possessions in the Caribbean and the Pacific, including the Philippines, which reacted with an armed revolt against the United States that took several years to suppress.

To protect its new empire and play its new world-power role, the United States expanded and modernized its armed forces in the early twentieth century. The reforms of Elihu Root gave the army a modern general staff organization and a system of advanced professional education on the European model. Spurred by Alfred Thayer Mahan's doctrines of sea power and its new imperial responsibilities, the United States had become by 1914 the third strongest naval power.

The European war that erupted in 1914 impinged on American interests in many ways—through the strangling of trade with European neutrals and the Central Powers, through the growth of a munitions industry fattened by foreign arms contracts, and through loss of American lives and property on neutral merchantmen attacked by German submarines. Responding to a popular clamor for "preparedness," the Defense Act of 1916 expanded the regular army and the NATIONAL GUARD and removed restrictions on federalization and use of the guard in an emergency, although it rejected the army proposal for a big volunteer federal reserve. In August 1916 Congress also voted a huge naval building program.

Although both sides in WORLD WAR I violated neutral maritime rights, the United States in April 1917 came in on the side of the Triple Entente. In the next nineteen months some 4 million men were mobilized, of whom about half were sent to France and played a part in the final battles of 1918. These forces were raised by a federally administered selective draft, which, as in the Civil War, served also to stimulate volunteering. Dependent on its allies for most of its armament, the United States supplied large quantities of small arms, ammunition, food, and raw materials to them and contributed substantially in warships and merchant shipping to the defeat of the German submarine.

In the succeeding two decades the development of the long-range bomber and naval aircraft carrier exposed the United States itself, for the first time since the disappearance of sailing navies, to the real possibility of attack from other continents. In the 1930s, moreover, the growth of Japanese power and ambitions threatened American interests in the Pacific and Far East, while the rise of Nazi Germany in alliance with Italy and Japan raised the specter of a hostile militarism wielding global power.

The navy was the nation's first line of defense during this period. But at the Washington Naval Conference of 1921–1922, the leading nations had agreed to limitations on naval strength and construction, which had the practical effect of giving Japan naval supremacy in the western Pacific. Meanwhile, in a climate of popular revulsion against war, meager appropriations and declining enlistments reduced the regular army, National Guard, and newly created Federal Organized Reserve far below authorized levels. The army's air forces embraced the new doctrine of strategic air power, and the ground forces and marines experimented with new techniques of mechanized and amphibious warfare. But on the eve of WORLD WAR II, the army had only a handful of modern aircraft and tanks.

During the 1930s the administration of Franklin D. Roosevelt (1933–1945) tried to foster hemispheric solidarity against Axis propaganda and economic penetration, and in 1938 it broadened national defense commitments to embrace the hemisphere. But in 1940, with the German conquest of most of western Europe, the United States suddenly faced the threat of German-Italian naval supremacy in the Atlantic and air attacks on South America from West African bases, while its fleet was pinned down in the Pacific watching Japan. Reacting to this threat, the United States instituted selective service and launched a massive rearmament program that year while negotiating with other hemisphere nations and Great Britain for base rights and military collaboration.

Hemisphere defense was closely linked with material aid to Great Britain, the Soviet Union (after June 1941), and other nations opposing the Axis. Under the Lend-Lease Act of March 1941, the United States eventually transferred to anti-Axis nations $50.2 billion in war matériel and services. During 1941, in collaboration with Britain, the United States occupied Iceland and other Atlantic bases, convoyed Allied shipping, exchanged shots with German submarines, ferried British troops, and helped plan the eventual defeat of Germany. In 1941, with German armies bogged down in the Soviet Union and with Great Britain apparently safe from invasion, the pace of American rearmament was slowing. At this juncture Japan, after fruitless negotiations for U.S. recognition of its regional hegemony, struck without warning on 7 December at U.S. bases at Pearl Harbor, Hawaii, and in the Philippines, and simultaneously moved against British, French, and Dutch possessions in Southeast Asia. Germany and Italy declared war on the United States a few days later.

In World War II the United States mobilized forces of 15 million men and women, about one-quarter of the total anti-Axis coalition; mounted large-scale campaigns in the Mediterranean, Europe, the Pacific, and Burma; and provided the backbone of a crushing material superiority over the Axis powers.

For a quarter-century after World War II the United States was the most powerful nation on earth. Yet its leaders perceived a threat to its very survival from a hostile and expansionist world communism. American fear of communism dated back to the 1920s, but its immediate source was the split with Moscow over the postwar settlement in Eastern Europe and Germany. Suspicious of its former allies and concerned for its future security, the Soviet Union after 1944 rapidly occupied and communized Eastern Europe, rejected an American proposal for international control of atomic energy, and in 1949 developed its own atomic bomb.

In 1947 Congress placed the armed services (including a separate air force) with the joint chiefs of staff under a single secretary and Department of Defense. In 1949 the United States joined with Canada and ten (eventually thirteen) European nations in a mutual defense pact, the NORTH ATLANTIC TREATY ORGANIZATION (NATO), bolstered by integrated forces organized under a single headquarters and an American supreme commander. NATO was the first in a global network of U.S.-sponsored regional mutual security pacts formed during the 1950s, embracing forty-two nations and supplemented by a vast system of military bases and communications and by permanent fleets in the Mediterranean and western Pacific.

In 1950 a Soviet-supported North Korean invasion of South Korea precipitated a major limited war (1950–1953) involving large-scale intervention by the Chinese Communists, who had been victorious in the Chinese civil war of 1947–1949, and deployment of U.S. forces to a peak strength of 350,000 in a combined UN force of 800,000.

During the administration of Dwight D. Eisenhower (1953–1960), Secretary of State John Foster Dulles proclaimed a strategy of "massive retaliation" to deter open or covert Communist aggression. The new strategy ostensibly relied primarily on strategic air power and nuclear weapons, elements favored in post-Korea military force structures. It also involved American aid to anticommunist governments in Taiwan, Thailand, South Vietnam, Iran, Israel, Turkey, Greece, and Pakistan.

In 1957 the Soviets developed their first intercontinental ballistic missile, ending the virtual immunity of the U.S. homeland to nuclear attack and creating a "balance of terror" between the two superpowers. With the advent of nuclear-powered missile-launching submarines and "hardened" missile sites in the 1960s, each side gained an "assured destruction capability" against the other's cities. The fragility of this deterrent standoff was demonstrated to a frightened world in October 1962 when U.S. intelligence discovered that the Soviets were attempting to offset American superiority in long-range missiles by secretly shipping shorter-range missiles to Communist-ruled Cuba. After a short, but tense confrontation, Moscow backed down and withdrew the missiles.

By the end of the 1960s the Soviet Union had achieved virtual parity with the United States in strategic nuclear weapons and was expanding its naval power. To avert an apparently imminent Communist takeover in South Vietnam in 1965, the Johnson Administration initiated heavy bombing of North Vietnam and large-scale deployment of combat forces in the south. North Vietnamese forces, supplied by the Soviet Union and China, began to move into the south at about the same time. Four years later, the United States had more than 600,000 troops in Southeast Asia, most of them in South Vietnam.

The turning point came in 1968, when the Communist Tet offensive convinced U.S. leaders that the war could not be won at acceptable cost. President Johnson halted the bombing of North Vietnam, initiated peace negotiations, and withdrew from the presidential election. After Richard Nixon's election to the presidency in 1968, he continued negotiations and gradually withdrew American forces from South Vietnam, while the Vietnamese were being trained and equipped to carry on alone. In 1973 the United States ceased military operations in Vietnam, and in 1975 Saigon fell to the North Vietnamese army. The war, the most unpopular in American history, cost 58,000 American lives, with annual expenditures that soared to $28.8 billion in 1969. American bombers dropped three times as much tonnage as in all of World War II. Use of the draft as the primary source of military manpower, reversing the Korean War policy of reliance on reserves, intensified popular antiwar feeling. In 1973 selective service was terminated, and the armed forces reverted to their traditional reliance on voluntary enlistments.

During the 1980s the Reagan Administration implemented the largest peacetime military buildup in American history. The end of the COLD WAR led many to question the need for such a large military and substantial defense cutbacks began. In 1991, however, the United States went to war in the Persian Gulf, and throughout the decade the use of American military force abroad increased, particularly in Somalia in 1992–1993 and the former Yugoslavia in 1995 and 1999.

In the wake of the terrorist attacks of 11 September 2001, the United States faced the most immediate threat to its national security since Pearl Harbor. The Bush Administration responded by attacking terrorist base camps in Afghanistan and commencing a massive defense buildup on par with the Reagan defense program of the 1980s. Most national security experts have concluded that terrorism poses a major threat to American security in the twenty-first century, and the military will increasingly be molded to respond effectively to that challenge.

BIBLIOGRAPHY

Millett, Alan Reed, and Peter Maslowski. *For the Common Defense: A Military History of the United States of America.* New York: Free Press, 1994.

Millis, Walter. *Arms and Men: A Study in American Military History.* New York: Putnam, 1956.

Perret, Geoffrey. *A Country Made By War: The Story of America's Rise to Power.* New York: Random House, 1989.

Weigley, Russell F. *The American Way of War: A History of United States Military Strategy and Policy.* Bloomington: Indiana University Press, 1977.

Richard M. Leighton / A. G.

See also **Air Force, United States; Air Power, Strategic; Army, United States; Cincinnati, Society of the; Fortifications; Frontier Defense; Missiles, Military; Navy, Department of the; Newburgh Addresses; 9/11 Attack; Preparedness; Roads, Military; War Powers Act.**

DEFENSE OF MARRIAGE ACT. President Bill Clinton signed the Defense of Marriage Act (Public Law 104-199) at 12:50 A.M. on 21 September 1996. It permitted any state to refuse recognition to any same-sex marriage performed in any other state. It also defined "marriage" as exclusively the union of one man and one woman for all purposes under federal law. Clinton signed it almost surreptitiously because he had won considerable lesbian/gay support in 1992 and hoped to do so again in 1996, but he feared the political cost of not opposing same-sex marriages.

A gay couple in Minneapolis first challenged the prohibition on same-sex marriages in 1970. Courts routinely dismissed such cases until 1993, when the Hawaii state supreme court, in *Baehr v. Levin,* found that denial of marriage licenses to same-sex couples violated the state constitutional prohibition on discrimination on the basis of sex. Along with similar decisions in Alaska and Vermont, the Hawaii case led conservative activists to push for state laws prohibiting recognition of same-sex mar-

In Defiance of the Defense of Marriage Act. Lesbian partners exchange a Certificate of Life Partnership, in Philadelphia, 1998. AP/WIDE WORLD PHOTOS

riages. The federal law reflected both conservative opposition to same-sex marriages and Republicans' desire to create political problems for President Clinton during an election year. The Defense of Marriage Act remains controversial, as lesbian/gay civil rights activists continue to push for same-sex marriage.

BIBLIOGRAPHY

Cain, Patricia A. *Rainbow Rights: The Role of Lawyers and Courts in the Lesbian and Gay Civil Rights Movement.* Boulder, Colo.: Westview, 2000.

Chambers, David L. "Couples: Marriage, Civil Union, and Domestic Partnership." *In Creating Change: Sexuality, Public Policy, and Civil Rights.* Edited by John D'Emilio, William B. Turner, and Urvashi Vaid. New York: St. Martin's, 2000.

Eskridge, William L. *Gaylaw: Challenging the Apartheid of the Closet.* Cambridge, Mass.: Harvard University Press, 1999.

William B. Turner

See also **Gay and Lesbian Movement.**

DEFENSE POLICY. The defense policy of the United States has evolved in response to the changing nature of America's culture, society, economic system, sense of national identity, public and private institutions, and perception of threat to its existence, and core values. Defense is a political function; that is, a choice to use state-sanctioned violence or the threat of violence to advance some particular communal goal. The term is usu-

ally applied to actions taken to prevent some entity from using death and destruction as a way of changing the political behavior of another entity. It includes force as an instrument of policy abroad. The term "military" is not quite synonymous since it can be applied to corporate bodies known as armed forces, which are instruments for the use of force. Defense policy suggests some system of anticipating various threats from other nations, non-state groups, and domestic insurgents and for making some provision for denying any prospective enemy with appropriate and proportional violence or war. The issues that cluster around the concept of defense policy include:

1. The question of who makes it. This can be analyzed by reference to level of government (national, state, local), political role (executive branch and legislative branch), functional role (political officials and military commanders), and a variety of institutional interactions.

2. The perception and analysis of threats and the relationship between the likelihood of conflict and the potential seriousness of conflict.

3. The cost of investing in standing and trained reserve forces and maintaining an industrial base with military potential—and of using money that might go to other social investments.

4. The degree to which a society is willing to subject itself to military regimentation and the sacrifices attendant to military service.

For the United States, the fundamental law for determining defense policy may be found in Article I, Section 8, and Article II, Section 2, of the Constitution; in the Second Amendment; and in the Militia Act of 1792. The clearest expression of defense policy may be found in the records of the annual congressional authorization and appropriation process; in the annual reports of the Secretary of Defense or his predecessors, the Secretaries of War and Navy; and in Title 10, U.S. Code.

Since its colonial origins, the United States has believed in civilian control of defense policy, but has divided control between the national and state governments. It regards senior military commanders as policy advisors and operational executives. The nation has tended to underestimate serious threats and to overreact to minor threats, in part because it is reluctant to spend public funds or subject itself to compulsory military service except in times of crisis. The nation depended upon its distance from the military powers of the Eastern Hemisphere (Great Britain, Continental European nations, and Japan) to discourage aggression or to allow adequate time for military mobilization. It did not depend upon allies between the end of an alliance with France (1778–1801) and the formation of the NORTH ATLANTIC TREATY ORGANIZATION (NATO) in 1949. Its temporary cooperation with other belligerents in nineteenth century punitive expeditions and the two World Wars were responses to pressing crises, not a reflection of defense policy. The United States also assumed that its affluence, its agricultural and industrial productivity, technological ingenuity, and population base guaranteed inevitable victory, even if the earliest stages of war might bring disasters due to unpreparedness.

The Origins

The settlement of North America in the sixteenth through eighteenth centuries created armed conflict between the entrepreneurial companies and sponsoring governments of England, France, Spain, and the Netherlands, some of which reached the level of international wars from 1689 until the conclusion of the American Revolution (1783). In addition, piracy was common along the Atlantic coastline and throughout the Gulf of Mexico and Caribbean. As the white settlers of the thirteen English colonies pushed out from the seaboard to the Appalachians and beyond, they fought warriors of the Native American woodland tribes, until white numbers and lack of European support doomed the surviving Native Americans to forced relocation beyond the Mississippi, a process that began in the 1790s and ended in the 1840s.

By the time of the last war with France (1755–1763), the English Crown had established a regular army in North America and protected its maritime lifeline with the Royal Navy. The colonies, however, also contributed volunteer forces and militia (men called to duty by law for short service) for frontier campaigns. Privateersmen (non–Royal Navy warships) conducted commerce raiding. This colonial experience shaped the defense policy of the United States for more than a century after independence.

The Revolution seemed to prove that the United States did not need a European-style military establishment. For defending the frontier—governed directly by the national government until it created states—a small army of light infantry and mounted forces would have to suffice, supplemented or substituted for by local militias of self-armed citizen farmers. For example, from 1789 until 1814 the Commonwealth of Kentucky could put larger (and often better) forces into the field against the Shawnees than the U.S. Army was able to. Two military giants of the time, the future presidents William Henry Harrison and Andrew Jackson, rose to prominence as the commanders of federal and state forces in regional anti–Native American, anti-British campaigns. The same scheme applied to the more heavily settled and developed coastal states; permanent coastal fortifications to defend ports and naval bases were built with federal funds and manned by regular soldiers, but the states had the responsibility of providing field armies to protect cities from invaders who chose land approaches. This system reached its highest development in the defense of Plattsburgh (New York), Baltimore, Norfolk, and New Orleans in the War of 1812. It failed only once—at Washington, D.C.

The Century of Continental Defense

The United States might have duplicated British defense policy and put its reliance upon an active fleet, at least large and expert enough (as Secretary of the Treasury Alexander Hamilton proposed) to hold the naval balance of power from the Caribbean to the North Atlantic. The states could not afford such a fleet, and Congress rejected the concept until after the War of 1812 when such a fleet was irrelevant. The only continuity in naval policy was the maintenance of squadrons of sailing ships capable of defending American merchantmen throughout the world from non-European naval forces, whether they were Barbary or Sumatran pirates, or belligerent Chinese, Fijians, or Samoans.

The U.S. Navy's finest hour in the era was the isolation of Mexico and the conduct of multiple amphibious landings on Mexico's coasts, a critical part of the overwhelming American victory in the Mexican-American War (1846–1848), the century's largest conflict related to North American territorial expansion. The Mexican-American War also showed that the traditional militia-based system of wartime mobilization was inadequate for creating an expeditionary force for extended service outside America's borders. The American armies still in the field in 1848 mustered about half the 100,000-plus soldiers who entered federal service.

The American Civil War saw the assumptions of defense policy played out at a level of bloodletting and destruction, and with a length of conflict, that made it the worst war in the nation's history The number of Union and Confederate combat dead (diseases not counted) was proportionately higher (as a percentage of the white male population, aged eighteen to forty-five) than the total number of American deaths during World War II.

Nations—especially democracies—do not normally design their armed forces to fight themselves, so the Civil War produced many false lessons or simply reinforced old assumptions. One, for example, was that the United States needed an internal transportation system adequate to move troops to its borders or threatened coasts; roads and navigable rivers again proved their usefulness in 1861–1865, and the railroads demonstrated a strategic importance that shaped national transportation policy for a century. Yet even as the national population grew and wealth accumulated in the late nineteenth century, the nation spent proportionately less and less for defense (perhaps 1 percent of the Gross Domestic Product, or GDP) and put fewer and fewer men in uniform (fewer than 50,000 in all three services) in relationship to the population. The volunteer militia, known as the NATIONAL GUARD, numbered around 100,000—or four times the regular army.

Since Mexico and Canada posed no military threat and the United States remained on good terms with Great Britain, the only foreign threat would be a fleet and invasion force from Asia or Europe, an unlikely danger. The national government assumed the lead in developing and funding the "first line of defense," which was an ocean-going fleet of modern battleships and a system of modern concrete fortifications with heavy coast defense guns, both supplemented with aircraft by 1920. The defense of the mainland forty-eight states went untested, but it was probably adequate. A revolution in Mexico produced a war scare in 1916–1917, and the regular army and National Guard placed more than 130,000 men along the border and sent a punitive expedition into Mexico of 12,000 regular soldiers.

The Mexican troubles dramatized a new strategic truth: the United States had developed international interests that required a larger, regular extracontinental expeditionary force (including aviation) and a naval force to protect it on its oceanic deployments. The military occupation of Alaska (after 1867) did not provide a test, but troubles in the Caribbean (Panama in 1885) and the Pacific (Samoa in the 1880s and Hawaii in the 1890s) gave the first hints that traditional defense policy would have to change. The War with Spain (1898), the annexation of the Philippines and the subsequent Filipino rebellion (1899–1902), the creation of the Canal Zone (1903), and the annexation of Guam and Hawaii, as well as a punitive expedition in China (1900), showed that any form of empire required imperial forces. Both the army and the U.S. Marine Corps of 1917 were five times larger than their counterparts of 1898. Expeditionary forces were viewed as essential in exercising American influence in China and the western Pacific and for preempting potential German and French intervention in the Caribbean. Militia forces, however, were barred from "peacetime" service outside the continental United States, and Congress would not create a competitive Federal Reserve ground force.

The World Wars

American participation in the two World Wars demonstrated that the assumptions of the Century of Continental Defense were not wrong, but simply not appropriate for a world at war. The system of the fleet-in-being, coastal defenses, and sea- and land-based air forces made attacks on the United States proper unlikely—at least with conventional forces. The challenge in 1917–1918 and 1941–1945 was to create massive air, land, and naval forces and then transport them to Europe and the Asia-Pacific Rim where the wars were fought. An allied coalition in both cases gave the United States the time to muster the will and to mobilize the forces for war. The nation put 4.8 million people into uniform in 1917–1918 and then quadrupled that figure in 1941–1945. It spent $32 billion in the first war and ten times that amount in the second.

In the first war, American troops appeared in England, France, Russia, and Italy. In the second war, they campaigned in Asia from India to China and in the Pacific from Hawaii to Okinawa; in the war against the Italian-German Axis, they fought in North Africa, Sicily, Italy, France, Holland, Belgium, and Germany. American aviation forces contributed little in World War I, but they became an essential part of every campaign in World War II and attempted to force Axis surrenders by strategic (urban-industrial) bombing. The United States started on the road to high technology warfare in the first war and became fully committed to the military exploitation of several important technologies: the electromagnetic spectrum (radios and radar), undersea sound-ranging (sonar), fuses for all sorts of munitions that did not require a direct hit (proximity and variable time fuses), the internal combustion engine for mechanized and motorized vehicles and aircraft, advanced medical treatment for wounds and illnesses, and food prepared and packaged for long travel and extended times. American engineers conquered every place and clime. If the United States did not always make the best weapons systems (as with, for example, the M-4 tank), it simply built more than the enemy. Its trucks and artillery were the envy of all the belligerents.

The Cold War

For five years after World War II, the United States attempted to come up with a new variant of its traditional policy, with one new addition: the fleet gave way to the nuclear-armed bombers of the Strategic Air Command as the first line of deterrence and defense. The potential foe was new, the Soviet Union, but its goals were old. It sought hegemony over Eurasia through Russian military forces and the subversion of European and postcolonial regimes in the Middle East and Asia, through local Communist revolutionary movements engaged in "wars of national liberation." The prospect of Russian influence spreading through international communism affected parts of Latin American and Sub-Saharan Africa as well.

American defense policy, however, reverted to old patterns: only one-plus million service personnel on active duty and spending in the range of 1 to 2 percent of the GDP. The Soviet nuclear weapons program and military pressure on Czechoslovakia and West Germany began to change estimates about an adequate force in 1948–1949 and spurred American entry into NATO. No changes in spending, force structure, modernization, and manpower levels occurred, however, until the outbreak of the Korean War in 1950. By 1953 the defense budget had become 13 percent of the GDP (it had reached 45 percent in World War II). By almost every measure of size and effectiveness, the armed forces increased by an order of three in terms of divisions, ships, aircraft wings, nuclear weapons, and logistical establishment. The Cold War defense policy had taken shape.

Although the end of the Korean War brought a one-third reduction of force structure, the policies of nuclear deterrence and forward, collective defense could clearly be seen in the post-1953 armed forces. The Strategic Air Command became a force of 2,000 aircraft, which declined in numbers as the air force added 1,054 intercontinental ballistic missiles to its inventory by 1967. The navy contributed a force of large, missile-firing submarines that reached 41 boats at its peak strength. The Russians developed their own "triad," but it was heavily weighted to large ballistic missiles with heavy warheads. Both sides calculated that 1,500 to 1,700 warheads used on each other's cities and military targets would put both nations back in the Stone Age. Concerned about having adequate forces for retaliation after absorbing a surprise first strike, both sides sought some source of stability, first by increasing the numbers of delivery vehicles and warhead power, then by increasing accuracy and warhead numbers, and then by negotiating arms control agreements. The Cuban Missile Crisis of 1962 showed how delicate the balance of terror might be. Keeping the threshold of nuclear war high also encouraged the development of theater and tactical NUCLEAR WEAPONS and conventional forces. The United States placed its greatest emphasis on the forward defense of Europe and northern Asia. Its air, ground, and naval force in England, Europe (especially Germany), and in the Mediterranean reached 300,000-plus while its forces in South Korea, Japan, and Taiwan numbered over 100,000. Strategic reserve forces were placed in Hawaii and the mainland United States, but the nation never created maritime and air mobility forces adequate to place even a fraction of these forces abroad rapidly. Pre-positioning of supplies and the creation of overseas bases helped some, but even in the Persian Gulf War (1990–1991) it took months to place a 500,000-person expeditionary force in the theater of operations.

The Vietnam War (1965–1973, as far as American combat participation is concerned) was another difficult test of power projection. By 1967, when the United States had adequate forces and base structure in Southeast Asia, the government and the general population had lost their taste for defending a people they did not understand or admire. The Vietnam War also increased the speed of the government's abandonment of the draft, reestablished in 1948 to aid the army, but exploited by all the services to attract recruits. When the draft expired, the services shrank by almost a third, which then forced the United States to spend as much money to recruit and train a single soldier as most people spent for a public university education. The manpower shortages did increase career opportunities for non-white service personnel and women, groups that soon made up 10 to 30 percent of the active duty forces. Sensitivity to the rising cost of defense (over $300 billion a year, despite its shrinking portion of the GDP) and the prospect of casualties did not completely inhibit American military intervention in trouble spots throughout the world before and after the Vietnam War. Conventional American forces fought and took casualties in Lebanon (twice), Panama, Grenada, Somalia, Kuwait, Iraq, and in the Persian Gulf "tanker war." Special operations forces and paramilitary forces supported by the Central Intelligence Agency fought in Iran, Cambodia, Laos, Nicaragua, El Salvador, Afghanistan, Colombia, Hungary, and the Philippines. Throughout the Cold War period, the planning for a conflict with the Soviet Union served as the foundation for force structuring with a few concessions for regional problems. After 1991 the planners tried to reconcile two approaches: meeting the demands of simultaneous regional wars in north Asia and the Middle East, and acting on the conviction that a "spectrum of violence" or "asymmetrical warfare" required a wide range of military capabilities not tied to a specific contingency plan. The promises of advanced technology for aerospace warfare complicated planning by raising the price tag and increased the risk of technology failure in "information warfare," where the first deaths are diskettes, not humans.

The Gulf War may have been the last war that can be traced to the defense policies of the Cold War. The September 2001 terrorist attacks on New York City and Washington, D.C., may have been the first battles in a new warfare in which conventional military forces may not be either targets or the instruments of victory. There are still, however, some continuities that go back to 1945, including a belief in the importance of coalition forces operating under some sort of international mandate, the essential requirement for appropriate technology in the hands of highly skilled service personnel, and a public demand to keep casualties as low as possible. The effectiveness of the operational forces of the army, navy, air force, and marine corps is far more important than the theoretical military strength of a mobilized America on the World War II model. Such a force will not be inexpensive. Even before 2001, it required almost $350 billion to maintain a force of barely 1.3 million (with a smallest portion of this force forward deployed since 1950). The requirements of peacekeeping under United Nations or NATO sanctions provide additional demands—with an endless number of future possibilities for such operations in the Middle East and Africa. Whatever American defense policy will be in the twenty-first century, it will not be the same as the policies of the two previous centuries.

BIBLIOGRAPHY

Baer, George W. *One Hundred Years of Sea Power: The U.S. Navy, 1890–1990.* Stanford, Calif.: Stanford University Press, 1994.

Carroll, John M., and Colin F. Baxter, eds. *The American Military Tradition: From Colonial Times to the Present.* Wilmington, Del.: Scholarly Resources, 1993.

Chambers, John Whiteclay, II, ed. *The Oxford Companion to American Military History.* New York and London: Oxford University Press, 1999.

Dawson, Joseph G., III, ed. *Commanders in Chief: Presidential Leadership in Modern Wars.* Lawrence: University Press of Kansas, 1993.

Drew, Dennis M., and Donald M. Snow. *The Eagle's Talons: The American Experience at War.* Maxwell Air Force Base, Ala.: Air University Press, 1988.

Hagan, Kenneth J., and William R. Roberts, eds. *Against All Enemies: Interpretations of American Military History from Colonial Times to the Present.* Westport, Conn.: Greenwood Press, 1986.

Hagan, Kenneth J., ed. *In Peace and War: Interpretations of American Naval History, 1775–1984.* 2d updated ed. Westport, Conn.: Greenwood Press, 1984.

Jessup, John E., with Louise B. Ketz, eds. *Encyclopedia of the American Military*. 3 vols. New York: Scribners, 1994.

Millett, Allan R., and Peter Maslowski. *For the Common Defense: A Military History of the United States of America*. Rev. ed. New York: Free Press, 1994.

Shuman, Howard E., and Walter R. Thomas. *The Constitution and National Security*. Washington, D.C.: National Defense University, 1990.

Weigley, Russell F. *The American Way of War: A History of United States Military Strategy and Policy*. New York: Macmillan, 1973.

Allan R. Millett

See also **Air Defense; Air Force, United States; American Expeditionary Forces; Army, United States; Civil Defense; Council of National Defense; Defense, Department of; Defense, National; Marine Corps, United States; Military-Industrial Complex; Navy, United States; Strategic Defense Initiative.**

DEFIANCE, FORT. Several different forts in American Indian Country were named "Defiance." The name itself clearly symbolized federal determination to quell Native resistance to westward expansion. The two most significant forts were constructed in Ohio and Arizona. Although the forts themselves did not survive, the communities Defiance, Ohio, and Fort Defiance, Arizona, did.

Fort Defiance, Ohio, is associated with General Anthony Wayne, who in 1794 ordered the structure constructed where the Maumee and Auglaize Rivers meet. Wayne is said to have chosen the name to defy not only the Indians but also the British and "all the devils of hell." His victory at the Battle of Fallen Timbers in 1794 constituted a significant defeat for the Shawnees and their allies, yet Tecumseh mobilized Native resistance again in the early 1800s.

Fort Defiance, Arizona, was built in the heart of Navajo country in 1851, a scant three years after the United States claimed the region under the terms of the Treaty of Guadalupe Hidalgo. The Navajos hoped to eliminate the fort's unwelcome presence but failed in several attempts to wrest it from the Americans. Christopher ("Kit") Carson and others used Fort Defiance as a base for their campaigns against the Navajos, which ultimately resulted in the Long Walk, a forced march of the Indians to exile at Fort Sumner, New Mexico.

The treaty of 1868 signed at Fort Sumner allowed the Navajos, who call themselves Diné, to return home. In time, Fort Defiance became a Navajo settlement called Tsehootsooi in the Diné language, meaning "green place among the rocks." After World War II, given its proximity to the Navajo capital of Window Rock, it emerged as a vital commercial and residential center.

BIBLIOGRAPHY
Frink, Maurice. *Fort Defiance and the Navajos*. Boulder, Colo.: Pruett, 1968.

Peter Iverson

See also **Indian Country; Indian Treaties.**

DEFICIT, FEDERAL. *See* **Debt, Public.**

DEFOLIATION. Defoliation involves the extermination of plant life that in military operations might conceal enemy armed forces, command centers, supply depots, or, less commonly, fields of crops. Such destruction is accomplished by three principal courses of action: setting fires; dropping napalm or phosphorus bombs; and spraying chemical agents from trucks, helicopters, or fixed-wing aircraft. During World War II and the Korean War the United States employed the former two methods, whereas during the Vietnam War chemical agents, chiefly Agent Orange, tended to be used. Defoliation generally produced the desired military objectives, but the human and ecological consequences remain controversial.

In Vietnam the American attempt to defoliate jungle growth and thus expose the enemy focused on the areas around South Vietnamese and later American base camps; along the Ho Chi Minh Trail; across the Demilitarized Zone separating North and South Vietnam; up and down rivers, canals, and railways; and on any suspected North Vietnamese or Vietcong concentration. In a July 1999 interview Elmo R. Zumwalt Jr., the commander of naval forces in Vietnam from 1968 to 1970, explained that he had ordered the use of defoliants because his personnel were taking casualties at the rate of 6 percent a month, which meant the average young man would have about a 70 percent probability of being killed or wounded during his year's tour.

The campaign to reduce that casualty figure was designated Operation Ranch Hand, which began officially in January 1962 and lasted until January 1971. During that period U.S. Air Force UC-123 aircraft flew thousands of sorties and sprayed nearly 10,000 square miles with roughly 19 million gallons of herbicide, about 11 million of which were AGENT ORANGE. The nonscientific names for the herbicides—Agent Orange, Agent White, and so forth—were derived from the color codes on the drums that contained the defoliants. These chemicals, mainly those tagged 2,4-D and 2,4,5-T, were combined and sprayed to fatally accelerate plant growth, causing destruction within days of the spraying.

From the outset the military use of herbicides generated negative responses from both Vietnamese and Americans, most particularly when crop destruction was involved. Although the spraying of crops succeeded in reducing the available food supply for the North Vietnamese and Vietcong, it also resulted in the destruction of innocent farmers' crops. State Department officials argued that what little advantage was gained in diminishing the enemy's food supply was vastly exceeded by the ill will generated from the unavoidable damage to non-enemy crops. Since crop destruction never constituted more than 15 percent of Ranch Hand's operations, defoliation advocates in the Defense Department grudgingly accepted sporadic political restrictions placed on crop eradication activities, down to the ending of all chemical operations in January 1971.

Other consequences—chiefly political, ecological, and medical—ensued. During the war many in the American media and scientific communities claimed that the use of herbicides constituted chemical warfare, outlawed by numerous treaties to which the United States was a signatory. At the very least this charge created a public relations problem and added to the opposition that the Vietnam War was generating. It also led to pointed questions about the ecological and human costs of defoliation, compelling the Defense Department to commission studies, the results of which caused further heated debates. One study, begun by the National Academy of Sciences in 1970, asserted in its 1974 report that no long-term damage, including birth defects or environmental degradation, could be attributed to the various herbicidal agents sprayed in Vietnam.

In the 1990s that same organization found connections between herbicides containing dioxin and several ailments, including sarcomas, non-Hodgkin's lymphoma, Hodgkin's disease, and chloracne. Congress, the Air Force, and the Veterans Administration (VA) commenced studies of Vietnam veterans who had possibly been exposed to herbicides. In 1978 the VA began conducting physical examinations, doing laboratory work, and launching a registry to study systematically the latent effects of exposure.

Perhaps the most notable case of an American soldier's illness being attributed to Agent Orange is that of Elmo R. Zumwalt III. His sickness and eventual death from cancer at age forty-two in 1988 attracted much attention, since his father had ordered the spraying of herbicides in areas where the son served from 1969 to 1970. Although a causal relationship could not be established, Elmo III believed one existed, particularly since his son, Elmo IV, had been diagnosed with a genetic disorder. In 2001 a University of Texas researcher, Arnold J. Schecter, produced a public health report on Bien Hoa, where seven thousand gallons of Agent Orange had spilled in 1970. His study revealed high levels of dioxin in children born after the war and in adults who moved to the city from locations where no herbicides containing dioxin were sprayed. Schecter concluded that the toxic substance migrated from soil to the groundwater to waterways, from which fish were caught and eaten. One gathers that some relationship exists between exposure to the various herbicidal agents and numerous health problems, since the VA has provided compensation to nearly two thousand

veterans and because the various chemical companies that manufactured the agents settled a class-action lawsuit out of court that provided almost $200 million in damages to veterans.

BIBLIOGRAPHY

Buckingham, William A., Jr. *Operation Ranch Hand: The Air Force and Herbicides in Southeast Asia, 1961–1971.* Washington, D.C.: Office of Air Force History, United States Air Force, 1982.

Schuck, Peter H. *Agent Orange on Trial: Mass Toxic Disasters in the Courts.* Cambridge, Mass.: Harvard University Press, 1986.

Texas Technical University. "Vietnam Archive." Burch and Pike collections. Available from http://archive.vietnam.ttu.edu/vietnamarchive.

Wilcox, Fred A. *Waiting for an Army to Die: The Tragedy of Agent Orange.* New York: Random House, 1983.

Zumwalt, Elmo R., Jr., and Elmo R. Zumwalt III. *My Father, My Son.* New York: Macmillan, 1986.

Thomas Reins

See also **Insecticides and Herbicides; Vietnam War.**

DEISM, a philosophy often termed "Enlightenment religion," was popular in the seventeenth and eighteenth centuries in England, France, Germany, and America. Unlike atheism, which denies the existence of God; polytheism, which recognizes the existence of many gods; and pantheism, which sees God in everything; deism recognizes the existence of a supreme being or God as revealed in Nature and perceived by human reason. While deism can be traced to the Stoics of ancient Greece, modern deism is generally traced to the writings of Faustus Socinus and other sixteenth-century Unitarian thinkers.

Deism, derived from the Latin "deus," or "God," differs from conventional Christianity, Judaism, and Eastern religions in that deism denies the necessity of any special revelation of the existence of God; likewise, it denies the sacred nature of any given text. Instead, deism requires only that the human mind apply logic and reason to come to a recognition and understanding of God, because God is innately logical and reasonable. Consequently, deism also denies the importance of sacred ritual and church tradition and the possibility of miracles, all of which it deems beyond the scope of reason and empirical possibility. Faith, according to deism, is the suspension or abandonment of reason and is therefore incompatible with a God who has created man to be a thinking, reasonable creature. Furthermore, while many deists acknowledge the wisdom and goodness of various traditional religious figures such as Jesus and the Buddha, deism denies the sacred or divine nature of these figures; for such persons to somehow share in God's divine nature would imply a favoritism or special dispensation on the part of God which deists deny as a possibility for a just and logical Creator. Man can exercise his free and rational will, according to deism; sin, defined as the failure to love others and to do good toward the furtherance of the human condition, is therefore possible. Perhaps the most pervasive image of the God of deism is that of God as "the cosmic watchmaker," one who created the universe and peopled it with thinking human beings, and then dissociated himself from his creation.

Early deism grew from the increased interest in natural science exhibited in the works of Copernicus, Galileo, Sir Francis Bacon, and others. Early deist thinkers sought to apply the same principles of the rational study of nature to the study of religion. In his *De Veritate* (1624; "On Truth"), Lord Herbert of Cherbury set forth Five Articles of English Deists:

1. There exists only one supreme God.

2. Mankind's duty is to revere this God.

3. Adoring worship of God must be practiced in conjunction with applied principles of morality.

4. If man repents his sins and improves his behavior, God will forgive.

5. Good works are rewarded both before and after death.

Anthony Collins (1676–1729) and Matthew Tindal (1657–1733) were prominent English deists; in France the philosophy was taken up and expanded by Jean-Jacques Rousseau (1712–1778) and Voltaire (1694–1778). By the late 1700s, deist philosophy came to include the belief that religious authority could only be derived by the application of reason to Scripture, not by an unquestioning reliance on the inerrancy of that Scripture; the denial of the doctrine of the Trinity; the belief that the teachings of Jesus, not the writings of St. Paul, were foundational; the idea that the importance of the resurrection was in its demonstration of the possibility of immortality, not as Christ's atonement for mankind's sins; the argument against the doctrines of Calvin (total depravity, unconditional election, limited atonement, irresistible grace, and the perseverance of the saints); a faith in the innate goodness and reasonableness of humans; and the belief that all religious thought should be free rather than coerced either by fear of threats or by the promise of rewards.

Deism in America

The influence of French and English deists on America's founders was immense. The vast majority of American leaders at the time of the Revolutionary War had read the works of Tindal, Rousseau, and Voltaire, and most of these founders considered themselves deists. John Quincy Adams, Ethan Allen, Benjamin Franklin, James Madison, George Washington, and Thomas Jefferson were among this group, as was Thomas Paine, who wrote extensively on the topic. Paine's *Age of Reason* (1794, 1796) has often been singled out as one of the most eloquent statements of advanced deist philosophy, although his blunt attacks on the orthodoxy caused him to be considered a heretic by many of his own day.

In addition to the principles they inherited from the Greeks and their European forebears, American deists refined and added to the list of beliefs they shared. One of the Americans' major refinements included a practical disavowal of any group being God's "chosen" people: they espoused a direct denial of American Puritans' notion of the new nation as the setting for a jeremiadic mission. Americans held a strong yet somewhat modified denial of the occurrence of miracles, although many did recognize and appreciate what they felt were occasional but inexplicable interventions of "Providence." The founders of the United States demonstrated a strengthened and identifiably democratic insistence on the need for practical morality and an increased belief in the obligation to prayerfully adore and offer thanks for the goodness shown by the beneficent Creator. Benjamin Franklin, Thomas Jefferson, and Thomas Paine were especially critical of the emphasis traditionally accorded the writings of Saint Paul of Tarsus. They also strongly disavowed the subsequent traditional Trinitarian theology concerning the substitutionary theory of atonement which states that Christ as part of the Godhead was required to die in payment of the death penalty of sin borne by all mankind as a direct result of their kinship to Adam. While Franklin, Jefferson, and Paine all recognized the necessity of doing good works, none saw this as a way to purchase salvation; however, neither did they accept the idea of original sin or the proxy of Jesus's death as substitution for man's own individual sins. Rather, they believed that each man must exercise his own thought and will to act appropriately toward others and that salvation could be gained by simply seeking God's forgiveness and forgiving others in turn. Such a concept of self-responsibility and independence rang true to many of the early American inhabitants.

In a similar fashion, American deists devoutly denied the necessity of any intercessory priesthood to mediate between God and man, not only in terms of receiving salvation, but also in terms of coming to an intellectual understanding of God and the universe he created. Rather than relying on church tradition, polity, or pronouncements, deists instead averred that God's true nature was obscured by what they saw as the pretensions of a traditional clergy or canonical hierarchy. By employing the gift of reason and examining the wonders of nature in the new land in which they had settled, American deists precluded their own dependence on traditional faith, preferring instead to question the workings of the world around them. They often referred to traditional constructions of faith as "superstition" or "magic" or as a reliance on "divine revelation" and saw this as being directly in opposition to the notion of all they believed about God. According to deism, it made no sense to posit a Creator who would have given man a mind with which to think and reason but who later would have arbitrarily punished man simply for not suspending that reason in the name of faith. By extension, not only the individual deist should exercise his own will and reason in making decisions, but every man should also do likewise. Each person, then, should depend on his own reason and free will, and should also take into consideration the fact that his fellow man was doing the same. As a result, the democratic ideals of the young nation were espoused in common with deist philosophy. That is, deists expressed virtually no preference for or prejudice against any organized religion, preferring instead to live in tolerance of all faiths and to give full play to each individual's decisions and actions.

America's founders had been raised in a Christian society, generally in orthodox Christian or Calvinist families; as a result, they came to deism with a strong knowledge of Christian ideology and of the practical workings of church polity. While deism does not advocate wholesale rejection of tradition, often these men's primary departure from Christian teaching was based in their studious consideration and subsequent rejection of the doctrine of the Trinity and of traditional Calvinist dogma. The deist commitments to social justice and individual responsibility were also attractive to the leaders of the young nation, as was the concept of religious tolerance. These ideals are most clearly illustrated in the First Amendment's insistence on the free exercise of religion, but the overarching concern of deism with man's exercise of reason as a free and thinking being is foundational to most of American legal, social, and cultural experience.

Deism's major attraction was to the well-read American intellectual of the late eighteenth century. While deism certainly never replaced orthodox Christianity as Americans' majority religion, it is telling that many of the nation's founders did indeed subscribe to this philosophy and incorporated it into the framework of the young republic. By the early- to mid-nineteenth century, deism in Europe and in America had become colored by skepticism, perhaps most notably as a result of the rapid spread of evangelical and fundamentalist Christianity. It has also been argued that Romanticism was a reaction to deism and was a possible cause for its decline by the 1830s. In the late twentieth century, deism appeared to undergo something of a revival, although the lack of an organized polity or structure renders precise measurements of the number of practitioners impossible. Many contemporary deists label themselves "practitioners of no religion" or align themselves with liberal Unitarian or Universalist congregations.

BIBLIOGRAPHY

Davidson, Edward H., and William J. Scheick. *Paine, Scripture, and Authority: The Age of Reason As Religious and Political Idea.* Bethlehem, Pa.: Lehigh University Press, 1994.

Koch, G. Adolf. *Religion of the American Enlightenment.* New York: Crowell, 1968.

May, Henry Farnham. *The Enlightenment in America.* New York: Oxford University Press, 1976.

McDermott, Gerald R. *Jonathan Edwards Confronts the Gods: Christian Theology, Enlightenment Religion, and Non-Christian Faiths.* New York: Oxford University Press, 2000.

Paine, Thomas. *The Age of Reason.* Design Philip Sheldon Foner. New York: Lyle Stuart, 1989 [rprt. 1792 ed].

Rinaldo, Peter M. *Atheists, Agnostics, and Deists in America: A Brief History.* Briarcliff Manor, N.Y.: DorPete Press, 2000.

Walters, Kerry S. *The American Deists: Voices of Reason and Dissent in the Early Republic.* Lawrence: University Press of Kansas, 1992.

———. *Rational Infidels: The American Deists.* Durango, Colo.: Longwood Academic, 1992.

Barbara Schwarz Wachal

DELANEY AMENDMENT. In 1958, U.S. Representative James Delaney of New York added a proviso to the 1938 Federal Food, Drug, and Cosmetic Act declaring that the Food and Drug Administration cannot approve any food additive found to induce cancer in a person or animal. The clause inaugurated the federal government's role in protecting the public from cancer and eventually affected other areas of regulation, such as the Environmental Protection Agency's control of pesticides. As cancer risk became better understood and carcinogens more easily detectable, the "zero cancer risk" limit was increasingly seen by scientists and industry as an impractical standard. In 1996, Congress replaced the amendment to require a less-than one-in-a-million lifetime risk threshold.

BIBLIOGRAPHY

Hollander, Earle. "The Delaney Era Ends." *Frontiers: A Chronicle of Cancer Programs at The Ohio State University* 5, no. 2 (Summer/Autumn 1997). Available from www.osu.edu/units/cancer/sa97front/Delaney.htm.

National Research Council, Committee on Scientific Regulatory Issues Underlying Pesticide Use Patterns and Agricultural Innovation. *Regulating Pesticides in Food: The Delaney Paradox.* Washington, D.C.: National Academy Press, 1987.

Stever, Donald W. *Law of Chemical Regulation and Hazardous Waste.* New York: C. Boardman, 1986.

Eric S. Yellin

DELAWARE. Nestled along North America's mid-Atlantic seaboard, Delaware is the second smallest state in the United States, with a land area of 1,954 square miles and a population of 783,600 according to the U.S. census of 2000. Belying its modest size, however, is the significant role that the state has played in the history of the United States. On 7 December 1787, Delaware became the first of the thirteen original states to ratify the U.S. Constitution, hence earning its nickname, "The First State." Since then, Delaware periodically has been in the national spotlight, and has played an important role in the nation's political, social, and economic development.

Delaware's earliest recorded history stretches back to 1609, when English explorer Henry Hudson discovered what became known as the Delaware River on his journey to find passage to China. In the following year, the river and its adjacent bay were named after Lord de la Warr, the then-governor of Virginia, by English sailor Samuel

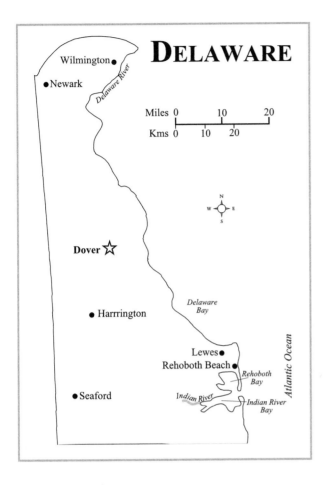

DELAWARE

Wilmington

Newark

Delaware River

Miles 0   10   20
Kms 0   10   20

N
W   E
S

Dover ☆

Harrrington

Delaware Bay

Lewes
Rehoboth Beach

Rehoboth Bay

Seaford

Indian River

Indian River Bay

Atlantic Ocean

Argall, who encountered the waterways when seeking shelter from a storm. Although English cartographers affixed the name Delaware to the river and bay, the land itself remained unsettled by Europeans for another two decades.

In the spring of 1631, a small Dutch settlement called Swanendael was established near what is known today as Lewes Creek, in the southern part of the state, marking the first time in which a European power staked a claim to the territory. The settlement itself utterly failed, as another Dutch expedition discovered in 1632 when it found Swanendael abandoned and its inhabitants missing or dead. It was not until March 1638 that a permanent settlement was successfully established farther north, near modern-day Wilmington, by Swedish colonists arriving on two ships, the *Kalmar Nyckel* and the *Vogel Grip*. The twenty-five men who remained behind called their settlement Fort Christina, in honor of the Swedish Queen Christina, and by 1643 Johan Printz was installed as the governor of New Sweden.

While the population of New Sweden never exceeded 1,000 inhabitants, it was a successful colony of farmers occupying sturdy wooden cabins. Despite its tranquility, however, New Sweden was threatened by Dutch interests claiming the territory due to the early settlement of Swanendael. On 15 September 1655, the poorly fortified colony was conquered by the Dutch and formally incorporated as a southern extension of New Netherland. Dutch rule itself proved to be relatively short-lived, however; in October 1664 the English conquered all of New Netherland, renaming the territory New York.

The English governed Delaware as part of New York until 1682, when William Penn was given a proprietary grant to the territory, which was divided into the three counties of New Castle, Kent, and Sussex. Since the land was not part of Penn's original Pennsylvania grant, the Delaware holdings were regularly referred to as the Lower Counties on the Delaware. Unlike the other English colonies, therefore, Delaware did not have a proper name until it was finally given independence from the Penn family on the eve of the Revolution in 1776.

Given its newfound status as an independent state, Delaware participated in the Continental Congress debates over independence from Great Britain. Delaware's three delegates to the Congress meeting in Philadelphia were Thomas McKean, George Read, and Caesar Rodney. At the Congress, each state was given one vote, although the delegates were polled individually. The poll taken on 1 July 1776 revealed a division among the Delaware delegates, with McKean voting for independence and Read voting against it. Rodney, who was absent from the 1 July vote, quickly rode to Philadelphia to cast the deciding vote for the Delaware delegation the next day, in favor of independence.

Throughout the colonial era, Delaware's economy was primarily agricultural. The Swedish, Dutch, English, Scots-Irish, and Welsh settlers who came to inhabit the land grew wheat, corn, fruits, and vegetables for personal consumption and sale in larger markets such as Philadelphia. Beginning as early as 1639, African slaves were also imported for labor, particularly into the southern counties of Kent and Sussex. By the end of the eighteenth century, Delaware's economy and social structure came to be increasingly divided, with the northern county, New Castle, focusing on activities such as shipbuilding, tanning, and flour milling, and Kent and Sussex counties remaining overwhelmingly agricultural. By 1790, the dual nature of Delaware's development could be seen in two different statistics: its flour mills near Wilmington were the largest in the nation, while at the same time African American slaves toiling in the fields composed nearly 25 percent of the state's population.

Once established as the first state in the new country, Delaware's social and economic patterns continued to develop along similar lines. Flour millers such as Joseph Tatnall and his son-in-law, Thomas Lea, were among the state's most prominent citizens, but wealthy slaveholders also wielded considerable power and influence. Along with the rest of the country, however, Delaware was transformed by advances in technology and transportation in the early decades of the nineteenth century. In 1802, for example, E. I. du Pont de Nemours & Company (here-

541

after referred to as DuPont) was founded along the banks of the Brandywine River outside of Wilmington as a manufacturer of gunpowder. Although the du Pont name was a new one to Delaware, the firm and the family behind it grew to be among the world's best known. The demand for powder in the United States was brisk, as explosives were used to clear forests and blast mines, and within a relatively short span of time the names of du Pont and Delaware were closely linked.

That Delaware had both manufacturing interests and slaveholding planters reflected the nation as a whole. Thus, when the Civil War erupted in 1861, Delaware was a microcosm of the North-South political divide. The urban and industrial northern part of the state overwhelmingly supported the Union cause, whereas the state's southern agriculturists often sympathized with the Confederacy. Delaware's top political figures appeared to reflect both sides of the conflict as well. Governor William Burton, U.S. Senators James Bayard and William Saulsbury, and U.S. Representative William Whitely all were on record as supporting the institution of slavery, yet none favored secession for Delaware. Likewise, when the matter of secession came to a vote at the state legislature, the lower house unanimously rejected the proposal, and the Senate did so as well by a vote of 5 to 3. Thus, Delaware became one of only four slave-holding states to remain in the Union during the Civil War.

Although military battles were not waged in Delaware, as a border state it did play an important role during the war. Fort Delaware, located offshore on Pea Patch Island, served as a prison for Confederate soldiers and officers, housing up to 12,500 men in squalid conditions. The state's industries also were important to the Union's war effort, with DuPont supplying one-third to one-half of all Union powder, and smaller firms supplying textiles, leather goods, rail cars, and ships.

In light of Delaware's small size and its loyalty to the Union, the Lincoln administration viewed the state as a potentially important test case in regard to emancipation. In the autumn of 1861, Lincoln proposed that Delaware slaveholders emancipate their slaves in exchange for U.S. government compensation. With some 1,800 slaves in the state at the time, it was estimated that the cost to the U.S. government would be approximately $900,000. When Delaware lawmakers rejected the proposal, the plan was dropped and Lincoln abandoned compensated emancipation, reasoning that if the plan was unacceptable to Delaware slaveholders, it would be even more vigorously opposed by other states. In part, therefore, Lincoln considered the Delaware case when he issued the more sweeping Emancipation Proclamation on 1 January 1863.

In the years following the Civil War, Delawareans cast aside disagreements that had arisen during the conflict and looked ahead to the remaining years of the nineteenth century with well-founded optimism. Since slavery was already a dying institution in Delaware before the war, former slaveholders adjusted to Emancipation with greater ease than their counterparts farther south. As for the state's manufacturing sector, the closing decades of the century marked a time of growth and consolidation. Although some traditional enterprises such as milling declined due to competition farther west, in general manufacturing expanded and provided employment for the state's growing population. Delaware was not known for any single industry, but instead was characterized by diverse firms involved in leather production, fiber and paper manufacturing, machine building, iron manufacturing, and shipbuilding.

Delaware's economy increasingly turned toward manufacturing and business throughout the nineteenth century, but the small size of the state and of its population meant that the state's economy was likewise smaller than that of other northeastern states. In 1897, however, the Delaware legislature enacted a new General Corporation Law that ultimately made the state a leading force in the American economy. With its flexible corporation statute, its attractive tax provisions, and its Court of Chancery, a tribunal dating back to the colonial era to hear business disputes, the incorporation law was specifically designed to attract companies to incorporate in Delaware, regardless of whether or not they actually operated within the state. In time, thousands of companies incorporated in Delaware.

As Delaware's profile in the national economy rose in the early years of the twentieth century, so did the fortune of its largest firm, DuPont. Despite having been broken up in 1912 due to antitrust violations, DuPont still possessed a government-sanctioned monopoly on military-grade smokeless powder. Not surprisingly, the firm profited handsomely from powder sales during World War I, supplying some 40 percent of all powder used by the United States and its allies. With the resulting capital it now had available, DuPont and the du Pont family members at its helm broadened the activities of the firm by the war's end. Increasingly the company turned toward the manufacture of chemicals and synthetic fibers, and soon Delaware housed numerous research, administrative, and production facilities of the corporate giant that made rayon, nylon, Dacron, Lucite, and cellophane household names. As DuPont rose to become the world's largest chemical company, its power and influence within the state became unrivaled.

As the twentieth century progressed, DuPont and the thousands of Delawareans it employed symbolized the modern face of the state. Still, Delaware retained elements of its agricultural past, particularly in its southern counties of Kent and Sussex. Poultry production, especially of broiler chickens, grew at a phenomenal rate in the 1920s and 1930s, such that by 1942 Delaware farms raised approximately 25 percent of all broilers in the United States. The dramatic growth in broiler production made Sussex one of the wealthiest agricultural counties in the nation by the onset of World War II.

By the middle of the twentieth century, Delaware continued to be characterized by a dual economy—urban and industrial in the north, rural and agricultural in the south—much as it had been 100 years earlier. There was a continuity in the state's social structure as well. Just as Delaware had been one of only four slave states to remain in the Union during the Civil War, race relations in the mid-twentieth century were a mixture of both southern and northern patterns. Whereas schools, restaurants, and theaters were segregated, for example, other types of public accommodations such as libraries, buses, and trains were not. Even before the U.S. Supreme Court's BROWN v. BOARD OF EDUCATION (1954) decision outlawed segregation in public schools, however, Delaware had begun the process of desegregation.

In 1950 Chancellor Collins J. Seitz of the Delaware Court of Chancery ordered that the University of Delaware admit African American students, a watershed event in the state's history that ultimately influenced the federal courts as well. Slowly, private institutions throughout Delaware abandoned segregation policies, including the YWCA in 1951, the Catholic school system in 1952, and the state's leading luxury hotel, the Hotel DuPont, in 1953. When the Brown v. Board decision was handed down in 1954, the state's attorney general, H. Albert Young, complied with federal law and oversaw the desegregation of public schools throughout the state.

Meanwhile, the state was undergoing a noticeable demographic transformation. Although the state's population growth exceeded national averages in the post–World War II era, the population of its largest city, Wilmington, was steadily declining. In 1940, Wilmington's population was 112,504; by 1999 that figure had dropped to 71,491 as increasing numbers of people sought life in the suburbs. In addition, Delaware's traditionally rural counties in the south also experienced population growth due to an increase in non-agricultural employment, as well as a willingness of commuters to travel greater distances to jobs. With suburban sprawl taking the place of urban concentration, Delaware became part of the larger megalopolis that extends from New York City to Washington, D.C., in the mid-Atlantic region.

At the close of the twentieth century, Delaware became best known as a center for American corporate business. More than 308,000 companies were incorporated in the state, including 60 percent of the Fortune 500 and 50 percent of the companies listed on the New York Stock Exchange. Although the vast majority of these firms did not have operations within Delaware, they nevertheless had an important impact on the state's economy through tax receipts and ancillary activities such as legal and financial services. Moreover, due to the Financial Center Development Act of 1981, the state had become a leading center for banking and credit card operations, with Delaware-based banks issuing some 43 percent of all credit cards in the United States by 1997, and providing employment to over 32,000 Delawareans.

Since its first European settlement in 1631, Delaware has transformed significantly. In a state once populated by a handful of Dutch and Swedish settlers, Delaware's population increasingly became more diverse by ethnicity and race, trends that are projected to continue. As the twenty-first century unfolds, new challenges and opportunities await the First State. Like other states in the region, manufacturing and industrial production are being replaced by service sector employment, particularly in fields of banking and corporate services. Despite its small size, Delaware has played an important role in the history of the United States; given its importance to American corporate business and the national economy, it will remain significant in the years to come.

BIBLIOGRAPHY

Delaware. Home page at http://www.delaware.gov.

Hoffecker, Carol E. *Corporate Capital: Wilmington in the Twentieth Century.* Philadelphia: Temple University Press, 1983.

Munroe, John A. *History of Delaware.* Newark: University of Delaware Press, 2001.

Williams, William H. *Slavery and Freedom in Delaware, 1639–1865.* Wilmington, Del.: SR Books, 1996.

Wolters, Raymond. *The Burden of Brown: Thirty Years of School Desegregation.* Knoxville: University of Tennessee Press, 1984.

Jonathan S. Russ

DELAWARE, WASHINGTON CROSSING THE.

Gen. George Washington's crossing of the Delaware River and defeat of the British in New Jersey checked the British advance toward Philadelphia and restored American morale. On Christmas Day 1776, Washington and 2,400 men with artillery crossed the Delaware from Pennsylvania to surprise British forces, chiefly Hessians (soldiers recruited from Germany), in their quarters north of Trenton, NEW JERSEY. They killed the Hessian commander, Col. Johann Rall, and took 946 prisoners and their weapons. The sick and wounded, as well as supplies left by other Hessian troops retreating to Princeton, were captured by Gen. John Cadwalader. On 29 December, Washington, who retired to Pennsylvania after his exploits, recrossed the Delaware and advanced to Trenton, where he was attacked by the British under Gen. Charles Cornwallis, then marched to Princeton hoping to capture British supplies at New Brunswick. After his victory at the Battle of Princeton, Washington prevailed in skirmishes at Springfield, Hackensack, and Elizabethtown. He headquartered at Morristown, and, for the moment, the American cause was saved.

More than sixty years after the campaign that solidified Washington's reputation, a German-born American painter, Emanuel Leutze, produced his famous *Washington Crossing the Delaware.* However stirring the image, it has been called absurd by many critics. The pose of Washington in the prow of a rowboat is ridiculous; the flag is

Washington Crossing the Delaware. A rendering of Emanuel Leutze's symbolic—albeit not entirely credible—1851 painting of the American commander's crucial surprise attack near Trenton, N.J., in 1776. ARCHIVE PHOTOS, INC.

an anachronism; and the river covered with ice is the Rhine, not the Delaware. Nonetheless, the painting has become a symbol of Washington's accomplishment and is perhaps the best known of Leutze's works and the most popular conception of the crossing.

BIBLIOGRAPHY

Bill, Alfred H. *The Campaign of Princeton, 1776–1777.* Princeton, N.J.: Princeton University Press, 1948.

Dwyer, William M. *The Day Is Ours!: November 1776–January 1777: An Inside View of the Battles of Trenton and Princeton.* New York: Viking Press, 1983.

Kammen, Michael. *Meadows of Memory: Images of Time and Tradition in American Art and Culture.* Austin: University of Texas Press, 1992.

Wilbur C. Abbott / A. R.

See also **German Mercenaries; Princeton, Battle of; Revolution, American: Military History; Trenton, Battle of.**

DELAWARE INDIANS, Native Americans who call themselves Lenape are the largest native group to survive from the mid-Atlantic region, primarily because they neither fought a major war nor fell victim to slave raids. Moreover, they held an annual rite of thanksgiving called the *gamwing* (big house rite), which provided a cultural focus that sustained them through continual adversity. Their aboriginal lifeline was the river named for them that has branch drainages covering New Jersey, eastern Pennsylvania, and adjoining sections of New York, Connecticut, and Delaware.

The Delawares' traditional culture was based in the village with farm fields and hunting territories within a watershed. Kinship was traced through the mother, and each local segment of a matrilineal clan belonged to one of three overarching units (a phratry) whose emblems were the Wolf, Turtle, and Turkey. Their economy mixed fishing and maize farming with hunting. The two largest political divisions that survived into the twenty-first century are the Monsi of the northern homeland and the Unami of the south. Survivors of coastal groups were briefly known as Unalachtigo.

While the Spanish, Swedes, Germans, English, and French all had contact with the Delawares, the religious influences of the Quakers and Moravians had the greatest impact. Some Delawares converted, but those religions also became foils for prophets periodically revitalizing their lifeways. John "Moonhead" Wilson continued this tradition into the 1900s as he simultaneously advocated Catholicism, the Ghost Dance, and the beginnings of the Native American Church (peyotism).

Forced into Ohio, the Delawares divided by 1800. Most Monsi moved into Ontario. The Unami continued to Indiana, where they went through a major religious revival, then to Missouri, Kansas, and Oklahoma, where they were forced to join the Cherokee Nation in 1867. The splinter "western" Delawares, who had allied with Caddos in Texas, were forced into Oklahoma in 1859. In

1996 the Delaware majority, with ten thousand enrollees, returned to sovereign status, though the Cherokees continued to oppose them in federal court.

BIBLIOGRAPHY

Goddard, Ives. "Delaware." In *Handbook of North American Indians*. Edited by William C. Sturtevant et al. Vol. 15: *Northeast*, edited by Bruce Trigger. Washington, D.C.: Smithsonian Institution, 1978.

Miller, Jay. "The Delaware as Women: A Symbolic Solution." *American Ethnologist* 1, no. 3 (1974): 507–514.

———. "The 1806 Purge among the Indiana Delaware: Sorcery, Gender, Boundaries, and Legitimacy." *Ethnohistory* 41, no. 2 (1994): 245–266.

Jay Miller

See also **Cherokee; Indian Religious Life; Indian Removal.**

DELEGATION OF POWERS

DELEGATION OF POWERS refers to the practice of empowering one part of government to act in the name of another. The extent to which any branch of government may delegate power, however, remains in question. For example, the courts have often said that Congress as a recipient of delegated power from the people through the Constitution may not further delegate its legislative powers to other agencies of government. At the same time they have admitted that Congress can adopt only a general policy, which must be implemented by others in unanticipated circumstances and contexts. The U.S. Supreme Court stated in 1940 that "delegation by Congress has long been recognized as necessary in order that the exertion of legislative power does not become a futility," and the Court has voided only three delegations of power by Congress: *Panama Refining Company v. Ryan* (1935), *Schechter Poultry Company v. United States* (1935), *Carter v. Carter Coal Company* (1936).

Three types of delegation can be identified. The first leaves to a person or agency the task of filling in the details and elaborating on the implementation of general policy. This, the most common type of delegation, is exemplified in the INTERSTATE COMMERCE COMMISSION being directed to ensure that railroad rates are "reasonable." A second type is contingency delegation. In this type, legislation is passed that will go into effect or be suspended when the executive branch determines that a specified situation exists. Tariff laws, for example, usually give the president power to change duties if other countries make specified changes in their duties. The third type of delegation of power occurs in the field of foreign affairs, where courts have approved broader delegations of power to the president than in domestic affairs because of the unique role he plays in this area.

Limits do exist on the ability of Congress to delegate legislative power to administrative agencies. Congress must define the subject to be regulated and must provide some standard to guide its agent's actions, even if that standard is no more exact than "just and reasonable." The delegation must be to public officials, not to private groups or individuals. Penal sanctions for violation of administrative orders can be provided only by Congress.

Strict judicial adherence to the nondelegation doctrine would have made virtually impossible congressional exercise of the powers conferred on the legislative branch by the Constitution. Judicial recognition of this fact contributed to the great growth of administrative agencies and independent regulatory commissions in the twentieth century.

BIBLIOGRAPHY

Barber, Sotorios A. *The Constitution and the Delegation of Congressional Power*. Chicago: University of Chicago Press, 1975.

FitzGerald, John L. *Congress and the Separation of Powers*. New York: Praeger, 1986.

*Robert H. Birkby/*A. G.

See also **Cabinet;** *Carter v. Carter Coal Company;* **Checks and Balances; Civil Service; Congress, United States;** *Panama Refining Company v. Ryan; Schechter Poultry Company v. United States;* **Separation of Powers.**

DE LIMA V. BIDWELL

DE LIMA V. BIDWELL, 182 U.S. 1 (1901), the first of the famous INSULAR CASES following the SPANISH-AMERICAN WAR. The protectionists' (those who advocate governmental economic protection of domestic products) claim that Puerto Rico was a foreign country, and so subject to the Dingley Tariff, was rejected by the Supreme Court. However, Congress was permitted on other grounds the power to regulate the tariff relations of dependent states.

BIBLIOGRAPHY

Cabranes, Jose A. *Citizenship and the American Empire: Notes on the Legislative History of the United States Citizenship of Puerto Ricans*. New Haven, Conn.: Yale University Press, 1979.

Kerr, James Edward. *The Insular Cases: The Role of the Judiciary in American Expansionism*. Port Washington, N.Y.: Kennikat Press, 1982.

*Harvey Wish/*A. R.

See also **Tariff; Trade, Foreign.**

DEMOBILIZATION

DEMOBILIZATION, the dismissal of troops to civilian life and the winding down of a war industry at the cessation of a national emergency. Because American wars have relied predominantly on volunteers, militia, and drafted civilians, the sudden return of these service people to civilian life often has had the proportions of an avalanche, particularly since Americans paid little attention to this phase of warmaking—except following WORLD WAR II.

In the first two American wars, the Revolution and the WAR OF 1812, short-term enlistments and limitations of transportation and communication made demobilization a continuous process. Mustered-out troops often went unrecorded, sometimes unpaid, and always had to find their own way home.

In the MEXICAN-AMERICAN WAR, Gen. Winfield Scott experienced a premature demobilization of 40 percent of his troops after the Battle of Cerro Gordo (18 April 1847) when their one-year enlistments expired. From then on, volunteers enlisted for the conflict's duration. At the end of the war, 41,000 men dispersed over the American southwest and Mexico before the military finally transported them to New Orleans by boat.

The problems of releasing 1,034,064 men after the CIVIL WAR dwarfed previous demobilization efforts but lacked a detailed demobilization plan. Corps and divisions were transferred to nine rendezvous areas, where officials prepared muster-out rolls and payrolls, released soldiers, and deactivated units. Demobilization took as long as eighteen months for volunteers, and even longer for regular troops.

The sudden victory of the United States in the SPANISH-AMERICAN WAR (1898) heralded the usual public outcry to bring the troops home, but changes to mustering-out procedures midway through demobilization caused much confusion. Some regiments were held in service until 1902 because of the continuing insurrection in the Philippines.

WORLD WAR I ended with an abruptness that again caught American military planners unprepared. More than 3 million service people were eligible for discharge. Officials considered discharge by military unit the most equitable and least economically disruptive alternative, and, at the same time, provided an effective force for occupation and other contingencies. Thirty demobilization centers in the United States processed troops out of service as close to their homes as possible.

A special division began planning WORLD WAR II demobilization in the last two years of the war. Even so, the sudden Japanese surrender and public pressure to return soldiers to civilian life released a deluge of veterans and caused concern among military strategists eyeing the threat of the Soviet Union to American security. Eight million soldiers—five million deployed abroad—had to be demobilized, and a four-year logistical buildup had to be liquidated. A point system governed the sequence of troop release by individual rather than by unit. The military released half of its 8 million service people by the end of 1945, but a slowdown early in 1946 prompted public outcry and even troop demonstrations. By June 1946, the army again halved its strength. This sudden reduction left the fully demobilized U.S. Army much weaker than its numbers implied.

After World War II, several factors altered the traditional problems of demobilization. The limited wars of this period used reserve call-ups and rotated drafted troops on an individual twelve-month basis, making de-

mobilization continuous. Moreover, peace did not come unexpectedly and demobilization could be planned in advance.

BIBLIOGRAPHY

Carroll, John M., and Colin F. Baxter, eds. *The American Military Tradition: From Colonial Times to the Present.* Wilmington, Del.: S. R. Books, 1993.

Matloff, Maurice, ed. *American Military History: 1775–1902* (Vol. 1) and *1902–1996* (Vol. 2). Conshohocken, Pa.: Combined Publishing, 1996. Earlier publication: Washington, D.C., Office of the Chief of Military History, U.S. Army, 1969.

Sparrow, John C. *History of Personnel Demobilization in the United States Army.* Washington, D.C.: Center of Military History, U.S. Army, 1994. (Distributed to depository libraries in microfiche.) Originally published: Washington, D.C.: Office of the Chief of Military History, Department of the Army, 1951.

Don E. McLeod/c. w.

See also **Army, United States; Mobilization; Revolution, American: Military History.**

DEMOCRACY. In the simplest sense, democracy is rule by the ruled. In a democratic political system, government power is legitimized by the consent of the governed. Consent is expressed in a variety of forms, including annual election of government leaders and citizen participation in governing processes. The roots of American democratic culture can be traced to the direct election of many colonial legislatures, as well as the practice of democratic governance in many localities. The American Revolution was animated by the idea that the colonists were defending the principle of democratic self-rule and that the American struggle was analogous to the English Parliament's struggle against the monarchy.

The formal mechanisms of democracy can vary, however, with direct democracy at one pole and representative democracy at the other. Direct democracy allows for unmediated citizen deliberation and decision making on public matters; representative democracy permits citizens to elect representatives who act on their behalf. American democracy is representative in design and function, yet it is clearly influenced by the ideology of direct democracy.

In *The Federalist Papers*, James Madison argued for representative democracy, because of its power to "refine and enlarge" public opinion and to control the intemperate passions of the people, who—if permitted to make government policy directly—would threaten individual rights. A balance between majority rule and individual liberty could be struck if the people's representatives, at a physical and psychological remove from citizens, ruled on their behalf. Representative democracy was best suited for an "extended Republic"—a large nation with a multiplicity of crosscutting interests. If sufficiently removed from the fray of constituent pressure, legislators would be able to discern a good for the nation that transcended the sum total of voter demands.

While Madison's vision of democracy was ultimately enshrined in the U.S. Constitution, Madison's opponents—the anti-federalists—charged that representative democracy was at too far a remove from citizens. On matters of importance power needed to reside closer to the people, if not exercised by their direct consent. While arguments for representative democracy carried the day, the tension between the two models of democracy is a theme that resonates throughout American political history.

Democracy and the American Party System

The development of democracy is closely related to changes in the American party system. The competition between political parties to win offices often generates interest among the electorate in politics and government policies. Political parties can also pursue demobilization strategies, designed to keep people away from the polls. In the early republic factional differences between rivals were rather quietly resolved in congressional caucus. When intense rivalry between Whigs and Democrats emerged in the 1840s, parties turned their efforts to getting out the vote with speeches, events, and policies tailored to win the long-term loyalty of voters.

The Civil War shifted the party system. Party politics became extremely sectionalized, with Democrats dominating offices in the South and many urban areas elsewhere, and the Republicans consistently winning elections in the East and West. After the election of 1896 Republicans dominated national politics until 1932. Sectionalism and weak competition had the effect of lowering voter turnout as well as general interest in politics. The Great Depression sparked a Democratic Party revival that pulled union members and Roman Catholics, among other groups, into a greater habit of voting and democratic participation than they had practiced previously. In the later decades of the twentieth century party loyalty among the electorate began to wane. Many analysts associated the decline in voter turnout with the loosening of ties between citizens and political parties.

Suffrage

While the theoretical debate over the nature and design of democracy was clearly elucidated during the founding of the United States, the extension of full democratic citizenship came much more slowly. The electorate in the years after the constitutional founding numbered only one out of every thirty Americans. Those without property, African Americans, and women were denied the franchise. Many states dropped the property-holding requirement during the great period of political mobilization and political party growth, the age of Jackson (1820s–1830s). But it was not until 1856 that the last state, North Carolina, eliminated the property-holding requirement. In 1966 the Supreme Court held that the poll tax—a

charge levied for voting—was unconstitutional. The poll tax had been commonly used in southern states to deter African Americans from voting.

The Fifteenth Amendment to the Constitution (1870) prohibits the denial of the right to vote based on race or color. While many African Americans exercised the new right during the reconstruction period, southern states eventually instituted a regime of legally enforced segregation known as "jim crow," which included laws designed to discourage African Americans from voting. As late as 1960, less than 10 percent of African Americans were registered to vote in Mississippi. A series of Supreme Court decisions in the 1950s and 1960s, as well as the Voting Rights Act of 1965 and its extensions, declared most of the jim crow practices to be unconstitutional.

The right of a woman to vote was most readily accepted in the American West. The Wyoming state government made federal acceptance of women's suffrage in the state a condition of its entrance into the Union in 1890. In 1920 the ratification of the Nineteenth Amendment extended voting rights to women nationally. In 1971 the Twenty-sixth Amendment lowered the voting age from twenty-one to eighteen.

Voter Turnout and Political Participation

The simplest form of democratic participation is voting. Since 1828 voter turnout among eligible voters in presidential elections has ranged from a high of 81.8 percent in 1876 (Republican Rutherford B. Hayes defeated Democrat Samuel J. Tilden) to a low of 48.9 percent in 1924 (Republican Calvin Coolidge defeated Democrat John W. Davis and Progressive Robert La Follette). During the period 1960–2000 voter turnout in presidential elections averaged 55 percent. Voter turnout rates are lower in off-year elections between presidential contests, when many congressional contests are held; during the second half of the twentieth century typically only about one-third of the eligible electorate voted in off-year elections. The degree of competition between candidates and parties, the salience of issues being discussed in a campaign, legal barriers that increase the difficulty of voting, and the demographic composition of the electorate all affect voter turnout. Americans also face a blinding blizzard of choices, electing hundreds of thousands of officials from posts ranging in importance from the U.S. president to local city and county representatives and school board members.

In the early 2000s the U.S. rate of voter participation trailed that of the major western European democracies, a cause of concern for those who fear that the legitimacy of the governance system is threatened if too few people vote. Nonvoting is sometimes interpreted as a symptom of widespread disgust with the American two-party system. By 2002 calls had been made for the emergence of alternative political parties and ideologies to capture the interest and passion of the disenchanted, as well as changes in electoral law to make the birth of alternative parties easier. The surprisingly robust third-party candidacy of the businessman Ross Perot in the presidential elections of 1992 and 1996 was to many an example of the power of outsiders to attract politically alienated citizens. (Perot won 19 percent of the vote in 1992.) Perot, like other third-party or independent candidates for president, flourished during a time of economic and social unrest. Among the few independent presidential candidates who captured voter attention were Congressman John Anderson in 1980, Senator Robert La Follette in 1924, and former President Theodore Roosevelt running with Progressive Party support in 1912. Low voter participation has also been interpreted as a sign of contentment with the status quo, a signal that Americans are fundamentally happy with the political order.

Voting is the most formal act of political participation, but not the exclusive form of citizen involvement in the political system. A 1995 study found that 10 percent of Americans were political activists, defined as those who voted, worked in and contributed to political campaigns, and lobbied elected officials; 15 percent limited their activity to voting and helping out in political campaigns; 20 percent voted but limited more extensive involvement in community affairs to nonpolitical matters; 20 percent did no more than vote; and 20 percent did not vote at all. This survey suggests that a few people do most of the work seemingly required for the maintenance of democratic institutions.

In the early 2000s attention was devoted to the loss in the United States of "social capital"—the pool of trust and reciprocity among citizens that can be drawn on to solve collective problems. With Americans working longer hours, watching more television, and more attached to their professional and workplace institutions than to their geographical community, participation in local political and civic organizations dropped off. Many worried that the vitality of democracy was threatened as a result.

Democracy and Trust

Despite America's long democratic tradition and the slow but steady enfranchisement of excluded groups of citizens, public opinion surveys showed that trust in the democratic process declined in the United States in the aftermath of President Richard Nixon's Watergate scandal and the fallout from the Vietnam War. Many called for reforms to renew the trust of citizens in democracy.

Campaign finance reform, aimed at capping the amount that candidates and parties can spend on elections, cycled off and on the public agenda from the 1970s to the early 2000s. In the 1990s many states and localities adopted term limits for elected representatives to encourage the participation of amateurs in politics. Other suggested reforms proposed using new communications technology to involve more citizens in politics, as well as make voting easier.

Calls for reform that seek to augment representative democracies with more direct forms have a long history. During the Progressive Era (c. 1890–c. 1920), many states adopted initiative and referendum procedures to bring policy proposals directly before citizens by placing proposals on the ballot. Citizens could thereby bypass representative institutions that were often under the control of urban political machines or state legislatures dominated by rural interests. In the 1990s direct democracy procedures were adopted at a fevered pace. By 2002 California's most important policy decisions were usually resolved by referendum vote rather than in the state legislature.

Political movements have also argued for more expansive notions of democracy. During the New Deal era many liberals argued for forms of economic democracy that would recognize the workplace as an important site of power, where citizens in their role as workers traditionally had little control. In the 1960s the New Left linked democratic participation with individual development, asserting that the communal activities of direct democracy fulfill human potential and cultivate virtue.

Within the framework of consensus about democratic ideals, Americans will continue to debate the merits of direct and representative forms of democracy, and contest the inclusiveness of democratic citizenship, as well as its duties and obligations.

BIBLIOGRAPHY

Gant, Michael M., and Norman R. Luttbeg. *American Electoral Behavior: 1952–1988.* Itasca, Ill.: F. E. Peacock Publishers, 1991.

Kammen, Michael, ed. *The Origins of the American Constitution: A Documentary History.* New York: Penguin, 1986.

Morgan, Edmund S. *The Birth of the Republic, 1763–1789.* Chicago: University of Chicago Press, 1992.

Putnam, Robert D. *Bowling Alone: The Collapse and Revival of American Community.* New York: Simon and Schuster, 2000.

Verba, Sidney, Henry E. Brady, and Kay Lehman Schlozman. *Voice and Equality: Civic Voluntarism in American Politics.* Cambridge, Mass.: Harvard University Press, 1995.

Richard M. Flanagan

See also **Suffrage, Woman's; Two-Party System; Voting.**

DEMOCRACY IN AMERICA, by Alexis de Tocqueville. The most influential study of the United States ever written, *Democracy in America* owes its enduring significance to the complexity of Tocqueville's analysis. This child of aristocracy was "a liberal of a new kind" (Tocqueville to Eugène Stoffels, July 24, 1836, in *The Tocqueville Reader,* p. 153): despite his personal passion for freedom and individual distinction, he conceded that equality and democracy were God's ideals for the future. In the United States, which he visited in 1831–1832, Tocqueville saw how liberty could be channeled by widespread participation in public life to prevent a potentially volatile "tyranny of the majority" from spilling over into anarchy or despotism. In the widely read and highly praised first volume of *Democracy in America* (1835), Tocqueville showed how boisterous local associations and a decentralized political system moderated the fractiousness of democratic life. In the second volume (1840), which reflects his growing anxiety about a new industrial feudalism (from a trip to Great Britain) and a stagnant mass culture anesthetized by prosperity (from developments in his native France), Tocqueville ventured a more abstract and ambitious meditation on the consequences of equality for freedom.

Differences of tone and emphasis marked the two volumes of *Democracy in America*, and interpreters' differing analyses of Tocqueville have reflected their own passions and perspectives. His first American reviewers, post-Federalists and proto-Whigs who were also among his most important informants, praised him because he took American democracy seriously (unusual for a European visitor) and because he emphasized—as these Americans did—the importance of distinguishing between the corrosive egoism of individualists on the make and the democratic virtue of "self interest rightly understood." Only through experiences such as serving on juries or participating in voluntary associations, Tocqueville argued, did Americans learn to cooperate with each other, to see things from other points of view, and to internalize the crucial ethic of "reciprocal obligation" (*Democracy*, p. 572).

From the Civil War through World War II, *Democracy in America* slipped into relative obscurity as conflict eclipsed cooperation as the most striking feature of American life. In the late 1930s, against the chiaroscuro of fascism and communism, American democracy again shimmered with promise; Tocqueville assumed the stature of sage that he has enjoyed ever since. If centralization and conformity bred totalitarianism, Tocqueville showed how America managed to avoid such perils. If Jefferson's Enlightenment rationalism and Marx's revolutionary positivism seemed too simple for a chastened age, Tocqueville provided—as did Max Weber—a more subtle, multidimensional alternative. If Dwight Eisenhower was the first President to quote Tocqueville, all of his successors have followed his lead because *Democracy in America* offered wisdom for everyone. Since the 1960s right and left alike have adopted Tocqueville as a sober prophet, who saw the hollowness of material prosperity either detached from tradition and authority (for conservatives) or detached from the promise of participatory democracy (for the communitarian left). But only readers alert to Tocqueville's delicate balancing of freedom and equality, of cultural stability and innovation, will avoid jamming him awkwardly into contemporary categories and see him, as he saw himself, perched between the old regime of privilege and the problematic future of egalitarian democracy.

BIBLIOGRAPHY

Schleifer, James T. *The Making of Tocqueville's "Democracy in America."* Indianapolis: Liberty Fund, 2000.

Siedentrop, Larry. *Tocqueville.* Oxford: Oxford University Press, 1994.

Tocqueville, Alexis de. *Democracy in America.* Edited by J. P. Mayer, translated by George Lawrence. Garden City, N.Y.: Doubleday, 1969.

Zunz, Olivier, and Alan S. Kahan, *The Tocqueville Reader: A Life in Letters and Politics.* Oxford: Blackwell Publishing, Ltd., 2002.

James T. Kloppenberg

See also **Individualism; Liberty, Concept of.**

DEMOCRATIC PARTY, the oldest mass-based political party in the world. The party traces its ancestry to the collaboration between Thomas Jefferson and James Madison of Virginia and Aaron Burr and George Clinton of New York. The four founders of the party may first have gathered in upstate New York in 1791 when Jefferson and Madison were allegedly on a botanical expedition to observe the vegetation and wildlife of the region. The fateful alliance between Virginia and New York, between the planters and small farmers of the South with the small farmers of the West and urban workers of the East, began a durable coalition of American politics that endured into the middle of the twentieth century.

Jeffersonian Origins

Jefferson, Madison, Burr, and Clinton began their party as an organized opposition to the politics of Alexander Hamilton. Hamilton and his supporters favored a strong central government, debt, credit, banking, and trade policies to further commercial and manufacturing interests, an expanded military and naval budget, and a conciliatory policy toward Great Britain. The Jeffersonian "Republicans" as they were then known, favored minimalist government, retirement of the national debt, no favoritism for banks or for manufacturing enterprises, and discriminatory trade policies that would favor France over Britain. The Jeffersonians conceived that they could make America's agricultural exports into a potent instrument of diplomacy. Jefferson, Madison, and Albert Gallatin, the ablest political economist among them, disdained military and naval expenditure as inherently wasteful and corrupting in peacetime.

The Jeffersonians gained power in both the executive and legislative branches in 1801 and they retained political power for a quarter century, the era known as the "VIRGINIA DYNASTY": Jefferson's two terms as president were followed by two terms each for his fellow Virginians James Madison and James Monroe.

Jefferson as president was not the minimalist that Jefferson the opposition leader had been. Although he reduced government expenditures, particularly the war and navy budget, his refusal to pay a "tribute" to the dey of Algiers resulted in the Tripolitan War, and a buildup of American naval forces that extended to the WAR OF 1812. Most importantly, Jefferson the "strict constructionist" of the Constitution dramatically expanded presidential power by negotiating the LOUISIANA PURCHASE, which he initiated and concluded without a specific constitutional warrant.

Jefferson's second term and Madison's first term marked a less successful period for the party that now called itself the "Democratic Republicans." The Jeffersonians tried to achieve their diplomatic ends peacefully, and this meant attempting to force diplomatic success through trade policy. Jefferson's Embargo Act and Madison's Non-Intercourse Act marked efforts to secure French and British recognition of America's neutral rights in the midst of their all-out struggle in the Napoleonic Wars.

In the upheaval of the war with Britain in 1812, the Jeffersonians found themselves severely hampered in their defense efforts, in part because of the cutbacks in naval and military budgets they had initiated a decade earlier. In the aftermath of the War of 1812, Madison and Monroe altered their approach to economic policy. Madison endorsed a protective tariff in 1816 and supported a new charter for a Bank of the United States. Madison even cautiously approved of federally initiated internal improvements, such as canals, roads, and river and harbor improvements. By the end of Madison's presidency and throughout Monroe's two terms, known as the "ERA OF GOOD FEELING," the Democratic Republican Party largely abandoned its minimalism and supported tariff, banking, and improvements policies originally supported by its Federalist opponents.

The Jacksonians

After the retirement of James Monroe, the newly renamed "Democratic" Party came to rally around the candidacy of Andrew Jackson. Jackson steered the party back toward its minimalist origins. Jackson vetoed the recharter of the Second Bank of the United States and expressed his hostility to federally funded internal improvements with a veto of the Maysville Road Bill. While Jackson favored tariff reduction in his first term, he would not countenance the efforts of states' rights extremists in South Carolina, under the leadership of John C. Calhoun, to nullify the existing tariff. Jackson reduced the tariff and used the threat of a Force Bill to compel South Carolina to retreat from its dangerous course. Jackson favored aggressive western expansion into Native American lands and he initiated the removal of the remaining Indian tribes in the Southeast—the Cherokees, Creeks, Choctaws, Chickasaws, and Seminoles—to much less hospitable lands more than 1,000 miles farther west in what today is the state of Oklahoma.

Jackson and his successor Martin Van Buren of New York favored the radical "HARD MONEY" policies advocated by labor reformers and some small farmers. Jackson initiated the Specie Circular, which required that all land transactions be conducted using coin rather than bank notes. In the aftermath of a severe downturn in the economy in 1837, Van Buren blamed "overspeculation" and called for a complete separation of bank and state. Hereafter all federal deposits would repose in an independent Subtreasury, immune from banking interference but also unavailable for investment to reflate the economy.

While the Specie Circular did not have its intended effect of reducing the power of banks and speculators, neither did it cause the panic of 1837, as many of the Democrats' Whig opponents charged. Nevertheless, the panic of 1837 and the economic discontent that lasted into the 1840s ended the Democratic dominance of the government after a dozen years. The Whig opposition to the Democrats succeeded in 1840 by imitating many of the aspects of Jacksonian Democracy that the voters found most appealing: in the "Log Cabin" campaign of that year they nominated a war hero and alleged log cabin dweller William Henry Harrison, known as "Old Tippecanoe" to supplant "Old Hickory" and his successor "Old Kinderhook." Van Buren may not have made much impression on the voters in 1840, but he left a lasting impression on American language: His nickname "O.K." came to stand for anything that had popular approval.

The Democrats came back into power in 1845 with the accession to the presidency of another Tennessean, "Young Hickory," James K. Polk. Polk, like Jackson, was an ardent expansionist, and he campaigned for the presidency with promises to annex the republic of Texas to the Union and to extend Oregon Territory to the border of Russian Alaska: "FIFTY-FOUR FORTY OR FIGHT!" In the latter affair, Polk accepted reality and abandoned northern expansion in favor of an equitable split of Oregon Territory between the United States and British North America. In the matter of Texas, Polk proved far more willing to resort to war. The successful conclusion of that war and the forced cession by Mexico of California, New Mexico, and the rest of its northern territory proved very popular. Polk's free trade policy, negotiated at a time when Great Britain was also abandoning protectionism, helped to generate significant economic expansion. Polk was sufficiently popular that he could easily have run for reelection. He had promised to serve only a single term, however. A Whig, the MEXICAN-AMERICAN WAR hero General Zachary Taylor, followed in office.

Polk's term as president marks the maturity of the Democratic Party in the antebellum era. The Democrats had succeeded in becoming the dominant party of the era by appealing to most planters in the South, small farmers in the West, and urban workers and immigrants in the Northeast. The Democrats were the party of minimal government and libertarianism on the domestic front. The party was consistently hostile to the causes of social reform, such as temperance, education reform, women's rights, and, most unequivocally, abolitionism. The party supported western expansion and after Polk's term this expansion was linked to extending territory for the expansion of slavery. Jefferson's notion that expansion into the West would extend the "empire of liberty" had given way to an idea condemned by antislavery reformers that further expansion would only further the "empire of slavery."

The Democratic Party in the Sectional Crisis and Civil War

By the mid-1850s the Democratic Party was the only significant national institution that united adherents both North and South. The Democrats accomplished this feat at a time when churches, professional associations, and fraternal organizations, to say nothing of the Whigs, had split over the issue of slavery. The party had achieved this unity by papering over its differences on the issue of slavery and, as a result, antislavery Democrats like David Wilmot, Charles Sumner, and even Martin Van Buren abandoned the party. Beneath the veneer of unity, there lurked a deep division between the wings of the Democratic Party. Northern Democrats like Stephen A. Douglas of Illinois favored popular sovereignty as a solution to the problem of slavery in the territories. Southern Democrats like John C. Breckinridge of Kentucky argued that slaveholders were entitled to full protection of their "property" wherever they should go in the federal territories, a view endorsed by the U.S. Supreme Court in the *Dred Scott v. Sandford* (1857) decision.

By 1860 the Democrats could no longer paper over their differences. In a four-way presidential contest with Republican Abraham Lincoln and Constitutional Unionist John Bell, both wings of the Democratic Party were resoundingly defeated. With the secession of the Confederate states, the Democratic Party lost its base and became a rump party, deeply divided between WAR DEMOCRATS like Montgomery Blair of Maryland, who served in Lincoln's cabinet, and Peace Democrats like Mayor Fernando Wood of New York, who were openly friendly to the aims of the Confederacy. With the Union victories of 1863 and 1864, General George McClellan, a War Democrat campaigning on a Peace platform, could not win the presidency away from Abraham Lincoln.

The Gilded Age

In the aftermath of the CIVIL WAR the Democrats drifted for nearly a decade, unsure of their identity, from the prosouthern urban politics of New York governor Horatio Seymour to the reformist zeal of Horace Greeley, once anathema to every organization Democrat North or South. Although the Democrats under Samuel J. Tilden won the popular vote and in all likelihood the electoral vote in the disputed election of 1876, the Republican Party emerged victorious in a compromise settlement. The Democrats gained by this Faustian bargain, however. With the withdrawal of federal troops from the southern states in 1877, the South became solidly Democratic and succeeded in disenfranchising African Americans almost completely within a decade.

The Democrats' fortunes revived in 1884 thanks to the reformism of New York governor Grover Cleveland. Dedicated to free trade and civil service reform and opposed to expansionism into the Caribbean and Hawaii, the Democrats attracted a significant coterie of reform-minded Republicans known as the "MUGWUMPS." These deserters left their party to support Cleveland and remained in the Democratic Party as the forerunners of the Democratic Progressives.

Populism and Progressivism

In the 1890s, however, the urban and agrarian components of the Democratic coalition drifted apart on the issue of an expansionist money supply. Cleveland and other eastern Democrats, known as "GOLD BUGS," favored remaining on the gold standard, a policy that benefited both Wall Street financiers and urban workers. Agrarian Democrats in the West and South, however, suffering severely from credit reduction after the depression of 1893, found a new eloquent champion for an expansionist money policy in the silver-tongued oratory of William Jennings Bryan.

Bryan's oratory left his southern and western listeners spellbound. His hostility to banks and to eastern financial interests had deep roots in Jeffersonian and Jacksonian ideology. Bryan's expansionist money policy engendered hostility, however, among the other key component of the Democratic coalition: urban workers in the East. His money policy and his endorsement of free trade in the depressed economy of the 1890s left wageworkers seeking prosperity under the protectionist policies of William McKinley and the Republicans. Bryan's religious fundamentalism gave his oratory tremendous moral power among those for whom biblical imagery was an appropriate metaphor for all problems of life. His famous peroration delivered at the Chicago Democratic Convention in 1896 electrified his supporters, "You shall not press down upon the brow of labor this crown of thorns, you shall not crucify mankind upon a cross of gold." Others found Bryan's speech more alarming than thrilling. Among liturgical Christians, particularly Catholics and Lutherans, Bryan's use of the crucifixion as political metaphor sounded blasphemous. To Jews, the fixation on Christian crucifixion and on the avarice for gold held unpleasant echoes of European anti-Semitism. The result was the alienation of non-evangelical Democrats from Bryan and from the party. The Republican Party thereafter dominated all sections of the United States except the South until the Great Depression.

The Democrats spent the following sixteen years as a political minority, identified with a kind of retrogressive agrarianism in the South and ethnocentric tribalism in the North. The election of Woodrow Wilson transformed the Democrats in 1912. He led the party away from its agrarian roots and toward an energetic form of progressivism. Wilson's progressivism was more concerned with promoting economic competition than with regulating monopolies. Wilson essentially abandoned the traditional minimalism of previous Democrats from Jefferson and Jackson through Cleveland. Only in one respect did Wilson retain a traditional Democratic approach: Wilson was a strict segregationist who re-segregated the civil service in Washington.

During WORLD WAR I, Wilson took an antitrust approach in foreign affairs. Like Jefferson and Madison one hundred years earlier, Wilson found it impossible to generate respect for American neutral rights when Europe was once again engaged in an all-out struggle. With America's entry into the war, the Wilsonians' agenda became ever more interventionist. The WAR INDUSTRIES BOARD regulated wages and prices in key defense industries, including steel, petroleum, and railroads.

The aftermath of World War I brought the Democrats new problems. Wilson sponsored the FOURTEEN POINTS as principles by which the victorious Allies might lay the foundations of a lasting peace at Versailles. These were hailed abroad and widely admired at home. Wilson's devastating stroke, his consequent lack of judgment, and his failure to cooperate with the Republican-controlled Congress doomed the Versailles Treaty's passage in the Senate, and the failure of the United States to participate in Wilson's cherished LEAGUE OF NATIONS. The war's aftermath brought other problems on the home front. The passage of the ESPIONAGE and SEDITION ACTS and the "PALMER RAIDS" led by Wilson's attorney general against domestic radicals tarnished the Democrats' record as the defender of civil liberties. It also harmed the party's image among those ethnic minorities, such as Italians and Jews, singled out for persecution.

The 1920s were a period of eclipse for the Democrats. The party was bitterly divided over ethnocultural issues, including Prohibition, immigration restriction, and whether or not to recognize the KU KLUX KLAN. The Democratic Party was deeply divided between Drys and Wets, Protestants and Catholics, Klansmen and their antagonists. Even among what Wilson called "hyphenated Americans," there were deep divisions between northern and southern Europeans, old and new immigrants, Catholics and Jews. With Al Smith's nomination for president in 1928, the latter divisions between non-Protestant immigrants disappeared and the urban Progressive Smith led a new generation of Italian and Jewish Americans into the Democratic fold, where they would later support Franklin D. Roosevelt and the NEW DEAL. Smith, however, proved too much of an urban stereotype for Protestant Democrats in the South and West. His accent, his Catholicism, and his antagonism to PROHIBITION alienated many Democrats in the South and West into voting Republican for the first time in their lives. In 1928 Smith carried only two heavily Catholic states outside the Deep South: Massachusetts and Rhode Island. The Solid South was no longer solid in the face of a Catholic running for president. Smith lost the Upper South, where fear of Catholicism triumphed over hatred of Republicans. Only in

the Deep South (including heavily Catholic Louisiana) did the loathing of Republicans prove stronger than fear of a Catholic in the White House.

The New Deal and the Fair Deal

In 1932, in the worst days of the GREAT DEPRESSION, the Democrats nominated another New Yorker for president: this time however, he had an impeccable old-line Protestant background and he hailed from a rural area in the Hudson River valley. Franklin D. Roosevelt united the Wets, Catholics, Jews, and urban Progressive reformers of the East and Midwest with the small farmers and miners of the West and the lily-white Democratic Party of the South. Roosevelt synthesized the trust-busting economic policy of the Wilsonians with the interventionist regulatory approach of his distant cousin Theodore.

In the midst of the Great Depression, Roosevelt launched the "alphabet soup" of government agencies instituted to help the American economy get going again. In agriculture, labor reform, securities trading, child labor restrictions, social security, unemployment relief, rural electrification, banking, and currency regulation, Roosevelt stamped the Democrats' vision of government as inherently interventionist.

WORLD WAR II drew the United States once again into an all-out European conflict, and Roosevelt sought an unprecedented third term because the nation required an experienced chief executive in the midst of such a grave worldwide crisis. In the midst of the war, the Democrats sponsored active intervention in the economy. As in World War I, government, industry, and labor found themselves in a sometimes-uneasy partnership directing a planned war economy. Wartime exigencies forced Roosevelt to break with another Democratic tradition: in the midst of the war, by executive order, Roosevelt prohibited racial discrimination in the hiring policy of federal contractors. African Americans reciprocated by giving their support to the Democrats, beginning in 1932 and accelerating in the 1940s. For the first time in American history, by the 1940s the majority of African American votes were cast for the Democrats.

With Roosevelt's death and the defeat of the Axis, the Democrats looked to Harry Truman to orchestrate the postwar strategic and economic order. The devastation of Western Europe and growing tensions with Joseph Stalin over the political complexion of Eastern Europe produced conflict with the Soviet Union in the early stages of formulating a postwar world order. The Soviet blockade of West Berlin and a Communist takeover of Czechoslovakia produced a siege mentality among Americans now in the early stages of the COLD WAR with the Soviet Union.

Truman and the Democrats supported interventionism and new mechanisms to promote international stability. The MARSHALL PLAN, the WORLD BANK, and the INTERNATIONAL MONETARY FUND produced economic aid and lent stability to the war-torn Western European economies. The TRUMAN DOCTRINE in the eastern Mediterranean produced "containment" of Communism in Greece and Turkey. American sponsorship of decolonization in India and the Middle East gave Americans greater leverage in those newly emerging states. The United States' recognition of Israel cemented a lasting relationship in the Middle East, despite the antagonism of European allies and the emerging Arab states.

East Asia proved more difficult for Truman and the Democratic Party. The successful Communist Revolution in China prompted Truman's Republican opponents to ask, "Who lost China?" American inability to halt the KOREAN WAR before it degenerated into a long, inconclusive stalemate also proved unpopular with the voters. When the Republicans nominated war hero Dwight Eisenhower in 1952, campaigning against "Korea, Communism, and Corruption," they made inroads into hitherto solid Democratic constituencies, including Southerners and Catholics.

In 1954 the Democrats regained their control of both houses of Congress after their losses in the 1952 Eisenhower landslide. The Democratic leadership was able to work with Eisenhower to promote a bipartisan approach to such issues as nuclear energy, federal aid to education, interstate highways, and limited civil rights legislation. The Democrats in Congress and the Eisenhower administration proved unwilling, or incapable, however, of opposing Senator Joseph McCarthy, until his own ruthless excesses destroyed him.

The New Frontier and the Great Society

In 1960 the Democrats broke with tradition and nominated a young, Harvard-educated Catholic, John F. Kennedy, for the presidency. Kennedy inspired a generation of young Americans with his idealistic rhetoric promoting sacrifice. Kennedy sponsored sweeping civil rights legislation, a tax cut to stimulate the economy, and a doctrine of "limited war" that would engage Communism in peripheral struggle without risking nuclear holocaust.

After Kennedy's assassination, President Lyndon Johnson inherited Kennedy's civil rights and limited war initiatives. In the hands of Johnson, widely considered the most effective majority leader of the Senate, sweeping civil rights legislation passed Congress for the first time since Reconstruction. The Democrats, once the party supporting white supremacy, inaugurated an era of Second Reconstruction with the CIVIL RIGHTS ACT OF 1964, the VOTING RIGHTS ACT OF 1965, and the Fair Housing Bill of 1966. These measures and Johnson's sponsorship of a WAR ON POVERTY brought to life the full promise of inclusion for African Americans. That this was achieved by a southerner, thanks to his extraordinary legislative abilities, was an irony lost neither on blacks nor on his fellow white southerners. The VIETNAM WAR, however, proved to be Johnson's worst nightmare. He would not withdraw and he could not escalate the war without risking a nuclear war with the Soviet Union and with China.

Johnson was left in a war he could not win, and he refused to run for re-election in a year in which the Democrats seemed bent on self-destruction.

The candidacies of Robert Kennedy and Eugene McCarthy in 1968, and the candidacy of George McGovern in 1972, fired the idealism of the youthful antiwar wing of the Democratic Party. The labor unions, the lower middle class, Catholics, and white southerners expressed their alienation from these new politics by staying away from the polls or defecting to the Republicans or to George Wallace.

The Post-Watergate Democrats

In the aftermath of WATERGATE, widespread disillusion with the Republicans produced dramatic gains for the Democrats in Congress and in the statehouses in 1974. Despite a four-year hiatus in which white southerner Jimmy Carter temporarily won the South back for the Democrats, the party once again seemed on the verge of convulsion in 1980. With the advent of Ronald Reagan's presidency in that year, the Republicans gained control of the Senate as well as the White House, while the Democrats—bitterly divided once again between the liberal wing supporting Edward Kennedy and the moderate wing supporting Carter—went down to a landslide defeat. The Democrats recovered their control of the Senate in 1986 but continued to govern largely in response to Republican initiatives in the Reagan years and in the PERSIAN GULF WAR of President George H. W. Bush.

The election of Bill Clinton in 1992 seemed to argue a return to more of the activist policies of the Democrats in earlier eras, but after the failure of his health care initiative and the ignominious defeat of the Democrats in both houses of Congress the party lost whatever initiative it had in leading the government. Although President Clinton easily won a second term in 1996 and Vice President Al Gore won the popular vote in 2000, after that time the Democratic Party exhibited the deep divisions between its diverse constituencies that marked its earlier errands in the political wilderness.

BIBLIOGRAPHY

Baker, Jean H. *Affairs of Party: The Political Culture of Northern Democrats in the Mid-Nineteenth Century.* Ithaca, N.Y.: Cornell University Press, 1983.

Banning, Lance. *The Jeffersonian Persuasion: Evolution of a Party Ideology.* Ithaca, N.Y.: Cornell University Press, 1978.

Benson, Lee. *The Concept of Jacksonian Democracy: New York as a Test Case.* Princeton, N.J.: Princeton University Press, 1961.

Burner, David. *The Politics of Provincialism: The Democratic Party in Transition, 1918–1932.* Cambridge, Mass.: Harvard University Press, 1986.

Cunningham, Noble E. *The Jeffersonian Republicans: The Formation of Party Organization, 1789–1801.* Chapel Hill: University of North Carolina Press, 1957.

———. *The Jeffersonian Republicans in Power: Party Operations, 1801–1809.* Chapel Hill: University of North Carolina Press, 1963.

Formisano, Ronald P. *The Birth of Mass Political Parties: Michigan, 1827–1861*. Princeton, N.J.: Princeton University Press, 1971.

Goodman, Paul. *The Democratic Republicans of Massachusetts*. Cambridge, Mass.: Harvard University Press, 1964.

Leuchtenberg, William E. *In the Shadow of F.D.R.: From Harry Truman to Bill Clinton*. 2d ed. Ithaca, N.Y.: Cornell University Press, 1993.

McGerr, Michael E. *The Decline of Popular Politics: The American North, 1865–1928*. New York: Oxford University Press, 1986.

Remini, Robert V. *Martin Van Buren and the Making of the Democratic Party*. New York: Columbia University Press, 1959.

Andrew W. Robertson

See also **Political Parties; Republican Party; Republicans, Jeffersonian; Two-Party System;** *and vol. 9:* **An Interview with Fannie Lou Hamer.**

DEMOGRAPHY AND DEMOGRAPHIC TRENDS.

Demography is the study of the growth, structure, and movement of human populations. It focuses on enumerations (censuses), which take stock of a population at a moment in time, and also flows of vital events—births, deaths, marriages, and migratory move-ments. These two sources furnish the basis for the statistical underpinnings of this article.

The Census

The demographic history of the United States can readily be divided into two segments based on the availability of "modern" demographic data, mainly before and after 1790, the date of the first federal census. The United States was the first nation to have mandated regular census enumerations. The Constitution specified a census every ten years for apportionment of the federal House of Representatives. From a very modest enumeration of heads of households with only a few questions in 1790, the census grew into a large-scale operation. In 1850, the census became nominal; that is, every person was enumerated separately by name, instead of a summary of information by household (as had been done for the censuses of 1790 to 1840). In 1820, a preliminary effort was made at an economic census of manufactures. From the 1840 census onward, censuses of manufactures and agriculture have been taken regularly. Mining and minerals were usually counted along with manufactures. Beginning in the late 1920s, wholesale, retail, and service establishments were also enumerated. Later, censuses of governments were undertaken. The population census is still

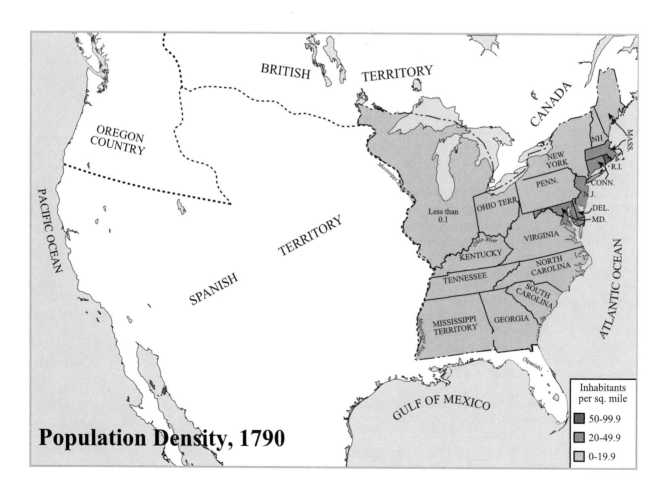

Population Density, 1790

taken decennially in years ending in zero, but the economic and government censuses are taken more frequently.

Vital Processes

The study of vital processes has been more difficult. Unlike census enumeration, registration of births, deaths, and marriages was left to state and local governments. Consequently, it was done unevenly. Some cities (New York, Boston, Philadelphia, Baltimore, and New Orleans) were already registering deaths by the early nineteenth century. Massachusetts was the first to institute statewide vital registration in 1842. A federal Death Registration Area was created in 1900 with ten states (the six New England States, New York, New Jersey, Indiana, and Michigan) and the District of Columbia, all of which were deemed to have had at least 90 percent completeness. A parallel Birth Registration Area was only set up in 1915 with ten states (the six New England states, New York, Pennsylvania, Michigan, and Minnesota) and the District of Columbia, again with the criterion of at least 90 percent registration completeness. Both areas were only completed in 1933 with the admission of Texas. By the 2000s, the nation still lacked comprehensive registration of marriages and divorces. For international migration, statistics have been collected at major ports of entry to the United States since 1819. Arrivals across land borders were not regularly counted until 1906, while alien departures were only reported from 1907 to 1957. No direct registration of internal migration has been undertaken. From 1850, the federal census has asked a question on place of birth (state within the United States, country if foreign-born) as well as current residence, which allows a view of "lifetime" migration to that point. A question on residence five years prior to the census was instituted in 1940. Since 1947, the Census Bureau has collected monthly data on a variety of detailed demographic, social, and economic topics with an interview system know as the Current Population Survey.

To determine demographic history before the "statistical era" (1790 to the present), other sources must be used. There were several dozen colonial and early national state censuses. In addition, family reconstitutions have been undertaken using parish records, genealogies, tax lists, muster rolls, and other such sources. We know more about the New England and Middle Atlantic colonies than those south of the Chesapeake. The population of the British North American colonies increased from several hundred Europeans in the early seventeenth century to about 2.5 million by 1780 (2 million whites and about half a million blacks). In contrast, the Amerindian population of the region experienced a serious decline, from about 1.1 million in 1650 to about 700,000 in 1780. This decline continued into the early twentieth century as a consequence of new diseases, warfare, loss of economic territory, and changes in way of life. (See Table 1.)

Since 1790, the American population grew from about 4 million (about 3.2 million whites and about

TABLE 1

Estimated Population by Race and Ethnicity, British North America and the United States, 1650–2000 (in Thousands)

Date	Total	White	Black	Other	Amerindian
1650	75	72	3	(NA)	1,152
1700	251	223	28	(NA)	987
1750	1,171	935	236	(NA)	780
1800	5,308	4,306	1,002	(NA)	600
1850	23,192	19,553	3,639	(NA)	370
1900	75,994	66,809	8,834	351	237
1950	150,697	134,942	15,042	713	343
2000	281,422	216,931	36,419	28,072	4,119

Implied annual % growth rates					
1650/1700	2.42	2.26	4.47		− 0.31
1700/1750	3.08	2.87	4.26		− 0.47
1750/1800	3.02	3.05	2.89		− 0.52
1800/1850	2.95	3.03	2.58		− 0.97
1850/1900	2.37	2.46	1.77		− 0.89
1900/1950	1.37	1.41	1.06	2.36	0.74
1950/2000	1.25	0.95	1.77	7.35	4.97

SOURCE: See Haines and Steckel (2000), Table A-1, 694. Based on data from U.S. Bureau of the Census (1975).

760,000 blacks, of whom about 700,000 were slaves) to about 281 million in 2000. This represents an average annual growth rate of 2 percent per year. Over the long run, natural increase (births minus deaths) has accounted for approximately three-quarters of this growth, while net in-migration contributed about one-quarter. Net in-migration is the difference between total gross in-migration and total gross out-migration.

Race and Ethnicity of the Population

The shares of the population by race and ethnicity have varied over time. Prior to 1860, only whites and blacks were enumerated. For the first several decades of the republic, whites comprised 81 to 82 percent of the population. This share began to rise as white immigrants from Europe contributed substantially to population growth, while the black population grew almost entirely through natural increase, since the slave trade was officially ended in 1808. In the decades of the 1850s and the 1900s, the contribution to population growth from immigration rose as high as 33 percent. The share of the white population peaked at about 90 percent in the period 1930 to 1950, after which it began to decline. This was related to shifts in immigration from Europe to Asia, Latin America, and Africa. The 2000 census indicates that whites constitute 77 percent of the population, blacks 13 percent, and other races 10 percent, of which Amerindians are 1.5 percent and Asians 4.5 percent. Also, Hispanics (of all races) are about 13 percent of the total, up from about 1 percent in 1910. (See Table 2.)

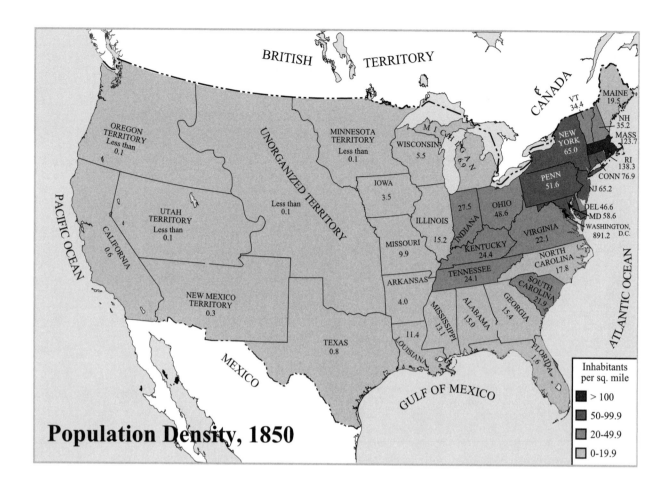

Population Density, 1850

Inhabitants per sq. mile	
▓	> 100
▓	50–99.9
▓	20–49.9
▓	0–19.9

A related issue is the foreign-born population. The 1850 census revealed that, at that moment, about 10 percent of the American population had been born abroad. This peaked at 15 percent in 1910, from which point the share diminished to 4.8 percent in 1970. Thereafter, changes in immigration legislation have resulted in large net inflows of migrants, such that the share of the foreign born as of 2002 was about 9.5 percent.

Population Distribution

An important feature of American history is the redistribution across space. In 1790, only 5 percent of the population resided in urban areas, defined as incorporated places of 2,500 persons and over. By the time of the Civil War (1861–1865), this had risen to 20 percent. The census of 1920 was the first to show that more than half of the American population was urban, a fact that led to such a protracted congressional conflict over reapportionment that the 1920s was the only decade in which the House of Representatives was not redistricted. The official urban proportion stood at 75 percent in 1990, but this tends to understate the true urban population because of as-yet-unincorporated areas growing up on the fringes of metropolitan areas and other urban places. (See Table 2.)

There have been shifts in regional shares of population. The original thirteen states were spread along the

Atlantic Coast, mostly east of the Appalachian Mountains. Population was about evenly divided between the Northeast (New England and Middle Atlantic States) and the South Atlantic and East South Central regions. The well-known westward movement to the frontier (mostly along east-west latitudes), as well as immigration from Europe, which went mostly to the North, began to shift the balance. By 1860 the North (the Northeast, Midwest, and West regions) had about 65 percent of the population, while the South had only about 35 percent. The westward movement ended in about 1890 and was replaced by an increasing rural-to-urban migration. In the late twentieth century this turned to a movement from central cities to suburbs and a regional migration to the "Sun Belt." About half of the American population lived in suburban places and another quarter in central cities. In 2000, 19 percent of the American population resided in the Northeast, 23 percent in the Midwest, 22 percent in the West, and 36 percent in the South. The state of California alone held 12 percent of the nation's people.

Immigration and Population

The United States has long been an immigrant destination. Overall, between 1821 and 1997, approximately 64 million immigrants officially entered the United States. Between 1820 and 1920, a period of virtually unrestricted

TABLE 2

U.S. Population by Race, Residence, Nativity, Age, and Sex, 1800–1990 (in Thousands)

Census Date	Total	Growth (% p.a.)	White	%	Black	Other	Urban	%	Foreign-Born	%	Median Age	Sex Ratio(b)
1790	3,929	—	3,172	80.7	757	(NA)	202	5.1	(NA)	—	(NA)	103.8
1800	5,308	3.01	4,306	81.1	1,002	(NA)	322	6.1	(NA)	—	16.0(a)	104.0
1810	7,240	3.10	5,862	81.0	1,378	(NA)	525	7.3	(NA)	—	16.0(a)	104.0
1820	9,639	2.86	7,867	81.6	1,772	(NA)	693	7.2	(NA)	—	16.7	103.3
1830	12,866	2.89	10,537	81.9	2,329	(NA)	1,127	8.8	(NA)	—	17.2	103.1
1840	17,070	2.83	14,196	83.2	2,874	(NA)	1,845	10.8	(NA)	—	17.8	103.7
1850	23,192	3.06	19,553	84.3	3,639	(NA)	3,544	15.3	2,245	9.7	18.9	104.3
1860	31,443	3.04	26,923	85.6	4,442	79	6,217	19.8	4,104	13.1	19.4	104.7
1870	39,819	2.36	33,589	84.4	4,880	89	9,902	24.9	5,567	14.0	20.2	102.2
1880	50,156	2.31	43,403	86.5	6,581	172	14,130	28.2	6,680	13.3	20.9	103.6
1890	62,948	2.27	55,101	87.5	7,489	358	22,106	35.1	9,250	14.7	22.0	105.0
1900	75,994	1.88	66,809	87.9	8,834	351	30,160	39.7	10,341	13.6	22.9	104.4
1910	91,972	1.91	81,732	88.9	9,828	413	41,999	45.7	13,516	14.7	24.1	106.0
1920	106,711	1.49	94,821	88.9	10,463	427	54,158	50.8	14,020	13.1	25.3	104.0
1930	122,755	1.40	110,287	89.8	11,891	597	68,955	56.2	14,283	11.6	26.5	102.5
1940	131,669	0.70	118,215	89.8	12,866	589	74,424	56.5	11,657	8.9	29.0	100.7
1950	150,697	1.35	134,942	89.5	15,042	713	96,468	64.0	10,431	6.9	30.2	98.6
1960	179,823	1.77	158,832	88.3	18,872	1,620	125,269	69.7	9,738	5.4	29.5	97.1
1970	203,302	1.23	178,098	87.6	22,580	2,883	149,325	73.4	9,619	4.7	28.1	94.8
1980	226,546	1.08	194,713	85.9	26,683	5,150	167,051	73.7	14,080	6.2	30.0	94.5
1990	248,710	0.93	208,704	83.9	30,483	9,523	187,053	75.2	21,632	8.7	32.8	95.1

(a) White population.
(b) Males per 100 females.

SOURCE: See Haines and Steckel (2000), Table A-4, 702–704. Based on data from U.S. Bureau of the Census (1975).

immigration, approximately 33.7 million immigrants were counted. Serious immigration restriction began with the Literacy Test Act of 1917 and continued with the Emergency Immigration Act of 1921 and the "National Origins" Act of 1924. Immigration quotas were established and continued, in modified form, until 1965. The depression decade of the 1930s was the only period in U.S. history to show net out-migration. After World War II (1939–1945), however, immigration once more picked up. With modification in immigration laws, notably the 1965 Amendments to the Immigration and Nationality Act, and with increasing numbers of undocumented aliens (especially from Mexico and other areas of Latin America), an estimated 25.5 million immigrants entered between 1945 and 1997.

There have been two major shifts in the composition of immigrants. The first took place in the 1880s when the focus of departures from Europe shifted from northern and western European nations (Britain, Ireland, Scandinavia, and Germany) to southern and eastern European nations and areas (Italy, Austria-Hungary, eastern Germany, Russia, the Balkans, Spain, Portugal). For the period from 1821 to 1890, northern and western Europe furnished 82 percent of immigrants, but for the following three decades (1891–1920), southern and eastern Europe contributed 64 percent. The second great shift occurred in the 1960s and 1970s, when the focus of departures

shifted from Europe (89 percent of all arrivals in 1821–1920) to Latin America, Asia, and Africa (83 percent of all immigrants in 1971–1997).

The Demographic Transition

Every developed nation has undergone a process known as the demographic transition from high to low levels of fertility and mortality. The United States began its transition at least in the early nineteenth century, but America was also distinctive. First, whereas its fertility transition began in the late eighteenth or early nineteenth century at the latest, other Western nations began their sustained fertility declines in the late nineteenth or early twentieth century. The sole exception was France, whose decline also began about the same time as the United States'. Second, the fertility rate in the United States commenced its sustained decline long before that of mortality. This may be seen in the fertility measures in Table 3, including the estimated crude birthrate and the wholly census-based child-woman ratios. This contrasts with the stylized demographic transition in which mortality decline precedes or occurs simultaneously with fertility decline. American mortality did not experience a sustained and irreversible decline until about the 1870s. Third, both processes were influenced by America's very high level of net inmigration and also by the significant population redistri-

TABLE 3

Fertility and Mortality in the United States, 1800–1990

Approx. Date	Crude Birth Rate(a) White	Crude Birth Rate(a) Black(f)	Child-Woman Ratio(b) White	Child-Woman Ratio(b) Black	Total Fertility Rate(c) White	Total Fertility Rate(c) Black(f)	Expectation of Life(d) White	Expectation of Life(d) Black(f)	Infant Mortality Rate(e) White	Infant Mortality Rate(e) Black(f)
1800	55.0		1342		7.04					
1810	54.3		1358		6.92					
1820	52.8		1295	1191	6.73					
1830	51.4		1145	1220	6.55					
1840	48.3		1085	1154	6.14					
1850	43.3	58.6(g)	892	1087	5.42	7.90(g)	39.5	23.0	216.8	340.0
1860	41.4	55.0(h)	905	1072	5.21	7.58(h)	43.6		181.3	
1870	38.3	55.4(i)	814	997	4.55	7.69(i)	45.2		175.5	
1880	35.2	51.9(j)	780	1090	4.24	7.26(j)	40.5		214.8	
1890	31.5	48.1	685	930	3.87	6.56	46.8		150.7	
1900	30.1	44.4	666	845	3.56	5.61	51.8(k)	41.8(k)	110.8(k)	170.3
1910	29.2	38.5	631	736	3.42	4.61	54.6(l)	46.8(l)	96.5(l)	142.6
1920	26.9	35.0	604	608	3.17	3.64	57.4	47.0	82.1	131.7
1930	20.6	27.5	506	554	2.45	2.98	60.9	48.5	60.1	99.9
1940	18.6	26.7	419	513	2.22	2.87	64.9	53.9	43.2	73.8
1950	23.0	33.3	580	663	2.98	3.93	69.0	60.7	26.8	44.5
1960	22.7	32.1	717	895	3.53	4.52	70.7	63.9	22.9	43.2
1970	17.4	25.1	507	689	2.39	3.07	71.6	64.1	17.8	30.9
1980	15.1	21.3	300	367	1.77	2.18	74.5	68.5	10.9	22.2
1990	15.8	22.4	298	359	2.00	2.48	76.1	69.1	7.6	18.0
1998	14.6	17.7			2.07	2.17	77.3	71.3	6.0	14.3

(a) Births per 1,000 population per annum.
(b) Children aged 0–4 per 1,000 women aged 20–44. Taken from U.S. Bureau of the Census (1975), Series 67–68 for 1800–1970. For the black population 1820–1840, Thompson and Whelpton (1933), Table 74, adjusted upward 47% for relative under-enumeration of black children aged 0–4 for the censuses of 1820–1840.
(c) Total number of births per woman if she experienced the current period age-specific fertility rates throughout her life.
(d) Expectation of life at birth for both sexes combined.
(e) Infant deaths per 1,000 live births per annum.
(f) Black and other population for CBR (1920–1970), TFR (1940–1990), e(0) (1950–1960), IMR (1920–1970).
(g) Average for 1850–1859.
(h) Average for 1860–1869.
(i) Average for 1870–1879.
(j) Average for 1880–1884.
(k) Approximately 1895.
(l) Approximately 1904.

SOURCE: See Haines and Steckel (2000), Table A-2, 696–699. Based on data from U.S. Bureau of the Census (1975).

bution to frontier areas and later to cities, towns, and suburbs.

In the late eighteenth century, birthrates for the white population were quite high by European standards, with the crude birthrate (births per 1,000 population per year) in the range of 40 to 55. This attracted comment by Thomas Malthus, Benjamin Franklin, and other observers. Mortality was moderate, with crude death rates (deaths per 1,000 population per year) likely in the range of 20 to 40. Table 3 shows the sustained decline in white birthrates from at least 1800 and of black fertility from at least 1850. Family sizes (as indicated by the total fertility rate) were large early in the nineteenth century, being approximately seven children per woman at the beginning of the century and between seven and eight for the mainly rural slave population around 1850. The decline continued uninterrupted until the late 1940s, when the United States experienced the rather unexpected postwar baby boom. Birthrates rose and peaked in the late 1950s (with total fertility rates in the range of 3.5 to 4.5 births per woman). Thereafter, the fertility decline began again until it reached relatively stable levels in the 1990s (with total fertility rates of about 2 births per woman).

Table 3 reveals that mortality did not begin to decline until about the 1870s or so. Previously, death rates fluctuated, being affected by periodic epidemics and changes in the disease environment. There is now evidence that death rates rose in the early nineteenth century, likely in response to rapid urbanization, the nationalization of the disease environment, and possibly worsening distribution of income. A measure of the biological standard of living, adult heights, exhibited declines for the age cohorts born in the 1830s and 1840s. Since a high incidence of infection early in life is related

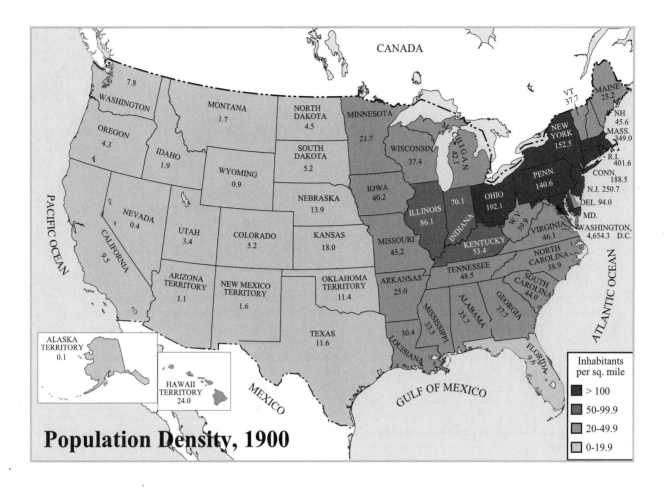

Population Density, 1900

to shorter final heights, this supports the view of a worsening disease environment.

Table 3 also shows that American blacks had differentially higher fertility and higher mortality relative to the white population, although both groups experienced the fertility and mortality transitions. Both participated in the baby boom as well as the subsequent resumption of birthrate declines in the 1960s.

Structural explanations for the fertility transition have involved the rising cost of raising children because of urbanization, the growth of incomes and nonagricultural employment, the increased value of education, rising female employment, child labor laws and compulsory education, and declining infant and child mortality. Changing attitudes toward large families and contraception, as well as better contraceptive techniques, have also been cited. Late twentieth century literature suggested that women were largely responsible for much of the birthrate decline in the nineteenth century—part of a movement for greater control over their lives. The structural explanations fit the American experience since the late nineteenth century, but they are less appropriate for the fertility decline in rural areas prior to about 1870. The increased scarcity and higher cost of good agricultural land has been proposed as a prime factor, although this is controversial. In addition, the increased secularization of social values has

been hypothesized as playing an important part in convincing families that they could have control over important processes such as fertility. The standard explanations also do not adequately explain the post–World War II baby boom and subsequent baby bust. More complex theories, including the interaction of the size of generations with their income prospects, tastes for children versus material goods, and expectations about family size, have been proposed.

The mortality decline since about the 1870s seems to have been the result particularly of improvements in public health and sanitation, especially better water supplies and sewage disposal. The improving diet, clothing, and shelter of the American population over the period since about 1870 also contributed to improving health behaviors. Specific medical interventions beyond more general environmental public health measures were not statistically important until well into the twentieth century. It is difficult to disentangle the separate effects of these factors. But it is clear that much of the decline was due to rapid reductions in specific infectious and parasitic diseases, including tuberculosis, pneumonia, bronchitis, and gastrointestinal infections, as well as such well-known lethal diseases as cholera, smallpox, diphtheria, and typhoid fever. Nineteenth-century cities were especially unhealthy places, particularly the largest ones. This began

559

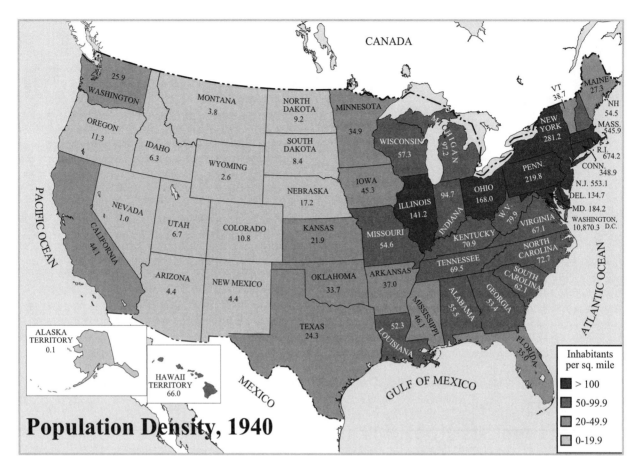

Population Density, 1940

Inhabitants per sq. mile

■ > 100
▨ 50-99.9
□ 20-49.9
□ 0-19.9

to change by about the 1890s, when the largest cities instituted new public works sanitation projects (such as piped water, sewer systems, filtration and chlorination of water) and public health administrations. They then experienced rapid improvements in death rates. As for the present, rural-urban mortality differentials have converged and largely disappeared. This, unfortunately, is not true of the differentials between whites and blacks.

Aging and Marriage

One of the consequences of the decline in fertility has been the aging of the population. Population age structure depends mostly on fertility rates: high-fertility populations are younger and low-fertility populations are older, provided that migration does not intervene in a major way. Table 2 shows that the median age of the population rose from about 16 years in 1800 to almost 33 years in 1990. Since male mortality is usually higher at all ages than female mortality, an older population tends also to have a preponderance of females. The final column of Table 2 indicates that the sex ratio (males per 100 females) declined during the twentieth century from well over 100 to about 95. The ratio was kept high through 1910 because of sex selectivity of immigration—more males than females entered as migrants up through World War I.

Although no data on marriage are presented in the tables, the United States has experienced some major

changes in nuptiality since 1800. Marriage in colonial North America was notable for being early (for women) and marked by low percentages never marrying. This was different from the distinctive northwest European pattern of late marriage and high proportions never married, although the underlying family formation pattern ("neolocal," in which newly married couples form new households) was the same in both colonial North America and the areas of origin of this population. Thus, Malthus was correct. Abundant resources rather than basic behavioral differences made early and extensive marriage possible in the colonies.

Between 1800 and the early twenty-first century there were long cycles in nuptiality. Since about 1800, female age at first marriage rose from relatively low levels to a peak around 1900. The female age at first marriage was less than 20 in 1800, but rose gradually to about almost 24 years (and about 27 years for males) in 1900. Thereafter, a gradual decline began, with a trough being reached about 1960 at the height of the baby boom, when the female age at first marriage had fallen to 20.3 years and the male age to 23.4 years. There then began another, and rapid, upswing in both male and female marriage ages. Proportions never married at ages 45 to 54 replicated these cycles with a lag of about 20 to 30 years. Male nuptiality patterns generally paralleled female patterns. Male marriage ages were higher than those of females

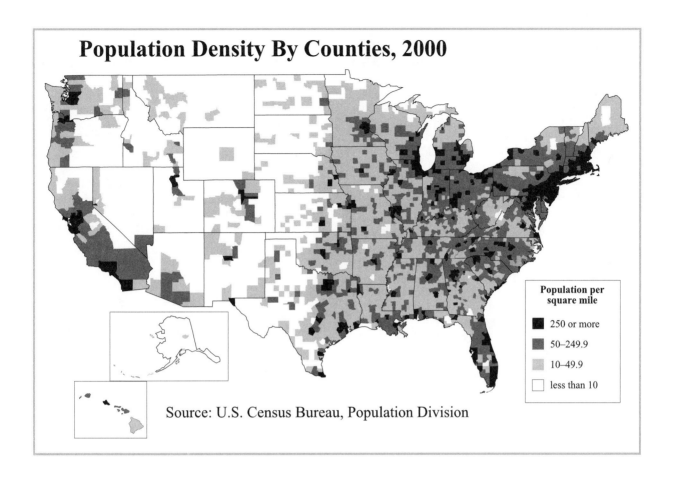

Population Density By Counties, 2000

Population per square mile

- 250 or more
- 50–249.9
- 10–49.9
- less than 10

Source: U.S. Census Bureau, Population Division

with proportions never marrying also usually higher. Black ages at marriage moved from being lower to being higher than those for whites. So, for example, in 1990 white females married for the first time at an average age of 24.8 years, while black females married at an average age of 28.7 years. Marriage behavior of the Hispanic population looked rather more like that of the white population. Much of the change was due to delayed childbearing, more single-parent households, and more couples living in nonmarital unions and for longer periods of time.

Much of the work of the discipline of demography involves creation, evaluation, and analysis of a variety of data sources. The creation of standard demographic measures, such as those found in Table 3, is a frequent goal. Historical demography, however, faces a number of different challenges. Historical demographers work in areas and on time periods for which regular censuses, surveys, and/or vital registration do not exist or are quite deficient in coverage, accuracy, or completeness. In the case of the United States, fortunately there have been records of decennial federal censuses from 1790, as well as some state and local censuses. With the exception of the 1890 census, the original manuscript schedules of the federal censuses have survived virtually intact in the National Archives. The Integrated Public Use Microsample (IPUMS) project at the University of Minnesota has created or improved microsamples for the censuses of 1850–1880,

1900–1920, and 1940–1990. As of 2002, samples of the 1930 census were under way, and the Census Bureau was producing samples for the 2000 census. These are enormously valuable resources for historical population research. But prior to 1850, the federal censuses were not nominal and hence have not been sampled. Before 1880, there were no questions on the schedules regarding marital status or relationship to head of household. As already mentioned, registration of births and deaths did not cover the entire nation until 1933. For the colonial period, while there were some censuses, they had quite limited information. Civil vital registration was not in place.

Consequently, a variety of sources and methods have been used. For data, parochial or town registers of births, deaths, and marriages; genealogies; wills and probates; military records; tax lists; and college and school records are among the sources used. The technique of family reconstitution, using parochial or local records and genealogies, was developed by Louis Henry and his colleagues in France in the 1950s and 1960s. Although it is enormously time-consuming and labor-intensive, it has been used for a variety of community studies. From these we know a good deal about fertility, mortality, marriage, and family structure in the New England colonies, rather less about the middle colonies and the Chesapeake, and least about the South.

Techniques of indirect estimation of fertility and mortality have also been created, originally for use in developing nations, which have missing or deficient data. These include "own children" methods, which have been applied to the microsamples of the federal censuses of 1900 and 1910 to estimate fertility and mortality for the whole nation. Age-specific marital rates and overall birthrates are estimated from the microsamples of the 1850–1880 censuses. Questions on deaths in the household in the year prior to the census in the censuses of 1850–1900 have been used to create life tables for the United States for that time period. Some of these indirect estimates appear in Table 3.

Work is continuing on such topics as fertility and marriage, migration, social mobility, rural and urban environments and their influence on demographic behavior, and differentials between blacks and whites, between the native born and the foreign born, and among specific ethnic groups in various settings. The availability of small area data (counties, cities, and towns) allows matching of macrodata to local conditions. These same small area data are being placed in a National Historical Geographic Information System (GIS) for aggregate analysis. Advances in computing technology and data storage and retrieval have made this work much easier and more accessible to a wider variety of researchers. And there can be expected to be further cross-fertilization from the disciplines of demography, sociology, history, economics, geography, anthropology, and others that should inform the work in historical demography methodologically and theoretically and with more and better data.

BIBLIOGRAPHY

Anderson, Margo J. *The American Census: A Social History.* New Haven, Conn.: Yale University Press, 1988.

Daugherty, Helen Ginn, and Kenneth C. W. Kammeyer. *An Introduction to Population.* 2d ed. New York: The Guilford Press, 1995.

Haines, Michael R. "Economic History and Historical Demography: Past, Present, and Future." In *The Future of Economic History.* Edited by Alexander J. Field. Boston: Kluwer-Nijoff Pub., 1987.

———. "Long-Term Marriage Patterns in the United States from Colonial Times to the Present." *The History of the Family: An International Quarterly* 1, no. 1 (1996): 15–39.

———. "The American Population, 1790–1920." In *The Cambridge Economic History of the United States.* Edited by Stanley Engerman and Robert Gallman. Vol. 2. New York: Cambridge University Press, 2000.

Haines, Michael R., and Richard H. Steckel. *A Population History of North America.* New York: Cambridge University Press, 2000.

Preston, Samuel H., Patrick Heuveline, and Michel Guillot. *Demography: Measuring and Modeling Population Processes.* Malden, Mass.: Blackwell Publishers, 2001.

Shryock, Henry S., Jacob S. Siegel, and Associates. *The Methods and Materials of Demography.* Washington, D.C.: Bureau of the Census, U.S. Government Printing Office, 1971.

U.S. Bureau of the Census. *Historical Statistics of the United States from Colonial Times to 1970.* Bicentennial Edition. Washington, D.C.: Department of Commerce, Bureau of the Census, U.S. Government Printing Office, 1975.

Thompson, Warren S., and P. K. Whelpton. *Population Trends in the United States.* New York: McGraw-Hill, 1933.

United Nations. *Indirect Techniques for Demographic Estimation.* Manual X. New York: United Nations, 1983.

Vinovskis, Maris A., ed. *Studies in American Historical Demography.* New York: Academic Press, 1979.

Wells, Robert V. *Revolutions in Americans' Lives: A Demographic Perspective on the History of Americans, Their Families, and Their Society.* Westport, Conn.: Greenwood Press, 1982.

———. "The Population of England's Colonies in America: Old English or New Americans?" *Population Studies* 46, no. 1 (March 1992): 85–102.

Willigan, J. Dennis, and Katherine A. Lynch. *Sources and Methods of Historical Demography.* New York: Academic Press, 1982.

Michael R. Haines

See also **Census, U.S. Bureau of the; Immigration; Migrations, Internal.**